THE OXFORD HANDBOOK OF

THE ATLANTIC WORLD

THE OXFORD HANDBOOK OF

THE ATLANTIC WORLD

c.1450–c.1850

Edited by

NICHOLAS CANNY

and

PHILIP MORGAN

OXFORD
UNIVERSITY PRESS

OXFORD
UNIVERSITY PRESS

Great Clarendon Street, Oxford OX2 6DP

Oxford University Press is a department of the University of Oxford.
It furthers the University's objective of excellence in research, scholarship,
and education by publishing worldwide in

Oxford New York

Auckland Cape Town Dar es Salaam Hong Kong Karachi
Kuala Lumpur Madrid Melbourne Mexico City Nairobi
New Delhi Shanghai Taipei Toronto

With offices in

Argentina Austria Brazil Chile Czech Republic France Greece
Guatemala Hungary Italy Japan Poland Portugal Singapore
South Korea Switzerland Thailand Turkey Ukraine Vietnam

Oxford is a registered trade mark of Oxford University Press
in the UK and in certain other countries

Published in the United States
by Oxford University Press Inc., New York

© Oxford University Press 2011

The moral rights of the authors have been asserted
Database right Oxford University Press (maker)

First published 2011

British Library Cataloguing in Publication Data
Data available

Library of Congress Cataloging in Publication Data
Data available

Typeset by SPI Publisher Services, Pondicherry, India
Printed in Great Britain
on acid-free paper by
MPG Books Group, Bodmin and King's Lynn

ISBN 978–0–19–921087–9

1 3 5 7 9 10 8 6 4 2

Acknowledgements

The authors thank Christopher Wheeler for inviting them to co-edit this volume. A particular debt is owed to the Moore Institute, at National University of Ireland, Galway, where the first conference leading to the preparation of this volume was convened, and to the Higher Education Authority, through its PRTLI instrument, The Irish Research Council for the Humanities and Social Sciences, and the Mellon Foundation, who have sustained the efforts of the Moore Institute to promote research in Atlantic History. The second preparatory conference was held in Baltimore, and for this we are indebted to the National Endowment for the Humanities, and Johns Hopkins University, especially its History Department and then chair Gabrielle M. Spiegel, for providing the necessary financial support. Marie Kennedy of the Moore Institute has done sterling work in keeping the volume on track. We also thank Jackie Pritchard, our copy editor; Mike O'Malley, map designer; and Seumas Spark, indexer. It has been a pleasure dealing with our contributors, who have been generous with their time and inordinately patient. Sadly one of our number, John Russell-Wood, died in August 2010 and will be missed by all who knew him. His helpful contributions along the way and his masterful essay will keep his memory alive.

CONTENTS

PART II: CONSOLIDATION

PART III: INTEGRATION

PART IV: DISINTEGRATION

ABBREVIATIONS

CHLA Leslie Bethell, *The Cambridge History of Latin America* (Cambridge, 1984)
GWC Geoctroyeerde Westindische Compagnie
HC *The History of Cartography* (Chicago, IL, 1987–)
LIA Little Ice Age
VOC Dutch East India Company
WIC West India Company

List of Figures

LIST OF TABLES

LIST OF MAPS

LIST OF CONTRIBUTORS

Ida Altman	University of Florida
David Armitage	Harvard University
Lauren Benton	New York University
Christopher Leslie Brown	Columbia University
Nicholas Canny	National University of Ireland, Galway. Appointed to the Scientific Council of the European Research Council in January 2011.
Joyce Chaplin	Harvard University
Matthew Edney	University of Southern Maine
David Eltis	Emory University
David Geggus	University of Florida
Ira D. Gruber	Rice University
David Hancock	University of Michigan
Tamar Herzog	Stanford University
Richard L. Kagan	Johns Hopkins University
Wim Klooster	Clark University
Robin Law	Stirling University
J. R. McNeill	Georgetown University
Elizabeth Mancke	Akron University
Silvia Marzagalli	University of Nice
Laura de Mello e Souza	Universidade de São Paulo
Kenneth Mills	University of Toronto
Philip Morgan	Johns Hopkins University
Craig Muldrew	Cambridge University
David Northrup	Boston College
William O'Reilly	Cambridge University
Anthony Pagden	University of California, Los Angeles
Susan Scott Parrish	University of Michigan
João José Reis	Universidade Federal da Bahia
Daniel K. Richter	University of Pennsylvania
N. A. M. Rodger	Oxford University
Jaime E. Rodríguez O.	University of California, Irvine
Emma Rothschild	Harvard University
Joan-Pau Rubiés	London School of Economics
A. J. R. Russell-Wood	Johns Hopkins University

Jean-Frédéric Schaub	École des Hautes Études en Sciences Sociales, Paris
Stuart Schwartz	Yale University
Carole Shammas	University of Southern California
David S. Shields	University of South Carolina
Kevin Terraciano	University of California, Los Angeles
Troy L. Thompson	University of Pennsylvania
Neil Whitehead	University of Wisconsin

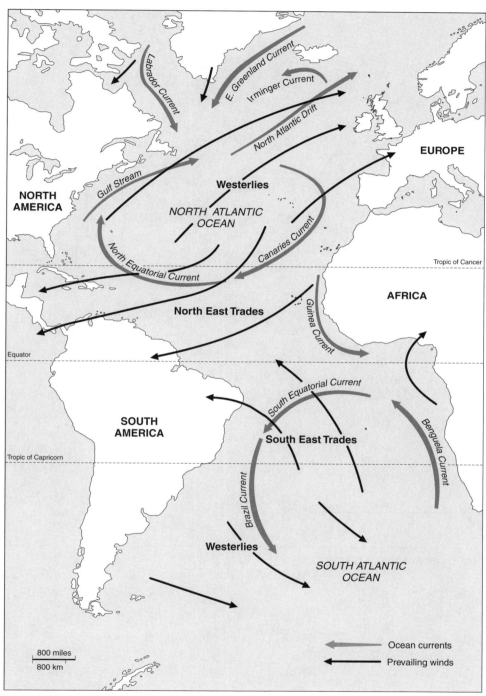

MAP 1 Atlantic winds and currents

MAP 2 The Americas, *c.*1500

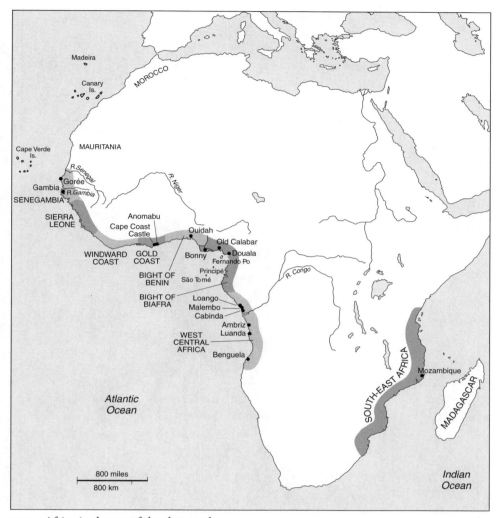

MAP 3 Africa in the era of the slave trade

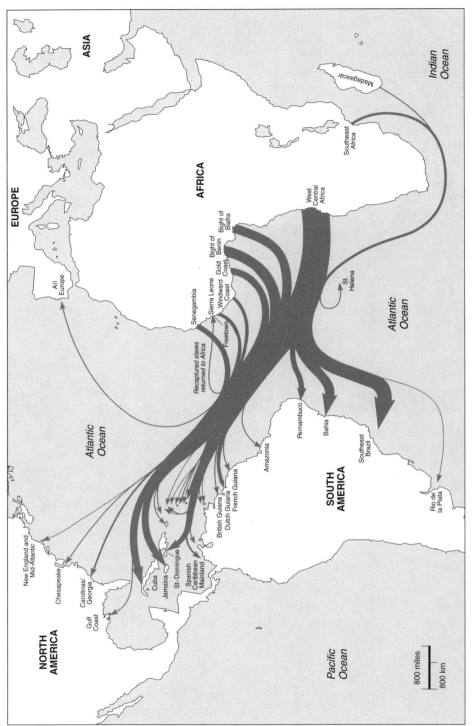

MAP 4 Volume and direction of the transatlantic slave trade

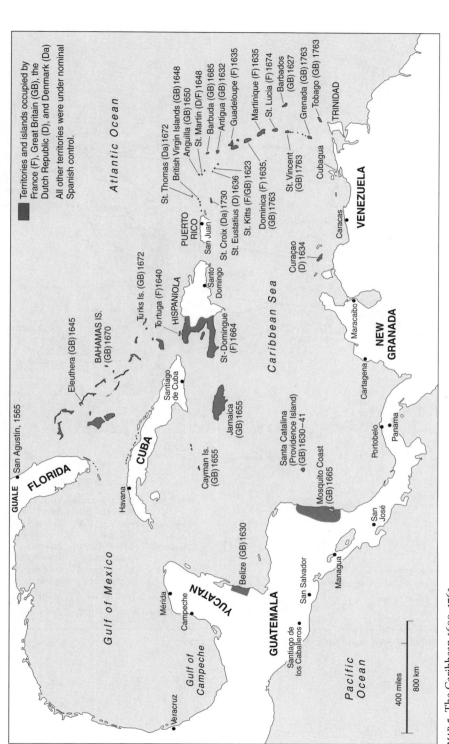

MAP 5 The Caribbean 1600–1763

Territories and islands occupied by France (F), Great Britain (GB), the Dutch Republic (D), and Denmark (Da). All other territories were under nominal Spanish control.

Atlantic Ocean

St. Thomas (Da)1672
British Virgin Islands (GB) 1648
Anguilla (GB)1650
St. Martin (D/F)1648
Barbuda (GB) 1685
Antigua (GB) 1632
Guadeloupe (F)1635
Martinique (F)1635
St. Lucia (F)1674
Barbados (GB)1627
Grenada (GB)1763
Tobago (GB) 1763

TRINIDAD

St. Croix (Da)1730
St. Eustatius (D)1636
St. Kitts (F/GB)1623
Dominica (F)1635, (GB)1763
St. Vincent (GB)1763
Cubagua

PUERTO RICO
San Juan

Curaçao (D)1634

Caracas

VENEZUELA

Caribbean Sea

Turks Is. (GB)1672
Tortuga (F)1640
HISPANIOLA
Santo Domingo
St-Domingue (F)1664

BAHAMAS IS. (GB)1670
Eleuthera (GB)1645

Maracaibo

NEW GRANADA

Santiago de Cuba

CUBA

Jamaica (GB)1655

Santa Catalina (Providence Island) (GB)1630–41

Cayman Is. (GB) 1655

Havana

Cartagena

Portobelo
Panama

Mosquito Coast (GB)1665

GUALE
FLORIDA
San Agustin, 1565

Gulf of Mexico

San José
Managua

San Salvador

Santiago de los Caballeros

GUATEMALA

Belize (GB)1630

YUCATAN

Mérida
Campeche

Gulf of Campeche

Veracruz

Pacific Ocean

400 miles
800 km

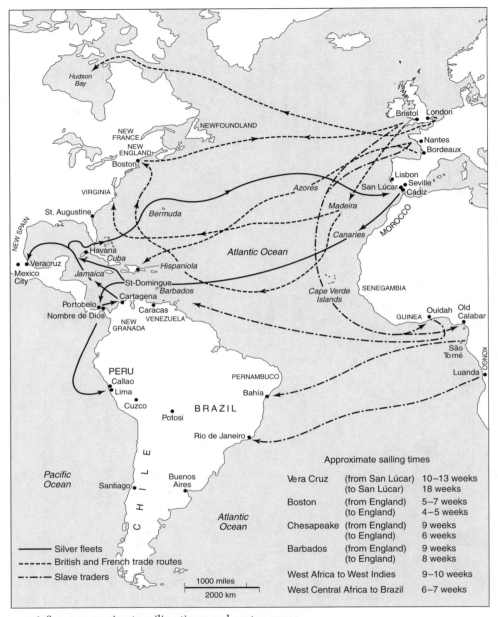

Approximate sailing times

Vera Cruz	(from San Lúcar)	10–13 weeks
	(to San Lúcar)	18 weeks
Boston	(from England)	5–7 weeks
	(to England)	4–5 weeks
Chesapeake	(from England)	9 weeks
	(to England)	6 weeks
Barbados	(from England)	9 weeks
	(to England)	8 weeks
West Africa to West Indies		9–10 weeks
West Central Africa to Brazil		6–7 weeks

—— Silver fleets
- - - - British and French trade routes
-·-·- Slave traders

1000 miles
2000 km

MAP 6 Some approximate sailing times and routes, c.1700

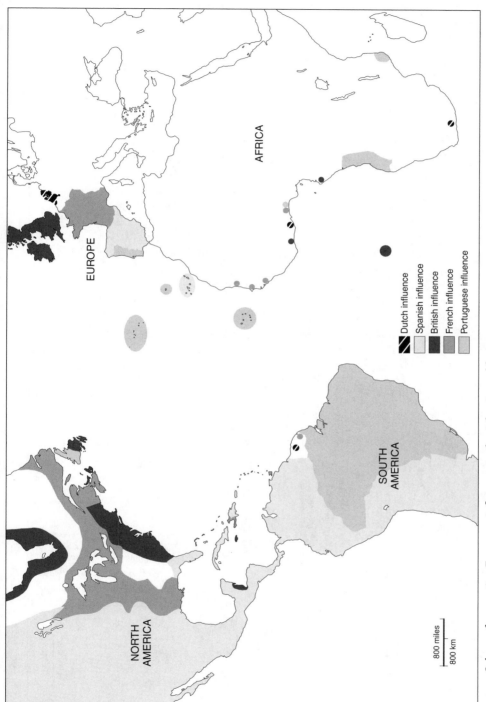

MAP 7 Sphere of competing European influences in the Atlantic world c.1750

Dutch influence
Spanish influence
British influence
French influence
Portuguese influence

EUROPE

AFRICA

NORTH
AMERICA

SOUTH
AMERICA

800 miles
800 km

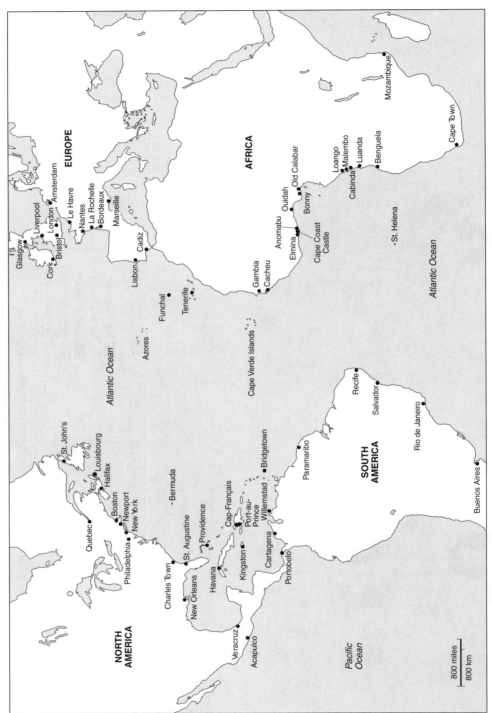

MAP 8 Ports of the Atlantic world, c.1750

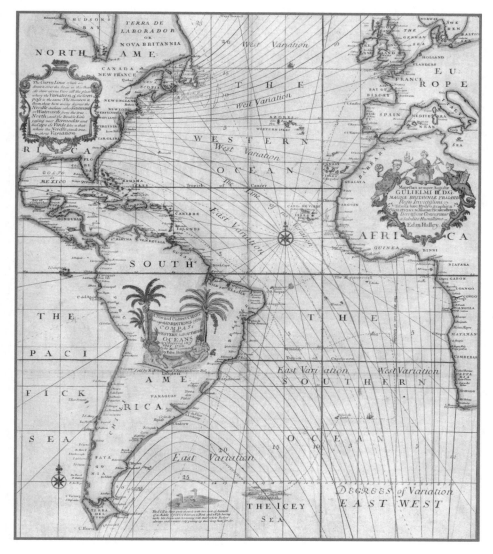

MAP **9** Edmond Halley, *A New and Correct Chart Shewing the Variations of the Compass in the Western & Southern Oceans as Observed in y^e Year 1700 by his Maties Command* (London: R. Mount and T. Page, 1706).

CHAPTER 1

INTRODUCTION

The Making and Unmaking of an Atlantic World

NICHOLAS CANNY
PHILIP MORGAN

BEGINNING in the fifteenth century, people, plants, pathogens, products, and cultural practices—just to mention some key agents—began to move regularly back and forth across the Atlantic Ocean. As the connections and exchanges deepened and intensified, much was transformed. New peoples, economies, societies, polities, and cultures arose, particularly in the lands and islands touched by that ocean, while others were destroyed. The several authors in this volume seek to describe, explain, and, occasionally, challenge conventional wisdom concerning these path-breaking developments from the late fifteenth to the early nineteenth century. While contributors benefit from an outpouring of recent scholarship devoted to Atlantic History, this volume is more ambitious than anything previously published, since it covers many themes and topics, spans a vast chronological spread, and operates on an extensive geographical canvas.[1] Also the editors have enjoined its thirty-eight authors to think comparatively when addressing their particular aspects of Atlantic History, in the hope of removing barriers that have tended to compartmentalize scholarly investigations into discrete 'national' involvements with an Atlantic world, even when its resources were shared.

Our appraisal opens when some people (mostly Christian people) were beginning to comprehend the extent of, and possibilities presented by, the ocean that had once divided the continents of Europe and Africa from the Americas, and it closes when the integrity that had emerged in the Atlantic world was threatened by novel political, economic,

---

[1] For examples of recent synoptic works, see Jack P. Greene and Philip D. Morgan (eds.), *Atlantic History: A Critical Reappraisal* (Oxford, 2009); Bernard Bailyn and Patricia L. Denault (eds.), *Soundings in Atlantic History: Latent Structures and Intellectual Currents, 1500–1830* (Cambridge, MA, 2009).

technological, and moral forces. It is arranged into rough, schematic periods—which we have labelled emergence, consolidation, integration, and disintegration—although some essays straddle a number of these stages. One of the goals of this introduction is to highlight some of the seminal developments within the Atlantic world during the period under review, thus providing a fresh narrative framework for the study of Atlantic history.

While bringing readers up to date with current scholarship, this volume also aims to be mould breaking, not least in adumbrating a narrative for the study of this broadly conceived subject. A sequence of essays shows how, over the course of the fifteenth, sixteenth, and seventeenth centuries, several Atlantic worlds, each with distinctive features but also sharing much in common, were fashioned. Later contributors make the case that each of these worlds, which had achieved a degree of self-sufficiency, was gradually absorbed into a larger unit of interdependency until a single functioning Atlantic world, shaped and continuously influenced to varying degrees by European, African, and American peoples, flourished through much of the eighteenth century. A final cluster of chapters suggest that the interconnectedness of this world explains why challenge and collapse in any given part usually led to significant disruption of neighbouring areas, if not of the entire system. This introduction brings this preferred narrative into focus while it also alludes to the Atlantic dimension that emerges when developments in any given area are considered comparatively or in a broad oceanic context.

The particulars discussed in this collection will be familiar to those acquainted with what was once known as the History of European Overseas Expansion. To this extent the established narratives remain in place: Europeans, and their relatively superior technologies, are credited with achieving mastery over an ocean that had previously acted as a barrier against human endeavour; Europeans are acknowledged to have been the driving force behind the overthrow of the Aztec, the Inca, and other Native American empires; Native American peoples succumbed disastrously to pathogens borne by Europeans and Africans; and African slaves were the most obvious victims and instruments of the European-dominated colonization that shaped the Atlantic world. However the dominant Eurocentric model is challenged by essays that demonstrate the persistent influence over their destinies exercised by Native Americans and Africans until well into the eighteenth century. Received wisdom is therefore modified in light of the better appreciation of the part played by Native Americans and Africans in shaping the course of events. Representations of 'Overseas History' as an extension of European history, and teleological delineations of transitions from 'colony to nation', are therefore emphatically rejected.[2]

These essays show that successive European conquests of Native American populations (in North and South America) succeeded only because small groups of determined, yet vulnerable, European adventurers who promoted them could form alliances

[2] Chapter by Elizabeth Mancke.

with native enemies of dominant groups. They also demonstrate that massive population losses suffered by Native American peoples were due as much to exploitation, maltreatment, and unthinking environmental destruction perpetrated by the conquerors, as to warfare and the impact of Old World diseases. But while they do nothing to conceal the tragic and the sordid, succeeding authors explain how some of the indigenous populations endured the onslaught. Thus, to cite cases where the challenge was extreme; on the West Indian islands where Spanish destruction was most complete, some of the native populations survived either by melding with the peoples of other islands, or by retreating and intermingling with inhabitants on the mainland, or by contributing their genes and values to the children born of interracial unions; similarly, in coastal Brazil many natives endured Portuguese intrusion by withdrawing into the Amazonian interior. The native populations of North America adopted comparable survival strategies when they, in turn, experienced European 'invasions'.

The history of native societies and habitats through our period is, therefore, one of continuous change and adaptation rather then termination. The changes that essayists identify are: the development of genetic intermixtures; shifts in territories; the formation of novel political alliances among Native American peoples, and sometimes between Native Americans and European partners; the adoption by Native Americans of European weapons and technologies; the increased involvement of Native Americans in exchanges triggered by European demand for American commodities; the destruction of traditional environments especially resulting from the introduction of European livestock, vegetation, and agrarian technologies; and massive population losses suffered by Native Americans, regardless of their geographic location, due to their exposure to the various crowd disease pathogens that Europeans and Africans carried with them unwittingly from the Old World. But the narrative is also one of survival since the essays collectively show that Native American loss of influence was seldom total or immediate, and that recovery and retrenchment proved possible for many who continued to shape their destinies throughout the period. One example of enduring Native American influence was the continued employment by Europeans of native legal codes to achieve conflict resolution, and the resort of astute Native Americans to 'forum shopping' to secure the best possible legal outcomes from contested disputes.[3] Also, in the religious sphere, where previous scholarly generations, and particularly those treating of encounters in Central and South America, sought to 'measure' the pace of Christian conversion, the concern here is to explain how everywhere the Christian message came to be 'naturalized and localized'.[4]

If some Native Americans contributed to the Atlantic trading world that flourished from the later seventeenth century onwards, rulers on the coast of West Africa (and African leaders more generally) succeeded in preserving their economic as well as their political independence—even dictating the pace of change—until well into the eighteenth century. Where much previous writing has sought to pinpoint when Portuguese,

---

[3] Chapter by Laurie Benton.   [4] Chapter by Ken Mills.

or English, or Dutch, or French traders first conveyed African slaves across the Atlantic, the relevant chapters here emphasize the tentative character of the European presence off the Atlantic coast of Africa to the end of the eighteenth century; the reliance of European merchants on the goodwill of those who ruled over the sequence of African polities abutting the Atlantic Ocean; and the prolonged primary interest of Europeans in African gold, textiles, and dyestuffs, rather than slaves, for half of our period.

Thus, while some African slaves were conveyed across the Atlantic from the early sixteenth century to meet labour shortages in Central and South America, it was not until after 1700 that trade in slaves became the principal interest of European merchants dealing with Africa. Then, an escalating demand for labour in America, occasioned principally by the demographic collapse of Native American workforces and a dramatic expansion of sugar cultivation and production in Brazil and the Caribbean, made it necessary to import slaves from Africa. Slaves, however, could be acquired only with the agreement of African rulers and with the cooperation of African traders, or traders of mixed African/European race associated with stations, factories, and castles on the African coast, or on islands offshore. As the demand increased so also did the geographic extent of slave stations along the coast, while African traders and those who supplied them with captives had to reach ever deeper into continental Africa for slaves to satisfy the increasing American appetite for bound labour. The cultural and linguistic range of the African peoples who were forced into slavery and conveyed to American plantations increased correspondingly, and particularly so in the later eighteenth century when the traffic was at its height. The traffic proved profitable for African-based merchants as for the European traders who conveyed Africans to the Americas, not least because African merchants also supplied provisions to European slave ships for the transatlantic crossing. Consequently, African opposition to the abolition of the slave trade proved more determined and persistent than that mounted by those Europeans who had a vested interest in slave trading, once both groups were put on the defensive when abolitionism became a humanitarian, evangelical, or political cause for influential groups in European and American societies.

Slaves on plantation estates managed their work rhythms as best they could, seized opportunities to escape to maroon societies where possible, and strove to retain something of their African languages, cultures, religions, and political aspirations. A sense of 'Africanness' may have emerged on the African coast, but the coming together of an ever greater range of Africans in America spurred the process of ethnogenesis and racial consciousness.[5] Once Africans and African Americans came to constitute a numerous or a majority population in many locations in the Americas, it became necessary for the dominant population to introduce slave codes which, in themselves, rendered these American societies different from anything in previous experience. Such codes did not prevent the sexual exploitation of women of African

---

[5] Chapter by Robin Law.

descent by white males which quickly gave rise to mixed populations everywhere that slavery flourished. In some locations people of mixed origin were accorded a separate legal status from African-born slaves, while intermingling between runaway slaves and Native American peoples created yet other configurations of racial and political mixtures.

Interminglings occurred on many other levels. Native Americans enriched the rest of the Atlantic world with their plants (the most important of which were the potato, maize, and manioc); Europeans contributed their domesticated animals primarily to the Americas, the numbers of which rose exponentially and the protein of which boosted people's height; Africans transferred to the New World their plants such as millet, yams, bananas, okra, sesame, watermelon, and African rice; while Europeans introduced to both Africa and America plants and commodities that were native to Asia. In the realm of medicine, Africans, and also Native Americans, had their Euro-American masters reliant on them because of their superior knowledge concerning the curative properties of plants.

Historians of the Atlantic world are generally at pains to explain how people shaped their destinies, not least because scholars of other dispersed worlds linked by a shared body of water have contended that outcomes were determined by the forces of nature. Prime among the determinists is Fernand Braudel, who depicted a Mediterranean world where social forms and trading patterns were dictated by climatic and geomorphologic constants, regardless of the cultural backgrounds of the peoples who resided within these environments.[6] More recently historians of the Indian Ocean, many of them admirers of Braudel, have implied that the predictable wind systems and water currents prevailing on either side of the sub-continent of India proved more important than the navigational, nautical, astronomical, and business acumen of Asian sailors and traders, in linking the various trading sectors of the Indian Ocean into a unified commercial world that long pre-dated European water-borne influence in that area.[7]

Current scholars of exploration and trade on the Atlantic are perhaps more aware than those of earlier generations how the endeavours of mariners in the age of sail were both aided and circumscribed by the prevailing winds and currents of the ocean in much the same way that travel on the Indian Ocean was enabled and limited by the forces of nature. Such factors, as much as the diverse interests that different Europeans had in the Atlantic, are advanced to explain the plurality of Atlantic worlds that were gradually mastered by European navigators during the course of the fifteenth century. But if the efforts of navigators of the early modern centuries (and earlier) were limited by natural forces, they also came to appreciate that there were two principal routes by which they could negotiate their way in the Atlantic Ocean during this era of sail: the

---

[6] Fernand Braudel, *The Mediterranean and the Mediterranean World in the Age of Philip II*, trans. Sian Reynolds, 2 vols. (London, 1972–3).

[7] K. N. Chaudhuri, *Trade and Civilization in the Indian Ocean: An Economic History from the Rise of Islam to 1750* (Cambridge, 1985); O. Prakash, *European Commercial Expansion in Early Modern Asia* (London, 1997).

northern route which was an extension of that plied by the Vikings in medieval times, and the southern route with which the Portuguese became acquainted when they sailed westwards into the Atlantic hoping to take advantage of the eastern trade winds to carry them south of the Cape of Good Hope into the Indian Ocean. The northern route brought Bristol fishermen to the Newfoundland Banks perhaps before Columbus crossed the Atlantic, while Columbus, in 1492 and in his subsequent voyages, exploited the southern route.

While they make allowance for such environmental determinants, scholars who study the halting penetration of the Atlantic Ocean by mariners associated with trading ports in Western Europe give principal credit to human agency. Thus they attribute the ultimate success of European mariners in mastering and comprehending that ocean to a slow accumulation of knowledge and experience of particular sections of the Atlantic Ocean by those searching for fishing grounds, or seeking the source of African gold, or tracing an all-water route to Asia by the African coastline. Historians of the Atlantic have shown how these various seafaring communities developed a knowledge of several Atlantics and of the islands and promontories associated with each; a better understanding of what ships and sails were appropriate for traversing the tempestuous Atlantic waters; an appreciation of how to travel ever-longer distances into the ocean and navigate a way home; and an accretion of information about the hazards associated with particular harbours. Attention is also given to how these groups benefited from improved scientific practice in navigation, ship construction, and in the making of navigational instruments and maps that had been advanced within the Mediterranean basin, and particularly in Italy. Credit is also given to pilots and ship captains from Italy (ranging from John Cabot to Christopher Columbus) who participated in the exploration of the Atlantic basin. But the presumption behind these essays, and the scholarship on which they are based, is that trial and error were more important than any scientific breakthrough in emboldening European seafarers to make increasing use of the Atlantic, in the same way that, 400 years previously, intelligent experimentation had enabled Viking explorers to negotiate regular journeys between their homeland and their settlement on Greenland, and to proceed as far as the American coastline from which they returned home. Despite their insistence upon the importance of human agency, historians of the Atlantic are sometimes forced to concede that impersonal forces could dictate outcomes. Thus, in a recent study, Stephen Behrendt has discerned that as the transatlantic slave trade expanded in scale and geographic range during the third quarter of the eighteenth century, environmental factors placed strict limits on where and when traders might pursue their business.[8]

The issue of predetermination also features in scholarship concerning encounters between different European and Native American peoples. Authors have long contended that Iberian interaction with the Moors, leading to their expulsion from Spain, prefigured how Iberians would relate to Native American peoples, and it has been

---

[8] Stephen D. Behrendt, 'Ecology, Seasonality, and the Transatlantic Slave Trade', in Bailyn and Denault (eds.), *Soundings in Atlantic History*, 44–85.

similarly argued that English responses to, and interaction with, Native American peoples during the sixteenth and the seventeenth centuries were conditioned by their previous experiences in Elizabethan Ireland.[9] Recent scholars, including authors in this volume, are more concerned than their predecessors of the past half-century to distinguish between parallels, verbal metaphors, and actual influences. This is exemplified by recent work on the interplay of Mediterranean Christian peoples with Muslim populations of the Iberian Peninsula and North Africa, indigenous populations of the Canary Islands, and the populations encountered by Columbus and his associates on various Caribbean islands. Comparison between these three interactions leads to the conclusion that the encounters were parts of a continuum, that prejudice and precedent influenced the actions of Christians, and that all three interventions were rationalized in similar, but not identical, fashion.[10] Also consideration in this volume of the 'universalization of brutality' recognizes that the increased incidence of mass violence, which unquestionably characterized the early modern centuries, was as much 'domestic as colonial', and that violence in Europe and in foreign locations influenced each other to the extent that real and imagined atrocities in both spheres were depicted together, and sometimes fused, in printed literature of the period.[11]

Another subject of general interest is the extent to which the previous experience of European groups at establishing settlements within Europe, in Africa, or on various Atlantic islands influenced their promotion of human settlement in America, or determined the shape of those settlements. Cases cited are the supposed tendency of Spaniards to locate themselves in towns from which they might dominate the surrounding countryside, and of English, French, and Dutch settlers to fashion rural villages or seigniories in colonial settings.[12] Such generalizations now carry less weight because of greater awareness of the diversity of settlements established by each European power in the Atlantic. On the other hand, greater respect is now being given to the extent to which the economic activity associated with any given colony shaped the pattern of settlement there. This has been demonstrated most effectively through the study of colonies dedicated to fishing or other maritime activity.[13] Similarly, European settlements (whether in the Americas or in Asia) closely involved with the production of high-value goods for European or world markets attracted greater state involvement in the conduct and protection of trade. Contrariwise, settlers devoted to the cultivation and processing of agricultural goods experienced less state oversight, and possibly cherished greater individual freedom. However, attachment to freedom was necessarily compromised by the fact that, for much of our period, business in most

---

[9] D. B. Quinn, *The Elizabethans and the Irish* (Ithaca, NY, 1966), esp. 106–22.

[10] David Abulafia, *The Discovery of Mankind: Atlantic Encounters in the Age of Columbus* (New Haven, CT, 2008).

[11] Chapter by Jean-Frédéric Schaub.

[12] D. W. Meinig, *The Shaping of America: A Geographical Perspective on 500 Years of History* (New Haven, CT, 1986–98); D. H. Fischer, *Albion's Seed: Four English Folkways in America* (Oxford, 1989).

[13] Michael Jarvis, *In the Eye of All Trade: Bermuda, Bermudians, and the Maritime Atlantic World, 1680–1783* (Chapel Hill, NC, 2010).

European countries was conducted by merchant companies who had the political connections required to negotiate state monopolies.[14]

Efforts to compare and thus arrive at generalizations have, up to now, brought similarities more than differences into focus. To overcome this bias, many of our essayists devote particular attention to difference, none more stark than that between the European and African migrations that contributed to the peopling, or more accurately the re-peopling, of America.[15] What they shared is that the overwhelming majority of the millions who crossed the Atlantic during our centuries were 'forcibly transported; coerced to move either by enslavement, violence, economic dislocation, social and religious persecution of unstable political conditions'.[16] Notwithstanding this commonality a fundamental contrast existed between European and African migrations over the question of volition. Essentially, the overwhelming majority of European emigrants to America, including indentured servants, but excluding convict migrants and those rounded up for expulsion in the aftermath of war, exercised some degree of choice concerning travel to America. Furthermore, some Europeans, increasingly so in the eighteenth century, made well-informed decisions about their American destinations. African migrants, on the other hand, were almost invariably people who had been enslaved after they had become captives in tribal warfare, or after slave raiders had forcefully taken them from their African villages. Captives then frequently passed through several hands before they eventually reached a slave-trading port on the Atlantic coastline where an African merchant would sell them to a European slave trader who, in turn, would convey his purchase to whichever American destination held out the prospect of best profit to the trader. European migrants (with the exception of convicts and war victims) usually made their own way to ports of embarkation, purchased or negotiated passage with ship captains, sometimes selected a ship heading for a particular destination, and enjoyed relative freedom of movement on the outward voyage. European migrants also frequently provided their own supplies of food and water for their crossing, or cooked their own food, whereas the captains of slave vessels assumed as much responsibility for the nurture, hygiene, and health of their human cargo as they did for keeping them in bondage.

Another fundamental difference related to gender balance. Men were in a distinct majority in all European migrations to America during the centuries in question and, in some instances, were overwhelmingly so. The sex ratio was however more evenly balanced in the African migration not least because in Africa more women than men were customarily forced into slavery, a function of field work in Africa being assigned to women workers, and African women slaves being required to satisfy sexual as well as labour appetites. Given that European traders were aware of the prejudice of planters against assigning harsh agricultural work to women, they had consistently solicited

---

[14] Chapter by David Hancock.

[15] The phrase comes from Bernard Bailyn, *The Peopling of British North America: An Introduction* (New York, 1986).

[16] Chapter by William O'Reilly.

their African suppliers for more young male slaves. Their requests produced some rectification of the gender imbalance, but the American demand for slaves was such that a considerable number of African women necessarily became field slaves in several locations in America.

The two population flows also differed due to the much wider range of cultural, religious, linguistic, and geographic backgrounds from which African slaves, as opposed to European migrants, were drawn.[17] Europeans who crossed the Atlantic usually went to colonies sponsored by their home country, and while some inclusivity was initially tolerated especially among the Iberians, exclusivity remained fairly rigid until the later decades of the seventeenth century. Thus, for example, people of Jewish or Irish Catholic lineage were considered different in Spanish and Portuguese Atlantic settlements, and individuals from the Channel Isles were considered strangers in New England towns. This closed character of migration began to ease somewhat after the mid-seventeenth century, and most conspicuously so in colonies of English and Dutch settlement which then began to draw people from more heterogeneous backgrounds to their Atlantic settlements. These included Scots, Irish, and Welsh from within the British monarchies, and settlers (Catholic and Protestant) from extensive areas of Germanic-speaking Europe, together with some Huguenots who had been exiled from France.

The societal contrast within the Atlantic world most frequently discussed is that between colonial British America and Iberian America, with British settlers allegedly remaining aloof from intermixture with other populations, and being more reluctant than others to engage in evangelization. The validity of all such generalities, including the supposition that the British were most active in building re-configurations of European social forms in an American setting, has been challenged by John Elliott, whose sustained comparison between experiences in the British and Hispanic worlds in America alludes to as many similarities as differences between the two experiences.[18] The commonality of the British range of colonial experience with that of Atlantic empires carved out by other European powers becomes even more apparent when account is taken of the British involvement with the Caribbean which has not always been given due weight. This was Britain's most consequential presence in the Americas for most of the colonial period, and racial intermixing there was as widespread as in any other colonial society. Indeed, one of the principal products of scholarly endeavour on colonial British America over the past generation is the better appreciation of the importance to Britain of their presence in the Caribbean relative to that in their colonies on mainland America whose only significant contribution to increasing the wealth of the home country—which remained the ultimate seventeenth-century justi-fication of all colonies—was fish from Newfoundland and tobacco from the Chesa-peake. The value of each of these commodities was small compared with the value of

---

[17] Chapter by David Eltis.

[18] John Elliott, *Empires of the Atlantic World: Britain and Spain in America, 1492–1830* (New Haven, CT, 2006).

sugar produced on the island colonies. Indeed the mainland colonies were to increase in relative importance in the minds of merchants and British officials over the course of the eighteenth century only because the demand for provisions to feed the escalating slave population in the Caribbean provided a new *raison d'être* for the mainland colonies. Also eighteenth-century commercial and communications factors made it possible for the mainland colonies to become suppliers of food to the expanding population of Western Europe. These developments explain the major expansion in the number of European agricultural and artisanal settlers who went to settle in Britain's mainland colonies over the course of the eighteenth century. However, it would be teleological to suggest that this important development, which transformed the character of settlement in parts of mainland British America, could have been anticipated in previous centuries.

Although national segmentation of the Atlantic basin became a reality, as Portuguese, English, French, Dutch, and other European groups tried to emulate the achievements of the Spaniards and create their own colonies—thus explaining why some of these essays explore those entities separately—over time, the Atlantic world became increasingly integrated, particularly so in the economic sphere. As the eighteenth century proceeded, the overall volume and range of products criss-crossing the Atlantic escalated; the number of ships moving back and forth in circular orbits—creating 'a common seaborne culture'[19]—rose enormously (1,500 vessels annually visited Saint-Domingue in the 1780s, for example, and more than twice that number were involved in the Atlantic wine trade); a significant fall in the ratio of crew to tons occurred; ships became bigger and sleeker; voyage times accelerated, and turnaround times in ports declined. Shipping also became more reliable and predictable, routes more regularized, and even though risk could never be eliminated, the probability of death on some maritime routes was less than on shore, and sea travel could be promoted as a health cure. Sophisticated marine insurance and financial services arose; harbour and dockside infrastructure grew apace; and transatlantic communication improved due to more reliable post, commercial press, and regular packet services. The density of economic exchanges deepened and thickened to the point where each 'national' development contributed to the enrichment of all.

A notable feature of this commercial system was the degree to which the informal, illicit, contraband sector evaded formal, regulated, and official constraints. In various parts of the Atlantic and at different times, one historian argues, 'contraband trade dwarfed legal exchange'. Similarly, state control via monopoly, licence, and restriction gradually and imperfectly gave way to looser arrangements and more self-organized, decentralized agents. The French relaxed their *exclusif*, the Spanish shifted to *comercio libre*, the Dutch persisted in the transit business, the English experimented with free ports, and if Portugal was odd man out because of its reliance on the Company of Grão Pará and Maranhão to develop new export commodities, it was in part because for

---

[19] Chapter by N. A. M. Rodger.

them 'mercantilism and protectionism were [always] conceits rather than attainable goals'. Different imperial models of trading relations obtained, but overall there was a trend to greater openness and porosity; and even the Portuguese developed a freer trade regime in the last quarter of the eighteenth century, which became open after 1808.[20]

The number of 'revolutions' that historians have posited for this period—a sugar revolution, a consumer revolution, and an information revolution, to name but three—suggests that economic transformation in the Atlantic world was dramatic. Whether a true consumer revolution, such as T. H. Breen has adumbrated for Britain's colonies on mainland North America, occurred throughout the entire eighteenth-century Atlantic world remains debatable, but tastes certainly expanded enormously, diets were transformed, luxuries became necessities, and consumption patterns were profoundly altered. Tobacco smoking became widespread; Atlantic wines, coffee, chocolate, rum, and tea became popular drinks, even if expenditures on them were always a small part of most household budgets; while, in all Atlantic colonies, pottery, clothing, jewellery, firearms, and metal goods were in great demand. The profits of Atlantic trade did not generate the European industrial revolution, but the Atlantic's edibles and consumables helped replenish European human 'energy systems', allowing the continent to overcome Malthusian constraints, and enabling African populations to sustain the Atlantic slave trade.[21]

Geography facilitated integration. Prevailing winds and currents—clockwise in the northern hemisphere and anticlockwise in the southern—help explain why Western Europe became the centre of the slave trade in the northern hemisphere and Brazil became its base in the southern hemisphere. Since the continental areas drained by rivers emptying into the Atlantic are about twice as great as those entering into the Pacific and Indian oceans combined, this single ocean's extensive riverine systems encouraged the deep penetration of hinterlands. Because ports on the Atlantic were always more tightly connected to oceanic-borne influences than interior locations, the distinction between 'near' and 'far' Atlantics, used in a Central American context, has more general applicability. In addition, islands were especially vital connectors and way stations. The prototype for plantation sugar production emerged on Atlantic islands such as Madeira and São Tomé off the coast of Africa; these same islands then became crucial places of exchange when their sugar booms faded; and yet other African islands, close to shore, sometimes located in rivers, became key centres of the slave trade; and

---

[20] Wim Klooster, 'Inter-Imperial Smuggling in the Americas, 1600–1800', in Bailyn and Denault (eds.), *Soundings in Atlantic History*, 141–80; Jorge M. Pedreira, 'From Growth to Collapse: Portugal, Brazil, and the Breakdown of the Old Colonial System (1760–1830)', *Hispanic American Historical Review*, 80/4 (2000), 839–64; Alan L. Karras, *Smuggling: Contraband and Corruption in World History* (Lanham, MD, 2010); chapter by John Russell-Wood.

[21] T. H. Breen, *The Marketplace of Revolution: How Consumer Politics Shaped American Independence* (New York, 2005); Kenneth Pomeranz, *The Great Divergence: China, Europe and the Making of the Modern World Economy* (Princeton, NJ, 2000).

the sugar-producing Caribbean islands, particularly in the French and British cases, became the hubs of empire.[22]

Integration was far from just economic or geographic. In the legal realm, institutions such as prize courts arose to deal with the rise of inter-imperial commercial competition; conversely, as planters grappled with the policing of their slaves, so they borrowed provisions of slave codes from neighbouring empires in a process of inter-imperial emulation. The scores of scientific expeditions as well as hundreds of individual engineers, botanists, architects, artists, and city planners who moved around the Atlantic collecting and forwarding useful data—experiencing, experimenting, eye-witnessing, and then regularizing, systematizing, and universalizing—contributed enormously to a circum-Atlantic exchange of knowledge, to which the rise of racial science was just one dimension. In familial arrangements, Atlantic migrations created in many places 'quasi marriage-free zones' or at the very least 'marriage-challenged zones'.[23] The 'consolidating and integrative' type of Atlantic polity embraces in its very name the absorptionist, expansionist, and incorporative forces that shaped the Atlantic world; and justifies consideration of, say, the Iroquois confederacy, the kingdom of Asante, and the Dutch empire in one analytical frame.[24] In terms of imperial governance, centralized authority was generally premised on delegation, on overlapping compromises, and above all on negotiation with local elites. Transatlantic exchanges even spurred a greater attention to the senses throughout the Atlantic world, leading some to propose a universal *sensus communis*.[25]

The existence of creoles, neither immigrants nor indigenes, but locally born peoples usually drawn either from newcomers alone or from mixtures of newcomers and natives, increasingly self-aware and conscious of themselves as separate and distinctive, contributed another distinguishing shared commonality to the Atlantic world. The word 'creole' (in Portuguese *crioulo* and Spanish *criollo*) originally referred to the offspring of Old World progenitors born in the New World (it even extended to plants and animals of Old World origin but produced in the New). More recently, linguists have appropriated the term to refer to the mixed languages that emerged among the native-born or slaves in contact situations; and increasingly the term has been more widely applied not just in the Americas but also in the Atlantic more broadly, to particularly cosmopolitan peoples noted for their cultural plasticity and social adaptability. The process of creolization in Africa is associated with cultural hybridity as people of mixed African and European ancestry, or Africans with no European antecedents but who worked closely with Europeans, became in effect bi-cultural people. Scholars term them Afro-Europeans or Eurafricans, and occasionally creoles. In the Americas creoles could be either slaves or members of the elite, as long as they were locally born. In the Hispanic world, by the eighteenth century the phenomenon of

---

[22] John R. Gillis, *Islands of the Mind: How the Human Imagination Created the Atlantic World* (New York, 2004).

[23] Chapter by Carole Shammas.

[24] Chapter by Elizabeth Mancke.   [25] Chapter by David Shields.

creole patriotism emerged, with local elites resenting the pretensions of *penisulares* (Spaniards), and lauding their combined indigenous and Hispanic pasts; the North American patriots who fought the British generally refrained from using a term with such Hispanic associations, preferring to describe themselves as 'American' or 'British-American', although those patriots who perpetrated the Boston Tea Party did attire themselves as Mohawk Indians. Whether local populations embraced or repudiated hybridity, it was a fact, and the emergence of creole populations throughout the Atlantic—however varied they were—was proof of commonality.[26]

War, always a catalyst of change, served to integrate as well as to divide, because, during wartime, empires often relaxed normal restrictions. Foreign ships might, for example, be welcomed for provisioning and trading purposes, thus encouraging inter-imperial cooperation, even as conflicts raged. The very word 'Atlantic' to describe the ocean became especially current during times of imperial warfare, precisely because awareness of that maritime space heightened during a crisis. Europeans as a whole waged war differently from Native Americans and Africans—on a larger scale, more lethally, and more unrestrainedly. Over time, however, convergence occurred as Native Americans and Africans adopted muskets as their principal armaments and engaged in more efficient killing along European lines. However, divergence was also apparent, as Europeans increasingly observed conventions for the conduct of warfare in their home theatre, even as it increased in scale, whereas smaller, unlimited, frenzied, frontier wars became more usual in the rest of the Atlantic. Also as warfare in Europe became more formalized and confined to discrete periods, it became a continuous feature of life in the rest of the Atlantic world.

While warfare in some respects rendered the Atlantic world of the eighteenth century a more integrated space, it (and particularly the Seven Years War, 1756–63, the first truly global war) also contributed to its re-segmentation into multiple polities, and in two phases. First this major conflagration involved most European powers, and conflict extended to overseas possessions because these were perceived to be contributing ever more significantly, and in many different ways, to the wealth of the states that competed for European hegemony. Then, in the interest of covering the costs of the debts that had accrued during the war, and of protecting territories that had been retained and/or gained, all Atlantic empires underwent a process of reorganization and reform. Metropolitan officials in Britain identified the looseness of imperial governance as a key problem and began efforts to tighten it. The French empire retooled and refocused on the Caribbean, which vigorously expanded. The Spanish Bourbons over-hauled their army and navy, modernized their bureaucracy, improved university education, boosted mineral yields, and wrested control over church property. Portu-gal's Braganza rulers, and especially the chief minister, the marquis of Pombal, oversaw a comprehensive reform of their empire, including the expulsion of the Jesuits. Renovation programmes, which included everything from information collecting to

---

[26] Charles Stewart (ed.), *Creolization: History, Ethnography, Theory* (Walnut Creek, CA, 2007).

agricultural improvement, and from better mapping to new penal codes, became part of the Enlightened state agenda.[27]

These reform programmes clarified the boundaries between the Atlantic empires of the various European powers whose governments became ever more determined to stamp out smuggling and other cross-border activity that had previously contributed to integration. To this degree war consciously contributed to segmentation of the Atlantic world, but it did so also in an unintended fashion because the reform programmes that were necessitated by the war produced resistance, revolt, and revolution almost everywhere. The first of these was the American War of Independence with its principal revolutionary outcome being the fashioning of a new republic from one large segment of what previously had been Britain's Atlantic empire. The origins of the American Revolution can be traced in no small measure to the attempt by the British Parliament to fund the 10,000 regulars stationed in North America at the end of the Seven Years War. In the Spanish world resentment of Bourbon policies designed to increase revenues and consolidate centralized control led to tax riots, culminating in the *Comunero* uprising in New Granada (modern Colombia) in the early 1780s. In the lusophone world, protests occurred in opposition to the expulsion of the Jesuits in 1759, which in turn owed much to the war fought by the Guaraní Indians who had settled in Jesuit missions.

Another factor accelerating segmentation was that imperial crises with resulting creole independence movements made it increasingly difficult for Native Americans to maintain whatever autonomy they had enjoyed in the past. Some Native American groups had been able to use balance of power diplomacy and diverse trading partners to maintain some cultural integrity, while those more deeply incorporated into the Atlantic economy through labour drafts or virtual enslavement had maintained some independence of action in their various engagements with Atlantic markets. As Native Americans were deprived of European protectors and dealt directly with white creoles who coveted both their labour and property, they became engaged with nativist movements that rejected all things Euro-American, and which were as much directed against mixed-race collaborators as they were against Euro-American oppressors. The emergence of American nation-states as one of the outcomes of segmentation therefore doomed the play-off system and generally forced two outcomes on Native Americans—subordinated incorporation or marginalized dependency—both of which cut them off from extensive participation in the Atlantic world.

How the American Revolution played out is well understood but it involved only thirteen mainland colonies, and the places in the British Atlantic empire that were most different from Britain—the West Indies, Nova Scotia, Quebec, and the Floridas—were the ones that remained loyal to the empire, from concerns either of security or of economic interest. Because the new state that emerged after its successful pursuit of war shared much with Britain in customs, laws, religion, and political economy, it was soon

[27] Gabriel Paquette (ed.), *Enlightened Reform in Southern Europe and its Atlantic Colonies* (Burlington, VT, 2009).

reincorporated into the world of Atlantic commerce with which North American merchants had been previously associated. One of its unforeseen consequences was that the pursuit of American independence advanced the antislavery agenda, but more so in Britain, where the loss of its thirteen colonies produced much soul searching, than in the newly emerged United States.

By way of contrast, the Revolution in Saint-Domingue was far more transformative than its American counterpart, because it involved a greater mass mobilization, saw more destruction, and resulted in the polity of Haiti determined to terminate the trade that underpinned the Atlantic commercial world. The 1791 slave uprising was the largest and most successful in history, and struck against slavery where the institution was strongest. Still it was replete with paradoxes. Although the Revolution was the worst nightmare of slave owners throughout the Americas, it stimulated a huge expansion of slavery elsewhere. Although slaves sometimes spoke in the language of republicanism, more often they presented themselves as defenders of church and king. In the beginning, the massive revolt furthered the abolitionist cause, but its excesses soon put abolitionists on the defensive. The example of Haiti might have encouraged slave resistance elsewhere in the Americas, but its immediate consequence was to make slave regimes more vigilant and stronger. Haiti, in the words of one historian, was 'both unforgettable and also unrepeatable'.[28]

If the American Revolution arose out of a crisis of integration, the Spanish American revolutions proceeded from a crisis of disintegration, when Napoleon's armies invaded Spain in 1808. And in the same way that most whites and free coloured activists in Saint-Domingue wanted self-rule and not independence, so most Spanish American creoles professed loyalty to the monarchy while seeking to expand their local autonomy. Although a plurality of creole patriotisms emerged within Spain's colonial empire all were too circumscribed to generate national movements for independence from Spain, and it was only the dissolution of the Spanish Monarchy that forced dissidents to move beyond seeking home rule within the traditional framework of the Spanish imperial monarchy. However, given the complex multi-racial composition of the populations within the several segments of Spain's Atlantic empire, the process of gaining independence proved almost as devastatingly costly in Spanish America as in Saint-Domingue. The savagery of civil war was, to a degree, related to the extent of ethnic divisions. Blacks and mulattos often formed the backbone of militia regiments drawn into the various conflicts; both sides armed slaves; and Indians and mestizos formed a majority of soldiers in some armies. The length and ferocity of the Spanish American revolutionary wars were notable, but once independence of the several new states had been achieved nobody could contemplate a return to the old regime given the sheer human cost of winning independence.

Historians frequently explain how all Atlantic revolutions were interconnected, with each one (and revolution also within France) successively influencing and informing the next. While not denying the importance of such linear influence, these essays point

---

[28] David P. Geggus (ed.), *The Impact of the Haitian Revolution in the Atlantic World* (Charleston, SC, 2001), 4, 13; Derek R. Peterson (ed.), *Abolitionism and Imperialism in Britain, Africa, and the Atlantic* (Athens, OH, 2010).

to the ways in which the totality of revolutions led to the disintegration of what had previously been a reasonably coherent Atlantic trading world. Also, while emphasizing revolution and nation-building, the essays also devote attention to places where the revolutionary message did not take hold, with, for example, the Haitian experience becoming an obstacle to decolonization in Cuba and other parts of the Caribbean. Brazil too proved largely impervious to Haiti's siren call, and its slave rebelliousness was inspired more by the discontent of the Muslim population of West Africa, many of whom were dispatched across the Atlantic as slaves in the aftermath of civil conflict there, than by Enlightenment ideology. In a reverse direction, the effects of the Atlantic revolutions on Africa were minimal. That the French abolition of slavery in 1794 did not extend to Senegal is telling, while Sierra Leone, conceived as an experiment in the viability of free labour in Africa, proved a failure. And while the abolitionist cause had advocates in almost every European and American polity, most African elites remained opposed to the abolition of the slave trade. Moreover, the shift from trading in slaves to so-called legitimate commerce probably increased demand for slaves in Africa, where they came to be employed in the production of the vegetable oils that became the staple of West Africa's exports. As a corollary, the adoption of revolutionary principles and the abandonment of the slave trade in various new states in the Americas did not necessarily bring an end to the institution of slavery; in fact, the number of people bound in slavery expanded greatly in the late eighteenth and early nineteenth centuries.

From the mid-fifteenth to the early nineteenth centuries, the Atlantic world formed a distinct regional entity. Its peculiar mix of idealism and exploitation, noble aspirations and brutal dynamism, had long coexisted in uneasy tension. But by the end of the period, the region's original integrity was breaking apart. The emergence of nation-states in some places and deepening colonialism in others was one major dichotomy. Those places where slavery was expanding and those where the institution was on the road to extinction constituted another fundamental division. The development of steam-powered transport in the nineteenth century meant that ever-increasing numbers of Europe's poor, including people from the eastern and southern extremes of that continent, could gain access to an Atlantic world for the first time. However, since the Atlantic world of this volume was one forged by trade, the overbearing factor is that by the early nineteenth century, American as well as European traders were able to (and did) operate on a global scale, and learned how to navigate the Pacific Ocean as readily as they did the Atlantic and Indian oceans. Consequently, the different commercial segments of the globe, which, with the exception of the Portuguese and possibly the Dutch overseas empires, had previously been linked to each other indirectly, principally through European hubs, became part of a single global market, which extended even to the market in human labour.[29] This

---

[29] Kevin H. O'Rourke and Jeffrey G. Williamson, 'When did Globalisation Begin?' and 'Once More: When did Globalisation Begin?', *European Review of Economic History*, 6 (2002), 23–50 and 8 (2004), 109–17.

shift was symbolized by the reluctant abandonment of slavery, as well as the slave trade (which together had been predominant characteristics of the Atlantic world) throughout the Americas as the nineteenth century proceeded, and the growing importation of a lowly paid primarily male work force from the more densely populated parts of Asia into the previous slave plantations.

BIBLIOGRAPHY

Armitage, David, and Michael J. Braddick (eds.), *The British Atlantic World, 1500–1800* (2nd edn. New York, 2009).

Bailyn, Bernard, *Atlantic History: Concept and Contours* (Cambridge, MA, 2005).

—— and Patricia L. Denault (eds.), *Soundings in Atlantic History: Latent Structures and Intellectual Currents, 1500–1830* (Cambridge, MA, 2009).

Benjamin, Thomas, *The Atlantic World: Europeans, Africans, Indians and their Shared History, 1400–1900* (New York, 2009).

Delbourgo, James, and Nicholas Dew (eds.), *Science and Empire in the Atlantic World* (New York, 2008).

Elliott, John, *Empires of the Atlantic World: Britain and Spain in America, 1492–1830* (New Haven, CT, 2006).

Greene, Jack P., and Philip D. Morgan (eds.), *Atlantic History: A Critical Reappraisal* (New York, 2009).

Hancock, David, *Oceans of Wine: Madeira and the Organization of the Atlantic World, 1640–1815* (New Haven, CT, 2009).

Schwartz, Stuart B., *All Can Be Saved: Religious Tolerance and Salvation in the Iberian Atlantic World* (New Haven, CT, 2008).

Thornton, John, *Africa and Africans in the Making of the Atlantic World, 1400–1800* (New York, 1998).

PART I

EMERGENCE

CHAPTER 2

......

THE WORLDS OF EUROPEANS, AFRICANS, AND AMERICANS, *c.*1490

......

JOAN-PAU RUBIÉS

INTRODUCTION

......

Writing about Western Sudan in the 1330s, the Arab historian Al-'Umarī told the story of an expedition of 200 ships sent by the king of Mali to discover the furthest limits of the ocean. From this only one man returned, describing a large river where all other ships were lost. This news inspired the sultan to personally lead a second expedition of 2,000 ships, which was never seen again. Hence Mansa Mūsā, the king's deputy, came to power.[1]

One might be tempted to identify this river across the ocean as the Amazon. It is however the utter implausibility of this story that lies at the heart of our understanding of how it came to be that Europeans alone, precisely in this period, began to discover and colonize Atlantic islands, persistently learning of the ocean's powerful winds and currents, and eventually establishing a complex system of trade, settlements, and forced labour that linked three continents across the vast sea. Mansa Mūsā's story, perhaps a legitimizing discourse for his irregular succession to the Mande kingdom of Mali, acquires a status similar to a fascinating 1960s novel concerning a fifteenth-century Mexican discovery of Spain: it illuminates what happened with reference to what did not, or could not, have occurred.[2] Hence, when in 1455 and 1456 the Venetian explorer

---

[1] *Corpus of Early Arabic Sources for West African History*, trans. J. F. P. Hopkins, ed. N. Levtzion and J. F. P. Hopkins (Cambridge, 1980), 268–9.
[2] Avel.lí Artís Gener, *Palabras de Opoton el Viejo* (Mexico, 1992).

Alvise Cadamosto sailed up the River Gambia hoping to establish trade with the Mandinkas, whose chiefs still owed residual allegiance to a now-declining sultan of Mali, he emphasized that whilst the 'black people' navigated the rivers skilfully and quickly with huge canoes (*almadie*), they were amazed by the European caravels with their masts, sails, and anchors: never before, Cadamosto judged, had they seen anything like that, although it soon became apparent that they had already heard unflattering reports about Europeans, who for some years had been buying slaves at the Senegal River.[3] It is rare to have such an early account of an African reaction to European visitors:

> Little by little the blacks drew nearer, gaining confidence in us, until at last they drew alongside my caravel; and one of them who could understand my interpreter boarded the ship, marvelling greatly at her, and at our method of navigating by means of sails, for they know of no method except by rowing with oars . . . He was overcome with astonishment at the sight of us white men, and marvelled no less at our clothing . . . [4]

In effect, the Atlantic system of the early modern centuries was primarily the creation of European navigation, trade, and colonization. Although the peoples of Africa and America were by no means passive spectators and played crucial roles in shaping the Atlantic system, it is the primacy of European agency that first needs to be addressed. Columbus' crossing of 1492 was the culmination of a period of Atlantic explorations rather than an isolated initiative, and those explorations were, in turn, the product of a number of structural conditions in late medieval Europe, conditions that made possible the careers of men like Henry the Navigator and Columbus himself. This essay will approach the issue in two ways. First, it will analyse the late medieval sources of the European dynamic involvement with the Atlantic. A second section will compare European conditions with those obtaining in Africa and America.

EUROPEAN EXPLORATION OF THE ATLANTIC 1300–1492

The voyages undertaken by the Portuguese in the Atlantic in the fifteenth century were extensions of those organized by the trading nations of the western Mediterranean. In effect, the Portuguese relied on colonial, cartographic, and some navigational techniques of Mediterranean origin, in order to pursue their Atlantic agenda. They also

---

[3] *Navigazioni di Alvise Ca' da Mosto* in Ramusio, *Navigazioni e viaggi*, ed. Marica Milanesi (Turin, 1978), i. 518–19. For a text with all the manuscript variants see Tullia Gasparrini Leporace, *Le navigazioni atlantiche del veneziano Alvise da Mosto* (Rome, 1966).

[4] *Navigazioni*, 526 (a passage referring to the subsequent voyage of 1456). I have also consulted the annotated translation offered by P. E. H. Hair, *The Discovery of River Gambra by Richard Jobson 1623*, The Hakluyt Society, series III (London, 1999), 251.

benefited from fourteenth-century oceanic voyages, mostly by Genoese and Catalan traders from the island of Majorca. These traders were active in the North African ports of Tunis, Bugie, and Ceuta, where they learnt that the sources of gold lay beyond the Sahara. Thus, information concerning the trans-Saharan caravan trade reached Europe. In the remarkable atlas made *c.*1375 for the princes of Aragon by Cresques Abraham, a Jewish Majorcan cartographer, the 'lord of the blacks of Guinea' Mansa Mali (of the same dynasty that elsewhere claimed to have crossed the Atlantic) achieved an almost mythical status as 'the wealthiest and noblest lord of those parts, for the abundance of gold that he orders to be gathered in his land'.[5] Despite some anachronisms in Cresques' illustrated world map, evidence from subsequent works of the same school suggests that information on the Sudan and on the Portuguese exploration of the Atlantic coast was regularly updated.[6]

Fourteenth-century Mediterranean traders had also sailed to Flanders and England, the Genoese using the Andalusian ports of Seville and Cádiz as bases. Others (such as the Venetian Cadamosto) followed in the fifteenth century, occasionally working with the princes of the house of Avis in Portugal, who also enticed Majorcan cartographers. By the 1480s some Italians were important investors in the licensed trade of the Atlantic islands and mainland Africa, as far as Benin, notably the Florentine Bartolomeo Marchionni, who had settled in Lisbon. Building on such connections, the Portuguese thus achieved the hybridization of the two largely distinct navigational and commercial traditions of the Mediterranean and the Atlantic.

The most enduring legacy of the explorers of the fourteenth century was the mapping and commercial exploitation of the Canary Islands, including some interesting attempts at colonization or even missionary work. Few episodes are as revealing of the deep economic, institutional, and ideological roots of the European conquest of the Atlantic.[7] The first expedition to the Canaries—quickly identified with the 'Fortunate Islands' of antiquity—by the Genoese Lanzarotto Malocello (possibly including Portuguese sailors) can be dated to 1336 and led to the island still today named Lanzarote. It was already represented (together with nearby Fuerteventura) in Angelino Dulcert's portolan chart of 1339, bearing the arms of Genoa. News of this expedition led to others, of which a number are documented. Giovanni Boccaccio, for example, wrote in some detail about the Canary Islands on the basis of reports brought by an expedition of 1341. Whilst the kings of Portugal and Castile soon engaged in rival claims to the rights to conquer the islands, the Catalans made the first sustained effort at colonization, with

---

[5] For a modern edition see *L´Atlas català de Cresques Abraham* (Barcelona, 1975).

[6] These illustrated *mappaemundi*, based on portolan charts, were non-Ptolemaic. Later in the fifteenth century there were hybrids that sought to combine new and classical information, such as the so-called 'Genoese' map of 1457, but most Iberian sailors made limited use of parallels and meridians and continued to rely on rhumbs and compass, as did Juan de la Cosa in his famous world chart of 1500 that first showed the lands of America.

[7] Felipe Fernández-Armesto, *Before Columbus: Exploration and Colonisation from the Mediterranean to the Atlantic, 1229–1492* (London, 1987); Robert Bartlett, *The Making of Europe: Conquest, Colonization and Cultural Change 950–1350* (London, 1993).

various expeditions recorded for the years 1342, 1346, 1352, 1360, 1369, and 1386. Their nature varied from conquest and commerce (mainly involving slave raiding) to missionary work. For example, the 1351 voyage to Gran Canaria included twelve native converts who spoke Catalan being taken back to assist a mission; even a bishop was appointed.[8]

While these fourteenth-century efforts led to relatively accurate mapping of the islands, they did not result in permanent settlement until King Henry III of Castile forced his sponsorship upon two French adventurers, Jean de Béthencourt and Gadifer de la Salle, who from 1402 colonized (or re-colonized) the islands of Lanzarote, Fuerteventura, and Hierro. Prince Henry sought repeatedly to reassert the Portuguese claim. However, a number of military disasters (especially against native resistance) and diplomatic miscalculations frustrated Portuguese efforts, and eventually the issue was solved by treaty to the benefit of Castile. In exchange for letting Castile complete the conquest of the Canaries unhindered, Portugal retained the Cape Verde Islands and a hard-won monopoly on South Atlantic trade along the African coasts, at a time when the sources of African gold had finally been found in the Gulf of Guinea.

Fifteenth-century ventures to the Canaries and elsewhere reveal that while early initiatives of exploration were often multinational, the consistency of political patronage was crucial for the colonizing success of particular nations and the consolidation of navigational breakthroughs. The Portuguese, led by Prince Henry and later by John II, excelled precisely in this capacity. Henry's activities were especially varied. Initially, his patronage of African exploration beyond Cape Bojador was secondary to a crusade against Morocco and to the colonization of Atlantic islands, mainly to create new sources of revenue. While the Moroccan enterprise proved a fiasco, the colonization of Madeira and the Azores compensated for failure in the Canaries. What mattered was the determination and consistency with which Henry pursued these ventures, rather than discovery for its own sake.

Fourteenth-century cartography suggests that Madeira and perhaps also the Azores were already known. The case of the Azores is uncertain because contemporary maps depicted both real and imaginary islands, often mixing mythical names with new ones, but by 1427 the Portuguese had certainly 'rediscovered' them, and Gabriel de Vallseca's chart of 1439 offered a reasonably accurate representation. Prince Henry made a success of the colonization of these two uninhabited archipelagos through a system of feudal grants, seigniorial monopolies, and temporary fiscal privileges, all inspired by well-tried medieval techniques of colonization in the Iberian Peninsula. Madeira was colonized quickly from the early 1420s; it was fertile and soon a successful settler economy was developed based on timber, wheat, wine, and (from the 1450s) sugar. The naturalized Italian Bartolomeo Perestrello, Columbus' future father-in-law, was an active leader of that process. The Azores were colonized over several decades, with a significant contribution by Flemish settlers. They also produced wheat and sugar, but on a lesser scale.

---

[8] Antonio Rumeu de Armas, *El obispado de Telde: misionarios mallorquines y catalanes en el Atlántico* (Madrid, 1960).

Through these experiences the Portuguese learned to navigate the Atlantic by mastering currents and winds and by adopting ships suited to Atlantic conditions. The square-rigged *naos*, a fifteenth-century Iberian hybrid of Mediterranean and Atlantic ships, could maximize carrying capacity and wind power in the open ocean, while the caravel, a light vessel usually reliant on lateen sails, was suited to exploring shallow waters, but required larger crews and had less cargo space.[9] The early exploration of the Atlantic by southern Europeans had largely relied upon navigational skills developed in the Mediterranean from the twelfth to the fourteenth centuries. For example, the Canaries could be reached by the traditional methods of coastal navigation, and were incorporated into portolan charts, which showed the coasts in great detail. They also appeared in contemporary world maps (*mappaemundi*), a richly illustrated and more aristocratic product, not meant to be taken on board, which incorporated political and ethnographic information, frequently extending its scope beyond the areas of European navigation. These charts and maps used a system of rhumbs which, through the use of the compass, allowed pilots to determine direction with reasonable accuracy. The lack of a significant magnetic variation in the Mediterranean made it possible to do this without recourse to latitude or longitude, and Italian and Catalan pilots also used traverse tables, useful for calculating distances on a plane chart provided the ship's speed was correctly estimated. The challenge was to learn to navigate the open and uncharted waters of the Atlantic, where reliance on dead reckoning was inappropriate. The astrolabe and quadrant were employed for astronomical observation but rarely used on board because it was difficult to make an accurate observation of the relative position of stars or the sun due to ship movement. For navigation in northern waters latitude was often calculated with naked-eye observations of celestial bodies like the Pole Star. In effect, although the Atlantic wind system was relatively stable, prevailing winds and currents made it difficult when using these Mediterranean methods to sail further south than Cape Juby and return safely. The great achievement of the Portuguese in the fifteenth century was, through experience, to master the winds and currents of the South Atlantic. Under Henry they did not use nautical astronomy—it was only after reaching Sierra Leone in 1460 that there is evidence of a quadrant being used by Diogo Gomes, and then only to correct the distances entered on a portolan-style chart, rather than to calculate absolute latitudes (latitude scales had not yet been introduced). Eventually, as they sailed south towards the equator and lost sight of the Pole Star, the Portuguese had to learn to calculate latitude by observing solar altitudes. This, in turn, required the use of astronomical tables (for solar declination) as well as the astrolabe—a complex application of late medieval science encouraged by John II in the 1480s.

Determination and political will, therefore, rather than any technological breakthrough, explain the rounding of 'Cape Bojador' in 1434. The idea was not novel since,

[9] These differences explain why the hybrid *nao* or the large carrack, often combining square sails with a lateen mizzen, would become the key vessel for long-distance oceanic voyages. See also Rodger in this volume.

already in 1291, two Genoese, the Vivaldi brothers, seeking to reach India by sea, had attempted to sail around Africa in a galley (and disappeared). By 1346 the Majorcan Jaume Ferrer sought to reach the 'riu d'or' or river of gold, possibly the Senegal River, a more modest aim that continued to inspire Europeans up to the time of Prince Henry. Although the name derived from classical geography, we have already noted that knowledge of the trans-Saharan trade in gold dust was transmitted to Europeans in the *mappamundi* of Cresques Abraham, which also recorded (and illustrated) Ferrer's voyage. The Majorcan Jews who dominated Catalan cartography had traditional connections to the ports of North Africa, and were able to obtain knowledge about 'the land of the blacks of Guinea' with remarkably few concessions to classical mythology. However, it is likely that Ferrer's *uxer* (a transport ship with oars and lateen sails) also failed to return, because ignorance of the powerful currents in that latitude and of the best ships to navigate the prevailing winds made it difficult to succeed with a single attempt. These failed sailings were not forgotten, and contributed to the belief that it was hazardous to navigate beyond 'Cape Bojador'.

Obviously, Gomes Eanes de Zurara, the chronicler of Prince Henry's African ventures (*Chronicle of the Deeds of Arms in the Capture of Guinea*, c.1457–1465), rhetorically elaborated the mythology of Cape Bojador to serve his chivalric panegyric. Whilst the practical difficulties of navigation were real enough, most cosmographers familiar with the largely empirical Italian and Catalan cartography would have rejected the idea that the lands beyond were uninhabited. Henry's real contribution was that he insisted on new attempts (as many as fifteen are mentioned by Zurara), until eventually the navigation was accomplished under the direction of Gil Eanes, who established that it was possible to continue sailing southwards and return. The river of gold—the Senegal—turned out to be further than expected, but the Atlantic was progressively opened up along the West African coast. By 1441 Nuno Tristão had reached Cape Blanco, and in 1444 Cape Verde had also been reached. The exploration of the Senegal and Gambia rivers soon followed, which made it possible to actually find some of the gold of the Sudan, although less than expected. The Portuguese were able to exploit the new route by abandoning their practice of kidnapping Berber and Black coastal peoples, which proved costly wherever West Africans could respond with canoe warfare and poisoned arrows, and by instead negotiating with local powers (as Cadamosto had tried to do) in order to buy slaves, ivory, and civet musk. In exchange, Europeans bartered horses, textiles, beads, and metal hardware (although the sale of arms to Muslims was theoretically forbidden). According to Diogo Gomes, a horse in 1462 would trade for twelve or even fifteen people.[10] The European market for slaves made all this trade possible. When Henry died in 1460, Portuguese sailors (or Italians under Portuguese patronage) were about to reach Sierra Leone, which opened up the

---

[10] Diogo Gomes de Sintra, *Descobrimento primeiro da Guiné*, ed. Aires A. Nascimento (Lisbon, 2002), 88. On the problems of the *De prima inventione Guinee* see Peter Russell, *Prince Henry the Navigator: A Life* (New Haven, CT, 2000), 327–33.

trade in malagueta pepper (albeit not comparable to Indian pepper), and the uninhabited Cape Verde Islands, that provided a base for a permanent colony.

The story of how between 1469 and 1474 Fernão Gomes, a private investor from Lisbon, paid an annual sum for a contract to explore 100 miles of coast each year beyond Sierra Leone, in exchange for a lease of a substantial portion of the crown's monopoly of trade, points to the flexible combination of private capital and state control that would distinguish many crucial phases of Atlantic exploration. In this case the formula proved effective, since the coast between Sierra Leone and the island of Fernando Po in the Gulf of Guinea—an unfamiliar stretch of tropical forests—included the long-sought access to supplies of gold in Ghana. By the end of the contract the monarchy was ready to take direct control, erecting a permanent fortress on the mainland in order to access the supply of gold—an unprecedented and risky move given the hazards to health and safety. The account of the founding of São Jorge da Mina in 1482 given by John II's court chronicler Rui de Pina reveals that despite Portuguese assertiveness (they even shipped pre-cut stones and mortar from Europe in order to speed up the building), a complex negotiation with local Akan rulers proved necessary. Pina noted, for example, that the local chief of Fetu 'Caramansa' (Kwamena Ansah) at first objected to the Portuguese building a fortress, and threatened that his people would abandon the area unless satisfied with the conditions of trade. It was soon understood that a system of presents and preferential prices, or bribes, was, here, as elsewhere in West Africa, part of the business.[11]

The advantages of long-distance maritime navigation meant that the Portuguese were not limited to trading between Europe and particular African locations such as Mina, but could also develop regional trades. These, in fact, lowered the costs of importing gold to Europe, whilst stimulating further exploration and contacts, even colonies. The kingdom of Benin on the western Niger Delta, for example, produced some excellent pepper that was being bought by Europeans in Gwato in the mid-1480s; Benin also became, for a few decades, a source of slaves for the Akan states of the Gold Coast. A few years later a sugar plantation based on slave labour was developed on the island of São Tomé, fed with slaves bought in Kongo by a special privilege issued in 1493 for that island's settlers. Therefore, by 1490 the Portuguese were not only tapping pre-existing regional trades in Africa for a European market, or merely diverting the old trans-Saharan caravan route, but were also creating new exchanges in West Africa. These trades were increasingly conducted through intermediaries of mixed ethnic origin; Luso-Africans who either lived in island settlements such as the Cape Verde Islands (sometimes doing business at odds with the monopolistic claims of the crown), or as *lançados* under the protection of African rulers, who found their services useful. Luso-African traders, quite a few of Jewish origin (some settled in São Tomé), also helped spread Portuguese-based creole languages which became a lingua franca for trade in the African Atlantic.

[11] John W. Blake, *Europeans in West Africa 1450–1560*, 2 vols., The Hakluyt Society (London, 1942), i. 71–8.

The discovery and exploitation of gold and new supplies of slaves in the Gulf of Guinea did not slow down exploration. Rather the contrary, a sense of urgency was apparent throughout the decisive decade of the 1480s. In the 1470s and 1480s the west Atlantic trading fleets were so regular, and the Portuguese mastered the wind systems of the Atlantic so quickly, that single expeditions could become ever more ambitious. In 1483 Diogo Cão, a squire of John II, reached the River Zaire, establishing an initial contact with the kingdom of Kongo (which soon proved fruitful), and went on exploring beyond Cape Santa Maria. The African coastline continued further than expected, and the long-cherished ambition to reach Prester John in Abyssinia had to be deferred again. It became apparent that the Portuguese could only hope to reach their semi-mythical Christian ally by circumnavigating Africa rather than by penetrating the river systems that supposedly connected the interior of West Africa with the Nile. The voyage by Bartolomeu Dias that finally reached the Cape of Good Hope in January 1488 probably reassured King John that he had been correct to dismiss Columbus' project to seek Asia by sailing westwards.

The European dynamic had a powerful religious aspect that went beyond the search for Prester John as a crusading ally. Papal bulls were solicited by the Iberian monarchies to provide them with a legal framework for negotiating the monopoly of trade and conquest in infidel areas. A bull such as *Romanus Pontifex*, granted by Nicholas V in 1455, left little room for ambiguity: all the lands and peoples of 'Guinea' (West Africa) were placed under the jurisdiction of the king of Portugal, and Castilian claims to the same rights were denied. Evangelization therefore became an inescapable obligation, although the Portuguese did little in practice until the 1480s, when John II took charge of business in Guinea. Despite this delay, evangelization was more than a pretext for plunder, trade, or conquest, and the possibility of conversion to Christianity occasioned high diplomatic encounters and novel cultural exchanges between the Portuguese court and various African kingdoms whose results were not necessarily negligible. The most remarkable success was the conversion in 1491 of the king of Kongo, an independent ruler, after only a few preliminary exchanges. Whilst commerce was still embryonic, there were early petitions for military assistance, and it seems obvious the process was driven by an African royal agenda that included access to unique European goods. There was another conversion attempt in Senegal, where the Jolof king 'Bemoim', whose succession was being contested, sought help from Portugal. In 1488 he became an exile at the court of John II, where, under duress, he converted to Christianity. Although the operation failed (the African pretender was actually murdered by a Portuguese captain as he was being conveyed by a fleet back to Senegal), the case remains remarkable because here Christianity was competing directly with Islam.[12]

Looking at Atlantic exploration as a process, it is worth emphasizing the strategic, economic, and cultural value that island colonization had for Europeans. Arguim, Cape

---

[12] Peter Russell, 'White Kings on Black Kings: Rui de Pina and the Problem of Black African Sovereignty', in *Medieval and Renaissance Studies in Honour of Robert Brian Tate* (Oxford, 1986).

Verde, and São Tomé were all secure bases for trade with the mainland, and the latter two were also suitable for sugar plantations sustained by a massive use of African slaves (unlike the sugar production in the Canaries and Madeira, where European labour remained important). The Cape Verde Islands, due to irregular rainfall, were more difficult to settle, until they were granted trading privileges in the Senegambia region, which led to a Luso-African commercial economy largely outside crown control. Islands also proved crucial for widening European navigational experience in the Atlantic. Columbus, for example, conducted business with his wife's relatives in Madeira, but had also to sailed north to Galway, and south to Mina not long after the Portuguese had built their fort there.[13] Moreover, powerful European myths stimulated the search for Atlantic islands. The Canaries were understood to be the Fortunate Islands of antiquity, and it seemed reasonable that other islands in the medieval cartographic tradition, such as Antilia, Brasil, or St Brendan's Island of the Blessed, would also be located. The difficulty of distinguishing between mythical and real islands helps explain the persistence of efforts to explore the North Atlantic, and various commissions can be documented from the 1460s to the 1490s. Rumours of sightings by sailors abounded (Columbus was a keen collector of such stories), and there were numerous Portuguese efforts to sail westward from the Azores to find 'Antilia' or the 'seven cities', including those of Luca di Cazana, a Genoese settler. Some voyages departed from Bristol in the 1480s, and perhaps the 1490s, in search of 'Brasil'.[14]

Whilst cartographic fantasy inspired these fruitless attempts, the idea of reaching Asia by sailing westwards was being advocated both in the 1470s by Paolo Toscanelli, a Florentine armchair cosmographer, and in the 1480s by Christopher Columbus, a Genoese sailor-entrepreneur. Columbus' genius, or luck, was that by starting from the Canary Islands (rather than the Azores) he found the correct winds for the crossing. One of the unintended consequences of Castilian success in the Canary Islands was that it enabled the Catholic monarchs to become the patrons of any such successful voyage. What Columbus eventually found was not the lands described by Marco Polo, but rather several previously unknown islands. Their naked inhabitants were obviously too uncivil to belong to urbanized Cathay, and could more easily be compared to the 'bestial' Canary islanders; although they proved less fierce, they were treated similarly. Whilst the colonization of Hispaniola proved more difficult than Columbus had led everybody to expect, he continued his explorations by sailing first around Cuba and, in a subsequent expedition of 1498, along a southern latitude that led him to the South American mainland. Until his death, he aspired to connect the islands he had found to the India and Cathay he had read about (he was encouraged by the mouths of the

---

[13] It was during these voyages that Columbus miscalculated the length of the degree, shortening the earth's circumference. By taking the altitude of the sun with a quadrant, Columbus thus sought to confirm Alfraganus' calculation of the degree to the meridian with a value of 56⅔ miles (not realizing that the Arabic miles were considerably longer than the Roman), where many other cosmographers assumed a value of 66⅔ miles.

[14] Perhaps these voyages involved some knowledge of Newfoundland or at least of some fisheries to the west of Iceland—see Rodger in this volume.

Orinoco River which to him suggested proximity to the terrestrial paradise). Meanwhile news of his achievements had spread, and other adventurers, notably John Cabot, were stimulated to offer their services to rival princes. In 1497 Cabot had reached Newfoundland and Cape Breton Island (in modern Canada), claiming them for Henry VII of England. He too was convinced he had been in the vicinity of Cathay, but unlike Columbus, who always found his way, Cabot was lost on a subsequent voyage.

European traders, navigators, and chart makers sought geographical knowledge for practical purposes, overwhelmingly favouring empirical methods, and towards the end of the fifteenth century pilots used tables of solar declination to calculate latitudes. However, it seems fair to conclude that the exploration of the Atlantic was never primarily a scientific exercise. On the contrary, from the fourteenth century onwards European motivations consistently combined economic, strategic, and ideological factors. Fishing, slaves, and the search for the sources of gold were crucial for the exploration of the West African coast, whilst the Atlantic archipelagos were settled to produce a variety of goods for export, and were also seen to have a strategic value for further exploration. However, for the princes who became patrons of voyages, all such activities were also conceived as elements of a 'crusade' against Islam. Such ideas proved especially useful to the monarchs of Portugal and Castile when soliciting papal support for monopolistic claims to discovery, colonization, and trade, but it was often more than that: in the millenarian atmosphere of the fifteenth century, influenced by the Ottoman threat upon what remained of the Christian empire of Constantinople, the war against Islam was a pious action which moved souls within aristocratic circles. Similarly, whilst the 'gentile' peoples encountered in the Canary Islands or in Africa were not directly the object of any crusade, they were soon subject to an ideology of evangelization and potential conquest which rarely excluded the immediate possibility of slavery, through violent raid or by purchase. In this context any supposed tensions between science and religion, or between religious mission and violence, were curiously limited. Columbus himself offers an example of how Europeans could combine religious ideology, even fanaticism, with economic calculations and practical know-how. That he was imbued with a sense of providential mission linked to the idea of financing the Christian reconquest of Jerusalem is well established. It remains striking how, in his written account of the naked Tainos he encountered in the Bahamas in October 1492, Columbus immediately, consistently, and effortlessly moved from the theme of a simple people without sect or religion who might easily be converted to Christianity, to the idea that these same people, who knew nothing of European weapons, would be easy to subjugate and should make good servants.[15] These thoughts, recorded in the journal that Columbus addressed to the Catholic monarchs, obviously sought to appeal with a single image of human innocence to both their distinct religious and economic concerns.

A second conclusion is that the ingredients of the later Portuguese and Spanish empires in the Atlantic were already present in the expeditions of the fourteenth and

---

[15] Christopher Columbus, *Journal of the First Voyage*, ed. and trans. B. W. Ife (Warminster, 1990), 28–30.

fifteenth centuries. Indeed, the way some peripheral European nations approached the Atlantic as a privileged area for economic opportunities with additional political and religious significance created the conditions for the great expeditions of Columbus and Vasco da Gama, by which Europeans almost simultaneously crossed the Atlantic and reached the trade of the East. Incremental knowledge of the seas, innovative development of ships and charts, an international network of merchant investment in maritime ventures, the legal model by which national monarchies could, with papal authorization, claim a monopoly of exploration and trade in particular regions, and, finally, well-tried methods of economic exploitation, either through selective colonization or peaceful factory trading, were all firmly in place by the end of the 1480s. It was therefore no accident that a successful Atlantic crossing took place towards the end of the fifteenth century, even though many of the specific circumstances (notably that the Catholic monarchs controlled the venture as rulers of Castile) might have easily been otherwise. Columbus was not the only person to have the idea; he was however the kind of experienced sailor who, crucially inspired by a massive miscalculation of the size of the earth, could, with arrogance and persistence, secure the necessary royal patronage, and skilfully find his way.

WESTERN EUROPE, WEST AFRICA, AND ATLANTIC AMERICA, 1300–1500: COMPARISONS AND CONTRASTS

The worlds of Europeans, Africans, and Americans c.1490 offered a complex mosaic of ethnic and cultural diversity. For millennia they had been isolated from each other, especially if we adopt an Atlantic perspective (the Mediterranean had since antiquity been an area of intense interaction between Africa and Europe).

Throughout the fifteenth century West Africa and Europe had become remarkably connected, whilst the Americas were about to be dragged violently into contact with them. At the same time, within each continental mass, levels of economic, political, and cultural integration varied enormously. Europe was by far the most integrated region. While the Mediterranean remained an area of continuing exchanges and shared heritages, it was also a shifting religious and military frontier. Latin Christendom, however, had brought together Mediterranean and Atlantic maritime traditions, and now reached unprecedented levels of economic development and cultural sophistication. By contrast, the world of Islam had its main focus in the East, encompassing a vast area of economic and cultural exchanges stretching into Asia by land and sea. Certainly, Islam also played a major role in the integration of North Africa with sub-Saharan Africa, although in Western Sudan (as opposed to the Indian Ocean) this was done almost exclusively through internal routes crossing the Sahara, and the kings of Mali and Songhai were more likely to travel to Egypt and Mecca than to gaze towards the sea with their remote Atlantic subjects.

Nevertheless, the three major economic and cultural areas of West Africa—Berber and Arab North Africa, upper Guinea (an ethnically complex region inhabited by speakers of Wolof, Fulbe, Mande, and West Atlantic languages), and the Kwa-speaking areas of lower Guinea (representing the family of languages that extended from the Akan in the west to the Igbo in the east)—were all connected, through the caravan route, the extensive river systems of the Western Sudan, and the activities of Muslim merchants.[16] Of all the Atlantic peoples encountered by the Portuguese, the western Bantu speakers of Kongo and Angola were perhaps the most culturally and economically isolated.[17]

The American Atlantic was not a significant centre for economic and cultural exchanges except for the Arawak-speaking Caribbean, where the Antilles were connected to South America and its huge river systems (which, as in Africa, served as key communication channels). The most integrated and culturally sophisticated region was Mesomerica, but although the late Maya developed a coastal trading route between the Gulf of Mexico and Central America, the imperial heartland was located firmly inland, in the Mexican plateau. Neither the numerous Algonquian-speaking peoples of coastal North America living between Florida and Canada, nor the Tupi-Guaraní of coastal Brazil, had an urban civilization, let alone a powerful system of maritime trade, although both lived a sedentary life in agricultural villages and under chiefdoms.[18] The Jesuit José de Acosta, in his overtly Eurocentric classification of barbarians, would have probably categorized them with the Tainos of Hispaniola, as small self-governing communities with elective war leaders. However, he placed the Tupi cannibals at the bottom of the scale as wild, lawless savages.[19]

How did these different worlds compare? One fundamental aspect that requires attention is religion. Europeans were militant Christians committed to a universalizing impulse, either through direct confrontation with Islam, or through the idea of converting gentiles. In sub-Saharan West Africa there existed an expanding frontier between Islam and polytheist or animist religions, roughly in the savannah, where courts and traders were agents of the spread of Islam and, with it, of literacy. Muslim traders, often operating as ethnic diasporas, penetrated southwards of the kingdoms of

[16] John Thornton, *Africa and Africans in the Making of the Atlantic World 1400–1800* (2nd edn. Cambridge, 1998).

[17] David Birmingham suggests that there was little trade between the Gulf of Guinea and the western coast of Central Africa: 'Central Africa from Cameroun to the Zambezi', *Cambridge History of Africa* (Cambridge, 1977), iii. 543.

[18] Compare Anna Roosevelt, 'The Maritime Highland, Forest Dynamic and the Origins of Complex Culture', in B. Trigger and W. Washburn (eds.), *Cambridge History of the Native Peoples of the Americas* (Cambridge, 1996), iii/1. 325; and John Monteiro, 'The Crises and Transformations of Invaded Societies: Coastal Brazil in the Sixteenth Century', ibid. 973–89.

[19] Acosta, *Historia natural y moral de las Indias* (Seville, 1590), book 6, ch. 19, and with slight variations in his *De procuranda Indorum salute* (1588). See also Anthony Pagden, *The Fall of Natural Man* (Cambridge, 1982), 162–8.

Songhay or Mali, as far as the Gold Coast and the Niger Delta. Given that the Portuguese sought to spread Christianity to these areas, the two monotheistic religions came into competition (although Christianity was not always perceived as purely monotheistic). At the same time commerce was usually conducted on the basis of mutual tolerance, for example in the Gambia River, where many Mande rulers and merchants were Muslims. Where Christian evangelization had potential, as in the Kongo kingdom south of the Zaire River, the initial process was largely driven by local agendas, in this case a royal elite with centralizing tendencies. However, a precondition for conversions was the existence of analogous beliefs in the power of the supernatural in Christian Europe, Muslim North Africa, and 'animist' Africa. This explains the possibility for rapid religious convergence in cultural areas never previously in contact.

Conditions were different in the Americas, where the arrival of the Spanish proved traumatic, and the conquests paved the way for a massive programme of acculturation. However, religious convergence sometimes occurred here too: when the Spanish led by Cortés reached Mexico, they spoke about God to people who believed in gods. Conceptions of the divinity might have been very different, but the importance attached to the role of spiritual forces in human affairs was widely shared (hence the prevalence of divination and magic rituals) and not always distinguishable from access to exotic technologies; this facilitated the creation of a common ground for a rather one-sided religious transformation which the military conquest could only accelerate. Unsurprisingly, over time, profound differences reasserted themselves, for example in the form of persistent 'idolatries' that the Church sought to extirpate.

From an Atlantic perspective, another aspect that invites comparison relates to attitudes to the sea, and in particular navigation. One under-explored question is why Arab sailors did not export their technology to the African coastline beyond coastal Morocco when, for centuries, they had controlled the straits of Gibraltar and much of the trade of the Mediterranean.[20] However, this hegemony was to collapse very quickly. Between the tenth and the twelfth centuries, Muslim navigation lost its technical superiority over that of European Christians. As the frontiers of Christendom expanded in Spain and Sicily, European sailors, especially the Genoese, established a maritime and commercial supremacy in the western Mediterranean that proved highly consequential for the exploration of the African Atlantic. As early as 1153 the Almohads (notwithstanding their militancy in Spain) had signed treaties granting trading privileges to the Genoese and, in 1168, to the Pisans, and these Italian traders created *funduqs* and operated as far as the Atlantic port of Massa. Subsequently, European maritime superiority only increased. When in 1339 some Genoese sold slaves from the Canary Islands to the sultan of Morocco, the latter sought information about their customs, but the navigation was entirely left to the 'Franks': as Ibn Khaldún explained,

---

[20] See however Raymond Mauny, *Les Navigations médiévales sur les côtes sahariennes antérieures à la découverte portugaise* (Lisbon, 1960), and, more recently, C. Picard, *L'Océan Atlantique musulman au moyen âge* (Paris, 1997).

'one only reaches the eternal islands by chance, never on purpose', because in the open Atlantic it was not possible to navigate with the use of compass and charts, besides which there were fogs, making the return voyage uncertain.[21] Despite occasional military setbacks, by the late fifteenth century the Portuguese monarchs had become masters of Morocco's Atlantic coast down to Safi, thanks largely to their use of artillery mounted on ships.

There were nevertheless a number of active regional networks of fishing and trade in various West African coastal areas. For example the fishing of the 'Azenegues' (Sanhadja), Muslim Berbers of the Saharan coast, was important enough for the Portuguese to want to tax it from their fortified trading post on Arguim island. The situation in Senegambia was perhaps typical of the way coastal trade by canoe was connected to the interior through river navigation—an approach European traders, bound to their ships, came to imitate. The largest canoes in Africa carried up to thirty men and could be effective also in war.[22] However, where Cadamosto noted the constant journeying of these *almadias* in the Gambia River, he also argued that Europeans could travel further because they were in less danger than local traders of being attacked and enslaved. The question of security was not the only limitation. The Niominka communities (a West African linguistic group related to the Serer of Senegal) fished and traded between the Senegal and Gambia rivers, connecting the southern ends of the desert caravan trade with local salt and fish, iron from the savannah interior, and products from the southern forest, notably malagueta pepper and cola nuts. However, their coastal navigation in canoes was geographically circumscribed by strong currents and winds. Hence the Niominka were unable to navigate north of Cape Verde, or south of the Gambia River, and needed to use creeks and portage to connect to the trade of the Casamance and Cacheu rivers further south.[23]

Therefore the advantage acquired by Europeans during the fifteenth century related to coastal as well as to oceanic navigation. It is significant that most Atlantic islands were not colonized from mainland Africa, unlike in the Caribbean, where the so-called Tainos and other Arawak-speaking peoples had settled the whole archipelago by canoe, probably navigating north from the Orinoco valley in a jerky process of colonization lasting centuries.[24] Given that the technology of African and Caribbean canoes, all made from single hollowed logs, was quite similar (Columbus and other early observers described the Taino boats as *almadias*, probably a word of Arabic origin, before the Arawak word *canoa* was generalized by Europeans), we should acknowledge the dangerous currents of the African coastline as a decisive factor in preventing travel in the open seas, although demographic pressures may also have been relevant. The Tainos, for example, seem to have practised a slash-and-burn method of cassava cultivation that explains why,

---

[21] Quoted from Ibn Khaldún's *Muqqadima* in Juan Vernet, 'Textos árabes de viajes por el Atlántico', *Anuario de estudios atlánticos* (1971).

[22] Even larger canoes were recorded in the Caribbean.

[23] George E. Brooks, *Landlords and Strangers: Ecology, Society and Trade in Western Africa, 1000–1630* (Boulder, CO, 1993), 87–95.

[24] Irving Rouse, *The Tainos: Rise and Decline of the People who Greeted Columbus* (New Haven, CT, 1992).

throughout the first millennium, they kept moving on, from Trinidad to the Lesser Antilles, and later Puerto Rico, Hispaniola, Jamaica, and Cuba; they also brought animals with them, such as dogs and *agouti* (edible rodents), and remained great fishermen. By contrast, in Africa, the inhabited Canary islands were exceptional. Here Berber-speaking natives seem to have arrived from the opposing mainland during the first millennium, although the Guanches of Tenerife and other island groups seem to have forgotten their navigational skills, because when the Europeans arrived they did not even travel between islands, and their dialects had diverged to the point of becoming mutually unintelligible. This facilitated the Spanish conquest of the largest islands, since they could enlist one island group against the other (for example, Gomerans helped reduce Grand Canary in the early 1480s). The other significant exception is Fernando Pó in the Gulf of Guinea, colonized from the relatively close mainland by the Bubi, a people speaking a Bantu language, centuries before the Portuguese arrived.

In the Americas, Tainos and Caribs might have been able to navigate effectively throughout the Caribbean, but as José de Acosta noted, no people in the New World had use of the compass, hence the peopling of the continent must have been achieved over a land-bridge.[25] As with the kingdoms of West Africa, from Mali to Benin to Kongo, the urban civilizations of Mexico and Peru were not maritime powers, although they ruled distantly over maritime areas, requesting tribute and service in an imperial fashion; even the Maya of Yucatán, some of whose cities—notably Tulum—were on the coast, did not look towards the sea for political expansion, although the Putun Maya conducted a vigorous regional trade with canoes and cargo rafts along the old Toltec coastal routes, connecting the Gulf of Mexico to Yucatán and Honduras.[26] As described by his son Ferdinand, who witnessed the event as a teenager, in 1502 Columbus encountered one of their trading canoes, as large as a galley and covered with a palm-leaf awning, which gave him an instant overview of the products of the mainland.[27] They traded with pottery, salt, obsidian knives, jade, copper hatchets, cacao, *pulque*, cotton textiles, quetzal feathers, and slaves; however, contact with Taino and other Arawak cultures was almost non-existent, despite the fact that the distance between western Cuba and the Yucatán was relatively short. Obsidian trade, so important to Mesoamerican culture, never reached the islands. Although the Maya were linguistically and culturally distinct from the Nahuas who dominated the Valley of Mexico in the centuries preceding the Spanish arrival, in reality they belonged to the old Toltec geopolitical and economic area of Mesoamerica that also included the Totonacs of the Gulf coast of Mexico, and even influenced central America along the Pacific coast, where Mexican *pochteca* traders established colonies. By contrast, the Caribbean was only directly connected to the Orinoco, and despite the importance of the great South American rivers for long-

[25] Acosta, *Historia*, i. 16–17.

[26] Eric S. Thompson, *Maya History and Religion* (Norman, OK, 1970), 3–47; David Drew, *The Lost Chronicles of the Maya Kings* (London, 1999), 359–62 and 372–80.

[27] Hernando Colón, *Historia del almirante*, ed. Luis Arranz (Madrid, 1984), ch. 89, 294. Also Las Casas, *Historia de las Indias*, ed. A. Millares Carlo, 3 vols. (Mexico, 1951), ii. 274–5.

distance trade, the only truly maritime people in the area were the island Caribs (an Arawakan-speaking people) who raided the Greater Antilles.[28]

The economic and political priorities of the most powerful kingdoms of West Africa and pre-Hispanic America also contributed to this shared lack of Atlantic vocation, which set them apart from their European contemporaries. In Mesoamerica there existed the militaristic empire of the Mexica, which forced tribute payments over many distant areas and benefited from the centralization of long-distance trade, although without promoting political or cultural integration (there was not even a homogeneous administrative elite). The Mexica of Tenochtitlan, who had arrived in the area relatively recently, were only the most powerful of a confederacy of city-states, and the memory of their nomadic existence remained alive. However, in Mesoamerica they enjoyed the benefits of a pre-existing urban civilization based on the cultivation of maize, and they had been able to claim the cultural inheritance of the Toltecs and other previous settlers who also spoke related Nahua languages (their main enemies, the Tlaxcalans, belonged to that same cultural world). Despite their urban achievements and imperial culture, in which the ritual sacrifice of captives was important, the world of the Aztecs was politically and economically self-centred, as was also that of the more centralized Inca state in the Andes: these two great urban empires were surrounded by more primitive peoples and lived in ignorance of each other. In Africa, by contrast, the Jolof rulers of Senegal, the Mande chiefs of the Gambia River, the various Akan states, and the kings of Benin or Kongo were all aware of a larger world of long-distance trade involving other centres of civilization. They were also commercially minded, even in those cases when (like the Edo of Benin) their main political concerns lay inland. Unsurprisingly, African political elites were often interested in trading with those Europeans who reached them from the Atlantic. When doing so they were either diverting the old trades of the interior river or caravan routes, or exploiting opportunities for new ones. They were not, themselves, organizers of trade, but powerful hosts, and had never been in a position to imagine themselves as patrons of maritime commercial ventures.

There was one other major difference between these two continents. The New World was, because of its global isolation, extremely vulnerable to any challenge coming from the Old World—not only in terms of military technology, although this was highly relevant, but primarily for ecological and biological reasons. By contrast, the extent to which the Portuguese forced their own terms of trade upon Africans can easily be exaggerated. African military power and a deadly disease environment both deterred a more significant European colonization of tropical Africa.

When Europe is considered from this perspective, what becomes apparent is not only the crucial role of navigational technology, but also the combination of economic

---

[28] Elizabeth Benson (ed.), *The Sea in the Pre-Columbian World* (Washington, DC, 1977); Louis Allaire, 'Archaeology of the Caribbean Region', *Cambridge History of the Native Peoples of the Americas*, iii/1. 668–733; contributions by Berend J. Hoff and others, in Neil Whitehead (ed.), *Wolves from the Sea: Readings in the Anthropology of the Native Caribbean* (Leiden, 1995).

pressures and political imagination that made possible, in a challenging environment, the continuity of patronage for maritime ventures. In other words, technological breakthroughs were the *outcome* of consistent maritime efforts, which in turn were largely driven by the desire to find alternative routes to existing trades with sub-Saharan Africa and India. Muslim traders, already operating in West Africa and the Indian Ocean, did not have such a motivation. The exceptional level of crown involvement in the peripheral kingdom of Portugal can be explained by reference to its particular circumstances: limited state resources and no potential for territorial expansion in Spain stimulated both Moroccan ventures and Atlantic exploration, albeit always within the context of a growing European demand for luxury goods, such as gold, slaves, spices, wine, or sugar. This economic context is what made exploration worthwhile—not simply a Portuguese initiative, but also a European demand that could be serviced by the Genoese and other trading nations.

In the light of these various arguments, it seems safe to conclude that the process by which c.1490 three different continents came to be connected by Atlantic navigation could only have been led from Europe.

BIBLIOGRAPHY

Abulafia, David, *The Discovery of Mankind: Atlantic Encounters in the Age of Columbus* (New Haven, CT, 2008).

Allaire, Louis, 'Archaeology of the Caribbean Region', in *The Cambridge History of the Native Peoples of the Americas*, iii: *South America* (Cambridge, 1996), part 1, 668–733.

Brooks, George E., *Landlords and Strangers: Ecology, Society and Trade in Western Africa, 1000–1630* (Boulder, CO, 1993).

Diffie, Bailey W., and George D. Winius, *Foundations of the Portuguese Empire 1415–1580* (Minneapolis, MN, 1977).

Fernández-Armesto, Felipe, *Before Columbus: Exploration and Colonisation from the Mediterranean to the Atlantic, 1229–1492* (London, 1987).

Mauny, Raymond, *Les Navigations médiévales sur les côtes sahariennes antérieures à la découverte portugaise* (Lisbon, 1960).

Parry, J. H., *The Age of Reconnaissance: Discovery, Exploration and Settlement 1450–1650* (Berkeley, CA, 1981).

Russell, Peter, *Prince Henry the Navigator: A Life* (New Haven, CT, 2000).

Thornton, John, *Africa and Africans in the Making of the Atlantic World 1400–1800* (2nd edn. Cambridge, 1998).

CHAPTER 3

....

AFRICANS, EARLY EUROPEAN CONTACTS, AND THE EMERGENT DIASPORA

....

DAVID NORTHRUP

ALTHOUGH Atlantic Africa was the last of the continent's shores to establish regular overseas connections, many aspects of its interactions mirrored those of East and North Africa. People along the Red Sea and Indian Ocean had been engaged in commercial and cultural contacts for more than fifteen centuries before the first Portuguese reached West Africa. North Africans had even older Mediterranean connections and, after the domestication of the camel and the rise of Islam, they increased their commercial and cultural intercourse overland with Africans along the southern edge of the Sahara. Early Muslim accounts write with awe of the empire of Ghana as 'the land of gold' in that *Bilad al-Sudan* (Land of the Blacks). Ghana's successors in the Western Sudan, the empires of Mali and Songhai, continued to assure safety, stability, and wealth to Arab and Berber traders from the north. As a result of these trans-Saharan connections, many Sudanese embraced Islam in the centuries after 1000, learning to speak and write the Arabic language.

Besides their fabled gold, the Sudanese shipped North Africans leather goods and cotton textiles and exchanged slaves for the horses needed for their empires' cavalry units. Trans-Saharan trade also supplied books and paper to the centres of Islamic learning at Timbuktu and elsewhere. In 1591, however, the power, wealth, and expansive policies of the Songhai rulers provoked a retaliatory invasion by the sultan of Morocco. The enslaved European musketeers who survived the desert crossing destroyed Songhai's political centre, but the Moroccan force was too small to recreate the imperial order and the security these states had so long provided. The trans-Saharan trade shifted east from the Niger bend to what is now northern Nigeria, just as new centres of commercial and cultural exchange were opening along the Atlantic.

Much like trans-Saharan contacts, the new Atlantic trade depended on existing regional trading networks and led to cultural as well as commercial interaction.

Observers on the Portuguese vessels in the fifteenth century described well-ordered societies large and small along West Africa's coast and hinted at the complex cultures (in places overlain with Islamic influences) that underpinned them. Coastal Africans' familiarity with regional and long-distance trading systems was evident in the speed and sophistication with which they established commercial relations with the Europeans. Indeed, the three stretches of coastal West Africa that responded strongly to the Portuguese (Upper Guinea, the Gold Coast, and the Niger Delta) all had prior links to the networks feeding the trans-Saharan trade. In other ways the new relations in Atlantic Africa also echoed those along the Sahara: mutually profitable trade (including gold and slaves), a strengthening of African authorities, and the opening of cultural influences (including Christianity, European languages, and education).

This chapter surveys the first two centuries of contacts in the African Atlantic under three interconnected and somewhat overlapping headings: the establishment of diplomatic relations, the growth of commercial exchanges, and the development of intercultural and cross-cultural relations. In each case it notes the different patterns that developed in Upper Guinea, the Gold Coast, the Niger Delta, and West Central Africa. African kingdoms and small states dominated these coastal connections, but people in less centralized societies also participated through the complex inland marketing networks. By 1650 Africa's Atlantic connections, though still of modest size, were beginning to rival in commercial and cultural importance the older overland ties to the Mediterranean.

DIPLOMATIC RELATIONS

Because sub-Saharan Africans were a common sight in the Mediterranean world, Portuguese explorers were not surprised at the appearance of the people they encountered along the Atlantic, but many coastal Africans initially reacted with shock and curiosity at the first sight of the strange ships and the even stranger-looking people who descended from them. Their apprehension flowed from fears that the Europeans might be evil spirits or alien creatures with superhuman powers. Suspicions of malice were reinforced by prejudices absorbed from North African Muslims. 'Christians ate human flesh, and . . . only bought blacks to eat them,' some people on the Gambia River charged in 1455. Even so, it took little time for cooler heads in powerful positions to conclude that the Portuguese were fellow humans who meant them no particular harm and could be the source of material benefits. Similarities in African and European notions of statecraft, markets, and cosmologies facilitated commercial and diplomatic agreements. In addition, both the Portuguese and their various African partners in these early centuries appeared sensitive to cultural differences and were willing to adapt.[1]

---

[1] David Northrup, *Africa's Discovery of Europe* (2nd edn. New York, 2008), 12–14.

Having established good connections with Africans along the lower Senegal and Gambia rivers, the Portuguese began efforts during the reign of King John II (1481–95) to open direct relations with the Muslim rulers of the still powerful inland Mali empire, efforts that were continued without success by his successors. Given Portuguese concerns at this time to find Christian allies in Africa or convert rulers to Christianity, the prospects for an alliance in this heavily Muslim region cannot have been great, but the one successful conversion is revealing even if it brought no lasting advantage. Bumi Jeleen, heir to the throne of the Senegalese kingdom of Jolof, had established advantageous commercial ties to the Portuguese, but in 1487, challenged for the throne by a half-brother, he sent his son to Lisbon to plead for horses, arms, and soldiers. King John sent horses but withheld other aid unless Jeleen agreed to become a Christian. By 1488, driven out of his kingdom by rivals, Jeleen himself was in Portugal, eloquently pleading for aid and expressing willingness to become a Christian. Jeleen acknowledged that the circumstances might put his sincerity in doubt, but King John did not doubt the genuineness of the conversion. Following an elaborate baptismal ceremony, Jeleen was returned to Senegal with military aid, missionaries to hasten the conversion of his kingdom, and materials for erecting a Portuguese trading fort in the kingdom. All ended badly with Jeleen's death, which aborted John's mission to Mali.[2] The episode is full of curious ambiguities, but the telling point is that intertwined religious and political motives seemed natural to both rulers, who were playing by the same diplomatic rules.

Further south along the coast, Akan-speaking Africans also negotiated early contacts with the Portuguese, who were eager to acquire some of the gold than came from inland mines. A coastal chief whom King John's agents called Caramansa agreed to the establishment of a permanent trading outpost on his land in 1482 at a place the Portuguese named São Jorge da Mina (St George of the Mine). In his welcoming speech Caramansa noted the mutual benefit such trade could bring, but he also warned the Portuguese that the trade would dry up if they failed to respect local authority and rights. The Portuguese had good reason to comply. A 1520 directive from the governor of Mina reminded newcomers of the need to give regular presents to the 'king of the Akan' and to another local authority who controlled the road inland.

During the first half of the sixteenth century local rulers at three other locations along the Gold Coast (at Axim, Shama, and Accra) agreed to the establishment of Portuguese trading posts. By 1600 English traders had secured African permission for three fortified outposts of their own (Fort Appolonia, Sekondi, and Dixcove). Over the next three decades the Dutch opened a trading fort at Mori and the English opened another at Kormantin. Like the Portuguese, the northern Europeans had no choice but to recognize their Akan landlords and pay them annual ground rents for their forts.[3]

Initially Europeans fortified these trading posts for protection from African raids, but as competition from other Europeans nations rose attacks from the sea became a

---

[2] John William Blake (ed.), *Europeans in West Africa, 1450–1560* (London, 1942), i. 33–4, 80–6.
[3] Blake, *Europeans*, i. 70–8, 130–1; Albert van Dantzig, *Forts and Castles of Ghana* (Accra, 1980), 1–20.

greater concern. Although relations between Europeans and Africans were generally peaceful, when amity broke down, local Africans made it clear who held the upper hand. Thus when some Portuguese trespassed on sacred ground while building the Mina fort, local residents forced the Portuguese to pay compensation. In retaliation for an offence in 1570, two coastal communities massacred over 300 Portuguese at Mina, decorating the grave of an African king with the skulls of fifty of them. A few years later another community took vengeance by razing the Portuguese outpost at Accra and slaying its inhabitants. By the end of the century both Europeans and Africans had learned the benefits of mutual cooperation. When an African impulsively beheaded a Dutchman for trespassing in a sacred grove in 1598, African authorities brought the hothead to the Dutch outpost and decapitated him publicly. 'From this we can see', commented a contemporary Dutch observer, 'how eager they were to maintain their friendship with the Dutch.'[4] After 1600 most conflicts were among Europeans, the most decisive being the wars between 1637 and 1642 by which the Dutch gained a dominant position on the coast by expelling the Portuguese and taking over the forts at Axim, Shama, and Mina.

Further down the coast rulers of the large, centralized kingdoms of Benin and Kongo sought to avoid the fragmented African positions on the Gold Coast by making Atlantic trade a royal monopoly. After the Portuguese made contact in 1486, the king of Benin dispatched a trusted official to investigate the strangers' country at first hand. The African delegate apparently learned Portuguese on the voyage to Lisbon, for the Portuguese account describes him as 'a man of good speech and natural wisdom'. Received as an ambassador, he was fêted, shown the sights, and sent back with fancy clothes for himself and his wife, along with a rich present for the king of Benin. The ambassador's report was evidently positive, since the king of Benin permitted the Portuguese to establish a coastal 'factory' or trading post for the pepper trade. Benin sent new embassies to Portugal in 1514 and 1515 to discuss trade relations as well as the linked topics of the ruler's conversion to Christianity and the sale of firearms. To enforce their royal monopolies the rulers of Portugal and Benin restricted trading to licensed individuals. As on the Gold Coast, European captains had to present rich gifts to the king and others before receiving permission to trade. For example, officers on a small Portuguese ship that arrived in May 1522 presented the ruler with '20 ounces of coral, four Indian caps, and ten and a half yards of red satin'. The two Benin officials in charge of trade with Europeans each received 20 yards of cloth, as did the chief of the port, while two African interpreters received 10 yards apiece. Over time, such 'customs' grew in value.

After the Portuguese withdrew from trade as the result of Benin's restrictions and competition from French 'interlopers', other Europeans sought to negotiate a share of the trade there. The king of Benin gave a warm welcome to the first English ships in 1553, even offering them credit if their cargo proved insufficient to cover their purchase

---

[4] Pieter de Marees, *Description and Historical Account of the Gold Kingdom of Guinea (1602)*, ed. and trans. Albert van Danzig and Adam Jones (Oxford, 1987), 44–97, quotation on 83.

of the kingdom's pungent pepper. High mortality among the English discouraged but did not completely deter visits to Benin. For the century after their first appearance in 1593, Dutch merchants dominated Benin's Atlantic trade. Although the market moved from the capital to more convenient coastal locations, Europeans continued to visit the capital and many wrote glowing accounts of the city's perimeter walls, broad avenues, immense palace (covering an area as large as Tübingen, a German account of 1603 asserted), and the palace's finely crafted bronze plaques that now hang in major museums.[5]

In West Central Africa, the kingdoms of Kongo and Ndongo became most adept at mastering European diplomatic culture, but that part of mainland Africa also became most subject to Portuguese hegemony. Beginning with first contacts in 1487, Kongo's rulers began to learn European diplomatic customs and to attempt to use them to better their positions. These efforts were deeply tied to the Kongo monarchy's adoption of Christianity as its official religion and the promotion of learning in Portuguese (see below). Kongolese letters and delegations sought to expand Atlantic exchanges while limiting Portuguese efforts to assert monopoly control over the kingdom's trade and Catholicism and influence its internal politics.

The first Kongo delegates to Portugal in 1488 (hostages taken by the Portuguese captain against the return of three priests who had gone inland to Kongo's capital city) were received in Portugal as ambassadors. As in the case of Benin's mission, they were fêted and sent back richly clothed. For their part, the Kongolese ambassadors learned Portugal's language and customs and adopted Christianity, as Kongo's ruler soon did too. Under the Christian King Afonso I (1509–42) a second delegation was dispatched, headed by his cousin and including his son Henry, who studied in Lisbon and was ordained a priest and consecrated as Kongo's first Catholic bishop. Henry and his uncle also gained an audience with Pope Leo X, and part of the skill displayed in subsequent diplomacy involved appeals to the papacy when direct relations with Lisbon were unsatisfactory. Afonso also dispatched many letters to Lisbon in the 1520s appealing for skilled technicians, teachers, and missionaries and seeking better regulation of the growing slave trade. Since the mail had to pass through the very Portuguese officials who were the cause of the problems, the letters were often delayed and the responses unsatisfactory. A 1535 delegation to the pope never got beyond Lisbon. During the 1540s and 1550s Kongo kept a resident ambassador in Lisbon.

Following a devastating attack by inland Africans in the 1570s, the kingdom's rescue was aided by a force of 600 Portuguese soldiers, but in the process Kongo rulers suffered diminished power and autonomy. The Portuguese had also begun cultivating the kingdom of Ndongo to the south and in 1575 established a new settlement at the port of Luanda, which grew rapidly in importance. In hopes of reclaiming their

---

[5] A. F. C. Ryder, *Benin and the Europeans, 1485–1897* (London, 1969), 44–57, 76–93; seventeenth-century descriptions of Benin are summarized in David Northrup, 'The Gulf of Guinea and the Atlantic World', in Peter C. Mancall (ed.), *The Atlantic World and Virginia, 1550–1624* (Chapel Hill, NC, 2007), 177–9.

kingdom's former primacy, Kongo authorities dispatched more delegations to Europe, including two that made it to Rome. In 1596 the papacy made the Kongo capital a new episcopal see, but the Portuguese monarch checked this move to greater autonomy by securing the right to name the bishops. During the seventeenth century Kongo rulers cultivated a Dutch alliance, especially during the period of Dutch occupation of Portugal's Angolan and Brazilian ports in the 1640s. Although the appointment of Italian and Spanish Capuchin missionaries as ambassadors opened a direct line to the papacy for a time, the Portuguese recapture of Angola in 1648 greatly diminished the autonomy of both kingdoms.[6]

The mutual diplomatic actions of the first century of contact persisted during the second. At one end of the spectrum, African rulers in coastal Angola had to share power with the Portuguese. Beyond the coastal enclaves of Angola and their much smaller counterparts on the Gold Coast, power rested in African hands. In the small chiefdoms along Upper Guinea, as in the large kingdom of Benin and its neighbours in the Niger Delta, African authorities continued to make it clear that in their lands Europeans guests were expected to be on good behaviour.

COMMERCIAL EXCHANGES

African chiefs and kings generally welcomed Atlantic trade, claimed monopoly rights over exchanges with Europeans, and designated the terms and locales of the trade, although they were not entirely successful in enforcing these conditions. The Portuguese crown also claimed exclusive control over all trade with Atlantic Africa, and that monopoly was similarly challenged by freebooting Portuguese and by others granted special privileges. To provide secure depots from which to trade, the Portuguese had colonized the uninhabited Cape Verde Islands from the 1460s and the islands of São Tomé and Príncipe in the Gulf of Guinea from the 1480s. The crown granted settlers special trading privileges with adjoining mainland African communities, a move that, by providing competition to the royal monopoly, helped drive up prices Africans received. After 1550 traders from other European countries broke the Portuguese monopoly, but European efforts to counter African trading strengths by multiplying the number of places they traded along the Atlantic coast produced mixed results.

The most valuable African exports into the Atlantic before 1650 were gold, sugar, pepper, and slaves, along with some manufactured goods and wild animal and forest products. From the beginning the Portuguese were eager to divert into the Atlantic some of the gold trade that for centuries had crossed the Sahara to Morocco and other parts of North Africa. Their efforts had little success in Upper Guinea but hit the jackpot on the appropriately named Gold Coast. In 1502, apparently one ship (of the

---

[6] Linda Heywood and John Thornton, 'Central African Leadership and the Appropriation of European Culture', in Mancall (ed.), *Atlantic World*, 201–17; Northrup, *Africa's Discovery*, 37–43.

twelve or fifteen King Manuel normally sent there each year) carried away 2,000 ounces of gold from Mina. Incomplete records from the middle of that decade suggest an official trade in excess of 20,000 ounces of gold a year from Mina, not including that which was smuggled. Other European nations were also drawn to the Gold Coast. The English managed to obtain 2,400 ounces of gold their first year (1553). Dutch trade grew to involve some twenty ships a year in the early seventeenth century, with gold the major export. By then, of course, the Portuguese were no longer participants. West Africa in this period was the principal source of gold for Western Europe, exports averaging between 25,000 and 27,000 ounces a year from 1471 to 1600 and over 32,000 ounces a year in the first half of the seventeenth century.[7]

The active cooperation of African miners and merchants was key to this gold trade. When production in gold-producing areas closer to the Sahara slowed as early as the fifteenth century, Juula merchants from the Western Sudan had moved south to link the locally important mines of the middle Volta River to supplement trans-Saharan trade. After the founding of São Jorge da Mina, the Juula and their local Akan associates collaborated in diverting gold southwards, since the route to the Atlantic was much shorter (and thus more profitable) than the long trek to the north. It is tempting to see the hand of the Juula Muslims as well in the change of the fort's popular name from Mina to Elmina, from the Arabic *al-minah* (the port). Northern Akan middlemen also positioned themselves in the fort's hinterland and by 1600 in the area north of the Accra fort, which was also a major participant in the gold trade to the Atlantic. Meanwhile, southern Akan people along the coast were consolidating their hold on the lands immediately surrounding the forts, ensuring that Europeans had to deal with them as middlemen to the interior.[8]

Sugar was another early African export that later became a defining feature of the larger Atlantic world. As they occupied uninhabited Atlantic islands, the Portuguese introduced sugar cane plantations and the system of African slave labour they had learned from Mediterranean Muslims. The Cape Verdes exported sugar, along with cotton, indigo, and American tobacco, but the centre of sugar production in the sixteenth century was the island of São Tomé, astride the equator. Canes were introduced to the island from Madeira, along with Portuguese and Italians familiar with sugar production. Settlers, including exiled Jews and convicts, were licensed to buy slaves from the mainland to grow and harvest the sugar cane. By the 1530s São Tomé had surpassed Madeira as the world's premier sugar producer. A few years later rich whites and mulattos there operated sixty to eighty large sugar plantations and the slave population of perhaps 10,000 produced enough sugar to fill ten vessels a year.

---

[7] Richard Bean, 'A Note on the Relative Importance of Slaves and Gold in West African Exports', *Journal of African History*, 15 (1973), 351–2; Ernst van den Boogaart, 'The Trade between Western Africa and the Atlantic World, 1600–90: Estimates of Trends in Composition and Value', *Journal of African History*, 33 (1992), 372.

[8] Van Dantzig, *Forts*, 9; Ivor Wilks, 'The Mossi and Akan States', in J. F. Ade Ajayi and Michael Crowder (eds.), *History of West Africa* (London, 1971), i. 360–6.

In addition to their backbreaking work in the fields, slaves were expected to supply all their own food. By 1600 the number of slaves reached 64,000. By then, however, Brazil's sugar production had leapt ahead both in quantity and quality, with enslaved Africans again constituting the labour force.[9]

During the same period free Africans in the mainland were cultivating another export commodity. The kingdom of Benin was a major supplier of a pungent indigenous pepper (*Piper guineense*), which was far superior to the malagueta pepper (*Amomum melegueta*) that came from the Windward Coast (later Ivory Coast) west of the Gold Coast and which held its own against the pepper (*Piper nigrum*) arriving in Europe in great quantities from India. Indeed, in 1506 the Portuguese king tried to ban further purchases of Benin pepper lest it compete with Indian pepper, but an illegal Portuguese trade from Benin continued for some time. It was this pepper that lured the first English ship to Benin in 1553. Despite the very high mortality among the crew due to deadly fevers, the English were pleased with the value of the eighty barrels of pepper they took away.[10]

In addition, Africans exported forest and wild animal products. The most valuable of these were elephants' tusks, which were obtained in greatest quantities from Senegambia, the Gold Coast, and Benin. Upper Guinea was a source of civet oil (from the musk glands of the civet cat), vegetable gums, and animal hides. Dyewoods and beeswax were also significant exports from Senegambia and the Gold Coast.

African textile manufacturers did a brisk business supplying Europeans with goods they needed to buy gold on the Gold Coast. A striped Moroccan cloth known as *hambel* was in high demand in the early sixteenth century as were Moroccan hooded gowns known as *jellabas*. Benin and its neighbours exported large quantities of indigo or blue and white cotton textiles for the Portuguese gold trade. These cloths became even more important to the Dutch and English in the first half of the seventeenth century. Benin was also the source of a stone bead highly esteemed on the Gold Coast.[11]

Because the export of slaves became so important a feature of Africa's engagement with the Atlantic during the two centuries after 1650, it is easy to forget that slaves made up a relatively modest share of African exports during the earlier two centuries, except from West Central Africa. Africans sold slaves into three distinct but interconnected Atlantic trades before 1650. The first supplied slaves to Iberia, supplementing and then displacing the trans-Saharan supply of slaves via North Africa. From small numbers in the 1440s this Atlantic trade to Europe grew to an average of 500 to 750 slaves a year by the turn of the century. Even though half of those reaching Lisbon were re-exported, mostly to the Spanish, Africans may have been 10 per cent of the city's population in the mid-1500s. The Portuguese managed a second slave trade between different parts of Africa, particularly to the Cape Verde Islands from Upper Guinea, to the islands of São

[9] Robert Garfield, *A History of São Tomé Island, 1470–1655: The Key to Guinea* (San Francisco, 1992), 65, 72–5; Blake, *Europeans* i. 157–60; Ryder, *Benin*, 74.

[10] Ryder, *Benin*, 31, 38–9, 77–85.

[11] Ibid. 94–5.

Tomé and Príncipe from the neighbouring mainland, and from the Niger Delta to the Gold Coast. The size of these trades is uncertain, but in the period 1490 to 1521 it is estimated that the trade to the Cape Verdes averaged about 800 a year, to São Tomé about 740, and to the Gold Coast about 300.[12]

Much more is known about the third slave trade, across the Atlantic. Some African residents of Iberia had accompanied Europeans to the Americas earlier, but the first slaves shipped directly from Africa to the Americas departed from the islands in Portuguese hands. In 1525 the *Santa Maria de Bogona* left São Tomé with a cargo of 300 slaves, of whom 213 survived the voyage to Santo Domingo. The next year two smaller ships left Cape Verde for Cuba with a total of 162 slaves. In 1532 three ships from São Tomé with a total of 692 slaves sailed for the Spanish Caribbean. The islands acted as bulking centres for these early voyages, most of the slaves having been purchased in small groups from neighbouring mainland areas. The first recorded slave passage from the African mainland to the Americas was the 1534 voyage of the *Conceição* from the Congo River to Santo Domingo and Jamaica.[13] Senegambia had a fairly steady transatlantic slave trade totalling over 200,000 by 1650, the greater part going to the Spanish Caribbean colonies up to the 1560s and thereafter to Spanish Central America (see Table 3.1). After 1550 slaves came primarily from West Central Africa, which in the first half of the seventeenth century accounted for 84 per cent of the entire transatlantic slave trade.

West Central Africa's exceptionally large position in the slave trade in this period (and long afterwards) was the product of a number of factors of differing orders of magnitude. Kongo and its neighbours were drawn into the Atlantic slave trade so early because they were eager to gain products from the Atlantic but lacked large supplies of ivory, gold, pepper, and other products that featured elsewhere. Moreover, the rulers of the younger and less centralized kingdom of Kongo quickly came to depend on the weapons and goods from the Atlantic to further its centralizing strategies, whereas the rulers of Benin had much greater internal control and were thus better able to control their involvement in the trade, as was evident in the king's decision to end the export of slaves in 1516. The often cited 1526 letters of King Afonso, seeking to end participation in the slave trade, reveal much more about his inability to control both Portuguese and Kongolese slave traders than about his moral opposition to enslavement. Perhaps also West Central Africans' greater participation in the Atlantic slave trade was connected to their isolation from the inland long-distance trade that shaped West Africans' engagement with the Atlantic. However important such factors may have been at the beginning, by 1650 new leaders and new kingdoms had emerged in inland West Central

---

[12] Ivana Elbl, 'The Volume of the Early Atlantic Slave Trade, 1450–1521', *Journal of African History*, 38 (1997), table 5.

[13] David Eltis, Stephen Behrendt, David Richardson, and Manolo Florentino, 'The Trans-Atlantic Slave Trade Database', www.slavevoyages.org, 20 May 2008, voyage nos. 46473, 11297, 11298, 11293, 46478, 46479, 46480.

Table 3.1. Estimated transatlantic slave trade from Africa by regions, 1525–1650

	Senegambia	Sierra Leone	Windward Coast	Gold Coast	Bight of Benin	São Tomé and Bight of Biafra	West Central Africa	Total
1525–50	57,200	0	0	0	0	2,100	4,900	64,200
1551–1600	90,100	1,400	2,500	0	0	6,400	113,000	213,400
1601–50	54,200	1,400	0	2,500	9,600	36,500	563,400	667,600

Source: David Eltis, Stephen Behrendt, David Richardson, and Manolo Florentino, 'The Trans-Atlantic Slave Trade Database', www.slavevoyages.org, 6 June 2008.

Africa, whose conflicts supplied ever larger numbers of captives to the Atlantic in return for the goods that leaders used to build new networks of power.

Africans in West Central Africa and elsewhere embraced Atlantic trade because of the imports they received. Had they not received desirable goods, they would never have parted with their gold, slaves, and other valuable products. Africans drove hard bargains and insisted on a great range of products, not just from Europe, but also from Asia, from the Americas, and from other parts of Africa. The early Portuguese brought Gold Coast Africans considerable quantities of goods, including textiles from Morocco and from Benin, along with Benin beads and slaves. A Portuguese account suggested that the Akan needed the slaves to carry inland the bulky trade goods they received in exchange for gold, though this was probably just the first of the tasks to which slaves were put. In the seventeenth century the Dutch had to draw upon their even broader global suppliers to persuade Africans to participate.

The proportions and type of goods varied considerably from coast to coast as well as over time. Overall, textiles dominated African imports during the first two centuries as well as later. Such strong demand suggests that local production did not saturate the African market and that the prices of Atlantic textiles were competitive. Some goods (e.g. silks and satins) were clearly aimed at an elite market while other, cheaper goods targeted a broader market. For example, between 1593 and 1607 the Dutch alone sold about 30 million yards of linen on the Gold Coast along with a great array of other textiles. Seventeenth-century cargoes included various textiles and clothing from Cyprus, India, Italy, Java, Hesse, La Rochelle, Leiden, Harlem, and Silesia, along with Turkish carpets.

Metals were also in great demand. Copper and brass found a strong market along the Gold Coast, where metals averaged at least 45 tons a year in the first half of the 1500s, a third of all the goods supplied by Portuguese traders. A century later the Dutch supplied ten times as much. Benin imported brass and copper *manillas* (wristlets) by the tens of thousands. Iron bars were also in great demand as were a variety of metal tools, utensils, and devices. Of these, firearms, though few in number, attracted great interest among Africans. The Portuguese had introduced firearms but were very reluctant to sell them to non-Christians. Even in Christian Kongo the musket trade was restricted. Protestant Europeans, though fearful of increasing Africans' strength, more readily caved in to African demand, selling enough muskets for some Gold Coast societies to become quite adept in their use by the early 1600s. The Dutch then restricted sales for some years but, under the pressure of English competition, resumed the trade by mid-century.

In contrast to all these consumer items, imports of cowrie shells are of particular interest since they had long functioned as a currency in parts of West Africa, and the large new imports suggest how the new Atlantic trade was promoting the expansion of commercial operations in inland areas. From an early date, Portuguese trading ships brought the shells back as ballast from the Indian Ocean and then reshipped them to West Africa. Benin imported cowries in considerable quantities from about 1520. *Manillas* also functioned as a currency unit in the Niger Delta, where many exchanges with Europeans were priced in them. Demand was not strong in Kongo, where people used a currency based on local shells and another one based on finely made palm cloths.[14]

These details about currencies, as well as the volume of exports and imports, suggest how much the involvement of coastal Africans in the new Atlantic trade depended on the existing commercial networks that criss-crossed inland areas. Marketing systems created to serve local and regional needs readily absorbed the new trade, making the necessary adjustments. The greater volume of goods moving to and from the Atlantic coast would have required additional transportation, but aside from the slaves imported along the Gold Coast, there is little evidence of innovations in these centuries. Except on the larger rivers, transport was by head portage in wooded areas, where endemic animal sleeping sickness precluded the use of beasts of burden (and thus of wheeled vehicles). In most cases, Atlantic trade's volume was probably not large enough by 1650 (or even 1800) to produce major changes in existing trading systems. The one notable exception was West Central Africa, where large new trade was stimulating new routes and trading professionals. Even there, however, despite the considerable misery that slave trading, and the conflicts that fuelled it, inflicted on individuals, the impact does not seem to have produced strongly dysfunctional changes, since the volume of slave exports continued to increase quite steadily, rising from an average of about 11,000 a year in the first half of the seventeenth century to over 38,000 two centuries later.

Cultural interactions

The cultural impact of Europeans before 1650 was strongest at the coast, although some influences spread inland along the trade routes. Within coastal communities acculturation varied. Many Africans employed by Europeans in menial positions acquired a basic understanding of European speech and customs. Some Africans, who interacted with Europeans on a more professional basis, became so familiar with European languages, manners, dress, and beliefs that they might be classified as bi-cultural. Those who became Christians went still further in the acculturation process, displacing many former practices and beliefs but also Africanizing their Christianity. The cultural impact of Africa on Europeans also varied. Most Europeans never learned an African language or gained more insight into African cultures than was expedient for trade, even though it often took months to complete transactions on an African coast. A few,

---

[14] For imports see Blake, *Europeans*, i. 92–3, 96–8, 100, 107; Eugenia W. Herbert, *Red Gold of Africa: Copper in Precolonial History and Culture* (Madison, WI, 2003), 125–40, 179–82; Ray Kea, 'Firearms and Warfare on the Gold and Slave Coasts from the Sixteenth to the Nineteenth Centuries', *Journal of African History*, 12 (1971), 185–213; Ray Kea, *Settlements, Trade, and Politics in the Seventeenth-Century Gold Coast* (Baltimore, MD, 1982), 154–63, 207–8; Ryder, *Benin*, 60–1, 300–4.

however, were drawn so deeply into African societies and family life that they made Africa their home.

Africans and Europeans shared common or compatible purposes but needed to develop a common language. Early Portuguese explorers kidnapped Africans, whom they trained as interpreters. Force soon proved unnecessary, as Africans recognized the utility of learning enough Portuguese to communicate with the Europeans—or with Africans outside their language group. Simple pidgins generally sufficed, but some Africans picked up a good command of standard Portuguese. The first English to reach Benin in 1553 were surprised when the ruler welcomed them in Portuguese, which he had learned as a youth. Many of the Kongolese elite learned to read and write Portuguese in the sixteenth century as did some Africans elsewhere. Initially English, Dutch, and French traders also used Portuguese as a lingua franca, but it was not long before some Africans mastered their languages as well. Thus, in 1614 an African ruler in Upper Guinea knew French while his wife spoke good Dutch. Competent African 'linguists' (interpreters) were highly valued for facilitating commercial exchanges and navigating cross-cultural relations.[15]

Besides facilitating exchanges between Europeans and elite Africans, versions of Portuguese were used by many Atlantic Africans to communicate among themselves. In the early 1600s the Jesuit missionary Alonso de Sandoval summarized what he had learned about acculturation in Africa from slaves he interviewed in South America. Slaves purchased directly from mainland ports in Upper Guinea 'come to Cartagena in great numbers every year', he reported, along with others born in the Cape Verde Islands or raised there from a young age. The latter groups spoke fluent Portuguese and were generally baptized Catholics. Other ships brought slaves of various origins from São Tomé. Anyone residing for a time on the island, Father Sandoval reported, picked up the 'language of São Tomé', a version of Afro-Portuguese pidgin that Jesuits in Cartagena also used to communicate with newly arrived slaves.[16] The language spread widely as the islands grew in importance in the transatlantic slave trade. The Portuguese-based pidgin remained important throughout the period before 1650, but was eventually displaced in West Africa by English-based pidgins that incorporated many Portuguese words.

Other more intimate contacts promoted deeper acculturation. According to a Dutch account, the Portuguese women who had accompanied their husbands to the Gold Coast had been miserable and often died, so it became the norm for resident Europeans to acquire African women who they treated as their wives. Such partners were also very useful as linguists and culture brokers. The account says husbands maintained these wives 'in grand style' and dressed them 'in splendid clothes' with abundant jewellery. The daughters of such marriages were preferred as wives by new European residents, while the sons were often successful culture brokers.[17]

---

[15] Northrup, *Africa's Discovery*, 64–5.

[16] Alonso de Sandoval, *Treatise on Slavery: Selections from* De instauranda Aethiopium salute, ed. Nicole von Germeten (Indianapolis, IN, 2008), 46–9.

[17] De Marees, *Description*, 216–17.

In the rivers of Upper Guinea, individual Portuguese known as *lançados* launched themselves into welcoming African societies, entering into traditional client relationships with local chiefs. Some carried acculturation to the point of wearing African clothing and Muslim amulets and undergoing facial scarification and circumcision, but most seem to have maintained a European identity out of personal preference or for prestige reasons. Their African landlords often provided the men with wives, who might be of servile status—perhaps an indication that the hosts regarded their Portuguese clients as of low social status. Marrying into their hosts' household connected the Portuguese to African trading networks, which their wives' linguistic and cultural skills helped them navigate. The many Europeans who succumbed to tropical diseases left their African widows considerable wealth and their offspring became part of a new Eurafrican class of intermediaries. *Lançados* also took on African apprentices, known as *grumetes*, who learned Portuguese ways as they were trained in the navigation of boats through the rivers. While the *lançados* operated in violation of Portuguese royal claim to monopoly over the trade of the region, they were too useful to be excluded from the trade with the Cape Verde Islands, Europe, and the Americas. These Eurafrican communities came to speak their own language, Crioulo, a mixture of Portuguese and West African languages, which was widely adopted on the mainland and became the spoken language of the islands.[18]

A new class of Eurafrican middlemen also arose in West Central Africa, where they played vital roles linking coastal Europeans and inland Africans. Known as *pombeiros* (marketeers, from the local word for market), they arose from the offspring of African women and Portuguese soldiers brought from São Tomé in 1571 and from Luanda after 1575 to defend Kongo against invaders. Their ability to communicate easily and effectively with both sides enabled the *pombeiros* to dominate trade routes into the interior by the early seventeenth century. As with other such groups, it was their bi-cultural identities that empowered them; their genetic mixture was simply the historical accident that led them to that position.

The spread of Christianity was a special element of the changing cultural identities in Atlantic Africa. Unlike most Protestant Europeans in Africa in the early modern period, the Portuguese actively promoted their religion. For the crown, missionaries and merchants spreading the Roman Catholic faith had both a religious goal and served to establish Christian allies south of the Dar al-Islam. Even Muslim rulers were not exempt, as the case of Jeleen illustrated. Some proselytizing efforts included Africans in Portuguese employ on the various coasts. However, the greatest efforts involved converting powerful African rulers, following a top-down conversion strategy that had been successful in spreading Christianity in Europe for many centuries. Thus, the Portuguese concentrated their efforts in the two large coastal kingdoms of Kongo and Benin, as well as the kingdom of Warri. For their part these African monarchs

---

[18] Walter Rodney, *A History of the Upper Guinea Coast, 1545–1800* (Oxford, 1970); George E. Brooks, *Eurafricans in Western Africa: Commerce, Social Status, Gender, and Religious Observance from the Sixteenth to the Eighteenth Century* (Athens, OH, 2003), 50–63.

showed great interest in the acquisition of new spiritual resources, though with quite different long-term outcomes.

The process in Kongo began with the conversion of the first delegates to Lisbon. The priests who accompanied the Kongolese embassy on its return in 1487 were warmly welcomed by the Kongo ruler and were soon summoned to the warfront, where they are known to have offered prayers for the success of the king's troops and supplied a religious banner to be carried into battle. Military success seems to have given credence to the power of the new religion and encouraged royal support. A royal son (baptized Afonso) was successful in claiming the throne on his father's death (with considerable support of the Catholic party) against a brother supported by traditionalists. Subsequently Afonso's son Henry underwent a long period of instruction in Kongo and then in Portugal, where he was ordained a priest and consecrated a bishop. After Bishop Henry returned to Kongo in 1521, an intensive programme to Christianize Kongo and Africanize Catholicism was undertaken. The political success of the Catholics in securing the throne in subsequent successions helped solidify the new religion in Kongo.

The Benin ambassador returning from Lisbon in 1486 was also accompanied by missionaries, who may have died soon afterwards of tropical fevers, but not, it would appear, without exciting some royal interest, since, in 1514, the monarch sent a second delegation to Portugal to discuss new missionaries and the sale of firearms. A Portuguese account affirms that the ruler was delighted when new missionaries arrived and summoned them to his war camp. After keeping them near the battle front for a year, King Ozolua returned to his capital, where he spent a month in discussion with the priests. Evidently as impressed as the Kongo king by the efficacy of the missionaries' prayers, he gave orders in 1516 for his son and some noblemen to be instructed in the new faith and for a church to be built. Christianity did not endure in Benin much longer than it had in Jolof, probably because the inauguration ceremonies held for the new king in 1517 dragged him back to the old religion. Later missionaries found King Ohogbua, a former convert, unsympathetic to their pleadings.

Rulers elsewhere formed more enduring attachments to Christianity. In 1600 the ruler of the Itsekiri kingdom of Warri sent his eldest son to Lisbon for religious instruction and other education. The heir, christened Domingos, returned in 1608 with a Portuguese wife, a Catholic chaplain, and a commitment to making Christianity the royal religion. He and his successors as kings kept up the adherence to Christianity well into the eighteenth century, despite a perennial shortage of priests. For most of the 1500s priests were in short supply in Kongo, which helped confine Christianity to the capital, São Salvador, and to the elite. As elsewhere in the Catholic world, services, prayers, and scriptures were in Latin. In the late 1500s a seminary to train indigenous priests functioned for a time on São Tomé, and Jesuit missionaries to Kongo in the early 1600s introduced a catechism printed in the Kongo language and established a school in São Salvador that turned out energetic catechists and teachers. The arrival of Capuchins at mid-century expanded the missionary efforts, recording large numbers of baptisms and marriages, even if Christian monogamy remained problematic among the elite and many pre-Christian beliefs and practices flourished among the masses—much as in Europe.[19]

The most pervasive cultural innovations from the Atlantic occurred in agriculture. Atlantic contacts brought new cultigens to Africa both deliberately and accidentally. On the Gold Coast the Portuguese introduced a number of domesticated animals (pigeons, fowls, pigs, and sheep) along with new cultigens (sugar cane, pineapple, and a South American banana). Even more important was Amerindian maize, which became an important food crop before 1600 on the Gold Coast. Apparently, both maize and sugar cane had reached the Gold Coast via São Tomé. In the early 1600s the Portuguese also introduced the Amerindian root cassava (manioc) to Angola, probably by accident. Despite some initial resistance, the new food plant was widely grown in lowland areas, where by mid-century it had become an important hedge against famine. The Portuguese also brought garlic and other vegetables to Angola. The Portuguese introduced Africans to tobacco from Brazil in the later 1500s, but Dutch traders played a greater role in increasing its availability. In the mid-1600s a German noted that people on the Gold Coast were eager smokers and hung little bags of tobacco around their necks at night 'as if it were a precious jewel'.[20]

Acculturation in coastal Africa was generally additive not substitutive. New languages did not displace old ones. New crops supplemented traditional staples. New weapons were used side by side with old ones. Even Africans who became Christians understood their new faith in terms of older cosmologies. That Africans were more likely to adopt European culture than Europeans were to become Africanized owes more to Africans' eagerness to embrace Atlantic opportunities rather than to the superiority of European culture. Moreover, the slave trade from West Central Africa extended aspects of this 'Atlantic Creole' culture to the Americas along with more traditional social practices, religious rituals, and other cultural institutions.[21]

By 1650 coastal Africans had forged strong links to the other Atlantic continents without being dominated by those connections. In contrast to the Americas, there was no widespread European conquest, no decimation of the population by unfamiliar diseases, and little subordination of native peoples to alien authority. In their diplomatic relations, commercial exchanges, and cultural adaptation, Africans engaged the Atlantic voluntarily and generally from positions of strength. Established rulers and merchants were best positioned to gain from these contacts, but the Atlantic also opened opportunities for clever and ambitious new people to become cultural and linguistic intermediaries, traders, or warlords. By 1650 sub-Saharan Africa's coast had joined those along the Sahara and the Indian Ocean as a conduit for political,

---

[19] Adrian Hastings, *The Church in Africa, 1450–1950* (Oxford, 1994), 71–102.

[20] De Marees, *Description*, 113–14, 216; Otto Freidrich von der Groeben in *Brandenburgh Sources for West African History, 1680–1700*, trans. and ed. Adam Jones (Stuttgart, 1985), 25; Anne Hilton, *The Kingdom of Kongo* (Oxford, 1985), 78–9; Heywood and Thornton, 'Central African Leadership', 199–200.

[21] Linda Heywood and John Thornton, *Central Africans, Atlantic Creoles, and the Foundation of the Americas, 1585–1660* (Cambridge, 2007), 169 ff.; James H. Sweet, *Recreating Africa: Culture, Kinship, and Religion in the African-Portuguese World, 1441–1770* (Chapel Hill, NC, 2003).

commercial, and cultural exchanges. The rapid development of plantation economies in the Americas after that date focused far more attention on the export of slaves.

BIBLIOGRAPHY

Blake, John William (ed.), *Europeans in West Africa, 1450–1560* (London, 1942).

Brooks, George E., *Eurafricans in Western Africa: Commerce, Social Status, Gender, and Religious Observance from the Sixteenth to the Eighteenth Century* (Athens, OH, 2003).

Garfield, Robert, *A History of São Tomé Island, 1470–1655: The Key to Guinea* (San Francisco, CA, 1992).

Hastings, Adrian, *The Church in Africa, 1450–1950* (Oxford, 1994).

Kea, Ray, *Settlements, Trade, and Politics in the Seventeenth-Century Gold Coast* (Baltimore, MD, 1982).

Northrup, David, *Africa's Discovery of Europe, 1450–1850* (2nd edn. New York, 2008).

Rodney, Walter, *A History of the Upper Guinea Coast, 1545–1800* (Oxford, 1970).

Ryder, A. F. C., *Benin and the Europeans, 1485–1897* (London, 1969).

Thornton, John K., *Africa and Africans in the Making of the Atlantic World, 1400–1800* (Cambridge, 1998).

CHAPTER 4

....

NATIVE AMERICANS AND EUROPEANS

Early Encounters in the Caribbean and along the Atlantic Coast

....

NEIL L. WHITEHEAD

THE first sustained encounters between Europeans and native peoples of America in the fifteenth century were temporally episodic and geographically uneven.[1] The prevailing winds and currents across the Atlantic nonetheless pushed European shipping repeatedly towards northern South America and the Caribbean region, as in the first voyage of Columbus. From this initial zone of contact European expeditions ranged to the south and west, enumerating rivers and assessing opportunities for trade and plunder. Within a decade of Columbus' first landfall under the flag of Spain, Portuguese expeditions had reported on the coastal regions of Brazil, followed in the 1530s and 1540s by reports from expeditions into the river basins of the Amazon and Orinoco.

Testimony from the accounts of these early voyages continually stresses the great abundance of mineral, floral, faunal, and human resources as well as the intensity with which they might be exploited. Evidence of the wealth and productivity of native agricultural techniques and economic organization thus emerges from the accounts of the trading and raiding for foodstuffs, gold, and minerals between native populations and Europeans. In time, as political relationships also emerged, such activities would ramify into a whole system of such exchanges, encompassing forest products (such as dyes, woods, animals), specially produced artefacts (such as ceramic wares, canoes, hammocks), and even persons in the form of slaves, concubines, and marriage partners. The Europeans offered metal tools, cloth, beads, mirrors, brass items, and,

[1] The short-lived Vinland settlements of the Norse in the period 985–1010 of course precede this fifteenth-century 'discovery'.

eventually, firearms and alcohol in return. However, there were also negative ecological impacts and wild cattle, pigs, and goats degraded ecosystems, making them less favourable to the indigenous species. Equally, European epidemic diseases could have locally devastating consequences amongst those native polities that incorporated populations into high-density settlement patterns, as was the case along the Brazilian coast, on the Caribbean islands, and the floodplains of the major rivers such as the Amazon and Orinoco. However, such effects were temporally extended and large populations persisted along the Orinoco and the Amazon well into the seventeenth century. Moreover, migration away from points of contact with the Europeans, as well as the new economic and political opportunities that European colonialism itself presented, must also be considered. An overemphasis on technology or biology as determining the fate of native peoples would be to ignore the clear evidence of demographic, political, and military persistence of native societies right up to the present day. This also ignores the widespread evidence for the emergence of new ethnic and political groupings in which both Africans and Europeans were incorporated into native political and economic structures.

The organization of production within native economies was largely domestically based and kinship relations were the basis for the organization of agriculture and hunting. Certain specialized craft products, such as ritual ceramic items, metalwork in gold and silver, lapidary, wood carving, weaving, and weaponry, were sometimes specialities of particular ethnic castes. Consequently key economic relationships were of necessity inter-ethnic and inter-village, since this specialization of collective domestic production implied supporting economic relationships with producers of more mundane items, and the regional integration of populations was far greater than conventional historical accounts have recognized. The distribution of the natural resources also influenced the local organization of processing and was often related to the commodities groups produced, there being little trade in raw materials, except rough hewn stone for the manufacture of stone axes and certain minerals as pottery temper. For these very reasons social and ethnic boundaries were not necessarily coextensive with particular economic, political, or linguistic systems. They might also be founded on a craft technique or specialization that was itself sustained by being part of a regional system of exchange.

Amerindians possessed developed military capabilities, but the threat of European aggression induced Amerindian groups to extend and refine their military practices. In many areas of the New World, neither guns nor horses were of a decisive strategic value and, as a consequence, a great reliance was put upon the political and military intelligence of the Amerindians themselves, as the pattern of European alliance making shows. It was not until the later colonial period that professional soldiery from Europe was deployed extensively, tribal mercenaries being preferred until this time. In this later period it was often those martial tribes that had been deliberately cultivated by the Europeans that were to become the object of these military campaigns.

The Caribbean Atlantic

The peoples of the Caribbean were the first to negotiate the new political and economic realities which European colonialism initiated, as well as to endure the ecological and demographic consequences of that arrival. In the islands of the Caribbean these processes were brief and brutal for the peoples of the Greater Antilles, where the native population had all but disappeared within a few decades, but were more attenuated and convoluted in the Lesser Antilles, whose inhabitants offered stout resistance to a succession of colonial powers. By the same token the impact of the Europeans on the native societies of the mainland was often locally disastrous but also allowed for more extended interactions, like those seen in the Lesser Antilles, to develop. This situation produced a wide range of novel political and economic responses on the part of the native population. Arguably none of the societies of the Caribbean region that were extant in 1492 survived unscathed, for, even where contacts were not direct, the impact of the Europeans on regional trade and alliance systems was significant. However, it is not sufficient to explain all population loss and cultural change by this means. The consequences of the introduction of European disease differed greatly according to the character of settlement size and social integration,[2] so that the first encounters with the natives of the Caribbean islands loom largest in the historiography of the region and in the ethnological schema of subsequent anthropologies, both colonial and modern.

The type of native societies the Europeans encountered thus strongly conditioned their political responses. The initial diplomacy exercised towards the *caciques* (kings or chiefs) of the Caribbean and Yucatán Peninsula strongly contrasts with the summary military invasions of Puerto Rico or Trinidad and the Venezuelan littoral, which were the early hunting grounds for slavers from the Greater Antilles. In such situations ethnological expectations and definitions became critical political factors, as is shown in the great debates between Las Casas and Sepúlveda concerning the humanity and rationality of the New World population. But these ethnological definitions were also responsive to the unfolding needs of the emergent colonial system and there were many more local exercises in defining and identifying friendly and hostile populations. In such a context the native population was itself polarized and the encounter with Europe was a dramatic disjuncture in native patterns of historical development, and it is the nature of that disjuncture and the new historical trajectories that were born of that encounter that went to make up the emergent identities and social processes of the new Atlantic world. The native survivors of the first decades of European occupation were therefore incorporated into the burgeoning colonial settlements of the region and the

---

[2] On the Caribbean islands the virulence of epidemic disease was enhanced by the physical circumscription of the native population, but this did not preclude migrations, by sea, towards the southern continent.

growing need for plantation and mining labour answered by the importation of Africans as slaves. What percentages of the aboriginal population had either fled the Greater Antilles or had died there during the initial contact is open to debate. However the overall consequence, as the colonial processes that had been unfolded on Española repeated themselves in Cuba, Jamaica, and Puerto Rico, was the complete dispersion and disappearance of a distinct 'native' element to the population in these regions.

These rapid conquests in the Greater Antilles, as well as the Bahamas, contrast strongly with the situation that unfolded on the Lesser Antilles, which became a refuge not just for native populations, but also for the *cimarrones* (escaped black slaves). Puerto Rico emerged as a southern frontier of Spanish settlement in the Caribbean islands, with the Lesser Antilles only being occupied during the seventeenth century by Spain's imperial rivals. During this hiatus between the end of new Spanish colonization and the onset of the French, Dutch, and English occupations, the native populations of the Lesser Antilles were able to take advantage of their position on the main shipping lanes between Europe and America to practise a profitable trade with the European vessels that stopped to replenish their drinking water and supplies after the Atlantic crossing. Geographically proximate to the Lesser Antilles and culturally integrated with them were those regions that the Europeans referred to as the Pearl Coast, Paria, and Trinidad. Although all these locations had been seen by Columbus in 1498 only the Pearl Coast was exploited initially, following the information gathered during the armed reconnaissance of Alonso de Hojeda and Cristobal Guerra.[3] As a result the political status of native populations of the rest of the Venezuelan coast and Antilles was contested between the missionary orders and those who saw a resource for slaves. This hiatus allowed the foundation of the first Franciscan monastery in the New World at Cumaná, as well as a Dominican mission at Chirivichi. But these pacific contacts were not to last and in 1519 the activity of the slavers recommenced. The native response was decisive: the religious foundations were destroyed and the Spanish settlements besieged; but the Spanish reoccupied the region in 1522, waging a deadly war a *fuego y sangre*. Thereafter followed a period of virtual anarchy during which various *doradistas* (gold-hunters) vied for access to the fabled wealth south of the Orinoco from their bases in the Cumaná and Trinidad. Along the Venezuelan coast the rule of the missions was gradually re-established, but only with the support of a series of military campaigns, most notably that of Juan de Orpín in the 1630s which definitively established Spanish dominance in this region. The native networks of gold trading that the *doradistas* so eagerly hoped to intersect, ultimately connected both the Caribbean islands and the western coasts of Tierra Firme to the heartland of the Colombian sierras. It was here that the dreams of encountering an El Dorado were

---

[3] With the discovery of the vast pearl fisheries off the island of Cubagua in 1512 European interests centred on the Venezuelan coast, rather than Trinidad, and it was not until 1531 that any sustained attempt was made to occupy and explore Trinidad and the Orinoco River, both these locations being occupied by Antonio de Berrio in the 1590s.

indeed realized and the occupation of the coastal region in order to gain access to those gold-working cultures was correspondingly brutal.

THE BRAZILIAN ATLANTIC

Apart from considerations of geography and navigation, the basic reason for the intensity of European trading activity along the Atlantic coast throughout the sixteenth century, particularly south of the Amazon, was the attraction of the timber resources of the Atlantic-coast forests, above all the red dye obtained from brazilwood. To the north of the Amazon the low-lying marshlands and mangrove swamps were an effective deterrent to landings by the early traders and the resources of the region were little investigated. Moreover, the native gold work that might be plundered in the Caribbean, as well as the exploitation of the pearl fisheries off the north Venezuela coast, effectively drew off any resources that might have been used for the exploration of the coastal zone between the Orinoco and Amazon deltas. It was for this reason that Spain's colonial rivals, especially the Dutch, found this region open to exploitation at the end of the sixteenth century.

In Brazil, particularly to the south of what was to become the captaincy of Rio Grande, the period from 1500 to the 1530s saw the development of an extensive trade with the coastal Amerindians, above all in brazilwood, from which a red dye could be extracted, but also including slaves, animal skins, and live parrots. The Europeans offered metal tools, clothing, and other 'trinkets' such as mirrors, combs, and whistles, in return for Amerindian labour in locating, cutting, and delivering the heavy brazil-wood. In the earliest phase of this trade the Portuguese employed the 'factory system' that had been successfully developed in their trade to the West African coast. Essentially this meant that a group of traders would secure a royal contract whereby the right to trade was leased for a fixed period. A group of vessels was then dispatched and a small fort cum warehouse (i.e. factory) would be erected. In 1506 the Portuguese crown became more directly involved by establishing a series of 'royal factories' along the coast, which private traders were then licensed to fill through the trade they conducted with the native population.

From 1504 onwards French traders had begun to seek brazilwood in defiance of Portuguese claims to a trading monopoly east of the Tordesillas Line, since they did not recognize the legitimacy of the papal grant. By 1530 the Portuguese crown had therefore decided that permanent occupation was necessary to interdict French attempts to trade with the native population. Fourteen captaincies were created, where only the Portu-guese residents could trade with the natives.[4] In this context the disposition of the native population was a key element, and dependence on them for both subsistence and

---

[4] Of these captaincies only ten were actually settled before 1550 and of these only two were considered a success, since there were chronic problems in attracting settlers and capital for their development.

military support was absolute in the initial years of settlement. From the native perspective, the presence of French traders was advantageous. The manner of French trading differed from that of the Portuguese in that they did not establish factories ashore, but traded directly off their ships. Once a ship had arrived the cargo would be traded only after negotiation with the local Amerindians. Resident traders frequently emerged amongst a number of coastal groups. Such individuals were not usually purposely planted among the natives but came there by means of shipwreck, or were effective cultural and economic brokers because of their mixed Euro-Amerindian ancestry. Nonetheless, they were an important avenue of communication for both the French and Portuguese, especially as reliance on the native population grew as trade turned to settlement under the captaincies.

Taking place against the background of a notable degradation of the brazilwood resources, this period of settlement from the 1530s into the 1550s required a different and less permissive strategy towards the native population. The native population had also changed in its attitude to the Europeans since their critical role in the brazilwood trade had made them less enamoured of the trinkets that they had earlier accepted for their labour in the cutting and carrying of logs. As a result they demanded better-quality goods, including weapons, for the delivery of the brazilwood, which had become more difficult and dangerous to extract as the coastal strip of forest had been utterly depleted in the immediate vicinity of the Portuguese factories.

In this context, and with a growing need for plantation land and the labour to work it, the Portuguese began taking slaves from native populations. As a result widespread attacks were made on the Portuguese settlements in the 1540s, only three of the captaincies escaping without major damage or destruction. Portuguese responses, to both these attacks and in subsequent dealings with the natives, were of necessity balanced by a military dependence on their native allies in face of continuing French incursions, which culminated in the occupation of the Bay of Guanabara (Rio de Janeiro) by Villegagnon in 1555. For both French and Portuguese alike the natives were thus an indispensable element in their overall military posture. As a result of the uncertainties of this transition from the brazilwood to plantation economy, the Portuguese crown took over the direct administration of Brazil in 1549, in the hope of bringing the native population under firm control and forestalling further French settlement. Accordingly, until 1580, military campaigns of pacification went along with evangelical campaigns of conversion, often indistinguishably so since resistance to conversion rendered a population liable to a 'just' enslavement. These military and religious actions led to a fundamental re-evaluation of Portuguese policy towards the natives resulting in a series of declarations in the 1570s concerning the legal status of the Amerindians. Although they could still be enslaved either in the course of a 'just' war, or for the practice of cannibalism, interest in the natives as a source of labour fell away as the importation of African slaves began. Many Amerindians retreated to the interior, compounding the appearance of population loss along the coast, but were there later pursued by the *bandeirantes* (slavers). In short, by the 1580s the Portuguese were definitively established in their coastal possessions south of Rio Grande and the Amerindians subjugated or dispersed from their original territories.

To the north of Rio Grande, in the captaincies of Ceará and Maranhão, which had never been occupied, the French had a briefly flourishing colony between 1612 and 1615. Despite the brevity of this occupation it left an enduring monument to the culture of the local Tupinambá since the Franciscan missionaries who accompanied the French force, Claude d'Abbeville and Yves d'Évreux, produced long texts on their evangelization that recorded many details of native life. The subsequent occupation of Maranhão by the Portuguese resulted in the total devastation of the Tupinambá and was to provide the Portuguese with their stepping stone into the Amazon basin proper from the fort at Belém, founded in 1616.

AMAZON, ORINOCO, AND ATLANTIC GUAYANA

The Spanish did not try to settle either the valley of the Orinoco until the 1580s or that of the Amazon until the seventeenth century, which is reflected in the fact that both the expeditions which first travelled the length of these rivers departed from the west: Francisco de Orellana leaving Quito in the expedition of Gonzalo Pizarro in 1541, Antonio de Berrio leaving Bogotá for the Orinoco in 1583. Certainly neither of these expeditions was the first European intrusion into the Amazon and Orinoco but they do signal the start of a serious interest in their exploitation. Up until this point these interior regions had been marginal to Spanish colonizing efforts which, in northern South America, had centred on Peru and the Caribbean littoral. In the event the Amazon River was to remain tangential to Spanish colonial interest, although parts of the upper Amazon were integrated with the *audiencia* of Quito, and it was the Portuguese, led by Pedro Teixeira, who initiated the occupation of the lower Amazon valley in the 1630s in defiance of the Line of Tordesillas. This occupation also swept away the trading posts and forts that the Dutch, Irish, and English had established in the river as part of their effort to develop trade with the Amerindians of the Amazon and Guayana, following on the expeditions of Robert Dudley, Walter Raleigh, and Lawrence Keymis in the 1590s and the establishment of the Dutch West India Company in 1616. The native population of these regions had therefore remained largely intact until the 1630s; this continued even into the eighteenth century outside the orbit of Portuguese slaving and missionary conquest.

The main base of European intrusion into the Guayana region in the sixteenth century was the Spanish colony on Margarita island, from where various *entradas* (armed incursions) were launched into the Orinoco basin and whose colonists developed significant trade links with some of the native groups of the Guayana coast, particularly the Lokono (Arawak). The pearl fisheries at Margarita certainly required significant numbers of native slaves, and the population of the Caribbean shore of Venezuela suffered accordingly, but there is little evidence to suggest systematic slave raiding either along the Orinoco River or the Guayana shore. Undoubtedly the occupation of Trinidad in 1531–2 by Antonio de Sedeño, as well as the rival expeditions led by Diego de Ordás to the mid-Orinoco in the same period, were accompanied by much bloodshed but they did not result in permanent settlement. Nevertheless, these kinds of expedition on the mainland, and the activities of Spanish slavers in the Caribbean islands, were the cause of a number of relocations by the native population, mirroring migrations of Brazilian groups following the Portuguese wars of conquest in the 1560s and 1570s.

In the Guayana Atlantic region there was no analogue for the intense brazilwood trade that developed along the Brazilian Atlantic shore. Military Spanish incursions into the Orinoco basin, as well as the first descent of the Amazon, were all carried out in pursuit of plunder, specifically gold work, and only later was permanent occupation envisaged, and then largely to forestall settlement by Spain's Protestant rivals. Trade led eventually to plunder and conquest in the case of Brazil; the reverse was true to the north of the Amazon, where relatively peaceful trade burgeoned despite prior military adventures in search of the land of El Dorado. Furthermore, there was no significant missionary activity, like the Brazilian Jesuit system of *aldeias*, in either Orinoco or Amazon, until the late seventeenth century and even later or not at all in the Guayana coastal zone. This created a situation where native autonomy persisted far longer. Even when the plantation economy developed in the late seventeenth century, Amerindian labour was redundant since the African slave trade had already been established to service the Brazilian and Caribbean markets. Indeed, the failure of the Dutch to colonize Brazil freed capital and resources for the development of their Guayana colonies, just as the French eventually turned to the Caribbean and Guayana after ejection from Brazil. Nonetheless, the political and ethnic character of the native population underwent a process of rapid change. The coastal population of Brazil did not have the opportunity to respond to European intrusion in the way that groups north of the Amazon did since it was extinguished or dispersed as a direct result of the character of occupation.

To the north of the Amazon, although many of the groups initially encountered disappeared, this was as much due to the series of political realignments made by native leaders, as to the effects of population loss following European conquest or the spread of epidemics. This sustained interaction between autonomous native polities and the small-scale European enclaves of the region produced a whole series of secondary social phenomena only intermittently glimpsed in the case of coastal Brazil; for example, the formation of new military elites, the emergence of new tribal divisions, and a fundamental reorganization of native trading networks.

Early contacts along the Amazon River, and the region of Maranhão at its mouth, resulted in many changes in native societies, leading to their ultimate destruction as autonomous entities by the end of the seventeenth century. Particular emphasis should be given to the changing character of the European colonial enclaves, which developed from trading into plantation and ranching economies. There was also diversity in indigenous responses to colonial intrusion which ranged from strategies of avoidance, or armed resistance, through to enthusiastic cooperation with the colonial intruders. Native groups surviving into the eighteenth century therefore showed equally variant continuity with the pre-colonial past, directly related to the character of colonial contact and indigenous response in this early period. First contacts were often much later along the Amazon than the coastal regions of Brazil and the Guianas since neither the Spanish nor Portuguese tried to settle the Maranhão region or the upper Amazon until the 1640s. Although other colonial powers were established throughout this region, their settlements were simply fortified trading posts.

The scale of Portuguese colonization in the Amazon valley was initially far less than that along the southern Atlantic shore of Brazil. Nonetheless, the impact on indigenous societies in this region, as elsewhere, was ultimately devastating, due mainly to the persistent slaving by the Portuguese from Belém. This resulted in a reorientation of many native trade and political networks from an interior to a coastal focus, where embroilment in the colonial regimes of the Europeans appeared to offer new social opportunities. However, the resulting demographic impact, as well as colonial policies concerning native groups, often forced social and political changes that aggregated remnant populations, enhanced the influence of native leaders with trading connections to the colonial economy, and reoriented military alliances. Native leaders actively sought economic and military alliances with colonial rivals of Spain and Portugal, hoping to impede attempts to dominate the region. By the beginning of the seventeenth century new native leaderships, appealing to new forms of ethnic sentiment, confronted the newly stabilized colonial regimes. These new native identities expressed these changing circumstances and so sometimes showed only a limited continuity with those that had preceded them.

These changing social and cultural patterns among the native population are reflected in missionary ethnologies of the period in which linguistic markers became a means to represent the distribution of native groups and how best to effect their conversion. Since the pre-colonial elite class of leaders was largely extinguished in the violence of initial colonial establishment, the power vacuum they left was filled either by the European missionaries and traders, or by the newly emergent trading and warring chieftaincies, such as the Manoa, Arawak, and Carib.[5] However, as the colonial economies of the region shifted from trade in forest products towards the laying out of plantations or other kinds of infrastructural activity, so commensurately the importance of native allegiance declined.

In line with their emergent role as foci for either indigenous resistance or cooperation with the colonial regimes of the region, such groups as the Carib, Manoa, and Arawak used their preferential trading relations with the Europeans to consolidate and extend their political and economic influence among the rest of the indigenous

---

[5] These groups, many still extant today, represent a complex historical inheritance from the ancient native polities, some being amalgams of highly divergent cultural traditions. Politically and economically, leaders of these neoteric groups were attuned to the political vagaries of colonial conflict and rivalry.

population. Against a background of local demographic decline the domination and even cultural incorporation of remnant populations was very successfully managed by such groups. This was particularly true where the complex rules of marriage and descent evident in the dynastic chieftaincies that had preceded them were abandoned in response to the changing conditions of socio-political life. It was therefore those groups who most actively sought contact with the Europeans, hoping to alter their relations with other native groups, as well as those who had already suffered from the slavers, who were the primary victims of the epidemics that were to sweep this area in the eighteenth century. Where direct military conquest had failed, missionaries were often able to accomplish the same ends more indirectly by the economic and political marginalization of regional leaders and traders.

Native leaders therefore were faced with an increasingly stable colonial system in which inter-colonial rivalry itself had somewhat abated. By the end of the seventeenth century, the Spanish occupied the Pearl Coast, Trinidad, and the Orinoco but had not advanced any further down the Amazon from their Andean colonies. The Dutch in Suriname, Berbice, and Essequibo were undoubtedly the dominant force along the Guiana coast, as Spanish governors fruitlessly warned their monarchs, and only finally abandoned their southern Brazilian colonies in 1654. The English and French held small sugar and tobacco plantations throughout the Lesser Antilles, as well as on the Atlantic coast of the Guianas, but had no further ambitions for outposts in the Amazon valley. However, the French had stabilized a colony between the Maroni and Oyapock rivers and had garnered sufficient native alliances to intermittently dispute the intervening zone with the Portuguese at Belém.

NORTH AMERICAN ENCOUNTERS

Exploiting the vast stocks of cod off the Newfoundland coast, European fishermen reached North America at about the same time as the Spanish and Portuguese discoveries occurred to the south. These expeditions also led to intermittent contacts with native coastal populations as the fishermen often landed to dry their catch in temporary camps. To the south, Juan Ponce de Léon claimed Florida for Spain in 1513 and led an abortive attempt at colonization in 1521. Several further attempts to settle Florida and to reconnoitre the resources and populations of the northern shores of the Gulf of Mexico as far as the Mississippi were launched from the Spanish Caribbean over the ensuing decades but all without success. In 1564 the French established a small colony on the Atlantic coast of Florida under the leadership of René Laudonnière only to have it destroyed by the Spanish, who themselves, in 1565, built a fort on the Florida coast to keep out foreign intruders. In 1570 Spanish Jesuits established a mission on the coast of present South Carolina and then in Virginia, but this represented the limit to Spanish activity on the Atlantic coast of North America, not least because they were already profitably engaged in the conquests of Mexico and Peru.

In the first decades of the seventeenth century the French, Dutch, and English began focusing on establishing colonies in North America rather than raiding Spanish settlements. One important feature of this period was the constantly shifting array of alliances with the native population, entailing commercial enterprises, particularly fur trading, but also involving their local native allies, and increasingly the wider political units, in direct military engagement in colonial rivalries. As a result, due to the more extended nature of European contacts, their impact extended to the demographic as well as to the social and economic domains, resulting in the spread of epidemic disease more virulently than had occurred during the early encounters. The French first established trade with the native population following the expeditions of Jacques Cartier to the region of Quebec and Montreal in the mid-1530s but it was not until the beginning of the seventeenth century that a burgeoning trade in furs drew the French back into the St Lawrence River valley. In this trade for furs first the Huron and then the Iroquois emerged as the key native groups for the French, although both the Huron and Iroquois, like the Mohicans, were ultimately to be destroyed by this active partnership in colonial economic and political development and military rivalries.

Only in the early seventeenth century did the Dutch take an interest in the Americas, having by then emerged as a major economic power based on the carrying trade. But, as in Brazil, their initial colonies lasted a relatively brief time. By the 1650s there was a general retrenchment of the Dutch presence in the Americas and their establishments in North America were no exception. This was due largely to various defeats by the English, their direct competitors financially and commercially. In 1614 the Dutch East Indian Company established Fort Nassau as a trading post on the Hudson River. Although the site was abandoned in 1617 the trade with native peoples continued, especially with the Mohicans, and eventually Fort Orange was established at present-day Albany. Also in the 1620s small farms were laid out on Manhattan island, eventually seized by the English and kept by them in return for the suspension of English claims in the Guyana region.

English interest in establishing permanent settlement in North America was roughly contemporary with that of the Dutch. Prior to 1600 they had made various futile efforts to establish outposts in the colder regions to the north, and on Roanoke island off the coast of present North Carolina sponsored by Sir Humphrey Gilbert and his half-brother Sir Walter Raleigh respectively. However, in 1607 a larger and more consistent effort was directed towards the establishment of Jamestown in Virginia in the territory of Powhatan (Wahunsonacock), paramount leader of a group of indigenous polities. The Jamestown settlement was tolerated by the Powhatans but there were sporadic outbreaks of violence and, in general, relations were ones of armed truce or hostile indifference. Matters took a different course once the English realized the possibility of producing tobacco in Virginia on a commercial basis, after which the sponsors in London determined to uphold the settlement even in the face of native onslaught initially in the 'massacre' of 1622 and continuing attacks through the 1640s. The settlement of English Protestant dissidents seeking a place of utopian refuge was well under way on the coast of Massachusetts by the 1620s and was further augmented by the so-called Great Migration of perhaps 30,000 settlers to New England during the 1630s. This migration differed from other English efforts at colonization in that it was organized about pre-existing family groups seeking to practise subsistence farming which would be augmented by fishing and trading rather than upon the production of speculative cash crops. However, the expansion of the area under settlement that resulted from a natural increase in population brought settlers into conflict with the natives of the region, resulting in the expulsion and the depletion of the native populations of the New England regions by the close of the 1670s.

Paralleling the establishment of these colonies in the north-east the Spanish ventured north from Mexico to encounter scattered nomadic hunting groups, from whom the Aztec themselves had originally derived, migrating south in the fifteenth century to become the masters of the Mexican plateau and the great city of Tenochtitlan. The Spanish also encountered the agricultural and urbanized Pueblo cultures of northern New Mexico and Arizona. The Puebloan cultures seemed to offer the best colonial prospects, due in part to hyperbolic reports deriving from the expeditions of Francisco de Coronado in 1541 and 1542. But the first colonizing effort did not occur for another forty years when Juan de Oñate led over 500 people some 800 miles north of the limits of Spanish settlement deep into the territory of the Puebloan cultures. Initial receptions were peaceful but the unbridled theft and violence of the Spanish expeditionaries had predictable consequences. They were attacked by the people of Acoma Pueblo losing eleven men, and responded by massacring the majority of the Pueblo inhabitants, selling the rest into slavery and turning over the remnants to the Franciscan missionaries. However, no gold or other form of quick wealth was apparent, although colonists frequently raided the nomadic groups, such as the Apache, Ute, and Navajo, for slaves to sell to the Spanish mining operations in northern Mexico. As a result most of the initial colonists drifted back to northern Mexico, making this part of the Spanish empire something of a neglected backwater, and even by 1680 the Spanish population of New Mexico barely exceeded 3,000 persons. The Franciscan missionaries therefore formed the real structure of administration in this region, although they were eventually also driven out by widespread Puebloan revolts of the 1680s. As in the rest of the Americas, there were epidemic occurrences, but no less significant was the introduction of sheep and horses. The iconic image of the North American Indian is indelibly associated with the horse, and the social and cultural revolution that was induced by the widespread adoption of horses can hardly be overstated. Likewise, although more limited in significance, the adoption of sheep-herding by the Navajo was a fundamental social and cultural reorientation directly associated with the time of Spanish intrusion and conquest.

CONCLUSION

For the native peoples of the Americas the arrival of the Europeans was a unique historic event as was this encounter for the Europeans. In the sphere of economic relations, the advent of metal tools had a fundamental impact. The desirability of these items was ubiquitous throughout the Atlantic littoral and new cultural possibilities certainly emerged as a result of their availability. The influx of metal tools greatly enhanced the ability to cut new gardens, and tropical and subtropical regions saw increasing reliance on swidden patterns of manioc agriculture, especially since such an agricultural system would be highly mobile and appropriate to a variety of ecological niches. Such considerations became critical as the Europeans later actively displaced the Amerindians from the most productive areas of the coastal regions and floodplains of the major rivers. Until active colonial settlement occurred along the whole Atlantic seaboard the Europeans were dependent on being supplied with the produce of native agriculture. This economic dependency also led the Spanish in Guayana into a series of military and political alliances with the Lokono against other local groups. For similar reasons, in the various captaincies of Brazil, access to Amerindian foodstuffs was critical to the survival of the colonists and even for the evangelization of the natives themselves. At the same time such a trade in foodstuffs may not have affected the extant Amerindian economy in the same way as the trade for brazilwood and other forest products. Native economies appear to have had notable capacities for production beyond a subsistence level and were very different from the small-scale, marginal subsistence systems described in modern ethnography, or observed in the aftershock of European conquest and occupation

The introduction of the new technological items by the Europeans was undoubtedly a source of great change in many aspects of native culture. At the very least the lithic technologies and their production sites, such as in highland Guayana, were marginalized by access to metal tools, and so a range of specialists and their skills in this sphere died out, as did the associated regional networks of trade, which collapsed or were reoriented to capture the European market. This is very evident from the intense brazilwood trade that the Europeans initiated along the Brazil shore, the axis of raiding and trading having previously been with the interior, as was also the case in Guayana. Here a similar pattern of reversal in the flow of trade is also suggested by the decline of the highland chiefdoms in Guayana, which had controlled the Amazon–Orinoco trade routes as well as the dispersion of gold and lapidary items from the mineral-rich upper reaches of the major rivers. These kinds of economic change were therefore accompanied by political and ethnic change also; a phenomenon well understood by the Europeans who actively worked to change native leadership using the lure of trade partnerships to reinforce the position of those leaders most receptive to their needs. To a degree the lessons learned in one part of the Americas were enthusiastically transported to other contexts and so the pattern of alliance and trading seen in South America recurs and is also fed by the tactics and strategies developed elsewhere, as in North America, and vice versa. The delicate nature of such alliances and the intricate process through which they were built up and preserved is vividly brought home in the account of Hans Staden, a German mercenary in Portuguese service, taken captive for nine months by the cannibalistic Tupinambá. At times this process also led to overt military alliances, as can be seen vividly from the history of the French and Portuguese rivalry along the Brazil shore, or that of the Spanish and Dutch in Guayana.

In the Guayana region local loyalties seem to have dominated over putative ethnic ones. Partly this may have been because, by the time of European settlement at the beginning of the seventeenth century, native polities had already undergone a series of changes in which the ancient elites had been marginalized or overthrown, either as a direct result of intermittent Spanish intervention, or as a consequence of them being disadvantaged in the struggle to capture the coastal trade with the Europeans. In either case the result was the formation of new political and military networks which themselves became the basis for new ethnic identities. Precisely because the material basis of these identities was so closely tied to the European trade, their range of incorporation closely followed the pattern of European occupation in the region, which was fragmented and localized in nature.

Generally the impacts on political organization were less dramatic than in the regions of highly centralized polities such as Peru and Mexico. Without doubt there were fundamental changes in the nature of leaderships, particularly where some form of dynastic or family inheritance of juridical or political rights and powers was involved, but the political formations that replaced them did not practise distinct political cultures but rather used these traditions to formulate new kinds of ethnicity, political and military alliance, and modes of economic interaction with both indigenous and colonial populations. In this way there were certainly secondary political developments and the emergence of new political formations, as was also the case in coastal West Africa.

In a similar vein, and again paralleling developments in West Africa, these types of alliances with the Europeans could also lead to changes in native military behaviours as well as to their associated ideologies. All along the Atlantic seaboard because of this relative persistence in native autonomy, there is reason to think that a general militarization of native groups took place as part of this same process by which the hinterland polities were marginalized; such factors were evident, for example, in the rise to dominance of the Guayana Caribs, and of the Huron and Iroquois in the regions of French trade. In the case of the Brazilian Tupi a vigorous tradition of war was utilized by the Europeans as they mobilized native armies, often numbering many hundreds, to assault the fortifications of their rivals.[6] At this time the sheer weight of native numbers more than offset the primitive musketry and cannonry of the Europeans. However, this kind of warfare, or more exactly its frequency, could not have been part of pre-European patterns so that, even in the instances where a martial tradition was highly developed, Native Americans were reluctant to become involved in warfare. However, the more directly they became involved in European rivalries the more frequently they became deployed as mercenaries. Such 'ethnic soldiering' became virtually institutionalized all along the Atlantic coast of the Americas, principally because of the longevity

---

[6] As in the Portuguese attack on the French fort at Rio in 1560 or the French aid given to the Potiguar in their attacks against the Portuguese settlement at Itamarcá in the 1540s; see also Neil Whitehead, 'Carib Ethnic Soldiering in Venezuela, the Guianas and Antilles: 1492–1820', *Ethnohistory*, 37/4 (1990), 357–85.

of interaction between autonomous native polities and a succession of European enclaves all dependent on native alliances to offset their lack of military resource from the metropolis. In the short run such conflicts certainly sharpened extant enmities and on occasion allowed a resolution of them in favour of one or other party; since native groups would receive European military support for the express purpose of totally annihilating their opponents—an outcome unlikely to have been achievable within the technological and social balance that pertained in earlier times.

Alongside these changes in the political and ideological context of warfare, native military technology also was altered. Fortifications and combat tactics were either adopted or elaborated under direct European influence while metal replaced bone or wood in pointed weapons and firearms were utilized if available, although their supply was very restricted, and of doubtful value, in the early period of contact. Nonetheless, eventually these technological changes were to induce alterations in the pattern of military organization as well, for the opportunity for specialized military activity was greatly facilitated by the long succession of wars, raids, and slave hunts that the Europeans carried out, always with native support. When such assistance was not provided in numbers of fighting men, as was the case in early Brazil, then it was supplied through the offer to Europeans of knowledge of the geographical and political landscapes.

Given such evidence of mutual impacts it is important not to counterpose a pristine pre-contact culture to a contaminated contacted one, for this would privilege a particular cultural moment—that of encounter with Europeans or Africans—which may not have been so privileged within indigenous cultures. Moreover, even where the moment of first encounter was of such cultural significance there are still a multiplicity of cultural meanings that may be assigned to it; and the meaning which eventually predominates is itself the outcome of a contested political process. This contested process becomes very evident as native groups showed great variety in their political and social responses to the encounter with Europe, and thus also began to diverge culturally. This variation was particularly provoked by the advent of missionary work, historically a very special feature of the American encounter. Such 'conversion', the results of which were aptly termed a *reducción* by the Spanish, says little about the presence or absence of individual faith, but does signal a clear political and social reorientation in the face of European intrusion that is often contested by more 'traditional' sections of native society; leading either to the formation of overtly hostile and physically separate factions, or to the persistent 'rebellion' of groups nominally collected within the mission system. The only other practical response to the wave of European evangelism was to migrate away from the shore, as did a section of the Bahia Tupinambá, facilitated by their own messianic tradition. Other such migrations, notably that of the Yao from Trinidad to Guyana, occurred in the region north of the Amazon. The Guayana region generally was the recipient of successive migrations from the islands of the Caribbean; suggesting again that not all population loss in this region can be automatically attributed to the action of epidemic disease.

Encountering Europeans and Africans was simultaneously an opportunity for the remaking of Amerindian cultures, as well as a cause of their destruction. So too the encounter with the native peoples of America profoundly altered European conceptions of themselves and others, as well as the religious, economic, and social world in which they lived out those consequences. 'Early Encounter' was thus a multifaceted event, not just a linear transition from 'tradition' to 'modernity', or from 'native' to 'colonial'. As such the 'New World' that encounter revealed was a disjunctural moment for natives and colonials alike, and it was also a world they went on to create. In part this was an 'Atlantic world' in which new identities, new regimes of economic and political exploitation, and new forms of social organization were born; but it was also, through the cultural experience of long-distance mobility, endemic warfare and slavery, epidemic disease, and ecological destruction, the first encounter with modernity.

BIBLIOGRAPHY

Adorno, Rolena, and Patrick Charles Pautz (eds.), *Álvar Núñez, Cabeza de Vaca: His Account, his Life, and the Expedition of Pánfilo de Narváez* (Lincoln, NE, 1999).

Carvajal, G. de, 'Discovery of the Orellana River', in J. T. Medina (ed.) and B. T. Lee (trans.), *The Discovery of the Amazon According to the Account of Friar Gaspar de Carvajal and Other Documents* (New York, 1934), 167–235.

Hakluyt, Richard, *Divers Voyages Touching the Discovery of America and the Islands Adjacent: Collected and Published by Richard Hakluyt in the Year 1582*, ed. John Winter Jones, Elibron Classics (New York, 2001).

Hulme, Peter, and Neil L. Whitehead (eds.), *Wild Majesty: Encounters with Caribs from Columbus to the Present Day. An Anthology* (Oxford, 1992).

Léry, Jean de, *History of a Voyage to the Land of Brazil*, trans. Janet Whatley (Berkeley and Los Angeles, CA, 1990).

Salomon, Frank, and Stuart B. Schwartz (eds.), *The Cambridge History of the Native Peoples of the Americas*, iii: *South America* (Cambridge, 2000).

Trigger, Bruce G., and Wilcomb E. Washburn (eds.), *The Cambridge History of the Native Peoples of the Americas*, i: *North America* (Cambridge, 1996).

Whitehead, Neil L. (ed.), *Of Cannibals and Kings: Christopher Columbus, Ramon Pané and Primal Anthropology in the Americas*, Latin American Originals Series 4 (University Park, PA, 2011).

—— *The Discoverie of the Large, Rich and Bewtiful Empire of Guiana by Sir Walter Ralegh*, Exploring Travel Series 1 (Manchester, 1997).

—— and Michael Harbsmeier (eds.), *Hans Staden's True History: A Tale of Cannibal Captivity in Brazil* (Durham, NC, 2008).

CHAPTER 5

....

ATLANTIC SEAFARING

....

N. A. M. RODGER

RATHER too often, 'Atlantic history' is history with a hole in the middle. The Atlantic is treated as a pre-defined, self-evident space which serves as a sort of rhetorical device to define the peoples living around its shores. It is not regarded as something requiring any historical analysis or explanation in itself. This sort of Atlantic history is history with the Atlantic left out.[1] Yet without the ocean—or rather, the two oceans, the North and South Atlantic—we cannot account for many of the basic facts of Atlantic history. Only ships and seafaring made possible the construction of the Atlantic world. It was shaped by the possibilities and impossibilities of long-distance voyaging under sail. It was the practicalities of seafaring that governed why different European peoples settled where and when they did. Without understanding the patterns of winds and currents, and the realities of navigation, we cannot explain, for example, why first the Portuguese and then the Dutch—but not the Spaniards or the English—settled Brazil. We cannot explain why the West Indies were the crucial theatre of war which determined the event of the American rebellion of the 1770s. Above all we cannot explain why the late medieval Europeans spread outwards from the Atlantic and eventually imposed their culture on the world, when other seafaring peoples elsewhere in the world appear to have been better qualified and equipped than they were to explore the world.

Two stages in the making of the Atlantic world need to be distinguished; the age of exploration, when the geography of the two oceans was yet to be determined, and the age of exploitation which followed. 'Exploration', however, is not a happy choice of word, for there was virtually no exploration of the Atlantic, as the term is popularly understood. Nobody put to sea from late medieval Europe to discover the geography of the unknown world, to fill in the blank spaces on the map. Voyages were undertaken into the Pacific in the eighteenth century and the Arctic in the nineteenth, with this among other motives, but the Atlantic world was explored by men who knew

[1] Cf. Alison Games, 'Atlantic History: Definitions, Challenges, and Opportunities', *American Historical Review*, 111 (2006), 741–57, at 745: 'the Atlantic history that many historians produce is rarely centered around the ocean, and the ocean is rarely relevant to the project.'

(or thought they knew) where they were going. When the Vikings sought lands to settle, when the English sought new fishing grounds, when the Portuguese sought to find the gold of Africa and to convert the heathen, when both Portuguese and Spaniards sought the wealth of the Orient, they were in every case seeking places or commodities of which they knew the existence for certain, and the whereabouts with a high degree of probability. It was only the new routes which had to be found out. Of all the explorers of the Atlantic, only Christopher Columbus was grossly mistaken in his basic geographical understanding, and only he blundered into a real discovery of an unknown world.[2]

For any voyage of discovery, on any scale, all the difficulty lies in the return. Any fool can sail into the unknown, and no doubt fools have done so in every century. The achievement of the first European voyagers was to discover the ways home. Because of the Atlantic wind systems the return voyages had to follow different courses from the outward, and required the mastery of new and difficult navigational techniques. It is a common modern mistake to conceive of navigation as a process of fixing a ship's position. For early modern navigators this was not only impossible, but essentially irrelevant, for there was no point in trying to fix the ship's position when the position of the land was unknown. ''Tis in vain to talk of the Use of finding the Longitude at Sea, except you know the true Longitude and Latitude of the Port for which you are designed,' as John Flamsteed, the first Astronomer Royal, told Samuel Pepys in 1697. Even when the outline geography of the Atlantic was more or less established, the exact position—in particular the exact longitudes—of places remained unsure, for surveyors were only slightly better able to fix positions than navigators. Well into the nineteenth century charts and navigation manuals gave seriously erroneous longitudes of major ports, and indeed whole continents.[3] To make landfall what ships needed was not so much a position as a course, and when longitude was the great unknown, the courses they sought were parallels of latitude, courses due east or west. In order to find their way across the oceans, and into the parallels they needed to make landfalls, what seamen needed to discover was not the physical geography of the islands and continents so much as the invisible geographies of the winds and currents and the earth's magnetic field, plus the strange seas of thought which had to be traversed to understand celestial navigation. None of these was mastered in the period we are studying. A complete knowledge of the Atlantic wind and current systems, of terrestrial magnetism and oceanic navigation, was not available before the late nineteenth century. The Atlantic world was opened up and exploited by navigators with only a rough and ready understanding of what they were doing.

Besides the intellectual constraints of navigation, seamen faced the practical constraints set by the capabilities of ships and rigs. The size and speed of ships governed their range, which was a function of the ratio of the crew's consumption to the ship's

---

    [2] William D. Phillips, 'Maritime Exploration in the Middle Ages', in Daniel Finamore (ed.), *Maritime History as World History* (Salem, MA, 2004), 47–61.

    [3] W. E. May, *A History of Marine Navigation* (Henley-on-Thames, 1973), 24–31.

stowage—of water and firewood more critically than of food, which is relatively compact and easy to preserve. Ships with large crews and small holds could not stray far from land. The mastery of the Atlantic world, and eventually the whole maritime world, depended on ships able to make long ocean passages, carrying enough to supply their own crews and a paying cargo. Successful solutions to this problem in the age of sail depended on a combination of hull, rig, and knowledge of the oceanic wind systems.[4]

Different people opened up different Atlantics, divided by space and time, which were not conceptually united until the sixteenth or even seventeenth centuries. Until then it is most realistic not to speak of a single Atlantic world, but of a series of Atlantic routes, outward and homeward. First came the Viking Atlantic to the north and west. Then there was the late medieval Mediterranean Atlantic, explored by Genoese, Catalan, Portuguese, and Spanish seamen reaching south and west to the Atlantic islands. From this grew both the Portuguese Atlantic to the south, and thence eventually the Portuguese route to the East, and the Spanish route westward to the Americas. In the same period, in the late fifteenth century, came the discovery of the English Atlantic route north-westward. Each of these Atlantic routes presented different challenges, met by different kinds of navigation and seamanship. In the long run, as we shall see, it was the Portuguese who developed the most advanced navigational techniques. Crucially, they went beyond a sufficient understanding of 'their' Atlantic to develop methods which worked anywhere on the surface of the globe. It was this which made it possible to unify the Atlantic world, and ultimately the whole world.

The first of all the European Atlantics was the Viking, and it was pioneered, even before the Vikings, by the Irish monks who first settled the Faeroes and Iceland. The Norwegian peopling of the Faeroes in the late eighth century, and Iceland in the ninth century, were the first mass long-range European overseas settlements. They were made possible by the extremely seaworthy Viking merchant ship, the *knörr, halfskip*, or *kaupskip*, capable of carrying up to forty or fifty tons of cargo—a capacity sufficient to carry whole households, with supplies and building materials, for voyages of hundreds of miles. Sailing to the north and west, Viking ships could use prevailing winds and currents.[5]

Once Iceland was settled, it was only a matter of time before ships voyaging to the west coast would sight the high land of Greenland barely 200 miles to the westward, and in 985 Eirík Rauði Thórvaldsson, 'Erik the Red', established the first permanent settlement there. Next year Bjarni Herjolfsson, son of one of the Greenland settlers, arrived in his ship from Norway to find his father gone west, and resolved to follow him.

---

[4] Richard Barker, 'Shipshape for Discoveries, and Return', *Mariner's Mirror*, 78 (1992), 443–5; id., 'Barrels at Sea: Water, Stowage and Guns on the Portuguese Ocean', in *I simpósio da história marítima 'As navegações portuguesas no Atlantico'* (Lisbon, 1994).

[5] Barry Cunliffe, *Facing the Ocean: The Atlantic and its Peoples, 8000 BC–AD 1500* (Oxford, 2001), 92–3; Felipe Fernández-Armesto, *Pathfinders: A Global History of Exploration* (Oxford, 2006), 51–6; G. J. Marcus, *The Conquest of the North Atlantic* (Woodbridge, 1980), 16–51.

In thick weather he lost his bearings completely—the dreaded condition of *hafvilla* so often described in the sagas—and came on an unknown shore, low and wooded. He knew then that he was far to the south of his intended destination—that is to say that he had a concept of latitude, to use the modern terminology, and at least a rough means of estimating it so long as the sky was clear. Since his coast trended northwards he worked up it until he came to a bare and stony land which he judged to be in the right latitude for Greenland, and then struck due east, until he sighted a high ice-covered country, and so made landfall at Herjolfsness (the modern Cape Farewell), the very spot where his father had built his farm. This voyage, successfully locating a destination which the navigator knew only by report, from an unexpected direction and an unknown departure, shows what Norse navigators could do so long as they had sight of the Pole Star to estimate their latitude and to 'divide the horizon' (*deila ættir*) and so steer a constant course.[6]

Still more impressive was the first direct passage from Greenland to Norway, made in 999 by Eirik's son Leif; an open-sea voyage of 1,200 miles across some of the stormiest seas in the world. It implies that he had correctly estimated that the latitudes of Cape Farewell and Bergen were about the same, and was confident of holding a course due east by 'latitude sailing', keeping the altitude of the Pole Star constant. For at least 400 years this passage was regularly made in both directions, by navigators who apparently had no instruments at all (apart from a magnetic compass in the late Middle Ages). This shows the confidence of accomplished mariners who preferred to trust their reckoning on a long ocean passage rather than risk the dangers of approaching the land. No southern Europeans reached this level of navigational skill until the Portuguese in the 1480s.[7]

By contrast Leif Eiríksson's more famous voyage in 1002, southward to investigate the unknown land which Bjarni Herjolfsson had sighted, involved a relatively short and simple voyage. His settlement of Leifsbúdir in Vinland (possibly that which has been excavated at l'Anse aux Meadows in Newfoundland) was soon abandoned in the face of native attacks. As long as their colony lasted, however, certainly well into the fifteenth century, the Greenlanders were accustomed to voyage to Markland (Labrador) to collect timber, and remained in touch with Iceland. It seems virtually certain that any Europeans who had contact with Iceland in the fifteenth century—which at a minimum included Danes, Norwegians, English, and Germans—could have heard of the existence of a wooded land lying in a temperate climate hundreds of miles south of Greenland.[8]

---

[6] Marcus, *Conquest*, 55–62, 106–12; Thorsteinn Vilhjálmsson, 'Norse Navigation', and Alan G. MacPherson, 'Norse Voyages of Exploration', in John B. Hattendorf (ed.), *The Oxford Encyclopedia of Maritime History*, 4 vols. (New York, 2007), iv. 278–89.

[7] Marcus, *Conquest*, 112–13.

[8] Marcus, *Conquest*, 74–94, 155–9; Kirsten A. Seaver, *The Frozen Echo: Greenland and the Exploration of North America, Ca. A.D. 1000–1500* (Stanford, CA, 1996), 24–8; ead., 'Norse Greenland on the Eve of Renaissance Exploration in the North Atlantic', in Anna Agnarsdóttir (ed.), *Voyages and Exploration in the North Atlantic from the Middle Ages to the XVIIth Century* (2nd edn. Reykjavík, 2001), 29–44; MacPherson, 'Norse Voyages of Exploration'.

Meanwhile the Atlantic islands had been explored, beginning with the Canaries. These islands had been known since classical times and their peaks and active volcanoes are visible from the Moroccan coast, but they were not explored by Arabs. Although Arabs were familiar with long-distance navigation in the Indian Ocean, the Muslims of the Atlantic shores feared the deep water of the 'Ocean of Darkness' and confined themselves to coasting.[9] The first Europeans in the Canaries were Genoese and Catalans in the early fourteenth century, and they clearly thought of their settlement as an extension of the western Mediterranean islands, particularly the Balearics, recently reconquered from the Muslims.

The Atlantic islands as settled by the Spaniards and Portuguese can be regarded in political, economic, and social terms as an extension of the Mediterranean world, but to reach them required the invention of quite new navigational techniques. By the fourteenth century Mediterranean navigation had been developed to a high degree of confidence, based on the magnetic compass, and portolan charts giving rough latitudes (though not longitudes) of ports, linked by a network of rhumb lines, or compass courses. In the Mediterranean sea passages are short and the mountainous coasts give easy landfalls, there are no tides or major surface currents, the range of latitude is only 14°, and dead reckoning by compass bearing, using plane charts with no allowance for magnetic variation, was sufficient for all passages out of sight of land. (Commercial airliners were navigating by identical methods until very recently.[10])

For the open Atlantic, however, this would not do. Since the positions of the islands were very imperfectly known, no charts usable to the navigator could be constructed. Seamen crossing hundreds of miles of sea swept by unknown currents could not possibly locate the islands or return to their home ports using dead reckoning alone. Moreover they now encountered for the first time part of the North Atlantic wind system, which gives north-east winds throughout the year in the eastern Atlantic. This made it easy to stretch down to the Canaries, but impossible to return the same way. Wind and current makes it very difficult to pass north between the Canaries and Africa, but the early settlers must quickly have discovered that on the seaward side of the islands there are winds allowing a north-westerly course. This would have carried them straight to Madeira, and 550 miles further to the north-west lie the Azores, which the Portuguese had reached by the early fifteenth century at the latest. To locate these islands required methods of fixing latitude at sea, initially using a cross-staff to take the

[9] Christophe Picard, L'Océan Atlantique musulman: de la conquète Arabe à l'époque Almohade (Paris, 1997), 31–47, 209, 293.

[10] David Waters, 'Columbus's Portuguese Inheritance', Mariner's Mirror, 78 (1992), 385–405; Luís Jorge Semedo de Matos, 'A navegação: os caminhos de una ciência indispensável', in Francisco Bethencourt and Kirti Chaudhuri (eds.), História da expansão portuguesa, 5 vols. (Lisbon, 1998–2000), i. 72–87; John H. Pryor, Geography, Technology and War: Studies in the Maritime History of the Mediterranean 649–1571 (Cambridge, 1988), 53–7; Susan Rose, The Medieval Sea (London, 2007), 54–9; Francis M. Rogers, 'Celestial Navigation: From Local Systems to a Global Conception', in Fredi Chiapelli (ed.), First Images of America: The Impact of the New World on the Old, 2 vols. (Berkeley, CA, 1976), ii. 687–704; May, Marine Navigation, 182.

altitude of the Pole Star. From the Azores there are northerly winds most of the year to carry a ship easily home to Portugal or Spain, whose principal Atlantic ports (Lisbon and Seville) lie in almost the same latitude as these islands. This discovery of the eastern Atlantic wind system, largely by Portuguese mariners, was the crucial first step in the European mastery of the Atlantic. It taught seamen to make long ocean passages by exploiting circular wind systems to get into the whereabouts, and latitudes, of their destinations. Like the Norwegians in the far North 400 years before, the Portuguese had discovered that the secret of long-distance passage-making is to keep far away from land.

The 'leap' west and north into the open Atlantic towards the Azores (the *volta do mar largo* or *volta do Sargaço*) sufficed to get home from the Canaries, but during the fifteenth century the Portuguese were pushing down the coast of Africa, initially in search of gold. By the 1450s they had reached the Senegal and Gambia rivers, in the 1460s they began to colonize the Cape Verde Islands, and in 1482 they founded the settlement of São Jorge da Mina at the mouth of the Volta. It was possible, slowly, to work down the African coast into the Gulf of Guinea, but to return required another, much longer 'leap', the *volta da Guiné*, far out into the South Atlantic and then north towards the Azores. The *volta da Mina* was longer still. By the 1440s Portuguese seamen were confident enough of their latitudes to keep far out of sight of land when voyaging south too, and only approach the African coast when they had got into the latitude of their destination. In 1475 the Portuguese crossed the equator, and by 1484 Diogo Cão had reached 13°S, beyond the mouth of the Congo. Here of course Polaris could not be seen, and a new method of fixing latitude was urgently needed. The king (John II) convened an expert panel of astronomers who proposed using an astrolabe to 'weigh' the noon altitude of the sun, and compiled the necessary declination tables. Now a method was available by which latitude could be fixed anywhere in the world; the crucial intellectual tool which allowed European seamen to break out of the Atlantic into the Indian Ocean and beyond. By now too the Portuguese had worked out the South Atlantic wind system, which is broadly circular anticlockwise. In 1487 Bartolomeu Dias crossed the Gulf of Guinea from Cape Palmas (4°25N) to the mouth of the Congo (6°S), a single passage of 10.5 degrees of latitude or 1,400 miles. In 1497 Vasco da Gama took his departure from Sierra Leone and sailed south-west, away from Africa, working across the south-east trade wind until he had gained enough southing to turn east towards the Cape. The Portuguese still did not know most of the physical geography of the Atlantic world, but they knew the essentials of its wind system, which was much more important.[11]

[11] Waters, 'Columbus's Portuguese Inheritance', 388–95; id., 'Reflections upon Some Navigational and Hydrographic Problems of the XVth Century Related to the Voyage of Bartolomeu Dias, 1487–88', *Revista de Universidade da Coimbra*, 34 (1987), 307–9; Semedo de Matos, 'A navegação', 75–80; Felipe Fernández-Armesto, *Before Columbus: Exploration and Colonization from the Mediterranean to the Atlantic, 1229–1492* (London, 1987), 162–6; Francisco Contente Domingues, 'Arte e técnica nas navegações portuguesas: das primeras viagens à Armada de Cabral', in Adauto Novaes (ed.), *A descoberta do homem e do mundo* (São Paolo, 1998), 209–13.

Besides knowledge of celestial navigation and the wind systems, there was one further key element of the Atlantic navigation system which was developed in the fifteenth century: the three-masted ship rig. In the early, coastal phase of their exploration the Portuguese appear to have relied heavily on the caravel, which in its simple form was a small lateen-rigged vessel with a deep hull and fine lines. The combination of the very tall and narrow lateen sail and a weatherly hull form gave excellent performance to windward, making it possible, slowly, to win ground against a headwind, and allowing navigators to approach strange coasts with some confidence that they would be able to work back to seaward. Unfortunately the lateen sail is difficult to handle in blowing or gusty weather and requires a large and expert crew. The large crew and fine lines (therefore limited stowage) of the caravel were the worst possible combination for a long passage. What was needed was a rig suitable for bigger ships, requiring fewer men, and adapted to the strong winds of the open ocean. This meant square sails, which draw effectively with winds on or abaft the beam, but this in turn was only feasible because the discovery of the ocean wind systems allowed seamen to make long passages with fair winds. The classic ship rig, well established in most European countries by the early sixteenth century, spread a single very large mainsail, which provided most of the power, in combination with smaller square sails on foremast and bowsprit, and a lateen mizzen whose function was as a manoeuvring sail to balance the sail plan and help the ship to tack in confined waters. These were the ships which carried the Portuguese down the South Atlantic and into the Indian Ocean. Caravels still formed part of their fleets, but now they were *caravelas redondas*[12] or *caravelas de armada*, partly or entirely square-rigged for long sea passages. Spanish Atlantic fleets also used caravels, but moved swiftly towards square rig as it became clear that it alone provided the combination of motive power with economy of manpower which was needed for oceanic voyaging. Sixteenth- and seventeenth-century shipbuilders achieved further savings in manpower by providing more but smaller square sails on main and foremasts. By the sixteenth century a typical Spanish ship of 300 tons in the *carrera de India* could be handled by a crew of fifty. Their victuals for a three-month transatlantic passage required 45 tons of stowage, leaving 250 tons or so for cargo.[13]

[12] There is a linguistic trap here, for *navio redondo* or *nau redondo* means 'square-rigged ship', not 'round ship' as modern Spanish- or Portuguese-speakers might naturally suppose.

[13] Martin Elbl, 'The Caravel', in Robert Gardiner and Richard Unger (eds.), *Cogs, Caravels and Galleons: The Sailing Ship 1000–1650* (London, 1994), 91–8; Quirino da Fonseca, *A caravela portuguesa a prioridade técnica das navegações Henriquinas*, 2nd edn. ed. João da Gama Pimental Barata (Lisbon, 1973); Leonor Freire Costa, *Naus e galeões na ribeira de Lisboa: a construção naval no século XVI para a rota do cabo* (Cascais, 1997), 144–6, 383; Domingues, 'Arte e técnica', 216–19; id., 'A prática de navegar: da exploração do Atlântico à demanda do Oriente: caravelas, naus e galeõs nas navegações Portuguesas', in Bethencourt and Chaudhuri (eds.), *História da expansão portuguesa*, i. 62–72; Ian Friel, 'The Three-Masted Ship and Atlantic Voyages', in Joyce Youings (ed.), *Raleigh in Exeter, 1985: Privateering and Colonisation in the Reign of Elizabeth I* (Exeter, 1985), 21–37; José Luis Casada Soto, 'The Spanish Ships of the Oceanic Expansion: Documentation, Archaeology and Iconography from the 15th and 16th Centuries', in Francisco Alves (ed.), *International Symposium on Archaeology of Medieval and Modern*

Portuguese Atlantic exploration was a long-term, centrally planned operation exploiting the best scientific knowledge of the day.[14] It is something of a shock to turn from the Portuguese navigators to Columbus. He adopted the 'narrow Atlantic' theories of cosmographers who accepted Ptolemy's estimate that the Eurasian land mass extends over 180° of latitude (instead of 100°). They advised him that the distance from Lisbon to Hangchow was only 6,500 miles. This, however, was still far beyond practicable sailing range, so by inflating the extent of Eurasia to 283° with various arbitrary assumptions, and confusing Arabic with Roman miles, Columbus persuaded himself that he could get from the Canaries to Cipango (Japan) in 2,400 miles: the true figure is 10,600. It is possible that he had a little more than wishful thinking to go on. Although Pedro Alvares Cabral in 1500 is the first navigator known to have sighted the coast of Brazil, Portuguese seamen had been voyaging far to the westward in their returns from the South Atlantic for a generation, and there is some evidence that it was known earlier. Likewise, as we shall see, Columbus might have learnt of the existence of Newfoundland or Labrador from Bristol merchants. He would have interpreted either piece of information as confirmation of the longitude of China or Japan. Columbus had learnt from the Portuguese enough about the Atlantic wind system to be confident that he could get home from a westward voyage by getting into the latitude of the Azores, but as he had only a rough idea how to observe the altitude of Polaris, and none at all of the sun (though he took an astrolabe for show), nor how to calculate easting and westing made good on a diagonal course, he had to sail from a port in the right latitude for his destination. This indicated Gomera, the westernmost of the Canaries, which were under Castilian rule. Columbus therefore had to seek Castilian patronage, but in any case there was little chance that the Portuguese king, who had the best scientific advice available, would have supported such an obviously ill-found proposal.[15]

Even when Columbus returned in 1493, loudly proclaiming that he had reached Japan, few experts were persuaded. From antiquity men had believed that the Western

---

Ships of Iberian-Atlantic Tradition: Hull Remains, Manuscripts and Ethnographic Sources: A Comparative Approach (Lisbon, 2001), 132–63; Cruz Apestegui, 'Arquitectura y construcción navales en la España Atlántica, el siglo XVII y primera mitad del XVIII: una nueva sistematización', ibid. 164–213; Richard Barker, 'Sources for Lusitanian Shipbuilding', ibid. 213–28; Clinton R. Edwards, 'Design and Construction of Fifteenth-Century Iberian Vessels: A Review', Mariner's Mirror, 78 (1992), 419–32; Pablo Emilio Perez-Mallaína Bueno, Los hombres del océano: vida cotidiana de los tripulantes de las flotas de Indias, siglo XVI (Seville, 1992), 77–8.

[14] Onésimo T. Almeida, 'Portugal and the Dawn of Modern Science', in George D. Winius (ed.), Portugal, the Pathfinder: Journeys from the Medieval Toward the Modern World, 1300–ca.1600 (Madison, WI, 1995), 341–61; Francisco Contente Domingues, 'Science and Technology in Portuguese Navigation: The Idea of Experience in the Sixteenth Century', in Francisco Bethencourt and Diogo Ramada Curto (eds.), Portuguese Oceanic Expansion, 1400–1800 (Cambridge, 2007), 460–79.

[15] Domingues, 'Science and Technology', 465–7; Waters, 'Columbus's Portuguese Inheritance', 404; Fernández-Armesto, Before Columbus, 205–52; id., Pathfinders, 156–64; Ilaria Luzzana Caraci, 'Columbus and the Portuguese Voyages in the Columbian Sources', Revista de Universidade da Coimbra, 34 (1987), 561–70; Helen Wallis, 'Cartographic Knowledge of the World in 1492', Mariner's Mirror, 78 (1992), 407–18.

Ocean was scattered with islands. Many had been discovered already, and no doubt Columbus had found another—as in fact he had. He did not sight the main land of South America until his third voyage in 1498, when a bungled altitude of Polaris persuaded him that he was sailing uphill and was about to enter the Earthly Paradise. By the time he came home from this voyage his reputation had been ruined by the return of Vasco da Gama from India, bringing news of a practicable route to the real Indies, and an accurate estimate of the size of the world which immediately exploded all Columbus' fantasies. He died still vainly defending his absurd claim to have reached Japan, leaving it to Vespucci and others to publicize the discovery of an unknown continent.[16]

Meanwhile the English too had been able to confirm the existence of land across the Western Ocean. In the 1470s both political and commercial obstacles tended to drive English ships from the Icelandic waters where they had fished for two generations. Soon afterwards there are indications that Bristol ships had discovered a rich fishery somewhere to the westward, possibly the Newfoundland Banks. Either from their own sighting, or by report from Iceland or Greenland, they may also have known of the existence of Newfoundland itself. It is therefore possible that the 1498 voyage from Bristol to Newfoundland by the Italian seaman known to English history as John Cabot was more in the nature of confirmation than exploration. Though not deceived by Columbus' miscalculations, Cabot did believe that in high latitudes he could reach northern China. At all events it is certain that Bristol and other English ports traded with Spain and the Azores, and the knowledge of this new English Atlantic route was soon available to Spanish and Portuguese mariners—possibly soon enough to have been of use to Columbus. Portuguese, Basque, Breton, and French ships were soon exploiting the cod and whale fisheries off Newfoundland and Labrador, though extensive European settlement did not follow until much later.[17]

By the mid-sixteenth century the Atlantic world was conceptually united. There was no more talk of reaching China or Japan across the Western Ocean; it was understood that new lands of unknown but vast extent barred the way, with another wide ocean beyond them (though straits through the Americas were still being sought in the eighteenth century). The last great geographic discovery of the Atlantic was the Gulf Stream, first reported in the Florida Strait by Juan Ponce de León in 1512, though not accurately plotted across the North Atlantic until the eighteenth century.[18] Though it

---

[16] Fernández-Armesto, *Pathfinders*, 183; Alfredo Pinheiro Marques, 'Epilogue: Triumph and Disgrace', in Winius (ed.), *Portugal, the Pathfinder*, 363–72.

[17] Brian Fagan, *Fish on Friday: Feasting, Fasting, and the Discovery of the New World* (New York, 2006), 205–26; Patrick McGrath, 'Bristol and America, 1480–1631', in K. R. Andrews, N. P. Canny, and P. E. H. Hair (eds.), *The Westward Enterprise: English Activities in Ireland, the Atlantic, and America 1480–1650* (Liverpool, 1979), 81–102; G. V. Scammell, 'The English in the Atlantic Islands c.1450–1650', *Mariner's Mirror*, 72 (1986), 295–317; Marcus, *Conquest*, 126–70; Evan Jones, 'The *Matthew* of Bristol and the Financiers of John Cabot's 1497 Voyage to North America', *English Historical Review*, 121 (2006), 778–95; Susan Rose, 'English Seamanship and the Atlantic Crossing, c.1480–1500', *Journal for Maritime Research* (2002).

[18] Fernández-Armesto, *Pathfinders*, 194; Ian K. Steele, *The English Atlantic 1675–1740: An Exploration of Communication and Community* (New York, 1986), 31.

was more than a century before the leading navigators in Spain, France, England, and the Netherlands had reached the sophistication of the Portuguese, the exploitation of the Atlantic world was now essentially a matter of using geographical and navigational information which was more or less common property among the seafaring nations. It is therefore time to sketch the world of Atlantic navigation under sail, as it existed from the sixteenth to the nineteenth centuries. Several fundamental conditions need to be understood at the start.[19] For practical purposes no ship (and from the sixteenth century almost all vessels engaged in deep-sea voyaging were ship-rigged) could point higher than six points (67.5°) off the wind, to which must be added at least another point of leeway to arrive at distance made good. This meant that it was always difficult and often impossible to win any ground to windward without a favourable tide or current. Added to the strain on crew and gear of constant beating, this meant that ships did not normally attempt to work to windward for any considerable distance except in emergency. The great difficulty of beating to windward made all approaches to the land, or shoal water, inherently dangerous. The nightmare of every seaman under sail was the lee shore, for if the wind was blowing towards the land there were many circumstances in which there was grave danger of shipwreck. At night or in thick weather a ship might be on or very near the coast before being aware of it, and unable to claw off. It was easy to become 'embayed'; trapped between two headlands neither of which the ship could weather. Then the anchors were the only hope, but in an onshore gale they were not likely to hold. Even if the wind were blowing offshore and the coast could be closed in relative safety, the wind might shift much faster than the ship could gain an offing. For all these reasons seamen constantly sought sea room, and regarded any approach to the land as their most dangerous moment. As the Vikings and the Portuguese were the first to realize, the key to safe long-distance voyaging was to keep away from land, in strong, fair winds, for as long as possible.

A large part of the danger and delay of an ocean voyage lay in getting in and out of port. Most ports lay inland, up rivers or inlets, which protected them from both the sea and the enemy, and exploited the commercial advantage of water transport to the maximum. To use them, however, vessels would ideally have been small, manoeuvrable, and shallow-draught, whereas ocean passages using the trade winds called for large square-riggers. The conflicting requirements made for awkward compromises, especially in trades whose home ports, like Seville or Amsterdam, were shallow or barred. Merchant ships were too clumsy to work quickly and safely in confined waters, and yet smaller than was desirable for long voyages. Not until the nineteenth century did two new technologies become available which liberated the sailing ship from many of the difficulties and dangers of entering and leaving port, and made possible the rapid increase in ship size which underpinned the last golden century of commercial sail: iron shipbuilding and the steam tug.

---

[19] There are surprisingly few convenient sources of reference on the general conditions of seafaring under sail. What follows draws heavily on N. A. M. Rodger, 'Weather, Geography and Naval Power in the Age of Sail', *Journal of Strategic Studies*, 22/2–3 (1999), 178–200.

The wind and current systems of the North Atlantic are broadly circular.[20] With only minor variations over the year, the winds blow from the north on the coast of Portugal, north-easterly around Madeira and the Canaries, and thence easterly across the southern part of the North Atlantic (roughly between 30°S and 10°S) and into the Caribbean basin. Off the Bahamas they blow south-easterly then southerly and south-westerly along the coast of North America, and so westerly back across the North Atlantic and across the British Isles. The currents, generated by the winds, follow the same pattern, the northerly drift of the Gulf Stream flowing at two or three knots out of the Florida Strait and up the American coast being especially powerful. For this reason the natural and normal route from European ports to North America traced a great arc to the southward, sometimes as far south as the Cape Verde Islands (15–16°N), and thence across the Atlantic and up the coast. To the modern eye the Caribbean appears to be marginal to the American War of Independence, whereas in the real terms of sailing passages, the islands lay on the easiest direct route from Europe to North America. Hence the strategic importance, but also the navigational danger, of the Bahamas, a great area of low-lying reefs and islands lying on the western edge of the normal route. Further north many ships bound for the middle or northern colonies were lost on the Carolina Banks, for they had to pass not far off this most dangerous coast, unmarked and invisible from a distance, with no good idea of their longitude. British ships bound to New England, and French ships going for Canada, were often tempted to halve their sailing distance by striking directly across the northern North Atlantic. This was best done in winter or early spring, when easterly winds are most common, but it was always risky, for a fair wind was far from predictable, the North Atlantic in winter is extremely hostile, and the drift was infallibly against them.

The Atlantic wind system gave the Spaniards a huge advantage in settling the Caribbean basin, for the transatlantic passage from Seville and back is swift and easy. Since both winds and currents set westward across the Caribbean, all shipping entered through the Windward Islands. Spanish ships generally gathered at Havana and left through the Florida Strait, continuing up the coast past Cape Hatteras before picking up the westerlies to blow them home across the central North Atlantic to the Azores and so on, due east for Cape St Vincent. The navigation was simple, predictable, and consequently dangerous in wartime. The early English colonies in Roanoke and Virginia were partly inspired by the hope of establishing privateer bases within easy reach of homeward-bound Spanish shipping.[21] In the seventeenth century Spain conceded a much more serious strategic advantage in permitting the French and

---

[20] Steele, *English Atlantic*, 6–9, is one of the few historians to show awareness of them. Basic sources are Boyle T. Somerville (ed.), *Ocean Passages for the World* (Admiralty, 1923 edn.), and James Clarke, *Atlantic Pilot Atlas* (London, 2nd edn. 1996). Note that winds are described by the direction from which they blow, currents by the direction to which they set, so a southerly wind goes with a northerly current.

[21] John C. Appleby, 'War, Politics, and Colonization, 1558–1625', in Nicholas Canny (ed.), *The Oxford History of the British Empire*, i: *The Origins of Empire: British Overseas Enterprise to the Close of the Seventeenth Century* (Oxford, 1998), 55–78, at 64.

English to settle the Windward Islands, and hence in due course to control the entrance to the Caribbean.

Just as the wind and current systems favoured the Spaniards in the Caribbean, they favoured the Portuguese in the South Atlantic. On the coast of Brazil and the northern part of the South Atlantic, the south-east trades blow throughout the year, providing an easy passage down to the latitude of Rio de Janeiro or even the River Plate, where a ship may pick up the westerlies which blow all round the world in high southern latitudes, often with great force. Portuguese settlement of Brazil (and Dutch rivalry for it) followed naturally from the fact that it was on the way to the East. Returning from the Indian Ocean, ships rounding the Cape had an easy run up the South Atlantic before the south-east trades before rejoining the North Atlantic wind system north of the equator.

The great challenge to the deep-sea navigator was the impossibility, before the mid-eighteenth century, of fixing longitude. A good observer with a good instrument could fix his latitude to within about ten miles, but this was an ideal figure. Errors of scores or even hundreds of miles were still common, and of course no observations were possible when the sky was overcast or the horizon obscured, that is, on the majority of days in the year around the British Isles.[22] Since the earth is symmetrical about its polar axis and in constant rotation, the problem of fixing the longitude of any point on the earth's surface relative to any other is the same as determining the difference of local time between the two. Several methods of doing so were theoretically available, and two became practicable more or less at the same time. The Göttingen astronomer Tobias Mayer published in 1755 tables which for the first time described the complex and irregular motions of the moon with sufficient accuracy to permit the calculation of longitude by lunar distances; that is, by inferring the rotation of the earth by measuring the movement of the moon against fixed stars. This called only for three straightforward observations with standard instruments, but the calculations were extremely lengthy and difficult. In ideal conditions this method allowed a good navigator to fix his longitude to better than one degree, though only with a clear sky for observations, and on about twenty days in each lunar month.[23]

The rival method was the chronometer, perfected by John Harrison in the 1760s, and soon imitated by other watchmakers in England and abroad. An instrument which can keep accurate time at sea over long periods permits an easy comparison between local sun time (so long as the sun can be observed) and the fixed or mean time of some datum meridian of longitude, the difference between the two representing the observer's easting or westing from the datum. For British navigators, and eventually for the whole world, the longitude of Greenwich Observatory was this datum. The accuracy required is considerable; to fix longitude to half a degree after a six-week voyage (a fast

[22] Taylor, *Haven-Finding Art*, 216–17; C. J. Sölver and G. J. Marcus, 'Dead Reckoning and the Ocean Voyages of the Past', *Mariner's Mirror*, 44 (1958), 18–34.

[23] Derek Howse, *Greenwich Time and the Longitude* (London, 1988; this is the 2nd edn. of *Greenwich Time and the Discovery of the Longitude*, London, 1980), 57–71.

transatlantic passage) the chronometer must lose or gain no more than three seconds a day.[24] Before Harrison no one had been able to make a clock which would keep accurate time in a constantly moving ship, subject to damp and rapid changes of temperature. The chronometer is a simple method of fixing longitude, and eventually it became the normal method, but initially chronometers were too expensive for most masters to buy them; 60 to 100 guineas in Britain in the late eighteenth century, plus five or ten a year for cleaning and repair. In 1802 only 7 per cent of British warships had a chronometer. Moreover, a single chronometer was not reliable: for real security a ship needed three, so that if one went wrong the error could be detected. Even the Royal Navy did not begin to issue official chronometers until early in the nineteenth century, and ships in home waters did not receive them until the 1840s.[25] Far into the nineteenth century many merchant ships crossed the Atlantic without any means whatever of calculating longitude. It is arguable that the great breakthrough in practical navigation was neither the chronometer nor lunars, but Thomas Sumner's method of obtaining a 'position line', first published in 1847, which allowed the navigator to get a working fix on the basis of fleeting observations of any two heavenly bodies (or the same body at intervals of time), at any hour of the day or night.[26]

Before the 'discovery of the longitude', all ocean navigation was a combination of observation of the latitude component and dead-reckoning for the longitude. When the sky was obscured and observations impossible, dead-reckoning had to serve for both, until the development of radio aids to navigation in the twentieth century. Uncertain both of their own longitude and that of the land, mariners making a passage across the Atlantic would try to make the land by getting into the latitude of a good landfall and running their easting or westing down (cautiously, at night or in thick weather) until they made landfall. The ideal port for oceanic trade in the pre-longitude era was one lying roughly midway along a coast trending north and south, with high land inshore and deep water offshore, the entry to the port itself marked by a prominent peak visible at a great distance—in a word, Lisbon. No other European seaport was as easy to find after a long ocean passage, but the ports on the Atlantic coast of Andalusia are nearly as satisfactory, for Cape St Vincent is a good landfall from which it is easy to make Seville, Cádiz, and the rest. This alone is a powerful explanation for the lead taken by the Portuguese and then the Spaniards in oceanic navigation. By contrast, English ports in general, and London in particular, are exceptionally difficult to reach under sail from the open sea.

In wartime, the necessity of closing the coast along a parallel of latitude was an important strategic factor, because it made the course of friendly or hostile shipping

---

[24] Howse, *Greenwich Time*, 71–8; David W. Waters, *The Art of Navigation in England in Elizabethan and Early Stuart Times* (London, 1958), 58.

[25] Howse, *Greenwich Time*, 71–8; id., 'The Lunar-Distance Method of Measuring Longitude', in William J. H. Andrewes (ed.), *The Quest for Longitude* (Cambridge, MA, 1996), 149–61; W. E. May, 'How the Chronometer went to Sea', *Antiquarian Horology*, 9 (1976), 638–63; R. W. Avery, 'The Naval Protection of Britain's Maritime Trade, 1793–1802' (Oxford D.Phil. thesis, 1983), 270, 291.

[26] May, *Marine Navigation*, 39, 172–5.

predictable. In the sixteenth century French and English pirates cruised off Cape St Vincent waiting to surprise inward-bound Spanish ships from the West Indies, knowing that the 'Indies trade' was a legal monopoly of the port of Seville, and the 'Cape of Surprises', as Spanish seamen nicknamed it, was their only likely landfall. Others lay in the Azores to catch the same ships earlier in their voyages. In the eighteenth-century wars French privateers from Martinique or Guadeloupe would cruise in the latitude of Barbados, fifty or a hundred miles to windward, waiting for British ships bound into the Caribbean to swim into their jaws. On the other side of the North Atlantic the British exploited the fact that the only safe landfalls for the French Atlantic ports (or the Spanish Cantabrian ports) are Cape Ortegal and Belle Isle. More difficult landfalls like the English Channel ports, which could not safely be approached on a parallel of latitude, were more dangerous to make but less vulnerable to enemy interception.

The social history of Atlantic seafaring, especially in its earliest phases, is largely unwritten. We can only guess what it meant to venture on long ocean passages for men who had never before been out of sight of land for more than a few days. We cannot tell how the decision to take such a risk might have been arrived at. Most historians assume a modern model of leadership by a charismatic commander who persuades or compels his men to follow him, but medieval ships seem very often to have been run on quasi-collective lines, with the whole crew involved in decision-making.[27] Perhaps the necessity of a skilled navigator to command on ocean passages helped to give the shipmaster the large authority he still has at sea. Some idea can be given of the risks of ocean voyages. It has been calculated that Spanish *flotas* homeward from the Americas between 1551 and 1600 were losing 7 per cent of their ships a year to marine causes or enemy action, but this average concealed wide fluctuations: in the worst year, 1591, more than a third of the ships perished. One-tenth of all losses occurred in the River Guadalquivir between Seville and the bar. Between 1500 and 1635 the Portuguese lost 16 per cent of ships outward-bound to India, and 15 per cent homeward.[28] This, however, was an exceptionally long and dangerous navigation, and the Spanish figures are from wartime. In terms of men rather than ships, a sample of 2,357 men who sailed on Spanish transatlantic voyages between 1573 and 1593 lost 290 dead (half of them in a single shipwreck), or 12.3 per cent, about three times the average mortality of the Spanish population ashore.[29] By the eighteenth century overall mortality aboard British merchantmen was about 0.5 per cent a year to accidents, 1 per cent to shipwreck and 4.5 per cent to disease, but losses were heavily concentrated in slavers and East India-men; the risk of dying on a North Atlantic voyage was well below 1 per cent a year,

[27] Dorothy Burwash, *English Merchant Shipping 1460–1540* (Toronto, 1947), 61–2; Jacques Bernard, *Navires et gens de mer à Bordeaux (vers 1400–vers 1550)*, 3 vols. (Paris, 1968), ii. 638–46; Sir Travers Twiss (ed.), *The Black Book of the Admiralty*, Rolls Series, 4 vols. (London, 1871–6), i. 94–7.

[28] Huguette and Pierre Chaunu, *Séville et l'Atlantique (1504–1650)* (Paris, 1955–9, 8 vols. in 11), vi. 866, VIII/i. 310; C. R. Boxer, *The Portuguese Seaborne Empire 1415–1825* (London, 1969), 219.

[29] Perez-Mallaína, *Los hombres del océano*, 186.

better than ashore. During the French Revolutionary War, British shipping worldwide was losing about 2 per cent of ships a year, half to enemy action', but in deep-sea voyages the ratio was 5–6 per cent.[30]

The study of Atlantic navigation raises as many questions as it answers. It seems to account for the early success of Portugal and Spain, but also seems to make almost impossible the rise to prominence in international trade of such remote and unfavoured ports as London and Amsterdam. It fails to explain the relative failure of such well-endowed maritime nations as France.[31] It does, however, point towards the reasons why the Europeans spread outwards from the Atlantic to the world, though in the fifteenth century the Polynesians were more experienced ocean navigators, the Arabs and Indians were accustomed to longer sea trade routes, and the Chinese built bigger and better ships. First it is clear that the Europeans had motives for expansion which others lacked. They came from an intellectually curious society, in which sea voyaging might be associated with chivalry, honour, and profit in this world or the next.[32] In China, by contrast, the famous voyages of Zheng He were 'essentially an urbane but systematic tour of inspection of the known world', mounted by a state which seldom took such interest in its surroundings, and never showed any curiosity about the barbarian world beyond.[33] The Arabs voyaged extensively in the benign marine environment of the Indian Ocean, where the biennial reversal of the monsoon allows every voyage to be made with a fair wind, but they never developed the navigational skill, or it seems the desire, to break out of the monsoon wind system. They certainly had no need to do so to reach Europe, most of which they conquered overland. Though both Arabs and Chinese knew the magnetic compass and the use of star altitudes, they did not discover the use of sun altitudes, and almost all their navigation was confined to the northern hemisphere.[34] More important was the nature of the winds. In a lapidary phrase, Felipe Fernández-Armesto declares that 'In most of our traditional explanations of what has happened in history, there is too much hot air and not enough wind.' The North and South Atlantic wind systems have two unique

---

[30] Peter Earle, *Sailors: English Merchant Seamen 1650–1775* (London, 1998), 130–1; Avery, 'Naval Protection', 242–7.

[31] Étienne Taillemite, 'Les Français à la découverte du monde: indifférence ou retard?', in Sylvia Marzagalli and Hubert Bonin (eds.), *Négoce, ports et océans, XVIe–XXe siècles: mélanges offerts à Paul Butel* (Bordeaux, 2000), 287–95.

[32] G. V. Scammell, *The First Imperial Age: European Overseas Expansion c.1400–1715* (London, 1989), 51–62; Felipe Fernández-Armesto, 'Maritime History and World History', in Finamore (ed.), *Maritime History as World History*, 20–30; id., 'Portuguese Expansion in a Global Context', in Bethencourt and Curto (eds.), *Portuguese Oceanic Expansion*, 480–511; Michel Vergé-Franceschi, 'Le Décloisonnement des mondes (1415–1492): de Dom Henrique à Cristofero Colombo', in Michel Le Bris (ed.), *L'Aventure de la flibuste* (Paris, 2002), 145–60.

[33] Joseph Needham, *Science and Civilisation in China*, iv: *Physics and Physical Technology*, pt. iii: *Civil Engineering and Nautics* (Cambridge, 1971), 479–529 (quoted 529).

[34] Dionisius A. Agius, *Seafaring in the Arabian Gulf and Oman: The People of the Dhow* (London, 2005), 130–62; K. N. Chaudhuri, *Trade and Civilisation in the Indian Ocean: An Economic History from the Rise of Islam to 1750* (Cambridge, 1985), 125 and 134; Kenneth McPherson, *The Indian Ocean: A History of People and the Sea* (Delhi, 1993), 16–75.

and extremely important characteristics. Once understood, they provide means for the navigator both to leave and to return: to pass from the North to the South Atlantic and thence to the Indian Ocean (but directly to the Pacific only with great difficulty). It is hard to escape from the monsoon wind system, and altogether impossible without the navigational breakthrough which only the Portuguese made.[35] Still more important for the creation of the Atlantic world is that the two Atlantic wind and current systems are circular, so that the ships of all nations easily and often passed to and from and by each others' ports. Though in the early stages of exploration the Atlantic was divided into different national routes, from the sixteenth century it was a unified world in which the ships of all nations voyaged together. Although this did not in the slightest reduce national rivalries, it created a common seaborne culture marked by the wide scattering of European settlements around the Atlantic rim, with Flemings in the Azores, Portuguese in New England, Bretons in Newfoundland, Gaelic-speakers in Nova Scotia and Sierra Leone. Without Atlantic navigation, there could have been no Atlantic world.

BIBLIOGRAPHY

Bethencourt, Francisco, and Diogo Ramada Curto (eds.), *Portuguese Oceanic Expansion, 1400–1800* (Cambridge, 2007).

Fernández-Armesto, Felipe, *Pathfinders: A Global History of Exploration* (Oxford, 2006).

Gardiner, Robert, and Richard Unger (eds.), *Cogs, Caravels and Galleons: The Sailing Ship 1000–1650* (London, 1994).

Howse, Derek, *Greenwich Time and the Longitude* (London, 1988; this is the 2nd edn. of *Greenwich Time and the Discovery of the Longitude*, London, 1980).

Marcus, G. J., *The Conquest of the North Atlantic* (Woodbridge, 1980).

Perez-Mallaína Bueno, Pablo Emilio, *Los hombres del océano: vida cotidiana de los tripulantes de las flotas de Indias, siglo XVI* (Seville, 1992).

Pryor, John H., *Geography, Technology and War: Studies in the Maritime History of the Mediterranean 649–1571* (Cambridge, 1988).

Rodger, N. A. M., 'Weather, Geography and Naval Power in the Age of Sail', *Journal of Strategic Studies*, 22/2–3 (1999), 178–200.

Scammell, G. V., *The First Imperial Age: European Overseas Expansion c.1400–1715* (London, 1989).

Waters, David W., *The Art of Navigation in England in Elizabethan and Early Stuart Times* (London, 1958).

[35] Fernández-Armesto, 'Portuguese Expansion', 493 (quoted); id., *Pathfinders*, 149; id., 'Maritime History', 30.

CHAPTER 6

KNOWLEDGE AND
CARTOGRAPHY IN THE
EARLY ATLANTIC

MATTHEW H. EDNEY

THE Atlantic has never been a natural, predefined stage on which humans have acted: like all spatial entities, it is a social construct that has been constituted through human activities.[1] Other chapters in this book explore the constitution of the Atlantic as a mutable and evolving field of seaborne exchange of people, biota, goods, and concepts; this chapter considers its configuration by Europeans through the production, circulation, and consumption of spatial information, specifically in the form of maps. Europeans slowly developed the idea of the Atlantic in order to organize and understand the waters, shores, peoples, and places that they encountered as they sailed westward and southward away from Europe.

Understanding the contributions of cartography to the formation of the Atlantic requires an appreciation of the historical limits to the various practices and institutions of making and using maps. Consider, for example, the way in which Columbus, when he headed out into the Ocean Sea in 1492, set aside one way of conceptualizing and representing the world and began working in another. He had conceived of his direct voyage to the Indies through participation in the general scholarly discourse of geography (then generally known as 'cosmography'), which understood the earth to be a sphere and already mapped it using latitude and longitude.[2] But once at sea he

---

[1] Jorge Cañizares-Esguerra and Erik R. Seeman (eds.), *The Atlantic in Global History, 1500–2000* (Upper Saddle River, NJ, 2007), pp. ix–x, citing Martin Lewis, 'Dividing the Ocean Sea', *Geographical Review*, 89/2 (1999), 188–214. This chapter relies heavily on *The History of Cartography* (Chicago, IL, 1987–), hereafter *HC*, especially: vol. i: *Cartography in Prehistoric, Ancient, and Medieval Europe and the Mediterranean*, ed. J. B. Harley and David Woodward (1987); vol. ii/3: *Cartography in the Traditional African, American, Arctic, Australian, and Pacific Societies*, ed. Woodward and G. Malcolm Lewis (1998); and vol. iii: *Cartography in the European Renaissance*, ed. Woodward (2007).

[2] Nicolás Wey Gómez, *The Tropics of Empire: Why Columbus Sailed South to the Indies* (Cambridge, MA, 2008).

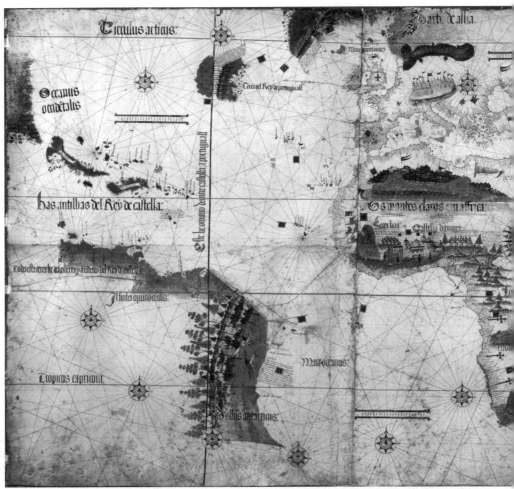

FIGURE 6.1 The 1502 world map (or 'planisphere'), almost certainly based on the Portuguese *carta padrão* that was smuggled out of Lisbon by Alberto Cantino, agent of the duke of Ferrara. It indicates clearly the line of demarcation established under the Treaty of Tordesillas (1494). Manuscript on three vellum leaves, 22 cm × 105 cm. By permission of the Biblioteca Estense, Modena (BE.MO.C.G.A.2).

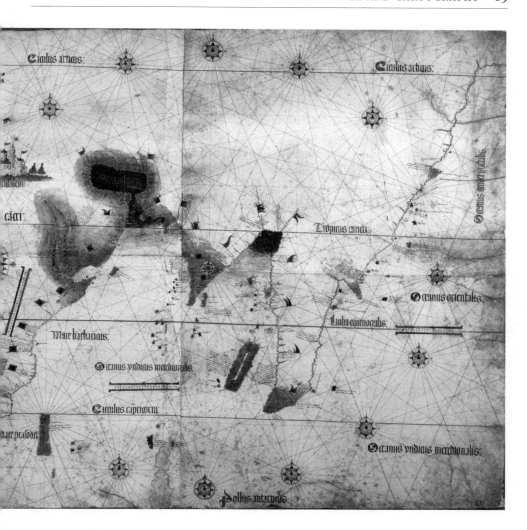

functioned like other pilots, by recording in his log the estimated distances travelled with directions measured approximately by magnetic compass in a manner that simply ignored the earth's curvature.

The two modes were so distinct that Columbus could not reconcile them. It was instead the Italian financier Amerigo Vespucci, with his scholarly interest in navigation and direct contacts with both mariners and court intellectuals, who would integrate Columbus' maritime experiences with geographical conceptions to recognize that Columbus had encountered an entirely 'new world'. Fundamental differences between early marine and geographical practices are similarly evident in the 1494 Treaty of Tordesillas, which demarcated Spanish from Portuguese spheres of activity in marine terms, by a 'line ... drawn straight ... at a distance of three hundred and seventy leagues west of the Cabo Verde islands' (Figure 6.1).[3] The difficulties of reconciling the nautical measure with a geographical framework, and of recasting the demarcation line as a meridian, would exercise Iberian diplomats and cosmographers for more than a century.

The domains of marine and geographical knowledge were thus circumscribed, their intersections contingent. The same holds true for other knowledges constructed of places and properties around the Atlantic's shores. Each knowledge domain featured its own particular set of representational strategies, whether performative or inscriptive, written or cartographic.[4] This chapter accordingly examines each of the several cartographies associated with the early modern Atlantic within their respective knowledge domains. It first examines the European charting of coasts and waters, revising common misunderstandings about the attempts made to control that knowledge, to regulate its dissemination, and to ensure its quality. Second, it analyses how marine knowledges were appropriated by geographers to create several oceanic regions including, by the end of the 1700s, the modern Atlantic in its full extent. Third, it summarizes the detailed terrestrial mappings which were marked by various blends of indigenous and European mapping traditions throughout the early modern period in a cartographic syncretism that was facilitated by significant cross-cultural similarities in traditional mapping practices. However, the self-conscious pursuit in Europe after 1650 of an overtly 'scientific' and 'universally applicable' cartography eventually negated those cultural commonalities.

MARINE NAVIGATION AND CHARTING

Codified marine knowledge derives ultimately from the experiences of the pilots responsible for guiding ships along coasts and across open waters. In both the Mediterranean and northern European waters, marine navigation developed as a craft

[3] Emma Helen Blair and James Alexander Robertson (eds.), *The Philippine Islands, 1493–1803*, 55 vols. (Cleveland, OH, 1903–9), i. 159–60.

[4] See Matthew H. Edney, 'Mapping Parts of the World', in James R. Akerman and Robert W. Karrow, Jr. (eds.), *Maps: Finding our Place in the World* (Chicago, IL, 2007), 117–57.

practice: pilots were trained through long apprenticeships in which they acquired knowledge of coastlines, ports, specific routes, currents, and hazards through oral lore and first-hand experience. Such orally constituted knowledge contained plenty of room for less-than-empirical components, such as belief in the existence of islands out in the Western Sea. Thus we know of attempts by Bristol pilots in the 1480s to find legendary Hy-Brasil only from a few ancillary legal documents: the craft of piloting was, in that time and place, strictly oral and left no direct archival trace.[5]

Some literate pilots did inscribe their accumulated knowledge as records of distances and directions to be sailed, perhaps illustrated by sketches of the appearance of coastal features, with descriptive statements of local conditions and, in northern waters, notes on the character of the sea floor. Such written itineraries were certainly well known to the ancient world and they were popular in the fourteenth-century Mediterranean, where the Italians called them *portolani* (*routiers* in French, eventually corrupted by the English as 'rutters'). Other mariners could then retrace known and codified routes, correcting their actual progress against the information provided in the rutter. In moving out into western waters, European mariners continued to use such simple technology (Figure 6.2). Of course, there is a great difference between following a well-sailed route and entering into unknown waters. On entering waters new to them, pilots generally sought to draw on the lore of local informants and to incorporate it into their own corpus, perhaps translating it from one mode of sailing (canoe) into another (caravel). Columbus famously seized several native mariners specifically to learn about the places he was to encounter and he particularly praised the sea knowledge of some of the indigenous peoples in the Caribbean; da Gama relied on Arab pilots in the Indian Ocean, while Drake relied on Spanish pilots in the Atlantic.[6]

The almost-closed circuits of the several basins that make up the Mediterranean and Black seas permitted some mariners, by the later 1200s, to graph out the *portolani* as charts, establishing a genre that would persist little changed until 1700. Such charts embodied the pilot's reliance on bearings and distances: a regular geometrical frame-work of intersecting rhumb (wind) lines was constructed within one or two circles; scale bars to measure distances were placed around the chart's margins; they had no need to take into account the curvature of the earth's surface. These Mediterranean charts would in turn provide the basic technology for mapping the shores of Western Europe and, after 1415, of western Africa (Figure 6.3). This is not to say that the European explorers made new charts while at sea: they recorded and communicated their routes by traditional means, which is to say orally and in written logs and rutters; the incorporation of new routes into existing charts was a complex task of shore-bound reflection and reconciliation. Indeed, charts provided navigators with a conceptual

---

[5] David Beers Quinn, *England and the Discovery of America, 1481–1620: From the Bristol Voyages of the Fifteenth Century to the Pilgrim Settlement at Plymouth* (New York, 1974), 5–87.

[6] Felipe Fernández-Armesto, 'Maps and Exploration in the Sixteenth and Early Seventeenth Centuries', in *HC* iii. 738–70, esp. 745; Eric H. Ash, 'Navigation Techniques and Practice in the Renaissance', in *HC* iii. 509–27.

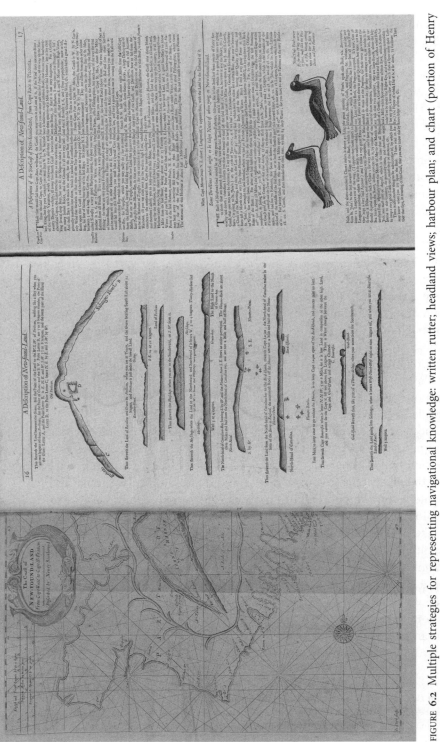

FIGURE 6.2 Multiple strategies for representing navigational knowledge: written rutter; headland views; harbour plan; and chart (portion of Henry Southwood, *Coast of New Foundland*). Letterpress, with woodcut insets, 46.5 cm high; (map) copper engraving, 42 cm × 102 cm, 1: c.310,000. From *The English Pilot. The Fourth Book. Describing the West-India Navigation, from Hudson's-Bay to the River Amazones* (London: Richard and William Mount, and Thomas Page, 1716), 16–17 (text) and between 10 and 11 (map foldout). Courtesy of the Osher Map Library and Smith Center for Cartographic Education, University of Southern Maine (OS-1716-1).

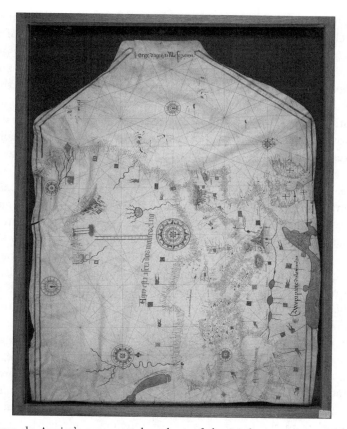

FIGURE **6.3** Jorge de Aguiar's 1492 portolan chart of the Mediterranean and Black seas and the Atlantic coasts is the earliest surviving dated chart of Portuguese origin. A decorative work similar in style to products of the Majorcan school of chart makers, it was meant for presentation rather than use at sea; the detail placed in the middle of the Sahara, below a scale bar, is the extension of the African coast from Senegal to the Niger. Manuscript on vellum, 77 cm × 103 cm. Courtesy of the Beinecke Rare Book and Manuscript Library, Yale University (Art Object *30cea 1492).

understanding of the overall organization of coasts and seas and were not directly used as instruments of navigation.[7]

Two competing communities of chart makers developed in the medieval Mediterranean: first, active and retired pilots made charts generally intended for practical use; second, specialized land-bound chart makers were more responsive to the intellectual and political needs of princes and so tended to think in geographical terms. The second group was the primary conduit for the flow of marine knowledge

[7] Tony Campbell, 'Portolan Charts from the Late Thirteenth Century to 1500', in *HC* i. 371–463; Corradino Astengo, 'The Renaissance Chart Tradition in the Mediterranean', in *HC* iii. 174–262; Fernández-Armesto, 'Maps and Exploration', 751–4; N. A. M. Rodger in this volume.

into geographical discourses, so that after 1498 the sporadic medieval attempts to reconfigure charts into world maps developed into a specific genre of manuscript world maps (as Figure 6.1).[8] The second group also sought to impose geographical concepts of latitude and longitude onto navigational practice. They did succeed early on in promoting the shipboard observation of latitudes, especially through new techniques based on solar observations that worked both north and south of the equator: latitude scales were being added to Portuguese charts by 1500, and the Spanish followed suit soon thereafter; the latitude scale was eventually extended across the rest of the map in the form of a square grid, the ordinate indicating latitude, the abscissa undefined, to produce a new form of chart, the 'plane chart'.

Otherwise, the two groups of chart makers remained at odds. In Spain, the Casa de la Contratación was divided by disputes between the more pragmatic pilots (notably Sebastian Cabot, pilot major 1518–26 and 1532–48) who repeatedly rejected the charts made by the geographically minded 'cosmographers' (such as Vespucci, the first pilot major, 1508–12) who sought to reconcile the curved geographical globe with the mariner's compass charts in complex and unwieldy charts.[9] Historians have made much of Gerhard Mercator's innovative projection that he used for his 1569 world map because it apparently resolved this conflict; after all, it became a common refrain among geographically minded chart makers in the 1590s and early 1600s that pilots should use charts made on this projection (as Figure 6.4). But what historians have overlooked is what English mariners found through experience, that to use charts made on Mercator's projection required highly difficult corrections for changes in magnetic variation and the nearly impossible determination of longitude while at sea.[10] Those who constructed charts on Mercator's projection either were largely divorced from the needs of pilots or intended their work for non-marine audiences. Conversely, chart makers continued to make and sell plane charts right through the eighteenth century.

European princes and corporations who underwrote marine activities hired the specialized chart makers to comprehend and combine the work of multiple pilots. Uncertain about the conflicting logs generated by the African voyages, the Portuguese crown had by 1433 reputedly hired away one or more of Majorca's chart makers (mostly members of the island's Jewish community) to reconcile the logs and establish a coherent archive of navigational data (see Figure 6.3). Eventually, geographical anxieties seem to have led to the formation of the Armazém de Guiné e Índia to control instruments and charts; the Armazém was especially tasked with maintaining a master *carta padrão de el-Rei* (royal pattern chart); its chart makers made copies of the *carta*

[8] Gaetano Ferro, *The Genoese Cartographic Tradition and Christopher Columbus* (Rome, 1996), 26–42; Fernández-Armesto, 'Maps and Exploration', 759–70.

[9] Alison Sandman, 'Spanish Nautical Cartography in the Renaissance', in *HC* iii. 1095–142.

[10] Sarah Tyacke, 'Geography is Better than Divinity: The Practitioners' Story' (second Sandars Lecture, Cambridge University, 2007), www.lib.cam.ac.uk/sandars/Sandars_Lectures_2007.html.

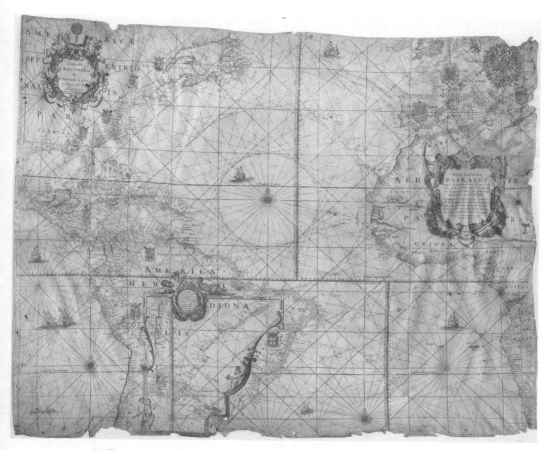

FIGURE **6.4** William Jansz. Blaeu, *West Indische Paskaert* (Amsterdam, *c.*1630). The second of Blaeu's small-scale charts of the Atlantic, prepared on the Mercator projection, intended to aid the African and American trade of the WIC. The southern portion of South America is in the inset filling the continental interior. This is a late impression, made *c.*1710. Copper engraving on vellum, hand coloured, 77.5 cm × 95 cm. By permission of the New York Public Library (Stokes C.1621-A-3).

padrão for use by Portuguese pilots although no direct copies survive (see Figure 6.1).[11] The Spanish crown followed suit with the creation in 1503 of the Casa de la Contratación in Seville; within the Casa, the pilot major was responsible for training and licensing pilots, maintaining the *padrón real*, and making copies for shipboard use. Again, few charts survive that were copied from the *padrón*. In the following century, the organization of the Dutch East India Company (VOC) in 1602 and West India Company (WIC) in 1621 led to concerted efforts by both companies to form centralized chart offices, with the result that Dutch chart production focused in Amsterdam; in

[11] Maria Fernanda Alegria et al., 'Portuguese Cartography in the Renaissance', in *HC* iii. 975–1068, esp. 977–87 and 1003–5.

turn, the WIC's bankruptcy in 1674 liberalized the production of charts of Atlantic navigation.[12]

Historians have also made much of the function of these several institutions to control cartographic information and to keep it secret; the Casa de la Contratación has especially been the subject of much overstatement in this regard. Official and corporate attempts to control marine knowledge could only encompass those portions amenable to inscription and archiving, which is to say logs, rutters, and charts. Other, oral portions of pilot lore remained in circulation beyond the ability of officials in the metropole to control and codify them.

Not that it was ever actually feasible for those officials to create a coherent cartographic archive. The Spanish crown issued no less than eleven royal directives during the sixteenth century to revise and update the *padrón real*. Pragmatic concerns eventually led to the abandonment of the geographically inspired ideal that a single world chart could hold all the attested information. After 1593, the *padrón* was reorganized into six separate parts, each reflecting a particular region of interest to Iberian mariners: least important, as rarely visited by ships under the Casa's direction, were the Mediterranean and the fishing grounds of the northern Atlantic; more important were the routes from Portugal to the East Indies, to Brazil and the Straits of Magellan, and from New Spain to the Philippines; most important was the transatlantic route to the West Indies, which henceforth was kept at a larger scale than the others. The Casa continued to train pilots and prepare charts after 1600, but it would seem that an unregulated trade in charts and logs flourished among pilots.[13]

More generally, the accretion of knowledge led to the proliferation of charts of specific coasts, gulfs, and primary routes that were made throughout the Spanish and Portuguese territories (Figure 6.5). In the Netherlands, the desire of both the VOC and WIC to keep marine information secret was effectively undone by the need to employ commercial map publishers to run their chart offices, so that a great deal of charted information was recast for published geographical atlases.

Control of knowledge and any claim to secrecy were also thwarted by the almost continuous exchange of pilots and chart makers between different polities. For example, after 1518, the Spanish hired a number of Portuguese chart makers to work in the Casa; again, after quitting as pilot major, Cabot went to England to train pilots. Furthermore, manuscript rutters and charts evidently circulated widely throughout the Western European marines. Thus, the few surviving French and Dutch oceanic and

---

[12] Sandman, 'Spanish Nautical Cartography'; Kees Zandvliet, 'Mapping the Dutch World Overseas in the Seventeenth Century', in *HC* iii. 1433–62; id., *Mapping for Money: Maps, Plans and Topographic Paintings and their Role in Dutch Overseas Expansion during the 16th and 17th Centuries* (Amsterdam, 1998).

[13] Sandman, 'Spanish Nautical Cartography', esp. 1142. See also her 'Controlling Knowledge: Navigation, Cartography, and Secrecy in the Early Modern Spanish Atlantic', in James Delbourgo and Nicholas Dew (eds.), *Science and Empire in the Atlantic World* (New York, 2008), 31–51.

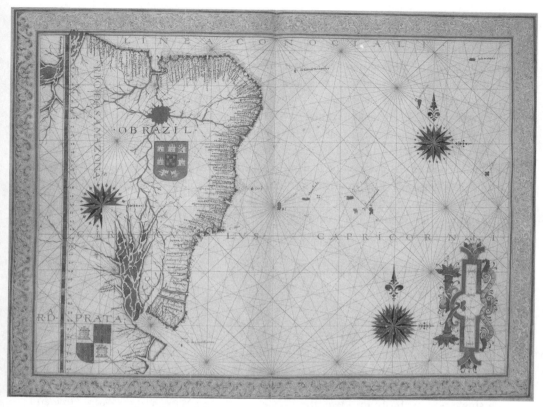

FIGURE **6.5** Presentation chart of the east coast of South America from an atlas compiled by Fernão Vaz Dourado in Goa, c.1570. By permission of the Huntington Library (HM 41, fo. 2).

regional charts of non-European waters made before 1600 are all manuscript copies of Portuguese charts.

A key Dutch innovation was to include charts in printed rutters; originally these were restricted to European waters, but smaller oceanic charts (*paskaarte*) of the Atlantic and the East India navigations began to be printed after 1630 (see Figure 6.4).[14] English chart makers followed the lead of the Dutch, even to the point of reissuing older Dutch charts, but without any concerted effort to control charting in the Atlantic. By the later seventeenth century, economic growth and increased amounts of shipping led London chart makers to publish detailed pilot books for the East and West India navigations (see Figure 6.2); the detailed maps in these books did not go through many subsequent revisions, being always secondary to the rutters. The publication of charts, and especially the widespread use throughout Western Europe of printed Dutch charts, did not

[14] Philip D. Burden, *The Mapping of North America: A List of Printed Maps [to 1700]*, 2 vols. (Rickmansworth, 1996–2007), nos. 194 and 233.

immediately replace older manuscript practices, which were preferred by many pilots well into the 1700s.[15]

We can thus discern the formation of a Western European practice of marine charting, originating in the Portuguese appropriation of medieval Mediterranean technologies but thereafter quickly diverging from those technologies. Oceanic charting remained a largely manuscript and practical craft, despite the attempts of geographically minded chart makers. While Europeans' initial navigation of strange shores often depended upon native guides, the knowledge of sand bars and tricky currents was soon incorporated into pilots' lore; the codification of that lore in charts soon elided the native presence. The practices and institutions of marine navigation and charting were all specifically European in nature. Yet this marine practice was global in scope, applied to and pursued in all oceans where Western Europeans sailed (see Figure 6.5). It only sustained a specific sense of the Atlantic through its connections to geographical discourses.

THE GEOGRAPHICAL CREATION OF 'THE ATLANTIC'

When the Portuguese began sailing down the African coast, they thought that they were skirting the fringes of the great Ocean Sea (*Mare Oceanus*) that encircled Africa, Europe, and Asia. Geographers had long applied specific, localized names to particular portions of this great sea. There was little consistency to these names, beyond the fundamental cosmographical divide of the equator that divided what we think of today as a single oceanic basin into two, the Western Ocean or Sea (*Oceanus/Mare Occidentalis*) off Europe and, south of the equator, the Southern Ocean or Sea (*Oceanus/Mare Australis/Meridionalis*). Otherwise, the history of oceanic concepts presents a highly complex narrative that intertwines marine practice, the self-conscious inheritance of classical ideas, proto-nationalistic trends, and intellectual inertia.[16] The complexity is evident in the work of one scholar, Martin Waldseemüller. In his famous world map of 1507, significantly informed by marine practices, he used the label only of 'Western Ocean', but in the accompanying cosmographical account, heavily informed by classi-

---

[15] In *HC* iii: Günter Schilder and Marco van Egmond, 'Maritime Cartography in the Low Countries during the Renaissance' (1384–432); Sarah Toulouse, 'Marine Cartography and Navigation in Renaissance France' (1550–68); and Sarah Tyacke, 'Chartmaking in England and its Context, 1500–1660' (1722–53). Thomas R. Smith, 'Manuscript and Printed Sea Charts in Seventeenth-Century London: The Case of the Thames School', in Norman J. W. Thrower (ed.), *The Compleat Plattmaker: Essays on Chart, Map, and Globe Making in England in the Seventeenth and Eighteenth Centuries* (Berkeley, CA, 1978), 45–100.

[16] I am especially indebted to Carla Lois and João Carlos Garcia, 'Do oceano dos clássicos aos mares dos impérios: transformações cartográficas do Atlântico sul', *Anais do Museu Paulista*, NS 17/2 (2009), 15–37.

cal texts, he drew on the classical label of 'Atlantic Ocean' for the waters off Africa at the end of the Atlas Mountains.[17]

Some early modern geographers did forgo the general scholarly obsession with the mapping of the continents and sought instead to frame various portions of the western and southern oceans as coherent regions. These oceanic framings manifested the navigational circuits and political claims of the several European maritime nations. To begin with, Italian and German geographers framed the circuit of Spanish voyages between Europe and the West Indies, mostly north of the equator (Figure 6.6). (Emphasizing their own maritime circuit, Spanish mariners progressively labelled the Western Ocean as *Mar del Norte* in opposition to southern waters.) This genre paradoxically culminated in Baptista Boazio's 1589 map delineating Drake's 1585–6 expedition against the Spanish in the West Indies. The same frame was resurrected after 1650 in French and English public discourse, to map the focal

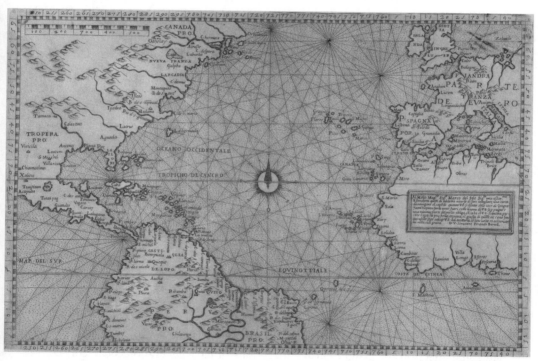

FIGURE 6.6 Ferrando Bertelli's *c.*1565 contribution to the genre of published maps framing the Spanish maritime circuit between Europe, Africa, and America. This map was published as a separate sheet in Venice and was included in 'assembled-to-order' atlases. Copper engraving, 24 cm × 36 cm. Courtesy of the Osher Map Library and Smith Center for Cartographic Education, University of Southern Maine (SM-1565-5).

[17] John W. Hessler, *The Naming of America: Martin Waldseemüller's 1507 World Map and the 'Cosmographiae introductio'* (London, 2008), 100–1.

arena of those nations' overseas mercantile interests; English maps delineating the routes of the Spanish treasure fleets in the northern Atlantic became common in the eighteenth century. (Previously, British printed maps of the Western Ocean had been fixated on the possibility of a North West Passage and so had framed only the northern waters.)[18]

For the Portuguese, the goal was to head south and get around Africa in order to reach India and other parts of the tropics that were believed to be the source of gold and spices.[19] It was, therefore, Portuguese charts of the routes to and through the Southern Ocean that first framed the oceanic basin, from the Cape of Good Hope to the British Isles and from Cape Horn to Newfoundland.[20] The consistent north orientation of the lettering on these charts, in distinction to the variable orientation of text on the Mediterranean charts, suggests that they were enlarged portions of world maps (as Figure 6.1). (Note that the famous 1513 chart of almost the entire Atlantic basin by the Ottoman admiral Piri Reis is in fact the surviving portion of a large world map.[21]) Indeed, Portuguese charts of the routes to southern waters were generally made in conjunction with charts of other parts of the great Southern Ocean. In the process, the Portuguese had by the 1530s displaced the descriptor of 'southern' to the waters washing the rich tropical shores of Asia, especially the Pacific ('South Seas'), and had begun to refer to the erstwhile Southern Ocean by the classical concept of *Mare Aethiopica*.

Ultimately, the Portuguese framing of the entire oceanic basin was adopted by the Dutch (see Figure 6.4) and then by the English. Both of these nations were similarly interested in the entire basin and in the further routes to Asia. At the same time, both Dutch and English geographers adopted the label 'Atlantic' and by 1650 they were using it as a synonym for the Western Ocean.

Only in eighteenth-century England was the cosmographical significance of the equator finally undermined and the entire oceanic basin mapped and named as a single entity. The key figure seems to have been the hack geographer Herman Moll. In 1701 he abandoned his previous adherence to a southern or Ethiopian sea and unambiguously wrote that Africa was completely bounded on its western side by the Atlantic; he then consistently mapped the Atlantic Ocean as broaching the equator in all his general maps.[22] Most other English geographers continued to derive their maps from Dutch or French sources and so generally failed to adopt Moll's innovation. But Moll's maps were reproduced in pedagogic texts for the rest of the century and seem to have had some effect on the geographical conceptions of later generations. The concept of the expanded Atlantic gained traction with the work of James Cook, the famous

[18] Pre-1700 printed maps of the Atlantic are all reproduced by Burden, *Mapping of North America*.

[19] Wey Gómez, *Tropics of Empire*, 159–228.

[20] See the charts reproduced by Armando Cortesão and Avelino Teixeira da Mota, *Portugaliae monumenta cartographica*, 6 vols. plus portfolio (Lisbon, 1960).

[21] Gregory C. McIntosh, *The Piri Reis Map of 1513* (Athens, GA, 2000), 8–18.

[22] Herman Moll, *A System of Geography* (London, 1701), 22.

navigator, who charted the 'South Atlantic Ocean'.[23] In incorporating the results of his great voyages of the 1770s into new maps, chart makers and geographers alike seem to have adopted and propagated the expanded Atlantic. The international adoption of the modern and internationally held concept of an extensive Atlantic thus probably stemmed from Britain's nineteenth-century cartographic hegemony.

TERRESTRIAL MODES OF MAPPING

Terrestrial modes of cartography are as bound up as marine charting with issues of control and power. The various practices of mapping the large extents of regions and countries, the landscapes of particular places (including towns and fortifications), and the precise bounds of real property are all inherently practices of cultural and social empowerment. As such they have been pursued by widely diverse institutions and communities that have sought to sustain or extend their territorial status and authority. In exploring the creation and dissemination of spatial knowledge about the lands around the Atlantic, the focus of enquiry inevitably shifts to the sheer variety of institutions and communities involved, to the cultural complexity of knowledge creation, and especially to the cartographic blending of indigenous and European representational strategies.

Indigenous mapping practices in North and Mesoamerica have received much historical attention; those in other parts of the world, especially sub-Saharan Africa, less so.[24] Such work has been sufficient to permit two broad and complementary generalizations concerning indigenous mapping practices, regardless of particular cultural formation. First, indigenous cartographies have emphasized performative mapping practices in which maps are constituted orally and through ritual, so that spatial knowledges are sustained by communal repetition and modification; if map artefacts are made, then they have generally been intended to be ephemeral, as part of speech and ritual, rather than to be free-standing and durable texts. This is not to argue that indigenous peoples were unable to create graphic maps of geographical space—a claim that has unfortunately contributed significantly to Western convictions of the intellectual and technological immaturity of non-European peoples—but that, like many people even in modern cultures, they had little need to do so.[25] Only in the highly articulated societies of the pre-Columbian American empires did there develop map-making traditions as complex and as persistent as those of pre-modern

---

[23] e.g. James Cook, *Chart of the Discoveries Made in the South Atlantic Ocean . . . 1775*, in his *A Voyage towards the South Pole, and round the World*, 2 vols. (London, 1777), map 4.

[24] In *HC* ii/3: the editors' introduction (1–10); Thomas J. Bassett, 'Indigenous Mapmaking in Intertropical Africa' (24–49); Lewis, 'Maps, Mapmaking, and Map Use by Native North Americans' (51–182); Barbara E. Mundy, 'Mesoamerican Cartography' (183–256); and William Gustav Gartner, 'Mapmaking in the Central Andes' (257–300). Also, G. Malcolm Lewis (ed.), *Cartographic Encounters: Perspectives on Native American Mapmaking and Map Use* (Chicago, IL, 1998).

[25] Denis Wood, *The Power of Maps* (New York, 1992), 28–43.

societies in Eurasia. For example, Mesoamerican scholars produced world maps that were as cosmographically and politically rich as Christian maps of the ecumene or Buddhist maps of Jambudvipal.[26] The cultural destruction associated with the Spanish conquests and demographic collapse makes it hard, however, to gauge the full extent of cartographic literacies in Mesoamerica and the Andes. Even so, works such as Guaman Poma's extraordinary, syncretic 'mapa mundi del reino de las In[di]as', which cast the Spanish domains in the Andes according to Incan cosmographical structures, remind us that those literacies must have been extensive.[27]

The second generalization is that most surviving indigenous map artefacts were produced through the active solicitation of Europeans; the remainder was almost all actively collected and preserved by Europeans in the eighteenth and nineteenth centuries. Interpretations of surviving indigenous maps and hints of mapping practices must accordingly take into account the particular ways in which Europeans interacted with indigenous peoples, which were in turn a function of the particular spatial conceptions within which Europeans acted. At the same time, in drawing upon indigenous knowledges, European map makers derived not just information and representational strategies but also spatial conceptions grounded in indigenous activities and cosmologies. These more fundamental conceptions permeate the subsequent maps, but are not easily read without careful ethnohistorical analysis.[28]

Geographical mappings of space

Knowledge about the lands beyond the shores of the Atlantic basin circulated in much the same way as did the marine knowledge of those shores and of the waters that washed them. Those who travelled the interior—both local inhabitants and European incomers—developed a corpus of functional information about rivers and roads that was transmitted orally and through performance. This applied as much to the self-conscious explorer who interrogated indigenous peoples about what to expect upriver or across the next mountain pass, as to a newly arrived colonist asking others about well-established routes between settlements. Some literate individuals recorded this information in diaries and itineraries; such itineraries were occasionally built up into sketch maps, perhaps also informed by coastal charts, which were then copied and shared in manuscript. Some educated officials and others wrote general descriptive accounts of the regions they had seen, with or without graphic maps, for the benefit of others. We have yet to study in detail the patterns of how these various geographical texts circulated around the Atlantic among officials and soldiers and among

---

[26] Denis Cosgrove, 'Mapping the World', in Akerman and Karrow (eds.), *Maps*, 65–115.

[27] Gartner, 'Mapmaking in the Central Andes', 294–9; Rolena Adorno, *Guaman Poma: Writing and Resistance in Colonial Peru* (Austin, TX, 2000), 89–119.

[28] See esp. Karl H. Offen, 'Creating Mosquitia: Mapping Amerindian Spatial Practices in Eastern Central America, 1629–1779', *Journal of Historical Geography*, 33/2 (2007), 254–82.

intellectuals and publishers, but it is certain that the flow of texts was never just one way, from colony to metropole, from official to public, from manuscript to print.[29]

The common reliance on itineraries permitted some degree of conceptual exchange. This was especially the case during the first Spanish incursions into the Aztec empire, when both cultures relied on a concept of space not as 'expanse' but as 'interval', as inscribed in itineraries, and only comparatively rarely made graphic maps (both still adapting terms such as 'depiction' or 'figure' for 'map') (Figure 6.7).[30]

In general, European explorers and administrators were ill equipped to interpret and inscribe oral and gestural testimony from indigenous informants. With their emphasis on the inscribed text, Europeans generally recorded only the bare bones of the

FIGURE 6.7 Antonio Asarti, 'Nova delineatio s[t]rictissimae S. Didaci Provinciae in Nova Hispania', in Baltasar de Medina, *Chronica de la santa Provincia de San Diego de Mexico, de religiosos descalços de N.S.P.S. Francisco en la Nueva-España* (Mexico City, 1682), following leaf 229. This view of the province of San Diego in New Spain combines a bird's-eye perspective with a spacing of towns and religious centres at constant intervals. Copper engraving, 16 cm × 26 cm. By permission of the John Carter Brown Library, Brown University (BA682 M491c/1-SIZE).

[29] Matthew H. Edney, 'John Mitchell's Map of North America (1755): A Study of the Use and Publication of Official Maps in Eighteenth-Century Britain', *Imago mundi*, 60/1 (2008), 63–85, gives initial comments on the circulation of geographical maps.

[30] Ricardo Padrón, *The Spacious Word: Cartography, Literature, and Empire in Early Modern Spain* (Chicago, IL, 2004), 45–91, esp. 243 n. 12; Mundy, 'Mesoamerican Cartography', 185–7; Richard L. Kagan, *Urban Images of the Hispanic World, 1493–1793* (New Haven, CT, 2000), 45–64.

information, such as redrawing on paper an ephemeral map sketched on the ground without also recording the associated oral performance. As such impoverished translations circulated among European geographers, they could be wildly reconfigured as they passed from white hand to white hand to meet the increasingly conventional spatial structures of European geographical maps; the fantastic interior drainage systems of early geographical maps of the Americas testify in particular to the manner in which Europeans routinely misinterpreted indigenous maps.[31]

Captain John Smith drew explicit attention to the processes of European exploration and interaction with indigenous peoples in his 1612 map of Virginia (Figure 6.8). He delineated the rivers with two weights—thick lines for the streams he and other Englishmen had followed in their explorations of the Chesapeake and its tributaries, thinner lines for the streams known to the English only through information gleaned from the Powhatans—and marked the points of transition by Maltese crosses, glossed in the legend as 'To the crosses hath bin discouered what beyond is by relation'.[32] Yet Smith actually showed relatively few precise details beyond the Maltese crosses (other than the western shore of North America that the English desired to be just a few weeks' journey from their new colony). The lack of interior detail manifests the manner in which the Powhatans were able for some time to keep the English on a tight rein, preventing them from meeting with neighbouring tribes and thereby controlling the distribution of English trade goods to those neighbours. Smith's map thus reminds us that indigenous peoples only gave away or sold information according to the advantage it would bring them (whether personally or communally) in their dealings with the Europeans and other indigenous groups.

European geographical discourses emphasized the Americas as the key locus of geography's intellectual drama.[33] The geographical mapping of the Americas was extensive and covered a wide range of formats and functions. A large number of regional maps were produced for a wide variety of administrative functions, from assigning mineral rights in Minas Gerais to defining the strategic location of new forts within the lands of the Iroquois; these administrative maps and their associated reports circulated in manuscript within the colonies, with copies occasionally being sent to the metropolitan authorities. Some of the regional maps ended up in print, mostly in promotional or propagandistic works, and after 1740 in some British and French journals to explain colonial wars to the burgeoning metropolitan publics; economic and political development in the British colonies in North America were sufficient to permit some regional maps to be printed there. At the same time, metropolitan

---

[31] Especially G. Malcolm Lewis, 'Indicators of Unacknowledged Assimilations from Amerindian Maps on Euro-American Maps of North America: Some General Principles Arising from a Study of La Verendrye's Composite Map, 1728–29', *Imago mundi*, 38 (1986), 9–34, and id., '*La Grande Rivière et Fleuve de l'Ouest*: The Realities and Reasons Behind a Major Mistake in the 18th-Century Geography of North America', *Cartographica*, 28/1 (1991), 54–87.

[32] This famous map has been frequently discussed, e.g. by Burden, *Mapping of North America*, no. 164.

[33] See Edney, 'Mapping Parts of the World', 139–41.

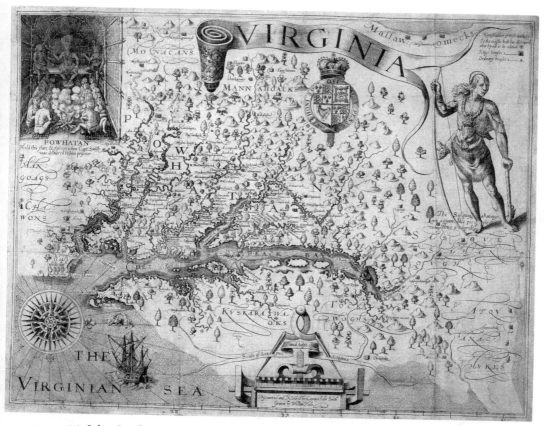

FIGURE **6.8** John Smith, *Virginia*, engr. William Hole, in Smith's *A Map of Virginia: With a Description of the Countrey, the Commodities, People, Government and Religion* (Oxford, 1612). Copper engraving, 32.5 cm × 41.5 cm. First state. By permission of the William L. Clements Library, University of Michigan, Ann Arbor (atlas E1b).

interests sustained the production of more general continental maps. Some of these were intended for official use, especially in terms of conceptualizing the wider spaces of colonial competition, assigning boundaries to large territorial patents, or comprehending how those patents overlapped one another. But most were prepared by commercial publishers in the Netherlands, France, and England, drawing upon a mixture of sources drawn from official and private archives, to address the intellectual interests of the educated classes. The sheer number and variety of all these geographical maps seems to defy any generalization beyond their basic function as geographical maps, to permit their readers to conceptualize, organize, and perhaps modify large swaths of the world.

By comparison, the geographical mapping of Africa was negligible. The character of Europe's economic engagement with Africa further dictated against any sustained engagement with its continental interior. The coastal polities restricted European traders to the coast, controlling the supply of slaves and other commodities, including knowledge of the interior. For most of the early modern era, European maps were restricted to highly generalized depictions of the entire continent; only in the mid-eighteenth century did chart makers reconfigure their detailed charts to make geographical maps for a general public and so added anything like detailed knowledge of interior peoples and polities (Figure 6.9).[34]

Topographical mappings of place

Topographical mapping sustains the conceptualization of discrete places, which is to say locales understood to be coherent and meaningful, including urban places. Topographical practices have varied depending on who undertook to describe a place (insiders or outsiders to a community), why they did so, and the criteria they used to construct meaning; for example, urban maps construe urban places as both built *urbs* and communal *civitas*.[35] Broadly speaking, we can distinguish two groups of topographers among early modern Europeans: first, local inhabitants tended to work within persistent traditions of 'sensuous' mapping that featured multiple viewpoints

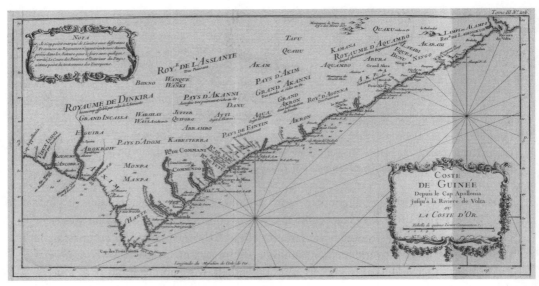

FIGURE 6.9 Jacques Nicolas Bellin, *Coste de Guinée depuis le Cap Apollonia jusqu'à la Rivière de Volta*, in vol. iii of *Le Petit Atlas maritime* (Paris, 1764). Hand-coloured copper engraving, 22.5 cm × 43.5 cm. Courtesy of the Osher Map Library and Smith Center for Cartographic Education, University of Southern Maine (SM-1764-4).

[34] See Jeffrey C. Stone, *A Short History of the Cartography of Africa* (Lampeter, 1995), 13–46.
[35] Kagan, *Urban Images of the Hispanic World*, 1–18.

and the goal of placing the map reader in the landscape itself;[36] second, landowners and governments employed more specialized surveyors who were increasingly trained after 1500 in the rules of perspective and geometrical measurement. In New Spain, the peoples of the former Aztec empire possessed a different set of abstract conventions for mapping topography, equally unconcerned with the geometries of modern cartography, so it can be hard for historians to distinguish the Spanish and Aztec components in sixteenth-century topographies.[37] The oft-reproduced map of Tenochtitlan that accompanied the publication in 1524 of Hernán Cortés' letters neatly illustrates the problem: once taken to be from a Spanish original, in large part because of the mediation of its European copyist, careful analysis reveals it to be more of a palimpsest derived from a Culhua-Mexica original that was in part misunderstood by the copyist.[38]

The communities of topographers tended to have different reasons for mapping places. On the one hand, local inhabitants mapped in order to assert the existence of a community and to preserve rights. Such mapping is limited in the Atlantic world beyond Europe to New Spain and the Andes, where a series of Spanish governmental initiatives led local aristocracies and communities to map their genealogies and rights into the landscape. The post-conquest reform of administrative districts led local lords to submit petitions to preserve their rights, often including maps at the request of the Spanish authorities;[39] sixteenth-century requests for information about the colonies from metropolitan administrations produced the remarkable array of representationally hybridized maps by indigenes and Europeans within the corpus of documents known as the *relaciones geográficas*;[40] and, throughout the colonial era and into the modern, indigenous communities have sought to assert their territorial rights *contra* Spanish land titles with, in part, maps of their communal lands often called *lienzos* (painted cotton sheets) (Figure 6.10). The highly variable nature of the *lienzos*, their scattered locations, and the secrecy with which they are often held means that little comparative work has been accomplished on this important genre of syncretic cartography.[41]

Surveyors from outside local communities mapped places in order to impose a sense of order and coherence on behalf of their employers. Following increasingly codified and increasingly international practices, surveyors and engineers planned and mapped

[36] The term is from David Harvey, *The Condition of Postmodernity: An Enquiry into the Origins of Cultural Change* (Oxford, 1989), 243. See P. D. A. Harvey, 'Local and Regional Cartography in Medieval Europe', *HC* i. 464–501, and much of *HC* iii.

[37] Barbara E. Mundy, *The Mapping of New Spain: Indigenous Cartography and the Maps of the Relaciones Geográficas* (Chicago, IL, 1996), 91–133; Padron, *Spacious World*, 75–82 and 247 n. 39; Kagan, *Urban Images of the Hispanic World*, 49–50.

[38] Barbara E. Mundy, 'Mapping the Aztec Capital: The 1524 Nuremberg Map of Tenochtitlan, its Sources, and Meanings', *Imago mundi*, 50 (1998), 11–33.

[39] Mundy, *Mapping of New Spain*, 180–211; Mundy, 'Mesoamerican Cartography', 241–3.

[40] David Buisseret, 'Spanish Colonial Cartography, 1450–1700', in *HC* iii. 1143–71, esp. 1145–6 and 1156; Mundy, *Mapping of New Spain, passim*.

[41] An exemplary study of a Mixtec *lienzo*, indicative of the problems in their analysis, is Ross Parmenter's 'The Lienzo of Tulancingo, Oaxaca: An Introductory Study of a Ninth Painted Sheet from the Coixtlahuaca Valley', *Transactions of the American Philosophical Society*, NS 83/7 (1993), 1–86.

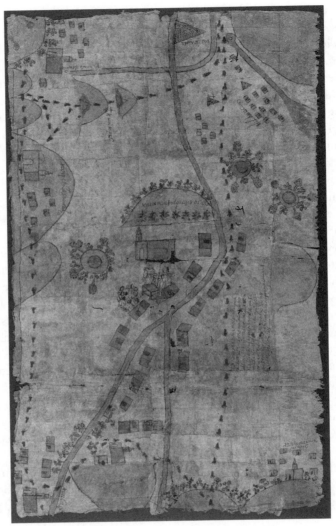

FIGURE **6.10** *Lienzo* of San Juan Tolcayuca (in the modern state of Hidalgo, Mexico), made in the seventeenth century as part of this indigenous community's assertion of its territorial rights against the encroachments of Spanish colonists, and presented in conjunction with a collection of other documents. The map is read from each side; the footprints probably represent the perambulation routinely undertaken by community members. Courtesy of the Special Collections Division, Library of Congress (Jay I. Kislak Collection).

fortifications, existing towns, new colonies, rivers and estuaries, and areas of plantations all around the Atlantic basin. From the views of slave-trading centres, notably Elmina, to more detailed plans of groups of sugar plantations in Saint-Domingue, such images circulated among officials and colonial elites; other than an occasional naivety of execution, these manuscripts were made in accordance with the same conventions as were used to map comparative features in Europe. Some were printed within promotional works or the great Dutch atlases consumed by Europe's elites, but most were instrumental, manuscript texts that rarely left their appropriate functional contexts.

Mappings of real property

The detailed mapping of real property is a function of complex societies with intense agricultural and urban systems. There is plenty of evidence that Mesoamericans undertook detailed cadastral and other property surveys, before and after the conquest,[42] and it seems likely given the similarities in techniques—estimation of area, simple measurement, laying out of 'new' lands in grids—that indigenous and European practices blended under colonial rule. Again, it must be remembered that relatively few maps of property were constructed in early sixteenth-century Europe. There, traditional practices persisted of marking boundaries in the landscape (with ditches, hedges, and monuments), labelling the areas thus enclosed with names of local significance, and recording them through frequent communal perambulations (see Figure 6.10) and in written 'metes-and-bounds' descriptions that simply inscribed the perambulation. In this respect, the significant difference between English colonists and native peoples in seventeenth-century New England in their delineation and representation of property was that the English also inscribed the metes-and-bounds descriptions in legal documents.[43] It was only after 1700 that English settlement became sufficiently dense in North America to require properties to be routinely mapped out in order to understand how they related one to another. The technologies employed by the English—compass, or primitive theodolite, and chain—were very basic, as they were throughout the Atlantic rim. Thus, a c.1700 treatise on land surveying from New Spain seems to have had little impact because the techniques it presented were just too complex and unnecessary for the colonial surveyor.[44] The resultant colonial property records, graphic and written, circulated tightly among only landowners, colonial administrators, and clerks in provincial archives, and very rarely crossed the Atlantic to metropolitan authorities.

Of course, the key difference between European property surveying in Europe and in the colonies was that the latter functioned less to record an existing patchwork of properties

---

[42] Mundy, 'Mesoamerican Cartography', 197–8, 203–4, and 223–5; Kagan, *Urban Images of the Hispanic World*, 48–51.

[43] See Margaret Wickens Pearce, 'Native Mapping in Southern New England Indian Deeds', in Lewis (ed.), *Cartographic Encounters*, 157–86.

[44] Herbert J. Nickel, 'Joseph Sáenz de Escobar y su tratado sobre geometría práctica y mecánica: um manual sobre geometría aplicada para personas no cualificadas en la materia, escrito en Nueva España (México) alrededor del año 1700', *Historia y grafía*, 15 (2000), 241–67. See also Miguel Aguilar-Robledo, 'Contested Terrain: The Rise and Decline of Surveying in New Spain, 1500–1800', *Journal of Latin American Geography*, 8/2 (2009), 23–47.

than to create one.[45] A variety of cultural, demographic, economic, and ecological factors determined the manner by which the colonial authorities divided up appropriated lands to create property: each new chunk of property could be a long lot, extending far back from a river frontage; part of an extensive grid, usually rather approximate than precise; part of some other roughly geometrical pattern; or a quite random pitch claimed by the putative owner. Even so, the basic process of land division gave rise to a common look to colonial property plans, once they were made, regardless of the colony or continent. Specifically, colonial property plans showed little more than the boundaries of a plot, with a minimum of landscape information, but generally recording the features that defined each corner of the property and its owner (Figure 6.11). At the same time, local inhabitants seem to have

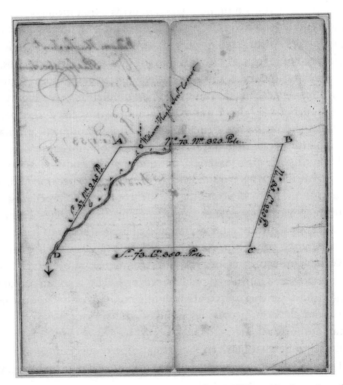

FIGURE 6.11 George Washington, plan of a survey for William Hughes, Jr. of 460 acres in Frederick County, Virginia, on the Cacapon River, accompanied by notes dated 4 April 1750 explaining the character of points AD. Manuscript, 18 cm × 16 cm (image). A rather extreme, but not uncommon, instance of the empty character of colonial property plans. Courtesy of the Geography and Map Division, Library of Congress (G3893.H2G46 1750.W3 Vault).

45 Roger J. P. Kain and Elizabeth Baigent, *The Cadastral Map in the Service of the State: A History of Property Mapping* (Chicago, IL, 1992), esp. 265–89, on English and French property surveys in the Americas and Caribbean.

remained a major source of surveying labour; in the middle colonies in North America, a number of African slaves seem to have been hired out as surveyors by their owners.

EUROPEAN ENLIGHTENMENT AND THE DECLINE OF SYNCRETIC CARTOGRAPHIES

Graphic mapping practices were just one part of the larger circulation of spatial knowledge around the Atlantic world. That circulation took the form of specific discourses addressing different spatial conceptions. At one end of the scale continuum, the highly focused conception of real property was sustained in legal and archival discourses that were almost entirely restricted to the colonies themselves. At the other, marine and geographical knowledge and maps circulated widely and, once in Europe and divorced from original context, could take on a life of their own. It was in this sense that European geographers first promulgated the idea of the 'Atlantic Ocean' and in which English geographers later popularized the idea of a single oceanic basin, relatively independently of the mariners who actually sailed the ocean. Within the Atlantic colonies, indigenous peoples and mestizos worked as map makers, or at least provided information to Europeans. The result was the establishment of several sets of syncretic mappings that at times departed substantially from established European practices.

The story is made all the more complex by Europe's increasing familiarity during the early modern era with all kinds of maps. As officials, traders, military officers, and landowners became progressively more interested in the geometrically correct representation of spatial relationships, at all scales, they progressively elided indigenous information and both indigenous and traditional mapping techniques. By the 1700s, even the non-specialist mappers of places, properties, and regions around the Atlantic were adopting the practices of the specialist surveyors, topographers, and geographers. This newly widespread cartographic culture was driven by increasing levels of education and familiarity with specialized cartographic products, but mostly by government activity.

On land, the growth of Europe's armies and the strategic shift from static fortifications to mobile columns and pitched battles led to a dramatic expansion of official perspectives: by the 1740s, military and some civil topographers were extending their precise mappings of places into detailed, systematic mappings of entire landscapes and territories.[46] These new processes delineated coastlines in great detail and ushered in a new era of hydrography, pioneered by the Dépôt de la Marine in France, in which coasts and coastal waters were mapped from the land outwards. These laborious surveys were mostly limited to Europe, but were applied to eastern North

---

[46] Edney, 'Mapping Parts of the World', 148–57.

America as part of Britain's post-1763 imperial consolidation. The basic technique of land-based determination of longitudes was also applied around the entire Atlantic basin by British, French, Dutch, and Iberian mariners and astronomers to correct coastal charts.

By the middle of the eighteenth century, the pursuit of cartographic science had developed within Enlightened discourses into a crucial ideological marker of difference between Europeans (the knowing, progressive Self) and non-Europeans (the unknowing, stagnant Other). As one Boston map maker declared, a predecessor's map of New England was 'as rude as if done by an Indian, or as if done in those Ages when Men first began to delineate Countries'.[47] The overt rejection of the role of indigenous peoples in creating spatial knowledge did not however mean that they ceased to have a role in mapping; much more work is needed to explore the fate of syncretic mappings in the later colonial and modern eras. At root, the history of mapping in the Atlantic world is one of complex and contingent cultural interactions across all cartographic modes.

Bibliography

Edney, Matthew H., and Mary S. Pedley (eds.), *The History of Cartography*, iv: *Cartography in the European Enlightenment* (Chicago, IL, in preparation).

Harley, J. B., and David Woodward (eds.), *The History of Cartography*, i: *Cartography in Prehistoric, Ancient, and Medieval Europe and the Mediterranean* (Chicago, IL, 1987).

Kagan, Richard L., *Urban Images of the Hispanic World, 1493–1793* (New Haven, CT, 2000).

Mundy, Barbara E., *The Mapping of New Spain: Indigenous Cartography and the Maps of the Relaciones Geográficas* (Chicago, IL, 1996).

Padrón, Ricardo, *The Spacious Word: Cartography, Literature, and Empire in Early Modern Spain* (Chicago, IL, 2004).

Wey Gómez, Nicolás, *The Tropics of Empire: Why Columbus Sailed South to the Indies* (Cambridge, MA, 2008).

Woodward, David (ed.), *The History of Cartography*, iii: *Cartography in the European Renaissance* (Chicago, IL, 2007).

—— and G. Malcolm Lewis (eds.), *The History of Cartography*, ii/3: *Cartography in the Traditional African, American, Arctic, Australian, and Pacific Societies* (Chicago, IL, 1998).

Zandvliet, Kees, *Mapping for Money: Maps, Plans and Topographic Paintings and their Role in Dutch Overseas Expansion during the 16th and 17th Centuries* (Amsterdam, 1998).

[47] William Douglass, *A Summary, Historical and Political, of . . . the British Settlements in North-America*, 2 vols. (Boston, MA, 1749–52), i. 362 n.

CHAPTER 7

VIOLENCE IN THE ATLANTIC

Sixteenth and Seventeenth Centuries

JEAN-FRÉDÉRIC SCHAUB

IN describing the process by which the 'brutalization' of humans became increasingly normalized in Western countries after the First World War, George L. Mosse indicated how human sensibility towards violence changed within particular historical contexts. Similarly, when Norbert Elias described the process by which 'civilization' progressed in early modern European societies he alluded to several mechanisms of coercion and to the violent impulses of individuals. Paradoxically for Elias, he traced the beginnings of the 'process of civilization' to a period when resort to violence appeared to be on the increase both in intensity and spread.

For historians, the concept of violence conjures up three principal meanings. First it invokes behaviour in quotidian social situations, such as brawls and fights, theft and rape. Second, it is associated with military operations, whether between opposing soldiers and militiamen, or the treatment of civilians by undisciplined or demobilized troops. A third meaning relates to the brutal methods sometimes employed to impose political or religious orthodoxy. Many historical experiences exemplify these diverse notions of political violence: the repression of populations by the legitimate authorities after local uprisings; the imposition through brutal methods of religious homogeneity in communities and countries; and the use of torture as an ordinary tool of a judiciary.

The shaping of an Atlantic world during the first two centuries of the Europe's overseas expansion saw an increase in the use and intensity of violence. Conquest, beginning with the Atlantic archipelagos (Canary Islands, Hispaniola, Santo Domingo), led to massacres and the elimination of populations. The diseases that Europeans brought with them may have done the most to wipe out the Canary Islanders during the fifteenth century, and the Tainos during the first decades of the sixteenth century, but harsh quasi-genocidal actions contributed to the indigenes' demise. These were certainly not the first massacres in history, but the obliteration of human societies was exceptional. The burgeoning Atlantic slave trade was also an especially violent phenomenon. Captivity and slavery by no means began with the exploitation of Atlantic space but the global dimensions of the pressure on African populations, during the sixteenth and particularly during the second half of the seventeenth century, escalated the practice. The threshold of tolerance for violence seems to have been lowered in Western society due to such Atlantic experiences.

Violence also disrupted the life of early modern populations not only through experience, but also as a series of images, fears, and fantasies. The spread of manuscripts and printed propaganda within Europe and its colonies enabled people to share vicariously in violent behaviour being enacted elsewhere. Consequently, as awareness of massacres and tortures invaded the consciousness of men and women in Europe, Africa, and America, distinctions were blurred between violence as a fact and violence as a construct. Reports about atrocities, and engravings describing tortures inflicted upon individuals, proved astonishingly popular during the first two centuries of print. These textual and graphic materials concerning conquest in America, wars of religion in Europe, and captivity in Africa and elsewhere created a unified web of representation.

This chapter will address both actual violent experiences and narratives of violence in the early modern Atlantic world. It will seek to explain how the creation of an Atlantic oceanic space rendered behaviour more brutal than previously.

CHANGE OF SCALE

The late fifteenth and early sixteenth centuries witnessed great violence. Civil wars devastated France, Castile, England, Portugal, Burgundy, and Flanders. Western African societies experienced the making and the collapse of military empires, they developed enhanced military techniques, and they suffered raids from North Africa. In America, Cortés and Pizarro successively destroyed two robust empires, which had themselves been conquering empires with elaborate military traditions. Increased use of gunpowder with its associated weaponry changed warfare radically. Battles and sieges produced ever-increasing casualties, and Western Europe was already a more violent place before European adventurers undertook the conquest of the Atlantic.[1]

The early modern period witnessed spectacular brutality in three poles of the Atlantic world. American societies suffered demographic and political collapse, as they proved unable to resist European disease, warfare, and greed. West African people

---

[1] Valentin Groebner, *Defaced: The Visual Culture of Violence in the Late Middle Ages* (New York, 2004); Paul Freedman, 'Atrocities and the Executions of Peasant Rebel Leaders in Late Medieval and Early Modern Europe', *Medievalia et humanistica*, 21 (2005), 101–13; Elena Benzoni, 'Les Sacs de ville à l'époque des guerres d'Italie (1494–1530): les contemporains face au massacre', in David El Kenz (ed.), *Le Massacre, objet d'histoire* (Paris, 2005), 157–70.

were captured, and sold by Africans to European traders who, in turn, sold them to work as slaves in plantations in the Iberian Peninsula, in the Atlantic archipelagos, and in America. In European countries, civil wars, foreign wars, and wars of religion sundered the former united Christendom into distinctive conflicting parts. Despite the optimism of the Renaissance, and despite the increasing importance attached to rational thinking by the close of the seventeenth century, the early modern era was one of intolerance and massacre throughout the Old World. Europeans developed an even greater sense of foreboding when they related their own experiences to what they heard and read of a larger world, particularly in the Atlantic where they were most involved. Thus discrete processes came to be viewed as parts of a single continuum.

None of the societies that were ultimately absorbed into the emerging Atlantic world was non-violent. Responsibility for the mass killings that did occur should not rest therefore either with the ultimate victors or the vanquished. Also, reactions to threats, oppression, and injustice were not necessarily passive or peaceful. Once elites were defeated or eliminated, popular revolts frequently persisted and proved extremely violent. Where local uprisings occurred and where popular memory of their suppression persisted, they frequently served as permanent threats to constituted authority in colonized areas. Prime examples of revolts justified by memory of past wrongs are the Morisco revolt in southern Spain in 1568–70, the assault launched by Powhatan upon Jamestown in 1622, the Irish rebellion in 1641, and the continued Araucan resistance in southern Chile during the seventeenth century. Revolts by maroons throughout the American plantation system also occurred frequently and were also justified both by memory of past wrongs and the reality of present injustice. Another permanent reality in the Atlantic world was the mutiny of starved crews, and occasional revolts by indentured workers. In most cases when such outbursts of violence perpetrated by weaker people were suppressed, the dominant authority mutilated and killed the leaders in exemplary fashion and inflicted collective and massive retaliation on the defeated populace.

The experience of violence must be framed in a Euro-Atlantic perspective, including the Mediterranean area. The actions of several actors shall be considered as exemplifying processes that took place in different territories at roughly the same time. The Spanish adventurer Hernán Cortés, who led the war against the last of the Aztec emperors, and was responsible for the total destruction of the city of Tenochtitlan (Mexico) in 1519, became, after his return to Spain, one of the captains of Charles V's fleet that laid siege in 1541 upon the corsair city of Algiers. In this, Cortés was bringing into play in North Africa his American experience of war against 'exotic' enemies. The French Calvinist shoemaker Jean de Léry first witnessed the practice of cannibalism in southern Brazil (1555), and later described cannibalism being practised by his own Christian followers in France during the siege of Sancerre (1573). In this case, de Léry's ability to describe what, for him, was something revolting in America steeled him to depict a somewhat analogous practice in Europe. In the English experience, Thomas Hariot, who was in charge of the English expedition to Roanoke Island (1585) and described the native people there, subsequently (1588) engaged in plantation settlement in Ireland, while Captain John Smith, the formidable governor of Jamestown and narrator of his experiences there, had previously been a traveller, soldier and adventurer within the Ottoman Empire. These two English protagonists related their experience of close 'otherness' with that of distant 'otherness'. These examples suggest that, from the beginning, the Atlantic space became a framework for shared experiences of brutality, enabling individuals to relate to each other atrocities witnessed or experienced in the New World and the Old.

The creation of an Atlantic world, during the sixteenth and the seventeenth centuries, introduced novel collective experiences. The conquest of huge territories in America, the destruction (if not genocides) of whole societies within only a few years, were the most striking episodes of these times. Portuguese merchants shaped the Atlantic slave trade almost a century and half before other European traders became seriously involved.[2] The slave trade, which already assumed a terrifying intensity during the seventeenth century, was another radical revolution in collective behaviour. American natives were also subjected to slavery as some were forced to work in mining in the Caribbean and the Andes, tobacco production in Virginia, and sugar cultivation and processing in the Caribbean and Brazil.[3] The Brazilian practice of manhunts in the wilderness was constant throughout the sixteenth and seventeenth centuries, and was imitated elsewhere.[4] The Peruvian mining system, which relied principally on native labour, was effectively a slave system, while in the British experience, Indian slaves from the American continent were sent to the Barbadian and Jamaican plantations.

These developments were all novel to Europeans, and took place against a European backdrop of the Wars of Religion, and a continuous struggle between states for political and military domination, where the destructions that European opponents inflicted on each other reached horrendous proportions. Another radical novelty, for Europeans at least, was the comprehension that the world was undergoing a process of unification, and that, despite Europe's Christian background, unification involved the universalization of brutality. Violence in Africa and in America mirrored European violence, and the frontier that had previously been perceived in Western society to have existed between civilized people and savages became blurred and hard to perceive. The apprehension that the world was entering a new dark age was widely shared by protagonists involved in the shaping of the Atlantic world. This was not the experience

---

[2] Roger Botte, 'Le Portugal, les marchés africains et les rapports Nord–Sud (1448–ca 1550)', *Cahiers des anneaux de la mémoire*, 3 (2001), 85–107; Bernard Vincent, 'Esclavage au Portugal: entre mer Méditerranée et océan Atlantique', in *Le Portugal et la Méditerranée, Arquivos do Centro Cultural Calouste Gulbenkian*, 43 (2002), 61–70; Antonio Almeida Mendes, 'Traites ibériques entre Méditerranée et Atlantique: le Noir au cœur des empires modernes et de la première mondialisation (ca. 1435–1550)', *Anais de história de além-mar*, 6 (2005), 351–87.

[3] Joyce E. Chaplin, 'Enslavement of Indians in Early America: Captivity without the Narrative', in Elizabeth Mancke and Carole Shammas (eds.), *The Creation of the British Atlantic World* (Baltimore, MD, 2005), 45–70.

[4] John Manuel Monteiro, *Negros da terra: índios e bandeirantes nas origens de São Paulo* (São Paulo, 1994); Pedro Puntoni, *A guerra dos bárbaros: povos indígenas e a Colonização do sertão nordeste do Brasil, 1650–1720* (São Paulo, 2002).

solely of the principal victims of European greed and brutality, but also of European settlers, sailors, merchants, soldiers, judges, and missionaries.

FROM EUROPE: THE DAWN OF A CIVILIZING PROCESS

A high level of insecurity prevailed in early modern Europe, symbolized by defence walls and gates, chains closing off streets, and locks on canals to constrain night circulation, while curfew regulations were enforced everywhere. These were, in fact, mechanisms for self-defence in a period when the enforcement of the law was local, amateur, and lacked a permanent police force. The control of violence was not exclusively a struggle against mobsters, thieves, and murderers, and many attempts to control the possession of weapons proved futile. Landlord courts and royal tribunals had limited capacity to offer solutions for the majority of interpersonal conflicts, while revenge killings and the killing of unfaithful wives were not always considered murders. The prohibition of duels—private ordeals to uphold the honour of individuals and their families—was, at best, gradual, and in France, Richelieu's famous measures to end the practice were spectacularly ruthless and occasioned the beheading of several disobedient noblemen.[5]

The trend, during the early modern period, towards a progressive control of the possession of arms and the regulation of conflicts by the royal authorities fell far short of reaching the ideal 'monopoly of the legitimate use of physical force within a given territory', which Max Weber considered the essential mark of modern statehood. The lack of state monopoly of violence meant that war—theoretically a sovereign activity par excellence—was partly in private hands. Noblemen and lesser lords frequently maintained private forces, often kinsmen or mobsters dressed in their master's livery. Although draft conscription increased, mercenary troops were still necessary, and the regular failure of royal administrations to provide pay, food, clothes, and supplies to the armies proved disastrous for civilians.[6] Soldiers frequently lived off the land, often at the expense of those they were commissioned to defend, and the billeting of soldiers in private houses during winter months was a continuing source of brutality and conflict. The traditional practice of pillaging cities after their surrender was not eradicated. Among many horrific episodes, the sack of Antwerp in 1576 was particularly traumatic. Its first cause was the uprising of the Spanish troops, because they had not received their pay for months, due to the disorder in Philip II's finances. The mutiny produced

---

[5] Pascal Brioist, Hervé Drévillon, and Pierre Serna, *Croiser le fer: violence et culture de l'épée dans la France moderne (XVIe–XVIIIe siècle)* (Seyssel, 2002); Stuart Carroll, *Blood and Violence in Early Modern France* (Oxford, 2006).

[6] Charles Tilly, *Coercion, Capital, and European States, AD 990–1990* (Cambridge, MA, 1990); Geoffrey Parker, *The Military Revolution: Military Innovation and the Rise of the West, 1500–1800* (Cambridge, 1996).

outrageous consequences: 1,000 buildings were burnt or destroyed, and around 8,000 citizens disappeared.[7]

If this was possible in the heart of the European territories of the Spanish Monarchy, is it surprising that matters were worse on the coasts of Africa, in the Caribbean, and in mainland America? During the creation of outposts in Africa, and the conquest of America, living off the country was the rule. From the beginning of the slave trade, interlopers challenged the authority of the kings of Portugal. The conquest of America was also largely achieved outside the control of successive Spanish and Portuguese monarchs. The arrest of Columbus and his brothers, the trial of Cortés, the civil war between *conquistadores* in Peru, the chaotic expedition of Lope de Aguirre: all these famous events demonstrate that the conquerors were less agents of a stately authority than war entrepreneurs. In Portugal, and later in the Low Countries and in England, webs of merchants and their companies regularly challenged the authority of the crown or the republic. In the late seventeenth century, English interlopers still fought against the monopoly of the Royal African Company, founded in 1672.

THE MAKING OF MASS MURDER

European outposts along the African coasts and settlements in the Atlantic archipelagos, the Caribbean, and American mainland were frontier societies. Despite the spectacular successes of the *conquistadores*, the conquest of America remained unfinished. In southern Chile, northern Mexico, and the Brazilian *sertão*, for instance, European authorities never controlled the land and its peoples. The continued resistance of Indians provided evidence of their resilience, and necessitated repeated military mobilization. The same proved true in the English colonies, particularly after Indian uprisings, from Jamestown in 1622 to King Philip's War in New England (1676). Resort to extreme violence was by no means limited to the Iberian colonial settlements. English, Scottish, and Dutch colonists in America killed and expelled local inhabitants from the lands they planned to settle, and sometimes became the victims of native retaliation.

Many natives and imported slaves became involved with the development of European settlements but were not considered full members of settler communities.[8] Indians in particular had a measure of autonomy in their relationship with European-created institutions and jurisdictions. However, since European colonists did not recognize the legitimacy of heathen authority, there were virtually no limits to the expansion of their settlements at the expense of indigenous populations.

---

[7] Geoffrey Parker, *The Army of Flanders and the Spanish Road, 1567–1659* (Cambridge, 1972).

[8] João Fragoso, Maria Fernanda Bicalho, and Maria de Fátima Gouveia (eds.), *O antigo regime nos trópicos: a dinâmica imperial portuguesa (séculos XVI–XVIII)* (Rio de Janeiro, 2001).

The experience of functioning on the border of civilized society was not limited to America and Africa. In Europe several internal conquests and processes of colonization occurred. The two most frequently cited cases in Western Europe were the kingdom of Granada in the crown of Castile and Ireland beyond the Pale. The last Muslim principality in the Iberian Peninsula was conquered between 1482 and 1492, and the Muslims who remained on the land were massively converted to Christianity by Cardinal Cisneros in 1500–6. Those who resisted or reverted to their ancestral faith were persecuted, particularly after a series of uprisings.[9] In 1568–70 a civil war broke out in the realm of Granada, when Moriscos—that is Christians of Muslim descent throughout the countryside and the Alpujarras mountains— attacked 'old Christian' communities and institutions. The repression was merciless: Morisco society was crushed, and many of the survivors were deported to other places in Castile. In Ireland during Queen Elizabeth's reign, several waves of new settlements, or 'plantations' of Protestant English subjects, took place. King James VI of Scotland, who succeeded Elizabeth as James I of England, continued the practice, and invited Scottish as well as English Protestants to settle on confiscated Irish land.[10] But attacks upon the Munster settlement in the 1590s and later the Irish Catholic uprising in 1641 fuelled a retaliatory ideology of extermination against those who opposed the British presence.[11] The two cases deserve to be compared, as they sometimes were at the time, especially because of the extreme violence and total solutions deployed by the two victorious states to restore order: transplantation and expulsion.[12]

As Europeans moved into the Atlantic, their actions proved even more disastrous. By the early sixteenth century, after 150 years of exploitation, slavery, and deportation, the Guanches of the Canary Islands had been exterminated.[13] Hundreds of them had been sold through Genoese and Portuguese commercial networks, and the last group of survivors suffered agonizing enslavement along the shore of southern Portugal, the Algarve. The process was even more rapid in the major Caribbean islands after Columbus' conquest, since, by the 1540s, the Tainos and Caribs had almost completely disappeared from most of their original locations. Efforts by the Spanish Monarchy to control and restrain the violence being inflicted upon natives had little effect. Charles V of Spain passed a series of laws to protect the Indians in the Caribbean, but they were seldom enforced. Slavery was theoretically prohibited, but the *encomienda* system used

---

[9] Antonio Domínguez Ortiz and Bernard Vincent, *Historia de los Moriscos: vida y tragedia de una minoría* (Madrid, 1985); David Coleman, *Creating Christian Granada: Society and Religious Culture in an Old-World Frontier City, 1492–1600* (Ithaca, NY, 2003).

[10] Nicholas Canny, *Making Ireland British, 1580–1650* (Oxford, 2001).

[11] Ciaran Brady, 'New English Ideology in Ireland and the Two Sir William Herberts', in Amanda J. Piesse (ed.), *Sixteenth-Century Identities* (Manchester, 2001), 75–111; Debora Shuger, 'Irishmen, Aristocrats, and Other White Barbarians', *Renaissance Quarterly*, 50 (1997), 494–525.

[12] Rafel Benítez Sánchez-Blanco, *Heroicas decisiones: la Monarquía Católica y los Moriscos valencianos* (Valence, 2001); Raphaël Carrasco, 'El tratado sobre los Moriscos de Pedro de Valencia', in *La Monarchie Catholique et les morisques (1520–1620): Études franco-espagnoles* (Montpellier, 2005), 237–305.

[13] David Abulafia, *The Discovery of Mankind: Atlantic Encounters in the Age of Columbus* (New Haven, CT, 2008); Alberto Vieira, *Os escravos no arquipélago da Madeira: séculos XV a XVII* (Funchal, 1991).

to exploit the labour of the native population continued and it was one of the major sources of their mass destruction.[14] From the beginning of the Spanish and Portuguese exploitation of the Caribbean islands and the American mainland, the leading adventurers were accustomed to disregarding royal orders. The motto 'obedezcáse pero no se cumple' ([the order] must be obeyed but not enforced), which was so popular in Latin America during the seventeenth century, accurately describes the behaviour of the first generation of *conquistadores*. They systematically broke royal regulations that favoured the Indians.

RELIGION AND VIOLENCE

Religious zeal, challenged only by avarice, proved to be a major source of violent behaviour in the Atlantic world. The struggle between Catholics and Protestants, which produced horrific civil conflict in several European countries, was frequently the context from which missionary activities in overseas outposts and colonies emerged. The two developments cannot be comprehended separately. The French Protestant corsair Jacques de Sores was already a legend by the middle of the sixteenth century. He burned part of the city of Havana in 1555 and raided the Canary Island of La Gomera in 1572, while in 1570 his men had slaughtered thirty-nine Jesuit clerics who had gone as missionaries to Brazil. Similarly, from his buccaneer hideouts in the Caribbean, the English adventurer Sir Francis Drake became the scourge of Spanish ports and cities in America and even in the Iberian Peninsula itself. Those raids were always violent against civilians, and when Protestant crews attacked Catholic communities, they often destroyed religious buildings and images throughout the three continents: in Trujillo de Honduras in 1570, in Cádiz in 1592, and in Arguin in 1595. Episodes of mass murder of religious opponents occurred in the newest French settlements of America even before the St Bartholomew's Day massacre of hundreds of French Protestants in Paris in August 1572. The killing of French Calvinist colonists in Florida by Spanish assailants in 1565 provided emblematic evidence in Protestant literature of the outrage of Spanish violence.

Religion was also invoked to justify Christian violence against the indigenous population. Iberian *conquistadores* and authors of New World chronicles, such as Gonzalo de Oviedo, condemned the natives for their brutal rites. Hernán Cortés, in his first reports to Spain of his achievements, alluded to the recent increase in the number of victims from human sacrifice within the Aztec empire, which became a trope for the increasing decadence of the Aztecs at the moment the Spanish reached them. The extent to which cannibalism, as described by André Thévet, Jean de Léry, and Hans Staden after their individual experiences in Brazil, was genuinely practised remains an open question, as scholars today debate whether these authors were actually

---

[14] Massimo Livi-Barci, 'Return to Hispaniola: Reassessing a Demographic Catastrophe', *American Historical Review*, 83 (2003), 3–51.

eyewitnesses to the rites they described relating to the consumption of human flesh.[15] In North America the practice of scalping defeated enemies was most frequently cited as evidence of the depravity of Native Americans. It seems to have been an indigenous practice, but one dramatically expanded as Europeans began to request tokens of loyalty from their Indian allies in local wars.[16] Contemporary Europeans never doubted such practices were widespread and used them to justify their harsh measures against the natives on the grounds that they were children of Satan.

One of the mechanisms used to investigate all such charges in the areas of the New World dominated by the Iberians was the Inquisition. It was not the only judicial institution specializing in religious crime known to Europeans, since every country, whether Protestant or Catholic, had developed its own system for investigating cases of heresy.[17] Nevertheless, the Iberian Holy Office and its Italian equivalents promoted an especially efficient persecuting machine.[18] Its operation relied on a web of informants, on the complete isolation of arrested suspects, and on the publicity given to the execution of its decisions. Inquisitors sentenced to death hundreds of Spaniards and Portuguese of Jewish and Muslim converted descent on various charges of backsliding. The Iberian colonists replicated in America this system of Inquisition control and repression. Throughout the western hemisphere, natives and slaves of African origins were accused of practising witchcraft or forbidden religious rites.[19] Inquisition courts were created in Lima in 1570 and Mexico in 1571. Even before then, Franciscan friars enjoyed authority to persecute Indian 'sorcerers'. Fray Juan de Zumárraga convicted many native people throughout the valley of Mexico between 1536 and 1543, as did Fray Diego de Landa in the Yucatán Peninsula through the 1560s.[20] Only the Inquisition of Lisbon was able to sue individuals in Brazil, but the Portuguese 'Holy Office' was very

[15] Frank Lestringant, *Une sainte horreur ou le voyage en Eucharistie, XVIe–XVIIIe siècle* (Paris, 1996); Frank Lestringant, *Cannibals: The Discovery and Representation of the Cannibal from Columbus to Jules Verne* (Berkeley, CA, 1997); Bernadette Bucher, *La Sauvage aux seins pendants* (Paris, 1977); H. E. Martel, 'Hans Staden's Captive Soul: Identity, Imperialism, and Rumors of Cannibalism in Sixteenth-Century Brazil', *Journal of World History*, 17/1 (2006), 51–69.

[16] James Axtell and William C. Sturtevant, 'The Unkindest Cut, or Who Invented Scalping', *William and Mary Quarterly*, 37 (1980), 451–72.

[17] Elena Brambilla, *La giustizia intollerante: inquisizione e tribunali confessionali in Europa (secoli IV–XVIII)* (Rome, 2006).

[18] Jean-Pierre Dedieu, *L'Administration de la foi: l'Inquisition de Tolède et les vieux-chrétiens (XVIe–XVIIe siècle)* (Paris, 1989); Francisco Bethencourt, *L'Inquisition à l'époque moderne: Espagne, Portugal, Italie, XVe–XIXe siècles* (Paris, 1995); Adriano Prosperi, *Tribunali della coscienza: inquisitori, confessori, missionari* (Turin, 1996).

[19] María Elena Martínez, 'The Black Blood of New Spain: Limpieza de sangre, Racial Violence, and Gendered Power in Early Colonial Mexico', *William and Mary Quarterly*, 63 (2004), 479–520; Irene Silverblatt, 'New Christians and World Fears in Seventeenth-Century Peru', *Comparative Studies in Society and History*, 2/3 (2000), 524–46.

[20] Patricia Lopes Don, 'Franciscans, Indian Sorcerers, and the Inquisition in New Spain, 1536–1543', *Journal of World History*, 17 (2006), 27–49; Inga Clendinnen, *Ambivalent Conquests: Maya and Spaniard in Yucatan, 1517–1570* (Cambridge, 1987).

active along the Atlantic shore of Africa from the sixteenth century. Here settlers of Jewish descent, and converted Africans suspected of being sorcerers, were persecuted.

Inquisitorial legal procedures usually included torture as the most effective way to reach the truth concerning the offences and crimes of suspects. In some cases, large communities were persecuted, and whole families put to death. The maintenance of jails presented a challenge during the early modern period because the Inquisition methods, based on absolute isolation of the suspects during the inquiry, required appropriate buildings. But lengthy jailing was not the favourite penalty.[21] Inquisition judges preferred public flogging, banishment, and death by burning at the stake. The execution of the sentences became a religious ceremony, with the convicted attired in clothes, the *sanbenitos*—symbols of their infamy—being exhibited in procession along with the procedure of 'autos da fé'. To ensure that the shame of conviction shrouded the relatives and descendants of the convicted, those uniforms were hung in the local churches, as reminders of the crime and its punishment.

The obscene violence of the Inquisition was criticized even in the sixteenth century, particularly by writers involved in the propaganda struggles against the Iberian crowns, in France, England, and the Low Countries.[22] Critics emphasized the contrast between the total secrecy of the inquiry and the open spectacle of humiliation and sacrifice. In the Portuguese experience of the sixteenth century, many Portuguese and Castilian Christians of Jewish ancestry fled to Latin America and Africa in order to escape persecutions by the Inquisition, but even there, networks of converted Christians in America had to protect themselves from informants.[23] Many suspects were hunted down and caught by the tribunals. Thus the violence of the Inquisition was exported from Europe to America and Africa, and information about converted, and supposed heretics, crossed the ocean with deadly efficiency.

VIOLENCE AND THE JUDICIARY

The Iberian Inquisitions were unique, but the royal justice and ecclesiastical courts of other Western European countries and overseas settlements shared many of the same techniques of repression. For example, the use of torture, or 'question', was the conventional way of interrogating arrested suspects everywhere, and was not confined to religious justice.[24] Generally, defendants who suffered judicial torture and did not

---

[21] Tamar Herzog, *Rendre la justice à Quito, 1650–1750* (Paris, 2001).

[22] William S. Maltby, *The Black Legend in England: The Development of Anti-Spanish Sentiment 1558–1660* (Durham, NC, 1971); Ricardo García Cárcel, *La leyenda negra: historia y opinión* (Madrid, 1998); Jocelyn H. Hillgarth, *The Mirror of Spain, 1500–1700: The Formation of a Myth* (Ann Arbor, MI, 2000).

[23] Nathan Wachtel, *La Foi du souvenir: labyrinthes marranes* (Paris, 2001).

[24] Lisa Silverman, *Tortured Subjects: Pain, Truth, and the Body in Early Modern France* (Chicago, IL, 2001); Francisco Tomás y Valiente, *El derecho penal de la monarquía absoluta: siglos XVI–XVII–XVIII* (Madrid, 1969).

confess were considered innocent of the charges brought against them, because, due to the pain inflicted, judges came to consider confessions as concrete evidence. Archival materials record the screams of the convicted during the questioning sessions as elements of the judicial procedure. In France and England, royal courts and church tribunals enforced religious persecution, as when, for example, Francis I convicted French Protestants in the 1530s, Mary Tudor persecuted suspected Protestants in the 1550s, and Queen Elizabeth pursued seminary priests in the 1590s. Mechanisms for pursuing witches in Protestant Europe were also exported to America, most notoriously in the witch trials in Salem, Massachusetts, of 1692.

European judicial penalties were also terrifying throughout the early modern period, with particular concern to inflict pain to the body and humiliate the convicted. Mutilation, such as cutting off thieves' hands or fingers, was not exceptional, nor was blinding, nor removing the tongue in the case of repeated blasphemy. Public flogging was another form of punishment, which mixed pain and shame, with judges frequently ordering hot-iron branding on the skin of the convicted. The mark could be on the shoulder of the offenders, but sometimes on the forehead, as a perpetual record of their guilt and dishonour. Such punishments became standard in the slave plantation system throughout the Atlantic world. In Spain and in Spanish America, potential runaway slaves were branded on the forehead or on the cheeks, thus reducing the possibility of escape. Penal servitude also linked judicial repression of crime with slavery, especially in Mediterranean countries where serving in the galley fleets became a frequent alternative to the death penalty. In the case of Spain, forced work in the poisonous mercury mines in Almadén, Andalusia, or residence in the Spanish outposts of northern Africa, were also alternatives to the death penalty.[25] Countries involved in colonization in North America—France, England, the Low Countries, and the Scandinavian kingdoms—also regularly commuted capital punishment into indentured servitude in their American colonies.

There was also a variety of methods employed for carrying out the death penalty. In many countries, noblemen enjoyed the privilege of being beheaded, by sword or axe, to differentiate them from commoners who were usually hanged. But judges had other options, such as burning the convicted at the stake, particularly in cases of witchcraft and the breach of religious constrictions like blasphemy, heresy, and sodomy.[26] More painful for the convicted, and more dreadful for the public, was the quartering of bodies, and execution on the wheel. Executions were usually conducted in public, in marketplaces and during festivals. Audiences attended the whole process from the procession of the convicted, frequently dressed in a white shirt and bearing a candle in sign of redemption, to the final execution, while clerics accompanied the convicted

---

[25] Julián Antonio Prior Cabanillas, *La pena de minas: los forzados de Almadén, 1646–1699* (Ciudad Real, 2006); Pedro-Alejo Llorente de Pedro, *El penitenciarismo español del Antiguo Régimen aplicado a su presidio más significativo: Orán-Mazalquivir* (Madrid, 2007).

[26] Alfred Soman, *Sorcellerie et justice criminelle: le Parlement de Paris (XVIe–XVIIe siècle)* (Aldershot, 1992); Robert Muchembled, *Le Roi et la sorcière: l'Europe des bûchers, XVe–XVIIIe siècle* (Paris, 1993); Robin Briggs, *The Witches of Lorraine* (Oxford, 2008).

along the way from confinement to the place of execution, encouraging public repentance and assisting them with prayer.

ALLIANCE, HYBRIDIZATION, AND RAPE

Atlantic history provides a framework particularly suited to research on the mestizo experience and about processes of racial and cultural hybridization.[27] The historiography of the 'first globalization' has presented these processes as proof of cultural openness on the part of Europeans, with Indian natives and Africans being defined as people who, under the tutelage of European settlers, might receive the grace of God and thus attain salvation. The destruction of 'idols' in Spanish America thus came to be considered a crusade against the devil on earth. Despite this positive premiss, missionary action in the sixteenth and seventeenth centuries resulted in a mixture of optimism and pessimism about the possible outcome. The prelapsarian hypothesis—which held that Native Americans lived in a state of innocence as had humanity in general before the Fall—made marriage with Indian women not only acceptable, but desirable, and such alliances were also considered a means to strengthen the social power and political authority of the *conquistadores* over local societies. But thinking of Native Americans as in thrall to Satan led to less positive attitudes.

In most colonies of European settlement in America, the sex ratio between male and female settlers was highly asymmetrical, leaving men to find women among native people or among slaves, resulting in Native American women and African slaves giving birth to thousands of mixed-blood children. Pregnancies often originated from sexual oppression, violence, and rape. In Spanish America new landlords, *encomenderos*, frequently imposed their sexual tyranny over native women placed under their authority, and the majority of those children were not recognized by their fathers. The situation was even worse in plantation societies, where the children of female slaves were usually categorized as slaves, or 'increases' in the slave livestock, initially by custom and later by law.[28] Rape, and other abuse of male authority over female victims, was a normal feature of everyday life of European families throughout the colonies in America and in Africa.[29] The birth of mestizo children can thus hardly be considered the prolegomenon of modern multiculturalism.

---

[27] Berta Ares Quejía, 'El papel de mediadores y la construcción de un discurso sobre la identidad de los mestizos peruanos (siglo XVI)', in Berta Ares Quejía and Serge Gruzinski (coords.), *Entre dos mundos: fronteras culturales y agentes mediadores* (Seville, 1997).

[28] Barbara Bush, 'Hard Labor, Women, Childbirth and Resistance in British Caribbean Slave Societies', in David Barry Gaspar and Darlene Clark Hine (eds.), *More than Chattel* (Bloomington, IN, 1996), 195–217; Jennifer L. Morgan, *Laboring Women: Reproduction and Gender in New World Slavery* (Philadelphia, PA, 2004).

[29] Kathleen Brown, *Good Wives, Nasty Wenches, and Anxious Patriarchs: Gender, Race, and Power in Colonial Virginia* (Chapel Hill, NC, 1996); Durba Ghosh, 'Gender and Colonialism: Expansion or Marginalization?', *Historical Journal*, 47 (2004), 737–55.

Children could also be innocent victims of religious persecution in the Atlantic. One of the most tragic episodes was the deportation of Jewish-born children who were taken away from their parents in 1496–7 and dispatched to Guinea, in fact to the island of São Tomé, by order of the king of Portugal Dom Manuel I.[30] Another horrifying example concerns Mexican children taken away from their villages by Spanish friars in the early 1520s to receive a Christian training and baptism, some of whom were subsequently killed by their own relatives after being returned to their homes.

Deportation of indentured workers, the sexual appetite of European settlers, rape, and brutal abductions produced hybridization far more effectively than mental openness, cultural curiosity, or sincere love. The current historiography on the creation of mestizo societies, as part of the process of globalization, cannot ignore the violent and brutal origins of seductive hybridization. For the most part the fuzziness of cultural or ethnic identities that did prevail during the early modern centuries, and the massive presence of citizens of mixed-blood descent in today's Latin American societies, derived more from the chaotic and brutal destruction of traditional societies in the Atlantic during early modern times than from any benevolence on the part of Europeans. During the early modern centuries the condition of slave labourers in the mines and sugar plantations of Spanish and Portuguese colonies was extremely hazardous, and sexual exploitation was possibly easier to pursue in Ibero-American societies than in later anglophone, or Dutch, plantation societies.

NARRATIVES OF CAPTIVITY AND VIOLENCE

The sixteenth century witnessed increasing corsair activities in the Mediterranean from Maghrib cities, like Salé, Algiers, Tunis, and Tripoli, so much so that becoming a captive in Muslim lands was perceived as a real threat by Christian sailors, soldiers, and merchants.[31] Pirates from Barbary not only attacked boats, but also sacked cities and villages along the coasts of Christian countries. The fear of Barbary pirates became obsessive in Western Europe and in the Atlantic archipelagos during the early modern period, and was not limited by the straits of Gibraltar. Many Spanish and Portuguese cities and fleets in the Atlantic suffered from Barbary aggression, most notoriously the 1617 raid on the island of Porto Santo, close to Madeira, which was pillaged, burnt, and almost all of its population brought to the Maghrib. In 1627, the famous Ottoman

---

[30] Antonio Almeida Mendes, 'Le Rôle de l'Inquisition en Guinée: vicissitudes des présences juives sur la Petite Côte (XVe–XVIe siècles)', *Revista lusófona de ciência das religiões*, 5/6 (2004), 138–55.

[31] Enrique Fernández, 'El cuerpo torturado en los testimonios de cautivos de los corsarios berberiscos (1500–1700)', *Hispanic Review*, 71 (2003), 51–66; Nabil Matar, 'Introduction: England and Mediterranean Captivity, 1577–1704', in Daniel J. Vitkus (ed.), *Piracy, Slavery and Redemption: Barbary Captivity Narratives from Early Modern England* (New York, 2001); Robert C. Davies, *Christian Slaves, Muslim Masters: White Slavery in the Mediterranean, the Barbary Coast, and Italy, 1500–1800* (Basingstoke, 2003).

expedition in the North Atlantic, conveying 3,000 men, abducted 242 captives from Iceland, while in 1631 Baltimore, in west Cork in Ireland, suffered a similar fate.[32] Captives taken in such raids were sometimes sold back to their relatives, given in exchange for Muslims captured by Christians, while some embraced the Muslim faith, or, more often, became slaves forever. At the same time, Muslim raids against the African population beyond the Saharan desert, and throughout the Niger after the decline of the Songhai empire, became a major source of chattel slaves, even to the point where Islamic lawyers debated during the sixteenth century whether the enslavement of Muslim black Africans was permitted.

Printed narratives of captivity and slavery in northern Africa became increasingly popular in Western European countries, and, in England, these became the most popular kind of printed material after sermons.[33] Readers in the sixteenth and seventeenth centuries are likely to have made a link between such experiences and the stories of captivity among Native American people. That of Hans Staden's captivity in Brazil was disseminated, first through the German edition of his 'real story' (Magdeburg, 1557) and later through Theodore de Bry, *America*. Both editions contained horrific woodcuts and engravings describing the methods for human flesh eating supposedly practised by Tupinamba tribes. A century later, as a consequence of King Philip's War in New England (1676), Mary Rowlandson was captured by Narragansett Indians from Lancaster, Massachusetts. After her liberation, she wrote a narrative of her three months in captivity.[34] This book, published in 1682, a bestseller in the American colonies as well as in England, asserted that a peaceful coexistence with Native Americans was impossible as she contrasted her piety and Christian faith with the absolute, unredeemable savagery of the Indian heathen.

Peter Martyr, Gonzalez de Oviedo, Bernal Díaz del Castillo, Girolamo Benzoni—the principal chroniclers of the Iberian conquest of America—also described the brutality of the native populations of the New World. The massacre of the French Protestant settlers in Florida by the Spaniards (1565), and the internal conflict of the settlement at Guanabara Bay (1566), were represented as extensions of the European Wars of Religion, which, in the memory of European Protestants, belonged with the sequence of horrific Catholic assaults upon Protestants, which were to culminate in the St Bartholomew's Day massacre and the sack of Antwerp. Thus colonial expansion provided Europeans with mirrors of their domestic violence: the rough savage on the one hand, and the pitiless *conquistadores* on the other hand became emblems of brutality in Europe itself. These atrocity stories had an impact as important as the

[32] Des Ekin, *The Stolen Village: Baltimore and the Barbary Pirates* (Dublin, 2006).

[33] Kenneth Parker, 'Reading "Barbary" in Early Modern England, 1550–1685', *Seventeenth Century*, 19 (2004), 87–115.

[34] Gary L. Ebersole, *Captured by Texts: Puritan to Post-Modern Images of Indian Captivity* (Charlotesville, VA, 1995), 15–60; Tiffany Potter, 'Writing Indigenous Feminity: Mary Rowlandson's Narrative of Captivity', *Eighteenth-Century Studies*, 36 (2003), 153–67.

production of silver, sugar, and tobacco for the further development of European countries and settlements.

Several clerics spoke in favour of the victims of the brutality of the Iberian conquerors. The most noted was the Dominican Fray Bartolomé de Las Casas (1472–1566), bishop of Chiapas, who bore witness to the greed and the violence of the *conquistadores* in the Caribbean and in the Yucatán Peninsula. In 1550, when pitted against Juan Ginés de Sepúlveda, he persuaded the clergy of Castile and the king that the native people of America would have to be freed from the servitude under which they had been placed by their Spanish masters. In fact, Las Casas' indictment of violence and massacre had begun much earlier with the *Memorial de remedios*, written in 1516, where he had pleaded that, in spite of the royal prohibition against enslavement of native people, the *encomienda* had imposed a system of indentured labour that had had a devastating impact on the physical as well as the moral life of the indigenous population.

Bartolomé de Las Casas' account of extermination and the cruelty of the behaviour of the Spanish *conquistadores* in the Caribbean and Central American mainland was printed in Seville in 1552, but the *Breve descripción de la destrucción de las Indias* probably had a greater influence in the Low Countries, in France, and in England, where the first translations of the short book were printed in Dutch (1578), French (1579), English (1583), and Latin (1598). The illustrated edition made by the engraver Theodore de Bry in Frankfurt in 1598 spread horrific pictures throughout Europe (and particularly throughout Protestant Europe) of the worst imaginable cruelty. A famous image displayed a Spanish soldier splitting an Indian baby to give the two halves to a pair of hounds. Depictions included pregnant women being killed, children having their heads smashed on rocks, and whole populations of villages being hanged and burnt at the stake. These series of images supported the propaganda campaigns against the Spanish crown, particularly in Protestant countries and Huguenot milieux.[35] Their popularity probably owed less to the solidarity they evoked with persecuted native peoples of America than to the analogy they drew between Spanish brutality in the Low Countries and in the New World. De Bry's engravings suggested connections with the archetypal image of the 'massacre of the Innocents', the sack of Flemish cities, and the 'destruction of the Indies'.[36] Previous series of horrific images had been published by de Bry's company in Antwerp in the 1570s, representing the violent repression led by the duke of Alba in the Low Countries, and his American publishing elaborated on the stock depictions. The model became so firmly imprinted upon the European imagination that Catholic indictment of the violence committed by Protestants upon Catholics,

---

[35] Michèle Duchet (ed.), *L'Amérique de Théodore de Bry: une collection de voyages protestante au XVIe siècle* (Paris, 1987); Thomas Scanlan, *Colonial Writing and the New World, 1583–1671: Allegories of Desire* (Cambridge, 1999).

[36] James Tanis and Daniel Horst, *Images of Discord: A Graphic Interpretation of the Opening Decades of the Eighty Years' War* (Bryn Mawr, PA, 1993); David Kunzle, 'Spanish Herod, Dutch Innocents: Bruegel's Massacres of the Innocents in their Sixteenth-Century Political Contexts', *Art History*, 24 (2001), 51–82.

as in the famous Richard Verstegan *Théatre des cruautés des hérétiques de notre temps* (Antwerp, 1587), seemed but a pale imitation of de Bry's output.

In the seventeenth century, the Jesuit António Vieira (1608–97) also pleaded in favour of Native Americans. He had first-hand knowledge of Brazil and of the penalties inflicted upon the native people there.[37] He supported the freedom of the Indians from illegal enslavement and general depredation. In Vieira's case, activism against the brutality of Portuguese settlers in America went together with an indictment of the Inquisition and a plea to ignore the non-Christian origins of converted people. He established de facto a link between the tradition of intra-European religious persecution and the violence of colonization overseas. His brilliant sermons were widely disseminated because print had become the best tool for spreading knowledge throughout the Atlantic world.

After a century dominated by Iberian and Italian accounts, and their translation into other European languages, sources composed in English, Latin, and French became popular. The violence inflicted upon African slaves in the British plantation system was described in remarkable books. Morgan Godwyn's *The Negro's and Indians Advocate* (London, 1680), Thomas Tryon's *Friendly Advice* (London, 1684), and the famous last chapter of *Gulliver's Travels* (Dublin, 1735) are certainly among the most poignant condemnations of the violence European colonizers spread abroad.

With the success of printing technologies, the spread of information concerning incidents of violence grew considerably. In different European countries printers sold broadsheets relating crimes, spectacular trials, and descriptions of massacres. These materials were relatively cheap and could be displayed on walls, to be read and commented upon abroad. Songs and ballads telling stories of crime and punishment also proved popular, many being printed and thus made available to a wider public. In the seventeenth century, almanacs and chapbooks, like the famous *Bibliothèque bleue* in France, yielded many sales, particularly those telling horrific stories of slaughters or monstrous events. Descriptions of capital punishments with songs sung during the executions were extremely popular. Later, weekly newsletters like the London *Weekly News* or the Paris *Gazette* gave their readers information about spectacular cases of violence.

FROM VIOLENCE TO RACE

During the early modern period, the experience of violence was intra-European and colonial. These realities mirrored one another. The 'others' could be described as not fully human beings, the revulsion deriving largely from their heathenism. But it was no

---

[37] Alcir Pécora, *Teatro do sacramento: a unidade teológico-retórico-política dos sermões de Antônio Vieira* (São Paulo, 1996); Thomas M. Cohen, *The Fire of Tongues: António Vieira and the Missionary Church in Brazil and Portugal* (Stanford, CA, 1998).

less the consequence of the legal necessity to legitimize hereditary servitude. Social and cultural violence fuelled the development of new conceptions of human races. At the beginning of the period, settlers, explorers, and missionaries shared still inchoate ideas about differences amongst people. But at the end of the seventeenth century, settlers and planters in America, slave traders in Africa, and their partners in Europe were able to promote new rules based on a racial conception of human diversity. The two-century experience of violence, destruction, failure in missionary activity, and the growth of the slave-based economy gave birth to the darkest conception of mankind one may imagine.

BIBLIOGRAPHY

Augeron, Mickaël, and Mathias Tranchant (eds.), *La Violence et la mer dans l'espace atlantique (XIIe–XIXe siècle)* (Rennes, 2004).

Crouzet, Denis, *Les Guerriers de Dieu: la violence au temps des troubles de religion, vers 1525–vers 1610* (Seyssel, 2005).

Hassig, Ross, *Mexico and the Spanish Conquest* (London, 1994).

Levene, Mark, and Penny Roberts (eds.), *The Massacre in History* (Oxford, 1999).

Parker, Geoffrey, *The Military Revolution: Military Innovation and the Rise of the West, 1500–1800* (Cambridge, 1996).

Ruff, Julius Ralph, *Violence in Early Modern Europe* (Cambridge, 2001).

Sandberg, Brian, 'Beyond Encounters: Religion, Ethnicity, and Violence in the Early Modern Atlantic World, 1492–1700', *Journal of World History*, 17/1 (2006), 1–25.

CHAPTER 8

THE ATLANTIC WORLD, THE SENSES, AND THE ARTS

DAVID S. SHIELDS

IN 1825, the father of gastronomy, Jean Anthelme Brillat-Savarin, proposed that the perfection of the senses in Western history coincided with the European encounter with America.[1] The fortuitous discovery that the West Indies, Mexico, and Peru possessed treasures (the potato, vanilla, and chocolate) that outshone Aztec gold and Potozi's silver occasioned the refinement of taste, for the press of new sensations led to a conscious effort to organize sense and explore pleasure. While Brillat-Savarin's claim that modernity gave the West a sense of the body may seem an expression of romantic audacity rather than proper historical hypothesis, the first chapters of *The Physiology of Taste* spur the imagination to conceive how the transatlantic exchanges of the sixteenth and seventeenth centuries moved people's sense of the world to a new consciousness, a new aesthetics.

How exactly did novel sensations of pleasure and pain change people on both sides of the Atlantic? We should not follow Brillat-Savarin by conceiving that the experience of the new led to a reorientation of human being away from spirit and towards the body, or concluding that the Old World's encounter with the New inspired a hedonism that led to a global economy predicated on the serving of appetite.[2] Nevertheless, smelling, tasting, hearing, seeing, and touching changed profoundly for those who experienced the opening of the Atlantic world. Here we will notice signal transformations of the sensorium by examining arts whose practices took up aesthetic innovations

---

[1] M. F. K. Fisher (trans.), *The Physiology of Taste: Or, Meditations on Transcendental Gastronomy by Jean Anthelme Brillat-Savarin* (New York, 1978).

[2] David S. Shields, 'The World I Ate: The Prophets of Global Consumption Culture', *Eighteenth-Century Life*, 25 (Spring 2001), 214–24.

explicitly, as well as some conditions of life in which they were concretized unthinkingly.

Because *novelty* brings to attention the qualities of sensation, our discussion favours early—often the earliest—experiences, rather than later. While this survey uses the classical 'five senses' organization of Western physiology as an organizing principle, it does so for convenience's sake, not to suggest that it operated as a universal structure of sensing in every culture of Europe, Africa, and the Americas. My materials were chosen to suggest the extent and penetration of aesthetic experiences on both sides of the Atlantic. For smelling I concentrate on the East Indies and West Indies, for hearing on Africa and Ibero-America, for tasting Central America and the West Indies (with a side glance at Africa), for seeing north Europe and North America.

I take up this enquiry cognizant that somewhat before 1492 Europe had begun to reconceive the materiality of things and the nature of experience as intellectuals began exploring antiquity, and merchants the Orient.

The nose

The primacy of the East can be seen in the art most closely associated with the sense of smell—perfumery. The Islamic Middle East placed a premium upon refined fragrances, whose value was certified in the Koran. Olfactory imagery dominates its representation of paradise. The faithful who cross the bridge Al Sirat in the Garden of Paradise gain access to the pool of Al Cawthar, where thirst is quenched forever with waters as fragrant as musk. In the Seventh Heaven the devout stroll through fields smelling of hyacinth, saffron, and musk and rest in bowers attended by perfumed Houris. The belief that perfume was food for the soul explained the energy of Islamic experiments in distilling natural odours. In the tenth century, Avicenna volatilized the oil of flowers, creating attar of roses and hyacinths, and adding liquid fragrance to the traditional gums and dried flowers. When the art of perfuming effloresced in Europe during the fifteen century, it burgeoned in Italy, first in Venice, the city-state with the most extensive trade relations with the Islamic world, then in Florence at the Dominican monastery of Santa Maria Novella, and finally in Rome in the household of the noble Frangiapani family.[3]

Before the influx of Eastern materials and techniques from the Islamic world, Europeans sweetened the odour of their rooms, clothes, and persons by a few traditional methods. Strewing flowers (cut or dried) or herbs in chests, on church pews, among linens, and on cadavers was the commonest way of brightening the smell of one's surroundings. Public houses customarily planted boxes of flowers at the windows to freshen those spaces in temperate months. In winter, fumigating spaces by smoking

---

[3] Aytoun Ellis, *The Essence of Beauty: A History of Scent* (New York, 1962), 70–3.

juniper, or some other resinous wood, masked the funk of human occupation.[4] Incense (frankincense and myrrh of the Scriptures, juniper, liquidamber) adorned the atmosphere of the grander of Europe's sacred spaces—visible prayer ascending to heaven. The Islamic East introduced rose waters, fragrant powders, animal musks, and gums. Inspired by Eastern examples the Dominicans at Santa Maria Novella introduced cosmetic unguents and lily water. The Frangipani family in Rome created a mixture composed of spices, orris root, civet, and musk (imported from India, home of the musk deer, via Turkey at great expense) and sold in a small perforated box, a cassolette, carried on one's belt or in one's pocket. The portable musk ball developed into the sine qua non of European courtiers, the pomander. The nobility of Italy, Germany, France, and England smelled of musk and citrus from the late sixteenth century to the eighteenth century.

Perfumer and botanist Mercutio Frangipani accompanied Christopher Columbus on his first voyage across the Western Ocean. His sensitive nose may have been the first on board that detected the perfume of land at sea. The nose was the sense organ by which the European first encountered the New World, and the literature of discovery is punctuated by scenes of detecting the western continent on the breeze as (to use the words of William Strachey) 'we smell a sweet savour'.[5] Frangipani entered world history when he detected Antigua as a cloud of perfume hanging over the Caribbean, isolated the source as the *Plumeria alba* (commonly called the Frangipani), brought it back to Europe, fixed the scent in spirits of wine, and naturalized the flower's growth in Italy.[6] A relative soaked glove leather in Frangipani spirits, lined the interiors with civet, and ignited in the Spanish court a craze for perfumed gloves among the titled classes of Europe.

John Stowe, the antiquarian, observed that perfume was not widely known in England before Edward de Vere's gift of perfumed gloves to Queen Elizabeth I in the fifteenth year of her reign. (*The Annales*—year 1585). Brought from Italy, the queen's gloves smelled of civet and Frangiapani . . . what came to be known as the earl of Oxford's perfume. Out of the ranks of England's alchemists Ralph Rabbards emerged to service the new courtly fashion for scent, concocting floral waters and sachet powders.[7] Sir Humphrey Gilbert sailed west in 1583 equipped with Rabbard's lotions and six pomanders when seeking the North-West Passage in the Arctic north. To the south Sir Walter Raleigh trekked with perfumes to scent his leather buskins. Neither would contribute anything to the olfactory enrichment of humankind, for Gilbert sought China beyond the expanse of ice, and Raleigh's eyes were so besotted with gold that his nose did not register the glories of Guiana. Their Spanish and Portuguese predecessors, however, were not so insensitive. Spaniards in the sixteenth century brought tobacco, sassafras, allspice, vanilla, West Indian Bay, Peruvian Balsam, Heliotrope, the Balsam of Talu, gum storax out of the West to join the traditional musks,

4 Roy Genders, 'The Scents and Smells of Early England', in *A History of Scent* (London, 1972), 136–57.
5 William Strachey, *The Historie of Travaile into Virginia Britainia* (London, 1849), 43.
6 Georg Schwedt, *Betörende Düfte, sinnliche Aromen* (Weinheim, 2008), 49–50.
7 C. J. S. Thompson, *Mystery and the Lure of Perfume* (Whitefish, MT, 2003), 111–13.

florals, and fragrant barks in the ingredients chest of Europe's perfumers. These new ingredients did not transform the art of perfumery, only enriched the range of scent. Yet because alchemy promoted a therapeutic value to fumigants and perfumes, the expansion of active elements in perfumers' mixtures inspired great hope in their medical efficacy.[8] The curative power ascribed to sassafras by natural historian Nicolas Monardes contributed to its incorporation in a wide variety of sachet powders.

Of all the aromatic substances that crossed the Atlantic during the sixteenth century, tobacco would have the greatest consequence. If the indigenous peoples of the Americas did not promote the pharmaceutical powers of sassafras greatly, they celebrated tobacco as a sacred substance vested with immense power to do good to body and spirit. In the earliest of all native medical codices, the Badianus manuscript,[9] the Aztec physician Martín de la Cruz described two kinds of tobacco, supplied their therapeutic applications, provided illustrations of their natural configurations, and indicated uses as an ingested medicine and an inhaled incense. The inhalation of fumes of henbane as a cure for pulmonary disorders had been a customary medicinal practice in Europe and the Middle East since antiquity. Consequently smoking a burning vegetable was not so great a novelty to prevent Europeans from embracing an America habit, particularly given the pronounced narcotic calm that smoking produced. Cortés brought the first sample to Spain in 1518. Europeans were cultivating tobacco crops in the West Indies for local consumption by 1531. Importation of seeds of *Nicotiana tobacum* by Franciscan friar André Thevet in 1555 and *Nicotiana rustica* by Jean Nicot in 1560 into France led to the production of both snuff and smoking tobacco as panaceas, curing headaches and clearing the 'superfluous humors of the brain'. By 1571, Monardes had discovered thirty-one maladies that tobacco cured, documenting them in *De hierba panacea* and inspiring an intense European demand for the plant. When he turned to the effects of the smoke, Monardes likened it to the oriental spice bague whose sweet smell and taste produced trances. 'In like sort the rest of the Indians for their pastime, do take the smoke of the Tobacco, for to make them selves drunk withal, and to see the visions, and things that do represent to them, wherein they do delight.'[10] The intoxicating effect of tobacco smoke explains the favoured characterization in English of 'drinking smoke' when describing inhalation of the fumigant. For those habituated to smoke, the scent of tobacco provoked as much pleasure as a floral scent.

Attention to native pharmacopoeia and ritual plant uses led to an expansion of the odoriferous materials imported from the New World. The fragrant sap of the Casarilla (*Croton eleutheria*) from the Bahamas found its way into soaps and unguents. The French in Martinique saw the natives adorn themselves with the aromatic blossoms of

---

[8] Richard Palmer, 'In Bad Odour: Smell and its Significance in Medicine from Antiquity to the Seventeenth Century', in William F. Bynam and Roy Porter, *Medicine and the Five Senses* (Cambridge, 1999), 61–9.

[9] Codex Barberini, 1552, Latin 241, Vatican Library.

[10] John Frampton, *Joyfull Newes out of the Newe Founde Worlde* (New York, 1925). 1577 English translation of Monardes.

the Talauma and exported it. The Spaniards did the same with the Rondeletia of Cuba and Mexico.[11] By 1700, the classical stock of ingredients employed by Italian perfumers of 1500 had increased 100 per cent by additions from America.

If perfumery was a Western art, the indigenous peoples of America possessed an aesthetic appreciation of odour commensurate with those of the *conquistadores*. José de Acosta observed, 'The Indians are great lovers of flowers, and in new Spaine more then in any other part of the world, and therefore they are accustomed to make many kindes of Nosegaies, which there they call Suchilles, with such prettie varietie and art, as nothing can be more pleasing . . . at this day they use the principall flowers of Castile, to that end, for that they grow better there than here, as Gilli-flowers, Roses, Jasmins, Violets, Orange flowers, and other sorts which they have transported out of Spaine.'[12] Like Europeans, the natives incorporated the best foreign scents into an established way of presenting odours, a customary method of floral arrangements.

Yet literary representations did not make agreeable fragrance the primary olfactory engagement between settlers and indigenous peoples. The tendency of various native peoples to use animal fat as an insulation applied to bare skin and the propensity of that fat to grow rancid led to ample comment throughout the colonial period on the malodorousness of Indians. The paradox was that the same accounts often ascribed extraordinary sensitivity to natives' olfactory sense—a capacity to smell game on the wind or distinguish between the various ethnicities of Europeans by the scent of their hands.[13] By the end of the sixteenth century, the rank odour of the native became so commonplace a judgement that it could be deployed in witty critiques of European excess. Pedro Oroz rebukes Spanish settlers in 1585: 'You are the ones who smell bad to me and cause my illness, for you live as though you were not Christians, and bear yourselves so foppishly that the Indians smell to me of heaven and console me and impart health to me.'[14]

THE TONGUE

Brillat-Savarin's maxim that human appetite rules the world finds confirmation in the history of early modern exploration. Indeed the idea that the hunger for spice drove world exploration became dogma over the twentieth century; so much so that

---

[11] John Charles Sawyer, *Odorographia: A Natural History of Raw Materials and Drugs Used in the Perfume Industry* (London, 1894), 459.

[12] Joseph de Acosta, 'Observations', in Samuel Purchas, *Hakluytus Posthumus, or, Purchas his Pigrimes*, 2nd part, 5th book (London, 1615), 116. The standard current edition: *José de Acosta, Natural and Moral History of the Indies*, ed. Jane E. Mangan, trans. Frances López-Morillas (Durham, NC, 2002).

[13] Peter Charles Hoffer, *Sensory Worlds in Early America* (Baltimore, MD, 2003), 33.

[14] Pedro Oroz and Angélico Chávez, 'Relación de la descripción de la Provincia del Santo Evangelio que es en las Indias Occidentales que llaman la Nueva España hecha el año de 1585', *The Oroz Codex: The Oroz Relación, Or Relation of the Description of the Holy Gospel Province in New Spain, and the Lives of the Founders and Other Noteworthy Men of Said Province* (Washington, DC, 1972), 72.

revisionists now feel obliged to insist that copper and other metals had equal influ-ence.[15] Yet Charles Corn in *The Scents of Eden* and Wolfgang Schivelbusch in *Tastes of Paradise* have kept the story of the construction of the first world drug culture across the Indian and Atlantic oceans current and popular.[16] Corn and Schivelbusch suggest that the effect of spice, sugar, tobacco, caffeine, and capsicum on the human body was so pronounced and pleasurable that these items were embraced immediately as a kind of biological response with a minimum of cultural mediation. This was not the case. Only sugar inspired this immediate universal desire. As with scents, new tastes had to be framed as remedies or combined in a familiar form of experience to become widely accepted.

Coffee, tea, and chocolate all became popular beverages in Europe within a short span of time during the first half of the seventeenth century. They did so by being consumed in a manner at odds with the original way they were prepared and ingested in the Islamic Middle East, China, and Central America. Coffee was brewed hot and straight in Turkey and Yemen. Tea was brewed for three minutes after a brief rinse of the leaves with hot water—no additives—in China. Chocolate was mixed with corn flour, hot chilli, vanilla, and spices and frothed in hot water in Mexico. In other parts of the Indies it was served cold. In northern Europe all would eventually be consumed with the addition of milk and sugar. Ignorance of the Chinese language can explain why Tom Garroway, the coffee purveyor who introduced tea into England in 1656, boiled his Hyson leaves several hours, then put leaves and liquor in a cask to steep several weeks, then drew off mugs of cold 'tea' to patrons to heat before the fire like cider. Given the tannic kick of the beverage there is little wonder why consumers wished to cut the bitterness with a sweetener and cream.

The English would not know how to prepare tea properly until Queen Catherine of Braganza taught the ladies of the court during the Restoration. Portugal's China traders had schooled the queen in the art of brewing and sipping.

Seventeenth-century Europeans knew about native ways of preparing coffee and chocolate. The cultivation, processing, and preparation of coffee became generally known with publication in 1583 of Bavarian Leonhard Rauwolf's account of 'Chaube'.[17] The special qualities of chocolate were announced to Europe in Hernán Cortés' second letter: 'una taza de este precioso brevaje promete un hombre de andaar un día sin tomar alimento'—'a cup of this precious drink enables a man to walk a day without eating' (*Cartas de relacíon de la conquesta de la Nueva España*). It remained an exclusive imported pleasure of the Spanish until 1606 when the Italian merchant Antonio Carletti secured some and spread its use to his native country. Consumption spread

---

[15] Lisa Jardine, *The New History of the Renaissance* (New York, 1998), 286–7.

[16] Charles Corn, *The Scents of Eden* (New York, 1998); Wolfgang Schivelbusch, *Tastes of Paradise* (New York, 1992).

[17] Dr Edward Pocoke's translation, *The Nature of the Drink Kaubi, or Coffee, and the Berry of Which it is Made* (Oxford, 1659), made Rauwolf's account the focus of medical debate upon the beverage. For Rauwolf and Pocoke, see Bennett A. Weinberg, *The World of Caffeine: The Science and Culture of the World's Most Popular Drug* (London, 2001), 99–100.

after courtiers sweetened the drink in the seventeenth century.[18] Thomas Gage's *The English American* detailed the drink in 1643 and again in 1648 in *A Survey of the West Indies*. When the first English chocolate house opened in Bishopsgate in 1658, it sold chocolate Spanish court style with sugar, not Aztec style.

Coffee, tea, and chocolate all tasted bitter to Europeans when first encountered. Yet Europeans registered the stimulation that caffeine and theobromine in the beverages produced, and ascribed great medical value to it. Early modern herbals regularly recommended that bitter decoctions be rendered palatable by dulcifying them with a sweetener (honey or sugar) and cream. The medicalization of the new placed new sensations into a familiar framework, and provided a warrant for revelling in novel tastes and somatic effects by connecting them with tried and true ingredients and recipes. Thus the English cup of Assam with milk and sugar, the latte, and the mug of sweet cocoa.

New things lodged themselves in other people's mouths and desires at different velocities. The chilli pepper sped around the equator before 1550, its heat being appreciated by a multitude of peoples in the tropic zone, yet incapable of supplanting pepper or ginger north of Hungary until the twentieth century. The acidity of tomatoes found favour in the Mediterranean, but the first 'pomo de oro' brought to England in the 1590s tasted 'rank' (i.e. rancid) to herbalist John Gerard. The embrace or rejection of novel tastes depended in great measure on the eating practices in place among a people—fish eaters chew a new variety of fish more readily than grain eaters. While sugar, particularly after the Brazilian plantations began mass shipments across the Atlantic, found immediate broad favour, transmuting from a royal delicacy to a common treat, other staple foods spread because of reasons beside their capacity to inspire human pleasure. Maize to European cultures raised on wheat and spelt seemed granular and crude. Its consumption in northern Italy as polenta tended to be restricted to the lower classes, despite the models of faro or buckwheat porridges. Yet livestock loved it, and the nutritional yield of maize was such that cattle could be sustained over winter on a harvest. This led to the revival of rural estates and contributed to the creation of the Palladian villa as a form.[19] Rice's blandness enables it to be eaten repeatedly without cloying and to serve as a backdrop for more pronounced flavours. West African peoples grew glaborina rice, those of Madagascar grew savita rices brought from Indonesia, and Italians, from the fifteenth century onward, japonica rice from India and South Asia. Rice crossed the Atlantic to Brazil and British America in the seventeenth century, becoming a trade commodity and a foundation of cuisine. West Africans in the New World worked with the non-glaborina varieties, installing them in their one-pot stews. When physician James Grainger in 1764 sketched the ideal diet for West Indian slaves, he sketched a transatlantic supply in which traditional

---

[18] Yolanda Gamboa, 'Consuming the Other, Creating the Self: The Cultural Implications of Aztecs' Chocolate from Tirso de Molina to Agustin Moreto and Pedro Lanini y Sagredo', in Mindy Badia and Bonnie L. Gasior (eds.), *Crosscurrents: Transatlantic Perspectives on Early Modern Hispanic Drama* (Lewisburg, PA, 2006), 28–31.

[19] Giovanni Gioconi, *The Villas of Palladio* (Princeton, NJ, 2003), 17–19.

West African staples were supplemented by wheat and beef: Carolina rice, English beans, Newfoundland cod, Pennsylvania flour, Scottish herrings, and beef. When Grainger's attention shifted to the garden plots of St Kitts' African labourers, he found a cosmopolitan range of plants:

> yams, and there cassada's root:
> From a good dæmon's staff cassada sprang,
> Tradition says, and Caribbees believe;
> Which into three the white-rob'd genius broke,
> And bade them plant, their hunger to repel.
> There let angola's bloomy bush supply,
> For many a year, with wholesome pulse their board.
> There let the bonavist, his fringed pods
> Throw liberal o'er the prop; while ochra bears
> Aloft his slimy pulp, and help disdains.
> There let potatos mantle o'er the ground;
> Sweet as the cane-juice is the root they bear.
> There too let eddas spring in order meet,
> With Indian cale, and foodful calaloo
> While mint, thyme, balm, and Europe's coyer herbs,
> Shoot gladsome forth, nor reprobate the clime.
>
> (*The Sugar Cane* (London, 1674), book IV)

The slave garden contained an international assortment of root vegetables, beans, and greens. From Africa came yams, okra, Angola bean (a field pea), and bonavist (Egyptian bean). The greens—West Indian Kale (*Xanthosoma atrovirens*) and Calaloo (*Amaranthus spinosus*)—grew native on the islands. Three root vegetables—sweet potatoes, cassava root (manioc), and edda (taro root)—hailed from the Central and South American mainland. The cuisine generated by this garden would have been syncretic, yet its enduring appeal to the taste of the gardeners is attested by the retention of these ingredients in West Indian foodways.[20] When we turn to those items that Grainger would add to the diet from the storehouse of empire, only Carolina rice would become a staple of West Indian cookery. Indeed arroz Carolina spread from the Indies to South America, where it remains the favourite long-grained white rice to this day. As to his other supplementations: fresh local fish would prove more convenient and palatable than Scottish herrings or salt cod. Pork, not beef, would become the favourite meat of the islands, thanks in part to the Spanish habit of releasing hogs on various islands throughout the Caribbean to supply sailors marooned by the periodic hurricanes. Goat would later join pork as a West Indian staple. Wheat flour would always hold a secondary popularity to maize and various 'bread roots'.

Though the slaves of St Kitts supped on the provender of five continents, desire cannot be said to have impelled this world of goods to the garden plot. Rice was introduced to the island diet, as Grainger suggests, by planters and officials as cheap nutrition for the bound workforce. The spread of coffee and cocoa, citron and cotton,

---

[20] See Lynn Marie Houston, *Food Culture in the Caribbean* (New York, 2005), 31–80.

served planter desires to naturalize those staples in the West Indies. Okra, Angola bean, and bonavist had been carried out of Africa by the slaves, a portable legacy. The local greens substituted for those of West Africa. Hunting feral hogs and fishing the local waters supplied animal protein. What Grainger did not see was the extent to which the roots and beans, grains and greens mixed into the cookpot in traditional ways, suiting the taste for stews, rice and bean mixtures, and roasts of West Africa. Nor did he notice that chilli had been added to the pot as well. Even in places where coercive power had greatest force, the tongue savoured the new primarily within the ambit of a familiar and traditional meals or food-sharing occasions.

THE EAR

European adventurers believed that music had special power to convey their being— their potency, their majesty, their spirituality, their gentility, and their violence. On coastal and transoceanic vessels instruments and instrumentalists sailed, conspicuous among them drummers and trumpeters, who awed strangers and enemies with noise. Recruited from the ranks of military musicians, these raucous bandsmen performed multiple functions. In obscure landscapes such as forests or smoke-choked battlefields, they alerted one's fellows of the whereabouts of the leader. Marc Lescarbout in *Histoire de la Nouvelle France* (Paris, 1609) related the unsuccessful attempt to recover a lost priest by fanfares and cannon fire. His narrative detailed the other uses of martial noises: mustering troops, sounding alarms alerting natives to one's proximity, punctuating the important moments in public life (the arrival of supply ships, the procession of officials, etc.).[21] The resonance of trumpets permitted them to be heard at distance, making them valuable heralds in travels upon land or sea. Instrumental proclamation of one's presence or incitement of one's company were not the only tasks music performed in the Atlantic world. It also enchanted the alien.

Europeans undertook a concerted effort to charm persons they encountered with music in the wake of a 1455 encounter by the Portuguese captain Alvise de Cadamosto with the Senegalese. A sailor began playing a bagpipe, inspiring a sensation among the auditors. 'They concluded that it was a living animal that sung thus in different voices, and were much pleased with it. Perceiving that they were misled, I told them that it was an instrument, and placed it, deflated, in their hands. Whereupon, recognizing that it was made by hand, they said that it was a divine instrument, made by God with his own hands, for it sounded so sweetly with so many different voices. They said they had never heard anything sweeter.'[22] Vasco da Gama in his voyage to India recorded the first musical conversation between Africans and Europeans near the Cape of Good

---

21 *Purchas his Pigrimes*, 18. 32.
22 Quoted in Ian Woodfield, *English Musicians in the Age of Exploration* (London, 1995), 95–6. This account epitomizes Woodfield's research.

Hope. The natives played on flutes; da Gama ordered the trumpets and drums to sound; a spontaneous dance among the sailors and the residents broke out.[23] The dance meeting became a fixture of Portuguese encounters. Pedro Alveres Cabral during his 1500 trip to Brazil has a piper on the expedition provoke a dance. When the Spanish attempted to provoke harmony between visitors and natives, following the Portuguese method, the outcome proved less successful. On Columbus' third voyage, the Spanish encountered a restive group of inhabitants. Columbus ordered his musicians break out shawms (a double-reed woodwind predecessor to the oboe) to quell their turbulent spirits, but the sound proved so odd that the hearers drew their weapons instead of breaking into dance. The magic exercised by European music had limits. Even when the magic worked to best effect, drawing natives near to hear the 'sweete harmony' of flutes, shawms, and drums, the listeners were never so wonderfully astonished that they declared themselves subject to its spell and the spell's makers, nor so enchanted that the power of their own songs diminished in their ears.

Indeed the songs of certain of the African and American peoples rivalled those of Spain and Lisbon in complexity and communicative piquancy, and the purposes to which music played resembled those of Europe. Gabriel de Rojas in 1581 noted that in the Mexican city of Cholula, home of the Quetzalcóatl cult, trumpeters and drummers sounded the hours, and a professional cadre of instrumentalists serviced the temple with ceremonial music.[24] (Certain of the distinctive drum patterns have been preserved in the manuscript *Cantares en idioma mexicano*.) The trumpets and drums performed the task of terrorizing would-be invaders, mirroring their use by Europeans. Their effectiveness was attested by Bernal Diaz del Castillo in *Historia verdadera de la conquista de la Nueva España*: 'Again there was sounded the dismal drum of Huichji-lobos and many other shells and horns and things like trumpets and the sound of them all was terrifying.'[25] The native instrumentalists could also perform lively and melliflu-ous tunes in their six-, seven-, and eight-note scales. When Emperor Charles V of Spain witnessed a native troupe assembled by Cortés at Vallodolid, he marvelled at the rhythmic perfection of the performances, the unison of the singing, and the ensemble of the dancers.[26] These attributes inspired comment in other witnesses at other times during the contact period: 'Illa verò tripudia sun inprimix memorabilia, nam cum tantus esset populi confluxus omne tamen ad eosdem numerous & sonos partier cantabant & saltabant nec obstabat varia soni mutation.'[27] Because this music existed within a ritual world of religion, because it was communal in expression, because it invoked a language of emotion intelligible to European as well as native listeners, because compositions were tied to occasions, because a professional caste of performers

[23] *Diário de viagem de Vasco da Gama*, ed. D. Peres, A Baião, and A de Magaháes Basto (Oporto, n.d.), 8.

[24] Gabriel de Rojas, 'Descripcion de Cholula', *Revista mexicana de estudios históricos*, 1/6 (November–December 1927), 162.

[25] *The True History of the Conquest of New Spain* (London, 1912), iv. 149.

[26] Robert Stevenson, *Music in Aztec & Inca Territory* (Berkeley and Los Angeles, CA, 1976), 89.

[27] Diego Valades, *Rhetoric Christiana* (Perusia, 1579), 169.

created and performed the music, the Roman Catholic missionaries who accompanied the conquest enlisted the entire caste into the service of the Christian religion. In 1532 the Royal Audiencia at Mexico City exempted native singers from tribute payments because they had, for the most part, attached themselves to the service of the Church. Since Spanish conquest resulted in one theopolity replacing another, the bureaucracy that served the old order could be fitted to the purposes of the latter, provided the leadership came from Spain. In both mission churches and cathedrals throughout New Spain, New Grenada, Peru, and Brazil, natives formed the bulk of the choir and instrumentalists, while musical priests from the peninsula served as choirmasters, organists, and instructors in the various musical schools in the New World. The music employed in the services was formally European, either Gregorian chant or *cano de órgano* (polyphony). Over the course of the sixteenth century, the growing influence of the polyphonic style in European church music was registered in Ibero-America, with Cristobal Morales' 1544 *Book of Masses* spreading from Rome throughout the colonies in two years.[28] Indeed, a healthy tradition of composition emerged through Spanish America in the polyphonic style, with composers such as Hernando Franco, Juan de Lienas, López Caillas, and Antonio de Salazar contributing to a New World tradition of liturgical music. String instruments, foreign to the indigenous musical cultures, were employed in the orchestras. Even chapels in pueblos had an ample contingent of instrumentalists—trumpeters, harpists, string players, bassoonists, and oboists in addition to the organist. While texts might be in native languages, (a Quechua text 'Hanacpachap' was the first work of American polyphony published in the New World in Peru in 1631) the music was decidedly new and European, and by all report a powerful force in attracting the native performers and auditors to Christian worship. In 1648, Thomas Gage, an English Catholic priest stationed in New Spain during the early seventeenth century, observed that 'the people are drawn to their churches more for the delight of the music than for any delight in the service of God' (*The English American*).

While the music of formal services may have maintained a rigorously European orientation, the blending of native and European qualities may be found in the spiritual songs ('alabanzas') employed outside of the *iglesia*, particularly in those areas of South America evangelized by the Jesuit order. In the missions of Brazil, particularly, musical and religious syncretism was allowed to occur side by side. While native motifs might insinuate themselves into the work of a European mission composer, such as the Italian Jesuit Dominico Zipoli in Argentina, more common was the communal creation of a body of folk performance popularized through informal gatherings. Musical *mestizaje*, the blending of sounds, had a peculiar capacity to influence traditional practices, whether European or indigenous, because the new blended with the familiar.

When African rhythmic sensibilities combined with already mixed forms, a singularly potent mixture came into existence. From the port cities of Spanish America, the

---

28 Gerard Béhague, *Music in Latin America: An Introduction* (New York, 1979), 6.

fandango, the habañera, the congo, the tango, and the calinda spread around the world, inciting feet to dance. From the southern region of North America, in the territory of Spanish Louisiana and the slave colonies, similar hybrid forms would emerge: gospel, ragtime, jazz, r & b. What is noteworthy about these mixed musics is that they never addressed the ear alone. Performance enlisted the body in dance and the eye in spectacle. The ear recruited one to communal action and installed one in a social gestalt. Historically, what compels attention is that the initial ambitions of Europeans carting their musicians with them when voyaging to communicate with others finds fulfilment repeatedly in the New World developments of both religious music and folk music. The ear was the organ than enabled newer and stranger forms of 'we'.

THE EYE

'I saw the things which have been brought to the King from the new land of gold (Mexico), a sun of all gold a whole fathom broad, a moon of silver of the same size, also two rooms full of the armour of the people there, and all manner of wonderous weapons of theirs, harness and darts, very strange clothing, beds and all kinds of wonderful objects of human use much better worth seeing than prodigies. These things are all so precious that they are valued at 100,000 florins. All the days of my life I have seen nothing that rejoiced my heart so much as these things, for I saw among them wonderful works of art, and I marveled at the subtle *ingenia* of people in distant lands.'[29] Here the great German artist Albrecht Dürer marvelled over the store of Mexican objects from King Charles V's collection on display in Brussels in 1520. Dürer's eye did not rejoice in prodigy—the demonstrations of nature's power to express itself in striking diversity—but in ingenuity, the creative mastery evinced in 'objects of human use' of 'people in distant lands'. Dürer's remark spoke a number of truths: when strange new things appeared as a plethora of difference, human imagination glutted and novelty's power to inspire wonder waned. By prodigies, Dürer meant natural prodigies, such as the huge square-headed fish he also examined in Brussels. The significance of a prodigy did not lie in its brute capacity to elicit sensation, but in its power of reference as a sign, portent, or omen. The novel plants, minerals, animals, and insects of distant lands demonstrated God's creative potency, and so they affirmed a truth already well known to believers in Christianity of the incomprehensible variety of provi-dential expression in nature. For experienced eyes such as Dürer's this lesson was too familiar to need repeated emphasis, but witnessing the power of human genius . . . *that* commanded attention, for people in distant lands were fallen, pagan, and strange, yet possessed subtlety and skill so telling that the greatest engraver in Germany stood before the Mexican artefacts astonished at their artistry. The wonder revealed to Dürer's eyes shone from the artistry of human genius. They revealed the ingenuity of humanity.

---

[29] W. M. Conway (trans.), *The Writings of Albrecht Dürer* (London, 1911), 101–2.

Dürer did not sketch the marvels he saw in Brussels. Five years earlier, however, he drew a Tupinamba warrior as an illustration to the great providential Psalm 24, 'The earth is the LORD's, and the fulness thereof; the world, and they that dwell therein,' in the margin of a book of hours prepared for Maximilian I. This portrait and those contained in Hans Burgkmair's 1516 woodcut illustrations for the triumph commissioned by Maximilian, suggest that the clothes, headdresses, weapons, and ceremonial objects of these Brazilian peoples were available for inspection in Maximilian's court in 1515–16.[30] The figures, while bare-chested and bare-legged, departed from Brazilian appearance, males sporting beards in Burgkmair's case, and a north European visage and hair in Dürer's image. These images demonstrate what Dürer's 1520 attestation would expect: a focus on the artefacts of human manufacture more than the humans themselves. Attention to the ethnographic characteristics of physiognomy and facial adornment can be seen in very few representations of American peoples in European depictions of the sixteenth century. Aside from Christoph Weiditz's eleven depictions made in 1529 of Aztecs brought to Spain by Cortés, the great body of accurate ethnographic portrayal was that made by John White of two bands of Algonquians living near the Roanoke settlement in 1585 Virginia.

Perhaps it is anachronistic to characterize White's portraits as ethnographic. They would better be termed anthropographic, representing the figures' human commonality as much as their distinctiveness. White's famous watercolours from Virginia represented two sorts of things—natural creatures (a terrapin, a swallowtail butterfly, a fish, a flower) and the Algonquian inhabitants of the territories he visited.[31] The former appeared as objects in themselves, isolated in a pictorial field, divorced from any environment or depicted context—the way a picture of a specimen would appear in a herbal. None of these would be engraved by Theodore de Bry for the illustrated version of Thomas Harriot's history of the colony, A Brief and True Report of the New Found Land of Virginia (1590). Only the portraits of the Algonquians were published. White's originals combined careful observation of significant figures in the native community with facial expression and details of dress clearly detailed in full-figure portraits, showing individuals with minimal background. As Karen Kupperman and others have suggested, the gestural language drew heavily upon European pictorial traditions, with attitudes conveying status, authority, and office.[32] One can detect classical precedents for some images, the shaman prefigured in the dance of the muses, and the circle dancers resembling Greek nymphs. The de Bry images removed the particularity of facial features and rendered the gesture language more emphatic, making the figures even more anthropographic, while fixing images in elaborated backgrounds meant to

---

[30] William C. Sturtevant, 'First Visual Images of Native America', in Fredi Chiappelli (ed.), First Images of America: The Impact of the New World on the Old, 2 vols. (Berkeley and Los Angeles, CA, 1976), i. 421–3.

[31] Housed in the British Museum, the watercolours were exhibited at Jamestown, VA, July–October 2008: 'A New World: England's First View of America.'

[32] Karen Ordahl Kupperman, Indians and English: Facing Off in Early America (Ithaca, NY, 2000), 64–6.

typify the natives' built environment. Theodore de Bry included White's supplement to the native portraits, five images of Picts and other inhabitants of the early British Isles, included 'to show how that the inhabitants of the Great Bretannie have been in times past as savage as those of Virginia'. In sum, the artist deployed a visual aid to recall the common humanity of Native Americans and Europeans, if readers could not recognize the resemblance themselves. The anthropographic visualization of Native Americans as beings tantamount to the viewers' European ancestors suggested difference among cultures inhered not in racial characteristics so much as different states of civil development. Humanist thought proposed acculturation into Christian civility as the means to bring peoples into common condition, a matter of education. Hariot and de Bry shared this assumption.

Theodore de Bry, a Protestant Walloon, established an engraving studio and publishing gallery in Frankfort that specialized in travels and voyages. He would become the single most influential image broker of the Atlantic world during the 1580s, publishing a series of illustrated relations that would remain the authoritative visualization of America and Native Americans for almost two hundred years. A friend and business partner of Richard Hakluyt, an avid collector of New World artefacts and images, he was a zealous enemy of the Spanish Catholic conquest of the western hemisphere as well as a humanist. De Bry visually played with the question, who is the savage?, by giving natives vaguely Mediterranean features, and showing them the victims of Spanish tortures, particularly in various illustrated versions of the Black Legend such as the popular picture book *Brief Explanation of the Horrible Deeds done by Spaniards in Various Parts of the New World 1599*. These images stand counterposed to the depictions of cannibalism of the Tupinambas in de Bry's *Americae tertia pars*.[33] In de Bry's engravings the New World oscillates between being a theatre of depraved violence and a pastoral world of Edenic naturals. Protestant humanism would not permit humankind, whether European or Native American, to escape from its fallen condition; nevertheless, it revelled in the creativity, ingenuity, and variety of the human condition. Any particular native also represented a number of general categories as well—priest, mother, warrior, child, king, physician, labourer. His desire to designate tribal identities within the native population appears to have been limited to illustrating distinctive features of the various material cultures.

Touch

In the historiography of the Atlantic world, touch has been the sense most fraught with consequence. The sensation of touching, the tactile moment of contact, has been entirely eclipsed by 'contact' as a metaphor communicating the irreversible

---

[33] Aucardo Chicangana Yobenj, 'El festin antropofágico de los indios tupinambá en los grabados de Theodoro De Bry, 1592', *Fronteras de la historia*, 10 (2005), 19–71.

convergence of cultures that led to the destruction of various indigenous traditions around the Atlantic, and the horrendous mortalities occasioned by the exchange of diseases in native and settler populations. Thus, when scenes of exploratory touching appear—such as the Caddoan-speaking people of the coast of the Gulf of Mexico feeling the face and body of Cabeza de Vaca in 1536—the voice of historical wisdom interposes to observe that 'invisible pathogens . . . carried off the populations of entire native villages'. An effort is made to forestall any recall of the pleasure, curiosity, doubt that may have attended episodes of contact between peoples. Historians grant priority to our present knowledge of the imperceptible agents of touch at work then over the palpable experience that filled their senses. Besides our historiographical reluctance to permit touch any 'innocence' in stories of the contact, there is a phenomenological problem surrounding touch as a means of adducing the new and strange; it is the sense least able to distinguish novelty, that quality so frequently announced as the distinguishing mark of perceptions of strange places, things, and persons around the Atlantic. Tactile sensations tend to be qualitatively of a piece. One can speak intelligibly about new intensities of feeling, for instance of the Arctic cold that the voyagers seeking the North-West Passage felt in the sixteenth century, or the discomforts of tropical disease and insect infestation that residents of temperate regions experienced when approaching the equator. Yet hot and cold, pain and pleasure, slick and abrasive, wet and dry, soft and hard, greasy and scratchy, springy and resistant—all of the discriminations of tactile sensation have always been available in experience without travel. So, curiously, touch, the most portentous of the sensations experienced in the Atlantic world, proves the least distinctive in sensation.

Touch, as the phenomenologist Maurice Merleau-Ponty argued in *The Phenomenology of Perception*, most often participates in a complex of feeling, a gestalt in which tactile sensation joins with input from other senses.[34] When Captain John Smith showed Opepechanconough his compass, the werrowance grew puzzled when he could not touch the moving needle because of the glass covering. Thomas Hariot, speaking of the Algonquian response to hearing the Bible in *A Briefe and True Report of the New Found Land of Virginia* (1588), indicated that they wish to absorb its power tactilely: 'yet would many be glad to touch it, to embrace it, to kisse it, to hold it to their brests and heades, and stroke over all their bodie with into shewe their hungrie desire of that knowledge which was spoken of' (p. 27). Yet the most emphatic whole-body sense of being registered in early European texts was that of space. The close confines shipboard in the Atlantic, the vast, sparsely populated overgrown terrains, the safe enclosure of the stockade, the uncertainty of the primeval forests were felt by hands, torso, legs, and feet, and registered with eyes, and measured acoustically with the ears. This sense of a new spatial dynamic is far more ubiquitous than the much more frequently studied attestations of pain, fatigue, hunger, and discomfort found in testimonies. Indeed, if anything can be said to be new in the feel of the New World

---

[34] Maurice Merlau-Ponty, *The Phenomenology of Perception* (London, 2002), 81–102, 122–56.

to Europeans, it was the spatial vacancy, the desertedness of the wild. We have few reliable testimonies of what the several Native American visitors to Europe felt upon experiencing the cities and countrysides there. If we can trust the testimony of Samuel Purchas, Powhatan's spy, Tomocomo, was forced to abandon his tally sticks registering the grain fields, forests, and population of England. He reportedly observed to Powhatan, 'Count the Stars in the Skys, the Leaves on the Trees, and the Sand upon the Sea Shore; for such is the Number of People in England.' This, however, may represent as much an English self-perception of population density as a native observation of profusion and density.

A historical dilemma emerges. Did the experience of the Atlantic world suggest the reality of a human *sensus communis*, the shared experience of the senses that had been asserted about persons of different cultures by philosophers since Archestratus of Gela accompanied Alexander the Great and Phyrro the Sceptic on the Greek world conquest, or did it introduce the possibility of some other way of feeling, seeing, tasting, smelling, hearing than the one 'I' experienced? While advantages accrue for imperial powers in proposing a universal *sensus communis* experienced by humankind, not every imperialist bought into this view. Consider Captain John Smith's admiration of the hypersensitive sight, smell, and touch of the Susquehanna Indians. In his representation we encounter vision of a sensorium more vitally engaged with the world than that available to European bodies. What enabled this amplification of sense? Training? Environment? Disparities in the providential design of human types? Perhaps the cultural relativism brought to view in exploring these questions accomplished something approximating what Brillat-Savarin believed, making aesthetics—the particularities and communal inflections of feeling, sense, and taste—philosophically important in Europe. Perhaps it *is* the precondition for the emergence of 'taste'—with all the emphasis upon 'discrimination'—as a regnant category of judgement in Europe. Concern with the cultural and communal particulars of sense and taste has dominated enquiry into the aesthetics of the Atlantic world since the rise of romanticism—visible in Brillat-Savarin's *Physiology of Taste* and the writings of the brothers Von Humboldt. Yet only in the work of the current generation of anthropologically influenced historians has enquiry truly taken up the unresolved issue: how did the possibility of experiencing the world differently influence the self-understandings of the myriad non-Western peoples of that Atlantic world? Just as the experience of the Americas may have inspired in Western observers a growing modal distinctness of sense, a greater attention to smelling, tasting, hearing, seeing, and touching as categories of sensing, the opening of the Atlantic world may have also brought to the attention of many peoples the possibility that the complex way the senses worked and the sensorium held together might be different for different peoples. Perhaps there was no unitary *sensus communis*, but rather multiple communities of sense that did not map neatly upon each other, yet coincided sufficiently to permit trade and the sharing of pleasure and pain.

BIBLIOGRAPHY

Baker, Geoffrey, *Imposing Harmony; Music & Society in Colonial Cuzco* (Durham, NC, 2008).

Corn, Charles, *The Scents of Eden* (New York, 1998).

Genders, Roy, *History of Scent* (London, 1972).

Hoffer, Peter Charles, *Sensory Worlds in Early America* (Baltimore, MD, 2003).

Houston, Lynn Marie, *Food Culture in the Caribbean* (New York, 2005).

Kupperman, Karen Ordahl, *Indians and English: Facing Off in Early America* (Ithaca, NY, 2000).

Schivelbusch, Wolfgang, *Tastes of Paradise* (New York, 1992).

Sturtevant, William C., 'First Visual Images of Native America', in Fredi Chiappelli (ed.), *First Images of America: The Impact of the New World on the Old*, 2 vols. (Berkeley and Los Angeles, CA, 1976).

Woodfield, Ian, *English Musicians in the Age of Exploration* (London, 1995).

Yobenj, Aucardo Chicangana, 'El festin antropofágico de los indios tupinambá en los grabados de Theodoro De Bry, 1592', *Fronteras de la historia*, 10 (2005), 19–71.

CHAPTER 9

··

THE IBERIAN ATLANTIC
TO 1650

··

STUART B. SCHWARTZ

THE Castilians and Portuguese were the first Europeans to create systems of continual communication, trade, and political control spanning the Atlantic. Following medieval precedents and moved by similar economic and demographic factors, these two kingdoms embarked in the late fifteenth century on a course of expansion that led to the creation of overseas empires and contact with other societies and peoples. This process produced a series of political, religious, social, and ethical problems that would confront other nations pursuing empire. Portugal and Castile were sometimes rivals, sometimes allies, and for sixty years (1580–1640) parts of a composite monarchy under the same rulers. Their answers to the challenges of creating empires varied according to circumstances and resources, but they were not unaware of each others' efforts, failures, and successes nor of their common Catholic heritage and world-view that set the framework of their imperial vision, their rule, and their social organization. It makes sense, therefore, to view the early creation of the Iberian Atlantic as a joint process and a dialogue, recognizing the differences, but emphasizing the common responses.

ATLANTIC ORIGINS

··

By the fifteenth century both Castile and Portugal had emerged as Catholic monarchies seeking to achieve religious unity. In both kingdoms a precocious move towards royal centralization and bureaucratization had taken place. Portugal had emerged from the shadow of Castile, its larger neighbour, as an independent and unified kingdom after 1385. In Castile, the process of unification took a century longer, and was facilitated by a dynastic marriage in 1469 that brought together Isabela, princess of Castile, and

Fernando, prince of Aragon. In the 1480s and 1490s, as monarchs of their respective kingdoms, they enacted religious and civil reforms and military campaigns against Muslim Granada, which finally fell in 1492. By 1500 religious unification of Iberia had ostensibly been achieved with the conversion or expulsion of Castilian Jews (1492), the forced conversion of Jews in Portugal (1497), and a programme of conversion of Muslims left in Iberia.

The chapter by J.-P. Rubies has explained how the pursuit of Portuguese interests in cereal and gold led to exploration down the African coast and resulted also in the occupation of Atlantic islands: Madeira (1418), the Azores (1427), and São Tomé (1471), and the creation of Portuguese 'factories' on the coast of West Africa from which gold, spices, ivory, and, after 1441, slaves were shipped to Europe. The presence of powerful African kingdoms and Portugal's own limited resources discouraged attempts at territorial acquisition. This push into the South Atlantic eventually became directed towards opening a sea route into the Indian Ocean, a dream realized in 1498 with Vasco da Gama's voyage. For a century thereafter, Portugal's preoccupations with the Indian Ocean and the spice trade meant that their interest in the Atlantic remained limited. This was in marked contrast to developments in Castile where its territories in the Americas rapidly became the heart of its overseas empire.

Castilians, although less inclined to maritime activities, had nonetheless contested control of the Canary Islands with the Portuguese, and, by 1480, after prolonged conflict, had wrested control of most of the islands from the indigenous Guanche population, and had been assigned responsibility by the papacy for their evangelization. Further papal intervention culminating in the Treaty of Tordesillas (1494) solidified a Portuguese sphere of influence in the eastern Atlantic and a Castilian sphere to the west, and previous essays have shown how Spain and Portugal as well as the papacy applied the theory and practice of these earlier experiments at exploration and settlement to subsequent endeavours in the Atlantic, aided always by foreign capital and personnel, especially from the Mediterranean basin, France, and Flanders.

Therefore the life and career of the Genoese Christopher Columbus reflected the continuity between the Mediterranean and Atlantic worlds and his own transitional position between them. His early career in the eastern Mediterranean had not only sharpened his maritime skills, but had exposed him to a variety of mercantile practices such as the use of merchant settlement outposts which in Europe had been strictly commercial bases, but in Africa had taken on certain military and political functions. While living and working in Portugal and Madeira, he had visited the outpost at El Mina in West Africa, a source of both gold and slaves; he had carried sugar from the Atlantic islands, and he had seen both the trades in sugar and slaves in the Atlantic islands as well as the arrangements for settlement under proprietary captains. These experiences seem to have influenced his own conception of his authority, his rights, and his goals, and the presence of foreigners like him, and of foreign capital, was a common aspect of the early Iberian experience in the Atlantic.

CARIBBEAN BEGINNINGS, 1492–1530

Sailing under Castilian auspices in 1492, but with the support of Aragonese courtiers and Genoese investors, Columbus' small fleet, seeking a sea route to Asia, made a landfall in the Bahamas and proceeded to further exploration of the Caribbean and its peoples in all his four voyages to America. His techniques of contact with native populations—trade in trinkets, seizing hostages, depositing convicts on shore who, if they survived, could become translators—recalled earlier Portuguese practices on the African coast. Columbus hoped to manage the full-blown settlement which he established on Hispaniola in 1493 like a Mediterranean or African commercial outpost under his personal control with colonists serving as employees. Tensions arose because the colonial model fostered by the colonists was the reconquest and settlement of lands taken from the Muslims in Spain, where individual, noble, municipal, and corporate privileges and opportunities were granted by grateful monarchs. Because gold was scarce in Hispaniola efforts were made to send slaves back to Spain, while in 1497 the Spanish colonists and employees revolted against Columbus' authority. The rebels were placated when they were conceded control over the indigenous population in a kind of vassalage that eventually developed into the *encomienda*, a system of labour and tribute extraction from the indigenous population that would be employed by Spain in all its American territories. The appointment of a royal governor, in 1502, placed a limit on Columbus' authority. Continued dissatisfaction of the colonists and a rapid decline of the native population meant that by 1520 the crown had assumed government of the islands. Nevertheless, Hispaniola was long known as 'another Portugal', and the vocabulary, techniques, and practices of the African coast persisted on the island, especially when African slaves began to be supplied there, principally by Portuguese merchants. From thenceforth to the mid-seventeenth century, Portuguese artisans, mariners, merchants, and settlers were the most prominent and numerous foreigners in the Spanish Caribbean.[1]

After sixteen years on Hispaniola, Spanish dominance and settlement extended over the Caribbean region, especially the other islands of the Greater Antilles (Puerto Rico, Cuba, and Jamaica) and the coasts of Panama and *Tierra Firme* (Venezuela). The Caribbean served as a crucible for the subsequent conquest of the Americas. Relations with the Tainos, the indigenous population of the larger islands, quickly moved from barter to mandatory labour in the gold washings, with devastating effects. Unlike the Portuguese experience in West Africa where gold and local products were acquired by trade, the Spanish found that gold, pearls, and later silver in the Americas could be obtained only by plunder or by mining, or, in the case of pearls, by collecting, always

---

[1] Marcel Bataillon, 'Santo Domingo "Era Portugal" ', in *Historia y sociedad en el mundo de habla español* (Mexico City, 1970), 113–20; Henry Keith, 'New World Interlopers: The Portuguese in the Spanish West Indies from the Discovery to 1640', *The Americas*, 25/4 (1969), 360–71.

enabled by exploiting indigenous workers. Demographic collapse, caused by disease, labour exploitation, and the disruption of indigenous society and economy, became widespread. The period of gold production on Hispaniola and Puerto Rico proved short-lived, and by the 1540s an agricultural economy based on sugar, livestock, and ginger had emerged.[2] On Cuba and Jamaica crop production and husbandry were established, and the introduction of new cultigens and livestock transformed the natural habitat, as would soon happen elsewhere in the Atlantic world. New economic activities created new labour demands which, as indigenous workers died off, were increasingly satisfied by African slaves from Portuguese African trading posts. The first arrivals came as house servants and artisans, but after 1520 Africans began to replace Indian workers on the sugar estates and other agricultural operations. A sense of permanency was conveyed by the arrival, about 1500, of the first Spanish women immigrants.

The forms and practices of Spanish government also took shape in the Caribbean. Spanish desire for urban living was symbolized in America by the city of Santo Domingo, which became an administrative and commercial centre. Smaller cities and towns quickly followed until, by 1540, there were thirty-four towns and cities on the islands and shores of the Caribbean, each, as in Spain, extending authority over the surrounding countryside. A basic city layout was developed that would also be extended to later Spanish conquests. Ships brought immigrants to the Spanish Indies at a rate of perhaps 2,000 a year who responded to changing economic opportunity within the Caribbean sphere. Meanwhile, the crown created the basic structures of civil life extending from a royal governor and treasury officials, to a court of appeals or *audiencia* in 1511, staffed by university-trained judges. The arrival of missionaries in the 1490s, the creation of three bishoprics in 1511, and the nomination of Santo Domingo as an archdiocese in 1545 pointed to Spain's intention to make this a part of Christendom.

Experience in the Caribbean shaped the Spanish Atlantic colonies in two other significant ways. Exploitation of indigenous labour interested the Spanish far more than the acquisition of land, and they adopted the hierarchical divisions in the society of the Taino to meet the purposes of the *encomienda* by assigning chieftains (*caciques*) and their villages to individual Spaniards. Thus indigenous leaders and communal organization were made to serve Spanish ends, and a pre-conquest category of dependent workers called *naborías* was enlarged and adapted to create dependent personal servants for the Spanish.

Since Castile claimed all the new lands, the inhabitants were theoretically vassals of the crown and their enslavement was prohibited in general, but those who resisted did not enjoy such protection. Spaniards made a distinction between Indians who were *guatiao* or friendly allies and those who were Caribs (*caribes*) and who resisted Spanish authority. That latter status was then associated with savagery and cannibalism that

[2] See Frank Moya Pons, *Despues de Colón: trabajo, sociedad y política en la economia del oro* (Madrid, 1986).

justified enslavement. The designation of Carib then was partly ethnographic, partly locational, and always political. The backdrop of all these developments was the vertiginous decline of the indigenous population. By the 1520s colonists on Hispaniola were petitioning to bring natives from other islands because there were none left. One Spanish response to this problem was a policy of resettlement or 'congregation', in which Indians would live in more easily controlled nucleated settlements where colonists, crown, and missionaries would have better access to them, and where in theory they could learn to live in a civilized manner like Spaniards. This technique of forced resettlement was used later throughout the Spanish conquests. The contact, exploitation, and decimation of the native peoples provoked questioning and debate as theologians, humanists, and lawyers sought to reconcile the otherness of the indigenous inhabitants and place them within the ideal of human universality and *ius naturae*. As early as 1504 a commission met in Spain to debate the legality of assigning Indians to Spaniards; by 1511 there were missionary voices raised in Santo Domingo against Spanish abuses, and in the Laws of Burgos of 1512 the first specific legislation to regulate Spanish control of Indians was issued. The debates begun in the Caribbean were extended throughout the rest of the Indies in the subsequent century.[3]

Finally, the Caribbean was also a proving ground for Spanish culture and social organization. Attempts to limit and restrict immigration to only Castilians of unquestioned Catholic orthodoxy proved unsuccessful. Both foreigners and descendants of Jews and Muslims found ways to evade the prohibitions. The shortage of European women and the sexual exploitation of indigenous women quickly led to the rise of a population of mixed origin that slowly was defined as a distinct intermediate category, neither Indian nor Spaniard. The full panoply of Spanish mental and material culture was winnowed and screened by distance, local conditions, indigenous practices, and eventually by earlier practices as successive groups of immigrants disembarked. What crystallized in the Caribbean was a streamlined, innovative 'conquest culture' that reflected a heavy dose of Andalusian and maritime influences and which incorporated local realities, vocabulary, and practices. This was then carried in the conquest to the rest of the Indies where it was again modified and reshaped by local human, geographic, and cultural realities.[4] It should be emphasized that in the matter of cultural transfer as in the matter of social organization, despite continuing attempts by the crown at control, most of the process was unplanned and undirected, the result of individual decision and local practice.

[3] Lewis Hanke, *The Spanish Struggle for Justice in the Conquest of America* (Philadelphia, PA, 1949); the excellent summary by John H. Elliott, 'The Discovery of America and the Discovery of Man', in Elliott, *Spain and its Empire, 1500–1700* (New Haven, CT, 1989), 42–64; Anthony Pagden, *The Fall of Natural Man* (2nd edn. Cambridge, 1986).

[4] George M. Foster, *Culture and Conquest: America's Spanish Heritage* (Chicago, IL, 1960).

CONQUEST AND SETTLEMENT TO 1570

The conquest of the mainland was rapid. With few exceptions, expeditions were organized locally, often as commercial ventures, and depended on private initiative, leadership, and financing although usually done with state approval and licence. Leadership was based on personal qualities, and kinship, regional, or personal ties often determined levels of compensation. The participants were a cross-section of Spanish society; a few with real experience in arms, but the vast majority peasants, artisans, labourers, and a few gentlemen, all of whom hoped to be rewarded for their services. Their expectations often went unrealized. Those men dissatisfied with their rewards were usually ready to organize the next expedition so that the conquest proceeded in a leapfrog fashion, but generally the process of conquest went from areas of dense indigenous population outwards to the more sparsely populated frontiers. Of course, in those frontiers, rumours of settled populations, gold, cinnamon, or lost cities often lay behind the original motive of conquest in regions such as New Mexico or the Amazon.

The conquest proceeded on two major fronts. Yucatán and Mexico were an extension of the Caribbean phase. Setting out from Cuba, Hernán Cortés carried out the conquest of the great Aztec confederation 1519–21, and established his capital of Mexico City on the ruins of Tenochtitlan. From there, Guatemala and Honduras were brought under Spanish control while expeditions moved northward, into Michoacan and New Galicia, and even further to the north. By the early 1540s, Francisco Vázquez de Coronado's men were raiding the Pueblo villages along the Rio Grande and venturing on to the great plains beyond. A second front began in Panama. A large expedition sent in 1514 directly from Spain under Pedrarias D'avila had taken over the Isthmus of Panama or what the Spanish called Castilla del Oro and then reached northward into Nicaragua. Marches southward by land were blocked by the impenetrable forests of the Darien, but the Pacific Ocean or 'Southern Sea' provided the way south, and rumours of great kingdoms in that direction quickly led to new expeditions. Francisco Pizarro's conquest of the Inca empire used Castilla de Oro as a springboard, taking Cuzco, the Inca capital, in 1533, and then extending control over the territory of the Inca state northward to Ecuador and southward to Chile, where Santiago was founded in 1541. The area of Colombia was disputed by expeditions from Peru and the Caribbean, both attracted by the considerable amounts of gold and relatively dense populations of the Muisca chiefdoms of the highlands. The Río de la Plata region was explored and settled directly from Spain, but Indian resistance and the difficulty of the conditions there led Buenos Aires to be abandoned for a while (1541–80) and the Spanish outpost in the region to be established upriver at Asunción, Paraguay, where villages of the agricultural Guaraní offered some support to Spanish settlement. Buenos Aires was re-established in 1580 mostly by the mestizo sons of the Spaniards who had settled at Asunción. In South America as in Yucatán, resistance of organized indigenous polities was stubborn and sometimes retreated into inaccessible areas where, like the neo-Inca state of Vilcabamba, it persisted. Elsewhere, in areas such as south of the Bío-bío River in Chile and in the north of Mexico, regions that were home to nomadic or part-time agriculturalists, an active military frontier persisted for centuries. In general, areas of dense indigenous populations like central Mexico and highland Peru became the centres of Spanish activity and rule, followed by areas that contained mineral wealth. The Hispanic population concentrated in the cities and towns of these regions. Between 1514 and 1540 Spanish forces had explored and seized control of the better part of two continents and an inland sea, overcoming tremendous environmental challenges and the resistance of the native inhabitants.

Portuguese explorations were concerned primarily with Africa and Asia until an accidental landfall of 1500 encouraged them to investigate the eastern coast of South America in parallel with the Spanish conquest we have just discussed. In the case of Brazil, while the cast of players—royal officials, merchants, settlers, prominent commanders, and missionaries—was similar to that involved with Spanish America, local conditions led to different outcomes and chronology. Since there was no dense indigenous population or large state in the interior of eastern South America, the Portuguese confined their exploration principally to the coast, where they established outposts on the African model for cutting dyewood. Gold was always sought but not immediately found, and the crown, preoccupied with the Indian Ocean route, conceded private contracts for the dyewood trade, but remained committed to preserving its claims from such foreign competitors as the French.

By the 1530s the monarchy introduced the instrument of proprietorships, or donatary captaincies, previously used for settlement of the Atlantic islands whereby nobles were granted tracts with authority to develop and settle them. These proved generally unsatisfactory in America due to poor relations with native peoples or to colonists objecting to seemingly feudal authority, and succeeded only in Pernambuco in the north and São Vicente in the south to which sugar cane cultivation was translated from Madeira and São Tomé. In 1549 a royal governor with officials occupied a newly created colonial capital at Salvador and missionary activities under the Jesuits began in earnest. Labour demands and disease led to Indian depopulation as the Portuguese sought workers for the growing plantation economy, and then, as on the Atlantic islands, the Portuguese began to import African slaves for the sugar mills, first as skilled workers, and increasingly as a workforce.

By 1570 the main outlines of the colony had been defined; foreign competitors had been eliminated, the indigenous population had been pushed from the coast or brought under Jesuit control, and an archipelago of port cities and towns, around which the Portuguese population concentrated, served a developing sugar export economy. There were then 60 sugar mills in operation, and by 1610, close to 200. Occasional expeditions in search of Indian labourers or precious metals brought Portuguese inland, but the population of 20,000–30,000 lived 'like crabs on the beach'. Royal government existed, but use was still made of seigniorial grants to keep costs low. Essentially, the crown was satisfied to tax private investment in sugar production and trade, and meddled little in social and economic matters.

In fact, neither the Spanish nor Portuguese crowns could control the process of overseas expansion, or explore or settle without private participation. Both crowns employed medieval precedents; concessions of lands, forms of lordship, grants of nobility or knighthoods, and monetary rewards or exemptions to encourage private initiative. Once an area was conquered, or gold was found, or an exploitable indigenous population was brought under control, earlier arrangements were cancelled. Columbus and his heirs sought unsuccessfully in the courts for almost a century to regain his original concessions, while Cortés, who did receive a noble title and extensive powers, later found his authority curtailed. The battle over the *encomienda* is a case in point. Intended to reward service, its destructive effects and promotion of semi-independent colonists moved the crown to revoke those grants over time, a policy that provoked anger, disobedience, and, in the 1540s, rebellion in Peru.

The Portuguese crown, as was noted, continued, until the late seventeenth century, to create donatary captaincies to encourage private conquest and settlement.[5] Yet the Iberian monarchies were concerned over the possible emergence of an overseas aristocracy of independent power and resources. Both crowns made use of an 'economy of grace', that is promises of social reward in return for 'services' rendered, but such remained limited. The Castilian crown awarded just two titles of nobility in the sixteenth century (to Cortés and Pizarro), and became more generous in subsequent centuries only because its financial situation worsened. The Portuguese monarchs granted no such titles in Brazil, and discouraged the development of a hereditary colonial nobility. Nonetheless, colonial oligarchies developed in control of local resources and thus could not be ignored by royal officers.

If the military conquests were impressive before the 1570s, the civil and ecclesiastical order was less so, since government was usually a negotiation between the crown and local interests whether these were former indigenous leaders and nobles, municipal councils whose members formed a kind of urban patriciate, or prominent *encomenderos*, merchants, or landowners. Cooperation was vital but the price was that personal and kinship relations often influenced, facilitated, or subverted the directives of the crown and its agents.

'Discoveries' and conquests necessitated institutions of empire in the metropoles. The fifteenth-century Portuguese clearing house and registry for its overseas trade (first called the Casa da Mina, later the Casa da India) was imitated in 1503 when Castile created a House of Trade (Casa de la Contratacción) to regulate and tax all trade with the Americas. After 1543 the Consulado or merchant guild of Seville controlled all shipping to the colonies, while in 1523, the Council of the Indies was created to administer and advise on all matters relating to the Indies. The Indies were incorporated into the crown of Castile

---

[5] António Vasconcelos de Saldanha, *As capitanias: o regime senhorial na expansão ultramarine portuguesa* (Funchal, 1992); Alberto Gallo, 'Aventuras y desventuras del gobierno señorial en el Brasil', in *Para una historia de América: los nudos 1* (Mexico City, 1999), 198–265.

and the laws of Castile applied there, but after 1516, when Charles V succeeded to both Castile and Aragon, the Indies were perceived as an extension of Spain. Portugal was less inclined to centralization and numerous councils, handling financial, judicial, and religious matters of all the overseas possessions, persisted until 1642 when a separate colonial council (Conselho Ultramarino) begin to function.

In both empires civil government reflected Iberia's precocious development of a professional bureaucracy composed of lawyers (*letrados*) who became essential to government. Councils were often staffed by a combination of *letrados* and nobles, and it was primarily from them, and in the case of Castile from prominent members of the regular clergy, that colonial crown officers were chosen. Balancing these elements of government was always delicate. In Spanish America the crown created two viceroyalties. Viceroys, drawn from families of the high nobility, with broad authority as representatives of the king, were established in Mexico City (1535) and Lima (1544), the first ruling the Caribbean, Central America, Mexico, and after 1570, the Philippines; the latter ruling all of South America except Venezuela (considered part of the Caribbean). The viceroys replaced the earlier form of delegated governance to leaders of expeditions analogous to donatary captains in Brazil.

The administration of justice was one of the Spanish monarch's primary attributes. All these lands were considered kingdoms of Castile, and Castilian law applied there, enforced by courts of appeal or *audiencias,* which exercised executive and legislative powers beyond those normally held by peninsular courts. Ten such courts were created for the Indies, their administrative districts becoming provinces of the viceroyalties. At the local level, governance became the responsibility of municipal councils dominated by local leading families whose interaction with the crown was often through the *corregedor* or district judge presiding over the municipal council, which was expected to guard royal interests and enforce laws and ordinances. In Indian communities, these officers also assumed the task of enforcing labour and tribute requirements. In Brazil, government was left under the control of a governor general and a single appellate judge rather than a court of appeals, a reflection of the colony's secondary position. As in Spanish America, the lower echelons of civil government were often bought or inherited—and were viewed as fee-earning sinecures. These went to Europeans at first, but, over time, came into the hands of settlers. As in Spanish America, municipal councils filled by local elites became a kind of urban patriciate with pretensions to nobility.

Ecclesiastical authority ran parallel to civil administration. Papal concessions allowed Spanish and Portuguese monarchs to nominate bishops and to control religious matters. Both monarchies took seriously their responsibility to evangelize as the primary justification of empire. Thus, especially in the densely populated areas of Mexico and Peru, spiritual responsibility was dominated by the great missionary orders, particularly the Franciscans, Dominicans, and Augustinians, with about 2,700 members, between 1493 and 1573, engaged on evangelization.[6] Later, especially after

⁶ Manuel M. Marzal, 'La evangelización en América Latina', in *Historia general de América Latina,* 9 vols. (Madrid, 2000), ii. 473–86.

1550, missionaries were pressured to assign responsibility for converts to diocesan priests and to move to frontier regions, and to this end there were by 1540 fourteen bishoprics throughout the Indies and archbishops in Mexico City, Lima, and Santo Domingo.

In Brazil, a bishopric was established in Salvador in 1551, but no archiepiscopal see was created in Brazil until 1676, and early bishops were frequently at loggerheads with the Jesuits' who were the principal missionary order. The early endeavours of the Spanish and Portuguese in the Atlantic took place well before the Council of Trent (1545–63) and so it was an 'unreformed' Catholicism that was carried from Iberia across the Atlantic. This, the Protestant challenge in Europe, and the persistence of perverse practices among the pagan populations of the Americas occasioned constant complaint from the clergy; criticisms that hardened as Spain moved from the Erasmian reformism of some of the early missionaries towards the rigid orthodoxy of the Catholic Reformation. One response was the creation of permanent tribunals of the Spanish Inquisition in Mexico (1571), Lima (1570), and Cartagena (1610). The same challenges existed in Portuguese Brazil but there cost and perhaps the influence of the many 'New Christians' (converts from Judaism) prevented the establishment of a permanent tribunal. All Inquisition cases from the Portuguese Atlantic were decided in Lisbon, once again reflecting the closer integration of Portuguese Atlantic colonies into metropolitan institutions.

Before 1570 the two burning issues of debate within the Iberian Atlantic were the indigenous population and the nature of the economy. The conquest had brought destruction and disruption everywhere, but Indian societies were remarkably resilient in the face of demographic disaster and the new demands for labour and tribute. In Mexico and Peru some continuity was maintained in leadership, cultural forms, and language, a process sometimes fostered for their own purposes by missionaries, *encomenderos*, and the state. Large-scale and rapid initial conversions fostered a certain millenarian impulse, but by the 1560s continued Indian 'superstition' and backsliding produced missionary campaigns to extirpate pagan beliefs, indigenous resistance, and to promote some accommodation between Spaniards and native peoples.[7] Throughout the Spanish Indies indigenous peoples accepted baptism, religious brotherhoods, and other aspects of the new faith, but altered and transformed their meanings while maintaining aspects of their former beliefs. Meanwhile the *encomienda* became the principal institution for exploiting Indian labour across the Indies, but in central areas, it faced increasing restrictions, especially after the New Laws of 1542 limited its longevity and eliminated personal service obligations. Although in marginal areas, like Chile and Yucatán, *encomiendas* persisted into the eighteenth century, they were gradually replaced in the core regions of central Mexico and Peru by state-managed labour service such as the *mita* or labour draft for mining. Native peoples also sought increasingly to become wage labourers as they migrated and sought employment in

---

[7] Kenneth Mills, 'The Limits of Religious Conversion in Mid-Colonial Peru', *Past and Present*, 145 (1994), 84–121.

cities or mines or on Spanish estates to avoid communal labour obligations. Such opportunities developed because as the Indian population contracted, colonists identified land rather than access to Indian labour as the basis of wealth. Partly in response to this decline, African slaves began to swell labour forces in cities, mines, and plantations.

These changes were related to the rise of the mining economy of the Spanish Indies. After the decline of the Caribbean gold fields, conquests opened new gold washings in New Granada and Chile in the 1540s, followed by major silver strikes in Mexico (Zacatecas, 1546; Guanajuato, c.1550) and in Peru (Potosí, 1545), which changed the nature of the Spanish enterprise in the Indies, especially with the discovery of a great mercury mine at Huancavelica in Peru and the introduction in 1571 of refining by amalgamation. Exports of precious metals far outweighed the combined value of all other American products, and while perhaps less than 15 per cent of the population was directly involved in mining, it created new population centres and regional markets, stimulated subsidiary activities, induced or forced migration, demanded a highly organized, expensive, and complex convoy system, and generally shaped the colonial economy. The state's role in stimulating, protecting, and supplying this industry became increasingly important to colonial life. If American treasure never exceeded a quarter of the crown's total revenues access to it maintained Spain's credit and allowed the monarchy to pursue a previously unthinkable foreign policy and imperial projects.

IMPERIAL SPACES AND TRADE

Relativities in pace and time influenced ease of contact, communication, and control of the two empires. Portuguese contact with north-eastern Brazil was relatively easy, with sailing time to and from Lisbon taking about thirty days on the outward and between forty and fifty on the return.[8] This temporal proximity encouraged close royal control and contact between metropolis and colony, and Brazil developed in many ways as an extension of Portugal. No separate colonial law code existed, no printing press or university was founded, and institutions such as convents that reinforced metropolitan social order were slow to develop. Colonial elites sent children to Portugal for education, hoping they would pursue careers in the metropolis and elsewhere in the empire. Proximity also meant that foreigners and privateers could outfit ships at relatively low risk and cost in hopes of gathering dyewood or of trading, or raiding, for sugar.

Castilian problems with communication were altogether greater. The major Caribbean island ports lay two months away from Seville, while it took seventy to eighty sailing days from Seville to reach Vera Cruz and Portobelo, the gateways respectively to New Spain and Peru, and perhaps a voyage of five to six months to return. While this

---

[8] Pierre Chaunu, 'Brésil et Atlantique au xvii siècle', *Annales*, 16 (1961), 1176–207.

time barrier discouraged interlopers and forced European competitors to organize larger and more expensive maritime incursions, it also contributed to the Castilian consciousness of the American territories as remote *reinos* with their own legal code, with viceroys enjoying considerable autonomy, and with the precocious growth of religious and social institutions that reproduced those of the metropole.

While both Spain and Portugal depended on maritime connection with their Atlantic colonies, the two empires approached commerce differently. Portugal had created a restricted system in the Indian Ocean in which spices returned to Lisbon under state control, but the Atlantic system was relatively open, mostly in private hands, and often dependent on foreign ships sailing under Portuguese licence. Spain developed an exclusivist policy prohibiting foreigners from direct trade and even forcing non-Castilian subjects to trade only through Seville. Spanish shipping moved quickly from loosely organized ventures of single ships or small groups of vessels to a more regularized commerce. The decisions to centralize all commerce to and from the Americas at Seville and its nearby ports, to have the state control all trade and immigration through the House of Trade, and to grant exclusive control over commerce to the Indies to the Consulado in Seville, all reflected the desire to keep contact with the Indies economically and politically exclusive. The Consulado, operating in concert with similar associations in Mexico City and Lima, eventually regulated all Spanish trade to the Indies and served as the point of collaboration between state and private enterprise. Until about 1540, outbound ships carried essential supplies such as metal tools, wine, and olive oil, but mostly immigrants. Over 200,000, perhaps two-thirds of them men, mostly from Andalusia and Extremadura crossed the Atlantic in the sixteenth century.[9] The conquests of Mexico and Peru created new demands for return shipping even though these areas were too distant to make most agricultural products profitable for transatlantic shipping. But the discovery of large silver deposits in both areas created new demands for cargo capacity and for maritime security, resulting eventually in a system of two large annual fleets, the *galeones de Tierra Firme* that sailed to Cartagena and Portobelo to pick up Peru's silver, and the *flota* which headed for Vera Cruz to trade for New Spain's production. These fleets, coordinated to link at Havana before return to Seville, formed the principal maritime link in the Spanish Atlantic, sailing under the protection of specially designed and heavily armed galleons which also carried the crown's share (about 20 per cent) of the silver. For the next century, almost 90 per cent of Spanish shipping from the Indies sailed as part of the fleets.

While cumbersome and plagued by graft and occasional incompetence, the system fulfilled its principal function. The major part of the silver fleet was rarely lost, even if

---

[9] John H. Elliott, *Empires of the Atlantic World* (New Haven, CT, 2006), 52. Portuguese immigration specifically to Brazil is difficult to establish but it is estimated that over 500,000 people left for overseas colonies between 1500 and 1640; Vitorino Magalhães Godinho, 'L'Émigration portugaise (XV–XX siècles): une constante structurale et les réponses aux changements du monde', *Revista de história económica e social*, 1 (1978), 5–32.

contrabandists, pirates, and European rivals were a constant problem. More serious was the irregularity of the fleets themselves. Of the seventy-nine convoys that sailed to New Spain between 1560 and 1650 only eleven actually arrived on schedule and the fleets to Panama were even more undependable. Contraband became endemic. By the 1560s French, Portuguese, and English ships were regularly visiting the Caribbean, combining smuggling and violence and often receiving tacit aid from the local population or suborned officials. This tension between an exclusivist royal policy and local economic interests remained the expensive Achilles heel of the Spanish commercial system.[10]

THE IBERIAN ATLANTIC 1580–1640

By the 1570s the general character of two Atlantic empires had been formed. The Portuguese had carried their Atlantic island experience to the Brazilian coast to create an extractive and plantation colony dependent on slave labour. Castilians had created island and mainland settlements based on the exploitation of indigenous populations and the production of mineral wealth. The Spanish had been attracted inland in a number of places by large and dense centres of indigenous population or by the discovery of precious metal deposits. In both empires administrative and social formations reproduced to an extent the institutions and practices of Iberia, although in Spanish America attempts were made to incorporate native systems of hierarchy and rank to facilitate control of the indigenous populations. Severe depopulation of native peoples had everywhere resulted in social, economic, and political readjustments, but by the 1570s, in some regions of Spanish America, a certain demographic equilibrium had been achieved. While the patterns of conquest, depopulation, and settlement continued on the peripheries, the conquest of the central areas had ended and a period of relative stability, bureaucratization, and evolution ensued. The state, appointing local administrators and village priests and incorporating native nobilities and leaders, became a mediator between indigenous populations and Spanish demands which fell differently on men and women. In the Andean region and Mexico these demands caused disruption and readjustments in native communities that varied from utopian religious movements and armed resistance to migration and accommodation.

The Spanish experience resulted in a population of mixed origin, the mestizos, the product first of sexual contact between Europeans and Native Americans, and increasingly of contact between those ethnicities and Africans. This new social category represented no more than 1 to 2 per cent of the population, but mestizos had originally acted as intermediaries, and they, especially women, continued to do so in marginal areas with scant European populations. There was also a growth in the American-born

---

[10] Murdo Macleod, 'Spain and America: The Atlantic Trade, 1492–1720', *CHLA* i. 341–88.

population of European descent, the *criollos*, who still considered themselves to be Spaniards, and whose existence transformed the meaning of Spaniard from a description of origin to one of colour. Slowly, they began to see themselves as distinct from Europeans: never able to secure positions as viceroys and rarely as archbishops or other high ecclesiastical offices, they coveted *audiencia* judgeships, minor offices, and, most importantly, grew in strength and influence as landowners and prominent citizens. In Spain the distinction between American-born Spaniards and persons of mixed heritage was blurred by the belief that all, having been corrupted either by blood or milk by Indians or Africans, were inferior to or less trustworthy than, persons from Spain itself. The response of creoles was to seek ways to emphasize their social position above those other groups.

These same processes operated in Portuguese Brazil, but were retarded since occupation and settlement was slower and European immigrants fewer. To the end of the seventeenth century, Portuguese-born dominated town councils, the merchant community, the Jesuit order in Brazil, and the ranks of the sugar planters. Their Brazilian-born children sought higher education, office, or advantage in Portugal. In the sugar plantation zones the presence of Native Americans was lower and of Africans higher so that patterns of miscegenation, especially the growth of a population of partly African heritage, resembled Santo Domingo or Cartagena more than Mexico City or Cuzco. In the frontier regions of São Paulo, Amazonia, and the cattle-raising areas of the north-eastern interior a large mixed population, called *mamelucos* or *mestiços*, developed with a role and importance similar to that on the fringes of the Spanish Indies. Indian admixture did not necessarily preclude elite status; African background almost invariably did. In both Spanish America and Brazil the restrictions of 'purity of blood' originally used to discriminate against descendants of Jews and Muslims were expanded to include blacks and mulattos.

The Iberian empires exceeded an Atlantic boundary. The founding of Manila in the Philippines in 1571, and developing regular contact across the Pacific to and from Acapulco, linked Spain's Atlantic system to the trade and markets of Asia. Peru, Chile, and the west coast of Central America were already geographically a 'far Atlantic'. Now an outpost of New Spain able to trade with China, matching the Portuguese presence in India, Manila laid the basis for a global imperial system.[11] America also became less Iberian once the initial Portuguese and Spanish successes provoked the envy and interest of other Europeans. Cupidity as well as European political and religious rivalries increasingly led to attacks upon the Iberian empires, while northern European competitors also attempted to create their own colonies.

The experiences of Spain and Portugal overlapped and ran in parallel until 1580 when Philip II of Spain resolved a dynastic crisis in Portugal by backing his claims to the Portuguese throne with money and troops. While Portugal remained a separate kingdom it was ruled by the Spanish Habsburgs, from 1580 to 1640, as part of a larger

---

[11] Serge Gruzinski, *Les quatre parties du monde: histoire d'une mondialisation* (Paris, 2004).

composite 'universal monarchy' whose extent far exceeded the boundaries of the Atlantic. Philip II was more interested in Lisbon's strategic location and its spice trade than in its Atlantic possessions where the sugar industry of Brazil was still modest, but Philip II's claims to Portugal had been supported by Portuguese merchants, groups of nobles, and other interests attracted by possible trade with the Spanish empire and access to American silver.

Although the two kingdoms were theoretically separate in law and practice, a good deal of contact, penetration, and exchange occurred, creating, in effect, a global empire. Habsburg reform of Portuguese administration and law resulted in a new legal code, the Philippine Ordinances (1603), and reforms and conformities were extended to the colonies, with a high court equivalent to the Spanish American *audiencias* established in 1609. The conquest and settlement of the northern Brazilian coasts and the mouth of the Amazon was promoted as the attacks of English, French, and Dutch enemies of Philip II increased. Spanish armadas sent to Chile or the Río de la Plata now stopped in Brazil, and sometimes assisted campaigns there. Some Spanish garrisons were stationed in Brazil despite Portuguese complaints, and where the Portuguese had been the largest foreign minority in the Spanish Indies, Spaniards played a similar role in Brazil. Spanish geopolitical planning extended to the coasts, fortifications and ports of Brazil, as conquest of the east–west coast of northern Brazil, elimination of foreign interlopers from the Amazon, and the foundation of the city of Belém (1614) were promoted for the security of Peru. Common threats merited collective responses. In 1625, Salvador was recaptured from the Dutch by a joint Spanish, Portuguese, and Neapolitan force, and in the 1630s Spanish-led armadas sought to dislodge the Dutch from Brazil. American colonial governors of the two empires shared information and sometimes collaborated in legal and illegal trade.

The hopes of discovering mineral wealth in Brazil as in Spanish America led to new explorations and administrative changes. Occasionally, Portuguese colonists in Brazil even petitioned for the introduction of the *encomienda*, but when the crown sought to limit the enslavement of Indians, the colonists objected that Spanish American precedents were not valid in Brazil. New demands for labour produced anomalous expeditions, or *bandeiras*, from São Paulo into the Spanish Jesuit mission fields of Paraguay and the Río de la Plata where they took captives from among the already Christian Guaraní. Such expeditions led to Portuguese activity well beyond the Line of Tordesillas, which had separated Spanish from Portuguese spheres.

The two Iberian empires in the Atlantic were linked fundamentally by economics. The sugar economy of Portuguese Brazil boomed from 1580 to 1630, producing some 120,000 tons a year. This was enabled by a South Atlantic system integrating the African ports and island settlements with Brazil and Spanish America. After 1580, Portuguese slaving in the Senegambia region was expanded and intensified. Hopes of discovering silver in Angola, first ceded as a captaincy in 1571, were fostered in the 1580s, but by the 1590s Luanda, its main port, had become a major terminal in the Atlantic slave trade, which by 1600 was sending some 10,000 slaves a year to Brazil and Spanish America. Although it had its own governors, Angola's administration was closely linked to Brazil. Portuguese and Luso-Africans who resided in the ports or travelled up country supplied slaves to Vera Cruz, Cartagena, and Buenos Aires. The contacts between Portuguese Africa and Spanish America were regularized after 1595 with the concession of a series of *asientos*, or exclusive contracts given to Portuguese merchants for the supply of slaves to Spanish America. Despite complaints from Seville merchants, about 1,000 licensed ships cleared Seville to carry slaves to Spanish America, and levels of contraband were probably three times greater. In Spanish America and later in Brazil, precipitous decline of the indigenous population, and legal prohibitions against its enslavement, increased the demand for imported labourers. During this period around 750,000 slaves reached Brazil and Spanish America as part of a broader commercial system controlled by members of the 'Portuguese nation' in many Atlantic ports, of whom two-thirds may have been 'New Christians'. During the 1580s, members of this community had created a system of familial and business links that transcended national boundaries.[12]

The Atlantic system, and also the Iberian trade in Asia, was enabled by the flow of American silver. In this period about 85 per cent of the world's silver was being produced in Spanish America, with production cresting between 1590 and 1620. In some years about 15–20 per cent of silver output was shipped from Mexico to the Philippines for trade in Asia. In the legal Atlantic slave trade alone, about 1.8 million pesos of American silver was transferred each year and levels of contraband were probably much higher. More and more was also going for the burgeoning government and the costs of defence in the Indies.

While the Portuguese benefited commercially from the union with Spain, there were associated costs. War with England (1585–1603) resulted in major losses of ships and cargoes; war in Flanders led, in 1591, to the prohibition of trade with the Dutch, traditional trading partners with Portugal, who began to acquire salt, sugar, and other commodities by contraband and force in the Caribbean region. Attachment to Spain also became less attractive when new taxes were imposed, and Spanish ambitions for an integrated empire were resented as Castilian impositions. After the formation of the Dutch West India Company in 1621, Portuguese shipping and possessions became primary targets for Dutch and English attacks. Moreover, in 1621, the creation of an inland customs house in the Río de la Plata also made the smuggling of silver through the 'back door' of Potosí more difficult for Portuguese traders. Also from the 1630s an inquisitorial campaign against 'Portuguese' merchants, sponsored partly by their competitors, made trade with the Spanish empire more dangerous and costly. The Dutch capture of Pernambuco and north-eastern Brazil (1630–54) and their seizure of the slaving ports of El Mina (1641) and Luanda (1641–8) was an attempt to create a rival South Atlantic system devoted to sugar production. Nor were Spain's own possessions exempt from these incursions as freebooters who, sometimes on their own, and sometimes with state sponsorship, established footholds in the Caribbean in the

---

12 Daviken Studnicki-Gizbert, *A Nation on the Ocean Sea* (Oxford, 2007).

1620s and 1630s. Demand and prices for slaves increased, and the selling price of sugar in Atlantic markets declined as Barbados, Suriname, Jamaica, and Guadeloupe began to produce sugar and tropical commodities. Thus, after 1650, the Iberians had to share the southern Atlantic with unwanted and bothersome neighbours and had to compete with them as sugar producers.

Foreign penetration of the Iberian Atlantic was one element of a broader problem. By the 1620s the Iberian Atlantic as part of this Habsburg universal monarchy was drawn into the more general political and economic turmoil of the seventeenth century.[13] In the South Atlantic, Spain's trade with the Indies had declined both because of contraction of demand and the reduction of silver flowing to royal coffers. For Spain, beset by economic stagnation, foreign wars, and fiscal problems, the contraction of colonial trade deepened its crisis and led to a questioning of the benefits and dreams of empire.

From a colonial perspective it was evident that contraction in Atlantic trade was resulting from the growth in the American economies and a diminished need for the metropolis. Greater self-sufficiency supported an increasingly autonomous political culture as local elites assumed greater roles in colonial institutions, created large estates, and exercised considerable influence over royal officials. The age of the hacienda had arrived and with it the growing strength of local interests and elites.[14] Theoretically, the indigenous population lived in an 'Indian Republic' (*republica de indios*) under their own leaders and protected by the state but subject to tribute and labour obligations, while the remainder, including mestizos and free people of colour, constituted the 'Spanish republic', expected to live and worship by the laws and customs of Castile. The reality was that in the social pyramid, the former supported the latter. As one viceroy put it, 'it is not silver that is carried from Peru to Spain, but the blood and sweat of Indians'. The economy and society of the Iberian Atlantic was inextricably bound together.

Spain's problems and its attempts to rectify them provoked a sequence of revolts during the 1640s, one of which in Portugal, led by a faction of nobles, placed the duke of Braganza on the throne as John IV. War persisted until 1668 when a Spain that had been distracted by many other challenges finally recognized Portuguese independence. To some extent Portugal's victory and its ability to reconstitute its South Atlantic system was made possible by its Brazilian sugar industry and its African slave trade, both of which, even during the war, continued to drain American silver from Madrid, provide income to Portugal, and attract the alliance and support of other European powers. Even in the midst of Portugal's independence struggle the old ties of interdependence and cultural borrowing were still visible as Portugal, following the Spanish model, created a fleet system in 1648 for its trade with Brazil. By the mid-century it was

---

[13] Geoffrey Parker, *La crisis de la monarquía de Felipe IV* (Barcelona, 2006), 19–53; Ruggiero Romano, *Coyunturas opuestas: la crisis del siglo xvii en Europa e Hispanoamerica* (Mexico City, 1993), 145–69.

[14] John Lynch, *Spain under the Hapsburgs*, 2 vols. (Oxford, 1969), ii. 184–228.

clear that Brazil and the South Atlantic, not the Indian Ocean spice trade, had become the keystone of Portuguese imperial hopes.[15]

By this point, the unity of the Iberian Atlantic had ended and its territorial integrity had been breached by the English, French, and Dutch. The costs of defending empire had been raised considerably, but while the hegemony of Spain in the South Atlantic had been weakened, the silver fleets continued to sail and there had been no real threat to the viceregal centres of its empire. The Portuguese South Atlantic system survived also, but at the price of making commercial concessions to England and the Netherlands. Foreign competition, falling sugar prices, and natural calamities made the following decades particularly difficult. As contemporaries viewed the situation, they could see that Iberian empires had been weakened, but failed to recognize growing strength and self-confidence within the empires themselves. Whether it was mulatto irregulars and herdsmen on Hispaniola who had turned back Cromwell's invasion in 1655, or the Brazilian rebels of Pernambuco who believed that they had ousted the Dutch and retaken the African slaving ports without much help from the metropolis, their growing self-confidence and pride was creating a sentiment of autonomy.[16] In both Spanish America and Brazil local elites played an increasingly important role in defence, governance, the enactment of colonial policy, and in the control of the complex social hierarchies that the Iberians had created in their Atlantic empires.

BIBLIOGRAPHY

Bakewell, Peter, *Miners of the Red Mountain: Indian Labor at Potosí 1545–1650* (Albuquerque, NM, 1984).

Fernández-Armesto, Felipe, *The Canary Islands Alter the Conquest* (Oxford, 1982).

Freire Costa, Leonor, *Imperio e grupos mercantis* (Lisbon, 2002).

Lockhart, James, *Spanish Peru, 1532–1560* (Madison, WI, 1968).

—— and Stuart B. Schwartz, *Early Latin America* (Cambridge, 1983).

Moya Pons, Frank, *Después de Colon: trabajo, sociedad, y política en la economía del oro* (Madrid, 1986).

Romano, Ruggiero, *Coyunturas opuestas: la crisis del siglo xvii en Europa e Hispanoamerica* (Mexico, 1993).

Schwartz, Stuart B., *Sugar Plantations in the Formation of Brazilian Society: Bahia 1550–1835* (Cambridge, 1985).

Studnicki-Gizbert, Daviken, *A Nation on the Ocean Sea* (Oxford, 2007).

Wachtel, Nathan, *Vision of the Vanquished: The Spanish Conquest of Peru through Indian Eyes 1530–1570*, trans. Ben and Sian Reynolds (New York, 1977).

---

[15] Rafael Valladares, *Castilla y Portugal en Asia (1580–1680)* (Louvain, 2001), id., *La rebellión de Portugal* (Madrid, 1998), and id., 'El Brasil y las Indias españolas durante la sublevación de Portugal (1640–1668)', *Cuadernos de história moderna*, 14 (1993), 151–72.

[16] Evaldo Cabral de Mello, *Rubro veio: o imaginário da Restauração pernambucana* (Rio de Janeiro, 1986).

CHAPTER 10

THE NORTHERN EUROPEAN ATLANTIC WORLD

WIM KLOOSTER

CONFRONTED with the establishment of Portugal and Spain as the hegemonic Atlantic powers, northern Europeans—French, English, and Dutch—initially tried to obtain African and American riches by raiding and trading. Successful colonization of the New World had to wait until the early seventeenth century, and settlements remained small until the 1640s. By then, northern Europeans held sway in various parts of North America, the Caribbean, and Brazil, and had captured Portugal's main West African trading station. As raiders, traders, and settlers, they had formed relations with native Africans and Americans, who had often enabled them to survive. But prejudice against their new neighbours intensified.

PRIVATEERS, MERCHANTS, AND FISHERMEN

After ships from ports in western France pioneered anti-Iberian actions by attacking Portuguese ships in the Cape Verde Islands in the 1480s, the northern European challengers of the Iberian powers combined trade and warfare in their quest for riches from the Atlantic world, starting in the 1520s. Originally, they did not plan to establish their own colonial empires. The entire English operation in the Atlantic prior to 1630, writes Kenneth R. Andrews, was a 'predatory drive of armed traders and marauders to win by fair means or foul a share of the Atlantic wealth of the Iberian nations'. This meant preying on shipping and conquering coastal towns for ransom. The marauders saw the Atlantic as an open sea in which they could seek riches as they pleased, unlike the Mediterranean or the Baltic seas, where regular trade prevailed. Especially alluring were the precious metals shipped from the New World.

French warrior merchants led the way in the maritime harassment of the Iberians, interspersing their transatlantic voyages with ruses for attacking Spanish treasure ships.

After the middle of the sixteenth century, single privateers gave way to whole squadrons harassing Spanish and Portuguese shipping or raiding settlements. In the 1560s and the early 1570s the English and the Dutch appeared on the scene for the first time, trying to hurt their mutual Spanish enemy, especially in the Caribbean and the Spanish Main. For Dutch expansion, this was a false start, since they would be conspicuously absent from Atlantic waters in the next two decades, but the English were there to stay, and more as privateers and pirates than traders. After England and Spain made peace in 1604, English privateers, many of them based on Bermuda, continued to harass the Spanish, but they now played second fiddle to the Dutch. Fuelled by their revolt against Habsburg rule, the United Provinces became the main champions of the fight with the Iberians, attacking ships, ports, and factories all over the world. As lucrative as their legalized piracy sometimes was—especially the capture in 1628 of the Spanish fleet en route from Veracruz to Seville—it proved so costly in the longer term that Dutch authorities curtailed its practice in the 1630s.

Military and commercial motives were often intimately linked, armed force enabling merchant vessels to opt for privateering if normal trade was prohibited or to break into the Spanish and Portuguese monopolies in Africa and the Americas. The French and English, whose exploratory voyages were frequently accompanied by ruses for attacking Spanish ships laden with treasures, set the tone. The Dutch joined them by the turn of the sixteenth century, when one-third of their ships in the Atlantic Ocean went on privateering expeditions. Soon, planters in the English and Dutch colonies also reaped the rewards of privateering, buying enslaved Africans from raiders who had stolen them from Portuguese slavers.[1]

The long-term impact of such predatory activities was limited, and by the early seventeenth century Spanish control of its American colonies still remained secure. In the northern maritime countries, the expansion of the Mediterranean and Baltic trades slowed down interest in transatlantic expeditions and thereby the whole American enterprise. In addition, environmental conditions prevented permanent occupation of Spanish American settlements. The nerve centres of the Spanish empire were located in interior uplands and were hard to conquer, while coastal places could only be held if the inhospitable hinterland was controlled. This proved too difficult.

The northerners' bid to challenge Portuguese dominance in the Africa trade had also failed by 1600. Small French ships began to sail to African destinations in the 1520s, followed by the English a decade later, some of them calling at the Grain Coast before crossing to Brazil. While Frenchmen were already residing seasonally in Senegambia and on the Gold Coast by the 1570s, English trips to Africa remained few, apart from the famous voyages by John Hawkins that introduced England to the slave trade. The

---

[1] Frédéric Mauro, *Le Portugal, le Brésil et l'Atlantique au XVIIe siècle (1570–1670): étude économique* (Paris, 1983), 538; Kenneth R. Andrews, *The Spanish Caribbean: Trade and Plunder, 1530–1630* (New Haven, CT, 1978), 82–3, 134; David B. Quinn, *Explorers and Colonies: America, 1500–1625* (London, 1990), 342–3; Linda M. Heywood and John K. Thornton, *Central Africans, Atlantic Creoles, and the Foundation of the Americas, 1585–1640* (Cambridge, 2007), 28–9, 37.

Dutch, for their part, did not venture to the African coast before the closing years of the century, when their trade suddenly took off. By 1610, twenty ships left the United Provinces annually to buy gold and ivory in Guinea with textiles, hardware, and increasingly merchandise bought at African coastal markets. Since Europe had a very modest internal supply, gold provided a powerful lure for European expansion in general. Throughout the seventeenth century, it was a more important trade item in Africa than slaves.[2]

What seduced some northern merchants to try their luck in the Americas, blazing trails for their countrymen, were changing commercial conditions in Europe. The shift in English trade from Antwerp to Spain and the Mediterranean set off a search for new trade goods, including Newfoundland cod. The forced Dutch removal from the Iberian Peninsula prompted voyages whose objective was to find alternative sources for the coveted salt, eventually leading to the capture of St Martin and Curaçao. There was also a military logic to the conquest of these two islands, which could serve as anti-Spanish bulwarks. Similarly, the French colony centred on Fort Caroline in Florida (1564–5) and the English ones in Roanoke (1585), Providence Island, and Tortuga (both founded in the early 1630s) were intended to hurt Spain.

Step by step, northern European pirates, explorers, and traders made inroads in the areas claimed by Spain and Portugal. Sometimes apprenticed in Iberian ports, they went in search of gold, silver, and more mundane riches from Africa and the Americas, thus preparing the way for regular maritime connections. Most ships venturing into the Atlantic sailed to what Pierre Chaunu has called a near New World, the area to which a ship could complete a voyage in about six months: the Azores, Canaries, Madeira, Cape Verde, virtually all the Antilles, the African coast up until Elmina (São Jorge da Mina), and northern Brazil. Such voyages did not require great technical resources or large investments and made it possible to use most of the ships' transport capacity for economic ends.[3] As Spain managed to protect its main administrative and commercial centres, the northern adventurers were bound to explore the marginal areas of the Americas. They displayed much activity on the Caribbean coasts of Central and South America, but often to little or no avail. There were few Spanish settlements, and contacts with the Indian groups encountered did not produce a lively trade. In all of the western hemisphere, trade between Europeans and natives remained minimal. Most exchange took place between communities of Europeans.[4]

---

[2] P. E. H. Hair and Robin Law, 'The English in West Africa', in Nicholas Canny (ed.), *The Oxford History of the British Empire*, i (Oxford, 1998), 243–4; Kenneth J. Banks, 'Financiers, Factors, and French Proprietary Companies in West Africa', in L. H. Roper and B. Van Ruymbeke (eds.), *Constructing Early Modern Empires: Proprietary Ventures in the Atlantic World, 1500–1750* (Leiden, 2007), 79–116: 86; Victor Enthoven, *Zeeland en de opkomst van de Republiek: Handel en strijd in de Scheldedelta, c.1550–1621* (Ph.D. dissertation, Rijksuniversiteit Leiden, 1996), 268.

[3] Ana Maria Pereira Ferreira, *Problemas marítimos entre Portugal e a França na primeira metade do século XVI* (Redondo, 1995), 177–8.

[4] Anne Pérotin-Dumon, 'The Pirate and the Emperor: Power and the Law on the Seas, 1450–1850', in James D. Tracy (ed.), *The Political Economy of Merchant Empires: State Power and World Trade,*

The only exception was the fur trade, in which the French were the pioneers. They relied on Indians supplying and treating the pelts, and in turn provided the Indians with European products that were used as weapons and tools. Like fish and tobacco, furs supplied the quick returns desired by entrepreneurs and easily paid for their transportation costs to Europe.[5] The fur business became the rationale for New France as well as for early New England and New Netherland.

Exploration and early trade were often the work of individual adventurers without connections to court or higher political echelons. Many of them simply tried their luck in what they saw as marginal speculations. National governments barely took notice of their activities. Colonization was another matter, requiring approval from above and forcing officials to formulate policies. The most ambitious of their plans—the grand designs for the New World—materialized, albeit briefly, in the case of the French colonies in Rio de Janeiro and Florida and the Dutch occupation of northern Brazil (1630–54). Dutch plans to conquer Peru and Mexico, thereby cutting off silver supplies to the Habsburg army in the Netherlands, never moved beyond the planning stage. Cromwell's Western Design did, but the addition of Jamaica to the English realm was unintended.[6] Overall, what is striking is the haphazard, uncoordinated, contingent nature of colonization, featuring immediate concerns and accidental openings, interrupted by warfare and internal strife. As anti-Iberian militancy was rarely matched by conquests, grand designs remained dead letters, and northerners had to resign themselves to settling places the Iberians had never occupied.

One way in which governments supported transatlantic exploits was by forming colonial chartered companies. These companies were granted trade monopolies, usually in a specific part of Africa or the Americas, although the area could differ from small (one French company was only allowed to deal with Senegal and Cape Verde) to medium (the English Guinea Company received a trade monopoly from Senegal to Nigeria) to large (the Dutch West India Company monopolized trade throughout the Atlantic world). The monopolies were intended to bring to an end the cut-throat competition among fellow nationals, which had considerably reduced profit margins, and their long duration was to compensate for the risky nature of transatlantic trade. Without incurring any expense—the state usually did not provide subsidies—the national governments benefited from such companies, which represented them in the arena of international politics. The monopolies, as it turned out, were no panacea. The chartered companies ran into ever deeper financial problems, which eventually

1350–1750 (Cambridge, 1991), 196–227: 206–7; M. G. de Boer, 'Eene memorie over den toestand der West Indische Compagnie in het jaar 1633', *Bijdragen en Mededeelingen van het Historisch Genootschap*, 21 (1900), 343–62; Murdo J. MacLeod, *Spanish Central America: A Socioeconomic History, 1520–1720* (Berkeley, CA, 1973), 354; David Eltis, *The Rise of African Slavery in the Americas* (Cambridge, 2000), 137.

[5] K. G. Davies, *The North Atlantic World in the Seventeenth Century* (Minneapolis, MN, 1974), 169.

[6] *Schaede die den Staet der Vereenichde Nederlanden, en d'Inghesetenen van dien, is aenstaende, by de versuymenisse van d'Oost en West-Indische Negotie onder een Octroy en Societeyt te begrijpen* (The Hague, 1644), 2, 8; W. Voorbeijtel Cannenburg, *De reis om de wereld van de Nassausche vloot, 1623–1626* (The Hague, 1964), 71–2.

forced them to license individual merchants to act on the company's behalf or to simply give up parts of their monopolies.

What made trade with the Spanish colonies risky was its illegal character. As early as the first half of the sixteenth century, much contraband trade took place in the Caribbean, site of the earliest Spanish New World settlements. Northern merchants sailing to the Caribbean without a licence risked confiscation and death, since Spain considered them to be pirates, at least until 1609, when the Dutch and the Spanish signed the Twelve-Year Truce. In order to bypass regulations, some northerners carried Spanish ship captains from the Canary Islands, while others bribed officials to obtain licences and sail from the Canaries to the Caribbean.

Prior to 1609, common interests sometimes made Spain's rivals join hands, as in Hispaniola, where a number of English, French, and Dutch ships conducted a brisk hides trade in 1602–3. The Dutch trade alone was impressive: twenty ships carrying 1,500 men were involved in the trade in Santo Domingo driven both here and in Cuba for the benefit of the Amsterdam leather industry. Another multinational trade took place in northern South America between Caracas and the Amazon River, where Englishmen and Dutchmen received tobacco through barter with natives in Cumaná and with Spanish settlers in Trinidad.[7]

In addition to these commercial pursuits, the northerners undertook the exploitation of natural resources. The chief extractive industry in which they engaged was fishing. The fisheries of Atlantic Canada, which produced the first American staple, were especially attractive, its trade accounting for a higher volume and perhaps value, by the late sixteenth century, than Spanish trade with silver-rich Mexico. European ships had started seasonal fishing at Newfoundland in the 1510s, their numbers multiplying in the following decades, until some 10,000 men made a living in this business by the 1570s. This was a truly international trade, Frenchmen (Bretons and Normans) fishing cod alongside Basques, English, and Portuguese; the Dutch only appeared as buyers of fish towards the end of the century. The 1580s formed a watershed in the Newfoundland fisheries. The French presence dwindled, due in part to the Wars of Religion, European economic setbacks, and the cooler climate. French ships diversified their activities, combining fishing with whaling and fur trading. The English presence increased, due in part to a strict new Danish system of licences that made it hard for the English to maintain their share in the Icelandic fishery. Crews from Portugal and the Basque country suffered a devastating attack by Englishman Bernard Drake in 1585 and then faced impressment of their vessels into the service of the Spanish Armada. The great beneficiaries were the English, whose maritime power grew along with the scale of the fisheries. Eager to procure cod to exchange for wine in France, they began to establish permanent communities in Newfoundland.[8]

[7] Engel Sluiter, 'Dutch–Spanish Rivalry in the Caribbean Area, 1594–1609', *Hispanic American Historical Review*, 28 (1948), 165–96: 184; Joyce Lorimer, *English and Irish Settlement on the River Amazon, 1550–1646* (London, 1989), 153.

[8] Peter E. Pope, *The Newfoundland Plantation in the Seventeenth Century* (Chapel Hill, NC, 2004), 13, 15, 17–19, 98; Laurier Turgeon, 'French Fishers, Fur Traders, and Amerindians during the Sixteenth

Besides fishing, other extractive industries lured adventurous men to cross the ocean. One was logging, but timber suffered from such high transport costs that it was impossible to compete with Baltic wood. The quest for salt deposits encouraged the Dutch to explore the Atlantic in the late sixteenth century, after Habsburg trade embargoes had sealed off their traditional sources in Spain and Portugal. Their subsequent search for alternative sources took them first to the Cape Verde Islands and then to coastal Venezuela, but a series of Spanish military expeditions put an end to the Dutch presence there.[9]

The impact of transatlantic activities on the metropolitan economies varied from trade to trade and place to place. The fisheries employed thousands of Frenchmen and Englishmen in the last decades of the sixteenth century, contributed to the development of shipbuilding industries and port cities, and offered many European consumers a viable alternative to the increasingly highly priced meat. Tobacco and sugar took longer to conquer the European markets, but once they had succeeded, their imports kept growing—shipments of Virginia leaf to England rose more than tenfold in the three decades after 1640—and their prices to decline, making these commodities available for a good part of the population.[10] Since their domestic markets were limited, the English and the Dutch both re-exported much to the Continent.[11]

The Atlantic not only rewarded enterprising merchants and created new customers, but also spawned whole new industries. Amsterdam boasted dozens of sugar refineries by the mid-seventeenth century, and Gouda developed into a major pipe-making centre, whose products were sold in the neighbouring countries, Russia, the East Indies, and the Americas. And both industries provided ample work for potters. National governments also benefited by levying import duties. In the 1660s, duties on Chesapeake tobacco accounted for around 25 per cent of England's customs revenues and 5 per cent of the government's income.[12]

Century: History and Archaeology', *William and Mary Quarterly*, 3rd Series, 55/4 (October 1998), 585–610: 590–2; Gilles Havard and Cécile Vidal, *Histoire de l'Amérique française* (Paris, 2003), 37; Stephen J. Hornsby, *British Atlantic, American Frontier: Spaces of Power in Early Modern British America* (Hanover, MD, 2005), 14.

[9] Jonathan I. Israel, *Dutch Primacy in World Trade 1585–1740* (Oxford, 1989), 138; Cornelis C. Goslinga, *The Dutch in the Caribbean and on the Wild Coast, 1580–1680* (Assen, 1971), 129–31, 135.

[10] Neville Williams, 'England's Tobacco Trade in the Reign of Charles I', *Virginia Magazine of History and Biography*, 65/4 (October 1957), 403–49: 419–20; Niels Steensgaard, 'The Growth and Composition of the Long-Distance Trade of England and the Dutch Republic before 1750', in James D. Tracy (ed.), *The Rise of Merchant Empires: Long-Distance Trade in the Early Modern World, 1350–1750* (Cambridge, 1990), 102–52: 141, 142.

[11] See for a very high estimate of the value of Dutch Atlantic trade: Victor Enthoven, 'An Assessment of Dutch Transatlantic Commerce, 1585–1817', in Johannes Postma and Victor Enthoven (eds.), *Riches from Atlantic Commerce: Dutch Transatlantic Trade and Shipping, 1585–1817* (Leiden, 2003), 385–445: 437.

[12] Jan de Vries and Ad van der Woude, *Nederland, 1500–1815: de eerste ronde van moderne economische groei* (Amsterdam, 1995), 361, 385; Edmund S. Morgan, *American Slavery, American Freedom* (New York, 1975), 193.

INFORMAL INTERMEDIARIES

The merchants actively exploring commercial opportunities in Ibero-America included Europeans who did not belong to any of the major nationalities in the Atlantic world. By the 1560s, a triangular trade developed between Antwerp, Lisbon, and Brazil, in which authorities in Lisbon allowed Flemish ships to leave for Brazil, as long as a Portuguese person had been designated as surety. This proviso was intended to ensure the ship's return to Portugal. After the Spanish conquest of 1585 had ended Antwerp's Atlantic heyday by setting off a massive emigration, other European merchants filled the void, including men from the Hansa cities of Hamburg and Lübeck, who owned ships that carried goods to Brazil on behalf of Portugal. The Dutch transatlantic trade was a similarly multinational affair. In the mid-seventeenth century, Italians, Irishmen, and Hanseatic merchants helped freight many a ship leaving Amsterdam for transatlantic voyages. Starting in the 1630s, Hanseatic ship-owners, often with the assistance of Dutchmen, also sent their own vessels to West Africa, Brazil, and Barbados, where they competed with the West India Company.[13] The Portuguese 'men of the Nation' were both rivals and supporters of Dutch activities. Made up of Roman Catholics and professing Jews, but also including men who displayed a hybrid religiosity, the members of Portuguese merchant houses connected numerous commercial nodes on both sides of the ocean. Although many reverted to Judaism in Amsterdam and hundreds moved to Dutch Brazil, where they were guaranteed freedom of religion, there is no evidence of Portuguese Jews conspiring with the Dutch against the Habsburg empire—Portuguese Jewish investment in the West India Company was actually quite modest.[14]

Dutchmen often moved beyond their traditional spheres. What set the Dutch apart from other Atlantic empires is the degree to which they functioned as intermediaries, exploiting commercial opportunities in all corners of the Atlantic world. The ubiquity of their vessels explains how the Dutch could be instrumental in the initial immigration of both Africans and Jews to North America and in the survival of both the Irish and English settlers on the Amazon River in the 1610s and St Christopher's French and

---

[13] Antwerp's trade: Eddy Stols, *De Spaanse Brabanders of de handelsbetrekkingen der Zuidelijke Nederlanden met de Iberische wereld 1598–1648* (Brussels, 1971). Hamburg's and Lübeck's trade with Brazil: Ernst Baasch, 'Beiträge zur Geschichte der Handelbeziehungen zwischen Hamburg und Amerika', in Hamburg Komité für die Amerika-Feier, Wissenschaftlicher Ausschuss (ed.), *Hamburgische Festschrift zur Erinnerung an die Entdeckung Amerika's*, 2 vols. (Hamburg, 1892), 1: 9–12; Hermann Kellenbenz, *Sephardim an der unteren Elbe: Ihre wirtschaftliche und politische Bedeutung vom Ende des 16. bis zum Beginn des 18. Jahrhunderts* (Wiesbaden, 1958), 109, 133. Hamburg's trade with Barbados: T.H., *A true and exact narrative of the proceedings of the Parliaments Fleet, against the island of Barbadoes, with the maner of the reducing thereof* (London, 1652), 4. Competition in West Africa: György Nováky, *Handelskompanier och kompanihandel: Svenska Afrikakompaniet 1649–1663, en studie i feudal handel* (Ph.D. dissertation, Uppsala, 1990), 76–84.

[14] Daviken Studnicki-Gizbert, *A Nation upon the Ocean Sea: Portugal's Atlantic Diaspora and the Crisis of the Spanish Empire, 1492–1640* (Oxford, 2007), 72, 74; Daniel M. Swetschinski, *Reluctant Cosmopolitans: The Portuguese Jews of Seventeenth-Century Amsterdam* (London, 2000), 116–17.

English settlements in 1629. In the Brazil trade, Amsterdam inherited Antwerp's role, although Flemish participation did not end. Some Flemish factors continued to operate in Brazil and Dutch ship captains heading for Brazil (by way of Portugal) sought after Flemish sailors, who were less suspect religiously, had a better command of the Portuguese language, and were more experienced on the coasts of the New World. Dutch ships en route to Pernambuco therefore frequently called at the Canary Islands, or Cádiz or Madeira, to take on Flemings.

The Canaries became an important hub for Dutch ships, their holds filled with textiles and provisions, partly for re-export to the American colonies, and the islands long remained an important gateway for the Dutch to Spanish America. After 1641, the Canaries attracted much foreign shipping after Spanish authorities allowed the archipelago to dispatch 700 tons of wine per year to the Americas in ships that did not have to be monitored by the House of Trade. English and especially Dutch merchants jumped at the opportunity, obtaining licences from local residents that enabled them to sail with sweet Canary wine to Cuba or other colonies, manning their vessels with largely Spanish crews and sometimes giving the ships Roman Catholic names.[15]

The Canaries were a gateway to the Spanish Indies, which Dutch merchants did not begin to explore in earnest until after the Peace Treaty of Münster (1648), which ended their war with Spain. Sailing with or without licences from the Canaries, ocean-going Dutch ships were involved in a massive trade with Buenos Aires and ports in the Spanish Caribbean until 1665. Annually, an estimated twenty large ships, often 400 tons or more, engaged in circuitous voyages that lasted over a year before returning to their home ports. This lucrative trade, with silver and dyestuffs in the holds of almost every returning ship, benefited from the Anglo-Spanish war of 1654–60, which saw all English vessels banned from Spanish colonial ports.[16]

Dutch merchants, known for their easy credit and low freight rates, also conducted an intensive trade with Anglo-America, targeting especially Barbados, St Christopher, and Virginia. Dutch tobacco shipments rapidly forged close ties between Rotterdam and Amsterdam (and, to a lesser degree, New Amsterdam), on the one hand, and Virginia, as can be gleaned from the indebtedness of Virginia planters to merchants in those ports. Dutch activities in the Chesapeake and Barbados were particularly important during the English Civil Wars.[17] Conclusive evidence is lacking, though, for the

15 Manuel Herrero Sánchez, *El acercamiento hispano-neerlandés (1648–1678)* (Madrid, 2000), 72; Fernando Serrano Mangas, *Armadas y flotas de la plata (1620–1648)* (Madrid, 1990), 366–7; Jonathan I. Israel, 'The Canary Islands and the Sephardic Atlantic Trade Network (1620–1660)', in id., *Diasporas within a Diaspora: Jews, Crypto-Jews and the World Maritime Empires (1540–1740)* (Leiden, 2002), 269–89: 280–2; George F. Steckley, 'The Wine Economy of Tenerife in the Seventeenth Century: Anglo-Spanish Partnership in a Luxury Trade', *Economic History Review*, 33/3 (August 1980), 335–50.

16 Wim Klooster, *Illicit Riches: Dutch Trade in the Caribbean, 1648–1795* (Leiden, 1998), 52–4.

17 *Documents Relative to the Colonial History of the State of New-York; Procured in Holland, England and France, by John Romeyn Brodhead*, ed. E. B. O'Callaghan (Albany, NY, 1856), 436–7; J. R. Pagan, 'Dutch Maritime and Commercial Activity in Mid-Seventeenth-Century Virginia', *Virginia Magazine*, 90 (1982), 485–501; April Lee Hatfield, *Atlantic Virginia: Intercolonial Relations in the Seventeenth Century* (Philadelphia, PA, 2004); Vincent T. Harlow, *A History of Barbados 1625–1685*

widespread theory that Barbados' successful start as a sugar producer or even its 'sugar revolution' was due to Dutch help. Experienced sugar planters in Brazil, the Dutch supposedly taught Barbadians how to grow sugar, loaned them capital to buy land and equipment and set up the sugar mills, supplied the slaves who worked the plantations and ground the cane, and shipped the end product to Europe. Proof is missing, for example, when it comes to the supply of capital goods and African slaves. Until 1645, Africans were supplied only to Dutch Brazil, and not until the 1650s, well after the start of the sugar revolution, are there signs of a restructuring of the Dutch slave trade that benefited the English colonies. At the same time, there is substantial evidence of a rapidly growing English slave trade to Barbados starting in 1640 and of plantation investments made exclusively by Englishmen.[18] More can be said for a crucial Dutch role in the French Caribbean colonies of Martinique and Guadeloupe, where 600 Dutch refugees from Brazil arrived with 300 slaves and sugar-mill equipment, where the Dutch virtually monopolized commercial traffic, and where planters were massively indebted to them.[19]

COLONIZATION

Once northern European exploration was under way or military and commercial pursuits were undertaken, the building blocks were in place for further expansion. The first temporary settlements of Frenchmen and Englishmen in the Caribbean were close to navigational passages, such as the islands east of Puerto Rico. The vain search for a north-western passage to China created expertise that was used to launch the English fur trade in North America. Likewise, the removal of the Iberians from Newfoundland in the late sixteenth century enabled English settlement of Virginia

(Oxford, 1926), 22; John C. Appleby, 'English Settlement in the Lesser Antilles during War and Peace, 1603–1660', in Robert L. Paquette and Stanley L. Engerman (eds.), *The Lesser Antilles in the Age of European Expansion* (Gainesville, FL, 1996), 86–104: 96.

[18] Cf. Richard Ligon, *A True & Exact History of the Island of Barbados* (London, 1657): 85. But see: K. Ratelband (ed.), *Vijf dagregisters van het kasteel Svo Jorge da Mina (Elmina) aan de Goudkust (1645–1647)* (The Hague, 1953), 6, 9, 11–12, 54, 117, 165–6, 169–71, 195, 211, 265, 282, 284–5, 292, 293–4; Ernst van den Boogaart and Pieter C. Emmer, 'The Dutch Participation in the Atlantic Slave Trade, 1596–1650', in Henry A. Gemery and Jan S. Hogendorn (eds.), *The Uncommon Market: Essays in the Economic History of the Atlantic Slave Trade* (New York, 1979), 353–75: 371–2; Larry Gragg, ' "To Procure Negroes": The English Slave Trade to Barbados, 1627–60', *Slavery and Abolition*, 16 (1995), 65–84; John J. McCusker and Russell R. Menard, 'The Sugar Industry in the Seventeenth Century: A New Perspective on the Barbadian 'Sugar Revolution', in Stuart Schwartz (ed.), *Tropical Babylons: Sugar and the Making of the Atlantic World, 1450–1680* (Chapel Hill, NC, 2004), 289–330: 294–303; and Heywood and Thornton, *Central Africans*, 45–6.

[19] Charles Frostin, *Histoire de l'autonomisme colon de la partie de St. Domingue aux XVIIe et XVIIIe siècles: contribution à l'étude du sentiment américain d'indépendance* (Lille, 1973), 31, 62, 65; Gérard Lafleur, 'Relations avec l'étranger des minorités religieuses aux Antilles françaises (XVII–XVIIIe s.)', *Bulletin de la Société d'Histoire de la Guadeloupe*, 57/58 (1983), 27–44: 29; Ernst van den Boogaart, Pieter Emmer, Peter Klein, and Kees Zandvliet, *La expansión holandesa en el Atlántico* (Madrid, 1992), 163.

and New England. The fisheries themselves were crucial for colonization by supplying 'a goodly share of the incentives, capital, and settlers for the most successful English efforts at colonization . . . '[20] Like exploring and fishing, privateering could unintentionally facilitate colonization. Not only were ships, men, and capital used and developed in the years after 1585 later used in colonization, a direct connection can also be made between English privateering in the Caribbean and colonization of Guiana. Besides, Dutch privateering helped guarantee the survival of infant French and English Caribbean colonies (as well as Bermuda) after 1621 (when the Twelve-Year Truce ended), while the most dramatic Dutch privateering success, the 1628 capture of the New Spain treasure fleet, strengthened the West India Company's financial position, which prompted the decision to invade and colonize northern Brazil.

Until 1640, the northern European colonies were small, not exceeding the summer population of 5,000–10,000 on Newfoundland's Eastern Shore. But migration to New England was substantial, and the Chesapeake and the Caribbean also began to receive large numbers of European settlers. Home to predominantly young, single males, the early northern settlements had a serious demographic imbalance during the first decades. Six times more men than women moved to the Chesapeake in the 1630s, and men migrating to Canada before 1650 outnumbered women by four to one. There was, therefore, little natural increase, and by the mid-seventeenth century, most colonists had still been born in Europe. Their background was not primarily in agriculture, most of them being urbanites, and for the most part, their migration cannot be explained by reference to economic downturns in their native countries. Nor were the colonies ethnically homogeneous. French colonies did mainly contain native Frenchmen, but Germans and Scandinavians came to the Dutch settlements, and Irishmen settled in numerous English colonies.[21]

Migration thus largely explains the increased size of the settlements by 1660, when some 8,000 Europeans had found a new abode in the Dutch settlements, around 16,000 in the French colonies, and more than 60,000 in the English. The Dutch reluctance to move to the New World can be explained by the relatively high incomes earned at home and the preference of sailors and soldiers to sign up for a destination in the East Indies. Among the French, only one in five migrants went to America—many instead leaving for Spain—against a majority of English migrants leaving their native soil. After their loss of Brazil, North America was where Dutchmen moved, Englishmen left for both the mainland of North America and the Caribbean, but six out of seven Frenchmen went to live in the Caribbean islands.[22] Except for some individuals, Indians were

---

[20] John J. McCusker and Russell R. Menard, *The Economy of British America, 1607–1789: with Supplementary Bibliography* (Chapel Hill, NC, 1991), 98.

[21] Pope, *Newfoundland Plantation*, 200, 205; Alison Games, *Migration and the Origins of the English Atlantic World* (Cambridge, MA, 1999), 83; James Horn, *Adapting to a New World: English Society in the Seventeenth-Century Chesapeake* (Chapel Hill, NC, 1994), 182; Leslie Choquette, *Frenchmen into Peasants: Modernity and Tradition in the Peopling of French Canada* (Cambridge, MA, 1997), 162 (table 6.6), 176 (table 6.9); Eltis, *Rise of African Slavery*, 30–2.

[22] Philip P. Boucher, *France and the American Tropics to 1700: Tropics of Discontent* (Baltimore, MD, 2008), 145, 157; Games, *Migration*, 20–1; Havard and Vidal, *Histoire de l'Amérique française*, 61.

not part of the European settlements, but Africans were. Their numbers may have been small in some places, but the short-lived English colonies of Tortuga and Providence Island already had a slave majority by the late 1630s. In those years, the English and Dutch slave trades took off, while the French relied on Dutch shipments, which expanded after mid-century. By 1660, Africans formed a sizeable minority in the French islands.[23]

If the men planning colonies proclaimed that the Americas would yield a wide range of products that would sustain an immigrant population, the conditions faced by the first settlers were often dismal. Internal strife contributed to the demise of the French colonies in Florida, Rio de Janeiro, and Guiana. Getting supplies also posed problems, dooming the early English colony in Roanoke and threatening the survival of Dutch Brazil two decades after its inception. In several new colonies, the lack of bread grains, meat, and legumes must have caused serious protein and vitamin B deficiencies. Various groups of men abandoned their colony after a brutally cold winter, while others became victims of deadly diseases—five English settlements in Guiana failed before Suriname succeeded. Indian attacks or the fear thereof could also delay or call off colonizing plans—in the Lesser Antilles, where only Barbados was spared Indian wars, Europeans exclusively moved to parts of the islands not inhabited by Kalinago (Carib) Indians.

Besides, there was the perennial threat of war with the Iberians. Spanish success in removing the northerners from the Americas began to falter in the early seventeenth century, when King Philip III called off expeditions against English settlers in Virginia and Bermuda. But Spain did defend its overseas provinces. Faced with protracted military and commercial harassment by the northerners, the crown after 1621 decided on a policy of privateering of its own, while expanding a programme of fortifications at key points in the New World and withdrawing some of its ships from Europe for service in the western Atlantic. However, such measures could not prevent the loss, one by one, to the northerners of the Lesser Antilles, which only belonged to Spain in name. Warfare with England (1624–8) and the Dutch (until 1648) only accelerated the loss of the islands. Nor did the occasional Spanish show of strength, such as the defeat of the English colony in Nevis, the French and English settlements at St Christopher (all in 1629), and those of the Dutch and the French in St Martin (1633), have much effect.[24]

In North America, Spain left the French in Newfoundland, Labrador, and the Maritimes alone, assuming that those areas were within Portugal's sphere as decided in Tordesillas, but tried to prevent English settlement further south, eventually failing to accomplish that. In Africa, where Spain had no colonies, the Portuguese resisted

[23] Games, *Migration*, 210; Boucher, *France and the American Tropics*, 157.

[24] Hilary Beckles, 'The Genocide Policy in English–Karifuna Relations in the Seventeenth Century', in Martin Daunton and Rick Halpern (eds.), *Empire and Others: British Encounters with Indigenous Peoples, 1600–1850* (Philadelphia, PA, 1999), 280–302: 286; Enrique Otero Lana, *Los corsarios españoles durante la decadencia de los Austrias: el corso español del Atlántico peninsular en el siglo XVII (1621–1697)* (Madrid, 1992), 258–9; Davies, *North Atlantic World*, 9–10; Carla Rahn Phillips, *Six Galleons for the King of Spain: Imperial Defense in the Early Seventeenth Century* (Baltimore, MD, 1986), 184.

tooth and nail as the northerners' commercial strength grew by leaps and bounds. Here the French were also the early challengers, accompanied after the mid-sixteenth century by English adventurers. From the 1590s onwards, a string of deadly encounters prevented the northerners from erecting their own trading stations. Not until the Dutch conquest of Elmina in 1637 did they establish a lasting foothold.

Collaboration between the northern Europeans at the strategic level was rare, although not for lack of plans. Still, joint operations of corsairs or smugglers were not uncommon, and the cooperation between Dutch merchants and English and Irish planters in the Amazon region in the early seventeenth century was very intensive. By the 1620s, however, competition over land in the insular Caribbean and over trade in West Africa and North America led to growing rivalry between the northerners. The French Compagnie des Cent-Associés, founded with Richelieu's backing, ran into immediate trouble in 1628, when its four vessels carrying 400 emigrants fell into the hands of an English privateering fleet.[25] After seizing Elmina, the Dutch were the established power in Guinea, facing commercial and military challenges from a host of European countries.

The volatile nature of international relations led to profound instability in some colonies. St Croix, one of several Caribbean islands that changed hands repeatedly, offers a good example. Englishmen and Dutchmen probably settled the island in 1625, six years before a Spanish expedition wiped out an English settlement there. The mid-1630s saw the establishment first of a French and then a second English colony, both of which were soon defeated by Spain. In 1642, the Dutch succeeded in carving out a settlement on the island after killing a dozen English settlers. A hundred and twenty Frenchmen settled on the island as well, but within three years, an invasion of Englishmen and Irishmen from St Christopher put an end to Dutch rule. A French expedition next captured St Croix. In West Africa, Senegambia offers a similarly unstable history. First the Portuguese dislodged the Dutch (1629), and then the English and French tried to end Dutch dominance, eventually successfully.[26] But Africa was not the site of northern European colonization in this period. Like in Asia, the northerners preferred establishing trading posts and factories there, not colonies.

While northern European governments needed guarantors of stable American colonies, colonial planners sought national grants of land. The solution was to establish

[25] Mickaël Augeron and Laurent Vidal. 'Refuges ou réseaux? Les dynamiques atlantiques protestantes au XVIe siècle', in Guy Martinière, Didier Poton, and François Souty (eds.), *D'un rivage à l'autre: villes et protestantisme dans l'aire Atlantique (XVIe–XVIIe siècles). Actes du colloque organisé à La Rochelle (13 et 14 novembre 1998)* (Paris, 1999), 31–61: 46; Wallace T. MacCaffrey, *Elizabeth I: War and Politics 1588–1603* (Princeton, NJ, 1992), 99–101; Quinn, *Explorers and Colonies*, 322; Paul E. Kopperman, 'Ambivalent Allies: Anglo-Dutch Relations and the Struggle against the Spanish Empire in the Caribbean, 1621–1641', *Journal of Caribbean History*, 21/1 (1987), 55–77: 65; Havard and Vidal, *Histoire de l'Amérique française*, 58.

[26] Alfredo E. Figueredo, 'The Early European Colonization of St. Croix (1621–1645)', *Journal of the Virgin Islands Archaeological Society*, 6 (1978), 59–64; Goslinga, *Dutch in the Caribbean and on the Wild Coast*, 258, 261–2; Philip D. Curtin, *Economic Change in Precolonial Africa: Senegambia in the Era of the Slave Trade* (Madison, WI, 1975), 102–3.

proprietary colonies, as had happened in Spanish and Portuguese America in the previous century. The proprietors, who ruled their colonies much like aristocrats and other landowners did in Western Europe, frequently locked horns with the crown (or, in the Dutch case, the West India Company) to whom they owed responsibility. At issue was usually the extent of their jurisdiction or their rights to local trade.[27]

Trade and settlement were indeed often at odds, and not only in proprietary colonies. Merchants wanted to keep overhead costs to a minimum, preferring to save on defence, desiring free trade, and often failing to see the advantages of colonization. Colonizers sought a trade monopoly and wished to pay for it by transporting migrants. They stressed, in the case of the Dutch, that immigration did more to guarantee the survival of a colony than the colonial presence of soldiers. Besides, without trade the military was bound to become a liability, since its salaries and rations would eat away the colonial budget. Settlers would create economic activity, pay duties, and bear the burden of the soldiery.[28]

In addition to economic interests, military motivation, and demographic strength, religion and religious policy shaped the early stages of the northerners' Atlantic pursuits, which overlapped with the Reformation and Counter-Reformation. The Inquisition of the Canary Islands, for example, had no mercy on foreign sailors, arresting a few dozen Englishmen, 'Flemings', Germans, and Frenchmen in the 1590s, not for smuggling but for their 'Lutheran' convictions. The French state and Church fashioned the Counter-Reformation by developing Quebec and Senegal's Petite Côte, both areas threatened by Protestant Englishmen and Dutchmen, as missions to pagan tribes in the 1620s and 1630s. French emigrants to North America, who frequently displayed religious indifference, were also subjected to the strict norms of the ubiquitous Counter-Reformation.[29]

At the same time, the Americas were the site of religious freedom, which, while always mixed with practical motives, encouraged significant numbers of Europeans to settle in the northerners' colonies in the New World. The familiar story of the Pilgrims' colony in New England is just one of many, Puritans also moving to Bermuda and Providence Island, while Huguenots were often left undisturbed not only in the English and Dutch, but also in the French colonies. Jews, most of whom belonged to the Portuguese Nation, were also granted freedom of conscience. They came to make up around one-third of the European population of Dutch Brazil, and by mid-century also

[27] Boucher, *France and the American Tropics*, 66–7; Jaap Jacobs, 'Dutch Proprietary Manors in America: The Patroonships in New Netherland', in Roper and Van Ruymbeke (eds.), *Constructing Early Modern Empires*, 301–26: 306, 324; L. H. Roper and B. Van Ruymbeke, 'Introduction', ibid. 1–19: 7.

[28] Davies, *North Atlantic World*, 9; Havard and Vidal, *Histoire de l'Amérique française*, 41; Wim Klooster, 'Failing to Square the Circle: The West India Company's Volte-Face in 1638–39', *De Halve Maen: Magazine of the Dutch Colonial Period in America*, 73 (2000), 3–9: 8.

[29] J. F. Bosher, *Business and Religion in the Age of New France, 1600–1760: Twenty-Two Studies* (Toronto, 1994), 43; George E. Brooks, *Eurafricans in Western Africa: Commerce, Social Status, Gender, and Religious Observance from the Sixteenth to the Eighteenth Century* (Athens, OH, 2003), 90–1; Choquette, *Peasants into Frenchmen*, 142, 144.

settled, albeit in small numbers, in the Caribbean (Curaçao, Barbados, Martinique), North America (New Amsterdam, Newport), and Guiana. Apart from money-lending, retail trade, and long-distance trade, they devoted themselves to plantation agriculture, a clear sign of their different status across the ocean.

Religion also provided a framework for relations with blacks and Indians. The main motive for settlement in North America, according to contemporary French propaganda, was France's obligation to preach the gospel to all creatures throughout the world, to expel idolatry, and to 'polish the barbarous ways of the Gentiles'. Likewise, Dutch and English ministers in the Americas tried to deliver the natives from their 'barbaric ways' by converting them simultaneously to a Christian and a 'civilized' life. Civilizing natives was considered easy, but experience soon exposed that idea as an illusion.[30]

The northerners soon entered into business relations with Africans and Indians, availing themselves of native 'brokers', who traded and/or translated on their behalf, and native allies in the wars with other European colonizers. In the New World, Europeans were sometimes left behind in or near Indian territories, while natives were taken to the metropoles and submerged in local culture. In many parts of coastal Africa, European trade only thrived due to the help of local rulers. Even on the Gold Coast, where they established long-lasting fortified trading posts, the northerners were dependent on the protection from local African authorities, whom they had to shower with gifts and show the respect due from subjects.

Relations with natives were often the key to survival. A topic still awaiting a comparative study is how the northerners' difficulties in feeding themselves changed their relations with neighbouring Indians and Africans. Virginia's first governors all intimidated Indians in order to guarantee food supplies, the French raided the gardens of their Kalinago neighbours or attacked them, while one group of New Englanders performed menial labour for Indians to get corn.[31]

The prevalent Dutch and English views of Indians stressed the natives' barbarity, treachery, and lasciviousness. Only in the French case was the creation of a bi-racial society supported by the authorities, although not without the fear that assimilation might jeopardize the social order. English and Dutch ministers often strongly condemned concubinage with Indians, Africans, or women of mixed race, yet everywhere northerners entered into sexual relations with natives, due in part to the demographic profile of the European immigrants. The propensity to miscegenation seems to have been greatest among the French in North America and smallest in the colonies of the English. Outside their American settlements and African factories, some Dutch males lived with native women and produced offspring in spite of official prohibitions.[32]

---

[30] Guillaume Aubert, '"The Blood of France": Race and Purity of Blood in the French Atlantic World', *William and Mary Quarterly*, 3rd Series, 61/3 (July 2004), 439–78: 450.

[31] Karen Ordahl Kupperman, 'English Perceptions of Treachery, 1583–1640: The Case of the American "Savages"', *Historical Journal*, 20/2 (June 1977), 263–87: 267–8, 273; Boucher, *France and the American Tropics*, 72, 122–3.

[32] Aubert, 'The Blood of France', 450–7; *British Guiana Boundary: Arbitration with the United States of Venezuela: Appendix to the Case on Behalf of the Government of Her Britannic Majesty* (London,

Economic activities outside the Iberian orbit spurred the northerners' Atlantic endeavours from the beginning, soon leaving an impact on the home countries. While cod became a staple in European cuisine, luxury goods from the Americas also found wide acceptance, as new demands were created—the trade in North American furs took advantage of the fashion for broad-brimmed hats, but tobacco and sugar were virtually unknown to most consumers when shiploads of these products began to arrive. Initially imported from Portuguese and Spanish America, these two cash crops hailed mainly from the northerners' own colonies by the middle decades of the seventeenth century. Increased consumption of these staples at home was thus closely connected to the transformation of the colonial economies.

Economic achievement was not matched by political success. By 1600, the northerners had as yet made little headway in their attempts to challenge the Iberian hold on the Atlantic world. To be sure, raids on enemy ships and ports were numerous and contraband trade at times lucrative, but the search for mineral wealth had been in vain and the Iberian monopoly of territorial power was still largely intact. When in 1655 the era of the challenge came to an end with the English capture of Jamaica, the balance-sheet looked better, with northern colonies growing rapidly in North America and the Lesser Antilles, and Portugal's commercial hold on Africa beginning to crumble. But little long-term harm was done to Iberian might. Spain's enemies, as one historian has put it, were 'driven to the fringes of Spain's American empire',[33] and Portugal eventually managed to expel the Dutch and restore its power over Angola and Brazil. Political tensions and contraband trade with the Iberian world would remain, but the northerners subsequently invested most time and energy in the development of their own colonies.

BIBLIOGRAPHY

Andrews, Kenneth R., *The Spanish Caribbean: Trade and Plunder, 1530–1630* (New Haven, CT, 1978).

Boucher, Philip P., *France and the American Tropics to 1700: Tropics of Discontent* (Baltimore, MD, 2008).

Davies, K. G., *The North Atlantic World in the Seventeenth Century* (Minneapolis, MN, 1974).

Games, Alison, *Migration and the Origins of the English Atlantic World* (Cambridge, MA, 1999).

Havard, Gilles, and Cécile Vidal, *Histoire de l'Amérique française* (Paris, 2003).

Pérotin-Dumon, Anne, 'French, English and Dutch in the Lesser Antilles: From Privateering to Planting, c.1550–c.1650', in P. C. Emmer and Germán Carrera Damas (eds.), *General*

1898), 39–43; Jaap Jacobs, *Een zegenrijk gewest: Nieuw-Nederland in de zeventiende eeuw* (Amsterdam, 1999), 329–30.

[33] Phillips, *Six Galleons*, 220.

History of the Caribbean, ii: *New Societies: The Caribbean in the Long Sixteenth Century* (London, 1999), 114–58.

Pope, Peter E., *The Newfoundland Plantation in the Seventeenth Century* (Chapel Hill, NC, 2004).

Postma, Johannes, and Victor Enthoven (eds.), *Riches from Atlantic Commerce: Dutch Transatlantic Trade and Shipping, 1585–1817* (Leiden, 2003).

Quinn, David B., *Explorers and Colonies: America, 1500–1625* (London, 1990).

Ratelband, Klaas, *Nederlanders in West-Afrika 1600–1650: Angola, Kongo en São Tomé* (Zutphen, 2000).

PART II

CONSOLIDATION

CHAPTER 11

THE SPANISH ATLANTIC, 1650–1780

IDA ALTMAN

DURING the years from the mid-seventeenth to the end of the eighteenth century the Spanish empire exhibited increasing economic diversity and robustness and maintained its dominant position among European empires in the Americas without serious challenge, notwithstanding Spain's eclipse as a military power in Europe and maritime power on the seas. Spain's economic difficulties and over-dependence on faltering silver revenues during the seventeenth century did not undermine the empire's viability as is sometimes suggested. In size alone Spain's possessions in the Americas dwarfed those of any other colonizing nation and indeed, despite some losses in the Caribbean, were growing both in territorial extent and in the size and density of populations. The diversity and complexity of those territories with their impressive cities, seminaries and universities, great cathedrals and ecclesiastical establishments, the patterns of trade that linked their commercial economies to one another or to Europe and sometimes all but circumvented the participation or intervention of Spain itself, and the increasing Americanization of institutions and enterprises made the provinces and kingdoms of the Spanish crown quite unlike the other European colonies in the Americas in many respects.

Spanish America loomed large in the Atlantic world, and its peripheries in particular fell within the orbit of other nations that increasingly participated in and profited from its potential both as a market, especially for African slaves and manufactured goods, and as a producer of desirable raw materials. Paradoxically, however, even as foreign participation—both legal and illegal—in Spanish America's trade grew in scale and frequency, and even though Spanish possessions and shipping were the preferred target of both the freelance and sanctioned attacks of buccaneers, corsairs, and privateers, the vast core of Spanish America remained relatively little touched or changed by developments that were largely confined to the islands of the Caribbean and the Atlantic and to a lesser extent Pacific rims. With the exceptions of key ports such as Havana and Cartagena, in the sixteenth century many of these peripheral areas had been fairly isolated or remote, slow to develop, and of little interest to the Spanish crown, as was the case for Venezuela, the Río de la Plata region of South America, or the far north of New Spain.

It was precisely in these places that the empire was most open to outside intrusion and influence, the foreign presence was most conspicuous, and Spanish subjects were most likely to come into direct contact with people who were not subject to Spanish rule—whether Indians, fugitive Africans, or other Europeans. Such elements were mostly absent in the core of New Spain or the Andean region, where the direct manifestations of the influence and operation of the larger (and not just Atlantic) world probably were to be found principally in the material culture—Asian silks and porcelain or fine Italian textiles, European paintings and décor, furniture, books, sacred objects—that graced the homes and bodies of the better-off members of society, the viceregal courts of Lima and Mexico City, and the churches, great cathedrals, and episcopal palaces. The principal exception to this generalization lay in the substantial numbers of African slaves who arrived via the transatlantic trade—captive foreigners travelling mainly on foreign ships. Yet Africans, like other foreigners in Spanish America, for the most part concentrated in the islands or along the peripheries (coastal Venezuela, Buenos Aires, the gold-mining region of New Granada, the coastal region of the viceroyalty of Peru) with relatively few exceptions, such as Mexico City or the sugar-growing regions of New Spain, where people of African descent rapidly were becoming creole (i.e. American-born), mixed, and Hispanicized.

This chapter roughly divides the period addressed here into two unequal parts. The earlier and longer one, from around the mid-seventeenth to the mid-eighteenth century, was relatively uneventful when compared to the era of contact, conquest, and establishment of Spanish rule that preceded it[1] and the period of the late eighteenth century reforms and late colonial revolts that followed. Developments of the mid-seventeenth to mid-eighteenth centuries, however, were closely connected to the more dramatic changes of the late eighteenth century.

MATURITY AND GROWTH

Population growth[2] probably was the most important factor driving change in these years. Even as indigenous populations began to recover from their lowest levels, more rapid growth took place in the Spanish and Hispanic sectors[3] that were the main consumers of commercially produced items—wheat, sugar, livestock, textiles, leather

---

[1] See Stuart Schwartz's article in this volume.

[2] From the mid-seventeenth to the mid-eighteenth century New Spain's population nearly doubled, from around 1.5 million to nearly 3 million. By 1810 it had doubled again. See Peter J. Bakewell, *A History of Latin America* (2nd edn. Oxford, 2004), 273–4 for these and other population figures.

[3] Charles Gibson, *Aztecs under Spanish Rule* (Stanford, CA, 1964), suggests that at least some of the recovery in the indigenous population might have been among mestizos incorporated into the indigenous sector.

goods. These sectors provided the proprietors of, and the entrepreneurial and mana-gerial personnel for, most of the enterprises that supplied the consumer markets of the towns and mines. The growth of the proprietarial and entrepreneurial groups, together with the greater availability of indigenous, and in some cases African, labour, meant that in many places production could expand as domestic markets grew. This growth of both population and production, notable in the second half of the seventeenth century, would continue almost unabated through the eighteenth century.

External events and pressures that both produced and reflected significant internal change framed the period from 1650 until around 1760 in the Spanish Atlantic world. Its beginning nearly coincided with the British conquest of Jamaica, an almost un-planned act (the expedition that Cromwell dispatched in 1655 was intended to take Hispaniola) that in time transformed significantly the balance of maritime, and eventually economic, power in the Caribbean. While Jamaica had been a minor, sparsely populated Spanish territory, its acquisition gave the British a significant toehold in the heart of the Spanish Caribbean and provided a base for buccaneers and privateers who preyed on Spanish ports and shipping. It also became an important centre for illegal trade, especially with Central America and New Granada.[4] In the eighteenth century Jamaica became one of the greatest sugar producers of the Carib-bean, as did the French colony of Saint-Domingue, carved out of Spain's first colony, Hispaniola. Only with the expansion of sugar production in Cuba starting around the middle of the eighteenth century would the Spanish Caribbean begin to participate fully in the commercial export economy that had yielded notable profits to British, French, and Dutch planters and merchants since the middle of the seventeenth century.

At the turn of the eighteenth century the death without heirs of the Spanish monarch Charles II set off a major European and international conflict and marked the end of the Habsburg dynasty in Spain. The disputed succession gave rise to an alliance between Spain and France, a war that pitted Spain and France against the British, Dutch, and their allies, and a new Spanish dynasty—the Bourbons—with French origins and connections. The war's conclusion guaranteed the independence of the new Spanish Monarchy, but Spain lost many of its territories in Europe and the Mediterranean and saw its naval power all but destroyed. Nonetheless, there are indications that Spain's economic, if not political, revival actually dated to the latter years of the Habsburg dynasty.[5] The nature of that economic revival, however, did not alter decisively the patterns of trade and supply that allowed—indeed at times encour-aged—foreigners to claim a large share in Spain's trade with its American possessions.[6]

---

[4] See Murdo J. MacLeod, *Spanish Central America: A Socioeconomic History, 1520–1720* (Austin, TX, 2008), 361. See also Kris E. Lane, *Pillaging the Empire: Piracy in the Americas, 1500–1750* (Armonk, NY, 1998).

[5] On the recovery of the Castilian economy after the mid-seventeenth century, see Carla Rahn Phillips, 'Time and Duration: A Model for the Economy of Early Modern Spain', *American Historical Review*, 92/3 (1987), 531–62.

[6] On this see Stanley J. Stein and Barbara H. Stein, *Silver, Trade, and War: Spain and America in the Making of Early Modern Europe* (Baltimore, MD, 2000).

In particular Spain's lack of access to sources of African slaves guaranteed its continued dependence for supplies of slaves on other nations—the Portuguese up until 1640, the French, British, and Dutch—which in turn facilitated direct foreign access to the trade of the Indies.

Another, if temporary, loss to the British, who occupied Havana for ten months in 1762–3, marked an era of accelerating change in Spanish America. This event is often seen as the catalyst for the extension to Spanish America of the administrative, military, and economic reforms that the Bourbon regime already had begun to implement in Spain itself. Yet the connection between the loss (and recovery) of Havana and the Spanish crown's decision to experiment more boldly with reform in the empire should not be made too mechanically, as the impact of reform and new policies began to be felt much earlier in some areas. As one example the wealth generated by the New Granadan gold fields, in this period primarily located in the inhospitable region of the Chocó, figured prominently in the crown's decision to create—after nearly two centuries—a third viceroyalty of New Granada in 1718–19. It lasted barely four years before being disbanded but was re-established in 1739. The creation of this viceroyalty might seem to have little in common with the better-known reforms of the later eighteenth century, harking back to the earliest years of the Spanish empire and the establishment of the great viceroyalties of New Spain and Peru. Yet the establishment of this viceroyalty and subsequently that of the Río de la Plata in 1776 both responded to factors associated with the Atlantic world—the greater threat and reality of both smuggling and potential foreign aggression—as well as to internal changes. As such they precipitated major jurisdictional and administrative shifts that would have significant repercussions for the alignment and functioning of bureaucratic arrangements and for the opportunities—or closing of such—available to the growing populations of creoles and *castas* (the mixed Hispanic sectors).

The first period considered here had begun with the dissolution of the union of the Spanish and Portuguese crowns in 1640. Portuguese merchants, who had circulated freely since the late sixteenth century and played a crucial role in the trade and shipping of the Spanish empire, especially the slave trade, were persecuted and suppressed. Yet contraband trade and contact between Spaniards and Portuguese hardly disappeared, and in many parts of the empire Portuguese immigrants had settled down and assimilated. Territorial disputes between Spain and Portugal, however, continued to plague Atlantic South America and led to the signing of the Treaty of Madrid in 1750. This treaty—later rescinded—had unanticipated repercussions in one of the more remote regions claimed by Spain. The terms of the treaty required the Guaraní who lived in the Jesuit *reducciones* of Paraguay to leave the flourishing mission communities where they had lived for generations; their response was to rebel.[7] Less than twenty years later, in 1767, also as part of the reform programme of the Bourbon monarchy, the Jesuits themselves faced expulsion from the Spanish empire, although many of those

---

[7] See Barbara Ganson, *The Guaraní under Spanish Rule in the Río de la Plata* (Stanford, CA, 2003).

expelled were American-born.[8] Thus wars, treaties, jurisdictional and administrative changes, and movement and displacements of people figured throughout the period.

Internally the kingdoms of Spain and Spanish America appeared to be mostly quiet, at least until the second half of the eighteenth century, fostering demographic growth and economic development and diversification. Certainly there were conflicts and even full-scale revolts, especially in the far north of New Spain (the great Pueblo revolt took place in 1680 and led to the temporary Spanish abandonment of New Mexico). In the earlier part of the period especially, however, almost none of these disturbances and rebellions had what might be characterized as an Atlantic component; indeed they often took place in areas remote from the Atlantic world and usually responded to internal strains and resentments.[9] Although quite different in its causes and repercussions from indigenous revolts in rural New Spain, the urban *tumulto* that shocked the upper classes in Mexico City in 1692 nonetheless arose from local conditions (bread and grain shortages) and perceptions of bad government.[10] Only later, in the second half of the eighteenth century, would external events and pressures come to figure in local protests and revolts.

Significant shifts in patterns of production and commercial activity did occur, resulting in rapid growth in some areas and relative decline in others. By the end of the seventeenth century New Spain's silver output had surpassed Peru's, a trend that would become definitive in the eighteenth century and would affect everything from transatlantic shipping to the accelerated growth of regional economies in New Spain. At the same time the increasing diversion of Peruvian silver from Panama or Cartagena to Buenos Aires helped fuel the growth of that formerly isolated port, although in fact from the later sixteenth century the connection between Buenos Aires and Potosí had become well established as a route for legal and contraband trade. Patterns of inter-colonial and international trade (both licit and illicit), rising demand, and royal policy meant that by the late eighteenth century a substantial percentage of Spanish American exports were agricultural—tobacco, cacao, hides, cochineal, indigo, and sugar—although precious metals still dominated. Caracas grew with the expansion of cacao production. Despite the near abandonment of the old fleet system[11] Havana played an important role in shipbuilding and remained a thriving port, especially with the expansion of Cuban sugar production.[12] In Spain Seville lost its old position as the

[8] Around the same time France and Portugal also expelled the Jesuits from their territories.

[9] On revolts in Spanish America during the earlier period, see Susan M. Deeds, *Defiance and Deference in Mexico's Colonial North: Indians under Spanish Rule in Nueva Vizcaya* (Austin, TX, 2003); William B. Taylor, *Drinking, Homicide and Rebellion in Colonial Mexican Villages* (Stanford, CA, 1979); Andrew Knaut, *The Pueblo Revolt of 1680: Conquest and Resistance in Seventeenth-Century New Mexico* (Norman, OK, 1995); and Susan Schroeder (ed.), *Native Resistance and the Pax Colonial in New Spain* (Lincoln, NE, 1998).

[10] R. Douglas Cope, *The Limits of Racial Domination: Plebeian Society in Colonial Mexico City, 1660–1720* (Madison, WI, 1994), chapter 7.

[11] Efforts were made to revive the fleet in the first half of the eighteenth century but the real increase in trade in the second half of the century was due to the increased use of specially licensed 'register' ships; see Bakewell, *A History of Latin America*, 282–3.

[12] The standard work on the development of Cuba's plantation economy is Franklin W. Knight, *Slave Society in Cuba in the Nineteenth Century* (Madison, WI, 1970).

fulcrum of movement of people and goods to and from the Indies to Cádiz. As ships grew larger and swifter and maritime power shifted, the Pacific rim of Spanish America also was drawn increasingly into the 'greater' Atlantic world, although Mexico had long acted as a bridge between the economies of the Atlantic and Pacific, with Mexican merchants to a great extent conducting the exchange of Mexican and Peruvian silver for Asian silks and ceramics through the port of Manila, which in turn acted as an entrepôt for trade with Asian ports such as Macao and Nagasaki.

NEAR AND FAR ATLANTICS

In his seminal book on economy and society in Central America in the sixteenth and seventeenth centuries, Murdo J. MacLeod compares the 'near' and 'far' Atlantics of Spanish and Portuguese America. These categories are useful in explaining the differing situations of various regions with regard to production, shipping, and markets in the seventeenth century; only gradually did circumstances begin to shift in the eighteenth century. The near Atlantic included the large islands of the Caribbean and coastal Venezuela as well as north-eastern Brazil, all of which enjoyed the geographic advantages of proximity to Europe as well as good ports and harbours, making the export of such bulky products as hides, tobacco, cacao, and sugar both viable and profitable. Exports from the territories of the 'far' Atlantic—Mexico, the Andean region of Peru, and New Granada—consisted almost entirely of the lucrative but relatively compact (by volume) mineral trade in silver, gold, and precious stones. By this reckoning Central America fell somewhere in between. While it could be reached more quickly from Spain than could Veracruz, it still took a week or so to sail from Havana to the Gulf of Honduras.[13] Furthermore, Central America suffered from the disadvantages of its lack of important sources of precious metals and its basically Pacific orientation in terms of both population and patterns of production, although it benefited from the possibility of relying on overland rather than seaborne transportation to Veracruz. The schema of near and far Atlantics also is useful in understanding the impact of foreign intervention in the form of legal and illegal trade and the vulnerability of different regions to both organized and freebooting attacks. With the exception of the military garrisons and forts to be found in the far north of New Spain or southern Chile, only Spanish America's most strategic ports—Havana, Veracruz, Cartagena—maintained serious fortifications and a military presence of sorts.

At the same time, however, the distinction between near and far Atlantics does not explain regional patterns of production and exchange. The viceroyalties of New Spain and Peru had diverse, well-developed regional economies that supplied their mines, towns, and cities with a nearly complete spectrum of goods and staples of domestic

---

[13] MacLeod, *Spanish Central America*, 199.

consumption, items that for the most part did not figure in the Atlantic exchange but instead formed part of intra- and inter-colonial as well as local and regional trade. Central America obtained wine from Peru in the seventeenth century, Mexico imported its cacao from Central America (whence much of it arrived on the backs of mules), Guayaquil, and Venezuela, Chile supplied Peru's mines with wheat, and Ecuador's textile industry primarily served the Peruvian market. Both Peru and New Spain produced sugar as well as wheat, maize, beef, wool, and cotton for their own consumption. In these areas domestic markets were sufficiently large to preclude any need to depend on an Atlantic exchange.

The maturity, diversity, and dimensions of local and regional production and exchange in the 'far' Atlantic regions were such that, in terms of essentials, they mainly depended on the transatlantic trade for iron, in both finished and unfinished forms, and mercury for refining silver. Mercury had become crucial to mining production in New Spain and Peru with the development of the amalgamation method of refining in the sixteenth century. Two of the major known sources of mercury in the world lay within Spanish territory—the Almadén mines in Spain itself, north of Córdoba, and Huancavelica in Peru. Although early Peruvian mining operations had the advantage of a local supply of mercury, Huancavelica was in decline by the middle of the seventeenth century. The Peruvian mines became more dependent on supply from Almadén, for a while to the detriment of Mexican mining production. Notably the other metal Spanish America did not produce for itself—iron—also could be supplied from Spain, as it had long been mined and refined in the Basque country. Although the fortunes of the iron mines and foundries of the Basque country varied considerably over time, they were on an upswing in the eighteenth century.[14] Apart from iron and mercury, African slaves, and to some extent wine and oil, Mexico and Peru largely depended on the transatlantic (and transpacific) trade for non-essential and luxury items—fine textiles, ceramics and porcelain, clothing, books, furniture, works of art, sacred objects (including the relics of saints)—that often did not originate in Spain itself. Spain's trade with its American possessions largely consisted of non-Spanish goods provided directly and indirectly by foreigners. The shift of the focus of the American trade from Seville to Cádiz, well under way by the middle of the seventeenth century, if anything exacerbated the trend towards replacement of Spanish merchants by foreigners. Already by the 1670s of the eighty-seven most important commercial firms in Cádiz, only twelve were Spanish, while the Genoese claimed seventeen, the French eleven, and the British ten; twenty were Flemish or Dutch and seven Hanseatic.[15]

The *flota* operated irregularly in the eighteenth century and all but ceased to function after 1748. Although legal trade expanded considerably in the second half of

---

[14] For a fascinating look at how the intertwined domestic and Atlantic economies of the Basque region affected local society, see Juan Javier Pescador, *The New World Inside a Basque Village: The Oiartzun Valley and its Atlantic Emigrants, 1550–1800* (Reno, NV, 2004).

[15] Louisa Schell Hoberman, *Mexico's Merchant Elite, 1590–1660: Silver, State, and Society* (Durham, NC, 1991). In 1717 the Casa de Contratación (House of Trade) officially moved from Seville to Cádiz.

the century, contraband and illegal trade flourished as well. Common in nearly all ports and coastal areas that had anything to offer in exchange, contraband played a central role in the Caribbean provinces of New Granada, where not only was official complicity commonplace but the revenues from the seizure, sale, and taxation of contraband more or less equalled the yields from legal trade.[16] Riohacha province in New Granada was home to the Guajiro Indians, who had rejected Christianity and Spanish rule but learned to keep the livestock Europeans had introduced. They traded horses, mules, and cattle along with brazilwood, salt, and pearls that they collected. In the almost complete absence of legal trade or of an effective Spanish military or civilian presence, contraband trade dominated the province's economy.

Before discussing the changes in the Spanish empire that are associated with the era of Bourbon reform, it is worthwhile to look more closely at the ways in which earlier patterns and practices in the 'near' Atlantic to some degree foreshadowed developments of the later eighteenth century. Venezuela probably offers the best early example of how a relatively peripheral part of the Spanish empire functioned in the context of both colonial and Atlantic worlds.[17]

From an early time Venezuela participated in both inter-colonial and Atlantic trades. Its early commercial development involved the production of wheat and flour exported mainly to Cartagena to supply the fleets and Caribbean ports. By the end of the sixteenth century wheat had lost ground to two other export crops, tobacco and cacao; already by 1650 the latter had become Venezuela's largest—and rapidly growing—export, with most of the cacao going to Mexico, underselling (and thus undercutting) Central American exports. In the early period of the expansion of the cacao trade Portuguese merchants played an important role, providing African slaves and buying up cacao for export to Mexico. At least in the first half of the seventeenth century the Portuguese were prominent in Venezuela not only as merchants but also as farmers and *encomenderos*. The early cacao producers, a diverse group with origins in Portugal, the Basque country, the Canary Islands, and Santo Domingo, not only had maritime and commercial experience but 'trading contacts in new regions, Africa, the Canaries, and Caribbean ports'.[18] Despite a decline in demand for Venezuelan cacao at mid-century, probably due to a combination of growing competition from Guayaquil cacao, currency problems,[19] and the withdrawal of the Portuguese merchants from the trade, the Venezuelan trade survived, as planters began dealing with Dutch merchants and obtaining African slaves from nearby Dutch Curaçao. Yet dependence on the Dutch for trade was no substitute for the access to New Spanish silver that planters had

---

[16] See Lance R. Grahn, 'An Irresoluble Dilemma: Smuggling in New Granada, 1713–1763', in John R. Fisher, Allan J. Kuethe, and Anthony McFarlane (eds.), *Reform and Insurrection in Bourbon New Granada and Peru* (Baton Rouge, LA, 1990), 123.

[17] This discussion is based on Robert J. Ferry's *The Colonial Elite of Early Caracas: Formation and Crisis, 1567–1767* (Berkeley and Los Angeles, CA, 1989).

[18] Ibid. 57.

[19] On the currency problems of the mid-seventeenth century and their impact on Central America, see Macleod, *Spanish Central America*, chapter 15.

once enjoyed and the fortunes of Venezuela's cacao planters revived only in the late seventeenth century, when they once again began to supply the Mexican market.

Here, then, Atlantic trends and personnel played a significant role in the commercial development of this part of the Spanish empire while at the same time it remained fully part of the imperial system of Spanish inter-colonial and transatlantic exchange. Jurisdictional changes underscore the complexity of Venezuela's situation, as in the second decade of the eighteenth century it became part of the new viceroyalty of New Granada and was placed under the authority of the *audiencia* (high court) of Santa Fe de Bogotá. At about the same time the establishment in 1728 of the Real Compañía Guipuzcoana de Caracas, which would enjoy a monopoly over cacao exports to Spain, signalled the growing economic activism of the Bourbons.[20] In authorizing the Basque company's ships to sail between San Sebastián (after a required stop in Cádiz to pay taxes) and Caracas, the chartering of the Guipuzcoana Company also anticipated a reform implemented much later in the eighteenth century, *comercio libre* (free trade), whereby a number of Spanish and Spanish American ports were permitted to participate in direct trade.

The lure of the booming cacao economy of the late seventeenth and eighteenth centuries brought new emigrants to the colony, especially Basques and Canary Islanders. Their presence in Venezuela—where their experience would differ considerably—reflects significant demographic and commercial shifts towards the Atlantic periphery of Spain and the continued diversity of Spain itself. Although Basques long were associated with mining and entrepreneurial activities in Spanish America, in Venezuela they combined commercial dominance with political clout, with Basques serving as governors in the 1730s and 1740s. Emigrants from the Canaries found themselves at almost the opposite end of the socio-economic spectrum. Hoping to become prosperous cacao growers, many ended up working as sharecroppers and came to be regarded in much the same light as African slaves, that is, as a potential labour pool, especially after the failure of a 1749 revolt against the company's monopoly.

Thus the reorganization of government and trade in eighteenth-century Venezuela had some unanticipated consequences. As long as the British South Sea Company[21] provided sufficient numbers of slaves and paid good prices for cacao to be sold in Mexico, both prices and slave supplies remained high and the cacao economy could continue to expand. The end of the *asiento* authorizing the British to supply African slaves had a negative impact on both, fostering discontent and economic contraction. Smuggling increased, with hundreds of Spaniards living on the Dutch islands of Bonaire and Curaçao and presumably involved in contraband activity, while Spanish sailors manned Dutch ships that brought cacao from Venezuela to the islands. Participants in the rebellion of 1749, led by *isleño* Juan Francisco de León, included Canary

---

[20] The crown had begun to regulate Cuban tobacco even earlier; see Sherry Johnson, *The Social Transformation of Eighteenth-Century Cuba* (Gainesville, FL, 2001), 26.

[21] The British received the monopoly, or *asiento*, for the slave trade by the terms of the Treaty of Utrecht of 1713; the contract expired in 1739.

Islanders as well as free blacks, fugitive slaves, and Indians. Members of the elite who resented the policies of the Guipuzcoana Company and of the Basque governors backed it as well. The revolt was suppressed, with lower-class participants predictably facing the harshest punishments. Although subsequent modifications in the relationship between the Company and the cacao planters satisfied some elite demands, a heavy-handed application of royal rule accompanied these changes. Thus a royal commercial monopoly and thoroughgoing change in the form and style of government brought the Habsburg-era mode of consensus-building and accommodation of local interests to an end, ushering Venezuela into the Bourbon age.

REORGANIZATION AND REFORM

Developments and events that had taken place in Venezuela by the mid-eighteenth century anticipated others that occurred later elsewhere in the Spanish empire. The Bourbon programme of reform in many ways responded to changes that already had taken place while producing further change. Had Venezuela not already developed a successful export economy, the crown would not have chartered a company to regulate the cacao trade. If the volume of transatlantic commerce and of both legal and contraband trade with foreigners had not increased exponentially, the *comercio libre* policy of opening more ports in Spain and Spanish America to direct trade similarly would have had little meaning. Incentives offered to mining entrepreneurs to invest in the renovation or opening of mines and expand production succeeded because the capital, expertise, and necessary pool of skilled labour existed in New Spain, where indeed the expansion of the mining sector and revenues sent to Spain already was under way. Reform to a great extent followed reality, but the new realities that the reforms produced did not always conform to expectations. Some measures proved a dead letter, others were introduced erratically and so late that their impact was limited, and yet others—particularly those involving new (or newly enforced) forms of taxation—set off strong, sometimes violent, reactions.

Scholars increasingly challenge the assumption that the Bourbon Reforms represented a thoroughgoing break with Habsburg practices and policies.[22] Neither the personnel nor the practices of the Habsburg era disappeared suddenly or definitively, and their retention often blunted and blurred the impact of change. The reforms, introduced most widely if not uniformly in the later eighteenth century, had complex if uneven effects throughout Spanish America. They helped to foster economic growth and institutional change as well as concomitant frustration on the part of Americans in their challenge to local interests and prerogatives. In some cases the reforms were ineffective or failed entirely to correct long-standing abuses. Thus while some of the

---

[22] See, for example, William B. Taylor, *Magistrates of the Sacred* (Stanford, CA, 1996).

late colonial revolts hinged on resentment of Bourbon policies designed to increase revenues through new or more efficient forms of taxation, others were rooted in much longer-standing problems. The massive uprising in Peru in 1780–1 known as the Tupac Amaru revolt was associated with the widespread practice of forced sale of goods to Indian communities (*reparto de bienes* or *mercancías*), a system that arose in part because salaries paid to the administrators (*corregidores*) of Indian districts were deficient. Their replacement by the *subdelegados* of the later Bourbon era did not rectify the problem, as the new officials were no more adequately compensated than their predecessors; indeed the Bourbons finally institutionalized the controversial practice by giving it legal sanction.

The reform programme, and the royal advisers and officials in Spain and Spanish America who were its greatest advocates and practitioners, reflected Spain's connections with the European intellectual milieu of the Enlightenment, which exercised a strong influence in the Spanish empire. While the 'French connection' established by the creation of the Bourbon monarchy played an important role in the introduction of Enlightenment ideas in Spain and the empire, as did the contributions of foreigners like Alexander von Humboldt, who travelled through much of Spanish America, Enlightenment thought and its practical and empirical applications took on a distinctly Spanish cast. The considerable influence exercised by members of the Gálvez family—committed Enlightenment thinkers and reformers—in both Spain and Spanish America underscores the simultaneously Spanish and Atlantic character of the ideas and motivations that underlay the reform programme.[23] Indeed the importance of men like José de Gálvez, Baylio Fray Julián de Arriaga, and the Marqués de Bajamar, all of whom served as secretary of state for the Indies, exemplifies the key roles that men with American experience would play in the formation of Spanish policy.[24]

The reforms targeted several principal areas: administration and government; the military and defence; economic life; and the Church. Committed reformers took a keen interest in measures affecting civic life as well. The discussion here, however, mainly concerns aspects of the reforms that had the greatest significance for the Spanish empire in the context of the Atlantic world.[25]

At one level the most general purpose of the reforms was to increase revenues to pay for the growing costs of defence in an era when the Spanish empire was expanding and, more than any time in the past, directly confronting and engaging other European powers over a very large area—the Atlantic and Pacific coasts of South America, North

[23] José de Gálvez spent six years (1765–71) in New Spain conducting an important general inspection and returned to Spain to serve as minister of the Indies from 1776 to 1787. His brother Matías de Gálvez served as viceroy of New Spain (1783–4), as did Matías's son Bernardo de Gálvez, who previously had governed Louisiana, where he married into a leading French family. The intendants of Puebla and Valladolid (and later Guanajuato) in New Spain were Bernardo's in-laws; see Johnson, *Social Transformation*, 100.
[24] On this see Mark A. Burkholder, 'The Council of the Indies in the Late Eighteenth Century: A New Perspective', *Hispanic American Historical Review*, 56/3 (1976), 404–23.
[25] For a succinct, useful overview of the reforms, see Bakewell, *A History of Latin America*, chapter 18.

America from Florida to California, and—as ever—the Caribbean. The creation of a new system of well-paid provincial administrators called *intendentes* (after the French *intendant*), who received broad (if somewhat ambiguous) powers over treasury, war, civic order, and justice, was meant at least in part to help regularize the collection of taxes as well as to extend the reach of royal government. Measures taken to limit the prerogatives and influence of the Church and clergy also bore a relationship to revenue concerns. The expulsion of the Jesuits from the Spanish empire meant the confiscation and sale (for the benefit of the royal treasury) of their properties, and the draconian *Consolidación de Vales Reales* of 1804, by which the crown required that church funds be turned over to the royal treasury and that people who owed money to the Church pay off their loans in short order, also was designed to raise revenue. Policies meant to stimulate mining and trade, and the establishment of new monopolies (such as those over tobacco and *aguardiente*), also reflected the crown's drive to expand economic production and tax revenues.

The crown's defence concerns certainly were real. Spain was at war, mainly with the British, during much of the second half of the eighteenth century. With their expanding naval power, the British, Dutch, and French even by the middle of the seventeenth century readily could reach once remote places in the South Atlantic. The British and French established short-lived bases in the Falkland Islands and demonstrated that they could regularly reach the Pacific coast of Chile and Peru. The British even began to show some interest in California—as did the Russians. In south-eastern North America Spanish Florida and British Georgia existed in close and tense proximity, and in the early eighteenth century Spaniards undertook the colonization of Texas at least in part to keep the French in Louisiana at bay.[26]

Military reforms, which had a varying impact, entailed several approaches to the problem of defence: the enormously expensive refurbishing of fortifications at strategic ports such as Havana and San Juan de Puerto Rico; the expansion of the navy; reorganization and militarization of some jurisdictions (such as the vast area of northern New Spain renamed the *Provincias Internas*) and expansion in the size and number of *presidios* (military garrisons); the creation of regular army units; and the reorganization and expansion of militias throughout Spanish America.[27] In many senses these measures were successful and accomplished their objectives. The Spanish navy became second in size only to the British, largely due to the productivity of Cuban

---

[26] The French on the Gulf Coast never proved a military threat to New Spain; indeed settlers at the isolated first Spanish capital of Texas, Los Adaes, often depended on the French settlement of Natchitoches, or even New Orleans, for trade and supplies.

[27] There is a substantial literature on military reform and its impact; see Johnson, *Social Transformation*; Allan J. Kuethe, *Cuba, 1753–1815: Crown, Military, and Society* (Knoxville, TN, 1986) and *Military Reform and Society in New Granada, 1773–1808* (Gainesville, FL, 1978); Christon Archer, *The Army in Bourbon Mexico, 1760–1810* (Albuquerque, NM, 1977); Leon C. Campbell, *The Military and Society in Colonial Peru, 1750–1810* (Philadelphia, PA, 1978); and Allan J. Kuethe and Juan Marchena F. (eds.), *Soldados del rey: el ejército borbónico en América colonial en vísperas de la Independencia* (Castelló de la Plana, 2005).

shipyards. Bernardo de Gálvez' 1781 victory at Pensacola contributed to the British loss of its North American colonies and the substantial reduction of a British military threat to Spanish territories. Yet it has been argued that Spain achieved its military and naval recovery at a crippling price, directing a huge portion of its colonial revenues towards defence rather than using them to invest in more productive kinds of development.[28]

Although the implementation of the military reforms was an imperial project, they enhanced the Atlantic aspects of imperial relations by bringing thousands of Spanish officers and soldiers to Spanish America. In some instances—notably in Cuba—Spaniards undercut creole dominance, although many Spanish military officers married into local families. The same might be said for administrative restructuring that allowed the crown to implement its policy of reducing creole influence in office-holding by appointing peninsular Spaniards, frequently military men, to new adminis-trative offices. At the same time the effort to maintain not only regular army units but well-trained and equipped militias had the paradoxical effect of creating groups that were granted a new form of privilege—the *fuero militar*—at a time when the enlightened monarchy was trying to eliminate enclaves of special privilege. Further-more soldiers could be a highly disruptive presence in ports and cities where Bourbons hoped to promote greater civil order and refinement of behaviour.[29]

International conflict had complex repercussions in Spanish American society and economy. The Spanish cession of Florida to the British at the end of the Seven Years War meant the evacuation of most of Spanish Florida's diverse residents—Canary Islanders, German Catholics, free blacks—to Cuba.[30] Interruptions in trade due to war created more opportunities for Spanish Americans to trade legally with other countries; for Mexico and Cuba this meant trade with the USA especially. The periodic flooding of the Mexican market with cheap goods undermined New Spain's flourishing textile industry. Rising textile exports from Catalonia in Spain accounted for some of the competition, although British textiles also entered the American market. British eco-nomic clout meant that British officials and traders could offer generous terms of trade to Indian groups that remained independent of Spanish rule but lived in close enough proximity that they could foment disorder and threaten outlying settlements; British dealings with the Creeks in south-eastern North America, the Miskitos and Cunas on the Caribbean coast of Central America, or the Guajiros of north-eastern New Granada often undermined Spanish security. The French, then the British, and later the Anglo-Americans armed the Comanches, while Cherokees, Chicasaws, and other groups also obtained arms from the British. Given their limited military successes in dealing with independent Indian groups, Spanish officials turned to giving gifts and medals and

[28] See Allan J. Kuethe, 'Carlos III, absolutismo ilustrado e imperio americano', in Kuethe and Marchena (eds.), *Soldados del rey*.

[29] Juan Marchena F., 'Sin temor de rey ni de dios: violencia, corrupción y crisis de autoridad en la Cartagena colonial', in Kuethe and Marchena (eds.), *Soldados del rey*, 48–51, identifies eighteen revolts by military units from 1710 to 1787, from Campeche to Chile. Soldiers usually demanded payment of back salary or better treatment and conditions of service.

[30] Johnson, *Social Transformation*, 47–8.

lavishly entertaining Indian leaders and their entourages, an expensive practice they copied from the British and French which was at odds with their traditional policy of not providing alcohol or arms to (or indeed negotiating with) Native Americans.[31]

Louisiana, acquired from France in 1763 in compensation for Spanish support (and losses) in the Seven Years War, in many ways exemplified the articulation of the Atlantic world on the periphery of the Spanish empire and the new direction set by the Bourbon reformers.[32] Louisiana was the first important Spanish American territory previously settled by another European power. The Spanish regime there in many ways proved to be moderate and flexible, fostering a fluidity in social relations and economic affairs that helped to transform New Orleans from an insignificant backwater of the French empire into a bustling, cosmopolitan port. Under Spain New Orleans increasingly linked the settlements of the Upper and Lower Mississippi River valley to the larger world of the Caribbean and Atlantic. New Orleans and Louisiana thus became integrated into the Spanish empire while still maintaining significant ties with France and the French empire and also forging enduring connections with the United States.

The realities of Louisiana's geopolitical situation fostered unanticipated accommodations. The Spanish crown hoped to attract more people to Louisiana to secure it against external challenges. Sponsoring colonization by Canary Islanders and other Spaniards proved prohibitively expensive, however, and often these settlement efforts fell short of expectations. With insufficient numbers of Spanish settlers, officials began to accept Catholics of any nationality. Spanish Louisiana welcomed French Acadians who had been expelled from Nova Scotia after the British conquest of Canada, as well as immigrants from France and later from Saint-Domingue. Immigration policy was further liberalized as Anglos and Anglo-Americans also were permitted to settle there and in Texas, initially in the expectation that they would convert to Catholicism. As it became clear that that hope was unlikely to be fulfilled, Spanish officials embraced a policy of religious laissez-faire in relation to the non-Spanish and non-Catholic residents of their territory, as long as the practice of Protestantism remained strictly private.

Thus the combination of pragmatic adaptation to existing circumstances and attempts to implement some of the reforms of the Bourbon era led to compromises. With regard to trade also the Spanish regime in Louisiana moved progressively towards greater flexibility and openness. In 1768 commerce between Louisiana and nine Spanish ports was officially endorsed, in keeping with the newly adopted Bourbon policy of 'free trade'. In 1782 direct trade between New Orleans and Pensacola and France also was permitted. Spanish attempts to limit commercial traffic in the lower Mississippi to Spanish ships were undermined by contraband, subterfuge, and the dispensing of

---

[31] David J. Weber, *Bárbaros: Spaniards and their Savages in the Age of Enlightenment* (New Haven, CT, 2005), 142, 161–2, 189–91.

[32] This discussion draws mainly on Gilbert C. Din (ed.), *The Spanish Presence in Louisiana*, The Louisiana Purchase Bicentennial Series in Louisiana History, 2 (Lafayette, LA, 1996); and Kimberly S. Hanger, *Bounded Lives, Bounded Places: Free Black Society in Colonial New Orleans, 1769–1803* (Durham, NC, 1997).

special licences. New Orleans in any case was becoming more dependent on imports of American staples produced upriver. The 1795 Treaty of San Lorenzo granted US citizens the right to navigate the Mississippi and ship their goods from New Orleans.

While the Spaniards were forced to make a series of concessions to French and American interests, these compromises by no means were unique to Louisiana, nor did they arise solely out of internal pressures within the colony. International conflicts caused major disruptions in transatlantic trade, and Spain had to make similar concessions in other parts of the empire in order to keep Spanish American ports supplied with needed goods. The neutrality and expanding productivity and markets of the USA made it the obvious choice to fill the supply gap. Louisiana's situation, of course, was unique because of its proximity to the USA and the increasing numbers of Americans who settled there, especially in the area around Natchez. Yet at the end of the eighteenth century Louisiana still was far from being (Anglo) Americanized, and indeed the largest numbers of residents there and in West Florida were African slaves.[33]

Military and naval expansion, growth in administrative and bureaucratic posts for which peninsulars were eligible and often preferred, and economic expansion brought significant numbers of immigrants from Spain to Spanish America in this period. In contrast to the earlier period, by the latter part of the eighteenth century many emigrants originated in northern Spain—Galicia and Cantabria. Basques, as seen, continued to figure prominently as merchants and miners, and the overcrowded Canary Islands sent people to destinations thought unlikely to attract many people on their own, such as Texas, Louisiana, and Florida, as well as to Cuba. Probably most emigrants headed to the rapidly developing, formerly peripheral parts of the empire— the Río de la Plata region, Venezuela, and Cuba. Spanish American societies became increasingly diverse demographically and economically as a result of immigration, internal migration, and burgeoning regional and international economies. The arrival of African slaves transformed the racial composition of places like coastal Venezuela and Colombia, Cuba, and Buenos Aires and contributed to population increase. The population of Buenos Aires, for example, rose from 12,000 to some 50,000 between 1750 and 1800.

Despite the secularizing tendencies of the Bourbon programme of reform, which sought to reduce clerical privilege and influence and strengthen civil authority, the many entities that constituted the Roman Catholic Church still figured largely in Spanish America; churches, monasteries, convents, seminaries, and their personnel continued to exercise great influence in colonial society and economy. In territories such as California and Texas, Franciscan missions played a key role in helping to establish a Spanish presence and working to bring indigenous groups under Spanish control.

---

[33] During the Spanish period, at least in lower Louisiana, slaves of African origin and descent constituted the largest segment of the population. The census of 1800, which included West Florida, counted nearly 20,000 free residents, compared to over 24,000 slaves; see figure 8 in Gwendolyn Midlo Hall, *Africans in Colonial Louisiana* (Baton Rouge, LA, 1992), 279.

REACTION AND REVOLT

The late colonial revolts were complex, seldom having a single cause.[34] They often took place in situations of economic stress or downturn that the innovations introduced by the Bourbon Reforms—especially those entailing more regular (and often rigorous) collection of taxes or the creation of new monopolies—exacerbated. For all that the late eighteenth-century economy appeared to be flourishing, indications are that real wages along with workers' leverage were diminishing in many instances, so the revolts often were grounded in economic insecurity. In Venezuela the Canary Islanders responded to the contraction of the cacao economy, for which they blamed the royally chartered Guipuzcoana Company, while in Paraguay the Guaraní who were ordered to vacate the mission communities resisted surrendering their homes, prosperous mate and cotton plantations, and cattle ranches.

The late colonial rebellions were similar to earlier protests, riots, and revolts in that they articulated discontent with changes in customary practices and policies that in the later eighteenth century might occur in a larger context of economic stress. They differed—as seen in León's revolt in Venezuela—from earlier events in that they often involved more than one ethnic or socio-economic group, including (at least initially) elites who felt aggrieved by the impact of certain reforms. Upper-class support, however, often evaporated in the face of burgeoning expressions of working- or lower-class discontent that seemed likely to shift in focus to target all the powerful economic and political groups of society (rather than, say, just peninsular Spaniards). This phenomenon characterized movements as dissimilar as the 1765 urban 'rebellion of the barrios' in Quito[35] (which became increasingly 'popular' and anti-peninsular) and the Túpac Amaru revolt, which initially had appealed to creoles and mestizos but soon became a largely indigenous revolt against the colonial order. The late colonial revolts also often were much more destructive and deadly than those of an earlier period and, in the case of the series of upheavals in the Andean region, more tenacious. Yet it is notable, despite all the changes that had taken place in the Spanish empire by this time, that as in earlier years these later revolts for the most part did not reflect developments and events of the Atlantic world but rather the internal strains and contradictions of the empire itself.

The chief exception to this generalization was the Guaraní rebellion. The 1750 Treaty of Madrid entailed the exchange of Spanish territory occupied by seven Jesuit missions

[34] The literature on the late colonial revolts is extensive; see, among others, John L. Phelan, *The People and the King: The Comunero Revolution in Colombia, 1781* (Madison, WI, 1978); Scarlott O'Phelan Godoy, *Rebellions and Revolts in Eighteenth Century Peru and Upper Peru* (Cologne, 1985); Steve J. Stern (ed.), *Resistance, Rebellion and Consciousness in the Andean Peasant World, 18th to 20th Centuries* (Madison, WI, 1980); Fisher, Kuethe, and McFarlane, *Reform and Insurrection*.

[35] See Anthony McFarlane, 'The Rebellion of the Barrios: Urban Insurrection in Bourbon Quito', in Fisher, Kuethe, and McFarlane, *Reform and Insurrection*.

east of the Uruguay River in return for Portuguese withdrawal from the area of Uruguay across the Río de la Plata from Buenos Aires.[36] The nearly 30,000 Guaraní living in the flourishing missions—many of them descendants of families who had settled there generations before—could remain under Portuguese rule or opt to move to Spanish territory on the other side of the river. Many Jesuits objected to the agreement and tried to delay its implementation, but none joined the armed rebellion, which began in February 1752. The resort to arms was not their only approach, however. Guaraní leaders wrote letters (in their own language), questioning why their loyalty and service to the king had brought undeserved punishment, and prepared and distributed printed leaflets in an effort to persuade the Indians on missions unaffected by the treaty to support their cause. Although poorly armed, the Guaraní had the advantage of their militia experience, as the threat from Portuguese slavers had necessitated that the missions have the means to defend themselves. A joint Portuguese-Spanish force finally brought the conflict to an end in early 1756. Many Guaraní fled the missions, some to work on Spanish farms or ranches or to live in towns, others to settle in Brazil. Several thousand more abandoned the *reducciones* after the expulsion of the Jesuits in 1767.

Despite its Atlantic dimensions and the Guaraní's use of modern tactics such as printed propaganda, the rebellion was conservative in ideology and intent; the rebels wanted to preserve what, under the Jesuits, had become their traditional way of life. Although the Jesuits had provided the direction for the missions, the Guaraní felt little strong loyalty towards them; their expulsion did not set off more violent protests. The late eighteenth-century revolts were conservative not only in intent but often in outcome as well. In Peru following the rebellions of Túpac Amaru and Túpac Katari the *corregidores* were eliminated and an *audiencia* was established for Cuzco, while in both Quito in the 1760s and New Granada following the Comuneros revolt of 1781 the official response was to back down on tax collection and royal monopolies. These outcomes again suggest that the tensions and protests of the late colonial period in most of Spanish America above all were a reaction to the measures imposed by the later Bourbon kings, especially in situations where longer-standing grievances went unaddressed. Rebels more probably looked inward and back to the consensual, corporate model of the Habsburg monarchy for their ideology and proposed solutions rather than outward to the revolutionary currents and rhetoric of the Atlantic world.

The Bourbon programme of reform aimed to foster closer integration of the Spanish empire with Spain itself by promoting the participation of Americans (or those with American experience) in government and policy-making in Spain while installing growing numbers of *peninsulares* in civil and military office in the colonies. Economic policies favoured at least some producers and entrepreneurs—miners in New Spain, tobacco farmers in Louisiana—and in some respects imperial rule responded to the particularities of regional variation. Nonetheless, aspects of the reforms proved

---

[36] This discussion is based on Ganson, *The Guaraní*. The rebellion is the subject of a 1986 British film, *The Mission*.

disruptive internally at a time when external forces—growing northern European commercial power and international economic competition, increasing size and complexity of international conflict, articulation of new political and social ideologies—also began to have an impact on Spanish America. The complex interplay of these forces underlay the movements for independence of the early nineteenth century.

BIBLIOGRAPHY

Bakewell, Peter, *A History of Latin America c.1450 to the Present* (2nd edn. Oxford, 2004).

Brown, Richmond F. (ed.), *Coastal Encounters: The Transformation of the Gulf South in the Eighteenth Century* (Lincoln, NE, 2007).

Elliott, J. H., *Empires of the Atlantic World: Britain and Spain in America, 1492–1830* (New Haven, CT, 2006).

Ferry, Robert J., *The Colonial Elite of Early Caracas: Formation and Crisis, 1567–1767* (Berkeley and Los Angeles, CA, 1989).

Ganson, Barbara, *The Guaraní under Spanish Rule in the Río de la Plata* (Stanford, CA, 2003).

Hanger, Kimberly S., *Bounded Lives, Bounded Places: Free Black Society in Colonial New Orleans, 1769–1803* (Durham, NC, 1997).

Johnson, Sherry, *The Social Transformation of Eighteenth-Century Cuba* (Gainesville, FL, 2001).

Kuethe, Allan J., and Juan Marchena F. (eds.), *Soldados del rey: el ejército borbónico en América colonial en vísperas de la Independencia* (Castelló de la Plana, 2005).

Lane, Kris E., *Pillaging the Empire: Piracy in the Americas, 1500–1750* (Armonk, NY, 1998).

Lynch, John, *The Hispanic World in Crisis and Change, 1598–1700* (Oxford, 1992).

MacLeod, Murdo, *Spanish Central America: A Socioeconomic History, 1520–1720* (Austin, TX, 2008).

Pescador, Juan Javier, *The New World Inside a Basque Village: The Oiartzun Valley and its Atlantic Emigrants, 1550–1800* (Reno, NV, 2004).

Stein, Stanley J., and Barbara H. Stein, *Silver, Trade, and War: Spain and America in the Making of Early Modern Europe* (Baltimore, MD, 2000).

Weber, David J., *Bárbaros: Spaniards and their Savages in the Age of Enlightenment* (New Haven, CT, 2005).

CHAPTER 12

···

THE PORTUGUESE ATLANTIC WORLD, C.1650–C.1760

···

A. J. R. RUSSELL-WOOD

AFTER sixty years of Spanish rule, Restoration in 1640 saw the accession to the Portuguese throne of the duke of Braganza as Dom João IV. This did not erase Portuguese guilt by association. Spain's enemies still harassed Portugal. The Dutch suspended trade with Portugal and sought spices, sugar, and slaves in their places of origin. By 1663, Portuguese holdings in Asia were severely reduced. In the Atlantic, the Dutch occupied the north-east of Brazil (1630–54), major ports of Angola (1640–8), and the archipelago of São Tomé and Príncipe. Portugal regained these. The only irrevocable Portuguese loss in the Atlantic was São Jorge da Mina on the Gold Coast. Dom João sought international support against Castile. Treaties were forged and tensions with European powers, including Spain, were resolved diplomatically by 1668, but at a price. Portugal's rivals obtained elsewhere goods originally supplied by Portuguese colonies, especially sugar and tobacco from Brazil. Dutch, English, and French corsairs, Turks, and Barbary pirates continued to challenge Portuguese vessels and harass settlements.

Continuity within the Atlantic, in contrast to disruption east of the Cape of Good Hope, underlines how deeply over two centuries Portugal had become entrenched in the Atlantic. At a time when Dom João, confronted by Dutch conquests in Asia and English predations in the Persian Gulf, refocused on the Atlantic, other Europeans were aggressively advancing their interests in the Atlantic and in Asia. The Dutch had the largest merchant fleet of any European nation. The Portuguese role must be seen in this international context of interaction with European and non-European states or kingdoms, and how the Portuguese Atlantic was irrevocably linked to lands and seas east of the Cape of Good Hope and west of the Strait of Magellan.[1]

---

[1] A. H. de Oliveira Marques, *History of Portugal*, i: *From Lusitania to Empire* (New York, 1972), 133–63, 217–70, 335–78.

MARITIME

A Portuguese sphere of influence in the Atlantic in this period extended from Morocco south to Benguela in Africa and from the River Amazon to Río de la Plata in South America. Portuguese holdings included extremes of physical features, climate, seismicity, soils, and vegetation. Each region was *sui generis*. At worst, this led to commercial and demographic isolation; at best, to complementary crops and exports, integration into commercial and migratory networks, and exchanges of peoples and cultures. The most dominant and all pervasive feature was the ocean. The Atlantic played a role in setting rhythms of empire, impacted on governance, communications, commerce, migration, cultural exchanges, movements of flora and fauna, and even how individuals identified themselves. Routes connected all points in the Portuguese Atlantic, and Portuguese archipelagos were points of articulation between North and South and East and West.

The Atlantic has always been central to the history of Portugal.[2] From the late seventeenth century there was intensive shipbuilding in private shipyards in Brazil. This accelerated in the eighteenth century with vessels for African and European routes. By century's end more vessels were built in Brazilian yards than in Portugal. Vessels for the India run were also built in royal shipyards in Brazil. Vessels for Atlantic trade were now better built, larger, with more capacity, and incorporated changes in design, rigging, and sails. The entry fee to be a player in Atlantic trade was much less than for the Cape route. No Atlantic route exceeded three months port to port. This was an incentive for individuals, merchant consortia, and businessmen to commission building of relatively cheap and speedy vessels. A combination of market conditions of supply and demand, bulkier cargoes, more trans-shipments, and a more sophisticated infrastructure—harbour facilities, banking/agents and insurance— contributed to ever more intensive use of the Atlantic by Portugal and its colonies.[3]

Time and distance exacted a toll on sailors and their families. Conditions on board were spare and rations barely adequate. Seasonally variable wind systems and out-of-season departures exposed crews to being becalmed in the doldrums outward-bound from Portugal or suffering heavy weather homeward-bound. Sailors were often in poor condition when signing on, susceptible to disease, and were hospitalized in Brazilian ports or in Luanda. Sailors jumping ship in Brazil and onboard mortality led to constant turnover and undermanned vessels. Crews included Africans, Afro-Brazilians, non-Portuguese Europeans, and Orientals.

---

[2] A. J. R. Russell-Wood, 'Portuguese Literature', in John Hattendorf (ed.), *The Oxford Encyclopedia of Maritime History* (Oxford, 2003), iii. 358–65.

[3] Patrick O'Flanagan, *Port Cities of Atlantic Iberia, c.1500–1900* (Aldershot, 2008); A. J. R. Russell-Wood, 'Ports of Colonial Brazil', in Franklin Knight and Peggy Liss (eds.), *Atlantic Port Cities: Economy, Culture, and Society in the Atlantic World, 1650–1850* (Knoxville, TN, 1991), 196–239.

When considering maritime policies and practices, Portuguese kings weighed commercial benefits against political interests and diplomatic relations with European and other rulers. It was not in the national interest to exacerbate sometimes prickly relations with England, but contraband by English vessels was rampant. English naval cover provided by the Methuen Treaty (1703) was a mixed blessing. Particularly sensitive was that Royal Navy vessels and the Falmouth Packet, immune to search by Portuguese authorities, spirited Brazilian bullion from the River Tagus to England. When the king of Dahomey expressed enthusiasm to governors and viceroys for more intensive trade between his kingdom and Brazil, and that acceptance could lead to concession of land for a fort and trading station, diplomatic and strategic factors became part of the decision-making equation. Portuguese kings weighed authorizing transatlantic voyages by individual vessels against the security provided by convoys or fleets. In 1706, vessels from Pernambuco, Salvador, and Rio de Janeiro combined into a single Lisbon-bound fleet of 150 vessels, larger than fleets on the India run. A Jesuit, António Vieira, enamoured of the Dutch and English India Companies, sold the idea of a Brazil Company to Dom João IV. Poor organization led to its transformation from a private stock-holding company into a crown company, which was dissolved in 1720. This did not dissuade private companies, of even shorter lifespans, from West African commerce.

During his reign (1706–50), Dom João V opened Santos to Portuguese vessels as a port of final destination, and banned vessels from Brazilian ports bound for Portugal from putting into African ports. Royal interventions were motivated by zealous protection of national interests, distrust of foreign interlopers, and abhorrence of contraband. Kings were aware of homeward-bound East Indiamen deviating from regular routes to put into Luanda to exchange oriental wares for African goods, cross the Atlantic to Brazil, and trade oriental luxury items and exotica and African goods for American gold, silver, diamonds, gemstones, and tobacco to take (often clandestinely) to Portugal. Coastal geography, distance between ports, ineffectual coastguards, smugglers' ingenuity, captains' intransigence, and rampant inter-colonial trade undermined regulations. Mercantilism and protectionism were conceits rather than attainable goals. French attacks and brief occupation of Rio de Janeiro and harassment of Bahia by English corsairs showed how vulnerable were even major ports during Brazil's 'golden age'.

People

Portuguese emigrated throughout the Atlantic. The period 1650–1760 saw a shift from emigrants who came principally from agricultural or artisanal backgrounds to emigrants with professional experience and more diverse skill sets. These included masters of their trades, pharmacists, lawyers, and physicians. Seasoned businessmen became commonplace. Metropolitan families dispatched relatives to Atlantic ports to acquire experience and build networks. Emigration was still predominantly of single males, but (depending on period, origin, and destination) there were more family units. Push factors included epidemics, famine, war, unavailability of adequate land to make a living, and laws of primogeniture. Pull factors included a spirit of adventure, opportunism, and unrealistic expectations. For some, to stay in Portugal meant a prison sentence, religious persecution, or the galleys. For others with liquid assets, a profession, skills, or aptitudes, the colonies presented opportunities for a more secure financial position, acquisition of prestige, and reinforcement of social status. Merely crossing the Atlantic induced self-ennoblement. To be a Portuguese-born living overseas carried a cachet unattainable to peers in Portugal. Circumstance of birth improved a male migrant's ability to find a partner in marriage or made him eligible for public office in a colony denied to locally born. Birthplace, religious orthodoxy, and racial 'purity' (white on maternal and paternal sides over three generations) could be more important overseas than in Portugal. In Brazil and Portuguese Africa a social hierarchy was based on a complex interweave of factors, including colour, perceptions, and personal 'qualities'.

Atlantic colonies ran the gamut from undesirable to highly desirable. West and Central Africa were undesirable. Climate and disease were hostile to Europeans. Madeira and the Azores were highly regarded but, by mid-seventeenth century, were overcrowded. Earlier migrants were moving to Brazil. The eighteenth century saw Brazil emerging in popular imagination as a land of opportunity. Between the 1690s and 1750, serial gold strikes spurred waves of migrants from Portugal and Atlantic islands. Together with massive internal migrations, these transformed settlement patterns in Brazil. Some migrants enjoyed great success; some eked out a livelihood; others died in poverty; still others were part of a reverse migration. Many expected to spend a few years overseas and return to bedazzle former neighbours with their riches. A few did return. Most died far from the land of their birth. Apathy, investment in land or commerce, a guaranteed livelihood, sense of achievement, a new family, or refusal to admit error led many to stay overseas. That, by the later seventeenth and eighteenth centuries, cities and towns in Brazil were comparable to those in Portugal, with religious and civil institutions, and systems of government, made newcomers feel comfortable. Towns in Madeira and the Azores had much in common with those in Portugal. Late eighteenth-century Luanda was a city of considerable style.

Portugal could not have created this Atlantic world without assistance, coerced and voluntary, of non-Europeans. This was less the case in the Madeiras and Azores where persons of European birth or descent were in the majority and where soil, rainfall, and topography favoured agriculture and stock raising. In the Cape Verdes, Upper and Lower Guinea, and Central Africa, Portuguese-born were an overwhelming minority. To build fortresses, trading stations, or settlements on the African continent, where there were established states and commercial systems, was best accomplished by diplomacy and with cooperation and forbearance of local rulers. Those inroads which the Portuguese made in Angola were invariably attributable to indigenous soldiers or middlemen. Africans provided labour and skills in planting, cultivation, harvesting, cutting timber, construction, transportation, sexual relations, and military assistance. The last two were linked in the royal mind in the hope that offspring would become soldiers and settlers. In Africa, local economies were mostly in African hands, as too was acquisition of commodities and their transportation to ports for export.

In Brazil, Portuguese ignored indigenous sovereignty and appropriated lands in the name of the king. They could not easily identify indigenous leaders or recognize evidence of organization, religion, or social hierarchy. Amerindian males were coerced into forced labour, regardless of inconsistent laws prohibiting this, and Amerindian women taken as concubines. Partly as a result of Portuguese need for Amerindian military assistance against the Dutch in the seventeenth century, and with eighteenth-century settlements in frontier regions in the north, south-east and west, Portuguese moved from describing Amerindian peoples generically and became aware of their individuality and distinctiveness. In eighteenth-century Minas Gerais and Mato Grosso governors made overtures to elders and tried to co-opt them or practised a policy of divide and rule. In Brazil, African and Afro-Brazilian slaves were the major source of labour or coexisted with Amerindians in some regions, whereas Amerindian labour was more common on the ever-moving frontiers. African women and women of African descent in Brazil became mistresses and concubines of Portuguese and Luso-Brazilians, but there was a higher incidence than in Africa of lasting bi-racial relationships and even marriage 'at the doors of the church'. Mulattos played a prominent role in Brazil as militiamen, soldiers, merchants, farmers, settlers, and mining entrepreneurs. Some made major contributions to baroque music and the arts.

Africa and Brazil presented challenges which the Portuguese lacked inclination, knowledge, or skills to confront. Africans and Amerindians were indispensable as scouts, guides on trails and rivers, and for knowledge of indigenous flora and fauna. Portuguese depended on Amerindians to share their knowledge of how to harvest and use indigenous plants as food or for their commercial potential. Some Africans had knowledge of mining and metallurgy crucial to Portuguese-born mining entrepreneurs in Brazil. Local economies and markets in Africa were the province of women, as too in Brazil where local marketing was dominated by African- and Brazilian-born slaves and free persons. In Africa and Brazil non-Europeans were visible in local economies and contributed to the Atlantic economy. The few Portuguese and Luso-Brazilian merchants in eighteenth-century Luanda or Benguela outsourced to Africans and to Luso-Africans the task of travel to the interior to round up individuals and take them to ports for embarkation on vessels bound for Brazil. *Mestiços* were empowered. They and African middlemen (*pombeiros*) took their cut on transactions, leading to higher costs to agents or merchants in Benguela or Luanda and to middlemen in Brazil, who passed on increases to purchasers.[4]

The Portuguese Atlantic counted individuals and groups denied full participation in the colonial enterprise. Some were seen as undesirables and, thus, disposables.[5] Roma

---

[4] Joseph C. Miller, *Way of Death: Merchant Capitalism and the Angolan Slave Trade, 1730–1830* (Madison, WI, 1988), 189–90, 242–3, 245–83.

[5] Timothy J. Coates, *Convicts and Orphans: Forced and State-Sponsored Colonizers in the Portuguese Empire, 1550–1755* (Stanford, CA, 2001).

were persecuted and harassed, but formed communities in Angola and Brazil. New Christians established themselves as businessmen, merchants, sugar planters, and mining entrepreneurs. Often they or their descendants married into Old Christian families. Some became Catholic priests; others reportedly held local and crown office in Angola and, possibly, Brazil. African slaves and their Brazilian-born slave offspring had their movements and activities circumscribed, but manumittees owned smallholdings, taverns, and shops, and may have held public offices. Native Americans were never free from abuse or harassment, but many made a living as craftsmen in close vicinity to towns or sold produce, and indirectly contributed to Atlantic commerce.

These individuals formed communities. Roma, self-isolated by language, culture, occupation, and marriage, lived in mobile and fixed communities in coastal areas and in the *sertão* of Brazil and Angola. New Christians engaging primarily in commerce, and known as 'The Portuguese Nation', built bridges between Portuguese and Spanish Atlantics, were part of diasporas reaching to Pacific America and to Asia, and remained active through the late seventeenth century.[6] Africans, Luso-Africans, and Afro-Brazilians—constraints of slavery notwithstanding—shared ethnic and cultural heritages which survived spatial distribution and, in Brazil, were nourished by regular influxes of new slaves. African diasporas throughout the Atlantic were, individually and collectively, transoceanic, transnational (in the European sense), and transcultural (in the African sense) and engaged in reciprocal exchanges between the New World and the Old. Some formed settlements. One such, Palmares in north-eastern Brazil, was eradicated in the 1690s after existing for almost a century. Native Americans formed their own enclaves, as too did Muslim slaves as in Salvador.[7]

These groups shared common features: fluency in languages other than Portuguese; interaction with Portuguese but having discrete communities; strong cultural traditions and ethnic identities not primarily European-based; faith systems existing independently, in parallel, or syncretically with Catholicism. All recognized that Portuguese was the 'official' language, Portuguese modes of behaviour the norm, and Catholicism the only acceptable religion. Speaking languages other than Portuguese, failure to adhere to Portuguese criteria of acceptable conduct and behaviours, and public expressions of faiths other than Catholicism, could result in prison or physical abuse. Such communities epitomized multiculturalism, exchange, interaction, and the anomalous situation of being within and without the Portuguese world. Senegambia, indeed the Upper Guinea coast, provides a case study of the complexity and variety of components which made up identity. Portuguese males, fugitives from the law, religious persecution, or creditors, and adventurers or scouts (*lançados*) had landed—voluntarily or coerced—on the coast. These included Jews and 'New Christians'. The latter often reverted to Judaism. They settled, married African

---

6 José Gonçalves Salvador, *Os Cristãos-Novos e o comércio no Atlântico meridional* (São Paulo, 1978); Daviken Studnicki-Gizbert, *A Nation upon the Ocean Sea: Portugal's Atlantic Diaspora and the Crisis of the Spanish Empire, 1492–1640* (Oxford, 2007), 13, 178–80.

7 Stuart B. Schwartz, *Slaves, Peasants, and Rebels: Reconsidering Brazilian Slavery* (Urbana, IL, 1992), 103–36.

women, and had children who mixed with local peoples. The bi-racial children called themselves 'Portuguese'. Various characteristics contributed to this self-identification: commerce as their major occupation; Portuguese-language speakers, later developing into hybrid creole; adherence to Catholicism, but interlarded with Islamic, Christian, and traditional African beliefs and practices; and material cultures, of which the most important were dwellings with distinctive architecture. Identity markers were not set in stone but were ever changing or reconfigured in new combinations. Initially, such settlers and their descendants were effectively beyond the limits of Portuguese influence. Depending on location, they opted to come under Portuguese jurisdiction rather than being at the mercy of local kings.[8] Settlers from Cape Verde were also of mixed race and, by definition, from within the Portuguese empire albeit speaking creole. French and English later settled in Senegambia, bringing further social and cultural interaction while preserving movement, change, and fluidity, which characterized the early modern Atlantic.

There were other Europeans in this 'Portuguese Atlantic world'. Transportation was frequently in Dutch vessels. French physicians in Brazil were reputed to have a cure for syphilis. There were settlements of English, Irish, French, and Spanish in the Amazon. In Brazil there were English consuls and Dutch families as legal residents. In the Gulf of Guinea and on the mainland in Central Africa, Europeans established trading posts in what Portuguese considered their bailiwick. That these handled an ever more intensive trade and diverse range of commodities made contraband attractive. This was conducted by Lisbon-based Portuguese merchants; by Portuguese merchants in Brazil; by Brazilian merchants in Rio de Janeiro and Salvador and associates in Central Africa; by Dutch, French, English, and Spanish merchants; and by Europeans gathering commercial intelligence under the guise of being travellers.

SETTLEMENTS, ECONOMIES, SOCIETIES

The geography of Portuguese Atlantic holdings in 1660 remained virtually unaltered a century later. Morocco lost its earlier importance for Portugal. Spain controlled Ceuta and Tangier was ceded (1661) to England. The fortress city of Mazagão grew, attributable in part to convicts and undesirables from Portugal, and counted a garrison, merchants, clerics, and artisans. Dependence on maritime lifelines for munitions and provisions, attacks and sieges by local rulers, and seaborne raids by corsairs and by the British, made a Portuguese presence untenable. In 1769, facing siege by 120,000 Moors and Berbers, Dom José I ordered abandonment of Mazagão.

---

[8] Peter Mark, *'Portuguese' Style and Luso-African Identity: Precolonial Senegambia, Sixteenth–Nineteenth Centuries* (Bloomington, IN, 2002); George E. Brooks, *Eurofricans in Western Africa: Commerce, Social Status, Gender, and Religious Observance from the Sixteenth to the Eighteenth Century* (Athens, OH, 2003).

By the late seventeenth and eighteenth centuries, archipelagos were the most densely populated, most commercially exploited, and most accessible of any place in the Portuguese Atlantic. They were valued for their intrinsic commercial, economic, and agricultural importance, for the comparative strategic and military advantage they gave Portugal, and for pivotal roles in intra-Atlantic free migration and forced African diasporas, in labour supply and demand, commerce, and circulation of information. They were the lifeblood of exchange between northern and southern hemispheres, between Europe, Africa, and America, and regular ports of call for Indiamen. These archipelagos call into question generic application of the model of cores and peripheries to the Atlantic.

The Madeiras and the Azores continued to play crucial roles in commerce between Europe, Africa, and America.[9] In Madeira new settlements sprang up on the coast and in the interior. Population increased by at least 60 per cent during this period. The island was famous for agriculture and high-quality wines, was a major player in what David Hancock refers to as the 'Madeira wine complex', and prospered despite recurring seismic activity in the mid-eighteenth century. Only Funchal had the title of city. The Azores shared some of the same characteristics: seismic activity, especially in Horta and São Miguel in the eighteenth century; population growth of some 25 per cent; increased immigration from Portugal leading to overcrowding; and new towns and boroughs. The port cities of Ponta Delgada and Angra dos Reis were centres of power, authority, wealth, social prestige, and commerce, and counted monasteries, magnificent houses, and civic buildings. Angra had the major fort of the Portuguese Atlantic, albeit Spanish-built. The nine islands of the archipelago varied in topography, soil quality, and rainfall. There were disparities between islands in terms of population, settlements, and prosperity. Azorean agricultural production for domestic markets and exports included cereals, vegetables, fruits, dyer's woad, stock farming, and harvesting timber in addition to fishing and whaling. Emigrants from the Madeiras and the Azores played prominent roles in the social and economic history of seventeenth- and eighteenth-century Brazil. They brought agricultural skills, a strong work ethic, and families. Social prominence and financial assets eased the entry of some into upper echelons of Brazilian society. They became merchants and sugar plantation owners, held elected office on municipal councils, and were prominent in prestigious Third Orders and Santas Casas de Misericórdia.

The complexion of the Portuguese Atlantic changes as we move to the Cape Verdes and São Tomé and Príncipe. The fourteen islands making up the two archipelagos had been uninhabited before the arrival of the Portuguese who brought Africans from the mainland. In the seventeenth and eighteenth centuries the crown still used the islands as dumping grounds for criminals and ne'er-do-wells. European settlement was

---

[9] Thomas Bentley Duncan, *Atlantic Islands: Madeira, the Azores, and the Cape Verdes in Seventeenth-Century Commerce and Navigation* (Chicago, IL, 1972); José Manuel Azevedo e Silva, *A Madeira e a construção do mundo Atlântico (séculos XV–XVII)* (Funchal, 1995); David Hancock, *Oceans of Wine: Madeira and the Organization of the Atlantic World, 1640–1815* (New Haven, CT, 2009).

problematic because of disease, climate, unpredictable farming conditions, and social and economic disruption. Both archipelagos had majority black or mulatto populations. African languages predominated. Creole was more widely spoken than Portuguese. Polyglot populations of African birth and descent included slaves and free persons.

Shared cultural and demographic characteristics notwithstanding, each archipelago had a distinctive history.[10] All islands in the Cape Verdes experienced seismic activity, notably Fogo with at least five major volcanic eruptions between the 1670s and 1760s. There were major droughts, famine, and epidemics. Climate, land degradation, and insect and rat infestations made farming precarious. Crops included vegetables, beans, potatoes, sugar cane, cotton, and tobacco for domestic consumption or export. Fishing and whaling gave predictable yields, as too did saltpetre, timber, and vegetable oils and dyes. Settlements mostly took the form of parishes. Urban nuclei were few. Ribeira Grande and Praia on the island of Santiago vied for pre-eminence. There was a strong religious presence. Capuchins and Franciscans were prominent in the second half of the seventeenth century, and a seminary was established. In 1754 a papal bull authorized an episcopal see. Internal tensions, feuding factions, threats of English and French attacks, hoarding, price gouging, and corruption made crown and local governance difficult. Impact of endemic contraband on local economies led the king to open ports to international trade. Sustained discord, physical violence, and virtual collapse of agriculture reached catastrophic proportions by the 1760s.

São Tomé and Príncipe also had a chequered history. Halcyon days as sugar producers were long past, but sugar was still exported to Europe, along with rice, vegetable dyes, cotton, timber, and salt. Soap was exported to Angola, Brazil, and Portugal. American plants, such as corn and manioc, were cultivated for domestic use. São Tomé counted a strong religious presence built up by Italian Capuchins, Jesuits, and religious orders who cooperated with secular clergy. Kings struggled to protect the islands from European raiders, especially French, but with limited success. In São Tomé, non-Europeans had their own social hierarchies and some achieved prominence and wealth. Black and mulatto women, island-born creoles, played prominent leadership roles and constituted a social elite. The city of São Tomé was famous for a seminary and a black and bi-racial secular clergy who exerted great influence in the archipelago, throughout the Gulf of Guinea, and as far south as Angola. São Tomé island was notorious for slave uprisings.

The Cape Verdes and São Tomé and Príncipe embody aspects central to the field of Atlantic history. Each was a hub for trade; each was situated closer to Africa than to Europe or America; each had a predominantly African population, mores, and

---

[10] Joaquim Veríssimo Serrão, *História de Portugal: a restauração e a monarquia absoluta (1640–1750)* (2nd edn. Lisbon, 1977), v. 280–7; Arlindo Manuel Caldeira, *Mulheres, sexualidade e casamento em São Tomé e Príncipe (séculos XV–XVIII)* (2nd edn. Lisbon, 1999); Charles R. Boxer, *The Church Militant and Iberian Expansion, 1449–1770* (Baltimore, MD, 1978); Walter C. Rodney, *A History of the Upper Guinea Coast, 1545–1800* (Oxford, 1970).

languages; each was privileged by strong cultural and commercial ties to the mainland. Here my focus is on the Cape Verdes. The archipelago was a way station for vessels between Europe and America, between northern and southern hemispheres, and for vessels voyaging beyond the Cape of Good Hope. By the mid-seventeenth century, the archipelago was the only major colonized island group in the eastern Atlantic south of the Tropic of Cancer but north of the equator and at about the same latitude as the Lesser Antilles. Location and current and wind systems ensured easy access to Portugal, the Azores and Madeiras, Upper Guinea, the Gulf of Guinea, Central Africa, and Brazil. Salvador and Luanda were roughly equidistant. Santiago, and its ports of Ribeira Grande and Praia, exemplify the inter-continental and inter-hemispheric dimension of commerce better than any other island in the Portuguese Atlantic. In addition to local products, imports from Africa, Europe, and America were repacked into cargoes for dispatch to destinations which included the West Indies, Spanish America and northern Europe. The archipelago was ideally located to test the viability of cultivating European and American flora. It was a vibrant offshore locus for African languages, customs, and belief systems of resident Africans and creoles. Africans from the nearby mainland and from as far away as Central Africa converged there prior to dispatch to America to be slaves.

The Cape Verdes also had a long-standing relationship with the mainland acknowledged by the creation of the captaincy of Cabo Verde e Rios de Guiné. In the later seventeenth century the crown authorized monopolistic trading companies linking the archipelago to Portuguese settlements at Cacheu and Bissau in Upper Guinea. The region between these towns was good for agriculture and cattle raising. Rivers transported goods from the interior to these two enclaves: vegetables, oils, skins, woods, ivory, cotton, and cloth; exotica such as feathers and tortoiseshell; and slaves. These ports and Portuguese holdings in Upper Guinea engaged in commerce with northern and southern Europe. Their products, via the Cape Verdes, found markets in the Caribbean, Spanish America, the state of Maranhão and Grão Pará, and the state of Brazil. Generations of merchants and ships' captains between the 1690s and 1760s created new markets for local produce, buttressed Upper Guinea as guarantor for the economic survival of the Cape Verdes, and promoted exchanges between the coast and interior in that part of Africa. They took advantage of Upper Guinea's proximity to northern Brazil, Europe, and the Caribbean, and that there was less competition than in Angola from other Europeans. These two ports constituted a northerly anchor on the African mainland for Portuguese interests, and enabled Portugal to bring a new dimension to commerce between the Old World and northern Brazil and the North Atlantic as well as with the mainland of Lower Guinea and, especially, with Angola. They illustrate how Atlantic commerce was more complex than a triangular or quadrilateral trade and that any single port or region could be a participant in multiple trading networks with or without a European, American, or African component. They disabuse the notion that African participation in Atlantic commerce was primarily in the context of the slave trade and vividly illustrate how African participation, by dint of its diversity, intensity, and reach, was an essential part of the history of continental Africa as well as of the Atlantic.

ANGOLA AND BRAZIL

In Central Angola, the Portuguese pressed eastwards and southwards from Luanda.[11] Markers of this effort were few: garrisons in forts, whose influence was symbolic rather than real and exerted little influence other than in their immediate vicinity; a fort built in 1680 at Caconda inland from Benguela; and markets (*feiras*) which were regional meeting places. A royal order of 1758 granted freedom to enter hitherto restricted areas of the interior to anyone engaging in trade, with implications for *feiras* and new regions for slaving expeditions. The governor succumbed to lobbying pressures by merchants in Luanda and obeyed but did not immediately or fully execute the royal intent of promoting free trade.[12] Luso-Africans, convicts, and criminal gangs flooded into instantaneous settlements, creating law and order problems, and demanding gubernatorial measures to regulate the new *feiras*. The Portuguese increased their presence in the Kwanza River valley. The river became the vehicle for Portuguese incursions to the interior. But, overall, this was a period of false hopes: failure to open a transcontinental route to the Portuguese colony of Mozambique; absence of anticipated mineral resources, and especially gold and silver; little progress in agriculture and stock raising; a dearth of Portuguese settlers; an economy dominated by labour demands of American colonies; and European captains and traders vying with the Portuguese for trade in coastal ports north of Luanda and into Kongo and southwards to Benguela and beyond. Two settlements inland from Benguela were short-lived. The governor in Luanda and the king in Lisbon must have been aware of the frailty of the colonial economy, possible challenges to Angola's key role in the slave trade, and even to its integrity as a viable colony, but remedial actions were absent, delayed, or ineffectual.

This century saw the emergence of Brazil onto the Atlantic stage as a major force demographically, socially, economically, and politically.[13] Radiating out from coastal areas with scattered pockets of settlement between the north-east and São Vicente there was extensive internal migration: from the coast to the interior; from traditional centres to the far north and far south; and, in the eighteenth century, from the coast and the

---

[11] David Birmingham, *Trade and Conflict in Angola: The Mbundu and their Neighbours under the Influence of the Portuguese, 1483–1790* (Oxford, 1966); José Carlos Venâncio, *A economia de Luanda e hinterland no século XVIII* (Lisbon, 1996); Phyllis M. Martin, *The External Trade of the Loango Coast, 1576–1870: The Effects of Changing Commercial Relations on the Vili Kingdom of Loango* (Oxford, 1972).

[12] Miller, *Way of Death*, 577–9, 581–3.

[13] Leslie Bethell (ed.), *Colonial Brazil* (Cambridge, 1987); Charles R. Boxer, *The Golden Age of Brazil, 1695–1750* (Berkeley, CA, 1962); John Hemming, *Red Gold: The Conquest of the Brazilian Indians, 1500–1760* (Cambridge, MA, 1978); Richard M. Morse (ed.), *The Bandeirantes: The Historical Role of the Brazilian Pathfinders* (New York, 1965).

interior to the far west. Mass internal migratory movements involved Europeans, Africans, Afro-Brazilians, and Amerindians. Camps became settlements, settlements became towns. A few towns became cities. Older coastal cities kept their commercial, social, and political pre-eminence, and new centres of population, urbanization, economic hubs, and markets came into being. Traditional hinterlands were reworked; new hinterlands were established; others were dissolved; and still others created new commercial networks without a coastal component. While Salvador and Rio de Janeiro enjoyed their core status because of a combination of administrative (secular and religious), commercial, and social circumstances, developments in Mato Grosso led to new hinterlands for São Paulo and for Belém do Pará or São Luís do Maranhão and changing relationships in response to new configurations of supply and demand. Monoculture continued but there was increasing agricultural diversification and blurring of distinctions between stock raising, agriculture, extractive industries, and commerce. Occupational categories became porous and fluid: plantation owners engaged in commerce, had town houses, and participated in urban social and economic life; merchants bought plantations and they, or their offspring, adopted the lifestyles of plantation owners; businessmen made up the financial services sector but also invested in land and urban properties; mining entrepreneurs had fields under cultivation for foodstuffs and tobacco. Some free-born and former slaves came to own a smallholding, horses, cattle and goats, and a shop or tavern.

This was a century of increasing social and economic mobility in the South Atlantic for some Portuguese, Luso-Brazilians, Africans, Luso-Africans, and Afro-Brazilians and Afro-Luso-Brazilians. It witnessed a slave trade growing by leaps and bounds and hundreds of thousands of individuals in bondage. Sobering is the realization that the Catholic Church and slavery were two institutions present throughout the colonial period whose influence permeated all sectors of Brazilian life, culture, society, economy, and politics, and neither was an instrument for change. But, change there was. Despite clerical displeasure and royal ambivalence, this period saw an increase in numbers of slaves who themselves bought their freedom or were manumitted by an owner. The incidence varied regionally, but this practice was most prevalent in Minas Gerais. Slaves born in Brazil were more likely to gain their freedom than African-born. They should not be confused with those Afro-Brazilians born free. The resulting increase in free or freed individuals of African descent had social and economic ramifications for the colony. Notwithstanding similar ambivalence to merchants and to creoles, there was an ever-growing class of Portuguese and Luso-Brazilian merchants who variously engaged in regional, interregional, oceanic, and transoceanic trade, became wealthy and highly influential, and had capital to invest in the colony's infrastructure as well as for discretionary spending on the arts, on churches and mansions, and on beautification of towns and cities.[14]

[14] James H. Sweet, *Recreating Africa: Culture, Kinship, and Religion in the African-Brazilian World, 1441–1770* (Chapel Hill, NC, 2003); A. J. R. Russell-Wood, *Slavery and Freedom in Colonial Brazil* (Oxford, 2002); João L. R. Fragoso, *Homens de grossa aventura: acumulação e hierarquia na praça mercantil do Rio de Janeiro (1790–1830)* (Rio de Janeiro, 1992).

South Atlantic exchanges

There were continuing exchanges between Brazil and Africa. American sweet potatoes were carried to Africa, maize and manioc became staples of African diets, and African plants were brought to Brazil. African preparation of foods spread to Brazil. Although the ingredients might be virtually identical, the same dish could differ between the two colonies. Salvador had such close ties with the Bight of Benin that connections and exchanges—of individuals, goods, cultures, culinary practices—between Salvador and African ports were more regular than between Salvador and towns in the interior of the captaincy of Bahia.[15]

The slave trade dominated exchanges between Brazil and Angola. Inherent to this traffic are less well-known aspects. Some few Brazilian products found a market in Angola. Brazilian sugar cane brandy (*cachaça*; *geribita*) replaced local African spirits and Portuguese wines and brandies in Central Africa. Bahian tobacco was in great demand in Central Africa for chewing and smoking. Both had negative health and social ramifications for Africans.[16] The impact of Africa on Brazil during this period reflected the most intensive period of the middle passage. Diseases or epidemics not indigenous to the Americas but which occurred in Brazil were attributed (spuriously) to African origins. The volume of the slave trade, its sheer numbers for the first half of the eighteenth century, and rapid redistribution of slaves after arrival, led to immediate dissemination of Central African languages in Brazil. This was accompanied by belief systems and practices associated with traditional African religions. These impacted in varying degrees on different regions of Portuguese America in terms of governance, physical security, marketing practices, public morality, and domestic life. That Christian rites and ceremonies were adopted and adapted in Kongo and Angola had ramifications for Christianity as practised by Africans in Brazil. Africans in Brazil also celebrated the annual coronation of kings and queens of Kongo.[17]

The slave trade was not static or monolithic. Ships' captains accommodated themselves to infra-African conditions (such as disease and warfare) affecting supply and demand. By the second half of the seventeenth century, it was common for Portuguese merchant families to place a young male relative in a Brazilian port to gain experience and be a local anchor. So too did it become standard practice for merchant families or joint partnerships in Salvador and Rio de Janeiro to dispatch relatives to check out the

---

[15] Pierre Verger, *Trade Relations between the Bight of Benin and Bahia from the 17th to 19th Century* (Ibadan, 1976).

[16] Jean-Baptiste Nardi, *O fumo brasileiro no período colonial: lavoura, comércio, e administração* (São Paulo, 1996); José C. Curto, *Enslaving Spirits: The Portuguese–Brazilian Alcohol Trade at Luanda and its Hinterland, c.1550–1830* (Leiden, 2004).

[17] Mary Karasch, 'Central Africans in Central Brazil, 1780–1835' and Elizabeth W. Kiddy, 'Who is the King of Kongo? A New Look at African and Afro-Brazilian Kings in Brazil', in Linda M. Heywood (ed.), *Central Africans and Cultural Transformations in the African Diaspora* (Cambridge, 2002).

African supply system and report back or to have a family member or agent resident in an African port. In this regard, *carioca* and Bahian families were to the fore. An innovation in the Angola–Brazil axis occurred in the 1720s. Bahian merchants initiated trade between Salvador and Benguela. Bahian merchants or agents took up residence in Benguela; *cariocas* favoured Luanda.[18] Another dimension was African and Afro-Brazilian participation in the Atlantic bullion trade. Branches of the Brotherhood of Our Lady of the Rosary in Luanda and in Brazil dispatched consignments of gold to Portugal, sometimes to pay for religious statues or works of art. Individual Africans and Afro-Brazilians—mostly male but occasionally female, mostly free but occasionally slaves—also sent consignments of gold in their own names to Lisbon.

A WORLD INVERTED

The years *c.*1650–*c.*1760 were crucially important to Portugal and its Atlantic colonies. They saw the concentration of royal attention and of national interests on the Atlantic. Some products of Portuguese Atlantic holdings enjoyed niche markets. Others were in direct competition in European markets with identical goods, especially from the West Indies. The Portuguese people benefited little from incoming cargoes from Brazil and elsewhere which were trans-shipped to northern Europe, Spain, and Italy. This situation was exacerbated by exemptions and privileges exacted by foreign nations. The Methuen Treaty was pernicious, politically and economically, to Portugal and its colonies. Inadequate investment in infrastructure and manufacturing in Portugal and royal extravagance forced Portugal to purchase basics—grains, foodstuffs, manufactured goods—from Britain. Portugal suffered a balance of payments problem. Discoveries of gold in Brazil between the 1690s and 1740s, and diamond strikes in the 1720s and subsequently, saved Portugal from disaster but at the cost of dependency on Britain. Decline of gold production, noted as early as the 1730s, and a vertiginous decline after 1750, was devastating to Portugal.

Contrasting with this reality was the public image of Portugal associated with the personage of Dom João V, who was the envy of his contemporaries; a Maecenas to an international army of artists, artisans, and architects; recipient of papal favour; builder *par excellence*; and creator of extravaganzas. The irony was that, during the age of absolutism (*c.*1668–1750) in Portugal, and notably during the reign of Dom João V, colonists in the Portuguese Atlantic world came to the realization that the metropolis was no longer central to their existence. There was de facto reversal of roles. The centre of gravity shifted from North Atlantic to South Atlantic, from metropolis to colonies.[19]

---

[18] Miller, *Way of Death*; Corcino Medeiros dos Santos, 'Relações de Angola com o Rio de Janeiro, 1736–1808', *Estudos históricos*, 12 (1973), 7–68.

[19] Kenneth Maxwell, 'The Atlantic in the Eighteenth Century: A Southern Perspective on the Need to Return to the "Big Picture" ', *Transactions of the Royal Historical Society*, 6th Series, 3 (1993), 209–36.

Acknowledgement of this reversal was implicit in the observation in the 1730s by a prescient courtier that Portugal's survival depended on Brazilian riches and his advice to Dom João that he would be more comfortable and safer in a land of abundance (Brazil) than in a country offering only privation (Portugal). Indeed, during his long reign substantially more Europeans left Portugal for Brazil than from Spain or Britain for the Americas.[20] When gold is factored in, the value of commodities sent during his reign from Brazil to Europe may have exceeded those from mainland British or Spanish America.

The year 1750 saw accession to the throne of Dom José I and the autocratic rule of his first minister, the marquis of Pombal, who devoted himself to reversing what he saw as erosion of Portugal's fortunes. The Atlantic was central to Pombal's strategic and mercantilist mindset. Transfer (1763) of the capital of Brazil from Salvador to Rio de Janeiro recognized the latter's strategic importance and intense engagement in Atlantic and transoceanic trade. In major Brazilian ports Pombal created inspection boards to monitor the quality of exports (notably, sugar and tobacco) and appointed intendants to oversee maritime matters. He created monopolistic commercial companies based on Lisbon to stimulate Brazilian agricultural exports and guarantee a regular supply of slave labour. One focused on Grão-Pará and Maranhão; another on Pernambuco. By so doing, Pombal sought to integrate northern Brazil into Atlantic commerce, curb European competitors and interlopers, reinforce a Portuguese presence in Upper Guinea, and strengthen ties between Portuguese archipelagos in the eastern Atlantic. His enlightened reforms included secularization of the University of Coimbra and outlawing of the distinction between Old and New Christians. In keeping with his advocacy of mercantilism, Pombal ousted nobles from positions of power and authority and replaced them by commoners with demonstrated financial acumen and commercial success.

The actions of Dom João V and Pombal's nationalist zeal failed to recognize that already the ground was shifting from under absolutist and autocratic governance based in Portugal. Overseas-born graduates eschewed remaining in Portugal, entering the royal service, or taking holy orders, but opted to return to the colonies and became part of a new, cosmopolitan, creole elite exposed to Enlightenment doctrines and ideas, and impatient with the structure and characteristics of the *ancien régime*. By favouring merchants, Pombal gave his imprimatur to individuals whose entrepreneurial initiative was more focused on furthering their own aspirations than on national goals. His mission to restore Portugal's standing in the Atlantic by promoting monopolistic commerce was doomed to failure. In 1808 the prince regent responded to the prevailing sentiment for free trade and opened Brazilian ports to international trade.

Two threads run through my narrative. The first is how individuals and changing attitudes, especially in the South Atlantic, forced through change despite royal decrees and metropolitan attitudes and which the crown was faced to acknowledge as a *fait*

---

[20] David Eltis, 'Free and Coerced Migrations from the Old World to the New', in Eltis (ed.), *Coerced and Free Migration: Global Perspectives* (Stanford, CA, 2002), 1–74, esp. appendix; table 1.

accompli. One such was migration. Notwithstanding attempts to regulate emigration from Portugal to Brazil, the passport system collapsed because of the sheer numbers of Portuguese who participated in colonization and commercialization of the Atlantic in numbers far in excess of those in Portuguese India (Estado da Índia). There was serial migration throughout the Portuguese Atlantic by sea, river, and land, a flow of humanity between the Old World (Europe, Africa) and the New, between islands and continents, and within continents. The crown was impotent to stem this flow, even when vital commercial interests, such as sugar cultivation, were threatened. The absence of a sustained policy on settlements meant that individuals essentially took this into their own hands. Royal approval, or at least acquiescence, came *ex post facto*.

The complexion of the Portuguese Atlantic changed incrementally. This led to the creation of a new lexicon to describe bi- and multi-racial individuals. Individuals and groups identified themselves in new ways, and there were pan-Atlantic creole and related cultures. Portuguese kings had made a distinction between Portuguese-born (*reinóis*), which—at least in terms of perception—included Madeira and the Azores, and creoles (persons born overseas, in Africa or Brazil). The former were preferred in appointments and advancements, and more likely to secure office in Church and state. The eighteenth century saw an easing of such restrictions in practice. Some Brazilian-born served as royal advisers, as governors, and crown magistrates within the Atlantic circuit. Kings adhered to the official line that, to be eligible for public or elected office, candidates should demonstrate 'purity of blood', namely be white. And yet Dom João V and Dom José I waived this and similar rulings in response to petitions by black soldiers to have the same degree of eligibility for promotion as their white counterparts, for some mulattos in Rio de Janeiro to carry swords, and black brotherhoods to enjoy privileges previously the exclusive preserve of white brotherhoods. A blind eye was cast on mulattos and creoles who, 'circumstances of birth' notwithstanding, were deemed qualified for municipal office. That porosity which existed in the commercial sector among merchants of different nationalities, or among persons of different religious beliefs, extended to bi-racial or multi-racial individuals. Crown officials in Brazil and Portuguese Africa yielded to local pressure to permit such appointments when faced by compelling demographic circumstances and the absence or reluctance of whites to hold some public offices.

This was a century characterized by ebb and flow, by constant movement, by change, and by reverses as well as advances. There were glaring disparities between localities and regions. Crown zeal to regulate was often ineffectual, royal instructions ignored, and the royal intent circumvented by the geography of the Atlantic, the plethora of inlets, bays, and estuaries for concealment, shortage of manpower, and the vastness of the ocean. Throughout this Portuguese Atlantic, new markets came into being; networks of trade developed, expanded, contracted, or were reformulated into new combinations; hinterlands gained a reputation, stimulated new markets or sources of raw materials, and waxed or waned.

The second thread running through the narrative is how, during this century, colonists exerted greater control over their activities, evaded traditional obligations to the crown, took collective and individual initiatives independent of kings or their agents, and engaged in exchanges which were inter-colonial and without a metropolitan component. Consolidation of merchant communities throughout the Portuguese Atlantic, the pan-Atlantic range of their activities, their access to capital, and unilateral decision-making led to creation of new networks, commercial practices, and organization independent of crown or official intervention or even a metropolitan component. A crucial development was that Brazilian merchants (including those engaged in the slave trade) amassed capital assets sufficient to allow them to act independently of metropolitan financing. This permitted greater adaptability to changing market conditions, independence of action, and innovation. The downside (from the crown's perspective) was that these developments led to unauthorized or clandestine commercial practices, exchange of commodities which were forbidden or did not meet quality criteria, use of unauthorized routes by land or sea, and failure to adhere to regulations specifying ports of call. At worst, commerce became part of a corporate 'endemic culture of evasion'. There was ample opportunity for individuals to participate in this culture: counterfeiting coins; mixing tin shavings into gold dust; dusting tobacco leaves with sand; avoiding licence fees and taxes.

Deference gave way to greater independence of thought and action, blind obedience gave way to negotiated agreements, and colonists or their elected representatives gained the royal ear. Colonial aspirations were more loudly voiced, colonial points of view more heard at court, and colonists had a greater say in setting colonial priorities rather than kowtowing to metropolitan interests. Royal opposition to a printing press or a university in colonial Brazil and constraints on the book trade did not prevent dissemination throughout the Portuguese Atlantic of Enlightenment ideas and texts on political economy and philosophy. There was a contrarian tone most in evidence in Portuguese Africa and Portuguese America. Surprisingly, this did not rise to the level of colony-wide revolution. A different perspective on unrest in Brazil, largely ignored in a historiography which saw Brazil from a coastal lookout rather than from the interior or far west, was provided by events in the Eastern Sertão where frontier migrants seeking to settle in the eastern forests of Minas Gerais clashed with Native Americans, thereby initiating eight decades of Indian resistance.[21] What defined 'frontier' in that region remained elusive, as was the case elsewhere in Brazil and Angola where hollow frontiers were the norm through the nineteenth century.

CONCLUSION

The Portuguese Atlantic was redolent with change during the years c.1650–c.1760. Some changes were measurable: demography, migration, commerce, settlement, urbanization,

---

[21] Hal Langfur, *The Forbidden Lands: Colonial Identity, Frontier Violence, and the Persistence of Brazil's Eastern Indians, 1750–1830* (Stanford, CA, 2006), 290.

trading networks, organizational structures, and revenues and disbursements. Others were qualitative: dissemination of ideas, changes of attitudes, reorientation of perceptions, emergence of new social groupings, creation of new identities and new vocabularies, and cadences of culture and language. One lesson to be learnt from the Portuguese Atlantic world is that these intangibles—their elusive, fluid, and permeable quality notwithstanding—ring louder across time and space and are more indicative of enduring change, especially in human relationships, than are written crown and official instructions, correspondence, and ledgers of the imperial enterprise.

BIBLIOGRAPHY

Alencastro, Luiz Felipe de, *O trato dos viventes: formação do Brasil no Atlântico Sul* (São Paulo, 2000).

Bethencourt, Francisco, and Diogo Ramada Curto (eds.), *Portuguese Oceanic Expansion, 1400–1800* (Cambridge, 2007).

Boxer, Charles R., *Salvador de Sá and the Struggle for Brazil and Angola, 1602–1686* (London, 1952).

Marques, A. H. de Oliveira, and João José Alves Dias, *Atlas histórico de Portugal e do ultramar português* (Lisbon, 2003).

Mauro, Frédéric, *Le Portugal et l'Atlantique au XVIIe siècle, 1570–1670: étude économique* (Paris, 1960).

Miller, Joseph C., *Way of Death: Merchant Capitalism and the Angolan Slave Trade, 1730–1830* (Madison, WI, 1988).

Russell-Wood, A. J. R., *The Portuguese Empire, 1415–1808: A World on the Move, 1415–1800* (Baltimore, MD, 1992).

Thornton, John, *Africa and Africans in the Making of the Atlantic World, 1400–1800* (2nd edn. Cambridge, 1998).

CHAPTER 13

....

THE BRITISH ATLANTIC

....

JOYCE E. CHAPLIN

THE phrase 'British Atlantic' brings together, without so much as a comma, two terms that emerged rather belatedly (and perhaps unhelpfully) in the history of English colonization, long after groups of people with some allegiance to a monarch and Parliament based in London had crossed the Western Ocean and established colonies in North America and the Caribbean. During these seventeenth-century developments, English colonization relied on private initiatives that did a great deal to convince colonists of their distinctive capacity for autonomy, even as they stoutly maintained themselves to be as English as the people at home. Then, from the late seventeenth century onward, the English colonies underwent unprecedented population growth, which inspired new faith in colonists' ability to adapt to and dominate the New World. While other European empires may also have had either a degree of colonial autonomy or rapid population growth, only English-speaking colonists gained confidence from both characteristics.

But this settler confidence was challenged, from the mid-eighteenth century onward, by the creation of a *British* empire with *Atlantic* dimensions. These new developments sequentially defined a new set of imperial interests, ones that relied more on centralized governance than on the voluntaristic impulses that had established an earlier English empire, and which conceived of the Atlantic Ocean as a conduit of that centralized authority. Because settlers in the English-speaking colonies had for a long time connected a non-British identity, meaning Englishness, to being an ocean away from England itself, the newly British and Atlantic empire was less inviting to them and the temptation to define Americans' political and natural interests as separate from Great Britain was eventually overwhelming.

In the beginning, there was no Atlantic Ocean, no Great Britain, no British empire, not even a single English-speaking colonizer who acted for a specific political entity. English overseas expansion began more humbly and informally. When fishermen from the western part of England ventured across the outlying ocean in the late 1400s, they were pursuing their trade, not any imperial agenda. If they thought about it, they probably did conceive of themselves as Englishmen, though ones who acted for their private gain. The nature of their enterprise, in which private actors occasionally acknowledged their Englishness, remained characteristic of English colonization for the next 200 years, at least.[1]

When the English authorities began to plan colonial projects in competition with Spain, the acknowledged great power in the Americas, they did not banish private effort but harnessed it. The 1496 patent that Henry VII gave to John Cabot was a logical, modest step from private Atlantic voyages to crown-sanctioned reconnaissance. Elizabeth I was even bolder than her grandfather in her decisions to encourage and even profit from the English privateers who raided Spain's colonies and ocean-going vessels.

And to a surprising extent, successful English colonies were products of private corporations chartered by the crown. Several small and ill-funded operations foundered in the late sixteenth century. From those failures, the crown took the lesson, not to contribute more, but to encourage the pooling of private funds. So, just as the Levant, Muscovy, and East India companies carried English trading interests eastward, into the Mediterranean, Russia, and South Asia, so to the west did several other commercial agencies, including the Virginia Company of London, the Plymouth Company, the Somers Isle Company, the Massachusetts Bay Company, the Providence Island Company, the Newfoundland Company, and the Bristol Society of Merchants Adventurers.[2]

These joint-stock companies yielded mixed results, especially for their investors, and several of them had remarkably short lives. Most of them were intended to foster trade, meaning establish small trading posts whose personnel were to identify and extract valuable American commodities; large settlements with commodity-producing settlers were only slowly accepted as necessary. It is all the more remarkable, therefore, that the trading corporations became the primary means to organize the first English colonies and colonial economies on the North American continent and on some Caribbean islands. The key enclaves at Jamestown, Bermuda, Plymouth Plantation, and Boston provided models for future ventures. Timber, tobacco, fish, and sugar began to flow out from these island and mainland outposts and across the Atlantic. And, in the 1630s, the disruptions which led into the English Civil War sent thousands of migrants flowing the other way and into the waiting colonies. Over 50,000 went to the three main areas of seventeenth-century English settlement: about 21,000 to Massachusetts, 10,000 to Virginia, and over 20,000 to the Caribbean. (Another estimated 20,000 went to Ireland.) This out-migration of private citizens was extraordinary. Compared to Spain, France, the Netherlands, Portugal, Ireland, and Scotland, early modern England sent a much larger proportion of its population to America.

From these experiences, the crown learned the merits of leaving colonization to private actors, whether individual or incorporated. Joint-stock companies fell from favour, but proprietary charters succeeded them, with the Courteen syndicate establishing tobacco planting on Barbados and the Catholic Calverts settling their

---

[1] David Harris Sacks, *The Widening Gate: Bristol and the Atlantic Economy, 1450–1700* (Berkeley, CA, 1991).

[2] Kenneth R. Andrews, *Trade, Plunder, and Settlement: Maritime Enterprise and the Genesis of the British Empire, 1480–1630* (Cambridge, 1984).

co-religionists in Maryland. The history of colonial trading companies and private charters underscores the extent to which England's monarchs were prepared to privatize the business of colonization. While the Spanish Monarchy and other European nations also avoided the work and expense of colonization, the English tendency to do so was extreme—and very oriented toward commercial profit. Even more striking was the English monarch's indifference to the form of government within each colony. When the Massachusetts Bay Company transplanted company headquarters to Massachusetts, it created a government with a particular sovereignty. English officials did not protest that or other colonial efforts at creating local governments. The quick institution of representative assemblies likewise indicated that officials gave their blessing to colonists' efforts to govern themselves.

To be sure, each colony eventually had a governor sanctioned, directly or remotely, by the monarch. These governors and a scattering of other colonial officials believed themselves to be agents within an imperial chain of command, acting under orders. This was especially the case once certain colonies, including Virginia, existed under royal government. But these imperial actors were exceptions and regarded as such, as they ruefully noted whenever they faced indifference or opposition, especially from the colonial assemblies. For the most part, instability within colonial governments had nothing to do with antipathy to crown interference but resulted from conflict among factions, each of which sought the upper hand in local government.[3]

It was perhaps most surprising that English authorities allowed propertied settlers so much power over their fellow colonists. Once tobacco became a lucrative crop in the Caribbean and the Chesapeake, planters scrambled for servants and exploited the indentured labourers who joined the Great Migration. Sold for the periods of their indentures, many servants were underfed, overworked, and beaten for minor infractions. The conditions of their life would not have been legal in England itself, where agricultural labourers had, since the Black Death, gained considerable ability to choose masters and protest unfair treatment. In the Caribbean and the Chesapeake, many servants died before they had served the total amount of their time—they were unable ever to enjoy the freedom (and landholding) they had hoped for in the New World.[4]

A freebooting atmosphere remained powerful in the English Caribbean. Colonies there had always been intended to harass the exposed edges of the Spanish empire and many early English settlers were happy to do their part. Although attempts to establish a foothold in the Amazon had failed, the English withdrew to the Leeward Islands, St Kitts, Nevis, and Barbados, where the prevailing wind and ocean currents allowed relatively quick transport to and from England yet kept these places out of easy reach of

---

[3] Stephen Saunders Webb, *The Governors-General, the English Army, and the Definition of the Empire, 1569–1681* (Chapel Hill, NC, 1979); Jack P. Greene, *Peripheries and Center: Constitutional Development in the Extended Polities of the British Empire and the United States, 1607–1688* (Athens, GA, 1986), chapters 1–2.

[4] Richard S. Dunn, *Sugar and Slaves: The Rise of the Planter Class in the English West Indies, 1624–1713* (London, 1973), 239; Edmund S. Morgan, *American Slavery, American Freedom: The Ordeal of Colonial Virginia* (New York, 1975), 108–30.

the Spanish on the mainland and to the west. Tobacco cultivation provided the first exports from these colonies, as in Virginia, to be succeeded by the much more profitable crop of sugar in the 1650s.

Meanwhile, buccaneering activities against the Spanish continued. The Treaty of Madrid (1670) outlawed privateering, but those activities began again, in earnest, in the 1690s. By the early 1700s, over 5,000 men were acting as pirates in the Caribbean and beyond. If the generally piratical spirit of early colonization was wearing away, actual piracy became a specialized practice and a strategic one for the expanding nation, until Britain initiated a war against these pirates in order to focus energies on regular maritime commerce during the first two decades of the eighteenth century.[5]

After the 1650s, a steadier trade in African captives to the Caribbean ensured a transition from indentured white labourers to enslaved blacks. In Barbados, the white servant population was over 13,000 in the early 1650s but fewer than 3,000 by 1680. By the late 1650s, in fact, Barbados had become the first permanent English colony with a black majority population. At the start of the 1700s, the enslaved black population of that island was over 50,000, at least three times the total of white settlers. Other plantation colonies followed suit, the Leeward Islands in the 1670s, and the Chesapeake and Jamaica from the 1680s onward. At this point, the plantation colonies embraced cultural patterns that set them apart from England, with its mixed agriculture and free labour. Moreover, the exoticism of the Caribbean and Chesapeake meant that English people tended to assume that all of America, even New England, was filled with black slaves and swaying palm trees.

The colonists' sense of physical separation from England was particularly apparent in the name which they and the stay-at-home English tended to use for the seas that divided them: the *Western Ocean*. Although other Europeans had already begun using the name 'Atlantic' for that body of water, English-speaking people tended not to, and maps and charts done for English consumers followed suit. *Western* Ocean clearly implied a geographical orientation in relation to England, and equally implied that those on the far side of that ocean were at the back of beyond.

Still, most of the English migrants who helped to establish the first colonies thought of themselves as tied back to their native land and a surprising number came and went for various reasons. Only the Pilgrim group at Plymouth, after all, had made a decision permanently to abandon England and its national Church; nearly all other settlers either intended to return or, at the least, maintain ties of some kind. The distinctive English nature of the early settlements is also apparent in their composition, which was overwhelmingly drawn from England. During the seventeenth century, the Protestant Irish only occasionally joined the English colonies and surprisingly few Scots, even Protestant ones, were willing to do so. Scottish migrants found Poland, Sweden, and, increasingly, Ulster in Ireland more enticing than Massachusetts or Virginia.[6]

---

[5] Robert C. Ritchie, *Captain Kidd and the War against the Pirates* (Cambridge, MA, 1986).

[6] David Cressy, *Coming Over: Migration and Communication between England and New England in the Seventeenth Century* (New York, 1987); T. C. Smout, N. C. Landsman, and T. M. Devine, 'Scottish Emigration in the Seventeenth and Eighteenth Centuries', in Nicholas Canny (ed.), *Europeans on the Move: Studies on European Migration, 1500–1800* (Oxford, 1994), 78–112.

The English colonies were, moreover, usually carefully set apart from the colonies of other nations, especially Catholic ones. A brief Jacobean rapprochement with Spain after the Treaty of London (1604), which enabled English colonization of Guiana, cheek by jowl with actual Spaniards, was atypical, as were Plymouth Plantation's cordial relations with the Dutch and Anglo-French cooperation on St Christopher, which the two nations managed to share during the seventeenth century. More often than not, English settlers from Massachusetts to Barbados regarded other Europeans as competitors and kept their distance. Xenophobia was a constant. Fervent English anti-Catholicism encouraged the leaders and even ordinary people in the Catholic enclave at Maryland to be very careful not to offend Protestants, whether within the colony, in neighbouring Virginia, or back in England.

Even more strikingly, military conflict brought out colonists' English patriotism. The pattern for this seems to have been set in Ireland, where the Elizabethan invasion sharply distinguished between English and others and generated violent conflict between those groups. Disdain for native Irish social forms, intolerance of Irish Catholicism, and disappointment over the general rejection of the Protestant message by the Old English (whose ancestors had arrived in Ireland in the twelfth century), all formed parts of English justification for the invasion of Ireland. The fact that the ventures into Ireland and into America overlapped in personnel, motivation, and methods underscored an early and important English assumption that military conquest was essential to colonization, which itself relied on an essential division between English and non-English. These distinctions were made apparent when, after the English Civil War, Cromwell arranged for 12,000 Scottish and Irish prisoners of war to be shipped to Barbados as servants-for-life.[7]

Little surprise, then, that during colonial wars, many colonists publicly described themselves in national terms, especially as militant Protestants, but sometimes just as militant Englishmen. Their identification made sense especially in cases when conflicts in America mirrored those within Europe and recruited colonial and metropolitan troops. The first Anglo-Dutch war (1652–4), for instance, included both military actions between England and the Netherlands and Anglo-American attacks on (and acquisition of) New Netherland, in a phase of conflict notable for its unusual Protestant versus Protestant dimension. Anti-papist sentiment was a more conventional rallying point. If Oliver Cromwell's Western Design was never quite the pan-Protestant assault on the Catholic monarchy the protector had intended, it did at least result in the English conquest of Jamaica in 1655. These two acquisitions inaugurated new phases of colonial expansion, into the middle-Atlantic section of the North American continent and into more of the Caribbean.

For every conflict dictated from the centre of empire, however, colonists undertook several on their own. Over the course of the seventeenth century, English settlers

---

[7] Nicholas P. Canny, 'The Ideology of English Colonization: From Ireland to America', *William and Mary Quarterly*, 3rd Series, 30 (1973), 575–98; Hilary McD. Beckles, *White Servitude and Black Slavery in Barbados, 1627–1715* (Knoxville, TN, 1989), 48.

battled Native Americans with ominous frequency and steadily took advantage of intra-African conflicts to obtain slaves. In these ways, English authorities continued to sub-contract much of the work of colonization to private persons. They sanctioned slave trading, mostly to the Caribbean, starting with the aggressive incursions of William and John Hawkins in the 1530s and 1560s and ending with a steadier if no less exploitative extraction of captives from Africa. The authorities also allowed free white colonists to make slave codes to suit themselves. Those laws maximized the autonomy of individual slaveholders, without the careful attention to the rights of the enslaved (especially their conversion, Christian marriage, and baptism of their children) that preoccupied the Spanish Monarchy. Above all, colonists were allowed to create a significant legal innovation when they decreed that enslaved status would follow in the mother's line, a custom radically at odds with the patriarchal forms of inheritance in England itself.[8]

England's rulers also approved or turned a blind eye to military ventures against Native Americans. They did so most dramatically in the Anglo-Virginian response to the 1622 Powhatan attack on settlers, where English reprisal was persistent, bloody, and indiscriminate, and in New England's horrific Pequot War of 1636, culminating in the attack on Indians at Fort Mystic, where the besieged natives were either burned alive or shot as they tried to escape.

In both instances, the English authorities benefited from settlers' firm assumption that they were different, not just from Catholics, but also from non-European idolaters. Militant Protestantism was in this way an important component of racism. Certainly, prohibitions against intermarriage, either with Indians or Africans, reinforced a strict separation between colonizers and colonized, a distinction intended to achieve a specific outcome, the non-existence of populations that blurred the boundaries. But the laws failed: interracial unions produced persons who blurred those boundaries, though census takers and other authorities tended not to record their existence, thus guaranteeing that historians would find it difficult to work such people into the story.[9]

And the practice of domestic slavery itself kept inserting non-English people into English settlements, with the result that colonial agriculture, language, cooking, and magical practices bore traces of the un-free people, Indian or African, who had cultivated crops, nursed children, prepared meals, and interpreted the cosmos for settlers, sometimes within their very households.

Perhaps because the hybridization was ongoing, most English settlers were determined to deny that it made any difference to their Englishness. They were always reluctant to compare themselves to Indians and bristled when others made the comparison; the same was true for any cultural similarity between themselves and

[8] Elsa V. Goveia, 'The West Indian Slave Laws of the Eighteenth Century', in Laura Fonger and Eugene Genovese (eds.), *Slavery in the New World: A Reader in Comparative History* (Englewood Cliffs, NJ, 1969), 113–37.

[9] Gary B. Nash, 'The Hidden History of Mestizo America', *Journal of American History*, 82 (1995), 941–64.

those of African descent. Robert Beverly's 1705 statement that he was an 'Indian' was the exception that proves the rule. Even more remarkably, colonists disliked being called *creoles* because that implied their similarity to Spanish-Americans, those American-born descendants of Spaniards whose Catholicism, presumed suitability for hot climates, and perceived amalgamation with Indians made them everything that English colonists did not want to be. Not for nothing did Cotton Mather decry the 'Criolian Degeneracy' that awaited Christians who, in America, might slide into spiritual lethargy or heresy.[10]

Thus a slight paradox: even as most English colonists considered themselves to be private actors, only some of whose behaviours were subject to metropolitan authority, they had a remarkable regard for their own Englishness. In describing themselves as English, they referred to a complex bundle of customs, beliefs, personal characteristics, and bodily aptitudes. We might distinguish between the cultural and natural phenomena, though that distinction made little sense to people in the early modern era. Rather, they assumed that customs were simply a second nature, a set of practices natural to a people who inhabited a particular physical place and themselves had distinctive physical features. Of course the reasoning was circular, but that made it no less powerful.

With stubborn and quite self-conscious conservatism, the first waves of settlers re-established in America many prized English folkways. From Boston to Bridgetown, everything from legal culture, housing stock, church practices, animal husbandry, social hierarchy, and food preferences was as distinctively English as the colonists could make it. There was no corner of the colonies, they believed, that might not be improved by apple trees, bee hives, and fields of wheat. Some of their decisions seem mad, as when well-off Caribbean settlers continued to wear English clothing, wigs, and boots in order to maintain social distinctions despite (or because of) the alien climate. Other preferences survived as intriguingly hybrid compromises, as when colonists gave up wheat for Indian corn, but combined the American grain with eggs and dairy products from the domestic fowl and ruminants they had brought from England—and with sugar or molasses from the island colonies.[11]

Given colonists' persistent identification with England and with English ways, it is not very surprising that they tended to see English government as mostly benevolent, not least because it was a faint, distant presence in their lives. Metropolitan authorities were nevertheless keen, from the 1650s onward, to better regulate the colonies that had proved such magnets for population and industry. The Navigation Acts of 1651 and

---

[10] Michael Craton, 'Reluctant Creoles: The Planters' World in the British West Indies', in Bernard Bailyn and Philip D. Morgan (eds.), *Strangers within the Realm: Cultural Margins of the First British Empire* (Chapel Hill, NC, 1991), 324–38; Joyce E. Chaplin, 'Creoles in British America: From Denial to Acceptance', in Charles Stewart (ed.), *Creolization: History, Ethnography, Theory* (Walnut Creek, CA, 2006).

[11] Dunn, *Sugar and Slaves*, 263–334; David H. Fischer, *Albion's Seed: Four British Folkways in America* (New York, 1989); Joyce E. Chaplin, *Subject Matter: Technology, the Body, and Science on the Anglo-American Frontier, 1500–1676* (Cambridge, MA, 2001), chapter 6.

1660 initiated such regulation. Royal charters were another new way to harness the private energies that went into the founding of Carolina (1663) and Pennsylvania (1681), as well as the not-so-successful Company of Royal Adventurers to Africa (1660) and the Royal African Company (1672). The post-Restoration shifts in power from periphery to centre, particularly in the wake of the simultaneous disruptions of King Philip's War and Bacon's Rebellion in 1675, were somewhat less decentralized. But there was remarkably little colonial dissent over rule from afar, except when the Dominion of New England deprived colonies in that region of their original charters after 1685.[12]

Overall, free white colonists and colonial administrators were content with a system of imperial governance that remained substantially sub-contracted, lightly supervised from the centre, and most responsive to the desires of men who lived and held property within the colonies. Perhaps because most colonists saw the Glorious Revolution (1688–91) as an event that restored their autonomy—again in sharp contrast to Ireland, with King William's military pacification of that much-battered part of the empire— they did not voice much discontent with the state of imperial affairs going into the eighteenth century. Their sense of a balance between their cultural similarity to the English yet distance from England still worked, at least for them.[13]

When did colonists—or anyone else—begin to think of themselves as British and as acting on behalf of greater British interests? And when did the *Atlantic*, as a concept, begin to temper their sense of physical distance from England, now Britain?

Whereas 'England' and 'English' had signified one nation with particular customs, politics, and language, 'Britain' and 'British' implied military and political subjection of one people by another, and therefore signified empire, though it originally did so only within the island that contained England, Scotland, and Wales. The supposed etymology of *Briton* was a person descended from Brutus, survivor and veteran of the Trojan War, whose wanderings took him far into northern Europe, where he left progeny. During the Tudor period, propagandists used the concepts of 'Britain' and 'British' on behalf of Henry VIII and Edward VI to sanction subjection of Scotland to England in what was clearly meant to be a form of empire. The Tudor family's origins in Wales, and English transfer of political authority over Wales from the native Welsh Marches to English Parliament, were taken as harbingers of a greater unification among the different kingdoms of the island.[14]

Scotland remained for the moment independent, despite the Tudor bluster, but the subsequent Elizabethan Conquest of Ireland signalled that future reduction of neighbouring territories might be even more violent and exclusionary than had been the case with Wales. In this way, the two words 'British' and 'Britain' continued to imply a legacy of conquest and empire, an implication that, for the moment, the Scots

    [12] Stephen Saunders Webb, *1676: The End of American Independence* (New York, 1984).
    [13] Jack P. Greene, 'The Glorious Revolution and the British Empire 1688–1783', in Lois G. Schwoerer (ed.), *The Revolution of 1688–1689* (Cambridge, 1992).
    [14] David Armitage, *The Ideological Origins of the British Empire* (Cambridge, 2000), 37–43.

vigorously resisted. And most Anglo-American colonists assumed they had avoided such a fate by making themselves into arms-bearing invaders of overseas territories, active participants in empire rather than objects of conquest.

After Elizabeth's death in 1603, the union of Scottish and English thrones under James VI and I initiated a definite if slow political amalgamation. It would take another hundred years to reach the next step, the union of Scottish and English parliaments. Under the Treaty of Union (1707), Scotland's legislature was abandoned and Scottish members and peers were inserted into the Parliament at Westminster. The Scots also agreed not to undertake independent colonizing or overseas trading activities, on the promise of free access to colonies, trading companies, and financial institutions that had once been labelled English but were now designated as British. Indeed, educated Scots quickly penetrated many parts of the empire, becoming overseers of West Indian plantations, tutors of colonial children, and doctors to imperial troops and sailors.[15]

But the bargain bore a high price, as two Scottish uprisings in 1715 and 1745 soon made clear. The perceived Protestant unity between Scotland and England failed to appease the Catholic Scottish aristocracy, including the now defunct Scottish royal line, with its ready supply of enraged 'Pretenders' to the throne. Nor were many ordinary Scots, especially poorer Highlanders, entranced by their purely hypothetical access to English trading companies and financial concerns. From the moment of its birth, Great Britain was gloriously imperial for some, humiliatingly imperious to others.[16]

It was for that reason that colonists did not know quite what to make of the bigger, more powerful British empire that now reigned over their several provincial centres. Would Britons regard British Americans respectfully or imperiously? Might the colonists, like the Scots, achieve representation in Parliament, for instance? The distance over the Atlantic was much greater than that between Edinburgh and Westminster, yet, during the eighteenth century, West Indian planters served as members of Parliament (representing English constituencies yet attuned to island concerns) and most of the continental colonies made sure they had agents, essentially lobbyists, stationed in London and ready to defend colonial interests.

Those arrangements were possible because of British perception that the colonies, and especially the sugar islands, were commercially valuable. And in general, British America was, from 1707 onward, more populous, prosperous, and expansive than ever before. Territorial expansion was dramatic. Old settlements like Virginia grew greatly; new settlements like Georgia (1732) and Nova Scotia expanded older colonial regions, the latter especially after the expulsion of French-speaking Acadians in 1755. By 1763, Britain controlled all of North America's coastline, from Canada to Florida, as well as many Caribbean islands. These successful colonies were now parts of an established trading network with footholds on either side of the ocean. British outposts in West Africa, for instance, helped guarantee the colonies' access to slaves; likewise, colonial

---

[15] David Armitage, 'Making the Empire British: Scotland in the Atlantic World', *Past & Present*, 155 (1997), 34–63.

[16] Linda Colley, *Britons: Forging the Nation, 1707–1837* (New Haven, CT, 1992), chapters 1, 2.

demand for Irish beef, dairy products, and linen showed the transatlantic integration of commercial exchanges done under the authority of a consolidated British empire.

Within the American colonies, and in sharp contrast to other parts of the empire, population soared and kept rearranging itself over a greater extent of territory. Much of the population growth was due to natural increase rather than immigration, in contrast to the seventeenth century. The exception was the slave trade, most of which still went to the Caribbean, and which vastly outpaced white immigration. Between 1701 and 1810, British slave imports totalled about 1.5 million human beings, 50 per cent of them bound to a single colony, Jamaica. (In all the New World, only Brazil imported more African slaves than the British Caribbean.) While slaves on the continent were increasing through natural reproduction, their island counterparts died faster than they could produce children. Between 1700 and 1780, the British islands imported 950,000 slaves but in 1787, the population of slaves numbered a mere 350,000; conversely, only about 250,000 African slaves went into British North America in the same period, but by 1790 the slave population had increased to 750,000.

The upward trend was true for all population on the mainland, and the constant growth reinforced British North America's difference from the British West Indies and from the other European empires in North America—as well as Britain itself. At the end of the Great Migration, in 1660, the mainland colonies had over 70,000 people, at a time when there were only 10,000 European souls in New Netherland and 3,000 in New France (and even fewer in Spain's borderland territories within North America). By 1700, the English/British colonies had about a quarter of a million people, by 1750, over 1 million, and by 1770, 2.3 million. Even before these developments, the population of New Netherland had shrunk and the French and Spanish regions had begun to lag behind the increase of English-speaking peoples, as would be true of the British West Indies, which had not quite 500,000 people in the 1770s. By that decade, the mainland colonies had 82 per cent of the total population of British America.

A greater number of colonists brought stability and even glory to the empire, even as the busily reproducing white creoles assumed they should enjoy a concomitant measure of autonomy. Indeed, the converging characteristics—the long-standing use of private initiative in colonial settlement and the new spurt in population on the continent—made British America distinctive. While the French kings may have permitted or even encouraged similar private initiatives, New France never grew in the way the English-speaking colonies did; the Spanish colonies did grow, but remained for the most part under Spain's centralized control. Only British America would have a large and rapidly growing free creole population that consciously gloried in its history of political and economic freedom.

The natural increase of population was the direct cause of increased economic output—over the eighteenth century, colonial exports soared. Despite variation in prices for colonial products, the general trend was upward. In 1700 the colonies had exported to Britain goods worth about £1,157,000 or almost 20 per cent of total British imports; by 1730, the relevant numbers had shot up to £2,241,000 and 30 per cent; by 1772, to £5,199,000 and 38 per cent. Within those totals, the West Indies contributed a rising proportion: 13 per cent of the total in 1700 but almost 24 per cent by 1772, and 62 per cent of the colonial American total.[17]

As colonial exports rose, so did imports, a trend that always indicated British merchants' growing reliance on a colonial market, especially for British manufactures and for exotics re-exported from Britain. If English exports to the colonies had comprised only £461,000 in 1700 (10 per cent of the total exports), British exports to the colonies mounted to £3,875,000 by 1772, a remarkable 38 per cent of the total exports. Although the West Indies contributed a disproportionate amount of colonial exports to Britain, the continental colonies accounted for most of the imports, over 68 per cent by 1772. A burgeoning consumer culture meant that white colonists who had the money to do so adopted British social customs (especially the drinking of tea), reading habits (everything from novels to political economy), and material culture (chinaware, cotton frocks, wallpaper, and much other stuff). If colonists had once thought themselves English because they could produce and consume American beer, apples, and honey, their wealthier descendants now identified themselves as British because they could import and consume Madeira, oranges, and chocolate.[18]

Still, the British at home did not believe colonists were much like them. Certainly, the gap between the colonial and British elites, in terms of wealth and consumer culture, remained tellingly wide. As well, eighteenth-century colonists would have surprised their seventeenth-century forebears with their greater tolerance for non-English peoples. Dutch, German, and Scottish populations, in particular, became more common in the colonies, especially in the mid-Atlantic. Protestants were still much more welcome than any other group, though an enclave of Catholic Minorcans in Florida and groups of Jews in Rhode Island, New York, the lower south, and Caribbean made the colonies seem, from a British perspective, rather mixed. The large populations of Africans, especially, set the colonies apart from Britain, though metropolitan cities, and London in particular, had considerable numbers of black people. By mid-century, there was clearly a polyglot British-Atlantic culture, though it was much more apparent and abundant on the western side of the Atlantic.

When ordinary people in Britain thought of the colonies, they probably thought of the colonial commodities they produced—trade fuelled the empire and brought American products into daily use in English households. If tobacco, fish, and sugar had made earlier generations of English consumers dependent on colonial trade, that development was accentuated by the constant upward rate of sugar consumption, which reached into the working classes by the latter part of the eighteenth century. As well, the use of pottery and textiles dyed blue with Caribbean indigo, the increased consumption of Carolina and Georgia rice, and the rage for furniture fashioned from

[17] B. R. Mitchell, *British Historical Statistics* (Cambridge, 1988), 496.
[18] Ibid.; T. H. Breen, '"Baubles of Britain": The American and Consumer Revolutions in the Eighteenth Century', *Past & Present*, 119 (1988), 73–104; Richard L. Bushman, 'American High-Style and Vernacular Cultures', in Jack P. Greene and J. R. Pole (eds.), *Colonial British America* (Baltimore, MD, 1984).

Honduras mahogany all made visible Britain's eager acceptance of American trade-stuffs. Above all, the use of slaves in port cities was a constant reminder of the non-English and extra-territorial peoples who made the empire work.

The volume and value of colonial trade prompted British officials to provide services meant to speed traffic across the Atlantic Ocean, then up and down the coast and around the islands. Transatlantic communication had long been a private affair—people entrusted their letters to ships' captains and others whose business sent them in the direction that the letters needed to go. Britain first experimented with an official packet boat service for correspondence early in the eighteenth century. Under the British Post Office, a regular transatlantic service commenced after 1745, and its continued expansion to new ports and over a spreading landscape made it clear that Britons and Americans now expected smooth transfer of information whatever the growth of the Atlantic empire. Yet even in this instance, Britons sub-contracted the work of empire by employing colonists to get the mail sorted and delivered; two deputy postmaster generals were, after 1763, delegated to standardize the continental American service and make it pay for itself.[19]

Much of the inbound postal service carried news and newspapers, so it showed a renewed belief among colonists that English-speaking people were distinctive for their interest in literacy and learning. The founding of Harvard College in Massachusetts Bay had revealed Puritans' determination to study and disseminate the gospel on the western side of the ocean. Subsequent colleges, from William and Mary and Yale to the College of Philadelphia (later Pennsylvania), College of New Jersey (later Princeton), and King's College (later Columbia), spread those aspirations through other regions of British America. While higher education was still very much reserved for white men of the propertied classes, libraries and even learned societies were open to larger numbers. The Library Company of Philadelphia, whose roots lay in Benjamin Franklin's Junto, a reading and debating society for young working men, was only the most famous of provincial organizations meant to display the extent to which colonials were enlightened. Clubs, Masonic lodges, and scientific demonstrations were also popular and pervasive, making the colonies resemble provincial society in Britain itself.

In every way, white colonists still considered themselves cultural equivalents of the English, and were not initially adverse to considering themselves British. To literate and urban colonists in particular, the Scottish case seemed somewhat promising as an example of how provincials might join and be an ornament to the metropolitan centre. Scotland provided a comforting analogy, especially for scribbling colonists who admired and wished to emulate Edinburgh's cosmopolitan thinkers and authors: from the empire's periphery, wisdom might flow.[20]

Great Britain's imperial warfare also provided new opportunities for colonists with varied ambitions. From King William's War (1689–97) to the Seven Years War

---

[19] Howard Robinson, *Carrying British Mails Overseas* (New York, 1964), chapter 4.
[20] Bernard Bailyn and John Clive, 'England's Cultural Provinces: Scotland and America', *William and Mary Quarterly*, 3rd Series, 11 (1954), 200–13.

(1756–63), Britain fought seven major wars against France, five of which also involved Spain. Colonists used every conflict to serve their own interests. New England merchants obligingly fitted out an invasion of French Louisbourg in the Atlantic Maritimes in 1745, for instance, an act both patriotic and self-serving. In similar fashion, Virginia settlers and land investors attacked a French outpost in the Ohio Valley in 1754 which would set off the Seven Years War. At this point, British officials did not merely subcontract colonial effort, but merged their formal military engagements with it.

It was at this militant stage of things that use of the word 'Atlantic' to describe the ocean between Britain and America became common. In colonial newspapers, the key decade when the term proliferated was the 1740s, meaning during the War of Jenkins's Ear (which began in 1739) and at the roughly chronological crescendo of eighteenth-century imperial warfare. And after the 1740s, use of 'Atlantic Ocean' in the papers increased still more. To some extent, this merely reflected how maritime imperial activity was becoming more common and more visible. But the new name for the ocean no longer implied, as 'Western Ocean' had done, that Britain lay in the default direction and America on the wrong side of things. 'Atlantic Ocean' was a neutral designation; its waters might connect Britain and British America as much as it divided them.

So, almost three centuries after those pioneering English fishermen had ventured out into western waters, there now was a *British Atlantic*. And that newly meaningful phrase might have signalled a new and more powerful convergence between British and colonial interests and aspirations, forged especially in the fires of imperial war, and indicated by the natural convergence of interests and currents that flowed equally across a connecting body of water, through newspapers, books, and pamphlets carried by the newly successful postal service, and through commodity exchanges that let Glaswegians savour Caribbean coffee while Charlestonians tippled London gin.

But it never quite worked out that way. When colonials fought alongside British troops (and, perhaps more significantly, subordinate to British officers) during the 1740s in the War of Jenkins's Ear, their metropolitan comrades called them 'Americans'. For a people who had long called themselves English, and who were perhaps beginning to consider themselves British, the designation was not entirely welcome. High-handed British command over colonial troops and officers in the Seven Years War confirmed a suspicion that Britons did not regard their settler cousins as equals. Colonists especially resented any suggestion that they might resemble the native Indians or forcibly imported Africans who made America seem, to Europeans, distinctively exotic. By not regarding colonists as equals, late eighteenth-century Britons were blind to all the careful, strategic cultural work that had gone into over a century of English-based colonizing ideology.[21]

---

[21] Fred Anderson, *A People's Army: Massachusetts Soldiers and Society in the Seven Years War* (Chapel Hill, NC, 1984); T. H. Breen, 'Ideology and Nationalism on the Eve of the American Revolution: Revisions *Once More* in Need of Revising', *Journal of American History*, 84 (1997), 13–39.

Moreover, it no longer seemed clear to colonists that Britons regarded them as distinct from peoples who had been subjugated by force. British efforts to regulate Indian affairs and to reform the slave trade may have been positive reforms, but they struck colonists as ominous ways to level out the different statuses of colonial populations. Pontiac's Conspiracy of 1763 made it seem to British officials that Indian affairs required a firm hand and consistent, centralized policy. But the resulting decision to forbid pell-mell colonial movement into western territory, lest conflict over Indian lands spark another frontier war, infuriated poorer westerners. In December 1763, in response to Pontiac's uprising and the proclamation, a group of Pennsylvania settlers brutally murdered twenty Indians who were Christian converts and in alliance with the colonial government. While a Pennsylvania delegation was able to prevent further violence, they never brought any of the vigilantes to justice, an omission that Indians and British officials thought showed continuing colonial inability to keep the peace.

Antislavery debates elicited more transatlantic divisions. Those discussions were, as with those over Indian affairs, meant to address real problems. It was not yet the case that very many white people had principled objections to slavery. But slave rebellions, rare in the seventeenth century, became a dangerously persistent feature of life in the eighteenth-century colonies, especially the West Indies, which brought public attention to the drawbacks of slave labour. Jamaica's Maroon Wars of the 1720s and 1730s were a dramatic case in point, in which runaway slaves or maroons built an autonomous subsistence economy in the mountainous interior of Jamaica, a constant invitation to other slaves to strike out and join them. When white militias were unable to crush the maroons, the authorities made a peace treaty with them in 1739–40, the first time that slaves anywhere in the British empire had gained their freedom through force of arms. Other slave rebellions were not as successful, but fear of a slave conspiracy in New York City in 1741 and reaction against an actual revolt, the Stono Rebellion, in South Carolina in 1739, kept slavery's dangers in the public eye. The instabilities of the Seven Years War then encouraged slaves on Jamaica to rise in 1760 in what became known as Tacky's Rebellion.

These and other incidents questioned the wisdom of continuing to introduce disaffected and alien outsiders to the British colonies. By the end of the war, publicity about the cruelties of the slave trade met with a more receptive audience than would have been the case earlier. In Parliament and beyond, Britons and British Americans discussed the problems of slavery and openly contemplated how the slave trade and forced labour might not have an indefinite future.

While some white colonists welcomed closer regulation of the slave trade, and a minority even wanted to abolish it, others saw these developments as implied criticisms of their way of life. The Somerset Decision of 1772 was especially galling. While Lord Mansfield had only judged, in that case, that slaveholders could not remove slaves from England against their will, and had not declared slavery illegal in England, it was nevertheless true that the decision gave property in humans full legal protection on one side of the Atlantic Ocean only. The decision implied that, whereas Britain was enlightened, America was benighted. However much slaveholders might point out that Britons profited enormously from plantations and slavery, and enjoyed the fruits of enslaved labour, a line had been drawn.[22]

Finally, mainland colonists were surprised to find that the empire was now supposed to be a haven for foreign Catholics. After Britain had obtained Canada, under the terms of the Treaty of Paris that concluded the Seven Years War, British government was extended over what had been New France. Under the Quebec Act (1774), Parliament guaranteed that French settlers could maintain their laws and religion. Protestant colonists, especially New Englanders, were outraged that Catholics who had only recently been loyal subjects of a Catholic king would so easily be drawn into the British empire, as if they were actually comparable to the English-speaking and Protestant subjects of George III.

The old arrangements, in which free colonists had had enormous discretion to deal with Indians, rule over African slaves, and exclude Catholics, were now a matter for reform, with British officials chiding colonists for their intolerance and inhumanity and making the non-European or Catholic residents of British America into objects of solicitous care. Suggestions that either Indians in alliance with Great Britain or slaves might be considered British subjects was the worst insult, again because the very idea hinted that colonizer and colonized shared the same status.

With the advent of new British policies to gather revenue from colonial trade, colonists were convinced that, indeed, their new status as British Americans meant loss of status and autonomy and that the Atlantic Ocean was an all too convenient highway for speeding British troops and tax officials to the colonies. While it would be impossible to determine whether colonists would have accepted new taxes had they believed themselves to be distinctively privileged members of a large polity in the same manner as their English ancestors, it is certainly the case that they saw most of Britain's mid-eighteenth-century policies as invasive innovations rather than reasonable developments. The *British Atlantic*, boldest of all imperial innovations of the eighteenth century, had proved much too bold to maintain the world that English settlers had created on the far side of the Western Ocean.

BIBLIOGRAPHY

Armitage, David, and Michael J. Braddick (eds.), *The British Atlantic World, 1500–1800* (New York, 2009).

Games, Alison, and Adam Rothman (eds.), *Major Problems in Atlantic History: Documents and Essays* (Boston, MA, 2008).

Gilroy, Paul, *The Black Atlantic: Modernity and Double Consciousness* (Cambridge, MA, 1993).

---

[22] Christopher Leslie Brown, *Moral Capital: Foundations of British Abolitionism* (Chapel Hill, NC, 2006).

Greene, Jack P., and Philip D. Morgan (eds.), *Atlantic History: A Critical Reappraisal* (New York, 2009).

McCusker, John J., and Russell R. Menard, *The Economy of British America, 1607–1789* (Chapel Hill, NC, 1985).

McFarlane, Anthony, *The British in the Americas, 1480–1815* (London, 1994).

Rediker, Marcus, *Between the Devil and the Deep Blue Sea: Merchant Seamen, Pirates, and the Anglo-American Maritime World, 1700–1750* (Cambridge, 1987).

Steele, Ian K., *Warpaths: Invasions of North America* (New York, 1994).

—— *The English Atlantic, 1675–1740: An Exploration of Communication and Community* (New York, 1986).

CHAPTER 14

THE FRENCH ATLANTIC WORLD IN THE SEVENTEENTH AND EIGHTEENTH CENTURIES

SILVIA MARZAGALLI

THE French were major actors in the creation of an Atlantic world. From the sixteenth century onwards, the Atlantic sphere provided employment for thousands of French sailors, sustained a large merchant community, and supplied much capital. In the following two centuries, cities and ports involved in Atlantic trade emerged and prospered. On the eve of the French and Haitian revolutions, many Frenchmen made their living by shipping and producing industrial and agricultural products, which circulated around the Atlantic basin.

During the seventeenth century, the involvement of French traders in the Atlantic world attracted the attention of chartered companies and the crown, leading to the establishment of a formal empire and permanent trading posts on the African coasts. The French monarchy repeatedly tried to construct and sustain its empire by bolstering its personnel, but ultimately depended on the strength of merchant networks. French imperial policy was a source of permanent tensions—between colonists and authorities in Versailles; planters, free coloured, and slaves; France and other European colonial powers—leading eventually to the progressive loss of the French empire in the course of the eighteenth century.

Although French colonial trade and movements of people increased considerably over this period—the French West Indies provided Europe with huge quantities of sugar and coffee produced by an increasing number of African slaves—the French Atlantic world was never confined within its imperial boundaries. French influence extended beyond the formal limits of empire.

SHAPING THE FRENCH ATLANTIC

By 1650 the French crown had successfully managed to build an empire both on the American mainland and in the West Indies. Effective French settlements in the Americas and on the African coasts followed a century of informal private enterprise both in the Newfoundland fisheries and in transatlantic trade with Africa and the Americas. Private ventures contributed to shape French perceptions of Atlantic opportunities and influenced royal decisions regarding the direction of French colonization.

In the early sixteenth century, Newfoundland was already a regular destination for fishermen from Normandy, northern Brittany, and south-western France. By 1580, with possibly 500 ships, Frenchmen dominated these fisheries.[1] The commercialization of cod required the organization of regular shipping linking Northern Atlantic French ports to catholic southern Europe, which absorbed most of the product. Due to the year-long duration required to complete a fishing campaign, this trade relied on loans. Newfoundland fisheries, thus, were a key element both in the rise of French Atlantic shipping and in the emergence of a class of major shipowners and merchants in French Atlantic ports, who progressively engaged in other sectors of the Atlantic economy.

Newfoundland fisheries contributed also to the establishment of first contacts with Native Americans. Captains and crew soon recognized the interest of adding trade to fishing. Bartering was well established by the time of Jacques Cartier's first expedition in 1534, when he was offered furs by Micmacs in Gaspé and by Montagnais near Belle Isle Strait.[2] Within a few decades, a tiny regular trade flow had arisen, with Frenchmen providing copper pans, knives, metal wares, and glass beads in exchange for Amerindians' furs. Not until the 1570s–1580s, however, did French merchants fit out ships specifically in order to procure furs. Their importance attracted royal attention, and in 1577 and again in 1598 royal representative Troilus de La Roche de Mesgouez obtained a trade monopoly. By the beginning of the seventeenth century, the lobby around the crown and the economic relevance of the fur trade influenced the colonial priorities of the French crown, as B. Allaire has convincingly argued. European diseases and Amerindian lack of immunities emptied the St Lawrence River of its local inhabitants, facilitating French settlement.

French merchants and ships' captains traded also with Native Americans and Iberian colonists who had settled in the 'Indies' (Spanish mainland, West Indies) and Brazil, where their presence is documented as early as 1504. They also turned to piracy and the slave trade. In the first third of the sixteenth century, Jean Ango, merchant and shipowner in Dieppe, fitted out at least thirty vessels for the Americas. In 1522, one of his masters, Jean Fleury,

---

[1] Laurier Turgeon, 'La Pêche française à la "terre neufve" avant Champlain ou l'avènement d'une proto-industrie: la place du Centre-Ouest?', in M. Augeron and D. Guillemet (eds.), *Champlain ou les portes du Nouveau Monde: cinq siècles d'échanges entre le Centre-Ouest français et l'Amérique du Nord* (La Crèche, 2004), 57–61.

[2] Laurier Turgeon, 'Les Français en Nouvelle-Angleterre avant Champlain', in Raymonde Litalien and Denis Vaugeois (eds.), *Champlain: la naissance de l'Amérique française* (Sillery, 2004), 98–108.

captured three Spanish ships carrying Cortés' booty. Less spectacular cargoes consisted of dyewoods and parrots. Although only a single French slave ship is documented for the sixteenth century, many others seem to have engaged in the trade. As early as 1548, the ships *Le Baudollier* and *La Rebarge* left Le Havre for Cap Vert and the Gambia River 'to pick up some Blacks if possible', before going to the West Indies 'to sell them with other goods of the country'.[3] Between 1571 and 1588, 165 ships left Le Havre for 'Peru' (a generic term for Spanish America) or, more frequently, 'Africa and Peru'.[4] French merchants did not wait for the crown to provide them with opportunities in the New World: in fact, they induced their king to sponsor exploration and settlement attempts. Both Verrazzano's and Cartier's first expeditions were largely co-financed by private capital.

The growing importance of the Atlantic induced the French crown to renew its attempts to impose its presence overseas. The rise of the first French overseas empire was the result of an increasingly consistent policy pursued throughout the seventeenth century by Henry IV, Louis XIII, and Louis XIV and their main ministers Richelieu, Mazarin, and Colbert. Nevertheless, economic interests rather than a carefully directed state policy determined both the directions and degree of success of French colonization. Both chronologically and spatially, French colonization of the Americas paralleled English efforts. Henry IV (1598–1610) continuously attended to North America, leading to Samuel Champlain's expedition and the foundation of Québec (1608). Louis XIII (1610–43) and Richelieu directed their main concerns to the West Indies (notably Martinique and Guadeloupe in 1635, Sainte-Lucie in 1637). Mazarin, the minister in charge during the minority of Louis XIV (1643–1715), continued these efforts after the end of the Thirty Years War (Saint-Barthélemy, 1648; Saint-Martin and Grenada, 1650). Both Richelieu and Mazarin encouraged colonization attempts in French Guyana, which came to nothing until the 1660s and 1670s.

In other instances, French settlements in the West Indies preceded the crown's official commitment. From the middle of the seventeenth century, Frenchmen settled on the western coast of Hispaniola. They used the island for privateering, grew tobacco, and traded smoked meat to ships' captains. But only in 1697, at the peace of Ryswick, did Spain officially cede this territory, which became Saint-Domingue.

In these early phases, the viability of French settlements depended on the possibility of attracting a sufficient number of settlers to replace those who died or returned. Attractiveness depended on economic resources rather than on state policy. Thus Saint-Domingue developed more consistently than Guyana, despite the latter's earlier status as a colony. By the end of the seventeenth century, French colonization in North America had developed along the St Lawrence River to the Great Lakes, and explorers, followed by soldiers, went down the Mississippi to the Gulf of Mexico. In 1682 Cavalier de la Salle took possession of what was to become French Louisiana—an area that

---

[3] http://www.slavevoyages.org/; Archives Nationales, Paris, Minutier Central des Notaires, Notaire Yves Bourgeois, 7 May 1548. I thank Bernard Allaire for this information.

[4] Philippe Barrey, 'Le Havre transatlantique de 1571 à 1610', in Julien Hayem (ed.), *Mémoires et documents pour servir à l'histoire du commerce et de l'industrie en France* (Paris, 1917), vol. v.

approximates to that covered by twenty states of the present United States—and Le Moyne d'Iberville initiated the first French permanent settlement.

Missionaries accompanied and sometimes preceded colonization. The collaboration of the crown and the Church to convert Native Americans to Christianity was part of a broader evangelization project which affected all parts of the kingdom.[5] It was also a means for the French crown to compete with the pretensions of the Spanish king to be the sole protector of Christianity overseas.

The building of a French empire was not confined to the New World, nor to the Atlantic. Parallel to the rise of the French West Indies, Frenchmen established permanent trading posts on the African coast in order to procure slaves. Merchants from Dieppe and Rouen obtained the monopoly of trade from Senegal and Gambia in 1626 (Compagnie Normande, 1626–58): two years later, they established the first French settlement in Senegal. Founded in 1658, Saint-Louis became, with Gorée (1677), the core of French permanent settlements in Africa. Frenchmen set foot also in the Indian Ocean, where they took possession of today's Reunion (1638) and Mauritius (1715) islands, and established various trading posts in India, notably Pondicherry.

The establishment of an empire compelled a rethinking of French sovereignty in such distant areas. From the 1660s, Louis XIV and Colbert put the colonies progressively under direct state control, instead of the previous policy of granting a monopoly to private chartered companies and letting them administer and defend the colony. As Minister of the Navy and of Public Finances, Colbert fought to restrict the presence of foreign merchants and ships—notably the Dutch—in the French colonies and, after the failure of the West Indian Company, which he initiated (1664–74), he encouraged French merchants to invest in transatlantic trade by protecting them from foreign competition. Although he was never completely successful, Frenchmen increasingly engaged in colonial trade. The growth of European demand in colonial goods created a further incentive to develop West Indian production, leading in turn to an increase in the slave trade and greater integration across the Atlantic.

The French empire, which reached its maximal extension at the end of the seventeenth century, was progressively lost during the 'Second Hundred Years War', an expression forged by historians to designate the frequency of warfare from 1689 to 1815.[6] Wars were the expression of increasing rivalry between Great Britain and France, which had developed colonies in the same geographic areas, and had competed also to gain a privileged access to the Iberian markets and American silver and gold.

The inefficiency of French naval and military bases, notably Louisbourg, which became an important trade and smuggling centre but was not effective, as its garrison surrendered both in 1745 and 1758, as well as growing British naval mastery led to the progressive loss of French North America in 1713 (Newfoundland, Hudson Bay, and

---

[5] Dominique Deslandres, *Croire et faire croire: les missions françaises au XVIIe siècle* (Paris, 2003).

[6] J. Meyer and J. Bromley, 'The Second Hundred Years War', in D. Johnson, F. Bédarida, and F. Crouzet (eds.), *Britain and France: Ten Centuries* (Folkestone, 1980), 168–71; François Crouzet, 'The Second Hundred Years War: Some Reflections', *French History*, 10/4 (1996), 432–50.

Acadia) and in 1763 (New France including Louisiana, the latter ceded to Spain). Contemporaries could minimize these losses, because peace treaties confirmed fishing rights in Newfoundland and preserved the French West Indies, the most valuable colonies. By the mid-1750s, French trade with the West Indies was twenty-five times greater than trade with New France.

Strategically, however, the loss of New France reduced French capacity to protect its West Indian possessions. Just as during the Seven Years War, when the British occupied Martinique and Guadeloupe after their conquest of Canada, so France could not prevent their occupation, as well as part of Saint-Domingue, in 1793–4. The absence of a permanent base on the American mainland also weakened France's capacity to counter the slave uprising in Saint-Domingue (1791), which ultimately led to the independence of Haiti (1804). The loss of New France, thus, undermined the whole French colonial empire in the Americas. The attempts to develop French Guyana as a substitute failed miserably and resulted in a human catastrophe (the Kourou expedition of 1763). Bonaparte's effort to recover Louisiana from Spain (in 1800) was just as fruitless, as he ultimately sold it to the United States both because the outbreak of war against Great Britain (1803) made it impossible to protect this colony from enemy attacks, and because he had failed to regain control over Saint-Domingue (Leclerc's expedition, 1802).

France's loss of influence in the Americas is the most visible part of its overall decline in the Atlantic—Senegal became British from the Seven Years War to 1783, and was occupied again by the British during the Anglo-French wars—and, more generally, outside Europe. The Seven Years War left France with only five trading posts in India, and in 1815, Mauritius became British. The vulnerability of the French empire is generally attributed to the relative weakness of the French navy, which in turn was the result of the desperate state of public finances as well as the more continental orientations of French foreign policy.[7] Warfare, however, was not an independent variable; it was the result in part of the exclusive, monopolistic way in which European countries organized their colonial trade across the Atlantic and ruled their empires.

The characteristics of the French Atlantic empire

Like British America, French America presented two major colonial patterns, but these were less integrated than in the British case. One was a predominantly rural society in North America, essentially consisting of free Europeans interacting with Amerindian

---

[7] Martine Acerra and Jean Meyer, *Histoire de la marine française: des origines à nos jours* (Rennes, 1994); James Pritchard, *Louis XVs Navy, 1748-1762: A Study of Organization and Administration* (Kingston, 1987); id., *The Anatomy of a Naval Disaster: The 1746 French Expedition to North America* (Montreal, 1995); id., *In Search of Empire*; Jonathan Dull, *The French Navy and the Seven Years' War* (Lincoln, NE, 2005).

groups.[8] The other was a plantation economy based on slave labour in the West Indies, and to a much lesser extent in Louisiana and French Guyana. In Africa, French slave trading posts such as Saint-Louis and Gorée coexisted with the development of a plantation economy in Bourbon (today's Reunion) and Île de France (Mauritius), which also served as a basis for slave trade in East Africa.

French Canada suffered from a chronic lack of settlers. About 70,000 French men and women crossed the Atlantic to New France, but two-thirds of them returned, often after completing the contract which bound them as indentured servants.[9] In 1700, after almost a century of efforts, the French population of New France totalled only 15,000 inhabitants. By sending to Canada 770 young adult women—mostly orphans—Colbert had succeeded in balancing the sex ratio (1 woman for 6 men at the beginning of the 1660s), thus allowing for significant population growth in the following decades.[10] But the number of inhabitants was modest, especially considering France's status as the most populated country in Europe (22 million inhabitants in 1715). Despite their dramatic decline in numbers, natives outnumbered newcomers, leading the French toward a policy of accommodation and alliance with Amerindian groups.

If land and resources in Canada seemed boundless, other constraints limited settlement. France exported both the seigniorial system, which weighed heavily on French peasants at home, and religious orthodoxy, to the New World. New France was not to be a refuge for French Huguenots,[11] nor did it represent the opportunity for migrants to create new models of social interaction, despite contemporary perceptions of a freer Canadian society. The small size of this society, the fact that it had to survive on its own—contacts to France being limited and on a yearly rhythm—made French Canada evolve autonomously and integrate elements of native societies, with a significant *metissage*.

Just as much as the harsh Canadian winters, a society allowing for little upward mobility within a generation probably accounts for the lack of enthusiasm of potential migrants to venture to New France. By the time the British conquered it, the Canadian population had grown to approximately 70,000 inhabitants, but it was still dramatically under-populated compared to the 2 million inhabitants of British North America. One positive feature of under-population, however, was that conflicts with Amerindians over land were rare in French America, certainly compared to the situation in British America.

French Canadian society was heavily land-oriented. Its scant demographic development, however, never allowed New France to play a role within the French Atlantic world similar to that played by the British mainland colonies. Canada provided no

---

[8] Throughout the French regime, 1,500 Amerindians lived as slaves in French Canada and 200 in Louisiana and Illinois. Additionally, a total of 300 African slaves were shipped from the West Indies; see further p. 245.

[9] Leslie Choquette, *Frenchmen into Peasants: Modernity and Tradition in the Peopling of French Canada* (Cambridge, MA, 1997).

[10] Yves Landry, *Les Filles du roi au XVIIe siècle: orphelines en France, pionnières au Canada* (Montreal, 1992).

[11] French trade to New France was however largely in the hands of Protestant merchant houses in France: J. F. Bosher, *The Canada Merchants, 1713–1763* (Oxford, 1987).

significant agricultural surplus to the mother country, nor was the integration between mainland and islands comparable to the British case. Industrial production was limited by the lack of skilled and abundant labour even more than by restrictive legislation imposed by the mother country, which aimed to ensure that French industry would not suffer from colonial competition and would, on the contrary, benefit from colonial demand.

New France exported some wood, livestock, and cereals to the French West Indies and furs to France, and imported manufactured goods as well as wine, brandy, and food for its soldiers. This trade occasionally provided extraordinary profit opportunities to French officers as well as to the merchant houses of Bordeaux and La Rochelle.[12] From its beginnings, public demand shaped the Canadian market. Contrary to the West Indian export-oriented economy, a few ships a year sufficed to undertake this commerce.[13]

In contrast to a largely self-sufficient Canadian society, the West Indies developed a plantation economy based on slave labour. Tobacco was the essential export until the 1660s, but declined thereafter. Sugar developed from the middle of the seventeenth century, and coffee from the 1730s–1740s. Together with indigo, these three products represented 90 per cent of the value of eighteenth-century colonial exports. By the 1720s, Saint-Domingue sugar production exceeded Jamaica's. France's major colony was the predominant sugar and coffee world producer until the early 1790s.

The development of the plantation economy was characterized by modest white immigration and a massive forced influx of Africans. By 1700 the French West Indies had approximately 27,000 black slaves and 21,000 white inhabitants. By 1790, those populations were respectively 650,000 and 60,000. The French colonies received about 1 million African captives over the course of the eighteenth century, compared to about 300,000 French migrants, most of whom died within a few months of their arrival or returned to France. Saint-Domingue, and to a lesser degree Martinique and Guadeloupe, represented the core of the French plantation system and by far its most populated areas.

Other French colonial possessions in the Americas were less successful than the West Indies. Mid-eighteenth-century French Guyana had 600 white inhabitants and 7,000 slaves in total. With 10,000 inhabitants, including 6,000 slaves of African descent, Louisiana was still under-populated in 1763.[14] Despite John Law's attempts in the late 1710s to promote migration through El Dorado-like descriptions of this region, Louisiana failed to develop to a significant export-oriented colony. Law, the minister of finances of the child king Louis XV, elaborated a plan to absorb the French public debt

---

[12] Jacques Mathieu, *Le Commerce entre la Nouvelle-France et les Antilles au XVIIIe siècle* (Montreal, 1981); Silvia Marzagalli, 'Bordeaux et le Canada, 1663–1773', in Augeron and Guillemet (eds.), *Champlain*, 207–12.

[13] James S. Pritchard, 'The Pattern of French Colonial Shipping to Canada before 1760', *Revue française d'histoire d'outre-mer*, 231 (1976), 189–209.

[14] The direct slave trade from Africa to French Louisiana started in 1719 and ended in 1743. Other slaves were introduced indirectly from the British colonies or the West Indies. The slave birth rate was higher than in the West Indies. Havard and Vidal, *Histoire de l'Amérique*, 164–7.

with the profit of the Mississippi Company—which merged soon afterwards into the Indian Company—to which he granted the trade monopoly to Louisiana. This speculation ended in 1720 in a colossal financial bubble. In 1731, the Indian Company abandoned its monopolistic rights and the state took the colony under its direct administration, in order to maintain a territory which had strategic value in preventing British expansion in North America. Once Canada was lost, France considered it useless to keep Louisiana and ceded it to Spain.

The French presence in Africa owed everything to the development of the plantation economy. Like other Europeans, the French sought secure bases for the slave trade. The crown directed its attention to Senegal and Gorée, and individual slavers established some trading posts from Senegambia to the Bay of Benin where a few dozen Frenchmen resided permanently (at Bissau and Judah). The French colonies in East Africa had varied goals: Reunion and Mauritius islands served both as ports of call for ships bound from and to the East Indies and for slave ships; and they developed coffee and sugar plantations, like the West Indies. In the 1770s, French colonies in the Indian Ocean were increasingly integrated into the Atlantic economy, as slave ships not only provided Reunion and Mauritius with slaves, but began carrying them to the West Indies. On the eve of the French Revolution, the population of the two islands was 48,000 and 45,000 respectively, mostly comprising slaves. In the 1780s, forty to fifty ships a year plied between Mauritius and France. From the French perspective, the economic value and the relations with its plantation colonies in the Indian Ocean did not differ from the West Indies. All of them were a part of its empire.

The system of colonial rule involved the delegation of authority to a governor and an *intendant*. Both posts existed in France, the former in charge of military defence in the provinces, the latter of finances, justice, and administration. Whereas the influential power of governors decreased in France after Louis XIV's reign, they still played a major role in the colonies, because the distance from Versailles gave them larger responsibilities and more immediate decision-taking. Moreover, they were one of the main sources of information for the crown and the minister of the navy and the colonies. The presence of an *intendant* was expected to counterbalance the influence of the governor. Their functions, in fact, overlapped in many instances.

When exerting control over the colonies, the French kings tried to avoid the difficulties they faced in continental France, where local privileges had produced much complexity and diversity in law, fiscal charges, and administration. The French crown aimed to produce rational and uniformly organized colonies. Whereas different inheritance practices coexisted in France, for instance, all colonies adopted the Parisian customary law. Contrary to France, judicial officers did not buy their positions and could not transmit them to their heirs; the crown, thus, had more direct control over its servants in the colonies than at home. Colonists did not pay the tax on salt (*gabelle*) or the *taille*, but they had to serve in the local militia to protect the colony. Colonies were conceived as experiments. In order to rule, the crown sought good information, dispatching engineers, botanists, scientists, architects, and city planners around the Atlantic to collect and forward useful data. These agents conveyed plants, seeds, and animals, to be analysed and eventually acclimatized in Europe and in other parts of the empire.[15]

French attempts to understand and to appropriate a different world aimed ultimately at shaping it according to French interests. The core of colonial ideology could be distilled into what Adam Smith would label later as 'mercantilism'. The crown promoted the establishment of colonies and paid for their protection because they were strategically well located and a source of prestige. Above all, they were potentially beneficial to French merchants and to the country's balance of trade. In order to increase the benefit for the mother country, the state obliged the colonists to trade exclusively with Frenchmen and to import and export goods on only French-owned ships, which were not allowed to sail from or to a foreign port.

The consequences of this system, which took shape under Colbert, were manifold. Most signally, merchants in France were protected from foreign competition in colonial markets. In addition, goods bound for and coming from the colonies systematically passed through a French port, although many were originally produced or were ultimately destined abroad. As a result, the economic activities of French ports benefited as did public revenues. By reserving profits to the mother country, however, the system created a permanent source of tension between centre and periphery. In practice, the exclusive system worked—despite its many leaks and endemic smuggling in the West Indies—in peacetime, but was entirely disrupted in warfare, when French ships were unable to provide colonists with sufficient stores and slaves because of the increased insecurity on the ocean. In such extremities, governors authorized the entrance of foreign ships, and it was a particularly delicate task to restore the exclusive system once the conflict was over. Dissatisfaction with the rule imposed by the mother country occasionally provoked revolt, as in Martinique in 1717 or in Saint-Domingue in 1769.[16] The crown accommodated in 1767 and again in 1784: foreigners were allowed a limited trade with the French West Indies, although not in essential commodities like sugar, coffee, fish, or meal. This half-measure merely encouraged smuggling. Further, colonists had to pay foreigners in specie, thereby making it more difficult to pay their French suppliers and reducing colonial trade's profitability.

The exclusive system reflects the subordinate status the crown assigned to its non-European territories. If colonies differed from the mother country, this was also because colonists were a minority compared to non-European populations living on the territory that the French king considered under its sovereignty. Relations to African descendants and Native Americans in the Americas gave rise to radically different societies. Nevertheless local specificities and privileges were an essential feature of the

---

[15] Charlotte de Castelnau-l'Estoile and François Regourd (eds.), *Connaissances et pouvoirs: les espaces impériaux, XVIe–XVIIIe siècles, France, Espagne, Portugal* (Bordeaux, 2005); François Regourd, 'Sciences et colonisation sous l'ancien régime: le cas de la Guyane et des Antilles françaises, XVIIe–XVIIIe siècles' (Ph.D. thesis, Bordeaux, 1999).

[16] Charles Frostin, *Les Révoltes blanches à Saint-Domingue aux XVIIe et XVIIIe siècles* (Paris, 1975; Rennes, 2008).

French monarchy, so that the integration of the peculiarities of colonial societies was not perceived as particularly problematic.

The establishment of slavery in French America introduced a fundamental disparity in the judicial status of individuals between France, where slavery had disappeared in the Middle Ages, and the colonies, where it was codified to face the new challenges of colonization. The Code Noir (1685) instituted a distinction between free people and slaves—a difference ostensibly founded not on race or colour, but on the legal status of the individual. But the 1724 version of the Code Noir formally introduced racial discrimination by prohibiting marriages between white and blacks—whatever their status—and increasing the social barrier between free people (white and coloured) and slaves, who could not intermarry. In theory the Code Noir determined the conditions of slaves in the French colonies and imposed some responsibilities and limits on masters. Concretely, however, slaves had little chance to obtain justice from colonial authorities.

The vast majority of French colonists in the West Indies were men, whose sexual exploitation of black concubines and female slaves produced an increasing number of children of mixed descent. On the eve of the French Revolution, one slave out of five in Guadeloupe was coloured. In Saint-Domingue, colonists freed many of their coloured children, so that the free coloured—free Blacks and mulattos—were almost as numerous as white colonists and possessed a third of plantations and a quarter of slaves in 1786, when one of their number, Julien Raimond, travelled to Paris to claim his people's civil rights. In Guadeloupe, free coloureds comprised less than a fifth of the free population (compared to 45 per cent in Saint-Domingue) and owned one plantation in four and 5 per cent of the slaves. Paradoxically, the emergence of this group of free coloured, many of whom were wealthy, educated, and vital to the functioning of the local militia, increased racist attitudes among white colonists, and contributed to the emergence of a racial discourse on both sides of the Atlantic.[17]

Interactions between races and people of different legal statuses were not confined to the colonies but affected France. Some planters sent their mulatto children to France for an education; others dispatched slaves to acquire specific skills. Sometimes domestic slaves accompanied their masters when they travelled home. The presence of slaves presented French society and judges with new challenges, particularly in major Atlantic cities. In 1777, for example, there were 208 slaves and 94 free coloured in Bordeaux. Formally, slavery did not exist in early modern France, with the exception of major Mediterranean ports, where Ottoman and black slaves were employed in the galleys and in the Marseille and Toulon arsenals alongside French convicts and free labour. But the development of a plantation economy in the West Indies led to an evolution of the legal status of slaves in France: by the second half of the eighteenth century, French

---

[17] Frédéric Régent, *Esclavage, métissage, liberté: la révolution française en Guadeloupe, 1789–1802* (Paris, 2004); Pierre Boulle, 'La Construction du concept de race dans la France d'ancien régime', *Revue française d'histoire d'Outre-Mer*, 89/2 (2002), 155–75.

authorities were inclined to accept the continuation of slave status for those slaves who came to France on a temporary basis.[18]

Although slaves were present in New France, they were never numerous and were usually Native American, an indication that the key encounter here was between French colonists and Amerindian groups. New France depended on Native Americans for intelligence, provisions, furs, and protection against British expansion. Entangled in alliances with native groups, the French took part in their struggles, as in the mid-seventeenth century, when they countered the expansion of the Iroquois on former Huron territories. By the end of the seventeenth century, French diplomacy had managed to impose the governor as an acknowledged protector of Amerindian nations. In 1701, more than thirty of these nations—Iroquois included—signed the great Peace of Montreal.

Maintaining good relations with Amerindian groups required French recognition of their relative autonomy. From the French point of view, assimilation was also possible. This policy depended on a patronizing pyramidal system in which the French governor acted as a benevolent father distributing gifts and carefully evaluating the strengths, influence, and faithfulness of each group. French jurisdiction did not extend to internal Amerindian affairs, and conflicts between natives and newcomers were generally resolved by the Native American principle of collective reparation rather than on the basis of the French principle of punishment for a guilty individual. Still, on occasion, as in the case of the Natchez in 1729, major native uprisings occurred. Yet both the nature of the economic relations between French and Amerindians based on the fur trade and the composite integrative character of the French monarchy facilitated a system of alliances which partially offset the demographic weakness of French America and allowed France to maintain a permanent presence in North America for a century, despite the superiority of the British American population.[19] These alliances made New France viable, but their consequences for Native Americans were extremely mixed.

THE ECONOMY OF THE FRENCH ATLANTIC IN ITS 'GOLDEN AGE'

French Atlantic trade increased throughout the eighteenth century until the French Wars (1793–1815), which are traditionally considered the end of a golden age of prosperity. Although the opulence of French ports is unquestionable, the system that enabled their growth was fragile. The French Revolution revealed its intrinsic

---

[18] Susan Peabody, 'There Are No Slaves in France': The Political Culture of Race and Slavery in the Ancien Regime (New York, 1996); Pierre Pluchon, Nègres et Juifs au XVIIIe siècle: le racisme au siècle des Lumières (Paris, 1984).

[19] Havard and Vidal, Histoire de l'Amérique, 61–5, 170–253.

weakness, more than representing a sudden disruption of imperial domination. The French Atlantic, however, was not confined to its imperial boundaries.

The development of permanent settlements in French America sustained a steady flow of people and goods across the Atlantic, which was shaped by the restrictive legislation imposed by the mother country. The value of imports from America grew from 16.7 million *livres tournois* in 1716 to 192 million in 1787; on the eve of the French Revolution, colonial trade represented a third of French total imports. Merchants, however, increasingly complained of shrinking profits and of colonists' outstanding debts. Arguably the rise of colonial trade from the end of the Seven Years War to the French Revolution represented the merchants' response to lowered profit margins rather than robust, healthy fundamentals. The colonists' indebtedness was in part the consequence of enhanced contacts with foreigners, who absorbed existing colonial funds in payment for their supplies.[20]

Despite inherent fragility, colonial trade sustained intensive and increasing shipping. In 1773 French ships sailing to the West Indies totalled 570, of which 296 went to Saint-Domingue alone. Fifteen years later, 677 vessels carried Caribbean goods back to France: one out of three sailed to Bordeaux, followed by Nantes and Marseille (19 per cent each) and Rouen–Le Havre (16 per cent). Among these vessels, 55 were slave ships. The French fitted out over 3,330 slave ships throughout the eighteenth century, four-fifths of which went to Saint-Domingue. Nantes launched 40 per cent of the slaving expeditions, but Bordeaux competed in the 1780s and outstripped Nantes during the 1802–3 peace of Amiens.[21]

On the eve of the French Revolution, about 15,000 seamen gained their livelihood on board ships bound either directly or via the African coasts to the French West Indies. Approximately the same number found employment in the 386 ships fitted out to Newfoundland—just as many as a century before.[22] Despite stagnation and strong Anglo-American competition, the French crown supported the fisheries, considered the best possible training for hard-working seamen. Protection included not only diplomatic efforts, but also heavy duties on the import of foreign cod. An essential part of French shipping and half of its fisheries depended on the Atlantic world. In fact, its impact stretched far beyond the coasts of France to their hinterlands.

A burgeoning transatlantic colonial trade contributed to a reordering of the hierarchy among French ports. Whereas a few emerged—four major ports garnered almost nine-tenths of colonial returns in 1788, and Granville and Saint-Malo fitted out about 60 per cent of French ships to the shores of Newfoundland in 1786—others were relegated to regional and local trades. Some fast-growing ports were favoured by a

---

[20] Michel Morineau, 'La Vraie Nature des choses et leur enchaînement entre la France, les Antilles et l'Europe (XVIIᵉ–XIXᵉ siècle)', *Revue française d'histoire d'Outre-Mer*, 84 (1997), 3–24.

[21] Pierre Pluchon, *Histoire de la colonisation française* (Paris, 1991), 1020; Tarrade, *Le Commerce colonial*, ii. 773; Eltis et al., *The Transatlantic Slave Trade*; Éric Saugera, *Bordeaux, port négrier, XVIIe–XIXe siècles* (Paris, 1995).

[22] Jean-François Brière, *La Pêche française en Amérique du Nord au XVIIIe siècle* (Montreal, 1990).

rich hinterland such as Bordeaux, which exported its wine and meal to the West Indies, or by the proximity of a major market, such as Rouen and Le Havre, which forwarded their imports along the Seine to Paris. Others specialized in colonial trade because of their strong merchant networks, connected to regions able to absorb colonial re-exports. Hanseatic and Dutch captains used to sail to Bordeaux, for instance, to procure wine; and they progressively added sugar and coffee to their return cargo. Merchants in Nantes had easy access to East Indian products arriving at Lorient which were necessary in the slave trade.

For these emerging ports, the eighteenth century was a golden age marked by significant population growth, the rise of a wealthy merchant elite, and important changes in their urban landscapes due to private and public expenditures, which are still evident in Nantes or Bordeaux today. French Atlantic cities prospered and attracted population from the surrounding countryside, thus redistributing merchant wealth to the rest of society.

Whereas foreign capital and foreign merchants—especially Dutch—initiated and financed the first French expeditions to the West Indies at the end of the seventeenth century, a group of wealthy, influential French merchants dominated colonial trade in the eighteenth century. Like their counterparts in other parts of Europe, they relied on their correspondents in major Atlantic ports to forward information and goods and to provide services. Their sons circulated within the network to complete their education, or sailed for some years on their father's or partner's ships in order to acquire a direct experience of markets and of the sea. On the eve of the French Revolution, merchants and shipowners in major French ports belonged to local elites and some of them, notably in Nantes, became part of the nobility.[23] The Atlantic world helped to disrupt traditional societal structures in France.

Despite its visible effects on Atlantic ports, the overall impact of colonial trade on the French economy is difficult to gauge. Colonial trade stimulated industrial and agricultural exports, as well as the shipping industry. But colonial goods were largely re-exported on foreign ships to consumers, especially to northern Europe, the Baltic, and to the eastern Mediterranean, and they did not initiate significant industrial activities in France. Historians of Nantes insist that, contrary to Eric Williams's thesis, profits from trade and particularly the slave trade did not finance French industrialization.[24]

National consumption of colonial goods was modest even if cities experienced new consumption patterns and fashions directly linked to imports from the Americas. Coffee houses, tobacco, textiles coloured with indigo, mahogany furniture, certainly made themselves felt. Nevertheless, although the Atlantic economy changed the everyday life of inhabitants of French Atlantic ports and their hinterlands, the majority of the 28 million Frenchmen in 1789 were probably not aware of or deeply affected by the existence of the Atlantic world. Indeed, its emergence probably increased the

---

[23] Olivier Pétré-Grenouilleau, *Les Négoces maritimes français* (Paris, 1997).
[24] Olivier Pétré-Grenouilleau, *L'Argent de la traite. Milieu négrier, capitalisme et développement: un modèle* (Paris, 1996).

differences between French provinces, rather than contributing to their integration. Seemingly, two economies—one Atlantic, confined to the coast and adjoining hinterlands; the other more inward-looking and continental—developed. Tensions within these two worlds produced an explosion when the poor crops of the late 1780s coincided with a major political crisis, provoked by immense war expenses and outstanding public debt. The French Revolution, which was in part the consequence of Atlantic warfare and colonial issues, produced major changes in the French Atlantic.

The impressive growth of French colonial trade came to an abrupt halt in the early 1790s, as a consequence of the 1791 slaves' revolt in Saint-Domingue and the beginning of the war between France and Great Britain (1 February 1793), which disrupted trade with the other components of French colonial empire. Because it was impossible to supply the colonies, France authorized neutral shipping to the West Indies. Martinique, Guadeloupe, and a part of Saint-Domingue were occupied in 1793–4, although the French recovered Guadeloupe shortly after, by promising freedom to slaves.

By opening colonial trade to foreigners, warfare temporarily eliminated the contradiction between an exchange system based on an imperial restrictive policy and broad international demand. Suppliers and clients could trade directly or via neutral carriers and bypass imperial legislation. The frequency of Atlantic warfare should challenge traditional descriptions of imperial trade systems, which consider peace the norm and war as the exception. Warfare, in fact, might have acted as a safety valve allowing the monopolistic system to function and perform in peacetime. The exclusive system and international competition over territories and markets created tensions leading to warfare. Warfare, in turn, allowed for regulation of structural imbalances of trade (through freight and the remittance of subsidy to French allies) between France and its northern markets, which absorbed most of its colonial re-exports, which in turn allowed France to pay for its imports from Great Britain, Central Europe, and Asia.[25] Nevertheless, warfare led to the progressive loss of the French empire. The French Wars (1793–1815) were the last episode of this story, rather than an unforeseeable fatality abruptly affecting a healthy system destined for continuous growth.

The importance of the French empire and its dramatic changes over time should not mask the existence of other forms of French participation in the opportunities provided by the Atlantic world. Franco-British rivalry was largely a struggle for the control of Iberian markets and access to Spanish silver and Brazilian gold. Such access could be obtained in the Americas—through intensive smuggling or official supply contacts with the Iberian monarchies—or indirectly in Spain and Portugal. Whereas British merchants enjoyed a dominant position in Portugal, their French counterparts largely controlled Spanish trade.

French merchants were numerous and influential in Cádiz even before the Spanish crown was awarded to the grandson of Louis XIV at the beginning of the eighteenth century. In 1686, French manufactured goods represented 40 per cent of total overseas

---

[25] For the idea that the imbalance in trade between France and the Netherlands was paid off during wars, see Morineau, 'La Vraie Nature', 18. His argument may apply more generally to the Atlantic world.

exports from Cádiz. Saint-Malo merchants were able to procure silver in return, which irrigated trade in France and made it possible to trade to Asia and to the Levant. French merchant houses in Cádiz dominated and financed a large part of Spanish overseas trade throughout the eighteenth century.

Frenchmen also penetrated the Spanish empire. During the War of the Spanish Succession, France obtained the *asiento* (1702–13), the contract to provide Spanish America with African slaves. French ships fitted out officially for the Spanish empire and Saint-Malo merchants ventured into the Pacific to Peru.[26] Frenchmen did not limit themselves to these legal trades within the Spanish Atlantic. The West Indies traditionally saw intense smuggling to the Spanish mainland—an activity encouraged by French authorities as it enabled Frenchmen to obtain badly needed silver coins.[27] Despite the monopolistic views of the European powers, intensive colonial production in French and British West Indies based on slave labour was only possible because other parts of the British and Spanish Americas provided food, wood, and cash for the plantations. In other words, the supposedly exclusive national colonial system relied on interconnections among its transnational components.

Such trades were the result of merchants' initiatives and constant adjustments rather than the product of a carefully planned policy. The state, in fact, had little impact on the actual development of trade, as the scant Franco-American relations after 1776 demonstrate. Despite France's position as a major market for Chesapeake tobacco, the Ferme Générale, which had the tobacco monopoly in France, kept on acquiring the product in Glasgow even when it was possible to organize direct shipments from the Chesapeake to France. French attempts to penetrate the American markets were a failure, and not until the end of the 1780s, when France's crops failed, did shipping between the United States and France increase. The war of 1793 provided an extraordinary opportunity for neutral American ships to carry goods to the French ports—hundreds of American ships sailed to France in 1795—but they deprived French shipping of the benefit of freight and transport.[28]

CONCLUSION

Whereas in the sixteenth century the French presence in Africa and in the Americas was informal, during the two succeeding centuries France created an empire overseas

[26] André Lespagnol, *Messieurs de Saint-Malo: une élite négociante au temps de Louis XIV* (Rennes, 1997).

[27] Wim Klooster, *Illicit Riches: Dutch Trade in the Caribbean, 1648–1795* (Leiden, 1998).

[28] Jacob M. Price, *France and the Chesapeake: A History of the French Tobacco Monopoly 1674–1791 and of its Relationship to the British and American Tobacco Trades* (Ann Arbor, MI, 1973); special issue: 'New Perspectives on the Atlantic', *History of European Ideas*, 34/4 (December 2008); Silvia Marzagalli, 'Establishing Transatlantic Trade Networks in Time of War: Bordeaux and the United States, 1793–1815', *Business History Review*, 79 (2005), 811–44.

and trading posts on the African coasts which intensified transatlantic links. Contacts with Amerindians on the mainland and interactions with an increasing number of slaves in the plantation colonies shaped new societies in the New World while also affecting France. Moreover, Frenchmen continued, legally or not, to carry on trade to other parts of America. Many manufactured goods sold in Spanish America were produced in France.

In the latter half of the eighteenth century, the French West Indies, and notably Saint-Domingue, were at the core of a production system based on slave labour which supplied Europeans with increasing quantities of sugar, coffee, indigo, while trade to Spain and the Spanish American mainland procured silver, which undergirded other sectors of French trade. About a thousand French ships and 30,000 French sailors crossed the Atlantic each year to fish, carry colonists and slaves, transport goods within imperial boundaries as well as beyond them. Thousands of foreign ships sailed to France to acquire colonial goods produced in America.

The French Atlantic was more centred on West Indian production, less diversified, and less integrated than the British Atlantic. The relative importance of the American mainland was radically different. The variety of goods produced in the British empire allowed for a greater degree of interaction not only within the empire itself, but also between Great Britain and the other parts of the Atlantic world, with a degree of sophistication which was never attained in France. Canada and Louisiana never played an economically significant role within the French empire, although their loss weakened French control over the West Indies. The increasing and almost exclusive importance of the West Indies reduced the French capacity to adapt to changes within the Atlantic world, notably the independence of former British, French, and Iberian colonies and the end of the legal slave trade.

After the loss of Haiti, the French empire in the Americas was reduced to Guadeloupe, Martinique, and Guyana, where slavery was abolished in 1848. Following the independence of the United States and Haiti, the independence of Brazil and Spanish America opened a new era in which markets relied on competitiveness rather than on imperial monopolistic rule. But after a quarter of a century of warfare, French industry was not competitive enough to impose its products on a free market across the Atlantic.

BIBLIOGRAPHY

Allaire, Bernard, *Pelleteries, manchons et chapeaux de castor: les fourrures nord-américaines à Paris (1500–1632)* (Paris, 1999).

Banks, Kenneth, *Chasing Empire across the Sea: Communications and the State in the French Atlantic, 1713–1763* (Montreal, 2002).

Brière, Jean-François, *La Pêche française en Amérique du Nord au XVIIIe siècle* (Montreal, 1990).

Butel, Paul, *Histoire des Antilles françaises XVIIe–XXe siècle* (Paris, 2002).

Cabantous, Alain, André Lespagnol, and Françoise Péron (eds.), *Les Français, la terre et la mer, XIIIe–XXe siècle* (Paris, 2005).

Harvard, Gilles, and Cécile Vidal, *Histoire de l'Amérique française* (Paris, 2003).

Mathieu, Jacques, *La Nouvelle-France: les Français en Amérique du Nord, XVIe–XVIIIe siècles* (Paris, 1991).

Meyer, Jean, et al., *Histoire de la France coloniale* (Paris, 1991).

Pluchon, Pierre (ed.), *Histoire des Antilles et de la Guyane* (Toulouse, 1982).

Pritchard, James, *In Search of Empire: The French in the Americas, 1670–1730* (Cambridge, 2004).

Tarrade, Jean, *Le Commerce colonial de la France à la fin de l'Ancien Régime* (Paris, 1973).

CHAPTER 15

....

VOICES FROM THE OTHER SIDE

Native Perspectives from New Spain, Peru, and North America

....

KEVIN TERRACIANO

EUROPEAN and African migrations brought waves of change to millions of people on the western side of the Atlantic world. This chapter examines indigenous responses to some of these changes in three regions of the Americas, from about the mid-sixteenth to the second half of the eighteenth centuries. Three sections consider the strategies of men and women who sought to protect and promote their interests by engaging settlers and colonial officials, criticizing existing practice, and affecting policies towards them. Each section highlights indigenous attempts to reach out across the Atlantic, to meet imperial authorities face to face, to speak to them through mediators and messengers, or to influence them with writings.

TROUBLES IN NEW SPAIN
....

When the lords of Tlaxcala decided to send a delegation to the king of Spain in 1552, they designed a painting depicting their role as allies of the monarchy in the conquest of New Spain. The purpose of the delegation was to 'lay Tlaxcala's troubles before the emperor'. The expedition required contributions from all Tlaxcalans because the city's assets could not meet the cost of an expedition to Spain. Two years earlier, they had sent letters to the king, to no avail. Finally, in 1554, they received a royal decree authorizing their voyage.[1] Tlaxcala's strategy of appealing directly to the emperor is recorded in the Nahuatl-language minutes of the meetings of the Spanish-style town council (*cabildo*) of Tlaxcala, a remarkable example of early native-language alphabetic writing in Mesoamerica. Tlaxcala was a confederation of four *altepetl*, the Nahua name for a local state. Its *cabildo* consisted of more than 200 men who represented the hereditary lordly establishments, or *teccalli*, of this large state in central Mexico.

Tlaxcala had never submitted to the dominant *altepetl* of the 'Aztec empire'—Mexico Tenochtitlan. Tlaxcalans gave valuable support to Spanish-led forces in the war against the Mexica, for which they received certain privileges. They were not placed in *encomienda*, for example, and thus did not pay tribute and labour directly to a Spaniard, as did most other *altepetl* immediately following the conquest. The painting proposed for the emperor in 1552 probably formed the basis for a pictographic text, known today as the *Lienzo of Tlaxcala*. An eighteenth-century copy of the original *lienzo* (painting on cloth), which is now lost or destroyed, shows that native artists painted a large principal scene and numerous smaller scenes below.[2] The top and centre of the main scene displays the imperial crest of Spain, held by a Habsburg two-headed eagle (Figure 15.1). A pre-conquest-style hill glyph occupies the middle, representing the *altepetl* (literally 'water' and 'hill'). Tlaxcala's coat of arms appears at the foot of the hill, above a cross and below the façade of a chapel dedicated to the Virgin Mary. Numerous *teccalli* in the corners, depicted in the traditional manner as palaces with lords seated inside, surround two new churches. Lords issue forth from the four parts to meet high-ranking Spanish officials who are seated on European-style chairs. Some eighty other scenes follow, most depicting Tlaxcalans fighting alongside Spaniards in their joint conquest of New Spain. The Tlaxcalan artists selectively adapted the content of the scenes to suit their strategy, omitting depictions of their own battles against the Spaniards before they were forced to make peace with Cortés, but including multiple images that commemorate Tlaxcala's loyalty and service to the king, and their immediate acceptance of Christianity.

The *cabildo* records reveal some of Tlaxcala's troubles in this period. In one of the first recorded sessions, the *cabildo* hired an attorney to represent the city in lawsuits before the *audiencia* or high court of New Spain, thus revealing the cost of working within the new legal system. The council sent a letter to the emperor complaining of the encroachment of Spanish livestock on the lands of the *altepetl*, an issue that was to be a constant irritant. Money too was a problem. When the *cabildo* lacked funds to pay for religious expenses, it was forced to sell land to meet the costs; this grievance was repeated the next year. The council complained that the constant sale of assets would impoverish a 'moneyless' city, and sought to raise additional taxes and borrow money. In 1553, the *cabildo* complained that the lordly houses were falling apart, due to depopulation and competition with Spaniards for labour, and that nobles had to sell

---

[1] James Lockhart, Frances Berdan, and Arthur Anderson, *The Tlaxcalan Actas: A Compendium of the Records of the Cabildo of Tlaxcala, 1545–1627* (Salt Lake City, UT, 1986), 45–55.

[2] Alfredo Chavero (ed.), *Lienzo de Tlaxcala* (Mexico, 1979).

FIGURE 15.1 Principal scene of the Lienzo of Tlaxcala. From Josefina García Quintana and Carlos Martínez Marín (eds.), *Lienzo de Tlaxcala* (Mexico, 1983), 56.

lands because they lacked sufficient workers to cultivate them. Only three months earlier, the Spanish viceroy had decreed to the *cabildo* that uncultivated lands were to be confiscated. The visit to Spain proved disappointing because in 1562 the members concluded that 'for all the trials' they had endured in serving the king they had 'been paid nothing'. That same year, the council prohibited Tlaxcalans from selling land to Spaniards, 'who have their own cities and should not live among the Tlaxcalans', and threatened offenders with a stiff penalty of 100 pesos and exile. This was not the first complaint concerning Spaniards living among them, and the *cabildo* contemplated sending another delegation to Spain to 'to bring the city's problems' to the king's attention, but had no money to do so.[3]

The Tlaxcalan nobility campaigned throughout the sixteenth century and beyond for tribute relief, sending several delegations to the viceroy in Mexico City and to the king in Spain. Campaigns for exemptions and privileges resulted in numerous royal decrees in favour of Tlaxcala, but most were violated by Spaniards or diluted by royal officials. In reality, Tlaxcalans were subject to many types of tribute in kind, money payments, and labour drafts. Throughout the century, they were required to deliver 8,000 *fanegas* (about 13,000 bushels) of maize kernels to Mexico City annually. The assessment remained constant even as the population declined precipitously. When, at century's end, Tlaxcala fell behind on payments, *cabildo* officials were jailed and community land was auctioned to Spaniards to meet payments. Besides the maize tribute, Tlaxcala also provided labour service to the Spanish city of Puebla, and other types of monetary tribute. Certain privileges were granted to individuals, but the community as a whole derived little benefit from the decrees of exemption. Despite their historic 'favoured' status as an armorial city, their claims to having assisted the conquest, and the assignment of privileges to certain lords, Tlaxcala declined in population and wealth as rapidly as most other *altepetl* in and around the Basin of Mexico.[4]

Tlaxcala was not alone in reaching across the Atlantic to appeal directly to the sovereign, and in constructing selective images of the past to promote present concerns. In 1560, for example, the *cabildo* of Huexotzinco urged the king in a reverential form of Nahuatl to recognize their plight and to reward them for their past service by relieving them from onerous taxation and tribute amounting to 14,800 pesos annually and an equal number of *fanegas* of maize.[5] Stressing the enormity of this exaction from a community that possessed no mineral wealth, they described themselves as the king's 'poor commoners' who bowed humbly before him 'from very far'. The lords asked plaintively, 'have we done something wrong?' 'have we committed some sin against almighty God?', and lamented that it would not be long before the king's city 'completely disappears and crumbles'. Three years later, the nobles of Xochimilco adopted the same strategy, and wrote in Spanish to request justice, particular privileges,

---

[3] *The Tlaxcalan Actas*, 52–62.

[4] Charles Gibson, *Tlaxcala in the Sixteenth Century* (2nd edn. Palo Alto, CA, 1967), 178.

[5] James Lockhart, *We People Here: Nahuatl Accounts of the Conquest of Mexico* (Berkeley, CA, 1993), 288–97.

and a reduction in tribute and labour service. They also complained of Spaniards who competed directly with them for resources, notably lands and labourers, and contended that they paid more taxes under Spanish rule than previously, 'even when Moteuczoma tyrannized this land'.[6]

As the Nahua *cabildo* of Tlaxcala appealed to the emperor, a Nahua man named Francisco Manuel complained to the Council of the Indies. Francisco, a slave from Mexico living in Spain, was among the hundreds of Indian slaves who, over the course of the sixteenth century, petitioned for manumission to the Council of the Indies, on the grounds that they had not been seized in a 'just war'. They took advantage of royal legislation in their favour, which did not apply to African slaves in Iberia. Francisco understood Nahuatl, his native language, but answered questions in Spanish, having lived in Spain since he was a child. Unlike most in similar circumstances, Francisco did, in fact, win his freedom in 1553.[7]

The Indian slave trade to Iberia went unchecked until the New Laws of 1542 prohibited Indian slavery in 'pacified' areas of the Indies. Precise figures are uncertain, but several thousand Indians were shipped to Spain during the sixteenth century, of whom as many as half died en route. The vast majority of Indian slaves to cross the Atlantic went to Lisbon and Seville and worked as unskilled labourers. They would have stood out even in the multi-ethnic milieu of cities such as Seville because they were branded on the forehead or face, and those who were granted freedom, whether by their owners or by the Council of Indies, worked for low wages or begged in the streets. Few returned to their homeland because they lacked the resources or royal licence to do so.

Despite the New Laws, slavery in Spanish America persisted among the 'unpacified' peoples, who remained subject to 'just war', especially on the military frontiers to the north. Whereas the conquests of the sedentary peoples in the centre and south of New Spain were quick and permanent, fighting in many areas of the north persisted, and indigenous groups resisted more successfully than the Mesoamericans because they were fewer, scattered, and more mobile. In contrast, sedentary peoples mounted few rebellions that unified communities across regions, and officials managed to suppress many local uprisings before they spread. If the Mesoamericans and Europeans had much in common, the northern groups seemed different and therefore threatening. Spanish institutions of coerced labour such as the *encomienda* did not work well in the north, where there was no precedent for organizing tribute payments and labour drafts. The region received little attention until Spaniards located silver mines which attracted thousands of settlers. The so-called Mixtón Wars of the 1540s against the Caxcanes and other groups marked a cycle of violence that continued for centuries. In the vast expanses of the north, native bands raided Spanish settlements and ambushed mule trains. In response, Spanish troops were stationed permanently in *presidios* or forts.

---

[6] Matthew Restall, Lisa Sousa, and Kevin Terraciano, *Mesoamerican Voices: Native-Language Writings from Colonial Mexico, Oaxaca, Yucatan, and Guatemala* (Cambridge, 2005), 66–71.

[7] Esteban Mira Caballos, *Indios y mestizos americanos en la España del siglo xvi* (Madrid, 2000), 72–3.

The soldiers supplemented their meagre salaries by selling Indians as slaves and sending them to other parts of New Spain or the Caribbean. Another northern adaptation was the mission, where people from a large surrounding area were congregated. The mission, usually located near *presidios*, was a typical feature of Spanish and Portuguese expansion into the under-populated regions of the Americas. Another tactic in the north was to use 'friendly Indians' as buffer populations. In 1591, after several appeals from the king and the viceroy, an expedition of some 400 Tlaxcalan families set out to settle in the north, accompanied by Franciscans. Subsequent expeditions to Saltillo, Coahuila, Texas, and Nuevo Mexico proceeded from the original 400 families and their descendants. The sedentary 'Pueblo Indians' of 'New Mexico' reminded the Spaniards of settlements in central Mexico, hence the names for the groups and place. Tlaxcalans built one of the first churches in Santa Fe, founded in 1609.[8]

According to a prolific Nahua historian who went by the name of Don Domingo de San Antón Muñón Chimalpahin Quauhtlehuanitzin, New Mexico was the probable site of Aztlan, the legendary place of origin of the Aztec people.[9] Born in 1579 in Amecameca, Chimalpahin moved to nearby Mexico City when he was young. From 1593 to the mid-1620s he was educated by, and lived among, Franciscans in Mexico City. Chimalpahin's writings treat both of the pre-conquest past and his own present times, focusing on events in and around Mexico City. He is known especially for his annals, a genre of Nahua writing that was continued after the conquest. Chimalpahin wrote a *Diario*, a 284-page Nahuatl-language text, which is a selective and personal rendering of references to the people, places, and events of his day, covering the period from the 1590s to 1615.[10] The text is organized into year entries that refer to both the Christian calendar year and its Nahua equivalent. He described public ceremonies involving high officials, religious feasts, and processions; recorded plagues and epidemics, earthquakes and floods, solar eclipses and comets, storms and other natural events; and reported crimes and executions, including inquisitorial *autos da fé* and sensational events such as an aborted black rebellion in Mexico City.

The *Diario* referred also to events in Europe, from the death of a Spanish king to papal affairs in Rome. Perhaps more than any other indigenous writer in this period, Chimalpahin understood the global nature of the Spanish empire, for he was attentive to both the Atlantic and Pacific worlds. The *Diario* made frequent mention of events in China (i.e. the Philippines) and Japan, and detailed a delegation of Japanese men passing through Mexico City on their way to Europe. New Spain was a bridge between the two oceans with the ports of Acapulco and Veracruz as its gates. He reported sightings of English or Flemish pirates waiting on the Pacific coast for ships coming

---

[8] Edward Spicer, *Cycles of Conquest: The Impact of Spain, Mexico, and the United States on the Indians of the Southwest, 1533–1960* (Tucson, AZ, 1962).

[9] Arthur J. O. Anderson and Susan Schroeder (eds. and trans.), *Codex Chimalpahin* (Norman, OK, 1997), i. 69.

[10] James Lockhart, Susan Schroeder, and Doris Namala (eds. and trans.), *Annals of His Time: Series Chimalpahin* (Palo Alto, CA, 2006).

from China, and seemed relieved that Portuguese troops were being moved to the fort in Acapulco to repel the thieves.

But Chimalpahin never lost sight of matters concerning indigenous people, especially the communities in and around the Basin of Mexico. His *Diario* demonstrated that the four-part *altepetl* of Mexico Tenochtitlan did not disappear when the Spaniards made it the capital city of New Spain. His consciousness of the city's many ethnic and racial groups reinforced his own firm Nahua identity. His purpose in writing the *Diario* in his own language was not to achieve some strategic objective in the manner of the *lienzos* but, as he said himself, to preserve memories of the past for future generations of Nahuas, often using older pictorial writings as the basis of his information.

Although the indigenous presence in Mexico City was still palpable nearly a century after the conquest, it is difficult to overlook the enormous consequences of the European presence in Mexico City. What could be more profound than the attempt to drain the water from the lake surrounding Mexico City? The *desagüe*, as the drainage project was called, sought to end the periodic floods that threatened the city. At one point, Chimalpahin related two separate but significant events. In 1604, in order to build a wooden wall to protect the city from water that descended from forests surrounding the Basin of Mexico, the viceroy paradoxically ordered several communities to chop down thousands of trees from the nearby mountain slopes, thus further deforesting the wooded areas that might have checked the flow of water. Ten years later, Chimalpahin reported that as many as 50,000 indigenous men were killed during the course of excavating a mountainside for the *desagüe* project. The drainage project was ultimately completed, at enormous human cost and with drastic environmental consequences for the Valley and City of Mexico.

The greatest consequence of the European presence that Chimalpahin chronicled in his annals, the gravest cause of trouble for indigenous peoples, was the introduction of unknown infectious diseases. Despite the severe implications of depopulation, most indigenous communities throughout New Spain managed to survive in some form throughout much of the viceregal period, protected by royal legislation that recognized *pueblos de indios* as corporate entities. Each of these thousands of pueblos, identified by both indigenous and patron saint's names, maintained a landholding base and a group of local governing elites. Most communities were reduced to smaller settlements that had undergone *congregación* and other Spanish attempts at reorganization. In more remote regions of New Spain, where native populations were large in comparison to non-Indians, where there was little profit potential (no mineral wealth) to attract many Spanish migrants, various indigenous customs and practices continued in altered but recognizable ways. In Oaxaca, for example, many Mixtec hereditary rulers, called *caciques* (male) and *cacicas* (female) by Spaniards, adapted to changes and maintained their high status, using the Spanish legal system to their advantage. Whereas the Nahua *teccalli* or lordly establishments in central Mexico had declined by the middle of the seventeenth century, its Mixtec equivalent continued to function and thrive in many places into the eighteenth century. Even in the Valley of Oaxaca, site of Hernán Cortés' *marquesado*, Mixtec and Zapotec caciques and communities were among the largest landholders by the end of the colonial period.[11]

By the middle of the seventeenth century, the native population of New Spain reached its nadir and began to increase gradually. Overall population growth in the colony led to an increased demand for land in more densely populated areas. In response, a programme called the *composiciones de tierras* restricted corporate land-holdings to a townsite measured from a pueblo's centre (usually its church). It established the limits of community holdings, raised revenue by granting titles to lands beyond the pueblo's townsite, and repossessed all 'vacant' land occupied without grant or title, which was legally royal domain. Officials auctioned off repossessed lands to the highest bidder, usually Spaniards. In general, Spanish haciendas (agricultural and livestock estates) accrued land at the boundaries of indigenous corporate landholdings. The programme forced pueblos and individuals to furnish or purchase proof of possession. Some resorted to producing their own titles, not fully aware of a legitimate title's format, content, or language, submitting their home-made 'primordial' titles to Spanish authorities as evidence of possession since 'time immemorial'. The *composiciones* prompted a fascinating genre of indigenous writing designed to protect communal resources from outsiders.[12] The law also gave constituent parts of a community incentive to seek autonomy as a separate 'pueblo' in order to claim its own townsite, contributing to the fragmentation of larger *altepetl* and the proliferation of small pueblos. Most of this fragmentation was based on pre-existing settlements and modes of organization, however. Nevertheless, European principles of private and communal property had profound long-term consequences for indigenous communities, as did the introduction of a money economy, which was fuelled by American silver.

'NO REMEDY' IN PERU

The Atlantic world spilled over into the 'South Sea' and reached the shores of the Andean region, where Spaniards encountered a large population and tremendous mineral wealth, which assured Spanish determination to incorporate it into the Atlantic world. As in the Caribbean and Mesoamerica, contact here was abrupt and dramatic. The collapse of the Inca empire was followed by conflict between Spanish factions and, in the highlands, where most indigenous people lived, a millenarian-style revolt against Spanish dominance called the Taqui Onqoy (Quechua for 'dancing

[11] James Lockhart, *The Nahuas after the Conquest: A Social and Cultural History of the Indians of Central Mexico, Sixteenth through Eighteenth Centuries* (Palo Alto, CA, 1992); Kevin Terraciano, *The Mixtecs of Colonial Oaxaca: Ñudzahui History, Sixteenth through Eighteenth Centuries* (Palo Alto, CA, 2001); William Taylor, *Landlord and Peasant in Colonial Oaxaca* (Palo Alto, CA, 1972).

[12] Paula López Caballero, *Los títulos primordiales del centro de México* (Mexico, 2003).

disease'). Native prophets in the 1550s predicted the end of Spanish rule and called for the return of ancient *huacas* or sacred spirits. In 1572, the Spanish viceroy captured Tupac Amaru, the last claimant of the Inca dynasty who ruled the remains of the empire in the highlands. The Inca lord was tricked into a truce, convicted of treason, and beheaded in the main square of Cuzco. The colonists consolidated power, organized massive labour drafts, and cleared the way for silver mining in and around Potosí, perhaps the world's richest mining site. In the formative years of Philip II's reign, specie began to flow across the Atlantic, enabling the crown to continue its ambitious foreign policy from Madrid and making the Atlantic overseas empire commercially attractive for Seville and other European financial centres.[13]

Don Felipe Guaman Poma de Ayala must have witnessed many of these sweeping changes in his lifetime. Born around 1534, Guaman Poma was a Quechua-speaking native of the Huamanga region of Peru. His mother had been a Spaniard's mistress, with whom she gave birth to a mestizo son who became a friar, and later married Don Felipe's indigenous father. Guaman Poma worked most of his life as a bilingual translator and aide for Spanish officials. In his own words, after working in the Andean countryside for nearly thirty years, he returned to Huamanga to find his home occupied and his land confiscated. When he protested, the Spanish *corregidor* (chief magistrate) and priest expelled him from the province. He then travelled to protest at Lima, the viceregal capital. On his journey he saw many injustices, including *mita* (a Quechua term for labour drafts) workers being exploited in the mines of Huancavelica and women being abused by Spaniards in Huarochirí. Once in the capital, he attempted to see the viceroy but was rejected. Around this time, he completed his *Nueva corónica y buen gobierno* and gave it to a viceregal official in Lima, who apparently sent it to Madrid.[14] The manuscript, completed about 1615, consisted of nearly 1,200 folio pages and 500 illustrations. It represents an unsponsored, unedited, and outspoken native perspective on the colonial system, informed by many years of interaction with Spaniards and colonial institutions (Figure 15.2).

Although there are many Quechua (and some Aymara) words and phrases sprinkled throughout the manuscript, Guaman Poma used Spanish rather than his native language because he wrote to a Spanish audience. In fact, he addressed the king. He utilized typical Spanish genres of the period—the chronicle, a standard medium, and the 'good government' discourse—in which he proffered complaints and remedies to the king. In the 'buen gobierno' part, which in some respects resembles the Nahua letters to the crown discussed above, Guaman Poma unleashed a diatribe against all Spaniards in the countryside. He complained of Spanish officials and priests who manipulated ethnic groups to maintain their power, and of mestizos as the undesirable

---

[13] Steve J. Stern, *Peru's Indian Peoples and the Challenge of Spanish Conquest: Huamanga to 1640* (2nd edn. Madison, WI, 1993).

[14] Felipe Guaman Poma de Ayala, *El primer nueva corónica y buen gobierno*, ed. John Murra and Rolena Adorno, trans. of the Quechua by Jorge Urioste (Mexico, 1980); Rolena Adorno, *Guaman Poma: Writing and Resistance in Colonial Peru* (Austin, TX, 2000).

FIGURE 15.2 Self-portrayal of Guaman Poma, speaking with Andean lords and elders. The heading contains phrases written in three languages (Spanish, Quechua, and Aymara), which refer to a dialogue between the author and his sources. Line drawing from *El primer nueva corónica y buen gobierno por Felipe Guaman Poma de Ayala*, ed. John V. Murra and Rolena Adorno, trans. of the Quechua by Jorge L. Urioste (Mexico, 1980), 338.

offspring of Spanish men and native women, who contributed to the decline of the native population. Ideally, he wanted a native world that kept its traditional authorities and made its own decisions, independently of Spaniards. This idea, advanced by Fray Bartolomé de Las Casas and other religious in the sixteenth century, had become anachronistic and unrealistic by the early seventeenth century. Guaman Poma favoured Spanish law and Christianity, but he considered that both were being ignored in Spanish Peru. He revealed the depth of his frustration by frequently punctuating his narrative with the phrase *y no hay remedio*, 'and there is no remedy'. The author died a poor, frustrated, and unknown man shortly after handing over his manuscript in Lima, and it is unlikely that the king or any important official ever read the work, which came to scholarly attention only in the twentieth century.

Guaman Poma finished his manuscript about the same time that a prominent mestizo Peruvian writer had completed a second volume on the history of Peru, but the two never met in person. Gómez Suarez de Figueroa was born out of wedlock in 1539 in Cuzco to an Inca noblewoman and a high-ranking Spanish *conquistador*. Typical of the sexual relations between Spanish men and indigenous women that Guaman Poma denounced (sexual unions between Spanish women and indigenous men were very rare), Gómez's father never married his mother, but he provided for their son, who was educated in Cuzco in the European, Christian tradition. As a boy, he observed the violent conflict between Spanish factions in Peru, in which his father was involved. He went to Spain when he was 21 years old and adopted his father's name, Garcilaso de la Vega. He approached the noble house of Figueroa but was rejected because he was considered an Indian, and was also rebuffed at court, largely because his father was implicated in Gonzalo Pizarro's rebellion that had resulted in the viceroy's execution, an unforgivable act of treason. In 1569 the younger Garcilaso served as a captain, at his own expense, in the campaign to suppress the revolt of the Moriscos of Granada, but having received no recognition for his service he retreated into the world of letters, and studied Italian, Renaissance philosophy, and humanism, using the name 'Inca' to distinguish himself from his father and his father's cousin, the famous writer Juan Garcilaso de la Vega.

Although 'Garcilaso Inca de la Vega', as he signed himself, was not an 'Indian' by the legal standards of the day, he knew the Quechua language and he celebrated his tangible connection to that heritage. Like many peoples of mixed European, African, and indigenous descent who lived among native peoples of the Americas, as Guaman Poma had attested, Garcilaso was profoundly influenced by his Andean experience. Neither a Spaniard nor an Indian, he referred to Peru as his homeland and called himself an Inca, even though he maintained little connection with his Inca relatives and lived twice as long in Spain as in Peru. He resembled many prominent mestizos in Spanish America by asserting both sides of his heritage. Mestizos like Garcilaso complicate the ethnic category of the 'Indian', suggesting the flexibility of the label throughout the colonial period, especially in cities and also in the so-called *pueblos de indios* or Indian towns, as indigenous peoples everywhere came into increasing contact with ethnic others.

Garcilaso Inca de la Vega wrote two published histories in his lifetime: the *Comentarios reales de los Incas* (Lisbon, 1609) and the *Historia general del Peru* (Córdoba, 1617).[15] The first was written in honour of his mother and to defend his Inca heritage. As a boy, he had enjoyed privileged access to both the Inca nobility and the Spanish *conquistadores*. His sources for the native past were Quechua-speaking relatives of his mother, herself the granddaughter of the Inca emperor Tupac Inca Yupanqui. He claimed that his uncle had told him legends and traditions handed down over generations. Until the *Comentarios*, little had been written about the Inca and most Spanish

---

[15] Garcilaso de la Vega, *Comentarios reales de los Incas*, ed. Carlos Araníbar, 2 vols. (Lima, 1991).

histories had justified colonial rule by portraying them as tyrants. He objected to such misrepresentations of native religion and culture on the grounds that Spanish historians did not know the language and misunderstood many concepts. Instead, Garcilaso likened the Inca to the ancient Romans and Greeks, also conveyers of great civilizations before Christianity.

The *Historia general*, written in honour of his father, was designed as the second part of the *Comentarios*, but was assigned a different title when published shortly after his death. For this he relied on information from his father's peers, relatives, and friends in Peru to praise the accomplishments of the *conquistadores* and the miracles worked by God. Garcilaso was proud to be the son of a conqueror, and while accepting the conquest as the inevitable divine prelude to a union of the Spaniard and the Indian that would be guided by Christian and Inca laws, he criticized the violence with which the Inca had been overthrown. At times, he struggled to reconcile the demise of the great Inca past with the greed and injustice of the conquest, and he was not afraid to challenge published Spanish histories. For example, in one of the final chapters, which concluded with the 'courageous' death of the Inca leader Tupac Amaru, Garcilaso departed from Spanish accounts of how the Inca ruler confessed to fraud and treason before his execution, and instead portrayed a hero who knew he was being murdered unjustly by the viceroy. The *Historia general* ends on a tragic note, in contrast to the utopian tone of the *Comentarios*. To Garcilaso, the Spanish conquest of Peru had not fulfilled the promise of the great Inca past.

The impact of Garcilaso's history is unclear but more than a century and a half after its publication it was cited to justify a major rebellion in the highlands of Peru, led by a *curaca* calling himself Tupac Amaru II. In 1780, he executed the Spanish *corregidor* for allegedly abusing the Indians of the area, recruited an army, controlled large parts of the highlands, and threatened to take over Cuzco, the old Inca capital. Tupac Amaru II had, apparently, read Garcilaso's writings, and colonial authorities then prohibited the circulation of his books, blaming them for inciting hatred against Spaniards. More immediately, Garcilaso's work and life evoke pity. He had envisioned a Holy Inca Empire, based on the marriage of conquerors and Inca noblewomen, governed by a Christian mestizo group, who would rule Inca people according to Inca and Spanish laws. But he was painfully aware of European prejudices towards Indians and of the controversy surrounding Spanish rule. He cited his knowledge of both sides as evidence that he would make a good colonial official—an idea that would have disturbed Guaman Poma—hoping to return some day to Peru as a *corregidor*. However, that day never came because he died in 1616 and was buried in the cathedral of Córdoba, inside the old *mesquitta*.

THE LIMITS OF NEGOTIATION IN NORTH AMERICA

As Guaman Poma and Garcilaso brought their writings to a close in 1614, an English captain sold as many as thirty Algonquian-speaking slaves in the port of Malaga, Spain.

One by the name of Squanto returned to his homeland, by way of London. He had completed at least two round trips to England, with a brief stay in Spain, by the time the *Mayflower* reached his village in 1620. The population of the area had then been decimated by a recent epidemic and the village was deserted. Massasoit, the Pokanoket *sachem*, relied on Squanto to negotiate a mutual protection plan with the Plymouth colony 'Pilgrims' against his enemies, the Narragansett. Squanto lived with the English and taught them how to plant corn seed.[16]

Meanwhile, the daughter of a powerful Algonquian leader to the south married an Englishman and travelled to England in 1616. Pocahontas and her husband, a tobacco planter in Virginia, their child, and at least ten other people from her village made the voyage. During her nine-month sojourn, Lady Rebecca Rolfe, as Pocahontas was known in England, met the king and queen and numerous high-ranking dignitaries. The entourage was financed in part by the Virginia Company, which sought to advertise its successful transatlantic ventures. To the English she represented the ideal outcome of Anglo-Indian relations, a Protestant Christian Indian princess who spoke English and dressed like a lady. But she fell ill and died on the return voyage in 1617, at Gravesend, on the bank of the Thames (Figure 15.3).[17]

These two transatlantic encounters signalled the rise of another imperial power in the Americas. The English presence at Jamestown in 1607 posed a military threat, but also offered tempting commercial and strategic opportunities for Powhatan, whose authority extended inland from the Chesapeake Bay over a large territory that included at least 10,000 people. The English traded manufactured goods for food in order to survive, while Powhatan hoped to incorporate them into his confederation and enlist them against his enemies. After a difficult start in which the settlers survived only with the assistance of indigenous people, they identified the commercial potential of tobacco that ensured the colony's success and encouraged continued immigration. The widespread cultivation of tobacco spurred a demand for land and labour among the English, which led to conflict in 1622, when the settlers expanded inland from the coast. The use of firearms and metal weapons and European practices of warfare transformed the violent nature of combat in this period. In 1646 Powhatan's brother and successor was captured and killed, leading to a treaty which recognized them as vassals of the monarch and hence subject to numerous English laws and demands. Land was the colonists' principal demand. In 1676, renegade colonists conducted raids on indigenous settlements, seizing lands and slaves and convincing colonial authorities to recognize the gains of 'Bacon's Rebellion'. Another treaty in 1677 created reservations for nearby indigenous

---

[16] Neal Salisbury, *Manitou and Providence: Indians, Europeans, and the Making of New England, 1500–1643* (Oxford, 1982), 101–25.

[17] Alden T. Vaughan, *Transatlantic Encounters: American Indians in Britain, 1500–1776* (Cambridge, 2006), 77–96. Daniel Richter, *Facing East from Indian Country: A Native History of Early America* (Cambridge, MA, 2001), 70–8.

FIGURE 15.3 Portrait of Pocahontas, also called Rebecca Rolfe. Engraved in London in 1616 by Compton Holland after an original by Simon van de Passe. Courtesy of the John Carter Brown Library at Brown University.

groups, required them to provide military support against unfriendly Indians, and regulated their trade activity.[18]

Further north in Plymouth, Puritans arrived after a full century of occasional contact between English explorers and fishermen with indigenous coastal groups that had distributed material goods and spread disease throughout the coastal hinterland. As in Virginia, most English settlers in New England were not as interested in trading with the Indians or converting them to Christianity as they were in acquiring more land by whatever means necessary, as more immigrant families arrived after 1630. The Pequots of eastern Connecticut suffered the most sensational loss of land and lives when they

[18] Helen Rountree, *Pocahontas' People: The Powhatan Indians of Virginia Through Four Centuries* (Norman, OK, 1990), 62–127.

resisted English expansion but failed to enlist the support of other indigenous groups. Combined forces from the Massachusetts Bay and Connecticut colonies, aided by Narragansett and Mohegan contingents, slaughtered an entire Pequot village by Mystic River in a pre-dawn surprise attack, killing all but the few who escaped. The rapid demise of this group was documented by a treaty of 1638, which divided all remaining captives among the victors and declared the Pequot 'nation' dissolved.[19]

By the second half of the seventeenth century, most indigenous groups in New England were reeling from the rapid expansion of the settler colonists, and had learned that signing treaties with them entailed some form of subjugation to their political designs. When the Wampanoag *sachem*, Metacom, the son of Massasoit, was forced to disarm and submit to Plymouth's government, he abandoned his father's strategy of negotiating with the Puritans. In 1675, he recruited Narragansett, Nipmuck, and others to fight the English settlers and their allies, the Mohawks, in a conflict known as King Philip's War. He was killed the following year, and many of his followers and other victims of the war took flight or were sold as slaves in the Caribbean. In the aftermath of the war ten 'praying towns', communities that were subject to English law and Calvinism, were disbanded, leaving only four remaining. Separate from Indian and Puritan settlements, the towns were part of a strategy to resettle Indians, confining them to small towns with restricted agricultural holdings, while Puritan settlers moved onto their former lands. One of these praying towns was Natick, founded in 1651 about 30 kilometres west of Boston. Continued epidemics, competition for land and fisheries, demands for military service, debt, and the division and sale of lands to English buyers led to the eventual dispossession and dispersal of indigenous people from Natick by the end of the eighteenth century.[20]

The English were not the only or even the first European power competing for resources in North America. Cartier's expeditions along the St Lawrence River had initiated direct contact between French and indigenous peoples as early as the 1530s. French traders established prosperous fur-trading bases by the early seventeenth century; Champlain founded Quebec City, the capital of New France, in 1608. Algonquian-speakers traded for manufactured goods and sought to enlist Champlain's men in their ongoing conflict with Iroquois to the south. At the same time, the five Iroquois nations—Mohawk, Oneida, Onondaga, Cayuga, and Seneca—developed their own fur trade with the Dutch along the Hudson River, from whom they acquired firearms and metal tools. The Dutch settled in New Amsterdam, on Manhattan Island, and travelled up the Hudson River to found Fort Orange, a fur-trading centre near Mahican settlements. The Iroquois, especially the Mohawk, supplied the Dutch with thousands of pelts a year in return for firearms, iron goods, cloth, and alcohol. Through the Dutch, the Mohawk supplied other groups with wampum, strings of bright white and

[19] Salisbury, *Manitou and Providence*, 203–25.
[20] Jean O'Brien, *Dispossession by Degrees: Indian Land and Identity in Natick, Massachusetts, 1650–1790* (Cambridge, 1997).

deep purple shells collected along the coastline that were prized for their exchange and prestige value.

Despite competition from the Iroquois and the Dutch, the French maintained a brisk fur trade by extending further into the interior of the continent and developing ties with the Huron, who lived around Georgian Bay and obtained pelts through trapping and trade with groups to the west. Smaller in number and eager to acquire raw materials, the French depended on maintaining good relations with their trade partners. From the 1620s onwards, Hurons paddled their canoes to Montreal to exchange pelts for copper pots, metal axes and knives, clothes, alcohol, and guns. Beginning in the 1640s, however, the Iroquois began to intercept Huron trading expeditions and harassed their settlements, dispersing them and adopting captives until they had undermined the group's influence in the Great Lakes region. In response, the French became more aggressive in fighting the Iroquois and their European allies, first the Dutch and then the English, who captured Fort Orange in 1664 and renamed it Albany. More than 1,000 French troops destroyed three Mohawk villages in 1666, forcing the five nations to negotiate a peace in Quebec. From the 1680s on, the English and French fought bitterly for control of the region. The French sent more than 2,000 troops against the Seneca in 1687; the Iroquois retaliated by attacking French settlements along the St Lawrence River.[21]

Continuous warfare, disease, and European alcohol had ravaged the indigenous population by the end of the seventeenth century, including the powerful Iroquois nations. In response, in 1701, the Iroquois signed separate treaties with New France in Montreal and New York in Albany, playing one against the other in the hope of peace and protection. This strategy worked as long as neither imperial power gained the upper hand, and Anglophile or Francophile factions within the complex councils of the Iroquois confederacy did not succeed in overrunning the neutralists. Peace and neutrality were fragile and tenuous because the French and English were not at peace.[22]

Despite the separate treaties, Britain and France continued to solicit the support of the Iroquois against their enemies. To pursue promises made in 1701, a Mohawk and Mahican delegation travelled to London in 1710. Queen Anne personally received the 'four Indian kings', as they were called by the English, lavished gifts on them, and arranged to meet their expenses. In reality, the four delegates had been recruited by English colonists who advocated an invasion of French Canada, and who hoped to use their entourage to convince the queen that they had the support of the Iroquois confederacy. However, the confederacy council chose not to identify too closely with the British or the French, and continued to pursue a policy of neutrality. None of the so-called kings was a member of this council; all were young Anglophiles, only one

---

[21] John Kicza, *Resilient Cultures: America's Native Peoples Confront European Colonization, 1500–1800* (Upper Saddle River, NJ, 2003).
[22] Daniel K. Richter, *The Ordeal of the Longhouse: The Peoples of the Iroquois League in the Era of European Colonization* (Chapel Hill, NC, 1992); Gilles Havard, *The Great Peace of Montreal of 1701: French–Native Diplomacy in the Seventeenth Century* (Montreal, 2001).

might have been considered a *sachem*. In other words, they did not represent the Iroquois in any official capacity, but the organizers of the trip concealed their identities, orchestrated their visit, and organized a full slate of diplomatic meetings and public appearances. The four men met with heads of state, military officers, and leading churchmen. They attended banquets, theatres, entertained crowds, and had their portraits painted. Most importantly, they met with members of the Board of Trade and the Hudson Bay Company, who sought to expand their role in the fur trade at the expense of the Canadian competition. For the imperialists, the visit was a sound investment. When the delegation returned to North America, plans were already under way for an invasion of Canada, supported by hundreds of Iroquois warriors. Anglo-Iroquois ties had been strengthened at the expense of the French. But the invasion failed miserably, and the peace agreements survived as neutralists within the Iroquois councils prevailed. The Iroquois continued to play a central role in the fur trade, and grew in number by adopting peoples who had been displaced from the coastal regions and Carolinas, where warfare continued unabated. For the next half-century, Iroquois delegates appealed to British and French authorities for arms, supplies, money, favourable trade agreements, and alliances to protect their territories from enemies, whether European or indigenous.[23]

Similarly, in 1730, seven Cherokee men left South Carolina for London, hoping to win concessions from the king. They met the royal family at Windsor Castle, where they were clothed, fed, and entertained. By way of recompense the Board of Trade hoped for a formal agreement of alliance and commerce with the Cherokees against their French and Spanish neighbours to the south. The resulting treaty promised the British government and its South Carolina colony a trade monopoly with the Cherokees and a commitment by them to uphold the crown's interests in the region. Thus, Britain effectively extended its imperial claim to Cherokee territory, while the Cherokees could count on Britain's friendship, defined in general terms, and the delegates received many gifts, especially weapons.[24]

Creek, Mohegan, and other delegations continued to visit London in the hope of obtaining royal favour, until the 'French Indian' war erupted. The British occupation of Canada in 1760 made it clear that the 'play-off' strategy was no longer viable. The English became stronger than ever, building forts and extending their control westwards throughout New York, into the Ohio River valley, and up to Lake Michigan. Most of the Iroquois nations supported the English crown in the War of Independence. After 1776, indigenous delegations no longer had occasion to go to London and were forced to come to terms with a new power that was all too close for comfort. Prospects for negotiation and compromise were limited. The 'middle ground' was lost.[25] When

---

[23] Erik Hinderaker, 'The "Four Indian Kings" and the Imaginative Construction of the First British Empire', *William and Mary Quarterly*, 53 (1996), 487–526.

[24] Vaughan, *Transatlantic Encounters*, 137–64.

[25] Richard White, *The Middle Ground: Indians, Empires, and Republics in the Great Lakes Region, 1650–1815* (Cambridge, 1991).

the British recognized the independence of the former colonies in 1783, they ceded all land south of the Great Lakes to the United States and abandoned their old friends, the Iroquois, leaving them exposed to settlers who coveted their lands. Many were forced onto reservations or fled into Canada. By this time, Anglo-American leaders set their sights on acquiring more land for an expanding population and pushed native peoples away from the Atlantic.[26]

Concluding Remarks

The three sections of this chapter outline some of the pragmatic strategies of indigenous groups and individuals who confronted changes in the Atlantic world, exemplified by the transatlantic voyages discussed in sections one and three. Unfortunately for us, none of the delegations from North or South America in this period left any written record of its experiences. We are left to imagine what they thought of the other side, or resort to the impressions of Europeans who wrote about their visits. The indigenous and mestizo authors discussed in the first two sections were among the few from their world to set down their words for future generations. Their texts represent rare, insightful commentaries from the two major viceroyalties of Spanish America, sites of intense inter-ethnic interaction, within a century after their incorporation into the Atlantic world. Many of these writings from Mexico and Peru reveal a tension between hope and despair, expectation and frustration, as possibilities for cooperation, trade, and alliance between colonists and indigenous gave way in many places to competition for resources and profit. The long-term costs of this competition to Native Americans were incalculable. Settlers and traders brought institutions and mentalities across the Atlantic that transformed the new world in the image of the old. European kingdoms, companies, and nation-states fought to control trade routes, resources, and populations in the Americas, engaging or enlisting native groups in the process, even when leaders of those groups sought to remain neutral. Many indigenous peoples were drawn into a maelstrom of violence, fighting other Indians as much as Europeans. In contrast to the global scale of imperial ambitions, the vast majority of Native Americans struggled to protect the livelihood of their local communities. Most indigenous views of the Atlantic world were shaped and bound by local perspectives. Delegations that crossed the ocean represented their specific interests and did not pretend to speak on behalf of other native groups or, in the case of Mexico, even nearby communities. They hoped to distinguish themselves and their local interests from other so-called Indians with whom they had little or no affiliation. For the same reason, indigenous writers rarely referred to themselves as 'Indians', a misnomer applied by Europeans to all native peoples of the 'Indies', with its juridical implications and pejorative connotations.

---

[26] Colin G. Calloway, *The American Revolution in Indian Country: Crisis and Diversity in Native American Communities* (Cambridge, 1995).

The consequences of some changes are as difficult to imagine as they are to document. How are we to assess the impact of epidemic diseases on thousands of native societies and cultures, the periodic plagues that decimated approximately nine-tenths of indigenous populations over the course of two centuries? Perhaps the most startling fact is that the total population of the Americas did not reach its pre-contact level again until the nineteenth century, despite the transatlantic migration of millions of Europeans and Africans before 1800. And yet 'Indians' still outnumbered other racial groups in many parts of the Americas by the end of the long colonial periods, while contributing untold numbers to the creation of multi-racial societies throughout the hemisphere. These facts attest to the powerful, enduring presence of indigenous peoples in the Atlantic world.

BIBLIOGRAPHY

Gibson, Charles, *The Aztecs under Spanish Rule: A History of the Indians of the Valley of Mexico, 1519–1810* (Palo Alto, CA, 1964).

Gruzinski, Serge, *The Conquest of Mexico: The Incorporation of Indian Societies into the Western World, 16th–18th Centuries* (Cambridge, 1993).

Kupperman, Karen Ordahl, *Indians and English: Facing Off in Early America* (Ithaca, NY, 2000).

Lockhart, James, *The Nahuas after the Conquest: A Social and Cultural History of the Indians of Central Mexico, Sixteenth through Eighteenth Centuries* (Palo Alto, CA, 1992).

Richter, Daniel K., *Facing East from Indian Country: A Native History of Early America* (Cambridge, MA, 2001).

Salisbury, Neal, *Manitou and Providence: Indians, Europeans, and the Making of New England, 1500–1643* (Oxford, 1982).

Spalding, Karen, *Huarochirí: An Andean Society under Inca and Spanish Rule* (Palo Alto, CA, 1984).

Stern, Steve J., *Peru's Indian Peoples and the Challenge of Spanish Conquest: Huamanga to 1640* (2nd edn. Madison, WI, 1993).

Terraciano, Kevin, *The Mixtecs of Colonial Oaxaca: Ñudzahui History, Sixteenth through Eighteenth Centuries* (Palo Alto, CA, 2001).

White, Richard, *The Middle Ground: Indians, Empires, and Republics in the Great Lakes Region, 1650–1815* (Cambridge, 1991).

CHAPTER 16

···

AFRICA, SLAVERY, AND THE SLAVE TRADE, MID-SEVENTEENTH TO MID-EIGHTEENTH CENTURIES

···

DAVID ELTIS

WHICH of the major components of the Atlantic world—the Americas, Africa, and Europe—was most immediately affected by the integration of the Old and New Worlds that Columbian contact triggered? On epidemiological grounds alone the Americas would be the choice of most scholars, with Europe, at least prior to the eighteenth century, the least affected. In terms of dramatic economic, demographic, and social consequences of the early stages of Atlantic integration, Africa lies somewhere between the two. Yet if we shift the focus to changes in the nature and size of connections between the continents as opposed to changes within them, the most striking developments between the 1640s and the 1770s relate to Africa, not Europe or the Americas.

The growth of those connections was very slow. By the time of the First World War about 70 million people had crossed the Atlantic to the Americas since 1492. But only about half a million of these, or less than 1 per cent, had made the voyage in the first century and a half. About half the early migrants were captives from Africa; the other half, largely free or indentured, were from Europe. The most recent estimate of the number of captives carried off across the Atlantic in the 1640s is 12,000 a year, when the population of sub-Saharan Africa was certainly several million. Moreover, the only products traded across the Atlantic after 150 years of the Iberian Americas were precious metals and sugar—the latter still a high-value luxury rather than a consumer

I am indebted to Robin Law for comments on earlier drafts of this chapter.

item. Commodities other than sugar and precious metals made it across the Atlantic as ancillary items in the sense that precious metals, especially, had a high value to weight ratio and freed up space for lower-valued goods. The basic inhibiting factor to stronger trade ties, therefore, was the high cost of long ocean voyages. Thus, Africa remained a source of luxury items for most Europeans. In aggregate terms gold exports from Africa exceeded the value of slaves traded until the beginning of the eighteenth century.

Epidemiology apart, the main impact of ocean-going technology did not begin to take effect until after the mid-seventeenth century. In the slave trade at least, voyage times shortened, the ratio of tons per crew fell, and slaves per crew increased, suggesting falling costs. While systematic data for branches of transatlantic commerce other than the slave trade do not exist, trends presumably were similar. The density of exchange, the packet ships, the huge increase in the range of products traded, the sophisticated development of marine insurance and financial services make the period covered in the present chapter as different from the preceding 150 years as this period was from the nineteenth century. The impact for the slave trade was a sevenfold increase in the volume of captives carried across the Atlantic between the decade of the 1640s and 1766–75—from 12,000 to 80,000 a year. Indeed, 1763 to 1776 was the peak fourteen-year period of the transatlantic slave trade and slaves accounted for more than 95 per cent of total trade.

Much of this expansion occurred because West Africa—the region north of Angola encompassing the modern countries from Senegal to the Cameroon Republic—which had been only marginally involved in the slave trade hitherto, became for nearly two centuries an equal partner with Angola in the supply of slaves to the Americas. It now seems likely that there were two underlying environmental structures to the transatlantic traffic and thus two, rather than one, slave trades. Map 1 shows two systems of wind and ocean currents in the North and South Atlantic that follow the pattern of giant wheels—one lies north of the equator and turns clockwise, while its southern counterpart turns counterclockwise.[1] The northern European slaving nations and their colonial merchants used mainly the first, and the Iberian nations and Brazil used mainly the second. The Netherlands, France, England, and the Scandinavian nations entered the slave trade in a systematic way only in the mid-seventeenth century, and the northern system expanded accordingly.

For Africa the entrance of these countries into the business meant an unprecedented expansion in the movement of enslaved Africans from north of the equator to the Americas. Prior to 1640 the Portuguese had assembled African captives from various parts of Upper Guinea—chiefly the southern rivers of Senegambia—in 'factories' (trading establishments) located initially at Arguim, and then at Santiago and Fogo in the Cape Verde Islands. These captives ended up in the Spanish Caribbean and Central America, though this branch of the slave trade had, early in the seventeenth century, been overtaken by the route from Angola. The Windward Coast, south and

[1] Daniel B. Domingues da Silva, 'The Atlantic Slave Trade to Maranhão, 1680–1846: Volume, Routes and Organization', *Slavery and Abolition*, 29 (2008), 477–501.

east to the Bight of Biafra, sent very few captives to the Americas before 1640. The Dutch, followed closely by the English, established their own 'factories' on islands south of Cape Verde—James Fort in the Gambia, Isles de Los, Bunce Island—and where there were no physical islands, they built islands of a different kind in the sense of heavily fortified factories, or castles, particularly on the Gold Coast. But, at this point, slaves were more likely to be sold to gold-producing Africans rather than bought for transportation to the Americas. However, from the second half of the seventeenth century, some slaves were dispatched across the Atlantic. The major slave-trading areas of West Africa lay to the east of the Gold Coast castles, in the Bights of Benin and Biafra, and eventually at markets north of the Congo River, Loango being the most important. Any European land-based presence was thin or non-existent between the Gold Coast and Luanda in Portuguese Angola, and African authorities laid down the rules.

On the Upper Guinea coast, non-human commodities dominated overseas trade until the 1740s. High-quality dyewood (called camwood after a Temne word) came from the Sherbro, and to a lesser extent from the Sierra Leone estuary region. It was probably the most valuable single export in the late seventeenth and early eighteenth centuries. Some gold was exported early in this period, and Senegal gum (also used for dyes) became important in the mid-eighteenth century. Small amounts of ivory were always traded. The major markets for captives taken directly to the Americas at this time were in the Senegal and Gambia rivers—the buyers chiefly British and French slave traders. Vessels of all nations sailing to the Bight of Benin and beyond obtained occasional slaves in this region as they coasted south and east. But all this activity accounted for no more than one in twelve of all captives conveyed across the Atlantic from sub-Saharan Africa prior to 1740. However, after 1740, the whole region of Upper Guinea began to engage in significant direct transatlantic trade; this expansion peaked in the second half of the eighteenth century. Captive Africans became the most valuable 'export' until 1807. Major centres for the slave trade appeared in the so-called southern rivers of Senegambia (now Guinea-Conakry), the Sierra Leone estuary, Cape Mount (mainly Liverpool vessels), and Cap Lahou (mainly Dutch vessels). In the second half of the eighteenth century just under one in six of all African captives drawn into the transatlantic traffic came from Upper Guinea.

Upper Guinea south of the Gambia River had no large-scale state-like structures, and in addition, population densities were relatively low compared to the rest of West Africa that lay within the forest zone. Ethnic diversity was considerable even by African standards. Languages and nations tended to live in mixed communities, or, if separate, the towns would be adjacent to centres where other peoples resided. Perhaps these characteristics, particularly the absence of empires, shaped the supply of victims for the slave trade. If later patterns (1820s and 1830s) are true for the eighteenth century, then no one group provided the majority of captives.[2] More than three-quarters of all captives originated within 150 miles of the Atlantic shore. Whilst Mende and Mandingo

---

[2] But, for the Balanta people, see Walter Hawthorne, *Planting Rice and Harvesting Slaves: Transformations along the Guinea-Bissau Coast, 1400–1900* (Portsmouth, NH, 2003).

were the largest source of captives, they provided little more than a third together of all those entering the Atlantic trade from this region. Wolof, Kissi, Fula, Temne, Vai, and Loma, and many others of lesser numerical importance, probably never came close to generating as many as 10 per cent each of Upper Guinea captives.[3]

At the beginning of our period the Gold Coast, comprising roughly modern Ghana, supplied very few captives to Atlantic merchants. The traffic in people leaving the Gold Coast comprised a little over 1,000 a year on average down to 1695 (compared to eight times that figure in the same period from the adjacent Slave Coast). However, it leaped to 7,000 a year between 1696 and 1705 and never fell below this figure for the rest of the eighteenth century.

Despite the prominence of peoples from the Gold Coast in the relatively well-documented early British Caribbean, an ethnic profile of deportees is harder to build here than for any region on which transatlantic slave traders drew. The major shifts in the fortunes of the Akan-speaking coastal societies such as Ahanta, Fetu (the location of Cape Coast Castle), Fante (where Anomabu was built), and Accra during the slave-trade era are known in outline.[4] The gold-producing states of Denkyira and Akani in the north struggled as production declined. Further east, the Akwamu empire rose and then fell in this era before relocating in much reduced form on the Slave Coast in 1730. All states felt the enduring pressure from Asante in the north, though Asante did not break through to the coast until the early nineteenth century.[5] Such conflicts undoubtedly yielded captives, and thus some of these events are associated with the expansion and contraction of slave departures from the three major Gold Coast embarkation points of Anomabu, Cape Coast Castle, and Elmina. Yet we know rather more about those selling the slaves than we do about the slaves themselves.

Some tentative inferences on ethnicity are nevertheless possible. Before 1700, both volumes of departures and prices were low enough—the years 1676–84 saw the nadir of coastal West African slave prices in the two centuries after 1650—that most slaves must have been drawn from coastal states such as Asebu, Fetu, Fante, Agona, Accra, and Adangme, or just beyond.[6] The rapid expansion of the traffic after 1700 and the associated rise in slave prices would have seen slaves travelling the paths to the coast from the north along with diminishing quantities of gold. The peak of the traffic after 1750, however, was linked to Asante expansion—the major Asante trade routes to the coast terminating at Elmina, Cape Coast Castle, Anomabu, and Accra. Most slaves in this period originated as tribute sent to Kumasi, the Asante capital, by Asante's neighbours, probably from Dagomba and Mossi country. Such slaves must have begun their journey to the Americas from the region where forest became savannah

---

[3] Philip Misevich, 'The Origins of Slaves Leaving the Upper Guinea Coast in the Nineteenth Century', in David Eltis and David Richardson (eds.), *Extending the Frontiers: Essays Based on the New Transatlantic Slave Trade Database* (New Haven, CT, 2008), 155–75.

[4] Ray A. Kea, *Settlements, Trade and Polities in the Seventeenth-Century Gold Coast* (Baltimore, MD, 1982), 11–50, 136–42.

[5] J. K. Fynn, *Asante and its Neighbours, 1700–1807* (London, 1971).

[6] David Eltis, *Rise of African Slavery in the Americas* (Cambridge, 2000), 293–7.

200 or more miles from the coast. They could have had little in common with the Fante through whose hands they passed.[7] Thus while slaves leaving Gold Coast in the second half of the eighteenth century continued to be called 'Coromantee' or 'Mina', they were probably culturally distant from the slaves assigned these same ethnic terms in the seventeenth century.

Produce exports into the Atlantic world—a little ivory and some African textiles called 'country cloths'—were of minor significance in the Bight of Benin. By contrast, more people left the Bight of Benin than any other region except West Central Africa. Nevertheless, the step up to large-scale and sustained volumes of slaves entering the transatlantic trade did not occur until after 1650 and was led by the Dutch and English until a Brazilian-based tobacco trade got under way in the 1670s. The term 'Slave Coast' for the region was not used until the 1690s.[8] The growth of the trade was astonishing, rising from about 1,000 a year in the 1650s to 8,000 in the 1680s, to a peak of over 19,000 a year in the 1720s. Departures were nearly double those of the adjacent Bight of Biafra. The broad patterns are clear. Ouidah accounted for well over half of all the region's captives sent to the Americas between 1650 and 1770. It reached its peak in the 1720s just before the king of Dahomey, who had already reduced the kingdom of Allada (1724), destroyed the independence of Ouidah. Nevertheless, despite the latter's prominence in the slave trade, down to the early 1680s four out of five captives had embarked not at Ouidah, but at Offra, the chief port of the state of Allada to the west. After the Dahomean conquest, smaller centres along the coast such as Porto Novo, Badagry, and Benin gained market share at Ouidah's expense, while departures from nearby Jakin, which had briefly emerged as a rival to Ouidah before 1727, collapsed when it also was destroyed in 1732.

Why was the Slave Coast such a major supplier of slaves to transatlantic markets? It seems unlikely that the hinterland of the region contained more people than these other regions. It had no forts to match those on the Gold Coast, few islands, and, for those approaching from the sea, dangerous surf. The basic explanation might be African political authority, necessary not so much for enslavement as for providing orderly markets and debt-collection institutions at the point where the African slave became the property of Europeans. Credit was the greatest single irritant in European–African slave-trade relations. This region developed African-controlled trading enclaves that offered security to outside traders, Europeans and Africans alike.[9] Thus African political authority made such features as fortifications and islands unnecessary, and effectively provided an ordered environment and a set of rules for carrying on business. In contrast to

---

[7] Fynn, *Asante and its Neighbors*, 116–17, 119, 125; Margaret Priestley, *West African Trade and Coast Society: A Family Study* (Oxford, 1969), 11–12, 73–4.

[8] Robin Law, 'The Slave Trade in Seventeenth-Century Allada: A Revision', *African Economic History*, 22 (1994), 63–76; see also id., *The Kingdom of Allada* (Leiden, 1997), 1, 85–9.

[9] Robin Law, *The Slave Coast of West Africa, 1550–1750: The Impact of the Atlantic Slave Trade on an African Society* (Oxford, 1991), 89–91, 217–18; id., *Kingdom of Allada*, 72–3; id., 'On Pawning and Enslavement for Debt in the Pre-Colonial Slave Coast', in Toyin Falola and Paul E. Lovejoy (eds.), *Pawnship in Africa: Debt Bondage in Historical Perspective* (Boulder, CO, 1994), 55–69.

the Gold Coast, Europeans were sideline observers of relations between African polities, not participants. The king of Ouidah successfully imposed his authority on competing national groups and, even during European wars, vessels trading in his waters would not engage in hostilities.[10] Dahomey continued to enforce this neutrality after the conquest and through most of the balance of the slave trade era. Ouidah was thus a port in the European sense in that it was open to the ships of all nations, but on its own terms.

The ethnicity of captives leaving the Bight of Benin is less well known than the military and political struggles among coastal communities that generated them. Two broad phases may be discerned down to the 1770s. The extremely rapid expansion of the slave trade to its peak in 1701–25 was funnelled through Ouidah, Popo, and Offra. There is no evidence of a strong Yoruba component in this first phase of the traffic so that Dahomey military expansion to the north and the fall of the Akwamu empire in the west were likely major sources. The majority of slaves before 1725 would have been Gbe speakers.[11] The second phase spanned the relative decline of Ouidah from the late 1720s. Thereafter, Dahomey's actions against lagoon-based rivals in the slave export business generated captives and shifted slave provenance southwards, closer to the coast. Dahomey also passed on tribute slaves and slaves obtained commercially, both from outside Dahomey, including Tapa (or Nupe), Bariba, and even some Hausa.[12] Eastern ports emerged towards the end of our period, and these drew slaves primarily from Yoruba-speakers in the east sent out by the Oyo empire rather than Dahomey. For these, one might hypothesize a mix of Gbe-speaking and Yoruba peoples.

While the Bight of Benin supplied the most slaves of any West African region, the Bight of Biafra hinterland (see Map 1) was subjected to the most concentrated pressure from Atlantic slave markets. A direct, regular, transatlantic traffic began in the mid-seventeenth century through English and occasional Dutch vessels, and built up to an average of 2,000 slaves a year by the 1660s. The traffic continued at this level for the next seventy-five years. The large rise in the volume of departures occurred in this region, with a 200 per cent increase between 1736–40 and 1741–5. Twenty-five years later, the region dispatched more captives to the west than the Slave Coast. Although the Slave Coast has a much higher profile in the literature, almost one-third more slaves left the Bight of Biafra in the second half of the eighteenth century—an average of 14,000 a year, almost all of them going to the Caribbean.

If the Slave Coast lacked the castles of the Gold Coast, the Bight of Biafra lacked permanent European shore-based establishments of any kind. From time to time the English maintained factory ships at Bonny and Old Calabar but no buildings. Yet there were no large African states or empires either on the coast or in the interior. The

---

[10] Charles Thomas to RAC, 22 November 1703, T70/13, fo. 44; Robin Law, *Ouidah: The Social History of a West African Slaving 'Port', 1727–1892* (Athens, OH, 2004), 123–5.

[11] Law, 'Ethnicity and the Slave Trade: "Lucumi" and "Nago" as Ethnonyms in West Africa', *History in Africa*, 24 (1997), 207; id., *Kingdom of Allada*, 101–4.

[12] Law, *The Oyo Empire c.1600–c.1836: A West African Imperialism in the Era of the Atlantic Slave Trade* (Oxford, 1977), 226–7.

emergence of trade with the Atlantic in this area, in slaves and small amounts of ivory, coincided with the spread westward of the Aro network from Arochukwu—primarily a prestigious trading diaspora with the ability to carry out some governmental, judicial, religious, and military functions. However, it was not, and did not result in, a centralized state, or in military conquest of what is now south-east Nigeria, or direct trading between the Aro and Europeans.[13] A range of Aro institutions, including dispute settlement mechanisms—ultimately connected to the Aro oracle—and the Ekpe society, came to be of central importance in areas into which the Aro diaspora expanded. All trading networks, of which the Aro was the most important, acquired slaves and sold them to intermediaries who, in turn, dealt with trading houses, or towns with locations along the Imo and Cross river estuaries.

Slave departures in every African coastal region were concentrated in just a handful of embarkation points, but in this region nearly all captives left from just three ports between 1650 and 1770—Bonny, New Calabar, and Old Calabar—four out of five of them on English vessels. These communities became specialized slave-trading emporiums over time, but never city-states in the sense of minor military powers forming alliances and marching against, or with, *neighbouring* powers in wars of conquest. Trading houses evolved that fostered close relationships between Bristol and Liverpool buyers on the one hand and African sellers, often Efik traders at Old Calabar, on the other. Ship accounts for both Bonny and Old Calabar show twenty to forty African traders selling slaves to large vessels, but typically two or three of these traders would be responsible for one-third or half the total shipment, a market structure not drastically different from what existed in the Bristol and Liverpool slave trader communities. The African traders would be heads of houses whose wards or towns would line the river banks and form the elements of the ports known as Bonny and Old Calabar. Because slave captains advanced goods on credit to African merchants, regulation and enforcement of debt was a central preoccupation of these houses. In Bonny, the king's power under the Pepple (or Perekuele) family was sufficient that he was able to act as both financial intermediary between African and European traders as well as enforcer. At Old and New Calabar, human pawnship became a central method of guaranteeing debts between Africans and Europeans. In addition, at Bonny and particularly at Old Calabar, a secret society—Ekpe—evolved to which all African slave merchants belonged. It, too, helped maintain orderly credit and market transactions and served much the same function as governments in the coastal states on the Slave Coast.[14] Igbo peoples formed the largest single group among captives who left the

---

[13] Law, *The Oyo Empire*, 114–45; Kenneth O. Dike and Felicia I. Ekejiuba, *The Aro of South-Eastern Nigeria, 1650–1980: A Study of Socio-Economic Formation and Transformation in Nigeria* (Ibadan, 1990), 54–93; G. Ugo Nwokeji, *The Slave Trade and Culture in the Bight of Biafra: An African Society in the Atlantic World* (Cambridge, 2010).

[14] Paul E. Lovejoy and David Richardson, 'Trust, Pawnship and Atlantic History: The Institutional Foundation of the Old Calabar Slave Trade', *American Historical Review*, 104 (1999), 333–55; eid., 'The Business of Slaving: Pawnship in Western Africa, *c.*1600–1810', *Journal of African History*, 42 (1999),

Bight of Biafra in these years, though, unlike the later period, they were probably a minority. Ibibio also had a strong minority presence.[15]

West Central Africa was by far the largest supplier of slaves to the Americas. It was also the only region in Africa where Europeans had some control over the routes by which slaves reached the coast. In these years 38 per cent of all slaves who crossed the Atlantic boarded ship in one of the ports between Cape Lopez and Benguela. The Portuguese-dominated South Atlantic wind and current system connected the region closely with Brazil, but Dutch, French, and British did break into the system. From an Atlantic perspective there were two distinct coastal segments within the region, the division between the two lying somewhere between Ambriz and Luanda. The Portuguese traded south of this line, mainly Luanda and Benguela, and, after 1700, carried all their slaves to Brazil. Beginning in the 1660s, other Europeans carried slaves to the Caribbean, the Guianas, and mainland North America from north of this line, mainly Loango, Malimba, and Cabinda. The impulse here was Dutch expulsion from Luanda a few years earlier and the explosive growth of the Caribbean plantation complex, though the northern area, especially Loango, also supplied dyewoods and some ivory, copper, and cloths.[16]

The division between the northern ports and the south extended to the organization of the trade. In the former, slaves moved from African to European control on the coast, much as in West Africa. During the peak slave-trade era, the three major ports north of the Congo were outlets for the states of Loango, Kakongo, and Ngoyo respectively. These states shared a language, had similar laws, customs, and government structures, but were also competitors. In each, European traders negotiated with agents of the king, called *mafouks*, using temporary factories on shore for which they paid what they viewed as rent. Jurisdiction always lay with the African authorities and the captain of a French vessel reported from Cabinda in 1702 that 'ships are more secure [here] than at Juda [Ouidah]'.[17] In Portuguese Angola, by contrast, a limited European territorial presence meant that trade routes to the interior were more susceptible to European control. The mid-seventeenth century witnessed the last Portuguese attempts at conquest prior to the nineteenth century as the African kingdom of Kongo fragmented. Ndongo came under Portuguese influence, and the Portuguese negotiated trading treaties with Matamba and Kasanje, major states

25–50; eid., ' "This Horrid Hole": Royal Authority, Commerce, and Credit at Bonny, 1690–1840', *Journal of African History*, 45 (2004), 363–92.

[15] Cf. David Northrup, *Trade without Rulers: Pre-Colonial Economic Development in South-Eastern Nigeria* (Oxford, 1978), 58–65, 237. See also Philip D. Curtin, *The Atlantic Slave Trade: A Census* (Madison, WI, 1969), 251–64.

[16] Phyllis C. Martin, *The External Trade of the Loango Coast, 1576–1870: The Effects of Changing Commercial Relations on the Vili Kingdom of Loango* (Oxford, 1972), 33–72.

[17] Sieur Hays to Asiento Company, 27 October 1702, Paris, *Archives Nationales, Section d'Outre-mer*, Colonial, C8A, 15, fo. 109.

250–300 miles to the east.[18] It was now possible to access slaves from the Lunda empire, located on the tributaries to the Kasai River, even further east.[19] After 1683, the Portuguese put more emphasis on trade, and the source of slaves for Brazil shifted eastwards. A central part of the trading system was the role of an intermediary group of peoples of mixed African and Portuguese ancestry called Pombeiros who created what colonial settlement there was in Angola outside Luanda, and who provided the transportation and credit links between Luanda and the slaving frontier. Some were even able to send slaves on consignment to Brazil.[20]

The West Central African hinterland was easily the largest of the eight African regions examined here. It comprises the whole of Equatorial Africa—a huge rainforest area about the size of arable West Africa, stretching from southern Cameroon to the Congo estuary and east to almost the great lakes—in addition to the woodlands and grasslands of central and southern Angola. The area east and north of the Congo River generated far fewer slaves than did central and southern Angola. No social organization in the hinterland of northern Equatorial Africa could match the Lunda empire on the Kasai in organizing slave production in what is now eastern Angola, or indeed, the Aro in the western and central Bight of Biafra hinterland, the Ashanti on the Gold Coast, and Dahomey in the Bight of Benin.[21] The group that came closest was the Loangan coast traders themselves, known south of the Congo as Mubiri. They operated caravans that set out from Loango, Ngoya, and Kakongo, travelled widely, formed something of a trading diaspora, and tapped many diffuse sources in addition to major markets such as Malebo Pool on the Congo. Like the Aro in Igboland, the Mubiri had prestige in areas they serviced.[22]

Overall, Cabinda sent out the greater number of slaves among ports north of the Congo. It was closer to both the mouth of the Congo and the supply networks south of the Congo, and had the best harbour on the coast. After 1725, the salient long-run port trends are the rise and fall of Malimba, and the gradual decline of Loango. These broad patterns correspond very well with long-run decline of the Vili kingdom of Loango from the seventeenth to the early nineteenth centuries. Former dependencies Kakongo and Ngoya, to the south, and Mayomba in the north had become competitors by the following century. The northern ports drew slaves from Equatorial Africa, including Gabon, and, as implied above, from points south. Overall, they drew on a wider

[18] Linda Heywood and John Thornton, *Central Africans, Atlantic Creoles, and the Foundation of the Americas, 1585–1660* (Cambridge, 2007), 109–68.

[19] David Birmingham, *Trade and Conflict in Angola: The Mbundu and their Neighbours under the Influence of the Portuguese, 1483–1790* (Oxford, 1966), 42–132; Joseph C. Miller, 'The Slave Trade in Congo and Angola', in Martin Kilson and Robert Rotberg (eds.), *The African Diaspora: Interpretative Essays* (Cambridge, MA, 1976), 84–102.

[20] Roquinaldo Amaral Ferreira, ' "Fazandas" em troca de escravos circuitos de crédito nos sertões de Angola, 1830–1860', *Estudos Afro-Asiaticos*, 32 (1997), 75–96; Joseph C. Miller, *Way of Death: Merchant Capitalism and the Angolan Slave Trade, 1730–1830* (Madison, WI, 1988), 245–83.

[21] Robert W. Harms, *River of Wealth, River of Sorrow* (New Haven, CT, 1981).

[22] Martin, *External Trade*, 70; Birmingham, *Trade and Conflict in Angola*, 131–2.

hinterland than probably any other group of neighbouring ports in Africa. That hinterland ranged from the Mboko, who lived on what is now the Gabon–Congo boundary, to Kasanje on the upper Kwango in eastern Angola, and encompassed, too, the Upper Congo drainage area.[23]

For the Portuguese trade from West Central Africa, the scale and steadiness of Luanda's contribution to the transatlantic slave trade is striking. In the early 1620s it had already reached a volume of trade in people that was not to be surpassed until after 1800. Conflict with the Dutch meant the slave trade collapsed temporarily, but it dispatched 8,000–10,000 slaves a year throughout our period. The direct trade from Benguela to Brazil did not begin until the 1710s (before this point, slaves from Benguela had been shipped to Luanda for transatlantic embarkation). Departures typically ran at about half those at Luanda after 1750.

The evidence on the provenance of slaves passing through Portuguese ports is known only in very broad outline. There is broad agreement that in the seventeenth and early eighteenth centuries, the Mbundu peoples of central Angola—living within 200 miles of the coast—were at the beginning of the chain that created deportees and that a slaving frontier moved steadily eastwards and to a lesser degree southwards as well. States on the Kwango, Matamba, and Kasanje, east of the Mbundu kingdoms, took over the Mbundu role and effectively blocked direct Portuguese access to the Lunda empire, which had, by the later eighteenth century, become the leading source of slaves. Other sources were the south-east Central Highlands and the Upper Congo basin.[24] They, and the Lunda empire, lay more than 700 miles away from Luanda and Benguela.

South-east Africa was a minor participant in the Atlantic world in this era. Beginning in the 1670s, after the English government established a monopoly company with sole rights to trade in West Africa, English and English colonial merchants who wished to skirt that monopoly began to seek African captives for the Americas in south-east Africa. In addition, throughout this period the Dutch engaged in a small slave traffic, as did the French. But for the Atlantic world, south-east Africa meant Madagascar, which, with the exception of occasional Portuguese vessels seeking slaves for Brazil at Mozambique Island, supplied all the captives from the region that ended up in the Americas before 1750. And because trade in commodities was minor, the slave trade was essentially the only significant commercial exchange between the Atlantic and south-east Africa. Malagasy captives emerged in small numbers from scattered points in the far south and the north-east, but especially from the north-west of the island. European trade with Madagascar (which was preceded by, and accompanied by, extensive Muslim merchant activity) was associated with the rise of the Sakalava empire in the north—probably the first imperial structure in East Africa—which

---

[23] Louis de Grandpré, *Voyage à la côte occidentale d'Afrique fait dans les années 1786 et 1787; contenant . . .* , 2 vols. (Paris, 1801), ii. x, 25, 37; Jan Vansina, *Paths in the Rainforests: Toward a History of Political Tradition in Equatorial Africa* (Madison, WI, 1990), 219; Martin, *External Trade*, 117–35.

[24] Birmingham, *Trade and Conflict*, 160–1; Miller, *Way of Death*, 148, 207–44.

became the most important single polity in the island, and most Malagasy captives were either from this empire or had been captured by it. For reasons as yet unexplained, Madagascar dropped out of Atlantic trade networks from 1760. It had never supplied even 1 per cent of all captives taken to the Americas.[25]

In summary, the slave trade expanded in Africa mainly by pushing regions across a threshold of supply. A large surge of departures marked the crossing of this threshold in most of the large regions examined here, followed by a plateau in the volume of the traffic. Except for West Central Africa, each region experienced a one-time increase after many years when slave departures averaged only a few hundred a year. One possible explanation of this pattern is the time, resources, and adjustment of social structures required to establish a supply network, or to break through to new sources in the interior, or perhaps to redirect an existing network for goods or slaves, towards the Atlantic. Upper Guinea in the mid-eighteenth century is one example. Aro activity in the Bight of Biafra hinterland is another. On the Gold Coast, the massive increase in slaving coincided with the exhaustion of deposits.[26] In the Bight of Benin, the key event appears to have been the reorganization of the trade associated with the emergence of Ouidah. The Dahomean conquest of that community appears to have brought expansion of the traffic to a close. In West Central Africa a doubling of departures occurred in the mid-seventeenth century, but the numbers continued to grow dramatically after that initial increase; here, a continually shifting frontier of slaving apparently did exist.[27] Given the lighter population densities, the shortage of continuously navigable waterways, and the length of trade routes, networks would have to be put in place and slave prices at the coast would have to rise sufficiently to cover the costs of travel. In the long run, then, this region's 'plateau' became much higher than elsewhere in Africa. In south-east Africa, the step up occurred after the period that concerns us here. Transatlantic slave trading thus expanded by pulling in new regions of the sub-continent each of which experienced a single dramatic increase in the scale of departures. Within each region two-thirds or more of total departures passed through just three or four ports. The rising demand for captives from rapidly expanding sugar production, and behind that, everyday demand for sugar from North Atlantic consumers, provides 50 per cent of the explanation for these broad patterns. Africanists still need to supply details on the other half of the story.

A great variety of regions and peoples were drawn into the Atlantic slave trade for the first time in this period of 120 years. Given that 5.2 million coerced migrants left Africa for the Atlantic world in just over a century, there is no precedent in world history for the scale of dislocation to the lives of ordinary people. Perhaps most extraordinarily from the perspective of the history of long-distance migration, almost 2 million were female. In fact, for this period, only 63 per cent of slaves moved across

---

[25] Jane Hooper, 'An Island Empire in the Indian Ocean: The Sakalava Empire of Madagascar' (unpublished Ph.D. dissertation, Emory University, 2010), especially chapter 2.

[26] Eltis, *The Rise of African Slavery*, 150–1.

[27] Miller, *Way of Death*, 140–53, 234–41.

the Atlantic were male. Never before had long-distance migration contained such a significant female component. Moreover, the movement was accompanied by what, from an African perspective, was a reconstruction of gender that affected all facets except the strictly biological. The gender roles of Africans and Europeans had evolved in isolation from each other until the revolution in ocean-going technology and differed in terms of both work and reproductive functions.[28] Much of the agricultural work in sub-Saharan Africa was, and is, performed by women. Women and children formed the majority of slaves exchanged and acquired in the internal African context. When Europeans attempted to purchase slaves on the African coast, they were taken aback by the number of females offered for sale. Their own conception of gender meant that they were looking for what they called 'prime males'.

One of the first 'new' experiences for African captives being assembled for transportation to the Americas must therefore have been the extraordinarily high proportion of men. What appeared high to Africans was, for Europeans, extremely low. Heavy field labour carried out in gangs was not women's work either in Europe or, initially, in the European Americas. This preference did not, of course, prevent slave owners in the Americas from making full use of female field labour. In the last years of slavery in the British Caribbean, the so-called first gangs on sugar estates frequently comprised only women. But for newly arrived Africans observing the plantation labour scene, the novelty lay in the number of males set to work. The adjustment required for those living in the hinterlands of the three Bight of Biafra ports must have been particularly severe. Over this long century as the slave traffic grew to its peak, sex ratios on vessels departing from these major ports were, on average, almost balanced. Indeed, one of the striking features of the slave trade at this time was the large variations across regions in the gender composition of the streams of people leaving for the Americas.

A more immediate concern for captives as they contemplated their predicament on the African coast was the horrendous conditions under which they were forced to travel across the ocean. Europeans were never subjected to such conditions as they moved to the New World. The horrors of the middle passage have become well known in the last few years, but historians have not yet appreciated the wide variations in slaves' shipboard experiences. Mortality decreased from nearly one-quarter of those embarked to around 14 per cent from 1651–75 to 1751–75, but in deaths per day it remained extremely high in comparison with other ocean-going routes. The variation across voyages was also enormous. Thus the high rates were due to the catastrophic experiences of particular ships, while three-quarters of all voyages experienced mortality well below the mean. Shipwreck and slave revolts were partly responsible for this pattern, but the major factor was the incidence of infectious disease. Gastrointestinal disease (dysentery was described as 'the bloody flux') accounted for most deaths and its particularly virulent forms appear to have been restricted to relatively few vessels

---

[28] Eltis, *Rise of African Slavery*, chapter 4.

where the effects were truly devastating.[29] Regional variation was also important. Mortality varied far more according to where the slave vessel began its voyage, as opposed to where it went. Thus, mortality and morbidity were much higher (almost double) on vessels leaving the ports in the Bight of Biafra than from the rest of Africa, and within the region; Old Calabar had a particularly bad record. As in the North Atlantic emigrant business in a later period, not just the conditions on the vessel, but conditions in the port and en route determined survival. Those who survived the passage from the Bight of Biafra to the Americas were almost invariably described as weak and emaciated.

Unlike mortality, sailing times changed little between the mid-seventeenth and late eighteenth centuries. For some major routes, such as that from the Gold Coast to Jamaica, they actually increased. In addition there was much less variation from one voyage to the next than for shipboard mortality on any given route. However, there was huge variation between routes. For those fortunate to be carried from Senegambia to the eastern Caribbean or Amazonia the middle passage typically lasted less than six weeks in this era. But captives leaving from the Gold Coast and sailing to Saint-Domingue spent an average of just under four months on board. No data survives for those leaving from Madagascar for North America, but their middle passages must have been longest. The fairly abundant records on provisions suggest that, contrary to the popular image, food shortages were not common, and small quantities of tobacco and alcohol were also distributed to slaves. The misery of the middle passage stemmed rather from the awful crowding, the disease, the periodic catastrophic outbreaks of violence, and the trauma of helplessness and the unknown.

Revolts were fairly common. About one in eight vessels in the mid-eighteenth century appear to have experienced attempts by captives to take over the vessel. The costs of controlling such resistance increased the price of slaves and thus reduced the number of slaves carried off from Africa. Most popular histories claim that rebellion was most likely while the vessel was off the African coast. In fact revolts per week were just as frequent during the middle passage and off the Americas as they were on the eastern side of the Atlantic. The very few successful revolts—in the sense of slaves escaping onto the African coast—were more likely to occur near Africa. How many were successful? The *Voyages* database has records of 361 African attacks on slave vessels between 1641 and 1770;[30] twenty-one of these resulted in some slaves escaping to the African coast, and of these, some would certainly have been re-enslaved. For another fifty or so of this group the outcome was an aborted voyage, but in these cases the captives were either all killed—usually because the vessel exploded during the uprising—or the ship was severely damaged and the slaves were transferred to other vessels. The major impact of resistance was thus not the freeing of slaves but rather on the cost structure of the business.

---

[29] Herbert S. Klein, Stanley L. Engerman, Robin Haines, and Ralph Shlomowitz, 'Transoceanic Mortality: The Slave Trade in Comparative Perspective', *William and Mary Quarterly*, 52 (2001), 92–118.

[30] http://slavevoyages.org/tast/database/search.faces?yearFrom=1641&yearTo=1770&resistance=1.2.3.4.5.6.

For the 85 per cent of captives that survived the voyage, the range of destinations in the Americas makes analysis a challenge. No less than 227 combinations of embarkation and disembarkation regions—in other words voyage routes—linked by transatlantic slave ships in this period can be isolated in the new *Voyages* database. Despite such complexity, some fairly clear patterns are evident. In these years, Amazonia drew two-thirds of its captives from Senegambia, and mainland North America obtained 40 per cent of its African peoples from Upper Guinea as a whole. No other region in the Americas came close to this ratio. In other words captives from Upper Guinea found themselves scattered across the Americas and for the most part they nowhere formed a large concentrated group—even supposing they had something in common at their point of origin. Almost one-third of all captives from the Gold Coast went to Jamaica, and a further one in six to Barbados, many of them in the early 1700s. In both places they met even larger numbers of people from the Bight of Biafra and northern Angola. Thus the greatest impact of captives from the eastern Gold Coast was in the much smaller Danish West Indies, which drew almost exclusively on this part of the African coast. The English carried far more slaves from the Gold Coast than any other national carrier, but as the English also supplied slaves to all parts of the Americas outside Brazil, Gold Coast captives were scattered almost as widely as those leaving the three Upper Guinea regions. Captives leaving the Bight of Benin experienced a quite different kind of diasporic pattern. In the seventeenth century the heavy English and Dutch presence in the slave trade here ensured a majority of those leaving disembarked in Jamaica, Barbados, and the Spanish Americas—via Curaçao. But in the eighteenth century the Portuguese and French replaced the Dutch and English slavers with the result that captives leaving Ouidah, Jaquin, Badagri, Benin, and Little Popo poured into Bahia, Saint-Domingue, and Martinique. Probably two-thirds of all slaves arriving in Bahia between 1710 and 1770 came from the Slave Coast and half the slaves from these ports went to Bahia, making the Bahia–Slave Coast connection one of the largest and strongest of all Atlantic slave routes. A short distance to the east, Bonny, New Calabar, and Old Calabar hewed to the Gold Coast pattern. Once more, English dominance in the slave trade ensured a wide dispersion of captives—exclusive of Brazil. The Río de la Plata, Spanish Central America and the Caribbean, every island in the English Caribbean, and British North America all drew heavily on these three embarkation points in this period. A minority Portuguese trade also connected these ports with Bahia. In fact the dispersal of captives from this region was the widest of all regions, which perhaps might account for the weaker cultural impact on the Americas of peoples from the Bight of Biafra than others that were less scattered.

West Central Africa during this period essentially experienced two diasporas. Captives from the northern ports went to the colonies of northern Europeans, those from Luanda and Benguela in the south went to Brazil. The Dutch were most important in shaping the northern system. Centring their activities on Loango, they carried one-quarter of the total exodus to Suriname, mainly in the eighteenth century, and another fifth to Spanish Americas under the Dutch West India Company, mainly in the seventeenth century. They were closely followed by the French, with Saint-

Domingue alone absorbing one-third of this large total outflow of captives. The English carried off only half the numbers of their French and Dutch rivals from this region before the 1770s, and, playing their usual role of selling slaves to all possible markets, dispersed their human wares over a very wide geographic range from New York to the Río de la Plata. The southern diaspora, centred overwhelmingly on Luanda, was much simpler and forged the strongest of all transatlantic links in the whole re-peopling of the Americas process. The Brazilian ports of Pernambuco, Bahia, and Rio de Janeiro took in 97 per cent of the captives leaving Luanda and Benguela, and almost all the remaining 3 per cent went to Amazonia. The most important destination for this diaspora was Bahia, despite its overall reliance on the Bight of Benin for its source of slaves. Pernambuco, likewise, drew on both the Slave Coast and Angola. Of the three major Brazilian ports, indeed of all the ports in the Americas, Rio de Janeiro had the strongest and most exclusive links with an African regional source of slaves. Over 500,000 captives arrived in Rio de Janeiro from Angola in these years, constituting 95 per cent of arrivals from all sources. The vast majority of these passed through the single port of Luanda. The size of Luanda's slave catchment area notwithstanding, the sugar plantations of south-east Brazil must have had the most homogeneous labour force in the Americas.

By the end of the third quarter of the eighteenth century, the transatlantic slave trade was close to the highest level it was ever to attain. For every seven people crossing the Atlantic from east to west, six were African. For every fifteen females following the same route in these years, fourteen came from Africa. Yet the cultural diversity of Africa is such that it is a gross distortion to refer to a single movement. What does 'African' mean in this context—something with much less meaning than 'European', surely. More specifically what does a Fulbe Muslim from the upper Senegal River valley who finds himself in Maryland have in common with an animist Malagasy carried into the Río de la Plata, and then on to Bolivia? Perhaps about as much as an eighteenth-century English agricultural labourer shared with a Chinese peasant. The transatlantic slave trade of course forces us into such aggregations, and by accepting the categories we are able to address the major paradoxes of freedom and coercion, wealth and poverty, and elite political authority and the agency of those without property that so preoccupy modern scholars of Atlantic history. Yet the final lesson from this survey is the vast diversity of the African experience in these tumultuous years.

BIBLIOGRAPHY

Eltis, David, *Rise of African Slavery in the Americas* (Cambridge, 2000).

Falola Toyin, and Matt Childs (eds.), *The Yoruba Diaspora in the Atlantic World* (Bloomington, IN, 2004).

Fynn, J. K., *Asante and its Neighbours, 1700–1807* (London, 1971).

Heywood, Linda, and John Thornton, *Central Africans, Atlantic Creoles, and the Foundation of the Americas, 1585–1660* (Cambridge, 2007).

Kea, Ray A., *Settlements, Trade and Polities in the Seventeenth-Century Gold Coast* (Baltimore, MD, 1982).

Law, Robin, *Ouidah: The Social History of a West African Slaving 'Port', 1727–1892* (Athens, OH, 2004).

—— *The Slave Coast of West Africa, 1550–1750: The Impact of the Atlantic Slave Trade on an African Society* (Oxford, 1991).

Martin, Phyllis C., *The External Trade of the Loango Coast, 1576–1870: The Effects of Changing Commercial Relations on the Vili Kingdom of Loango* (Oxford, 1972).

Northrup, David, *Trade without Rulers: Pre-Colonial Economic Development in South-Eastern Nigeria* (Oxford, 1978).

Nwokeji, G. Ugo, *The Slave Coast and Culture in the Bight of Biafra: An African Society in the Atlantic World* (Cambridge, 2010).

Richardson, David, 'The British Empire and the Atlantic Slave Trade, 1660–1807', in P. J. Marshall (ed.), *The Oxford History of the British Empire*, 5 vols. (Oxford, 1998–9), ii: *The Eighteenth Century*, 440–64.

PART III

INTEGRATION

CHAPTER 17

THE ECOLOGICAL ATLANTIC

J. R. McNEILL

INTRODUCTION

This chapter presents a vision of the Atlantic world in which pigs and plasmodia share the stage with people. In environmental history, nature is not merely the backdrop against which human events play out. It provides unconscious participants in the drama, who, although they left no memoirs, took part in shaping human history. In the Atlantic world in the centuries from 1450 to 1850, tumultuous changes in ecology had outsized impacts on human affairs.

Environmental historians have already laid useful foundations for an ecological history of the Atlantic world.[1] But whereas historians have already tried to synthesize environmental histories of some other sizeable bodies of water, to date no one has attempted this for the Atlantic. The macro-histories of the Atlantic world ignore ecological considerations.[2] One reason historians may have shied away from offering a conspectus of the environmental history of the Atlantic is because it presents vexing problems of selection, theme, and organization.

One could present the story regionally. The ecological experience of the fifteenth to eighteenth centuries suggests four major regions of the eastern Atlantic and another four on the western side. From Scandinavia to Seville, Atlantic Europe participated in

---

[1] e.g. Alfred Crosby, *The Columbian Exchange: Biological and Cultural Consequences of 1492* (Westport, CT, 1972); William Cronon, *Changes in the Land* (New York, 1984); Richard Grove, *Green Imperialism: Colonial Expansion, Tropical Island Edens, and the Origins of Environmentalism, 1600–1860* (Cambridge, 1995).

[2] e.g. Bernard Bailyn, *Atlantic History: Concepts and Contours* (Cambridge, MA, 2005); Paul Butel, *The Atlantic* (London, 1999).

the ecological Atlantic by fishing its northern quarter, by organizing most of its long-distance trade, by systematizing and circulating new information about nature, by contributing its animals, plants, and pathogens to other shores, and by absorbing a few American crops, notably potatoes and maize, into its agriculture and diet.

Just to the south, from the Málaga–Motril coast to the Moroccan river valleys, another region took part in the ecological Atlantic by refining the format of plantation sugar production, which between 1430 and 1550 leapfrogged to Madeira, the Canary Islands, the Cape Verdes, São Tomé, and Brazil. This region has no name, and is rarely conceived as one, but in the commercial plantation it provided one of the foremost forces for ecological change on Atlantic islands and in the zone from Bahia to the Chesapeake.

Atlantic West Africa from Senegambia to the Gulf of Guinea participated in the ecological Atlantic by providing a few cultigens to the Americas, its share of pathogens (notably malaria and yellow fever), and above all by supplying the majority of the workforce—several million slaves and their descendants—who would remake the ecology of the Atlantic. In a world with minimal inanimate energy, the human muscle power of Atlantic Africa must have ranked high among energy sources of the Atlantic world (on which more later). In addition, slaves brought to the Americas the practice of variolation, a shield against smallpox, and knowledge of wet rice-growing techniques. Atlantic West Africa also absorbed American foods, maize and peanuts for example.

Kongo-Angola is a fourth region of the eastern Atlantic. It had a particularly close link with Brazil, and welcomed maize and especially manioc warmly. Maize and manioc proved great improvements, at least in terms of calories and drought resistance, over existing African crops.[3] And manioc, a root crop from Brazil, had the further appeal that it could be left in the ground for a year or two before harvesting, ideal for people expecting to be scattered from time to time by slave raiders.[4] The Cape and South Africa generally I think more properly belong to the Indian Ocean world than to the Atlantic, despite their colonization by the Dutch.

Shifting to the western Atlantic, the northern realms formed a fish province from Greenland to the Grand Banks. Few people lived here year-round, but visiting fishermen caught tons of the fish, chiefly cod, that made an impact on diet in Europe and America as far south as Barbados. The protein acquired reduced the pressure to use land for livestock elsewhere. This was a region where land scarcely mattered; it was a mere appendage to the sea. Its role in the ecological Atlantic was perhaps the simplest of any region's.

To the south of the fish province lay a region from Quebec to Baltimore which played many roles in the ecological Atlantic. Its ecosystems provided timber, furs, and after 1720 or so copious grain. Its traders had a hand in almost every sphere of Atlantic commerce, from slaving to whaling. For people with the portfolio of disease immunities routine in Atlantic Europe and Africa, this was the healthiest part of the Atlantic

---

[3] Maize requires water early on but maturing crops handle drought well.
[4] Jan Vansina, 'Histoire du manioc en Afrique centrale avant 1850', *Paideuma*, 43 (1997), 255–79.

world, and thus (in part) the region where, after the early catastrophes, population grew fastest.

From the Chesapeake to Bahia spread a giant plantation region. Its ecological diversity was such that one might easily divide it into several regions—the Chesapeake, the Low Country, the Caribbean, the Wild Coast, north-eastern Brazil. But the whole region featured a broad unity in its orientation to export agriculture based on slave plantations. São Tomé, Cape Verde, and Madeira, although in the eastern Atlantic, might logically be included in the plantation Atlantic too.

To its south stood what is now southern Brazil and Argentina, a region affected by the disruptive currents of ecological change in the Atlantic, and after 1750 or so making a substantial contribution in the form of hides, tallow, and other animal products. Its broad grasslands served as a new home for great herds of horses, cattle, and sheep, all new to the Americas; prolific colonizers in their own right, and a useful basis for a new way of life for Amerindian peoples dislodged from their former homes and habits.

Another way to think about the ecological Atlantic is in terms, not of regions, but of processes. Consider, for example, the intellectual ferment and cultural change brought by the welter of new observations in natural history. From the European perspective, inquiring minds had to make sense of manatees and moose, creatures unknown to them before 1492 and not mentioned in sacred or ancient texts. In some intellectual spheres such as medicine, the cross-currents of the Atlantic brought challenges to every tradition, whether Galenic, Angolan, or Iroquois. New ailments mystified healers. Some admitted it and probed rival traditions for useful knowledge. A few European doctors in the eighteenth-century West Indies, for example, aware that their remedies against yellow fever proved powerless, turned for help to Africans—whose herbs and salves, as it happened, worked no better. Amerindian concepts of nature and disease must have changed considerably under the impact of repeated epidemics and the arrival of several unfamiliar animal species. Amerindians who saw spiritual qualities in animals must have puzzled over how to understand new creatures, cattle for example, loosed on their shores after 1492. Those Africans for whom food crops figured centrally in religious ritual had adjustments to make when they took up the cultivation of maize and manioc.

Or consider the mobilization of commodities for transoceanic trade, replete with ecological consequences. Leaving aside the plantation crops for the moment, probably the most ecologically consequential commodity trades were those involving silver, timber, grain, beaver fur, and deerhide, all flowing mainly from the Americas to Europe. After the silver boom began, say in 1580, mining's ecological effects ranked among the greatest in the Americas, especially in Mexico and the Andes. Silver miners piled up small mountains of slag, cut forests for pit props and fuelwood for smelting, and poured mercury-tinged wastes into waterways. The beaver fur trade, which by 1800 stretched to the Rockies, nearly eliminated the chief architect of North America's waterscape, changing streamflow, sedimentation, and erosion regimes on most of the waterways north of the Mason–Dixon line. Many other commodity trades were locally important: the green turtle hunting in the West Indies, for example, which brought a large tasty creature to the brink of extinction by 1800, and reshuffled the undersea ecology of Caribbean reefs.[5] Markets for whale oil and whalebone brought Atlantic whales near extinction too by 1850. Maize became a commodity in Atlantic Africa, with remarkable consequences.

In this chapter I will present several angles of vision. I begin with pan-Atlantic processes, such as climate change. Then, I will summarize the important themes which strike me as the most central to the whole subject: the Columbian Exchange, including its often-neglected African components, and the ecology of plantations, slavery, and slave trades. This will provide some sampling of the ecological regions of the Atlantic, as well as of the commodities and cultural processes involved.

PAN-ATLANTIC ENVIRONMENTAL HISTORY

Climate change touched the entire Atlantic world. The Little Ice Age (LIA), lasting roughly 1300 to 1850, reduced average temperatures by about 1°C in the northern hemisphere, and more in northern Europe (where the data are best). Its coldest decades came in 1590–1610, the 1640s, 1690s, and 1780s. Throughout, it brought expansion of glaciers in the north and in high mountains, occasionally scraping villages away and covering upland pastures. The onset of LIA cold may have helped end the Norse settlement of Greenland around 1450 (although this is disputed). The Ebro in Spain froze over now and again. The LIA shortened the growing season, with occasionally disastrous consequences in places such as Sweden, Scotland, and along the St Lawrence, where in the best of circumstances climate made grain farming marginal. In the 1750s, Iceland's harbours disappeared within a ring of ice, fishing and farming became nearly impossible, and a local population crash (15 per cent) followed. On the more cheerful side, wintry scenes of peasants frolicking on ice enriched Dutch landscape painting, and especially dense maple, willow, and spruce from the cold decades of 1660–1720 allowed Stradivarius to make his glorious violins.[6]

At lower latitudes the Little Ice Age was often a big drought age. Central Mexico, for example, was scorched by drought, which may have set off epidemics, in the form of rodent-borne diseases, and sharpened conflicts over irrigation. In Africa, the southern fringe of the Sahara moved southward, reducing densities of both bush and tsetse fly, thereby expanding the belt in which horses could survive. This opened new scope for equestrian slave raiding and state building, severely punishing populations without cavalry. Correlations between drought and expanded slave raiding seem to exist in

---

[5] James J. Parsons, *The Green Turtle and Man* (Gainesville, FL, 1962); J. B. C. Jackson, 'Reefs since Columbus', *Coral Reefs*, 16, suppl. (1997), S23–S32.

[6] Jean Grove, *The Little Ice Age* (London, 1988); Wolfgang Behringer, Hartmut Lehmann, and Christian Pfister (eds.), *Kulturelle Konsequenzen der 'Kleinen Eiszeit'* (Göttingen, 2005). A more popular take is Brian Fagan, *The Little Ice Age* (New York, 2000).

Angola too. On a smaller scale, if the tree rings are to be trusted, Walter Raleigh's effort to colonize the (water-scarce) Outer Banks of North Carolina in 1585–6 coincided with the deepest drought of the past 800 years. Even had all else gone right with the Lost Colony, this alone might well have sealed its fate. Early Jamestown settlers had luck almost as bad, landing in the midst of the driest seven-year spell in the last 770 years, which contributed mightily to their travails.[7]

Even the ocean felt the LIA, shallow estuaries more so than deep water. The average temperature of Chesapeake Bay, for example, fell by as much as 2 to 4 °C in the depths of the LIA, playing havoc with its rich marine life. Reef waters off Puerto Rico in the eighteenth century likewise seem to have been 2–3 °C cooler than today. Codfish migrated southwards during the LIA, attracting fishermen to more welcoming waters off New England and Nova Scotia during the late fifteenth and sixteenth centuries. It is also likely, although uncertain, that hurricanes were fewer and weaker during the LIA, making shipping slightly less hazardous. The LIA was pan-Atlantic, although apparently stronger in the northern hemisphere than in the southern. That, however, may be an impression left by paucity of information.[8]

A second pan-Atlantic feature was tumult. Ecological history, like biological evolution, proceeds at a variable clip, with periods of stately serenity punctuated by hurricanes of creative destruction. In the Atlantic world, while of course things changed in the millennia before 1450, they changed far faster in the few centuries following. That is because, as Alfred Crosby explained, biological provinces long put asunder (by plate tectonics) were suddenly united. Squadrons of invasive species were loosed upon all participating continents. Several native species went extinct. The history of life on earth has few if any parallels.[9]

The cultural processes that historians now describe with the word 'hybridity' had parallels in ecology. This is most obvious in the human realm, where populations of mestizos, métis, and mulattos resulted from sexual encounters among Amerindians,

---

[7] Georgina Endfield, *Climate and Society in Colonial Mexico* (Oxford, 2008); James Webb, *Desert Frontier: Ecological and Economic Change along the Western Sahel, 1600–1850* (Madison, WI, 1995); George Brooks, *Landlords and Strangers: Ecology, Society and Trade in Western Africa, 1000–1630* (Boulder, CO, 1993); Joseph Miller, *The Way of Death* (Madison, WI, 1988); David Stahle et al., 'The Lost Colony and Jamestown Droughts', *Science*, 280 (1998), 564–7.

[8] On sea temperatures, T. M. Cronin et al. (2004), 'Medieval Warm Period, Little Ice Age, and 20th Century Temperature Variability from Chesapeake Bay', USGS webpage: www.geology.er.usgs/gov/eespteam/Atlantic/GPCabs.htm (visited 25 August 2008); T. Watanabe, A. Winter, and T. Oba, 'Seasonal Changes in Sea Surface Temperature and Salinity during the Little Ice Age in the Caribbean Sea Deduced from Mg/Ca and $^{18}O/^{16}O$ Ratios in Corals', *Marine Geology*, 173 (2001), 21–35; Amos Winter, Hiroshi Ishioroshi, Tsuyoshi Watanabe, Tadamichi Oba, and John Christy, 'Caribbean Sea Surface Temperatures: Two-to-Three Degrees Cooler than Present during the Little Ice Age', *Geophysical Research Letters*, 27 (2000), 3365–8; J. M. Grove, 'The Initiation of the "Little Ice Age" in Regions Round the North Atlantic', *Climatic Change*, 48 (2001), 53–82.

[9] Australia after 1788 perhaps comes closest. The trans-Pacific traffic after Magellan, or the circum-Indian Ocean traffic, had smaller biological effects, as did the trans-Saharan crossings. The opening of the Suez Canal in 1869 is another parallel: it instantly united the Indian Ocean and Red Sea aquatic biota with that of the Mediterranean.

Europeans, and Africans. Genetic reshuffling also took place among other species from carp to hawks. Most of this was accidental, but human direction was involved at times, especially with dogs. Thus several 'hybrid' species emerged in the Atlantic world after 1492, and still more hybrid ecosystems. Even without genetic intermixing, wherever species formerly an ocean apart commingled they remade environments, producing a 'creole ecology'. Such recombination, on the genetic and ecosystemic level, happens all the time, but rarely with the fury that characterized the Atlantic after 1492.

THE COLUMBIAN EXCHANGE (AUGMENTED)

In 1972 Alfred Crosby introduced the concept 'The Columbian Exchange'. It gradually colonized the lexicon of historians and became routine shorthand for the massive biotic exchange between the two sides of the Atlantic in the centuries after Columbus. A menagerie of animals, plants, and microbes criss-crossed the Atlantic with Columbus and his successors. Crosby could not do justice to the African roles in the process, which decades of subsequent Africanist historiography have illuminated more clearly.[10]

First the microbes: Amerindians in the fifteenth century did not live especially long or healthy lives, judging by the skeletal evidence. In South America there was Chagas' disease and leishmaniasis, carried by insects. In North America, Rocky Mountain spotted fever and Lyme disease, both tick-borne. Amerindians may have hosted typhoid, syphilis, and almost surely tuberculosis. Those communities that took up maize in preference to other foods grew more numerous and less healthy: maize is excellent at turning sunshine into calories but poor in vitamins, and especially in niacin.

But Amerindians did not have the acute infections sometimes called the 'crowd diseases'. These almost all derive from pathogens of Afro-eurasian herd animals. After millennia of living cheek by jowl with pigs, camels, dogs, ducks, and more, humans came to host a welter of highly infectious and lethal diseases: smallpox, measles, influenza, whooping cough, mumps, among others. They spread from human to human easily. They usually appeared as searing epidemics, but once they had infected all available people, they 'burned out' and disappeared for years, until a new population of susceptibles grew up. Eventually, where populations were large and dense enough, they became childhood diseases, which everyone encountered in the first few years of life, and to which the survivors carried resistance or immunity thereafter. By the fifteenth century all the densely settled parts of Eurasia and probably most of Africa north of the Kalahari hosted most of the crowd diseases most of the time. Thus most adults carried hard-won portfolios of immunities and resistance.

Microbial life in Africa co-evolved with humans and hominid ancestors far longer than anywhere else. Thus Africa presented an especially rich disease environment,

---

[10] What follows draws heavily from Crosby, *The Columbian Exchange*, and less so from his *Ecological Imperialism* (Cambridge, 1986).

including yellow fever, dengue, filiariasis, hookworm, falciparum malaria among many others, all unfamiliar to Amerindians. By contrast, microbial life in the Americas had had only 14,000 years or so to 'figure out' how to exploit the niches presented by human bodies, and far fewer microbial species had done so. Amerindian immune systems remained unprepared for what hit them after 1492.

Despite the difficulties of getting microbes over the sea, all the crowd diseases and aforementioned African infections crossed to the Americas. Fishermen chasing cod probably brought some of the crowd diseases to the Amerindians of north-eastern North America (Vikings may have too). Columbus and those trailing in his wake introduced and re-introduced them to the Caribbean. Once the slave trade geared up, by 1550 or so, African infections added to the calamity. Malaria and, though it may have arrived only in the 1640s, yellow fever accounted for the more thorough depopulation of lowland and low-altitude Atlantic America as opposed to chillier elevations in Mexico and the Andes where indigenous people and culture survived in larger proportion.

The full effect took roughly 150 years to play out. Population declines of 50–90 per cent over six or eight human generations were routine. As Crosby and others recognized, this was not merely a matter of exotic introduced infections. Amerindians suffered from violence, enslavement, loss of land and livelihood, and other misfortunes (or crimes), all of which killed many and weakened the immune response of many more. However, given that smallpox normally kills about 30 per cent of those (non-immunes) it infects, and that yellow fever often claims an even higher toll, the fate of Amerindians exposed to wave after wave of different infections would have been only slightly less calamitous even were they well fed and left in peace.[11]

In the microbial realm, the Columbian Exchange was rather one-sided. It is possible but uncertain that an American variety of syphilis travelled to Europe with Columbus' returning crew. No other pathogens of any consequence made the trip. The diseases of the Americas, comparatively few in any case, often depended on insect, tick, or other vectors that could find no place in African or European ecosystems. It seems, however, that Africans south of the Gulf of Guinea acquired new strains of tuberculosis, pneumonia, and smallpox, because the (sparse) sources indicate epidemics, especially of smallpox, in the seventeenth century.

The exchange in animals was one-sided too. Before 1492, America had few domesticated animals, Africa more, and Eurasia more still. Amerindians raised turkeys, kept dogs, and in the Andes also alpacas and llamas—all in all not much to work with. No human population ever did more with less animal help than Mesoamericans.

In the Columbian Exchange, the Americas acquired horses, sheep, goats, cattle, and pigs—a mixed blessing. An ark load arrived with Columbus' second voyage. They found the Americas to their liking, with few predators, few diseases, and lots of room to roam. As diseases emptied the lands of people, animals rushed in. When De Soto

---

[11] For a recent argument to the contrary, see Paul Kelton, *Epidemics and Enslavement: Biological Catastrophe in the Native Southeast, 1492–1715* (Lincoln, NE, 2007). Kelton sees the English slave trade (of Amerindians) as a necessary precondition for the disease disaster.

landed in Florida in 1539 he brought thirteen pigs with him; the pigs flourished, numbering 700 by De Soto's death in 1542. In Mexico and especially on the Argentine pampas, horses and cattle formed feral herds, sometimes so large they might oblige one to wait a day while an animal parade passed. Pigs and goats ran wild too, and reproduced with an abandon that astonished observers.[12]

It did not take long for people—Amerindians, Africans, Europeans—to take to the new livestock. Horses and cattle provided traction, making ploughs and wheeled vehicles practical for the first time, opening new possibilities in agriculture. All five animals provided hides more easily than had deer. Sheep and goats gave wool, a welcome addition. Animal fat rendered tallow for candles, required for the underground mining of Zacatecas and Potosí. All but the horse became important as food, providing more protein. With domestic herds available, hunting slowly declined in significance, which brought adjustments in gender roles. The new herds brought social conflict between pastoralists and farmers, a long-standing feature of life in Africa and Eurasia previously almost unknown in the Americas. Lastly, horses allowed equestrian society to emerge in suitable environments, such as the pampas, where Amerindians and mestizos created a new way of life broadly analogous to that of the 'Plains Indians' of North America: mobile, militarized, and very male-dominated. Cattle, sheep, and horses opened up new terrain to human occupation. Dry grasslands, or the wet *llanos* of Venezuela, were hard to put to human use without ruminants to convert grass into milk and meat. Thus the immigrant animals changed the nature of human society and its spatial extent in Atlantic America.

Some species found the Americas tough going. Europeans brought camels across the Atlantic several times but they never prospered. By accident, the world's most dangerous animal, the *Anopheles gambiae*, by far the most efficient vector of falciparum malaria, made it across the ocean from time to time, but never found a good foothold—to the great good fortune of all in the Americas.

The African contribution to the animal invasion of the Americas seems modest. Most of the founding fathers and mothers of the new herds came from Iberia and Britain. However, in Brazil it is likely that Angolan goats and cattle contributed strongly to the mix. The zebu cattle breeds, widespread in Brazil, are originally South Asian, but might have come to Brazil via Africa. So might some of the pigs ancestral to the Brazilian porcine population. Perhaps the most consequential of African animal immigrants was the *Aedes aegypti* mosquito, the vector of yellow fever and dengue.[13]

The exchange of plants was a true exchange. The Americas acquired cereals such as wheat, oats, barley, and rye. Citrus fruits, grapes, melons, figs, and dozens of other crops made the crossing. Only a few Eurasian species, generally from South or

---

[12] R. A. Donkin, *The Peccary—with Observations on the Introduction of Pigs to the New World*, American Philosophical Society Transactions 75 (Philadelphia, PA, 1985), 40–5.

[13] The animal exchange: Crosby, *The Columbian Exchange*; Elinor Melville, *A Plague of Sheep* (Cambridge, 1994); Virginia DeJohn Anderson, *Creatures of Empire: How Domestic Animals Transformed Early America* (Oxford, 2005); Donkin, *The Peccary*.

South-East Asia such as citrus and banana, prospered in the Caribbean and Brazil, where African crops did better. On the slave ships from Angola and West Africa came millets, sorghums, yams, bananas,[14] okra, black-eyed peas, sesame, watermelon, and African rice. These suited the warm lowlands from Brazil to South Carolina, and became important foods of the slave populations, and in some cases of others too. Medicinal and religious plants, like kola nut used in Yoruba and Afro-Brazilian ceremonies, also crossed the Atlantic. So did several African grasses.[15]

Unlike the livestock, most crops could not easily find niches on their own. Only a few succeeded as weeds (e.g. clover, peach trees). Spaniards tried wheat, olives, and grapes everywhere, but with modest success until they reached lands with Mediterranean climate in Chile and California. Wine, indispensable to Catholic religious ritual, had to be imported to Spanish America. It took decades, even centuries, of trial and error before the immigrant crops found their most suitable locales in the Americas. As they did, they raised the Americas' food-producing potential. Many of them, such as wheat in North America and Argentina, yielded well in places where indigenous crops had not. But before 1800 these immigrant crops paled in significance next to the immigrant animals—and next to the drug crops of sugar and coffee.

The spread of American crops was another matter. By 1492 the Americas hosted perhaps 100 cultigens, several of which attained world historical importance in modern times. They included a drug crop, tobacco, which, although often regarded as medicinal in Europe and China, in the fullness of time killed more people around the world than new diseases did in the Americas. The food crops Amerindian farmers gave to the world included maize, manioc, potatoes, sweet potatoes, beans, tomatoes, pumpkins, pineapples, squashes, peanuts, and cocoa.

Potatoes, although originally despised in Europe, spearheaded an agricultural, nutritional, and demographic revolution in the cool and humid lands from Ireland to Russia. They produced far more calories per acre than could cereal grains, and enough nutrition so that together with milk they allowed families to survive (in misery), as millions of Irish and Scots did. That of course left them vulnerable to famine should the potato harvest fail, as it did in Ireland after 1845. In lands where inheritance custom divided farms into ever-smaller parcels, Spanish Galicia for example, the caloric yield of potatoes was irresistible. Like manioc in Angola, potatoes appealed to peasants (and lords) who anticipated marauding armies, because they can be left in the ground for weeks, whereas grains must be harvested

---

[14] Bananas, of South-East Asian origin, arrived in south-eastern Africa perhaps 2,000 years ago, and thence came to the Americas.

[15] Torciso de Souza Filgueiras, 'Africanas no Brasil: gramineas introduizadas da Africa', *Cadernas de geociências*, 5 (1990), 57–63; Judith Carney, *Black Rice* (Cambridge, MA, 2001); Carney, 'African Plants in the Columbian Exchange', *Journal of African History*, 42 (2001), 377–96; Judith Carney and Richard Rosomoff, *In the Shadow of Slavery: Africa's Botanical Legacy in the Atlantic World* (Berkeley, CA, 2009); J. J. Parsons, 'The "Africanization" of New World Tropical Grasslands', *Tübingen geographische Studien*, 34 (1970), 141–53. Peter Wood, *Black Majority* (New York, 1974) emphasized the African origins of South Carolina rice. David Eltis et al., 'Agency and Diaspora in Atlantic History: Reassessing the African Contribution to Rice Cultivation in the Americas', *American Historical Review*, 112 (2007), 1329–58.

when ripe and thus made an easy target for quartermasters. Monarchs appreciated potatoes too: both Frederick the Great and Catherine the Great sponsored potato-farming, perhaps thinking that more peasants meant more infantry. For reasons of climate, potatoes had almost no impact on Africa outside of uplands such as the High Atlas or the Drakensberg.[16]

Maize transformed southern Europe. Its yield both per acre and per labourer recommended it highly. Its stalks could serve as trellises for beans, food for livestock, or fuel for fires. It got a quick start in Morocco and Egypt and then southern Europe generally. It flourished anywhere from sea level to mountain valleys, and in the right conditions could zoom from seed to harvest in six to eight weeks, allowing two crops a year. Braudel says maize saved south-western France from the famines that ravaged the rest of the country in the seventeenth and eighteenth centuries.[17]

Maize had a still stronger effect on Atlantic Africa. It appeared in Kongo soon after 1548, and over the next two centuries became a staple from Senegambia to Angola. Maize yielded much more than millets or sorghum. Different varieties fit different local ecologies, especially the rhythms of wet and dry seasons. Maize stored much better than tubers and root crops, making an ideal food for the sustenance of slave ships and caravans. Around Whydah, maize found a place in seasonal crop rotations (after millets and before yams). Farmers turned to it along long-distance trade routes. Its portability helped professional armies from maize regions roam far afield, build states where none existed before, and extend the power of forest kingdoms such as Asante northward towards the West African savannah. Maize became integral to Atlantic African culture, especially for the Yoruba, who invoked it in personal and political ritual.[18]

Africans also took up manioc, peanuts, sweet potato, cocoa, pumpkins, and other American crops. Manioc's indifference to soils, drought, and pests made it suitable to many environments from Nigeria to Angola—almost anything but swamp. It arrived in Kongo around 1600, and became a staple in equatorial regions in short order, and in the kingdoms of Angola before 1750. In West Africa it spread widely along the coast, but hardly at all inland. As noted earlier, like maize it had a special compatibility with slave raiding, but in a different way: it allowed vulnerable populations to flee and survive, whereas maize allowed slavers to operate more efficiently. Manioc came with costs too: Its most pervasive variant, bitter manioc, is spiced with poisonous prussic acid. Making it edible required skilled and laborious work, which fell to women.[19]

Thus Amerindian farmers enriched the rest of the Atlantic world, and indeed the whole world, with the cultigens they had developed over the centuries before 1492. To some (unquantifiable) extent, the early modern population growth of Atlantic Europe

---

[16] John Reader, *Propitious Esculent: The Potato in World History* (New York, 2008) on potato history.

[17] Fernand Braudel, *The Identity of France*, ii: *People and Production* (New York, 1991), 269.

[18] Robert Harms, *The Diligent: A Voyage through the Worlds of the Slave Trade* (New York, 2002), 159; John Iliffe, *Africans: The History of a Continent* (Cambridge, 1995), 138; James McCann, *Maize and Grace: Africa's Encounter with a New World Crop, 1500–2000* (Cambridge, MA, 2005), 19–55; Nicou Ldjou Gayibor, 'Écologie et histoire: les origines de la savane du Bénin', *Cahiers d'études africaines*, 26 (1986), 13–41.

[19] Iliffe, *Africans*, 138.

(indeed all of Europe) may be attributed to potatoes and maize, their higher yields, and their suitability to otherwise low-value soils. Whether population grew or not in Atlantic Africa in the early modern period is unknown, but because of maize, manioc, and peanuts, among others, it was higher than it otherwise would have been.

PLANTATION ECOLOGY

One of the hallmarks of the early modern Atlantic was the slave plantation system. Transferred from the Mediterranean and Morocco, it eventually extended from Bahia to the Chesapeake. In commercial and business terms the plantation system was a genuinely Atlantic enterprise. So it was also in ecological terms, as a sketch of its 'metabolism' shows.

The output of the plantation system consisted chiefly of marketable foods and drugs:[20] sugar first and foremost (both a food and a drug), rice, coffee, tobacco, indigo, and cotton. Sugar cane is a grass from New Guinea; the skills and technologies needed to refine cane juice into sweet crystals were honed in India, Egypt, and the Levant before sugar spread to the western Mediterranean and the Americas. Rice grows wild in many parts of the world, but some of the plantation rice of the Americas came from West Africa. Coffee is a small tree native to Ethiopian forests. Commercial production of its caffeinated beans began in Yemen, but as a plantation crop its career began in the Caribbean, Guiana, and Brazil in the eighteenth century. Tobacco is the only important plantation crop of the Atlantic world native exclusively to the Americas.[21] Indigo is a shrub with leaves that, if fermented properly, provide an ingredient for a deep blue dye. The plant is found throughout the world's midsection, and the species grown on plantations came both from the Americas and the Old World. Cotton too grew naturally around the world at low latitudes, and the skills needed to grow it and weave its fibres into cloth developed in many settings. The cottons raised on plantations were usually American varieties with long, strong fibres. With the right amounts of sunshine, water, soil nutrients, and skilled labour, these plants could be turned into money.

Sugar, coffee, rice, and cotton make heavy demands on soil nutrients. Growing them as monocultures, year in and year out, made near impossible demands on soil nitrogen and phosphorus. Indigo, or more accurately a bacterium that grows amid its roots, fixes nitrogen from the air to the soil, and thus actually restores one of plant life's limiting nutrients. Indigo aside, these plantation crops could not have loomed large in the history of the Americas without two conditions only recently fulfilled: an abundance of livestock and of tall forest.

---

[20] Among the first to emphasize drugs as plantation crops was the Jesuit Andre João Antonil in his aptly titled *Cultura e opulencia do Brasil por suas drogas e minas* (Lisbon, 1711), half of which is devoted to sugar and tobacco.

[21] The genus has representatives elsewhere but these never served as the basis for commercial production.

Livestock provided manure, which replenished soil nitrogen and phosphorus. On the rice fields of Suriname and South Carolina, for example, as in Senegambia and the inland Niger, cattle grazed on stubble after the harvest in what amounted to a rotation of pasturage and rice. All plantations raised livestock. Animals were often encouraged to browse on scrubland or forest, but sometimes pampered with their own dedicated pastures. Their manure served as storehouses of nutrients for distribution to the fields. Without the big introduced domesticated animals, soil nutrient depletion would have limited the scope of plantation agriculture in the Americas severely.[22]

Tall forest too helped make the plantation regime possible. Amerindians had routinely burned vegetation to make room for their gardens and fields, and to open land to sunshine to make grass for herbivores which they liked to hunt. Instead of raising domestic livestock, they managed ecosystems with fire so as to maximize the deer and bison herds for easier hunting. But after 1492 the burning abated. Thus tall forest grew up in places it had not existed for centuries.

By the seventeenth and eighteenth centuries, this looked to Europeans like forest primeval. For those carving out plantations in Atlantic America, this forest seemed an obstacle but was a godsend. For a century or two before felling, tree roots had been pulling nutrients up from deep beneath the surface; depths which neither sugar cane nor cotton roots could ever reach. These nutrients then remained in trees' wood and bark. With each passing year, more and more nitrogen, phosphorus, and potassium were stored in these giant nutrient towers. When felled and burned, much of this stockpile entered the soil among the ashes. Hence sugar, coffee, and cotton planters liked to seed fields that had recently been forest, sometimes sowing while the ashes were still warm. If they did not have plenty of animals for manure, they could raise crops only for a few years before they needed to deforest new land to unlock more stored nutrients. Even with manure, they usually found that their yields declined over time, and their plantations grew less profitable and less competitive against newer ones on the frontiers of deforestation.[23]

Thus the various processes of the Columbian Exchange brought together the cultigens and nutrients that underlay the plantation system. But the system needed water and energy too. Water usually came from the skies, but when and where it was required in specific quantities at specific times, as in rice cultivation, irrigation came into play. The greatest challenge there was labour, moving millions of tons of earth around and keeping it in the right places against the forces of gravity and erosion. Energy too came from the skies, in the form of sunshine to power photosynthesis, but equally indispensable was energy in the form of human muscle power, in other words, labour.

The plantations all made enormous demands in terms of labour; felling trees, digging (and maintaining) irrigation ditches, spreading manure, planting (transplanting in cases), weeding, and harvesting, feeding sugar boilers with cane and firewood,

---

[22] Carney, *Black Rice*, mentions livestock's role in rice cultivation.

[23] Warren Dean, *With Broadax and Firebrand* (Berkeley, CA, 1995) emphasizes the importance of forest soils; Charles Mann, *1491: New Revelations of the Americas before Columbus* (New York, 2005), 243–326 on Amerindian forest burning. Sugar planters also needed wood to fire sugar boilers.

husking rice, suckering tobacco, herding cattle. Sugar and rice plantations made limited use of windmills for energy, and most plantations used animal power. But most work had to be done by human hands, almost always slaves. About 11 million of the slaves were nourished on the foods and nutrients of the regions of their birth from Senegambia to Angola. They and their descendants provided the mechanical energy that made the plantations run. Their food (that is their energy) came from gardens, fields, and fisheries on and around the plantations for the most part, although in the West Indies, especially the smaller islands where land was scarce, refuse cod and menhaden from the North Atlantic supplemented their diet. As the scale of the plantation system grew from around 1550 to 1800 (and beyond), billions and trillions of calories of chemical energy cycled through the slave population, whose bodies transformed it into mechanical energy, in the service of raising commercial crops, whose owners could transform that into money. The whole system rested on a wasteful and unsustainable double exploitation of soils and slaves, but while supplies lasted, it supported the linchpin of the Atlantic economy.

Three significant ecological aspects of the plantation system are not captured in this metabolic approach. First, the plantations required knowledge and skill to put all the plants, nutrients, and water together in just the right ways, to nurture the crops, harvest them, process them, and pack them on their way to market. In most cases those skills were acquired mainly through trial and error on plantations themselves. Tobacco knowledge, however, came substantially from Amerindians, whose ancestors had raised tobacco for fifteen centuries before Jamestown. Rice knowledge in some measure—scholars debate how much—came from West African slaves. Many planters adopted a scientific approach to their business, and sought what knowledge they could find from around the world, adopting Chinese technology for pressing cane juice from sugar cane, or imitating Egyptian and Indian irrigation practices.

Second, procuring slaves had ecological effects. In Africa, slaving extended the domains of maize and manioc, and maize helped extend the domain of slaving. In general, the heightened security risks people faced in an era of pervasive slaving put a premium on mobility. Pastoralism increasingly made more sense than sedentary farming; clearing new land more rarely justified the effort. Perhaps population declined in some regions, allowing resurgent forest to grow up. Probably the transportation of slaves from one zone to another and the flight of peoples from slave raiders brought people into contact with unfamiliar infections with predictable results. One can generate many hypotheses but few firm conclusions about the ecological effects of slaving in Africa. Slaving in the Americas, which took place on a far smaller scale, apparently hastened the spread of smallpox and other diseases among Amerindians.[24]

---

[24] See Paul Kelton, *Epidemics and Enslavement: Biological Catastrophe in the Native Southeast, 1492–1715* (Lincoln, NE, 2007). Kelton argues that the slave trade to South Carolina and Virginia, 1660–1715, which involved a few tens of thousands of captives, was decisive in spreading smallpox. While uncertain, this is suggestive, and might well also apply to *bandeirante* slaving in Brazil.

Third, the Atlantic slave trade brought malaria and yellow fever to the plantation zone. Gradually, these diseases became widely endemic. They had long been hyperendemic in West Africa, so all those who survived childhood there were fully immune to yellow fever and maximally resistant to malaria. Many West Africans were genuinely immune to falciparum malaria by virtue of carrying the sickle-cell trait, a genetic adaptation to the world's most highly malarial environment. Thus West Africans in particular, and Angolans to some degree, suffered less acutely from these two lethal infections than did other populations in the plantation zone. Atlantic Europeans, for example, if born and raised in temperate climes, proved highly susceptible to both yellow fever and malaria. Europeans born in the West Indies (after the 1690s at least), on the other hand, if they survived childhood were also likely to be immune to yellow fever, and resistant, although not as much so as West Africans, to malaria. Amerindians proved as vulnerable as anyone.[25]

These differentials in resistance to malaria and yellow fever helped make African slavery more economic in the plantation zone than any other labour regime. They also made it extremely difficult for Europeans to establish settler colonies in the Caribbean or Guyanas, and scuttled several attempts. A Scottish effort to colonize Darien, in Panama (1697–8), came to grief amid gruesome epidemics, as did a French one at Kourou in Guyana (1763–4). Moreover, military expeditions intended to take territory from Spain routinely fell afoul of yellow fever and malaria, keeping Spanish America Spanish after 1655 despite determined predation.[26]

Europe's Atlantic ecological footprint

Among the world historical consequences of the ecological history of the Atlantic may be the rise of modern Europe—or at least its remarkable failure to settle into Malthusian stagnation. Long ago scholars suggested that money made in the slave trade and on slave plantations helped finance the industrial revolution in Britain. A newer argument puts the matter in ecological terms: Atlantic American ecosystems subsidized the overstrained ones of Atlantic Europe after 1600, allowing escape from stagnation and eventually encouraging a sustained economic growth that made the tiny societies of north-western Europe the most dynamic and soon the most powerful in the world.

In the sixteenth and seventeenth centuries, Atlantic European societies recovered from the population decline begun with the Black Death and once more began to press,

---

[25] See Kenneth Kiple, *The Caribbean Slave: A Biological History* (New York, 1984). Kiple may overstate the resistance of Africans somewhat, and loosely uses the term 'blacks' where he means 'people born and raised in the endemic malaria and yellow fever zones of Africa'. Disease resistance and vulnerability are not correlated with race or skin colour, despite impressions to the contrary among people, black and white, living in the plantation zone, and among some scholars as well.

[26] J. R. McNeill, *Mosquito Empires: Ecology and War in the Greater Caribbean, 1620–1914* (New York, 2010). See also James Webb, *Humanity's Burden: A Global History of Malaria* (New York, 2009).

in Malthusian fashion, upon available resources. Shortages of food and fuel came more frequently and severely (abetted by the Little Ice Age). Forests in particular were shrinking from Scotland to Spain. Peat in places such as the Netherlands helped with fuel, and imports from the Baltic helped with food.[27] But long-term stagnation punctuated by periodic crises loomed because, ultimately, there was not enough land for forests and fields to supply fuel and food. The energy system of Atlantic Europe was approaching its limits.

The enlistment of Atlantic ecosystems averted Malthusian scenarios. The fish, grain, and timber from the Americas, and to a lesser extent the calories in sugar as well, permitted escape from the growth constraints in Atlantic Europe in ways available nowhere else on the planet. In today's vocabulary, Atlantic Europeans expanded their 'ecological footprint'. They exploited, in Eric Jones' words, 'ghost acreage'.[28] In terms of energetics, they expanded their catchment of solar energy and photosynthesis. Thus Atlantic Europe sidestepped the constraints of the pre-industrial organic energy regime until the subterranean forest, coal, helped to shatter them. What began as an energy subsidy from another place, America, led to an energy subsidy from another time, the Carboniferous.[29] If this argument is only partly true, it is the most important feature of Atlantic Europe's involvement with ecosystems on other Atlantic shores.

CONCLUSION

The centuries from 1450 to 1850 in the Atlantic world witnessed one of history's greatest ecological tempests. Climatic turbulence forced adjustments in ecosystems and brought calamities to societies. A surge of biological globalization recast Atlantic ecosystems. The migration of people, pathogens (and mosquitoes) fundamentally reshuffled the demography of the Atlantic world, especially on its oceanic islands and in America. The exchanges of animals and plants revised agro-ecosystems, improving nutrition here and there, but also bringing new sources of social conflict. Perhaps the most sudden and thorough ecological revolutions took place in the plantation zone of the Americas, where African and Eurasian people, plants, livestock, and diseases combined with American soil and sunshine to create the most distinctive and characteristic ecosystems and social institutions of the Atlantic world, and one of the most unhappy and unsustainable regimes in world history. At the same time, American resources,

[27] For the Dutch fuel situation, Jaap Buis, 'Historia forestis: Nederlandse Bosgeschiedenis', *AAG Bijdragen*, 26 (1985), 1–472 and 27 (1985), 473–1058; M. A. W. Gerding, *Vier Euew Turfwinning: De Ververeningen in Groningen, Friesland, Drenthe, en Overijssel tussen 1550 en 1950* (Wageningen, 1995).

[28] E. L. Jones, *The European Miracle* (Cambridge, 1981).

[29] See Rolf-Peter Sieferle, *The Subterranean Forest* (Cambridge, 2001); Kenneth Pomeranz, *The Great Divergence* (Princeton, NJ, 2000).

mobilized by European entrepreneurship and often by African labour, probably helped Atlantic Europe bend and then break the constraints of the ecological Old Regime.

BIBLIOGRAPHY

A number of sixteenth- to eighteenth-century books contain accounts of natural history that help scholars grasp the ecological history of the Atlantic: José de Acosta, *Historia natural y moral de las Indias* (Seville, 1590); Richard Ligon, *A True and Exact History of the Island of Barbadoes* (London, 1657); J.-B. Du Tertre, *Histoire générale des isles de Christophe, de la Guadeloupe, de la Martinique, et autres dans l'Amérique* (Paris, 1667–71); Ambrósio Fernandes Brandão, *Diálogos das grandezas do Brasil* (Lisbon, 1618). Scholars also use textual archives, bio-archives (pollen analysis for example), and geo-archives (e.g. soil profiles).

Important recent scholarly works include:

Álvarez Peláez, Pedro, *La conquista de la naturaleza Americana* (Madrid, 1993).

Brailosky, Elio, *Historia ecológica de Iberoamérica: de los Mayas al Quijote* (Buenos Aires, 2006).

Cronon, William, *Changes in the Land* (New York, 1984).

Crosby, Alfred, *The Columbian Exchange* (Westport, CT, 1972).

—— *Ecological Imperialism* (Cambridge, 1986).

Curtin, Philip, Grace Brush, and George Fisher (eds.), *Discovering the Chesapeake: The History of an Ecosystem* (Baltimore, MD, 2001).

Dean, Warren, *With Broadax and Firebrand: The Destruction of the Brazilian Atlantic Forest* (Berkeley, CA, 1995).

Grove, Richard, *Green Imperialism: Colonial Expansion, Tropical Island Edens and the Origins of Environmentalism, 1600–1860* (Cambridge, 1995).

Kiple, Kenneth, *The Caribbean Slave: A Biological History* (Cambridge, 1984).

McNeill, J. R., *Mosquito Empires: Ecology and War in the Greater Caribbean, 1620–1914* (New York, 2010).

Melville, Elinor G. K., *A Plague of Sheep: Environmental Consequences of the Conquest of Mexico* (Cambridge, 1994).

Miller, Shawn, *An Environmental History of Latin America* (Cambridge, 2007).

Watts, David, *The West Indies: Patterns of Development, Culture, and Environmental Change since 1492* (Cambridge, 1987).

CHAPTER 18

··

MOVEMENTS OF PEOPLE
IN THE ATLANTIC WORLD,
1450–1850

··

WILLIAM O'REILLY

THE movement of people in the Atlantic world in the period 1450–1850 is a story of categorization, organization, and exploitation of labour in a time of global transformation. The precipitous peopling of the Americas might also be considered a process of impopulation, the uprooting and seeding of populations in new environments. Over 25 million people were transported from east to west, to be planted in South, Central and North America, the Caribbean, the Atlantic islands, and the West African littoral. The fruits of this seed labour came irrevocably to transform the demographic composition of the Americas and Africa, and to a lesser extent Europe. Almost half of those who crossed the Atlantic were forcibly transported; coerced to move either by enslavement, violence, economic dislocation, social and religious persecution, or unstable political conditions. Some migrants were slaves, or unfree white colonists, notably convicts and prisoners, or indentured servants whose liberties were severely limited. Others still emigrated by choice, often intending a short period of time abroad but frequently remaining for the duration of their lives. Many migrants had previous experience with semi-free labour in Europe, and crossing the Atlantic was one, albeit significant, journey in a quest for employment and opportunity. This massive transplantation of Africans and Europeans to new locations resulted in the grafting of old and new ideologies of master–servant relationship thus creating politically, socially, and racially hybrid communities in Atlantic contexts. The impopulation of America took place at the expense not just of Africa and parts of Europe, but (see Whitehead's chapter in this volume) also of the resident populations of the Americas, since many of those who endured European violence and disease were enslaved or forcibly relocated. The movement of people in the Atlantic world is thus overwhelmingly a history of the sourcing, transportation, plantation, and exploitation of labour. Improving technologies—particularly of transportation—a European appetite for precious metals and plantation commodities, an African desire for textiles and metals, and the need of a labour force to enable these requirements, impelled a repositioning of Atlantic populations.

Migration was, and is, a natural constant of the human condition.[1] The dynamics of Atlantic world migration of the period 1450–1850 made it different from anything previously experienced. Force, magnitude, distance, and outcome distinguished this from all previous human migrations, whether the westward passage into Europe of Celts, Romans, Goths, Huns, and others, or the migrations associated with the spread of Christianity and Islam, or the rise of the European city. Responding to constant flux within Europe, lords and leaders had long striven to inhibit and even prohibit the emigration of subjects and the immigration of strangers. Frontiers were created, legal and moral determinations on what constituted a native and a stranger were reached, and the often-peaceful *convivencia* of different religious, ethnic, and native-born groups in most places came to an end. In this context regional violence was silenced or redeployed to the service of centralizing states, leading to the emergence of coherent monarchies, principally along the Western European seaboard, many of which became associated with the colonization of overseas acquisitions. Colonization, in turn, created the need to facilitate migration overseas, in the interest of furthering a new European economic system, in which trade dominated.[2] This episode in human history was novel principally because mercantilist European states involved in the transportation of African slaves participated in a process of forced migration on a greater scale than previously witnessed.[3] Migration in the Atlantic world can be seen in terms of a number of opposing possibilities: internal or domestic as opposed to external migration; forced versus free transportation; individual versus familial movement; settler versus labour migration; temporary versus permanent migration; illegal versus legal migration; and planned versus unplanned movement.[4]

A variety of factors encouraged and enabled the movement of people in Europe from the late fifteenth century forward. A growing population in parts of Europe produced intermittent food shortages and price increases, while efforts to enclose common land and to place restrictions on the poor rendered emigration an attractive option. So also did religious and political developments which produced particularized ethnic, linguistic, and religious regions which some found constrictive. The growth of towns and cities provides evidence of internal migration, as cities offered opportunity and liberties. The European migratory trend was typically from the country to towns, from towns to riverside or port cities, and from cities into the wider world. Commerce dictated the terms and conditions of movement, balancing human resources with

---

[1] Bernard Bailyn, *The Peopling of British North America: An Introduction* (New York, 1988), 36.

[2] Immanuel Wallerstein, *The Modern World System: Capitalist Agriculture and the Origins of the European World-Economy in the Sixteenth Century* (New York, 1974), 15.

[3] Joseph Inkori and Stanley L. Engerman (eds.), *The Atlantic Slave Trade: Effects on Economics, Societies and Peoples in Africa, the Americas, and Europe* (Durham, NC, 1992).

[4] Robin Cohen (ed.), *The Cambridge Survey of World Migration* (Cambridge, 1995), 5–6.

commercial and colonial interests. From Western Europe, emigration in the period 1450–1850 was predominantly westward, with occasional and region-specific sorties to Central and Eastern Europe and to Asia. In Africa (see Northrup's chapter in this volume) intra-continental migration also loosely followed labour needs. A trans-Sahara slave trade brought sub-Saharan Africans to Muslim North Africa and beyond, while southern African peoples were pushed to the interior by European settlement in the south. More broadly, attitudes to migrants generally changed at this time. Borders were defined, and in Europe the bureaucracies associated with the placing of restrictions on human movement now incentivized 'desirable' in- and out-migrations. By the mid-seventeenth century, many European states discouraged emigration and encouraged immigration, recognizing, with William Petty, that a strong domestic population furthered economic success.[5] Charles Davenant pronounced in 1699: 'It is not extent of territory that makes a country powerful, but numbers of men well employed.' Others saw advantage in having some employed in overseas colonies.[6]

Over half the migrants who crossed the Atlantic before 1850 went involuntarily, the overwhelming majority enslaved Africans, and the remainder European convicts and prisoners. Many others were indentured servants, or were otherwise contracted under terms of labour debt, which meant that only 10 per cent of migrants enjoyed total independence.[7] Three factors contributed to the transformation of migratory patterns in the Atlantic world, particularly from the mid-seventeenth century: the dramatic reduction in the Amerindian population; the introduction on the Caribbean sugar islands of gang-labour practices; and the frequency and cheapness of travel which enabled people, produce, and print to cross the Atlantic with unprecedented efficiency and proclivity,[8] were the factors that helped to create a 'hemispheric' Atlantic community in which contact between peoples around the Atlantic reshaped values and redefined the global labour market.[9] The earliest European migration to the Americas, composed of soldiers, artisans, professionals, and clergy, was indisputably free, and represented, both militarily and ideologically, the front line of colonial and imperial ambition.[10] Where possible, Amerindian slaves were used as labour by the first European colonists, but, by the end of the sixteenth century, disease had

[5] *The Economic Writings of Sir William Petty*, ed. Charles Henry Hull, 2 vols. (Cambridge, 1899), i. 22.

[6] *The Political and Commercial Works of . . . Charles D'Avenant*, ed. Charles Whitworth (London, 1771), ii. 192.

[7] Matthew Frye Jacobson, *Whiteness of a Different Color: European Immigrants and the Alchemy of Race* (Cambridge, MA, 1998); Winthrop D. Jordan, *White over Black: American Attitudes Toward the Negro, 1550–1812* (Chapel Hill, NC, 1968).

[8] David Eltis, 'Identity and Migration: The Atlantic in Comparative Perspective', in Wim Klooster and Alfred Padula, *The Atlantic World: Essays on Slavery, Migration, and Imagination* (Upper Saddle River, NJ, 2005), 108–25, here 115.

[9] Ira Berlin, *Many Thousands Gone: The First Two Centuries of Slavery in North America* (Cambridge, MA, 1998), 29–63; Eltis, 'Identity and Migration', 110.

[10] Ida Altman and James Horn (eds.), *'To Make America': European Emigration in the Early Modern Period* (Berkeley, CA, 1991), 39–47.

dramatically reduced indigenous numbers.[11] Older European solutions to the problem of work shortage, such as hiring labourers, or engaging prisoners or criminals, were attempted but proved expensive and unsatisfactory. Failure on these fronts necessitated the escalation of African slave importation into the Americas. The Atlantic economy would never have flourished, certainly not in the era of sail, without coerced migration.

SOURCING OF MIGRANTS

Writing in 1709, Daniel Defoe expressed a commonly held belief that 'people are indeed the essential of commerce, and the more people the more trade; the more trade, the more money, the more money, the more strength; and the more strength, the greater the nation'.[12] Increasingly, emigration to the settler colonies was also identified as a solution to social problems at home and a means of expanding domestic interests. In practice, the first century of migration from Europe was largely voluntary, composed of notables, professionals, military, and clergy, and was predominately male and short-term in intent. Guidelines were quickly established, permitting some to emigrate and prohibiting others, like Jews and Moriscos from the kingdom of Spain, and Roman Catholics from England and Ireland. Transportation to and from colonies was confined to particular ports, such as Seville in Spain, and initially Plymouth, Bristol, and London in England. Later, European states recognized new Atlantic colonies as sites for economic advancement, for the alleviation of domestic problems, like the poor, the destitute, and minorities, and for the establishment of new markets. By encouraging emigration, remarked Francis Bacon in 1606, England would gain 'a double community, in the avoidance of people here, and in making use of them there'.[13]

Once established, the principle of encouraging migrants was liberally extended. Scots, Irish, Levellers, convicts, indigents, orphans, and child migrants would all be shipped from England to the colonies. A royal proclamation of 1617 advocated the transportation of London's poor and destitute; Sir Edwyn Sandys asked for a warrant to have 100 children sent to Virginia from London, the first in a long line of child shipments which would persist for centuries. Sandys argued that residents 'of whom the Citie is especially desirous to be disburdened' might best be sent to Virginia, where they would be gainfully employed. In English, but curiously not in Spanish, Portuguese, Dutch, or French debates, it was claimed that emigration would relieve poor rates and overpopulation and that idlers, vagrants, and criminals would be put to good use in the colonies. Migrants were raised 'by beat of drum' with print, ballads, and encouragers promising limitless opportunity in new lands where every knave might be a master.

---

[11] Noble David Cook, *Born to Die: Disease and New World Conquest, 1492–1650* (Cambridge, 1998).
[12] Daniel Defoe, *A Review of the State of the British Nation*, 2 July 1709.
[13] Eric Williams, *Capitalism and Slavery* (London, 1964), 10.

Maps and pamphlets were published, seamen's reports distributed, true and false travelogues circulated, written correspondence read aloud and passed between friends, and sermons preached encouraging Christian settlement. All communication methods were employed to spread news of opportunity abroad. Newly established trading companies were also licensed to source, recruit, cajole, or even pressgang migrants into venturing abroad.

Religion and language, as well as flora and fauna, travelled with these first colonists; one accident of Spanish and general European colonialism was the environmental and ecological transformation of the Americas. Unlike their English counterparts, Spanish *conquistadores* had few inhibitions about having sexual relations with indigenous women, possibly because the right of Spanish women to emigrate was restricted. Consequently, Spanish emigrants, certainly in the first generations of colonization, became more localized or 'creolized' than English colonists.[14] The number of emigrants from Portugal was large relative to the population of the kingdom and far exceeded comparable figures for England.[15] Emigration from Portugal was never strongly directed by the state, except in the case of the occasional use of Angola, and other sites, as penal colonies. The scale was so great that emigration was seen not as beneficial, but as a threat to domestic well-being. Essentially it was lack of opportunity at home that drove so many Portuguese to migrate, and the Portuguese state and economy derived relatively little profit from its Atlantic and global empire. Administrative reform, new attitudes to emigration, and a change in heart towards the colonies came too late to benefit Portugal. In France, schemes for colonization were, initially, more ambitious than those of the English colonial companies, and frequently included the offer of free passage and grants of land to would-be colonists in the Americas. As in England, the pressganging of criminals and orphan girls also took place, but France failed to raise sufficient colonists to consolidate its holdings in the Americas, and the European population of French Canada was only 55,000 in 1750.

By the eighteenth century, a *rabies Carolina* swept through parts of Europe spreading the fever of emigration. Between 1683 and the end of the eighteenth century, over 100,000 German-speaking migrants were shipped from Dutch ports to Pennsylvania, New York, New England, the Carolinas, and Georgia, leading to the accusation that European states were offloading a 'swarm' of destitute continental migrants who, according to Benjamin Franklin, threatened to turn Pennsylvania into a 'colony of aliens'.[16] Nationals of other European states—Danes, Swedes, Finns, Swiss, Bohemians, amongst others—travelled to smaller settlements or to those of friendly states.[17]

---

[14] Altman and Horn (eds.), 'To Make America'.

[15] Vitorino Magalhães Godinho, 'Portuguese Immigration from the Fifteenth to the Twentieth Century: Constants and Changes', in Emmer and Mörner (eds.), *European Expansion*, 13–48, esp. 28–30.

[16] Benjamin Franklin, *Observations Concerning the Increase of Mankind* (Philadelphia, PA, 1751).

[17] James H. Cassedy, *Demography in Early America: Beginnings of the Statistical Mind, 1600–1800* (Cambridge, MA, 1969).

Migrants commonly travelled with relatives, retaining kinship connections and communitarian practices in the New World. The free movement of Europeans was an extension of, rather than a deviation from, customary social and familial obligations. Social conventions within Europe sometimes propelled migrants to leave home, and migration secured career mobility for young men of the middling and higher orders such as *hidalgos* in Spain, and younger sons in Britain and France, for whom inheritance possibilities were limited. Emigration into the Atlantic world thus became a career choice for many Europeans, especially in the eighteenth century.[18] Freedom to move depended on a number of factors, including age, marital status, social rank, occupation, and gender. Unmarried men made up the bulk of all European migrants in the pre-eighteenth-century period. Few women, other than servants, moved unaccompanied to the Atlantic colonies before the nineteenth century, which is unsurprising given that women had traditionally left home only to marry or to take up employment in prearranged locations. Families who moved as units responded to different variables. They usually expected to establish a new household in an environment hospitable to a particular religion, or to migrants with particular skills, but families sometimes transplanted themselves because of desperate circumstances at home.

Some new communities assumed a superficial resemblance to those left behind, in political, social, and economic organization, in size and design, and in administration. Emigrants to settlements with residents of different ethnic, religious, social, and linguistic background reached unspoken understandings concerning what cultural and social interactions and diversity would be tolerated by the dominant group, which, in turn, influenced levels of endogamy and exogamy.[19] 'Temporary' and 'permanent' were always relative terms in the story of migration, and while rates of return to Europe varied across time and location, emigration from Europe was never as absolute as from Africa. Before the transportation of some 1,200 African American 'Nova Scotians' to Sierra Leone in 1792 and the later establishment of Liberia, return migration to Africa was paltry. Return to Europe in the pre-steamship era was higher than previously thought. Many migrants who intended to re-establish themselves in elevated positions at home once they had made good in America were disappointed, but others who planned to remain in the Americas returned to Europe for positive, or negative, reasons. Return was important not least because positive news of America was more plausible when circulated by return migrants. Not all enjoyed the possibility of returning, but the successful who did so played a crucial role in stimulating the subsequent departure of relatives and acquaintances, and perhaps more effectively so than any state or regional authority could have done.

---

[18] Ida Altman, 'Spanish Migration to the Americas', in Cohen (ed.), *World Migration*, 28–32, here: 30.

[19] Ibid. 31.

FIRST NATIONS, AFRICANS, AND EUROPEANS
AND THE PEOPLING OF THE ATLANTIC WORLD

America in the pre-Columbian period, like all other continents, was populated by hundreds of peoples distinct in language, ethnicity, social and cultural practice, religious belief, and methods and means of community maintenance. The vast differences in climate, landscape, and natural resources from Tierra del Fuego to the northern ice-cap contributed to the emergence of widely divergent societies as surviving native American populations interacted with European colonists and African slaves.

Without doubt, the movement of enslaved Africans (see Eltis's chapter in this volume) was the largest movement of people across the Atlantic until the middle of the nineteenth century, as enslaved Africans became a central dynamic of the resettlement of the Americas after the disastrous decline in the Native American population. Between 1500 and 1860, about 12 million people were transported from the shores of Africa to America and the Caribbean, and to a much lesser extent to the Atlantic islands and Europe. Slaves were taken on the earliest Spanish and Portuguese expeditions and were used to cultivate sugar in Brazil in the 1540s as well as to assist in the farming of land seized from the peoples of central Mexico.[20] Fewer than one in twenty Africans transported across the Atlantic disembarked in North America; almost half were shipped to Brazil and a near-comparable number were transported to the Caribbean islands. Enslaved Africans were present almost everywhere that European settlement was established, working on farms and plantations and as domestic servants.

The organization of the slave trade changed over time, but can be broadly divided into three periods (1450–1650, 1650–1807/8, and 1807/8–67). The formative period was dominated by the Portuguese; the second, which witnessed the greatest exploitation of African labour, sequentially by Dutch, French, and British traders; and the third phase saw slaves transported within the Caribbean and the United States, with ongoing transportation from Africa to Cuba, Puerto Rico, and Brazil. National and commercial-venture companies were contracted to supply slaves. The majority of slaves were men, but far more African than European females migrated, with the result that those plantation societies which employed most slaves were largely African in demographic composition. In some places, the settlement of Europeans and Africans overlapped, but even here African women, because of their numbers, exerted most impact on demographic growth. While Africans may, in particular locations, have been most influential in demographic terms, it was Europeans who determined the form and composition of settlements in the Americas and controlled the transatlantic slave trade.

---

[20] Paul E. Lovejoy, *Transformations in Slavery: A History of Slavery in Africa* (Cambridge, 2000), 19; Eltis in this volume.

SPAIN

....

Basque and Galician fishermen had sailed the North Atlantic for centuries before Columbus, but the *reconquista* and expansionist ambition gave impetus to Spanish overseas interest. Spanish migration to the Indies began with Columbus in 1493, but in the 1520s the movement of people gained in size and momentum. Following the conquest of Mexico (New Spain) in 1521 and Peru in 1532, fresh colonial destinations emerged, including New Granada (Colombia), Guatemala, Chile, Santo Domingo (the first Spanish city established in the Indies), and Havana. Spanish migration was almost exclusively from Castile and was tightly regulated from the outset. The Casa de Contratación (House of Trade) in Seville, established in 1503, acted as the checkpoint for the traffic of both people and commerce, and Seville retained its privileged position until displaced by Cádiz. In theory, legislation deterred undesirables, such as gypsies, Moriscos, and *converses*, from emigrating. Destinations perceived as remote and dangerous experienced difficulty in attracting settlers, and *Entradas* (expeditions) were sometimes required to induce colonists from places already settled, for example from Peru to settle Chile. Taken together, Mexico and Peru received the greatest number of primary and secondary migrants in the sixteenth century. The high ratio of persons of African descent to white colonists on Cuba, in particular, exemplified what would become the racial characteristic of plantation society in all European settlements in the Caribbean and Brazil.

Until the eighteenth century Spanish migration was primarily from Castile, especially from Andalusia, Seville, and its hinterland, but some migration from the kingdom of Aragon proceeded thereafter. Another change was the increase in the number of women and families among the migrants. Women constituted about 5 per cent of emigrants in the period to 1519, but 25–35 per cent during the last third of the sixteenth century.[21] Estimates of the total size of the migration remain speculative: the figure of 450,000 is offered for the period 1500–1650 and was dominated by members of the middle ranks of Castilian society.[22] For the eighteenth century, best estimates posit 53,000 Spanish emigrants to America, with the balance more heavily male than previously. This emerges from the 1790 census for New Spain, where but 279 of the 5,779 *peninsulares* recorded were women.[23] Extra-legal and non-Spanish migrants to the Americas were not included in such data; Portuguese (particularly from Algarve), Italians, Irish, and other nationalities may have accounted for 3 per cent of all European-born residents of the viceroyalty of New Spain between 1700 and 1760. In general,

---

[21] Peter Boyd-Bowman, *Patterns of Spanish Emigration to the New World (1492–1580)* (Buffalo, NY, 1973), 25, 49, 72.

[22] Magnus Mörner, 'Migraciones a Hispanoamérica durante la época colonial', *Suplemento de anuario de estudios americanos*, 43/2 (1991), 3–25.

[23] Nicolas Sanchez-Albornoz, 'The Population of Colonial Spanish America', in *The Cambridge History of Latin America* (Cambridge, 1984), 3–35, here: 31.

emigration from sixteenth-century Spain reflected the political and social dominance of Old and New Castile, and the existence of roads from Andalusia and Extremadura leading to urban centres and ports of departure for the Americas. The source of emigrants was broader in the eighteenth century, when the importance of Spain's maritime provinces (including the Canary Islands), demographic dynamics (as in Galicia), and commercial expansion (in Catalonia) coalesced to draw migrants from across Spain.[24]

Emigrants to the Atlantic colonies included people of different levels of wealth, and not just *hidalgos*; over time those who wished to emigrate and could not, or did not, obtain a licence, or could not pay their way, travelled as servants or employees.[25] These *criados* were similar to indentured servants from Britain, and elsewhere. Except for African slaves and Moriscos, all migrants from Spain into the Atlantic world were free.

PORTUGAL

The sea connected Portuguese communities around the world as did river systems and roads for other nationalities. The Portuguese (see Russell-Wood's chapter in this volume) already had an empire in Africa and Asia before an empire based on trade in slaves, gold, and sugar emerged in the Atlantic.[26] *Reconquista* policies brought Portuguese *fidalgos* (knights) across the straits to North Africa, first garrisoning the Moroccan port of Ceuta in 1415, and, encouraged by clerical, noble, and royal support, piracy and slave raiding became the foundation of a Portuguese Atlantic empire. Portuguese sailors first settled Madeira and the Canary Islands, and later Cape Verde and São Tomé, cultivating sugar, wheat, and vines. Prince Henry (the Navigator) established a monopoly over trade with Guinea, and crown monopolies marked Portuguese activity in the sixteenth-century Atlantic. Trading factories (*feitorias*) and forts (*fortalezas*) came to symbolize the formal empire along the West African coast and in the East. The commercial empire in Africa was run by a creole community, born and raised in Africa, after the manner of Portuguese activity in Asia, at least in the first century of contact.[27]

By the late fourteenth century migration was already part of the pattern of Portuguese life, with privileged and poor moving from rural to urban areas, when the opportunity

---

[24] Magnus Mörner, 'Spanish Historians on Spanish Migration to America during the Colonial Period', *Latin American Research Review*, 30/2 (1995), 251–27, here: 261–2.

[25] Ida Altman, *Emigrants and Society: Extramadura and Spanish America in the Sixteenth Century* (Berkeley, CA., 1989), 196–7.

[26] Malyn Newitt (ed.), *The First Portuguese Colonial Empire*, Exeter Studies in History 11 (Exeter, 1986), 1–2.

[27] Ibid. 4–6.

presented.[28] Estimates of emigration from Portugal in the period 1415–1760 range between 1 million and 1.5 million persons, with totals of 50,000 in the fifteenth century; 280,000 in 1500–80; 360,000 between 1580 and 1640; 150,000 in 1640–1700; and 600,000 emigrants in the period 1700–60.[29] This scale of emigration seriously disrupted the fabric of rural life, and labour shortages, sexual imbalance, and demographic collapse were frequent, if not regular, occurrences.[30] Portuguese emigration to sites in the Atlantic world and beyond was not from the mother country alone, but involved the Portuguese Atlantic islands and those areas in Africa, South America, and Asia over which Portugal claimed jurisdiction. Cape Verdeans moved to Portuguese Africa, and Portuguese Brazilians settled areas of Mozambique and the Gulf of Guinea, where they encountered men and women of Portuguese descent who had moved from west-coastal India. In Brazil, particularly, a significant internal migration of persons of Portuguese and African descent took place. Major trends in Portuguese settlement in the Atlantic included a move from Portugal to Madeira and to a lesser extent to the Azores in the period 1450–1500; increased emigration to the Azores and a decline in movement to Madeira, 1500–50; steady emigration to Brazil but much greater numbers of emigrants to India and Ceylon and beyond, 1530–1600; and a significant increase in the number of emigrants from the Azores and Madeira to Brazil 1560–1700.

Push and pull factors alone do not explain the high level of emigration from Portugal and the Portuguese Atlantic islands into the wider Atlantic world.[31] News of opportunity abroad reached all levels of Portuguese society. With such prevalent emigration it is curious that neither the word 'emigrant' (*emigração, emigrante*) nor 'emigrant agent' (*engajador, aliciador*) features in Joseph Marques' Portuguese dictionary of 1764, while the words 'colony' and 'colonist' do.[32] Movement abroad was experienced, or was represented, as a state activity. Chain migration was especially prevalent in the Portuguese case, with strong parochial, district, and regional ties surviving the Atlantic crossing and supporting new community formation. The majority of Portuguese emigrants originated in the north of the country and were disproportionately unmarried men, although couples emigrated in significant numbers to the Azores and Madeira. The shortage of white women was a recurrent complaint of Portuguese administrators in the seventeenth- and eighteenth-century colonies. When asked whether she was a spinster or married, one Portuguese woman in the early eighteenth-century comedy *Guerras do Alecrim e Mangerona* answered: 'I have a

---

[28] Malyn Newitt, *A History of Portuguese Overseas Expansion, 1400–1668* (London, 2005), 9.

[29] A. J. R. Russell-Wood, 'Patterns of Settlement in the Portuguese Empire, 1400–1800', in Francisco Bethencourt and Diogo Ramada Curto (eds.), *Portuguese Oceanic Expansion, 1400–1800* (Cambridge, 2007), 161–96, here: 168.

[30] Ibid. 163.

[31] David Higgs, 'Portuguese Migration before 1800', in David Higgs, *Portuguese Migration in Global Perspective* (Toronto, 1990), 7–28, here: 23.

[32] Joseph Marques, *Novo diccionario das linguas portugueza . . .* (Lisbon, 1764), ii. 170, cited in Higgs, 'Portuguese Migration', 7–8.

husband who has been in Brazil for forty-seven years.'[33] In the seventeenth century, Brazil rather than India became the destination of choice, and while Africa, especially Mozambique, continued to attract emigrants the numbers remained small.[34]

Portuguese traders continued to be heavily involved in the trafficking of Africans. Between 2.5 and 4 million slaves were settled in the Portuguese empire before 1800. From 1511, when 200 Africans fought with Albuquerque, Portuguese traders pioneered a global, and globalizing, African slave labour market, moving Africans not only to the Americas, but also to the East Indies, Japan, and Ceylon, where they were forced to serve as slaves, soldiers, sailors, servants, traders, and, not least, mistresses and wives for Portuguese men.[35] Africans were transported not just from east to west, but by 1500 as many as 100,000 Africans had been relocated to Portugal proper, as well as to Cape Verde, São Tomé, and Príncipe. The European and slave populations of Brazil increased fiftyfold between 1540 and 1620.[36] From an initial European community in 1540 of fewer than 2,000, the population rose significantly to 25,000 in 1580 and 30,000 in 1600. The total of African slaves numbered half that of European settlers. By 1620, the population had reached a racial equilibrium with perhaps as many as 50,000 African and Indian slaves and a similar number of Portuguese settlers. Sugar production in Portuguese Brazil escalated the demand for African slaves. Until 1530 African slaves had been recruited, almost exclusively, for the Portuguese Atlantic islands, but thereafter Portuguese traders, many of them New Christians, supplied slaves for the Spanish Atlantic colonies, too. The opening of the New World silver mines increased demand for slaves, and together with the Angolan wars both fed a growing Portuguese demand for slaves; 40,000 were transported to Brazil in the period 1575–1600, and five times that number were conveyed into the Atlantic during the first quarter of the seventeenth century, half the total to Brazil.[37] In time, Brazil would become home to the second-largest population of persons of African descent in the world, which tells as much about Portuguese-induced migration as it does about the creation of an Atlantic labour system.

BRITAIN AND IRELAND

English, Irish, Scottish, and Welsh navigation and migration in the North Atlantic pre-dates the period of transatlantic exploration by centuries. While relatively few English, besides fishermen, had contact with the Americas before the close of the sixteenth

---

[33] Higgs, 'Portuguese Migration', 18.

[34] A. J. R. Russell-Wood, 'Ritmos e destinos de emigração', in Francisco Bethencourt and Kirti Chaudhuri (eds.), História da expansão portuguesa, ii: Do Índico ao Atlântico (1570–1697) (Navarra, 1998), 114–25.

[35] Newitt, A History of Portuguese Overseas Expansion, 262–3.

[36] Ibid. 181.

[37] Hugh Thomas, The Slave Trade (London, 1997), 144–5.

century, English adventurers and investors were deeply involved in Ireland, where plantations were seeded and colonists, principally from England, were tasked with making Ireland British.[38] Methods of colonization and of engaging with natives were tried and tested in Ireland and later applied to mainland North American and the Caribbean colonies. And some inhabitants, of Ireland and later Scotland, would become colonists and agents of empire in the western Atlantic under the aegis of both the British and Spanish monarchies.

The first attempts at English settlement in North America, at Roanoke (1584/1587), Jamestown (1607), and Plymouth (1620), met with limited success. Commercial entrepreneurs and religious separatists sought to establish factories or refuges in America, but inauspicious environmental conditions and hostility with natives frustrated progress. Many of these first migrants had spent time away from England at sea, or as soldiers or religious refugees on continental Europe. Subsequent migration from Britain and Ireland can be distinguished from this earlier movement by magnitude and destination. Three consecutive episodes in the story of this migration can be discerned: the first, from the establishment of the Plymouth colony until 1681; the second, from the establishment of Pennsylvania until the American Revolution; and the third, from 1780 into the era of steamship emigration. In the first phase of migration, ships, particularly from Bristol and London, carried perhaps 400,000 migrants to the British American colonies. Various chartered companies recruited colonists for the new settlements where cash crops including sugar, tobacco, cotton, and dyestuffs were cultivated for market. Of those who crossed the Atlantic before 1680, over 200,000 went to the Caribbean islands, 120,000 to the Chesapeake, and another 20,000 went to New England. Over three-quarters travelled under terms of indenture, most were under the age of 25, and most were from the lowest socio-economic sector of society. Migrants were typically unskilled or semi-skilled men or servant women; those with means paid for their passage and sought to establish themselves as planters or merchants. This latter group were usually young, unmarried men from southern England, who had migrated to London prior to emigrating. After arrival, all faced a hostile disease environment (especially in the Chesapeake and the Caribbean), and in the first decades of settlement as many as 40 per cent died soon after arrival.[39] Migrants with financial resources, or with connections through family, marriage, or rank, could (when they endured) make modest progress acquiring a plantation, slaves, and a household.[40] Natural population growth was impeded, however, by the highly disproportionate sex ratio of English migrants; even by the 1660s, men outnumbered women by three to one in the Chesapeake. Although encouraged by the colonial

[38] Nicholas Canny, *Making Ireland British, 1580–1650* (Oxford, 2001).
[39] James Horn, *Adapting to a New World: English Society in the Seventeenth-Century Chesapeake* (Chapel Hill, NC, 1994), 23–6.
[40] Allan Kulikoff, *From British Peasants to Colonial American Farmers* (Chapel Hill, NC, 2000), 20–2, 57–8.

assemblies and the trade companies, emigration was dependent on opportunities at home and the price of American commodities on European markets. By the late 1670s, the Chesapeake and Caribbean colonies were less attractive for would-be English migrants as opportunities opened up elsewhere. Scots and Irish migrants now featured more prominently, but plantation owners, denied a steady stream of white settlers, increasingly turned to slave labour to maintain productivity and increase exports.

Unlike on the islands and in the Chesapeake, migrants to New England created settlements that were more balanced, in gender terms, and population increased naturally after the Great Migration of the 1630s. Thanks to a more favourable gender balance and health environment, 5 per cent of all migrants from England to North America in the 1600s had, by 1700, produced 40 per cent of the entire population of English stock.[41] These colonists migrated more frequently in family groups than their counterparts elsewhere, were disproportionately skilled, and typically more religiously devout than migrants moving to the Caribbean or the Chesapeake. The Caribbean islands were the most favoured destination in the pre-1660 period; at this time 40 per cent of all colonists in the English colonies lived in the Caribbean. The English presence was augmented in the 1650s by émigrés from Scotland and Ireland rounded up in the wake of Cromwellian military victories in both jurisdictions. Barbados and Jamaica attracted large numbers of settlers and the Irish presence became significant on several islands; Scottish entrepreneurs also featured prominently in Jamaica. With the change in the later seventeenth century from cotton and tobacco to sugar, island settler communities were transferred into slave societies over the course of two generations. By 1700 the islands were no longer attractive to British and Irish labourers. Sugar cultivation altered the demographics of the British Caribbean, with a disproportionate ratio of African slaves to white settlers, especially on Barbados and Jamaica, more akin to the ratios in the French Caribbean plantations than elsewhere in the English world. Thereafter, British and Irish migrants were more attracted to the mainland than to island colonies, although the settlement pattern that emerged in the Carolinas more resembled that on the islands than elsewhere on mainland British America.

In the second phase of emigration from Britain and Ireland, 1700–80, the most evident change from the preceding period was the staggering increase in the number of Irish and Scottish migrants, Roman Catholic and Presbyterian, crossing the Atlantic. Ten times more Scots and at least three times more Irish immigrated to the Americas in the eighteenth than in the seventeenth century.[42] At the same time, the number of

[41] Stephen Innes, *Creating the Commonwealth: The Economic Culture of Puritan New England* (New York, 1995), 23–4.

[42] James Horn, 'British Diaspora: Emigration from Britain, 1680–1815', in P. J. Marshall, *The Eighteenth Century* (Oxford, 1998), 30–2.

English and Welsh migrants declined, dropping from 350,000 in the seventeenth century to 80,000 in the eighteenth. Convicts, too, were transported from England; perhaps as many as 36,000 were shipped before 1776.[43] The port of Philadelphia grew in importance, as more migrants arrived to populate Pennsylvania and the middle colonies more generally, moving steadily southwards from settlements along the valleys of the Appalachian mountains. Eighteenth-century migrants were more likely than their seventeenth-century predecessors to travel in family or community groups, and were usually more skilled or better informed on how to establish a household once their contracts of indenture had come to an end. By 1776, ships under English flag were carrying more non-English than English migrants. The British colonies were demographically, culturally, and linguistically less English than they had ever previously been (see Figure 18.1 below).

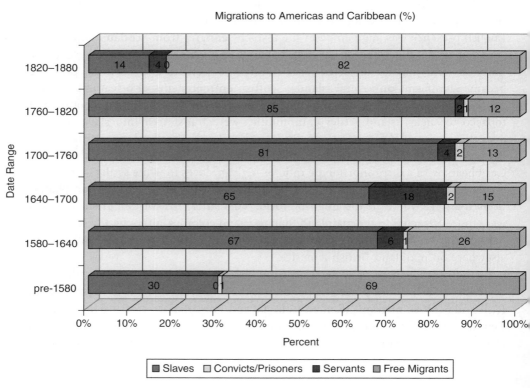

FIGURE **18.1** Migrations to Americas and Caribbean

43 A. Roger Ekirch, *Bound for America: The Transportation of British Convicts to the Colonies, 1718–1775* (Oxford, 1987), 112–15.

THE NETHERLANDS

The United Provinces was unusual among European states in that it was more associated with immigration than emigration. There was a tradition of Dutch men and some women engaging in seasonal labour migration (similar to the German *Hollandgänger*) and of men joining the army and navy, even if the choice to emigrate from a country with a thriving economy appeared curious. With the establishment of the Dutch East India Company (VOC) in 1602 a new demand emerged for sailors, soldiers, and traders to travel to Asia. Many who responded were neither immigrants to, nor emigrants from, the Netherlands, but were trans-migrants from other parts of Europe, using Amsterdam (in particular) as a stopping point to employment overseas. This pattern was repeated with the Dutch Atlantic colonies, which drew heavily on willing German migrants from the Rhineland. Dutch emigrants to settlements in the West Indies and the Americas probably numbered no more than 25,000 people and by 1800 the population of free burghers at the Cape of Good Hope was some 16,000.[44]

The Dutch West India Company (WIC), established in 1621 and abolished in 1795, failed to gain a monopoly from the Netherlands for Atlantic trade. It was also distracted from its commercial activities by having to battle the Spanish and Portuguese and to develop the slave trade. Settlements along the north-east coast of Brazil and in North America were initially most important for the WIC. New Holland, with its largest settlement at Recife, was taken by the Dutch in 1630 and was held, with difficulty, for a quarter of a century.[45] At the outset, the white and mixed population of mestizos and mulattos numbered some 40,000 persons. There was little permanent emigration from the United Provinces; *vrijlieden* (ex-WIC employees and other immigrants) grew from 1,100 to some 3,000 by 1645 and were attracted by Company offers of land and of religious toleration for Jews, who came to form one-third of the *vrijlieden*. But there was little permanent settlement. With the loss of the colony in 1654 most immigrants left for Dutch settlements in North America and the Caribbean.[46]

Settlement in Suriname, conquered in 1667, was never extensive, but it did have the oldest and largest Jewish community in the Americas; by 1811 there were 2,029 European settlers of whom 1,292 were Jews.[47] These numbers were augmented by a small number of soldiers that increased in times of crisis, as in 1773 when 2,300 troops were garrisoned in the colony. Plantations were worked by hundreds of African slaves and a small number of white supervisors; most whites expected their period of residence to be short-term. In western Guyana, including Demerara, most of the

---

[44] F. S. Gaastra, 'De VOC in Azie', *Algemene Geschiedenis der Netherlanden*, 9 (1980), 24–67, here: 44.
[45] Adriana Lopez, *Guera, açucar e religião no Brasil dos holandeses* (Senac, 2002).
[46] E. van den Boogaart, 'De Netherlandse expansie in het atlantisch gebied 1590–1674', *Algemene Geschiedenis der Netherlanden*, 7 (1980), 220–54.
[47] R. Cohen, *Jews in Another Environment: Surinam in the Second Half of the Eighteenth Century* (Leiden, 1992).

settlers were British, and few Dutch migrants chose to put down roots. Settlement on the Dutch Windward Islands (Saba, St Eustatius, and St Martin) was initially in the hundreds, with larger numbers moving to Aruba, Bonaire, and Curaçao. Perhaps as few as 15,000 migrated from the United Provinces to Dutch settlements in the Caribbean, South America, and along the West African coast, with most moving in the second half of the eighteenth century. Dutch settlement in the Atlantic was little more than a footnote to the larger story of emigration to the East Indies.

Emigration to North America was similarly small-scale, and the number of emigrants hardly exceeded 10,000 prior to 1840. New Netherland had a population of some 2,500 people in 1645; by 1660 the population of New Amsterdam on Manhattan Island was 1,500 inhabitants. New Netherland grew as Dutch migrants relocated from other colonies, particularly New Holland and Recife as well as from the United Provinces. Not all colonists from the United Provinces were Dutch; a Company policy encouraged thousands of Jews, Mennonites, and Dutch Quakers to cross the Atlantic. Dutch America was short-lived, however. New Netherland was lost to the English in 1664 and ambitions in North America ceased in 1667.[48] In all, about 15,000 Dutch-sponsored migrants moved to South America and the Caribbean and another 10,000 to North America, and as many as half of those who moved may have been trans-migrants, mainly from neighbouring German states. When compared with the 500,000 people who migrated to the Dutch East Indies, the Dutch Atlantic seemed a low priority to the United Provinces.

FRANCE

French emigration into the Atlantic world was small in scale and modest in settlement. Despite the efforts of pioneering religious communities such as the Huguenots and the Jesuits, the number of French colonists remained small, partly because the all-important French fur trade, with its widely dispersed trappers, was not conducive to a settled agricultural economy.[49] Emigration from France to the American colonies continued, to a varying degree, until the Revolution; thereafter, Africa became the first site of French colonial interest. From the mid-sixteenth century, French commerce expanded from the St Lawrence River and ultimately dominated a large area known as New France, stretching from Acadia (Nova Scotia) to the Great Lakes. Fur trading was the dominant activity for French settlers, coordinated through fortified settlements at Quebec (established in 1608), Ville-Marie (Montreal, 1642), and Detroit (1701). French influence gradually expanded southwards along the Mississippi to the Gulf of Mexico, where settlements were established at Mobile (1701) and New Orleans (1718). French

---

[48] Jaap Jacobs, *New Netherland: A Dutch Colony in Seventeenth-Century America* (Leiden, 2005).

[49] Leslie Choquette, *Frenchmen into Peasants: Modernity and Tradition in the Peopling of French Canada* (Cambridge, MA, 1997).

merchants also established tobacco plantations on several Caribbean islands and gained a strategic foothold on the South American coast at Guiana. Under the mercantilist policies of Jean-Baptiste Colbert, Caribbean tobacco was superseded by more lucrative sugar, indigo, and cotton production.

The nature and scale of French colonial migration, while determined by economic and demographic factors, was greatly influenced by domestic political upheavals and shifts in colonial policy. Emigration was, as elsewhere, a political matter and the subject of considerable debate; civilian colonization was encouraged to consolidate the tenuous grip on the American colonies. Free passage and generous allocations of land were offered to army veterans, and official propaganda celebrating the richness of the colonies circulated widely. Orphan girls were forcibly transported to redress the colonial gender imbalance and press gangs roamed the streets of French cities 'recruiting' petty criminals and the unemployed as pioneer colonists. Between 1665 and 1672, the number of settlers more than doubled from 3,200 to 7,000.[50] After the 1670s, however, incentives were reduced, though high fertility rates in Canada maintained a limited population increase.

After ceding Acadia and Newfoundland to England at the Treaty of Utrecht (1713), the French state launched a propaganda campaign to raise colonists for Louisiana. Some 4,000 convicts and volunteer *colons* arrived between 1718 and 1721, but the wildly optimistic claims about the region proved fraudulent and most survivors returned to France.[51] Between 1725 and 1750, the European population of New France increased from about 20,000 to 55,000, with perhaps 70,000 French settlers reaching Quebec in the seventeenth and eighteenth centuries. In all, perhaps as many as 75,000 migrants moved to French Canada in this period.[52] This compares poorly with the British colonial experience. Already by the late 1600s there were 250,000 settlers in British America, and indeed by 1750 Massachusetts alone was more populous than all New France. French Guiana, which had about 600 settlers in 1760, was also the focus of a propaganda campaign after the Treaty of Paris (1763); Cayenne was depicted as an earthly paradise of richness and abundance. In the mid-1760s, 15,000 colonists, mainly from Alsace and Lorraine but also Germans and Swiss, set sail for Guiana, but within months 9,000 had died of disease.

The Caribbean islands proved more attractive to French migrants; in 1645, there were 8,500 settlers in the Caribbean compared with just 300 in New France, and numbers increased steadily thereafter. On Martinique, the white population rose from 4,770 in 1683 to 14,000 in 1756. The island economies remained increasingly dependent on African slave labour. During the eighteenth century French slave traders transported 1 million Africans to the Caribbean with 270,000 arriving in the 1780s

[50] Philip P. Boucher, *Les Nouvelles Frances: France in America, 1500–1815: An Imperial Perspective* (Providence, RI, 1989), 54.

[51] Mathé Allain, 'Not Worth a Straw': French Colonial Policy and the Early Years of Louisiana* (Lafayette, LA, 1988).

[52] Choquette, *Frenchmen into Peasants*, 20–2.

alone. Between 1713 and 1753, the slave population of Martinique and Guadeloupe increased fourfold from 14,500 to 65,000. On Saint-Domingue, there were 9,000 slaves in 1700, 172,000 in 1752, and 480,000 in 1790, with some 25,000 white and a similar number of free coloured settlers, a ratio of almost ten slaves to every free resident.[53] A rigid social and racial pyramid emerged, characterized by a small number of plantation owners and increasing numbers of *petits blancs* (small white farmers), *engagés* (descendants of forcibly transported Europeans who arrived before the slave trade commenced), mulattos of mixed race, and African slaves.

French colonial emigration, especially before the Third Republic, was part of a broader pattern of population movement. Migrants to non-colonial areas of Europe, North America, and Latin America normally outnumbered those leaving for the colonies. Of the 26,000 people who left France each year in the 1840s, for example, 8,000 were bound for other European countries, 7,700 for the USA, 5,500 for South America, and only 4,500 for new French Algeria.[54] France proved too attractive, and the Atlantic colonies too different, for the French to venture *à l'étranger*.

CONCLUSION

Migration in the Atlantic brought large parts of the world into European spheres of influence and Europeanized them in terms of language, religion, ideologies, and political and judicial institutions. But some Europeans began to question their achievements in the Atlantic world just when it was proving most profitable, and slavery was challenged on moral grounds and then by legislation in the nineteenth century. By then those countries most involved in Atlantic trade and settlement were beginning to act globally. However, people at the farthest reaches of Eastern Europe who had previously had little contact with the Atlantic were now belatedly, in the age of steam, drawn into a growing trade in human capital, supplying necessary labour for the cities and the countryside of South, Central, and North America.

BIBLIOGRAPHY

Altman, Ida, and James Horn (eds.), *'To Make America': European Emigration in the Early Modern Period* (Berkeley, CA, 1991).
Bailyn, Bernard, *Voyagers to the West* (New York, 1986).
—— *The Peopling of British North America: An Introduction* (New York, 1988).

[53] Boucher, *Nouvelles Frances*, 71, 90.
[54] Louis Chevalier, 'L'Émigration française au XIXe siècle', *Études d'histoire moderne et contemporaine*, 1 (1947), 127–71.

Cohen, Robin (ed.), *The Cambridge Survey of World Migration* (Cambridge, 1995).

Eltis, David (ed.), *Free and Coerced Migrations: A Global Perspective* (Palo Alto, CA, 2002).

Games, Alison, *Migration and the Origins of the English Atlantic World* (Cambridge, MA, 1999).

Hansen, Marcus Lee, and Arthur Meier Schlesinger, *The Atlantic Migration 1607–1860* (1941; New York, 2001).

Inkori, Joseph, and Stanley L. Engerman (eds.), *The Atlantic Slave Trade: Effects on Economics, Societies and Peoples in Africa, the Americas, and Europe* (Durham, NC, 1992).

Lovejoy, Paul E., *Transformations in Slavery: A History of Slavery in Africa* (Cambridge, 2000).

Manning, Patrick, *Migration in World History* (New York, 2005).

CHAPTER 19

··

ATLANTIC TRADE AND
COMMODITIES, 1402–1815

··

DAVID HANCOCK

IN 1402, the city of Mocha was the principal port for the export of coffee, supplying communities around the Red Sea, Arabian Sea, and Gulf of Aden, but not to Europe, where it remained rare through the seventeenth century, or to America where it was unknown. By 1815, coffee had become a common drink on all four continents fronting the Atlantic, but Mocha's dominance had faded, and the West Indies had become its major source.

The experience with coffee was far from unique, and this chapter reviews the transfer of goods and services between the continents bordering the Atlantic Ocean. It will show that the demands of long-distance trade, particularly but not solely across the Atlantic, encouraged innovation in technologies and methods, transformed commercial institutions, and required traders to develop novel ways of managing their businesses. Trade was probably the crucial factor in creating and integrating a cohesive oceanic community that coexisted with national and imperial regimes.[1]

I

···

Atlantic exchange, as J.-P. Rubiés's chapter demonstrates, flourished long before Columbus reached the Americas. The first valuable export crops from the Canary Islands were *orchilla*, an indigenous lichen yielding a highly prized violet dye, and sugar, which the

---

[1] This definition of 'Atlantic', focusing on European trading because Europeans were the principal *transoceanic* traders, narrows the scope of enquiry considerably. This chapter does not address coastwise and inland trading, nor the indigenous Africans and Americans who played large roles in them. Nor does it consider non-voluntary 'exchanges', like piracy and the trade in slaves.

Castilians introduced.[2] Portuguese settlers cultivated wheat on Madeira and Porto Santo. In time, Madeirans, using African slaves, exported sugar, highly valued for its whiteness, sweetness, and fineness. The Portuguese also used the Azores as a stopping point on the return voyage from Africa and a production zone for wheat, while extending the Madeira sugar/slave plantation model to the Cape Verdes, São Tomé, and Princípe.[3]

The first century of Iberian Atlantic trading was tentative: production was uncertain, shipping was erratic, and monarchs provided little support. Nonetheless, overseas trading grew. Horses, maize, and cloth from Morocco, sugar from Madeira, the Cape Verdes, and São Tomé, *orchilla* from the Canaries, wheat from the Azores, and gold, slaves, and pepper from West Africa arrived in Iberia in increasing volume. In return, mainland merchants supplied islanders with foodstuffs, textiles, and hardware.

Early trading

Columbus' 'discoveries' were transformative rather than innovative. From the outset, people traded the exotic commodities he had carried back.[4] Each region of the Americas settled by explorers had something to offer, but Spain's primary interest lay with bullion. Spaniards took gold from indigenous peoples and tapped alluvial deposits. After 1519, mining spread to New Spain, Peru, and New Granada. Gold exported to Europe peaked in the 1550s, when silver surpassed it. Mines produced over 16,000 tons of export silver between 1500 and 1650. The crown directed that bullion be coined quickly and so erected five mints to convert annual yields into nearly pure coin.[5]

Even if not 'the singular product most responsible for the birth of world trade', bullion transformed Atlantic trade. It became 'a harvested exportable' that lubricated several European economies. In America, it both brought 'monetization and commercialization to the colonial economies', and forged an early link 'between the mining and commercial sectors'. Given its potential, the Habsburgs devised a complex commercial system to guarantee that the wealth of America became Europe's.[6]

---

[2] Charles Boxer, *The Portuguese Seaborne Empire, 1415–1825* (New York, 1969); Jose Castellano Gil and Francisco Macias Martin, *History of the Canary Islands* (Santa Cruz de Tenerife, 1993).

[3] Alberto Vieira, *O comércio inter-insular nos séculos XV e XVI (Madeira, Canárias e Açores)* (Funchal, 1987); Celso Batista de Sousa, 'São Tomé e Príncipe, do descoprimento aos meados do seculo XVI: desenvolvimento interno e irradiaçao no golfo da Guiné, 1473–1550' (Ph.D. thesis, Universidade de Lisboa, 1990); Robert Garfield, *A History of Sao Tomè Island, 1470–1655: The Key to Guinea* (San Francisco, CA, 1992).

[4] C. H. Haring, *The Spanish Empire in America* (New York, 1947); John H. Parry, *The Spanish Seaborne Empire* (New York, 1970); Henry Kamen, *Spain's Road to Empire: The Making of a World Power, 1492–1763* (London, 2002).

[5] Stanley J. Stein and Barbara H. Stein, *Silver, Trade, and War: Spain and America in the Making of Early Modern Europe* (Baltimore, MD, 2000), 24–5.

[6] Dennis O. Flynn and Arturo Giráldez, 'Born with a Silver Spoon: The Origin of World Trade in 1571', *Journal of World History*, 6 (1995), 201; Stein and Stein, *Silver*, 51, 27; Haring, *Spanish Empire*, 294.

Their approach promoted a 'mercantilist' mindset that argued for national self-sufficiency, augmentation of military and naval power, state control of gold and silver reserves, and protection of the economy—all sustained by laws and institutions. The Spanish Monarchy monopolized commerce, created an organization to manage it, established a fleet system to protect it, and gave Seville merchant guilds the charge of—and profit from—exploiting trade. Under laws passed early in the 1500s, commodities were to flow from Spain to Spanish America, and vice versa. Ships were to be owned and operated by Spaniards; they were generally restricted to servicing the ports of Seville and Cádiz (in Spain) and Vera Cruz, Cartagena, and Nombre de Dios (in the Americas). Cargoes were to be handled by Spaniards. The re-export of certain goods like bullion was forbidden, while that of others like cochineal could be.

Central to Atlantic commerce was La Casa de Contratación, founded by the crown in 1503. The Casa managed transatlantic shipping: it licensed and supervised merchants, vessels, crew, equipment, cargoes, and migrants, enforced regulations concerning voyagers, vessels, and goods, and collected revenue, particularly convoy taxes and import/export duties. Tightening its grip in 1526, the crown forbade merchants to sail the ocean unchaperoned, without heavily armed convoy. Protecting the increasing outflow of bullion from America became the crown's chief concern. It regularized the obligatory, protected fleets, usually sending two annually. Later, in 1543, it allowed the large commercial traders of Seville to form a guild and, through it, control the imperial trading community through a monopoly of flows between Spain and America.[7]

It proved impossible to enforce such control, however, and the grant of licences to supply slaves to Spanish Americans (*asientos*) to non-Spanish Europeans, notably the Portuguese and English, only worsened the flouting of rules, as foreigners could legally penetrate crown-set barriers. In time, German and French houses acquired controlling interests in some of Spain's largest mercantile firms.[8]

Portugal's trade was less organized and more slight compared to Spain's, since the Portuguese regarded trade with the East as more desirable. In fact, it was only after Pedro Álvares Cabral accidentally landed in 1500 in Brazil that Portuguese merchants established trading posts there for collecting brazilwood. Later, they imported African slaves to cultivate the plant that produced both the red dye *brazilin* and a wood especially suited to making string-instrument bows.[9] After the introduction of African slave labour revolutionized sugar cultivation there, Brazil attained commercial prominence. The industry was located in its north-eastern settlements, primarily Pernambuco and Bahia. The 60 sugar mills operated by Brazilian planters in 1570 had risen to

---

[7] Enriqueta Vila Vilar, Adolfo González Rodríguez, and Antonio Acosta Rodríguez (eds.), *La Casa de la Contratación: la navegación y el comercio entre España y América* (Seville, 2003).

[8] Philip Curtin, *The Atlantic Slave Trade: A Census* (Madison, WI, 1970), 47.

[9] C. R. Boxer, 'Padre Antonio Vieira, S.J. and the Institution of the Brazil Company in 1649', *Hispanic American Historical Review*, 29 (1949), 474–94; Vitorino M. Godinho, *L'Économie de l'empire portugais, XVe–XVIe siècles* (Paris, 1968); Leonor Freire Costa, *O transporte no Atlântico e a Companhia Geral do Comércio do Brasil (1580–1663)* (Lisbon, 2002).

195 by 1600, while gross output increased from 600,000 *arrobas* in 1600 to 960,000 by 1624.[10]

Despite such growth, the Portuguese never imposed a monopoly over American possessions, possibly because their mining output was comparatively small and their agricultural commodities less valuable. Also their monarchy was poorer and less bureaucratized than Spain's, conceding leasing rights over trade to reap short-term profit. In controlling African slaving, Portugal preferred private contractors and indirect means to raise revenue. Only during the union with Spain (1580–1640) were monopoly and exclusion attempted. Thereafter, the Companhia Geral do Comércio do Brasil received a monopoly over flour, oil, wine, and cod in 1649, but there was neither *Casa* nor privileged guild to manage all Atlantic trade.[11]

Seventeenth-century diversification

Atlantic trade increased in volume and diversified during the seventeenth century. At its end, fish and crops, rather than metals and dye, were the principal goods shipped from the Americas, where plantation slavery had become entrenched. In tandem, as more Europeans settled new colonies, a significant reverse trade evolved to bring them European produce and manufactures.

The efforts of Europeans to control Atlantic trade produced conflict both between jurisdictions and between segments within a jurisdiction, notably between the Spanish Habsburg monarch and his Protestant subjects in the Low Countries. Military over-reach led ultimately to the weakening of Spain, which increasingly could not harvest the fruit of its empire. On the other side, the Dutch, constituted as the United Provinces, sustained their interests in Europe and overseas with a formidable navy and the chartered Dutch West India Company (Geoctroyeerde Westindische Compagnie or 'GWC'), which enjoyed a monopoly on traffic with West Africa, the Atlantic, and the Americas. In the short term, the GWC erected trading posts in New Netherland, the Dutch Antilles, and Africa's Gold Coast. New Netherland exported furs and skins to Amsterdam, while African settlements shipped slaves to Caribbean plantations. Such exchanges unwittingly forged a Dutch Atlantic community and loosened the Iberian stranglehold over trade and settlement. Other Dutch trades engaged other empires, notably that in sugar, tobacco, and brazilwood from Portuguese Brazil, sugar from the English Caribbean, and tobacco from the English Chesapeake, while individual Dutchmen participated in illicit exchanges and in attacks on the Spanish treasure fleets.[12]

---

[10] Stuart B. Schwartz, *Sugar Plantations in the Formation of Brazilian Society: Bahia, 1550–1835* (Cambridge, 1985), 17–19, 165, 168, 176–7.

[11] H. B. Johnson, 'The Leasing of Brazil, 1502–1515: A Problem Resolved', *The Americas*, 55 (1999), 481–7; Herbert Klein, *The Atlantic Slave Trade* (Cambridge, 1999), 74–5; Curtin, *Atlantic Slave Trade*, 47.

[12] Jan De Vries and A. M. van der Woude, *The First Modern Economy: Success, Failure, and Perseverance of the Dutch Economy, 1500–1815* (Cambridge, 1997); Wim Klooster, *Illicit Riches: Dutch*

After regaining independence from Spain in 1640, the Portuguese created a transatlantic trading system that was more vigorous than what had existed before 1580.
Foreign trade became the most vibrant sector of their economy and, despite crown
efforts to promote domestic activity, people invested most heavily in developing
international traffic in Asian spices, Brazilian produce, and Portuguese wines. The
number of overseas traders and vessels increased, revenues grew, and overseas interests
became more diverse, and less Asia-focused, not least because the Portuguese lost
ground to Dutch and English rivals in Asia. To compensate, they expelled the Dutch
from Angola in 1648 and Pernambuco in 1654. As they increased their slaving in Africa
and moved towards a land-based empire in America, Portuguese traders exported
mainland wine and olive oil to Angola and Brazil, moved slaves from Angola to Brazil,
and imported Brazilian sugar, tobacco, gold, and gems into Portugal. They also re-
exported American sugar, grains, and fish to European markets, and European grains
and manufactures to Brazil.[13]

Following initial successes, the GWC lost many forts in America and Africa to
European rivals, and suffered from the effects of England's anti-Dutch trading legislation. Its two large colonization schemes faltered: New Holland in 1654, and New
Netherland in 1674. With the latter's demise, the GWC gradually collapsed, its successor abandoning conquest and piracy and focusing instead on marketing Dutch plantation produce. As it did so, the Dutch developed a role as the ocean's premier
commercial intermediaries. Peace with Spain in 1648 enabled Dutch merchants to
funnel northern European goods to Iberia, and Spanish and Spanish American goods
to northern Europe; simultaneously, other merchants sent 'register ships' to Brazil free
of the convoys. The intermediation was dominated by traders who focused on the
Caribbean, supplying the needs of Portuguese plantations in Suriname and river
settlements in South America and exporting the Americans' sugar, coffee, cacao, and
cotton. Others supplied slaves (and general northern European goods) to Spanish
America, usually via Curaçao, which they exchanged for colonial produce. Such
middleman business generated most of the Netherlands' Atlantic revenue.[14]

France and England also experimented, without entirely adopting either the 'Spanish
imperial model' or the 'Dutch intermediation model'. Each relied on monopolistic
control but encouraged private trading within a mercantilist regulatory framework that

Trade in the Caribbean, 1648–1795 (Leiden, 1998); Johannes Postma and Victor Enthoven (eds.), *Riches
from Atlantic Commerce: Dutch Transatlantic Trade and Shipping, 1585–1817* (Leiden, 2003).

[13] José Vicente Serrão, 'O quadro económico: configurações estruturais e tendências de evolução', in
José Mattoso (ed.), *História de Portugal*, vol. iv (Lisbon, 1993), 97; Kenneth Maxwell, *Pombal: Paradox of
the Enlightenment* (Cambridge, 1995), 43; Joaquim Veríssimo Serrão, *História de Portugal*, vol. v (Lisbon,
1982), 403; Carla R. Phillips, 'The Growth and Composition of Trade in the Iberian Empires, 1450–1740',
in J. Tracy (ed.), *The Rise of Merchant Empires* (Cambridge, 1990), 69.

[14] Wim Klooster, 'An Overview of Dutch Trade with the Americas, 1600–1800', and Victor Enthoven,
'An Assessment of Dutch Transatlantic Commerce, 1585–1817', in Postma and Enthoven (eds.), *Riches*,
365–83, 385–445.

the French codified in *l'exclusif* and the English in the Navigation Acts. The goal was to encourage private initiative and privilege national entrepreneurs and home ports, while using the apparatus of regulatory protection to raise money for the state. Despite their similarity of approach, each regarded the other as its principal rival.

Fleets regularly left northern and western French ports for the Newfoundland fisheries from the 1630s and returned with wet green cod and occasionally beaver and otter furs. The cod fishers of the Bay of Biscay and Brittany developed a profitable triangular trade between France, Newfoundland, and Iberia.[15] To better order its Atlantic commerce, the crown devised a restrictive arrangement whereby French merchants and ships monopolized colonial trade. First articulated in 1625 after the Spanish model, *l'exclusif* was reiterated and expanded in 1664, 1698, 1717, and 1727. While designed to oblige French colonists to buy from and sell to French merchants, it ultimately, unwittingly, encouraged smuggling.[16]

The English of the sixteenth century viewed the Atlantic much as did the French—a site for extending North Sea and Icelandic fishing to the north-west Atlantic and raiding the Spanish bullion fleet. From 1604, as other chapters have described, they began to establish permanent settlements along the North American coast and in the Caribbean. They produced staple crops, but exportation was subjected to scanty surveillance: population was thin, production small, and demand for manufactures slight. Instead, the crown granted charters for management to private joint-stock companies.[17] A more consistent policy in relation to Atlantic extraction, importation, and protection was enacted by Parliament between 1651 and 1696 to eliminate the role of the Dutch as intermediaries and channel the flow of goods within the expanding empire.[18] The Atlantic became the pivot of empire, as the scale of overseas trade escalated between 1675 and 1700. Output accelerated in industries like iron production and salt harvesting, and a variety of their manufactures went overseas. Imports grew by one-third. Goods once viewed as luxuries—tobacco, sugar, wine, and calico—become commonplace during the late 1600s. But exports and re-exports rose by over one-half, with re-exports increasing more dramatically than exports. By 1700, the English economy had come to depend upon the Atlantic marketplace to a remarkable extent.[19]

---

[15] Paul Butel, *The Atlantic* (London, 1999), 115.

[16] Ibid. 117–18, 127; Bernard Schnapper, 'La Fin du régime de l'exclusif: le commerce étranger dans les possessions françaises d'Afrique tropicale, 1817–1870', *Annales africaines*, 5 (1959), 261–82.

[17] Lawrence A. Harper, *The English Navigation Laws: A Seventeenth-Century Experiment in Social Engineering* (New York, 1939).

[18] Stanley L. Engerman, 'Mercantilism and Overseas Trade, 1700–1800', in R. Floud and D. N. McCloskey (eds.), *The Economic History of Britain Since 1700: 1700–1860*, vol. i (2nd edn. Cambridge, 1994); John J. McCusker, 'British Mercantilist Policies and American Colonies', in Stanley L. Engerman and Robert E. Gallman (eds.), *The Cambridge Economic History of the United States: The Colonial Era*, vol. i (Cambridge, 1996).

[19] Ralph Davis, 'English Foreign Trade, 1700–1774', *Economic History Review*, 15 (1962), 78, 92–4; Peter Mathias, *The First Industrial Nation: An Economic History of Britain, 1700–1914* (London, 1983), 84.

The great eighteenth-century struggle

The long eighteenth century witnessed a precipitate decline of France as an Atlantic commercial power and a steady rise of England. Fighting three wars on land and sea, France lost most of its overseas possessions other than those in Africa. Paradoxically, its Atlantic trading burgeoned, at least at first. The Grand Banks fisheries, which it retained in 1713, continued to prosper. Saint-Domingue, Martinique, and Guadeloupe exported greater quantities of sugar and coffee than ever before, and, from the 1740s, foreign merchants in France re-exported their bulk to the Netherlands and the Baltic states. France's African trade also flourished, with merchants from Le Havre, Nantes, La Rochelle, and Bordeaux carrying increasing numbers of slaves to French Caribbean planters. France's overseas trade was exuberant in the first three quarters of the century: while the value of its total trade quadrupled between 1720 and 1790, the value of specifically colonial trade increased tenfold. By the 1780s, colonial imports constituted four-tenths of all imports.

Such dominance was challenged by Britain's War for America, the Caribbean slave revolts of 1791 and 1793, and the naval superiority that Britain attained during the Revolutionary and Napoleonic wars. The War for America and the independence of Haiti in 1804 resulted in the destruction and loss of plantations and colonies, crushing both production and distribution. By the time France recovered Guadeloupe and Martinique in 1814 and peace was declared in 1815, colonial exports were insignificant. Equally debilitating to French dominance was the loosening of l'exclusif in 1767 and 1784, after which Caribbean merchants traded directly with Britain and the United States.[20]

As France's Atlantic commerce fell away, Britain's grew. Imports expanded more than sixfold, and exports and re-exports more than sixfold and tenfold, respectively, outstripping English agricultural output and domestic consumption of manufactures. Overseas markets waxed important: around 1700, 80 per cent of England's exports and re-exports went to the unprotected markets of continental Europe, and 15 per cent to overseas dependencies in America, Asia, and Africa; by 1775, only half went to Europe, but over a third to overseas dependencies. The American sector had become the most valuable for British trade, even if the War of Independence temporarily stagnated it.[21]

Throughout, sugar was the empire's most valuable commodity, as David Eltis notes in his chapter, and slaves its chief source of labour. The organization of trade in sugar

[20] Jean Tarrade, Le Commerce colonial de la France à la fin de l'Ancien Régime: l'évolution du régime de l'exclusif de 1763 à 1789, 2 vols. (Paris, 1973); Philippe Haudrère, La Compagnie française des Indes au XVIIIe siècle, 4 vols. (Paris, 1989); Pierre Pluchon, Histoire de la colonisation française (Paris, 1990); Jean Meyer, Jean Tarrade, and Annie Rey-Goldzeiguer, Histoire de la France coloniale, i: La Conquête, des origines à 1870 (Paris, 1996); Butel, Atlantic, 127, 166.

[21] N. F. R. Crafts, British Economic Growth during the Industrial Revolution (Oxford, 1985), 45, 132–3; E. L. Jones, 'Agriculture', in Floud and McCloskey (eds.), Economic History, 66–86; Davis, 'English Foreign Trade, 1700–1774', 83, and The Industrial Revolution and British Overseas Trade (Leicester, 1979), 89, 94, 97, 102, 105; Mathias, First Industrial Nation, 89, 91, 92.

was emblematic of the extensive and intricate nature of much trading. African slaves were conveyed to the West Indies, Caribbean sugar and its by-products were exported to North America and Britain, and New English rum and English guns were shipped to West Africa. Bilateral schemes were common, such as codfish for wine or gold, engaging Newfoundland, Massachusetts, Portugal, and Spain. As more blacks and whites arrived in Anglo-America, and as natural increase there rose, there were more mouths to feed, bodies to clothe, and homes to fill with European-made products, as well as more commodities produced to use for payment. Private initiative trumped monopoly power, even as protective regulatory schemes persisted.

While Britain and France struggled for Atlantic control, the Netherlands flourished, albeit in slightly different channels than before. 'Still seen as the cheapest carriers', the Dutch, with more ships deployed and more investors enrolled, profited in the transit trade. The value of their commerce in 1780 was nearly twice what it had been in 1636, servicing both Ibero- and Anglo-America, as well as the European continent. Symbolizing their middleman position, the free port of St Eustatius became an entrepôt of critical international importance.[22]

Similarly, the Iberian empires advanced, if erratically. Imports into Brazilian settlements from Europe rose sixfold between 1685 and 1796, wine, oil, and sugar being the most important. Brazilian sugar and tobacco exports also rose, while Brazilian gold and diamond exports both grew and transformed mainland fortunes. Portugal became Europe's principal bullion supplier, albeit indirectly, for re-exports from the kingdom were largely handled by British traders.[23] While some Portuguese grew wealthy from this relationship, hostility grew, and so, in the 1760s and 1770s, the chief minister, Pombal, sought to wrest Portuguese trade from the British, to introduce stricter commercial regulations, and to charter monopoly companies that would promote mainland production and supply Brazil. Due to its reforms as well as its neutrality during the French Revolutionary and Napoleonic struggles, Luso-Brazilian trade improved, as did the re-export of sugar and cotton, but the 1807 French invasion and the removal of the court to Rio disrupted the entire colonial commercial system.

Spain's Atlantic trade was likewise buffeted by the revolutionary winds of the century. In 1700, Spain possessed an ineffective financial bureaucracy, a paltry navy, and an economy that was heavily based on agriculture and dependent on northern European manufactures. At home, the *consulados* controlled overseas commerce, while, abroad, the government could neither launch annual fleets nor protect individual vessels. In 1713, the new Bourbon dynasty set out to regain national and imperial solvency, disbanding dysfunctional fleets and allowing individually licensed vessels; it weakened the *consulados* by extending similar privileges to traders in northern Spain.

---

[22] Klooster, 'Overview', 377, 379; Enthoven, 'Assessment', 436, 440, 400, 390, 410.

[23] Mattoso (ed.), *Historia*, iv. 104; José Bacelar Bebiano, *O porto de Lisboa* (Lisbon, 1960), 42, 55, graphs 1–3; Virgílio Noya Pinto, *O ouro brasileiro e o comércio anglo-português* (2nd edn. São Paulo, 1979), 296–7; Jorge Borges de Macedo, 'Portugal e a economia "pombalina": temas & hipóteses', *Revista de historia (Sao Paulo)*, 19 (1954), 81–97.

But it was not until 1759 that customs duties were reduced and tax concessions given. The crown tightened old monopolies and created new ones, appointed officials to manage them, and refused to allow their work to be delegated. It also resumed and regularized annual ship convoys, and initiated a packet service between Spain and Cuba. Most boldly, it pronounced *comercio libre* in 1778: all ports in Spain could thenceforth trade freely by licence with all Spanish American ports, and all colonies except New Spain and New Granada could trade with each other.[24] But in the end the reforms were not enough to resuscitate trade. The empire's core continued to rot, while its periphery flourished.

II

The intensification of transoceanic trading after 1492 engendered commensurate institutional changes. Transformations were most radical after 1675, when conventions supportive of trade and regulative principles were introduced in three key areas—shipping, finance, and information.

Atlantic trade required substantial investments and innovations in shipping. The first big change was in scale. The size of Atlantic-going vessels increased between 1550 and 1800, although, as ships grew larger, they became more expensive to maintain. Merchant fleets also grew in size. Between 1600 and 1800, the Dutch Republic's tonnage rose fivefold, France's ninefold, and England's thirty-onefold—striking inasmuch as France and England did not become significant transatlantic traders until the second half of the seventeenth century. Between 1670 and 1787, when Dutch tonnage fell by a third, that of France and England each increased ninefold. Between 1585 and 1787, the combined tonnage of Spain and Portugal remained reasonably constant; by 1787, it was roughly half of the Netherlands', a third of France's, and a quarter of England's.[25]

New ship designs were introduced to expand the fleets' capabilities. The Dutch first launched the *fluyt* in the late sixteenth century, and its capaciousness was quickly perceived and copied by non-Dutch traders and mariners.[26] During the seventeenth century, Bermuda shipwrights modified the Dutch *sloep*, enhancing its speed, although

---

[24] Laura Nater, 'Colonial Tobacco: Key Commodity of the Spanish Empire, 1500–1800', in Steven Topik et al. (eds.), *From Silver to Cocaine* (Durham, NC, 2006), 106–7; Haring, *Spanish Empire*, 320–2; Stein and Stein, *Silver*, 114–15.

[25] Richard W. Unger, 'The Tonnage of Europe's Merchant Fleets, 1300–1800', *American Neptune*, 52 (1992), 259–60; Jan Glete, *Navies and Nations: Warships, Navies and State Building in Europe and America, 1500–1860*, vol. ii (Stockholm, 1993), 551–3, 576, 579, 619–30, 639, 641; John J. McCusker, Jr., 'The Tonnage of Ships Engaged in British Colonial Trade during the Eighteenth Century', *Research in Economic History*, 6 (1981), 73–105; Carla Rahn Phillips, 'Galleons: Fast Sailing Ships of the Mediterranean and Atlantic, 1500–1650', in *Cogs, Caravels and Galleons: The Sailing Ship, 1000–1650* (London, 1994), 98–114.

[26] Charles R. Boxer, *The Dutch Seaborne Empire, 1600–1800* (New York, 1965), 20, 68.

not its capacity. A highly manoeuvrable fore-and-aft rig, and a single mast situated farther forward than on competing fast boats, allowed it to negotiate crowded ports and manage strong Atlantic coast winds more deftly.[27]

The work of mariners and traders improved in other ways. Sheathing of wooden hulls to minimize the drag created by seaweed and barnacles attaching to the hull or the destruction by *teredo* worms occurred widely in the second half of the eighteenth century, drawing frequently upon ancient techniques using copper, lead, or even a 'second skin' of wood.[28] Improvement of coastal and riverine navigation accelerated, too: building lighthouses, dredging rivers and ports, refurbishing natural harbours, erecting man-made ones, training cadres of specialized longshoremen and transporters, and extending them greater legal rights. Such developments helped shippers and traders cope more effectively with higher shipping levels, greater distances, and needier vessels and crews.[29]

Improvements arising in two general areas also enhanced overseas shipping and trading: finance, and information. The medium of exchange became 'dematerialized' as, over four centuries, interested parties supplemented commodity money and base money (coin) with more refined, abstract forms of payment. Commodities had long been used as money—in Europe, Asia, and Africa—and the practice persisted into the nineteenth century, and even increased in certain places, notably tropical Africa. As the international demand for African slaves grew, so also did the use as money of precious goods, including white cowrie shells, brass *manilla* bracelets, and highly decorated textiles. Iberian Americans do not seem to have made much use of commodity money, but their Anglo-American counterparts were more receptive, using indigenous manufactures (like wampum) and agricultural crops (like tobacco) to good effect. At the same time, base money proliferated, as gold and silver flowed from Mexico and Peru, and the *reale* and *peso*, made from silver mined and minted in Spanish America, became the coin most frequently used in all Atlantic empires.[30]

The progression from commodity to coin and beyond was not linear. Specie remained scarce, even in the bullion-rich Iberian empires. In the seventeenth century, overseas traders started using paper forms (bank notes, bills of exchange, and the like). Such new 'invisible money' gradually dominated the world of payments as allowable credit expanded and further engendered change in new requirements for security,

[27] Michael Jarvis, '"The Fastest Vessels in the World": The Origin and Evolution of the Bermuda Sloop, 1620–1800', *Bermuda Journal of Archaeology and Maritime History*, 7 (1995), 31–50.

[28] Randolph Cock, '"The Finest Invention in the World": The Royal Navy's Early Trials of Copper Sheathing, 1708–1770', *Mariners' Mirror*, 87 (2001), 446–59.

[29] Dolores Romero and Agustín Guimerá (eds.), *Puertos y sistemas portuarios (siglos XVI–XX): actas del coloquio internacional el sistema portuario español, Madrid, 19–21 octubre 1995* (Madrid, 1996); Carlos Caetano, *A ribeira de Lisboa na época da expansão portuguesa (séculos XV a XVIII)* (Lisbon, 2004); R. C. Jarvis, 'Metamorphosis of the Port of London', *London Journal*, 3 (1977), 55–72; David Stevenson, *The World's Lighthouses before 1820* (Oxford, 1959).

[30] Stein and Stein, *Silver*; Philip D. Curtin, 'Africa and the Wider Monetary World, 1250–1850', in J. F. Richards (ed.), *Precious Metals in the Later Medieval and Early Modern Worlds* (Durham, NC, 1983), 231–68; Jan Hogendorn and Marion Johnson, *The Shell Money of the Slave Trade* (Cambridge, 1986).

observation, and warrant and forms of contract. Especially important, the use of bills of exchange, drawing upon practices developed in Antwerp during the late sixteenth century, became commonplace among overseas traders a century later. Users innovated in three areas: making bills payable to the bearer, transferable to another party, and negotiable, by which was meant capable of being assigned or endorsed multiple times. Over time, Atlantic traders came to view these bills not only as an asset and a means of payment but also as a form of credit.[31]

Similarly, another form of finance—marine insurance—became more precise, tailored to individual needs, reliable, and available. Its evolution was vital because shipping and trading were notoriously risky endeavours. How to manage the threats of sinking and seizure was a persistent problem, and certain innovations were introduced in the late seventeenth and early eighteenth centuries to mitigate it. First, specialist marine underwriters emerged in Amsterdam, London, and Lisbon. Secondly, underwriters standardized the forms of contract until, by 1675, only three types of policy prevailed. Finally, the understanding of risk grew deeper, and the imposition of premium became commonplace; even as the type of risk against which insurance protected widened, 'the techniques for the calculation of risks and premium rates' for contract and premium gained precision and reliability.[32] One related significant development was the expansion of the insurance market, with a 'trend towards economic convergence'. Portuguese merchants, for instance, became as likely to insure in Amsterdam or London as in Lisbon, depending on what was most appropriate and economical. The relationship of the European marine insurance markets to the Americas was likewise thick, if complex: a large share of Western European policies were designed to protect against Atlantic risk or loss, yet increasingly insurers there confronted New World competition, as creole insurers emerged and flourished in most large American ports.[33]

One final set of changes—aptly captured in the phrase 'Information Revolution'—transformed Atlantic commerce, as the world moved from communication that was largely oral—at least barely recorded—to one that was not only written but printed. By 1800, maritime news was published, disclosing information that had been largely secret a century before.[34] The impact is incalculable. For merchants working in London, Amsterdam, Paris, Lisbon, Seville, and their American analogues in 1675–1700, letters were the normal source of information on overseas matters, and information from the

---

[31] John McCusker, *Money and Exchange in Europe and America: A Handbook* (Chapel Hill, NC, 1978), 18–23; James S. Rogers, *The Early History of the Law of Bills and Notes: A Study of the Origins of Anglo-American Commercial Law* (Cambridge, 1995).

[32] Violet Barbour, 'Marine Risks and Insurance in the Seventeenth Century', *Journal of Economic and Business History*, 1 (1928–9), 592, 595; Florence Edler de Roover, 'Early Examples of Marine Insurance', *Journal of Economic History*, 5 (1945), 172–200.

[33] Frank C. Spooner, *Risks at Sea: Amsterdam Insurance and Maritime Europe, 1766–1780* (Cambridge, 1983).

[34] John J. McCusker, 'The Demise of Distance: The Business Press and the Origins of the Information Revolution in the Early Modern Atlantic World', *American Historical Review*, 110 (2005), 295–321.

press was always ancillary to that from mail. As the century advanced, newspapers became equal partners with letters. The exchange of information expedited the transatlantic trades and the exchange of New and Old World commodities, assisted by the rise and spread of newspapers and the increase in frequency and regularity of posts in most European states and overseas settlements.[35] That Europe and the Americas were regularly linked by packet services profoundly changed expectations of information exchange—and enterprise.[36]

III

The increase in the efficiency of shipping, the dematerialization of finance, and the spread of information were, by themselves, substantial results of a burgeoning Atlantic trade. They also forced changes in traders' and governments' ideas about how commerce should be managed. In short, early systems of trade in the Atlantic that privileged state control through monopoly, licence, protection, restriction, and regulation—the Spanish model and variations of it—gave way by 1700 to approaches allowing for the primacy of independent and decentralized agents.

The short-term fiscal benefits of the state controlling trade through monopoly were great and obvious, but experience alerted people to considerable drawbacks. A state could not keep other states—or even its own subjects—from encroaching on its monopolies. Even as they wished to control trade, northern rulers resignedly introduced varying degrees of competition and decentralization into the management of overseas commerce. Regulated and, later, joint-stock companies were bespoke for the work. Externally, they exercised a quasi-state power that allowed them to stand up to foreigners and gather commercial information. Internally, they possessed an organization that was better capitalized and serviced than a monopoly, their ties to employees being non-familial, formal, and even-handed.[37]

Regulated companies were first deployed to meet the challenges of long-distance, seaborne commerce. For the most part, they dealt with the 'near abroad'—areas reachable by land and short sea voyages—as did the London and Bristol merchants chartered by James I to develop the fishery off Newfoundland. Such companies endured beyond the death of grantees and governed in a corporate manner, with subscribing merchants deciding who could be a member and how members would

---

[35] Ian K. Steele, *The English Atlantic: An Exploration of Communication and Community* (Oxford, 1986), 131.

[36] Ibid. 183–8; Kenneth J. Banks, *Chasing Empire across the Sea: Communications and the State in the French Atlantic, 1713–1763* (Montreal, 2002); McCusker, 'Demise of Distance', 295–321.

[37] P. R. Milgrom, D. C. North, and B. R. Weingast, 'The Role of Institutions in the Revival of Trade: The Law Merchant, Private Judges, and the Champagne Fairs', *Economics & Politics*, 2 (1990), 1–23.

conduct trade. Capital came from fees and levies imposed upon member traders to whom the company provided shipping services.

The longer distances involved in Atlantic trading ultimately exceeded the capacity of regulated companies to meet their obligations, because the greater expanse of water necessitated larger ships (requiring more capital) and longer voyages (requiring more credit). Accordingly, to meet Atlantic challenges, monarchs and traders came to favour the joint-stock form, under which each member of the company acquired a share in the whole vessel and cargo, rather than just a portion of a particular hold. As merchants progressed from wanting a share in a ship or a voyage to owning a share in a company over the course of the seventeenth century, the company gained a steady working capital. As distances stretched well beyond the near-beyond—notably the voyage to India—northern European rulers granted joint-stock charters. But the joint-stock form ordered Atlantic trade as much as it did Asian, establishing an exclusive trade to and from America and founding colonies.[38]

Despite the obvious benefits, the idea of vesting absolute control in the ruler over trade fell into disrepute in almost every Atlantic empire, albeit more rapidly in northern than in southern Europe. During the seventeenth century, overseas traders challenged legal or de facto monopolies by promoting a more associational approach to transatlantic enterprise. Proprietors, family firms, and partnerships rose to the fore. Largely free of state control, they pushed into the Atlantic in pursuit of riches, even as monopolizing monarchs, privileged guilds, and chartered companies struggled to shut them out.

Sole proprietors had a smaller presence and influence in southern Europe's empires; crowded out by large port *consulados*, they did not enter much into Spanish overseas trading until the first half of the eighteenth century. In Portugal, private merchants were allowed freer rein overseas, but that was squelched in 1649 with the founding of the Lisbon-based Companhia Geral, which strove to bar them from Brazil, their most lucrative Atlantic market. Over a century later, Pombal established similar monopolies over trade between the mainland and Brazil to keep the English from dominating Brazilian commerce. In contrast to their southern peers, French, Dutch, and English merchants always operated more independently and prominently in the transatlantic marketplace, as in their respective Newfoundland fisheries during the sixteenth century and their thinly settled American colonies in the seventeenth. Monopoly sustained none of these endeavours.[39] By the eighteenth century, private initiative was generally considered effective and desirable, and individual traders had come to dominate

---

[38] E. E. Rich, *Hudson's Bay Company, 1670–1870*, 3 vols. (New York, 1960); Leonard Blusse and Femme Gaastra (eds.), *Companies and Trade* (Hingham, MA, 1981); Ann M. Carlos and Stephen Nicholas, 'Theory and History: Seventeenth Century Joint-Stock Chartered Trading Companies', *Journal of Economic History*, 56 (1996), 916–24.

[39] Jorge Miguel Pedreira, 'Tratos e contratos: actividades, interesses e orientações dos investimentos dos negociantes da praça de Lisboa (1755–1828)', *Análise social*, 31 (1996), 355–79; António Barros Cardoso, *Baco & Hermes: o porto e o comércio interno e externo dos vinho do Douro (1700–1756)*, 2 vols. (Porto, 2003).

Atlantic commerce. Sole proprietors were independent agents who controlled most decision-making and possessed sufficient capital; they constituted the most numerous set of overseas traders.[40]

A firm or partnership was little more than a group of proprietors that represented a pooling of talent, effort, property, capital, and connection. In its simplest form—the family firm—members were linked by blood or marriage, and, during the course of the eighteenth century, family firms became 'the outstanding force in private economic enterprise'. The virtue of the family firm was that it was ad hoc in inception, indeed in legality, for no legal documents spelled out its creation, management, capitalization, and duration. It was generational in organization and succession, its head the source and dispenser of capital and the arbiter of disputes. In principle, all members were expected to contribute, with profits being ploughed back into firm capital or apportioned among members according to tradition or need. But the family firm was also beset by problems, principally discord between close relatives.[41]

Compared to family firms (and large companies), private partnerships were managed with 'more facility, and frequently . . . skill, prudence, and economy'. In large measure, they were more malleable: they could be 'general' (contracted 'for a long course of dealing and extending to a large stock or capital in trade') or 'special' (formed for 'a particular concern' or 'a single dealing or adventure').[42] Their most striking feature was size: few had more than four partners. Furthermore, neither licence nor charter was needed to form them—merely 'the bare consent' of those involved. A variety of partnerships were struck: some were combinations of equals, with tasks and returns evenly divided; others divided shares, responsibilities, or profits unevenly; still others were dominated by one individual in association with passive or 'dormant' senior or junior partners. Complementarity of business strengths—either geographical or operational—was probably the strongest force binding them together, enabling them to vie effectively with quasi-state organizations. In a world roiled by fluctuations in demand and supply, merchants wanted regular outlets and sources. They accordingly chose as partners other merchants who had knowledge of regions, commodities, and services of which they knew little.[43]

---

[40] K. G. Davies, *The Royal African Company* (London, 1957); John Carswell, *The South Sea Bubble* (London, 1960).

[41] Frederic C. Lane, *Venice and History: The Collected Papers of Frederic C. Lane* (Baltimore, MD, 1966), 36–7; Mary B. Rose, 'Networks, Values and Business: The Evolution of British Family Firms from the Eighteenth to the Twentieth Century', *Entreprises et histoire*, 22 (1999), 16–30.

[42] William Watson, *A Treatise of the Law of Partnership* (2nd edn. London, 1807), xxiii, 1, 3–6, 11, 17, 46, 54–5, 63.

[43] David Hancock, *Citizens of the World: London Merchants and the Integration of the British Atlantic Community, 1735–1785* (Cambridge, 1995), 9–10; Richard B. Sheridan, *Sugar and Slavery: An Economic History of the British West Indies, 1623–1775* (Baltimore, MD, 1974), 299, 389–486; Philippe Gardey, 'Négociants et marchands de Bordeaux de la guerre d'Amérique à la Restauration (1780–1830)' (Ph.D. thesis, Université Paris IV-Sorbonne, 2006); Bernard Bailyn, *The New England Merchants in the Seventeenth Century* (Cambridge, MA, 1955), ix; Phyllis W. Hunter, *Purchasing Identity in the Atlantic World: Massachusetts Merchants, 1670–1780* (Ithaca, NY, 2001), 3; Cathy Matson, *Merchants & Empire: Trading in Colonial New York* (Baltimore, MD, 1997), 3–4, 334 n. 5.

Even so, traders' ideas of how overseas trade should be managed changed. In the late seventeenth century, there was seldom enough business to specialize by commodity or type of goods; so, even if merchants had a general focus or interest, realistically they traded whatever was available. After acquiring some capital and attaining some custom, merchants typically integrated downstream, buying and selling shares in ships and cargoes. This pattern persisted through the early nineteenth century. But, by then, some merchants, especially those in cities, had definitely begun to specialize in commodities or regions.[44]

In managing increasingly complex business operations, overseas merchants maintained correspondences with supplier-purchasers and purchaser-suppliers around the Atlantic rim and deep into its hinterland. Much of the initiative for correspondence came from Europeans, who had several options. A firm could form a transactional relationship with a merchant overseas, who would conduct business for it and then charge the firm a small percentage for doing so. Alternatively, if no trusted correspondent was found, it could send a partner or factor to America to manage the transaction, thereby forgoing payment of any commission fee. A third option developed after 1675: the firm could bypass merchants and directly form quid pro quo relations with customers. During the eighteenth century, specialist brokers dealing in shipping, insurance, and bills also emerged and facilitated the work of the commission houses proliferating in Europe. As the eighteenth century closed, American traders gained increasing amounts of capability and parity, adopting many of the roles that Europeans had traditionally played. However, in one-on-one relationships with Europeans they seldom gained the upper hand.[45]

How did Atlantic commodity trading change between 1402 and 1815? Commerce was initially tied to commodity extraction, and products were precious metals, rare dye-stuffs, and the like—all goods with high value-to-volume ratios. Moreover, the organization was highly centralized, either nationalized or ordered through crown-sponsored companies. Given the large amounts of capital required to extract metals and dyestuffs and their high market value which invited foreign predation, state support was required to defend the trade. Iberians dominated early Atlantic commerce, and the Spanish developed the overarching imperial model. Portuguese products were less valuable and therefore less attractive to predators, which may explain why they adopted Spain's model only fitfully in the first and second centuries of Atlantic empire.

---

[44] Jacob M. Price, 'What Did Merchants Do? Reflections on British Overseas Trade, 1660–1790', *Journal of Economic History*, 49 (1989), 267–84; Hancock, *Citizens*.

[45] Sheridan, *Sugar and Slavery*, 319, 322; Linda R. Baumgarten, 'The Textile Trade in Boston, 1650–1700', in Ian M. Quimby (ed.), *Arts of the Anglo-American Community in the Seventeenth Century* (Charlottesville, VA, 1975), 224–6; Jacob M. Price, *Capital and Credit in British Overseas Trade: The View from the Chesapeake, 1700–1776* (Cambridge, MA, 1980); Jacob Price, 'The Rise of Glasgow in the Chesapeake Tobacco Trade, 1707–1775', *William and Mary Quarterly*, 11 (1954), 179–99; Dennis J. Maika, 'Commerce and Community: Manhattan Merchants in the Seventeenth Century' (Ph. D. thesis, New York University, 1995), 83, 91, 93, 96; Kenneth Morgan, 'The Organization of the Colonial American Rice Trade', *William and Mary Quarterly*, 52 (1995), 441; David Hancock, *Oceans of Wine: Madeira and the Emergence of American Trade and Taste* (New Haven, CT, 2009).

The Spanish imperial model imploded after 1600, when the focus of empires shifted from extraction to cultivation. Sugar, tobacco, rice, wheat, fur, and fish now comprised the mainstay of traders and policy-makers alike, bullion having receded. American agricultural productivity rose dramatically, as more European settlers tilled more cropland. The products of note were no longer mined but farmed, and their value-to-volume ratio was lower. Without denying its staying power for Spain, the viability of the imperial model elsewhere was constantly questioned, allowed to collapse, and gradually replaced. By 1815, the requirements of cultivation were not so much capital-intensive as labour-intensive, colonial agriculture demanding a fairly high range of labour, which was performed by a mix of free adventurers, indentured servants, free blacks, and enslaved blacks and indigenes. The organization of the trade in products like coffee had become less centralized by the nineteenth century and, in many cases, markedly decentralized. Spain's model had been developed in response to sixteenth-century conditions; its trade was a function of the value of, the capital intensity of, and the security requirement of, metals and dyestuffs. In contrast, the trades of the northern European states and empires, which became of equal consequence only some centuries later, were built on goods less valuable per ton. Since their crop production in America was less capital-intensive but more labour-intensive than earlier Iberian endeavours, they had both less need for protection of trading vessels and routes and less requirement of complex trading organizations.

Ultimately, the logic of agriculture led to a looser form of regulation. Even when the empires competed heavily with each other and enacted contravening legal systems in the seventeenth century—l'exclusif and the Navigation Acts—the systems were less regulatory, their management less thoroughgoing, and their implementation less heavy-handed than had been the case with Spain. But it was not just a case of commercial agriculture dictating organizational looseness and openness and tolerating, indeed promoting, individual initiative. The rather hybrid approach adopted by both Britain and France—the former more successfully than the latter—was a product both of their earlier experiences with the North Atlantic fishery, and of their emergence at a time of great innovation in shipping, capital, and communication. Those fishing off Newfoundland and Massachusetts had enjoyed independence from the outset since they had set out to make their fortunes without assistance or interference from any crown. The effect of this experience continued to unfold gradually as the northern European Atlantic empires experimented with monopoly organizations only to discard them in favour of privileging private traders, who were better able to respond quickly and flexibly to, and flourish in, a situation which demanded more cultivation, more labour, less capital, and attracted fewer predators.

BIBLIOGRAPHY

Boxer, Charles R., *The Dutch Seaborne Empire, 1600–1800* (New York, 1965).
—— *The Portuguese Seaborne Empire, 1415–1825* (New York 1969).

Coclanis, Peter (ed.), *The Atlantic Economy during the 17th and 18th Centuries: Organization, Operation, Practice, and Personnel* (Columbia, SC, 2005).

Davis, Ralph, *The Rise of the English Shipping Industry in the Seventeenth and Eighteenth Centuries* (London, 1962).

Godinho, Vitorino, *L'Économie de l'empire portugais, XVe–XVIe siècles* (Paris, 1968).

Hancock, David, *Oceans of Wine: Madeira and the Emergence of American Trade and Taste* (New Haven, CT, 2009).

McCusker, John, and Russell Menard, *The Economy of British America, 1607–1789* (Chapel Hill, NC, 1985).

Meyer, Jean, Jean Tarrade, and Annie Rey-Goldzeiguer, *Histoire de la France coloniale*, i: *La Conquête, des origines à 1870* (Paris, 1996).

Parry, John, *The Spanish Seaborne Empire* (New York, 1970).

Postma, Johannes, and Victor Enthoven (eds.), *Riches from Atlantic Commerce: Dutch Transatlantic Trade and Shipping, 1585–1817* (Leiden, 2003).

Price, Jacob, *Capital and Credit in British Overseas Trade: The View from the Chesapeake, 1700–1776* (Cambridge, MA, 1980).

Sheridan, Richard, *Sugar and Slavery: An Economic History of the British West Indies, 1623–1775* (Baltimore, MD, 1974).

CHAPTER 20

....

PEOPLE AND PLACES
IN THE AMERICAS

A Comparative Approach

....

RICHARD L. KAGAN

WRITING in the wake of King George's War, Edmund Burke, together with his cousin, offered the first comparative analysis of European settlement patterns in the New World in his *Account of the European Settlement of America* (1757). Although Burke never crossed the Atlantic, he was still able to provide insights into the 'comparatively weak' state of Spanish settlement in New Mexico, the lack of 'towns and villages' in New France, together with the defects in James Oglethorpe's plan in Georgia to create a colony based on small, independent farms.

As it happens, Burke was not necessarily interested in settlement per se, but rather how patterns of settlement related to his ideas about liberty—one of his favourite subjects— and the state of commercial relations between colony and metropolis. However, his comments on the subject constitute a convenient starting point for this chapter, which, in addition to North America, will examine patterns of European settlement in selected portions of South and Central America.

The only comprehensive study of this subject is that found in D. W. Meinig's *The Shaping of the Americas* (1986), a brilliant geographical analysis of the peopling of North America in the course of the colonial area. Meinig had little to say about other parts of the Americas. On the other hand, his idea of comparing the 'blueprints' of particular areas of settlement—his choice was Jamestown, Quebec and Santa Fe, all settled in the opening years of the seventeenth century—is perhaps the best way to approach a topic that, given the diversity of settlement patterns, is difficult to summarize in the compass of a short essay.

The one inter-imperial study of settlement patterns in the Americas is Ralph Bennett's edited volume *Settlements in the Americas: Cross-Cultural Prospects* (1993). Bennett defines the 'act of settlement' as synonymous with 'cultural expression', whether English, Spanish, or French. The proposition is risky because it rests on cultural stereotypes such as the 'rigidity' of the Spaniards as opposed to the more 'ad hoc', free-wheeling English. The emphasis on 'national culture' in this analysis tends also to overwhelm the importance of other, more local factors relating to the environment, commerce, defensive considerations, relations with indigenous peoples, let alone the ability of colonial governors to implement policies relating to land use and the creation of towns.

John H. Elliott offers a far more nuanced approach to settlement in *Empires of the Atlantic World* (2006), a comparative study of the Spanish and British empires in the Americas. In a brilliant chapter, 'Occupying American Space', Elliott separates 'symbolic' from 'physical' occupation. He also avoids using 'national culture' as the basis of comparison. Rather, he argues that settlement was conditioned by a variety of local and regional factors that include existing patterns of indigenous settlement and land use, access to water and overseas markets, and the presence of important sources of mineral wealth, which, in the case of Peru, served to create a 'plunder economy' as opposed to one based on agriculture and trade. Elliott also recognizes differences conditioned by property law, royal policies regarding the emergence of large landlords, the role of chartered companies—virtually absent in Spanish and Portuguese America—and the impact of such institutions as the *encomienda* which granted the original Spanish settlers possession of people, in the sense of labour services and tribute, as opposed to land, and which required these settlers to live in towns. On balance, Elliott's book offers what is arguably the most imaginative and far-reaching comparative analysis of settlement patterns in the New World, yet he does so with a relatively broad brush.

Given the enormity of the subject, and as Elliott rightly suggests, the seemingly endless variety of local and regional settlement patterns, no single essay can do justice to the topic of comparative settlement in the Americas. Following Meinig, however, it is possible to identify certain overarching patterns—blueprints—that typified the different ways different empires organized American space. Few of these blueprints worked out as planned, although at the outset it was expected that settlers, following Old World practices, would organize themselves into contiguous communities—'ordered' towns in the case of the Spaniards; a 'compact and orderly village' as in Jamestown, or the type of 'compact' settlement that Champlain and others envisioned for New France. Very quickly, however, these plans went awry as settlers went off on their own, whether to engage in lucrative trade with the natives, as with much reviled 'bush-lopers' in New France, to hunt for slaves in the case of Brazil's notorious *bandeirantes*, or in Tidewater Virginia, where settlers, hoping to cash in on the lucrative trade in tobacco, dispersed in order to establish plantations of their own. In general, the Spanish and Portuguese colonies, and, to a certain degree, those of the Dutch, fared better with the problem of dispersion than either those of the English or the French, where, despite repeated attempts to establish nucleated settlements, the pull of the land proved irresistible. The question: why were the Iberians better able to maintain their original settlement blueprints than either the British or the French?

SPANISH AMERICA: PRIMACY OF TOWNS

Various theories have been adduced to explain this difference, including the strength of Iberia's deep-seated urban tradition, which stretched back to the time of the Romans, and which was neatly summarized at the start of the sixteenth century by one Spanish nobleman with the phrase: 'The country is a nice place to visit but not to live in.'[1] Only rarely, therefore, did noblemen live permanently on their estates. Instead they resided in towns, enjoying the benefits of urban life while leaving the day-to-day management of their holdings to others. Dispersed patterns of land ownership reinforced the strength and vitality of this urban tradition as noblemen were content to manage their estates through surrogates rather than abandon the palaces they constructed in towns.

Such was the tradition that Spanish settlers, starting in the 1490s, carried with them to the New World. It helps also to explain why these settlers, unlike their British counterparts in New England, had little inclination to establish themselves as small-holders residing in villages similar to those they left behind. The famed Dominican friar Bartolomé de Las Casas envisioned this kind of settlement society as the best way to protect native rights and end the abuses associated with the *encomienda*, but his attempt in 1519 to create such a colony ended in failure, as did others the monarchy sought to promote. Most Spanish émigrés gravitated towards towns, leaving the countryside to natives from whom they exacted labour services and tribute.

From the outset, therefore, Spain's New World empire was destined to became an 'empire of towns', the majority of which, following the grid-iron design of Puerto de Santa María and other towns in southern Spain, were built, chequerboard fashion, around a central plaza and endowed with a measure of self-government. The first of these 'ordered' towns was Santo Domingo (founded 1501) on the island of Hispaniola. Others soon followed—over 240 by 1580—and by the end of the sixteenth century the majority of Spanish émigrés to the Americas—a number somewhere between 200,000 and 250,000 by 1600—were living in, or immediately adjacent to towns, the largest of which were Mexico City and Lima (Figure 20.1). The creation of new towns lasted well into the eighteenth century, by which time even what is now the south-western United States was dotted with towns, each serving as places of refuge as well as vital centres of government, religion, commerce, and exchange.

In most cases, these Spanish towns appropriated existing indigenous settlements, as in the example of Mexico City, which was built atop the ruins of the Aztec capital of Tenochtitlan, and Cuzco, in the highlands of Peru, which stood astride the former Inca capital. In these cities, as in other towns established in areas previously subject to Aztec or Inca rule, *encomenderos* (holders of *encomiendas*), with the help of native chieftains (*caciques*), established themselves at the receiving end of tribute systems that were already in place at the time of their arrival. Spaniards, therefore, had little reason to

---

[1] As cited in Richard L. Kagan, *Urban Images of the Hispanic World, 1493–1793* (London, 1999), 19.

FIGURE 20.1 Starting with the foundation of Santo Domingo on the island of Hispaniola in 1501, Spain's possessions in the Americas took the form of an 'empire' of self-governing towns. The majority of people lived in or immediately adjacent to these communities. This map illustrates the principal town settlements in the Spanish New World. After Richard L Kagan, *Urban Images of the Atlantic World, 1492–1793* (New Haven and London: Yale University Press, 1999), p. 29.

abandon these safe urban havens. It follows that in such areas as Oaxaca in Mexico, efforts to persuade Spaniards to live outside the city of Antequera brought few results.

Starting in the 1540s, the monarchy extended its town-based model of empire by herding natives living in scattered hamlets into larger, more urbanized communities. The rationale underlying these native settlements—called *reducciones*, after the Spanish verb *reducir*, to reduce and thus perfect, as if a cook was preparing a fine sauce—was to promote the conversion of natives to Christianity and a more Spanish way of life. As in the case of the *reducciones* created by the Jesuits in what is now Paraguay (and immortalized in the 1986 British film *The Mission*), the religious orders envisioned resettlements as part of a separate 'Indian republic' subject only to their jurisdiction and control. In most instances, however, authorities established *reducciones* near (or, in the case of Lima, inside of) Spanish towns with an eye towards supplying town-dwellers with easy access to native labour, a much-valued commodity at a time when the indigenous population was in rapid decline. Yet few of these *reducciones* worked as planned, as natives abandoned them to return to their traditional habitats, or, more commonly, moved into neighbourhoods (*barrios*) located on the outskirts of towns occupied primarily by Spaniards. Over time ready access to native labour served to prevent Spaniards from abandoning towns and drifting off into the countryside, as many of their counterparts in both New France and British America were so inclined to do. They also imparted to Spanish towns a multi-racial flavour lacking in such places as Boston, Philadelphia, or Montreal. At the end of the seventeenth century, for example, the population of Lima, capital of Spanish Peru, stood at *c*.80,000, two-thirds of which consisted of natives, mestizos, and blacks.

Environmental factors also served to keep Spaniards—and their American-born descendants, the creoles—living in towns. In North America, climate, fertile soil, and easy access to riverine and maritime transport combined to foster the movement of the settler population into the back country. Such factors were absent in much of Spanish America. Yet the discovery of abundant mineral resources in northern Mexico and the highlands of Peru did serve to draw settlers into the interior, and led to the emergence of various mining towns, the most famous of which were Potosí (in the Andes) and Zacatecas (in northern New Spain). Making use of native labour, and to a lesser degree imported African slaves, Spanish mine owners had few incentives to surrender the comforts and camaraderie, not to mention the sense of security and protection, offered by urban life.[2]

The preferences of Spanish ranchers were much the same. Starting already in the sixteenth century the monarchy sought to promote the rural economy in such regions as the Bajío in central New Spain as well as coastal areas of Peru. Here, and elsewhere, small farmers and ranchers, many of whom were mestizos—that is, Hispanic rather than Spanish—did live in small towns and villages, generally in close proximity with natives. However, Spaniards who acquired large *estancias* rarely lived permanently on

---

[2] For the importance of towns in colonial Mexico, see Ida Altman and James Lockhart (eds.), *Provinces of Early Mexico: Variants of Spanish Regional Evolution* (Los Angeles, CA, 1976).

their estates. Rather, in keeping with tradition, they shunted back and forth between their ranches and their town houses, generally spending as much time in the latter as in the country. Even then, ranchers brought the city into the country by marking the entrances to their holdings with post-and-lintel constructions that mimicked city gates. Presumably, these entrances were there to remind would-be intruders, especially 'barbaric' Indians still leading nomadic or semi-nomadic lives, that the rules governing these ranches were essentially those found in towns. In this way, Spaniards managed to urbanize even the frontiers of their empire and by the end of the colonial era their town-based model of the settlement was found well into the interior of the Americas, both North and South.

LUSO-AMERICA: CRABS ON THE SHORE

Portugal, like Spain, also had a strong urban tradition that manifested itself in such institutions as the *senado de câmara* (town or municipal council) and various charitable brotherhoods among which the most important was the Santa Casa de Misericordia (or Holy House of Mercy). But whereas Spain's empire in the Americas was predicated on territorial conquest and the creation of towns, Portugal's was rooted in trade. Thus with the exception of the small agricultural settlements established on Madeira and the other Atlantic islands in the course of the fifteenth century, the initial organizational node of Portugal's empire was the fortified trading 'factory', or *feitoria*, of which Arguim, São Jorge da Mina, and other places along the coast of West Africa were among the first. Serving principally as ports of call rather than nodes for conquests, *feitorias* were not very imposing, as they generally constituted little more than a stockaded enclave housing a garrison, a chapel, storehouses, and a few residences. Symbolically, however, they represented places of power, strongholds from which the Portuguese brokered what they called 'treaties of peace and friendship' with local chiefs. *Feitorias* also served as points of exchange, places where Portuguese traders could acquire slaves, spices, and other precious commodities.

Feitorias also marked the beginnings of Portugal's foothold in Brazil. It did not take long, however, before the monarchy decided to create a settlement colony similar to the one that Las Casas had envisioned for Venezuela. The policy began in 1532 when King John III empowered twelve noblemen—known as donatary captains—to administer portions of the colony, establish villages, and issue land grants (*sesmerias*) meant to attract settlers (or *moradores*) to coastal lands previously occupied by natives, many of whom, fearing enslavement, fled into the bush (*sertão* in Portuguese). In 1549, however, the lack of *moradores* prompted this same ruler to replace the donatary captains with a royal governor—Tomé da Sousa—who, in addition to having the power to grant *sesmerias*, was instructed to promote the local economy through the creation of sugar plantations. He was further instructed to promote the development of towns, and promptly did so by transforming an existing *feitoria* of Salvador da Bahia into the colony's capital.

What followed was a pattern of settlement—call it a blueprint—that lasted for well over a century and is best characterized by Fray Vicente do Salvador's seventeenth-century description of Portuguese settlers as crabs who rarely ventured beyond the shore. In this instance, what the crabs liked was sugar—Brazil's El Dorado—and they migrated principally to the narrow coastal belt between Pernambuco and Bahia where this crop was most easily cultivated, albeit with the assistance of increasing numbers of slaves imported from Africa. By 1587 the Portuguese who had moved to Brazil lived mostly in coastal settlements scattered along the coast from Maranhão in the north to São Vicente in the south. The largest concentration, numbering some 10,000–12,000 inhabitants, lived in Bahia. Of these at least one-half resided in Salvador, the remainder—planters (or *senhores de engenhos*), sharecroppers known as *lavradores*, and their retainers—lived in the *Recôncavo*, the name for lands immediately adjacent to All Saints Bay and connected to Salvador by water. Here, as one observer wrote, 'The majority of people live outside [the town] on their *engenhos* and *haciendas*.' Yet very few of the largest *senhores de engenhos* resided on their estates outside the busy harvest season or *safra*. Rather they gravitated towards Salvador, where, in addition to maintaining a residence, they took part in the affairs of the *senado de câmara*, the Casa de Misercordia, and, starting in the seventeenth century, the construction of that city's elaborate array of Baroque churches and convents. The residence patterns of planters in Pernambuco, centred on the town of Olinda, were much the same.[3]

In this respect, the settlement colony that emerged in coastal Brazil had much in common with that of the Carolina Low Country, another plantation society where planters divided their time between the port of Charlestown, the regional entrepôt, and their plantations, most of which were easily accessible by water.[4] Towns in this sense occupied a position in Portuguese America comparable to that in Spanish America. Unlike the Spaniards, however, who established towns throughout their colonies, the Portuguese were relatively slow to move inland and establish towns in the *sertão* until the discovery of gold at the end of the seventeenth century in the region that came to be known as Minas Gerais (Figure 20.2).

To be sure, the settlement of the *sertão* did not occur overnight. Starting already in the sixteenth century, the coastal belt depended upon the *sertão* for meat, hides, and other products such as cacao, many of which were obtained through barter from natives. Itinerant traders were therefore a regular presence in the interior while other, more adventurous types prospected for gold, silver, and other sources of mineral wealth. There were also the fearsome *bandeirantes*, who ventured inland in search of Indian captives to be sold as slaves. Sustained penetration of the interior proceeded

[3] For Bahia, see Stuart B. Schwartz, *Sugar Plantations in the Formation of Brazilian Society, 1550–1835* (Cambridge, 1985).

[4] For South Carolina, see Max S. Edelson, *Plantation Enterprise in Colonial South Carolina* (Cambridge, MA, 2006).

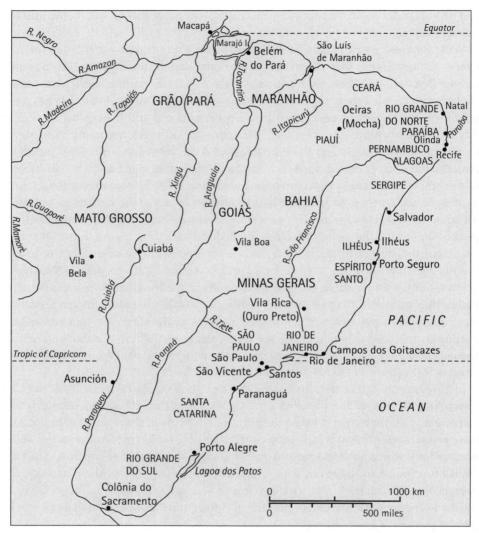

FIGURE 20.2 Until the late seventeenth-century, most Portuguese Settlers in Brazil resided in a long ribbon that stretched along the colony's Atlantic Coast. The Late seventeenth-century discovery of gold in Minas Gerais drew them into the interior and led to the foundation of Vila Rica and other inland towns. After *Cambridge History of Latin America*, ed. Lesley Bethell (Cambridge: Cambridge University Press, 1984), vol. 2 p. 422.

slowly, and only in the seventeenth century did émigrés from Bahia push inland and establish a series of thinly populated cattle ranches along the banks of rivers such as São Francisco. At this stage, the only signs of urbanization in the *sertão* were the mission settlements (*aldeias*) that the Jesuits had established with royal support, and the communities of runaway slaves known as *quilombos*. The *aldeias* resembled

Spain's *reducciones*, as well as the 'praying towns' established by John Eliot in seventeenth-century New England, to the extent that they aimed at hastening the natives' conversion to Christianity and to a more European way of life. As for the *quilombos*, most were small, itinerant communities; others, notably the 'Negro republic' of Palmares, were relatively stable and housed several thousand inhabitants spread over a considerable area.

The first truly Portuguese towns established in the interior formed part of the monarchy's effort to instil a degree of order into the California-like gold rush sparked by gold strikes in Minas Gerais in 1693. Between 1700 and 1760, more than 500,000 settlers from Portugal and the Atlantic Islands emigrated to Brazil, and of these tens of thousands, accompanied by slaves and free persons of colour, pushed into the interior hoping to strike it rich. These newcomers soon clashed with existing prospectors. Violence ensued, and in an effort to end the fighting, as well as the smuggling that denied the monarchy its rightful share of gold, the governor of Rio de Janeiro transformed a series of mining camps into the townships, the largest of which, Vila Rica (founded 1711), became the region's first capital. Mariana (founded 1745) and other towns followed, but given its enormous size, the *sertão* remained thinly settled. Farmers, or *roceiros*, were relatively few as compared with adventurers and itinerants practising native-style slash-and-burn agriculture, let alone the inhabitants of the *quilombos*, whose livelihood centred on smuggling, raiding native villages for captives, and occasional dealing in cocoa beans, vanilla, and the so-called *drogas de sertão*. The presence of these itinerants, collectively known as *vadios*, the Portuguese term referring to individuals 'not rooted in the land', prompted the monarchy in 1766 to issue a decree compelling all 'vagabonds' in the *sertão* 'to live together in civil townships' of at least fifty households. Small land grants were to serve as the lure, while those who refused to join these communities were to be treated as 'highwaymen and common enemies'. This decree, together with others designed to shepherd natives into *aldeias*, met only with limited success, but it speaks directly to the continuing importance of towns in Portugal's imperial *imaginaire*.[5]

The wealth and excitement generated by the *sertão* in the course of the eighteenth century was certainly important, but compared to the ongoing strength of the colony's sugar-based economy, it did little to alter the basic pattern of settlement that dated from Brazil's earliest years. At the end of the eighteenth century at least half of the Portuguese residing in Brazil still lived in coastal areas. There, true to Fray Vicente do Salvador's description of his fellow countrymen, they still lived like crabs, huddling close to the shore, but this blueprint had less to do with natural instincts than environmental factors and the power of sugar to keep settlers close to the coast.

---

[5] Hal Langfur, *The Forbidden Lands: Colonial Identity, Frontier Violence, and the Persistence of Brazil's Eastern Indians, 1750–1830* (Palo Alto, CA, 2006).

THE FRENCH ATLANTIC: THE LURE
OF THE WOODS

The French, in comparison, proved more adventurous, especially in North America or what is now Canada. In this region El Dorado wore fur. Just as gold lured Spaniards to venture far from the coast, the lucrative trade in pelts persuaded French settlers to move inland. It also led to a string of fortified trading posts along the banks of the St Lawrence, the most important of which were Quebec, established by Samuel de Champlain in 1608, and Montreal. Champlain's dream was to find a North-West Passage to China, but in the interim he suggested that the French monarchy create a 'compact' settlement colony centred on Ludovica, a town he named in honour of France's ruling monarch, Louis XIII.

Champlain's dream, known as New France, went unrealized. To begin with, settlers were scarce. In 1627, for example, fewer than 100 Frenchmen, working primarily as fur traders, lived in the colony. The monarchy's response was to charter the Compagnie de Nouvelle France, and grant its shareholders a perpetual monopoly over the fur trade upon the condition that they convert the 'sauvages' to Christianity and populate the colony with 4,000 peasant farmers in the course of fifteen years. So began a scheme whereby the new company granted wealthy *seigneurs* large tracts of land fronting the St Lawrence. Numbering about seventy, these *seigneurs* were to recruit 'natural-born Frenchmen' of Catholic origins by subdividing their holdings into smaller tracts (*cenistaires*) with access to a mill, storehouses, and a church. The company, however, was not much better at persuading settlers to move to Canada than Champlain, nor to create the kind of town-based pattern of settlement the monarchy had envisioned. What emerged was an elongated pattern of settlement, stretched narrowly along the banks of the river between Quebec and Montreal, a distance of less than 200 miles. Compact settlements, however, were few, as settlers lived mostly in isolated dwellings and used the river as the chief means of transport, trade, and exchange.

Even then, the colony, especially when compared with contemporaneous developments in nearby New England, failed to prosper. In 1663, the settler population stood only at 4,000, and, organizationally too, the colony was in disarray. The Company attempted to protect its monopoly over the fur trade by forging alliances with the Huron and other local tribes, but its officials could do little to prevent individual settlers from going off into the woods to barter directly with the natives. Such was the origin of 'bush-lopers' or *couriers de bois*, many of whom, lacking French women to marry, 'went native', dressing and living like Hurons and even taking Huron women as wives, much to the dismay of Jesuits and other friars seeking to 'Frenchify' the natives and convert them to Christianity. According to one royal official, bush-loping served also to 'depopulate the country of the best men ... [It also] renders them indocile, incapable of discipline, debauched, and causes their children to be brought up like savages.'[6]

To provide a remedy for bush-loping and also provide the colony a much needed boost, in 1663 Louis XIV abolished the Compagnie de Nouvelle France, appointed a governor general who was to reside in Quebec, and ceded overall responsibility for the colony's management to his energetic minister Jean-Baptiste Colbert. So began a new plan to downplay the fur trade and reorganize the colony's economy around forest products, seal oil, and fish, much of which was to be exported to the monarchy's newly established French colonies in the Caribbean. As for the shortage of population, Colbert believed that 'the greatest obstacle to the peopling of Canada had its roots in the freedom of the settlers to live where they pleased'.[7] In his view 'scattered settlements', were also dangerous because they needlessly exposed their inhabitants to indigenous attack. He therefore returned to Champlain's idea of a 'compact' settlement and proposed that New France be reorganized around several large, ordered villages (or *bourgades*) established on lands expropriated from the Jesuits. As for settlers, Colbert proposed recruiting them from the ranks of the bush-lopers, whose free-wheeling trading practices were to be stopped. In Roman fashion, Colbert also instituted a scheme through which French soldiers would be rewarded with lands in the colony and another to export orphan girls—the so-called 'filles de France'—to Canada so that the new settlers would have French women to marry.

In the end Colbert succeeded in bringing more settlers to New France, although nothing on a scale comparable to the 'Great Migration' that New England enjoyed. Yet he failed to create anything that remotely resembled a compact settlement, let alone the development of any sizeable towns. At the end of the seventeenth century, Quebec, the colony's largest urban enclave, remained a ramshackle community with just over 600 inhabitants that, according to one visitor, was more like a 'humble village' than a city.

The main reason for the lack of urban development was the pull of the woods. The fur trade was far too profitable to be stopped, and several of the colony's governors, rather than forcibly resettling bush-lopers in towns, did just the opposite and encouraged their movement to the west and south-west by creating a string of fortified outposts-cum-trading posts in what are now Ontario, Ohio, Michigan, Illinois, and the Mississippi Valley as far south as St Louis, and eventually New Orleans. Yet this westward movement was never a mass movement and was minuscule in comparison to that of Minas Gerais. The core of New France remained the ribbon-like line of settlement along the banks of the St Lawrence. This line consisted of independent farmsteads—'straggled villages' according to one formulation—that were spaced about 100 to 200 metres apart and responsible for the tillage of lands that stretched back into the interior, eventually giving way to meadow and woods (Figure 20.3). These farms

---

[6] P. F. X. de Charlevoix, *Journal of a Voyage to North America* (London, 1761), 3: bk. 9, p. 93.
[7] Ibid. 93. For more on New France, see R. Cole Harris, *The Seigneurial System in Early Canada: A Geographical Study* (Madison, WI, 1961).

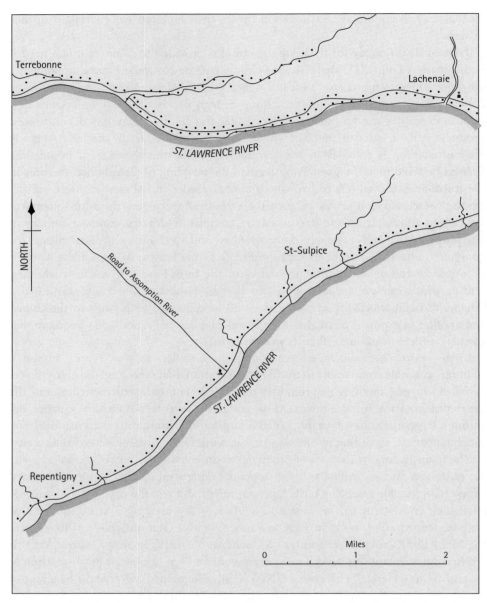

FIGURE 20.3 Despite efforts by the governors of New France to gather the colony's settlers in large, easily governed towns, many continued to reside in individual homesteads in a thin ribbon of 'straggled' villages located on both sides of the St Lawrence River. The map represents two of these villages in the mid eighteenth-century. After Richard C. Harris, *The Seigneurial System in Early Canada. A Geographical Study* (Madison: University of Wisconsin Press, 1961), p. 185.

were loosely connected to eight 'villages' that functioned as centres of worship, points of exchange, and the seat of government to the extent that they occasionally hosted a seigniorial court to resolve local disputes.

In 1763, when France ceded this colony to Britain, the total European population in New France stood only at 45,000, a number that paled in comparison with that of New England; nor could its farm- and timber-based economy even begin to compete with that of France's profitable, plantation-based island colonies in the Caribbean. Here too the original idea was to cluster settlers in a compact, well-defended town, but the relatively small size of both Martinique and Guadeloupe allowed for a settlement pattern that resembled those of the planters in Bahia to the extent that landowners could live independently on the estates yet still have access to the port towns of Fort-de-France (Martinique) and Basse-Terre (Guadeloupe). According to Pérotin-Dumon, the latter had important administrative and religious functions, but the town's white population—a measly 320 in 1671—accounted only for a minuscule fraction of the roughly 9,000 whites then living in Guadeloupe.[8] The distribution of settlers in Saint-Domingue, the largest French colony in the Caribbean, was much the same. In 1789, whites in this colony numbered just over 30,000 (as compared to well over 400,000 slaves), but, again, most lived on their estates. The island's capital, Port-au-Prince, with only 1,800 whites was a 'Tartar Camp' in the eyes of one visitor whereas the largest town, Cap-Français, with 3,600 (out of a total population of 16,000) was hyperbolically described as the 'Paris of the Antilles'.

In the end, the settlement patterns that developed in France's New World colonies had little to do with their original blueprints. Local adaptations prevailed, and the differences between the 'straggled villages' of New France and the dispersed plantations of the Caribbean suggest that the role of national culture and inherited tradition had little influence upon the ways in which émigrés occupied the land. Other 'on the ground' factors proved far more important, especially those relating to ecology, the presence (or absence in the Antilles) of an indigenous population, and finally the availability and accessibility of open land.

DUTCH AMERICA: ISLANDS OF SETTLEMENT

Dutch merchants and traders made their presence felt in the Americas well before the West Indies Company or WIC (created in 1621) elected to establish settler colonies of its own. The first but by no means the most successful of these colonies was New

---

[8] Anne Pérotin-Dumon, *La Ville aux îles, la ville dans l'île: Basse-Terre at Point-à-Pitre, Guadeloupe, 1650–1820* (Paris, 2000), 120. For Saint-Domingue, see David Geggus, 'The Major Port Towns of Saint Domingue in the Later Eighteenth Century', in Franklin W. Knight and Peggy Liss (eds.), *Atlantic Port Cities: Economy, Culture and Society in the Atlantic World, 1650–1800* (Baltimore, MD, 1991), 87–116.

Amsterdam, in what is now New York, but the WIC also created New Holland, in north-eastern Brazil, and, following the end of that colony in 1654, others in Guyana (after 1656) and several Caribbean islands, the most prosperous of which was Curaçao. Settlement patterns differed in each, although, as they developed, settlers lived mostly in protected enclaves or 'islands' rather than fanning out, in the style of English settlers in colonial North America, across the land. Traditionally related to issues of national character, these 'islands', in many scholars' estimation, represent an offshoot of the WIC's initial refusal to embrace 'the conquest of land and people', a policy that was predicated in part by the relatively small size of the Netherlands as compared to Europe's other imperial powers. The founding charter of the WIC referred to the 'peopling of fruitful and unsettled parts', but the 'advancement' of trade, whether in slaves or any number of natural products, merited greater attention. In addition, the company, in keeping with the importance of maritime commerce in the Dutch early modern economy, favoured the establishment of coastal-based trading outposts as opposed to agriculture and prospecting for silver and gold.

The WIC first implemented this policy in New Netherland (established 1624). Having been granted a monopoly over the lucrative trade in furs and beaver pelts, the WIC established a series of fortified trading posts, among them one at Ft Amsterdam, at the southern tip of Manhattan Island, the other, Ft Orange, near Albany, but accessible to the sea via the Hudson River. The original inhabitants of these forts were soldiers and company employees, some of whom, while living inside or in close proximity to the forts, became farmers. The WIC, however, was singularly unsuccessful in attracting settlers to the colony, and in 1629, Ft Amsterdam had less than 300 inhabitants, Ft Orange no more than thirty.

That same year, in a move reminiscent of Portugal's decision to divide Brazil into hereditary captaincies, the WIC voted to offer large grants of land, in perpetuity, to individual landlords (or *patroons*) upon the condition that they recruit a specified number of settlers to the struggling colony. In exchange, the *patroons* received exclusive fur-trading rights within their particular domain. But of the six patroonships granted, only three were actually settled, and of these, only one, Rensselaerswijck near Ft Orange, succeeded in attracting more than a handful of settlers. Further reforms came in 1638, when, again with an eye towards bringing more Dutchmen to the colony, the trading monopolies granted the *patroons* were abolished, and individual settlers were allowed to traffic in furs. At this point, emigration from the Netherlands began to climb, although in 1674, when the Dutch ceded control of New Netherland to the British, the European population had only reached 9,000.

The decision to surrender New Amsterdam (as opposed to Curaçao and Guyana) speaks to the WIC's difficulties in 'peopling' the northern reaches of New Netherland, let alone the lands immediately adjacent to the Delaware River. The Dutch never developed a settlement blueprint, and certainly nothing comparable to Spain's ordered towns, or France's idea of a 'compact' settlement, or the patchwork of self-governing towns that the English, starting in the 1620s, were busily creating in New England. Except for those émigrés engaged in the lucrative fur trade with the Iroquois, most of the Dutch who settled in New Netherland were farmers living in independent home-steads clustered around fortified trading posts. Even then, settlement was haphazard, and only after a series of Indian raids in 1655 did the WIC order 'the colonists [to] settle themselves . . . in the manner of villages, towns, and hamlets as the English are in the habit of doing, and who thereby live more securely'.[9] The first tangible result of the new policy was Esopus (later Wiltwijck), the palisaded settlement established in 1657 by Peter Stuyvesant near what is now Kingston, NY. Yet even this little settlement failed to prosper, and when, in 1674, the Dutch ceded New Netherland to Britain, the colony's only real population centres were New Amsterdam with 2,500 inhabitants, and Beverwijck, near Ft Orange, with just short of 1,000.[10]

The history of New Netherland dovetails neatly with the experiences of Dutch colonies established in other parts of the Atlantic world. Consider, for example, the short-lived (1630–54) colony the WIC carved out by force of arms in Pernambuco in north-eastern Brazil. The predominantly Catholic Portuguese population had little sympathy with these Calvinist interlopers, let alone the Jews who were brought to the colony at the invitation of Johan Maurits, the colony's inspirational leader from 1637 until 1644. For this reason, few of the Dutch merchants who emigrated to Brazil—and there were never very many—showed much interest in living outside Recife, or Mauritsstad, the new town he created on a nearby island.

A similar pattern of settlement emerged in Curaçao, where the town of Willemstad served as the home of most of the Dutch merchants who emigrated to the island starting in 1634. It was much the same in Suriname (a Dutch colony established in 1667), a plantation colony inhabited mainly by African slaves. In 1684 the colony's European population was only about 1,000, most of whom were merchants and land-owners living in or immediately adjacent to Paramaribo, the port city that developed in the shadow of the fortified trading post known as Ft Zeelandia. The one exception was the cluster of Sephardic Jewish householders—some 232 by 1684—living in Jodens-avanne, a small settlement established on the bank of the Suriname River some fifty miles south of Paramaribo. The founders of this community were Jews who left Recife following that city's takeover by the Portuguese in 1654, but once in Jodensavanne, these Sephardim created yet another Netherlandish town, albeit one that was distinctly Jewish in character and governed by a *mahamad* (Jewish religious council) as opposed to a WIC official. Moreover, the Jodensavanne's largest landowners, the so-called 'plantation Jews', replicated the settlement patterns found in other Dutch colonies to the extent that they resided primarily in the town proper as opposed to their estates. It is tempting to attribute this clustering to the 'island' mentality that is supposedly

[9] As cited in Albert E. McKinley, 'English and Dutch Towns of New Netherland', *American Historical Review*, 6 (October 1900), 1–18: 5.

[10] For this colony, see Donna Merwick, *The Shame and the Sorrow: Dutch-American Encounters in New Netherland* (Philadelphia, PA, 2006), and Oliver A. Rink, *Holland on the Hudson* (Ithaca, NY, 1986).

characteristic of the Dutch, but in this instance it is best explained by religious factors together with the absence of inland forts whose presence might have offered Jodensavanne's inhabitants shelter from the occasional raids mounted by runaway slaves (*bosnegers* in Dutch).

BRITISH AMERICA: AMBITION AND ADJUSTMENT

Towns—and the absence of towns—loomed large in the 'planting' of British North America. Colonial planners, starting with Walter Raleigh, envisioned that towns, as in England, would serve as the basic organizational unit of colonial society, providing settlers with a measure of security against native raids in addition to serving as places of residence, commerce, government, and religion. As in Spanish America, towns also served as symbolic markers of civilization in what was otherwise regarded as a 'desert-wilderness'. And in the case of John Eliot's 'praying towns' in western Massachusetts, they doubled as places in which 'savage' Indians could more easily be taught to live, work, and worship like Englishmen.

Yet colonial planners had to contend with local and regional factors that reduced the importance of towns in some areas, notably Tidewater Virginia, but guaranteed them a key role in New England. Even then, almost nothing worked out as planned. The Massachusetts Bay Company originally envisioned a colony organized around a single town in which settlers would be essentially servants, working lands on the company's behalf. Settlers, however, saw themselves as 'sole proprietors', independent farmers who, in keeping with the ideals of England's enclosure movement, endeavoured to 'improve' the land through agriculture, an ideal that the Company promoted by granting small groups of settlers permission to hive themselves off from existing towns and establishing others on lands emptied of their native inhabitants, either through purchase or forcible seizure. So began a somewhat ad hoc process of serial town settlement that, in the absence of a standardized blueprint, was largely determined by such environment factors as the suitability of the land for tillage or access to riverine transport. Otherwise, the only real constraint on this hiving-off process was the danger of native attack, but even this threat diminished starting in the 1660s with the establishment of the strategic alliances with native groups and construction of a string of frontier forts along the Connecticut River and other inland sites (Figure 20.4). These forts were originally designed to ward off incursions by the French and their native allies, but land-hungry New Englanders took advantage of the protective shield they offered by pushing further inland and establishing 'incorporated' towns wherever they chose to settle.

These 'towns' had little in common with those established either in Spanish America or Brazil, most of which were compact, densely settled communities and, especially in Spanish America, 'ordered' in terms of the layout of their streets and location of their main buildings. These towns were also polychromatic to the extent

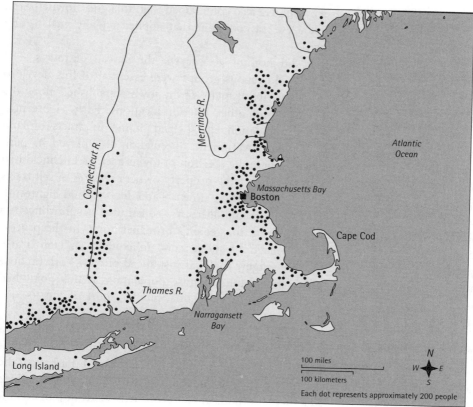

FIGURE 20.4 Having moved out of their original settlements around Massachusetts Bay, the expanding settler population in colonial New England founded new townships along coastal lowlands and accessible river valleys. Subsequently, the remainder of the region was 'filled in' on lands cleared of their native inhabitants. This map represents English settlements in New England *c.* 1675. After Stephen J. Hornsby, *British Atlantic, New Frontier. Spaces of Power in Early Modern British America* (Hanover and London: University Press of New England, 2005), p. 130.

that Iberians and their creole offspring were commonly outnumbered by an ever-increasing and changing mixture of natives, mestizos, and blacks. In contrast, New England towns, similar to the 'townlands' that English settlers established in Ireland, are best described as 'townships' whose inhabitants—most of whom came from European stock—occupied independent homesteads spread out over a large area as opposed to a well-defined urban centre with a distinct shape. New Haven (founded 1638) was planned in accordance with a grid, but with the exception of a town green, the New England town was less of an *urbs*, or built structure, than a *civitas* or *res publica*, a political-cum-juridical community that gathered periodically in the town hall to conduct business, resolve disputes, and to socialize. Churches also served as gathering points, but with reference to Watertown (Massachusetts) Edward Johnson recognized that the town's 'fruitful plat' allowed its 609 families to 'scatter', leaving its 'sabbath assemblies . . . very thin'. He also complained that 'this great towne has to shewe nothing delightful to the eye', a comment that applied equally well to any number of New England towns.[11]

Lack of planning, however, did nothing to prevent the spread of towns. The alliances that settlers forged with indigenous groups were essential to this development. So too was the relative prosperity of many of the towns established along the reaches of the Connecticut Valley and other interior locations. Early eighteenth-century increases in the settler population also helped 'filling in' tracts of land previously outside the orbit of town government. Speculation also played its part, especially in western Connecticut, where the creation of towns such as Litchfield had less to do with collective enterprise than large property owners seeking to sell tracts of land to individual settlers. Together these towns—and by the mid-eighteenth century most of New England was already 'filled-in'—constituted a sprawling network of trade and exchange centred on the region's principal ports. In the process Boston evolved from an 'urban village' of about 7,000 inhabitants in 1700 into a respectable town of 25,000 in 1760, a figure that was just ahead of New York (21,000) and the North American giant, Philadelphia, whose population at this point had reached 30,000, a figure comparable to that of Lima, but far short of the 100,000 inhabitants then residing in Mexico City.

Despite the many legends surrounding the much celebrated 'city on a hill', New England's town-based pattern of settlement was hardly typical of the British Atlantic world. In the Caribbean, especially the important sugar islands of Barbados and Jamaica, the settlement blueprint had far more in common with Bahia than anything north of Chesapeake Bay. Even then, no two islands were exactly alike. In Jamaica, the largest planters tended to be absentees who managed their estates with the help of 'attorneys', the majority of whom lived either in Spanish Town, the island's inland capital, or, increasingly, in Kingston, the major port.[12] In contrast, settlement in Barbados was quite different. Here plantations were not only smaller, but planters, starting soon after the colony's creation in 1627, fanned out across the land accompanied by servants and slaves. In 1647 Richard Ligon counted 285 adjacent plantations that climbed up, 'one above another, like several stories in stately buildings', along the island's sloping leeward coast. Planters in Barbados tended also to live on their estates, the most prosperous ones in large, elegant residences similar to those constructed along the Ashley and Cooper rivers in the Carolina Low Country. Carolina's planters lived primarily in Charleston, relying on overseers to manage their estates, whereas their counterparts in Barbados tended to avoid Bridgetown, the island's main port. According to Ligon, the 'bridge' had more taverns and warehouses than people, and he attributed its truncated development to its insalubrious location, but it also reflected

---

11 Edward Johnson, *A History of New England* (London, 1653), chapter xxii.
12 For this town, see James Robertson, *Gone is the Ancient Glory: Spanish Town, Jamaica, 1534–2000* (Kingston-Miami, FL, 2006).

the ability of planters, even those with inland properties, to use mule-drawn carts to transport goods to the sea with relative ease.[13]

The one place in British North America whose settler blueprint most closely resembled Barbados was Tidewater Virginia, and other lands immediately adjacent to Chesapeake Bay. In this region initial attempts at organizing a settlement colony around Jamestown ended, starting in the 1620s, with the introduction of tobacco and emergence of a series of riparian plantations that exported their harvests directly to Bristol, London, and other English ports. Abetting this changeover from a settlement to a plantation colony was the so-called 'head right' system, which initially granted 50 acres to each settler and an additional 50 for every family member or indentured servant who accompanied him.

To be sure, not every settler who went to Virginia became a planter. Some became hunters; others traders in the backwoods; a few even became 'white Indians' and lived in the 'sauvage's towns'. Yet the principal reason for settlers' failure to establish towns in Virginia was the ready availability of land along the James River and its tributaries, something that Edward Waterhouse recognized when he reported that ' the plantations . . . were placed straglingly and scatteringly, as a choice vein of rich ground invited them, and the further from neighbors held the better'.[14] Indian massacres of the 1620s brought a temporary stop to this development, but it picked up again by the middle of the seventeenth century, by which time the tobacco-based plantation economy encompassed those portions of Maryland bordering the Chesapeake. As a result the entire region shared what one observer described as an 'unhappy form of settlement' that, as Roger Green recognized in 1662, contributed to the lack of 'Christian neighborhood . . . [and] the benefit of Christian and civil conference and commerce'.[15]

The antidote: repeated but singular unsuccessful attempts on the part of Virginia's colonial managers to herd settlers into towns—first Jamestown, then Henricus (1622)— similar to those found in New England. In 1705, Robert Beverley attributed the planters' reluctance to abandon their 'straggling and distant habitations' to 'ambition', a term equivalent to what has been more recently characterized as the peculiar kind of 'possessive individualism' that separated settlers in Virginia (and the Caribbean) from the more communal-minded Puritan settlers of colonial New England. However, the patchwork design of the Tidewater probably had more to do with a regional ecology that facilitated direct trade between planters, both large and small, and ocean-going vessels that doubled as warehouses and stores. The kind of direct trade rendered towns, together with many of the services traditionally provided by merchants and

---

[13] Richard Ligon, *A True and Exact History of the Island of Barbados* (London, 1673), 21, 25.

[14] Edward Waterhouse, 'A Declaration of the Colonie and Affaires in Virginia' [1622], in S. M. Kingsbury (ed.), *Records of the Virginia Company of London* (London, 1906–39), iii. 550.

[15] Robert Beverley, *History and Present State of Virginia* (London, 1705), 47–8, and Roger Greene, *Virginia's Cure* (London, 1662), as cited in William S. Gaustad (ed.), *A Documentary History of Religion in America to 1877* (Grand Rapids, MI, 2003), 61.

shopkeepers, somewhat redundant. All this would change, however, once the Privy Council designated Williamsburg as the colony's capital in 1699. Government in turn worked as a magnet and served to transform what had been the somewhat sleepy former 'Middle Plantation' into the first Virginia settlement that approximated a town.

By the time of Williamsburg's creation, Virginians had embarked on a seemingly relentless march to the west into a somewhat protected pale of settlement that resulted from a series of strategic alliances with indigenous groups, and, secondarily, the establishment of a line of frontier forts along the Appalachian chain. In Virginia, however, the settlement of the back country followed a pattern markedly different from that of New England. In the Shenandoah Valley, for example, settlement began with hunters and traders whose livelihood and reputation—*banditti* in the view of George Washington—closely approximated the 'bush-lopers' of New France and the *vadios* of Minas Gerais. Settlers soon followed, although rather than create townships, the first homesteaders moved into widely dispersed independent farmsteads which constituted 'open-country' villages whose inhabitants occasionally gathered at a mill, roadside tavern, or ferry crossing to exchange goods and barter with itinerant traders. Eventually, barter gave way to more organized trade, sedentary merchants and shop-keepers, a few nucleated villages, and, starting in the eighteenth century, the appear-ance of incorporated towns—Winchester, founded in the 1720s, was one—that served as collection points, seats of local government and places of worship, and permanent places of residence. Compared with settlement blueprints of New England, not to mention Spain's 'empire of towns', the belated appearance of towns in Virginia rendered this colony distinctive.[16]

CONCLUSION

A brief essay cannot do justice to the seemingly endless variety of ways in which European settlers took possession of the Americas, both North and South. Imperial blueprints for settlement existed, and in most cases they called for compact, town-based colonies predicated on European practices. At the same time, these blueprints were adjusted, even rejected, as settlers gradually adapted themselves to both the challenges and the opportunities that new environments posed. As they developed, therefore, the patterns of settlement that emerged throughout the Atlantic are best viewed as a part of a protracted process of adaptation and adjustment as opposed to something 'hard-wired' into settlers' heads. Tradition mattered, but tradition, as in most things human, is the product of both invention and change.

[16] On the settlement of Virginia backwoods, see Warren Hofstra, *The Planting of New Virginia: Settlement and Landscape in the Shenandoah Valley* (Baltimore, MD, 2004).

BIBLIOGRAPHY

Bennet, Ralph, *Settlements in the Americas: Cross-Cultural Perspectives* (Newark, DE, 1993).

Burke, William, *An Account of the European Settlements in America* (London, 1777).

Daniels, Christine, and Michael V. Kennedy, *Negotiated Empires: Centers and Peripheries in the Americas, 1500–1820* (New York, 2002).

Elliott, John H., *Empires of the Atlantic World: Britain and Spain in America 1492–1830* (New Haven, CT, 2007).

Gerhard, Peter, *A Guide to the Historical Geography of New Spain* (Cambridge, 1972).

Hornsby, Stephen J., *British Atlantic, American Frontier: Spaces of Power in Early Modern British America* (Hanover, MD, 2005).

Lorimer, Joyce (ed.), *Settlement Patterns in Early Modern Colonization, 16th–18th Centuries* (Aldershot, 1998).

Meinig, D. L., *Shaping of America*, i: *Atlantic America, 1492–1800* (New Haven, CT, 1986).

CHAPTER 21

HOUSEHOLD FORMATION, LINEAGE, AND GENDER RELATIONS IN THE EARLY MODERN ATLANTIC WORLD

CAROLE SHAMMAS

HOUSEHOLDS did not figure prominently in the early Atlantic migration to the Americas. For military adventurers, planters, and free and unfree labourers, household formation had to begin anew, and that process frequently involved disrupting the domestic lives of indigenous populations who experienced either a conquest or an invasion of their territory. The opportunity for innovation in household structure, given the ethnicities, economies, and colonial regimes involved, was great. Western Europeans, West Africans, and American Indians differed among one another and among themselves over who should be in a household, under what terms, and even what a household was. Rules taken for granted in one society seemed a major deviation to another. How these differences got resolved in the Americas is not always clear and may have varied significantly depending on region. For many of us, the information we have is largely based on knowledge of one part, sometimes a very small part, of the two continents and nearby islands. Like the proverbial blind men and the elephant, how we conceptualize the colonial household depends heavily on what region we study.

The potential for differing versions of the early modern American family can be grasped best by looking at how the population had evolved towards the end of the colonial period. In Table 21.1, I present my best guess as to the racial classification of the population in each of the regions of the Americas circa the 1770s. The exact percentages offered here are debatable, as information on population is scanty and the evidence that

Table 21.1. Racial classification of the population in the Americas by region c.1770–1775

	Population in millions	% Indian	% European descent	% African descent and mulatto	% Mestizo
All Regions	15.155	48.3	25.1	21	5.6
North American mainland North of New Spain					
Canada	0.120	10	89	1	0
Northern British colonies	1.157	2	94	4	0
Southern British colonies	1.061	5	57	38	0
Settler-free North America	0.672	100	0	0	0
Mainland Latin America					
Settled borderlands[a]	0.138	87	11	2	0
Mexico[b]	3.091	65	16	9	10
Central America	0.900	60	18	4	18
Brazil	1.711	34	23	43	0
S. Amer. Sp. Colonies	4.725	70	15	7	8
Caribbean[c]	1.580	0	15	85	0

[a] Louisiana, Texas, Nuevo Mexico, and Alta California.
[b] Euromestizos and Afromestizos are included in the European descent and African American descent columns. Indomestizos are classified as mestizos.
[c] Also includes Suriname, French Guiana, and British Honduras.
Source: Michael R. Haines and Richard H. Steckel (eds.), A Population History of North America (Cambridge, 2000), passim; 'Colonial Statistics', in Susan B. Carter et al., The Millennial Edition of Historical Statistics of the United States (New York, 2006), v. 627–772; Robert V. Wells, The Population of the British Colonies in America before 1776 (Princeton, NJ, 1975), passim; Russell Thornton, American Indian Holocaust and Survival: A Population History since 1492 (Norman, OK, 1987), passim; Daniel H. Usner, 'American Indians in Colonial New Orleans', in Gregory A. Waselkov et al. (eds.), Powhatan's Mantle (Lincoln, NE, 2006), 176; Ramon A. Gutierrez, When Jesus Came, the Corn Mothers Went Away (Stanford, CA, 1991), 167; Steven W. Hackel, Children of Coyote, Missionaries of St Francis (Chapel Hill, NC, 2005), 21, 40–1; Colin McEvedy and Richard Jones, Atlas of World Population History (New York, 1978), passim; and Dauril Alden, 'The Population of Brazil in the Late Eighteenth-Century: A Preliminary Study', Hispanic American Historical Review, 43/2 (May 1963), 173–205.

exists depends upon how the authorities at the time identified the population and also how people chose to identify themselves. Despite the millions who had crossed the Atlantic over the preceding 280 years and the enormous population loss suffered by indigenous peoples, Indians in the 1770s still constituted almost half of the population. Those of European and African descent represented a quarter and a fifth respectively, with the rest in the mestizo category. Mestizos were undercounted because Brazilian sources do not report European-Indian mixtures and estimates of Spanish-speaking mestizos in Mexico are lumped in with those of European descent on the assumption that they usually followed colonial and church norms on marriage, kinship, inheritance, and gender roles. The non-existence of mestizos in North America above New Spain and in the borderlands areas reflects a failure in the sources to identify them as such, not an absence of racial mixing. While European empires claimed most of the Americas at this time, and their officials along with the Christian churches laid down rules for household formation, one has to wonder about their impact on the ground level in such regions as the Caribbean, where almost nine out of ten inhabitants were of African descent, or in Spanish South America where, 70 per cent of residents were Indians. In mainland Latin America, Indians constituted a majority except in Brazil, where the presence of a large population of Africans and African creoles reduced their share. These percentages confirm that Europeans and their offspring outnumbered Africans and Indians in only a relatively small geographical area of the Americas. For all the attention lavished on the history of the New England family and gender relations, that area turns out to have been part of a region that was strikingly unique racially and not as populous as most of the other regions.

For most of the Americas, the conquest of Indian nations and the implementation of plantation slavery made such a drastic impact that the story of household formation has primarily become a narrative of how colonial officials, creole (e.g. native-born) elites, and the Catholic and other Christian Churches exerted control over racially diverse populations and the extent to which those populations became victims of or outlaws from household government. Some colonies evolved into quasi marriage-free zones and colonial authorities increasingly concerned themselves with preventing what they considered misalliances between men and women of different racial and ethnic backgrounds. Scholars wonder whether the long-standing 'non-marrying behaviours' that can be traced back to the colonial period do not in fact 'cast serious doubt on the conventional demographic assumption that nuptiality is the basis of the family'.[1]

Colonial policies and reactions to them, however, did not occur in a vacuum. Any discussion of household formation in the Americas has to deal with the assumptions of the Atlantic migrants about marriage, lineage, and gender relations and those of the indigenous populations they encountered. Investigations of lineage and kinship have declined in popularity in recent years,[2] yet even a cursory reading of anthropological journals and historical travel narratives makes abundantly clear that households are not synonymous with domestic units everywhere and that one has to know something about the authority of lineage groups to determine the nature of the household and ultimately to gauge the changes that occurred as the Atlantic migration to the Americas proceeded.

---

[1] Nara Milanich, 'Whither Family History? A Road Map from Latin America', *American Historical Review*, 112 (2007), 451.

[2] David Warren Sabean and Simon Teuscher, 'Kinship in Europe: A New Approach to Long Term Development', in David Warren Sabean et al. (eds.), *Kinship in Europe: Approaches to Long-Term Development (1300–1900)* (New York, 2007), 1–32; Sylvia J. Yanagisako, 'Bringing it All Back Home: Kinship Theory in Anthropology', ibid. 33–50, and Jack Goody, 'The Labyrinth of Kinship', *New Left Review*, 36 (November–December 2005) www.newleftreview.org/?view=2592.

Maintaining an even lower profile in recent times have been investigations of the role played by the American physical environment in promoting or discouraging household formation. Since the eighteenth century, commentators have cited the importance of land availability in allowing couples in what later became the United States to marry early and increase the size of their families, but just how the resources of the Americas and the uses to which they were put affected the domestic arrangements of non-Europeans or those in other regions has not been explored to the degree that it deserves.

I begin, therefore, with a reconsideration of the pre-contact situation and then move on to what we know about the impact of the natural environment on all regions of the Americas, before looking at the evolving role of colonial governments and Christian churches in household formation and dissolution. The conclusion will point out the issues I could not examine due to lack of space or research and discuss how what happened in the Americas affected the Atlantic world as a whole.

Transatlantic comparisons of domestic organization at the time of contact

Arguments for profound differences in the household organization of Atlantic migrants and Native Americans date back to Lewis Morgan and the beginning of professional kinship studies. His mid-nineteenth-century examination of the Iroquois nation led him to conclude that their lineage system, which he found other Indian cultures shared, provided insight into 'the history and experience of our own remote ancestors *when in corresponding conditions* [italics added]'.[3] The Iroquois reckoned descent through the female line and seemingly collapsed the distinction between direct descendants and collateral kin by making the children of all sisters and brothers the brothers and sisters of one another. In Morgan's view, they offered a glimpse into an earlier developmental stage of society from which Europeans and other civilized peoples had already emerged. Social critics such as Friedrich Engels turned this story of evolutionary progress on its head, praising the Iroquois as more communally oriented than the money-obsessed bourgeois family of nineteenth-century Europe; but even this reinterpretation retained the presumption of a great gap existing between the two.

The majority of the woodland Indians of eastern North America—the Indian groups most commonly encountered by the French, Dutch, and English—followed the practice of matrilineal rather than patrilineal descent; that is, property and preferments came to children through the mother's kin group not the father's. They also exhibited matrilocal characteristics, the main domestic space for children being the house of the

[3] Lewis H. Morgan, *Ancient Society* (New York, 1878), p. vii.

mother and her lineage. European perceptions that women in Indian communities did all the work can be partially explained by the fact that the fields and the home belonged to the wife's kin not the husband's. The husband had to maintain his relations with his mother's lineage group, even after marriage. Thus matrifocality prevailed. Women married early, soon after puberty, and serial monogamy appeared more common than polygyny, which was primarily associated with elites. Despite their seemingly inferior position in the lineage, most scholars emphasize that males ruled these nations, and matrilinearity, matrilocality, and matrifocality should not be confused with matriarchy, female political domination. Needless to say, researchers today also avoid equating matrilineal with barbarism and patrilineal with civilization.[4]

Matrilineal kinship existed in parts of West Africa as well. Muslim and Christian visitors to the Gold Coast and Upper Guinea during the medieval and early modern periods commented disapprovingly about female sexual freedom, the frequent dissolution of marriage, and the father's lack of responsibility for maintenance of children. Similar to European travellers' descriptions of matrilineal Native American societies, these male observers marvelled at the hard-working women and the alleged idleness of the husbands. In contrast to most Indian nations, African polygyny seemed more deeply entrenched, as did slavery. Men in matrilineal societies could claim for their lineage only children conceived with slave women. This arrangement probably explains why some Europeans observed wives hoeing fields for husbands and fathers selling children: these wives and children were slaves lacking lineage protection.[5]

From Senegambia down to Angola, however, most West African peoples favoured a strong patrilineal kinship system featuring brideprice payments. A generation ago, anthropologist Jack Goody drew attention to what he saw as a major contrast between sub-Saharan African kinship and that of Europe—reliance on brideprice rather than dowry.[6] In sub-Saharan Africa, Goody argued, the emphasis fell on obtaining rights over labour rather than realty. Thus the groom's lineage, seeking to grow, paid a brideprice to a woman's kin in exchange for her labour and reproductive services

---

[4] Carole Shammas, *A History of Household Government in America* (Charlottesville, VA, 2002), 39–43; Jane T. Merritt, *At the Crossroads: Indians and Empire in a Mid-Atlantic Frontier 1700–1763* (Chapel Hill, NC, 2003), 52–7; and Alan Gallay, *The Indian Slave Trade: The Rise of the English Empire in the American South, 1670–1717* (New Haven, CT, 2002), 113, 168–9.

[5] Said Hamden and Noel King (eds.), *Ibn Battuta in Black Africa* (Princeton, NJ, 1994), 37–9; Pieter de Marees, *Description and Historical Account of the Gold Kingdom of Guinea* (1602), trans. and ed. Albert van Dantzig and Adam Jones (Oxford, 1987), 19–27, 182; William Bosman, *A New and Accurate Description of the Coast of Guinea* (1702) (London, 1967), 196–206; Ward Stavig, 'Living in Offense of Our Lord: Indigenous Sexual Values and Marital Life in the Colonial Crucible', *Hispanic American Historical Review*, 75 (1995), 597–622; Stephanie E. Smallwood, *Saltwater Slavery: A Middle Passage from Africa to American Diaspora* (Cambridge, MA, 2007), 110–18; and Susan Herlin Broadhead, 'Slave Wives, Free Sisters: Bakongo Women and Slavery c.1700–1850', in Claire Robertson and Martin Klein (eds.), *Women and Slavery in Africa* (Portsmouth, NH, 1997), 161–2.

[6] Jack Goody, *Production and Reproduction: A Comparative Study of the Domestic Domain* (Cambridge, 1976).

and she became part of his lineage group, removing any threat of conflicting allegiances such as males faced in a matrilineal system. Her kin in turn could use the brideprice to purchase wives for her brothers. Buying female slaves also strengthened the patri-lineage. In contrast, European societies considered rights over land paramount and patrilineal households relied upon dowries to form a conjugal fund that had to be protected from too many heirs through enforcement of monogamy, celibacy, and primogeniture. With land not labour scarce, bound servitude withered.

Questions have been raised about Goody's theories linking marriage strategies to economic development. One aspect, though, receives strong support from a wide range of experts: the household as conceived in Western European societies proves to be an elusive target in West Africa. Scholars stress the difficulty in identifying what is the domicile within the kin assemblage and seem particularly unenthusiastic about equat-ing the West African household of any period with a family firm where members work as a unit. Textbook descriptions of African household systems remind one of Russian nested dolls: pull apart the larger lineage and it gives way to smaller and smaller family groups until one reaches the uterine domestic unit of mother and children. Patrilineal kinship turns out to be compatible with matrifocal domiciles in which each adult female lived in a separate dwelling. While patrilineage affiliation might have significant political implications for children, their material inheritance depended upon their mother's rank in the queue of wives and her own resources. Both polygyny and slavery tightened bonds between mother and children.[7]

Scholars of European kinship and family have no difficulty identifying the household and considering it a firm. Western Europe had a bilateral system of descent with brides coming into the marriage with a dowry that either got folded into the conjugal fund (as in England) or remained somewhat separate (as on the Continent), yet in both cases it ultimately devolved on the children of the marriage in the same way as the inheritance of the patrilineage.[8] The latter, however, clearly held the favoured position having not just naming rights but control over the family firm that was created with variations depending upon nation and century.[9] The Christian Church was a sometime facilitator, doing its part to streamline and narrow the lineage for what some have argued were its own interests. Its early opposition to polygyny and serial monogamy has been described alternatively as a populist manoeuvre to win over to the faith lovelorn bachelors shut out of the marriage market by women-hoarding elite males and as a

---

[7] Joseph Miller, *Way of Death: Merchant Capitalism and the Angolan Slave Trade, 1730–1830* (Madison, WI, 1988), 161; de Marees, *Description*, 19–22; Bosman, *New and Accurate Description*, 199–200. Ernest Osas Uglagbe et al., 'An Evaluation of the Principles of Primogeniture and Inheritance Laws among the Benin People of Nigeria', *Journal of Family History*, 32/1 (January 2007), 90–101; Sandra E. Greene, *Gender, Ethnicity, and Social Change on the Upper Slave Coast: A History of the Anlo-Ewe* (Portsmouth, NH, 1996), 5–12, 108; and Jane I. Guyer, 'Household and Community in African Studies', *African Studies Review*, 24/2–3 (June/September 1981), 87–127.

[8] Space constraints make it impossible to deal with kinship differences among Western European countries.

[9] Sabean and Teusher, 'Kinship in Europe', 1–32.

strategy to garner bequests for itself by improving the odds that the patriline would not produce an heir. In addition, it rid households of excess heirs by accepting them into religious orders at more attractive prices than could be found on the apprenticeship or marriage markets and by eliminating the baseborn. The Church's ban on polygyny did not ensure the fidelity of husbands to their wives, but it did cut down on legitimate heirs.

The Church often found itself in conflict with patrilineal ambitions and proved a fickle friend to dynastic strategies. Marriage being a sacrament, the Church adjudicated household formation and dissolution. The priority it gave to consent of the couple over the wishes of the parent in judging the validity of a son's or daughter's marriage angered many a patriarch. It also stands accused of encouraging the use of wills so that men might alienate property from the patrilineage and put it to more divine uses.[10]

Youth had its issues with dynastic planning too, as patriarchs sometimes put obstacles in the way of early marriage and household formation. Western Europeans postponed marriage longer than did any other society for which records existed. Women commonly wed for the first time in their mid- to late twenties, and a relatively high proportion, 15–20 per cent, never married. Late ages at marriage depressed fertility and also reduced a couple's reliance on the patrimony as their own labours in their single years could fund more of their portions. When a couple did wed, the customary practice dictated the formation of a neolocal (i.e. new) household rather than taking up residence with parents, siblings, or a large lineage group.[11]

Western European uniqueness, however, should not be taken too far. While neolocal marriages of women in their late twenties was not the West African or Native American pattern, studies of Mesoamerican households and kinship show a household economy not that remote from European models, especially if one looks to Eastern and southern Europe where marriage ages were earlier and stem (adult married child living with parents) and joint (more than one married child living with parents) family arrangements appear. In fact, Spain, the nation that invaded Mesoamerica, had regions that possessed these characteristics. Nahua (Aztec) and Mayan families resided in a household complex of adjacent structures around a hearth or patio where parents and married children pooled their resources and labour, a pattern also found in South America among Andean peoples.[12] As in Western Europe, the patriline dominated, but

[10] Jack Goody, *The Development of the Family and Marriage in Europe* (Cambridge, 1983); David Herlihy, *Medieval Households* (Cambridge, MA, 1985); and Michael Sheehan, *The Will in Medieval England* (Toronto, 1963), 303–6.

[11] J. Hajnal, 'European Marriage Patterns in Perspective', in D. V. Glass and D. E. C. Eversley (eds.), *Population in History: Essays in Historical Demography* (London, 1965), 101–43.

[12] Marzio Barbagli and David I. Kertzer, *Family Life in Early Modern Times, 1500–1789* (New Haven, CT, 2001), pp. xiv, xvi; Susan Kellogg, *Weaving the Past: A History of Latin America's Indigenous Women from the Prehispanic Period to the Present* (New York, 2005), 24–30, 148–9, 190–1; Robert McCaa, 'The Nahua Calli of Ancient Mexico: Household, Family, and Gender', *Continuity and Change*, 18 (2003), 23–48; Matthew Restall, 'The Ties that Bind: Social Cohesion and the Yucatec Maya Family', *Journal of Family History*, 23/4 (October 1998), 355–82.

property descended to children through both parental kin groups. Polygyny was primarily confined to the elite. The bilateral source of property did not preclude the exercise of patriarchal power, although that might be said of the Western European household as well.

The distinction here is between those populations that had easily identifiable households centred around the establishment of a conjugal fund and those where matrilocality, patrilocality, brideprice, or slavery or some combination of them meant bride and groom did not pool their resources, might maintain separate domiciles, or owe services to a lineage group outside the domestic unit. In Western Europe, the Christian Church, older age at marriage, and inheritance law changes eliminating mandatory endowment of children allowed the household head considerable independence from the lineage system. In Mesoamerica, the joint family arrangement appears to have strengthened the resources of the household and diminished the role of the lineage. In contrast, woodland Indian couples of North America relied more heavily on their respective matrilineages for support. West African patrilineages gained strength from the addition of wives gained through payment to the women's patrilineage or through the slave trade. Each segment of the patrilineage had within it matrifocal domestic units.

So what happened when these practices came together in the resource-rich Americas? Economic historians have always looked to the physical environment, specifically, the high land/labour ratio and untapped natural wealth in the Americas, as an important determinant of change. It is to those factors that I will now turn.

THE HOUSEHOLD AND LAND AVAILABILITY: TAKING ANOTHER LOOK

By the later eighteenth century the transatlantic commentary on American households took on a celebratory tone. Colonists and Europeans alike proclaimed that abundant natural resources, especially land, allowed young couples to form their own households at an early age and raise large families. They marvelled at the fast rate of population growth, which they considered a mark of economic vitality. On one point almost everyone agreed: the average size of households expanded in America from what it was in Western Europe. The America they referenced, though, was specifically the northern part of North America, largely populated by European religious dissidents who originally migrated in family units. Recent demographic studies of New France, New England, and the mid-Atlantic confirm that women married four to five years earlier than in Europe and as a consequence had more children. Over the course of the eighteenth century, as density increased, age at marriage rose and fertility dropped in the longer settled areas, but those eager for early unfettered procreation moved on to territories further inland.[13]

Other areas of European settlement in the Americas did not have quite the same happy tale to tell regarding household formation. In fact, the neolocal household turned out to be a problematic site in many places for production and reproduction. A combination of high sex ratios, high mortality due to tropical diseases, and high proportions of mostly male indentured servants forbidden to marry until their service had been completed meant that not until the eighteenth century did the Chesapeake population experience natural increase rather than having to rely upon immigrants for growth. Native-born girls married young, but they represented too small a percentage of the population and died at too early an age to spark population growth initially. The high incidence of parental death meant households dissolved at a rapid rate leaving children in a vulnerable position.[14]

In areas where the plantation economy drove in-migration, profitable staple crops increased the demand for labour that neither family members nor free nor even indentured labour could meet. No matter how much of an earth mother the wife of a householder may have been, she could not produce a workforce fast enough nor could the offspring grow quickly enough to make a household competitive. The planter had to buy labour and hold on to it. Free labour moved off to start new households and so eventually did indentured workers. Brideprice and polygyny would add workers as would slavery, the solution eventually adopted by large numbers of households in the Chesapeake, the Lower South, the Caribbean, and Brazil. By subjecting Indians and then much greater numbers of Africans to perpetual servitude, those of European descent in the Americas created domestic sub-units in their households.

The domestic sub-units represented a major departure for most early modern Europeans. Unlike indentured servants and apprentices who signed a contract not to marry or fornicate during their term of service, slaves lived under the umbrella of the master's household forever and were expected or even encouraged to procreate.

---

[13] Wilson H. Grabill, Clyde V. Kiser, and Pascal K. Whelpton, 'The Long View', in Michael Gordon (ed.), *The American Family in Social-Historical Perspective* (New York, 1973), 374–7 and J. Potter, 'The Growth of Population in America 1700–1860', in Glass and Eversley (eds.), *Population in History*, 633–88; Peter Laslett, *Family Life and Illicit Love in Earlier Generations* (Cambridge, 1977), 20–1; Robert V. Wells, *The Population of the British Colonies in America before 1776* (Princeton, NJ, 1975), 299–300; Hubert Charbonneau et al., 'The Population of the St. Lawrence Valley, 1608–1760', in Michael R. Haines and Richard H. Steckel (eds.), *A Population History of North America* (New York, 2000), 143–90; Robert V. Wells, 'The Population of England's Colonies in America: Old English or New Americans?', *Population Studies*, 46 (1992), 85–102; Daniel Scott Smith, 'A Malthusian-Frontier Interpretation of United States Demographic History before c.1815', in Woodrow Borah, Jorge Hardoy, and Gilbert A. Stetler (eds.), *Urbanization in the Americas: The Background in Comparative Perspective* (Ottawa, 1980), 15–24; Philip J. Greven, Jr., *Four Generations: Population, Land, and Family in Colonial Andover, Massachusetts* (Ithaca, NY, 1970).

[14] See the essays by Lorena S. Walsh, Carville Earle, and the Rutmans in Thad W. Tate and David L. Ammerman (eds.), *The Chesapeake in the Seventeenth Century: Essays on Anglo-American Society* (Chapel Hill, NC, 1979).

Whether or not household heads took on slaves as concubines, the structure of households with female slaves and children resembled that of African polygynous patrilineages more than households in the countryside of Western Europe, because of the domestic sub-units which were frequently matrifocal. Moreover, no fertility boom occurred in the most densely populated plantation colonies in the Caribbean, and not until the mid-eighteenth century did the slave population of the southern colonies experience natural growth. Instead high mortality and a low birth rate meant households had to be resupplied constantly with new slave immigrants.

Some economic historians have argued that not only the availability of land and the plantation complex affected household formation but also the type of staple being grown. Large plantations like those established to produce sugar and rice provided more opportunities for slaves to form two-parent households. The harsh work regime of sugar plantations, heavier than for other crops, however, apparently depressed slave women's fertility. Tobacco plantations often employed fewer workers and they dispatched them to quarters of just a few people, making it difficult for conjugal units to develop and thus creating another barrier to reproduction.[15]

For the indigenous population in regions with heavy Western European inmigration, like the east coast of North America, the story was land loss not land availability. While woodland Indian women had children at a young age, fertility appears to have been low and greater contact with the European population drove it down further. Disease decimated the Indian population in most places, but, unlike in Europe after the Black Death, no rebound occurred for centuries. Captives taken as slaves had been one way victorious Indian nations recouped losses after wars. When Indians operated as slave traders to whites in order to obtain goods, however, the Indians lost this source of population replacement.[16] The matrilineal system of kinship, which in most woodlands groups meant women controlled and cultivated fields, greatly distressed colonial officials and settlers, and missionaries tried to change the gender roles to conform to European norms. Their success is unclear. Colonists considered the aversion of Indian men to field work as symptomatic of their generally hands-off approach to the family economy. Commentators complained that men did not take charge of their wife and children. They attributed the 'isolation and numerical weakness of the race' to their household system.[17]

---

[15] Philip D. Morgan, *Slave Counterpoint: Black Culture in the Eighteenth-Century Chesapeake and Low Country* (Chapel Hill, NC, 1998); Allan Kulikoff, *Tobacco and Slaves: The Development of Southern Cultures in the Chesapeake, 1680–1800* (Chapel Hill, NC, 1986), 330–2; Kenneth Morgan, 'Slave Women and Reproduction in Jamaica ca 1776–1834', in Gwyn Campbell, Suzanne Miers, and Joseph L. Miller (eds.), *Women and Slavery: The Modern Atlantic* (Athens, OH, 2008), 27–43; and Richard Follett, 'Gloomy Melancholy: Sexual Reproduction among Louisiana Slave Women 1840–1860', ibid. 54–75.

[16] Russell Thornton, *American Indian Holocaust and Survival: A Population History since 1492* (Norman, OK, 1987), 31, 53–4; Brett Rushford, ' "A Little Flesh We Offer You": The Origins of Indian Slavery in New France', *William and Mary Quarterly*, 3rd Series, 60 (2003), 777–808; and Gallay, *Indian Slave Trade*, 294–300.

[17] Shammas, *Household Government*, 40–4.

In Mesoamerica and South America, Indian populations rebounded from seventeenth-century lows, but it cannot be attributed to land availability or the adoption of a European household economy. According to the estimate in Table 21.1, the *total* population of the Americas 1770–5 fell far below the current calculations of demographers as to the number of Indians in 1492.[18]

In addition to the issue of how land availability affected early household formation and population growth, there is the question of its impact on household stability and dissolution, even in those areas of mainland North America where the European and creole population multiplied due to early marriage and relatively low mortality. British America lacked an established church. Sects proliferated and no central register of marriages existed in most communities. While England in the 1750s acted to shore up the holes in its registration system, no equivalent steps occurred in the colonies where multiple denominations and low density made it difficult to police weddings and force couples to marry. The problem only grew over the course of the eighteenth century when the creation of church congregations and county governments could not keep pace with the migration to the interior. It is conceivable that a significant portion of couples living in the more recently settled locales were not legally married. In fact, such communities might attract such households. This sort of environment made serial monogamy a feasible alternative. As late as the Progressive period in the United States, reformers bemoaned the nation's lax marital regime and its countenance of the mis-named 'common law' marriage.[19] So it turns out that land availability and the resultant low density facilitated not only easy household formation of certain segments of the population but easy dissolution as well.

MARRIAGE-CHALLENGED ZONES

While the resources of the Americas may have allowed free European migrants and their heirs to marry early and increase the size of their households, these same resources precluded most African immigrants, who outnumbered their European counterparts by a ratio of over 3 to 1, from having to deal with marriage at all. The majority of the residents of the Caribbean and Brazil as well as large pockets along the North American mainland's tidewater could not marry or had little incentive to do so. Atlantic migrations created densely populated marriage-challenged zones where nothing like a household economy emerged.

In British America, monogamy and legitimacy had little real meaning as enslaved peoples could not legally wed. The master's household included slaves and their children,

---

[18] Thornton, *American Indian Holocaust*, 23.

[19] Shammas, *Household Government*, chapter 4. Fischer, *Albion's Seed*, 423 has figures for the number of churches for years 1650 to 1850. Dividing these numbers by the population at the time shows the slower pace of church growth through the colonial period.

living in the main house, cabins, or barracks. The sexually explicit diary of Thomas Thistlewood, overseer and later slave owner on Britain's largest sugar-producing colony, Jamaica, exposes better than any abolitionist tract the irrelevancy of marriage, monogamy, and legitimate birth on this island with a population in 1774 greater than New York's. According to biographer Trevor Burnard's calculations, Thistlewood recorded over a thirty-seven-year period sexual relations with 137 different women, nearly all slaves, while also maintaining a long-term relationship with the creole slave Phibbah, the mother of his only son.[20] Neither Thistlewood nor most of the other whites mentioned in his journal, married or single, respected the integrity of black unions, and not surprisingly these unions frequently dissolved. The Anglican Church, weddings, and parish life which played such a large role in the diaries and novels of eighteenth-century English writers might as well not have existed as far as they figure in Thistlewood's world.

In the Spanish and Portuguese empires, the Catholic Church would marry slave couples and baptize slave children whether legitimate or not. Outside of the Caribbean, Brazil contained the biggest concentration of slaves. Despite a more pro-marriage policy by these churches, very few of the enslaved wed, judging by the overwhelming percentage of slave babies, 80–90 per cent in plantation areas, mining regions, and cities, whose baptism records showed their parents were not married. Among creole slave populations in rural areas of early nineteenth-century Brazil more couples married, but still half of slave babies baptized had unknown fathers and lived in matrifocal domestic groups.[21]

Masters and less evangelical priests may have discouraged weddings, but it appears at least some enslaved also lacked enthusiasm for Christian marriage,[22] as it so little resembled the institution that they remembered and mandated a foreign code of sexual behaviour. In West African patrilineal societies, like those of Benin and Angola, unmarried women reportedly enjoyed considerable sexual freedom, and the demonstration of the ability to conceive made a woman more desirable as a wife. Once married, though, they faced a much more restrictive existence, as husbands, who had paid brideprice, expected fidelity and substantial labour from their wives.[23] In America, slave status and absence of a lineage group meant males of African descent had little means to replicate brideprice or polygynous unions or control a wife's labour. The examples of polygynous slave families are few, at least if one relies on plantation lists, where about one domestic unit out of twenty had a man with two wives. The demographics where immigrant men outnumbered women by a two to one margin did not help nor did the unequal competition from white men. One study of a maroon society where African men could exert more control over household arrangements, however,

---

[20] Trevor Burnard, *Mastery, Tyranny, and Desire: Thomas Thistlewood and his Slaves in the Anglo-Jamaican World* (Chapel Hill, NC, 2004), 156–7 and *passim*.

[21] James H. Sweet, *Recreating Africa: Kinship, Culture, and Religion in the African-Portuguese World, 1441–1770* (Chapel Hill, NC, 2003), 36. Alida C. Metcalf, 'Searching for the Slave Family in Colonial Brazil: A Reconstruction from San Paulo', *Journal of Family History*, 16 (1991), 290.

[22] Burnard, *Mastery, Tyranny*, 163–4; Sweet, *Recreating Africa*, 34–5, 39–44; Morgan, *Slave Counterpoint*, 553–4.

[23] Sweet, *Recreating Africa*, 35, 37; Marees, *Description*, 238; Bosman, *Description*, 342–6, 441–7, 462–3.

found 20 per cent of families to be polygynous. On the other hand, African-born and creole women in the Americas may have had more choice in their sexual partners than their counterparts across the ocean.[24]

In the eighteenth-century Caribbean, births per woman remained very low and some scholarly attention has been devoted to explaining the reason. Slave owners blamed the promiscuity of the slave population which led to venereal disease. Sexually transmitted illnesses seem to have been common among both whites and blacks, aided no doubt by the behaviour of the islands' Thistlewoods who had the opportunity to infect more females than any enslaved male. Most scholars, however, downplay the impact of venereal disease and point to the exhausting work regime female slaves endured in the sugar fields and the insufficiency of the diet they received.[25] Everywhere creole slave women had higher fertility rates than African-born women, probably an important reason mainland black fertility far exceeded that in the West Indies. The question is whether creole women's advantage can be attributed to an African woman's later age at birth of first child, her higher probability of being a sugar-field worker, or whether some of the problem can be ascribed to her disorientation over the household system, marriage, and gender roles.

THE COLONIAL STATE AND INDIAN NATIONS
CONFRONT THE THREAT OF MISALLIANCES

The refusal of the British and the uneven efforts of those in the Iberian empires to include slaves in the marriage system were not the only way colonial and imperial authorities affected household formation in the Americas. Slowly but surely they acted to curb racial intermixing or what they came to view as misalliances. Though the various colonial empires dealt with the issue differently, in the end all came to view such marriages with disapproval. The drive to control who could marry whom increased the proportion of female-headed households and of children who had no rights to inheritance.

At the time of invasion and conquest, most Western European governments and the Catholic Church encouraged intermarriage of their soldiers and settlers with American Indian women to solidify their colonial position and spread Christianity. Yet a significant proportion of the free population avoided a Christian marriage and Indian kinship groups might have been no more eager for large-scale intermixing unless the European

---

[24] Morgan, *Slave Counterpoint*, 535–6, 553–4; Burnard, *Mastery, Tyranny*, 187–90, 296; and Sweet, *Recreating Africa*, 238 n. 53.

[25] Kulikoff, *Tobacco and Slaves*, 67–73; Morgan, 'Slave Women and Reproduction in Jamaica', 27–43; Henrice Altink, 'Proslavery Representations of Jamaican Slave Women's Sexuality ca. 1780–1834', in Campbell, Miers, and Miller (eds.), *Women and Slavery*, 209–30; Follett, 'Gloomy Melancholy', 54–75; and Verene A. Shepherd, 'Ethnicity, Colour, and Gender in the Experience of Enslaved Women on Non-Sugar Properties in Jamaica', in Paul E. Lovejoy and David V. Trotman (eds.), *Trans Atlantic Dimensions of Ethnicity in the African Diaspora* (London, 2003), 195–217.

male joined their lineage. The assumption that most offspring of European and Indian unions were illegitimate was widely held. Later, creoles, knowing metropolitan theories about the physical inferiority of those born in the western hemisphere and smarting about preferment being monopolized by *peninsulares*, increasingly supported measures that would separate those of European descent from not only the enslaved population but the rest of the free population as well, making it more difficult for prospective grooms and brides who wanted to contract a legitimate marriage to do so, if either party had any Indian, mestizo, or African ancestry.[26]

In the Iberian empires, it was the transfer of the *limpieza de sangre* (purity of blood) policy adopted in Reconquista Spain to root out of government, and preferably the nation, Christian converts descended from Jews and Muslims that led to the creation of a race/caste system in the Americas and the erection of barriers to interracial household formation. By the late sixteenth century the ideology of purity of blood had created a Spanish society 'obsessed with genealogy'.[27] Offices in Church and state and entry into colleges and professions depended on obtaining purity of blood documentation, which materialized only after Inquisition officials investigated a person's lineage including claims to nobility, legitimate birth, and Christian parentage. In the Americas the interrogations increasingly came to focus upon race. Even though the imperial authorities reaffirmed that only a lineage with African ancestors not Indian ones was impure, parishes from the early seventeenth century kept separate vital records for those of mixed ancestry. The Inquisition officials used these records in their investigations of *limpieza de sangre* and some institutions requiring the certification began to discriminate against mestizos on the basis of having strains of illegitimacy in their background. Such evidence might not be that difficult to trace given that one study of parish registers in seventeenth-century Guadalajara shows, depending on decade, that 40–64 per cent of baptisms were babies of unwed mothers and that females headed nearly half of all households. Similar statistics surface in other New Spain communities and also in Spanish Peru.[28] Seventeenth-century Mexico City marriage records rarely denote mixed-race unions.[29] The Church had procedures for legitimating a birth, but few petitioned, perhaps because the investigation could extend back many generations.

---

[26] Milanich, 'Whither Family History?', 439–58; Amos Megged, 'The Social Significance of Benevolent and Malevolent Gifts among Single Caste Women in Mid-Seventeenth-Century New Spain', *Journal of Family History*, 24/4 (October 1999), 420–40.

[27] Maria Elena Martínez *Genealogical Fictions: Limpieza de Sangre, Religion, and Gender in Colonial Mexico* (Stanford, CA, 2008), 1.

[28] Thomas Calvo, 'The Warmth of the Hearth: Seventeenth-Century Guadalajara Families', in Asuncion Lavrin (ed.), *Sexuality and Marriage in Colonial Latin America* (Lincoln, NE, 1989), 279–31; Megged, 'Social Significance', 420–40. For Lima, Bianca Premo (*Children of the Father King: Youth, Authority, and Legal Minority in Colonial Lima* (Chapel Hill, NC, 2005), 51) finds that in 1700 54% of Lima households with children had no men in them. Out of all households, females headed one-quarter.

[29] Ann Twinam, *Public Lives, Private Secrets: Gender, Honor, Sexuality, and Illegitimacy in Colonial Spanish America* (Palo Alto, CA, 1999); R. Douglas Cope, *The Limits of Racial Domination: Plebeian Society in Colonial Mexico City, 1660–1720* (Madison, WI, 1994), chapter 4; and Richard E. Boyer, *Lives of Bigamists: Marriage, Family, and Community in Colonial Mexico* (Albuquerque, NM, 1995).

The Bourbon Reforms of the later eighteenth century placed further barriers in the way of potential brides and grooms. The 1776 Royal Pragmatic on Marriage issued in Spain and applied to the colonies in 1778 required sons under 30 and daughters under 25 to obtain parental approval before marrying. The grounds parents could use to stop nuptials included unequal status of the bride and groom, and in America that could mean interracial unions. Resort to the Inquisition court that handled the legitimation of children also increased in this late eighteenth-century period. The greater concern about marriage and racial purity may be due to higher incidence or simply the status anxieties of creole families.[30]

The Portuguese empire, with a high proportion of its subjects African slaves, had its own version of purity of blood investigations. Record keepers in Brazil often lumped Indians in with Africans, as they had colonized them before moving on to the Americas. The use of the term 'bastardo' to describe persons of mixed ancestry assumes that parents of different races seldom married. Baptismal records of free children showed lower illegitimacy rates than those of the enslaved, but the percentages, as reported in several eighteenth-century parish registers, still ranged between 25 and 50 per cent. While Portuguese law made a distinction between illegitimacy due to parents simply not marrying and illegitimacy due to an 'impediment'—usually a euphemism for the existence of a wife—the censuses reveal female headship rates of 28–45 per cent, indicating that the problem involved more than couples not bothering with legal niceties.[31] Considering the limited number of Portuguese who emigrated to Brazil and the degree of illegitimacy recorded in parish registers, the Inquisition authorities in Brazil charged with issuing purity of blood certification did not have an easy job. Faced with something of a crisis by the late eighteenth century, the crown issued a resolution that abandoned children should be considered legitimate and also confirmed Indian juridical equality with whites. Despite these actions, rumours of racial mixing and illegitimacy could ruin a person's bid for public office or a splendid marriage.[32]

Initial metropolitan receptivity giving way to hostility toward racial intermarriage occurred in the French empire as well. The programme of government-funded dowries for Indian women championed by Louis XIV's minister Colbert stands as the most frequently cited example of such enthusiasm. Others—Champlain, Richelieu, and later Cadillac—also spoke approvingly of Indian–French unions to speed colonial growth

[30] Patricia Seed, *Love, Honor, and Obey in Colonial Mexico* (Stanford, CA, 1988), 146, 178; Susan M. Socolow, 'Acceptable Partners: Marriage Choice in Colonial Argentina, 1778–1810', in Lavrin (ed.), *Sexuality and Marriage in Colonial Latin America*, 209–51; and Twinam, *Public Lives*, 8.

[31] Muriel Nazzari, 'Vanishing Indians: The Social Construction of Race in Colonial Sao Paulo', *The Americas*, 57/4 (2001), 497–524; Sweet, *Recreating Africa*, 36; Donald Ramos, 'Single and Married Women in Vila Rica, Brazil, 1754–1838', *Journal of Family History*, 16/3 (1991), 261–82. Most notably, where no impediment occurred, fathers could allow illegitimate children to inherit from them. See Linda Lewin, 'Natural and Spurious Children in Brazilian Inheritance Law from Colony to Empire: A Methodological Essay', *The Americas*, 48/3 (January 1992), 351–96.

[32] James E. Wadsworth, *Agents of Orthodoxy: Honor, Status, and the Inquisition in Colonial Pernambuco, Brazil* (Lanham, MD, 2007), 109–12.

and conversion. Weddings in the Caribbean between Europeans and those of African descent elicited fewer positive comments, but during the seventeenth century priests occasionally married such couples and one island governor suggested the French follow the example of the Iberians and use this method of increasing the population. The architects of the 1685 Code Noir probably intended to discourage French–African relationships by confiscating the concubines of married planters and requiring bachelor slave owners to marry their slave mistresses, but technically interracial marriage was not banned.

By the eighteenth century creole settlers and governors rejected interracial marriages of Europeans not only with Africans but with Indians too, charging that their women and fur traders lived in disorderly and licentious households. Indians, still numerically dominant in the Mississippi River valley, also considered the unions problematic, and offenders along with their children faced ostracization from their lineage group. Because of Indian opposition, most Indian–French couplings involved enslaved women, apparently a growing social group in French America. By 1709, New France sanctioned Indian slavery. Louisiana authorities stopped short of taking that step, but nonetheless it existed within the territory. They did prohibit all interracial marriages, including those between whites and Indians. While the French Caribbean islands never formally barred mixed marriages, they punished grooms by stripping them of their honorary titles and the right to hold government or military office.[33]

The British position on interracial marriage shows more consistency over time. Aside from the Pocahontas moment, nary a flicker of support can be detected from the beginning of the colonial period to the end, although over time legal sanctions replaced verbal disapproval. The lack of official encouragement of interracial unions and the higher level of family migration to British colonies have led to long-standing assumptions of little sexual mixing between the British and those of other races. Certainly evidence of such weddings is scarce, and British colonies led the way in enacting laws prohibiting their occurrence. No record of a colonial marriage between a New England male and an Indian woman has yet been found. In the 1660s, Bermuda and Barbados pioneered the anti-miscegenation movement in the Caribbean. Virginia in 1691 and North Carolina in 1715 banned whites from marrying anyone non-white, even if free. The ban in the later colony specified that even those with only one grandparent of Indian or African descent would be ineligible to take vows with a white person.[34] Free white women faced severe fines or bound servitude if they consorted with African American men, and their children had to serve as slaves to their thirtieth birthday. At the same time, sexual relations of a non-marital nature

---

[33] Guillaume Aubert, ' "The Blood of France": Race and Purity of Blood in the French Atlantic World', *William and Mary Quarterly*, 3rd Series, 61 (2004), 439–78, and Kathleen DuVal, 'Indian Intermarriage and Métissage in Colonial Louisiana', ibid. 65 (2008). Gallay does not find the same hostility to incorporation of those of mixed race among the Indians of the south-east, *Indian Slave Trade*, 356.

[34] Shammas, *Household Government*, 44; Kathleen Brown, *Good Wives, Nasty Wenches and Anxious Patriarchs: Gender, Race, and Power in Colonial Virginia* (Chapel Hill, NC, 1996).

between the races were not the rarity once believed, especially in plantation colonies and urban areas.[35] Thus the inability of mixed-race couples to marry and children to inherit was an issue of some consequence throughout the Americas.

CONCLUSION

'The stage of the largest scale assault on marriage in history', 'non-marrying behaviors have been so widespread in the region as to cast serious doubt on the conventional demographic assumption that nuptiality is the basis of the family', 'monogamy was as unfashionable among slaves as it was among whites'.[36] These recent quotations from scholars about Atlantic household formation indicate how in their view large portions of the Americas diverged from the prescribed patterns of marriage in the Western European empires that had laid claim to the territory. This diversion makes some sense, however, when one considers the racial and ethnic composition of the population and the pre-contact traditions of those bordering the Atlantic. The importance of lineage allegiances and polygyny to Africans and Native Americans and their reluctance to accept the primacy of the monogamous conjugal household have perhaps been underestimated. Lineages provided a refuge for both wives and husbands seeking a respite from or the dissolution of a marriage. Polygyny denoted status among males and assured women of a defined place, albeit highly subordinated, in a greater household. Even for those of Western European descent, the monogamous conjugal fund presented problems when transferred to the Americas.

The Western European pattern favoured a single couple-centred household economy using children and waged labour and policed by the Christian Church to maintain monogamy. High land/labour ratios favoured the proliferation of that system in only select circumstances, such as those where Protestant religious dissidents came over to the north-eastern portion of the North American mainland as part of a family group, removing the indigenous population. Even then, a preference for lower ages at marriage continually pushed young couples into the interior where policing marriages and preventing household dissolution proved challenging. In plantation areas, this household form appeared to be ill suited to economic objectives. Instead a household

---

[35] Burnard, *Mastery, Tyranny*, Philip D. Morgan, 'Interracial Sex in the Chesapeake and the British Atlantic World, 1700–1820', in Jan Ellen Lewis and Peter S. Onuf (eds.), *Sally Hemings and Thomas Jefferson: History, Memory, and Civic Culture* (Charlottesville, VA, 1999), 52–84; Kulikoff, *Tobacco and Slaves*, 386–7, 395–6; Brown, *Good Wives, passim*; Clare A. Lyons, *Sex among the Rabble: An Intimate History of Gender and Power in the Age of Revolution, Philadelphia 1730–1830* (Chapel Hill, NC, 2006). Trevor Burnard, 'A Failed Settler Society: Marriage and Demographic Failure in Early Jamaica', *Journal of Social History*, 28 (1994), 80, finds about one in nine children baptized in an eighteenth-century parish to be of mixed parentage.

[36] Goran Therborn, *Between Sex and Power: Family in the World 1900–2000* (London, 2004), 157, Milanich, 'Whither the History of the Family', 451, and Burnard, *Mastery, Tyranny*, 163.

structure prevailed that Western Europeans found foreign: a patriarchal figure presid-ing over a family core surrounded by other, often matrifocal, domestic sub-units, a structure not so dissimilar from African patrilineal polygynous households, except that polygyny was not instituted and African men had no lineage to help them acquire wives. Whites were the household heads. In short, what evolved in the Americas offended almost everyone.

But were some less deeply offended than others, either because of remoteness from colonial bureaucracies or because their household system differed less dramatically from that of the invaders? Of all the groups discussed in this essay, the situation of Mesoamerican and Peruvian Indians living in rural, non-plantation areas might benefit most from further investigation. Though heavily decimated by the aftermath of conquest, Indian populations of these areas were still large. How did their multi-household system fare and what exactly were its features? Were polygyny, corporate lineages, and indigenous slavery of any importance to that system at all? What in this case accounts for what has been observed as a growth in the proportion of female-headed households and a heavier work load for women?[37] Was it just the burden of tributes, an often summoned-up explanation?

Left unexplored in this chapter is whether late eighteenth-century intellectual and political movements originating with Western Europeans—the Enlightenment, repub-licanism, and liberalism—changed the authority of the household head over children, free women, and slaves or whether only household heads benefited from the seemingly more individualistic and egalitarian values being put forward. A tremendous literature relating primarily to British America and the early United States exists on this subject, and I cannot do any justice to it here, since I have primarily apportioned space on the basis of demographic importance and the subject also exceeds the chronological boundaries of this chapter. Elsewhere I have suggested that the effect of these ideas depended heavily on the degree to which parents had lost or ceded control over the marriage of their children.[38] In a recent book, Mary Hartman has tried to move discussions beyond just a consideration of disembodied ideas of liberty, taking the position that the more individualistic behaviour of household dependents can be traced in Western Europe to their need to postpone marriage. She underscores the importance of the superannuated European bride, whom she considers not only responsible for triggering the long-term drop in fertility but who, by marriage postponement, went to school longer, worked longer, and when married could deal with her husband on a more egalitarian basis.[39] Later marriage made men and women more alike—both left their parental household in their early teens to work elsewhere. The greater similarity in spousal ages and the smaller number of children made women less subservient than in other cultures. In the Americas, the phenomenon of a rising female age of marriage in north-eastern coastal areas of what became the United States coincided with the

---

[37] Kellogg, *Weaving the Past*, 63–81.
[38] Shammas, *Household Government*, chapter 4.
[39] Mary S. Hartman, *The Household and the Making of History* (New York, 2004).

surfacing of Enlightenment ideas of women's education and revolutionary republican ideology.

Finally, what also needs further investigation is how household formation in the Americas affected the 'donor' nations in Western Europe and West Africa. To date, the impact discussed the most in regard to the latter is demographic and economic. Overall, the number of men shipped to the Americas exceeded the number of women sent by over a two to one margin, resulting in an exceptionally low sex ratio in many parts of West Africa. Ship manifests, when combined with contemporary comment from Catholic religious orders scattered in enclaves along the coast, have led historians to speculate that this export pattern intensified the practice of polygyny, somewhat countering the expected effect of lowered fertility, and increased the work load of prime-age women, as they had to bear a larger proportion of the support for those too young or too old to labour. The lack of balance in the sex ratio, it is theorized, may have even depressed brideprices and expanded slave concubinage.[40]

The demographic effect on Western European household formation has been more or less shrugged off, at least in regard to England, where male out-migration peaked in the mid-seventeenth-century Civil War era and declined thereafter. Only from 1651 to 1681 might it have been responsible for reducing women's marriage possibilities and partially account for a decline in fertility.[41] And of course not all out-migration was over the Atlantic. Many of those fleeing repressive policies or seeking new opportunities migrated east.

Knowledge about the marriage and gender practices of other peoples bordering the Atlantic seeped gradually into the consciousness of the literate classes of Western Europe. By the eighteenth century, this knowledge had resulted in a widely held belief that adherence to monogamy proved the superiority of their civilization over those peoples who placed little value on a girl's virginity and allowed the taking of more than one wife.[42] There was another kind of sexual freedom though that might have been viewed in a more positive way by certain segments of the population: can any relationship be discovered between the greater freedoms associated with early household formation among colonists in parts of the Americas and the last half of the eighteenth-century drop in Western European marriage ages as well as the rise in illegitimacy in certain parts of Western Europe, phenomena which usually are attributed to urbanization and industrialization?[43] Young people in European villages were not

---

[40] Miller, *Way of Death*, 159–67; Patrick Manning, *Slavery and African Life* (New York, 1990); and John Thornton, 'Sexual Demography: The Impact of the Slave Trade on Family Structure', in Robertson and Klein (eds.), *Women and Slavery*, 39–7.

[41] Ida H. Altman, *Emigrants and Society: Extremadura and America in the Sixteenth-Century* (Berkeley, CA, 1989), and E. A. Wrigley and R. S. Schofield, *The Population History of England 1541–1871: A Reconstruction* (Cambridge, 1989), 232–3.

[42] Shammas, *Household Government*, 8–11, and Barbara Taylor, 'Feminists versus Gallants: Sexual Manners and Morals in Enlightenment Britain', in Sarah Knott and Barbara Taylor (eds.), *Women, Gender and Enlightenment* (New York, 2005), 35–6.

[43] Edward Shorter, *The Making of the Modern Family* (New York, 1975), 80–3, and Wrigley and Schofield, *Population History*, 255 and 266.

necessarily reading Benjamin Franklin, Edward Wigglesworth, or Count Buffon, but they might know from those contemplating going to the Americas that inhabitants found it easier to marry because the kinds of restraints they experienced in Europe were not holding them back. Certainly Christian Utopian groups such as the Shakers and Moravians viewed America as the place to go to practise innovative forms of household organization.

In the end, early modern Atlantic migration changed the process of household formation in the Americas. It spread the practice of household slavery, instituted monogamy, and severely limited the influence of corporate lineage groups. Any generalization about the degree to which it affected power relations between men and women is almost impossible given the diverse demographics of different regions. Earlier marriage favoured the young over their parents but has only been documented for the free population in certain geographic areas.

In the Atlantic world as a *whole*, which of the changes brought about by the European and African migration to America made a lasting impact? Slavery was destined gradually to disappear. Polygyny and corporate lineage influence became rarer over time but so did monogamy. All in all, in the Americas we may see the first steps being taken to diminish the importance of marriage in the forming of households everywhere.

BIBLIOGRAPHY

Burnard, Trevor, *Mastery, Tyranny, and Desire: Thomas Thistlewood and his Slaves in the Anglo-Jamaican World* (Chapel Hill, NC, 2004).

Goody, Jack, *Production and Reproduction: A Comparative Study of the Domestic Domain* (Cambridge, 1976).

Hajnal, J., 'European Marriage Patterns in Perspective', in D. V. Glass and D. E. C. Eversley (eds.), *Population in History: Essays in Historical Demography* (London, 1965), 101–43.

Hartman, Mary S., *The Household and the Making of History* (New York, 2004).

Kellogg, Susan, *Weaving the Past: A History of Latin America's Indigenous Women from the Prehispanic Period to the Present* (New York, 2005).

Milanich, Nara, 'Whither Family History? A Road Map from Latin America', *American Historical Review*, 112 (2007), 439–58.

Morgan, Philip D., *Slave Counterpoint: Black Culture in the Eighteenth-Century Chesapeake and Low Country* (Chapel Hill, NC, 1998).

Shammas, Carole, *A History of Household Government in America* (Charlottesville, VA, 2002).

Smith, Daniel Scott, 'A Malthusian-Frontier Interpretation of United States Demographic History before c.1815', in Woodrow Borah, Jorge Hardoy, and Gilbert A. Stetler (eds.), *Urbanization in the Americas: The Background in Comparative Perspective* (Ottawa, 1980), 15–24.

Sweet, James H., *Recreating Africa: Kinship, Culture, and Religion in the African-Portuguese World, 1441–1770* (Chapel Hill, NC, 2003).

Thornton, John, 'Sexual Demography: The Impact of the Slave Trade on Family Structure', in Claire Robertson and Martin Klein (eds.), *Women and Slavery in Africa* (Portsmouth, NH, 1997), 39–47.

CHAPTER 22

··

POLITY FORMATION
AND ATLANTIC POLITICAL
NARRATIVES

··

ELIZABETH MANCKE

FROM a global perspective, the Atlantic basin was an extremely dynamic arena of political change in the early modern era. Polity formation, re-formation, and collapse occurred as collateral consequences of European expansion, whether the spread of infectious diseases, the establishment of settler colonies, or commercial opportunities. Thus new polities arose in West Africa to engage in maritime trade with Europeans, Comanches came to the fore on the southern Plains of North America by dominating the market for horses, and the St Lawrence Iroquoians collapsed in the face of over-whelming pressures. Yet these diverse examples of political change tend to be pushed to the margins of the historical narrative of governance in the Atlantic world which is still stalwartly Eurocentric, bracketed, as it were, with the European settlement of colonies, their maturation, and their bids for independence in the Age of Revolution.[1]

General accounts of political change have failed to come to terms with specialist findings. Africanists document the political consequences of the shifts in trading systems, both overland and maritime, that reconfigured power from the Mediterranean to Madagascar.[2] Scholars write brilliant studies of indigenous Americans resisting Europeans, refusing to disappear, and insisting on governing themselves. These studies accumulate in ever greater numbers and with ever greater sophistication in analysis. Nevertheless, the political narrative of 'colony to nation', or state formation, is largely unchallenged. We also are analytically uncertain about European colonies that retain

---

[1] A. J. R. Russell-Wood (ed.), *Government and Governance of European Empires, 1415–1800*, 2 vols. (Aldershot, 2000), and id., *Local Government in European Overseas Empires, 1450–1800*, 2 vols. (Aldershot, 1999) provide introductions to the scholarly literature on European polity formation overseas.

[2] See chapters by David Northrup and Robin Law in this volume; and Emmanuel Kwaku Akyeampong (ed.), *Themes in West African History* (Athens, OH, 2006).

imperial associations, whether the Falklands and St Helena in the South Atlantic, Saint Pierre and Miquelon in the North Atlantic, or diverse island colonies and overseas *départements* in the Caribbean. Poor fits with the dominant historical narrative, they become not just the 'confetti of empire', but the confetti of political history.[3]

By stepping back from the question of Atlantic state formation to look more broadly at polity formation, it becomes possible to incorporate more kinds of autonomous and semi-autonomous polities into our analyses. We can begin by distinguishing among three basic forms: diasporic, niche, and consolidating and integrative polities;[4] categories which emphasize that polities function in geopolitical systems to which they respond. A consolidating and integrative polity competed with, dominated, or absorbed other polities. A niche polity distinguished itself from surrounding polities and did not have, or abandoned, expansionist agendas. A diasporic polity was dispersed and positioned among multiple polities. These categories shift our focus away from questions of internal polity development—the 'colony to nation' (or state) paradigm— and towards polity responses to external pressures and contestations among Amerindians, Africans, and Europeans that figured so prominently in the early modern era. Consequently, these categories differ from, but are not exclusive of, conventional polity definitions that give greater priority to internal structure and development than to geopolitical dynamics. Furthermore, the emphasis on relations among polities means there is no optimum, much less essential or normative, size or kind of polity.

Diasporic polities were far-flung networks of culturally alien people to whom local authorities granted self-governing privileges, and were generally based on ethnic and/ or religious affiliations, for example, Jewish, Armenian, or Mande.[5] Often associated with trading and financial networks, many diasporic polities had no autonomous territorial base where they constituted the majority population. Commercially oriented diasporic polities were widespread in the Afro-Eurasian world and many eschewed the use of armed force—an expectation, if not requirement, of local hosts—except for limited defensive purposes. Indeed, the eschewing of violence contributed to the idea that commerce was a peaceable enterprise; in Montesquieu's phrasing, 'The natural effect of commerce is to lead to peace.'[6] In exchange for the privilege of living and trading among other nations, members of diasporic polities were often prohibited from controlling land, though many merchants married local women to connect with local kinship networks. Merchants from territorially based polities, such as the English Merchant Adventurers, negotiated diasporic privileges with foreign rulers, most especially religious toleration and governance of their own members by their own laws. Similarly the governments of some niche polities, such as Genoa and Venice, adopted

---

[3] Robert Aldrich and John Connell, *The Last Colonies* (Cambridge, 1998), 238.

[4] These categories are of my own devising based on extensive consideration of geopolitical change in the early modern era. But I am indebted to Alec Haskell for recommending that I analyse in terms of polities not states.

[5] Philip D. Curtin, *Cross-Cultural Trade in World History* (Cambridge, 1984).

[6] Charles de Montesquieu, *The Spirit of the Laws*, ed. and trans. Anne M. Cohler, Basia C. Miller, and Harold Stone (Cambridge, 1989), 338.

diasporic practices and developed skills associated with diasporic polities, such as expertise in finance, commercial law, diplomacy, and navigation; skills which made them attractive clients of consolidating and integrative polities, such as the kingdoms of Portugal and Castile.[7]

Niche polities and consolidating and integrative polities were opposites, though no polity is static and any may take on characteristics of another type. Niche polities, for example, generally shaped their external policy to the expansionist agendas of neighbouring consolidating and integrative polities. These latter could become niche polities for strategic or survival purposes; Sweden shifted from being a consolidating and integrative polity with trans-Baltic and overseas ambitions to becoming a niche polity in the decades after the Great Northern War (1700–21).[8] Niche polities were of varying sizes. Swiss cantons have long been determinedly niche polities that confederated to protect themselves from neighbouring consolidating and integrative polities, whether the Holy Roman empire, the Austro-Hungarian empire, or Napoleonic France. In North America, the Hopi living in mesa-top towns are a pre-Columbian niche polity. The Channel Islands remain centuries-old niche polities, eschewing full incorporation into the United Kingdom, France, or the European Union. With the collapse of the Aztecs and Incas in the sixteenth century, many former tributary groups retained their local identities and governing status within Spanish viceroyalties, while others sought refuge as niche polities in parts of Mesoamerica and South America at some remove from the centres of Spanish and Portuguese colonization.[9] Escaped slaves in the Americas formed autonomous polities—maroon communities—some of which negotiated treaties with Europeans, as did, for example, maroon communities in sixteenth-century Peru and eighteenth-century Jamaica.[10] This category of niche polity covers the broadest spectrum, from communities of former slaves, to royal domains that resisted integration into the greater realm, to African kingdoms, to newly independent republics, such as Venezuela.

Consolidating and integrative polities had agendas for bringing together people and resources at the expense of the autonomy of other polities. They could destabilize both individual polities and the geopolitical systems within which they operated, as happened when the Spanish conquered the Aztecs and Incas, or when Louis XIV invaded the Low Countries and precipitated war across Europe. The Iroquois league, in North America, was such an entity, but parts broke away, as did the Catholic Mohawks who, in the seventeenth century, established the niche polities of Akwesasne and Kanesatake

---

[7] E. M. Carus-Wilson, *Medieval Merchant Venturers: Collected Studies* (2nd edn. London, 1967), 143–5; G. V. Scammell, *The World Encompassed: The First European Maritime Empires c.800–1650* (Berkeley, CA, 1981), 86–220.

[8] The transition from consolidating and integrative polities to niche polities is probably as important as the colony-to-nation transition, yet is largely unstudied as a phenomenon in state development.

[9] See chapters by Neil Whitehead and Kevin Terraciano in this volume.

[10] Jane Landers, 'Leadership and Authority in Maroon Settlements in Spanish America and Brazil', in José C. Curto and Renée Soulodre-La France (eds.), *Africa and the Americas: Interconnections during the Slave Trade* (Trenton, NJ, 2005), 173–84.

near Montreal. All five Atlantic powers—Spain, Portugal, France, Britain, and the Netherlands—meet the definition, although all utilized diasporic practices and had dependencies that exhibited niche tendencies. The same applies to many West African polities that engaged in the Atlantic slave trade, such as the kingdoms of Asante and Dahomey. These consolidated in the seventeenth and eighteenth centuries, but not to the exclusion of African diasporic polities, which remained vital in moving goods long distance within Africa.[11]

These categories of diasporic, niche, and consolidating and integrative polities allow us to orient ourselves away from the analytic limitations of existing categories of polities. They are applicable to both European and non-European polities without the strong cultural associations attached to categories such as state, non-state, chieftaincy, and tribe. They are useful for assessing geopolitical dynamics more than internal development. Finally, they do not imply teleologies of political development, such as the non-state and state distinction implies. A niche polity, for example, is not an early stage in the development of a consolidating and integrative polity. And consolidating and integrative polities may become niche polities, as happened with the Powhatan Confederacy in eastern North America or the successor republics of the Spanish empire, albeit some of them had expansionist aspirations; Argentina, for example, engaged in aggressive wars against Brazil. In short, these basic categories can help us analyse the political volatility of the early modern Atlantic world, and how groups of people chose polity forms to confront the era's tumultuous challenges.

One distinctive feature of European expansion is the projection of power across vast maritime spaces. Europeans launched bold ventures to build consolidating and integrative polities in strikingly new ways, conquering and dismantling similar polities in the Americas, absorbing niche and diasporic polities, and creating new societies of their transplanted subjects, which grew sufficiently mature to rebel against their dependent status and establish themselves as autonomous polities. Europeans articulated narratives of governance to explain and legitimize their actions, and by turn to delegitimize polities they wished to subordinate or absorb, narratives that contributed to the embedding of the state/non-state dichotomy in political discourse. Three narrative forms were essential. One involved the projection of European sovereignty into the extra-European world. A second concerned the overseas extension of European-derived legal systems, both domestic and international; those legal narratives intersected with and influenced the emerging narratives of sovereignty in the Atlantic world. Narratives of civility are the third type. They operated at many levels and became embedded in international discourse so that Europeans could concur that their political, legal, and social systems were sufficiently advanced beyond non-Europeans' systems of governance to justify subordinating other polities. Pivotal to the European articulation of a hierarchy of polities and a teleology of political development, these narratives were also critical diplomatic tools for the emergent European international

---

[11] Curtin, *Cross-Cultural Trade*, 15–59.

community to legitimize some polities as states and eligible for membership and to deem others as either non-states or states with despotic systems of law and government that needed to be subordinated to a civilized state. These European narratives of sovereignty, law, and civility were formative in contestations that defined the political dialectics of the early modern Atlantic world and that both validated the elevation of European polities over others in the world, and legitimized the subordination of some small European polities to larger ones.

In the Afro-Eurasian world, diasporic polities had for centuries, if not millennia, been the sinews of long-distance trade and conduits through which knowledge, belief systems, and technology were transmitted among cultures. Scholars interpret these networks as primarily commercial phenomena, but they also had distinct political qualities. Europe's expanding powers adopted myriad diasporic practices: commercial diplomacy, financial management, legal pluralism, ethnic accommodation, applied literacy, map making, and advanced travel skills. Their ability to co-opt and combine them with the powers of consolidating and integrative polities eventually distinguished Europe's overseas empires from Eurasia's territorially contiguous empires, such as the Ottoman, Safavid, Mughal, or Qing.

In early Atlantic forays, the Portuguese and Castilian crowns contracted with Genoese and Venetians for their money and maritime skills. After the Portuguese mastered navigation to West Africa, they limited foreign involvement, choosing to consolidate control of increasingly far-flung enclaves in Portuguese hands.[12] While successfully establishing settlements on the Azores, Madeira, Cape Verdes, São Tomé, and Príncipe, the Portuguese did not initially conquer territory in West Africa; they took considerable territory in Angola only in the late sixteenth century after the emergence of a Luso-African population there. Instead, West African rulers facilitated them, and subsequent Europeans, with negotiated diasporic privileges: Europeans could establish factories on land leased from African rulers; practise their own religion; and govern their own associates under their own law. While Europeans effectively exercised sovereign powers within a factory and its yards and over commercial employees, their land claims in West Africa were limited.[13]

Prior to the maritime arrival of Europeans, long-distance trade into and from West Africa moved along overland routes, and large consolidating and integrative polities formed around critical junctures in those systems of contact and exchange, for example the Sudanic kingdoms/empires of Mali, Ghana, and Songhai.[14] The West Africans' success in obliging Europeans to continue centuries-old Afro-Eurasian commercial

[12] Charles Verlinden, *The Beginnings of Modern Colonization* (Ithaca, NY, 1970), 98–180; Scammell, *The World Encompassed*, 177–83.

[13] George E. Brooks, Jr., *Eurafricans in Western Africa: Commerce, Social Status, Gender, and Religious Observance from the Sixteenth to the Eighteenth Century* (Athens, OH, 2003); John Thornton, *Africa and Africans in the Making of the Atlantic World, 1400–1800* (2nd edn. Cambridge, 1998).

[14] Ghislaine Lydon, *On Trans-Saharan Trails: Islamic Law, Trade Networks, and Cross-Cultural Exchange in Nineteenth-Century Western Africa* (Cambridge, 2009), 49–106.

practices cautions against interpreting West Africa proper as being overly defined by the emerging Atlantic trades. West Africans adapted maritime trade to existing exchange networks that already connected West Africa to the Mediterranean and Indian Ocean worlds. As transatlantic trade intensified over the seventeenth century and eclipsed overland trade, new West African consolidating and integrative polities, such as the Asante, Dahomey, and Oyo kingdoms, emerged nearer the Atlantic coast; polities with enslaved military forces for procuring slaves for the Atlantic trade and for protection.[15] At the same time, new niche polities coalesced: some, such as the quasi-independent ports of Ouidah and Lagos, engaged in the growing slave trade; others formed to advance protective strategies such as walling villages which might insulate them from the deleterious impacts of the Atlantic slave trade.[16]

The social, economic, cultural, and ecological factors shaping sub-Saharan polities differed in striking ways from European polities, but with parallels in the Americas. People were valued over land, what Africanists call wealth-in-people and the related wealth-in-knowledge, meaning that political power was measured by the number and quality of people under someone's authority.[17] Animistic religions, which many West Africans practised, required a keen knowledge of local ecologies and family lineages, reinforcing the socio-political emphasis on wealth-in-people and wealth-in-knowledge. Religions with universalist theologies, such as Islam and Christianity, which provided ideological legitimization for political integration in Europe, Asia, and North Africa, had difficulty in winning acceptance among many West Africans. However, pockets of Islam flourished among several diasporic merchant communities under Sufi influences, while, among Christian religions, Catholicism made greater inroads than Protestantism. Localized knowledge reinforced localized political control; in contrast, the European shift toward generalized knowledge, associated with overseas expansion and the scientific revolution, reinforced political integration and consolidation. Lineage strongly influenced African socio-political relations, and identities were often matrilineal and matrilocal. Women exercised considerable local political and economic power, even in Eurafrican communities, while men handled affairs beyond the locality: trade, warfare, diplomacy, law, or simply the production of agricultural commodities for export, such as palm oil. Thus, the dialectic between consolidated and niche polities in Africa (with a similar pattern in many Amerindian polities) had a gendered component.[18]

While sub-Saharan Africa had large urban places, archaeological studies show that few had monumental architecture and other markers of social hierarchy that scholars associate with urbanization in Eurasia, Mesoamerica, and South America. Rather,

[15] John Thornton, 'Armed Slaves and Political Authority in Africa in the Era of the Slave Trade, 1450–1800', in Christopher Leslie Brown and Philip D. Morgan (eds.), *Arming Slaves: From Classical Times to the Modern Age* (New Haven, CT, 2006), 79–94.

[16] Sylviane A. Diouf (ed.), *Fighting the Slave Trade: West African Strategies* (Athens, OH, 2003).

[17] Jane I. Guyer et al., 'Wealth in People: Wealth in Things', *Journal of African History*, 36/1 (1995), 83–140.

[18] The spatial expressions of gendered power among Africans and Amerindians deserve further analysis.

urban spaces were apparently organized as heterogeneous composites without marked hierarchy among constituent parts. People organized communities within urban centres by occupational or knowledge expertise, such as merchants, blacksmiths, or spiritual leaders.[19] This composite, rather than hierarchical, ordering of complex societies preserved considerable governing discretion within constituent parts and provided a plasticity that allowed diverse groups to shift, relocate, and coexist. Land occupation through usufruct agreements rather than ownership enhanced plasticity and the interspersing of multiple ethnic groups, as was particularly apparent from Senegambia to the Slave Coast. The West African tendency for niche polities to retain local control as they were incorporated into consolidating and integrative polities would subsequently legitimize the modern European tribalization of Africa.

Europeans operated successfully on this African political terrain. Local control allowed diverse commercial enterprises to negotiate land leases for slave-trading forts. Intimate contact between European men and African women sometimes resulted in ethnogenesis, most strikingly the Luso-African groups who became the majority populations on the Cape Verdes, São Tomé, and Príncipe, and were influential in Senegambia and Angola. European-controlled slave-trading forts along the Atlantic coast were among the most monumental structures in West Africa and emblematic of Europe's rising global power and the more integrated political systems that undergirded Atlantic commerce. The passage of slaves through them helped strip captives of their nuanced ethno-political identities. While Europeans recognized differences among Africans depending on their region of origin, they also contributed to making 'Negro', 'Black', and 'African' (and their equivalents in Spanish, Portuguese, French, and Dutch) interchangeable terms in the Atlantic world. 'Atlantic Africans' resisted apolitical constructions and, over the centuries, attempted to recover some political influence, whether through involvement with maroon communities, the Haitian Revolution, the founding of Sierra Leone as a British colony for freed blacks, the pan-Atlantic African merchant network that American Paul Cuffee imagined in the nineteenth century, or simply citizen rights within the several American republics constituted in the Age of Revolution.[20]

The European adoption of diasporic political practices in most of West Africa checked their deployment of narratives of sovereignty, law, and civility, except for Portuguese-controlled Angola and a few other enclaves. Europeans did deploy these narratives against Africans caught in the maelstrom of Atlantic slavery, contributing to emergent racist ideologies. It would take three centuries of slavery and political upheavals among Europeans in the Atlantic world before social movements emerged to abolish the slave trade and then Atlantic slavery itself. Ironically, that Atlantic shift contributed to new European territorial footholds in West Africa, notably Sierra Leone,

---

[19] Roderick J. McIntosh, 'Clustered Cities of the Middle Niger: Alternative Routes to Authority in Prehistory', in David M. Anderson and Richard Rathbone (eds.), *Africa's Urban Past* (Oxford, 2000), 19–35.

[20] James Sidbury, *Becoming African in America: Race and Nation in the Early Black Atlantic* (Oxford, 2007); and the essays in Curto and Soulodre-La France (eds.), *Africa and the Americas*.

and concomitantly a new projection of the Atlantic narratives of civility, law, and sovereignty against West Africans; narratives which, by the late nineteenth century, helped justify the division of Africa among Europeans who asserted sovereignty over most of the continent. Europeans, however, projected those narratives onto the Americas and then the Antipodes before they appreciated their full utility for politically controlling Africa.[21]

European ambitions to bring the Americas under their control began with Columbus' first voyage, and then intensified as they realized that they shared no history with the continents' peoples, no precedents to guide interactions with them, no myths to test in face-to-face encounters, no customary practices that would mediate interactions as they had in West Africa. To fill that ethnographic void, they drew on a battery of biblical, medieval, and classical legends, imagining Amerindians variously as a lost tribe of Israel, as Amazons, or the people among whom St Thomas laboured. In an uneasy and unstable tension between on-the-ground engagements and more detached considerations—scholarly debates, royal decrees, judicial decisions, and international agreements—Europeans imagined indigenous Americans into a Euroamerican world, and thus into the consolidating and integrative reach of Europe's expanding powers. Nothing illustrates these acts of imagination more simply than the repeated diplomatic swaps and partitions of American territory made at treaty tables in Madrid, Ryswick, Utrecht, Paris, London, without consulting Amerindians, and often in woeful ignorance of the peoples and territories being traded. In 1608, Hugo Grotius chided the Portuguese for the hubris of their claims in Africa and Asia, noting that Europeans had known about those lands for centuries, and knew they were inhabited. A sea route to Asia, he observed, did not justify the Portuguese overriding that history with grandiose claims. As for the Americas, Grotius, like commentators before and after him, was more ambivalent.[22]

Our comprehension of Amerindian political systems is complicated by the ways in which history has been conceptualized over the last half-millennium.[23] Indigenous Americans did not exist in biblical history, and Europeans debated their humanity, whether they had souls, whether they could be saved, how they were to be Christianized and civilized. In the absence of a history that included the Americas, even a flawed and distorted one, Europeans projected futures that paid little heed to American pasts. To the extent that those projections included indigenous Americans, they were optimistically imagined as Christians, loyal subjects of European monarchs, and willing labourers for European enterprises. By the eighteenth century, Europeans' understanding of history underwent significant secularization, and a narrative of political and economic

---

[21] Stuart Banner, *Possessing the Pacific: Land, Settlers, and Indigenous People from Australia to Alaska* (Cambridge, MA, 2007).

[22] See the chapter by Anthony Pagden in this volume.

[23] Gyan Prakash (ed.), *After Colonialism: Imperial Histories and Postcolonial Displacements* (Princeton, NJ, 1995); and Jack Goody, *The Theft of History* (Cambridge, 2006).

maturation increasingly replaced a biblical narrative of redemption. As biblical history gave way to secular history, Amerindians remained outside history, sometimes in an Aristotelian state of natural inferiority, sometimes imagined as noble savages, but increasingly located in a prehistory which they could only exit with the assistance of more advanced societies located already in historical time. The study of prehistoric cultures was not the domain of historians, but of a new category of scholars, anthropologists, who, like natural scientists, were cataloguing the natural world, including human cultures, using methodologies deemed scientific and objective, notwithstanding the fallacy that some human societies were outside history. Included in this new anthropological domain, along with indigenous Americans, were scores of other human societies, including most African ones, now deemed in this reorganization of knowledge to be outside history and thus denied the possibility of autonomous change without the intervention of their cultural superiors, most particularly Europeans. This epistemological division of human communities assumed the political immaturity of 'prehistoric' societies whose political systems were labelled tribal or chiefdoms. They contrasted, at least implicitly, with the political dynamism and sophistication of European and Euroamerican political systems organized around states. In this structure of knowledge, European empires became a vehicle to convey civilization and political development to much of the world.[24]

A half-century of scholarship has eroded the idea that Amerindians existed in an unchanging prehistory and that Europeans introduced them to historical change. Yet 'tribe' as a social and political category is so ingrained in our conceptions of Amerindian political structures—and has not undergone the scrutiny that Africanists have applied to that same term—that escaping its thrall is difficult.[25] So it is best to begin with the greatest contrasts to 'tribes', which are the numerous, and more normative, consolidating and integrative polities in the Americas within which the majority of indigenous Americans lived: the Aztec and Inca systems on which the Spanish imposed their governance; or the League of the Iroquois that eluded European domination until the late eighteenth century; or entities that emerged in the aftermath of European contact, such as the Comanche or the expanding Araucanians in southern Chile.[26] These systems varied enormously in material culture, yet each was expansive and attempted to absorb or displace other polities; each was the dominant power over an extensive territory, controlled the movements of goods and peoples through their

[24] Anthony Pagden (ed.), *Facing Each Other: The World's Perception of Europe and Europe's Perception of the World*, parts I and II (Aldershot, 2000); Eric R. Wolf, *Europe and the People without History* (Berkeley, CA, 1982); and Gyan Prakash, 'Introduction: After Colonialism', in *After Colonialism*, 3–17.

[25] Leroy Vail, 'Introduction: Ethnicity in Southern African History', in Vail (ed.), *The Creation of Tribalism in Southern Africa* (London, 1989), 1–19; Steven Feierman, 'Africa in History: The End of Universal Narratives', in Prakash (ed.), *After Colonialism*, 40–65.

[26] See the chapters by Terraciano and Whitehead in this volume; Pekka Hämäläinen, *The Comanche Empire* (New Haven, CT, 2008); and Tom D. Dillehay, *Monuments, Empires, and Resistance: The Araucanian Polity and Ritual Narratives* (Cambridge, 2007).

territory, and influenced the allocation of resources. All were eventually brought under the sway of Euroamerican integrative polities through varying strategies for fragmenting the indigenous equivalents into niche polities, assisted, of course, by population decimation wrought by newly introduced diseases. The nature of indigenous polities, whether primarily sedentary, semi-sedentary, or nomadic, influenced how Europeans incorporated them, with the nomadic ones generally being the most difficult to assimilate.

The Spanish toppling of the pinnacles of Aztec and Inca power brought approximately half of the indigenous population of the Americas (conservatively estimated at 50 million inhabitants in the entire western hemisphere) under Spanish control.[27] The dominant underlying social structures were sedentary and highly resilient, composed of ethnically differentiated and socially complex cities, towns, and villages, which, under successive overlords, retained considerable internal governing autonomy, and were called by the Spanish *repúblicas de indios*. Too numerous for the Spanish to police effectively, they partially restructured them to fit Spanish governing practices and objectives, frequently with the cooperation of indigenous leaders, many initially drawn from local nobility. Beyond the sedentary regions of the former Aztec and Inca domains, Spanish claims to sovereignty were tenuous and were achieved not through the conquest and subordination of the indigenous inhabitants, but rather through the projection of an Atlantic narrative of sovereignty upon them. In 'frontier' regions, whether mountainous or plain, arid or tropical, Spanish control continued to be contested. Rather than colonize such areas, the Spanish designated frontiers as zones of missionization, hoping to achieve pacification through Christianization and promotion of indigenous settlements.[28]

Spain's European rivals in the Americas encountered similar difficulties in bringing indigenous peoples under their governance. At the end of the eighteenth century, after three centuries of European colonization, much of the arable territory of the Americas remained under indigenous control.[29] Among semi-sedentary and nomadic Amerindians various practices of polity formation reinforced their autonomy. Shared strategies for accommodating cultural heterogeneity allowed groups under pressure to disperse and reorganize elsewhere, and villages of different ethnicities often lived in close proximity to one another. As in Africa, the negotiation of land use through usufruct arrangements rather than ownership facilitated the interspersing of diverse ethnic groups. The documentary record is replete with examples of groups fleeing pressure in one place and settling in another, sometimes invited by host groups, such as the Tuscarora relocation from the southern to the northern Appalachian region to join the League of the Iroquois as the sixth nation. At the local level, Amerindian women had considerable political

---

[27] Amy Turner Bushnell, 'Indigenous America and the Limits of the Atlantic World, 1493–1825', in Jack P. Greene and Philip D. Morgan (eds.), *Atlantic History: A Critical Appraisal* (Oxford, 2009), 192.
[28] David J. Weber, *Bárbaros: Spaniards and their Savages in the Age of Enlightenment* (New Haven, CT, 2005).
[29] Bushnell, 'Indigenous America', 310–12.

and economic power, as women did in many parts of Africa, while men controlled diplomacy, war-making, hunting, and long-distance trade, and Europeans commented on the leadership of women in re-establishing displaced communities.[30]

In the myriad zones where the claims and interests of European powers over-lapped—notably between Brazil and Argentina, Texas and Louisiana, Florida and the Carolinas, New York and Canada—Amerindian polities evolved sophisticated strate-gies to protect their interests in the face of persistent European pressure. By the late seventeenth century, some indigenous polities began to send agents and emissaries to Europe to circumvent colonial officials and negotiate directly with metropolitan officials (as had Africans, such as the king of Kongo). Competition among Amerindian integrative polities, many allied with one or other European power, could also limit European expansion. On the vast open grasslands of South America's pampas and North America's Great Plains, new and powerful Amerindian polities coalesced in response to the possibilities presented by access to horses and firearms.[31] One of the last parts of eastern North America that Europeans penetrated was the upper Ohio River valley and the eastern Ohio Country, which they entered only in the 1740s. That area lay between three large native polities—the Iroquois to the north-east, the Wendat-Algonquian system to the west, and the Cherokees to the south-east—who contended among themselves for influence in the area.

From their first arrival in the Americas, Europeans projected their own concep-tions of sovereignty, law, and civility over the peoples and land of the continents, manifesting possession by planting crosses, raising pillars, enacting rituals in which native leaders ostensibly swore fealty to a distant European monarch, or baptizing entire Amerindian communities.[32] In some areas, settlements, the most effective manifestation of possession, displaced indigenous people and replaced them with Europeans, thereby transforming, and often lessening, the continents' cultural het-erogeneity, partly as a consequence of indigenous population declines wrought by epidemics and warfare, but also because Europeans in the Americas tended towards greater cultural conformity—primarily religious, linguistic, and legal—than existed in Europe. Local and regional identities that were important in Europe attenuated in the Americas, as European migrants realized the importance of being subjects of a particular European monarchy, and having access to the administrative and judicial systems of a European overseas empire. And involuntary African migrants were defined by Europeans more by their continent of origin, legal condition, or skin colour than by their diverse African ethnic or political identities.

---

[30] Rebecca Kugel and Lucy Eldersveld Murphy (eds.), *Native Women's History in Eastern North America before 1900: A Guide to Research and Writing* (Lincoln, NE, 2007).

[31] Alden T. Vaughan, *Transatlantic Encounters: American Indians in Britain, 1500–1776* (Cambridge, 2006); Kristine L. Jones, 'Comparative Raiding Economies: North and South', in Donna J. Guy and Thomas E. Sheridan (eds.), *Contested Ground: Comparative Frontiers on the Northern and Southern Edges of the Spanish Empire* (Tucson, AZ, 1998), 97–114.

[32] Patricia Seed, *Ceremonies of Possession in Europe's Conquest of the New World, 1492–1640* (Cambridge, 1995).

Nevertheless most Amerindians, confronted with catastrophic socio-political disruptions, preferred merging with other Amerindian groups over joining Euroamerican communities. Among indigenous peoples, ethnic blending and ethnogenesis were common, and new entities attempted to remain self-governing. While native polities that formed through consolidation of collapsed polities tended to be niche polities concerned more with maintaining their distance from Europeans than with expansion, many nonetheless allied, if not confederated, with other native polities. The Catawbas in the Carolinas emerged in the seventeenth century as a new native nation composed of fragments from collapsed polities. In a few instances, new Amerindian polities with broad ambitions coalesced in response to European pressure; some assumed consolidating and integrative characteristics, for example, the movement led by Tupac Amaru in southern Peru, which aspired to have native overlordship replace Spanish rule. In the eighteenth and early nineteenth centuries a growing number of nativist movements emerged with agendas either to overturn European overlordship—the case of Tupac Amaru—or to block the expansion of Euroamerican settlements—such as the movement led by Tecumseh and Tenskwatakwa in the trans-Appalachian West.[33]

When these nativist movements began to manifest themselves, European empires and their Euroamerican successor polities had developed logistical infrastructures with transatlantic reach to suppress them. This sometimes took decades, and required steady infusions of men, matériel, and, especially, Euroamerican settlers. At the international level, the transatlantic narratives of sovereignty, law, and civility ostensibly validated European sovereignty over the entirety of the Americas, and not just where they settled. These narratives characterized indigenous peoples as lacking sufficient 'civilization' to justify them being accorded an international identity independent of any Euroamerican power. Transatlantic political upheavals of the Age of Revolution disposed European empires and Euroamerican successor polities to negotiate treaties, such as the 1795 Spanish–American Treaty of San Lorenzo, that curbed the long-standing practice of using native allies against European rivals.[34] That development made it easier to fragment native alliances and to assign groups to reservations, often at a distance from former homelands and allies, which, in turn, undercut wealth-in-people and wealth-in-knowledge, which among semi-sedentary and nomadic Amerindians were critical elements of their socio-political systems.

Amerindian strategies for accommodating ethnic differences—social systems that tolerated relocations, and political practices to negotiate wide-reaching alliances for military cooperation, resource sharing, trade, and land use—provided for cultural and political resilience and regeneration for three centuries after 1492. Ironically, with the rise of the nation-state and the privileging of cultural homogeneity, they became marks of primitivism and tribalism.

---

[33] Ward Stavig, *The World of Túpac Amaru: Conflict, Community, and Identity in Colonial Peru* (Lincoln, NE, 1999); Gregory Dowd, *A Spirited Resistance: The North American Indian Struggle for Unity, 1745–1815* (Baltimore, MD, 1992).

[34] See the chapter by Daniel Richter in this volume.

The annals of early Atlantic exploration are replete with the names of Venetians and Genoese working under contract for Portuguese, Castilian, French, and English monarchs. Italians captained many early voyages of exploration, traded into West Africa, and financed settlements on the Canaries, Azores, Madeira, and Cape Verde Islands. Yet by the early sixteenth century, as already articulated in the 1494 Treaty of Tordesillas, the Portuguese and Castilians were seeking to monopolize African and American markets despite their continued reliance upon foreign bankers. The restrictions they imposed upon other Christian merchant competitors sufficiently breached established commercial practices that they elicited diplomatic protests from English and French monarchs who emphasized the unwarranted limits on their subjects' customary liberty of transit and trade, which, they argued, was protected by natural law. Ironically, once the English and French established overseas territorial claims, they too imposed restricted trading zones which officially were limited to their own subjects; indeed, in the early seventeenth century France even excluded French Protestants from trading in some territories.[35]

The imposition of restricted trading zones was a development that sharply differentiates early modern trading practices in the Atlantic world, except those in West Africa, from ancient and ongoing practices in the Mediterranean, the Indian Ocean, the China Seas, and across the caravan routes of the Sahara and Central Asia, where a wide diversity of diasporic polities were actively involved in long-distance trade.[36] These new Atlantic practices had profound governance and geopolitical implications. Restrictive commercial zones required a modicum of centralized control and governmental reach, and they reinforced an emerging emphasis on cultural homogeneity within a political system and an integration of landed and commercial power, which, by the late eighteenth century, found expression in the nation-state. These Atlantic changes also reconfigured the relation between conquest and commerce in expansionist endeavours. Where, previously, merchant networks had financed the military adventures of princes and kings, increasingly the militaries of some central governments were supporting the commercial adventures of their subjects. Finally, in some systems, notably Britain's, merchants were claiming vast tracts of land in historically unprecedented ways; the commercialization of land became more common and with it increasingly defined as a natural economic resource.

While the Spanish and Portuguese imposed the initial exclusions, the long-term consequences derived from the interactions between the five Atlantic empires. Thus the eclipse of diasporic polities (though not non-political diasporic networks) in the Atlantic was not a consequence of their internal development but of the actions of non-diasporic polities, in particular Atlantic empires over which diasporic polities had virtually no control. The principles of overseas expansion that the French and English

---

[35] Elizabeth Mancke, 'Empire and State', in David Armitage and Michael J. Braddick (eds.), *The British Atlantic World, 1500–1800* (Basingstoke, 2002), 175–95.

[36] Significantly, Spain, honoured the terms of the Treaty of Tordesillas by not trading in Africa and contracted with other Europeans to supply slaves until 1750.

articulated to challenge the Spanish and Portuguese, and the distinctive ways they implemented those principles, ultimately had profound consequential impacts for Atlantic, and then global, forms of governance and regulation.

In challenging the Iberians, the French and English repeatedly emphasized two customary practices with centuries-old antecedents. First was liberty of trade and transit—a liberty in the sense of a privilege customarily granted by a ruler—and which evoked ancient Afro-Eurasian practices. But in the French and English iterations, this liberty, rather than being negotiated between a merchant network and a landed ruler, was being negotiated between landed rulers for their own subjects. Second, the French and English asserted that Spanish and Portuguese claims of discovery, and their subsequent treaty agreements, were insufficient grounds for sustaining their wholesale claims to the extra-European world. If they had no natural-born subjects on the ground, their rivals could authorize the settlement of their own subjects, a principle that spurred European invocations of Roman law that property is created through the investment of labour.[37] In domestic contexts this principle concerned relations between a prince and subject, such as when peasants moved into marchlands or resettled land after periods of depopulation. Its invocation to challenge the Iberians' hegemonic claims shifted it from domestic to international contexts, and articulated it as a 'natural law' principle that Europeans applied to the Americas, albeit with some unease and equivocation, to justify taking land from the native inhabitants.

A number of far-reaching socio-political shifts occurred as these two ideas were entrenched in international negotiations over the extra-European world. Making liberty of trade and transit a matter of state-to-state negotiation shifted the structure of power of a few landed European states: domestically in terms of their commercial classes, and internationally in relation to other polities. They became arbiters of international trade, not just concerning who could trade in their kingdoms, but who could trade in vast parts of the world. Diasporic polities with no central landed government had to operate under land-based governments, as Sephardic Jews did from the Netherlands and Dutch overseas territories.[38] Niche polities with diasporic characteristics, such as Venice and Genoa which had risen to international prominence through trade, found their influence gradually eclipsed by Europe's new commercial powers. For most of the early modern era, the totality of commerce in the Afro-Eurasian world kept the impact of Atlantic developments modest, but by the late eighteenth century, the Atlantic practice of creating zones of protected commerce was making itself felt also in Indian Ocean and Pacific arenas of trade. Concerning the second principle, the elevation of improvement of land from a domestic negotiation between a prince and subject to a principle in international relations over how landed powers could claim land outside of their boundaries was new.

---

[37] Ken MacMillan, *Sovereignty and Possession in the English New World: The Legal Foundations of Empire, 1576–1640* (Cambridge, 2006), 17–48.

[38] Richard L. Kagan and Philip D. Morgan (eds.), *Atlantic Diasporas: Jews, Conversos, and Crypto-Jews in the Age of Mercantilism, 1500–1800* (Baltimore, MD, 2009).

The conjoining of the two principles was probably even more consequential, in that while they arose out of distinct political applications something totally distinctive emerged once they were combined. The principle of liberty of transit had applied to merchants, missionaries, scholars, and pilgrims, and was generally attributed to natural law or the law of nations; in other words it arose out of customary practices that were not from the legal tradition of any particular political system. The second principle, that claims to territory had to be confirmed by establishing a property claim through the settlement of subjects and their improvement of land, can be traced back to Roman law as found in Justinian codes, but had variations in different landed societies. French and English officials who authorized companies to trade in the Americas combined liberty of transit and trade with the right to claim and improve American land. In exchange for the expense of creating settlements, merchants could claim land that their monarch would acknowledge. French and English merchants, who customarily had limited access to landed property at home and especially in foreign contexts, now had access to vast tracts of American land. In contrast, as we have seen, European merchants in West Africa leased land from African rulers and could not claim ownership of it through royal charter or discovery. Similarly in Asia, French and English companies could not claim land through royal charter, but initially established trading factories on land leased or acquired through negotiations with Asian rulers. In the Americas, however, French and English companies acquired land through royal charters, the basis, for example, of the claims to Canada of the Compagnie des Cents-Associés.

Land acquisition in the Americas created powerful centrifugal momentum, and all five Atlantic empires grappled with the socio-political implications of wide availability of land for distribution to their natural-born subjects, because in European societies, land ownership was closely associated with governing powers. The questions that immediately arose were as follows: what would be the terms and mechanisms of distribution? how would systems of governance be structured in response to land acquisition? who would be entitled to own land, and with what attendant social obligations? And finally, what would be the terms of the alienation of lands from the indigenous inhabitants? At some stage each Atlantic empire adapted the institutions of European landed society, with distributions of land (though not necessarily freehold ownership) that carried governance obligations, ranging from the donatary captaincies and military orders of the Portuguese, the *encomiendas*, and later the haciendas, of the Spanish, the *seigneuries* of the French, the patroonships of the Dutch, to the proprietary colonies of the English. In the Portuguese, Spanish, and French cases, the institutions of landed society associated people with place. In Spanish America, for example, people had two political identities: one, citizenship based on membership in a city or town; and two, subjecthood to the monarch.[39] The Portuguese, Spanish, and French also used

---

[39] L. H. Roper and B. Van Ruymbeke (eds.), *Constructing Early Modern Empires: Proprietary Ventures in the Atlantic World, 1500–1750* (Leiden, 2007); Tamar Herzog, *Defining Nations: Immigrants and Citizens in Early Modern Spain and Spanish America* (New Haven, CT, 2003).

noble rank and the ecclesiastical offices and orders of the Catholic Church to project known institutional arrangements upon unknown territory. These institutions organized people by place, whether in relation to a landed elite or by parish.

The English and Dutch, however, tended to implement practices more reflective of merchant culture, including high levels of mobility, a legal system that allowed for contractual arrangements over great distances, and the lack of a regularized system of ranked society overseas. Instead status based on wealth became widely acknowledged, and was more transferable over great distances than landed status. For the English, the easy transferability of land became widespread, and in British North America became a favoured way of dispossessing native peoples of their land because it ostensibly was peaceful and non-coercive. Trading was deemed a natural human activity, although for many societies, including Amerindian ones, it did not include land. Indeed, in Europe landownership and land transfers by foreigners were severely restricted. Thus in British America, and to varying degrees elsewhere in the Americas, it was not just the higher incidences of landownership, and thus political participation, that were new, but also the close association of commerce and landownership, the greater ease of selling land, and the converting of landed wealth into mobile wealth and status.

These new practices of expansion differentiated political and economic developments in the early modern Americas from those in the Indian Ocean world and in West Africa. Their articulation, legitimization, and application occurred not just by coincidence among the five Atlantic powers, but through diplomatic debates and multilateral negotiations and agreements, some of which became embedded in treaties, others of which became accepted as customary international practice. When France and England challenged Spain and Portugal's hegemonic claims, they recalibrated the intellectual debate concerning overseas expansion from an Iberian emphasis on relations with non-Christian and previously unknown peoples to an English and French emphasis on equity of access to the extra-European world among Europeans. That shift, which privileged intra-European concerns, was often framed in terms of natural law or the law of nations, thereby obscuring its European bias.

The emerging multilateral conventions for negotiating competing overseas interests can be seen as a set of shared imperial practices within European international relations that survived Atlantic realignments in the Age of Revolution and subsequently found articulation elsewhere in the world. Britain justified its claims in Australia and the Pacific by echoing older arguments about claiming unimproved and underutilized land in the Americas. While France lost most of its overseas territories in the wars and revolutions of the long eighteenth century, it retained extensive privileges in the extra-European world through international cooperation; privileges normally associated with imperial powers. France and Britain negotiated their claims to Pacific islands, and collaborated in getting China to grant French and British citizens extraterritorial rights. When the British decided to recognize the independence of the Latin American republics and to influence control through economic investments, they were capitalizing on changes that made it possible for commercial interests to invest in land and fixed capital in foreign countries. While many countries resisted foreign investments and invoked the right of a country to restrict foreign ownership of land, nineteenth-century British and French investors could now argue that commercial exchange of land was a liberty protected by natural law. The new United States, while eschewing participation in European international relations, operated as an expanding territorial and commercial power in the lee of British foreign policy and using the principles of expansion that were articulated in the early modern era.

West Africa illustrates how new Atlantic political practices came to define global political practices. For three centuries, trade along the Atlantic coast of Africa shared similarities with the eastern Mediterranean where maritime and caravan routes converged and a diversity of ethnic groups engaged in commerce. In Atlantic Africa, Europeans could not impose the trading restrictions they imposed in the Americas. West African polities underwent transformations wrought by greater Atlantic engagement, but they mediated those changes for themselves. In the late eighteenth century, however, Europeans began to intervene more frequently in West African affairs, establishing Sierra Leone for former slaves, abolishing the slave trade, and advising Africans about other trading opportunities. Nevertheless, across most of the continent, African polities kept European involvement limited. Finally, in the 1880s, European governments were to argue about Africa being a *terra nullius*, a land without significant human improvement, thus justifying the division of Africa amongst themselves. This was a variant on arguments used to dispossess indigenous peoples in the Americas, Australia, and the Pacific, one that Europeans had knowingly not used for Africa in the early modern era.

Atlantic political history is far more than a repackaging of colony-to-nation narratives. Rather it offers a way to reassess critical developments in modern history: the linkages between commerce and colonization; the resilience of non-European political systems; the role of international relations in supporting and mediating Atlantic expansion; and the deployment by Europeans of Atlantic practices in other parts of the world.

BIBLIOGRAPHY

Akyeampong, Emmanuel Kwaku (ed.), *Themes in West African History* (Athens, OH, 2006).
Aldrich, Robert, and John Connell, *The Last Colonies* (Cambridge, 1998).
Curtin, Philip D., *Cross-Cultural Trade in World History* (Cambridge, 1984).
Greene, Jack P. (ed.) *Exclusionary Empire: English Liberty Overseas, 1600–1900* (Cambridge, 2010).
—— and Philip D. Morgan (eds.), *Atlantic History: A Critical Appraisal* (Oxford, 2009).
McCabe, Ina Baghdiantz, Gelina Harlaftis, and Ionna Pepelasis Minoglou (eds.), *Diaspora Entrepreneurial Networks: Four Centuries of History* (Oxford, 2005).
MacMillan, Ken, *Sovereignty and Possession in the English New World: The Legal Foundations of Empire, 1576–1640* (Cambridge, 2006).

Russell-Wood, A. J. R. (ed.), *Government and Governance of European Empires, 1415–1800* (Aldershot, 2000).

—— (ed.), *Local Government in European Overseas Empires, 1450–1800*, 2 vols. (Aldershot, 1999).

Weber, David J., *Bárbaros: Spaniards and their Savages in the Age of Enlightenment* (New Haven, CT, 2005).

CHAPTER 23

ATLANTIC LAW

Transformations of a Regional Legal Regime

LAUREN BENTON

LEGAL histories have often been placed within studies of intra-imperial or national political ordering. In Atlantic history, law also functioned as an element of regional formation. Legal practices and discourses circulated widely, and similar patterns of legal politics produced parallel regulatory shifts around the region. While continuing to trace changes within separate systems of law, recent scholarship in comparative and colonial legal history reveals these elements of regional legal continuity.

Three overlapping historical processes guided the formation and change of an Atlantic legal regime between 1450 and 1820. First, legal actors across the Atlantic world, especially but not exclusively Europeans, drew on elements of a shared legal repertoire, in the process helping to circulate familiar discourses and practices of law. Second, patterns of legal pluralism and reform were widely replicated, producing synchronous shifts and the emergence of an inter-imperial regulatory order. Third, inter-imperial relations in the Atlantic world helped to shape a regionally circulating discourse about the connections between imperial constitutions and international law.

This chapter cannot treat these elements of Atlantic law comprehensively but instead highlights processes contributing to each trend. The first section considers some similarities in strategies for extending sovereignty and notes the prominence of often indirect references to Roman law by European sojourners and settlers. I then turn to repeating patterns of legal pluralism, discussing in particular the regional effects of maritime conflicts and of decentralized legal authority, including control over slaves. This point leads to the observation that, particularly in the late eighteenth century and into the early nineteenth century, legal conflicts in the Atlantic world stood at the centre of new discourses of imperial, constitutional, and international law. While noting the most salient differences between legal systems within the Atlantic world, the chapter emphasizes shared features contributing to the formation and transformation of an inter-imperial Atlantic legal regime.

Imperial legal repertoires

Colonial legal histories have often focused on tracing and defining the continuities and discontinuities of metropolitan and colonial law. For the legal history of British North America, the degree to which English common law was carried into the colonies has formed a central research question. For Spanish America, historians have emphasized the Spanish crown's efforts to streamline legal administration in the empire and, even, to engineer jurisdictional tensions in the empire that would serve to strengthen the crown as the ultimate legal arbiter. These approaches have a very long pedigree. Imperial officials from the earliest days of Atlantic empire were preoccupied with defining the nature of legal difference in the colonies. British colonial legal histories often begin with an analysis of Calvin's Case in 1608, which occasioned Sir Edward Coke to offer the ruling that English subjecthood and the king's legal authority, but not the protections of the common law, extended beyond England to the crown's other realms. For Spanish America, the crown's decree that Castilian law would be the law of the colonies, or the insistence on controlling ecclesiastical appointments in empire, provided similar points of divergence. Such arrangements positioned Atlantic colonies as realms of clearly defined legal difference. The efforts were associated, at times more prominently than at others, with a broader discourse contrasting Europeans as bearers of law and civility with barbarous inhabitants of an extra-European sphere rendered as a sphere of lawlessness.[1]

A story of stark legal contrasts between metropole and colony is overly simplistic, however. Three aspects of European Atlantic law in particular lead us to complicate this narrative. First, European sojourners and settlers in the Atlantic world carried law with them everywhere. Efforts to render colonies as legally exceptional coexisted with an insistence that subjects of the crown retained their subjecthood wherever they went. Christians were expected to remain Christians, a status that had legal as well as religious implications. This dimension of 'personal law' had important implications for the way sojourners and settlers invoked the law. A discourse about subjecthood pervaded early Atlantic projects and also influenced colonial legal conflicts. Ties of subjecthood could be strategically claimed from the top, by officials seeking gains for the crown through the actions of informal imperial agents, and they could be activated from the bottom, by sojourners eager for crown protection and by settlers positioning themselves for future patronage.

References to subjecthood had clear juridical meaning. Though historians have tended to cite Jean Bodin's writings on sovereignty in the sixteenth century as an expression of early absolutist ideology, Bodin's ideas also built upon a construction of sovereignty that emphasized the ties of sovereign to subject as its foundational quality.

---

[1] Eliga Gould, 'Zones of Law, Zones of Violence: The Legal Geography of the British Atlantic, circa 1772', *William and Mary Quarterly*, 60/3 (2003), 471–510.

This relation framed the unchecked prerogatives of sovereigns and permitted the imagination of empires as entities constructed out of the extension of sovereignty through the actions of individual subjects travelling or settling in regions very far from home. Each subject, in effect, carried law with him; each could at times make explicit claims about promoting crown interests.

We see the influence of this way of thinking about sovereignty as a juridical tie in the earliest sojourns into the wider Atlantic world. The Portuguese sought commercial advantage in West Africa in the sixteenth century by emphasizing the subjecthood of Luso-Africans when it was convenient to do so and repudiating them as subjects when it was not. Individual Portuguese agents cited evidence of their own status as loyal subjects in chronicles designed to bring them favour, and cast aspersions on the loyalties of rivals and new subjects. Such strategies continued to flourish on the other side of the Atlantic, with conflicts over subjecthood surfacing especially in the context of newly forming political communities. Even European settlers with rebellious tendencies strategically celebrated the ties of subject to sovereign. Spanish subordinates who overthrew their commanders presented their actions as those of loyal subjects rooting out corruption and misrule. In Virginia, Nathaniel Bacon proclaimed his loyalty and called into question the legitimacy of the government of Governor Berkeley, accused of usurping the king's authority; Berkeley in turn charged Bacon and his followers with treason.[2]

Indians in the New World were very quick to learn this language of subjecthood. In New England on the verge of the outbreak of King Philip's War, Indian leaders wrote to the king to remind him of their loyalty and his duty to protect them as his subjects. In Spanish America, Indians exercised their right to petition the king directly. They also became active litigants in the courts, suing both other Indians and Spaniards. Two centuries later, Indian litigants engaged in forum shopping in the Andes to appeal to royal over local officials, citing loyalty to the distant crown. Royalism is perhaps best understood as part of an array of legal strategies rather than simply a strain within colonial politics. Even pirates, with an eye on possible future cases in prize courts or criminal prosecutions, went out of their way to assert their loyalty to particular sovereigns and to construct paper trails that would support those claims.[3]

Empires' reliance on structures of delegated legal authority also worked to carry law into supposedly lawless parts of the Atlantic. Ships' law is an example. Ship captains operated as delegated legal authorities who presided as legal officers over their ships, with the expectation, common across European maritime empires, that capital cases

---

[2] For more on Atlantic treason, see Lauren Benton, *A Search for Sovereignty: Law and Geography in European Empires, 1400–1900* (Cambridge, 2010), chapter 2.

[3] Jenny Pulsipher, *Subjects unto the Same King: Indians, English, and the Contest for Authority in Colonial New England* (Philadelphia, PA, 2005); Brian Owensby, *Empire of Law and Indian Justice in Colonial Mexico* (Stanford, CA, 2008); Sergio Serulnikov, *Subverting Colonial Authority: Challenges to Spanish Rule in Eighteenth-Century Southern Andes* (Durham, NC, 2003); Lauren Benton, 'Legal Spaces of Empire: Piracy and the Origins of Ocean Regionalism', *Comparative Studies in Society and History*, 47 (2005), 700–24.

should be referred to metropolitan courts for action. The recognition that ships acted as vectors of metropolitan law coexisted with an emerging vision of the seas as a common space regulated by natural law. This argument, developed especially by Hugo Grotius in the early seventeenth century to defend Dutch trading interests in the Indian Ocean, was repeated in ways that also supported European commercial expansion in the Atlantic, particularly challenges to Spanish control over the South Atlantic. The ties of ships to sovereigns, and the legal authority held by captains, meanwhile continued to structure shipboard relations and influence inter-imperial legal disputes.

In early colonizing ventures, leaders' shipboard legal prerogatives were effectively transferred to land, either to rule over garrisons or to affirm authority over reconnaissance forces. Sir Humphrey Gilbert, at the head of an expedition in 1583 to settle in Newfoundland, and Samuel de Champlain, on his 1609 reconnaissance in the St Lawrence region, merged their shipboard command with legal authority over men under their charge once their expeditions moved on land. Some legal posts were structured in ways to make this flexibility possible. For example, the Spanish adapted a category of legal officials first used in the Reconquest to travel with strike forces in Muslim territories and adjudicate disputes among co-religionists. In the New World, these *adelantados* had the authority to found new towns, hold hearings, order punishments, or create municipal governments anywhere along the routes they travelled. Even as settlement changed the structure of delegated legal authority across the New World, the line between law-on-the-move and settled law remained blurred in places. An especially intriguing example occurred in Newfoundland, where the commodore of the Royal Navy Squadron sent to patrol the fishery in summer gradually took on the authority of commander-in-chief on land.[4]

Alongside subjecthood and the delegation of legal authority, a third element of continuity in Atlantic law resided in the replication of familiar practices across European Atlantic empires. Often the roots of these practices lay in the shared repertoire of Roman law. Europe in the eleventh and twelfth centuries had experienced an enthusiastic revival of interest in Roman law sources, and the core texts of this reception, the writings produced under the Emperor Justinian and known as the Justinian Digest, were made widely available. Legal training in late medieval Europe had been centred in regional universities, most notably at Bologna, and focused on Roman and canon law. By the sixteenth century, the explicit emphasis on a shared legal tradition had faded to some degree, but continuities deriving from this connection remained. The important Spanish compendium of laws called the *Siete partidas* contained many Roman law elements. Even in places such as England, where common law courts expanded their jurisdiction at the expense of parts of the legal system that relied more closely on sources shared with continental law, jurists and other legal elites still had knowledge of Roman law and, indeed, relied heavily on classical sources in legal writing.

---

[4] Jerry Bannister, *The Rule of the Admirals: Law, Custom, and Naval Government in Newfoundland, 1699–1832* (Toronto, 2003).

We can see this pan-Atlantic legal discourse most clearly in actions and pronounce-ments directed by European actors at other Europeans. In making and defending claims to New World enclaves and territories beyond them, sojourners and settlers knew to draw on legal symbols that could be readily understood by other imperial agents. Ceremonies of possession had mainly similar characteristics across European empires. Voyagers placed markers and settlements at prominent places, often near the mouths of rivers, to signify inchoate claims to territories beyond. Mapping was often intended as another way of marking claims, and, when possible, the markers were supplemented or replaced with settlements and forts indicating occupation. These moves drew on knowledge, probably conveyed through familiarity with the Justinian Digest, of ways of acquiring private property in Roman law. Rituals of possession represented creative interpretations of Roman law, filtered through many influences and often imperfectly understood. It is significant that the acts were selected in part precisely because they were intelligible across imperial orders.[5]

Roman law as a flexible source of law in the European Atlantic did not by itself determine the continuity of practices across empires. In the same way that imperial agents drew creatively from localized metropolitan legal sources such as Germanic codes, the English common law, and Spanish *fueros* (unwritten or written local law codes), they invoked Roman law selectively, in declaring or challenging ties of subject-hood, defining new political entities in empire, or establishing claims before rivals. In the early Atlantic world, this repertoire was available in different forms to Portuguese, Spanish, French, Dutch, and English actors, and the strategic adoption and adaptation of its elements around the Atlantic represented one aspect of an emerging regional law.

JURISDICTIONS AND 'JURISPRACTICE'

Legal continuities were not restricted to Europeans' citing of familiar practices and doctrines. European legal systems shared with those in Africa and the Americas structural qualities that in turn facilitated cross-cultural movement and negotiation. In particular, legal systems around the early modern Atlantic world housed multiple, sometimes overlapping jurisdictions. Many arenas of law were relatively sheltered from the direct control or influence of imperial state law. This high degree of legal pluralism, and the jurisdictional tensions it engendered, formed an important dimension of a regional legal regime.

At the time that European Atlantic powers entered into long-distance trade and Atlantic colonizing, they were structured as 'composite' states featuring complex

---

[5] Ken MacMillan, *Sovereignty and Possession in the English New World: The Legal Foundations of Empire, 1576–1640* (Cambridge, 2006); Lauren Benton and Benjamin Straumann, 'Acquiring Empire by Law: From Roman Doctrine to Early Modern European Practice', *Law and History Review*, 28/1 (2010), 1–38.

jurisdictional orders.[6] Royal or secular state law operated forums that competed with ecclesiastical and merchant courts. Spain's multi-layered and intricate legal order invited individuals to manoeuvre legally by claiming exemptions from crown prosecutions under local or ecclesiastical law. Regions within Spain had their own *fueros*, and the Church claimed rights to jurisdiction over certain classes of people—in addition to clergy, widows, orphans, and other 'wretched people'—and over particular spheres of social action. In England, a complex jumble of jurisdictions also promoted forum shopping by litigants, while civil law courts and lawyers tried to protect civil jurisdictions from the steady encroachments of the common law. Ecclesiastical prerogatives were under attack in Protestant Europe, but the distinction between secular and religious law remained salient. Whilst jurisdictional complexities underwent change in colonial settings, they were sometimes exacerbated as colonial factions jockeyed for influence. Europeans relied on the jurisdictional split between canon and state law as an analogy upon which to draw in structuring the relations between imposed law and the law of non-Christian inhabitants or Christian converts in conquered territories.[7]

Europeans encountered familiar patterns of jurisdictional complexity in African and New World societies. The multi-jurisdictional structure of African polities and the layered sovereignty of American Indian political communities offered legal routines for incorporating subordinate groups, hosting merchant diasporas, and even accommodating conquerors. The prevalence of multicentric legal orders provided an element of institutional continuity in a world divided by many legal authorities. In West Africa, host polities had long been accustomed to extending limited jurisdictional prerogatives to diasporic merchant communities in their midst. This receptivity to semi-autonomous minority communities allowed the Portuguese to establish trading posts and to order their own affairs within them. Iberians, for their part, had experience with managing a legal order in which various religious groups (Christians, Jews, and Muslims) held different legal status, lived apart, and enjoyed a degree of legal autonomy. Similarly, in the Americas, the Spaniards recognized and even promoted Indians' subjecthood, but they also allowed and in many ways encouraged Indians' separate conflict resolution. Much like minority groups within other large empires, Indians could adjudicate some disputes while opting to bring others to imperial courts, especially complaints against other Indians over access to resources. A traveller moving from the Mediterranean to the Atlantic in the sixteenth or seventeenth centuries would have found such practices unsurprising. Forum shopping, the appeal to royal or imperial justice over local courts, the strategic use of labelling (for example, subjects defining themselves as Indian, mestizo, or Spanish in different forums in New Spain), certain legal protections for captives, and the reserved rights of imperial sovereigns or

---

[6] J. H. Elliott, 'A Europe of Composite Monarchies', *Past and Present*, 137 (1992), 48–71.

[7] James Muldoon, *Popes, Lawyers, and Infidels: The Church and the Non-Christian World, 1250–1550* (Philadelphia, PA, 1979); Lauren Benton, *Law and Colonial Cultures: Legal Regimes in World History, 1400–1900* (Cambridge, 2002).

host polities to intervene in capital cases—these features were repeated across (and, indeed, beyond) the Atlantic world.

Alongside familiar forms of legal pluralism, commerce and conquest inspired new, mainly disaggregated attempts at devising imperial legal policy. The Atlantic colonies became legally different both by design and through politics; fashioned as jurisdiction-ally simpler realms than those at home, they were also nurseries for new laws, and for the studied ignorance of imperial decrees. Some differences lined up along imperial or religious lines, while others reflected peculiar local interactions; most variations com-bined these influences. In the Portuguese trading-post empire, captains had consider-able latitude in administering justice and could appoint *ouvidors* (magistrates) in the Portuguese empire. The crown periodically sought to tighten its reins, issuing the Ordenações Manuelinas in 1521 and appointing judges (*juizes da fora*, or judges from outside, and *corregidores*, superior court judges) to oversee magistrates. A High Court (Relação) was established in Bahia in 1609, following a pattern begun with the founding of a Relação at Goa in 1544. Transfers of convicts from Brazil to Angola and vice versa, and even the placement of parts of West Africa under Brazilian court jurisdiction, show the degree to which Portuguese officials considered the Atlantic settlements and posts as part of a single legal sphere. In the Spanish empire, a key institution was the municipality, whose councils carried some judicial authority and could determine membership in local communities, a status that came with certain legal prerogatives.[8] By the end of the sixteenth century, the Spanish Americas housed ten *audiencias* (high courts), whose officials straddled the imperial bureaucracy and local elite factions. Both Spanish and Portuguese empires established offices of the Inquisition, which func-tioned as courts under a special jurisdiction formally separate from both *audiencias* and ordinary ecclesiastical courts. In Spanish America, this move generated further jurisdictional complexity as Indians were soon made exempt from prosecution under the Inquisition, classified as 'wretched persons' (*miserables*) requiring special legal protections, and given access to a special court and to legal officials (*protectores de indios*) to assist in preparing their cases.

English colonies were inserted within a less centralized legal order. They continued to defer to the crown on some matters of law and to refer to England for models of court practice, but the colonies also diverged, both from English law and from one another, soon after their founding. Some of the divergence reflected differences in their relation to crown authority. The crown delegated legal authority by issuing letters patent, relying also on corporate legal forms to assign jurisdiction to companies (such as the Virginia Company) and to other formal corporate structures in Plymouth, Connecticut, New York, and Rhode Island. Proprietary settlements such as Maryland and Pennsylvania offered yet another pattern in which at first lawmaking was con-centrated in the hands of proprietors. At the end of the seventeenth century, the crown

---

[8] Tamar Herzog, *Defining Nations: Immigrants and Citizens in Early Modern Spain and Spanish America* (New Haven, CT, 2003).

converted most governments into royal colonies, and governors became central agents in the legal systems in conjunction with assemblies.

Within this diversity of imperial and intra-imperial institutions, some elements of legal conflict were repeated. Legal officials everywhere learned quickly to position themselves as loyal subjects while also establishing and protecting their own authority. The Spanish quip 'Obedezco pero no cumplo' ('I obey but do not execute'), intended to describe colonial officials' responses to unwelcome crown directives, found parallels in the strategies of officials in other empires who relied upon slow communications and multi-layered bureaucracies to respond selectively and incompletely to metropolitan mandates. Across the Caribbean, prize court officials ignored unofficial news about new treaties in order to condemn captures supposedly made in time of war. In New France and the French Caribbean, as one historian remarks, colonists 'normally questioned, evaded, or modified laws' and only obeyed them 'as a last resort'.[9]

Even when they did not intentionally alter the law, legal actors far from home often introduced innovations. One historian has offered the term 'jurispractice' to describe the combination of legal culture and strategy followed by Indians in their interactions with colonists.[10] The term could equally apply to settlers engaged in legal conflicts. Despite the circulation of law books from Europe and a growing capacity for training lawyers in the Americas, settlers and emerging creole elites had a varied and often flawed understanding of how the law operated in metropolitan centres, where jurisdictional complexity and doctrinal confusion were the norms. Even as they struggled to establish and document legal positions that would be upheld on appeal, colonists operated on the basis of impressions, hearsay, and often vague instructions about what constituted proper legal forms. This posturing often resulted in colonists' actions being recognized as legally valid.

Conditions in the colonies also prompted innovation because they presented new challenges. The legal treatment, incorporation, or marginalization of indigenous peoples within and near European-controlled enclaves created further intra- and cross-imperial differences while also replicating patterns of conflict. The elaborate institutions and debates of the Spanish empire regarding the legal treatment of Indians have no precise counterpart in British or French colonies. These debates concentrated in the first half of the sixteenth century and, especially in the writings of Fray Bartolomé de Las Casas and Francisco de Vitoria, produced a sustained critique of the Spanish conquest and its aftermath, based on the argument that Indians possessed rights under natural law. This line of critique had important practical results, in particular an end to legal enslavement of Indians and the protection of a distinctive legal status for Indians. Historians often note the contrasting situation in British North America, where several turning points in the legal treatment of Indians—particularly

---

[9] James Pritchard, *In Search of Empire: The French in the Americas, 1670–1730* (Cambridge, 2004), 260.

[10] Katherine Hermes, 'The Law of Native Americans, to 1815', in Michael Grossberg and Christopher Tomlins (eds.), *The Cambridge History of Law in America I* (Cambridge, 2008), 32–62.

the late seventeenth-century conflicts of King Philip's War and Bacon's Rebellion—
seem to have foreclosed the possibility of a plural legal order in which Indian jurisdictions would nestle within or operate alongside colonial courts. Yet even here, the events
did not eclipse Indian legal authority or end Indian participation in colonial legal
conflicts in the definitive way sometimes imagined. Especially on the margins of white
settlement, as occurred over the broad area of the Pays d'en Haut, where neither French
settlers nor Indians secured a monopoly on violence, hybrid legal practices were
common.[11] Strikingly similar adaptive legal systems characterized African zones of
encounter, from West Africa to Angola and near the nascent Cape Colony.

While guiding local differences in the law, these conditions also produced similar
patterns of conflict which in turn urged parallel institutional responses, including an
increasing interest on the part of imperial officials in centralizing and lending greater
consistency to legal institutions. Because European empires were global enterprises,
information about jurisdictional conflicts and the ambition of formulating imperial
legal policies did not initially mark the Atlantic as a separate or distinctive legal region.
That shift began to occur toward the end of the seventeenth century, when a thickening
of imperial legal institutions in the Atlantic corresponded to the growth of commerce
and contraband, as well as to intensifying inter-imperial competition.

In response to a surge in piracy and privateering in the last decades of the seventeenth century, new systems of colonial prize courts, with distinctive Atlantic variants,
were established. Paradoxically, this shift did not mark an expansion of maritime law
but occurred in the context of a widespread trend toward the absorption of maritime
law into other jurisdictions. Admiralty law was losing ground to the common law in
England, and maritime law was blending with non-specialized merchant law in Spain,
France, and the Netherlands. These institutional fixes at home were unsettled by
imperial expansion. In the Spanish empire, for example, the crown decreed in 1674
that prizes should be taken to the nearest *audiencia* and pirates might be tried in
colonial courts. This adjustment was intended to weaken incentives for local communities to provide cover for contraband trading. In England, by the second half of the
seventeenth century, the process of shrinking admiralty jurisdiction had culminated
with its loss of authority over maritime disputes arising on land and over acts in non-
tidal waters. Admiralty courts retained jurisdiction over prize cases and formal jurisdiction over piracy, and trials of pirates were shifted to special courts where they were
conducted with the common law institution of juries. Vice-admiralty courts had
already developed in the colonies, mainly to deal with local concerns such as sea
wrecks in Bermuda and piracy and prize in Jamaica. In the last decades of the
seventeenth century, these courts gained stature, and other vice-admiralty courts
were founded. A 1673 reform required pirates to be tried in admiralty courts, and the
1700 'Act for the More Effectual Suppression of Piracy' created a special procedure
allowing for a seven-person commission to be established to try pirates anywhere in the

---

[11] Richard White, *The Middle Ground: Indians, Empires, and Republics in the Great Lakes Region,*
1650–1815 (Cambridge, 1991).

empire.[12] Imperial officials meanwhile increasingly turned to the vice-admiralty courts to enforce the Navigation Acts. The French empire was slower to erect functioning prize courts, but the ambition to create an imperial network of forums emerged in the same years, with the crown's announcement in 1672 that it would establish admiralty courts in the empire.

Such parallel intra-imperial changes began to add up to something more, an apparent shift toward a regional regulatory order. Mariners seizing ships could still expect rulings both to reflect local interests and to refer to treaties and states of war. The difference was that after the end of the seventeenth century, a network of courts existed around the Atlantic with jurisdiction to try matters that had formerly been referred back to metropolitan centres, studiously ignored, or dealt with in idiosyncratic ways by local forums. We see the effects of this new state of affairs only a few decades later when, in the lead-up to the War of Jenkins's Ear, Spanish *guardacostas* hauled captured English ships to Havana and announced that they had been declared good prizes. While Spanish officials claimed that they were merely doing what the English admiralty courts did, English officials were left to complain through diplomatic channels about irregularities in seizures and lax procedures. They accused the Spaniards of piracy, but in a legally infused discourse that recognized separate but interrelating networks of imperial law.[13] Another example of rivals adjusting legal strategies in tandem unfolded in the middle decades around the Dutch entrepôt of Curaçao, where the Dutch West Indian Company responded to Spanish laws offering freedom for runaway slaves from Protestant empires by regulating more closely the movement of blacks and mulattos on ships entering and leaving the harbour. Though working at cross-purposes, the Spanish and Dutch legal policies produced a thickening of trade regulation at the micro-regional level.[14] Such partial and oddly constructed regulatory matrices did not reduce violence—the Seven Years War and the naval seizures of the Napoleonic era were yet to come—but they did mark a new insistence that sea raiding, and inter-imperial conflicts over property, could and should be contained and controlled by law.

This expansion of legal infrastructure was visible not only in the maritime world but in other practices, on both sides of the Atlantic. English and French settlements multiplied in North America, and both empires blended civil and military authority in frontier garrisons. In the French empire, a programme of imposing royal justice included the founding of nine Colonial Sovereign Courts in New France and the French Caribbean between 1663 and 1717. As Iberian rule solidified in regions like the River Plate and the interior of Brazil that had been on the margins of empire, a geographically broader legal and institutional net included new courts; the formation and decline of semi-autonomous legal spheres such as the Jesuit missions; and the rise

---

[12] See Robert Ritchie, *Captain Kidd and the War against the Pirates* (Cambridge, MA, 1986).

[13] Benton, *A Search for Sovereignty*, chapter 3.

[14] Linda Rupert, 'Marronage, Manumission, and Maritime Trade in the Early Modern Caribbean', *Slavery and Abolition*, 30/3 (2009), 361–82.

of politically influential, legally trained creole elites. The expansion of colonial court systems was accompanied by imperial legal codification. The Spanish crown ordered the collection and publication of all laws applying to the Indies in the *Recopilación de los reynos de las Indias*, which appeared in 1661. The French crown took actions beginning in the 1660s to impose the same body of customary law (the Custom of Paris), common civil procedure, a criminal code, and the Slave Code or Code Noir (1685).

Synchronous shifts in law in European states also affected the wider region. Vagrancy legislation gripped all the Atlantic European polities, part of a broad-scale criminal-ization of the poor that influenced perceptions of voluntary and involuntary migrants to the colonies. An overhauling of legal instruments in European finance altered the calculation of the risks and costs of long-distance trade, while the threat of large losses during wartime promoted marine insurance and related litigation. Newly forming fiscal-military states depended on the expansion of navies, and on large-scale systems of recruitment, impressments, and labour discipline under military command—a cross-regional legal system nestled within the imperial order.

COERCED LABOUR AND LEGAL AUTHORITY

Late eighteenth-century imperial law featured the intensification of state-sanctioned labour coercion over vast areas. Authority over subordinates encompassed a wide array of prerogatives to discipline workers and administer summary punishments, including often very harsh sentences of corporal punishment, while in theory courts retained the power to inflict capital punishment. Coerced labour appeared in new forms, like debt peonage on the haciendas of New Spain, and intensified in older forms, for example with increasing penalties under British master–servant law.[15]

The expansion of convict transportation across the Atlantic formed a part of this larger trend. After the end of the Seven Years War, the Spanish shipped convicts and deserters to work on fortifications in *presidios* in Havana, San Juan, and the Philip-pines, and the French began sending political prisoners, and later common criminals, to French Guiana.[16] The Portuguese already possessed a well-developed imperial system of convict transportation, sending about 50,000 convicts overseas, to destina-tions in the Indian Ocean and the Atlantic, including Brazil, Angola, and São Tomé, before the middle of the eighteenth century.[17] The English transported about 60,000

---

[15] Douglas Hay and Paul Craven, *Masters, Servants, and Magistrates in Britain and the Empire, 1562–1955* (Chapel Hill, NC, 2004).

[16] Ruth Pike, *Penal Servitude in Early Modern Spain* (Madison, WI, 1983); Miranda Spieler, 'Empire and Underworld: Guiana in the French Legal Imagination c. 1789–1870' (Columbia University doctoral dissertation, 2005).

[17] Timothy Coates, *Convicts and Orphans: Forced and State-Sponsored Colonizers in the Portuguese Empire, 1550–1755* (Stanford, CA, 2001).

convicted men and women to North America and the Caribbean between the 1660s and 1770s, with the vast majority going to just two colonies, Maryland and Virginia.[18] The greatest expansion came after 1718, when Parliament passed the Transportation Act, allowing the courts to make transportation a sentence rather than a conditional pardon substituting for another punishment. Although banishment overseas and the exploitation of convicts in colonial ventures had been common practices in the earliest years of colonizing, the new systems were distinguished by a systemic quality that connected policing measures in Europe to the creation of new and harsher disciplinary regimes for transported convicts.

Systems of slave labour were structurally similar to these legal arrangements, but the law of slavery was also distinctive in two main ways: the degree of power conferred on slave owners and the legal treatment of slaves as property. Like other forms of delegated authority, the master's role was one of control over a semi-autonomous sphere, a system of 'plantation justice' in which he had discretion to judge and punish.[19] When slaves were tried in courts, the system was stacked against them; judges were usually slaveholders and slave testimony was not formally admitted. Punishments ranged from whipping, the most common, to capital punishment, though courts held formal jurisdiction over capital cases and were in general hesitant to deprive masters of their investments. The underlying view that slaves constituted property meant that civil suits, particularly over damage to slaves that were the property of another, routinely arose and made up a significant portion of legal cases involving slaves. Commercial law and slave law also intersected because slaves were used as divisible property, with shares divided among owners and creditors.[20]

Patterns of litigation and the degree to which criminal courts operated as a control on masters' prerogatives varied with such factors as the goods being produced, slave owners' perceptions of the dangers of slave insurrections, and slaves' own strategies. Slave law in the Atlantic world operated on several levels as an element of regional legal continuity. Upholding slavery in particular places depended on the recognition of a regional system protecting the legal prerogatives of slave owners. We see this dimension in the borrowing of slave code provisions across imperial legal orders. We see it, too, in litigation over slaves in courts of adjacent colonies as, for example, in New Orleans cases brought by exiled slave owners seeking to regain or retain control over their slaves after fleeing Haiti, or to recover insurance losses after slave mutinies. We see it in a general sense in the 'compensatory expansions' of plantation slavery after the Haitian Revolution.[21]

---

[18] G. Morgan and P. Rushton, *Eighteenth-Century Criminal Transportation: The Formation of the Criminal Atlantic* (New York, 2004), 12.

[19] Philip Morgan, *Slave Counterpoint: Black Culture in the Eighteenth-Century Chesapeake and Lowcountry* (Chapel Hill, NC, 1998), 277.

[20] Ariela Gross, *Double Character: Slavery and Mastery in the Antebellum Southern Courtroom* (Princeton, NJ, 2000).

[21] Seymour Drescher, 'The Fragmentation of Atlantic Slavery and the British Intercolonial Slave Trade', in Walter Johnson (ed.), *The Chattel Principle: Internal Slave Trades in the Americas*

While regional continuities were interrupted by formal differences between metropolitan and colonial slave law, historians have shown recently that the distinctions were not precisely between 'free' and 'unfree' parts of the empire. French crown edicts in 1716 and 1738 sought to regulate conditions under which French subjects might transport slaves to France and continue to hold them as property, and even these regulations were flouted by planters.[22] In England, the celebrated 1772 Somerset case, in which the Court of King's Bench ruled that James Somerset, a slave who escaped after being brought by his owner from Jamaica to England, could not be sold back into slavery and forcibly shipped to Jamaica, followed a long period in which English courts had protected 'near servitude' or 'slavish servitude' in England.[23] Mansfield's ruling in the Somerset case also did not challenge the legality of slavery elsewhere. The ruling was less a harbinger of emancipation than an attempt to inject flexibility into the imperial legal order by recognizing the legality of servitude while restricting the geographic range of laws protecting the disciplinary power of slave masters.[24]

Africans and African captives were not passive actors within this legal regime. Although they ultimately produced a small proportion of slaves for the Atlantic trade, judicial mechanisms for enslaving Africans pre-dated the arrival of European traders in Africa and expanded in response to growing demand for slaves. Captives, for their part, adopted strategies in the New World based in part on expectations about the legal order. Maroon communities, for example, pursued and sometimes secured a status in relation to plantation societies that was similar to that of a subordinate jurisdiction. In Jamaica, maroons agreed in the peace treaty of 1739 to refer capital cases and cases involving whites to the colonial judiciary. We can surmise that some slaves understood that they were being used as collateral for debts and sold or awarded in part-shares to multiple owners in property or credit transactions, though it was usually impossible for them to defend against these actions. Even in their most disadvantaged role in courts, as defendants in criminal cases, slaves sometimes managed to adopt postures designed to deflect the worst outcomes.[25] Such strategies both changed the course of individual cases and, over time, produced systemic results, as when, for example, British military courts ruled in 1809 that they would begin accepting into evidence the testimony of slaves.

Taken together, historians' findings show that eighteenth-century Atlantic law presents an apparent contradiction. On the one hand, metropolitan powers began to attempt to exert greater control and influence over colonial legal systems, so that we can refer in this

(New Haven, CT, 2004), 235; Walter Johnson, 'White Lies: Human Property and Domestic Slaving aboard the Slave Ship Creole', *Atlantic Studies*, 5/2 (2008), 237–63.

[22] Sue Peabody, *There are no Slaves in France: The Political Culture of Race and Slavery in the Ancien Régime* (New York, 1996).

[23] George Van Cleve, 'Somerset's Case Revisited: Somerset's Case and its Antecedents in Imperial Perspective', *Law and History Review*, 24/3 (2006), 601–64.

[24] Daniel Hulsebosch, 'Nothing But Liberty: Somerset's Case and the British Empire', *Law and History Review*, 24/3 (2006), 647–58.

[25] Thomas Morris, *Southern Slavery and the Law, 1619–1860* (Chapel Hill, NC, 1996).

period to 'imperial legal policy', an elusive objective for empires before the late seventeenth century. On the other hand, it is precisely in this period that we see a sharper divergence between legal administration and practice in metropolitan centres and their colonies, as well as increasing variability across colonies. A result of this tension between imperial consolidation and divergence was to highlight a series of legal problems connected to constitutional questions about the legitimacy, viability, and structure of empires.

ATLANTIC LAW AND IMPERIAL CONSTITUTIONS

At key moments, trends and events in the Atlantic world raised to prominence issues that stood at the intersection of imperial constitutional law and an emerging 'international' law. They included questions about the right relation of colonies to metropolitan centres, the configuration and authorization of delegated legal authorities within empires, and the rights of subjects across imperial realms. They simultaneously bore on the formation of international law and on discourses of constitutionalism.

Because the organization and legal cultures of the Atlantic empires varied, imperial constitutions also differed. Most striking in this regard is the long record of colonial debate and conflict over whether and to what degree the 'rights of Englishmen' extended into the colonies, and about the definition of these rights. Colonists in English North America advanced in various ways from at least the middle of the seventeenth century on a 'minimalist version' of the constitutionalism of England.[26] Although common law jurisdiction did not extend to the colonies, an abstract version of the common law linked to natural liberties could be represented as following English subjects everywhere. The English doctrine of 'repugnance' also opened the door to fluid interpretations of what was meant by 'English law'. Many colonial charters provided that no laws could be made in the colonies that were repugnant to the laws of England. Colonial litigants and officials on both sides of the Atlantic referred to repugnance in crafting and challenging colonial legislation and in court cases. The built-in autonomy of local law in the English empire meanwhile nurtured understandings of colonial governments as incipient 'empires' in relation to frontiers, Indian communities, and imperial rivals.[27]

Some constitutional issues crossed empires. From the sixteenth century on, European Atlantic colonies invoked variants of martial law. Military legal authority was in some cases structurally blended with civil authority, as it was in French colonies where governors held civil and military judicial authority prior to the establishment of sovereign courts, and with *adelantados* in the Spanish empire at the head of armies of

---

[26] Daniel Hulsebosch, *Constituting Empire: New York and the Transformation of Constitutionalism in the Atlantic World, 1664–1830* (Chapel Hill, NC, 2005), 57.

[27] Ibid.; Mary Sarah Bilder, *The Transatlantic Constitution: Colonial Legal Culture and the Empire* (Cambridge, MA, 2004).

reconnaissance. In other cases, elites drew on martial law as a temporary measure, though one with sometimes lasting consequences. In Virginia, Dale's Laws imposed martial discipline on English settlers between 1612 and 1619, influencing after they expired the colony's acceptance of a harsh disciplinary regime for servants. Across European Atlantic empires, martial law gained importance during the late eighteenth century as part of global militarization. Declaring martial law had become less salient by then as a routine emergency measure within Europe, and its increasing use in the empire marked a noticeable contrast. In the British Atlantic empire, martial law was declared in wartime New York during the Revolution and in response to slave rebellions in Barbados in 1805 and 1816, and in Demerara (British Guiana) in 1823, following a wider pattern in the global empire. Both the Barbados and Demerara cases raised constitutional concerns, in Barbados about the authority to execute rebellious slaves once martial law had lapsed, and in Demerara about the constitutionality of extending martial law beyond a moment of crisis when whites were in actual danger of attack. Martial law in these and other cases provoked constitutional uncertainties about the authorization of delegated legal authority. They also pointed to the fact that martial law was itself poorly understood and defined. Its declaration seemed an invitation to improvisation on the part of local officials.[28]

Military and martial law also featured in the constitutional debates within the Spanish empire and the republics of South America. In Spain, liberal constitutionalists supported separating military and political power everywhere but in the colonies, where many thought that this blending was a necessary evil. Both in fledgling republics and in colonies that remained loyal to Spain, governance tended increasingly to merge civil and military power. Most new constitutions enshrined the 'state of siege' as a tool of governance. Even liberal forms of constitutionalism increasingly privileged order over rights.[29]

Across the Atlantic world, the unsettled decades at the turn of the nineteenth century produced conflicts over how to constrain the power of subordinate jurisdictions in systems that continued to depend upon delegating legal authority. We are most familiar with this problem in constitutional debates about slavery. Emancipationists favoured legal reform as a strategy to curb Atlantic slavery, but they could not effect change without grappling with constitutional questions about the authority under which slaveholders held their legal prerogatives or could be stripped of them.

Revolutionary discourse across the Atlantic approached issues of imperial ordering by imagining the formation of new sovereignties from within empires. As a document of both international law and regional imperial constitutionalism, the American Declaration of Independence portrayed the creation of new sovereignties as legitimate under certain circumstances. The Haitian Revolution pushed this logic further by

---

[28] Rande Kostal, *A Jurisprudence of Power: Victorian Empire and the Rule of Law* (Oxford, 2005); Nasser Hussain, *The Jurisprudence of Emergency: Colonialism and the Rule of Law* (Ann Arbor, MI, 2003).

[29] Jeremy Adelman, *Sovereignty and Revolution in the Iberian Atlantic* (Princeton, NJ, 2006).

showing that non-elite actors could take responsibility for the formation of new states. Taken together, the revolutions introduced the historically novel claim that empire could spawn new polities while also foreshadowing the idea that such polities might then claim membership in an international legal society composed of nation-states. An emerging positive law doctrine of international law, usually situated in the nineteenth century and in Europe, can be found in formation in late eighteenth-century Atlantic conflicts. As in earlier centuries, when invoking a natural law basis for freedom of the seas coexisted with assertions of control over particular sea lanes, the new understanding of international law based on the rise of nation-states did not eclipse a discourse about rights based in natural law.[30]

Conclusion

Law in the Atlantic world structured the relations of imperial agents to crown sponsors, provided language and rituals for the formation of new political communities, and formed a repertoire for improvising settlers and sojourners. Atlantic polities delegated legal authority to ship captains, military commanders, and local governments, mainly following widely shared and long-established routines for decentralizing legal authority. Jurisdictional complexity across large and small states of the Atlantic world meanwhile created an element of continuity for travellers and traders. Legal politics altered some of these familiar features and, combined with the changing Atlantic political economy, produced new forms of layered sovereignty, from Jesuit missions to slaveholding plantations. Local variations multiplied, guided by the legal strategies of colonial elites and indigenous legal actors, even as a regional legal regime took shape.

Inter-imperial relations guided parallel shifts in legal policies within empires. At the turn of the eighteenth century, Atlantic European empires sought to define a clearer and more consistent legal structure, multiplying colonial forums and restructuring their relation to metropolitan courts. Unlike jurisdictional complexity, a dimension of legal systems that extended well beyond the Atlantic, these imperial policies were applied in distinctive ways in the Atlantic world and began to mark it as a separate regulatory sphere.

Yet we must take care not to exaggerate the coherence of imperial law and its integrating effects. Law in the eighteenth-century Atlantic undergirded the intensification of labour coercion, in turn exacerbating constitutional tensions. Once again, legal actors at very different parts of the socio-economic order invoked legal discourse in support of strikingly different positions. The language of natural rights could be mobilized in support of colonial elites facing off against imperial bureaucracies, impoverished settlers opposing

---

[30] David Armitage, *The Declaration of Independence: A Global History* (Cambridge, MA, 2007).

indigenous interests, and, as in Haiti, slaves in revolt. The upheavals of the late eighteenth and early nineteenth centuries are perhaps best understood in legal terms as struggles to define the limits of authority within layered legal orders. Participants adopted complex strategies involving law. Andes Indians simultaneously revolted and appealed to royal judges to contain local judges' abuse of power; merchants profiting from contraband trade sometimes favoured expanded regulation of trade; and, in embracing martial law, colonial officials suspended law but continued to struggle to define legal procedures and the relation of martial law to imperial constitutional orders.

Because law mattered so profoundly in the Atlantic world, its history deserves to be extracted from the national and intra-imperial casings that have traditionally contained it. The regional study of law is essential to understanding trade networks, relations between European colonists and indigenous peoples, slave regimes, revolutionary movements, and other subjects that have long held the attention of Atlantic historians. Legal cultures infused Atlantic social formations, and strategic use of law by social actors at all levels influenced the course of institutional change. Studying law as a regional phenomenon helps us to identify and understand when and how the Atlantic world became a distinctive region.

BIBLIOGRAPHY

Armitage, David, *The Declaration of Independence: A Global History* (Cambridge, MA, 2007).

Benton, Lauren, *A Search for Sovereignty: Law and Geography in European Empires, 1400–1900* (Cambridge, 2010).

—— *Law and Colonial Cultures: Legal Regimes in World History, 1400–1900* (Cambridge, 2002).

Coates, Timothy, *Convicts and Orphans: Forced and State-Sponsored Colonizers in the Portuguese Empire, 1550–1755* (Stanford, CA, 2001).

Hulsebosch, Daniel, *Constituting Empire: New York and the Transformation of Constitutionalism in the Atlantic World, 1664–1830* (Chapel Hill, NC, 2005).

MacMillan, Ken, *Sovereignty and Possession in the English New World: The Legal Foundations of Empire, 1576–1640* (Cambridge, 2006).

Owensby, Brian, *Empire of Law and Indian Justice in Colonial Mexico* (Stanford, CA, 2008).

Peabody, Sue, *There are no Slaves in France: The Political Culture of Race and Slavery in the Ancien Régime* (New York, 1996).

Pritchard, James, *In Search of Empire: The French in the Americas, 1670–1730* (Cambridge, 2004).

Serulnikov, Sergio, *Subverting Colonial Authority: Challenges to Spanish Rule in Eighteenth-Century Southern Andes* (Durham, NC, 2003).

CHAPTER 24

ATLANTIC WARFARE,
1440–1763

IRA D. GRUBER

In the early fifteenth century, the peoples of the Atlantic basin lived and fought in relative isolation. Whether Europeans, Africans, or Americans, the inhabitants of each continent waged war mainly among themselves. But in the ensuing three centuries, when Europeans spread across the Atlantic in search of plunder, converts, trade, and colonies, they frequently went to war with other peoples of the Atlantic world—with Africans and Americans as well as Europeans. The resulting wars were shaped by the methods and intentions of all who fought in them, and those methods and intentions were often contradictory: to defeat the enemy and to limit the effects of war. This chapter explores those contradictions, to see how making and limiting war changed across space and time and to consider how changes in methods and intentions affected conflicts in the Atlantic world from the fifteenth to the eighteenth centuries. If the perspective is more European than African or American, it is because Europeans did more than others to initiate, shape, and record Atlantic warfare in these centuries and because historians have studied European warfare far more intensively than African or American.

Our first concern will be to define war in this era—specifically, to distinguish between acts of war and other types of violence that occurred in the Atlantic world between 1440 and 1763. Such a distinction becomes particularly important for the two centuries after 1440 when many Europeans, West Africans, and Americans lived in loosely organized communities and when the line between private and public violence was often blurred; and such a distinction remained important for the century after 1648 when peoples of the Atlantic were drawn increasingly into empires and imperial conflicts. This chapter begins, therefore, with the understanding that war was 'a collective and public phenomenon', an expression of social or political will. Men living in the Atlantic basin might routinely have used force to make others do their will, but they waged war only when sanctioned by a community, ruler, or state. Gradually between 1440 and 1763, as the peoples of the Atlantic became better organized and more tightly linked together, their wars became more clearly distinguishable from 'particular, private, and individual forms of violence'. By the eighteenth century their wars had become—in both a domestic and an international sense—primarily political or, as Carl von Clausewitz was to say, 'a continuation of political activity by other means'.[1]

Although the peoples of the Atlantic world made war idiosyncratically in this era—shaping their uses of force to suit their particular social, technological, political, and cultural circumstances—all were to be touched by what historians term the Military Revolution. Soldiers used the phrase as early as 1761 to describe the impact of gunpowder on warfare; but not until the second half of the twentieth century did scholars employ 'Military Revolution' to connect gunpowder to the development of military power, European states, and global empires. At present, many scholars agree that the Military Revolution involved short bursts of rapid development within long periods of incremental change occurring from the fourteenth to the eighteenth centuries, or as Clifford Rogers has most persuasively described it, a 'punctuated equilibrium evolution'. According to Rogers, this Military Revolution began in the fourteenth century when infantry used manpowered weapons to defeat heavy cavalry; moved substantially forward once Europeans developed effective gunpowder weapons in the fifteenth century; proceeded with the application of those weapons to war in the sixteenth and seventeenth centuries; and culminated in the seventeenth and eighteenth centuries with the creation of standing armies and navies, centralized states, and global empires.[2]

During the first phases of the Military Revolution, Europeans made war more deadly, expensive, and exportable—if not more decisive. They were most successful in developing artillery that altered war on land and sea. By the middle of the fifteenth century, they had created cast-bronze guns using improved gunpowder that could fire cast-iron shot capable of bringing down the walls of a medieval castle. These smooth-bore guns remained inaccurate and short ranged for more than a century, but when they were cast with trunions and mounted on wheeled carriages, they greatly increased the power of an army. The French and Spanish used such guns during the Italian Wars (1494–1559) to accelerate the pace of sieges and to improve their chances of winning battles. To offset these new guns, architects designed massive new fortifications with thick low walls, sharply angled bastions, wide ditches, and extensive outworks that allowed a garrison to cover its walls with defensive fire and that kept besiegers from firing directly at the main defences. These works, which appeared first in Italy in the fifteenth century and spread to Spain, France, and the Netherlands by the 1540s, were expensive to build and garrison; and they greatly slowed the pace of war.

---

[1] Philippe Contamine, *War in the Middle Ages* (Oxford, 2002), p. xiii; Carl von Clausewitz, *On War*, ed. and trans. Michael Howard and Peter Paret et al. (Princeton, NJ, 1976), 87.

[2] Campbell Dalrymple, *A Military Essay* (London, 1761), 56. Clifford J. Rogers, 'The Military Revolutions of the Hundred Years War', and Geoffrey Parker, 'In Defense of the Military Revolution', in Clifford J. Rogers (ed.), *The Military Revolution Debate: Readings on the Military Transformation of Early Modern Europe* (Boulder, CO, 1995), 55–93 (quoting 77), 337–65; Geoffrey Parker, *The Military Revolution: Military Innovation and the Rise of the West, 1500–1800* (Cambridge, 1988).

It took somewhat longer for Europeans to put heavy guns on ships, but those guns eventually transformed warfare at sea. Europeans had to build sailing ships that could support the weight and recoil of cast-bronze guns capable of smashing an enemy vessel. They also had to design watertight gun-port hatches that would permit the mounting of such heavy cannon near the waterline where they would be most effective and would not impair the stability of the ship. By about 1500, and with the support of their king, who helped them bear the costs, the Portuguese had ships and guns capable of fighting their way into the Indian Ocean. These were relatively small, fast, sailing ships with perhaps a heavy gun or two, mounted in the bow. Not until the 1540s did the English succeed in casting iron cannon that were cheap and reliable enough to arm a fleet. Within a quarter of a century, European ships with cast-iron guns mounted broadside would fight off the coasts of Africa and of Central America; and by the early seventeenth century the Dutch would be building and arming such warships for service throughout the Atlantic. But Dutch and English fleets would not fight in line-ahead formations, broadside to broadside, until the 1650s.[3]

It took well over a century to develop guns and ships that would transform war at sea; it took even longer to develop handguns and tactics that would transform war on land. Infantry equipped with pike, longbow, and lance had been able to defeat cavalry in the fourteenth century, encouraging kings to invest more heavily in infantry. Yet kings were relatively slow to equip their infantry with handguns, which were for much of the fifteenth century less effective than crossbows and longbows—less accurate and reliable and more difficult to reload. By the beginning of the sixteenth century, the Spanish and Venetians were replacing the crossbow with an improved handgun that, together with pike, helped Spanish infantry defeat French cavalry at Pavia in 1525. Even so, the matchlock harquebus of 1525 was soon to be replaced by the matchlock musket. The new musket was scarcely an ideal weapon; but it was more powerful than the harquebus, had a greater range (well over 100 yards), and was easier to learn to use (better suited to expanding armies). The musket had to be used in conjunction with other arms (to protect the musketeer while he was reloading), and it was most effective when used in volley fire (to offset the inaccuracy of each individual weapon). Yet by the end of the sixteenth century it was the most common of all infantry weapons, and as such, it would contribute significantly to the growth and power of European armies in the seventeenth century.[4]

The initial phases of the Military Revolution had then produced larger and more powerful forces; they had also made war much more destructive of life and property.

    [3] Parker, *Military Revolution*, 6–16, 86–103; John F. Guilmartin, Jr., 'The Earliest Shipboard Gunpowder Ordnance . . .', *Journal of Military History*, 71/3 (2007), 650–69; John F. Guilmartin, Jr., *Gunpowder & Galleys: Changing Technology & Mediterranean Warfare at Sea in the 16th Century* (London, 2003), 55 n. 39, 104–9, 167–83, 280–8, 319–26; Jan Glete, *Navies and Nations: Warships, Navies, and State Building in Europe and America 1500–1860*, 2 vols. (Stockholm, 1993), 168–72.
    [4] Gordon R. Mork, 'Flint and Steel: A Study in Military Technology and Tactics in 17th Century Europe', *Smithsonian Journal of History*, 2 (1967), 25–52; Guilmartin, *Gunpowder & Galleys*, 158–61; Parker, *Military Revolution*, 16–18.

As long as heavy cavalry had been superior to infantry, aristocratic values shaped warfare: victorious soldiers took prisoners for ransom. But once infantry was able to defeat cavalry, and once states began to rely on ordinary men to fill their ranks, soldiers were more likely to kill their enemies. The development of gunpowder weapons not only confirmed the superiority of infantry over cavalry and the increasing lethality of war but also, with the spread of angled-bastion fortresses, further encouraged the growth of armies. European states increased those armies from roughly 25,000 to 30,000 men during the Italian Wars of 1494–1525; to 65,000 in the 1570s; to over 100,000 in the early seventeenth century. Because most states were as yet unable to conscript men, most relied on mercenaries to enlarge their forces; and mercenaries added significantly to the destructiveness of war. Without firm governmental control or regular logistical support, mercenary forces killed civilians, sacked cities, and committed atrocities. They were particularly unrestrained in the religious and civil wars of the second half of the sixteenth century—prolonged conflicts between Catholics and Protestants in Germany and the Netherlands, between Christians and Muslims in the Mediterranean, and between political and religious factions within France. European wars of the sixteenth century clearly cheapened life and weakened international order.[5]

At just the time that Europeans were experiencing the first phases of their Military Revolution and beginning to wage war more destructively, they were also venturing into the Atlantic. When the Portuguese pushed south to Africa and Brazil and the Spanish west to the Caribbean, Mexico, and Peru, they encountered a variety of native military traditions, none as technologically advanced as their own but each formidable in its own way. West Africans shaped their forces to different climates and customs: cavalry for the savannahs of Mali; infantry for the forested coastal regions of Senegambia, Sierra Leone, Gold Coast, Kongo, and Angola; and combinations of cavalry and infantry for the Gap of Benin. If few wore armour, all Africans relied on hand-powered weapons (clubs, swords, javelins, bows and arrows, and sometimes pikes and axes); and nearly all, on some kind of fortification (hedges, ditches, and palisades). Americans, lacking horses and steel swords, fought as infantry with clubs, stone-edged wooden swords, spears, bows and arrows, and slings; and with wooden and earth fortifications to secure their communities. Although the native peoples of West and Central Africa and of the Americas did not have firearms, and although they lacked the resources for extended campaigns, most were able to raise large, communal forces for short periods of service and small, elite forces for year-round duty.

However they chose to fight, the polities of Africa and the Americas had customarily striven to limit the effects of war. Rarely did any native people seek to destroy an enemy. Most treated war with fear and respect, shaping war aims to preserve themselves and to benefit from capturing rather than killing their enemies. Throughout West and Central Africa in the fifteenth and sixteenth centuries, there were far more

---

[5] Rogers, 'Military Revolutions', 58–64; J. R. Hale, *War and Society in Renaissance Europe, 1450–1620* (Leicester, 1985), 46–56, 63–94, 179–204.

skirmishes, raids, and ambushes than pitched battles. Local rulers fought to acquire slaves, weaken potential enemies, and take prisoners for ransom. Much the same was true in the Americas. The natives of eastern North America fought to teach a lesson, have revenge, or gain prestige—and only after thorough debate and ritualistic preparations. Once committed to war, they sought to surprise their enemy, making prisoners who might be adopted into their community, offered for ransom, held hostage, or sacrificed. They avoided costly battles and attacks on fortifications; and they killed prisoners mainly to hasten withdrawal after a raid or skirmish. In Mexico, the Aztecs sought to avoid war, maintaining specially trained troops to intimidate their subjects and potential enemies, especially those living beyond their frontiers. In north-eastern South America native peoples preferred skirmishing, defensive warfare, and even withdrawal to battle; and they too took prisoners for ransom. But on the coasts of Brazil, native warfare was exceptionally violent: early European reports suggest that the victors regularly roasted and ate their prisoners.[6]

When Europeans first ventured across the Atlantic in the fifteenth and sixteenth centuries, they and the peoples of Africa and the Americas had well-established and very different ways of making and limiting war. How then did those several military traditions come together to shape Atlantic warfare in the early stages of European expansion and of the Military Revolution? Specifically, how did the Portuguese and Spanish who led Europeans overseas affect warfare as it developed throughout the Atlantic in this era? Both the Portuguese and the Spanish had the benefit of kings who supported overseas exploration and trade, who agreed initially to separate spheres of exploitation, and who subsidized the building of ships and guns that gave their subjects maritime supremacy in their first encounters overseas. What was the result?

In this era—in the fifteenth and sixteenth centuries—the Portuguese had less influence on Atlantic warfare than the Spanish—in part because the Portuguese devoted smaller forces to their portion of the Atlantic and in part because they faced stronger opposition in Africa than they or the Spanish did in the Americas. By the middle of the fifteenth century the Portuguese had gone ashore in West Africa, fought with the inhabitants, and been defeated. They withdrew to the Cape Verde Islands, where they established a base and began trading with Senegambia. They subsequently went farther south along the coast of Africa, creating a post at Elmina and negotiating an alliance with the kings of Kongo. Within three-quarters of a century, they were able

---

[6] John K. Thornton, *Warfare in Atlantic Africa, 1500–1800* (London, 1999), 19–125; John F. Guilmartin, Jr., 'The Cutting Edge: An Analysis of the Spanish Invasion and Overthrow of the Inca Empire, 1532–1539', in Kenneth J. Adrien and Rolena Adorno (eds.), *Transatlantic Encounters: Europeans and Andeans in the Sixteenth Century* (Berkeley, CA, 1991), 50–7; Alida C. Metcalf, *Go-betweens and the Colonization of Brazil, 1500–1600* (Austin, TX, 2005), 71–3, 198–201, 209; Wayne Lee, 'Peace Chiefs and Blood Revenge: Patterns of Restraint in Native American Warfare, 1500–1800', *Journal of Military History*, 71/3 (2007), 701–41; Ross Hassig, 'Aztec and Spanish Conquest in Mesoamerica', Neil L. Whitehead, 'Tribes Make States and States Make Tribes…', in Brian Ferguson and Neil L. Whitehead (eds.), *War in the Tribal Zone: Expanding States and Indigenous Warfare* (Santa Fe, NM, 1992), 83–102, 148.

to use their warships and guns to control coasts and rivers of Central Africa, establish a colony in Angola, and join with native troops to win an occasional battle against other native forces. But they could not conquer an African state; and with the exception of artillery, European weapons and tactics made little impression on African warfare. The matchlock harquebus and musket with their low rates of fire and fragile firing mechanisms were simply not effective enough to displace traditional African weapons; and the Portuguese were ever dependent on African troops for operations ashore. The Portuguese did have a greater impact on American than on African ways of war—perhaps because Native American forces were more fragmented and less well equipped than African and because the Portuguese were more willing to settle in Brazil than in Angola and to become a part of an emerging Euro-American military culture. The Portuguese made one additional and unintentional contribution to Atlantic warfare: by taking a principal part in the slave trade, they injected African military practices into the Americas, practices that would emerge conspicuously in slave rebellions.[7]

By comparison with the Portuguese, the Spanish had a much more substantial impact on Atlantic warfare of the sixteenth century. Beginning in 1494 in the West Indies and with the support of the crown, Spanish adventurers explored and conquered vast stretches of Central and South America. In so doing they exploited not just the European Military Revolution but also American ways of war. In initial encounters with native peoples, the Spanish benefited from combined arms tactics developed in the Italian Wars (1494–1525), tactics that integrated firearms and hand-powered weapons and that allowed infantry and cavalry to act together. But those tactics were not always successful in engagements with Americans, and it was not until the Spanish attracted native allies and waged war against the dominant peoples of Mexico and Peru that they had their greatest success. In conquering the Aztec empire, 1519–21, the Spanish employed some 500 disciplined European troops equipped with handguns, artillery, and steel-thrusting weapons, and were supported by much larger native forces armed with traditional wooden and stone weapons. This mixed force defeated an enemy weakened by disease, defections, and the deaths of its leaders. The Spanish conquered Peru, 1532–9, much as they had Mexico, except with fewer European soldiers and less reliance on firearms. In both Mexico and Peru, the Spanish exploited a population accustomed to a centralized government, a population that could be persuaded to accept a new centralized administration and church. By the middle of the sixteenth century, New Spain and Peru were exporting large quantities of silver to Spain— eventually in regular convoys and through ports that were protected by fortifications and heavy guns.

In establishing their empire in the New World, the Spanish had significantly increased the destructiveness of Atlantic warfare. Before the Spanish reached the New World, Americans rarely tried to destroy one another. The Spanish showed no such restraint. In addition to pacifying some tribes and enlisting others as allies or

---

[7] Glete, *Navies and Nations*, 120–4; Thornton, *Warfare in Atlantic Africa*, 23–4, 64, 98–102, 112–13, 139; Metcalf, *Go-betweens*, 111–12, 209–11.

surrogates, the Spanish sought to eradicate tribes they considered barbarous or intractable. Even when they did not intend to destroy an enemy, their weapons and tactics made battle more lethal for Native Americans. Harquebuses, muskets, crossbows, and cannon were more powerful and more likely to inflict deadly wounds than arrows or stones; and steel swords or steel-sheathed pikes were more effective than wooden or even obsidian-edged clubs. Beyond that, the Spanish were able to combine their arms so as to allow each soldier to make the most of his weapons, to allow each harquebusier or crossbowman time and protection to use his weapons without fear of being overrun by the enemy. Body armour also gave Europeans an advantage when closely engaged with Native Americans who had only hand-powered weapons. Americans sometimes inflicted heavy casualties on the Spanish—as on Hernando de Soto's men as they made their way through Alabama in 1542—but the natives paid a disproportionate price until they too were able to acquire firearms.[8]

The Portuguese and Spanish were not the only Europeans to use force in the sixteenth-century Atlantic. The French, English, and Dutch all contested Iberian claims to West Africa and the Americas; and all used force in trying to break into the Portuguese and Spanish empires. Because many of these French, English, and Dutch incursions were privately funded, they often seemed more like piratical raids than acts of war. But when the raids were encouraged by kings and queens and accompanied wars in Europe, they foreshadowed imperial conflicts of the seventeenth and eighteenth centuries.

The French were the earliest and most persistent in pursuing plunder, trade, and colonies in the Iberian Atlantic. Between the 1520s and 1560s, while the kings of France and Spain were intermittently at war, French adventurers claimed the coasts of North America from Florida to Cape Breton, began a settlement in Brazil, explored the St Lawrence River, and tried to establish colonies in Brazil, West Africa, and Florida. Although driven out of Brazil and Florida, met by force on the coast of Africa, and subsequently diverted from the Atlantic by civil war at home (1562–98), the French would return to West Africa, Nova Scotia, and Brazil at the turn of the seventeenth century. The English were later than the French but no less persistent in preying on the Atlantic empires of Portugal and Spain. Beginning in the 1560s and 1570s, the English justified piracy (privateering in wartime) as legitimate resistance to an oppressive Spanish crown and Catholic Church. They sank Spanish warships in the harbour at Vera Cruz, captured a pack train in Panama, and raided Spanish shipping in the Pacific Ocean. In the 1580s they shifted their efforts further east, plundering Santo Domingo and Cartagena, attacking the Spanish in Florida, and trying to establish a colony in North America on the flank of shipping lanes between New Spain and Iberia. By then, the Dutch, who had been in rebellion against Spain since 1567, needed no excuse to

[8] Guilmartin, 'Cutting Edge', 40–69; John F. Guilmartin, Jr., 'The Military Revolution: Origins and First Tests Abroad', in Rogers (ed.), *Military Revolution Debate*, 307–13; Ian K. Steele, *Warpaths: Invasions of North America* (New York, 1994), 6–20, 25–33; J. H. Elliott, *Empires of the Atlantic World: Britain and Spain in America 1492–1830* (New Haven, CT, 2006), 3–5, 17–23, 56–62, 64–87, 97–101, 108–11, 123–33; Hassig, 'Aztec and Spanish Conquest', 96–100.

attack the Spanish and Portuguese empires (united from 1580 to 1640). From the 1590s the Dutch were building warships to protect the Netherlands and their trade and to support private ventures overseas from Africa to the Americas.[9]

As long as the French, English, and Dutch concentrated on raiding Portuguese and Spanish overseas possessions, they contributed little to Atlantic warfare. But in the seventeenth century, when they made determined efforts to establish trading posts and colonies, they had a much greater impact on warfare throughout the Atlantic world. The Portuguese and especially the Spanish had established themselves in some of the most hospitable places in the Atlantic: places where the environment was favourable to Europeans, where native peoples, organized in structured societies, were amenable to being incorporated within a centralized state and church, and where Europeans could forge satisfying and profitable lives. The French, English, and Dutch adventurers still hoped to break into the Portuguese and Spanish empires of the Atlantic, but in the seventeenth century, they were often driven to establish colonies on the peripheries of European settlements where the native peoples proved less willing to submit peacefully to colonization. The French, English, and Dutch adventurers did have the overt support of their European governments and of state-chartered commercial companies; and with such support they were able to recruit settlers and sustain them overseas. But permanent new settlements provoked strong reactions not just from older Spanish and Portuguese colonies and from native peoples but also from rival new French, English, and Dutch colonies. The ensuing conflicts brought increasingly intense fighting, sometimes fuelled by religious and cultural differences, conducted with improved firearms and tactics, and carried out with a determination to destroy enemies. Such fighting transformed Atlantic warfare in the seventeenth century.

The Dutch made important contributions to warfare in this era, developing both an army that maximized the firepower of infantry and a navy that was able to project power overseas. But they had less impact on Atlantic warfare than either France or England—in large part because they were unwilling to fight for many of their Atlantic settlements. In the first half of the seventeenth century, they moved aggressively into Africa and the Americas. They created the Dutch West India Company to establish trading posts and naval bases in West Africa; plant settlements in Guiana (including Suriname), Brazil, and New York; and capture Curaçao and St Martin in the West Indies. But, overcommitted, the Dutch were driven from Angola and Brazil and defeated in the first of their maritime wars with England (1652–4). After two more wars with the English (1665–7, 1672–4), the Dutch terminated their first West India Company, founded another that was not a war machine, and surrendered their North American colony, New Netherland, to the English. Dutch traders remained at Albany, selling firearms to Native Americans under loose English supervision; the Dutch

⁹ Glete, *Navies and Nations*, 120–2, 125–32, 168–70; W. J. Eccles, *France in America* (East Lansing, MI, 1990), 1–14; Edmund S. Morgan, *American Slavery American Freedom: The Ordeal of Colonial Virginia* (New York, 2003), 6–43; C. R. Boxer, *The Dutch Seaborne Empire: 1600–1800* (New York, 1965), 16–24; Steele, *Warpaths*, 16–33.

retained Curaçao and Suriname; and the Dutch government continued to support one of the most formidable navies in Europe. But the Dutch influence on Atlantic warfare had been relatively transitory.[10]

Like the Dutch, the French sought trade and colonies in the seventeenth-century Atlantic. But they were more willing than the Dutch to pursue settlements that brought them into conflicts, particularly in the West Indies and North America. At the beginning of the century, the French sought trading posts in West Africa as well as colonies in Brazil, Guiana, the West Indies, and Canada. But the Portuguese drove them from Brazil; the English destroyed their settlement in Nova Scotia; and friendly natives drew them into war on Lake Champlain. Although the English and the Iroquois continued to attack their outposts in Canada, the French remained in Nova Scotia and on the St Lawrence River; and during the Thirty Years War, they added four Spanish islands to their colonies in the West Indies. In the 1660s and 1670s, Louis XIV made a sustained effort to develop an American empire, to use the resources of the state in support of merchants and settlers overseas. He took over the government of Canada, organized a company to manage French trade in America, sent troops to the West Indies, and launched an offensive to secure settlements on the St Lawrence. French regulars succeeded in bringing peace to the St Lawrence by systematically burning Iroquois villages, by making war with greater intensity than any rival during a half-century of chronic skirmishing on the Canadian frontier. French regulars also succeeded with less force in evicting Dutch traders from the French West Indies and Dutch forces from Guiana.[11]

Like the French and Dutch, the English ventured into the Atlantic in the seventeenth century in search of trade and colonies; and like their rivals, they drew upon private and public resources in their ventures. But to a greater extent than either the French or Dutch, the English were willing to settle overseas and to use force in establishing and defending colonies—particularly against the native peoples and other European colonists of North America. Beginning with their first permanent settlement in the Chesapeake in 1607, the English learned that they would have to fight for the land they claimed and that even with firearms their militia were not tactically superior to the natives of Tidewater Virginia. When the natives attacked in 1622 and 1644, the English responded with prolonged and brutal campaigns that defeated the natives by burning their crops, stores, and villages. The English did much the same in New England. In 1637 they punished one tribe with a ferocity that exceeded anything that the natives had known, killing women and children as well as men in arms. Three decades later, when many other natives of New England rose against them, the English resorted to the same brutal warfare. With a larger population, far greater resources, and improved weapons,

---

[10] Parker, *Military Revolution*, 18–23, 99–104, 118; Boxer, *Dutch Empire*, 24–6, 49, 87–9; Glete, *Navies and Nations*, 180–97; Steele, *Warpaths*, 110–30; and Wim Klooster for his critical reading of this paragraph.

[11] Glete, *Navies and Nations*, 120, 127–9, 187–9; Eccles, *France in America*, 14–100; Steele, *Warpaths*, 63–79.

the English were still not tactically superior to the natives. They prevailed once again first by starving and then by killing, deporting, and enslaving their enemies. The English felt fully justified by the laws of war and by their Protestant faith in destroying or dispossessing all who contested their settling in North America, not just the native peoples who lived along the Atlantic seaboard but also the Dutch who established posts in New York, the French who colonized their northern and western frontiers, and the Spanish who claimed Florida. The English were less brutal but no less successful in capturing some fifteen of Spain's islands in the West Indies in the course of the seventeenth century.

Whether in North America or in the Caribbean, the English had clearly altered Atlantic warfare, both by their actions and by their example. Native Americans had been exposed to Europeans well before the English arrived, yet few had experienced warfare as waged by the English. Those who fought the English along the Chesapeake and in New England soon learned to do more than skirmish with an enemy. By 1649 the Iroquois were destroying Huron and French posts along the Great Lakes, and within thirty years, the Algonquians threatened to do the same to the English in New England. In the interim many natives had acquired the flintlock fusil, a weapon that was particularly well suited to their tactics and that greatly increased their firepower. An experienced soldier could load and fire a flintlock fusil two or three times a minute or about three to six times faster than he could fire a matchlock musket. He could also hope to surprise an enemy while armed with a flintlock, which, unlike the matchlock, did not require a lighted fuse. The native peoples of North America were quick to appreciate the advantages of the flintlock and to learn how to repair and employ it. Although they could not manufacture gunpowder—in the 1670s they remained dependent on European suppliers—they made better use of the new weapon than their English opponents; and that weapon made warfare more deadly for all. Nor were Americans the only native Atlantic peoples to see the advantages of the flintlock: West Africans who had shown little interest in the matchlock musket began adopting the flintlock in the 1680s—particularly on the Gold Coast and in Senegambia. In short, the flintlock complemented the new emphasis on killing and made warfare more lethal for all in the late seventeenth-century Atlantic.[12]

The increased lethality of war had by then moved Europeans to seek security in ever more powerful armed forces and centralized governments—in forces and governments that would, within a century, bring Europeans global empires and complete what historians have called the Military Revolution. During the Thirty Years War, Sweden had shown how much military power a relatively small state could generate with a

---

[12] Steele, *Warpaths*, 37–58, 80–109; Daniel K. Richter, *Facing East from Indian Country: A Native History of Early America* (Cambridge, MA, 2001), 18–26, 47–50, 75, 90–109; Eccles, *France in America*, 17; Lee, 'Peace Chiefs', 702–9, 729, 738–41; Glete, *Navies and Nations*, 131–3; Patrick M. Malone, *The Skulking Way of War: Technology and Tactics among the New England Indians* (Lanham, MD, 1991), 1–2, 22–4, 32–41, 52–98. Robin Law, 'Warfare on the West African Slave Coast, 1650–1850', in Ferguson and Whitehead (eds.), *War in the Tribal Zone*, 111–24; Thornton, *Warfare in Atlantic Africa*, 10–11, 25, 31, 45, 62–3.

national standing army supported by a strong government, efficient bureaucracy, and controlled economy. Other states soon began to invest in standing forces, in disciplined national fleets and armies that increased security at home and abroad by ending dependence on mercenaries. In raising such national forces Europeans accepted larger and stronger governments, governments that would soon have the power to consolidate Atlantic and global empires. Although some native peoples of Africa and the Americas had been able to make excellent use of European weapons, nearly all were to become victims of the Military Revolution. Nearly all lacked that combination of economic, political, and cultural resources that allowed Europeans to go beyond a tactical application of new weapons to enhance the power and security of their states and establish global empires.

In the second half of the seventeenth century, England took the lead in creating a fleet of specialized warships to defend its home waters and to protect its overseas trade and colonies. English leaders were able to draw on popular support for parliamentary government and fears of Catholic France to assemble by 1715 the foremost navy in the world. That navy was supported by strong public credit; administered by bureaucrats who were responsible to Parliament; built and maintained by a combination of private and public dockyards; and led by officers who made the navy a career and were increasingly knowledgeable and responsible in their service. By the beginning of the eighteenth century, the British had warships with the heavy guns and the seaworthiness both to take their place in a line-ahead engagement in the Channel and to keep the sea for months along the coasts of Africa or the Americas. Within another fifty years, they would have a fleet of more than 300 warships as well as bases in the West Indies and North America to clean and refit those ships. The French and Spanish governments responded to Britain by building rival fleets so that by 1760 those three European states had more than two-thirds of the world's sailing warships.[13]

While England was leading at sea, France was building the largest and most powerful standing army in Europe. Although he did not have the popular support or the public credit of England's parliamentary monarchy, King Louis XIV had the largest population in Europe and substantial revenues from agriculture and commerce. He was determined to use those resources not just to secure France with a standing army and belts of angled-bastion fortresses but also to extend his frontiers to the Rhine, Alps, and Pyrenees. Beginning with an army that had not exceeded 125,000 men during the Thirty Years War (scarcely enough to garrison France's fortresses), Louis expanded that army to 253,000 for his war with the Dutch in the 1670s and to 340,000 for the War of the League of Augsburg in the 1690s, increases that far outstripped the growth of his population in those years, 172 per cent to 13 per cent. He also appointed commissaries to encourage discipline, check corruption, and

[13] Parker, *Military Revolution*, 4, 23–4, 39–45, 100–3, 117–21, 146–68; Glete, *Navies and Nations*, 173–273; Paul M. Kennedy, *The Rise and Fall of British Naval Mastery* (London, 1976), 45–107; John Brewer, *The Sinews of Power: War, Money and the English State 1688–1783* (London, 1989), 11–13, 29–63, 137–61, 167–90.

subordinate all officers to the state. When he equipped his army with the latest weapons, when he furnished every infantryman with a flintlock fusil and bayonet, the French army became the most powerful as well as the largest in Europe. (The invention of a bayonet that could be fixed to a fusil made it possible for armies to dispense with pike, thereby increasing firepower without leaving infantry vulnerable to cavalry.) Other states, fearing Louis XIV, invested in comparable forces, bringing more than a million men under arms for the War of the Spanish Succession.

While creating ever larger and more powerful armed forces, Europeans were also attempting to limit the costs and risks of war. The Thirty Years War, 1618–48, had brought nearly unrestrained violence to the Low Countries and parts of Germany— violence initiated by sectarian passions and sustained by mercenaries who served in every army and plundered indiscriminately. That war persuaded kings and ministers to seek not just tighter controls over their own forces but also greater restraints on every aspect of warfare. They undertook to replace mercenaries with standing armies and navies, with forces that could be kept subordinate to the state. They wanted to make sure that the rank and file were thoroughly disciplined and that officers put service before personal ambition. They also wanted to use their armed forces to promote peace and stability in Europe, to check monarchs who threatened existing boundaries and lines of succession. If war became unavoidable, most governments wanted their generals and admirals to act prudently, to be wary of the general engagements that might destroy an army or a fleet and to rely on sieges, skirmishes, and manoeuvres to exhaust the enemy. They clearly sought to spare the lives of civilians and to treat prisoners with restraint. They did not end war, but for much of the eighteenth century they succeeded in damping the effects of war in Western Europe and in creating an international community of soldiers with shared values and prudential approaches to warfare.[14]

At first, at the turn of the eighteenth century, raising standing armies and limiting war had a greater effect in continental Europe than in the Atlantic world. When Louis XIV undertook to extend his frontiers and to link the thrones of France and Spain, he provoked two prolonged wars: the War of the League of Augsburg, 1689–97, and the War of the Spanish Succession, 1701–14. Although he and his enemies, England, Austria, and the Netherlands, had massive forces, they chose to concentrate those forces in Western Europe and to wage limited war—mainly sieges and manoeuvres with a few great battles—for what became a limited end, the containment of France. England, the Netherlands, and Austria succeeded at last through superior public credit, more powerful navies, and combined armies that had the skill and coherence to exhaust their enemies.

The wars of Louis XIV did spill into the Atlantic. But for more than half a century after the beginning of the War of the League of Augsburg, European states waged

---

[14] Robert A. Doughty and Ira D. Gruber et al., *Warfare in the Western World*, 2 vols. (Lexington, MA, 1996), i. 29–41, 61, 63–76, 100–1; John A. Lynn, 'Recalculating French Army Growth during the Grand Siecle, 1610–1715'; and Colin Jones, 'The Military Revolution and the Professionalisation of the French Army under the Ancien Régime', both in Rogers (ed.), *Military Revolution Debate*, 117–36, 149–67.

limited war at sea, keeping their fleets largely in home waters and placing the security of European trade and ports before those of overseas commerce and colonies. Although warships were becoming ever more seaworthy—capable of remaining overseas for months on end—no one state had sufficient ships to control simultaneously the seas at home and abroad; and until the middle of the eighteenth century, Europeans consistently chose continental over colonial interests (in 1750 'more than three quarters of British commerce was still with Europe'). During the War of the League of Augsburg, the combined fleets of England and the Netherlands were able to dominate the English Channel and the Mediterranean, but they could not keep French cruisers and privateers from capturing more than 4,000 allied merchantmen, and they were unable to inflict comparable damage on French commerce. Much the same was true during the War of the Spanish Succession: while British and Dutch warships were superior in European waters, their colonies and commerce remained vulnerable (the French severely damaged the Newfoundland fishery and captured some 3,250 merchantmen). Not until the middle of the eighteenth century was Britain more successful than France at raiding commerce.[15]

While European fleets and armies waged large-scale limited wars, their colonists in the Americas fought one another and native peoples in small, unlimited wars along their frontiers. Fighting in America was sometimes linked to wars in Europe but was rarely limited by European military conventions; Americans fought to dispossess or destroy their enemies. At the beginning of the War of the League of Augsburg, the Iroquois of New York attacked New France, expecting to be supported by English colonists. The English, acting under secret instructions from their king, refused to help the Iroquois, who were left alone to fight a debilitating war and accept a humiliating peace. At the same time, New Englanders burned Port Royal in Nova Scotia and in 1690 sent expeditions to conquer Canada, expeditions that proved too ambitious for inexperienced forces weakened by smallpox and unsupported by the English navy. Because neither the English nor the French colonists received much help from their governments, the war soon degenerated into sporadic frontier clashes that favoured the French—that allowed them and their native allies to survive a long war against far more numerous enemies. Most of these frontier clashes were connected to the war in Europe, and some were clearly shaped by decisions made in London or Paris. But there were many other Atlantic conflicts in this era that were quite local in origin: Spanish campaigns against native peoples in New Mexico, Chile, and Texas; and similar campaigns by the Portuguese in Brazil; the Dutch in Suriname; the English in the Carolinas, and the French on the Mississippi—all concurrent with the War of the League of Augsburg but none closely related to it.

The ensuing War of the Spanish Succession included Spain as an ally of France and brought more European forces into the Atlantic. But it was waged in North America

---

[15] Glete, *Navies and Nations*, 206–8, 215–28, 256–9; Kennedy, *Rise and Fall of British Naval Mastery*, 75–94; Brendan Simms, *Three Victories and a Defeat: The Rise and Fall of the First British Empire, 1714–1783* (London, 2007), 74–6, 250–89, and quoting 366.

much as the War of the League of Augsburg had been: primarily by European colonists and native peoples in small violent encounters without conventional European limits. At the outset, South Carolinians launched unsuccessful attacks on Spanish colonists in Florida; New Englanders fought the French and their native allies on the frontiers of Maine and Acadia; and English, French, and Spanish privateers raided commerce at sea. The Iroquois and New York remained neutral for eight years, allowing trade to continue between Albany and Montreal until New Englanders persuaded the Iroquois, New York, and the British to join in an invasion of Canada. Delayed by negotiations in Europe and bickering among the allies, that invasion did not take place until 1711 when a squadron of British warships and transports carrying some 12,000 regulars and provincials sailed up the St Lawrence while another force of 2,300 provincials advanced across Lake Champlain. The offensive collapsed when eight ships and nearly 500 men were lost in the St Lawrence, and the British withdrew. The war continued with fighting on the frontiers of New England and South Carolina and ended in 1713 with a peace that brought modest territorial gains for the British in North America.

For forty years after the War of the Spanish Succession—through a quarter-century of peace and the ensuing War of the Austrian Succession—Europeans were content to let their colonists do most of the fighting in the Atlantic world. European governments did build bases and fortifications in the West Indies and North America in the first half of the eighteenth century; they responded with force when merchants complained about foreign competition and foreign restraints on trade; and they sent fleets and contingents of troops to the colonies during the War of the Austrian Succession. Yet European governments did little more. Colonists had to defend their frontiers during the long peace from 1713 to 1739: the French fighting the Foxes on the Great Lakes and the Natchez and Chickasaws in Louisiana; the English, the Abenakis in Maine and the Yamasees in South Carolina. The colonists also had to supply most of the troops for the war in North America from 1739 to 1748—particularly, the English for expeditions to St Augustine, Cartagena, and Louisbourg and for the defence of their frontiers against attacks by French and Spanish colonists and native allies. Neither the British nor the French government tried to capture the other's islands in the West Indies during the War of the Austrian Succession—merely to destroy sugar plantations and disrupt trade. Both sought to limit the aims, the conduct, and the results of the war. It remained for their colonists to go beyond those limits as they had done so often in the past.

So too in the last of the Anglo-French wars in America, the Seven Years War. When their colonists fought over the Ohio River valley in 1754, neither the British nor the French government wanted war. Each would have used as little force as possible to sustain its claims to the Ohio. The colonists—at least, many British colonists—wanted more: to conquer Canada so as to stop French and Indian attacks on their frontiers and open the west to British settlers and speculators. Only gradually were European governments—British, French, and eventually Spanish—drawn into a war of conquest, a war with unlimited aims that was waged in limited ways. By 1756 the war had spread to Europe; and both Britain and France were devoting most of their resources to the

Continent. But with a powerful navy and strong public finances Britain was better able than France or Spain to support the war overseas; and in time British offensives achieved decisive results, particularly in the Atlantic. British commanders, employing the techniques of limited war (sieges and blockades more often than great battles), conquered French and Spanish possessions from Canada to the West Indies. At the Peace of Paris, Britain acquired Canada, Florida, Dominica, Grenada, St Vincent, and Senegal—extinguishing nearly all French and Spanish claims to North America east of the Mississippi River, diminishing French holdings in the West Indies, and leaving the native peoples of eastern North America to face gradual destruction by aggressive European colonists.[16]

The conquest of Canada represented a culmination of prolonged European efforts both to make war effectively and to limit the effects of war. Since the fifteenth century, Europeans had been searching for ways to make their armed forces more powerful: to improve handguns and artillery, build better fortifications and ships; and create ever larger and better disciplined armies. They had used their increasingly powerful forces to establish colonies in the Americas and, unintentionally, to make warfare more deadly among many native peoples. By the seventeenth century, Europeans were also suffering from their more powerful armies, particularly from the ill-disciplined mercenaries who roamed Central Europe during the Thirty Years War. To improve security, Europeans created standing fleets and armies, stronger central governments, and international customs limiting the risks and costs of war. For nearly a century, Europeans kept their new standing forces close to home, waging limited wars on the Continent and relying on their colonists to fight small, unlimited wars with one another and the native peoples of the Americas. Not until the Seven Years War were Europeans drawn overseas into a war of conquest, a war that demonstrated not just their capacity to project military power around the earth but also their ability to make war prudentially, even toward unlimited ends.

BIBLIOGRAPHY

Eccles, W. J., *France in America* (East Lansing, MI, 1990).

Elliott, J. H., *Empires of the Atlantic World: Britain and Spain in America 1492–1830* (New Haven, CT, 2006).

Glete, Jan, *Navies and Nations: Warships, Navies, and State Building in Europe and America, 1500–1860*, 2 vols. (Stockholm, 1993).

Parker, Geoffrey, *The Military Revolution: Military Innovation and the Rise of the West, 1500–1800* (Cambridge, 1988).

---

[16] Richter, *Facing East*, 155–88; Eccles, *France in America*, 100–15, 182–229; Steele, *Warpaths*, 137–225; Elliott, *Empires of the Atlantic*, 267–77, 292–5; Glete, *Navies and Nations*, 263–73; Simms, *Three Victories*, 423–95.

Richter, Daniel K., *Facing East from Indian Country: A Native History of Early America* (Cambridge, MA, 2001).

Rogers, Clifford J. (ed.), *The Military Revolution Debate: Readings on the Military Transformation of Early Modern Europe* (Boulder, CO, 1995).

Steele, Ian K., *Warpaths: Invasions of North America* (New York, 1994).

Thornton, John K., *Warfare in Atlantic Africa, 1500–1800* (London, 1999).

CHAPTER 25

....

RELIGION IN THE
ATLANTIC WORLD

....

KENNETH MILLS

WRITING on the diffusion of artistic forms in a transoceanic context, the art historian George Kubler likened an important work of art to a lighthouse emitting 'signals', which might be transferred officially, but might also be carried by 'unexpected bearers' to be 'relayed' to diverse people, including unintended recipients.[1] Kubler allowed that a 'deformation' of the 'original signal' might occur at various points of relay. This chapter adapts his model of diffusion and transformation to the transatlantic afterlives of a broader set of European forms and ideas, particularly those relating to religion.

Kubler's seems a useful tool to assist understanding of the transmission and fruition of religious forms to the outer reaches of the Atlantic world during the early modern centuries, enabling us to escape from traditional value judgements related to any 'weakening' of the light or any 'decline' in its richness, complexity, or value. His method insists on the original relay and the new form being accepted as equals, thus disallowing the possibility of religious ideas, forms, and practices of peoples across the Atlantic zone being categorized as imitations, copies, satellites, or subsidiaries. This challenges the presumption of European authors of the early modern centuries, and many authors since then, writing on the spread of Christianity.

What is most vital within Kubler's approach is that it recognized the possibility of a novel creation becoming 'its own signal', without being described as either derivative or degenerated. Almost as important is Kubler's openness to what might be called naturalization or localization, with the new form being understood as a 'composite' creation of people and circumstances at its new points and in its new places of transmission. By 'composite' Kubler meant that the object was 'composed . . . in part of the message as it was received, and in part of the impulses contributed by the relay itself'. Process is all-important within his frame of thinking, with the form in question

[1] George Kubler, *The Shape of Time: Remarks on the History of Things* (New Haven, CT, 1962), 17–24.

being characterized not as imperfection but as re-creation with the capacity to become more powerful, locally, through its own 'consequent agitations'. Focusing on the re-creation makes it possible to disregard, at least for a time, the circumstances associated with the creation of the original signal. What matters for Kubler is the new signal, which, in turn, grows, sets out on its own paths, attracts its own communities, and generates its own stories and re-creations. Recent publications on the vibrant propagations and unsanctioned adaptations of influential prints depicting important religious themes by artists across the early modern Spanish world suggest the explanatory power and applicability of Kubler's idea.[2]

In this chapter I contend that episodes suggesting religious transformation across the Atlantic world can be fruitfully studied in similar terms. I highlight moments in which religious participant-tellers and commentators found themselves at various kinds of interpretational impasse, face to face, as it were, with the often-disconcerting outcomes of unsanctioned religious change. Indeed, because sculpted and painted religious images were sometimes at the centre of such encounters, the connection is especially apt. Even Kubler's attention to some people's continuous striving after what they maintained was religion's 'pristine signal' is usefully instructive of historical contexts. Essentially, desires and efforts to authorize and direct, however powerful they might have been, were doomed, because religious ideas and forms—like the people who carried them—proved impossible to control, and frequently encouraged the fusions and fruitions their carriers and promoters most feared.

In 1569, Gregorio González de Cuenca, a judge of the royal district court in Lima, Peru, bewailed that, while 'the new church and the conversion of all these native peoples' had begun well, much backsliding had occurred. Dr Cuenca was a learned Spaniard of fourteen years' experience in Spanish America, who had visited the Peruvian provinces and reported on conditions of the native peoples. What he had witnessed pained him, and he attributed the spiritual regression to the laxity of poorly trained parish clergy and to the generally scandalous behaviour of Spanish Christians. As he wrote to the Father General of the Society of Jesus, he solicited him to send more *padres* who might act as regional supervisors in a redoubled evangelization effort.[3]

Cuenca's preoccupation was the spiritual condition of the indigenous peoples, of whom he wrote collectively in paternalistic terms describing them as 'the principal treasure and resource of this land'. He particularized their rampant 'errors', contending that these native peoples were even more 'vice-ridden' than their pre-Hispanic ancestors.[4] What he, like many of his Spanish and Hispanicizing contemporaries, wanted

---

[2] See, for example, essays by Javier Portús, William A. Christian, Jr., and Luisa Elena Alcalá in Ronda Kasl (ed.), *Sacred Spain: Art and Belief in the Spanish World* (New Haven, CT, 2009).

[3] Universidad Antonio Ruiz de Montoya, Biblioteca Felipe McGregor SJ, Colección Vargas Ugarte (hereafter Colección Vargas Ugarte), MSS Tomo. 20/2/fos. 4^r–5^r. Dr Cuenca, oidor de la Real Audiencia de Lima al P. Francisco de Borja, Prepósito General de la Compañía de Jesús, Los Reyes, 1 de abril de 1569.

[4] Colección Vargas Ugarte, MSS Tomo. 20/2/fos. 4^r–5^r.

was a convenient bifurcation between peaceful, Christian, and Hispanicized indigenous peoples—*indios de paz*—in contrast to bellicose indigenous peoples—*indios de guerra*—who had not *yet* been reached by Spanish civilization and religion. Thus Cuenca, like many like-minded contemporaries, hankered after a clear progression; a conversion with no 'difficult middle'.[5]

Yet lived religious life was rarely like that of a well-choreographed public procession, and Cuenca's vagueness and silences beg attention. As the reports of others who got closer to indigenous people reveal, this indeterminacy occasioned the most discomfort. Cuenca was therefore hardly alone—either in Peru or in an increasingly interconnected world that came to encompass a great many ethnicities and a great many interactive processes of becoming—in his inability to face and articulate the 'problem' of change and heterogeneity on the ground.[6] In religious terms, the Atlantic world between the late fifteenth and early nineteenth centuries became defined by the ways in which those who were determined to change others frequently found the evidence of religious transformation painful, if not impossible, to behold.

In 1572, possibly because of Cuenca's solicitation, a Jesuit was on his way to Peru who would write regularly of his experiences. He was José de Acosta, who, after fourteen years in Peru and a few more in Mexico, would pen two of the most influential texts ever written about the Americas. The José de Acosta who wrote from the Panamanian isthmus en route to Lima was a man of limited extra-European experience, dedicated to preaching and administering the sacraments, and reporting to Rome.[7]

Acosta was exercised by the condition of the so-called *cimarrones* in Panama; that vital commercial link between the Peruvian ports of the South Sea and Europe through which tons of silver and other commodities passed in either direction. The *cimarrones* were escaped slaves and otherwise rebellious peoples of African, mixed Afro-Indian, and sometimes Afro-European descent, and offspring of the same.[8] Acosta was as taken aback by the size and number of the communities, which might 'do harm to Indians and Spaniards', as he was by their growing reputation for daring raids. But worst of all was how the *cimarrones* unsettled his mind.

'These Blacks live a bestial life', Acosta explained, yet they were 'baptized', and he found among them one who christened the babies who were born. Moreover he discovered that they maintained some semblance of Christianity, with churches and crosses, and did no evil to priests or friars. The more Acosta thought over what he witnessed and heard, the more horrified he became with a *cimarrón* religious reality he

---

[5] Jeffrey Jerome Cohen, *Hybridity, Identity, and Monstrosity in Medieval Britain: On Difficult Middles* (Basingstoke, 2006).

[6] Matt Cohen, *The Networked Wilderness: Communicating in Early New England* (Minneapolis, MN, 2009).

[7] Colección Vargas Ugarte, MSS Tomo 20/6/fos. 12^r–13^r, P. Joseph de Acosta to P. Francisco de Borja, Panamá, 20 February 1572, fo. 13^r.

[8] A. Fortune, *Obras selectas*, ed. G. Maloney (Panamá, 1993); E. Vila Vilar, 'Cimarronaje en Panamá y Cartagena: el costo de una guerilla en el siglo XVII', *Caravelle*, 49 (1987), 77–92.

called 'a monstrous thing'. On the altar in one of their churches, 'in place of the missal', lay 'a book of aphorisms of medicine'. Acosta speculated that because the object was a book, the *cimarrones* assumed it 'belonged in a church'. That he went no further to ascertain what was the meaning of a book for the *cimarrones*, or of the intentions of those who put it on the altar, reveals much more about Acosta and contemporary Spanish Christian attitudes than about these ostensible Christians. Acosta went no further because he considered their self-Christianizing and unsupervised mixing of secular and sacred beyond remedy. He warned against having such people armed and languishing in 'dense and inaccessible hinterlands' on this crucial isthmus.[9]

Acosta's contentions concerning the inaccessibility of these *cimarrón* Christians, and his readiness to ridicule, rather than attempt to comprehend, their beliefs and practices, is suggestive on several levels. First, the Jesuit's reactions—his casting about for a simple explanation, his resort to guesswork, his ready despair and dismissals—were common early modern responses to local evidence of unsanctioned religious and cultural change that produced un-tethered processes of nascent self-Christianization. Acosta could reflect no further about *cimarrón* religious specialists who interpreted, re-created, and administered sacred rites and systems as they saw fit, with books of their choosing, on their own altars, and in their own churches. Second, these reactions came not only from a European mind fresh to America, but from one of the finest minds ever to apply itself to the histories, to the human and natural realities, and to the Christianization of the inhabitants of those lands.

What might have been considered first fruits by the *cimarrones* were judged first deformities by Acosta. The religiosity of many other people of African descent, whether under conditions of enslavement or not, was frequently treated thus by Christianizing agents across the Atlantic world. God's plan was thought to permit enslavement, and even his most talented preachers counselled Africans to be content with their lot, recognizing that if they converted in their hearts to Christianity, eternal salvation would be theirs.[10] Even in the case of Alonso de Sandoval—another Jesuit who followed Acosta and did much, in his way, to draw attention to the doleful condition and the spiritual neglect of African peoples in the Americas—there was a tipping point beyond which he might squint but not proceed. Sandoval worked most intensely in the great Caribbean port city of Cartagena de Indias in the early seventeenth century, a place in which an African majority of 7,000 people outnumbered Spaniards by more than half.[11] As the title of his *De instauranda Aethiopum salute* (1627) captures, Sandoval was one of many who believed that an apostle—St Thomas—had evangelized African

---

[9] See n. 7.

[10] Nicole von Germeten, *Black Blood Brothers: Confraternities and Social Mobility for Afro-Mexicans* (Gainesville, FL, 2006); 'Two Slaveries: The Sermons of Padre Antônio Vieira, Salvador, Bahia (ca. 1633), and São Luis do Maranhão (1653)', in Kenneth Mills, William B. Taylor, and Sandra Lauderdale Graham (eds.), *Colonial Latin America: A Documentary History* (Wilmington, DE, 2002), 218–33.

[11] Nicole Von Germeten, 'Introduction', in *Treatise on Slavery: Selections from De instauranda Aethiopum salute* (Indianapolis, IN, 2008), p. x.

(as well as indigenous American) peoples, and that he was therefore seeking to rescue a once-righteous people who had fallen prey to Satan. 'Restoring' the 'Ethiopians' to a state in which they would deserve salvation was even more urgent in the Americas than in Africa because so many of them there suffered in slavery. Insistent that peoples of African descent were wayward but not damned, Sandoval blamed their spiritual condition on incompetent clergy and he paternalistically prescribed patience and firm correction.

Whether on the isthmus of Panama, in Cartagena de Indias, in Massachusetts, on the island of Cuba, or in Brazil, the beliefs and practices that obtained among people of African descent throughout the Atlantic world often come to our attention because individuals and groups were investigated for purported errors, or because deviations from supposed norms were reported upon by concerned missionaries and clergy. Their beliefs and practices were judged to be everything from excessively exuberant to diabolical witchcraft. African religious transformations in the Americas were frequently composed of multiple dimensions at once—re-creating what Kubler might have called signals, signals with origins in Africa, Europe, and in the Americas themselves.[12]

In the case of the religiosities Africans conveyed to, developed, and lived in the Americas, those originating among the Yoruba and Igbo are two of many that scholars have investigated both for their resilience and complex fusions with aspects of Christianity, especially the Catholic cult of the saints.[13] Religious transformations into Vodou in Haiti, and Santería (or Lukumí) especially in Cuba, are prime examples.[14] In the case of the African diaspora, the dynamic presence of Islam—already a transplant and re-creation among a great number of Islamicized African peoples before the slave trade—added yet another heterodox dimension. Brazil became home to the largest number of Muslim African slaves in the Americas, where efforts to convert all African peoples to orthodox Roman Catholicism were uneven at best.[15]

Charting the interpenetration of religious systems in Brazil, Roger Bastide has argued that even when Catholicism took root as a living religious reality among Afro-Brazilians, a separation from 'Portuguese Catholicism' was distinguishable. What began in the enforced segregation of religious observances in the patriarchal atmosphere of plantation chapels, he argues, became racially divided observances of the

---

[12] See, for example, Albert J. Raboteau, *Canaan Land: A Religious History of African Americans* (Oxford, 1999); Kathryn Joy McKnight, 'The Diabolical Pacts of Slavery: The Stories of Two Mulatto Slaves before the Inquisition in New Spain', *Revista de estudios hispánicos*, 37 (2003), 509–36; Laura de Mello e Souza, *The Devil and the Land of the Holy Cross: Witchcraft, Slavery, and Popular Religion in Colonial Brazil*, trans. Diane Grosklaus Whitty (Austin, TX, 2003).

[13] John Ryle, 'Miracles of the People: Attitudes to Catholicism in an Afro-Brazilian Religious Centre in Salvador Da Bahia', in Wendy James and Douglas H. Johnson (eds.), *Vernacular Christianity: Essays in the Social Anthropology of Religion Presented to Godfrey Lienhardt* (Oxford, 1988), 40–50.

[14] Laurent Dubois, 'Voudou and History', *Comparative Studies in Society and History*, 43/1 (2001), 92–100; and Joan Dayan, 'Vodoun, or the Voice of the Gods', *Raritan*, 10/3 (1991), 32–45.

[15] Paul E. Lovejoy and Mariza C. Soares (eds.), *Muslim Encounters with Slavery in Brazil* (Princeton, NJ, 2007).

Catholic festival cycle.[16] Not unlike the *cimarrones* encountered by Acosta in Panama, African Brazilians created Catholic Christianities of their own. Recent scholarship on remarkable lay saints of African descent—many of them women—from across the Americas suggests the extent of such religious re-creations.[17] Moreover, Jon Sensbach's study of the ideas, actions, and mobility of the evangelical Protestant Rebecca Protten, who was converted by German Moravians, and became an itinerant preacher on the island of St Thomas (a Dutch sugar colony in the Caribbean), reminds us vividly that African religious transformations in the Atlantic world crossed confessional divides.[18]

Little more than a decade after Acosta's experiences in Panama, the Englishman Thomas Harriot and gifted illustrator John White encountered the religious beliefs and practices of the Algonquian peoples of the Carolina Outer Banks. Harriot, an established scientist and mathematician with a metaphysical bent, ostensibly created with his *Brief and True Report of the New Found Land of Virginia* (1588) an eyewitness account to further profitable colonization. Convinced of English superiority, and thus of the correctness of England's civilizing and Christianizing mission, Harriot's interpretative path seems familiar. Accounts from the Caribbean, and from Spanish and Portuguese America more broadly, had, for their own reasons, found similarly ingenious ways to present indigenous belief systems as simultaneously filled with error and an opportunity for Christian evangelization. Those approaching their responsibilities positively sought evidence that a pre-Hispanic apostle had worked among the Indians, or suggested that while the peoples they encountered had strayed into erroneous ways they still possessed the glimmer of Christianity's 'natural light'. Indeed, as Karen Kupperman has recognized, what Harriot and White identified and catalogued on Roanoake—all the flora and fauna included—was a 'quest for knowledge' akin to 'a religious search'.[19]

Nonetheless, Harriot presented native 'religion' as mistaken, if salvageable over time. He saw the Algonquians through a decidedly Protestant Christian lens: he could admire their civility and moral system, their general ceremoniousness around death and burials, and notions of a spiritual afterlife. Also, while Harriot bewailed their veneration of a distressing plurality of 'pettie gods' (called *montoác*) as idols in secluded temple-like structures, he rejoiced over their belief in 'one onely chiefe and great God, which hath bene from all eternitie'.[20] This reassuring northern version of an alluring

---

[16] Roger Bastide, *The African Religions of Brazil: Toward a Sociology of the Interpenetration of Civilizations*, trans. Helen Sebba (Baltimore, MD, 2007), 109–25.

[17] For example, Joan Cameron Bristol, *Christians, Blasphemers, and Witches: Afro-Mexican Ritual Practice in the Seventeenth Century* (Albuquerque, NM, 2007); Leo J. Garofalo, 'Conjuring the Coca and the Inca: The Andeanization of Lima's Afro-Peruvian Ritual Specialists, 1580–1690', *The Americas*, 63/1 (2006), 53–80.

[18] *Rebecca's Revival: Creating Black Christianity in the Atlantic World* (Cambridge, MA, 2005).

[19] *Roanoke: The Abandoned Colony* (Lanham, NJ, 2007), 94; Kim Sloan et al., *A New World: England's First View of America* (London, 2007).

[20] Harriot, 'A Briefe and True Report of the New Found Land of Virginia', in David Beers Quinn (ed.), *The Roanoke Voyages 1584–1590: Documents to Illustrate the English Voyages to North America under the Patent Granted to Sir Walter Ralegh in 1584* (London, 1955), i. 372–3, 345.

monotheistic principle, identified just as needfully by Catholic observers in Central and South America, might have satisfied Harriot that conversion was assured were it not for the dances and trance-like activities presided over by figures whom both Harriot and his illustrator White characterized as 'conjurors' and 'flyers', healers and sorcerers who invoked the devil.

These Algonquian religious specialists wore little more than a breechcloth and pouch for tobacco which, when ingested quickly in large quantities, provoked their visionary trances. Smoking the tobacco, they cast it 'into the air . . . with strange gestures, stamping, sometime dauncing, clapping of hands, holding vp of hands, & staring vp into the heavens, vttering therewithal and chattering strange words & noises'.[21] White's watercolours, which were intended as plates to accompany Harriot's text, informed the copper engravings by Theodore de Bry illustrating the 1590 edition of the work. One plate, inscribed 'the flyer', depicted a specialist in full trance 'verye familiar with deuils, of whome they enquier what their enemys doe, or other suche things. . . . The Inhabitants giue great credit vnto their speech, which oftentimes they finde to bee true.'[22] Another engraving depicted people gathered around a fire, shaking rattles and engaged in prayer, presumably to Satan.

Joan Pau Rubiés has warned that Harriot's 'cold, detached' presentation of an indigenous religion with some semblance to Christianity might have been to convince his readers how easy it would be to create a profitable colony.[23] Yet Harriot's purposefulness is significantly disrupted by his own written, and by White's visual, depictions of the conjurers and their ceremonies. The author's insecurities and fearful wonder about what he was observing and hearing were to be repeated in a startling string of later, and steadily more worried and negative, English Protestant descriptions of indigenous religious gatherings and their minister-healers compiled through the seventeenth century.

These other 'uncomprehending observers', as Catherine Albanese has dubbed them, who follow upon Harriot and White, begin with Captain John Smith and, among others, include Roger Williams, William Wood, John Josselyn, William Bradford, and Daniel Gookin. The features of Algonquin ritual that all found arresting were the 'strange' gestures and mutterings by the Indian practitioners, alleged familiarity with Satan, and perverse 'exorcisms' in the guise of curing the sick, and identifying these seemed more important than fresh observation to succeeding commentators. What we ultimately learn about Algonquin religious transformation from all such reportage is slight and tangential to their promotional purpose, but they make explicit the real targets of their disapproval: a dynamic native religiosity, centred upon prophecy, divination, and healing, that endured through change. Later, Algonquin processes of

---

[21] Harriot, 'A Briefe and True Report', 345.

[22] Thomas Harriot, *A Briefe and True Report of the New Found Land of Virginia*, introd. Paul Hulton (New York, 1972), 54, 62–5; Sloan, *A New World*, 128–9, and 118–19, 116–17.

[23] 'Texts, Images, and the Perception of Savages in Early Modern Europe: What we can Learn from White and Harriot', in Kim Sloan (ed.), *European Visions, American Voices* (London, 2009), 130 n. 26.

mixing would engage both with elements of Christianity and with African American folk beliefs and practices.[24]

Many Christian missionaries and commentators across the Americas worked among peoples whose first contact with Christian religion had commenced generations before. These later-generation encounters were frequently unsettling in that evangelizers were confronted with how indigenous peoples had made their own what earlier Christian missionaries had left them. Perspectives on these joint creations of lived religious realities are illuminating.

Prime examples come from the two pairs of Jesuits who, in 1621, climbed from their residence on the outskirts of Lima, Peru, for a two-month stay in the town of Huarochirí and its mountainous environs just south-west of the capital.[25] Theirs was a 'flying mission' (*misión volante*), regularly conducted by priests from Jesuit colleges across Catholic Christendom. Pertinently, this mission to Huarochirí was a return visit in that a team of specially appointed Jesuits had ministered there in 1570. These missionaries had devoted two years to intensive evangelizing of native Andean peoples in the province, becoming their regular priests and establishing schools for children in a number of towns, before they proceeded from the *doctrina*, which (in their view) produced mixed results, to work elsewhere. Those who followed them in 1621 were to witness some of what had developed in the aftermath of the earlier missionary drive.[26]

Fathers Juan Vásquez and Juan de Cuevas arrived to the sight and smell of *coca* leaf and animal blood sacrifices, and to the appearance of blood smeared upon the doors of the priests' and local magistrates' houses. They also discovered, on arrival, that a visiting idolatry inspector had imprisoned 'eleven famous sorcerers' and planned to investigate their errors. Then, after they had retired, one of the Jesuits was aroused by the 'very devout and elegant singing' of the imprisoned Indians. Enquiring how people 'so devoid of Christianity, and so given to the worship of demons' could know such songs and sing in such a manner, the 'sorcerers' explained that they had learned the hymns as children, 'almost forty years before, when *padres* from the Society [of Jesus] had been their priests'. The Indians admitted to having been subsequently 'deceived by the Devil who made them his ministers', while reassuring that they now felt the deception lifting, as the hymns had returned to their hearts and minds.[27]

This evocation of the earlier implantation of Christianity by Jesuits having been rekindled by this return visit became the subject of the annual letter for 1621 to the

---

[24] Catherine L. Albanese, *A Republic of Mind and Spirit: A Cultural History of American Metaphysical Religion* (New Haven, CT, 2007), esp. 102–4.

[25] 'Letras anuas de la Provincia del Perú de la Compañía de Jesús, Lima, 24 de abril de 1621', in *Revista de archivos y bibliotecas nacionales* (Lima), 3/5, primera entrega, 30 September 1900, 58–61, transcribed and republished by Laura Gutiérrez Arbulú and Javier Flores Espinoza, 'Dos documentos', 202–4.

[26] Rubén Vargas Ugarte, *Los jesuitas del Perú, 1568–1767* (Lima, 1941), 15; Francisco Mateos (ed.), *Historia general de la Compañia de Jésus en la Provincia del Perú, crónica anónima de 1600 que trata del establecimiento y misiones de la Compañia de Jesus en los paises de Habla Española en la America Meridional* (Madrid, 1944), i. 149.

[27] Arbulú and Espinoza (eds.), 'Dos documentos', 202.

Jesuit Father General in Rome. Less salutary reports were to follow because, as Jesuits persisted with their mission, they discovered both obstinate attachments to ancestral ways and signs of unsupervised Catholic Christianity.[28]

After an interlude away from the region, Fr de Cuevas returned, accompanied this time by Fr Rodrigo de Ávila. They worked first in San Juan de Chaucarima, a high settlement which the priests considered worryingly removed from the regular mass and doctrinal instruction available in the resettlement town (reducción) in the valley which Spanish officials had ordered into existence a generation earlier. Cuevas and Ávila were particularly perplexed by a 'large rock' which loomed in the Indians' consciousness, as if guarding the banks of their rushing stream, and which one indigenous witness insisted was known as 'the Devil's house'. The witness may have hoped to please his inquisitor. But just as plausibly, the rock's name suggests that the man was familiar with contemporary iconography of Satan, Hell, and the Last Judgement from his previous exposure to Christian evangelization, and that these had become transformed into authentically seventeenth-century Andean ideas.[29] The 'Fiend', the Jesuits learned from their witness, appeared at this large rock 'like a viper' but 'with big ears and a beard, killing whoever gazed upon him'.[30] The Jesuits responded by erecting a cross at the great boulder, hoping this would banish the devil.

The next reported experience of Frs Cuevas and Ávila related to a nearby town where they met a woman who carefully guarded in her home no fewer than 'fifteen saint's medals'. Their elation at this seeming witness of devotion was eclipsed as she explained how she had come by the medals and what they meant to her. The devil, she pronounced, had been in the habit of coming for her, whisking her off to a high mountain and, from there—much as contemporary preachers would have explained to her and the other townspeople the devil's temptation of Jesus—enticed her with 'such delightful gardens and flourishing meadows' that it took her breath away. When she had returned, still disoriented and afraid, from one of these visionary experiences she had confessed the occurrence to some Jesuits who had been passing through the town, who later 'had given her the medals, counselling that she confess her sins and receive communion frequently'. Subsequently, she had guarded the medals and followed their advice, so that 'even though the Devil still appeared to her, he kept his distance'.[31]

Ávila and Cuevas were even more perplexed when, on a small window within the humble church at Chaucarima, they found two small sculpted 'little animal' figures which had long been 'held in great veneration', because in times past, according to a sacred tradition ('una fábula'), these animals had proven their worth to the people's ancestors, especially by opening an important irrigation channel 'for one of their

[28] Ibid. 203.

[29] Kenneth Mills, 'The Naturalization of Andean Christianities', in R. Po-chia Hsia (ed.), *The Cambridge History of Christianity*, vi: *Reform and Expansion, 1500–1660* (Cambridge, 2007), 508–39; Andrew C. Redden, *Diabolism in Colonial Peru, 1560–1750* (London, 2008).

[30] Arbulú and Espinoza (eds.), 'Dos documentos', 203.

[31] Ibid. 203–4. See also Kenneth Mills, *Idolatry and its Enemies: Colonial Andean Religion and Extirpation, 1640–1750* (Princeton, NJ, 1997).

goddesses'. For this reason, these representations of the animals had been placed in a niche in the church they had built, in the hope of keeping their sacred structure secure. Meanwhile, the Jesuit visitors found, nearby, the mummified bodies (*malquis*) of ancestors with evidence of offerings, which they immediately either burnt publicly or threw off cliffs. Even more sinister for the Jesuits was a 'chapel' that the Indians had constructed, and within which were 'four idols at the foot of a cross'. This place seems to have been something of a cultic headquarters with which 'four sorcerers' were associated, one of them analogous to an itinerant preacher who 'wandered throughout the province, consulted by everyone', and 'led people into deception with spells and superstitious dogmas'.

Such information provoked further concern when it was connected to the reported discovery on 13 September 1621, by Dr Alonso Osorio, the idolatry inspector, of two sacred images that had become central to Andean Christian devotions in this locality.[32] These were representations of Ignatius Loyola and Francis Xavier, two Jesuit *beatos* who had not yet been canonized and whose images were therefore not strictly appropriate for general Christian veneration. A statue of the Jesuit founder rested on the altar, while on the wall was an evidently half-erased painting of Francis Xavier, the missionary to the East. This veneration by indigenous parishioners scandalized the *visitador*, so he demanded that the sculpture be removed and the painting fully erased.

Like many of his contemporary Catholic churchmen in the Atlantic world, Dr Osorio reflected concern for devotional propriety around sacred images, especially when it involved the association of indigenous people whom he, and others, regarded as perpetual neophytes. Yet Osorio was a visitor in more ways than one. The evidence of his investigation reveals that he held no monopoly on religious thought and activity in Huarochirí, and much less on what ought to be local people's spiritual concerns. Rumours had fast begun to swirl in the town about the *visitador*'s intentions for the sculpted Ignacio. The *kuraka* and governor of the province voiced the thoughts of many: that because Ignacio was not a saint Osorio planned to burn his image, as if he was a *huaca* or one of the Indians' ancestral *malquis* currently being incinerated and tossed into surrounding ravines. Various town notables, *principales*, and sometimes local office-holders testified. One thought 'that the *visitador* meant to burn the image and that everyone asked if it was *huaca*'. Perhaps attempting some damage control while saying mass in the cemetery, Osorio insisted that, while the sculpture of the *beato* Ignacio might be displayed in a Jesuit church, it was not appropriate for a parish church serving a 'town of Indians'.[33]

The inspector's explanations for his actions did not impress the local witnesses. When the sacristan carried out the inspector's orders, taking the sculpted image and locking it away, some indigenous parishioners reacted with anger and defiance. People were 'up in arms', affirmed one witness. Most others spoke less of violence and more of emotion. People 'had wept', remembered one, 'thinking that they wished to burn it [the

---

32 Arbulú and Espinoza (eds.), 'Dos documentos', 204–16.
33 Ibid. 210, 212, 213.

image of Ignacio de Loyola]'. For a *kuraka* principal (a regional governor and town notable) the prospect that Ignacio's image would be thrown into the fire was quite personal, because he as an Andean Christian had been the patron who had commissioned the image. For this reason, 'he and all the Indians cried in pain'.[34]

More than a century later, in the north-eastern portion of what is now the United States, David Brainerd, Bible in hand, was concealed near a town he called 'Juncauta' on an island in the Susquehanna River. It was 'the Lord's Day', 21 September 1745. Brainerd was 'not more than thirty feet' away from a massive gathering of indigenous peoples whose rituals he observed for hours, struggling to comprehend what he was witnessing and pondering how to defeat it. For nearly two years, this Connecticut-born preacher had been a missionary in the region, often assisted by native interpreters, but his days in Juncauta suggested to him that native curiosity about Christianity which he had enlivened had resulted only in their rejection of the word.[35]

Brainerd's trials in Juncauta had begun the evening before when an 'idolatrous revel' was enacted, and he was clearly frustrated by his inability to dissuade people from participating in rituals of nearly two days' duration and his inability 'to discourse privately' with people about Christianity. Because of his previous associations, Brainerd was allowed privately to witness 'nearly a hundred' people participate in a 'sacred dance' around a fire of 'prodigious height . . . yelling and shouting in such a manner that they might easily have been heard [for] two miles or more', where they sacrificed 'ten fat deer'.[36]

Brainerd's method of 'discoursing about Christianity' followed a three-stage process: selecting a potent passage of Scripture as a point of departure; summoning the force of God's word to descend 'like a mighty raging wind'; and moving his hearers' souls. At Juncauta, as at most places, Brainerd's intended hearers were indigenous people where he was partially or fully reliant on native interpreters to communicate. Yet at other times he sought the ears and hearts of 'white heathen' Euro-Americans 'of diverse denominations'.

Like other missionaries Brainerd found much to criticize and degrade in native religious culture, but he feared the signs of change even more. And like other religious participant-tellers across the Atlantic world, Brainerd feared what he felt the Indians were becoming, and particularly feared their degeneration as a result of interaction with unregenerate newcomers. The Indians of Juncauta, he contended, 'live so near the white people that they are always in the way of strong liquor, as well as of the ill

[34] Ibid. 206–7, 208, 209, 213, 214.

[35] Sandra M. Gustafson, *Eloquence is Power: Oratory and Performance in Early America* (Chapel Hill, NC, 2000), esp. 81–9 and chapter 2 *passim*.

[36] Brainerd, 20 September 1745, from the online edition of Jonathan Edwards, *The Life of David Brainerd*, ed. Norman Pettit at the Jonathan Edwards Center at Yale University. http://edwards.yale.edu/ archive? path=aHR0cDovL2Vkd2FyZHMueWFsZS5lZHUvY2dpLWJpbi9uZXdwaGlsby9YZXpZ2Fo ZS5wbD93amVfLjLjY.

examples of nominal Christians'; he found this developing situation made 'it so unspeakably difficult to treat with them about Christianity'.[37]

While particularly exercised concerning degeneration and corruption, Brainerd did not permit these concerns to overwhelm his critique of broader indigenous responses to changing circumstances and of the place of religious specialists within this process of change. He noticed that the people gathered with a special urgency and in response to the terrible spread of illness among them, and he concluded that his discourses on Christianity had been ignored because of the counter-attraction of half a dozen 'conjurers . . . playing their juggling tricks, and acting their frantic distracted postures, in order to find out why they were then so sickly upon the island, numbers of them being at that time disordered with fever and bloody flux'.[38]

Having decided that what he observed was a religious response to a social crisis, Brainerd turned his attention, as did Harriot, White, and others, to what they all perceived to be the grotesque extravagance of the religious specialists. With only the mention of sickness to serve as context, the narrator focused upon what, for him, was the strangeness of the Indians' faces and bodies, their gestures and movements, and particularly the religious specialists who 'were engaged for several hours':

making all the wild, ridiculous and distracted motions imaginable; sometimes singing, sometimes howling, sometimes extending their hands to the utmost stretch, and spending all their fingers . . . sometimes stroking their faces with their hands, then spurting water as fine as mist; sometimes sitting flat on the earth, then bowing down their faces to the ground; then wringing their sides as if in pain and anguish, twisting their faces, turning up their eyes, grunting, puffing, &c.

Brainerd's interpretation of these 'monstrous actions'—hours and hours of 'hideous charms and incantations' that were 'peculiarly suited to raise the devil, if he could be raised by anything [so] odd, ridiculous, and frightful'[39]—also bring to mind José de Acosta's response to *cimarrón* religious and cultural complexity in Panama at the end of the sixteenth century. Each concluded that what seems strange is diabolical, or ridiculous. Taken together, they explode any easy account of what Brainerd (or any other) was measuring as a failure or success of evangelization.

Although he does not state it explicitly, Brainerd's understanding of the Indians' 'disordered' health explains his rendering of a meeting he had with one of the religious specialists, a practitioner of the very actions he had characterized as 'monstrous'. As with Acosta on the isthmus, so for Brainerd on his island, 'monstrous' becomes the cross-temporal, pan-Americas code for the difficult religious and cultural middle which particularly worried our recording narrators but which they could not fully comprehend. In his account of their meeting, Brainerd invoked his authority as a first-person eyewitness, the

[37] Brainerd, 22 September 1745.
[38] Brainerd, 21 September 1745.
[39] Ibid.

one who had been there and thus possesses the right to inform.[40] Drawing upon this authority, he concluded that no sight 'ever excited such images of terror' in his mind as this particular specialist. His appearance suggested radical otherness, as readily animal as human in nature. He appeared in 'a coat of bear skins, dressed with the hair on, and hanging down to his toes' with 'a pair of bear skin stockings; and a great wooden face painted, the one half black, the other half tawny, about the colour of an Indian's skin, with an extravagant mouth, cut very much awry; the face fastened to a bear skin cap, which was drawn over his head'. The specialist shook a tortoise-shell rattle, 'and danced with all his might, but did not suffer any part of his body, not so much as his fingers, to be seen'. As the specialist approached Brainerd, 'his appearance and gestures were so prodigiously fright-ful' that he 'could not but shrink away from him'.

Brainerd's describing the specialist's dress as 'pontifical garb' is the first hint that he respected as well as mocked and feared the individual, and the continuing narration underscores that the specialist impressed and surprised Brainerd in equal measure. He had a 'house consecrated to religious uses, with divers images cut upon the several parts of it . . . [and] the ground beat almost as hard as a rock, with their frequent dancing upon it'. Even more significantly, he engaged Brainerd in lengthy conversation, seem-ingly without aid from an interpreter.[41] The man emerged from beneath the hairy cloak of a frightening and diabolic other to reveal himself as more than the simple custodian of 'pagan' authenticity. He proved himself capable of discoursing with Brainerd about Christianity, some of which he seemed to approve, but more of which 'he disliked extremely'. At this point in the narration, the specialist—or at least Brainerd's render-ing of him—was permitted to make a number of interjections and, arguably, to take over the conversation for a time. A sense of their parallel experience emerged. As Larzer Ziff has put it, it was as if 'David Brainerd [had] met his double'.[42]

The specialist turned out to be a convert—not of the kind Brainerd was meant to be seeking, but a man very like himself, a convert on his own terms. As recently as 'about four or five years' earlier, he 'had been inattentive and lax, just like most others around him', but was now steadfast in a belief system from which he would never waver. Disgusted with those around him, including wicked-living white people, and with 'his heart . . . very much distressed', the Indian had gone 'away into the woods, and lived alone for some months' during which time God had 'comforted his heart, and show[n] him what he should do'. Since then, according to Brainerd's narration, 'he had known God, and tried to serve him; and loved all men, be they who they would'.

The man was 'a devout and zealous reformer', Brainerd declared, 'or rather [a] restorer of what he supposed was the ancient religion of the Indians'. Brainerd thus revealed by his very conclusion, that he could not conceive of any belief system being in flux, in the process of being created or fashioned anew by people such as the specialist,

---

[40] Anthony Pagden, *European Encounters with the New World: From Renaissance to Romanticism* (New Haven, CT, 1994), chapters 1 and 2, 17–87; Rolena Adorno, *The Polemics of Posssession in Spanish American Narrative* (New Haven, CT, 2008).

[41] Brainerd, 21 September 1745.

[42] Ziff, *Writing in the New Nation: Prose, Print, and Politics in the Early United States* (New Haven, CT, 1991), 10.

regardless of what they themselves perceived themselves to be doing. However Brainerd appeared both to sympathize with the man, and even to perceive in him a mirror of himself who was struggling to restore Protestant Christianity among an unreceptive people as frequently of European as of Native American descent. Brainerd observed that the specialist was 'derided among most of the Indians' because he was 'a precise zealot . . . who made a needless noise about religious matters'.

As Brainerd further detailed the man's religious position he unknowingly illuminated a selective indigenous convergence with Christianity. Perhaps this illumination was purely the function of Brainerd's own needs and self-absorbed manner of understanding and telling.[43] But perhaps it was also rather more. The specialist revealed that he had his own mind, and was no agent of the devil, because, as Brainerd pointed out, 'there was no such creature known among the Indians of old times, whose religion he supposed he was attempting to revive'. Moreover, when the specialist discussed with Brainerd the spiritual fate of people after death, he pushed the case for an emerging religious convergence even further, outlining his belief that the souls of the dead Delawares 'went southward', 'and . . . the difference between the good and the bad was this: that the former were admitted into a beautiful town with spiritual walls; and that the latter would for ever hover around these walls, in vain attempts to get in'.

The religion of the specialist, according to Brainerd, was based upon a number of unbending principles about which this man was impressively informed and reflective, not least because they were presented in disciplined terms that a Protestant Christian might admire: 'a set of religious notions which he had examined for himself, and not taken for granted upon bare tradition.' Indeed Brainerd came to respect the Indian specialist as a courageous man who 'relished or disrelished whatever was spoken of a religious nature', according to how it 'either agreed or disagreed with his standard'. The specialist's critical and high 'standard' became the key component of his integrity: 'he seemed to be sincere, honest, and conscientious in his own way, and according to his own religious notions; which is more than I ever saw in any other pagan.' Moreover, he exhibited 'uncommon courtesy', and opposed the Indians' 'drinking strong liquor with all his power'. Whenever he failed to reform people, he went off crying into the woods.

At least three things appear simultaneously to be true about the specialist in mid-eighteenth-century Juncauta: first, he plausibly communicated to David Brainerd both something of his life story and of his perspective on the changes which beset his people and world; second, he became, for Brainerd, a vehicle for exploring *his own* perspective on this same world in motion; and thus third, Brainerd's description of the specialist as a 'reformer' or 'restorer', and in terms evoking the Christian virtues of lay sanctity, not only obscures but also enables our ability to understand the man and his perspective in his highly interactive, transforming environment.

David Brainerd's conclusion about his native interlocutor 'that there was something in his temper and disposition which looked more like true religion than anything I ever observed among other heathens' reveals that once they began to communicate, the

---

43 Gustafson, *Eloquence*, 81, 84–6.

specialist became for Brainerd another man finding himself, often and increasingly, alone in a mostly disappointing world. At the culminating point in Brainerd's narrative arc about his experiences in Juncauta in late September 1745, the specialist is a shunned figure in the wilderness, sharing his fear with Brainerd—a fellow outsider—about the transformations of his own people, about the Indians all around him 'growing very degenerate and corrupt'. The two are fellow-travellers in an early modern Atlantic world—reflective, doubting, worried men of faith, spiritual specialists with peripheral and penetrating perspectives upon the far broader middle ground of religious change of so many other people around them.

Appreciation for the global entanglements and interdependence which began in the late fifteenth and early sixteenth centuries is growing. Students of the outward flows of people, objects, goods, ideas, and behaviours across an Atlantic world are more likely to recognize their limits than were those of their predecessors a generation ago. Yet in the realm of 'religion'—or perhaps more appropriately religious change—notions of 'spiritual conquest', conversion, Christianization, evangelization, and missionization retain much of their power, pretending completion and thus obfuscating more complex and illuminating realities on the ground. Even proponents of 'syncretism' and 'mixture'— while arriving on the scene with considerable theoretical flourish and explanatory potential—can too often assume a passive, mix-and-match fusion accomplished by this or that set of heroes and thus opposed or ignored by another set of villains.[44]

Through a series of episodes featuring unsanctioned religious change that troubled their original commentators I have suggested an alternative manner of exploring the religious history of the Atlantic world of the early modern centuries. The Kublerian thinking tool of a lighthouse emitting complex signals that are not only relayed to other places but also made powerfully anew, gaining new resonances and meanings, assists understanding of this religious history. My alternative pathway has several defining characteristics. The most important is an insistence upon dynamic and individual actions viewed from as many perspectives as possible.[45] I stress interactive religious frameworks of appropriation and innovation, and I highlight the often unintentional processes of transformation and untethering of original ideas and forms beneath judgements of imperfection, chaos, and failure. I suggest through concrete examples that religiosities can be both tenaciously held and continuously renewed, and that they are, by their very nature, in motion and thus incomplete. I argue that it is illuminating to get beyond 'first contact' in colonial scenarios, to points in time when that which persists is that which adapts, when people are

---

[44] Inga Clendinnen, 'Ways to the Sacred: Reconstructing "Religion" in Sixteenth-Century Mexico', *History and Anthropology*, 5 (1990), 109–10; William B. Taylor, *Magistrates of the Sacred: Priests and Parishioners in Eighteenth-Century Mexico* (Palo Alto, CA, 1996), 47–73; and Bastide, *The African Religions of Brazil*, esp. 339.

[45] William B. Taylor in 'Two Shrines of the Cristo Renovado: Religion and Peasant Politics in Late Colonial Mexico', *American Historical Review*, 110/4 (2005), 944–74; Stanley Brandes, 'Conclusion: Reflections on the Study of Religious Orthodoxy and Popular Faith in Europe', in Ellen Badone (ed.), *Religious Orthodoxy and Popular Faith in European Society* (Princeton, NJ, 1990), 185–200.

Christianizing without a sense of conversion.[46] That many of these transformations shocked and dismayed commentators and investigating officials is a sign that we are exploring in the right ways and in the right places.

The sprouting shoots of religious re-creation in a vast transatlantic space reflect my enthusiasms and limitations, and these choices will not be every reader's. I disrupt the general scholarly tendency towards repeating hemispheric separatisms in matters of religion, and also explore similarities and resemblances across the Americas and their broader Atlantic world.[47] While my focus has fallen more fully on religious transformations among indigenous Americans in interaction with people of European and mixed descent, I do not discuss African religious agency as something distinct from the principal patterns of transformation and vital polycentrism I have traced across an Atlantic world. Finally, I have not presented the religious and cultural experiences of the largely Iberian Catholic (and thus more southerly American) zones as defined by a centrally controlled, integrated, and monolithic nature, in contrast to a more diverse, splintering and ultimately tolerant set of religious realities of the largely Protestant northerly Americas. My aim has been to account for meaningful and dynamic religious lives in a great number of places which were new found for all.

Bibliography

Axtell, James, *The Invasion Within: The Contest of Cultures in Colonial North America* (Oxford, 1985).

Christian, Jr., William A., *Local Religion in Sixteenth-Century Spain* (Princeton, NJ, 1981).

Clendinnen, Inga, 'Ways to the Sacred: Reconstructing "Religion" in Sixteenth-Century Mexico', *History and Anthropology*, 5 (1990), 105–41.

Greer, Allan, *Mohawk Saint: Catherine Tekakwitha and the Jesuits* (Oxford, 2005).

—— and Kenneth Mills, 'A Catholic Atlantic', in Jorge Cañizares-Esguerra and Erik R. Seeman (eds.), *The Atlantic in Global History, 1500–2000* (Upper Saddle River, NJ, 2007), 3–19.

MacCormack, Sabine G., '"The Heart Has its Reasons": Predicaments of Missionary Christianity in Early Colonial Peru', *Hispanic American Historical Review*, 65/3 (1985), 443–66.

Mills, Kenneth, 'The Naturalization of Andean Christianities', in R. Po-chia Hsia (ed.), *The Cambridge History of Christianity*, vi: *Reform and Expansion, 1500–1660* (Cambridge, 2007), 508–39.

—— and Anthony Grafton (eds.), *Conversion: Old Worlds and New* (Rochester, NY, 2003).

Pestana, Carla Gardina, *Protestant Empire: Religion and the Making of the British Atlantic World* (Philadelphia, PA, 2009).

Taylor, William B., *Magistrates of the Sacred: Priests and Parishioners in Eighteenth-Century Mexico* (Palo Alto, CA, 1996).

[46] Peter Brown, *Authority and the Sacred: Aspects of the Christianisation of the Roman World* (Cambridge, 1995).

[47] Compare J. H. Elliott in *Empires of the Atlantic World: Britain and Spain in America, 1492–1830* (New Haven, CT, 2006), esp. chapters 3 and 7 and Carla Gardina Pestana, *Protestant Empire: Religion and the Making of the British Atlantic World* (Philadelphia, PA, 2009).

CHAPTER 26

··

THE CHALLENGE
OF THE NEW

··

ANTHONY PAGDEN

I

··

The European incursion into the Atlantic—the 'occidental break out'—after the mid-fifteenth century created many challenges and generated many kinds of 'newness' for all of those caught up in it.[1] For the peoples of the African littoral, of the Canary Islands, of the Caribbean, and of the American mainland, the contact with Europeans throughout this period was inevitably, if not always initially, violent. The Europeans, furthermore, were unlike anyone who had preceded them. Ocean-going vessels were infrequent in the Atlantic (unlike in the Pacific) before the fifteenth century. So, too, were steel and gunpowder. Both Africa and America had been the site of large political structures which the Europeans called 'empires', Zimbabwe and Benin, Aztec Mexico and Inca Peru, before the fifteenth century. But none of these, so far as we know, harboured universalistic notions of exclusion and inclusion, nor did any of them seek to transform the religious, social, and intellectual life of their conquered peoples. By contrast the European interlopers came with monotheistic religious beliefs, which they sought to impose, along with their own political and legal systems, on the peoples they were able to conquer. We know something of how the peoples of Mesoamerica responded to a monotheistic system, which made hard and disturbing distinctions between 'good' and 'evil'.[2] We know how some of the peoples of Africa and America adapted not only to European technology (whose novelty soon wore off) but more significantly to European jurisprudence and European conceptions of

···

[1] The phrase is John Darwin's, *After Tamerlane: The Global History of Empire* (London, 2007), 51.
[2] See Fernando Cervantes, *The Devil in the New World: The Impact of Diabolism in New Spain* (New Haven, CT, 1994).

hierarchy. We know, or think we know, how the Aztecs reacted to European methods of warfare.[3] We know, or think we know, how the Wolof of Senegal exploited the Portuguese presence in Africa, in their own internal struggles.[4] The trouble is we know almost all of this only through the veil of European accounts. Very few indigenous peoples in either Africa or the Americas had the means to record their own experiences of the 'newness' which would eventually destroy their worlds forever. And most of those who did were engulfed and silenced or suborned long before they had any chance to do so. Such 'indigenous voices' as we do have, in particular from the Americas, are late, and written for the most part by authors of mixed origin, using a language which, even when it is not Spanish, is still predominantly that of their conquerors.[5]

The only people to register the 'discovery' of the Atlantic as challenge, the only peoples so far as we know to possess intellectual traditions in which novelty had any significant place as an agent of change, were the Europeans themselves.

For them, as the philosopher David Hume put it in 1757, the fifteenth century had been the 'Period modern history commences'. It had been then that 'America was discovered: Commerce extended: The Arts cultivated: Printing invented: Religion reform'd; And all the Governments and Empire almost chang'd'.[6] By the mid-eighteenth century not only had it become a commonplace to look upon the 'discovery' of America as a turning point in European, if not world, history; it had also become a commonplace to link that event closely to the other changes with which Hume associates it: the Reformation, the Renaissance, the invention of printing (and also of gunpowder and the compass), the emergence of global commerce, and a widespread transition in forms of government. The modern age was one associated with constant change, with the destruction of all the boundaries and the limits, geographical, physical, and intellectual, which had enclosed humanity, since antiquity. It was, as Hume's contemporary, the Scottish historian William Robertson, expressed it, the age

when Providence decreed that men were to pass the limits within which they had been so long confined, and open themselves to a more ample field wherein to display their talents, their enterprise and courage.[7]

For Hume and Robertson, as for the German naturalist and explorer Alexander von Humboldt and the French historian Jules Michelet in the following century, Columbus' 'encounter' with what he supposed to be the outer fringes of 'Cathay' had led inexorably, in Michelet's celebrated phrase, to 'the discovery of the world and the discovery of

---

[3] Inga Clendinnen, ' "Fierce and unnatural cruelty": Cortés and the Conquest of Mexico', in Stephen Greenblatt (ed.), *New World Encounters* (Berkeley, CA, 1993), 12–47.

[4] Peter Russell, 'White Kings on Black: Rui da Pina and the Problem of Black African Sovereignty', in *Portugal, Spain and the African Atlantic, 1343–1490* (Aldershot, 1995), XVI.

[5] See Kevin Terraciano this volume.

[6] Hume is in fact referring to the 'Reign of Henry the 7th'. *The Letters of David Hume*, ed. J. Y. T. Greig, 2 vols. (Oxford, 1932), i. 249.

[7] *The History of America* (1777), 4 vols. (London, 1800), i. 55.

man'.[8] It had also secured the future for Europe, a hitherto rather neglected peninsula of Asia, as the conqueror and occupier of much of the planet. The 'Atlantic world' in which these momentous events had occurred did not for contemporaries, however, have much, if any, significance. It was land which bound peoples together. Water, as the Roman poets Horace and Claudian had famously insisted, existed only to divide them. Until Magellan's circumnavigation in 1522, no one had any precise idea of the relationship between the Atlantic and the other oceans and bodies of water of the world, in particular the Pacific. All were still thought of, as they had been in antiquity, as one vast, encircling ocean—the 'Ocean Sea' of which Columbus had had himself made admiral. It was this which had hitherto bound together the three continents, Europe, Asia, and Africa. Columbus' discovery among other things had had the effect of detaching the two ends of the Euro-Asian landmass in a quite unexpected way, and of reorienting the perception of the relationship between earth and water. 'Hence we can see', wrote the Portuguese cosmographer Duarte Pacheco Pereira in 1508, 'that the Ocean does not surround the earth as the philosophers have declared, but rather the earth surrounds the sea that lies in its hollow and centre.'[9]

It was this unsettling of the premises on which ancient geography had been based which for later generations made the discovery into a foundational moment in world history. 'All that has appeared great up until now', wrote Voltaire in 1754, 'seems to disappear before this species of new creation.'[10] The continent on whose outer islands Columbus had stumbled on the morning of 12 October 1492 was 'new' in quite a different way from either Asia or Africa. Sub-Saharan Africans had been a familiar sight in the Mediterranean for centuries, and although the precise outline of the Atlantic coast of Africa south of Cape Bojador had been entirely unknown to Europeans before the Portuguese began steadily working their way south after 1434, Africa itself had been a part of European geographical knowledge since about 500 BC. As early as 146 BC, the Roman general Scipio Aemilianus had sent a fleet under the command of the Greek historian Polybius to explore the west coast, although it does not seem to have got very far. Ever since at least the first century AD Africa had also been assumed to be both circumnavigable and triangular in shape.[11] For all that the interior of the continent itself remained unexplored and filled with imaginary or semi-imaginary peoples and places until the nineteenth century, 'Africa' was conceptually at least a known quantity, largely indistinguishable from Europe and Asia. Why, Herodotus had asked, should 'three names, and women's names at that [Europa, Asia, and Africa], have been given to a tract which is in reality one?'[12]

[8] *Histoire de la France* (Paris, 1855), vii, pp. ii–iii; and see John Elliott, 'The Discovery of America and the Discovery of Man', *Proceedings of the British Academy*, 58 (London, 1972), 101–25.

[9] *Esmeraldo de situ orbis*, quoted in W. G. L. Randles, 'Classical Models of World Geography and their Transformation Following the Discovery of America', in Wolfgang Haase and Meyer Rheinhold (eds.), *The Classical Tradition and the Americas*, i: *European Images of the Americas and the Classical Tradition*, part I (Berlin, 1994), 5–76, at 63.

[10] *Essai sur les mœurs*, ed. René Pomeau (Paris, 1963), ii. 330.

[11] Strabo, *Geographia*, 17. 3. 1.

[12] *Histories*, 7. 104.

In 1497 Vasco da Gama rounded the Cape of Good Hope and sailed into the Indian Ocean, thereby proving that there did exist a serviceable westward sea route, if not all the way to 'Cathay', then at least to India, and demonstrating conclusively that Columbus' 'small-earth' theory was wrong. Thereafter the Portuguese began to claim to have 'discovered' India, as the Spanish claimed to have 'discovered' America, and thus to enjoy exclusive sailing rights in the Indian Ocean, as the Spanish did in the western Atlantic. It was, as the Dutch humanist Hugo Grotius pointed out in 1608, an obvious historical absurdity. Both Asia and Africa had been 'frequently visited' in antiquity by both the Greeks and the Romans. All the Portuguese had done was to establish new sailing routes across the Atlantic and Indian Oceans *for Europeans*. For this, Grotius acknowledged, they deserved praise. But even these achievements were, in his view, the outcome of an irresistible historical cycle. Even if Vasco da Gama had not been the first to find a sea route to India, then sooner rather than later someone else would have done so. 'For', Grotius concluded, 'the times were coming on a pace in which along with other sciences the geographical locations were being better known each day.'[13]

America was different, and its discovery, unlike those which had preceded it (but like the discoveries in the Pacific which would follow it), had, or so it seemed, resulted in the recognition of an entirely 'new' world—'cet autre monde' as Montaigne significantly called it.[14] True the recognition that America was indeed 'new' and 'other' was not immediate. Maps showing Cuba as 'a part of Asia' were being produced well into the early sixteenth century, and as late as 1533, the Nuremberg astronomer Johann Schöner could still claim that the so-called 'New World' was in fact a part of the Asian landmass and that the Mexica city of Tenochtitlan, destroyed by Hernán Cortés in 1521, was the Chinese commercial city of 'Quinsay' (Hang Zhou)—of which Marco Polo, and Columbus himself, had made so much. (This would, of course, have made Charles V master of the Ming Empire, which not even he ever claimed.) Nor was Schöner alone. As late as 1604 the Mexican Creole Baltazar Dorantes de Carranza concluded his account of the wonders of his native land—the *Sumario relación de las cosas de la Nueva España*—by saying that 'all that I have said about the fertility and happy condition of these Indies, demonstrates and confirms that they are the outmost parts of the true India'.[15] But in most respects these are exceptions. From the moment Columbus' first letter arrived in Spain announcing his landfall on the shores of Asia, it was clear to most that, in the words of the gossipy court humanist Peter Martyr, 'this Columbus is the discoverer of a New World'.[16] And by the time he had returned from

---

[13] *Mare liberum: The Freedom of the Seas, or the right which belongs to the Dutch to take part in the East India Trade*, trans. with a revision of the Latin text of 1633 by Ralph van Deman Magoffin (Oxford, 1916), 42.

[14] 'Des cannibales', *Essais*, I. xxx. 1. *Essais de Michel de Montaigne*, ed. Albert Thibaudet (Paris, 1950), 239.

[15] Serge Gruzinski, *Les Quatre parties du monde: histoire d'une mondialisation* (Paris, 2004), 119.

[16] *Opus espitolarum, patri martyris Angleria* (Alcalá de Henares, 1530), fo. xxxiv[r]. Letter to Ascanio Sforza, 1 November 1493.

his third voyage in 1500 it was obvious that what lay between Europe and Asia was not merely, or only, a scattering of islands but an entire continent.

The terms 'new' and 'discovered', however, were by no means uncontentious, and already by the mid-sixteenth century their exact status had become a topic of heated debate. Nor was this only a squabble over semantics or etymology. It carried with it serious legal and political implications, for discovery could be said to convey rights of occupation. Under Roman law, it was legitimate for anyone to take possession of a territory which was quite literally 'unknown'. (The designation was *res* or *terra nullius*, a 'thing' or 'land of no one', and the example most commonly cited, which is directly analogous to the 'discovery' of America, was that of an island which emerges in the middle of a river.[17]) If then the Spanish could claim that America was 'new', in that prior to 1492 it had been unknown to anyone who might be in a position to claim rights in it, the Spanish crown would be in a good position to claim, against any other European power, to be the sole possessor. The Portuguese had used a similar argument to assert their supposed rights of occupation over areas of the African, and even the Indian coast, on which they had set up stone columns, known as *padrões*, asserting the sole rights of the kings of Portugal frequently not only to the land but also to the sea itself.

There were, however, two words in play in these debates: the late ecclesiastical Latin *disco-operire*, which means literally to 'take the lid off' or 'reveal to the gaze', and the far more troubling classical term *invenire*. The question was: did *invenire* mean only something like 'see for the first time'—or did it imply something more: possession and occupation, that is some kind of creative *act*? And if it was land which was being 'discovered' in this sense could any place which was inhabited be said to have been 'discovered' by any one other than its original inhabitants? The outcome of these debates was inevitably inconclusive. But it is not insignificant that in the European vernaculars *disco-operire* obviously became 'to discover' and *invenire*, 'to invent', and only the latter carried with it any legal implications. As Grotius argued, if the Portuguese claims to have 'discovered' India were to be made good, they would have indeed to have occupied it, and this they clearly could not do because it was already fully occupied. What territories they did possess there, and in Africa, he pointed out, they had, in fact, leased from local rulers. *Invenire*, he remarked caustically, 'is not merely to seize with the eyes, but to apprehend'.[18] To claim, as the Portuguese had done, that their mere presence in Indian territorial waters meant that they exercised sovereignty there was as absurd as claiming that any Japanese fleet cruising in the Atlantic could claim sovereignty over the kingdom of Portugal.

---

[17] Justinian, *Institutes*, 2. 1. 12. See Anthony Pagden, 'Law, Colonization, Legitimation and the European Background', in Michael Grossberg and Christopher Tomlins (eds.), *Cambridge History of Law in America* (Cambridge, 2008), 1–31.

[18] *Invenire enim non illud est oculis ursupare, sed apprehendere* (*Mare liberum*, 11–12) citing *Digest*, Lex 3 of *De adquirendo dominio*.

Most Europeans were prepared to accept that the same argument applied to the Americas. The continent had been unknown to the ancients, but it was nevertheless clearly inhabited, and by the mid-sixteenth century it was clear also that it was inhabited by a great variety of peoples many of whom lived in large urbanized societies. No one could, therefore, suppose that by virtue of 'discovery' they might exercise any sovereign rights there. Francisco de Vitoria (1492–1546), one of the earliest of the Spanish theologians to raise the whole question of the legitimacy of the Spanish occupation of the Americas, briskly dismissed what he termed the title by 'right of discovery' (*in iure inventionis*)—with which 'pretext alone Columbus of Genoa first set sail'—on the grounds that although 'the law of nations expressly states that goods which belong to no owner pass to the occupier . . . the goods in question here had an owner [and thus] they do not fall under this title'.[19]

If America was 'new', therefore, it was clearly new only to the Europeans. In 1556, one of Vitoria's successors, the great Dominican theologian Domingo de Soto, in discussing the right of the Holy Roman Emperor to be 'Lord of all the World', and therefore also of the Americas (a right which he firmly denied), rejected any claim that the term 'new' when used in the by then familiar phrase 'new world' meant anything like 'newly created', which might thereby imply that the Spanish could claim rights of 'discovery' (*invenio*) over it. When, Soto observed, the Roman poet Lucan had written the line 'Arabs you have come to a new world unknown to you', what he meant, and what all his Latin-speaking readers knew he meant, was simply: 'you find yourself in an unfamiliar place.' The same applied, he went on, 'When we speak of a New World or a New Earth of islands and a continent which encompasses vast spaces.'[20] No one, Soto was arguing, had ever supposed that these places were literally 'new'. They were simply unknown to *us*. It was precisely the autochthonous identity of the New World—its existence prior to its 'discovery'—which made that 'discovery' at all remarkable. For this reason there was considerable unease over the appropriateness of referring to places in America as 'new' versions of places in Europe, 'New Spain', 'New England', etc. The earliest of the natural historians of the Americas, Gonzalo Fernández de Oviedo, in his account of Nuño de Guzmán's expedition to the region in north-western Mexico which he named 'New Galicia', objected forcibly to this apparently indiscriminate use of the adjective for 'the Spaniards called this New Galicia, not because it is more or less ancient than Old Galicia, but simply because the Christians have recently found (*hallaron*) it'.[21]

The discovery, furthermore, had not only revealed the existence of a 'new' or 'other' world. It had also opened up the possibility of still more worlds to discover. 'Who can say',

---

[19] *De Indis*, 2. 3–4, in Anthony Pagden and Jeremy Lawrance (eds.), *Francisco de Vitoria: Political Writings* (Cambridge, 1991), 264.

[20] *De iustitia et iure* (Salamanca, 1556), 306, and see Anthony Pagden, 'La Découverte de l'Amérique et la transformation du temps et de l'espace en Europe', *Revue de synthèse*, 129 (2008), 1–16.

[21] *Historia general y natural de las Indias*, ed. Perez de Tudela Bueso, *Biblioteca de autores españoles*, vols. cxvii–cxxi (Madrid, 1959), iv. 269 and 278.

wrote Montaigne in 1572, 'if there might not be another [world] to be discovered in the future, so many people greater than we are, having been mistaken about this one?'[22] By then, the possibilities of those other worlds had taken concrete shape in the Pacific. The fabled Southern Continent, the *Terra australis incognita*, would eventually turn out not to exist (although 'Australia'—not at all the same place—of course, would). But the very possibility of its existence carried with it a continuing challenge to the limits of European science: as well, of course, as the promise of further scope for European domination.

Under these conditions of uncertainty, wrote the Spanish jurist Fernando Vázquez de Menchaca (1512–69), the word *mundus*, which the Romans had used to describe what they took to be a fixed and immutable space, could now only be understood in the indefinite mode, as limited to a condition which was still only potential. And to claim to 'possess' something which was potential was, he said, to be compared to 'the tales of children, to the advice of the aged and to the shadows of an unquiet sleep'.[23]

It was still possible, however, to argue that even if America was new only in the sense of being 'unknown to us', even if it was recognized as having been inhabited for centuries by peoples who clearly exercised full rights both of possession and sovereignty over the territories on which they lived, those peoples, like the Africans and the Chinese, could still be said to have occupied no significant place in human history before the arrival of the Europeans. As early as 1512, the German humanist Johann Cochlaeus dismissed Columbus' entire enterprise (which he attributes to Amerigo Vespucci) as having nothing to do with 'Cosmography and the knowledge of History . . . for the peoples and places of that continent are unknown and unnamed to us'.[24] If history was, as it was for most Christians, the working out in time of God's plans for his creation—a view which Voltaire later compared to writing the history of Rome from the perspective of Wales—then any people who had not been the beneficiaries of Christ's redemption, who 'were unknown and unnamed to us', could have no part in it. As Galileo's opponent Cardinal Roberto Bellarmino put it: 'one could say that these provinces do not belong to the world.'[25] Or had not until evangelization had brought them into History and thus into the 'world'. Similarly for Bartolomé de Las Casas, the most outspoken defender of the autonomous identity and rights of the American Indians, Columbus' voyages had constituted an expression of God's favour to the moderns which because of their paganism he had denied to the ancients. Columbus' great contribution had been not to bring the Spanish to America—for which Las Casas could only revile him—but for having brought 'so many countless peoples' into history, and by so doing having 'broken the locks that had held the Ocean Sea fast ever since the Flood'.[26]

[22] 'Des cannibales', *Essais*, I. xxx. 1. *Essais de Michel de Montaigne*, 239.

[23] *Controversiarum illiustrium aliarumque usu frequentium, libri tres* [1563], ed. Fidel Rodriguez Alcalde, 3 vols. (Valladolid, 1931), i. 17; ii. 30.

[24] Quoted in J. H. Elliott, 'Renaissance Europe and America: A Blunted Impact?', in Fredi Chiappelli (ed.), *First Images of Americas: The Impact of the New World on the Old* (Berkeley, CA, 1976), i. 14.

[25] *Disputationes de controversii christianae fidei*, in *Scritti politici*, ed. Carlo Giacon (Bologna, 1950), 117.

[26] *Historia de las Indias*, ed. Augustin Millares Carlo, 3 vols. (Mexico, 1951), I. 47.

II

This, however, failed to address the problem which no amount of juggling with sacred histories seemed able to resolve. For on all the ancient, and Christian, accounts, the American Indians should not have existed at all. Until 1492, it was widely believed that the regions around the equator, the so-called 'Torrid Zone', were impassable, and since all humanity had to have been descended from Adam, the 'Antipodes', all the lands which lay to the south of the equator, must, therefore, be uninhabited. St Augustine had concluded, in what was taken to be the most authoritative utterance on the subject, that it was unthinkable that in those lands, 'where the sun rises when it sets to us, [there should be] men who walk with their feet opposite ours'.[27] The discovery of life in both America and southern Africa seemed to have demonstrated the falsity of this claim, and with it the authority not only of ancient geography, but also of one of the most authoritative of the Fathers of the Church.

An inhabited Torrid Zone however posed another, more troubling, problem. For if the integrity of the biblical account of the peopling of the world were to be maintained, the American Indians still had to have been descended from one of the sons of Noah, which meant that they had to have originated in some region of the Old World. Could they possibly be the descendants of shipwrecked Carthaginians, or Vikings, or, as Hugo Grotius supposed, Tartars, or—one of the most popular and enduring suppositions—the descendants of the Ten Lost Tribes of Israel? And if they were any, or all, of these how had they got there? Had they drifted across the Atlantic on rafts or primitive boats, or been carried by angels, eager to correct an oversight in God's plan for the re-peopling of the earth after the Flood? None of these hypotheses seemed very probable. And even if some such explanation might account for a human migration, how was one to explain the proliferation of non-human life, the anacondas and the pumas, not to mention a thousand different kinds of venomous snakes? Surely no man, nor angel, in his right mind would have taken the trouble to transfer such creatures from the Old World to the New.

One solution to the problem provided by a number of writers, the most influential being the Jesuit historian José de Acosta, was that the presence in the American continent of any life form which could not be accounted for by spontaneous generation could only be explained by the existence of a northern land bridge—whose precise location was yet to be discovered—which joined, or had once joined, America to Asia.[28]

---

[27] *City of God* Cap. XVI. 9.

[28] *Historia natural y moral de las Indias* [1590], ed. Edmundo O'Gorman (Mexico City, 1962), 324–30. As Joan-Pau Rubiés has pointed out, Acosta's account, despite his claim to originality, in fact follows that of the chronicler-royal Juan López de Velasco's *Geografía y descripción universal de las Indias* of 1574. A northern land bridge also appears on maps from 1550 by the Venetian cosmographer Giacomo Gastaldi. ('Hugo Grotius', 'Dissertation on the Origins of the American Peoples, and the Use of Comparative Method', in *Travellers and Cosmographers: Studies in the History of Early Modern Travel and Ethnology* (London, 2007), p. xi). But almost every learned man in Europe had read Acosta, whereas very few had read Velasco, and fewer still had seen Gastaldi's maps.

Today we know, from the fossil record, that this is, broadly speaking, true—a striking case of a true hypothesis being derived from entirely false premises. The peoples who settled the Americas did indeed come, as Acosta had supposed, from Asia, and they arrived across what is now called the Bering Strait in successive waves beginning sometime, probably, although this is hotly contested, around 12,000 to 13,000 years ago.

Although the Bering Strait theory gradually gained acceptance and became indeed the basis for a substantial diffusionist literature throughout the eighteenth century, it did not entirely dispel the suspicion that the peoples of America might be some quite different species of human being altogether. What if the biblical account of the peopling of the earth were simply wrong or incomplete? And, if they were not the descendants of any of Noah's sons, who then were they?

There were two possible answers. Aristotle had argued that certain lower creatures, insects, reptiles, and fish, might be generated either from the soil or from putrid matter.[29] The orthodox view was that this excluded all higher animals and in particular humankind—a point on which Aquinas had insisted—since man was the only creature, of course, to be endowed with an immortal soul. But there were those who thought otherwise. One was the Mantuan Aristotelian Pietro Pomponazzi. Had not God himself made Adam out of 'the dust of the ground'?, he asked. And if that were the case why should not humanity also have been created, as Plato had claimed, from rotting matter? Plato, knowing nothing of the Bible, had assumed that it had been the stars which had been responsible for the final act of generation. We, Pomponazzi assumed, now knew better. But the fact that Adam and his descendants had been created by the hand of God did not necessarily exclude the possibility of later non-divine acts of creation. 'That man is perfect and thus cannot be generated out of rotting matter', he told his students, 'is only a probable argument, but that does not exclude the possibility that it might occur.'[30]

The theory of spontaneous generation was taken up by the doctors who found in it a satisfyingly economical solution to the problem of polygenesis, by the German doctor Theophrastus Bombast, known as Paracelsus, in 1537–8, by Girolamo Cardano, by Andrea Cesalpino—who believed that the climate had something to do with it—'in the torrid zone', he claimed, 'perfect animals are constantly generated spontaneously'—and by the arch-magus Giordano Bruno, who was burned at the stake in part for harbouring such beliefs.

There was, however, another explanation for the origins of the American Indians which linked them to another equally 'remote' and equally troubling people: the Chinese.

What if there had, in fact, been not one but two Adams? It was, of course, a wildly heretical proposition. But it gained considerable support in the mid-sixteenth century and set off a controversy about human origins which continued well into the nine-teenth. 'We are all', wrote Paracelsus,, 'descended from Adam, and are those creatures

---

[29] *De generatione animalium*, 762a10. *Meteorologica*, 381b10.
[30] Bruno Nardi, *Studi su Pietro Pomponazzi* (Florence, 1964), 319.

called men, whose ancestor was generated directly by God, without the intervention of the stars?' But, he went on,

We must not forget those who have been discovered on remote islands, many of which are still hidden, and are still to be discovered. . . . It cannot be demonstrated that the men that occupy these unknown lands derive from Adam [for] no one can easily believe that they are of the line of Adam, since the sons of Adam could not have reached such remote places.

Therefore he concluded, it must be accepted that 'the sons of Adam do not occupy all the earth'.[31] This did not, he added, deny them a soul, only a common ancestor with the rest of the species.

Paracelsus' arguments were only tentative. But in 1655 a nominally French Huguenot, of Jewish descent, Isaac La Peyrère, published in the Netherlands a treatise entitled *Prae-Adamitae*. Based on a detailed analysis of the account of the creation in Genesis— and a stray comment from St Paul's Epistle to the Romans—La Peyrère pointed out that Genesis contained not one but two accounts of human creation: the first (1: 27) speaks of the simultaneous creation of Adam and Eve, 'male and female created he them'; the second and better-known one (7: 21–2) describes the creation of first Adam and then of Eve from Adam's rib.

It followed, La Peyrère argued, that these two separate acts of creation must have been divided by a vast period of time. The races of Europe and of western Asia were the obvious descendants of the better documented of the two Adams—that is the later one—the other peoples, who lived in both the extreme West and the extreme East, of the other earlier Adam. (He also claimed that the Old Testament, as history, could only apply to the past experiences of the Jews.) This theory proved to be instantly controversial and immensely popular. Within a year of its publication *Prae-Adamitae* had been translated into English, elicited at least a dozen refutations, been condemned by the Parliament of Paris, and burnt by the public executioner. La Peyrère himself went on to become perhaps the most celebrated heretic of his day, and although his work has now been entirely forgotten the controversy it aroused rumbled on well into the eighteenth century.[32] Its popularity is not difficult to explain. It provided an answer to those who were already beginning to recognize that no species could have been created from a single pair whose only recorded offspring were both male.

'Pre-Adamite' theory evidently led nowhere, as far as any scientific understanding of human origins was concerned. But it had the effect of destabilizing the Church's hold over human history, and of seriously undermining the belief in the Bible as an unquestionable historical source. In doing so, it contributed to the emergence of an entirely new, and vastly extended, conception of time which, together with the

---

[31] Quoted in Giuliano Gliozzi, *Adamo e il nuovo mondo* (Florence, 1977), 309–10.

[32] Richard Popkin, *Isaac La Peyrère (1596–1676)* (Leiden, 1987), 14, 80–1. For a detailed account of the debate over La Peyrère's work see Colin Kidd, *The Forging of Races: Race and Scripture in the Protestant Atlantic World, 1600–2000* (Cambridge, 2006), 62–7.

discovery of the fossil record in the nineteenth century, would finally discredit all forms of sacred history.

III

The discovery of America had seriously undermined both classical geography and the traditional Christian accounts of the creation and subsequent peopling of the world. It offered, however, other, less direct, challenges to the ancient understanding of the world which in the end, were to be even more devastating for the subsequent history of Europe.

The intellectual world of the late fifteenth century was one which was very largely bounded by reference to a canon of sacred and ancient authors, most notably Aristotle, to the point where all of what was then called 'natural philosophy'—that is the natural sciences—was largely limited to a series of textual commentaries.[33] The discovery of a hitherto unknown continent posed an obvious immediate and inescapable threat to the sovereignty of the text. For if the ancients had proved to be defective in this geographical respect, who could know, as Erasmus pointed out as early as 1517, in what other as yet undiscovered ways they might also turn out to have been in error?[34] Might their astronomy, their physics, their medicine and biology, even their ethics and politics— the entire basis on which the curricula of the universities of Europe rested—also turn out to be wrong? Over sixty years later, standing on the stern of the ship which was carrying him to America, and finding himself cold at midday with the sun directly overhead—an impossible situation according to ancient meteorology—José de Acosta had 'laughed and made fun of Aristotle and his philosophy'.[35]

The discovery of America as an event in the intellectual history of Europe was not, however, an isolated, instance. It was, as Hume was not alone in seeing, linked inescapably to the Reformation. Both, in their very different ways, had contributed to the collapse of the old intellectual order, which in the eighteenth century would be called scathingly 'the spirit of the system'. Both belonged to a new epoch in which, in Alexis de Tocqueville's brisk history of the origins of European modernity, 'philosophy properly speaking' had abolished 'received formulas, destroying the empire of tradition and overthrowing received authority'.[36]

Into this unravelling world there streamed an ever-increasing body of information about the New World and its inhabitants. Here, apparently, were worlds in which there existed peoples who ate and sacrificed each other; who, some claimed, mated with their

---

[33] See Anthony Grafton, with April Shelford and Nancy Siraisi, *New Worlds, Ancient Texts: The Power of Tradition and the Shock of Discovery* (Cambridge, MA, 1992).

[34] In a letter to the duke of Saxony, *Opus epistolarum Des. Erasmi roterodami*, ed. P. S. Allen, 12 vols. (Oxford, 1906–56), ii. 584.

[35] *Historia natural y moral de las Indias*, ed. Edmundo O'Gorman (Mexico, 1962), 77.

[36] *De la démocratie en Amérique* (Paris, 1961), ii. 15–16.

siblings, who knew far too many gods—and left the bodies of their dead to rot in the open air. More unsettling still, here were peoples who, without any knowledge of either European civilization or the Gospels, had created societies which in their structure, their order, their sheer wealth, were often remarkably similar to those to be found in Europe and Asia.

All of this flatly contradicted the traditional Christian view that there could really only exist one type of person and one kind of society, a society which, despite enormous differences in customs, dress, languages, and even beliefs, nevertheless conformed, unquestioningly, to certain moral, sexual, religious, and cultural rules. These rules made up the 'law of nature', and the law of nature was, on the most widely accepted account, innate, inscribed on the human mind, by the creator.

Faced with such evidence of human diversity, the only possible conclusion to which any reflective person could come was that the current understanding of the law of nature as a set of universal principles binding upon all mankind was seriously defective. God might indeed have created a pattern in the universe but it could not simply be equated with the customs and practices of the peoples of Europe. The general assumption that certain things were 'natural', others 'unnatural', was therefore an error. The natural law, to which every generation since Aristotle had made appeal as the ultimate measure of all human behaviour, had, at best, only a very limited foundation in nature. In reality, it was only a matter of collective opinion, masquerading as demonstrable certainty. To call something 'unnatural' was merely to condemn it as different, as 'other', alien, and frightening. As the French philosopher and mathematician Blaise Pascal put it, all the word 'natural' now meant was that something was generally accepted 'on this side of the Pyrenees'—if that is you were French.[37] On the other side another kind of 'nature' reigned. And if 'nature' could no longer be relied upon to be consistent between France and Spain, who could know what might be natural in America or Africa, China or Ceylon?

The subsequent historical re-evaluation of the significance of the discovery of America became, therefore, part of a story of the transition from an early largely irrational past to a new bright rational present (and it was hoped future). It had, wrote the great German naturalist Alexander von Humboldt—one of the most influential thinkers of the early nineteenth century—been Columbus' 'thoughts' which had been responsible for the 'unexpected thrust forward to the march of civilization' which had occurred in the fifteenth century, on that 'uncertain border where the Middle Ages and the modern world merge with one another'.[38] And the long-term consequences of that 'thrust' had been monumental. Before what Humboldt calls the 'epoch of Columbus', Europeans had conceived time, and their progress though it, as a set of responses to 'external circumstances'. With the addition of America to mankind's 'objects of contemplation', the European intellect 'henceforth produces . . . Grand results by its own peculiar and internal power in every direction at the same time'. 'Since that grand era', he wrote in his

---

[37] *Pensées*, 294.
[38] *Examen critique de l'histoire de la géographie du nouveau continent*, 5 vols. (Paris, 1836–9), iii. 9, 12, iv. 6.

magisterial history of the cosmos, *Kosmos*, 'a new and active state of the intellect and feelings, bold wishes and hopes scarcely to be restrained, have gradually penetrated into the whole of civil society.'[39]

In this history, the 'newness' of America underwent a final transformation. Now the 'new' world became not only a challenge to the comfortable intellectual assumptions of the old; it became a possible replacement for it. By the time Humboldt was writing a new transatlantic community, now called 'the West' had come into being. It included not only 'old' Europe, but the 'new' societies which Europe's own settler populations had created for themselves across the Atlantic, a community of peoples with similar origins who all belonged to what was thought of as a single 'civilization' (a term which also came into use at about this time).[40] But in this 'West' it was the 'new' which would dictate the future. It was, said Alexander Hamilton in 1787, now the duty of the Union of the United States to aim at 'an ascendant in the system of European affairs', to counterbalance a Europe which had for too long been able to 'plume herself as Mistress of the world and to consider the rest of mankind as created for her benefit', and to erect 'one great American system superior to the control of all transatlantic force or influence and able to dictate the terms of the connections between the old and the new world'.[41]

Nor was it only the Americans themselves who held the belief that somehow the capacity for regeneration lay no longer in Europe, not even in Revolutionary France, but somewhere on the far side of the Atlantic. As Georg Friedrich Hegel, lecturing in 1830 on the past, present, and future of humanity, explained in over-extended geographical terms, History, properly understood as the narrative of the victors, had begun in the East—'the region of origination'. It had then moved to Europe, the 'uniting element' of the 'three quarters of the globe'. The future, however, lay across the Atlantic, in this still new 'New World', 'where in the ages that lie before us, the burden of the World's History shall reveal itself'.[42]

BIBLIOGRAPHY

Cervantes, Fernando, *The Devil in the New World: The Impact of Diabolism in New Spain* (New Haven, CT, 1994).

Chiapelli, Fredi (ed.), *First Images of America: The Impact of the New World on the Old*, 2 vols. (Berkeley, CA, 1976).

---

[39] *Cosmos: Sketch of a Physical Description of the Universe*, 4 vols. (London, 1846–58), ii. 299.

[40] Marie Jean Antoine Nicolas de Caritat, marquis de Condercet, *Esquisse d'un tableau historique des progrès de l'esprit humain*, ed. Alain Pons (Paris, 1988), 208, 266. Conacrect was, however, thinking primarily of France, England, and the United States. Spain and the new republics of Spanish America were, in his view, still too mired in the superstition and tyranny of the world of the ancient regime.

[41] *Federalist* XI in Alexander Hamilton, James Madison, and John Jay, *The Federalist Papers*, ed. Isaac Kramnick (Harmondsworth, 1987), 133–4.

[42] *The Philosophy of History*, trans. J. Sibree (New York, 1956), 99.

Darwin, John, *After Tamerlane: The Global History of Empire* (London, 2007).

Grafton, Anthony, *New Worlds, Ancient Texts: The Power of Tradition and the Shock of Discovery* (Cambridge, MA, 1992).

Greenblatt, Stephen (ed.), *New World Encounters* (Berkeley, CA, 1993).

Gruzinski, Serge, *Les Quatre parties du monde: histoire d'une mondialisation* (Paris, 2004).

Jackson, Anna, and Jaffer, Amin (eds.), *Encounters: The Meeting of Asia and Europe, 1500–1800* (London, 2004).

Kidd, Colin, *The Forging of Races: Race and Scripture in the Protestant Atlantic World* (Cambridge, 2006).

Lupher, David A., *Romans in a New World: Classical Models in Sixteenth-Century Spanish America* (Ann Arbor, MI, 2003).

Pagden, Anthony, *The European Encounters with the New World, from Renaissance to Romanticism* (New Haven, CT, 1993).

Rubiés, Joan Pau, *Travel and Ethnology in the Renaissance: South India through European Eyes, 1250–1625* (Cambridge, 2000).

Schwatrz, Stuart (ed.), *Implicit Understandings: Observing, Reporting, and Reflecting on the Encounters between Europeans and Other Peoples in the Early Modern Era* (Cambridge, 1994).

CHAPTER 27

SCIENCE, NATURE, RACE

SUSAN SCOTT PARRISH

In 1670, Henry Oldenburg, secretary of the Royal Society of London for the Improvement of Natural Knowledge, writing to John Winthrop, governor of the colony of Connecticut, optimistically envisioned the transit of science across the North Atlantic whereby:

within a little time wee shall heare, that the ferment of advancing real Philosophy, which is very active here and in all our neighboring countrys, will take also in your parts, and there seize on all that have ingenuity and industry for the farther spreading of the honour of the English nation, and the larger diffusing of the manifold advantages & benefits to y[e] must proceed from hence.

Oldenberg further believed that:

the savage Indians themselves, when they shall see the Christians addicted, as to piety and virtue, so to all sorts of ingenuityes, pleasing exp[erimen]ts usefull inventions and practises, will thereby insensibly, and the more chearfully subject themselves to you.

Oldenberg, here, associates Europeans with the advancement of national pride, experimental science, Christian virtue, and superior knowledge, and non-Europeans with submissive intellectual backwardness. He thus locates science at the centre of an empire 'diffusing' its benefits to a grateful periphery of colonials and indigenous people. This attitude, called 'diffusionist' today, was sustained by historians of science well into the twentieth century. For example in 1967, George Basalla formulated a thesis about 'The Spread of Western Science', suggesting that as science moved to multiple peripheries in the shadow of empire, it first induced dependency, then an adolescent stage of growth, and finally a mature and autonomous national science. Anti-colonialist scholars, while opposed to Basalla's concept of 'diffusion', did little to unseat it as an explanatory model. They challenged the suggestion that Europe had 'produced' scientific truth for the rest of the world, but did not question the rubric of uni-directional domination itself.[1]

Other scholars have interpreted 'imperial' science in related fashion by analogy to trading interactions between centres and peripheries. When applied to Atlantic experiences this model has non-European peripheries supplying raw materials such as ivory, gold dust, sugar, tobacco, fish, lumber, and pelts, with the centres converting these commodities into (or exchanging them for) finished trade products. Thus, raw scientific 'things' arrived from Brazil, or New Spain, or Angola, or Charles Town (animals, plants, indigenous artefacts, observations, measurements) and were given increased epistemological value once processed at such European 'centres of calculation' as Seville, Lisbon, London, Uppsala, Paris, Antwerp, or Leiden.[2] In some cases, scientific specimens, once their marketability was determined favourably, became important materials for trade: cocoa, tobacco, and Peruvian bark (quinine), for example, began as curiosities, but became big business.

Telling the history of Atlantic science from this 'centre–periphery'—or 'tributary'—model would go something like the following. Various institutions were founded in these cities to collect, identify, judge, plant, and codify such 'new' material. These included the Casa da India (late fifteenth century) in Lisbon and the Casa de la Contratación de las Indias (1503) and Council of the Indies (1520s) in Seville; botanical gardens, established across Italy in the early sixteenth century and later copied in northern cities like Vienna, Leiden, Paris, Oxford, and Uppsala; publishing centres across Europe but especially in the Netherlands; princely cabinets of curiosities or *Wunderkammern* which were proto-museums; scientific societies, operating under royal imprimatur, notably the Royal Society of London (1660), the Académie des Sciences (1666) in Paris, and the Royal Academy of Sciences (1779) in Lisbon. All these, and more, comprised the various learned places in Europe where news (in the form of incoming letters, answered questionnaires or *relaciones*, and visiting travellers) and specimens were housed, transplanted, tested, secreted, engraved, described, exhibited, and categorized.

Since these institutions were as curious to collect biota from trading outposts in Asia as from outposts and colonies around the Atlantic rim, their development cannot be considered an exclusive Atlantic phenomenon but rather the product of, and further catalyst to, European global expansion. What distinguished the Iberian centres from the Dutch and English models was the monopolistic (and hence secretive) nature of their 'houses of trade'. In the Iberian experiences, all intelligence about the East and West Indies (plants, ports, indigenous behaviour, minerals) which could lead to

---

[1] Oldenburg to Winthrop, 26 March 1670, Royal Society of London MS, in microfilm collection of American Philosophical Society, 'Letters and Communications from Americans', reel 2, item 903; George Basalla, 'The Spread of Western Science', *Science*, 156/1775 (5 May 1967), 611–22; Mary Louise Pratt, *Imperial Eyes: Studies in Travel Writing and Transculturation* (London, 1992).

[2] Bruno Latour, *Science in Action: How to Follow Scientists and Engineers through Society* (Cambridge, MA, 1987), 215.

strategies by which the natural world could be transformed into merchantable commodities—an integral part of colonial venturing—was directed through, and tightly
controlled by, these governmental institutions. Moreover, information was recorded in
manuscript form, perhaps copied and circulated to a few trusted people, and then safely
archived, often never becoming public via a print medium. (Scholars of Iberian science
have pointed to this preponderance of manuscript materials as the reason why the
Spanish and Portuguese foundations of modern empiricism—a methodology often
believed to be instigated by Francis Bacon in 1605—have been overlooked.) The Dutch
East and West Indian Companies as well as the various joint-stock companies
operating British colonial ventures (Somers Island Company, the Virginia Company,
for example) were decentred and corporate rather than monarchical and monopolistic,
though centralizations under Cromwell and after the Restoration would bring the
British colonial ventures under greater central supervision. Because these companies
consistently needed to recruit extensive private capital, they used print, often with a
promotional rather than 'objective' slant, to publish American findings.

Along with the institutions (which physically embodied 'centres of calculation') were
the travellers, missionaries, doctors, military men, merchants, and trained naturalists
who gathered information and specimens and brought or sent them back to Europe.
Among others, Portuguese travellers Francisco Alvares (in Ethiopia, 1520s), Pero de
Magalhaes Gandavo and Gabriel Soares de Sousa (in late sixteenth-century Brazil);
Spanish travellers Gonzalo Fernández de Oviedo y Valdes (in Santo Domingo and
other parts of the Spanish New World, 1514–57), and Francisco Hernandez (in New
Spain, 1571–7); Dutch travellers Georg Markgraf and Willem Pies (or Piso) (in north-
eastern Brazil, c.1640s) and Maria Sibylla Merian (in Suriname, 1699–1701); British
travellers Thomas Harriot (in 'Virginia', 1585–6), Sir Hans Sloane (in the Caribbean,
c.1687), and Mark Catesby (in southern colonies and the Caribbean, c.1712–26);
travelling disciples of Carl Linnaeus, such as the Swedish-Finnish Peter Kalm (in
north-eastern North America, 1748–51), brought back to Europe their experience of
seeing new specimens, as well as the specimens, or sketches and watercolours of them,
which these travellers (and their patrons) could print in illustrated natural histories,
maps, and taxonomies.

Furthermore, a host of European virtuosi (these could be university professors,
doctors, ministers, wealthy merchants, or aristocrats) who never left Europe
incorporated the knowledge and material caches of travellers into their collections
and writings. These include the Sevillean physician Nicholas Monardes and the Leiden
botanist Carolus Clusius. Both through his medical practice and his Atlantic commercial ventures, Monardes had extensive contact with travellers returning from New
Spain through Seville (the only legal city of transatlantic trade embarkation) between
the 1530s and 1560s; these patients and informants told him of, and brought back,
medicinal herbs, and explained how they had learned to use these in America. Included
was the 'Michoacan root' (probably *Ipomaea jalapa*), which Monardes experimented
with in clinical trials, and soon became the main distributor of throughout Europe. His
Historia medicinal provides extensive accounts of *materia medica* retrieved from the

New World that had been explained to him by travellers, and experimented with by himself. Leiden naturalist Carolus Clusius (Charles de l'Écluse), who encountered Monardes' book on a trip to England, translated it into Latin as *De simplicibus medicamentis ex Occidentali India delatis, quorum in medicina usus est* (Antwerp, 1574). Another translation of Clusius incorporated Monardes' New World botanical knowledge with an account of *materia medica* in India compiled by Garcia da Orta, a Portuguese traveller. Besides being a translator who extended the reach of fellow European naturalists, Clusius also participated in the domestication of the (sweet) potato from the New World and tulips from Istanbul, and the establishment of botanical gardens in Vienna and Leiden.[3]

Other Europeans belong in this category of men who translated, compiled, annotated, and systematized in print the work of travellers to non-European places, or of natural histories written in a given vulgate. Among these were Martin Waldseemuller, the German map maker who transposed Amerigo Vespucci's name to the western hemisphere on his 1507 globular map of the world; Samuel Purchas and Richard Hakluyt, the great travel narrators of early modern England; and the publicist Theodore de Bry working in the 1590s in Frankfurt-am-Main. In the eighteenth century, Carl Linné (Carolus Linnaeus) through his network of travelling informants, through botanical gardens in Uppsala and in the Low Countries, and working from prior printed natural histories, established a system of binomial nomenclature that attempted to lay out the proper relations amongst all biota. And in Paris, the keeper of the Jardin du Roi, Georges-Louis Leclerc, comte de Buffon, especially in his thirty-six-volume *Histoire naturelle, generale et particuliere* (1749–78), outlined a theory and compiled a history of the biogeography of the planet. Along with maps, natural histories, and planetary systems composed by individuals, the scientific societies published journals which acted as clearing houses for travellers' information, turning manuscript sketches and descriptions into printed 'knowledge'.

Well-placed curious individuals willing to send back non-European biota enabled one variety of scientific outreach. Another critical source of scientific gathering was the global human network created by Catholic religious orders, particularly the Society of Jesus, beginning in the sixteenth century. Wherever any Catholic empire existed so did the Jesuits, establishing missions, botanical gardens, educational institutions, communication networks, and access to indigenous knowledge. As a network without particular nationalist loyalties, the Jesuits offer a significant counter-model for modernizing science. European curiosity about non-European nature was also satisfied by the scientific expedition, especially from the eighteenth century forward. Between 1735 and 1805 alone, Spain sent fifty-four expeditions to the Americas. In 1737 Philip V,

---

[3] Daniela Bleichmar, 'Books, Bodies, and Fields: Sixteenth-Century Transatlantic Encounters with New World *Materia Medica*', in Londa Schiebinger and Claudia Swan (eds.), *Colonial Botany: Science, Commerce, and Politics in the Early Modern World* (Philadelphia, PA, 2005), 84–91; Harold J. Cook, *Matters of Exchange: Commerce, Medicine, and Science in the Dutch Golden Age* (New Haven, CT, 2007), 84–110.

the new Bourbon monarch of Spain, dispatched a mixed group of Spanish and French geometers, technicians, map makers, and botanists, including Charles-Marie de la Condamine, to the mountains near Quito in the Spanish viceroyalty of Peru to disprove Isaac Newton's hypothesis that the earth was flatter at its two poles. Sadly for them, their measurements proved Newton to be correct. The Malaspina expedition (1789–94), devised to assess the Spanish empire in America, generated 4,000 documents. A botanical expedition to New Granada led by Jose Celestino Mutis, and employing physicians, plant collectors, artists, and enslaved labourers, created a herbarium of 20,000 specimens and numerous illustrations.[4]

Reflecting the cosmopolitan rhetoric of the Enlightenment, these sponsored expeditions were often represented as solely for the pursuit of knowledge: to collect unknown plants, or to establish the shape or varying biogeography of the globe. However, the identification of natural resources for trade, and the more general pursuit of inter-imperial political and economic rivalries, were enmeshed with the stated scientific goals, thus underlining the fact that science, from the perspective of the various European powers and their emissaries, remained a strategic component of competitive empire building. Sometimes, the strategy could be material and practical—discovering the best routes to secure materials for trade—while occasionally it could be more symbolic—creating a royal collection to showcase the natural splendour of imperial possessions or securing the intellectual prestige associated with a major discovery.

This dramatically abridged history of Atlantic science in the early modern world has been presented solely from the perspective of the European 'centres of calculation'. It is a sparse chronology of how Europeans 'internalized' the natural world they encountered through extra-European travel. In providing examples it has proven difficult to separate European scientific activity based on New World and African travels from that based on exchanges with Asia, because map makers, compilers of *materia medica*, and planetary theorists, along with traders from several European nations, were deeply involved in both spheres. (It would be interesting, albeit beyond the scope of this chapter, seriously to contemplate how the various sciences would have developed had there, in fact, *been no* western hemisphere. Then, presumably, the novel biota of the vast non-European parts of the globe would have fed the development of the natural sciences with copious enough matter for it to have 'matured'. But, one wonders, without the New World settler colonies and cultivars, which J. R. McNeill in his chapter in this volume shows to have replenished European energy systems that were reaching their limit, would there have been the prosperity in Europe to support such dramatic 'advancements in learning'?). Suffice it to say that when the history of science is written from a metropolitan perspective, as was done until the 1980s, the category 'Atlantic Science' is a problematic one.

---

[4] Neil Safier, *Measuring the New World: Enlightenment Science and South America* (Chicago, IL, 2008); David Goodman, 'Science, Medicine, and Technology in Colonial Spanish America: New Interpretations, New Approaches', in Daniela Bleichmar, Paula De Vos, Kristin Huffine, and Kevin Sheehan (eds.), *Science in the Spanish and Portuguese Empires, 1500–1800* (Palo Alto, CA, 2009), 18–22.

Examples of Atlantic science thus far have been drawn mainly from the field of botany, and to a lesser extent from geography, metallurgy, and zoology. Further examples could come from entomology, ichthyology, geology, and ethnology; all still chosen from the various fields comprising 'natural history'. If using the Basalla diffusion model, moreover, one could make the point that around the time the British colonies in North America were contemplating political independence, they had achieved a parallel scientific independence by producing, as Jefferson would patriotically pronounce in his *Notes on the State of Virginia* (1787), 'in physics ... a Franklin, then whom no one of the present age has made more important discoveries, nor has enriched philosophy with more, or more ingenious solutions of the phenomena of nature'. What Jefferson's pronouncement underlines is a hierarchy in the traditional estimation of the sciences, which has persisted in historiography, with laboratory and theoretical sciences, including mathematics, on the top, and the collection-based 'field' sciences on the bottom. Within this traditional historiography, a nation, or a people, can claim full epistemological maturation only when it produces predictive theories, or, as Jefferson put it, 'solutions', concerning universal laws of nature. Because of this, early modern science undertaken outside of Europe (especially before 1750) has traditionally been viewed condescendingly as the 'leg work' required to provide raw material for the true 'mental work' conducted in European cities.[5]

This model of Atlantic science—seen from a metropolitan perspective—is deficient because some people, indeed whole continents of people, drop out of the story as producers, or even possessors, of knowledge. When the book, the museum, the 'solution', and the printed map become the defining evidence of knowledge, Africans in the early modern Atlantic disappear from the story until the end of the eighteenth century, while Amerindians *may* appear only in Jesuit-redacted codexes. Occasional educated mestizos and creoles receive mention, but for some authors only Montezuma's gardens and the meticulously organized marketplace at Tenochtitlan would qualify as the (albeit doomed) 'centre of calculation' of the Aztec empire. Thus, a metropolitan rendition inevitably re-enacts the imbalances of power in the early modern Atlantic world, while the 'centre–periphery' model of Basalla, and others, is methodologically insufficient for narrating much of the knowledge of the natural world that existed around the Atlantic rim.

Basalla's model was first challenged in the 1980s by scholars working on the history of science in colonial or post-colonial Asia, Australia, and Africa, particularly concerning regimes of nineteenth- and twentieth-century science, technology, and empire, frequently while explaining how collusive science and empire have been. More recently, the early modern period has come into focus, with its emergent global

[5] Thomas Jefferson, *Notes on the State of Virginia* (2nd edn. Philadelphia, PA, 1794), 94; Roy MacLeod, 'Introduction' to special issue of *Osiris*, 2nd Series, 15, *Nature and Empire: Science and the Colonial Enterprise* (2000), 1–13; Michael A. Osborne, 'Introduction: The Social History of Science, Technoscience and Imperialism', *Science Technology Society*, 4/2 (1999), 161–70; Londa Schiebinger, 'Forum Introduction: The European Colonial Science Complex', *Isis*, 96/1 (2005), 52–5.

circuitries of exchange. In the last decade or so, scholars of Anglo-, Franco-, and Ibero-America have drawn attention to spheres of knowledge creation and knowledge contestation in the New World amongst Amerindian, African, and European creole populations. Also, since the onset of decolonization, Africanist scholars have been debunking Eurocentric suggestions of African inferiority, or belatedness in the fields of medicine, technology, and agriculture, but again with a focus on the nineteenth and early twentieth centuries in Africa. Independently of these trends, historians of European science have shifted from a teleological story of advancement to sociological histories of knowledge production. Despite these discrete scholarly developments in each continent, a truly circum-Atlantic history of knowledge exchange in the early modern centuries has yet to be written, and this chapter outlines a framework for such a history.

Undertaking a circum-Atlantic history requires that we question some traditional terms, starting with 'science' and 'nature', which signify concepts that would have been alien to many subjects of such a history. In English usage alone, it was not until the mid-nineteenth century that the term 'science' assumed its modern, restricted meaning as when, in 1867, William G. Ward employed the word 'expressing physical and experimental science, to the exclusion of theological and metaphysical'. By contrast, in the early modern era, 'science' (or *scientia*) referred variously to God's own knowledge, knowledge of the divine or supernatural, learning in general, or learning divided into the branches of the liberal arts, or to applied crafts and skills. Shifts in the meanings of the word 'nature' (or *Natura*) in Europe and Euro-America between 1500 and 1800 are also many and complex. Generally, notions of a protean, unfixed realm in which God could intervene to make dramatic changes and which adept humans could manipulate began to give way, about 1700 in learned circles, to a belief in 'Nature' as a self-consistent and orderly realm (some would say machine-like, others would say female and provident) which God had made available for the use of humans but did not erratically interrupt. On the other hand, at the moment when indigenous peoples of North America came into contact with Europeans and Africans, they did not, as one recent historian has put it, 'live in a *natural* world, but in a *social* world' inhabited by humans and 'other-than-human kinds of people' (plants, rocks, weather, skies, water, animals). When account is taken of such contrasting concepts, it seems appropriate to describe our zone of enquiry as the study of *exchanges and changes in knowing about and making things with the natural world*, thus abandoning both the terms 'science', which now has positivist, applied, and specialist associations, and 'nature', which still rings of the sentimental, maternal, and consumable.[6]

Before examining particular exchanges, we must think broadly about the shared understandings of Africans, Amerindians, and Europeans of the sixteenth and

---

[6] William G. Ward, in *Dublin Review*, 12 (April 1867), 255 n.; Lorraine Daston and Katharine Park, *Wonders and the Order of Nature, 1150–1750* (New York, 2001). George R. Hamell, 'The Iroquois and the World's Rim: Speculations on Color, Culture, and Contact', *American Indian Quarterly*, 16/4 (1992), 452–3.

seventeenth centuries concerning cosmology, epistemology, and technology. To mark off cognitive milestones in this way, one needs to conceptualize more like an anthropologist than a traditional historian of science. Thinking about commonalities does not mean that European technological advantages in ocean navigation and vessel construction, in firearms, and in the printing press are not a significant part of the story of Atlantic interaction, particularly in explaining why (coupled with infectious diseases and favourable oceanic currents) Europe came to dominate this interaction. It does however assist our understanding of on-the-ground, specific exchanges.

Though there were major differences in their understandings of the cosmos, most peoples around the Atlantic believed in an invisible or supernatural world, either one 'God' or a panoply of spiritual forces who controlled the visible, tangible world. In each society, special humans were set apart and trained to act as intercessors between the mundane and hidden realms. These humans often possessed special skills and knowledge having to do with earthly materials like plants and metals; they guarded the knowledge by which these materials could harm or help the human community; and they saw their relationship with the spiritual forces as a part of this knowledge and its efficacy. Practitioners of harming medicines, or sorcerers, were present amongst each of these groups. Humans around the Atlantic understood that the health of their bodies was related to their local environments; they all saw their bodies as porous and locally vulnerable; and they believed that a knowledge of surrounding conditions (plants, climate, water, air, and spirits) was essential to maintaining well-being. Technology for the great majority of people was artisanal; only the sugar *ingenios* (or *engenhos*) and some ironworks became quasi-industrial in scale, and even those were maintained through artisanal know-how.

So far, historians of botany (and by extension of early modern medicine and agriculture), geography, ecology, astronomy, electricity, and zoology have described, for the Americas, how knowledge was increased through complex interactions between Amerindians, travelling Europeans, creoles, mestizos, and Africans. Historians of European science have found their own 'contact zones', if you will, within Europe; the contact being less proto-racial and more regional, and class-based. Historians of Africa have studied exchanges of technological and medical knowledge, and have shown that West Africans in particular brought knowledge of rice cultivation, smallpox inoculation, riverine navigation, and an ingrained cultural practice of herbal-medicinal study to the Americas, all of which was noted, relied upon, and exploited by plantation owners, colonial authorities, and naturalists. While some of this knowledge was directly co-opted into furthering European colonial goals, herbal knowledge in particular was both heeded and feared by whites. Whites frequently used the practical knowledge of African informants, while seeking to extricate it from a 'superstitious' religious frame, without acknowledging that white Christians themselves placed their own botanical knowledge within a larger spiritual world-view. Scholars have also described how, with varying degrees of volition and openness, Amerindians communicated their own knowledge about geography, animal locations, botanical cultivars (maize, tobacco, the potato) and cures (ipecacuanha, Jesuit's Bark). Because naturalists in both colonies and metropoles wanted access to this knowledge, they were often willing to give Indian and African informants an epistemological authority—basically, that is, to treat them as credible experts—where they otherwise gave them little or no political authority.

What many of these recent studies convey in common is a complication of the idea of a straightforward, or uni-directional, 'diffusion' of 'science'. They also challenge the notion that information and scientific goods moved in some untroubled way from peripheries to centre. Many examples also illustrate what Daniela Bleichmar calls 'the fragility of information in motion'. In particular, when examining the circuits of travel and knowledge that lay behind Nicholas Monardes' *Historia medicinal*, Bleichmar contrasts Monardes' view from Seville with the experience in Lima of his informant, the Spanish soldier Pedro de Osma. While Monardes presumed that information from helpful Indians came easily and clearly, Osma considered himself threatened by the spiritual matrix out of which this information flowed, and by the actual hostility of his native informants. As Osma said:

I write your mercy about these things so that you may consider how many more herbs and plants possessing great virtues, similar to these, our Indies must have. But they are out of our reach and knowledge because the Indians, being bad people and our enemies, will not reveal to us a secret, not a single virtue of an herb, even if they should see us die, or even if they be sawed in pieces. If we know anything of the matters I have treated, and of others, we learned it from the female Indians. Because they get involved with Spaniards, and reveal to them all that they know.

Clearly, information about plants was of life and death importance to both Spaniards and Indians in this New World 'biocontact zone'. Coercion, whether sexual or military, and resistance to the point of death was the social truth around herbs which Osma and Peruvian Indians experienced and which Monardes did not appreciate.[7]

Historians of imperial/colonial science today are interested in the ways that knowledge both travelled and did not travel, in short, how it moved within scenarios of cultural unintelligibility, suspicion, and violent conflict. Moreover, very few people around the Atlantic rim could afford to be interested in knowledge-for-knowledge's-sake or lived in cultures where such a concept existed; in Leiden as much as in Suriname, knowledge of the natural world operated as a social, or political, lever.

Evidence of 'Atlantic science' is often drawn from European colonies in the Americas. Because the western hemisphere provided the meeting ground for Indians, Europeans, and Africans, it has tended to become the part-for-the-whole *locale* of Atlantic science ever since scholars have tried to draw attention away from European 'centres of calculation'. In thinking of what line of enquiry, or what topic, might necessitate a more polycentric and truly circum-Atlantic approach, it seems that a study of metals—or, more properly, the technologies and spiritualities associated with their transformation—would provide an opportune case study. What makes the case of metallurgy (mining, smelting, metalworking, metallurgical medicine, and alchemy)

---

[7] Bleichmar, 'Books, Bodies, and Fields', 87, 95.

distinctive is that peoples in Africa, Europe, and the Americas each had long and separate histories of developing metallurgical technologies before an 'Atlantic world' was born. Though metallurgical knowledge is portable, it is also associated with large instruments and sites which did not travel. Thus, while a blacksmith might travel he could not bring with him the location that defined his practice. The Atlantic story of metallurgy then seems comprehensible only through multiple, evolving locations of action, disruption, and change. Even to measure which parts of these fields of action were altered by Atlantic reorientations, and which were not, offers a new kind of opportunity for measuring how pervasive Atlantic world effects actually were. Moreover, a great deal of archaeological and historical work has been done on this topic, separately for each continent, thus making feasible the arduous comparative work of a truly polycentric Atlantic approach.

One would begin by describing the isolated and ancient African, European, and western hemisphere metallurgical practices and then trace how each indigenous metallurgical practice did or did not change as the Atlantic world became a zone pulled together through commerce, the slave trade, and empires. A few examples of the Atlantic phase of this story must suffice. In eastern North America, indigenous peoples found their material and technological world drastically changed by the introduction of iron. A first phase of this contact saw Native Americans adapting European metal products (kettles, for example) so they might continue to make their own traditional artefacts; the precision and strength of the new iron tools (knives, chisels, and awls) allowed their traditional crafts to grow and flourish, and become more intricate and elaborate (especially in the area of sacred wampum beads). Eventually, however, with large settler colonies established and the ensuing increased volumes of trade, Indians began to absorb European goods wholesale, without adapting them to traditional forms. In this way, indigenous crafts gradually disappeared and a dependence on European manufactures transpired.

The story of how, after contact, West Africans incorporated metal goods of European derivation was originally narrated by world system theorists as a story of African 'dependency'. More recent research shows the selective absorption by Africans of European firearms and a rejection of other metal products, and indicates that African steel-making was 'productive relative to its pre-industrial European counterpart'. Apparently local smelting continued to be very active despite European imports, and hence the blacksmith retained an important ritual and technological function in communities throughout West Africa.[8]

How the influx of gold and silver bullion into the Iberian Peninsula after the conquest changed the balance of power in Europe is well known. More recently,

---

[8] Daniel K. Richter, *Facing East from Indian Country: A Native History of Early America* (Cambridge, MA, 2001), 43–51; John Thornton, 'Precolonial African Industry and the Atlantic Trade, 1500–1800', *African Economic History*, 19 (1990–1), 1–19, quote 9; L. M. Pole, 'Decline or Survival? Iron Production in West Africa from the Seventeenth to the Twentieth Centuries', *Journal of African History*, 23/4 (1982), 503–13.

historians have been revealing the contributions made by Amerindians, in the first decades of Spanish conquest, to the technical knowledge of prospecting, assaying, and refining metals. The English competitive hunt for New World metals proved fruitless, despite many trials on samples of rock and earth brought back from America, and much talk of gold by such as Sir Walter Raleigh. The English reacted to this failure by demonizing the underground mining activities of the Spanish as part of the 'Black Legend', and began to tout their own, putatively more humane practice of planting and harvesting (what Thomas Hariot would call) 'vegetable gold'. Despite English failure to discover gold and silver in eastern North America, ironworks were established throughout the Chesapeake region by the late colonial period, which employed as many as 4,500 slaves, who functioned not only as low-skilled woodcutters but also in specialized roles as 'forgemen', 'hammermen', and 'finers'. A wrought-iron figure dating to the late eighteenth century in Virginia and found buried in the earthen floor of a blacksmith's shop, with stylistic similarities to Bamana artefacts, points to the persistence of some blacksmithing traditions from across the Atlantic. Presumably though, considering the exalted spiritual-technological positions of blacksmiths in West African society, they may have been traded into slavery less frequently. Perhaps skills newly acquired in the New World allowed Africans to fashion remembered forms.[9]

This inchoate sketch of mining and metalworking in the early modern Atlantic world indicates possible ways for historians of science to narrate a circum-Atlantic—rather than a metropolitan, or colonial American, or African—story. All such narrations require the historian to pull together materials from existing, including regional, studies in the fields of ethnohistory, history of art, history of technology, anthropology, and (what Africanists call) 'archaeometallurgy', and to consider the ways in which knowledge, artisanal skill, rituals surrounding technology, and the cultural place of the technologist existed before and after an 'Atlantic world' came into existence.

Thus far attention has been confined to the various kinds of knowledge of the non-human world that were practised and exchanged around the Atlantic. Intertwined with these circuits there developed what eventually grew, in Europe and Euro-America, into 'racial science', by which is meant ways of knowing human groupings and their differences. Because evaluation of what another human knew—and how one might use that knowledge—was wrapped up in each group's political treatment and construction of the other, understanding the narratives and emerging scientific categories that made these constructions 'natural' is a key part of the study of Atlantic science. While one might expect that there would be an exact correlation between the value one group placed on the worth of another and the value given to the scientific testimony or know-how of a member of that other group, one finds, in fact, an inconsistent correlation between the two.

    [9] Goodman, 'Science, Medicine, and Technology in Colonial Spanish America', 23; Philip D. Morgan, *Slave Counterpoint: Black Culture in the Eighteenth-Century Chesapeake and Lowcountry* (Chapel Hill, NC, 1998), 230–1; Sharon F. Patton, *African-American Art: The Evolution of a Black Aesthetic Timeline* (Oxford, 1998), 38.

At the time of Columbus' contact with the western hemisphere, peoples around the Atlantic held some ideas in common concerning embodiment. Bodies, as was mentioned, were considered products of their local environments—susceptible to the helps and harms of local natural and supernatural forces. These forces, moreover, could be manipulated by specially trained human adepts. Knowledge of a local environment, then, was understood to be critical to maintaining human physiological balance and health. This issue of the health or illness of bodies was a major way in which different peoples encountered each other across previous Atlantic divides. How contact with Europeans changed the bodily health of western hemisphere peoples for the worse— and made the curative knowledge of their healers suspect—was a major fact of changing embodiment. Europeans sometimes took this higher mortality of bodies that were indigenous to America to be a sign of their own physical superiority. Curiously, though, greater African imperviousness to diseases in America did not suggest to Europeans that Africans were physically superior to themselves; they argued rather that it made Africans fitter for hard physical labour.[10]

Because bodies were seen as products of local environments, migration out of one's native zone was cause for physiological concern, and presented the need to learn from those who were native to one's new environment. Europeans, inheritors of classical humoral theory, believed that certain types of bodily complexes (or complexions) existed in varying climatical bands that girdled the planet. Classical theory held the Mediterranean region to create an optimal physical balance; northern Europeans and sub-Saharan Africans would have both been equally, but differently, imbalanced according to this body-mapping. As the English, in particular, contemplated trading in, and then migrating in large numbers to, more southerly latitudes, they had to adjust, and then ultimately reject these climatic theories of bodily difference. Even before much empirical information filtered back to Britain about climates of the Indies (and how they did not correspond with theoretical projections), English promoters of westward and eastward colonization reached for explanations of difference that would transcend geography. In 1578, George Best, in his *True Discourse of the Late Voyages of Discoverie*, ventured the concept of an inherited biblical curse to explain Ethiopian embodiment: because Noah's son Cham had transgressed a paternal edict, 'all his posteritie [was] accursed'. 'Thus you see', he reasoned, 'the cause of the Ethiopians blacknesse is the curse and natural infection of bloud, and not the distemperature of the clymate. We may therefore very well be assured, that under the Equinoxiall [equator] is the most pleasant and delectable place of the world to dwell in.' Best's latching onto a theory of skin coloration as an inherited curse represented, in 1578, only one avenue of thinking about human difference, and not yet the dominant one it would later become. Global or Atlantic maps produced by Europeans well into the seventeenth century do not focus on skin colour as a key marker; instead, morphological differences (tails, heads in chests, giant stature, etc.), the practice of cannibalism,

---

[10] Chaplin, *Subject Matter*.

dress and self-ornamentation, technology (and especially, possession of weaponry), and spirituality comprised the many ways Europeans marked off non-Europeans from themselves.[11]

It was in the Americas, with the experience of the immigration of Europeans and Africans to new environments, and the displacement of Amerindians from old environments and locally embedded physiological practices, that people most struggled to understand, and cope with, new embodiments. Africans used old practices of orientation—learning about local plants and minerals and spiritual forces—both from empirical observation and from Indian informants. Ethnic African differences were both encountered and modulated in American settings. European creoles spent a great deal of energy diagnosing how their European bodies were changing amidst different airs and soils, under new stars (in South America), and on land which had produced Indian bodies heretofore. In some European natural histories of American locales, descriptions of creole mores tended towards constituting Euro-Americans as a separate, changed—even degraded—people. Indians faced the physical crisis of infectious diseases and the epistemological-spiritual crisis of seeing older healing practices fail. In Ibero-America and Caribbean Franco-America, sexual relations and intermarriage across human groupings produced new kinds and categories of people. As time went on, elaborate taxonomies of difference, complete with linguistic terminology and scales of status, based on an individual's relative proportion of Spanish, African, or Indian parentage, were established. Though the English had practised intermarriage as a source of building trade networks in the East, where their power was weak, initial moves in that direction in Virginia were abandoned as the (Eastern) trade model of contact there gave way to one of settler plantations, a form of colonization which necessarily created greater animus between English and native peoples and which destroyed the more subtle forms of Eastern-learned diplomacy. This by no means halted the practice of sexual contact between English and non-English in America, though legislation discouraging 'miscegenation' began to appear later in the seventeenth century.[12]

Differences, in short, between the various peoples of the Atlantic would have been read in complex ways in the early stages of contact, based on both appearance (skin, dress, bodily markings, bearing, portable weaponry) and behaviour (religious practices, language, sexual mores, wealth and property concepts, forms of knowledge). As long as Europeans in Africa and the Americas needed the diplomatic or trading partnerships with non-Europeans, evaluations of human difference remained somewhat open and malleable. Moreover, both European and African newcomers to the western hemisphere could not be sure that their own bodies were not going to change dramatically amidst new biological and spiritual conditions. However, as European domination of the Atlantic increased gradually over the course of the sixteenth and seventeenth

---

[11] George Best, *A True Discourse of the Late Voyages of Discoverie* (London, 1578), 30–2.

[12] Alison Games, *The Web of Empire: English Cosmopolitans in an Age of Expansion, 1560–1660* (Oxford, 2008), 131–4.

centuries—especially as large-scale plantation, mining, and settlement models became dominant in the Americas—and as new climates did not dramatically alter embodiment, markers of difference came, for Europeans, to function as justifications of perpetual enslavement (of Africans and Indians) or of exterminating war (against Indians). Because behavioural differences could be modulated—'heathens' could be Christianized, 'savages' could be 'civilized', technology could be transferred, languages could be learned—bodily variation gradually achieved an all-important status as the key signifier guaranteeing an essential difference and, from European and Euro-American perspectives, superiority. Thus, corporeal difference needed to be safe-guarded (by laws against miscegenation, or schemata mapping castes based on blood lines and skin colour), and, as science came to hold a privileged place in the European imagination in the late seventeenth century as the guarantor of truth, 'race' needed to be scientifically 'proven'. In Spanish America in the mid-seventeenth century, creole intellectuals Salinas y Cordova and Leon Pinelo independently (and defensively) took up the same line of reasoning which George Best had used to encourage colonization to Englishmen in the 1570s—a notion of inherited, biblically originated, and environmentally impervious human difference.[13]

By the end of the eighteenth century, European encroachment into the South Pacific allowed for a new, global schema of human geography. This stage of racial science focused on physiognomy, but, still more essentially, on skeletal 'proof' of morphological difference in human bodies and brains. Along with Petrus Camper, Georges Cuvier, and John Hunter, a representative figure was Johann Friedrich Blumenbach, author of *On the Natural Variety of Mankind* (3rd edn. 1795), in which he laid out his 'collection of the skulls of different nations'. In the mid-eighteenth century, before the turn to the skeletal domain, Linnaeus' many editions of *Systemae natura* (1735 forward) represented an influential taxonomic plotting of humanity. Linnaeus ranked humans within the broader field of animal life, with gradations between humans and animals (*Homo sapiens ferus*, *Homo troglodytes*), and divided the human animal into four varieties (*europaeus albus*, *americanus rubescens*, *asiaticus fuscus*, and *africanus niger*), suggesting categorical differences (with geography *and* colour as key markers) and even potentially polygenetic origins. By contrast, Buffon, in his *Histoire naturelle* (1749–67), argued that there was only one species of human, though widely diversified by geography across the planet. What especially interested Buffon was how particular bio-geographic zones had worked, over time, to the degeneration of one original human form, and his theory of historical and geographical racialization, particularly in his earlier writings, singled out the western hemisphere as a particular zone of biological, and hence necessarily cultural, degradation.[14]

[13] Jorge Canizares-Esguerra, 'New World, New Stars: Patriotic Astrology and the Invention of Indian and Creole Bodies in Colonial Spanish America, 1600–1650', *American Historical Review*, 104/1 (1999), 34.

[14] Johann Friedrich Blumenbach, *On the Natural Variety of Mankind* (3rd edn. 1795), prefatory letter, quoted in Christopher Fox, 'Introduction', in Fox, Roy Porter, and Robert Wokler (eds.), *Inventing Human Science: Eighteenth-Century Domains* (Berkeley, CA, 1995), 11; Phillip Sloan, 'The Gaze of Natural History', ibid. 122–3, 135–8.

Thomas Jefferson, writing amidst the turmoil of national formation, would, in his *Notes on the State of Virginia* (1787), defend this castigation of hemispheric inferiority by aligning the nativized white body with Indians and showing the indigenous human's physical and cultural integrity. By contrast, and as a deflective move, he singled out 'blacks' in their midst as the inferior race, stating that 'blacks, whether originally a distinct race, or made distinct by time and circumstances, are inferior to the whites in the endowments both of body and mind'. Jefferson wanted to have it both ways: for whites and Indians, embodiment was geographic (and, he reasoned through other biological evidence, positive); for the black people in America, however, embodiment was innately inferior and impervious to geography.[15] Like Spanish-American creoles of the seventeenth century, Jefferson, as a creole needing to defend Euro-Americans against castigations of environmentally induced inferiority, articulated a theory—concerning Africans in America—of inherited difference and inferiority.

Writers of the black Atlantic attempted to dislodge the category of 'whiteness' from its 'natural' perch of superiority. Olaudah Equiano, for example, deployed an African child's perspective at the beginning of his *Interesting Narrative* (1789) to register the violent strangeness of white bodies bearing down on coastal Africa, describing these whites as 'bad spirits' and wondering 'if we were not to be eaten by those white men with horrible looks, red faces, and long hair?' He then showed how he himself was acculturated gradually (and simultaneously) to Christianity, literacy, and a belief in the shameful ugliness of blackness, and he explained how, while living with an English family at about 12 years of age, he 'tried oftentimes myself if I could not by washing make my face of the same colour as my little play-mate (Mary), but it was all in vain; and I now began to be mortified at the difference in our complexions'.[16]

In British North America and then the United States, people of Indian and African descent responded to the racialization of difference, which had grown steadily over the course of the eighteenth century, either by racializing their own resistance, or by insisting, using the logic learned through Christianization, that the key locus of identity was spiritual and not corporeal. After the resolution of the Seven Years War in 1763, and after the inter-imperial rivalry in North America (between the French, Spanish, and English) resolved itself into a westward pushing of British hegemony, Indian resistance took on a racially conscious character. Prophetic messages inspiring a trans-Appalachian revolt led by Pontiac 'called all Indians to a cleansing war against "the Whites" '. In the violence that followed, 'enslaved African Americans were often spared'. Those who sought rhetorical and intellectual, rather than physical, resistance, like the Mohegan preacher Samson Occom and the enslaved African poet Phillis Wheatley who engaged in published correspondence with each other, condemned the 'strange absurdity of their [white Christians'] Conduct whose Words and Actions

---

[15] Jefferson, *Notes on the State of Virginia*, 209.

[16] Olaudah Equiano, *The Interesting Narrative of the Life of Olaudah Equiano, or Gustavus Vassa, the African* (London, 1794), in Vincent Carretta (ed.), *Unchained Voices: An Anthology of Black Authors in the English-Speaking World of the Eighteenth Century* (Lexington, KY, 1996), 203, 211.

are so diametrically opposite'. And finally, imagining nature's own display of deep-hued beauty, Wheatley wrote in 'An Hymn to Evening':

> Through all the heav'ns what beauteous dies are spread!
> But the West glories in the deepest red:
> So may our breasts with ev'ry virtue glow,
> The living temples of our God below!

If science had made 'white' and European superior, Nature, claimed Wheatley, if apprehended with true Christian perception, showed God's handiwork in every hue.[17]

If one were to write a comprehensive circum-Atlantic history of the creation and experience of 'race', one would need to consider the West Indies and those parts of South America with majority black populations, and ask how independence movements across the Americas changed racial concepts. One would also need to consider the construction of 'whiteness' in Europe, and whether, or how, that category transcended national lines. And finally, one would need to study Africa to understand how Atlantic trade networks, in the period before nineteenth-century colonization, began to alter Africans' own sense of embodiment.

In conclusion, it is clear that the 'diffusion' and 'centre–periphery' models with which we began do not reflect the complex on-the-ground realities by which ideas about the human and other-than-human worlds were created and exchanged. While some technologies, forms of knowledge, and biota were imposed from the eastern to western hemispheres, many travelled in the other direction; and many were created anew out of an Atlantic world being drawn together. Peoples around the Atlantic in the era of early contact had enough in common with each other that epistemic and technological trade could flow in many directions. Strange knowledge could also be resisted or one's own group knowledge could be jealously guarded—whether you were an African metallurgist or a Spanish naturalist in the Caribbean. And finally, the 'science' of 'race' was not the invention of Enlightenment systematizers, but slowly accreted—in fairly contingent and unsystematic ways—in the context of colonization and in the space of the colonies.

BIBLIOGRAPHY

Bleichmar, Daniela, Paula De Vos, Kristin Huffine, and Kevin Sheehan (eds.), *Science in the Spanish and Portuguese Empires, 1500–1800* (Palo Alto, CA, 2009).
Canizares-Esguerra, Jorge, *Nature, Empire, and Nation: Explorations of the History of Science in the Iberian World* (Palo Alto, CA, 2006).

---

[17] Richter, *Facing East*, 200; Phillis Wheatley to Samson Occom, 11 February 1774, printed in the *Connecticut Gazette* (11 March 1774) and cited in Carretta (ed.), *Unchained Voices*, 69; Carretta, *Unchained Voices*, 63.

Carney, Judith, *Black Rice: The African Origins of Rice Cultivation in the Americas* (Cambridge, MA, 2002).

Chaplin, Joyce, *Subject Matter: Technology, the Body, and Science on the Anglo-American Frontier, 1500–1676* (Cambridge, MA, 2001).

Cook, Harold J., *Matters of Exchange: Commerce, Medicine, and Science in the Dutch Golden Age* (New Haven, CT, 2007).

Delbourgo, James, *A Most Amazing Scene of Wonders: Electricity and Enlightenment in Early America* (Cambridge, MA, 2006).

—— and Nicholas Dew (eds.), *Science and Empire in the Atlantic World* (London, 2008).

Fox, Christopher, Roy Porter, and Robert Wokler (eds.), *Inventing Human Science: Eighteenth-Century Domains* (Berkeley, CA, 1995).

Isis, 96/1, Focus: Colonial Science (2005).

Osiris, 2nd Series, 15, Nature and Empire: Science and the Colonial Enterprise (2000).

Parrish, Susan Scott, *American Curiosity: Cultures of Natural History in the Colonial British Atlantic World* (Chapel Hill, NC, 2006).

Safier, Neil, *Measuring the New World: Enlightenment Science and South America* (Chicago, IL, 2008).

Schiebinger, Londa, *Plants and Empire: Colonial Bioprospecting in the Atlantic World* (Cambridge, MA, 2004).

—— and Claudia Swan (eds.), *Colonial Botany: Science, Commerce, and Politics in the Early Modern World* (Philadelphia, PA, 2005).

Wheeler, Roxann, *The Complexion of Race: Categories of Difference in Eighteenth-Century British Culture* (Philadelphia, PA, 2000).

CHAPTER 28

IDENTITIES AND PROCESSES OF IDENTIFICATION IN THE ATLANTIC WORLD

TAMAR HERZOG

WE tend to think about the inhabitants of the Atlantic world as members of discrete groups. We thus argue that 'Spaniards' had encountered 'Indians', 'Europeans' competed with one another, and 'Africans' were imported as slaves. Although these categories may be meaningful to us, like all identities and processes of identification, they were dynamic constructions in constant flux. Having gradually emerged during the early modern period and to a great extent because of the engagement with the Atlantic world, their creation involved both confrontation and dialogue and it allowed for competing interpretations.[1] Not only were these identities and processes of identification highly complex, other group solidarities that were just as important—such as the division between people of different religions, nobles and commoners, local citizens and foreigners—mediated between them, on occasions breaking them apart.

'EUROPEANS'

Europeans is a key word we use to designate all those who originated in that continent. We now know that some European identities may have been forged during the Middle

---

[1] S. N. Eisenstadt, 'The Construction of Collective Identities and the Continual Reconstruction of Primordiality and Sacrality: Some Analytical and Comparative Indications', in id., *Comparative Civilization and Multiple Modernities* (Leiden, 2003), 75–134, and Rogers Brubaker and Frederick Cooper, 'Beyond "Identity" ', *Theory and Society*, 29/1 (2000), 1–47, on 14–15.

Ages, but that the main impetus to distinguish Europeans from non-Europeans occurred during the phase of European expansion, and was intensified after Christendom had become divided through the processes of conflicting religious reformations. As a result of these developments, Europeans, who had previously thought of themselves as 'Christians' and who perceived their community as potentially universal, began to identify theirs as a particular civilization, linked to a classical past, that they came to classify as superior to all others. This process culminated in the eighteenth and nineteenth centuries when authors like Montesquieu argued that Europe was a nation made of many nations and when others sustained that all Europeans shared not only a common culture but also a common ethnicity, perhaps even race.[2]

During this period, a more restricted view of Europeans that divided them into Spaniards, Englishmen, French, Dutch (and so forth) also made its appearance. Coinciding with the birth of modern states and with the consolidation of more centralized political structures, in some European countries membership in these emerging communities designated subjection to a monarch (as was the case in England and France); in others it signalled citizenship and eligibility for rights (as in Spain and the Netherlands). Historians disagree whether these developments brought about the coming of nations or proto-nations. Some gesture in this direction, pointing out that although united by what was until the mid-sixteenth century a common religion, people living in Europe cared about linguistic, cultural, political, and legal differences. Competition in both Europe and overseas strengthened these feelings and guaranteed the persistence of distinctions as well as rivalries among Europeans. Other historians stress, on the contrary, the degree by which during the early modern period European entities were still flexible and permeable. Weak state structures and the constant incorporation and loss of territories were matched by the frequent move of populations. Whether as merchants, missionaries, soldiers or day labourers, many Europeans moved away from their region of birth, sometimes within the confines of the same political jurisdiction ('England,' 'France,' 'Spain', and so forth), but often outside it. Similar processes happened to Europeans abroad. 'Discoverers', 'explorers', and 'conquerors' were often hired guns. Although they may have worked for a monarch, they rarely worked for a nation. Those immigrating to the New World were also a varied crowd. In 1640, when Portugal separated from the Spanish Monarchy, authorities in both Madrid and Lisbon were unsure whether the inhabitants of Brazil would follow its example. By that time, Brazil was populated by many individuals who were either Spanish or had tighter connections to Spain and Spanish America than to Portugal.[3]

---

[2] Montesquieu, 'Reflexions sur la monarchie universelle', in *Œuvres complètes* (Paris, 1989–90), ii. 34 and Colin Kidd, 'Ethnicity in the British Atlantic World, 1688–1380', in Kathleen Wilson (ed.), *A New Imperial History: Culture, Identity, and Modernity in Britain and the Empire* (Cambridge, 2004), 261–77, on 275–6.

[3] Charles R. Boxer, *Salvador de Sá and the Struggle for Brazil and Angola, 1602–1686* (London, 1952), 144–52; Rafael Valladares Ramírez, 'El Brasil y las Indias españolas durante la sublevación de Portugal (1640–1668)', *Cuadernos de historia moderna*, 14 (1993), 151–72, on 155–61 and 171; and Rodrigo Bentes Monteiro, *O rei no expelho: a monarquia portuguesa e a colonização da América, 1640–1720* (São Paulo, 2002), 33–72.

The so-called English colonies included many individuals who were not English. Gradually co-opted de facto or de jure to the status of Englishmen (in order to enjoy the rights and privileges associated with it), these individuals nevertheless spoke an endless number of languages, practised different religions, and followed various social customs. How they turned into English, perhaps Britons, is a story still fairly unknown.[4] Pursuing such a story would require that historians accept that, rather than English, these colonies were European and that they adopt a vision that would transcend the nationalist narratives that made empires into 'English', 'Spanish', 'Portuguese', or 'French'.

Another issue confronting historians is the question whether local identities trumped all others. Some conclude that during the early modern period Spain, France, and England only existed in theory. In practice, most people living in parts of these jurisdictions considered themselves Catalans, Bretons, or Welsh. Others point out that the encounter with the outer world, as well as inter-European rivalries, enabled the cohesion of Scots, Irish, and Welsh into Britons, Basques, Aragonese, and Castilians into Spanish. They argue that disparate polities in Europe did not become homogenized into recognizable European states identified by a single language, legal system, and identity until some of their populations took up residence outside of Europe. European identities were thus born in the colonies and because of colonialism.[5] For some historians, this move designated the coming of nations. For others, it referenced the appearance of civilizations whose members were defined according to whether they obeyed the 'right' code of behaviour.[6] It is thus fair to say that rather than nationalized, during the expansion European identities were universalized. If Europe became different and superior in the process of being exported, its individual components (as well as Christianity) lost their European specificity. They became world cultures that could support the appearance of a commonwealth that, under the rubric of Britons or Hispanics, united peoples who did not necessarily originate in Europe and who hardly shared anything else.

Europeans were also divided by those who remained in the 'metropolis' and those who migrated to the new territories that had been acquired or settled by their country or monarch. For many years, historians have assumed that members of these two

---

[4] Bernard Bailyn and Philip D. Morgan (eds.), *Strangers within the Realm: Cultural Margins of the First British Empire* (Chapel Hill, NC, 1991). Also see James Horn and Philip D. Morgan, 'Settlers and Slaves: European and African Migrations to Early Modern British America', in Elizabeth Mancke and Carole Shammas (eds.), *The Creation of the British Atlantic World* (Baltimore, MD, 2005), 19–44, on 42–3.

[5] Nicholas Canny, 'The Origins of Empire: An Introduction', in id. (ed.), *The Origins of Empire: British Overseas Enterprise to the Close of the Seventeenth Century* (Oxford, 1998), 1–33, on 24–5; Henry Kamen, *Empire: How Spain Became a World Power, 1492–1763* (New York, 2003), 331–3; Irene Silverblatt, *Modern Inquisitions: Peru and the Colonial Origins of the Civilized World* (Durham, NC, 2004), 19–20; and Silvia Marzzgalli, 'The French Atlantic', *Itinerario*, 23/2 (1999), 70–81, on 74.

[6] Jack P. Greene, '"By their Laws Shall Ye Know Them": Law and Identity in Colonial British America', *Journal of Interdisciplinary History*, 33/2 (2002), 247–60, on 253–5; Colin Kidd, *British Identities before Nationalism: Ethnicity and Nationhood in the Atlantic World, 1600–1800* (Cambridge, 1999); and M. J. Rodríguez-Salgado, 'Christians, Civilised and Spanish: Multiple Identities in Sixteenth-Century Spain', *Transactions of the Royal Historical Society*, 8 (1998), 233–51.

groups, which were initially united, gradually distanced themselves from one another. While the first Europeans to arrive in the New World were very European, their descendants no longer were. Acculturation, matched by a growing awareness of the different interests of colony and homeland and by complaints about discrimination and marginalization within the political, social, cultural, and economic system, led to a gradual parting that matured with independence. The loyalty of colonists, in short, was transferred to the Americas, this process involving, among other things, the portrayal of Europeans as foreigners, even enemies. This transformation was matched by similar developments in Europe, where *colonists* were initially seen as fellow citizens, but were gradually portrayed as either degenerate, or disloyal, or both. Mostly invoked in order to explain, perhaps justify, why independence happened and in order to enable North, Central, and South Americans to portray themselves as victims of a European oppressor rather than as people who had profited from colonization and had oppressed the local and slave population, this portrait silenced the intellectual, social, economic, and political effort that was necessary to make those who were once similar different.[7] To take just one example, most vindications by American Spaniards insisted on their equality with Europeans, not their distinction from them. Many Americans may have been loyal to the New World, but they also maintained allegiance to their place of origin in Europe that, by the second and third generation, no longer depended on personal acquaintance but was re-enacted through family memory and the experience of forming part of networks of 'countrymen'[8]. Campaigns to expel Spaniards from Spanish America after independence mostly failed because even the most ardent republicans found it hard to define Spaniards as enemies if they were willing to swear allegiance to the new political order.[9] And, while people in Spain may have vilified the colonists, characterizing them as second-rate Spaniards (because they were impure, because they were acculturated, and so forth), returning migrants (*Indianos*)—even second- and third-generation settlers—could meet with a high degree of acceptance and acclaim. Many ended up reinserting themselves into their original communities, which they could modify greatly, transporting with them not only their fortune, but also their religious, social, cultural, and political practices.[10]

Although similar processes may have happened in the Portuguese, French, and British Atlantic, the literature on France and Portugal insists that most immigrants

---

[7] Stephen Conway, 'From Fellow-Nationals to Foreigners: British Perceptions of the Americans, circa 1739–1783', *William and Mary Quarterly*, 59/1 (2002), 65–100.

[8] Ida Altman, *Transatlantic Ties in the Spanish Empire: Brihuega, Spain and Puebla, Mexico, 1560–1620* (Stanford, CA, 2000); and Tamar Herzog, 'Private Organizations as Global Networks in Early Modern Spain and Spanish America', in Luis Roniger and Tamar Herzog (eds.), *The Collective and the Public in Latin America: Cultural Identities and Political Order* (Brighton, 2000), 117–33.

[9] Tamar Herzog, 'Communities Becoming a Nation: Spain and Spanish America in the Wake of Modernity (and Thereafter)', *Citizenship Studies*, 11/2 (2007), 151–72.

[10] Juan Javier Pescador, *The New World Inside a Basque Village: The Oiartzun Valley and its Atlantic Emigrants, 1550–1800* (Reno, NV, 2003); and Gregorio Salinero, *Une ville entre deux mondes: Trujillo d'Espagne et les Indes au XVIe siècle* (Paris, 2006).

to the New World were transients whose ability or wish to develop a local identity in the Americas was fairly restricted.[11] The same may have been partly true in the British Atlantic, where perhaps as many as one in four immigrants abandoned the New World to return to Europe.[12]

'INDIANS'

The people who inhabited the New World before Europeans arrived belonged to multiple formations. Although their grouping under the rubric 'Indians' was a European invention, what began as a mere fiction ended up representing at least a certain reality. Whether this happened because all Indians were treated similarly by Europeans, because of massive dislocation and destruction, because of inter-Indian miscegenation and acculturation, or, on the contrary, inter-Indian rivalries and animosity, native search to reconstruct a native culture, the introduction of new technologies and goods, or all of the above, by the time the colonial period was over many natives became 'Indians'. In many parts of North America, Indians affected by marginalization, enslavement, and extermination developed a pan-Indian movement.[13] In the Andes, under pressure from missionaries, a new pan-Andean religion made its appearance and Quechua, which was the language of one of the various indigenous groups, became the Indian lingua franca.

Although many Indian groups, demonstrating a cultural resiliency, survived the conquest and maintained a great deal of autonomy, other groups were eliminated. The reasons for elimination could vary: mortality because of diseases, warfare, forced immigration (to missions or settlements), territorial reduction, assimilation with other Indian groups, or miscegenation. Yet, while some groups disappeared, others made their appearance. Born out of inter-ethnic alliances, mutation of the original identity, changes in culture and places of residence, contact with Europeans, or the division of existing groups, many new Indian ethnicities were formed during the colonial period and because of colonialism. In some cases these formations represented genuine processes of adaptation and ethnogenesis.[14] In others, they were deliberately

[11] Gilles Havard and Cécile Vidal, *Histoire de l'Amérique française* (Paris, 2003), 207–8, Saliha Belmessous, 'Être français en Nouvelle France: identité française et identité coloniale aux 17e et 18e siècles', *French Historical Studies*, 27/3 (2004), 507–40.

[12] Susan Hardman Moore, *Pilgrims: New World Settlers and the Call of Home* (New Haven, CT, 2007).

[13] Evans Dowd, *A Spirited Resistance: The North American Indian Struggle for Unity, 1745–1815* (Baltimore, MD, 1992), Alan Gallay, *The Indian Slave Trade: The Rise of the English Empire in the American South, 1670–1717* (New Haven, CT, 2002); and Sabine MacCormack, *Religion in the Andes: Vision and Imagination in Early Colonial Peru* (Princeton, NJ, 1991).

[14] Nathan Wachtel, 'Note sur le problème des identités collectives dans les Andes méridionales', *Homme*, 122/124 (1992), 39–52; Colin G. Calloway, *New Worlds for All: Indians and Europeans, the Remaking of Early America* (Baltimore, MD, 1993); Patricia Galloway, *Choctaw Genesis, 1500–1700*

and consciously constructed. The Tlaxcalans of central Mexico constantly insisted that they were *conquistadores* rather than conquered peoples. Actively participating from the sixteenth to the late eighteenth century in the subjection of other native groups and sending colonists to settle northern Mexico, Tlaxcalans were exceptional, yet not completely unique, in their effort to blur distinctions between 'us' and 'them' and in the transformation of what had been originally a local identity into an ethnic one. In other cases, the new indigenous groups that appeared during the colonial period were practically invented by outside observers. Europeans who arrived in the Americas attempted to classify and thus understand the people they encountered. Dividing them into groups, ethnicities, or tribes, these classificatory efforts, even when they were based on misunderstanding, nevertheless created a geographical and mental map that persisted during the colonial period and thereafter and was to a large degree shared by both natives and Europeans.[15] Missionaries who acted as linguists and pre-ethnologists also registered, at times enhancing, at others inventing, what native communities were all about. The state intervened by classifying people into new groups, as happened, for example, with immigrant Indians who, in the Andes, ended up forming a new community literally called 'foreigners' (*forasteros*). State and church agents also divided the Indians into friends and foes, savages, cannibals, barbarians, and civilized (or semi-civilized). These divisions gave raise to new 'ethnic groups'. Capturing pre-Columbian designations, used by those who allied with Europeans to marginalize those who were external to their community, in northern Mexico these designations justified the formation of the 'Chichimecas', and in Brazil they gave rise to the distinction between Tupi (coastal Indians who shared a cultural and linguistic heritage) and Tapuai (all others).[16]

While processes of ethnogenesis are relatively easy to imagine, the question how were Indians distinguished from Europeans is one of the most difficult to answer. Initially, Indians were the natives who inhabited the New World. Yet, soon after colonization began, descent and place of origin no longer played a major role in the way people were classified. Either because they were unknown, or because they were considered less important, over time external and behavioural traits became the most persistent proof of membership. In North, Central, and Southern America, the English, the Spanish, the French, and the Portuguese often classified people as Indians or Europeans according to their skin colour but mainly according to their dress, their manners, their social contacts, and their reputation. These classifications could be

(Lincoln, NE, 1998); and Matthew Restall, 'Maya Ethnogenesis', *Journal of Latin American Anthropology*, 9/1 (2004), 64–89.

[15] Christophe Giudicelli, *Pour une géopolitique de la guerre des Tepehuán (1616–1619): alliances indiennes, quadrillage colonial et taxinomie ethnographique au nord-ouest du Mexique* (Paris, 2003), and Cecilia Sheridan, 'Social Control and Native Territoriality in Northeastern New Spain', in Jesús de la Teja and Ross Frank (eds.), *Choice, Persuasion and Coercion: Social Control on Spain's North American Frontiers* (Alburquerque, NM, 2005), 121–48.

[16] Susan Schroeder, *Chimalpahin and the Kingdoms of Chalco* (Tucson, AZ, 1991), 172–3; and Charlotte M. Grandie, 'Discovering the Chichimecas', *The Americas*, 51/1 (1994), 67–88.

contested, allowing for a conversation (not necessarily a dialogue) between classifier and classified over the meaning of certain terms and the way to approach them.[17] Because Europeans and Indians were treated differently (socially, economically, politically, and legally), these discussions involved not only, perhaps not even mainly, identity. Concerned with determining the rights and duties of individuals, the practical results of identifying certain people as Indians often overshadowed the discussion, influencing its outcome. Also determinant was the identity of the parties to the discussion, and the circumstances of each case. As a result, it is often hard to tell whether the designation as Indian or European was imposed or adopted voluntarily, was invented or represented existing structures, was purely strategic or reproduced an inner conviction. Nonetheless, the need to classify people in order to know whether they were eligible for certain rights or could be obliged to certain duties encouraged a constant elaboration of the differences between Europeans and Indians.[18]

Miscegenation and acculturation only made these processes more complex. Where in the early period individuals of mixed lineage could be adopted by either the European or the indigenous group, this was no longer true once the initial contact period was over. The literature often described mixed individuals (mixed either by descent or by culture) as people who did not belong. They could be portrayed negatively (as free agents) or positively (as cultural mediators), but it took a while before they came to form their own communities, made of mestizos or *métis*. By the eighteenth and nineteenth centuries, the members of such groups came to symbolize either the failure or the success (depending on who was speaking) of the colonial enterprise. This appreciation, which made miscegenation into a symbol, failed to acknowledge the degree by which all cultures and peoples were hybrid, none ever existing in 'an authentic' or 'pure' form.[19]

Whether Indians and their mixed offspring were considered racially different from Europeans is one of the hottest controversies. Many would claim that they were not: that they were considered equally human, with the same potential for progress and civilization as Europeans.[20] To argue otherwise, these scholars maintain, would be heretical in an early modern society still dominated by Christian dogma because it would either limit the universal appeal of the Church or sustain a theory of multiple creations (polygenesis). These historians explain that during the early modern period

[17] Douglas Cope, *The Limits of Racial Domination: Plebeian Society in Colonial Mexico City, 1660–1720* (Madison, WI, 1994), and Rebecca Earle, ' "Two Pairs of Pink Satin Shoes!!" Race, Clothing and Identity in the Americas (17th–19th Centuries)', *History Workshop Journal*, 52/2 (2001), 175–95.

[18] Martin Minchom, *The People of Quito 1690–1810: Change and Unrest in the Underclass* (Boulder, CO, 1994), 153–71, and Cynthia E. Milton, 'Poverty and the Politics of Colonialism: "Poor Spaniards," their Petitions and the Erosion of Privilege in Late Colonial Quito', *Hispanic American Historical Review*, 85/4 (2005), 595–626.

[19] Carolyn Dean and Dana Leibsohn, 'Hybridity and its Discontents: Considering Visual Culture in Colonial Spanish America', *Colonial Latin American Review*, 12/1 (2003), 5–35.

[20] Anthony Pagden, *The Fall of Natural Man: The American Indian and the Origins of Comparative Ethnology* (Cambridge, 1982), and Colin Kidd, *The Forging of Races: Race and Scripture in the Protestant Atlantic World, 1600–2000* (Cambridge, 2006), 25.

ethnicity and race could be best described as a theological problem involving the need to reconcile the common origin of men with the diversity of human groups. Explanations mainly focused on the effect of food and environment (on the one hand), sin and redemption (on the other), on human bodies and human societies. For these historians, in short, racism was a modern phenomenon, tied to growing secularism, to the intensification of competition for resources between Europeans and natives, to a growing European hegemony (that enabled the discrimination, even the annihilation, of Indians), as well as the development of modern science. Other historians argue on the contrary that the colonial experience (the failure of assimilating policies that hoped to make Indians English, French, or Spanish) and early modern scientific developments (that sought to explain, for example, Indian mortality versus European survival rates) led to the birth of racial categories that explained differences between people in terms of biological inherited traits.[21] Yet a third group of historians advances an explanation that is both surprising and intriguing. It points out that racial categories (although not necessarily racism) may have slowly evolved out of differences in religion or even rank precisely when the importance of these was fading away.[22] In the Spanish Atlantic, religious differences, expressed in the purity of blood regulations (*limpieza de sangre*), were mapped onto the *indigenous* and African populations, explaining the differences between them and Europeans also in terms of their heterodoxy, as implied in the fact that they were new or old converts, infidels (who had refused to become Christian), or innocent pagans (who never had the opportunity to embrace the Church). Similar processes may have also happened in the British Atlantic, where ethnicity initially defined religious alterity, not a distinction in race or nation. In the French Atlantic, a discourse distinguishing older from newer nobility and nobility from commoners was applied to both Indians and Africans, thus extending what had initially been an exclusionary policy of the French aristocracy to the colonial situation, making blood and lineage—both hereditary and unalterable—a marker for both physical and moral superiority. This development was partially present also in Spanish America, where, because they enjoyed a tax exemption while residing overseas, Spaniards refashioned themselves as nobles. This allowed them to claim that they were distinguished from Indians—who did pay taxes—not only by origin, but also by estate. The same claims also enabled the members of the indigenous nobility to argue that they were not only nobles, but also Spaniards. In the British Atlantic, physical and mental capacities were

---

[21] Saliha Belmessous, 'Assimilation and Racialism in Seventeenth and Eighteen-Century French Colonial Policy', *American Historical Review*, 110/2 (2005), 322–49, and Joyce E. Chaplin, *Subject Matter: Technology, the Body and Science on the Anglo-American Frontier, 1500–1676* (Cambridge, MA, 2001).

[22] Karen Ordahl Kupperman, *Settling with the Indians: The Meeting of English and Indian Cultures in America, 1580–1640* (Totowa, NJ, 1980), 3; Silvia Sebastiani, 'Race as the Construction of the Other: "Native Americans" and "Negroes" in the 18th Century Editions of the *Encyclopedia Britannica*', in Bo Strath (ed.), *Europe and the Other and Europe as the Other* (Brussels, 2000), 195–228, on 222–5; Guillaume Aubert, ' "The Blood of France": Race and Purity of Blood in the French Atlantic World', *William and Mary Quarterly*, 61/3 (2004), 439–78; and María Elena Martínez, *Genealogical Fictions: Limpieza de Sangre, Religion, and Gender in Colonial Mexico* (Stanford, CA, 2008).

thought to depend on social role. Non-European 'others' were compared to the British domestic lower classes and were made a target for exploitation not because they were racially different, but because they were part of a 'plebs'.

Very few Indians crossed the Atlantic and settled in Europe. Most of them arrived as slaves (in the sixteenth century) or as curiosities, put on display. A few travelled voluntarily as students, on diplomatic missions, or to present themselves in the court.[23] The very rare historians who have studied their experiences tend to describe these Indians as individuals rather than as members of groups. Apparently, those who stayed in Europe integrated into its society fairly rapidly and thus 'disappeared'. To my knowledge, there are no studies of a Native American presence in Africa.

'AFRICANS'

The Atlantic world also included a great number of Africans. Called 'Negroes', 'Moors', or 'Blacks' during the late seventeenth and eighteenth centuries; the term African also made its appearance. As happened with other groups, African experience in the Atlantic was highly diversified. Some Africans remained in the old continent, others emigrated, yet a third group was forced into exile by slavery. Today we know much more than previously about how slavery was organized and what some of its consequences may have been. Recent research stresses that the experience of slavery and emigration may have been radically different for different individuals. While many Africans were transported against their will and were made into slaves, others, who were familiar with European languages, practices, and norms, were involved in the slave trade as rulers, merchants, or middlemen. Their intense contact with Europeans generated new structures, identities, alliances, and rivalries.[24] New settlements were founded along the new trading routes, linking African regions and communities that previously had been less frequently connected. Villages along these routes underwent important transformations due to economic reorientation and growth, but also because of contact with new individuals and communities in both Africa and overseas. Enhanced relationship between different African communities—now tied to one another by the slave trade—gave rise to inter-African acculturation mixing. These processes—which expanded some languages, cultures, and religions over a larger space—transformed what had been separated communities into new, wider political and or cultural formations. The slave trade also intensified, prolonged, or extended conflicts among the different African communities. The opening of new markets also affected patterns of slavery in Africa, as well as influencing family structures, gender

---

[23] Esteban Mira Caballos, *Indios y mestizos americanos en la España del siglo XVI* (Madrid, 2000), and Gallay, *The Indian Slave Trade*, 350–1.

[24] Patrick Manning, *Slavery and African Life: Occidental, Oriental, and African Slave Traders* (Cambridge, 1990), 126, and Robin Law, *The Slave Coast of West Africa, 1550–1750: The Impact of the Atlantic Slave Trade on an African Society* (Oscof, 1991), 220–1.

roles, and the way warfare was conducted. It shifted the balance of wealth and power between and within local societies, perhaps even increasing social inequalities.

During this period many African enclaves were transformed into centres in which Europeans and Africans coexisted. The most famous example (although not the only one) is that of Kongo, whose king converted to Christianity in 1491 and adopted for his court and kingdom Portuguese names, manners, dress, laws, court etiquette, architecture, and even urban planning.[25] Young Kongo men were sent to study in Portugal and the Portuguese were allowed residence in local settlements. In other places, new communities comprising individuals of mixed ancestry and or mixed culture made their appearance.[26] Among them were the so-called Atlantic Creoles. These were persons who either travelled in the Atlantic as soldiers, sailors, merchants, and artisans or who had developed a cosmopolitan culture. Living in societies that were often multiracial, they were linked to one another not only economically, but also socially, linguistically, religiously, and culturally. By the late eighteenth century there were also individuals living among Atlantic Creoles who had been to the Americas and returned to Africa (although not necessarily to their place of origin), bringing with them what they had acquired economically, socially, culturally, and religiously, elsewhere. These developments introduced to Africa African elements, which were re-created and had metamorphosed in the New World.[27] In short, rather than bilateral, the African diaspora was multilateral: influences moved back and forth inside and outside Africa, towards the Americas and Europe, and between them.

This said, it is generally agreed that, while the slave trade had greatly affected some communities, others were barely influenced by it. Furthermore, during this period there was no consciousness of being African. According to some, an 'elementary pan-Africanism' may have arisen in response to the contact with Europeans, but this identity, if and where it existed, was very limited in scope. Historians of Africa thus stress that there was nothing odd about Africans enslaving Africans: after all, for those involved in the trade those whom they enslaved were aliens.

While this was happening in Africa, in the Americas arriving Africans originating in many different regions formed new communities. Although some of these communities

---

[25] A. J. R. Russell-Wood, 'Before Columbus: Portugal's African Prelude to the Middle Passage and Contribution to Discourse on Race and Slavery', John Thornton, 'Perspectives on African Christianity', both in Vera Lawrence Hyatt and Rex Nettleford (eds.), *Race, Discourse and the Origin of the Americas: A New World View* (Washington, DC, 1995), 134–68 and 169–98 respectively, and Linda M. Heywood and John K. Thornton, *Central Africans, Atlantic Creoles, and the Foundation of the Americas, 1585–1660* (New York, 2007).

[26] Ira Berlin, 'From Creole to African; Atlantic Creoles and the Origins of African-American Society in Mainland North America', *William and Mary Quarterly*, 3rd series 53/2 (1996), 251–88, and Robin Law and Kristin Mann, 'West Africa in the Atlantic Community: The Case of the Slave Coast', *William and Mary Quarterly*, 3rd series 46/2 (1999), 307–44.

[27] The ethnic designation of people as Yoruba, for example, had first appeared in the Americas and was than transported to Africa: Robin Law, 'The Port of Quidah in the Atlantic Community, 17th to 19th Centuries', in Horst Pietschmann (ed.), *Atlantic History: History of the Atlantic System, 1580–1830* (Göttingen, 2002), 349–64, on 363. Also see Rodolfo Sarracino, *Los que volvieron a Africa* (Havana, 1988).

may have respected differences in ethnicity, language, and religion, and these differences may have been validated by external observers who may have distinguished Africans according to their origin (or, more accurately, according to where they were shipped from), most of the older literature on Africans in the Americas stresses that, separated from their family and place of birth and under the compelling circumstances of slavery, in the Americas Africans were both creolized and Africanized. They were Africanized because, rather than identifying with a specific location or culture, they constituted pan-African communities, in which people and practices originating from different areas were gathered together and in which the influence of European values was also determinant. And, rather than retaining specific traditions, these communities kept 'cultural principles', which were shared by many Africans. Yet, these communities were creolized because these processes led to a growing homogenization that gradually made separate individuals and groups into one. In some cases, the new community was indeed designated as 'creole'. In others, it was identified as continuing a certain African tradition or nation. Yet, these new communities—even when adopting an African appearance—did not simply reproduce pre-existing structures. Although they used certain African traits as a reference point, these groups were created through the aggregation of different units that were thereafter designated with a new name. Some of this happened in the Americas, but the gathering of various peoples together could also be a designation made by slave traders that could be adopted not only by slave masters, but also by the slaves themselves. Thus, people originating in different villages or districts in the Bight of Biafra came to accept their common designation as Ibo, a term never used in Africa. The same happened with the Bambara, a name that in Louisiana designated a vast range of people, including both the Bambara and those captured and enslaved by the Bambara.[28] While the creation of new groups (and their constant evolution) was the most common phenomenon, in some areas Africans assimilated to the local society to such a degree that they practically disappeared from the records.[29]

Criticizing the earlier literature that studied Africa and African communities abroad separately and that perceived Africans as a collection of anonymous almost stereotyped individuals and searched for the survival of 'things African' in the Americas, the newest literature on Africa and Africans stresses how 'routes' became 'roots'.[30] Focusing on the personal experience concrete individuals may have had, it looks at this experience from

[28] James Horn and Philip D. Morgan, 'Settlers and Slaves: European and African Migrations to Early Modern British America', in Mancke and Shammas (eds.), *The Creation of the British Atlantic*, 19–44, on 42, and Gwendolyn Midlo Hall, *Slavery and African Ethnicities in the Americas: Restoring the Links* (Chapel Hill, NC, 2005), 46–51. The mutation of African identities in the Americas is also studied in James Sidbury, *Becoming African in America: Race and Nation in Early Black Atlantic* (Oxford, 2007).

[29] Thomas Fierhrer, 'Slaves and Freedmen in Colonial Central America: Rediscovering a Forgotten Black Past', *Journal of Negro History*, 64/1 (1979), 39–57, on 42.

[30] Dylan C. Penningroth, 'The Claim of Slaves and Ex-Slaves to Family and Property: A Transatlantic Comparison', *American Historical Review*, 112/4 (2007), 1039–67, on 1041, and Kristin Mann, 'Shifting Paradigms in the Study of the African Diaspora and of Atlantic History and Culture', *Slavery and Abolition*, 22/1 (2001), 3–21.

the perspective of African history (where it began) rather than American history (where it ended), wishing to reconstruct the journey of slaves from the interior of the continent to the coastal areas and from those to the New World. It thus insists that besides being slaves, Africans were also immigrants who, like all immigrants, made sense of their present in terms of their past. Conditioned not only by slavery, but also by their African experience, this literature argues for the need to study African culture not only as a culture of resistance but also as a culture that could support collaboration and that allowed expressing identity by forming part of society rather than by resisting it.[31]

The impact of African presence in Europe is the least documented of all. There is plenty of evidence that Africans were present, at times in large numbers, in port and capital cities in Spain, Portugal, England, and France.[32] Some arrived as slaves, but many were free individuals; some only remained in the continent for a short period, others made it their home. While the experience of a few eminent individuals, mainly famous authors, as well as African involvement in the struggle for abolition are somewhat studied, how most Africans influenced and were influenced by society and how they 'disappeared' from the history and even the records of most European countries is still largely a mystery. What is clear, however, is that by the end of the eighteenth century the memory of their existence was sufficiently gone to allow Spaniards to assume that Spaniards of African descent (a legal figure defined in the Constitution of Cádiz in 1812) only existed in the Americas.

While debate persists whether or not 'Indian' was a racial category, most people seem to agree that 'African' was one, if not immediately, than at least from the seventeenth century onwards. Although slavery could be divided into different categories depending on which labour was demanded of slaves and whether masters treated their slaves as goods (as in English common law) or humans (in the countries that practised Roman law) and whether they cared for their conversion and allowed their manumission, slavery, and most particularly plantation slavery, most historians argued, stigmatized Africans even after they were freed. Stigmatization was such that in some places the assumption was that if you were African you were a slave. Nonetheless, it is clear slavery not only produced new categories, but it was also based on existing ones. African slavery, we know, was introduced at a time in which

---

[31] Matthew Restall, 'Black Conquistadors: Armed Africans in Early Spanish America', *The Americas*, 57/2 (2000), 171–205, and Ben Vinson III, *Bearing Arms for His Majesty: The Free Colored Militia in Colonial Mexico* (Stanford, CA, 2001).

[32] William D. Phillips, *Slavery from Roman Times to the Early Transatlantic Trade* (Minneapolis, MN, 1985), 154–70; A. C. de C. M. Saunders, *A Social History of Black Slaves and Freedmen in Portugal, 1441–1555* (Cambridge, 1982); Peter Fryer, *Staying Power: The History of Black People in Britain since 1504* (London, 1984); Norma Myers, *Reconstructing the Black Past: Blacks in Britain c.1780–1830* (London, 1996); Philip D. Morgan, 'British Encounters with Africans and African-Americans, circa 1600–1780', in Bailyn and Morgan (eds.), *Strangers within the Realm*, 157–219 on 159–60; José Luis Cortés López, *La esclavitud negra en la España peninsular del siglo XVI* (Salamanca, 1989); and Didier Lahon, 'Esclavage, confréries noires, sainteté noire et pureté de sang au Portugal (XVIe et XVIIIe siècles)', *Lusitania sacra*, 15 (2003), 119–62.

Europe turned away from coerced labour.[33] And, while Indian slavery was prohibited in Spanish and eventually Portuguese, French, and English domains, African slavery was allowed. The issue therefore is not only how slavery stigmatized the Africans, but how Africans became slaves when other groups were gradually exempt from slavery. The normal argument is that they were enslaved because they were considered inferior, yet historians of medieval and early modern Europe on the one hand, African historians on the other, insist that initially slavery was not tied to racism. Often widespread among people of the same ethnicity, religion, or even territory, the connection between slavery and race emerged at some point in time as a possible, but not a foretold conclusion. Moreover, contemporaries did not justify slavery, or the discrimination of Africans, on the basis of racial distinctions. Early modern Spanish and Portuguese authors studying the slave trade framed their discussion by reference to the Roman law doctrine of 'just war': if Africans were taken as captives in a just war their enslavement was legal and thus permitted. Africans could also be enslaved because enslavement gave them the benefits of Christianity and civility. This was an important point, as some authors explained that Africans were enslaved as divine punishment for their sins. Theoretically, if they stopped sinning and became Christian, they would be saved both religiously and politically. In seventeenth- and eighteenth-century Spain and Spanish America, the exclusion of Africans was also justified by reference to their foreignness as, in their condition as forced immigrants, Africans never made the decision to attach themselves to the community.[34] For English interlocutors, the justness of slavery was largely encoded in religious difference: Africans were enslaved not because of their colour but because they were available and were non-Christians.[35]

OTHER CATEGORIES OF BELONGING

Besides being designated as Europeans, Indians, and Africans, people inhabiting the Atlantic world were also differentiated according to other criteria. Most important among *these* was religion. Depending on place and circumstances, religion could unite or divide people, be meaningful or not. Take for example the case of people of different religious creeds. There are abundant examples of hostility between Christians, Muslims, Jews, and 'pagans' (a Eurocentric denomination including all those who were not Christians, Muslims, or Jews). This hostility allowed scholars to understand the encounter between Muslims and Christians in Africa as jihad on the one side, crusade

[33] David Eltis, *The Rise of African Slavery in the Americas* (Cambridge, 2000), 7 and 58, and Sue Peabody, '"A Nation Born to Slavery": Missionaries and Racial Discourse in Seventeenth-Century French Antilles', *Journal of Social History*, 38/1 (2004), 113–26.

[34] Tamar Herzog, *Defining Nations: Immigrants and Citizens in Early Modern Spain and Spanish America* (New Haven, CT, 2003), 158–62.

[35] Eliga H. Gould, 'Entangled Histories, Entangled Worlds: The English-Speaking Atlantic as a Spanish Periphery', *American Historical Review*, 112/3 (2007), 764–86, on 774–5.

on the other.[36] Yet, there are also examples of how business relationships, common residency, or even common origin tied people of different beliefs together. The outstanding example involves the Sephardic diaspora, whose members, living in Africa, Europe, the Americas, and Asia, were tightly connected despite the fact that among them were practising Christians, practising Jews, many go-betweens who constantly changed their religious adherence, and a few proto-atheists.[37] Religion could also unite or divide Christians of different denominations. Inter-Christian solidarities were clear in the designation of Europeans as 'Christians' and in the common reference that European made to a system of law and morality that originated in Rome but was taken on, conserved, and developed by the Church. Yet, inter-Christian rivalries were just as strong. Obvious during the Reformation and Wars of Religion, anti-Catholicism was a more pronounced feature of eighteenth-century British discourse than was racism. Similar affirmations were made in the Dutch case, in which the struggle against Spanish sovereignty was also justified as the affirmation of a religious difference. The Dutch could thus identify with the plight of American Indians who, according to them, also suffered from Spanish intolerance and sense of superiority. In the process, America and its inhabitants on the one hand, Spain on the other, became key components in defining who the Dutch were. Corresponding to these images, contemporaries in Brazil presented the struggle against Dutch occupation as one confronting Catholics with Protestants, heretics, Jews, and atheists.[38] Inter-denominational solidarities were clear in the rescuing of Catholic prisoners from Muslim hands and in the willingness of Spain to give refuge to persecuted Catholics and England to allow the entry of French Huguenots. Religion, however, also divided. Spaniards were distinguished according to their 'purity of blood', that is, according to whether they descended from Jewish or Muslim families, or from families whose members were convicted of heresy up to three generations. In England, discussions among different Protestant denominations were often fierce, leading to persecution. Interreligious tensions were also evident in the division of people into orthodox or heretic. This division often transformed those suspected of dissent not only into marginal individuals, but also into foreigners.

On a more intimate scale, family identities could connect people of different extraction, origin, race, or even religion. Some families dedicated time and energy to maintain and consolidate their networks; others marked their boundaries by referencing a common ancestor, or a place of origin. Families were also sites of contestation regarding who would be included and who not. Recent literature argues that slavery, for example, also included a debate about what family meant and what were the

---

[36] Charles R. Boxer, *Race Relations in the Portuguese Colonial Empire, 1415–1825* (Oxford, 1963), 4.

[37] Daviken Studnicki-Gizbert, *A Nation upon the Ocean Sea: Portugal's Atlantic Diaspora and the Crisis of the Spanish Empire, 1492–1640* (Oxford, 2007), and Peer Schmidt, 'Les Minorités religieuses européennes face à l'espace atlantique à l'époque moderne', in Pietschmann (ed.), *Atlantic History*, 83–96.

[38] Benjamin Schmidt, *Innocence Abroad: The Dutch Imagination and the New World, 1570–1670* (Cambridge, 2001), and António Vieira, *La Mission d'Ibiapaba*, trans. João Viegas (Paris, 1998), 33, and in id., *A invasão holandesa da Bahia* (Bahia, 1955), 55.

consequences of family relations.[39] Other scholars have noted that, like all other social institutions, families were also in constant flux: according to need they could include blood or political relatives, people living in the household, godparents and godchildren. They could even include all those bearing the same surname even if their degree of parentage—if one ever existed—was completely unknown.

Another important factor likely to produce identities in the Atlantic world was the differentiation between nobles and commoners. Recent literature on the French state demonstrates that concepts of miscegenation, as well as purity of blood, could operate not only vis-à-vis subjected populations (native Indians and Africans) or competing ethnic groups (*conversos* in Spain), but also with regard to the domestic population. Justifying the privileges of nobles, during this period blood and inheritance were constituted as guarantors of a moral and bodily superiority that also found expression in the argument that the French nobility descended from the Franks, while commoners descended from the *Gauls*. In Spanish America, because of their nobility, descendents of Incas were classified not as Indians, but instead as Spaniards.[40] And, as noble status gradually lost ground to other types of social distinctions, the most meaningful differentiation now marked the boundaries between 'elites' and 'commoners' or 'plebs'. [41] While elite culture gradually converged, tying people of different regions, even different states, religions, and races to one another, popular culture seemed to have localized.

Europeans, Indians, and Africans were also divided between local citizens and foreigners. During this period, most people lived within the confines of their particular community, which served as their immediate point of reference. Cultivating stories about their glorious origins and nobility, early modern settlements in both Europe and the Americas often imagined themselves as corporate bodies or closed communities.[42] Although in some instances they restricted membership to people of the same origin, creed, or allegiance, this was not always true. In both Spain and Spanish America, non-Spaniards (although not non-Catholics) could easily become members of local communities. Their association with a local community was often deemed so complete that it was considered also a method of naturalization: it implied, by extension, that they had become not only local citizens but also Spanish.[43] Similar processes may have

[39] Penningroth, 'The Claim of Slaves', and Karin Wulf, ' "Of the Old Stock": Quakerism and Transatlantic Genealogies in Colonial British America', in Mancke and Shammas (eds.), *The Creation of the British Atlantic*, 304–20, on 314–15.

[40] Ruth Hill, 'Teaching the Pre-History of Race along the Hispanic Transatlantic', *Dieciocho*, 30/1 (2007), 105–18, on 105.

[41] John E. Elliott, 'Introduction: Colonial Identity in the Atlantic World', in Nicholas Canny and Anthony Pagden (eds.), *Colonial Identity in the Atlantic World, 1500–1800* (Princeton, NJ, 1987), 3–13, on 6; Michale J. Braddick, 'Civility and Authority', in David Armitage and Michael J. Braddick (eds.), *The British Atlantic World, 1500–1800* (London, 2002), 93–112.

[42] Peter Burke, 'Foundation Myths and Collective Identity in Early Modern Europe', in Stroth (ed.), *Europe and the Other*, 113–22, and Adeline Rucquoi, 'Des villes nobles pour le roi', in id. (ed.), *Realidad e imágenes del poder en España a fines de la edad media* (Valladolid, 1988), 195–214.

[43] Herzog, *Defining Nations*.

occurred in British North America, where foreigners who were admitted to local communities may have also been recognized not only as free but also as deserving the rights of Englishmen.[44] Strong local identities connecting people of different origin, ethnicity, or otherwise membership condition were particularly clear in frontier situations, in which the making as well as the crossing of boundaries was especially frequent.

Returning to my point of departure, it seems fair to say that although identities and processes of identification were extremely important in the Atlantic world (as elsewhere) they were always, by definition, contingent, depending on the identity of actors and audience and the circumstances of each case. This is not to say that identities and identification were not genuine. But, even when they were—which was often the case— and even when they were not imposed but instead came from within, they still depended on a certain dialogue—verbal or non-verbal—between observers and observed, a person and those around him or her.

BIBLIOGRAPHY

Altman, Ida, *Transatlantic Ties in the Spanish Empire: Brihuega, Spain and Puebla, Mexico, 1560–1620* (Stanford, CA, 2000).

Bailyn, Bernard, and Philip D. Morgan (eds.), *Strangers within the Realm: Cultural Margins of the First British Empire* (Chapel Hill, NC, 1991).

Belmessous, Saliha, 'Être français en Nouvelle France: identité française et identité coloniale aux 17e et 18e siècles', *French Historical Studies*, 27/3 (2004), 507–40.

Canny, Nicholas, and Anthony Pagden (eds.), *Colonial Identity in the Atlantic World, 1500–1800* (Princeton, NJ, 1987).

Herzog, Tamar, *Defining Nations: Immigrants and Citizens in Early Modern Spain and Spanish America* (New Haven, CT, 2003).

Kidd, Colin, *British Identities before Nationalism: Ethnicity and Nationhood in the Atlantic World, 1600–1800* (Cambridge, 1999).

—— *The Forging of Races: Race and Scripture in the Protestant Atlantic World, 1600–2000* (Cambridge, 2006).

Martínez, María Elena, *Genealogical Fictions: Limpieza de Sangre, Religion, and Gender in Colonial Mexico* (Stanford, CA, 2008).

Pagden, Anthony, *The Fall of Natural Man: The American Indian and the Origins of Comparative Ethnology* (Cambridge, 1982).

Sidbury, James, *Becoming African in America: Race and Nation in the Early Black Atlantic* (Oxford, 2007).

---

[44] Cora Start, 'Naturalization in the English Colonies in America', *Annual Report of the American Historical Association* (1893), 319–23; Edward A. Hoyt, 'Naturalization under the American Colonies: Signs of a New Community', *Political Science Quarterly*, 67 (1952), 248–66; and James H. Kettner, *The Development of American Citizenship* (Chapel Hill, NC, 1978), 83 and 86–9.

PART IV

DISINTEGRATION

CHAPTER 29

....

SEVERED CONNECTIONS

*American Indigenous Peoples
and the Atlantic World in an Era
of Imperial Transformation*

....

DANIEL K. RICHTER
TROY L. THOMPSON

SCHOLARS often portray indigenous people's interactions with the Atlantic world in linear terms: European expansion engulfs native communities and enslaves them to a global capitalist system. The mid-eighteenth to early nineteenth centuries, however, tell a more complicated tale. By the 1750s, many native peoples had learnt from decades of experience how to engage the Atlantic world on their own varied terms, often to their own advantage. Those engagements were disrupted by the British, French, and Spanish imperial crises spawned by the Seven Years War and especially by the creole independence movements born during those crises. The process worked out differently north and south of the Rio Grande, but, throughout the Americas, the collapse of European empires severed connections that had once guaranteed indigenous autonomy.

In the middle of the eighteenth century, most North American areas controlled by colonial governments were hostile places for native people. Spanish La Florida and French Canada were partial exceptions, but the native population of each was small. La Florida had once been home to more than forty Catholic mission towns with perhaps 35,000 native people accepting Spanish suzerainty to some degree, yet by 1720 all of the missions had been destroyed and their people enslaved or dispersed by native enemies allied with English Carolina. In New France, several communities of what the French called *sauvages domiciliés* dotted the banks of the St Lawrence River, enjoying considerable autonomy despite their origins in Catholic missions. Indians living within the confines of British colonies in such places as southern New England, Long Island, and the tidewater Chesapeake were not as fortunate. Some of these communities controlled most of their day-to-day affairs and retained tenuous ownership of small land holdings, but others melted into larger racially mixed populations of servants, day labourers, and former slaves.[1]

Beyond the boundaries of European colonies, however, in the heartland of North America north of La Florida, east of New Mexico, west of the Appalachian Mountains, and south of the Great Lakes, powerful autonomous Indian nations capitalized on their economic and military value to competing European Atlantic empires. 'To preserve the balance between us and the French', observed one colonial official, 'is the great ruling principle of the modern Indian politics.'[2] Thus, in the far north-east, Wabenakis balanced close economic and military connections to New France with regular, if sometimes violent, flirtations with New England. To their west, the Six Iroquois Nations of the Haudenosaunee manoeuvred among New France, New York, and Pennsylvania. Another variant on balance-of-power politics prevailed in the Great Lakes region, where trading posts and Jesuit missions anchored a network of Wyandot, Miami, Potawatomi, Ojibwe, and other villages that acknowledged the governor of New France as their 'Father' while dealing also with British 'Brothers' of New York. To the south, in the 'Ohio country', Shawnees, Delawares, and others depended on Pennsylvania traders but frequently welcomed French and Virginian visitors to their villages while struggling to avoid domination by the Iroquois confederacy, which asserted ownership of their lands. Cherokees trafficked mostly with Virginians but kept options open with Carolina and French-allied natives to their north, while Creeks balanced their strong Carolina trading relationships with links to both La Florida and French Louisiana. Choctaws did the same, but with the French as their primary partner.[3]

If balance was the principle of 'modern Indian politics', trade was its glue. 'A modern Indian cannot subsist without Europeans; And would handle a Flint Ax or any other rude utinsil used by his ancestors very awkwardly,' a South Carolinian wrote 1761. Native North Americans purchased not just the iron axes that replaced the flint of their ancestors but metal tools, brass kettles, woollen cloth, linen shirts and dresses, firearms and ammunition, jewellery, liquor, and tobacco—luxuries and necessities large and small.[4] Native American need of Atlantic trade explains why it was vital for them to maintain a balance among the imperial powers. If they were to avoid turning the corner from *dependence* towards the grim condition that economists call *dependency*, they must trade in multiple

---

[1] Daniel K. Richter, *Facing East from Indian Country: A Native History of Early America* (Cambridge, MA, 2001), 171–4.

[2] Peter Wraxall, *An Abridgment of the Indian Affairs Contained in Four Folio Volumes, Transacted in the Colony of New York, from the Year 1678 to the Year 1751*, ed. Charles Howard McIlwain (Cambridge, MA, 1915), 219 n.

[3] Richard White, *The Middle Ground: Indians, Empires, and Republics in the Great Lakes Region, 1650–1815* (Cambridge, 1991), 1–222; Michael N. McConnell, *A Country Between: The Upper Ohio Valley and its Peoples, 1724–1774* (Lincoln, NE, 1992), 5–158; Allan Gallay, *The Indian Slave Trade: The Rise of the English Empire in the America South, 1670–1717* (New Haven, CT, 2002), 199–344.

[4] Kathryn E. Holland Braund, *Deerskins and Duffels: The Creek Indian Trade with Anglo-America, 1685–1815* (Lincoln, NE, 1993), 30 (quotation); James Axtell, *Beyond 1492: Encounters in Colonial North America* (Oxford, 1992), 125–51.

markets, deploy their military strength to keep rival empires guessing about their intentions, and maintain a diplomatic system that featured substantial annual transfers of arms,
cloth, and tools. These ceremonial gifts, redistributed by chiefs to their people, were
tangible proof that natives exercised power over the Atlantic empires. What looked to
Europeans like handouts were, in native eyes, evidence of their leaders' ability to extract
tribute from imperial governments.[5]

West of the Mississippi, native people were not as engaged with the Atlantic economy
as those to the east. Still, tenuous links with Louisiana and New France on the one hand
and with New Mexico on the other brought trade goods through the countries of such
peoples as the Osages and Quapaws of the Arkansas valley to the Great Plains. There
people were domesticating the progeny of European horses that had migrated northwards from Mexico, while other animals and goods filtered in from the *presidios* and
missions that had grown up across Texas since the 1690s and from long-established
Spanish missions among the Puebloan peoples of New Mexico. The latter engaged in a
far-flung commerce, in which Utes, Comanches, and others attended annual trade fairs
where Hispanics and local native people bartered foodstuffs, horses, and firearms for
buffalo hides, furs, and slaves captured in indigenous wars.[6]

Multiple trade routes and balance-of-power diplomacy, then, created complicated
ties between North American native people and the Atlantic world. In that world,
Indians were not just consumers but producers. Native peoples proffered not just furs
and hides, when the market allowed, but exotic specialities such as ginseng or mundane
items such as maple sugar. Production for this system placed a heavy demand on
labour within villages; turning a deer-hide into leather, for example, occupied at least a
week of women's work. Native economies and work routines thus became ever more
oriented toward Atlantic markets. Yet, for all the toil that went into them, furs and
hides were minimally processed raw materials; their transformation into more valuable
finished products such as felt hats or leather goods took place in Europe. There, and on
the books of merchant middlemen on both sides of the Atlantic, capital accumulated,
while Indians principally consumed and produced. The lopsided economic relationship was captured well by a native spokesman who admitted that the trading post at
Oswego was 'a vast advantage . . . because we can get there what we want or desire.' Yet,
he told New York's governor, 'we think . . . that your people who trade there have the
most advantage by it, and that it is as good for them as a Silver mine.'[7]

[5] Daniel K. Richter, 'Stratification and Class in Eastern Native America', in Simon Middleton and
Billy G. Smith (eds.), *Class Matters: Early North America and the Atlantic World* (Philadelphia, PA,
2008), 35–48.

[6] Kathleen DuVal, *The Native Ground: Indians and Colonists in the Heart of the Continent*
(Philadelphia, PA, 2006), 63–118; David J. Weber, *The Spanish Frontier in North America* (New
Haven, CT, 1992), 147–98.

[7] E. B. O'Callaghan and B. Fernow (eds.), *Documents Relative to the Colonial History of the State of
New York* (Albany, NY, 1853–87), vi. 177 (quotation).

It is unclear whether the speaker was aware of the riches extracted from actual silver mines far to the south. There, over the course of two centuries, Spain had constructed a system to mobilize the labour of thousands of Indians for work in mines that injected millions of pesos of precious metal into the Atlantic economy. The Spanish had adapted pre-Columbian Inca and Aztec tribute networks, co-opted indigenous nobles through clientage and marriage, deployed a phalanx of Catholic missionaries, and consolidated indigenous populations wracked by epidemics into 'reduced' munici-palities (*pueblos de indios*) or mission towns (*reducciones*). Labour drafts (*reparti-miento* or *mita*) often required long-distance travel to mines and cities in Peru, Bolivia, Ecuador, or Mexico. Thus, the Spanish imperial system integrated roughly 6 million indigenous people into Atlantic markets on terms that were more onerous than those prevailing in North America. But here, too, relationships had reached equilibri-um by the mid-eighteenth century.[8]

In north-eastern Mexico and in Bolivia, thousands of Indians migrated to silver mines, others provisioned miners, and still others conveyed the precious metal to coastal cities. For example when, in the 1590s, silver deposits were discovered in Zacatecas, Topia, and Durango, authorities had encouraged Nahuatl-speakers of central Mexico to resettle in the territories of nomadic nations to the north. There, the newcomers raised sheep, cultivated beans, corn, and squash, grew *pulque maguey* to be fermented and sold to native miners, and cut mesquite trees to provision the mines with lumber and fuel. Similarly, Mixtecs and Zapotecs of Oaxaca grew wheat, cultivated silkworms, and raised livestock to trade for wine, linen, and other European luxuries. Native lords continued to own tracts of land and participated in a vibrant market economy, while commoners tended small ranches and harvested cochineal. Such diverse engagement with Atlantic markets allowed indigenous peoples of both Oaxaca and north-eastern Mexico to navigate the Spanish legal system and fund communal organizations such as *cofradías* (spiritual brotherhoods) crucial to their survival as indigenous communities.[9]

Such beneficial accommodations with the Atlantic world had little meaning for the majority of the native populations of New Spain and Peru who, by mid-century, no longer lived in such communities. Devastated by disease and the *repartimiento*, they rented land as peasants, served as wage labourers, or succumbed to virtual enslavement on haciendas (large estates), intermixed with African slaves and Hispanic peasants. The racial kaleidoscope theoretically resolved into an elaborate hierarchy of *castas* defined by various proportions of Hispanic, indigenous, or African bloodlines as documented by carefully recorded, if sometimes artfully invented, family genealogies. Yet *Mestizaje* (or mixture) characterized not just the broad bottom of society but the highest levels of

---

[8] Cheryl English Martin, 'Indigenous Peoples', in Louisa Hoberman and Susan Socolow (eds.), *The Countryside in Colonial Latin America* (Albuquerque, NM, 1996), 187–212.

[9] David Frye, 'The Native Peoples of Northeastern Mexico', in Richard E. W. Adams and Murdo MacLeod (eds.), *The Cambridge History of the Native Peoples of the Americas*, ii/2: *Mesoamerica* (Cambridge, 2000), 54; Susan Deeds, 'Legacies of Resistance, Adaptation, and Tenacity: History of the Native Peoples of Northwest Mexico', ibid. 118–23; María de los Angeles Romero Frizzi, 'The Indigenous Population of Oaxaca from the Sixteenth Century to the Present', ibid. 308–19.

indigenous communities in the viceroyalties of Peru and New Spain. Mestizo elites with kin ties to Spanish officials walked a fine line between being indigenous leaders and agents of empire.[10]

If kin ties, hereditary claims to indigenous office, and the complications of *mestizaje* mediated engagement with the Spanish empire and the Atlantic economy, so too did the Catholic Church. Subsidized by the state and endowed with the *repartimiento*, Jesuits, Franciscans, Carmelites, and Dominicans turned their missions into flourishing enterprises. Jesuits proved especially successful in regions of intensive slave raiding, such as western Amazonia, southern Brazil, and Paraguay. *Reducciones* provided protection from slave raiders at the cost of coercive paternalism and an often-oppressive labour regime. Yet the picture was not unrelievedly grim. By 1730, Jesuits had transformed indigenous economies in much of present-day Ecuador, Paraguay, and Argentina, most notably among some 100,000 Guaraní people living in thirty missions along the Río Uruguay. These missions supplied Atlantic markets with tobacco, cotton, sugar, wheat, beef, and iron and wood manufactures in exchange for iron implements, clothing, and firearms. Profits funded mission upkeep, religious festivals, and emergency food stores, and thus protected the Guaraní from land-hungry colonists.[11]

The protection that Jesuits provided offers a counterpoint to the experience of indigenous peoples in Portuguese Brazil. There, despite royal prohibitions, *bandeirantes* continued enslaving Indians, creating an environment perhaps even more hostile to Indians than that in British North America. At mid-century an estimated 250,000 indigenous people lived within the borders of modern-day Brazil, concentrated in the south from the Paraguayan border to the Atlantic coast, in the north-east on Amazon floodplains, and in the centre on the coast. Despite Portuguese efforts to exploit the natural resources of the latter region, it remained a refuge for Airomé and Botocudo people. Pockets within the Amazon floodplains also remained in Indian hands. Elsewhere the Portuguese were more successful in subjugating and enslaving Indians and converting their lands into cattle ranches and plantations.[12]

To the south, between the realms of Portuguese slave raiding and Spanish imperialism, were two powerful indigenous societies, the Guaykuru and the Payaguá. Their interactions with each other as well as with Iberian colonists created a balance of power not unlike that of native North America. Equestrian Guaykuruan peoples, such as the Toba and Mocoví of present-day north-western Argentina and the Mbayá of northern Paraguay, struck regularly against the Guaraní missions and Spanish cities. Plunder and slaves gained from such raiding were components of a multifaceted engagement

---

[10] María Elena Martínez, *Genealogical Fictions: Limpieze de Sangre, Religion, and Gender in Colonial Mexico* (Palo Alto, CA, 2008).

[11] Robin Wright, 'Destruction, Resistance, and Transformation: Southern, Coastal, and Northern Brazil (1580–1890)', in Solomon and Schwartz (eds.), *Cambridge History*, iii/2. 304–11; James Schofield Saeger, 'Warfare, Reorganization, and Readaptation at the Margins of Spanish Rule: The Chaco and Paraguay (1573–1882)', ibid. 266–79; Barbara Ganson, *The Guaraní under Spanish Rule in the Río de la Plata* (Palo Alto, CA, 2003), 61–83.

[12] Wright, 'Destruction, Resistance, and Transformation', 295, 299.

with the Atlantic economy. Slaughtering wild cattle and other game produced hides that, with surplus horses, could be sold to the Spanish. Mbayá people raised sheep, spun wool, and harvested forest goods such as honey and *yerba maté*. Such activity as well as the ransoming of captives and the sale of booty sustained an active, if sometimes dangerous, commerce with Europeans. Meanwhile, the Payaguá acted variously as brokers, kidnappers, thieves, spies, commercial fishermen, and diplomats.[13]

Still further beyond the reach of European sovereignty, indigenous inhabitants of present-day Nicaragua, Panama, and Columbia also exploited opportunities of the Atlantic world, trading on the margins of Spain's imperial control with British, French, and Dutch merchants. On the Caribbean coasts of Venezuela and Honduras, the incorporation of African populations gave new life to Caribs and Miskitos. Meantime, Miskito, Cuna, and Guajiro peoples negotiated trade alliances to secure markets for their hides, animal and vegetal dyes, slaves, gold, pearls, cocoa, hardwoods, cattle, and tortoise shells. Similar patterns emerged in what is now Chile and Patagonia, where, by 1750, Araucanian people had, for at least five generations, raised horses, used metal tools to grow wheat and barley, and produced other commodities for the Atlantic market. Here, as throughout the Americas, native peoples reinvented themselves as 'modern Indians'.[14]

After mid-century, the equilibria of indigenous connections to the Atlantic world began to collapse everywhere. The key event was the Seven Years War, which removed the French empire from North America and forced both Britain and Spain to attempt major imperial reforms.[15] The war had many roots in Europe and its far-flung colonies, but the fighting began in North America's Ohio country. In the long run, the British— or rather the metastasizing agricultural populations of Pennsylvania and Virginia— were responsible. In the short run, the French provoked conflict by staking a formal claim to territory coveted by the British and by building a line of forts connecting the Great Lakes to the site of modern Pittsburgh. Nursing grudges against British officials who had deprived them of lands further east, the majority of the Shawnees, Delawares, and others in the region took up arms with the French. Supplied from Fort Duquesne, warriors killed squatters and burned cabins wherever Pennsylvanians and Virginians had settled on lands that Indians—despite words on British treaty documents—still considered their own.[16]

In doing so, many of those warriors were inspired by religious prophets who, at least since the late 1740s, had been preaching rejection of the European Atlantic world, its

---

[13] Wright, 'Distruction, Resistance, and Transformation', 324–8; Saeger, 'Warfare, Reorganization, and Readaptation', 260–3.

[14] Kristine Jones, 'Warfare, Reorganization, and Readaptation at the Margins of Spanish Rule: The Southern Margin, 1573–1882', in Solomon and Schwartz (eds.), *Cambridge History*, iii/2. 139–59; David J. Weber, *Bárbaros: Spaniards and their Savages in the Age of Enlightenment* (New Haven, CT, 2005), 54, 75.

[15] Eliga H. Gould, 'Entangled Histories, Entangled Worlds: The English-Speaking Atlantic as a Spanish Periphery', *American Historical Review*, 112 (2007), 779–80.

[16] Fred Anderson, *Crucible of War: The Seven Years' War and the Fate of Empire in British North America, 1754–1766* (New York, 2000), 5–73.

goods, and its empires. 'This land where ye dwell I have made for you and not for others,' the Master of Life told the most famous of the prophets, the Delaware known as Neolin; 'as to those who come to trouble your lands—drive them out, make war upon them'. In preparation for the great struggle, Neolin enjoined his followers 'to quit the use of fire arms, and to live entirely in [your] original state that [you] were in before the white people found out [your] country'. Neolin's followers probably did not literally believe that war against Europeans could be won without guns, but his call to ritual cleansing repudiated all that the Atlantic world had come to represent.[17]

For half a century after the Seven Years War, prophets throughout the eastern North American continental interior preached similar messages seeking to unify 'Red people' across ethnic and linguistic lines. Some of these figures, such as Tenskwatawa, the early nineteenth-century 'Shawnee Prophet', were well known to whites, while others functioned behind the scenes. Purists among them had no patience for balance-of-power politics or accommodations with Europeans, and they gained widest hearing when the possibilities for playing white people off against each other were bleakest.[18]

The Treaty of Paris of 1763, which ended the Seven Years War, made New France and La Florida British, while it transferred French Louisiana to the Spanish. Already before the treaty had been signed, British commander-in-chief Sir Jeffrey Amherst asserted British hegemony when he announced that trade with Indians would be confined to army posts, that no weapons, ammunition, or rum would be sold to native customers, and that the expensive custom of diplomatic gift-giving would cease. Indians responded by resuming their warfare against the British. In 1763, during 'Pontiac's War', nativists destroyed most British posts west of the Appalachians and killed, captured, or evicted colonial squatters who had entered their lands since the conquest of New France.[19]

In 1764 and 1765 with relatively little bloodshed, British military forces regained some control, principally by reversing Amherst's approach and negotiating with native leaders while restoring the flow of trade goods and diplomatic gifts. In effect, the British military and a small group of crown-appointed officials assumed the role that the French had formerly played, providing some counterbalance to land-hungry creoles. Key to the new British approach was the Proclamation of 1763, which attempted to ban settlement west of the Appalachian Mountains. The Proclamation—and the Quebec Act, which in 1774 expanded the boundaries of that province southwards to the Ohio River—denied to British agriculturalists and land speculators access to the lands that many saw as the rightful fruits of war. In the eyes of many

---

[17] [Robert Navarre?], *Journal of Pontiac's Conspiracy*, ed. M. Agnes Burton, trans. R. C. Ford (Detroit, MI, [1912]), 28–30 (first quotation); 'A Narrative of the Captivity of John M'Cullough, Esq.', in Archibald Loudon, *A Selection of Some of the Most Interesting Narratives of Outrages, Committed by the Indians, in their Wars with the White People* (Carlisle, PA, 1808), i. 1, 321 (second quotation).

[18] Gregory Evans Dowd, *A Spirited Resistance: The North American Indian Struggle for Unity, 1745–1815* (Baltimore, MD, 1992).

[19] Gregory Evans Dowd, *War under Heaven: Pontiac, the Indian Nations, and the British Empire* (Baltimore, MD, 2002).

Euro-Americans, the Proclamation placed the British crown on the side of Indians and thus seemed to reward the violence of Pontiac's War. Unsurprisingly, the Proclamation and the Quebec Act became major grievances in the imperial crisis that produced the US War of Independence. Also unsurprisingly, as in the Seven Years War, most native people resumed their own war of independence. Where previously they had relied on French support against the British, now they depended on the British against the nascent United States.[20]

In 1783, when another Treaty of Paris ended the conflict between the United States and Great Britain, the leaders of the newly independent nation, like Amherst before them, tried to treat Native Americans as conquered nations. The treaty did not mention native people at all; it simply transferred to the United States all territory south of the Great Lakes, east of the Mississippi, and north of the Floridas, which were returned to Spain. As one US official crowed, 'We are now Masters of this Island, and can dispose of the Lands as we think proper'; if the Indians were to retain any territory east of the Mississippi, it would be only through the benevolence of the conquerors. In a series of coerced treaties between 1784 and 1786, the United States claimed nearly all of present-day western New York and Pennsylvania and eastern Ohio. Similar seizures, with scant effort to legitimize them by treaty, occurred south of the Ohio, as US citizens poured into Kentucky (designated a state in 1792) and Tennessee (1796).[21]

The Indian people being expelled from these lands, together with their allies throughout the Great Lakes region, inflicted humiliating defeats on the US armies and settlers in 1790 and 1791. While the British governors of Quebec and the newly organized province of Upper Canada remained officially neutral, they proffered material support to the Indians from Detroit and other forts that, contrary to the Treaty of 1783, they continued to control south of the lakes. British agents led their allies to believe that royal troops could be counted on if needed. Yet the failure of such help in August 1794, when troops under Anthony Wayne invaded Indian country, turned a relatively minor US victory at the Battle of Fallen Timbers into a triumph. Within months, word arrived that, in Jay's Treaty of 1794, Britain had agreed to withdraw from the posts in the north-west, leaving the Indians to confront the United States alone. At the Treaty of Greenville in 1795, their leaders made peace.[22]

In that treaty, the United States had to conform to Indian conventions of diplomacy and gift-giving that it had once scorned. In spectacle and numbers of participants— more than 1,000 attended—nothing like the Greenville Treaty had been seen since the Seven Years War. The negotiations were protracted and, if ultimately disadvantageous to the Native Americans, they followed a process that most of them considered

---

[20] Richter, *Facing East from Indian Country*, 206–23.

[21] Samuel Hazard et al. (eds.), *Pennsylvania Archives* (Philadelphia, PA, 1852–1949), 1st Series, x. 45 (quotation); Reginald Horsman, 'The Indian Policy of an "Empire for Liberty" ', in Frederick E. Hoxie, Ronald Hoffman, and Peter J. Albert (eds.), *Native Americans and the Early Republic* (Charlottesville, VA, 1999), 37–8.

[22] Wiley Sword, *President Washington's Indian War: The Struggle for the Old Northwest, 1790–1795* (Norman, OK, 1985).

legitimate. Thereafter, as long as the British remained in Upper Canada and the Spanish in Louisiana, the return to diplomacy and trade held out the prospect that balance-of-power politics might work once again.[23]

But the Treaty of Greenville, like many others the United States negotiated in the 1790s and early 1800s, revealed fundamental ways in which native North Americans had lost the ability to engage autonomously with the Atlantic world of empires. Greenville invalidated the controversial treaties of 1784–6 and purchased from the Indians the southern and eastern two-thirds of the present-day state of Ohio for goods worth $20,000 and perpetual annual annuity payments of $9,500. Such annuity payments became typical in subsequent years. At first glance, the old system of diplomatic presents seemed restored, in that annuities were left to chiefs to dispense. Yet by becoming a routine annual subvention rather than the product of specific negotiations between particular chiefs and imperial powers, annuities converted Indian nations into recipients of handouts rather than extractors of tribute.[24]

The trading arrangements enshrined in the new republic's Indian treaties similarly disempowered native communities. Licensing requirements for traders and centralization of distribution in Federal 'factories' gave US officials, not native people themselves, control of Indian engagement with the Atlantic economy. Even more disempowering were the terms under which the Greenville treaty and its successors guaranteed native ownership of land. 'When those tribes...shall be disposed to sell their lands', the Greenville document said, 'they are to be sold only to the United States.' Indians had no right to proffer their lands to the highest bidder, or, according to subsequent decisions by US courts and state and federal governments, no right to lease them to private citizens or in any other way turn them to profitable gain on their own terms.[25]

All of this went hand in hand with a broader federal strategy formulated by US secretary at war Henry Knox. His 'civilization' programme, which remained influential well into the nineteenth century, pressured Indian people to abandon their traditional economy of male hunting, female hoe agriculture, and communal landholding in favour of male plough agriculture and animal husbandry, female domesticity, and private property. Administered by federal agents and Christian missionaries, given at least lip-service by chiefs increasingly dependent on federal annuity payments, and funded by those same payments, this move towards a 'civilized' way of life was also designed to have Indians prosper on a much smaller land base, thus opening up surplus territory for white farmers.[26]

---

[23] Andrew R. L. Cayton, ' "Noble Actors" upon "the Theatre of Honour": Power and Civility in the Treaty of Greenville', in Cayton and Fredrika J. Teute, (eds.), *Contact Points: American Frontiers from the Mohawk Valley to the Mississippi, 1750–1830* (Chapel Hill, NC, 1998), 252–67.

[24] Charles J. Kappler (ed.), *Indian Affairs: Laws and Treaties*, vol. ii (Washington, DC, 1904), 39–45.

[25] Ibid. ii. 42 (quotation); Alan Taylor, *The Divided Ground: Indians, Settlers, and the Northern Borderland of the American Revolution* (New York, 2006), 403–7; Stuart Banner, *How the Indians Lost their Land: Laws and Power on the Frontier* (Cambridge, MA, 2005), 112–90.

[26] Bernard W. Sheehan, *Seeds of Extinction: Jeffersonian Philanthropy and the American Indian* (Chapel Hill, NC, 1973), 119–81.

The civilization programme did ultimately achieve the last goal—particularly as chiefs and individuals ran up debts for consumer goods, sold off lands to pay the bills, and thus fulfilled the prophecy that they no longer could rely on large hunting territories to participate in the fur and hide trades. But the emphasis on subsistence agriculture for men and homespun cloth for women had the paradoxical effect of *disengaging* native North Americans from Atlantic connections. Had the civilization project succeeded in turning Indians into self-sufficient farmers and spinners, they would have become virtually the only nineteenth-century North Americans (apart from a handful of utopian religious communalists) completely uninvolved in the Atlantic economy.[27]

As long as tensions remained high and borders porous between Canada and the United States, and as long as the Spanish of Louisiana and Florida remained a potential counterbalance in the south, native leaders could hope to find alternative markets and remain in control of their engagement with the Atlantic economy. The Louisiana Purchase, which transferred to the United States most of the trans-Mississippi west, including the important trading centres of New Orleans and St Louis, dashed those hopes. The grim reality was brought home to native leaders in a series of treaties they were forced to accept in the years before 1810, ceding what is now southern Indiana, most of Illinois, and parts of Wisconsin, Missouri, Tennessee, Georgia, Alabama, and Mississippi to the only entity to which they were permitted to sell.[28]

These developments inspired a new upwelling of nativism, through the interconnected movements of Tenskwatawa and his brother Tecumseh in the north and the Creek 'Red Sticks' in the south—movements that took advantage of the outbreak of war between the United States and Great Britain in 1812 to wage one last continent-spanning crusade for native independence. Like their predecessors in Pontiac's War, those who took up arms heard calls to reject the goods and influences of the Atlantic world, but, for the Red Sticks at least, 'mixed blood' accommodationists among the Creeks increasingly became the most reviled enemies.

Tecumseh was killed in battle in October 1813. Five months later, Andrew Jackson waged a scorched-earth campaign against the Red Sticks. These defeats were sealed in Euro-American diplomacy by the Treaty of Ghent in 1814, which made final peace between the USA and Great Britain, and by the Adams–Onís Treaty of 1820, which ceded Spanish Florida to the United States. Left to face a sole imperial power alone, native people strove to preserve their autonomy in countless ways. The most successful initially were those among the Creeks, Cherokees, Choctaws, Chickasaws, and Seminoles who attempted to beat their would-be conquerors at their own game,

---

[27] Daniel K. Richter, ' "Believing that Many of the Red People Suffer Much for the Want of Food": Hunting, Agriculture, and a Quaker Construction of Indianness in the Early Republic', *Journal of the Early Republic*, 19 (1999), 601–28.

[28] Reginald Horsman, *Expansion and American Indian Policy, 1783–1812* (East Lansing, MI, 1967), 104–69.

drafting written constitutions, electing their own governments, moving towards private property, and establishing cotton plantations worked by enslaved African labourers.

In every case, these developments (not entirely accurately associated with a 'mixed blood' elite that elsewhere in the western hemisphere would be called mestizos) were resisted by those who (also not entirely accurately) saw the advocates of 'civilization' as betrayers of traditional values who continued to embrace communal landholding and older gender and economic roles. Such internal divisions—which sometimes led traditionalists to argue paradoxically for exchanging eastern territory for lands west of the Mississippi where they could be left alone—further weakened the ability of Indian people collectively to resist the relentless pressure of US officials, of traders with their mounting books of debts, and of opportunities to profit personally by selling out. These trends set the stage for the Jacksonian era's Removal policy, whereby most Indians east of the Mississippi lost their lands.[29]

As revolutionary movements swept through the former Spanish empire, newly independent nations often treated indigenous communities in ways that would have been familiar in the early nineteenth-century United States. The similarities emerged, however, from quite different late eighteenth-century experiences. In 1762, Spain belatedly entered the Seven Years War as an ally of France, with disastrous results. Unable to collect adequate funds or mobilize effective defence of Caribbean and South Atlantic coasts, Latin America showed itself imperilled. Eyeing a continent where half the landmass was still effectively ruled by independent Indians, where 400 state-subsidized Jesuit missions operated untaxed and uncontrolled by the crown, and where an underground economy thrived because of ineffective bureaucratic controls, the crown accelerated the centralizing and modernizing programme known as the Bourbon Reforms.[30]

Central to that effort was the policy of *comercio libre*, or free trade. By multiplying legal channels for Spanish trade, and breaking monopolies in both Seville and the Americas, *comercio libre* stimulated economic growth and boosted tax revenue. It also shifted trade and political power eastwards, away from Quito and Lima towards the Atlantic coast. These developments spurred the growth of such eastern seaboard cities as Buenos Aires in Argentina and São Paulo, Rio de Janeiro, and Colónia do Sacramento in Brazil. At the same time, the wealthy *criollo* merchants who had controlled former trade routes had to look elsewhere for income. Some invested in silver mines in northern Mexico, while others diversified into producing wheat, maguey, cocoa, cochineal, cattle hides, tobacco, or wool for urban consumers in both Latin America and Europe. In northern Mexico, Peru, Bolivia, Paraguay, and Argentina haciendas expanded, expropriating indigenous lands and placing enormous pressure on indigenous labour.[31]

[29] R. David Edmunds, *Tecumseh and the Quest for American Indian Leadership* (Boston, MA, 1984); William G. McLoughlin, *Cherokee Renascence in the New Republic* (Princeton, NJ, 1986).

[30] J. H. Elliott, *Empires of the Atlantic World: Britain and Spain in America, 1492–1830* (New Haven, CT, 2006), 292–324.

[31] Adrian Pearce, *British Trade with Spanish America, 1763–1808* (Liverpool, 2007), 53–5, 62–5; Weber, *Bárbaros*, 192–3.

Accompanying the economic transformations was a new approach to relations with independent native peoples, one modelled after that of France in North America and influenced by experiences in newly Spanish Louisiana. This approach stressed coexistence through commerce, treaty negotiations, and diplomatic gifting. The impact was most dramatic on the northern frontiers of New Spain where, beginning in the 1780s, Navajos, Apaches, and Comanches benefited from the policy and, particularly in the case of the Comanches, exploited it to become the strongest powers in the region.[32]

In general, indigenous communities in New Spain initially found little to fear from the Bourbon Reforms. Through sophisticated engagement with the Spanish legal system and the mercantile economy, Indians in Oaxaca and central and north-eastern Mexico defended their territorial integrity and remained largely autonomous. Nahuatl-speakers in the north-east welcomed growing mining complexes, while, to the south, in Oaxaca, imperial reform, especially that concerning credit, as well as urban growth, shored up Mixtec and Zapotec economies. These developments gave native elites capital to expand production of cochineal, while indigenous smallholders gained markets for grains and beef in Puebla and other expanding cities.[33]

Chiapas and the Yucatán Peninsula as well as the north-western provinces of Mexico fared less well. Mining expansion threatened the arable lands of the Yaquis, Mayos, and Pimas, as creole ranchers spread westwards to provision urban markets. Meanwhile, the demand for workers in these enterprises embroiled Yaquis, Jesuits, and provincial Spanish governors in a struggle over the control of Indian labour tribute. This controversy, coupled with drought and poor harvests, provoked rebellions in 1740 and again in 1751. Ultimately, however, the rebels came to terms with colonial authorities. After 1751, most Yaquis and Mayos immersed themselves in the market economy, raising mules, importing Atlantic goods, and working in the mines for modest wages. Pimas were more resistant to change, many choosing flight over incorporation. To the south, the Mayan communities of Chiapas and the Yucatán Peninsula also withdrew beyond the reach of the state. From forest refuges, lowland Maya funnelled Atlantic goods, such as cocoa and cotton, to *pueblos de indios*. This intra-Mayan trade mitigated the impacts of colonial tribute, as it allowed many Indians to pay in kind rather than labour.[34]

Some communities more unambiguously profited from Spanish imperial policies, notably the Guaykuru-speaking Mbayá people of the Gran Chaco. The reorientation of trade towards Buenos Aires not only widened the buffer zone between Spanish Chile and Portuguese Brazil but also fostered trade between Bolivia, the Argentine interior, and Buenos Aires. To encourage settlement in the region, Bourbon officials built forts

---

[32] Pekka Hämäläinen, *The Comanche Empire* (New Haven, CT, 2009); Brian DeLay, *War of a Thousand Deserts: Indian Raids and the U.S.–Mexican War* (New Haven, CT, 2009).

[33] Frye, 'Native Peoples of Northeastern Mexico', 121–3.

[34] Susan Deeds, *Defiance and Deference in Mexico's Colonial North: Indians under Spanish Rule in Nueva Vizcaya* (Austin, TX, 2003); W. George Lovell, 'The Highland Maya', in Solomon and Schwartz (eds.), *Cambridge History*, iii/2. 417–19; Grant D. Jones, 'The Lowland Mayas: From the Conquest to the Present', ibid. 367–74.

near existing towns and along river routes. These put the Mbayá people in a position to play off imperial powers much as their counterparts in North America had long done. Some Mbayá *caciques* allied with the Portuguese, traded appropriated Spanish livestock, and harvested *yerba maté* to trade for guns and ammunition. Others made alliances with Spain, exchanging intelligence about the Portuguese for gifts and official recognition of Mbayá independence.[35]

Guaraní-speakers, meantime, suffered from another facet of the Bourbon Reforms, the expulsion of the Jesuits from Latin America in 1767. The era's economic and political changes had already disrupted the world of the mission Guaraní. To rein in the unregulated trade of the South Atlantic, Spain's Ferdinand VI ceded all lands east of the Río Uruguay to Portugal in the 1750 Treaty of Madrid. In return, Portugal yielded Colónia do Sacramento and the northern shore of the Río de la Plata. The treaty stipulated the forced eviction of some 30,000 Guaraní from the newly acquired Portuguese territory. The Guaraní resisted, first through peaceful appeals to the two crowns, and then through a military uprising that was quashed in 1756 by a combined Spanish–Portuguese force.[36]

Iberian officials blamed the Jesuits for inciting the insurrection, thus providing further ammunition for plans to expel the order from Spanish domains. More than 2,000 priests and missionaries were affected by the Spanish edict of 1767. (The Portuguese had already expelled the order in 1759.) Approximately 400 *reducciones* reverted to the crown and ultimately wound up in the hands of opportunistic *hacendados*, peasants, ranchers, and recent immigrants hostile to native interests. Unscrupulous officials stole mission herds, illegally sold Indian land to peasants and speculators, and forced Guaraní people to labour on nearby haciendas. Artisanal and husbandry skills acquired under Jesuit tutelage allowed several thousand people to abandon the *reducciones* for the cities of Argentina and Paraguay. The malnourished and overworked Indians who remained suffered all the depredations of mission life with none of the countervailing benefits of the Jesuit regime.[37]

The situation was equally grim for other indigenous people. Many of the arrangements the Guaykuru, Payaguá, and Guaraní had made with officials, settlers, and merchants had already been upset by the general reorientation of regional trade and population flows during the 1740s and 1750s. Spanish encroachment on Indian lands destroyed the wild herds and forest commodities that the Guaykuru had depended upon. Within the past generation or so over-hunting had exhausted stocks of feral cattle, while smallpox and other epidemic diseases along with wars of attrition had devastated Guaykuru populations.[38]

[35] Weber, *Bárbaros*, 162–201.
[36] Wright, 'Destruction, Resistance, and Transformation', 310–11, 322–4.
[37] Saeger, 'Warfare, Reorganization, and Readaptation', 275–80; Ganson, *Guaraní*, 93–102, 125–9.
[38] James Schofield Saeger, 'Another View of the Mission as a Frontier Institution: The Guaycuruan Reductions of Santa Fe', *Hispanic American Historical Review*, 65 (1985), 496–500.

Even greater woes befell the native peoples of Peru and Bolivia. For people of the Andean highlands, the troubles stretched back to the 1720s, when epidemics, catastrophic weather, and two earthquakes had left more than one-third of the population dead. In the 1730s administrative reforms and commercial expansion pushed many highland people to the brink of annihilation. The implementation of *padrones de tributarios* (lists of tributaries) shifted colonial obligations from communities to individual households, shattering communal bonds that had mitigated imperial pressures. The system of *reparto de mercancías* (forced sale of goods), which emerged informally about the same time and was legally enshrined in 1754, was intended to shuttle excess goods from Lima's saturated ports to under-served rural markets. In practice, however, it saddled indigenous people with un-payable debts to both merchants and the colonial state. Under these circumstances, many Indians abandoned their communities to work as wage labourers for nearby haciendas, *obrajes* (textile manufactories), or mines. Others rebelled, considering the *reparto* and tributary lists egregious betrayals of reciprocal obligations that delegitimized colonial authority.[39]

Most eruptions of violence were spontaneous local affairs that ended with either the murder or eviction of abusive *caciques* or colonial officials. The messianic leader Juan Santos Atahuallpa, however, envisioned more sweeping transformation. From 1742 to 1756, this Jesuit-educated distant descendant of the last Inca ruler executed by the sixteenth-century *conquistadores* ruled a rebel kingdom in the eastern Amazonian jungles of northern Peru. For Santos and his followers, 'the Spaniards' time [was] up'. Like the nativists of North America, Santos severed his realm from Atlantic trade networks and rid his territory of all things Spanish, favouring the bounty of the jungle and the manufactures of his indigenous subjects over imported goods. The prophecy of an end to Spanish hegemony and the millenarian return of Incan rule resonated among Andean societies long after 1756, when Spaniards finally suppressed Santos's rebellion.[40]

These themes exploded in the Andean Insurrections of 1780 to 1783, which led to the loss of perhaps 10,000 Spanish and 100,000 Indian lives. A man born with the name Juan Gabriel Condorcanqui had, like Santos, been educated by Jesuits and similarly traced his ancestry to the last Inca. Assuming the title of his supposed forebear, he proclaimed himself 'Túpac Amaru II' and created a movement that attracted peasants of varied ethnic backgrounds oppressed by taxes and economic dislocation. As defeats mounted and Túpac Amaru failed to win to his side the region's mestizo elite, he called for the extermination of all who rejected his authority. In this respect, the Andean Insurrections less resembled Pontiac's War than the Creek Red Stick movement, which would similarly focus much of its wrath on a mixed-race elite and ultimately identify mestizos among its enemies.[41]

[39] Saignes, 'Colonial Condition in Quechua-Aymara', 38–48.

[40] Luis Miguel Glave, 'The "Republic of Indians" in Revolt (*c.*1680–1790)', trans. Eileen Willingham, in Solomon and Schwartz (eds.), *Cambridge History*, iii/2. 508–24 (quotation from 521).

[41] David Garrett, '"His Majesty's Most Loyal Vassals": The Indian Nobility and Túpac Amaru', *Hispanic American Historical Review*, 84 (2004), 575–7.

And, as would be the case with the Red Sticks, the Andean movement provoked a brutal military conquest. Captured and sentenced by a royal court in 1781, Túpac Amaru witnessed the public execution of his wife and son before being drawn and quartered in the city of Cuzco. To the south-east in La Paz, a rebel, born Julián Apasa, proclaimed himself Túpac Catari and assumed the mantle of the slain Inca king, who, he claimed, had ordered him 'to put the knife to all *corregidores*, their ministers, *caciques*, collectors, and other dependents; likewise all *chapetones*, Creoles, women, and children without regard for sex and age, and every person who may be or seem to be Spanish, or at least dressed in imitation of such Spaniards'. Within a year, however, that rebellion too was crushed, and the immensity and virulence of the insurrections caused *criollo* elites in Peru and Bolivia to cling to the security of Spanish protection.[42]

In scale and carnage, the Andean Insurrections dwarfed anything in North America during the late eighteenth and early nineteenth centuries. But as was the case with Pontiac's War, the Andean Revolt was followed by creole independence movements and civil wars throughout Latin America that, for a time, created opportunities for autonomous native groups to play sides off against each other. Unlike in North America, the choice between rebels and royalists was seldom clear-cut. As in North America, however, once the creole regimes consolidated power, they systematically curtailed the ability of indigenous people to engage autonomously with the Atlantic world.

The process reached similar ends by different means in former Portuguese and Spanish possessions. In 1808, to escape Napoleon's invading armies, Dom João VI, king of Portugal, fled Lisbon and transferred his court to Rio de Janeiro. His arrival triggered a campaign to pacify frontiers and expand European occupation that continued after Brazil became an independent monarchy in 1822. Wars against the Botocudo, the Mura, and other indigenous peoples reinvigorated the slave trade, which devastated native populations. Repeatedly, indigenous peoples confronted a difficult choice: accept Brazilian suzerainty, which entailed forced relocation, settlement, and onerous labour obligations; or retreat deep into the Amazon where, into the twenty-first century, their hopes for survival would depend on isolation from the Atlantic world.[43]

Policy and ideology varied greatly across the many new nations that emerged from the ruins of the Spanish empire. In the wake of the Andean Insurrections, Peruvians and Bolivians paid little heed to indigenous rights. Elsewhere, juridical equality and *mestizaje* were proclaimed as ideals, but nonetheless the practical result for indigenous people was a relentless assault on communal rights won under the Spanish regime. After Mexico won its independence in 1821, for example, legislators expanded the definition of *terreos baldíos* (vacant lands that could be auctioned off to new owners) to include communal property that either lay fallow or was held for ceremonial

---

[42] Tupac Catari, 'Order to Kill Officials and Spaniards, Including Women and Children', in Ward Stavig and Ella Schmidt (eds.), *The Tupac Amaru and Catarista Rebellions: An Anthology of Sources* (Indianapolis, IN, 2008), 224.

[43] Wright, 'Destruction, Resistance, and Transformation', 308, 328, 371.

purposes. By 1830, Mexico discontinued the practice of diplomatic gift-giving that had prevailed since the 1780s, joining the United States in depriving indigenous communities of political power as well as land. Similarly, in the 1820s, the Argentine regime of Juan Manuel Rosas had resettled what it called *indios amigos* in frontier locations and paid them annuities in the form of foodstuffs, clothing, livestock, and alcohol. In subsequent decades, Uruguayans, Chileans, and Paraguayans conquered autonomous peoples, resettled or enslaved the survivors, and expanded cattle production into their lands. Nearly everywhere autonomous Indian nations increasingly came to be described as irredeemable 'savages'. To conquer the long-independent Araucanians, a Chilean commentator would say in the 1850s, meant 'the triumph of civilization over barbarism, or humanity over bestiality'.[44]

Throughout the Americas, then, creoles who proclaimed themselves civilized arrogated to themselves the terms on which native peoples could, or could not, engage with the Atlantic world. Everywhere, government policies forced peoples who had once managed their own dealings with Atlantic markets either into subordinated incorporation into the creole order or into a position of economic dependency on unproductive lands. Both fates meant disengagement from the systems of Atlantic production and consumption in which they had once participated. In the connections thus severed lie the roots of the ongoing dilemmas of twenty-first-century indigenous peoples who are once again seeking sovereignty in a global world.

BIBLIOGRAPHY

Baskes, Jeremy, *Indians, Merchants, and Markets: A Reinterpretation of the Repartimiento and Spanish-Indian Economic Relations in Colonial Oaxaca, 1750–1821* (Palo Alto, CA, 2000).

Braund, Kathryn E. Holland, *Deerskins and Duffels: The Creek Indian Trade with Anglo-America, 1685–1815* (Lincoln, NE, 1993).

Cohen, Paul, 'Was There an Amerindian Atlantic? Reflections on the Limits of a Historiographical Concept', *History of European Ideas*, 34 (2008), 388–410.

Dowd, Gregory Evans, *A Spirited Resistance: The North American Indian Struggle for Unity, 1745–1815* (Baltimore, MD, 1992).

Elliot, J. H., *Empires of the Atlantic World: Britain and Spain in America, 1492–1830* (New Haven, CT, 2006).

Gallay, Allan, *The Indian Slave Trade: The Rise of the English Empire in the American South, 1670–1717* (New Haven, CT, 2002).

Langfur, Hal, *The Forbidden Lands: Colonial Identity, Frontier Violence, and the Persistence of Brazil's Eastern Indians, 1750–1830* (Palo Alto, CA, 2006).

[44] Weber, *Bárbaros*, 267–8, quotation from 275.

Taylor, Alan, *The Divided Ground: Indians, Settlers, and the Northern Borderland of the American Revolution* (New York, 2006).

Van Young, Eric, *Hacienda and Market in Eighteenth-Century Mexico: The Rural Economy of the Guadalajara Region, 1675–1820* (Berkeley, CA, 1981).

Weber, David, *Bárbaros: Spaniards and their Savages in the Age of the Enlightenment* (New Haven, CT, 2005).

White, Richard, *The Middle Ground: Indians, Empires, and Republics in the Great Lakes Region, 1650–1815* (Cambridge, 1991).

CHAPTER 30

THE AMERICAN REVOLUTION IN ATLANTIC PERSPECTIVE

DAVID ARMITAGE

WHILE there is general agreement that the American Revolution was the first Atlantic revolution, eighteenth-century observers, transatlantic revolutionaries, and recent historians have differed over what it might mean to put the Revolution into Atlantic perspective. For some, it marked the first time any European overseas dependencies had cast off metropolitan rule to secure self-government: this was a new form of revolution, secessionist in form and anti-imperial in purpose, and it had originated in the British Atlantic world. For others, it marked the beginning of a sequence of fundamental social and political transformations in the Americas and Europe that would come to include the American and French Revolutions, the Haitian Revolution, and the civil wars and independence movements of Iberian America. And historians writing in the aftermath of the Second World War saw the American Revolution as the first act of a 'Democratic Revolution' which spawned a distinctive 'Atlantic Civilization' encompassing North America and much of Western and Central Europe, though not Latin America or the Caribbean.[1] Despite obvious differences of emphasis and ideological intent, these visions of the American Revolution shared two assumptions: that the Atlantic world shaped the Revolution, and that the Revolution shaped the Atlantic world.

These Atlantic perspectives on the Revolution implicitly or explicitly challenged accounts of it as a specifically *American* sequence of events, of defining relevance only to the history of United States. Beginning in the early nineteenth century, American historians of the Revolution had lionized the patriots who secured American freedom, mythologized their leaders as 'Founding Fathers', and reduced the history of colonial

---

[1] R. R. Palmer, *The Age of the Democratic Revolution: A Political History of Europe and America, 1760–1800*, 2 vols. (Princeton, NJ, 1959–64); Bernard Bailyn, *Atlantic History: Concept and Contours* (Cambridge, MA, 2005), 4–30.

settlement in mainland North America to the long-drawn-out prelude to independent nationhood. Such self-affirming stories ignored many key features of the Revolution and its history. By emphasizing the growth of American identity, they ignored the close links between Britain and its colonies before 1776. By concentrating on the Thirteen Colonies that seceded in 1776, they consigned the colonies in North America and the West Indies that did not rebel to the histories of Canada, the Caribbean, and the British empire. By hymning heroism and sacrifice, they suppressed the spectre of revolutionary violence along with the anti-libertarian tendencies of the Revolution, particularly for the hundreds of thousands of the enslaved. And, more generally, they failed to tease out those aspects of the causes, course, and consequences of the Revolution which overflowed what became the national borders of the United States.

Beginning in the 1770s, revolutionary ideologues such as Thomas Jefferson and Thomas Paine had portrayed the unfolding Atlantic crisis as one of *disintegration*. Jefferson related how 'the free inhabitants of the British dominions in Europe' established 'new societies, under such laws and regulations as to them . . . seem[ed] most likely to promote public happiness'. These white settlers created creole communities distinct from, and increasingly morally superior to, the corrupted Old World they had left behind. An era of 'salutary neglect' by Britain in the mid-eighteenth century encouraged this flourishing of colonial distinctiveness. However, the aftermath of the Seven Years War (1756–63) demanded greater regulation from the centre along with increased fiscal exactions. These external impositions expanded the sense of physical and psychological distance between the settlers and the metropole which Britain's use of military force against the colonists only exacerbated. Loyalty to Britain led to the voicing of grievances and inevitably to exit from the British empire in 1776. 'Every thing that is right or reasonable pleads for separation,' Paine concluded in January 1776: 'The blood of the slain, the weeping voice of nature cries, 'TIS TIME TO PART.' This linear history of liberty, first forged in the pre-revolution, remains the standard American narrative of national origins to this day.[2]

More recent historians have described the American Revolution rather as a crisis of *integration* within the British Atlantic world. In this version of events, over the course of more than a century and a half, free white settlers in the mainland colonies implanted English laws, institutions, religion, and customs into landscapes that they shaped according to practices imported from Britain and distinguished from those of native peoples. They brought similar norms to the Lower South and the Caribbean. Settlers in these colonies increasingly deployed the unfree labour of Africans while still congratulating themselves, like other British Americans, on their attachment to English liberties.[3] By the 1730s, the increasing speed and frequency of commerce,

---

[2] [Thomas Jefferson,] *A Summary View of the Rights of British America* (Williamsburg, VA, 1774), 6; [Thomas Paine,] *Common Sense: Addressed to the Inhabitants of America* (Philadelphia, PA, 1776), 38.

[3] T. H. Breen, 'Ideology and Nationalism on the Eve of the American Revolution: Revisions *Once More* in Need of Revising', *Journal of American History*, 84 (1997), 13–39; John M. Murrin, '1776: The Countercyclical Revolution', in Michael A. Morrison and Melinda Zook (eds.), *Revolutionary Currents:*

communications, and migration had united the American colonies, Britain, and Ireland into a single imperial community around the North Atlantic basin. Provincial subjects from the Caribbean and North America and later the inhabitants of the metropole promoted an ideological definition of this British Atlantic empire as uniquely Protestant, commercial, maritime, and free. The cycle of transatlantic warfare from the 1730s to the 1760s confirmed this common Britishness by uniting Atlantic Britons in a sense of shared victory over Spain and France. At the same time, a consumer revolution assimilated patterns of gentility, emulation, and modernity in the colonies ever more closely to those back in Britain. In the two decades before the American Revolution, the various white British communities around the North Atlantic rim were in fact more alike, in cultural practices, economic integration, political ideology, and distinctive self-conception, than they had ever been before. Metropolitan administrators in the 1760s had some reason to believe they were pursuing a logic of transatlantic incorporation which had begun in Britain and Ireland and was quite naturally being expanded to include the American colonies. When their colonial opponents protested against what they saw as novel and unbearable fiscal exactions, they did so 'in terms of fundamental English rights and the British constitution' and thereby only 'underscored the English-speaking Atlantic's growing political unity'.[4]

Institutional diversity within Britain's possessions in the Americas belied that unity. On the eve of the American Revolution, British interests in the western hemisphere stretched from Hudson Bay in the north to the Mosquito Coast in the south. They comprised long-settled colonies such as Virginia and Bermuda as well as the more recently acquired territories of Quebec, Cape Breton, East and West Florida, and the Ceded Islands of Dominica, St Vincent, Grenada, and Tobago, all of which had come to Britain in 1763 from France and Spain after the Seven Years War. They also included the lands overseen by the Hudson's Bay Company, the sparsely populated islands of the Bahamas, logging camps in the Bay of Honduras, and a protectorate over the Miskitu Indians in present-day Nicaragua. Despite many shared norms and experiences, the differences among Britain's various American settlements appeared to be greater than distinctions between the settlements and Britain itself. This differentiation can help to explain why the Revolution occurred at all and also why only some Atlantic Britons joined it in 1776.

Different criteria for counting Britain's disparate possessions yield different aggregate numbers; yet, whether the total is taken to be twenty-six, twenty-nine, or thirty-two, it remains the case that at the very most only half of Britain's American settlements

Nation Building in the Transatlantic World (Lanham, MD, 2004), 65–90; Jack P. Greene, 'Liberty and Slavery: The Transfer of British Liberty to the West Indies, 1627–1865', in id. (ed.), *Exclusionary Empire: English Liberty Overseas, 1600–1900* (Cambridge, 2010), 50–76.

[4] Ian K. Steele, *The English Atlantic, 1675–1740: An Exploration of Communication and Community* (New York, 1986); David Armitage, *The Ideological Origins of the British Empire* (Cambridge, 2000); T. H. Breen, *The Marketplace of Revolution: How Consumer Politics Shaped American Independence* (Oxford, 2004); Eliga H. Gould, 'Revolution and Counter-Revolution', in David Armitage and Michael J. Braddick (eds.), *The British Atlantic World, 1500–1800* (2nd edn. Basingstoke, 2009), 226 (quoted).

seceded from the empire in July 1776. The thirteen colonies that did leave formed a contiguous band hugging the eastern seaboard of North America from New Hampshire to Georgia. None of the islands of the British Atlantic or the Caribbean joined them nor did Nova Scotia, Quebec (which was invited to send delegates to the Continental Congress), and Newfoundland to the north, or the Floridas to the south. Moreover, Native Americans, who had little reason to trust the colonists, mostly remained neutral or allied with Britain during the conflict.[5]

The American Revolution occurred amid an explosion in population and migration, both free and unfree. In the years after 1760, almost a quarter of a million migrants reached British North America from Britain, Ireland, Europe, and Africa, and from 1751 to 1775 an estimated 668,000 people moved to the more demographically destructive British Caribbean. By 1775, some 2.6 million of the roughly 3 million people of British America were living in the territory that would become the United States after independence; one-fifth of them, or some 500,000, were enslaved, the great majority in the southern colonies. The years 1750–1830 marked the zenith of the Atlantic slave trade, when some 4 million Africans were transported to the Americas. The American War disrupted transportation to the mainland colonies, but the trade to the British Caribbean accelerated in the four decades after 1770. New territories had opened up for settlement after the Seven Years War and others, like Nova Scotia, had also become more attractive destinations for free migrants. But such innovations did not translate into revolutionary fervour: quite the opposite. 'The pace of . . . migration had unintended consequences: those colonies that received migrants at the highest rate'—the Floridas, Nova Scotia, and the West Indies, for example—'were those least likely to join the revolutionary colonies'.[6] To explain these patterns, it will be necessary to retrace the course of the Revolution from its beginnings in the aftermath of the Seven Years War and to place its events into the context of Britain's Atlantic empire and the shifting fortunes of the other European empires of the Atlantic world.

CONTESTING SOVEREIGNTY

After the 1760s, all the major European Atlantic empires, British, French, Spanish, and Portuguese, undertook major projects of imperial reform. Defeat in the Seven Years

---

[5] Andrew Jackson O'Shaughnessy, *An Empire Divided: The American Revolution and the British Caribbean* (Philadelphia, PA, 2000), pp. xi, 250 n. 1 (twenty-six); Jack P. Greene, 'Introduction: Empire and Liberty', in id. (ed.), *Exclusionary Empire*, 6 (twenty-nine); Lawrence Henry Gipson, *The British Empire before the American Revolution*, 15 vols. (Caldwell, ID, 1936–70), xiii. 172, 206 (thirty-two); Colin G. Calloway, *The American Revolution in Indian Country: Crisis and Diversity in Native American Communities* (Cambridge, 1995), 29–42.

[6] Bernard Bailyn, *Voyagers to the West: A Passage in the Peopling of America on the Eve of the Revolution* (New York, 1986); Alison Games, 'Migration', in Armitage and Braddick (eds.), *The British Atlantic World, 1500–1800*, 49 (quoted).

War drove France from North America and pressed the French government to reconstitute its navy, to overhaul its commercial policy in the Atlantic world (now centred on the vastly profitable sugar islands of the Caribbean), and to look for means to take vengeance on Britain in any future war. France's cession of Louisiana in 1763 had left Spain as the only European power in North America alongside Britain, though the British capture of Havana during the war had exposed the Spanish Monarchy's vulnerability in the Americas. Spain's new king, Charles III (who ascended the Spanish throne in 1759), and his ministers had initiated a wide-ranging overhaul of his American possessions, with greater oversight from the centre and increased fiscal demands to support much strengthened measures for security. They also looked to British commercial policy in America as a model for greater freedom of trade around the Spanish Atlantic. Such reforms helped to open up divisions in the Americas between long-settled creoles and peninsular Spaniards, but they produced competing visions of the empire rather than any incipient movements for independence. In Portugal, the marquis of Pombal's policy for restructuring the Luso-Brazilian Atlantic empire was distinctly more accommodationist and based on cooperation with Brazil's elites. Pombal watched the course of events in British America closely and drew cautionary lessons for the control of his dominions from Britain's more confrontational strategies. Such mutual surveillance and imperial imitation revealed how deeply entangled the Atlantic empires had become.[7]

Defeat and retreat had forced France and Spain to reform, while the cost of victory compelled Britain to renovate its imperial governance. As Adam Smith noted in 1776, 'The common advantages which every empire derives from the provinces, subject to its dominion, consist, first, in the military force which they furnish for its defence; and, secondly, in the revenue which they furnish for the support of its civil government.' By 1763, the British national debt stood at £132 million and Britain now had to defend new territories in North America, especially the Floridas and Quebec. It also had to police a wide-open western frontier across which the colonists were itching to move and along which Native Americans were determined to protect their own lands. Ministers needed to find ways to make the empire pay at least part of the cost of what Smith called the century's 'colony quarrel[s]' and to share the burden of imperial security, now based for the first time on stationing British troops permanently in North America. In 1764–5, George III's chief minister, George Grenville, put forward measures to strengthen the vice-admiralty courts, regulate the issuance of paper money in the colonies, amend the existing duties on sugar (thereby protecting the British Caribbean economy as well as raising revenue for continental defence), and bring the colonies 'into line with current

---

7 J. H. Elliott, *Empires of the Atlantic World: Britain and Spain in America, 1492–1830* (New Haven, CT, 2006), 292–324; Kenneth Maxwell, *Pombal, Paradox of the Enlightenment* (Cambridge, 1995), chapter 5; Gabriel B. Paquette, *Enlightenment, Governance, and Reform in Spain and its Empire, 1759–1808* (Basingstoke, 2008); 'AHR Forum: Entangled Empires in the Atlantic World', *American Historical Review*, 112 (2007), 710–99.

British practice' in the metropole by levying a stamp duty on legal documents and other printed papers.[8]

The burdens of the Stamp Act (1765) fell unevenly on Britain's various colonies in the western Atlantic. For example, it was to be lightly applied in Quebec, with a five-year grace period before documents in French were to be taxed; the mostly francophone Quebecois paid the duty with relatively little complaint. It weighed heaviest on the West Indies, where rates were higher, the number of potentially taxable transactions was often greater (due to the documentation associated with accelerating land transfers in the Ceded Islands), and the security benefits from the increased revenues were not as immediately obvious. There were disturbances in the Leeward Islands of St Kitts and Nevis against the enforcement of the Act; the two richest British islands, Barbados and Jamaica, complied with the duties, though not without issuing some pamphlets of protest against it. The Act was in force for less than five months before it was repealed. During that time, Jamaica alone generated more revenue than all the other colonies combined.[9]

Repeal of the Stamp Act came in response to violent protests in the mainland colonies. Such opposition had not been widely anticipated in Britain, despite some earlier colonial protests against the Sugar Act (1764). A few voices had been raised in warning, notably that of the Dublin-born MP Isaac Barré, who unwittingly affirmed the unity of the Atlantic empire when he called the protesting American colonists 'Sons of Liberty', a term first used in Irish politics of the 1750s. Opponents of the Stamp Act adopted his appellation as they organized themselves from Massachusetts to Georgia into cells of resistance against 'taxation without representation'.[10] Irish precedent again loomed when the short-lived Rockingham ministry (which succeeded Grenville's) responded to colonial pressure by repealing the Stamp Act in 1766, but issued a Declaratory Act—modelled on similar legislation applied to Ireland in 1720—affirming that Parliament 'had, hath, and of right ought to have, full power and authority' to legislate for the American colonies 'in all cases whatsoever' (6 Geo. III, c. 12).

This Declaratory Act facilitated the next suite of taxes that inflamed the mainland colonists, the so-called Townshend duties of 1767. They comprised a British declaration of independence from the mainland colonial assemblies and their revenue-raising powers by proposing to fund the salaries of royal governors and judges from levies on imports into the colonies, including paper, paint, glass, lead, and tea. In the eyes of the Pitt ministry (successor to the Rockinghamites), these measures were above all necessary to assert Parliament's continuing right to tax the colonies. Protests from the mainland colonies, notably Massachusetts and Virginia, led to menacing British troop

---

[8] Adam Smith, *An Inquiry into the Nature and Causes of the Wealth of Nations*, 2 vols. (London, 1776), ii. 193–4, 223, 585–7; John Derry, 'Government Policy and the American Crisis, 1760–1776', in H. T. Dickinson (ed.), *Britain and the American Revolution* (London, 1998), 50.

[9] Philip Lawson, *The Imperial Challenge: Quebec and Britain in the Age of the American Revolution* (Montreal, 1989), 91–3; O'Shaughnessy, *An Empire Divided*, 84–96.

[10] Neil Longley York, 'The Impact of the American Revolution on Ireland', in Dickinson (ed.), *Britain and the American Revolution*, 231.

movements against possible armed dissent. Tensions in the mainland colonies peaked with the Boston Massacre on 5 March 1770, in which rattled British soldiers killed five members of a jeeringly hostile crowd. On the very same day, on the other side of the Atlantic, Parliament had begun debating repeal of the Townshend Acts. All were ultimately abandoned, except for the duty on tea. The retention of the tea tax saved Britain's rulers from abandoning their right of colonial taxation altogether, while also maintaining the one tax that had brought in significant revenue—estimated at £12,000 a year—even though Dutch smugglers, operating through the West Indies, brought in perhaps three-quarters of the tea the colonies consumed.

In retrospect, the period 1770–3 looks like the calm before the storm. Turbulence was quietly gathering around the globe in credit markets and financial institutions in ways that would have profound consequences for the course of relations between Britain and its American colonies. The early 1770s were boom years across Europe and in the Atlantic world. Credit had become cheap, widely available, and increasingly subject to speculation. In 1772, the bubble burst, bringing ruin to Scottish bankers, British Atlantic merchants, and Virginia tobacco farmers alike. That same year, the East India Company also fell into financial distress brought on by its declining revenues in famine-stricken Bengal, the mounting costs of warfare in South Asia, unrealistic dividend payments on its stock, and vast unsold supplies of China tea. Under the Tea Act of April 1773, the North ministry permitted the Company to ship its tea directly to North America at reduced cost, leading to one of the few moments in history when falling prices have caused public disturbances. American merchants and consumers who were used to trading or drinking smuggled tea had other ideas about this plan to unite the Company-controlled East Indian and the state-sponsored West Indian wings of the British empire. Writing in Patna in the early 1780s, the Persian chronicler Ghulam Husain Khan Tabataba'i observed that the origins of the Revolution could not be disentangled from the imperatives of the East India Company: 'the king of the English [had] maintained these five or six years past, a contest with the people of America . . . on account of the Company's concerns.' Tabataba'i also saw how quickly the ensuing conflict became a world war, as it drew in the Spanish, French, and Dutch, with consequences felt as far away as India.[11]

The gathering global storm had finally hit the colonies when the first East India tea shipments arrived in December 1773. The Company managed to land cargo only in Charleston, while in Boston the consignment stayed on board ship. Protesters, some dressed as Mohawk Indians, pitched 90,000 pounds of tea into the harbour. This was a witty but unignorable affront to Britain's authority in its most combustible American

---

[11] Richard B. Sheridan, 'The British Credit Crisis of 1772 and the American Colonies', *Journal of Economic History*, 20 (1960), 161–86; P. J. Marshall, *The Making and Unmaking of Empires: Britain, India, and America, c.1750–1783* (Oxford, 2005), 211–12, 330–2; Ghulam Husain Khan Tabataba'i, *A Translation of the Sëir Mutaqherin; or View of Modern Times*, trans. Haji Mustafa, 3 vols. (Calcutta, 1789–90), III 331 (quoted), 332–6.

colony.[12] Lord North's government soon made an example of Massachusetts with punitive legislation designed to rule the Atlantic empire by dividing the colonies from one another, and even more specifically by separating Boston from the rest of Massachusetts. The so-called Coercive or Intolerable Acts closed the port of Boston until the East India Company had been reimbursed for its losses; gave greater powers to the governor in appointing judges and a colony council; made provision to move trials out of the colony or to England; and opened the way for troops to be compulsorily billeted in Boston. Within three years, reactions to all of these measures would find their way into the Declaration of Independence as grievances voiced collectively on behalf of all thirteen secessionist colonies, not just by Massachusetts alone.

FROM BRITISH CIVIL WAR TO AMERICAN REVOLUTION

The road from local protests in 1773 to the independence of thirteen colonies in 1776 was far from predetermined. What Jeremy Adelman has written in regard to the Iberian Atlantic empires of the early nineteenth century applies just as well to the British Atlantic empire of the mid-1770s: 'it was not so much separation from empire that was at stake, but how to reconstitute it on new foundations, even by giving it a new centre, or multiple centres'. In an 'age of imperial revolutions', sovereignty was less a source of jurisdictional certainty than a site of fevered contestation within the empires of the Atlantic world from the 1760s to the 1840s.[13] In the case of the British American colonies, including Quebec and Ireland, the decades after 1774 would be a pivotal moment for the elaboration of novel conceptions of sovereignty, within, against, and— for the colonies that rebelled—finally outside of empire. The question of Parliament's right to tax the colonies, and hence the distribution of authority and consent between metropolitan and colonial institutions, was the tinder for this explosive movement.

On each side of the Atlantic, incensed creole settlers, uncomprehending ministers, and their various supporters saw the gathering conflict as a collision of conspiracies. The exploding print culture of the Atlantic world had carried to the colonies a canon of late seventeenth- and early eighteenth-century British political writings which divided the political world into virtuous, commonwealth-minded patriots, and corrupt, self-interested courtiers. That vision would make much sense to angry colonists in the 1760s and 1770s and gave them a ready-made explanation for what might otherwise have

---

[12] Benjamin Carp, *Defiance of the Patriots: The Boston Tea Party and the Making of America* (New Haven, CT, 2010).

[13] Jeremy Adelman, 'Iberian Passages: Continuity and Change in the South Atlantic', in David Armitage and Sanjay Subrahmanyam (eds.), *The Age of Revolutions in Global Context, c.1760–1840* (Basingstoke, 2010), 76; Adelman, 'An Age of Imperial Revolutions', *American Historical Review*, 113 (2008), 319–40.

seemed to be British ministerial incrementalism or simple incompetence. As the crisis heightened, so the conspiracy theories grew more pervervid. By July 1775, Jamaica's Assembly heard from the mainland colonists that there was a 'deliberate plan to destroy, in every part of the empire, the free constitution, for which Britain has been so long and so justly famed'. Later that year, in October 1775, George III himself expressed an equally paranoid reading of the colonists' intentions in a speech to Parliament lambasting the alleged 'authors and promoters of this desperate conspiracy' that was 'manifestly carried on for the purpose of establishing an independent empire'. This was a collision of incompatible but structurally parallel world-views, an ideological struggle on a pan-Atlantic scale.[14]

The redistribution of authority within the Atlantic empire, and not the creation of an authority outside the empire, was the main item on the agenda for the first Continental Congress, which met in Philadelphia in September 1774. Massachusetts took the lead in calling this strictly extra-constitutional meeting. Representatives of the British West Indian islands barely engaged in the debate on the question of rights within the empire, and even condemned the 'folly, madness, and ingratitude' of their 'Northern Brethren'. Quebec's inhabitants would also not be drawn into resistance: indeed, their status became another grievance after Parliament had passed the Quebec Act in June 1774, under which the French settlers retained civil law, were allowed to continue practising Catholicism, had the boundaries of their province extended as far as the Ohio River, and were denied a representative assembly. What else could this betoken to alarmed and increasingly embattled colonists but what one loyal British veteran of the Seven Years War, George Washington, called a 'regular, systematic plan' to substitute tyranny for freedom in North America?[15]

To expose and repel the ministry's alleged tyrannical design, the Continental Congress proposed to enumerate colonial rights, to specify the acts of Parliament that clashed with those rights, and to devise measures rolling back coercive legislation. To exert pressure on the imperial economy, they revived a non-importation movement that had first sprouted in the responses to the Stamp Act and the Townshend duties, now accompanied by a scheme for domestic production. The Continental Association signed by representatives of twelve colonies in October 1774 protested against 'a ruinous system of colony administration . . . evidently calculated for inslaving these Colonies'. It banned the import or consumption of British and Irish goods and the export of American goods to Britain, Ireland, or the British Caribbean. It also specified that the colonies would not 'import any East-India tea from any part of the world; nor any molasses, syrrups, paneles [unrefined sugar], coffee or piemento, from the British

---

[14] Bernard Bailyn, *The Ideological Origins of the American Revolution* (rev. edn. Cambridge, MA, 1992), chapters 3–4; 'Address to the Assembly of Jamaica' (25 July 1775), in James H. Hutson (ed.), *A Decent Respect to the Opinions of Mankind: Congressional State Papers, 1774–1776* (Washington, DC, 1975), 135; *His Majesty's Most Gracious Speech to Both Houses of Parliament, on Friday, October 27, 1775* (sc. 26 October 1775) (Philadelphia, PA, [1776]), broadside.

[15] O'Shaughnessy, *An Empire Divided*, 128; George Washington, 4 July 1774, quoted in Elliott, *Empires of the Atlantic World*, 339.

plantations, or from Dominica; nor wines from Madeira, or the Western Islands; nor foreign indigo'; they would also suspend the slave trade. By listing commodities from China, the Caribbean, the Atlantic islands, Bengal, and Africa, even in the act of abjuring them, Congress affirmed that the colonies' connections extended to every part of Britain's formal and informal empire around the world.[16]

The Association presented a thoroughgoing attack on the commercial foundations of that global empire: by 1772–3, roughly a quarter of Britain's exports had been going to the colonies. It also had tangible consequences for economic circulation around the British Atlantic world, as Ireland gradually became the major source of supplies for the West Indies. The white plantocracy of the islands had feared that the loss of their supplies would create famine and possibly encourage slave rebellions, leading them to lean ever more heavily on Britain for military and other support. Anxiety and dependency further divided the Caribbean elites (who were anyway more culturally disposed to see Britain as home) from those of the mainland colonies. The boycott's effects were also felt throughout those colonies, as local committees of inspection policed the ban by intruding into many aspects of daily life, from what people wore to what appeared on their tea tables. Women became frontline political actors by forswearing tea and creating home-spun clothing. Domestic production and consumption in the continental colonies thereby became increasingly aligned with virtue and a sense of moral distance from both Britain and its Caribbean colonies.[17]

Few colonists may have envisaged political independence in 1774 but the non-importation movement helped to make independence conceivable in the longer term. Even after British troops had fired on colonial militiamen at Lexington and Concord in Massachusetts in April 1775, the members of the Second Continental Congress, which met in Philadelphia in May 1775, continued to protest that they had no intention of exiting the empire. On 6 July 1775, Congress issued its first Declaration, to justify taking up arms in self-defence. In that document, they assured their 'friends and fellow subjects in any part of the empire' that they had 'not raised armies with ambitious designs of separating from Great-Britain, and establishing independent states' but only 'to relieve the empire from the calamities of civil war'. From then on, in the eyes of even the most aggrieved colonists, this would be an armed struggle carried on within a single political community, the British Atlantic empire, and hence in fact a 'civil' war. However, across the Atlantic, Lord North wrote to his king on 26 July 1775 that 'the war is now grown to such a height, that it must be treated as a foreign war'. The following month, George III duly declared the mainland colonies to be in open rebellion and no longer under his protection. With this proclamation, what had begun as a typical early modern provincial tax revolt became 'the American War',

---

[16] 'The Association &c.' (18 October 1774), in Hutson (ed.), *A Decent Respect to the Opinions of Mankind*, 11, 12.

[17] O'Shaughnessy, *An Empire Divided*, 137–47; T. H. Breen, 'Narrative of Commercial Life: Consumption, Ideology, and Community on the Eve of the American Revolution', *William and Mary Quarterly*, 3rd Series, 50 (1993), 471–501; Breen, *The Marketplace of Revolution*, 207–10, 229–34, 263–5.

though not yet an 'American Revolution': that term would not appear until the Continental Congress issued its official *Observations on the American Revolution* in 1779.[18]

On each side of the Atlantic, both Britain and the rebellious colonies needed to mobilize internal and external support. In Britain, each turn of the conflict brought a flurry of petitions and addresses from the British public, with every bout of loyalism and support for coercion of the colonists being met with an equal and opposite reaction towards conciliation. The ministry could therefore not count on public opinion to back its policies, especially when editors, pamphleteers, and political activists used the issues at stake in the American War as proxies for their own local or national grievances in Britain and in Ireland.[19] Britain was also diplomatically isolated: it would in fact prosecute the war until defeat at Yorktown in 1781 without any European allies, a unique—and uniquely debilitating—position for it among the great conflicts of the Second Hundred Years War Britain fought intermittently between 1688 and 1815.[20] The ministry had to scramble to provide the military muscle necessary for confronting the colonists. The quest for manpower was Atlantic in scope, and netted Hanoverians, Hessians, Highland Scots, Catholics from Ireland and Quebec, and, most controversially, Native Americans and slaves from within the colonies. This mustering of auxiliaries from Britain's various subject populations foreshadowed the restructured British empire that would emerge after the American War, in which there was greater recognition of diversity within and among Britain's global possessions but a reinforced emphasis on authority and hierarchy.[21]

Loyalists within the colonies were crucial to Britain's war aims. These were the people who, at the very least, retained their allegiance to the crown but were otherwise quite politically and ethnically diverse. They included British colonists, Native American groups like the Cherokee and Mohawk, and an estimated 20,000 slaves who gained their freedom by crossing British lines during the course of the war. The best estimates for the total number of white Loyalists suggest that about 20 per cent of the population, or roughly 500,000 colonists, were still loyal to the crown at the end of the war in 1783: some 60,000 of them, along with 15,000 slaves, left the United States as part of a global

[18] 'A Declaration . . . Seting Forth the Causes and Necessity of Taking Up Arms' (6 July 1775), in Hutson (ed.), *A Decent Respect to the Opinions of Mankind*, 96, 97; Lord North to George III, 26 July 1775, quoted in Marshall, *The Making and Unmaking of Empires*, 338; *Observations on the American Revolution: Published According to a Resolution of Congress* (Philadelphia, PA, 1779).

[19] From a vast literature see especially James E. Bradley, *Popular Politics and the American Revolution in England: Petitions, the Crown and Public Opinion* (Macon, GA, 1986); Kathleen Wilson, *The Sense of the People: Politics, Culture and Imperialism in England, 1715–1785* (Cambridge, 1995), chapter 5; Stephen Conway, *The British Isles and the War of American Independence* (Oxford, 2000), chapter 4.

[20] H. M. Scott, 'Britain as a Great Power in the Age of the American Revolution', in Dickinson (ed.), *Britain and the American Revolution*, 180–204; Brendan Simms, *Three Victories and a Defeat: The Rise and Fall of the First British Empire, 1714–1783* (London, 2007), chapters 21–3.

[21] Stephen Conway, *The War of American Independence, 1775–1783* (London, 1995), 44–6; P. J. Marshall, 'Empire and Authority in the Later Eighteenth Century', *Journal of Imperial and Commonwealth History*, 15 (1987), 105–22.

diaspora that reached Canada, East and West Florida, the Bahamas, Sierra Leone, British India, and Australia. During the war, British ministers had hoped that Loyalists in the Thirteen Colonies might provide a large fifth column ready to welcome British forces intent on liberating Charleston, Philadelphia, and New York, for example, as bridgeheads for the reconquest of the mainland. Such a strategy succeeded briefly in coastal Georgia and in South Carolina in 1779–80 but proved unworkable elsewhere. However, those colonies, such as South Carolina, Georgia, and New York, where there were vigorous Loyalist minorities, experienced the American War as a series of local civil wars, amid the larger transatlantic conflict that divided the anglophone population of the Atlantic world within and among its various different communities.[22]

The true nature of those divisions would only become clear after the Continental Congress had taken the momentous decision to declare independence in 1776. The Declaration of Independence announced to 'a candid world' that the former colonies were now 'Free and Independent States'. It aimed to convert a civil war within the British Atlantic empire into a war between sovereign states and to introduce into the Atlantic world the first modern republics in the Atlantic world. It also informed 'the Powers of the Earth'—that is, the great diplomatic powers of Europe—that the United States was now open for business and available for alliances. Discussions continued behind the scenes with France but a public declaration of support for the colonists was not forthcoming until after they had shown their ability to defeat British forces at the Battle of Saratoga in September 1777. The Franco-American treaties of alliance and commerce of February 1778 opened the way to a French declaration of war on Britain in June of that year. Spain also declared war in April 1779, thereby transforming a British colonial war into an international conflict of hemispheric, Atlantic, and ultimately global proportions which became a rematch of the Seven Years War, with France and Spain hoping to recover at least some of their recent losses.[23]

Conjuring states out of colonies was the single most radical act of the American Revolution: indeed, it was precisely what turned that sequence of events from a civil war into a revolution as it began the transformation of the Atlantic world into an arena hospitable, first, to independent states on its western shores, then to republicanism (in the sense of non-monarchical government), and finally to the creation of federal republics—the United States, Venezuela, and Mexico, for instance—on a scale un-dreamed of by classical and early modern thinkers. As Edmund Burke wrote after the Peace of Paris in 1783 confirmed British recognition of American independence,

[22] Keith Mason, 'The American Loyalist Diaspora and the Reconfiguration of the British Atlantic World', in Eliga H. Gould and Peter S. Onuf (eds.), *Empire and Nation: The American Revolution in the Atlantic World* (Baltimore, MD, 2005), 239–59; Maya Jasanoff, 'The Other Side of Revolution: Loyalists in the British Empire', *William and Mary Quarterly*, 3rd Series, 65 (2008), 205–32; Jasanoff, *Liberty's Exiles: American Loyalists in the Revolutionary World* (New York, 2011).

[23] David Armitage, *The Declaration of Independence: A Global History* (Cambridge, MA, 2007); Carolyn Kinder Carr and Mercedes Águela Villar (introd.), *Legacy: Spain and the United States in the Age of Independence, 1763–1848/Legado: España y los Estados Unidos en la era de la Independencia, 1763–1848* (Washington, DC, [2007]).

'A great revolution has happened—a revolution made, not by chopping and changing of power in any one of the existing states, but by the appearance of a new state, of a new species, in a new part of the globe. It has made as great a change in all the relations, and balances, and gravitation of power, as the appearance of a new planet would in the system of the solar world.'[24]

Not every observer, then or now, would have agreed with Burke that the successful creation of a new state (or states) was what made the American Revolution revolutionary. In the early twentieth century, the so-called Progressive historians had found beneath the constitutionalist veneer of the American Revolution a transformative class struggle comparable to the classic scripts of conflict associated with the French and Russian Revolutions. Neo-Progressive historians have recently revived this account of the contested course of the Revolution, but they have not supplied a general explanation of its causes (because cross-class alliances against Great Britain were more common) or of its consequences (as other divisions, especially between sections of the country and later the emergent party system, shaped the faultlines of the Early Republic). Even an influential account of the Revolution's radicalism that portrays it as the event, 'more than any other . . . that made America into the most liberal, democratic, and modern nation in the world', describes the results of the Revolution better than its roots. It overlooks the fact that 'America' did not exist before 1776 and confines its analysis of what preceded the alleged revolutionary transformation to the Thirteen Colonies alone. This amounts to a neo-nationalist narrative of the Revolution whose origins can be traced back to the ideological propaganda of Jefferson, Paine, and others more than two centuries ago. Yet without independence and statehood, no such national story could ever have found favour, nor could the processes of economic and social transformation have unfolded in the decades after 1776. Independence was the indispensable innovation from which all the Revolution's other effects flowed.[25]

When the American Revolution is placed in Atlantic perspective, it is clear that this was not a nationalist revolution. No burgeoning national distinctiveness had inspired self-identifying 'Americans' to cast off British rule: the authors of the Declaration of Independence still spoke of their 'British brethren' in the act of proclaiming that they were no longer fellow subjects. The Revolution produced Americans, it was not produced by them; indeed, it would not be until the aftermath of the second American Civil War that an American nation emerged to encompass the majority of the

---

[24] Alison L. LaCroix, *The Ideological Origins of American Federalism* (Cambridge, MA, 2010); *The Works and Correspondence of the Right Honourable Edmund Burke*, ed. Charles William, Earl Fitzwilliam and Sir Richard Bourke, 7 vols. (2nd edn. London, 1852), ii. 453. Sir William Herschel's discovery in 1781 of the 'Georgian star'—better known as Uranus—presumably inspired Burke's remark.

[25] Woody Holton, *Forced Founders: Indians, Debtors, Slaves, and the Making of the American Revolution in Virginia* (Chapel Hill, NC, 1999); Michael A. McDonnell, *The Politics of War: Race, Class, and Conflict in Revolutionary Virginia* (Chapel Hill, NC, 2007); Gordon S. Wood, *The Radicalism of the American Revolution* (New York, 1992), 7 (quoted); 'Forum: How Revolutionary was the Revolution? A Discussion of Gordon Wood's *The Radicalism of the American Revolution*', *William and Mary Quarterly*, 51 (1994), 677–716.

population within its borders. To understand the Revolution as a strictly American event would demand not the broader spatial perspective of the Atlantic world, but the much longer temporal perspective of 1765–1865, from the Stamp Act to the Confederate surrender at Appomattox.[26]

THE ATLANTIC AND BEYOND

An Atlantic perspective highlights the manifold ambivalences of the American Revolution. The successful introduction of thirteen new states, soon to be united for external purposes under a single federal government, into the international order for the first time in two centuries was a revolutionary act. So, too, was the creation of what in European terms would appear to be a decapitated social order, lacking a hereditary monarchy and aristocracy. This feature inspired egalitarians on the other side of the Atlantic as they sought to fulfil the promise of 'democracy' against 'aristocracy', particularly during the French Revolution, but disappointment, frustration, and anger at American failure to take the axe to slavery—the third, and most opprobrious, form of hereditary status prevalent in the period—tempered sympathizers' enthusiasm for the achievements of the Revolution. Most subsequent Atlantic revolutions, first in Saint-Domingue and then in Spanish America, would rapidly bring emancipation in their wake, with radical implications for race relations in the new republics of the Americas. Splitting so many of the former British colonies on the North American mainland from the islands of the British Caribbean made the prospect of an empire without slaves thinkable for British abolitionists, who could now conceive of different regimes of labour, property, and governance amid the reconfigurations of the British empire. The American Revolution may thus have hastened British abolition of the slave trade in 1807 and then of slavery itself in 1833, even as it would take a great civil war for the latter to be achieved in the United States.[27]

Unlike the French Bourbons, who allegedly learned nothing and forgot nothing, the Hanoverian monarchs, their ministers, and their Parliament did derive some salutary

[26] John M. Murrin, 'A Roof without Walls: The Dilemma of American National Identity', in Richard Beeman, Stephen Botein, and Edward C. Carter III (eds.), *Beyond Confederation: Origins of the Constitution and American National Identity* (Chapel Hill, NC, 1987), 333–48; Charles Royster, 'Founding a Nation in Blood: Military Conflict and American Nationality', in Ronald Hoffman and Peter J. Albert (eds.), *Arms and Independence: The Military Character of the American Revolution* (Charlottesville, VA, 1984), 25–49.

[27] William Doyle, *Aristocracy and its Enemies in the Age of Revolution* (Oxford, 2009), chapter 4; Gary B. Nash, 'Sparks from the Altar of '76: International Repercussions and Reconsiderations of the American Revolution', in Armitage and Subrahmanyam (eds.), *The Age of Revolutions in Global Context, c.1760–1840*, 1–19; Christopher Leslie Brown, *Moral Capital: Foundations of British Abolitionism* (Chapel Hill, NC, 2006), chapter 4; David Brion Davis, 'American Slavery and the American Revolution', in Ira Berlin and Ronald Hoffman (eds.), *Slavery and Freedom in the Age of the American Revolution* (Charlottesville, VA, 1983), 262–80.

lessons from the loss of the Thirteen Colonies. Parliament continued to claim that its sovereignty was unlimited but in practice it never again attempted to levy taxes on its colonies as a source of revenue after the American War. It treated established colonial assemblies with greater deference but was also careful not to allow representative institutions to take root where they had not existed before, for example in Trinidad after it fell to Britain in 1797 during the Napoleonic War. Parliament was fearful that Ireland might go the way of the rebellious colonies but responded to demands for legislative independence, first by relaxing economic restrictions and then in 1782 by repealing the Declaratory Act of 1720 and dropping the procedure by which all Irish legislation had to be reviewed by the Privy Council: 'Ireland is reaping a large share of the harvest produced by our labours,' James Madison remarked in July 1782. Ireland secured its place, at least temporarily, within a federal restructuring of the British empire on the eastern side of the Atlantic, but when the United Irishmen rose in arms in 1798, the British authorities suppressed them ruthlessly. Lord Cornwallis, the vanquished general at Yorktown in 1781, was lord lieutenant of Ireland at the time: he had clearly learned another important lesson from defeat at the hands of rebellious British colonists.[28]

The ripple effects of the American Revolution on the eastern side of the Atlantic and beyond were not easily predictable. It set off what John Adams called a 'contagion of liberty' around the Atlantic world. British authorities at the slave entrepôt of Cape Coast Castle on the Gold Coast reported in 1784 that American sailors were instilling in the local African population a dangerous 'spirit of republican freedom and independence' rendered more toxic by another potent spirit: rum. Meanwhile, in France, American anti-nobilism, the revolutionary language of natural rights, and the structural innovations of the state constitutions were all eagerly received among radicals during the early stages of the French Revolution, though disenchantment soon set in and the 'mirage in the West' faded rapidly from the French scene. After the French Revolution, the example of white American creoles throwing off metropolitan rule was not lost on similar elites in Saint-Domingue, even if their insurrection would set off a chain of consequences much more violent and transformative than anything experienced in British America. In this regard, the Haitian Revolution was part of a contagion of sovereignty in which imitative anti-colonial and secessionist movements followed the American example by declaring and securing their own independence within a gradually expanding world of states.[29]

---

[28] Eliga Gould, 'Liberty and Modernity: The American Revolution and the Parliamentary History of the British Empire', in Greene (ed.), *Exclusionary Empire*, 129–31; J. R. Ward, 'The British West Indies in the Age of Abolition, 1748–1815', in P. J. Marshall (ed.), *The Oxford History of the British Empire*, ii: *The Eighteenth Century* (Oxford, 1998), 434–45; York, 'The Impact of the American Revolution in Ireland', in Dickinson (ed.), *Britain and the American Revolution*, 222–8 (Madison quoted ibid. 228).

[29] Bailyn, *The Ideological Origins of the American Revolution*, chapter 6; Ty M. Reese, 'Liberty, Insolence and Rum: Cape Coast and the American Revolution', *Itinerario*, 28 (2004), 26; Durand Echeverria, *Mirage in the West: A History of the French Image of American Society to 1815* (Princeton, NJ, 1957), chapter 5; Armitage, *The Declaration of Independence*, 103.

An enlarged Atlantic perspective would not, in the end, be sufficient to encompass the historical ramifications of the American Revolution. For that, a global perspective would be necessary.[30] To be sure, there were parts of the world apparently unconnected to the fortunes of a tiny number of settlers perched on the edge of a faraway continent. For example, writing of Japan during its closed *Sakoku* period, a Dutch East India Company official recalled that as late as 1799, 'we truly had a lot of difficulty . . . in making clear to the Japanese that the Americans were *not* English . . . they had never heard the news of their declaration of independence'. The results of the American Revolution penetrated more rapidly, though indirectly, into the South Pacific: 'the creation of the independent United States of America had no conceivable meaning to the natives in Australia and the warm islands of the South Seas, but it was to disturb the isolation of their lives' in the wake of Cook's voyages and the British government's search for new penal colonies after the Revolution had closed American conduits for convicts. The global diaspora of Loyalists also carried the first people of African descent to Australia, some of whom might have witnessed the arrival of the first supply ship to reach Sydney from Calcutta in June 1792. This emblem of imperial integration had a fitting name: the *Atlantic*.[31]

By this moment, an independent United States had already entered the circuits of inter-regional trade around the globe with its first voyages to China and India. The president of Yale College, Ezra Stiles, exulted in May 1783:

This great american revolution, this recent political phænomenon of a new sovereignty arising among the sovereign powers of the earth, will be attended to and contemplated by all nations. Navigation will carry the american flag around the globe itself; and display the thirteen stripes and new constellation at *bengal* and *canton*, on the *indus* and the *ganges*, on the *whang-ho* and the *yang-tse-kiang*.

Not all Americans were quite so triumphant. In May 1788, Eliza Farmer of Philadelphia gave a desultory account of local and global events: 'as for News from this place there is not much stirring they are all busy in forming a new Constitution likewise the Merchants in setling a Trade to China and the East Indies'. Between Stiles' enthusiasm and Farmer's nonchalance lay a common understanding that transformations in sovereignty were inseparable from those in political economy. That characteristic discovery of

[30] 'Forum: Beyond the Atlantic', *William and Mary Quarterly*, 3rd Series 63 (2006), 675–742; Lauren Benton, 'The British Atlantic in Global Context', in Armitage and Braddick (eds.), *The British Atlantic World, 1500–1800*, 271–89; Nicholas Canny, 'Atlantic History and Global History', in Jack P. Greene and Philip D. Morgan (eds.), *Atlantic History: A Critical Appraisal* (Oxford, 2009), 317–36.

[31] Hendrik Doeff, *Recollections of Japan* (1833), ed. and trans. Annick M. Doeff (Victoria, BC, 2003), 93; Geoffrey Blainey, *The Tyranny of Distance: How Distance Shaped Australia's History* (rev. edn. Sydney, 2001), 17; Alan Frost, *The Atlantic World of the 1780s and Botany Bay: The Lost Connection* (Bundoora, 2008); Cassandra Pybus, *Epic Journeys of Freedom: Runaway Slaves of the American Revolution and their Global Quest for Liberty* (Boston, MA, 2006); Suzanne Rickard, 'Lifelines from Calcutta', in James Broadbent, Suzanne Rickard, and Margaret Steven, *India, China, Australia: Trade and Society, 1788–1850* (Sydney, 2003), 65–6.

the Age of Revolutions was the product of the novel perspectives, Atlantic and ultimately global, opened by the American Revolution.[32]

BIBLIOGRAPHY

Armitage, David, and Sanjay Subrahmanyam (eds.), *The Age of Revolutions in Global Context, c.1760–1840* (Basingstoke, 2010).

Billias, George Athan, *American Constitutionalism Heard Round the World, 1776–1989* (New York, 2009).

Calloway, Colin G., *The American Revolution in Indian Country: Crisis and Diversity in Native American Communities* (Cambridge, 1995).

Conway, Stephen, *The British Isles and the War of American Independence* (Oxford, 2000).

Dickinson, H. T. (ed.), *Britain and the American Revolution* (London, 1998).

Elliott, J. H., *Empires of the Atlantic World: Britain and Spain in America, 1492–1830* (New Haven, CT, 2006).

Gould, Eliga H., and Peter S. Onuf (eds.), *Empire and Nation: The American Revolution in the Atlantic World* (Baltimore, MD, 2005).

Jasanoff, Maya, *Liberty's Exiles: American Loyalish in the Revolutionary World* (New York, 2011).

Lawson, Philip, *The Imperial Challenge: Quebec and Britain in the Age of the American Revolution* (Montreal, 1989).

Marshall, P. J., *The Making and Unmaking of Empires: Britain, India, and America c.1750–1783* (Oxford, 2005).

O'Shaughnessy, Andrew Jackson, *An Empire Divided: The American Revolution in the British Caribbean* (Philadelphia, PA, 2000).

---

[32] Ezra Stiles, *The United States Elevated to Glory and Honor* (New Haven, CT, 1783), 52; Eliza Farmer to John Lewis Stephens, 9 May 1788, Eliza Farmer Letterbook, 1774–89, Historical Society of Pennsylvania; Leonard Blussé, *Visible Cities: Canton, Nagasaki, and Batavia and the Coming of the Americans* (Cambridge, MA, 2008); James Fichter, *So Great a Proffit: How the East Indies Trade Transformed Anglo-American Capitalism* (Cambridge, MA, 2010).

CHAPTER 31

THE HAITIAN REVOLUTION IN ATLANTIC PERSPECTIVE

DAVID GEGGUS

OF all the Atlantic revolutions, the fifteen-year struggle that transformed French Saint-Domingue into independent Haiti produced the greatest degree of social and economic change, and most fully embodied the contemporary pursuit of freedom, equality, and independence. Between 1789 and 1804, the Haitian Revolution unfolded as a succession of major precedents: the winning of colonial representation in a metropolitan assembly, the ending of racial discrimination, the first abolition of slavery in an important slave society, and the creation of Latin America's first independent state. Beginning as a home-rule movement among wealthy white colonists, it rapidly drew in militant free people of colour who demanded political rights and then set off the largest slave uprising in the history of the Americas. Sandwiched between the colonial revolutions of North and South America, and complexly intertwined with the coterminous revolution in France, Haiti's revolution has rarely been grouped with these major conflicts despite its claims to global significance.

AN ATLANTIC COLONY

For much of the eighteenth century, Saint-Domingue was Europe's main source of tropical produce. At the height of its importance in the late 1780s, it was exporting more than the United States, far more than Mexico or Brazil, and it was the largest single market for the Atlantic slave trade. Saint-Domingue was never 'the richest colony in the world', as some have claimed; the slaves who made up nearly 90 per cent of its population possessed little and generated little demand for imports or infrastructure. But it was a dynamo of the Atlantic economy. Besides accounting for one-third of France's overseas trade, it had commercial links through its free ports or through smuggling with many parts of the Americas. The farm produce, fish, and lumber that its colonists purchased from Yankee skippers in 1790 amounted to one-tenth of US exports. Most of Saint-Domingue's livestock and currency came from neighbouring Spanish colonies. It purchased slaves from British, Danish, and Portuguese, as well French, merchants. Because France could absorb only a fraction of the colony's enormous output, its produce was sold from Scandinavia to the Middle East, in England and New England, Louisiana and Mexico, and thus achieved far wider distribution than usually was possible under mercantilist restrictions.

On the eve of the Revolution, about 1,500 vessels visited the colony each year, bringing more than 1,500 passengers, perhaps 20,000 seamen, and 30,000 enslaved Africans. Schooners and brigs making the two-week run from Philadelphia and New England, and smaller vessels from Venezuela, Curaçao, and Cartagena, arrived more frequently than the big merchantmen from France that usually took two months to cross the Atlantic. On a fast ship, news could arrive from Europe in four weeks, and the latest Paris fashions, it was said, took only a little longer to appear in Cap Français, Saint-Domingue's elegant main seaport. Colonists flocked to recent French plays and operas in the colony's six theatres; many participated in the network of international freemasonry; a few intellectuals corresponded with learned societies in Europe and North America.

By 1790, the colony's resident population consisted of about 30,000 whites, a similar number of free people of colour, and close to half a million slaves. Most were migrants. More than half the slaves had been born in Africa and roughly three-quarters of the whites in France. Among local merchants, there was a scattering of cosmopolitan Jews with transnational families. A few planters had Irish Catholic origins, and Italians were prominent among the seafarers who thronged the colonial waterfront. The rest were 'creole', meaning locally born. Among the whites, creoles did not form a distinctive group, but in the slave community, they constituted a sort of upper class and increasingly monopolized the positions of slave driver, domestic servant, and artisan craftsman. One in three adult slaves was creole. The most unusual feature of Saint-Domingue society was the relative wealth and size of its free coloured sector. As elsewhere in the Americas, it was victimized by discriminatory laws and extra-legal harassment, but it included (along with indigent ex-slaves) many free-born and prosperous planters of mixed racial descent, some of whom were educated in France. Insofar as a sense of creole or American identity existed in Saint-Domingue, it was probably most developed among the free people of colour, although they remained an extremely diverse group.

Saint-Domingue's social structure was typical of Caribbean colonies. The free coloured sector was proportionately larger than most, but small by Hispanic standards. Although the slave population was almost as large as that of the US South, the colony was not densely settled for a West Indian island. The imbalance between slave and free, and between white and black, was extreme but not unique. The slave population grew at unusual speed on the eve of the Revolution but so did that of some other colonies. The combination of extreme demographic imbalance and rapid growth, however, was exceptional.[1]

---

[1] David Geggus, 'Saint Domingue on the Eve of Revolution', in D. Geggus and N. Fiering (eds.), *The World of the Haitian Revolution* (Bloomington, IN, 2009), 29–56.

A COMPLEX REVOLUTION

The Haitian Revolution, like the French, was several revolutions in one. Because the whites, free coloureds, and slaves each pursued their own separate struggles, the Revolution had a social and political complexity not found in the mainland independence movements. Whereas in France a briefly successful aristocratic revolt against the monarchy opened the way for a bourgeois revolution propelled forward by peasant and popular insurrections, in Saint-Domingue the actions and mutual apprehensions of whites, free coloureds, and slaves stimulated and impeded by turns their respective pursuits of autonomy, equality, and freedom. And just as events in Saint-Domingue shaped the simultaneous revolution in France, the Haitian Revolution evolved from beginning to end in constant interplay with the metropolitan revolution. How much it was influenced by the French Revolution, rather than internal factors, is a central question in its interpretation.

Both revolutions began with the bankrupt monarchy's decision to call the States-General in 1789, which opened up the prospect of sweeping change in public life. Although the colonies were not invited to participate, wealthy planters organized secretly to choose representatives, who, once in France, argued their way into seats in the new National Assembly. As the absolute monarchy yielded to the democratic thrust in France, planters, lawyers, and merchants formed regional assemblies in Saint-Domingue's three provinces and converted the militia into a national guard. The royalist administration—till then all-powerful—could only acquiesce. In April 1790 a colonial assembly met in the town of Saint-Marc that declared itself sovereign. It drew up a constitution that entirely ignored the French National Assembly and accorded very limited roles to the king, French merchants, and the royal governor. Its most radical deputies supposedly discussed making the colony independent.[2]

The autonomist spirit of the propertied classes had deep roots. Saint-Domingue's planters had long envied their British counterparts their legislative assemblies and they resented the mercantilist restrictions that hobbled their trade, especially as they received neither the commercial advantages nor more effective naval protection enjoyed by British colonists. In the 1720s and 1760s, colonists had rebelled against metropolitan misrule, and in the 1780s they chafed against a new wave of reforms that alienated a wide spectrum of white society. The fiscal question was less prominent than in the other Atlantic revolutions; colonists paid little tax but they considered themselves victims of a 'ministerial despotism' that ignored their needs. While claiming loyalty to the French crown, some argued that their seventeenth-century forebears had conquered the colony and offered it to France. To make the point, the Saint-Marc Assembly opened with a small pageant in buccaneer costumes. The colonists also drew

---

[2] Blanche Maurel, *Cahiers de doléances de la colonie de Saint-Domingue* (Paris, 1933); Gabriel Debien, *Les Colons de Saint-Domingue et la Révolution française: essai sur le Club Massiac* (Paris, 1953).

inspiration from the long conflict in France between aristocratic bodies and the royal government. Like the metropolitan *parlements*, Saint-Domingue's appeal courts, known as *conseils supérieurs*, sometimes obstructed new legislation and acted as spokesmen for popular discontent. Finally, the successful revolt of the United States was an example that could not be ignored in the 1780s, when US seamen and merchants were a constant presence in the colony's main ports. The American Revolutionary War had given Saint-Domingue a tempting experience of free trade that was soon curtailed, and it helped drive the French state to the bankruptcy that began the Revolution. Its ideological impact is hard to gauge but in 1791 the US constitution was published in Cap Français.[3]

Saint-Domingue's white settler revolution that unfolded in the years 1788–92 fits well into R. R. Palmer's model of an 'aristocratic reaction' leading to democratic revolution.[4] The elite individuals who first sought to establish colonial self-government had socially exclusive aspirations. In late 1789, however, the protests of white wage earners and small proprietors inspired by the popular revolution in Paris compelled them to accept an exceptionally broad white male franchise. This added a radical element to the spectrum of local politics, which remained nonetheless an affair of factions and regions more than of class. When a new colonial assembly was elected in August 1791, its radical majority changed its name from 'Colonial' to 'General' Assembly and it quickly assumed executive functions.[5]

It is unlikely that outright independence ever attracted many serious supporters. Island colonies with tiny white populations were infinitely more vulnerable to naval blockade, foreign invasion, and slave revolt than those of the mainland. However, a British protectorate or takeover was an alternative that could appeal to several con-stituencies: not just liberals and planters indebted to French merchants, but also conservatives who opposed the French Revolution and its perceived threat to the slave regime and white supremacy. Colonists made the first of several secret overtures to the British government in September 1791, in the aftermath of massive rebellions by slaves and free people of colour.[6]

The August rebellion of free men of colour in the centre and south of Saint-Domingue had no connection with the simultaneous slave uprising in the Northern Plain, although both grew out of a failed revolt in the north led the previous October by the freeman Vincent Ogé. Ogé and his more militant successors demanded that the colonial government accord them the equality with whites that the National Assembly seemed implicitly to have promised in its 1789 Declaration of the Rights of Man.

---

[3] Charles Frostin, *Les Révoltes blanches à Saint-Domingue* (Paris, 1975); Gabriel Debien, *Esprit colon et esprit d'autonomie à Saint-Domingue au XVIIIe siècle* (Paris, 1954).

[4] Robert R. Palmer, *The Age of the Democratic Revolution*, 2 vols. (Princeton, NJ, 1959, 1964).

[5] For participant histories written respectively from radical and conservative perspectives, see Chotard, aîné, *Précis de la Révolution de Saint-Domingue, depuis la fin de 1789, jusqu'au 18 juin 1794* (Philadelphia, PA, 1795), and Antoine Dalmas, *Histoire de la révolution de Saint-Domingue* (Paris, 1814).

[6] David Patrick Geggus, *Slavery, War, and Revolution: The British Occupation of Saint Domingue, 1793–1798* (Oxford, 1982), 33–67.

Discrimination against free non-whites in Saint-Domingue had worsened in the previous decades at the same time as their numbers and wealth grew rapidly. As they made up close to half of the militia and most of the rural police, the situation was more explosive than in other French colonies. The participation of a free coloured battalion in the American Revolutionary War (as part of a French expeditionary force) boosted their self-confidence, and in the 1780s some discreetly lobbied the colonial minister for minor adjustments in the colour bar. Then the French Revolution changed everything.

Within days of the Declaration of Rights, free coloureds visiting or living in Paris formed the Society of American Colonists to campaign for representation in the National Assembly and for equal access to jobs and to public assemblies in the colonies. Free men of colour in Saint-Domingue soon followed suit, petitioning local authorities to be included in the political process as taxpaying men of property. The Friends of the Blacks abolitionist society in Paris also took up their cause. The Revolution thus gave free men of colour a forum and won them allies, but it also increased their opponents' hostility. Before the Revolution, racial equality meant the right to become a doctor or lawyer; after 1789 it meant access to political power. Moreover, the claim that concessions to free non-whites would undermine the slave regime was much more compelling now that abolition was on the agenda of the French Revolution. Pressured by the colonial lobby, the National Assembly's response to the race question, and to antislavery, was embarrassed prevarication and dishonest manoeuvring. The government secretly tried to prevent men of colour from crossing the Atlantic and it opened their mail.[7]

In Saint-Domingue, the predominant white response was intransigence and violent repression. Many colonists were probably willing to co-opt the wealthiest and lightest-complexioned men of colour with honorary white status, if they could control the process, but the foregrounding of egalitarian ideology in the revolutionary crisis soon ruled out such compromise measures. With racist poor whites gaining influence in local politics, the moment for conciliation passed. In some regions, whites demanded an oath of respect from men of colour, and there was a series of violent confrontations, murders, and property seizures that culminated in Ogé's rebellion in October 1790.

After some initial panic, Ogé's gathering of 300 armed men in the northern mountains was quickly dispersed. Despite the urging of more militant companions, he refused to recruit slaves. Most free coloureds sought racial equality, not slave emancipation. Many were slave owners. Yet some had relatives living in slavery, and all were descended from slaves. Ogé himself had previously evoked an eventual ending of slavery, and free coloured activists often called for the freeing of slaves of mixed racial descent, probably to boost their own numbers. It was therefore difficult to separate the race question from that of slavery. When news of Ogé's capture and barbarous execution finally shamed the National Assembly into granting political rights to a limited number of free coloureds (15 May 1791), it threw Saint-Domingue into uproar. The governor refused to implement the decree; some whites plotted secession, and the

[7] John Garrigus, *Before Haiti: Race and Citizenship in French Saint-Domingue* (New York, 2006); Yvan Debbasch, *Couleur et liberté: le jeu du critère ethnique dans l'ordre juridique esclavagiste* (Paris, 1967).

free coloureds went into rebellion in the south and west regions where they were as numerous as whites. The fighting was vicious, and the atrocities committed by both sides made future reconciliation difficult. Yet, when the French government eventually decreed racial equality (4 April 1792), most white colonists accepted the decision.

This was because they now confronted a more dangerous enemy, whom they were unable to defeat without the military skills of the free men of colour. The slave uprising that took over much of the North Province in the autumn of 1791 was the largest, longest, and most destructive in the history of the Americas. In just the opening month, hundreds of whites were killed and a thousand plantations were burned. The uprising drew strength from the rapid growth of the slave population in the 1780s, and the long-term evolution of the creole language and Vodou religion that knit together the diverse cultures that composed it. Ogé's rebellion helped prepare the way in perhaps two respects. Free coloured militiamen, who helped police the plantations, were disarmed in some districts in the rebellion's wake, and a number of free black rebels who went into hiding after their defeat later resurfaced in the slave insurgents' ranks. Their role was not critical, however. The August uprising's main leaders were all black creole slaves, notably coachmen and slave drivers. They took advantage of the way the French Revolution had divided and distracted colonial society and weakened its government and garrison. They mobilized support by exploiting false rumours of slavery's abolition by the king, which were becoming widespread in the Caribbean and probably were distortions of news of French reforms and of the recent antislavery trend in Britain and the United States.[8]

The slaves faced a deeply divided opposition. Free coloureds in the North Province were split between those who fought against the slave uprising under white leadership; those who temporarily cooperated with the insurgent slaves in separate units until racial equality was conceded; and a smaller number of free blacks, like Toussaint Louverture, who were or became integrated into the slaves' army. White radicals and conservatives each blamed the other, as well as free coloureds, for fomenting the slave revolt. Although some insurgents used libertarian language, most of their leaders presented themselves as opponents of the French Revolution and as loyal subjects of the French king. It is possible they knew that, in the American Revolution, slaves who had fought for the English king against their masters had been offered their freedom. More certainly, they cast themselves as counter-revolutionaries so as to obtain aid from the conservative Spanish in neighbouring Santo Domingo. Local and usually brief insurrections broke out elsewhere in the colony, but the main uprising remained confined to part of the North Province. There it remained impossible to suppress,

---

[8] Carolyn Fick, *The Making of Haiti: The Saint Domingue Revolution from Below* (Knoxville, TN, 1990), 85–117; David Geggus, *Haitian Revolutionary Studies* (Bloomington, IN, 2002), 11–13, 62, 84, 170; Geggus, 'Slavery, War, and Revolution in the Greater Caribbean, 1789–1815', in D. B. Gaspar and D. Geggus (eds.), *A Turbulent Time: The French Revolution and the Greater Caribbean* (Bloomington, IN, 1997), 7–12.

because of the sheer numbers involved and because the whites had to fight simultaneously free coloureds in the west and south as well as slaves in the north.

By early 1793, free coloureds and whites had united in a tense alliance, and the 12,000
troops France sent to Saint-Domingue finally were making major advances. At that
point, however, the entrance of Britain and Spain into the French Revolutionary War
tipped the balance of power in Saint-Domingue. Drawing on its lengthy experience of
dealing with maroon communities in Spanish America, the Spanish government
successfully recruited most of the insurgent slaves with offers of freedom for themselves
and their families, and it sent forces across the Santo Domingo frontier. War with
England meant that France could no longer safely send troops across the Atlantic, and
the prospect of foreign intervention encouraged white colonists to rebel against the
authoritarian representatives of the new French Republic, *commissaires* Sonthonax and
Polverel. Imposing racial equality in the autumn of 1792, they had closed the colonial
assembly and assumed dictatorial powers. In the summer of 1793, they tried to outbid
the Spanish invaders by offering terms to the insurgent slaves and then, between
August and October, by abolishing slavery throughout Saint-Domingue in a desperate
bid to maintain French rule.[9]

This landmark decision emerged from the conjuncture of three developments. Most
immediate was the dire military situation confronting the republican officials. Yet slave
emancipation was not just a political calculation, for Sonthonax had been one of the
rare radicals to express abolitionist views early in the French Revolution and, although
he had no authority to end slavery, he was aware that support for abolitionism had
been growing in France. French libertarian ideology, therefore, was a second factor.[10]
The third, and most obvious, was the undefeated slave insurrection.

This raises the controversial question of the insurgents' aims: whether they themselves had sought a complete elimination of slavery, or just their own freedom, or
merely their leaders' freedom combined with some reform of slavery. The evidence is
mixed and unclear, because filtered through the passions of contemporary observers,
and complicated by fraudulent documentation. Expectations probably varied among
the tens of thousands in revolt and fluctuated according to military fortunes. Certainly
the principal leaders of the insurgents, Jean-François and Biassou, displayed little
commitment to a generalized abolition of slavery beyond freeing their own families
and principal followers. They twice attempted to negotiate a peace that would have
returned most of their followers to slavery; they rounded up women and children on
the plantations and sold them to their Spanish allies; and they refused to join the

---

[9] David Geggus, 'The Arming of Slaves during the Haitian Revolution', in Philip Morgan and
Christopher Brown (eds.), *The Arming of Slaves in World History: From Classical Times to the
Modern Age* (New Haven, CT, 2006), 220–4; Robert Louis Stein, *Léger-Félicité Sonthonax: The Lost
Sentinel of the Republic* (Rutherford, NJ, 1985).

[10] Jean-Daniel Piquet, *L'Émancipation des noirs dans la Révolution française (1789–1795)* (Paris, 2002),
219–94.

French Republic after its adoption of freedom for all. They would maintain their 'church and king' rhetoric down to their deaths in the early nineteenth century.[11]

The emancipation decrees of Sonthonax and Polverel aligned the forces of black self-liberation and French libertarian ideology but, at first, very few insurgents rallied to the commissioners' new regime of liberty and equality. Neither in Europe nor the Caribbean did the French Republic look as though it could defeat its enemies, and most insurgents continued to play the role of committed royalists. The civil commissioners and their free coloured allies, therefore, raised armies among the ex-slaves to fight the original slave insurgents and their Spanish allies, who were joined by British invaders in September 1793. Sonthonax's initiative, however, did cause the number three insurgent leader, Toussaint Louverture, to discreetly adopt his own emancipationist discourse at the same time as he captured much of northern Saint-Domingue for Spain. Competing with the republicans as a liberator, Toussaint acted independently of his proslavery Spanish patrons, just as Sonthonax had abolished slavery without permission from France. Until then, he had shared Jean-François's equivocal stance on slave emancipation. Yet he differed in that he personally had not sold captives and, already a freedman, he was obviously not fighting for his own freedom. It remains uncertain whether he was a pragmatic altruist and secret originator of the slave uprising, or an opportunist who belatedly took his cue from Sonthonax.[12]

In February 1794, at the radical highpoint of the French Revolution, France's legislature welcomed the black, white, and brown deputies Sonthonax sent from Saint-Domingue and, after lengthy debate, extended the abolition of slavery to all French colonies. The emancipated slaves were declared citizens with full constitutional rights. Slave owners were not compensated and slave emancipation was hailed as a new weapon of war to be wielded against the colonies of Britain and Spain. It was the first time a sovereign state had abolished slavery. Henceforth black militancy in the Caribbean was backed by the resources of a major power. The Constitution of the Year III, drawn up in 1795, ended colonial status and incorporated the ex-colonies into a unitary French state. The egalitarian promise of these epoch-making reforms was never fully realized, however. Emancipation was extended to only two other colonies, Guadeloupe and Guyane, and former slaves who did not serve as soldiers were everywhere subjected to forced labour, so as to maintain plantation production. Electoral arrangements for Saint-Domingue were held up in Paris until January 1798, and the administration in Guadeloupe simply refused to hold elections.[13]

---

[11] David Geggus, 'Print Culture and the Haitian Revolution: The Written and the Spoken Word', *Proceedings of the American Antiquarian Society*, 116/2 (October 2006), 297–314; Geggus, 'Toussaint Louverture et l'abolition de l'esclavage à Saint-Domingue', in Liliane Chauleau (ed.), *Les Abolitions dans les Amériques* (Fort de France, 2001), 109–16; Geggus, 'The Exile of the 1791 Slave Leaders: Spain's Resettlement of its Black Auxiliary Troops', *Journal of Haitian Studies*, 8/2 (2002), 52–67.

[12] David Geggus, 'Toussaint Louverture and the Haitian Revolution', in R. William Weisberger (ed.), *Profiles of Revolutionaries in Atlantic History, 1750–1850* (New York, 2007), 115–35; Geggus, 'Toussaint Louverture avant et après le soulèvement de 1791', in Franklin Midy (ed.), *Mémoire de révolution d'esclaves à Saint-Domingue* (Montreal, 2006), 112–32.

[13] Yves Benot, 'Comment la Convention a-t-elle voté l'abolition de l'esclavage en l'An II?', *Annales historiques de la Révolution française*, 293–4 (1993), 349–61; Miranda Spieler, 'The Structure of Colonial Rule during the French Revolution', *William and Mary Quarterly*, 66/2 (2009), 365–407; Laurent Dubois,

Even before the emancipation decree of 4 February 1794 was known in Saint-Domingue, several insurgent leaders shifted their allegiance from the Spanish and British invaders to the embattled republican administration. By far the most important was Toussaint Louverture. His transfer of support was deviously slow but, once assured that France had abolished slavery, he turned on the Spanish, their black allies, and the English in quick succession and inflicted heavy defeats. The balance of power tipped against the alliance of slave owners, foreign invaders, and their ex-slave mercenaries, and French rule in Saint-Domingue was secured for another decade, but henceforth the black revolution held centre stage.

Spain abandoned all of Hispaniola to the French Republic in 1795, but the British continued to send troops to Saint-Domingue, where they occupied most of the west and the tip of the southern peninsula until 1798. In collaboration with a mixture of conservative royalist and radical autonomist whites and propertied free coloureds, they kept the slave regime functioning with dwindling success. These years of continuous warfare enabled Toussaint Louverture to forge a larger and stronger army. At least half of his troops must have been African-born. His officers included a sprinkling of free coloureds and whites but the most important were creole ex-slaves like Jean-Jacques Dessalines. Toussaint's skills proved to be political as well as military. He out-manoeuvred a succession of white officials sent from France as well as rival generals among the former slaves and free coloureds, now called *anciens libres*. In April 1796, he was declared deputy governor after foiling an *anciens libres* plot against the French governor, Étienne Laveaux. In 1797, Sonthonax made him commander-in-chief, but a few months later Toussaint had Sonthonax deported on trumped-up charges.

After the British were expelled in 1798, the black general faced off against André Rigaud, who had emerged as leader of the free coloureds. His power base was the south; Toussaint controlled the north and west. Rigaud was a radical republican who had favoured slave emancipation; most of his soldiers were former slaves, and he and Toussaint had cooperated in fighting the British. Without a common enemy, however, they soon turned on each other. The War of the South (1799–1800) was a power struggle coloured by class and ethnic tensions. Although Rigaud and other *anciens libres* commanders had flouted French rule just as much as had Toussaint, French officialdom discreetly backed Rigaud for fear that Toussaint's autonomy was developing into outright independence.

The ex-slave crushed the *anciens libres* in the south and those in his own army who rebelled against him. Their leaders fled to France. In 1793 the free coloureds had seemed set to dominate Saint-Domingue as the power behind French officials, but the British occupation had divided them politically and geographically, just when slave emancipation undermined their wealth and created a latent mass movement that the ex-slave generals were best able to exploit. By 1800, the influence of the white colonists had been

A Colony of Citizens: Revolution and Slave Emancipation in the French Caribbean, 1787–1804 (Chapel Hill, NC, 2004).

long eclipsed. Most had emigrated or died in the local massacres that punctuated the Revolution's history. Toussaint Louverture now governed the entire colony.[14]

Toussaint maintained the forced labour system that Sonthonax had introduced, which compelled ex-slaves who did not join the army to continue working on their plantations in return for a share of the revenue. Most *cultivateurs*, as they were now called, preferred to become independent peasants rather than profit-sharing serfs, but protests were met with corporal punishment and military executions. Only plantation agriculture and an export economy could finance the black army that guaranteed their freedom. Toussaint and his fellow officers took over many estates whose owners had emigrated, and they formed a new black landholding class, alongside the *anciens libres* and surviving white planters. Toussaint encouraged refugee planters to return and resume running their estates, and he consulted white advisers. Agriculture began to revive. Admirers praised the new regime as a multi-racial experiment, imbued with the humane and egalitarian values of republican France. Critics condemned a black dictatorship that paid only lip-service to France and allowed generals to amass personal fortunes while their unpaid troops exercised a petty tyranny over the rural masses.

Most disturbing for the French government was the independent foreign policy Toussaint Louverture pursued while posing as a loyal servant of the state. In 1798–9, he signed secret trade treaties and non-aggression pacts with Britain and the United States despite their being at war with France. They had become Saint-Domingue's main trading partners and Toussaint depended on their supplies. He then expelled from the colony French privateers that attacked their shipping. Preoccupied with war in Europe, the Republic could do little, but at the end of 1799 France acquired its own military strongman. Napoleon Bonaparte hoped to rebuild France's colonial empire, and he had no commitment to slave emancipation or racial equality. At first, it seems, he was undecided whether to overthrow Toussaint Louverture or to enlist him in France's war effort. As soon as he came to power, Bonaparte placed the colonies outside the French constitution, but this may have been to accommodate those colonies (like Martinique and the Mascareignes) that had maintained slavery. It did not necessarily mean that he intended to restore the pre-revolutionary status quo in all of them.[15]

Relations between Louverture and Bonaparte deteriorated in 1801 when the black general annexed neighbouring Santo Domingo, contrary to French instructions, and then promulgated his own constitution for Saint-Domingue to fill the legal void left by Napoleon. Drawn up by white colonists with an autonomist background, Toussaint's constitution declared the ex-slave governor general for life with the right to name his successor. It accorded France no role in the legislative process, and foreshadowed Bonapartist militarism with its rubber-stamp political institutions. While maintaining

---

[14] The best studies of Toussaint, written from left- and right-wing perspectives, are C. L. R. James, *The Black Jacobins: Toussaint L'Ouverture and the San Domingo Revolution* (New York, 1963), and Pierre Pluchon, *Toussaint Louverture: un révolutionnaire noir d'Ancien régime* (Paris, 1989).

[15] For opposing views, see Pluchon, *Toussaint Louverture*, 445–75, and Yves Benot, *La Démence coloniale sous Napoléon* (Paris, 1992).

the forced labour system on the plantations, it declared all Saint-Domingue's inhabitants free and French, and was put into effect immediately. If Louverture was willing to antagonize Bonaparte to this degree, some think he should have declared outright independence and rallied the black population against France. Yet this would have made French retaliation certain and might have caused the British and Americans to blockade the island, fearful of the effect on their own slave populations of an independent black state. Louverture wanted the substance of independence more than its trappings and he gambled that France would accept Saint-Domingue's evolution into a de facto associated state or dominion.

Bonaparte, however, wanted French merchants to control Saint-Domingue's trade, and vengeful planters lobbied him to restore slavery. Britain's naval superiority made it too risky to send a large expedition to the Caribbean until peace negotiations cleared the way, in the autumn of 1801, and the British signalled their approval of a French reconquest of the colony. Although Toussaint had in 1799 secretly betrayed to the British, as a goodwill gesture, a French attempt to raise a slave rebellion in Jamaica, his regime was widely perceived as a potential threat to other slave colonies. The British and American governments assisted Toussaint Louverture during the period 1798–1800 as a means of weakening their French enemy, but neither encouraged Toussaint to seek independence, despite persistent allegations. For the British especially, it meant choosing the lesser of two evils, and calculations changed once war ended. In the United States, Thomas Jefferson's replacement of John Adams as president brought to power a ministry more concerned with the fears of southern slave owners than the interests of northern merchants. In July 1801, Jefferson assured the French that he would embargo the black regime. Thus encouraged, Bonaparte mounted a large expedition that landed in Saint-Domingue in February 1802. France's allies, the Spanish and Dutch, agreed to provide the expedition with ships, cash, and supplies. All the major powers with Caribbean interests were implicated in the French attempt to reconquer Saint-Domingue.[16]

Unlike his French, British, and Spanish predecessors, Bonaparte succeeded in deploying a large military force during the colony's healthy season. The French commander, Victor-Emmanuel Leclerc, managed to co-opt several of the black generals, and he defused resistance among the rural masses by proclaiming slave emancipation to be inviolable. Toussaint surrendered after three months of desperate fighting and was soon deported to France. The tide turned against the French during the summer, when it became clear that Bonaparte's intention was indeed to restore slavery, and when tropical fevers began to destroy his army. Popular resistance spread in the countryside and the black generals who had collaborated with Leclerc progressively deserted him. They were joined by *anciens libres* like Alexandre Pétion who had formed part of Leclerc's expedition but now realized that neither racial equality nor slave emancipation could be guaranteed without colonial independence. By the spring of

[16] Geggus, *Haitian Revolutionary Studies*, 176–7; Rayford W. Logan, *The Diplomatic Relations of the United States with Haiti, 1776–1891* (Chapel Hill, NC, 1941); Claude B. Auguste and Marcel B. Auguste, *La Participation étrangère à l'expédition française de Saint-Domingue* (Quebec, 1980), 75–126.

1803 the French were fighting the majority of the colonial population grouped under the leadership of Jean-Jacques Dessalines, the senior black general. Several autonomous African leaders in the mountains fought a brief 'war within the war' against the black creole generals, whose control they resented, but were successively eliminated.[17]

Although massacre, torture, and mutilation were common features of the Haitian Revolution from its beginning, the war of independence of 1802–3 was exceptionally brutal. Atrocities were widespread and the French military veered toward a strategy of genocide. Expected to live off the land, as in its European campaigns, the army had difficulty coping with its enemy's scorched-earth tactics and its guerrilla combat. The situation became hopeless for France once war with Britain resumed in May 1803. The British blockaded French positions in Saint-Domingue and prevented further reinforcements crossing the Atlantic. In Washington as well as London, fear of an aggressive French imperialism ultimately trumped fear of a successful black revolution. President Jefferson's growing concern about French ambitions in Louisiana quickly dampened his enthusiasm for the Leclerc expedition and, throughout the conflict, he allowed North American merchants to trade with both the French and their black opponents. After losing perhaps 40,000 soldiers in less than two years, the French army evacuated the colony in late 1803.

Dessalines proclaimed independence on 1 January 1804 and adopted the Amerindian name 'Haiti' as a symbolic erasure of the colonial past. Most of the few thousand whites who chose to chance their luck in the new state were systematically massacred in the following months. Dessalines hoped thereby to assuage a widespread desire for revenge and to issue a warning against another French invasion. The country's new elite was a volatile mixture of *anciens libres* of mixed racial descent and former slaves who had risen through the army. They and their descendants would compete for power throughout the nineteenth century.

REPERCUSSIONS

The Revolution's international impact remains controversial because it was diverse and ambiguous. It destroyed the main slave mart in the Americas but did little to reduce the volume of the Atlantic slave trade; liberating half a million from bondage, it simultaneously encouraged the spread and intensification of slavery elsewhere. Dominguan refugees developed coffee cultivation in Jamaica and Cuba, and sugar manufacture in Louisiana along with francophone culture. Louisiana's sale to the United States in 1803 was partly due to Napoleon's defeat in Saint-Domingue. The triumph of black over white alarmed slave owners across the Americas and emboldened their slaves. Events in

---

[17] Claude B. Auguste and Marcel B. Auguste, *L'Expédition Leclerc, 1801–1803* (Port-au-Prince, 1986).

Saint-Domingue or the hope of Haitian assistance inspired several conspiracies, revolts, and assertions of black pride from Brazil to the USA.[18]

The heroics and violence of the Revolution fed contradictory attitudes to race, which pro- and antislavery forces each used in their propaganda. Fear of slave revolt was probably not a major influence on the abolition movement's success. However, by ending French commercial rivalry, the Revolution did make it easier for British legislators to abandon the slave trade in 1807. The logistical assistance President Pétion gave to Simón Bolívar in 1816 made a major contribution to ending slavery and colonial rule in northern South America, but fear of Haiti's example helped keep Cuba a colony through the nineteenth century.

COMPARISONS

Although modest in its geographic and demographic dimensions, the Haitian Revolution might be considered the most transformative of the Atlantic revolutions, partly because of its relative cost and partly because of its multiple achievements: independence, racial equality, and slave emancipation.

In the contemporary European revolutions, national independence was not an issue except in the Austrian Netherlands. Nor were slavery or racial equality important questions in Europe, although it is usually forgotten that blacks were enfranchised in France and slavery was abolished there in September 1791 (quite independently of the slave uprising in Saint-Domingue).[19] Slavery was a favourite metaphor for revolutionaries everywhere, but it was an omnipresent reality only in the Americas, where the Haitian Revolution directly freed about one-sixth of the enslaved population and, because of its repercussions on Guadeloupe and Guyane, it freed in total one in five American slaves.[20] The American Revolution undermined slavery in diverse ways but, in comparison, it had a very limited impact on the institution, and none at all on race relations. The Spanish American revolutions had a more substantial influence in both areas. Yet, as they established a technical racial equality almost at their outset, they gave rise to relatively little racial conflict, and their contribution to eradicating slavery amounted to little more than a belated concession of gradual emancipation that was in large measure a response to Haitian pressure.[21]

---

[18] D. Geggus, 'The Influence of the Haitian Revolution on Blacks in Latin America and the Caribbean', in Nancy Naro (ed.), *Blacks, Coloureds and National Identity in Nineteenth-Century Latin America* (London, 2003), 38–59; Geggus, 'French Imperialism and the Louisiana Purchase', in Paul Hoffman (ed.), *The Louisiana Purchase and its Peoples* (Lafayette, LA, 2004), 25–34.

[19] Jérôme Mavidal (ed.), *Archives parlementaires de 1789 à 1860* (Paris, 1862), xxxi. 442.

[20] Around 1790 nearly 1 in 4 American slaves lived in a French colony, but the emancipation decree of February 1794 was not implemented in all of them.

[21] Paul Verna, *Petión y Bolívar: cuarenta años de relaciones haitiano-venezolanas* (Caracas, 1969), 87–298; Robin Blackburn, *The Overthrow of Colonial Slavery* (London, 1988), 348.

The price of success in the struggle for freedom, equality, and independence was, in relative and often absolute terms, far greater in the Haitian Revolution than in any of its counterparts. Newly independent Haiti exported about a quarter as much as pre-revolutionary Saint-Domingue. To judge from the Haitian census of 1805, the colonial population fell by one-third during the Revolution, a decrease of 180,000 people, far more than even Venezuela lost in twelve years of violent revolution. Some contemporaries thought the population had already declined that much by 1798. The number of refugees is hard to estimate, as many exiles returned home and fled again, but as a proportion of the total population their numbers were approximately twice as high as those of the American Loyalists (or exiled Dutch Patriots) and almost ten times as high as those of the French émigrés. The value of the property they abandoned—according to the French government, 272 million dollars—was much higher than for any other group of exiles. The three colonial powers, in attempting to suppress the Revolution, lost close to 70,000 European soldiers and many thousands of seamen.[22] It is nonetheless somewhat bogus to depict the Revolution as a transformation of the Americas' 'wealthiest' colony into its poorest state: the standard of living of most of its inhabitants almost certainly improved, as the rapid growth of the ex-slave population suggests.

In view of its claims to international prominence, it is striking that the Haitian Revolution was largely ignored in the seminal texts of the Atlantic turn, R. R. Palmer's *Age of the Democratic Revolution* and Jacques Godechot's *France and the Atlantic Revolution of the Eighteenth Century*. Whether an oversight or a calculated exclusion, this raises the question of the conceptual unity of these revolutions 'of the West', as the French and the American scholar called them. How much did they have in common? The issue of causation offers probably the least fruitful line of approach. Palmer and Godechot themselves disagreed: the former stressing ideas and politics; the latter, demography and economics. The collapse of state power, essential to launching the French, Haitian, and Spanish American revolutions, was absent in the case of the American Revolution. A cycle of war, fiscal reform, institutional protest, and popular resistance was visible everywhere between the 1760s and 1780s but only in France and the Thirteen Colonies did it lead to revolution.

Godechot and Palmer probably felt that Haiti's revolution would be out of place in their grand narrative of liberal, republican democracy. Although the struggles of Saint-Domingue's white colonists and free people of colour might easily be incorporated into their revolutionary paradigm, the black revolution whose origins lay in the slave uprising of 1791 and which produced Haiti's first heads of state fits less well because

---

[22] Figures from Drouin de Bercy, *De Saint-Domingue* (Paris, 1814), appendix; James Leyburn, *The Haitian People* (New Haven, CT, 1966), 33, 320; Service Historique de la Défense, Vincennes, Armée de Terre, MS 592, ii. 15; John Lynch, *The Spanish American Revolutions, 1808–1826* (London, 1973), 221; Palmer, *Age of the Democratic Revolution*, i. 188; Jacques Godechot, *France and the Atlantic Revolution of the Eighteenth Century, 1770–1799* (London, 1965), 60; *État détaillé des liquidations opérées par la commission . . . de l'indemnité de Saint-Domingue*, 6 vols. (Paris, 1828–33); Geggus, 'Slavery, War, and Revolution in the Greater Caribbean', 24–5.

of its authoritarian and later 'ethno-national' character.[23] Such a judgement is at odds with some modern scholarship that presents the slave revolution as a pursuit of 'democratic ideals' and 'republican rights' and claims for it an important role in the creation of modern democracy.[24] Its rhetoric, however, was overwhelmingly counter-revolutionary and never republican. Insurgent slaves used *citoyens* as a smearword to describe their opponents. The French Republic never really followed through in its extension of citizenship to ex-slaves, and the few elections held in Saint-Domingue in the 1790s, to name deputies to the French legislature, were very localized and, according to critics, hardly free and fair.[25] Toussaint Louverture, Jean-Jacques Dessalines, and Henry Christophe, the main leaders who rose from slavery, were unashamedly dicta-torial in their politics, as each of their constitutions makes clear. The country's unique declaration of independence justified secession as an act necessary to prevent the restoration of slavery but otherwise made no mention of rights. The État d'Haïti founded in 1804 was not a republic, although historians persist in calling it one. Dessalines arrogated all power to himself and took the titles governor general and then emperor. When his *anciens libres* opponents assassinated him in 1806 and drew up a republican constitution, Henry Christophe created a secessionist northern state that soon became a monarchy.

The Latin American revolutions also produced a few monarchs, and the French Revolution similarly ended in military dictatorship, but Haiti was unique in its blending of race and nationalism. Contrasting the complexions of the Haitians and French, and stressing the latter's cruelty and vulnerability to tropical disease, the declaration of independence vowed 'eternal hatred of France' and called for vengeance against those French who remained in the country. Most were massacred in the following months. Dessalines' constitution forbade landowning by 'whites' and man-dated that all Haitians be designated 'blacks'. Notwithstanding Simón Bolívar's *guerra a muerte* against metropolitan Spaniards, the nationalism of the Americas' white revolutionaries expressed little animosity toward the colonial rulers they much resem-bled, but Haitian nationalism, forged in enslavement and an exceptionally vicious war, was defined by race and born in bitterness.

Haiti's revolution also differed from the other colonial revolutions in that indepen-dence was not its central goal. Whereas the mainland revolutions more or less began with a declaration of independence, in the Haitian Revolution it was the final act. The concept of colonial independence had almost no support among France's revolution-aries, whose sense of national interest overrode their libertarianism. In Saint-Domingue, most white and free coloured activists wanted self-rule rather than independence. The

[23] D. Geggus, 'The Caribbean in the Age of Revolution', in David Armitage and Sanjay Subramanyam (eds.), *The Age of Revolutions in Global Context, c.1760–1840* (New York, 2010), 244 n. 51; Leslie Manigat, *Évolution et révolutions* (Port-au-Prince, 2007), 88, 96.

[24] Laurent Dubois, 'An Enslaved Enlightenment: Rethinking the Intellectual History of the French Atlantic', *Social History*, 31 (2006), 11–12; Dubois, *Avengers of the New World* (Cambridge, 2004), 3; Dubois, *A Colony of Citizens*, 2–7.

[25] *Histoire des désastres*, 363–4; Dubois, *Avengers of the New World*, 205.

wealthiest planters tended to live in France, and those in the Caribbean were greatly outnumbered by slaves; they could not contemplate secession in the same way as their Virginian or Venezuelan counterparts. The age-old tensions caused by metropolitan control of trade never reached flashpoint during the Revolution, because the colonists in France decided to bury the issue so as to build a proslavery alliance with French merchants, while those in the colony were able to ignore mercantilist restrictions as government authority declined.[26] When they did seek to throw off French rule in 1791–4, it was primarily to maintain slavery and white supremacy, and they sought, not independence, but a British protectorate.

The place of independence among the goals of Saint-Domingue's slaves is unclear. One of the earliest documents to issue from the 1791 uprising summoned the French to pick up their jewellery and leave the colony to the slaves, whose sweat and blood had earned them title to the land. Common sense also might suggest that the slaves would not have rebelled unless they expected to live afterwards free from the possibility of French revenge.[27] Such expectations, however, seem to have been quickly scaled back and, as noted above, the leadership of the insurrection generally displayed a rather limited commitment to the idea of general emancipation, let alone independence. Once the French Republic abolished slavery, most former slaves found their interests best served by remaining subjects of the French state, while most of the insurgents had already opted for a career as mercenary troops of the king of Spain. Certainly, the polity that Toussaint Louverture ruled by 1800 was a colony only in name; some contemporaries thought he would declare Saint-Domingue independent, and some Haitian historians have argued this was only a matter of time. Yet Toussaint never took that step, even when attacked by General Leclerc. It was Bonaparte's attempt to restore slavery and racial discrimination that finally led to independence.

The winning of independence benefited somewhat from British naval support in 1803—just as the US navy helped Toussaint defeat Rigaud in 1800—but foreign military intervention in the Haitian Revolution was for the most part hostile, at least in intent. Spain's intervention may have revived the slave insurgency and indirectly led to emancipation, but, like Britain's intervention, it was intended to restore the status quo. The Haitian Revolution differed in this respect from the mainland colonial revolutions and resembled the French Revolution, in which foreign invaders also unintentionally radicalized developments. Whereas the North Americans received crucial assistance from the French state, as did Spanish Americans from the Haitian government and various foreign sympathizers, Haiti's revolutionaries, like those in France, triumphed largely in spite of the outside world.

Foreign powers similarly took far longer to recognize Haiti's independence than that of the mainland colonies. None did so until 1825, when France imposed a large indemnity as reparations for its colonists. The United States and the Vatican withheld

---

[26] Debien, *Les Colons de Saint-Domingue*, 53.

[27] Geggus, 'Print Culture', 88–92; Yves Benot, 'The Insurgents of 1791, their Leaders and the Concept of Independence', in Geggus and Fiering (eds.), *The World of the Haitian Revolution*, 153–71.

recognition until the 1860s. The country was never isolated, as sometimes claimed, but the USA imposed a trade embargo between 1806 and 1810, and Haitian ships were excluded from British colonies until the 1840s. Transformed into a peasant economy, Haiti remained an important coffee exporter.

BIBLIOGRAPHY

Ardouin, Beaubrun, *Études sur l'histoire d'Haïti* (1853), 3 vols. (rev. edn. Port-au-Prince, 2005).

Benot, Yves, *La Révolution française et la fin des colonies* (Paris, 1987).

Dubois, Laurent, *Avengers of the New World: The Story of the Haitian Revolution* (Cambridge, MA, 2004).

Fischer, Sibylle, *Modernity Disavowed: Haiti and the Cultures of Slavery in the Age of Revolution* (Durham, NC, 2004).

Garrigus, John D., *Before Haiti: Race and Citizenship in French Saint-Domingue* (New York, 2006).

Geggus, David, *Haitian Revolutionary Studies* (Bloomington, IN, 2002).

—— (ed.), *The Impact of the Haitian Revolution in the Atlantic World* (Columbia, SC, 2001).

—— and Norman Fiering (eds.), *The World of the Haitian Revolution* (Bloomington, IN, 2009).

Madiou, Thomas, *Histoire d'Haïti* (1847–8), 8 vols. (rev. edn. Port-au-Prince, 1989–91).

Piquet, Jean-Daniel, *L'Émancipation des noirs dans la Révolution française (1789–1795)* (Paris, 2002).

CHAPTER 32

POPULAR MOVEMENTS IN COLONIAL BRAZIL

LAURA DE MELLO E SOUZA
JOÃO JOSÉ REIS

To speak of popular movements in Brazil before 1822 raises problems, especially if European and Atlantic contexts are considered. Who are the people, and how would they manifest themselves in a social formation marked by three centuries of slavery that not only deeply influenced the lives of Brazil's inhabitants but also articulated all economic and social relations, and radically demeaned the value of manual labour? What in this social formation would be the nature of popular struggles?

Colonial society in Portuguese America was, like all contemporary European and Euro-American societies, based on inequality and privilege. However, it presented additional elements that provoked dissatisfaction and conflict: the Portuguese rules of blood purity and the widespread use of slave labour. Bondage in Brazil involved millions of slaves from Africa, and before that, the enslavement of thousands of indigenous peoples; this diversity occasioned much tension and conflict. Similarly, since Portuguese America was a group of colonial territories subject to a monarchical regime located on the other side of the Atlantic, animosities developed between those who lived in the kingdom (*Reino*) and those who lived and, more particularly, were born in America. Consequently numerous social movements gained an anti-metropolitan, even anti-colonial, character without, until the early nineteenth century, mobilizing any significant popular participation. It is, therefore, important to differentiate between social movements and popular movements; among the latter we decided to include slave rebellions.

Although the Portuguese empire was increasingly interconnected, the motivation and logic of popular protest did not always have an imperial dimension. While some movements were specifically related to local events, issues, and processes, others were local expressions of broader, often revolutionary developments common to the Atlantic world—Africa included—which became more potent from the later eighteenth century onward.

INDIANS AND COLONISTS IN CONFLICT

After 1570 the crown repeatedly prohibited the enslavement of indigenous peoples in Portuguese America, more strictly during the period of Spanish dominion (1580–1640). Yet the crown and the Church, particularly the Jesuits—the most active missionary order operating in the colony since 1549—considered that indigenous peoples taken prisoner in 'just' wars (those fought against rebellious, non-assimilated Indians) could be enslaved. As colonization took root, the Portuguese often raided Indian villages to 'rescue' prisoners of internecine wars who might be legally enslaved because they were otherwise destined to be killed. This justification of indigenous enslavement provided colonists with a precedent for revoking royal orders ever more frequently and for vetoing obstacles to Indian enslavement.

As colonization advanced and sugar plantations in the north-east became the main economic activity in Portuguese America, the increased need for labour led to greater conflict between slave-hungry colonists and Jesuits. In places with limited access to African labour, notably the southern captaincies of Rio de Janeiro and São Paulo, and the northern captaincy of Pará, the most remarkable battles were fought over the Indian question. In the late sixteenth century, when Portugal was under Spanish rule, the Jesuits put pressure on Madrid to enforce legislation against Indian enslavement and to prohibit colonists' predation on Jesuit missions. The priests obtained orders from Philip IV that reiterated previous prohibitions of Indian enslavement. As a result, they were almost lynched in Rio de Janeiro, where they were permitted to remain only on the promise that they would not interfere with such matters. In São Paulo, the announcement of the antislavery edict incited the crowd to launch an attack on the Jesuit College, resulting in the expulsion of the Jesuits from both the city and the neighbouring port of Santos.

In 1680 in Pará, a further Jesuit reiteration of the rights of Indians provoked a rebellion of colonists against the Portuguese government. Planter dissatisfaction intensified when a company, created in 1682 and enjoying a significant trading monopoly in return for importing African slaves, failed to fulfil its obligations. Thus deprived of labour, planters incited street riots, abolished the company's monopoly, authorized Indian slavery, and expelled the Jesuits. A brief period of self-government followed, and when a new governor restored order, he had Lisbon permit Indian slavery, thus conceding the rebels' principal demand.

Indian resistance to colonization and enslavement had been a feature of Brazilian life since the first century of Portuguese conquest. In the second half of the sixteenth century, for instance, in the sugar plantation region known as the Recôncavo of Bahia, Christianized indigenous groups rose up in arms under the command of a young Indian from a Jesuit mission. The rebels professed religious justifications in which elements of Christian doctrine combined with millennial myths typical of coastal South

American indigenous peoples.[1] This movement was eventually suppressed, but it was a precursor to a long cycle of late seventeenth-century indigenous uprisings known as 'Guerra dos Bárbaros'—'War of the Barbarians' (1651–1704)—one of the largest and long-lasting social conflicts in Brazil's colonial history. The cycle divides into two phases: clashes in the Recôncavo of Bahia (1651–79), and the wars of the Açu River valley in the present-day state of Rio Grande do Norte (1687–1704).

The War of the Barbarians occurred in the aftermath of the expulsion by the Portuguese of the Dutch, who had occupied the Brazilian north-east between 1630 and 1654. As the Portuguese took over, cattle ranching intensified and penetrated further into the interior, and indigenous peoples responded with violent attacks in Bahia, beginning in 1651, and in Pernambuco, Rio Grande and Ceará, beginning in 1687. The conflict went beyond the coastal strip, where the original colonial settlements had been founded, and spread into the immense semi-arid backlands, extending from the east of Maranhão to the north of Bahia, where cattle ranches proliferated and where government and colonists hoped to remove the region's native inhabitants and open up new trails and find saltpetre mines. The war against the Indian resisters was won by Paulista (people from São Paulo) Indian hunters who had been brought to the northern region following promises of land and entitlement to take prisoners as slaves with disastrous consequences for the vanquished.[2]

Indian slavery and freedom continued to be an issue throughout the eighteenth century. Between 1765 and 1785, the decline in mining in the eastern backlands of Minas Gerais forced the colonial administration and colonists to find economic alternatives, putting pressure on densely forested areas inhabited by indigenous peoples. The main clash occurred between colonists with small parcels of land (*posseiros* or squatters) and Indian groups, such as the warlike Coroado, Botocudo, and Pataxó, who reacted violently to land encroachment and often took the initiative in attacks. Nevertheless, many Indians ended up living in colonial settlements, where they mixed with whites, becoming the victims of an uncertain, loose legal and social status that fluctuated between freedom and slavery. But they often proved to be zealous guardians of their status as free persons, to which they could lay claim by using existing legal instruments to claim their freedom.[3]

Other notable episodes of Indian resistance include the war fought by the Guaraní Indians, settled in the Jesuit missions of the Seven Peoples (*Sete Povos de Missões*), from 1752 to 1757 against a joint Portuguese and Spanish army. The Guaraní War, as it became known, was a prelude to the expulsion in the following years of the Society of

---

[1] Ronaldo Vainfas, *A heresia dos índios* (São Paulo, 1995).

[2] Pedro Puntoni, *A guerra dos bárbaros: povos indígenas e a colonização do sertão nordeste do Brasil—1650–1720* (São Paulo, 2002), 46; John Monteiro, *Negros da terra: índios e bandeirantes nas origens de São Paulo* (São Paulo, 1993), 7–8.

[3] Maria Leônia Chaves de Resende and Hal Langfur, 'Minas Gerais indígena: a resistência dos índios nos sertões e nas vilas de El-Rei', *Revista tempo*, 23 (2007), 15–32; Hal Langfur, *The Forbidden Lands: Colonial Identity, Frontier Violence and the Persistence of Brazil's Eastern Indians, 1750–1830* (Stanford, CA, 2006).

Jesus from the majority of Europe's Catholic kingdoms and their overseas possessions. Yet other Indian movements represented new chapters in the struggle against colonial encroachment, as in the 1770s and 1780s, when the Mura in the Amazon attacked forts, pillaged crops, and killed riverside dwellers.[4] Indian resistance thus remained endemic, usually provoked by the colonists' appetite for land and slaves.

AFRICAN SLAVES AS REBELS

Different forms of African slave resistance occurred in colonial Brazil, but rarely large-scale movements intent on destroying the reigning order. Slave resistance would rather range from work slowdowns to sabotage, and from magical-religious practices to suicide. Most commonly, slaves fled their captors, often organizing runaway communities— known in Brazil as *quilombo* or *mocambo*—some of which constituted sizeable villages.

African slave resistance decisively influenced the colonial mindset. In the tension between slaves and the free population it was impossible to distinguish real from imaginary danger, but both terrified colonists. Slave flight was endemic and runaway communities formed the most constant internal enemy threatening slave owners' hegemony. Quotidian slave resistance, however fragmented, proved effective at least symbolically, and coexisted with slave–master negotiation to ease oppression and exploitation.[5]

Large-scale resistance tended to happen on those occasions when masters relaxed control. Festive occasions, particularly Christmas and Easter, provided slaves with an opportunity to engage in their own collective celebrations, giving them a chance to conspire against masters. In Minas Gerais, for example, slaves planned an uprising to take place at Easter 1719. Plotters sent messengers to different parts of the captaincy to recruit rebels. It failed principally because the leaders belonged to two different 'nations', Angola and Mina, and disagreed about who would take command. Slave rebels also took advantage of political divisions among white colonists provoked by political and military crisis, as during the war against the Dutch in the mid-seventeenth century, and the anti-colonial movements at the turn of the nineteenth century.[6]

Probably founded in the early seventeenth century, the famous Palmares *quilombo* arose when a group of slave rebels from a sugar plantation settled on the Barriga

---

[4] Tau Golin, *A guerra guaranítica: como os exércitos de Portugal e Espanha destruíram os Sete Povos dos jesuítas e índios guaranis no Rio Grande do Sul (1750–1761)* (2nd edn. Passo Fundo, 1999); Francisco Jorge dos Santos, 'Descimento dos Mura no Solimões', in Patrícia Melo Sampaio and Regina Carvalho Erthal (eds.), *Rastros da memória: histórias e trajetórias das populações indígenas na Amazônia* (Manaus, 2006), 73–95.

[5] João José Reis e Eduardo Silva, *Negociação e conflito: a resistência negra no Brasil escravista* (São Paulo, 1989).

[6] Pablo Luís de Oliveira Lima, 'Marca de fogo: o medo dos quilombos e a construção da hegemonia escravista (Minas Gerais, 1699–1769)' (Ph.D. dissertation, Universidade Federal de Minas Gerais, 2008).

mountain range (Serra da Barriga), then a dependency of the captaincy of Pernambuco. It flourished during the Dutch occupation and kept growing after the 1640s when Portugal recovered control of the region. The several communities within the Palmares federation perhaps totalled as many as 10,000 former slaves and their offspring in the 1670s when it was at its height; it represented the major internal threat to Portuguese colonial society in the Americas before the anti-colonial movements of the late eighteenth century. Some scholars contend that it was an African re-creation in the heart of Portuguese America, but it was instead a community that had adopted many local customs and created new ones in order to survive, although elements of African cultural and institutional life can be identified. The term *quilombo* itself was a reference to a warrior society or *kilombo* found in the backlands of Angola. Overcoming several expeditions sent to crush it and signing a peace treaty negotiated in 1678 by Ganga Zumba, one of its leaders, the Palmares was finally defeated in 1695, when its most famous chief, Zumbi, was killed.[7]

This experience intensified slave owners' fears of runaways to the point where they thought a slave insurrection could destroy colonial authority. To counter possible successors the crown created a body of slave hunters called *capitães-do-mato* or bush captains, but there were already other *quilombos* in existence in old colonial areas, notably Cairu, Camamu, and Ilhéus, mostly dedicated to manioc production (and modest sugar undertakings), in southern Bahia, as well as in the Recôncavo area, the heart of Bahian sugar production. Also, smaller versions of Palmares continued to be created in Pernambuco in the early eighteenth century, some apparently offspring of the original federation.

Fears of slave resistance therefore had a basis in reality. Throughout the eighteenth century, small and medium-size *quilombos* featured in areas of difficult access but close to urban centres, mining fields, and plantations. Colonial authorities in Minas Gerais reported around 160 runaway communities over the century; in Mato Grosso, the Piolho *quilombo* lasted for over fifty years (1740–95); and in Goiás, near the capital, Vila Boa, small *quilombos* proliferated. The better-organized and stable communities produced most of what they needed to survive, and traded their surplus with nearby merchants and tavern owners. Because they rarely conspired to overthrow the slave system, these *quilombos* adapted to, rather than denied, slave society, and in a way constituted a safety valve circumventing a social explosion.[8] However, slave runaways, especially those organized in *quilombos*, were more than a nuisance and were perhaps

---

[7] Stuart B. Schwartz, *Slaves, Peasants and Rebels: Reconsidering Brazilian Slavery* (Urbana, IL, 1992), 104–36; João José Reis and Flávio dos Santos Gomes (eds.), *Liberdade por um fio: história dos quilombos no Brasil* (São Paulo, 1996); Flávio Gomes, *Palmares: escravidão e liberdade no Atlântico Sul* (São Paulo, 2005); Silvia H. Lara, 'Palmares e Cucaú: o aprendizado da dominação', (titular dissertation, Universidade Estadual de Campinas, 2009); and John Thorton, 'Les États de l'Angola et la formation de Palmares', *Annales: histoire, sciences sociales*, 4 (2008), 769–97.

[8] Donald Ramos, 'O quilombo e o sistema escravista em Minas Gerais no século XVIII', 164–92; Volpato, 'Quilombos em Mato Grosso', 222; Mary Karasch, 'Os quilombos do ouro na capitania de Goiás', all in Reis e Gomes (eds.), *Liberdade por um fio*, 240–62.

the main cause of the endemic instability of the slave system. Runaways disrupted transportation networks, pillaged crops, kidnapped slave women, and resisted armed forces sent against them. They were a threat to the residents of the big house and a bad example to the occupants of slave quarters.

COLONIAL INSURRECTION

Movements of a formal political nature enjoyed significant support from elements within the elites, which, even when there was popular participation, always controlled the protest. Over time, a North–South Atlantic connection became more markedly visible in these movements, which were anti-colonial in administrative more than in systemic terms. Planters and merchants were increasingly linked to the Atlantic world through economic activity. Those living in colonial ports frequently interacted with ships' captains and sailors, mostly Portuguese, but some foreign, who often smuggled in forbidden books and, by the late eighteenth century, seditious pamphlets. Well-off families sent their sons to be educated overseas, chiefly to Europe, since colonial Brazil lacked a university, and they frequently returned with enlightened ideas.

Protests from within colonial elites flourished at two interludes in the eighteenth century.[9] The first began with the War of the Spanish Succession (1711–13) and lasted until 1736. Actions ranged from anti-taxation or fiscal rebellions to confrontation with representatives of the crown to social struggles. Protagonists varied from descendants of the original colonists (particularly landed aristocrats) to the more recently arrived groups (traders, gold miners, public officers). The second coincided with colonial and social unrest between the American and the French revolutions (including both Revolutionary and Napoleonic wars). Participants in this second insurgent phase included the Brazilian and Portuguese-born elites as well as more popular groups, including free mulattos and even black slaves. Between these two periods of intense activity, a wave of written and verbal protests arose against the king, Dom José I, and his minister the marquis of Pombal for their banishment of the Jesuits from the Empire. This opposition may be described as a confrontation rather than an insurgency.

The reign of Dom João V (1706–50) inaugurated a shift in Portuguese imperial policy, not least because the discovery of gold in Brazil earned the Atlantic renewed importance in royal priorities. As the presence of the king, his administrators, and exactions was felt more strongly, uprisings and mutinies mushroomed in various parts of Portuguese America, manifesting either separately or in combination the following three characteristics: (1) conflicts between older aristocratic groups and groups of more recent settlers; (2) disputes between 'the people' and the government because of more

---

[9] Laura de Mello e Souza, 'Motines, revueltas y revoluciones en la America Portuguesa de los siglos XVII y XVIII', in Enrique Tandeter and Jorge Hidalgo Lehuedé (eds.), *Historia general de América Latina* (Brussels, 2000), iv. 459–73.

efficient fiscal policies; and (3) circumscribed opposition from the military rank and file protesting poor rations and denial of back pay.

The war of *Emboabas*—meaning non-Paulistas—in areas of Minas Gerais and São Paulo from 1707 to 1709, and that of the *Mascates*—literally, merchants, but in this case residents of Recife—in Pernambuco, between 1710 and 1711, combined elements of the first and second types. The former resulted from transformations deriving from the enormous dislocation of people during the gold rush in Minas Gerais, starting in 1695, that pitted the first discoverers, generally from São Paulo, against latecomers from other regions—such as Bahia—and especially from Portugal. It also expressed disgruntlement of miners at efforts of the metropolitan government to control the region more tightly, founding towns and organizing taxation, and the dissatisfaction of the people over monopolistic control of certain staple foods by merchants. The second conflict positioned traders in Recife—a village dedicated to maritime commerce to Europe and Africa founded during the Dutch occupation of the north-east—and sugar planters in the city of Olinda, the original, more aristocratic, colonial settlement. As in Old Regime European societies, tensions developed between an established society of orders and an emerging society based on merit and money, but local groups also protested against the king's representatives. The merchant class won the dispute and the Portuguese government awarded Recife city status, thus displacing Olinda and the sugar planters politically.[10]

In both episodes, the crown swung between the two sides, always fearful, with some justification, that conflict between powerful colonial interests would result in the loss of the colony. This fear was especially true for Pernambuco, where the struggle against the Dutch had increased the confidence of local people, producing hints of proto-nationalism and strong regional allegiances, which were rekindled by various dissatis-factions with representatives of royal power. In the Emboabas War, the Paulistas took advantage of contractualist theories then in fashion, articulating protests against the royal power whenever the interest of the people was thought under threat.[11]

In 1711, two revolts occurred in the city of Salvador, the capital of the sugar-producing captaincy of Bahia, and an important urban centre. They were multifaceted in their actions and social composition, but were directed particularly against taxes imposed on slaves imported from Africa, other import tariffs, and a salt tax. Soldiers, public officials, and sailors from the Portuguese royal fleet joined the protests and ransacked merchant stores. Leaders posted broadsheets threatening to become vassals 'to a different master unless the new taxes were suspended'.[12] Thus confronted, the local government reversed the tax hike and pardoned the rebels.

---

[10] Adriana Romeiro, *Paulistas e emboabas no coração das Minas* (Belo Horizonte, 2009); Evaldo Cabral de Melo, *A fronda dos mazombos—nobres contra mascates: Pernambuco, 1666–1715* (São Paulo, 1995).

[11] Luciano Raposo de Almeida Figueiredo, 'O Império em apuros: notas para o estudo das altercações ultramarinas e das práticas políticas no Império colonial português, séculos XVII e XVIII', in Junia Ferreira Furtado (ed.), *Diálogos oceânicos: Minas Gerais e as novas abordagens para uma história do Império Ultramarino Português* (Belo Horizonte, 2001), 197–254.

[12] Alberto Lamego, 'Os motins do "Maneta" na Bahia', *Revista do Instituto Histórico e Geográfico Brasileiro*, 55 (1929), 357–66.

In 1720, in the mining region of Minas Gerais, the magistracy confronted the governor, the local oligarchy protested against the crown, and there was general dissatisfaction with the levying of taxes on gold. In Vila Rica, several of the region's most important miners and merchants, including participants in the Emboabas War, led violent popular protests. The governor first indicated he would ease taxation, but later occupied Vila Rica militarily and resorted to strong-arm methods.

Between this cluster of early eighteenth-century rebellions and those towards century's end, a series of movements occurred in the central-eastern regions of Brazil— Minas Gerais, Mato Grosso, Goiás, Espírito Santo—led by cultivated men linked to the legal and ecclesiastical apparatuses. These were people trained by the Jesuits who, in the absence of universities in the colony, monopolized the education of boys and young men and enjoyed high esteem among elite groups. When the metropolitan government decreed the expulsion of the Jesuits in 1759, protests began. These conflicts, as with the Emboabas War, were justified by reference to contractualism, a principle dear to the Jesuits. However, the classic terms of contractualist rebellions of the Old Regime—'long live the King and death to bad government'—were inverted, since Jesuit supporters criticized the king and his minister, even if they did not deny the legitimacy of monarchy. Effectively, they implied 'long live good government and death to the king', thus uniquely targeting the royal persona.[13]

Most of the pro-Jesuit protests never went beyond meetings, the distribution of pamphlets, murmurings, and rumours. But given that words alone were considered seditious, there were investigations and accusations, especially in various locales in Minas Gerais between 1760 and 1776, and rumours circulated that Jesuit priests might facilitate an invasion of Brazil.

The second insurgent wave, at the end of the century, represented a rupture with the previous dissident tradition. It involved social groups and objectives closer in character to those that came to the fore in Europe at the close of the Old Regime. They were different from prior movements, because their deployment of enlightened ideals converged with a desire for radical change which, in the last resort, challenged both absolute monarchy as a form of government, and the colonial condition as a political and economic system. The so-called *inconfidências* (conspiracies) of 1789, in Minas Gerais, 1794, in Rio de Janeiro, and 1798, in Bahia, were the most notable, each reflecting the impact of the American and French Revolutions.

These conspiracies have frequently been identified in Brazilian historiography as the first steps towards independence from Portugal. Today, in the light of an emerging Atlantic History paradigm, they tend to be seen differently. Undoubtedly, they reflected a crisis in the old colonial system but, with the exception of the Bahian movement, the refusal of the rebels to renounce slavery, in spite of their professed enlightened ideas,

---

[13] Figueiredo, 'O império em apuros'; Leandro Pena Catão, 'Sacrílegas palavras: inconfidência e presença jesuítica nas Minas Gerais durante o período pombalino' (Ph.D. dissertation, Universidade Federal de Minas Gerais, 2005); id., 'Jesuítas, inconfidência(s), contestação e cultura política no Estado do Brasil nos tempos de Pombal' (unpublished essay, 2008).

severely limited the change they could promote. Tensions between the civilizing goals of the conspirators, many of whom were learned slaveholders, and their fear of 'barbarism' as represented by a majority population that was racially mixed, black and indigenous, meant no serious consideration of the abolition of slavery. In some cases, as happened in the 1789 Minas Gerais conspiracy, leaders sought to adopt reformist plans. However, defence of private interests—pardoning of debts, and free access to Atlantic trade networks, for example—gained precedence over ameliorative measures for the underprivileged. In general—especially in Minas and Rio de Janeiro— conspiracy apparently reflected the desire of local elites to gain political representation in metropolitan government bodies as well as in colonial administration. These movements therefore sought redistribution of power and economic gains rather than a disruption of the colonial relationship, as evidenced by the conspiracy in Rio de Janeiro which was limited to private discussions of enlightened and seditious ideas.

What transpired in Minas Gerais was different because, after becoming the most important region in the Portuguese empire with the discovery of gold (c.1694) and diamonds (1729), it developed a highly urbanized society, and a significant intellectual elite, whose sons attended universities in Europe and included some of the most celebrated eighteenth-century Luso-Brazilian poets, notably Cláudio Manuel da Costa and Tomás Antonio Gonzaga. Literary meetings and book lending were habitual, and included prohibited literature; private libraries displayed works by Raynal, Montesquieu, and Voltaire. Enlightened ideas acquired a dangerous potential after 1784, when a new governor altered the system used to appoint individuals for administrative positions. The indebtedness of some of those being displaced, all members of the local oligarchy, and the repression of illegal trade in diamonds increased dissatisfaction.

Influenced by the events of 1776 in North America, independence in the region became an issue debated over dinner tables and in private meetings, leading eventually to a seditious plan. The conspirators, who expected to attract popular support, acted when the governor launched the *derrama*, a fiscal instrument designed to bring more gold into the king's coffers. Aware that a rebellion was imminent, governor Viscount Barbacena suspended the *derrama* and moved to suppress the rebellion on 14 March 1789, charging with sedition anyone who had favoured measures of an anti-colonial nature, which included separation from Portugal, the promotion of free trade, the establishment of a constitutional, republican regime in Minas Gerais, and the creation of a gunpowder factory and a mint. Those charged were good-standing citizens, including not only poets, but the region's main military commander, large ranch owners, holders of the most important mining contracts, and senior clergy. Arrests began in May 1789, but the harsh punishments initially intended were later attenuated, possibly due to knowledge of what was happening in Revolutionary France.[14]

---

[14] Kenneth Maxwell, *Conflicts and Conspiracies: Brazil and Portugal, 1750–1808* (Cambridge, 1973); João Pinto Furtado, *O manto de Penélope: história, mito e memória da Inconfidência mineira de 1788–9* (São Paulo, 2002).

In Rio de Janeiro, capital of the viceroyalty of Brazil with a population of 40,000, trials and punishments produced a profound impression, as also did the attempt of the viceroy in 1794 to dissolve a literary society, accusing its members of embracing anti-monarchical ideas, of being sympathetic to French principles which justified subjects in rebelling against the king, and of condemning religiosity at the Portuguese court. These people were arrested, but after almost two years of investigation, the group's meetings and preaching were found to be non-conspiratorial, no evidence having emerged of treason or of a plan to ignite an armed revolt against the government.[15]

In this case French ideas seem not to have extended beyond a limited group, but a potentially explosive combination of French ideas and popular dissatisfaction occurred in Bahia in 1798. The captaincy was at the time undergoing a period of economic growth, and its capital, Salvador, included the largest urban concentration of blacks in Portuguese America. Bahia´s prosperity at the time was largely due to the revolution and economic debacle in Saint-Domingue, which provided unprecedented opportunity for other Atlantic sugar colonies. In Bahia the number of plantations multiplied, slave imports almost doubled, and sugar exports more than doubled between 1789 and 1795. Although most imported Africans were sent to sugar plantations, many were also employed in the city as domestics, tradesmen, and porters. By that time, the City of Bahia, as Salvador was more often called, also had a large population of Brazilian-born free and freed blacks and mulattos, who provided the backbone of the conspiracy.

On 12 August 1798, notices to the 'Bahian People' were posted in the city's public places promising great social changes, economic and professional advantages for the soldiers, racial equality in the recruitment for civil and military services, freedom for slaves, the elimination of absolutism, the creation of a republican regime, the reduction of taxes, and free trade. The programme responded to the interests of a vast constituency, ranging from slaves to export merchants, from soldiers to free blacks. The French Revolution clearly inspired the movement, and it was systematically invoked in several pamphlets. This movement was later called the Tailors' Revolt, because twelve of forty-eight defendants were tailors, but they also included soldiers and some officers.[16] Widespread rebellion was pre-empted by early arrests, but four men, all poor, black, or mixed-race, were condemned to death on 8 November 1799, and a further six, also poor, were exiled.

This Bahian conspiracy drew support from several segments of society, deployed a yet unheard-of revolutionary sensibility, and managed to span public and private arenas. Before 1798, sedition and enlightened protest had been contemplated behind closed doors, but public manifestos were now taken to the streets as in Salvador to promote a truly popular movement.

---

[15] Afonso Carlos Marques dos Santos, *No rascunho da nação: Inconfidência no Rio de Janeiro* (Rio de Janeiro, 1992).

[16] Katia M. de Queirós Mattoso, *A presença francesa no movimento democrático baiano de 1798* (Salvador, 1969); id., *Da revolução dos alfaiates à riqueza dos baianos no século XIX* (Salvador, 2004), 46.

Remarkably, French Revolutionary principles were invoked persistently throughout the investigation into the Bahian plot, but no analogy was drawn in any source to the Saint-Domingue Revolution, which had then been in progress for seven years. A mulatto soldier named João de Deus even considered it 'fitting that everybody should be like Frenchmen, to live with equality and plenty...eliminating the difference between the colours white, black, and brown', but he expressed no aspiration to be like Saint-Domingans.[17] Apparently, he also identified Bonaparte, not Toussaint Louverture, as a potential ally of the 'República Bahiense'.

The well-informed mulatto artisans and soldiers who constituted the backbone of the Bahian conspiracy were undoubtedly aware of the great Caribbean revolution, but perhaps could not contemplate its potential consequences for slavery and racial discrimination in Brazil. They seemed far more comfortable with French Revolutionary principles, such as the declaration of racial equality in France of April 1792, and the abolition of slavery in French colonies, including Saint-Domingue, in February 1794, both measures prompted by revolutionary events in the Caribbean. However, the Haitian Revolution, which was obliquely present in the Bahian conspiracy, exerted a greater influence in other Brazilian contexts.

HAITI AND POPULAR REBELLION

The impact of the Haitian Revolution was particularly felt in Brazil's northern frontier, where Luso-French territorial disputes had a long history. Soon after the outbreak of revolution in France, Portuguese authorities feared that the Brazilian frontier with French Guiana would provide access to revolutionary ideas. In 1792 the Portuguese accused the French there of 'flattering the slaves with the idea of pretended liberty and equality', and of encouraging maroons to flee across the border. Although no serious slave uprising occurred, the Portuguese remained fearful, particularly after 1808 when Napoleon's France had occupied Portugal and when, under pressure from Britain, the Portuguese court had fled to Brazil. As a precautionary measure the Portuguese occupied Cayenne in 1809, and its terms of French surrender included the requirement that slaves from both sides should be disarmed and returned to their masters. The 'French blacks' who had fought on the Portuguese side were ordered to leave the colony because they were considered potentially subversive.[18]

What transpired in northern Brazil was less relevant elsewhere in the Portuguese colony, other than in the minds of those who feared the spread of *haitianismo*

---

[17] Ignácio Accioli de Cerqueira e Silva, *Memórias históricas e políticas da Província da Bahia*, ed. Braz do Amaral (1835–7; Bahia, 1931), i/2. 17 n. 86.

[18] João José Reis and Flávio dos Santos Gomes, 'The Repercussions of the Haitian Revolution in Brazil, 1792–1830', in David P. Geggus and Norman Fiering (eds.), *The World of the Haitian Revolution* (Bloomington, IN, 2009), 284–313.

(haitianism); an expression coined in the early nineteenth century after which it featured regularly, particularly in the press, every time a revolt by blacks and/or mulattos threatened or materialized. Thus for the nineteenth century Haiti became what Palmares had been for the eighteenth century: the nightmare of Brazil's master class. Nevertheless, reports of Haitian reverberations in Brazil point to the potential, rather than reality, of large-scale black revolts. Thus while the 1817 rebellion in Pernambuco was primarily an anti-colonialist movement led by elite groups, it also mobilized popular support, meaning free blacks and mulattos who constituted the vast majority of the protesters and threatened to direct it to more radical goals. Groups that included free people and slaves attacked and killed Portuguese-born individuals in the opening act of the conflict. The rebel forces, who called themselves patriots after the French Revolutionary Convention, occupied Recife for almost three months, established a provisional government formed by elite members, and extended their control over a large area in the interior as well as neighbouring provinces. The Pernambuco movement represented the most serious challenge to Portuguese rule in the Americas to that point in time, precisely at the moment when Brazil had ceased formally to be a colony, because, since 1808, it had become the seat of metropolitan government and, since 1815, had been elevated, on paper at least, to the status of *Reino Unido* (United Kingdom) to Portugal and Algarves (the southern part of Portugal). Convinced that these were only symbolic concessions, the 1817 rebels, tired of political centralization and over-taxation by the crown, declared a complete autonomy of the north-eastern part of Brazil, where they planned to establish a republican regime, partly modelled on the US federation.

Other captaincies to the south failed to follow the example of Pernambuco. The anticipated support of Bahia never materialized, and rumours of local endorsement were quickly suffocated by the captaincy's governor, who also spearheaded repression of the movement in the north. Even in Pernambuco, while support for the rebellious party was strong and crossed class and colour lines, the property-owning elements reasserted control of the movement, which they had always intended to be a political rebellion, not a social revolution. Leaders then directed that all kinds of property, slaves included, were to be respected under the new regime, except for a few slaves who had been incorporated into the rebel forces, and had thus been manumitted. The possibility of a more radical, antislavery move was always present but the leaders deflected it. Interest in Haiti seemed muted, but after the movement had been defeated, the new governor general of Pernambuco claimed that 'men of colour embraced the rebel cause in an excessive and insulting manner' and reminded the local inhabitants of the bloody scenes in Saint-Domingue. As a result, enslaved and freed blacks/mulattos (and a few poor whites) received punishment without trial.[19]

---

[19] Jeffrey C. Mosher, *Political Struggle, Ideology and State Building* (Lincoln, NE, 2008), 35; Mota, *Nordeste 1817*; Glacyra Nazari Leite, *Pernambuco 1817: estrutura e comportamento sociais* (Recife, 1989); Evaldo Cabral de Mello, *A outra independência: o federalismo pernambucano de 1817 a 1824* (São Paulo, 2004), chapter 1.

In the 1820s, when anti-Portuguese feelings increased, fears of black rebellion heightened. Following the 1820 liberal revolution in Portugal—when the Portuguese Parliament called Dom João VI back to Lisbon to lead a constitutional monarchy—government juntas were organized in the several Brazilian provinces to temporarily replace governors appointed by the crown, now represented by the king's son Pedro as regent. Tensions between Portuguese and Brazilian-born people developed all over the country, in part because of fears that the Parliament in Lisbon—dubbed The Sovereign Congress—planned to 're-colonize' Brazil. The fundamental issue was the nature of the link that Brazilians would have with the *Reino Unido*. Some preferred the status quo, others demanded more autonomy under the crown itself, and still others favoured a republican government independent of Portugal. The leaders of these different options came from upper- or middle-class backgrounds but hoped for support from the masses with 'the people' becoming citizens rather than mere subjects.

The anti-colonial discourse necessarily encouraged black rebellion. Echoing Montesquieu's concept of 'political slavery', patriots described Brazil rhetorically as the 'slave' of Portugal; contended that the Portuguese Parliament would 'enslave' Brazilians; and professed that independence would 'free' Brazil from Portuguese 'shackles'. Slaves listened attentively and many began to compare the rhetoric of whites to their own experience. In 1821, in Itu, the rumour circulated that the Portuguese Parliament (or the king—there was some doubt) had allegedly proclaimed the end of slavery, but that slaveholders and local authorities had suppressed this information. Also in Minas Gerais in 1822 one local authority observed that blacks were actively meeting and 'spreading the voices of liberty'. There, as in other regions, slaves were joined by free and freed blacks, mulattos, and a few whites, in anti-Portuguese protests which often included demands for citizenship for all.[20]

Again, the northern region gave rise to the most intense independence process, both because of divisions within the elite and the response of the masses to the call for freedom and citizenship. In 1821 in São Luís, the capital of the northern Maranhão province, the mostly black and mulatto soldiers who accused a newly created junta of being pro-Portuguese were themselves accused of attempting to incite slaves to rise, with one witness asserting he had heard 'some blacks' praise Saint-Domingue. Later, in the village of Caxias, during the course of civil strife between elite factions, 'several Negroes met to talk about the Liberty of the Enslaved', while on the island of Marajó, Indians and blacks supposedly professed that 'until now we have been ruled by whites, now it is time for us to rule the whites'.[21]

---

[20] Magda Ricci, 'Nas fronteiras da Independência' (master's thesis, UNICAMP, 1993), 222–6, 258; Ana Rosa Cloclet da Silva, 'Identidades politicas e a emergência do Estado nacional: o caso mineiro', in Jancsó (ed.), *Independência*, 548–53 (quote on 542).

[21] Iara Lis Carvalho Souza, *A pátria coroada: o Brasil como corpo político autônomo, 1780–1831* (São Paulo, 1999), 150–2; Matthias Röhrig Assunção, 'Miguel Bruce e os "horrores da anarquia" no Maranhão, 1822–1827', in István Iancsó (ed.), *Independência: história e historiografia* (São Paulo, 2005), 345–78 (quote on 362); André Roberto de A. Machado, 'As esquadras imaginárias: no extremo norte, episódio do longo processo de independência do Brasil', in Jancsó (ed.), *Independência*, 338 (quote).

On the eve of independence, Maria Graham, an English traveller, observed insight-fully that, in Pernambuco, the Portuguese 'now, no doubt, look forward with dread to the event of a revolution, which will free their slaves from their authority, and... declare them all men alike'. With the unfolding of a political movement and the growing division between those who adhered to the liberal revolution in Lisbon—which initially promised a looser association of Brazilian provinces to Portugal—and those who supported an independent but centralizing government based in Rio de Janeiro, slaves intensified traditional forms of resistance, and inaugurated new ones. The number of *quilombos* multiplied in the woods around Recife and Olinda, the two largest urban centres in Pernambuco. Slaves mixed with poor free people, mostly blacks and mulattos, to protest in the streets against Portuguese rule. The crowds insulted and stoned Portuguese troops, while fresh troops sent from Portugal could not disembark in Recife due to popular protests in the streets.[22]

In Bahia, tensions between local and Portuguese forces became a fully fledged war because the commander of the Portuguese garrison refused to obey the local govern-ment, and later rebuffed Brazil's independence declared in 1822 by the future emperor Dom Pedro I. The black masses, including slaves, supported overwhelmingly the anti-Portuguese movement, both protesting against the Portuguese in Salvador, and enlisting in the Brazilian forces. Local and foreign observers feared that a 'Black party' was in the making to dispute political hegemony with whites in an independent country. A consul, an admiral, and a spy for Portugal—all of them French—inspired by events in their former Caribbean colony, warned on different occasions that the ideals of liberty and equality had already 'infected' Brazilian-born blacks and mulattos and even 'seasoned' Africans.[23] Although the experience of Saint-Domingue was not repeated, fears of another cataclysm were not just political propaganda or the hallucinations of desperate men, since Bahian slaves had repeatedly presented violent challenge to the slave regime.

SLAVE REVOLTS AND THE SOUTH ATLANTIC CONNECTION

A cycle of revolts and conspiracies produced by African-born slaves in Bahia during the first three decades of the nineteenth century suggests that rebellious ideas did not emanate solely from political turmoil associated with the struggle for independence. If

[22] Maria Graham, *Journal of a Voyage to Brazil and Residence there etc* (1824; New York, 1969), 126; Marcus Joaquim M. de Carvalho, 'O quilombo de Malunguinho, o rei das matas de Pernambuco', in Reis and Santos (eds.), *Liberdade por um fio*, 411; Souza, *Pátria coroada*, 161–2; Mello, *A outra independência*, 75.
[23] Glacyra Lazzari Leite, 'A confederação do Equador no processo de independência do Brasil: aspectos das relações internacionais (1822–1825)', in Manuel Correia de Andrade (ed.), *Confederação do Equador* (Recife, 1988), 34; João Reis, 'O jogo duro do Dois de Julho', in João Reis and Eduardo Silva, *Negociação e conflito* (São Paulo, 1989), 90–1, 94.

the Era of Revolutions was primarily an Atlantic phenomenon originating in Europe, North America, and the Caribbean, the ideologies of protest in the Bahian slave rebellions came mainly from West Africa. Most slave rebels in the region were Hausa- and Yoruba-speakers who had experienced devastating conflicts in their homeland, particularly the civil wars that led to the fall of the powerful Oyo kingdom, and the Fulani-led jihad, begun in 1804 in Hausa territory, that led in 1809 to the creation of the Sokoto caliphate. Indisputably an Era of Revolution in this part of West Africa, these wars led to the collapse of centuries-old kingdoms and the formation of new states, one of them a powerful Islamic federation. They had political repercussions in Brazil, particularly Bahia, not least because the African conflicts, which lasted for decades, occasioned the death, migration, displacement, and enslavement of thousands of people captured in battle and kidnapped from their villages, many of whom were sold to slave traders on the ports of the Gulf of Benin on the Atlantic coast.

Most of these slaves were conveyed to Bahia, because Bahian merchants practically monopolized the trade from the Bight of Benin to Brazil. Between 1791 and 1850, at least 354,100 captives, including a significant number of Muslims, reached Bahia from the Bight of Benin hinterland; many of them participated in revolts that shook Bahia. Some revolts were local affairs in the sugar plantation area of the Recôncavo, near Salvador, carried on by recently arrived, young, warlike, uncompromising Africans in protest against specific working or living conditions, but others were organized, bolder attempts to overturn the system. Both smaller, short-lived rebellions and more extensive and sophisticated conspiracies and uprisings were frequently, but not always, organized and implemented by Muslim slaves. The language and the inspiration of these rebels can often be traced to both Allah and the Orishas—the Yoruba gods and goddesses—who gave direction and promised protection to African rebels.[24]

In Brazil, African Muslim slaves were known by the Hausa term *musulmi*, or by the more popular Yoruba term *malê*, from the Yoruba word *imale* for Muslim, a tribute to the greater number of Africans from this group in the Bahian Muslim community in the 1820s and 1830s. These slaves' religious culture became interwoven with their political history. There is evidence of Muslim participation and leadership in at least two rebellions and two important conspiracies, but they were probably present in other African movements as well.

In 1807 an extensive conspiracy involving urban, suburban, and plantation Hausa slaves of Salvador and the surrounding region was detected. Organized under a complex hierarchy of leaders, some of whom were in charge of mobilizing adepts in different quarters of the city and on sugar plantations, the rebels planned to surround Salvador, conquer it, establish contact with Muslim slaves in Pernambuco, and organize a kingdom in the country's backlands. In Salvador, Catholic churches would be stormed, whites massacred, while black creoles and mulattos would serve the victorious

---

[24] On the Bahian revolts, see João José Reis, *Rebelião escrava no Brazil: a história do levante dos malês em 1835* (São Paulo, 2003), or a shorter English version, *Slave Rebellion in Brazil: The Muslim Uprising of 1835 in Bahia* (Baltimore, MD, 1993).

rebels as slaves. A Muslim leader would take political and religious command of the new regime. The plot was denounced by a loyal slave, the police arrested the main leaders, and the revolt was aborted just as the Tailors' Revolt had been nine years earlier.

In 1814, fugitive slaves gathered on the outskirts of Salvador and joined slave fishermen in a whaling station on the coast. They burnt fishing nets and warehouses, attacked a nearby village, and killed some residents. From there the rebels tried to reach the plantation area, killing more than fifty people before being overpowered by troops sent from the capital. Rebel ranks were overwhelmingly Hausa. Their principal leader, a man called João, was described as '*malomi* or priest', *malomi* being a Hausa term for a Muslim preacher/teacher. Some months later, the Hausas plotted another rebellion intending to combine urban slaves-for-hire and suburban *quilombos* where again a *malomi* was mentioned. Apparently other African 'nations' and even Indians had been invited to participate in the insurrection.

Slave rebels struck again in Bahia in 1816. In the Recôncavo, they burned several sugar plantations and killed whites and non-cooperative slaves. The uprising occurred in the aftermath of a religious, probably a Catholic, festival, lasted four days, and was obviously planned before it was snuffed out by force. This brought an end to Hausa-led rebellions in Bahia; Nagôs (Yoruba-speakers) then became the vanguard of the struggle against slavery in the region, as Brazil turned into an independent country, immersed in a state-building process. But this is another story.

CONCLUSION

The Atlantic dimension of popular movements in Portuguese America intensified as colonization advanced, and even more so during the process of decolonization. In a slave society, tension and the potential for conflict were ever-present, but restricted to certain regions. With the formation of strong groups of merchants and educated followers of the Enlightenment, the critical ideas of Atlantic revolutionary movements began to echo on Portuguese American soil, affecting even the subaltern classes. Enslaved Africans fought their own battles in a rather different arena, except when, at the time of independence, or before that, in 1798 or 1817, they raised hopes of experiencing freedom.

But slavery was the great divide, stifling any possibility of real change, unless promoted by slaves themselves. The various sectors of the subordinate classes had fluid boundaries and fluctuating interests, which often included slavery, making the formation of common strategies and plans difficult. The war against Indians and maroons were frequent and engendered imaginary panic but no unrestricted common cause united the excluded. Indian warriors played important roles in the war against escaped slaves, and creole and African slaves did not join forces to rebel. The Africans themselves were divided by their various nations, as events in Bahia demonstrated.

The territorial fragmentation of Portuguese America, as well as the regionalization of interests, could not lead to the rise of a more encompassing awareness on the part of the elites. The Minas and Rio *inconfidências* were localized protests, unable to bind together the various regions of the colony. Certain sectors of the royal administration most feared the potential strength represented by the union of these parts.[25] The colonists, however, did not yet think of Brazil as a unit; something that materialized only as part of the process of creating a national state. Even when independence from Portugal was achieved, Brazil remained a monarchical and slave society for most of the nineteenth century.

BIBLIOGRAPHY

Mello, Evaldo Cabral de, *A outra independência: o federalismo pernambucano de 1817 a 1824* (São Paulo, 2004).

Puntoni, Pedro, *A guerra dos bárbaros: povos indígenas e a colonização do sertão nordeste do Brasil—1650–1720* (São Paulo, 2002), 46.

Reis, João José, *Slave Rebellion in Brazil: The Muslim Uprising of 1835 in Bahia* (Baltimore, MD, 1993).

—— and Flávio dos Santos Gomes (eds.), *Liberdade por um fio: história dos quilombos no Brasil* (São Paulo, 1996).

Romeiro, Adriana, *Paulistas e emboabas no coração das Minas* (Belo Horizonte, 2009).

Santos, Afonso Carlos Marques dos, *No rascunho da nação: Inconfidência no Rio de Janeiro* (Rio de Janeiro, 1992).

Souza, Laura de Mello e, 'Motines, revueltas y revoluciones en la America Portuguesa de los siglos XVII y XVIII', in Enrique Tandeter and Jorge Hidalgo Lehuedé (eds.), *Historia general de América Latina* (Brussels, 2000), iv. 459–73.

[25] Laura de Mello e Souza, *O sol e a sombra: política e administração na América Portuguesa do século XVIII* (São Paulo, 2006), 78–108.

CHAPTER 33

REVOLUTION IN THE HISPANIC WORLD, 1808–1816

JAIME E. RODRÍGUEZ O.

THE bicentennial of the independence of Spanish America has prompted historians, public officials, and the general public to reassess that complex historical period. Most historians who study the era reject the 'official' interpretations of the events which will be celebrated during the coming years. These traditional interpretations of Spanish American independence, which continue to be widely accepted, use a variety of arguments to justify separation from the Spanish Monarchy. Generally, they maintain that Spain had been a backward, oppressive colonial power and that independence was the only means to free Americans from oppression. They also argue that nations existed before the state and that emancipation merely recognized the existence of these independent polities. While agreeing with many of the arguments of the traditional interpretations, the English historian John Lynch launched a new period of scholarship in 1973 with his *The Spanish American Revolutions,* which maintained that economic exploitation by the metropolis and class struggle in Spanish America had been the catalysts for the independence movements. The work, which also appeared in Spanish, is the most widely read volume on the subject.[1] In 1992 the French historian François-Xavier Guerra and I published works that refocused emphasis on the political aspects of Spanish American independence.[2] Unfortunately Guerra died before he could write a general history of the process of independence. As a result, my 1996 book *The Independence of Spanish America* currently represents the most complete version of this new general interpretation.[3]

---

[1] John Lynch, *The Spanish American Revolutions, 1808–1826* (New York, 1973).

[2] François-Xavier Guerra, *Modernidad e independencias: ensayos sobre las revoluciones hispánicas* (Madrid, 1992); Jaime E. Rodríguez O., 'La independencia de la América española: una reinterpretación', *Historia mexicana,* 42/167 (1992), 571–620. For the historiography of interpretations see Mónica Quijada, *Modelos de interpretación sobre las independencias hispanoamericanas* (Zacatecas, 2005).

[3] The work first appeared in Spanish as *La independencia de la América española* (Mexico, 1996).

The independence of Spanish America did not constitute an anti-colonial movement but formed part of the *political revolution* within the Spanish world and the *dissolution of the Spanish Monarchy*. Although a very radical political revolution occurred, it did not transform the social structure of Spanish America. Members of the complex socio-ethnic groups that existed in the continent based their participation in those processes on political and economic interests rather than on their membership in a particular class or race. Individuals from all groups participated on all sides of the complex struggle and were willing to modify allegiances as circumstances changed. Indians, blacks (both enslaved and free), mulattos, mestizos, and creoles sided with the royalists while many of their counterparts supported the varied insurgencies. These shifting coalitions formed to defend particular social, political, and economic interests rather than to advance the interests of these poorly defined heterogeneous socio-economic classes and racial groups.

The collapse of the Spanish Monarchy in 1808 precipitated a political revolution that shattered that worldwide polity into new nation-states, among them Spain itself. In the wake of the French invasion of the Iberian Peninsula, three broad movements emerged in the Spanish world: the struggle against the invaders, the great political revolution that sought to transform the Spanish Monarchy into a modern nation-state with one of the most radical constitutions of the nineteenth century, and a fragmented insurgency in America that relied on force to secure home rule. These three overlapping processes influenced and interacted with one another in a variety of ways. None of them can be understood in isolation. Historians have largely ignored the revolutionary political process, preferring to concentrate instead on Spain's 'War of Independence' against the French invaders or on the armed struggles in Spanish America, distorting our understanding of the formation of the nation-states that emerged from the break-up of the Spanish Monarchy.

Although the governing elites in Spain capitulated to the French in 1808 and acquiesced to the transfer of the crown to Napoleon Bonaparte's brother Joseph, the people of the Peninsula and the New World were virtually unanimous in their opposition to the invaders. The external threat underscored the factors that united them: the composite Spanish Monarchy, state-mediated Catholicism, and a flexible juridical and political culture. They were members of what soon came to be known as *la Nación española*, a nation consisting of the Peninsula and the overseas kingdoms. The people of both areas drawing upon a common political culture sought similar solutions to the evolving crisis. In keeping with Hispanic political theory most agreed that in the absence of the king, sovereignty reverted to the people who possessed the authority and the responsibility to defend the nation.[4]

The crisis galvanized Americans to defend the monarchy and expand their rights within that polity. The people of Hispanic America had exercised a high level of political autonomy. Only very late, during the reign of Carlos III (1759–88), did the

---

[4] Jaime E. Rodríguez O., *The Independence of Spanish America* (Cambridge, 1998), 7–59.

crown attempt to centralize the monarchy. That effort consisted of a series of economic and political changes known as the Bourbon Reforms. Americans opposed the political and economic innovations that restricted local control and modified many to suit their interests. Thus, on the eve of independence, the leaders of the New World retained a significant degree of autonomy and control over their regions.[5]

In the Peninsula, juntas, originally formed to govern their provinces and to oppose the French, established a Supreme Central Governing Junta, which convened on 25 September 1808 to govern the nation and to coordinate the struggle against the invaders. That body soon realized that it needed the support of the American kingdoms to conduct the war against the French. On 22 January 1809, it decreed that each of the ten kingdoms of America and Asia—the viceroyalties of New Spain, New Granada, Peru, and the Río de la Plata and the captaincies general of Puerto Rico, Cuba, Guatemala, Venezuela, Chile, and the Philippines—elect a deputy to represent them in the national government. Thus, the Junta Central explicitly acknowledged the Americans' claims that their lands were not colonies but kingdoms, that they constituted integral parts of the Spanish Monarchy, and that they possessed the right of representation in the national government. The act was profoundly revolutionary since it recognized the equality of Americans and Spaniards. It created a relationship between a metropolis and its overseas territories that no other European monarchy ever granted its possessions.[6]

As Americans held elections to the Junta Central, the French renewed their drive to conquer the Peninsula. French armies reoccupied Madrid and during 1809 and 1810 defeated Spanish forces throughout the country. News of these calamities alarmed Americans, many of whom believed that the Spanish Monarchy would not survive as an independent entity. They also worried that the authorities in Spain might surrender America to the French. The climate of fear profoundly influenced New World actions. It is not surprising, therefore, that in 1809, even as they were electing their representatives to the Junta Central, movements for autonomy erupted in the two South American kingdoms that had not been granted individual representation to the Junta Central because they were subordinate *audiencias* (high courts of justice that also exercised some administrative authority), Charcas in May and July and Quito in August 1809. The uncertain political situation provided the two kingdoms with the opportunity and the justification to seek independence from their viceregal capitals, Buenos Aires and Santa Fe de Bogotá. Although Charcas and Quito insisted that they were acting in the name of the imprisoned king, Fernando VII, the royal authorities rapidly crushed both movements.[7]

In an attempt to create a more effective government, the Junta Central, which had been unable to halt the French invasion, decreed on 1 January 1810 that elections be held

---

[5] Rodríguez O., *The Independence*, 19–35.
[6] Jaime E. Rodríguez O., 'La naturaleza de la representación en la Nueva España y México', *Secuencia: revista de historia y ciencias sociales*, 61 (2005), 6–32.
[7] Rodríguez O., *The Independence*, 64–9.

for a national *Cortes* (parliament). It subsequently appointed a five-member Council of Regency that included an American representative and dissolved itself at the end of January 1810.

According to the decree issued by the Council of Regency 14 February 1810, the *ayuntamientos* of *capitales de partido* (city councils of district capitals) of America were to elect three individuals of well-known probity, talent, and learning and select one by lot. Thus, the requirements for election and the electoral process were to be similar to those used in 1809 for elections for deputies to the Junta Central. There were, however, two major differences. The candidates had to be natives of the province, thus eliminating European Spaniards residing in America, and a deputy would be elected for each *ayuntamiento* rather than for each kingdom. No other European metropolis granted its overseas territories comparable representation. The English Parliament, generally believed to be the most advanced in the world, never granted its North American colonies representation.[8]

THE ELECTIONS

Elections for the new representative government occurred while warfare engulfed the Peninsula and parts of America. Because many of the occupied provinces of Spain could not hold elections, and because distance delayed the arrival of many American deputies, the regency decreed that fifty-five *suplentes* (substitutes), among them thirty from America and the Philippines, be elected by individuals from those areas who were in Cádiz. New World *suplentes* were a varied group; they included military men, lawyers, academics, clerics, and government functionaries. Two were *grandes* of Spain and one, Dionisio Inca Yupangui, was a Peruvian Indian who had served as a lieutenant colonel of dragoons in the Peninsula. The *suplentes* played a major role in the Cortes on behalf of their *patrias* and America as a whole. Moreover, when the proprietary deputies from America arrived, most *suplentes* remained in the Cortes representing New World realms that had failed to send proprietary deputies.[9]

Elections to form a representative government for the Spanish world were held in the midst of a crisis of confidence. By 1810, most Americans expected the French to triumph. Napoleonic armies, after all, controlled the majority of the Peninsula. Fear of French domination strengthened the desire of many in the New World to seek autonomy. Home rule movements re-emerged in Charcas and Quito and erupted in other kingdoms in 1810: Caracas in April, Buenos Aires and Charcas in May, Santa Fe de Bogotá in July and three areas in September—the Bajío in New Spain on the 16th, Santiago de Chile on the 18th, and Quito on the 20th. All these regions sought to

---

[8] Jaime E. Rodríguez O., '"Equality! The Sacred Right of Equality!" Representation under the Constitution of 1812', *Revista de Indias*, 58/242 (2008), 107–9.

[9] Ibid. 107–9.

establish caretaker governments to rule in the name of King Fernando VII. The autonomy movements of 1810, unlike those of 1809, inadvertently unleashed other social forces. Discontented groups and regions capitalized on the opportunity to redress their grievances. Within a short time, civil wars consumed large parts of the American continent.[10]

Elections for proprietary deputies to the Cortes were held in America during late 1810 and the first half of 1811. Although insurgencies had erupted in various parts of the continent, most kingdoms, with the exception of Chile and parts of Venezuela, New Granada, and the Río de la Plata, participated in the elections, which had a profound impact throughout the New World. The capitals of most of the provinces eligible to elect deputies consulted widely with the towns and villages of their regions. Each urban centre prepared lists of notables by consulting prominent individuals of the area. During the consultation process, there was widespread discussion in public places, such as plazas, markets, government buildings, parks, inns, and taverns. Curas discussed the significance of the event at mass and outside of church, emphasizing the importance of opposing the godless French—who were a threat to the Holy Faith, the king, and the *patria*—by participating in the new government of the Spanish nation. The elections in the provincial capitals were generally conducted in public and were accompanied by ceremonies that usually began with a mass of the Holy Spirit and ended with a Te Deum, the ringing of bells, and other public celebrations. Cities, towns, and villages decorated the centre of the town to commemorate the festive occasion. In large capital cities, the celebrations were accompanied by the firing of cannon and fireworks. These events created a spirit of optimism and gave Americans a sense that they could overcome the grave political crisis.

THE CORTES OF CÁDIZ

As their first act, the deputies to the Cortes of Cádiz declared themselves representatives of the nation and assumed sovereignty. When the Cortes convened, 104 deputies were present; thirty of them represented the overseas territories: a proprietary deputy from Puerto Rico and twenty-seven Americans and two Filipinos who were selected as *suplentes* in Cádiz. The other proprietary deputies were admitted as they arrived. Approximately 220 deputies, including sixty-seven Americans, eventually participated in the General and Extraordinary Cortes in Cádiz. The delegates to the Cortes were one-third clergymen, about one-sixth nobles, and the remainder members of the third estate who, because of their professions, might be called middle class.

The new Parliament faced the enormous task of restructuring the government while prosecuting a war in Spain and preserving the overseas kingdoms. The Cortes

---

[10] Rodríguez O., *The Independence*, 107–68.

appointed a commission of fifteen individuals, including five Americans, to prepare a project of the constitution of the Spanish Monarchy. The commission, which acted with great care, took months to complete the project that was submitted on 18 August 1811. In the ensuing debates, which lasted several months, the deputies addressed fundamental issues, such as the role of the Cortes, the king, and the judiciary; the attributes of provincial and local government; the nature of citizenship and political rights; and trade, education, the military, and taxation. In the process of debating the articles of the proposed constitution, the deputies were forced to make political compromises among competing interest groups and ideologies represented in the Spanish Monarchy. The extensive parliamentary debates were widely disseminated by the press and significantly influenced those Spanish Americans who supported as well as those who opposed the new Hispanic government.[11]

Despite strongly held opposing convictions that resulted in heated debate, the delegates from Spain and America to the General and Extraordinary Cortes produced a document that transformed the Spanish Monarchy. The Constitution of 1812 was not a Spanish document; it was a charter for the entire former Spanish Monarchy. Representatives from the New World played a central role in shaping the Constitution of Cádiz. Their arguments and proposals convinced many Spaniards to embrace substantial change in America as well as the Peninsula. American deputies were responsible for the creation of a new institution that formed the basis of the constitutional system: regional administrative bodies called provincial deputations. With the creation of these provincial bodies, the Cortes abolished the viceroyalties, transformed the *audiencias* from judicial and quasi-administrative bodies into high courts of appeal, and divided the Spanish world into provinces that dealt directly with the national government in Spain. Americans also played a key role in the establishment of the second home rule institution created by the Cortes, the constitutional *ayuntamientos*, which substituted popularly elected officials for the hereditary elites who had heretofore controlled city government. Deputies from America also successfully argued that constitutional *ayuntamientos* be established in cities and towns with at least 1,000 inhabitants; formerly in Spanish America, city governments existed only in major cities. This decision transferred political power from the centre to the localities by incorporating vast numbers of people into the political process.[12] The constitution, therefore, provided Americans who desired autonomy a peaceful means of obtaining home rule.

The Constitution of 1812, one of the most radical charters of the nineteenth century, abolished seigniorial institutions, the Inquisition, Indian tribute, forced labour—such as the *mita* in South America and personal service in Spain—and reasserted the state's control of the Church. It created a unitary state with equal laws for all parts of the Spanish Monarchy, substantially restricted the authority of the king, and endowed the legislature with decisive power. When it enfranchised all men, except those of African

11 Rodríguez O., *The Independence*, 64–92.
12 Manuel Chust, *La cuestión nacional Americana en las Cortes de Cádiz* (Valencia, 1999).

ancestry, without requiring either literacy or property qualifications, the Constitution of 1812 surpassed all existing representative governments, such as Great Britain, the United States, and France, in providing political rights to the vast majority of the male population.[13]

The most revolutionary aspects of the Constitution of 1812 were making the executive and judiciary subordinate to the legislature and introducing mass political participation. The Charter of Cádiz created three unequal branches. The judiciary received little independent power and the executive was subservient to the legislature. National sovereignty was entrusted to the Cortes. Mass political participation was accomplished by granting all males, except those of African ancestry, the franchise without requiring either literacy or property and by expanding the number of constitutional city governments. Thus, the constitution placed the Spanish Nation in the forefront of the broader movement transforming *antiguo régimen* societies into modern nation-states.

The Constitution of 1812 founded representative government at three levels, the city or town (constitutional *ayuntamiento*), the province (provincial deputation), and the monarchy (Cortes). The new constitution was widely introduced in those regions of the monarchy that recognized the government in Spain. It is striking that New Spain and Guatemala, lands that contained more than half of the population of Spanish America, implemented the new constitutional order more fully than any other part of the Spanish Monarchy, including Spain itself. Other areas of the New World under royal control that included more than half of the remaining population of Spanish America—the Caribbean, Quito, Peru, and Charcas—as well as parts of Venezuela, New Granada, and the Río de la Plata also introduced the charter. Despite the confusion, conflict, and delay inherent in the implementation of a new system, the first constitutional elections in Spanish America contributed to the legitimization of the new political culture. Spanish Americans established more than 1,000 constitutional *ayuntamientos* and a dozen provincial deputations during 1812–14. In some areas as many as three successive *ayuntamiento* elections were held. Several areas completed two elections at the provincial level, first to establish and then to renew their provincial deputations. Americans also elected more than 100 deputies to the Cortes in Madrid. Over a million citizens, including Indians, mestizos, *castas*, and blacks, participated in the elections and in government at the local, the provincial and the monarchy-wide levels. Although the constitution excluded men of African ancestry from the suffrage, recent studies demonstrate that they voted and, in many cases, elected officials of African ancestry in regions of New Spain, Guatemala, Guayaquil, and Peru. It is ironic that scholars have tended to ignore this great political revolution and instead have focused almost exclusively on the insurgencies. By any standard, the political revolution was more profound and extensive than the insurgencies, which have primarily occupied historians.

---

[13] For a comparison of the US, the French, and the Hispanic constitution see Mónica Quijada, 'Una constitución singular: la Carta gaditana en perspectiva comparada', *Revista de Indias*, 58/242 (2008), 15–38.

The new constitutional elections of 1812–13 were the first popular elections held in the Hispanic world. Relatively free elections occurred in those areas dominated by the royalists. Although the elite clearly dominated politics, more than a million middle- and lower-class men became involved in politics in a meaningful way and made their presence felt. An analysis of the 1813 election census in Mexico City, for example, concludes that 93 per cent of the adult male population of the capital possessed the right to vote. Indians participated actively. In a number of regions, such as Cuenca and Loja in the kingdom of Quito, Indians not only won control of their local towns they also formed inter-ethnic coalitions to participate in the government of the larger provincial capitals.[14] Ironically, the new Hispanic political system forced many insurgent governments to enhance their legitimacy by drafting constitutions and holding elections. Their constitutions, however, were less revolutionary than the Constitution of Cádiz; they often restricted suffrage by imposing literacy and property qualifications.

The first constitutional era ended in 1814 when King Fernando VII returned from France. The monarch's return provided an opportunity to restore the unity of the Spanish world. Virtually every act that had occurred since 1808—the struggle against the French, the political revolution enacted by the Cortes, and the autonomy movements in America—was taken in his name. Initially it appeared that he might accept moderate reforms, but ultimately the king opted to abolish the Cortes and the Constitution of Cádiz. His autocratic government relied on force to restore royal authority in the New World. There followed a five-year period in which, unfettered by the constitution, the royal authorities in the New World crushed most insurgent movements. Only the isolated Río de la Plata remained beyond the reach of a weakened Spanish Monarchy.

CIVIL WAR IN AMERICA

The insurgencies and civil wars that engulfed some regions of Spanish America were a response to the same events that generated the constitutional political revolution. Both movements sought to maintain the Spanish Monarchy as an independent political entity and to expand local political authority and representation. The disastrous Spanish defeats of 1809 and 1810 convinced most Americans in the New World that authorities in the Peninsula were incapable of defending the Spanish Monarchy. Some responded by forming local autonomous juntas to rule in the name of the imprisoned King Fernando VII. Most historians assert that these armed movements sought independence, that is, separation from Spain. In their view, American claims that they acted in the name of the king were a device to mask their true intent. In making these arguments, those scholars assume that nations existed in Spanish America before

---

[14] Jaime E. Rodríguez O., *La revolución política durante la época de la independencia: el reino de Quito, 1808–1822* (Quito, 2006), 103–23.

states were formed, a view rejected by most historians of nationalism. I maintain that the residents of those territories, or kingdoms as they were called, sought autonomy in order to preserve their *independence* from the French and to expand the scope of local authority.

The kingdoms of America reacted with great patriotism when they received the news that the French had invaded the Peninsula and imprisoned the king. They rejected the invaders and supported the new government of national defence, the Junta Central. As time passed, however, and as they learned of the disastrous defeats of Spanish forces, they increasingly favoured establishing local governments. The Americans, who formed local juntas, relied on the same juridical principle invoked by their peninsular counterparts: in the absence of the king, sovereignty reverted to the people. Although that principle justified the formation of local governments in the name of the king, it did not support separation from the monarchy. Since the regency and the Cortes could not constitutionally accede to the separation of New World kingdoms, when reforms and negotiations failed to restore the American juntas to compliance with the royal government, the authorities in Spain resorted to the use of force.[15]

The subsequent struggle erupted because Spanish Americans disagreed about the legitimacy of the government in Spain and the locus of sovereignty in the absence of the monarch. Spaniards and Americans in the New World, who believed that the Council of Regency and the Cortes were, indeed, the legitimate government, opposed the formation of local juntas. Others believed that the removal of the monarch by the French required the establishment of juntas in the Americas. The group favouring the formation of local governments gradually expanded as news reached America of the disastrous defeats of Spanish forces in the Peninsula. The autonomists disagreed among themselves about whether only capital cities of the American kingdoms possessed the right to form local governments or if the provincial capitals of the various realms enjoyed the same privilege. When the capital cities resorted to force to maintain political control, some insurgent groups began to form to defend provincial autonomy. Divisions among elites within the various provinces also led to intra-elite conflict. In some instances, violence broke out between the cities and the countryside. Occasionally, these power struggles led to civil wars that pitted the supporters of the Spanish national government against American juntas, the capitals of kingdoms against the provinces, the elites against one another, and urban against rural groups.

An intra-elite conflict in New Spain heightened divisions that resulted in an insurgency. Fearing that *novohispanos* (the people of New Spain) would use the crisis in the Peninsula to expand their political and economic influence, segments of the Spanish community opposed their proposal to hold a congress of cities in Mexico City to address the crisis in Spain. When Viceroy José Iturrigaray sided with the *novohispanos*, the Spaniards overthrew him on the night of 15 September 1808 and assumed control of the government. The *golpe* and the subsequent actions of the illegal regime exacerbated

---

[15] Rodríguez O., *The Independence*, 13–19 and 47–9.

the divisions in New Spain and convinced some Americans that they could only achieve self-government through force.

The authorities discovered a serious plot in the city of Valladolid in the autumn of 1809. The conspirators had supporters in other provincial centres, such as Guanajuato, Querétaro, San Miguel el Grande, and Guadalajara. They prepared an uprising for 21 December 1809, and expected backing from the army and the militia. They also hoped to attract thousands of supporters among the Indians and *castas* by promising to abolish tribute. The plan differed from the early peaceful autonomy movement in Mexico City only in that the conspirators planned to employ force because the Spaniards had seized the government. When the movement was exposed, the authorities chose to exercise leniency because many important people openly declared that the conspirators were guilty only of seeking to redress legitimate grievances in an inappropriate manner.[16]

Another conspiracy subsequently formed in the city of Querétaro. Influenced by the Valladolid plot, militia captains Ignacio Allende and Juan Aldama and *corregidor* Miguel Domínguez began informal talks to organize a similar movement. By March 1810, the plotters had recruited Father Miguel Hidalgo and other disaffected Americans. They, like the Valladolid group, sought to remove the illegitimate government imposed by some European Spaniards, with the aid of the rural and urban workers, and to establish an American junta to govern in the name of King Fernando VII. The conspirators planned the uprising for October 1810, but the authorities exposed the plot and arrested the Querétaro group on 13 September 1810. This pre-emptive action did not halt the revolt. Conspirators who eluded capture, Hidalgo, Allende, and Aldama, launched the insurgency from the prosperous town of Dolores on the morning of 16 September 1810.

Elite support for the revolt led by Hidalgo, which began as a movement for autonomy, ended when it became evident that the rebel leaders could not control their followers. The sack of the city of Guanajuato constituted the turning point in the revolt. The looting, carnage, and destruction of that city clearly demonstrated that the insurrection promoted uncontrollable class conflict. The elite feared that a revolution would spark a race war, while Indians and *campesinos* with communal lands feared that the landless poor in Hidalgo's forces might dispossess them. The royal army and most of the militia, which were 95 per cent American, remained loyal to the crown. Ultimately, the royalists defeated the insurgents. Hidalgo was subsequently captured, tried, degraded from the priesthood, and executed.[17] Ignacio López Rayón, a lawyer who assumed leadership of the movement after Hidalgo's execution in 1811, initially attempted reconciliation with the royal authorities. When they rejected his overtures, López Rayón and other insurgent leaders organized the Supreme National American Junta as an alternative government. In January 1812, royalist forces captured the town of Zitácuaro where the Junta was based. Although López Rayón escaped, he gradually lost

---

16 Rodríguez O., *The Independence*, 51–64 and 71–4.
17 Hugh M. Hamill, *The Hidalgo Revolt: Prelude to Mexican Independence* (Gainesville, FL, 1966).

his position as leader of the rebels. Father José María Morelos, who had been waging a guerrilla campaign in the south, emerged as the most important insurgent chieftain.

The Morelos insurgency flourished because he directed an orderly movement that reduced the spectre of race and class warfare. During 1811 and 1812, Morelos and his commanders concentrated on cutting the capital's lines of communication, thereby gaining control of the south. Morelos' greatest success came in 1812 when he captured Oaxaca. The following spring, he initiated a seven-month siege of Acapulco. Despite his military achievements, he could not claim authority merely by force of arms, particularly since the Hispanic Cortes had ratified the notion of popular sovereignty and representative government. After the promulgation of the Hispanic Constitution of 1812 and the holding of popular elections throughout New Spain, Morelos' urban supporters urged the convening of a congress to form an alternative government. In June 1813, the regions controlled by the insurgents, parts of Oaxaca, Puebla, Veracruz, and Michoacán, the insurgent province of Tecpan, and possibly a few secret groups in Mexico City and other urban centres, held elections for a congress to be held at Chilpancingo, a small, easily defended, and friendly town. Unlike elections under the Constitution of Cádiz, the insurgent elections were manipulated by the insurgent leaders and were less popular, involving less than 10,000 voters.[18]

Conflict ensued from the outset between the insurgent executive and the eight-member legislature. Although congress ratified Morelos' command as *generalísimo* and declared the independence of North America, the legislative body, like the Cortes in Spain, assumed national sovereignty and attempted to exercise supreme power. On 22 October 1814, congress issued the *Constitutional Decree for the Liberty of Mexican America*, known as the Constitution of Apatzingán, named after the town where it was promulgated. The new charter established a republic with a plural executive and a powerful legislature. Congress rejected Morelos' pretensions to power and stripped him of supreme authority, but it retained his support by appointing him a member of the executive triumvirate. On 5 November 1815, however, royalist forces defeated Morelos. He was captured, tried, degraded from the priesthood, and executed on 22 December 1815. Earlier that month, other insurgent leaders dissolved congress.[19] The Constitution of Apatzingán was not implemented and exercised no influence on subsequent constitutional development in New Spain/Mexico. Although the insurgents in North America were able to wage a guerrilla war for a few years and to introduce briefly an alternative government, the insurgency did not result in the creation of an independent nation-state.

Unlike North America where the royal government retained control of the capital and the institutions of government, in parts of South America the royal government collapsed and autonomous juntas were formed. The Supreme Junta to Conserve the Rights of Fernando VII was formed in Caracas on 19 April 1810. The Supreme Junta, which faced

[18] Virginia Guedea, 'Los procesos electorales insurgentes', *Estudios de historia Novohispana*, 11 (1991), 222–48.

[19] Ana Macías, *Génesis del gobierno constitucional en México, 1808–1820* (Mexico, 1973).

opposition from other cities and provinces, convoked a congress, the Body to Conserve the Rights of D. Fernando VII in the Provinces of Venezuela, in an attempt to establish legitimacy. The Parliament, which met on 2 March 1811, followed many of the precedents established by the Cortes of Cádiz. It arrogated authority to itself and created a weak executive by naming a triumvirate. Support for the Caracas government declined when young radicals who favoured emancipation pressured the congress to declare independence on 5 July. The Parliament subsequently wrote a federal constitution with a strong legislature and a weak triumvirate as the executive. The Venezuelan Charter was more conservative than the Constitution of 1812 then being drafted by the Cortes of Cádiz. The Venezuelan Constitution decreed legal equality for free men but unlike the Constitution of Cádiz retained property requirements for active citizenship. Drawing on Hispanic traditions, the Venezuelan Constitution granted considerable authority to the provinces while seeking to balance their power with that of the national government.[20] The regime was rejected by pro-royalist provinces and royalist forces from the Caribbean. Although it granted extraordinary power to the executive by appointing Francisco Miranda dictator with full civil and military power, the Republic collapsed in July 1812. The fall of the First Republic, as the first regime was later called, marked the end of widespread civil political participation and the rise of military leaders in Venezuela.[21]

Simón Bolívar, one of Miranda's original supporters, drew a number of conclusions from the failure of the First Republic that would have wide-ranging repercussions in the subsequent struggle in South America. In his view, the First Republic failed because it adopted a weak federal constitution, was too tolerant of dissenting opinions, held elections that provided the weak and incompetent with too great a voice, and failed to recruit an effective military force and successfully manage the economy.[22] Later, when he gained power, Bolívar preferred to govern as an autocrat; he assumed the title of dictator on various occasions and limited civilian participation.

New Granada, present-day Colombia, carried the principles of confederalism and strong legislatures to extremes. There the provinces splintered into three coalitions during 1810–15. Cartagena formed a governing junta on 8 May 1810 upon learning that the Junta Central in Spain had dissolved and established a Council of Regency. Other provinces followed. On 20 July, Santa Fe de Bogotá, the capital of the viceroyalty of New Granada, formed a Supreme Junta. However, many other provinces, which possessed conflicting economic interests, resented the capital's attempt to dominate them. Cartagena proposed establishing a federal government which would grant each province equality and autonomy. Santa Fe countered by convening a congress in the capital. In March 1811, that assembly created the state of Cundinamarca, which recognized Fernando VII as the constitutional monarch. The new government consisted of a strong legislature and a

[20] Caracciolo Parra Pérez, *Historia de la Primera República*, 2 vols. (Madrid, 1959), i. 367–487.

[21] Michael P. McKinley, *Pre-Revolutionary Caracas: Politics, Economy, and Society 1777–1811* (Cambridge, 1985), 161–74, 41–116.

[22] Simón Bolívar, 'Memoria dirigida a los ciudadanos de Nueva Granada por un caraqueño', in *Proclamas y discursos del Libertador* (Caracas, 1939), 11–22.

weak executive. The new 'centralist' state consisted of Santa Fe de Bogotá and other provinces of the sierra. Five other autonomous provinces, led by Cartagena, formed the United Provinces of New Granada, an extremely weak confederation. The United Provinces determined that if a separate executive power was created it would be completely subordinate to the congress of the confederation.[23] Each of the provinces proceeded to write its own constitution.

Three contending political coalitions existed at the end of 1811—the royalist provinces, such as Santa Marta and Panama, the state of Cundinamarca, and the United Provinces of New Granada. A bitter civil war erupted among the three groups. Most of the conflict, however, occurred between the two autonomous states, Cundinamarca and the United Provinces. After years of warfare, Santa Fe de Bogotá fell to the armies of the United Provinces on 12 December 1814. By that time, however, Fernando VII had abolished the Constitution of Cádiz and dispatched an army under the command of Marshal Pablo Morillo to restore order in northern South America. After a prolonged struggle, the United Provinces collapsed in May 1816.

In the southern cone, a conflict between the capital and the provinces erupted in the viceroyalty of the Río de la Plata. Established in 1776, the viceroyalty was still in the process of integrating its numerous distant provinces when Napoleon invaded Spain in 1808. The attempt by the city of Buenos Aires to play a dominant role in the formation and functioning of an autonomous government to address the crisis in the Iberian Peninsula unleashed a period of intense political instability that fragmented the viceroyalty. The response of the residents of the Río de la Plata to events in Spain underscores the tensions between viceregal capitals seeking to maintain their status in the new political context and the determination of provincial cities and their hinterland to assert their autonomy.

News arrived in Buenos Aires on 13 May 1810 that the Junta Central had disbanded after fleeing to Cádiz. The leaders of the city decided not to recognize the Council of Regency. After heated debate, on 25 May, the *porteños* (the people of the port of Buenos Aires) organized the Provisional Governing Junta of the Provinces of the Río de la Plata to rule in the name of Fernando VII. The provisional government swore to conserve the region for Fernando VII and his legitimate successors and to retain the Hispanic legal system. The following day, the Provisional Governing Junta dispatched a letter to the provincial capitals informing them of recent events and requesting that they recognize the body as the provisional government. On 27 May, it issued a decree instructing the cities to elect a deputy to the Provisional Governing Junta of Buenos Aires. The change of name from Río de la Plata to Buenos Aires clearly indicated that the *porteños* intended to control the government of the viceroyalty. To ensure its dominance, the Junta organized an army to impose the authority of the provisional government and its resolutions in all the provinces of the viceroyalty.

The leaders of the provinces of the Río de la Plata doubted that the Provisional Governing Junta represented their interests. Montevideo and its interior competed

---

[23] Manuel Antonio Pombo and José Joaquín Guerra, *Constituciones de Colombia*, 3 vols. (Bogotá, 1986), i. 281–8.

with Buenos Aires for control of seaborne trade, including livestock exports. Isolated Paraguay had little in common with the *porteños*. Charcas, which had fallen under the control of the viceroy of Peru after the 1809 autonomous movements in La Paz and Chuquisaca, considered Buenos Aires a threat. The interests of the interior provinces of the Río de la Plata, such as Córdoba, Salta, Tucumán, Mendoza, and San Juan, also clashed with those of Buenos Aires because they depended on commerce with Charcas and Chile and required protection for their manufactures, while the *porteños* insisted on free trade. Thus, many provinces rejected the Provisional Governing Junta. Montevideo, Paraguay, Charcas, Córdoba, and Salta decided to support the Council of Regency in Spain. The Buenos Aires government was also weakened by ideological struggles between moderate and radical factions. The moderates supported expanded self-government for the provinces and favoured many of the reforms, including freedom of the press, that had been adopted by the Cortes in Cádiz.

Attempts by the government in Buenos Aires to use military force to maintain control of the provinces frequently failed and hardened separatist sentiments in many regions. The policies of the government in Buenos Aires prompted some provincial leaders to discuss forming coalitions without the port city. *Porteño* leaders responded to the growing crisis by strengthening the executive and disbanding the assembly before it drafted a constitution and formed a new government. In January 1814, they appointed Gervasio Antonio Posadas supreme director and named José de San Martín commander of the Army of the North.[24] The diverse regions that formed the viceroyalty of the Río de la Plata might have united had Buenos Aires been willing to accept the creation of a confederation of equal provinces. It would not. Instead, the *porteños* sought to impose their rule by force. Despite the continuing stalemate between Buenos Aires and the other provinces, the region's isolated geographic position made it relatively safe from royalist forces.

The conflicts between the capitals of viceroyalties, *audiencias*, and captaincies general and their provincial capitals erupted not only in Venezuela, New Granada, and the Río de la Plata but also in Chile and Quito. These upheavals convinced insurgent leaders, such as Bolívar, that only strong centralized governments would succeed in winning independence and establishing order in South America. The centralist-provincial struggles, however, were difficult to contain; they continued for decades, profoundly affecting governmental stability and constitutional development in Spanish America.

THE CONSTITUTION RESTORED

Autonomists in America and Spanish and American liberals grew increasingly dissatisfied with the autocratic government of Fernando VII, which failed to conform to *antiguo régimen* government practice. In March 1820, liberals in Spain forced the king

---

[24] Rodríguez O., *The Independence*, 123–30.

to restore the Constitution of Cádiz. The return of constitutional government elicited disparate responses from Spanish America. New Spain and the kingdom of Guatemala conducted elections for countless constitutional *ayuntamientos*, provincial deputations, and the Cortes. Political instability in the Peninsula during the previous dozen years, however, convinced many *novohispanos* that it was prudent to establish an autonomous government within the Spanish Monarchy. They pursued two courses of action. New Spain's deputies to the Cortes of 1821 proposed a project for New World autonomy, which would create three American kingdoms allied with the Peninsula and governed by Spanish princes under the Constitution of 1812. At the same time, fearing that their proposal might be rejected, they organized a movement throughout New Spain to establish an autonomous monarchy under the Constitution of 1812. Confronting political, social, and economic crises in the Peninsula, the Spanish majority in the Cortes rejected the proposal to create autonomous American kingdoms. As a result, the leaders of New Spain chose to secede and established the Mexican empire. Central America also declared independence and joined the newly formed Mexican empire.[25]

The Río de la Plata obtained its autonomy and ultimately its independence in 1816 by default; the Spanish Monarchy lacked the resources to mount a campaign to regain control of the area. The three provinces that had refused to accept the domination of Buenos Aires became the independent nations of Bolivia, Uruguay, and Paraguay.[26] Chile endured only limited combat in the struggle for emancipation, and the military forces that liberated the Andean nation in 1818 quickly departed to secure the independence of Peru. As a result, civilians played a central role in the Chilean government.

In contrast to the rest of America, the independence of northern South America was achieved by military force rather than political compromise. In 1816 the insurgents renewed the struggle to take control of Venezuela and New Granada. The restoration of the Hispanic Constitution provided insurgents favouring independence with the opportunity to press their campaign to liberate the continent. They accepted the armistice offered by the Cortes in order to strengthen their forces, confident that the monarchy would not send a new expeditionary army to restore royal order in the region. However, those favouring independence faced strong resistance because the majority of the population of Venezuela, Quito, Peru, and Charcas as well as segments of New Granada eagerly implemented the restored constitutional system. They elected hundreds of constitutional *ayuntamientos*, but most were unable to complete elections for provincial deputations and deputies to the Cortes in Madrid because the insurgents violated the truce in 1821 and began a military campaign to subdue their opponents.

The conflict in northern South America enhanced the power of military men. Colombia provides the clearest example of that phenomenon. Convened by Simón Bolívar in February 1819, the Congress of Angostura legitimized his power and in December created the Republic of Colombia, incorporating Venezuela, New Granada, and Quito. Although a few regions of Venezuela and New Granada possessed

---

[25] Ibid. 169–237.
[26] Jorge Siles Salinas, *La independencia de Bolivia* (Madrid, 1992).

representation at Angostura, Quito and the most heavily populated parts of Venezuela and New Granada had none. Later in 1821, the Congress of Cúcuta, pressured by President Bolívar and intimidated by the army, ratified the formation of the Republic of Colombia, again without any representation from Quito. Bolívar also used force to compel large parts of Venezuela and New Granada to join the Republic because most people in those regions preferred the Hispanic Constitution to the Colombian Charter of 1821, which created a highly centralized government and granted vast authority to the president.

Bolívar's actions in the kingdom of Quito demonstrated his disdain for civilian rule and his willingness to subjugate other independent governments and impose martial law in his drive to expel royalist forces from the continent and consolidate power. Guayaquil declared independence and formed a republican government on 9 October 1820; in the following months, it attempted without success to free the highland provinces of the kingdom of Quito. Guayaquil subsequently requested help from San Martín and Bolívar in liberating the highlands. General Antonio José de Sucre, commanding a force consisting mainly of local troops, Colombians, and men from San Martín's army, finally defeated the royalist forces in Quito on 24 May 1822, at the Battle of Pinchincha. Bolívar, who arrived from the north in June with more Colombian troops, incorporated the region into the Republic of Colombia despite opposition from both Quito and Guayaquil. Subsequently, Bolívar imposed martial law in the former kingdom of Quito to impress men as well as to requisition money and supplies for the struggle against the royalists in Peru, the last bastion of royal power in America.[27]

Attempts to defeat the royalists in Peru began in August 1820, when San Martín landed in Lima with a liberating army composed of Chileans and *rioplatenses* (people from the Río de la Plata). Although he controlled the coast, San Martín could not overcome the royalists in the highlands. In an effort to win the loyalty of the population, liberal officers in the royal army forced the viceroy to abdicate on 29 January 1821, implemented the Hispanic Constitution of 1812, and named General José de la Serna captain general. The constitutionalists reorganized the royal army and nearly drove San Martín's forces from the coast. But divisions within the royalist ranks prevented them from expelling the republican forces.

Unable to secure additional resources to pursue the Peruvian campaign, San Martín ceded the honour of final victory to Bolívar. Although the Colombians arrived in force in 1823, they made little progress. Divisions among Peruvians, shortage of supplies, and strong royalist armies kept them pinned down on the coast. However, the royalists also were divided. In Charcas the absolutist general Pedro Olañeta opposed La Serna and the liberals. After the king again abolished the Constitution of Cádiz in 1823, General Olañeta took up arms against the liberals on 25 December 1823. This internecine conflict contributed to the royalists' defeat. For nearly a year, while Bolívar and his

---

[27] Rodríguez O., *La revolución . . . de Quito*, 179–86.

men recovered, royalist constitutional and absolutist armies waged war against each other in the highlands. Ultimately, General Sucre defeated the royalist constitutional army in the decisive Battle of Ayacucho on 9 December 1824. Olañeta's absolutist forces, however, remained in control of Charcas. Political intrigue finally settled the struggle. The assassination of Olañeta in April 1825 marked the end of royal power in Charcas. Subsequently, General Sucre formed the new republic of Bolivia in the territory of the former *audiencia* of Charcas. By 1826, when the last royalist forces surrendered, Bolívar dominated northern and central South America as president of Colombia, dictator of Peru, and ruler of Bolivia.[28]

CONCLUSION

By 1826 the overseas possessions of the Spanish Monarchy, one of the world's most imposing political structures at the end of the eighteenth century, consisted only of Cuba, Puerto Rico, the Philippines, and a few other Pacific islands. Having achieved independence, the countries of the American continent would henceforth chart their own futures. Most entered a prolonged period of economic decline and political instability. The break-up of the monarchy destroyed a vast and responsive social, political, and economic system that functioned effectively, despite its many imperfections. For nearly 300 years the worldwide Spanish Monarchy had proven to be flexible and capable of accommodating social tensions and conflicting political and economic interests. After independence, the former Spanish Monarchy's separate parts operated at a competitive disadvantage. In that regard, nineteenth-century Spain, like the American kingdoms, was just one more newly independent nation struggling to survive in an uncertain and difficult world. During the first half of the nineteenth century, the new nations experienced economic decline and political instability. The stable, more developed, and stronger countries of the North Atlantic, such as Britain, France, and the United States, flooded Spanish America with their exports, dominated their credit, and sometimes imposed their will upon the new American nations by force of arms. Consequently, the members of the former Spanish Monarchy were forced to accept a secondary role in the new world order.

BIBLIOGRAPHY

Anna, Timothy E., *The Fall of Royal Government in Peru* (Lincoln, NE, 1979).
Collier, Simon, *Ideas and Politics of Chilean Independence, 1808–1833* (Cambridge, 1967).

---

[28] Rodríguez O., *The Independence*, 215–19 and 228–34.

Costeloe, Michael P., *Response to Revolution: Imperial Spain and the Spanish American Revolutions* (Cambridge, 1986).

Dym, Jordana, *From Sovereign Villages to National States: City State and Federation in Central America, 1759–1839* (Albuquerque, NM, 2006).

Earle, Rebecca A., *Spain and the Independence of Colombia, 1810–1825* (Exeter, 2000).

Guerra, François-Xavier, *Modernidad e independencias: ensayos sobre las revoluciones Hispánicas* (Madrid, 1992).

Lynch, John, *The Spanish American Revolutions, 1808–1826* (New York, 1973).

Rodríguez O., Jaime E., *The Independence of Spanish America* (Cambridge, 1998).

—— *La revolución política durante la época de la independencia: el Reino de Quito, 1808–1822* (Quito, 2006).

—— '*Nosotros somos ahora los verdaderos españoles': La transición de Nueva España de un reino de la Monarquía Española a la República Federal de México, 1808–1824* (Zamora, 2009).

CHAPTER 34

AFRICA IN THE ATLANTIC WORLD, C.1760–C.1840

ROBIN LAW

THE transatlantic slave trade attained its peak volume in the third quarter of the eighteenth century, when over 80,000 slaves annually were being shipped from Africa for the Americas (see Chapter 16). This overshadowed the older-established trade in slaves northwards from West Africa across the Sahara Desert to the Muslim world, which was probably under 10,000 annually.[1] It also dwarfed trade in other African commodities, such as gold, ivory, dyewoods, and gum arabic; slaves now accounted for over 90 per cent of transatlantic exports.[2] The slave trade extended all the way down the Atlantic coast of Africa from the River Senegal to Angola, and even into the Indian Ocean coast of south-eastern Africa (Mozambique), which became a significant supplier of slaves for the Atlantic trade in the early nineteenth century. The volume of slave exports varied regionally, and in some areas other commodities remained relatively important: notably in Senegambia, in the extreme west, where slave exports remained limited or even declined over the eighteenth century, and were exceeded in value by exports of gum.[3] South Africa occupied an anomalous position, as the site of a European settlement colony (Cape Colony, initially Dutch, but taken by Britain in 1806), which was an importer rather than exporter of slaves, and drew these slaves from the east, across the Indian Ocean, rather than from Atlantic Africa.

---

[1] Slaves were also imported to the Muslim world down the Nile valley via Egypt, and by sea from East Africa. For an analysis integrating these various trades, see Patrick Manning, *Slavery and African Life: Occidental, Oriental and African Slave Trades* (Cambridge, 1990).

[2] Statistical information from David Eltis and Lawrence Jennings, 'Trade between Western Africa and the Atlantic World in the Pre-Colonial Era', *American Historical Review*, 93 (1988), 936–59; David Eltis, 'Precolonial West Africa and the Atlantic Economy', in Barbara L. Solow (ed.), *Slavery and the Rise of the Atlantic System* (Cambridge, 1991), 97–119.

[3] This raises problems for the emphasis on the impact of the Atlantic slave trade in some modern studies of Senegambia: here, in fact, the trans-Saharan slave trade was probably still a more important factor.

DEPENDENCE OR MARGINALITY? THE IMPORTANCE OF THE ATLANTIC SLAVE TRADE FOR AFRICA

Although the crucial importance of enslaved African labour in the European colonies in the Americas is clear, the significance of this trade for Africa itself is more difficult to grasp. A large part of the difficulty is that, while the volume and value of the transatlantic trade are well established (within generous margins of error), there is a lack of hard quantitative data on African domestic economies, against which the significance of overseas trade has to be measured. For some scholars, the Atlantic slave trade represented an important stage in the establishment of Africa's 'subordination and dependence' in relation to the European-dominated capitalist world economy;[4] while for others, it was quantitatively simply too small to have had much effect on the economic development of African societies. One analysis calculates that even by the end of the eighteenth century per capita earnings from overseas trade in coastal western Africa were only around 2 shillings (£0.10) annually, which is suggested to represent just 1 per cent of total domestic product.[5]

Generalization about western Africa as a whole, however, may obscure the fact that the level of involvement in the Atlantic economy was very uneven, as between different regions and even between different communities within particular regions. Overseas trade was certainly not of marginal significance for maritime entrepôts, such as Elmina, Cape Coast, Anomabu, and Accra on the 'Gold Coast' (modern Ghana), Ouidah, Porto-Novo, and Lagos on the 'Slave Coast' (the modern Republic of Bénin and south-western Nigeria), Bonny and Old Calabar on the Bight of Biafra (south-eastern Nigeria), or Luanda in Angola. The impact of the trade on such coastal communities is measured most obviously in their demographic growth, from small fishing or salt-making villages prior to European contact, to urban settlements of several thousands. Many of these Atlantic ports were not even self-sufficient in their basic foodstuffs, which they purchased from the interior, partly with local produce (especially salt) but mainly with the re-export of goods obtained from trade with Europeans. Such coastal communities, at least, literally lived by Atlantic trade.

For societies in the interior, the importance of Atlantic trade was evidently less, since these remained basically agricultural communities, and again variable from case to case, according to the scale of their participation. For Dahomey, the major power in the hinterland of the Slave Coast, one analysis calculates per capita export earnings in the eighteenth century as averaging just over 12 shillings (£0.61) annually.[6] What proportion of total domestic product this represented is debatable, depending on the assumptions

---

[4] Walter Rodney, *How Europe Underdeveloped Africa* (London, 1972), chapter 4.
[5] Eltis and Jennings, 'Trade', 955–6.
[6] Extracted from Patrick Manning, *Slavery, Colonialism and Economic Growth in Dahomey, 1640–1890* (Cambridge, 1982), 3, table 1.2.

made about the size of the domestic economy—suggestions have ranged between 2.5 per cent and 15 per cent. But earnings of this order were far from insignificant, representing the standard subsistence allowance for one person (at 2½ pre-decimal pence per day) for over eight weeks.[7]

The economic impact of the slave trade has to be assessed, not only in terms of its aggregate size, but also of the nature and extent of its linkages to the rest of the economy. On this, the general view has been that the 'multiplier' effects of overseas trade in western Africa in the eighteenth century were limited, not only because of its small size but also because the slave trade was restricted to a small elite of rulers and wealthy merchants, with the mass of people excluded from direct participation. By this analysis, overseas trade became an engine of economic growth in western Africa only in the nineteenth century, when the slave trade was replaced by the export of agricultural produce, in which the mass of ordinary people could engage.[8]

While there is some force in this argument, it is necessary, contrariwise, to guard against underestimating the degree of linkage between overseas trade and African domestic economies even in the slaving era. The goods imported were certainly not consumed exclusively by ruling/commercial elites, since they were regularly observed on sale in local markets, in the interior as well as at the coast. Moreover, a significant category among imported commodities comprised items which served as currencies for local exchange, including brass bracelets (*manillas*), copper rods, and above all cowrie shells, which were fished in the Indian Ocean but brought to western Africa via Europe. Cowries served as the circulating currency on the Slave Coast, and also in a large area of the West African interior.[9] This importation of massive amounts of cowries evidently implies an expanding domestic exchange economy, which in part fed off the overseas trade.

The importance of overseas commerce is in any case not restricted to its narrowly economic impact. The fact that imported European goods remained relatively rare does not mean that they were of little political or social significance, since their very rarity made access to them a source of social distinction, and the management of their distribution a means of reinforcing political authority. For example, when the first European explorer travelled into Yorubaland (south-western Nigeria) in 1825, he met a military officer of the then dominant kingdom of Oyo, who pointed to various items of his dress, declaring, '[t]his cloth is not made in my country; this cap is of white man's velvet, these trowsers are of white man's nankeen, this is a white man's shawl; we get all good things from the white man'.[10] From the perspective of the ruling elite, the value of such imported goods was enhanced, rather than diminished, by the fact that they remained beyond the reach of the generality of the population.

---

[7] Subsistence was paid in the local currency of cowrie shells, at 80 per day, cowries being valued at 4,000 to 10 shillings (£0.50) sterling: Robin Law, 'Posthumous Questions for Karl Polanyi: Price Inflation in Pre-Colonial Dahomey', *Journal of African History*, 33 (1992), 387–420.

[8] A. G. Hopkins, *An Economic History of West Africa* (London, 1973), chapter 3.

[9] Jan Hogendorn and Marion Johnson, *The Shell Money of the Slave Trade* (Cambridge, 1991).

[10] Hugh Clapperton, *Journal of a Second Expedition into the Interior of Africa* (London, 1829), 3.

The specific role of imported firearms and gunpowder should also be noted. It has been calculated that firearms imports into western Africa in the late eighteenth century may have amounted to no more than one gun per 118 persons annually.[11] But the point is that access to guns was not evenly distributed across the region; those societies (or groups within societies) which had guns, provided they learned to handle them effectively, could enjoy a decisive military advantage over those which did not. By the eighteenth century, the armies of several major states had adopted muskets as their principal armament, including Asante (Ashanti), inland from the Gold Coast, and Dahomey. Yorubaland was in this respect a late developer, but firearms were adopted there also from the 1810s, in the context of wars associated with the collapse of Oyo. In those parts of the coast where navigable lagoons and rivers afforded the opportunity of a naval form of warfare, as at Porto-Novo, Lagos, Bonny, and Old Calabar, canoes were regularly armed with cannon. The adoption of imported firearms affected the strategy, as well as the tactics, of African warfare, making the securing of access to or control over trade to the coast (and denial of them to enemies) a paramount military objective.

In the final analysis, the best evidence for the importance of the Atlantic trade for Africa is the demonstrable concern of rulers of major states to control and exact revenue from it, seen in the efforts of hinterland powers to extend their authority over the coastal entrepôts. Dahomey had conquered the port of Ouidah already in the 1720s, but Oyo established its control over Porto-Novo only in the 1770s, and Asante overran the Gold Coast in 1807. European abolitionists regularly argued further that the wars of these states were motivated by the desire to take slaves for sale, but this is more doubtful. More probably, the taking of slaves was generally a by-product rather than the origin of African wars, although the existence of a market for captives presumably increased the profitability of war, and hence the readiness of states to resort to it.

Western Africa as a participant in the 'Atlantic community'

Despite the long history of commerce, direct European involvement in Africa remained limited. In contrast to the Americas, European colonial occupation of African territory was minimal before the later nineteenth century. The Portuguese had settled the major offshore islands—the Cape Verde Islands in the west and São Tomé, Príncipe, and Fernando Po off equatorial West Africa—but very little of mainland Africa was formally colonized, the only major exceptions being Cape Colony in South Africa and the Portuguese colonies in Central Africa, Angola on the west coast and Mozambique on the east. Elsewhere, European occupation was restricted to coastal trading posts, sometimes fortified. Where possible, these were also situated on islands close to

---

[11] Eltis and Jennings, 'Trade', 954.

the shore, as with the French forts on Saint-Louis and Gorée in Senegal, and the British fort on James Island in the River Gambia. On the Gold Coast, and also at Ouidah on the Slave Coast, although forts were established on-shore, there was no occupation of any significant areas of territory; indeed, in most cases even these forts remained legally under African sovereignty, occupied with the agreement of (and often on payment of tribute to) the local authorities.

Further, there was little physical penetration by Europeans of the African interior, European traders generally remaining at the coast and waiting for slaves and other commodities to be delivered to them there. The only exceptions were some of the major rivers, by which Europeans penetrated by boat to trade in the interior, as on the Senegal and the Gambia, and the lower reaches of the Congo (but not on the Niger until the 1830s). Likewise, and again in contrast to the Americas, Christian missionary enterprise made little impact in Africa before the nineteenth century. Although the Roman Catholic Church had undertaken evangelization in the early centuries of European contact, this had largely faded out by the eighteenth century, leaving little lasting impression beyond the offshore islands and the Portuguese colony of Angola (where there were bishoprics at Santiago in the Cape Verde Islands, on São Tomé, and at Luanda), and in the Central African kingdom of Kongo. Protestant churches, by contrast, undertook little missionary activity before the end of the eighteenth century.

Nevertheless, the cultural impact of Europe, at least in coastal areas, was not insignificant, and not restricted to the few formal colonial enclaves. Three centuries of commercial contact, by the late eighteenth century, had produced a (partly) Euro-peanized population in many coastal communities. This was of heterogeneous origins, including both persons of mixed European and African ancestry, and others of purely African descent who had assimilated European culture either through travel abroad or in Africa. These people were distinguished by their knowledge of European languages, sometimes including literacy, and sometimes (though by no means always) also by allegiance to Christianity. The terminology which historians have applied to these Europeanized elements in African societies is problematic. They have often been called 'Afro-Europeans' (or 'Eurafricans' and other variants), which captures their cultural hybridity, but is of course a retrospectively invented term, not one that they themselves used; the currently fashionable term 'creoles' is also difficult in West Africa, because there it has a specific and narrower application, to the community of descendants of freed slaves resettled in the British colony of Freetown, Sierra Leone, from 1787.[12] In the eighteenth and nineteenth centuries, many of the people we now call 'Afro-Europeans' were called (and called themselves) 'whites' (or equivalents in African languages), this term being commonly constructed locally in cultural rather than narrowly racial terms; even persons who were entirely African in their biological ancestry, but who spoke

---

[12] Also called 'Krio', though whether this is a version of 'Creole' is disputed: Akintola Wyse, *The Krio of Sierra Leone* (London, 1989). 'Créole' was also applied in the French colony of Senegal to persons of mixed Afro-European ancestry; and 'crioulo' to the pidgin form of the Portuguese language spoken in the Cape Verde Islands and the adjacent mainland.

European languages, wore European dress, and otherwise affected European culture, were 'whites'.

These people not only maintained and identified with European culture, but also, in many instances, were involved in familial and social networks, as well as purely business links, which spanned the Atlantic, for example sending their children for education overseas. The Atlantic system thus involved not simply a one-way transfer of enslaved Africans into the diaspora, but continuing reciprocal interaction. The scale and intensity of these transoceanic linkages were such that it seems legitimate to regard West African coastal communities, or at least their commercial and political elites, as participating in an 'Atlantic community'.[13]

The character of this 'Atlanticized' population differed in different sections of the coast, according to the varied nature of their overseas links. Indeed, they are perhaps better conceptualized as belonging, not to a single 'Atlantic community', but rather to a number of discrete communities, which linked individuals in Africa with their counterparts in particular European (or American) countries. Although they had much in common, their varied external links meant that they were divided by language, and to some extent also by religious affiliation, between Roman Catholicism and Protestantism. On the upper (north-western) section of the West African coast, outside the French sphere of Senegal, the predominant influence in what was later to become Portuguese Guinea (modern Guinea-Bissau) was Portuguese and Roman Catholic, linked to the Cape Verde Islands rather than directly to metropolitan Portugal. In Sierra Leone, transatlantic links were mainly to Britain (even before the establishment of the Freetown colony in 1787); on the Gold Coast, to all three European nations which maintained permanent establishments there—Britain, the Netherlands, and Denmark; on the Slave Coast, mainly to Brazil, especially the province of Bahia; and in the Bight of Biafra, again, mainly to Britain. The Portuguese colony of Angola was also linked to Brazil, though to Rio de Janeiro rather than Bahia.

The variety of antecedents and experience among these 'Afro-European' populations is best conveyed by concrete examples. In some cases, they derived from the settlement of European (or American) traders, who took African wives and fathered descendants. In Sierra Leone, for example, the prominent merchant families of Rogers, Caulker, and Tucker were descended from men who served as local agents of English trading companies in the late seventeenth century.[14] On the Gold Coast, a noted case was the Irish trader Richard Brew, who lived on the coast from 1745 until his death in 1776, establishing his own private 'castle' at Anomabu.[15] On the Slave Coast, the major example was the Brazilian slave trader Francisco Felix de Souza, who resided on the

[13] Robin Law and Kristin Mann, 'West Africa in the Atlantic Community: The Case of the Slave Coast', *William and Mary Quarterly*, 3rd Series, 56 (1999), 307–34; Robin Law, 'The Port of Ouidah in the Atlantic Community, 17th to 19th Centuries', in Horst Pietschmann (ed.), *Atlantic History: History of the Atlantic System 1580–1830* (Göttingen, 2002), 349–64.

[14] Walter Rodney, *A History of the Upper Guinea Coast 1545–1800* (Oxford, 1970), 216–20.

[15] Margaret Priestley, *West African Trade and Coast Society: A Family Study* (London, 1969).

coast permanently from 1800 until his death in 1849, and in 1818 supported a *coup d'état* which overthrew the reigning king of Dahomey in favour of his brother Gezo, and was in reward installed as the latter's commercial agent at his port of Ouidah.[16]

In other cases, it was returned former slaves (or descendants of slaves) who settled in Africa. The best-known examples are the organized repatriation of free blacks to Freetown from 1787 (from Britain, Canada, and Jamaica), and Liberia from 1821 (from the USA). But many other ex-slaves returned to Africa on their own individual initiative, mainly to the Slave Coast, and principally from Brazil. Although the Afro-Brazilian re-emigration attained a large scale only from the 1830s, there were numerous cases of individual returnees already in the eighteenth century. As an illustrative example, a leading merchant in Ouidah in the 1780s was Dom Jeronimo, who was in origin a prince of Dahomey, but sold as a slave, and spent twenty-four years in slavery in Brazil, before being redeemed by the Dahomian King Kpengla (acceded 1774), with whom he had been friends in childhood.[17]

Other instances of the acquisition of overseas experience and education through enslavement and repatriation involved persons who had been enslaved illegally, but were eventually able to reclaim their freedom. A celebrated example was that of two 'princes' (actually, sons of prominent merchants) of Old Calabar, who were captured in a civil war in 1767 and sold to British traders who took them into slavery in Dominica, but succeeded in escaping to England in 1773, where they sought their freedom through the courts. They were eventually redeemed through the intercession of some Liverpool slave merchants, and returned to Calabar, having meanwhile acquired literacy and been converted to Methodist Christianity through their residence in England.[18]

In other cases, free Africans were sent abroad for the specific purpose of education. A notable example was Philip Quaque, originally taken as a hostage for a treaty between the British authorities on the Gold Coast and the local state of Fante in 1753, educated and ordained as an Anglican priest in England (where he also acquired an English wife), who returned to the Gold Coast in 1765 and served as chaplain of Cape Coast Castle until his death in 1816.[19] An example from the Slave Coast is the Lawson family of 'Little Popo' (nowadays Aného, in modern Togo). The founder of the family, Latévi Awoku (d. 1795), is said to have been a 'servant' of the English in his youth; this was probably in Africa (perhaps on the Gold Coast, from where the family originated), but in the 1780s he had two of his own sons being educated abroad, one in England and one in Portugal. The son in England was presumably Akuété Zankli, alias George Lawson (d. 1857), who took his English name from a trader who dealt with his father. In

---

[16] Robin Law, 'Francisco Felix de Souza in West Africa, 1820–1849', in José C. Curto and Paul E. Lovejoy (eds), *Enslaving Connections: Changing Cultures of Africa and Brazil during the Era of Slavery* (New York, 2004), 187–211.

[17] Robin Law, *Ouidah: The Social History of a West African Slaving 'Port', 1727–1892* (Oxford, 2004), 117, 149.

[18] Randy J. Sparks, *The Two Princes of Calabar: An Eighteenth-Century Atlantic Odyssey* (Cambridge, MA, 2004).

[19] Margaret Priestley, 'Philip Quaque of Cape Coast', in Philip D. Curtin (ed.), *Africa Remembered: Narratives by West Africans from the Era of the Slave Trade* (Madison, WI, 1967), 99–139.

addition to being educated in England, he is also said to have served as steward on a
Liverpool slaver on a voyage to Jamaica, before returning to resettle at Popo in 1812.[20]
The Lawsons are an example of a family which rose to prominence in part through its
European connections. In other cases, members of existing ruling elites acquired
similar experience abroad. Joe Aggrey, who became king of Cape Coast in 1816, had
previously served 'several years' in the British navy, and in consequence was literate in
English, and his house was 'furnished in the European style'.[21] At Old Calabar, sons of
prominent merchants were regularly sent for education to England, where they lodged
in the houses of their English business partners; this produced an unusually high level
of literacy among the ruling elite, who conducted written correspondence with England, and one of whom in the 1780s even kept a diary, providing a unique African
perspective on the operation of the slave trade.[22]

Some African states also maintained diplomatic relations with their trading partners
across the Atlantic. On the Slave Coast, there is record of no less than seven embassies
which arrived in Brazil from the African states of Dahomey, Porto-Novo, and Lagos
between 1750 and 1812, some of which also went on to Portugal before returning to
Africa.[23] As a curiosity (but an illuminating one) it may be noted that the first recorded
recognition of the independence of Brazil by any foreign state, in 1824, was transmitted
by a Portuguese claiming to serve as ambassador for the king of Lagos.[24]

LOCAL DIMENSIONS OF THE
AFRICAN 'ATLANTIC COMMUNITY'

The operation of the Atlantic trade had the effect of linking up different parts of Africa
with each other, as well as with Europe and the Americas. Europeans regularly took
Africans from one region for employment in another. The slaves employed in European
factories on the Gold Coast, for example, included persons brought from the Gambia to
the west and the Slave Coast to the east. Conversely, European factories on the Slave
Coast employed slaves imported from the Gold Coast. The logic of this practice was,
explicitly, that slaves moved away from their home areas were less likely to escape.

---

[20] Silke Strickrodt, 'Afro-European Trade Relations on the Western Slave Coast, 16th to 19th
Centuries' (Ph.D. thesis, University of Stirling, 2003), 184–7, 191–4.

[21] John Duncan, *Travels in Western Africa in 1845 and 1846* (London, 1847), i. 29.

[22] Paul E. Lovejoy and David Richardson, 'Letters of the Old Calabar Slave Trade, 1760–1789', in
Vincent Carreta and Philip Gould (eds), *Genius in Bondage: Literature of the Early Black Atlantic*
(Louisville, KY, 2001), 89–115; Diary of Antera Duke, in Daryll Forde (ed.), *Efik Traders of Old Calabar*
(London, 1956), 27–115.

[23] Pierre Verger, *Flux et reflux de la traite des nègres entre le Golfe de Bénin et Bahia de Todos os
Santos du XVIe au XIXe siècle* (Paris, 1968), 251–85.

[24] Alberto da Costa e Silva, *As relações entre a Brasil e a África negra de 1822 a la Guerra Mondial*
(Luanda, 1996), 7.

Africans were also extensively recruited as freemen for service outside their home-lands. On the Slave Coast, Europeans found that the indigenous people had no tradition of navigation on the sea (as opposed to the inland lagoons), and so hired canoes and canoemen from the Gold Coast to land goods and embark slaves there. Such canoemen normally returned home on completion of their contracts, but some settled permanently on the Slave Coast.[25] After the British colony of Freetown was established in 1787, numbers of Kru people (from what is nowadays Liberia, 300 miles along the coast to the south-east) came there to seek employment on the docks and in other work; and subsequently many Kru were recruited as sailors, initially by the British navy and later also by merchant shipping.[26] Improvements in marine technology introduced by Europeans (especially the sail) also enabled Africans to extend the range of their navigation by canoe along the coast. African merchants from the Gold Coast, for example, travelled by sea to trade on the Slave Coast.

This raises the question of how this movement of people along the coast may have affected questions of identity. It is usually thought that the idea of a collective 'African' (or 'black') identity emerged originally in the diaspora in the Americas, and was only fed back into Africa at a second stage, from the nineteenth century. But it may be that it emerged in local consciousness earlier than commonly assumed, and as a result of experiences in Africa, as well as in the diaspora. It seems clear, at least, that persons in coastal communities were aware that their encounter with Europeans was not unique, but shared with others elsewhere in Africa. There is also evidence that European racial usage was adopted by Africans in coastal areas, who commonly employed the contrasting categories of 'whites' and 'blacks' (and the 'white men's land'/'black men's land') in their own discourses.[27]

Autonomy and interconnection: the Muslim interior

There is clearly a danger that the foregoing account, by concentrating on those parts of western Africa (those along the coast) which were most directly and intensively involved in Atlantic trade, has conveyed an exaggerated impression of the significance of the latter for the history of Africa. It might be argued that much of West Africa, and in particular the interior, was only marginally, if at all, affected by the Atlantic trade, and more influenced by older commercial and cultural linkages, across the Sahara to

[25] Robin Law, 'Between the Sea and the Lagoons: The Interaction of Maritime and Inland Navigation on the Pre-Colonial Slave Coast', *Cahiers d'études africaines*, 19 (1989), 207–37.

[26] Diane Frost, 'Diasporan West African Communities: The Kru in Freetown and Liverpool', *Review of African Political Economy*, 29 (2002), 285–300.

[27] e.g. the Gold Coast myth of God's creation of 'whites' and 'blacks', explaining the former's possession of literacy and the latter's of gold, reported by William Bosman, *A New and Accurate Description of the Coast of Guinea* (London, 1705), 146–7.

the Muslim world. The autonomous (or northern-oriented) character of the West African historical process might seem to be self-evidently illustrated by one of the major developments of this period, a series of jihads, or 'Islamic Revolutions', in which Muslim clerics seized power from existing ruling groups: beginning with Futa Djallon (in modern Guinea-Conakry) in the 1720s, then Futa Toro (Senegal) in the 1770s, and the jihad in Hausaland (northern Nigeria) which created the Sokoto caliphate, from 1804. These movements drew their inspiration from a well-established West African tradition of Islamic scholarship, and can also be seen as a local variant of the phenomenon of fundamentalist revivalism which was also visible elsewhere in the Muslim world at this period (paralleling, for example, the Wahhabiyya in Arabia).

Yet is clear that these movements were not totally disconnected from the Atlantic world, since the areas where they arose were all by the eighteenth century involved in the supply of slaves for sale at the coast, and they were obliged to square this with their understanding of Islamic law. The rulers of Futa Djallon, for example, continued to supply slaves for the Atlantic trade, but justified this on the grounds that these were captives taken in what were represented to be 'holy wars' against neighbouring 'pagans'.[28] The later jihadist leaders were more fastidious about participation in the Atlantic slave trade, placing more emphasis on the need to enforce provisions in Islamic law which forbade enslavement of fellow Muslims. In 1787 the ruler of Futa Toro was reported to have 'enacted a law, that no slave whatever should be marched through his territories';[29] although contemporary European observers interpreted this as a total prohibition of slave trading, it was more probably an attempt to curb the enslavement and sale of Muslims. The leaders of the Sokoto jihad also condemned the sale of slaves from Hausaland to the coast, on the grounds that it involved the transfer of slaves, including some who were Muslims, into the ownership of infidels. Moreover, among offences against Islamic law current there prior to the jihad of 1804 which they particularly emphasized was the enslavement of Muslims. Although this issue had been a matter of concern in West African Muslim circles since at least the fourteenth century, it may be that its salience in Hausaland at this time reflected the impact of the Atlantic trade.[30] In 1824 the ruler of Sokoto agreed with emissaries of the British government to prohibit the supply of slaves to the coast; although this agreement was abortive, it serves to illustrate the potential convergence of Muslim concerns to regulate and restrict the process of enslavement with European abolitionism.[31]

---

[28] Walter Rodney, 'Jihad and Social Revolution in Futa Jallon in the Eighteenth Century', *Journal of the Historical Society of Nigeria*, 4/2 (1968), 269–84.

[29] C. B. Wadström, *Observations on the Slave Trade* (London, 1789), 4, 34.

[30] Humphrey Fisher, 'A Muslim William Wilberforce? The Sokoto Jihad as Antislavery Crusade: An Enquiry into Historical Causes', in Serge Daget (ed.), *De la traite à l'esclavage: Actes du Colloque International sur la Traite des Noirs, Nantes 1985* (Paris, 1988), iii. 537–55.

[31] Paul E. Lovejoy, 'The Bello-Clapperton Exchange: The Sokoto Jihad and the Trans-Atlantic Slave Trade, 1804–1837,' in Christopher Wise (ed.), *The Desert Shore: Literatures of the Sahel* (Boulder, CO, 2001), 201–28.

Transformations from the
Late Eighteenth Century

The revolutionary transformations which occurred elsewhere in the Atlantic world from the late eighteenth century had only limited immediate impact in Africa. The direct effects of the French and American Revolutions were minimal. In the French colony of Senegal, the local community, which included persons of mixed descent (*métis*) and Africans, as well as Europeans, unlike their counterparts in Saint-Domingue/Haiti, were only marginally involved in the Revolution in France. In the preparations for the summoning of the Estates General in 1789, a local meeting drafted a *cahier* calling for abolition of the monopoly privileges of the Senegal Company, but the colony was not represented in the subsequent revolutionary assemblies. The decree of 1794 abolishing slavery, and extending French citizenship to all inhabitants of overseas colonies, in theory applied to the Senegalese colony, but in fact it was not until the later Revolution of 1848 that slavery there was abolished, and provision made for representation in the French Assembly. The tenuousness of Senegal's linkage to the metropolitan Revolution is illustrated by an incident in 1802, when a rising by the African and *métis* population invoked the slogan 'Vive la Convention, Vive Robespierre!,' in seeming unawareness that this cause was long lost.[32] In Cape Colony in South Africa, the 'Patriot' agitation against the regime of the Dutch East India Company from 1778 onwards, and a frontier insurrection in 1795, drew some inspiration from the American and European revolutionary movements, but had their basic roots in the local situation.[33]

The Haitian Revolution, although it had no discernible political influence in Africa, had a major, albeit temporary, disruptive impact on the transatlantic slave trade, by removing what had latterly been a principal market for slaves. The European wars arising out of the French Revolution, between 1792 and 1815, also had the effect of disrupting transatlantic commerce. By the time peace was restored in Europe, the situation was complicated by the legal abolition of the slave trade. Although the French abolition of slavery (and, by implication, of the slave trade) was rescinded in 1802, the trade was then outlawed by a series of European and American nations, beginning with Denmark from 1803, followed by Britain in 1807, the USA in 1808, the Netherlands in 1814, and France again in 1818. The process of abolition was completed only in 1836, when Portugal, which had initially accepted only geographical restriction of the slave trade, finally agreed to a total ban. Legal abolition, however, proved to be a different thing from effective suppression. Although the British navy maintained patrols (based at Freetown) to intercept illegal slave ships, these were of limited effectiveness. The scale of the slave trade dipped in the immediate aftermath of British/US abolition in 1807/8, but subsequently recovered to around 60 per cent of its earlier peak, and

---

[32] John D. Hargreaves, *West Africa: The Former French States* (Englewood Cliffs, NJ, 1967), 76.
[33] Hermann Giliomee, *The Afrikaners: Biography of a People* (London, 2003), 54–6, 72–4.

remained at high levels for some time, now principally directed to Brazil and Cuba. The slave trade to Brazil was ended only in 1850, and that to Cuba not until the 1860s.

Although legal abolition thus had only limited immediate impact on the scale of the slave trade, it had significant effects on its organization in Africa. Most obviously, it affected the regional distribution of the trade, as slave ships gravitated towards areas where the geography of the coast or (in Portuguese Angola) the connivance of the local authorities afforded the best chance of evading British naval patrols. Within West Africa, for example, slave exports were ended early on the Gold Coast, but initially continued at a high level on the Slave Coast. West Africa overall declined in relative importance, with West Central Africa (especially Angola) recovering the overwhelming dominance in slave supply which it had had before the eighteenth century. Illegality also encouraged the accumulation of slaves on shore, so that they could be embarked *en bloc*, so as to minimize the time in which ships had to remain in port and vulnerable to arrest. Slaves therefore now spent less time on board ship, but more on shore awaiting shipment. This may account for an increase in shipboard mortality in this period, reversing the earlier trend of decline; the explanation possibly being that, having spent longer in the insanitary conditions of onshore 'barracoons' (stockades), they were in poorer health when embarked. There was also an increase in the proportion of children among slaves exported, to double the level of the eighteenth century (and reaching over 40 per cent of the total). The explanation for this is uncertain: it may possibly have reflected a strategy to anticipate the suppression of the trade by purchasers in America, to extend the working life of the slaves imported, but, given the existence of regional variations within Africa, there may also have been supply-side factors originating from within the exporting societies.

The story of the ending of the Atlantic slave trade is usually told from a European perspective. The role of Africans remained that of passive spectators, or indeed active opponents of the abolitionist project. Although the British made sustained efforts to enlist the alliance of African rulers in the suppression of the slave trade, the latter generally remained unconvinced that proposed alternatives would prove an adequate substitute, and continued to sell slaves as long as buyers presented themselves. The suppression of the Atlantic slave trade was effected through the closing down of markets in the Americas, rather than the shutting off of supplies of slaves from Africa.

African rulers were, however, clearly aware of the abolitionist agitation, even before the legal enactment of abolition, and the views of some of them on it were recorded by European observers. A British explorer visiting Old Calabar in 1805, for example, found that the leading merchant-chief, Egbo Young, was suspicious of his motives, declaring 'if I came from Mr Wilberforce they would kill me'.[34] In Bonny, 'King' Halliday, on receipt of news of British abolition in 1807, was sceptical about its feasibility: 'we think trade no stop, for all we Jew-Jew men [ju-ju men, i.e. priests] tell we so, for them say you country no can never pass God Almighty.'[35] The king of Asante, resisting British

[34] Nicholls to African Association, Old Calabar, 15 February 1805, in Robin Hallett (ed.), *Records of the African Association 1788–1831* (London, 1964), 198.
[35] *Memoirs of the Late Captain Hugh Crow of Liverpool* (London, 1830), 137 (spelling modernized).

pressure for his cooperation in suppressing the slave trade in 1820, insisted that the abolitionists 'do not understand my country', expressed puzzlement that Europeans should condemn the slave trade when Muslims, who worshipped the same god, accepted it, and asked, reasonably enough, 'if they think it bad now, why did they think it good before?'[36]

THE NEW ECONOMY OF 'LEGITIMATE' TRADE

The abolitionist project involved not only the suppression of the slave trade, but also the promotion of alternatives to it, which it was hoped would be both more profitable to Europe and more beneficial to Africa. After the slave trade became illegal, trade in other commodities was commonly called in contrast 'legitimate' trade. Although a wide range of commodities was developed or projected, in practice attention was concentrated on the promotion of agricultural exports. To some degree, initially, this was conceived within a colonial framework. The Danes on the Gold Coast, in anticipation of the abolition of the slave trade, experimented with plantations (mainly for the production of cotton), using slave labour locally, from 1788 onwards.[37] This was also an important element in the development of the British settlement at Freetown. Although its original establishment in 1787 was mainly intended to solve the perceived problem of a free black population in Britain, by resettling them in Africa, the Sierra Leone Company, which took it over in 1791, sought also to promote commercial agriculture (especially the production of sugar), in this case with free labour, as a substitute for the slave trade, albeit with limited success.[38] In the long run, however, the successful new trades were developed mainly by the inhabitants of independent African societies exploiting changing market opportunities, especially the production of palm oil, which was in demand mainly as a raw material in the manufacture of soap and candles. The import of palm oil into Britain for industrial purposes had begun already from the 1760s, but expanded rapidly and substantially in the abolitionist era.[39] Initially, the oil trade was concentrated in the 'Oil Rivers' (i.e. the delta of the River Niger and neighbouring areas of the Bight of Biafra), but eventually spread along the entire coastal forest area of western Africa, from Sierra Leone in the west to Angola in the south. From the 1830s, groundnuts, likewise initially used mainly for the manufacture of soap, also became a significant export, from Senegambia.

---

[36] Joseph Dupuis, *Journal of a Residence in Ashantee* (London, 1824), 163–4.

[37] Georg Nørregård, *Danish Settlements in West Africa 1658–1850* (Boston, MA, 1966), 172–85.

[38] Suzanne Schwarz, 'Commerce, Christianity and Civilization: The Development of the Sierra Leone Company', in David Richardson, Suzanne Schwarz, and Anthony Tibbles (eds.), *Liverpool and Transatlantic Slavery* (Liverpool, 2007), 252–76.

[39] Martin Lynn, *Commerce and Economic Change in West Africa: The Palm Oil Trade in the Nineteenth Century* (Cambridge, 1997).

This shift from slaves to vegetable oils as the staple of Africa's transatlantic exports involved a reorientation of its commercial links away from the Americas towards Europe, since the principal markets for the new staple were located in the industrial economies of Western Europe, although some palm oil was also traded to the USA and Brazil. This was compounded by the introduction of the steamship into Atlantic navigation from the 1830s, which freed shipping from the constraints of local winds and currents, and facilitated a return journey from Africa direct to Europe, rather than via the Americas, as was standard for sailing ships.

The rising produce trade probably already exceeded the declining slave trade in value by the 1840s, and continued to expand thereafter. The new trade in fact attained a higher value than the slave trade had ever reached: the value of Africa's Atlantic trade by the 1860s was over twice that in the 1780s. In terms of volume of imports, the increase was even greater, since this period saw significant reductions in the prices of many European manufactures; the terms of trade, that is, moved in favour of African producers. The new trade also appeared to hold out the prospect of a more positive impact on Africa's development. First, as noted earlier, it was open to participation by the mass of small-scale farmers and petty traders, rather than (like the slave trade) restricted to a narrow elite, and thus was potentially capable of forming stronger and more beneficial linkages to the wider economy. Since it was commonly thought that the European demand for slaves had stimulated warfare and disorder in Africa, it was also anticipated that a more peaceful era should now ensue.

In practice, these benefits were only partially realized. Although much of the oil exported was indeed produced by small-scale farmers, much was also produced by wealthy entrepreneurs, employing slave labour on large-scale plantations. In effect, slaves were diverted to export production within Africa, rather than being themselves exported. The ending of the overseas market for slaves was therefore offset by an increase in domestic demand.[40] Insofar as the existence of a market for slaves operated to encourage warfare, as abolitionists argued, this pressure presumably continued into the era of 'legitimate' trade. Certainly, there is little evidence for any decline in the incidence of warfare in Africa over the nineteenth century. Yorubaland, for example, following the collapse of Oyo, remained in a state of endemic internecine warfare throughout the century, which was fuelled in part by the continuing demand for slaves.[41] It may indeed be that disorder was exacerbated by the difficulties which African elites encountered in maintaining their position in the face of the strains of the commercial transition, although this idea of a 'crisis of adaptation' is contested.[42]

[40] Paul E. Lovejoy, *Transformations in Slavery: A History of Slavery in Africa* (2nd edn. Cambridge, 2000), chapter 8.

[41] Funso Afolayan, 'Warfare and Slavery in 19th Century Yorubaland', in Adeagbo Akinjogbin (ed.), *War and Peace in Yorubaland 1793–1893* (Ibadan, 1998), 407–19.

[42] Robin Law (ed.), *From Slave Trade to 'Legitimate' Commerce: The Commercial Transition in Nineteenth-Century West Africa* (Cambridge, 1995).

Moreover, the new trade in produce was subject to significant limitations. Most obviously, it involved higher transport costs than the slave trade, since produce had to be moved in large quantities, where possible by water but more generally by human porterage. Direct involvement in production for export was therefore necessarily restricted to a narrow area close to the coast, while the further interior could participate only indirectly, by supplying slaves to work in oil production in coastal areas. The full integration of the interior into international commerce would have to await the introduction of modern mechanized forms of transport, with the construction of railways in the colonial period.

It should also be noted that, although the expansion of the oil trade was impressive by comparison with earlier levels of trade from Africa, it did not match the general expansion of world trade at this period. If western Africa's overseas trade by the 1860s had doubled in value since the 1780s, total world trade during the same period had increased over fourfold. Africa's share in world trade had therefore declined, and was indeed never to recover the proportionate importance which it had enjoyed in the era of the slave trade.[43] While the importance of overseas commerce for Africa was growing, that of Africa within the world economy was declining. From a longer-term perspective, therefore, the ending of the slave trade might be regarded as marking the beginning of the combination of dependency and marginalization which has characterized the economic development of Africa down to the present.[44]

TOWARDS EUROPEAN DOMINATION

The suppression of the slave trade was associated with a more general increase in the level of European involvement in Africa. Most obviously, there was increased interest in exploration of the interior, associated in Britain with the establishment of the Association for the Discovery of the Interior Parts of Africa in 1788, motivated by a combination of scientific, humanitarian, and commercial interests. Although this was a private body, the enterprise of exploration soon attracted support from the British government also. Attention was initially concentrated on the main river systems (especially the Niger), which were thought to hold the key to the commercial development of the interior, by affording a cheap means of transport. A series of expeditions established the course of the Niger and its termination on the Atlantic coast between 1795 and 1830. Commercial exploitation, using steamships to navigate upriver, began soon afterwards, though with limited success before the 1850s.

This period also saw the revival of Christian missionary effort in Africa, now led by Protestant churches, especially in Britain, with the establishment of new bodies such as

---

[43] Eltis and Jennings, 'Trade', 941–2.
[44] Ralph A. Austen, *African Economic History: Internal Development and External Dependency* (London, 1987).

the London Missionary Society (1795) and the Church Missionary Society (1799). Initially efforts were concentrated on existing colonial or semi-colonial enclaves, such as Cape Colony and Freetown, extending into the Gold Coast from the 1820s. The decisive movement of missionary enterprise beyond existing colonial boundaries occurred only in the 1840s, with the organization of missions to what is nowadays southern Nigeria. The conversion of any large numbers of Africans to Christianity hardly occurred before the colonial period.

The Abolitionist era also saw an increased level of European political interference in Africa. The abolition of the slave trade put in question the value of retaining trading posts in Africa, and some were abandoned, including those at Ouidah on the Slave Coast. Most of the existing establishments, however, including those on the Gold Coast, were retained, and assumed the new role of bases for the promotion of 'legitimate' trade. The overall trend was for increasing state involvement, with the British government in particular taking over direct control of African possessions previously in private hands. Following the failure of the Sierra Leone Company, its settlement at Freetown was taken over as a crown colony in 1808, mainly to safeguard its humanitarian project, but also because of its potential as a naval base, for action against the now illegal slave trade, as well as the threat of French competition. Likewise, the Company of Merchants Trading to Africa, which had managed most of the British establishments in West Africa since 1752, was wound up in 1821 and its possessions on the Gold Coast taken over by the government. This involved the latter in relations with the hinterland power of Asante, which had conquered the coastal area in 1807, leading to military conflict in 1824–7—the first war fought by Britain against a major African state. The cost and embarrassment of this episode led to the transfer of the Gold Coast forts back into private hands in 1828, but crown rule was re-established from 1843. The British campaign to suppress the slave trade also involved intervention in (and coercion of) African states along the coast, though mainly after 1840.

The ending of the slave trade can thus be seen as an important step towards the extension of European rule over almost the entire continent, consummated in the later Partition of Africa. By the mid-nineteenth century, formal annexation remained restricted to a few coastal areas, and the conquest of the interior was not yet seriously envisaged, the general assumption still being that European enterprise would continue to operate within a framework of African independence. Nevertheless, the crucial precedent of a European right of intervention and disregard for African sovereignty had been set, establishing a necessary though not sufficient condition for the subsequent Partition.[45] In several respects, therefore, abolition marked an important transition in the history of western Africa, and of its involvement in the wider Atlantic world. These processes were, however, as yet still in an early stage by 1840.

---

[45] Robin Law, 'Abolition and Imperialism: International Law and the British Suppression of the Atlantic Slave Trade', in Derek R. Peterson (ed.), *Abolitionism and Imperialism in Britain, Africa and the Atlantic* (Athens, OH, 2010), 150–74.

BIBLIOGRAPHY

Barry, Boubacar, *Senegambia and the Atlantic Slave Trade* (Cambridge, 1998).

Brooks, George E., *Eurafricans in Western Africa: Social Status, Gender, and Religious Observance from the Sixteenth to the Eighteenth Century* (Athens, OH, 2003).

Eltis, David, *Economic Growth and the Ending of the Transatlantic Slave Trade* (New York, 1987).

Feinberg, Harvey M., *Africans and Europeans in West Africa: Elminans and Dutchmen on the Gold Coast in the Eighteenth Century* (Philadelphia, PA, 1989).

Law, Robin, *Ouidah: The Social History of a West African Slaving 'Port', 1727-1892* (Oxford, 2004).

—— and Kristin Mann, 'West Africa in the Atlantic Community: The Case of the Slave Coast', *William and Mary Quarterly*, 56/2 (1999), 307–34.

Miller, Joseph C., *Way of Death: Merchant Capitalism and the Angolan Slave Trade, 1730-1830* (Madison, WI, 1988).

Priestley, Margaret, *West African Trade and Coast Society: A Family Study* (London, 1969).

Rodney, Walter, *A History of the Upper Guinea Coast 1545-1800* (Oxford, 1970).

Thornton, John, *Warfare in Atlantic Africa 1500-1800* (London, 1999).

CHAPTER 35

··

SLAVERY AND
ANTISLAVERY, 1760–1820

··

CHRISTOPHER LESLIE BROWN

THE Age of Revolutions would seem to mark a watershed in the history of slavery in the Atlantic world. In the year 1760, the ownership of African slaves was common across the Americas, ubiquitous in Atlantic Africa, and tolerated if not always officially permitted in much of Western Europe. The trade in slaves, in the commodities produced by slaves, and in the goods produced for and sold to the American colonies drove the Atlantic economy. By 1820, though, this system had come under pointed attack in some quarters and, in others, had begun to experience severe strains from within. A new moral critique of colonial slavery and the Atlantic slave had led to the first organized efforts for their abolition. At the peripheries of the slaveholding world, in those places where the use of slaves was useful but not critical to the economy, the institution of slavery either had been banned or set on course for extinction. Four of the principal slave-trading nations, Britain, France, the Netherlands, and the United States, formally had abolished the Atlantic traffic by 1820. The former slaves of Saint-Domingue, the most valuable plantation colony in the Americas in the late eighteenth century, not only had overthrown slavery but had created as well the second independent republic in the Americas after the United States. It would seem that the revolutionary era brought with it the beginning of the end for slavery in the Atlantic world.

Yet, at the same time, there had never been more slaves in the Americas than there were in 1820. The slaving frontier expanded dramatically in these years, with hundreds of thousands of new acres brought under cultivation across the Caribbean and North America. The Atlantic slave trade approached a new peak. An estimated 488,000 captives embarked for the Americas between 1826 and 1830.[1] Only once before had more slaves been sent from African shores during a five-year period in the entire history of the Atlantic slave trade. This, then, was an era of extraordinary growth for

---

[1] All estimates on the size of the slave trade, both here and hereafter, are drawn from Voyages Database. 2010. Voyages: The Trans-Atlantic Slave Trade Database. http://www.slavevoyages.org

the institution of slavery as well as for the ethos of antislavery. Any general interpretation of the era, therefore, needs not only to acknowledge both trends but also to establish their relationship to each other.

THE EXPANSION OF SLAVERY IN THE AGE OF REVOLUTIONS

At the time of the Seven Years War, there were perhaps 1.5 million enslaved men, women, and children of African descent in the European colonies of the Atlantic world. The vast majority, no less than 80 per cent, lived, worked, and died on the plantations scattered across the American tropics, from the Bahamas in the north to Rio de Janeiro in the south. Nearly half resided in the Caribbean, where, in 1750, they outnumbered the free population by more than three to one. A second sizeable cohort, a third of all African slaves, toiled in the vast and varied territories of Brazil. Most of the remaining slaves laboured in the subtropical plantation zones of North America. By then there were perhaps 250,000 slaves in North America, with more than six of seven resident in the Chesapeake, the Carolinas, and Georgia. Perhaps another 50,000 worked alongside native, mestizo, and free coloured labourers in mainland Spanish America.[2]

Most of these captives produced staple crops for growing consumer markets in Europe. Sugar and its by-products predominated, particularly in the Caribbean. Probably three-quarters of enslaved men and women brought from Africa in 1750 went to work on sugar plantations. Some regions, though, came to specialize in other crops: tobacco in Bahia and the Chesapeake, cacao in Venezuela, rice in the Carolinas, and coffee in São Paulo. In Brazil, by 1750, gold and silver mining in Minas Gerais had surpassed sugar production as the leading employer of slaves. Most of the enslaved miners in Brazil worked for small-scale industrialists, for slaveholders who possessed fewer than ten slaves and allowed to them a much greater opportunity for manumission than was typical of other lucrative enterprises in the Americas dependent on slave labour. An important minority of the slave population in the Americas, therefore, worked at the peripheries of the plantation world in 1750. Others laboured in the growing number of cities and port towns scattered across the Americas. There the work

---

[2] Stanley L. Engerman and B. W. Higman, 'The Demographic Structure of the Caribbean Slave Societies in the Eighteenth and Nineteenth Centuries', in Franklin W. Knight (ed.), *General History of the Caribbean*, iii: *The Slave Societies of the Caribbean* (London, 1997), 48–9; Robin Blackburn, *The Making of New World Slavery: From the Baroque to the Modern, 1492–1800* (London, 1997), 486; Ira Berlin, *Many Thousands Gone: The First Two Centuries of Slavery in North America* (Cambridge, MA, 1998), 369–70. Herbert Klein and Ben Vinson report that Native American slavery in South America had come to an end by the late seventeenth century. Klein and Vinson, *African Slavery in Latin America and the Caribbean* (Oxford, 2007), 171. In North America, the enslavement of Native Americans persisted after 1760 on the North American borderlands, at the peripheries of the Atlantic world. See, most recently, Alan J. Gallay (ed.), *Indian Slavery in Colonial America* (Lincoln, NE, 2009).

included household service, manufacturing, or the provision of transportation over-land or through regional waterways. Everywhere, the work of slaves often served the local economy as well as the export sector. This was particularly the case, though, in South America where slaves grew both food and staple crops for regional consumption not international markets. If slave labour was concentrated in the plantation zones in 1750, it also had become entwined with every sector of the colonial economies across Atlantic America.[3]

The years 1750 to 1830 witnessed an extraordinary growth in the slave population of the Americas, which perhaps tripled from 1.5 million to approximately 4.5 million in an eighty-year period.[4] This rapid increase took place in the face of significant counter-vailing trends—the overthrow of slavery in Saint-Domingue, an increasing rate of manumission particularly in Brazil and mainland Spanish America, and emancipation at the peripheries of the slaveholding world, in the northern United States and in Chile, Mexico, and Uruguay. Most of this growth may be attributed to the natural increase of the slave populations of the United States and Minas Gerais in Brazil, where, unusually, in both instances, births outnumbered deaths.[5] But the number of slaves increased dramatically too in the Caribbean and in the plantation zones of Brazil where fertility rates were much lower and where the Atlantic slave trade provided the only means for increasing the number of slaves. In these regions, the slave population doubled between 1750 and 1830.[6]

An estimated 4 million slaves were carried to the Americas between 1750 and 1830. Almost half of all African captives landed in the Americas during the entire history of the Atlantic slave trade arrived in this period. In these years, the Atlantic slave trade passed through three distinctive phases.[7] From 1764 to 1790, the average number of slaves imported to the Caribbean accounted for more than three-quarters of the Atlantic slave trade and nearly all of the average increase. From 1790 to 1805, during the Haitian Revolution, the average number of slaves arriving in the Americas declined marginally. The distribution of those imports, however, shifted quite dramatically with Brazil accounting for nearly half of the market for slaves in these years. That southward shift in the Atlantic slave trade continued after Haitian independence. Thereafter, from

---

[3] Herbert S. Klein and Ben Vinson III, *African Slavery in Latin America and the Caribbean* (2nd edn. Oxford, 2007), 66–71, 77–81; Jeremy Adelman, *Sovereignty and Revolution in the Iberian Atlantic* (Princeton, NJ, 2006), 59–64; Verene Shepherd, *Slavery without Sugar: Diversity in Caribbean Economy and Society since the 17th Century* (Gainesville, FL, 2002).

[4] These estimates are based principally upon Engerman and Higman, 'The Demographic Structure of the Caribbean Slave Societies in the Eighteenth and Nineteenth Centuries', 50–2, and Laird W. Bergad, *The Comparative Histories of Slavery in Brazil, Cuba, and the United States* (Cambridge, 2007), 117–21.

[5] The recent research is summarized helpfully in Bergad, *The Comparative Histories of Slavery in Brazil, Cuba, and the United States*, 109–11.

[6] Engerman and Higman, 'The Demographic Structure of the Caribbean Slave Societies in the Eighteenth and Nineteenth Centuries', 48–52.

[7] This sequence is described in greater detail in David Eltis, *Economic Growth and the Ending of the Transatlantic Slave Trade* (Oxford, 1987), 34–43.

1806 to 1830, seven of ten slaves landing in the Americas disembarked in Brazil, with Caribbean ports taking by contrast only a quarter of the trade.

This expansion of the Atlantic slave trade and its increasing concentration on Brazil had profound consequences for the peoples and societies of West Africa. By 1750, in those places where the Atlantic slave trade had thrived (the Gold Coast, the Bight of Benin, the Bight of Biafra, and West Central Africa), there had developed an elaborate network of markets and credit networks, African intermediaries and warlords, which, together, facilitated the capture and sale of vulnerable peoples, many of whom had been seized in time of war. After 1750, formerly minor regions in the Atlantic slave trade acquired new importance. Exports from Senegambia and Sierra Leone increased dramatically. Elsewhere, where the Atlantic slave trade was well established, the slaving frontier extended inland, further north in the Niger valley, and further east and north along the Zaire. The growth of plantation production in the Americas led to an extension of the catchment area for slave taking across Africa, and, as a side-effect, further encouraged the employment of slaves within Africa.[8]

This steady demand for African captives followed from broader changes in the economy and political economy of the Atlantic world during the Age of Revolutions. In the first place, a growing demand in Europe for sugar, coffee, and cotton stimulated new efforts to increase plantation production, and not only in the established colonies.[9] Migrants in the new United States took slaves to the new territories in the south-west. A disproportionate number of African captives went to colonies where plantation economies scarcely had existed before. One-third of the increase in the slave trade to the Caribbean after the Seven Years War may be attributed to the British effort to populate the Ceded Islands of Dominica, St Vincent, Grenada, and Tobago. Fully half of the slave trade to the Caribbean during the era of the Haitian Revolution from 1794 to 1806 served the islands of Trinidad, St Lucia, and Guiana, new British colonies opened to plantation production during the course of the war with France. The Iberian states also invested more extensively in plantation production in the late eighteenth century. Spain encouraged coffee and sugar cultivation in Cuba, cacao production in Colombia and Venezuela, in part by removing all restrictions on the slave trade to the Spanish colonies in 1789. Portugal deepened its commitment to the plantation economy in Brazil by chartering new companies to promote cotton production after the Seven Years War.[10]

---

[8] Paul Lovejoy, *Transformations in Slavery: A History of Slavery in Africa* (2nd edn. Cambridge, 2000), 68–152.

[9] For recent overviews that provide a useful guide to earlier research, see Anne C. McCants, 'Exotic Goods, Popular Consumption, and the Standard of Living: Thinking about Globalization, in the Early Modern World', *Journal of World History*, 18/4 (2007), 433–62, and Jan De Vries, *The Industrious Revolution: Consumer Behavior and the Household Economy, 1650 to the Present* (Cambridge, 2008), 154–64. World cotton production increased by 75% between 1791 and 1830. Douglas A. Farnie, 'The Role of Merchants as Prime Movers in the Expansion of the Cotton Industry', in Farnie and David J. Jeremy (eds.), *The Fibre That Changed the World: The Cotton Industry in International Perspective, 1600–1900s* (Oxford, 2004), 18.

[10] Klein and Vinson, *African Slavery in Latin America and the Caribbean*, 72–3, 76.

If a growing European demand for staple crops largely accounts for the growth of the Atlantic slave trade after 1750, the Haitian Revolution from 1791 to 1804 and British slave trade abolition in 1807 help explain its southward shift. By destroying the most valuable sugar colony in the Americas, a colony that, as of 1790, produced nearly half of the world's sugar, the slave insurrection in Saint-Domingue opened new opportunities for competitors elsewhere in the Atlantic world. In the long run, Brazil perhaps benefited most. Sugar production doubled in Brazil between 1790 and 1807, by which time the colony had become again what it had been once before—the largest sugar producer in the world. By 1830, Brazilian coffee dominated European markets as well, assisted by both the growth in European demand and the rapid decline in coffee production in the French and British West Indies after the Haitian Revolution and British abolition. Only Brazil and Cuba enjoyed unfettered access to slave imports from 1815 to 1830; everywhere else in the Americas the importation of slaves was nominally illegal by 1820. Cuba, like Brazil in these years, as a consequence, quickly acquired a pre-eminent place in the production of sugar and coffee in the Atlantic world.[11]

The Age of Revolutions, then, was an era of spectacular growth in the institution of slavery in the Americas, when considered from a hemispheric perspective. It witnessed the dramatic expansion of the slave population in the colonies, the extension of the Atlantic slave trade, an increase in captive taking across Africa, and a diversification of the plantation economy in the Americas. If some regions in the Americas experienced absolute or relative decline, others grew swiftly enough not only to take their place but also to surpass the performance of earlier eras.

War and slavery in the Age of Revolutions

This brief summary should suggest that the history of warfare has particular relevance to the history of slavery, and, as will become apparent, antislavery, in the Atlantic world. In the Age of Revolutions, wars were fought not only between rival empires but also between political factions within them. Combatants divided along lines of political and economic interest, sometimes more than along national identities or dynastic allegiance. Slaveholding elites in the Americas, as a consequence, often showed more loyalty to the institution of slavery than to empire, state, or nation. On the eve of the American Revolution, for example, slaveholders in Virginia and South Carolina joined in the resistance to British rule in part to secure the plantation order. The slaveholding elite in Saint-Domingue (detailed in the chapter by Geggus) responded to the calling of the National Assembly in 1789 by demanding political representation in France, political

---

[11] Klein and Vinson, *African Slavery in Latin America and the Caribbean*, 85–107; Eltis, *Economic Growth and the Ending of the Transatlantic Slave Trade*, 40–3.

autonomy in the colonies, and guarantees for the principle of white supremacy.[12] Spanish American wars for independence first proved most 'vigorous', in Robin Blackburn's words, where slaveholding aristocracies enjoyed particular prominence, as in New Granada for example.[13] Most plantation owners in the Americas chose not to rebel, to be sure. The slaveholders of Brazil and the British Caribbean, who, together, owned at least half of the slave labour force in the Americas, remained loyal to the empires that nourished them. Yet, at the same time, the leading role of plantation owners in many of the colonial uprisings during the Age of Revolutions would mean that the suppression of rebellion required an attack on the owners of slaves, if not upon slavery itself.

Imperial authorities sometimes responded to these independence movements by inviting slaves to defend the colonial order. British officials offered liberty to slaves most consistently in these years, most notably during the American Revolution and the War of 1812. Spanish royalists followed the British example when they suppressed patriot independence movements in New Granada and Venezuela between 1812 and 1814 with substantial help from armed slaves. In the Haitian Revolution, European armies with an interest in the West Indies scrambled to win the favour of the insurgents who had liberated themselves in 1791 and after. Between 1793 and 1798 in particular, Spain, Britain, and France each sought an alliance with the former slaves in order to establish political supremacy in the Antilles. In this regard, the leaders and agents of Jacobin France succeeded spectacularly by embracing the slave insurrection in 1794 and casting it as an expression of revolutionary principles and thereby, for a time, winning the allegiance of the former slaves. For these officials, in times of crisis, enslaved men and women could serve as a useful counterweight to restive colonists. They could, at once, relieve pressures on money and manpower and reduce the number of slaves available to colonial rebels.[14]

At the same time, arming slaves often brought with it significant risks. Throughout the period, metropolitan governments lost the allegiance of colonists alienated by the decision to put slaves in arms. Arming slaves frequently undermined the plantation economies that had made these colonies worth fighting for in the first place. Colonial officials, moreover, sometimes lost control of the former slaves whom they called in to service and risked, as a consequence, destabilizing the institution of slavery as a whole. Therefore, in each of these conflicts, those who would arm slaves in the service of empire hoped to cow colonists into submission without, at the same time, wrecking the

---

[12] Sylvia Frey, *Water from the Rock: Black Resistance in A Revolutionary Age* (Princeton, NJ, 1991), 56–69; Laurent Dubois, *Avengers of the New World: The Story of the Haitian Revolution* (Cambridge, MA, 2004), 73–90.

[13] Robin Blackburn, *The Overthrow of Colonial Slavery, 1776–1848* (New York, 1988), 337.

[14] This paragraph and the next draw upon the following: Philip D. Morgan and Andrew Jackson O'Shaughnessy, 'Arming Slaves in the American Revolution', David Geggus, 'The Arming of Slaves in the Haitian Revolution', Peter Blanchard, 'The Slave Soldiers of Spanish South America: From Independence to Abolition', all in Christopher Leslie Brown and Philip D. Morgan (eds.), *Arming Slaves: From Classical Times to the Modern Age* (New Haven, CT, 2006), 187–92, 224–6, 261–3. Roger Norman Buckley, *Slaves in Red Coats: The British West India Regiments, 1795–1815* (New Haven, CT, 1979); John McNish Weiss, 'The Corps of Colonial Marines, 1814–1816', *Immigrants and Minorities*, 15/1 (1996), 80–90.

social order or plantation production. Some imperial officials proved more successful than others in this balancing act. During the American Revolution and during the French Revolution, the agents of empire in South Carolina and in Guadeloupe, for example, restored the labour regime on the plantations even as they laid enemy property to waste.[15] In the Caribbean, the British government defended British plantations and conquered neighbouring colonies with the assistance of the British West India regiments, slave men purchased from traffickers in West Africa and then enlisted for military service. France, by contrast, lost all influence in Saint-Domingue after 1802, when French officials attempted, and failed, to rescind the Jacobin emancipation decree of 1794 that had confirmed the insurgents' liberty. Then and thereafter, the Haitian Revolution provided a powerful argument for colonial elites against taking the security of the plantation regime for granted.

Plantation owners across the Americas, by contrast, opposed the arming of slaves in almost every instance from 1775 to 1826, from the American Revolution to the end of the Spanish American Wars for Independence. Outside of the plantation colonies, however, the pattern was quite different. In the temperate zones of British North America and Spanish South America, in places where the slave population was significant but not substantial, colonial leaders sometimes enlisted slaves in wars for independence. In the middle and northern states of British America, this choice reflected a response to shortages of manpower. The enlistment of slaves helped fill the ranks of colonial militias, especially in those states that struggled to recruit a sufficient number of volunteers. Some bondsmen in the new United States received their liberty as a consequence.[16] In Spanish America, too, manpower shortages often prompted creole leaders to bring slaves into the ranks. In these instances, though, the patriot leadership sometimes ennobled the offers by presenting them as the fulfilment of republican principles. That tendency became particularly apparent in Buenos Aires, where the revolution of 1810 against what remained of royal authority led to the extensive recruitment of slaves. Patriot slave-holders made a show of their commitment by donating slave labour to the war for political liberty. In 1813 the Buenos Aires government created the Regiment of Libertos, the freedmen of the state, who received liberty from slavery after five years of service. Their enlistment was cast as a 'rescue' from bondage. Some who provided distinguished service to the republic received public approbation as well as their liberty. The Argentine commander José de San Martin led an army that contained hundreds of slave soldiers to conquests of Chile in 1817 and to Peru from 1820 to 1822.[17]

---

[15] In addition to the works cited above, see Frey, *Water from the Rock*, 123–7; Laurent Dubois, '"The Price of Liberty": Victor Hugues and the Administration of Freedom in Guadeloupe, 1794–1798', *William and Mary Quarterly*, 56/2 (1999), 380–90.

[16] Benjamin Quarles, *The Negro in the American Revolution* (Chapel Hill, NC, 1961), 51–93.

[17] This paragraph and the next draw principally from what is now the best detailed account of the subject: Peter Blanchard, *Under the Flags of Freedom: Slave Soldiers and the Wars of Independence in Spanish America* (Pittsburgh, PA, 2008), 37–112. Also see Seth Meisel, '"The Fruit of Freedom": Slaves and Citizens in Early Republican Argentina', in Jane G. Landers and Barry M. Robinson (eds.), *Slaves, Subjects, and Subversives: Blacks in Colonial Latin America* (Albuquerque, NM, 2006), 273–305.

Similar trends were at work in the viceroyalty of New Granada, which presented the rare instance in which slaveholders armed slaves *en masse* to win political independence. Republican leader Simón Bolívar believed in the economic and political importance of colonial slavery and disliked, and often distrusted, enslaved men and women. At the same time, after the brutal suppression of the first attempts to establish independent republics in Venezuela in 1812 and 1814, he recognized the ways in which an alliance with free and enslaved blacks could shift the balance in time of war, especially once he understood that liberated slaves could be useful soldiers, and once he determined that it was better to exploit slave unrest then become a victim of it. Bolívar famously won arms and supplies from the Republic of Haiti in 1816 by promising to turn the creole campaign for political independence into an attack on slavery as well. His public declarations against the institution of slavery often disguised a more calculating aim to, at once, defeat Spain and preserve the social and economic order. But his offer of freedom to those who would join his army helped tilt the balance against royalist forces across the northern provinces and trouble the distinction between slave and citizen. War, more than antislavery, was the engine of change for slavery in Spanish South America.

For their own part, the enslaved looked for and seized upon opportunities for independent action. Sometimes this meant seeking the favour and patronage of one of the principal combatants in order to acquire refuge, protection, and liberty. Many sought self-advancement by declaring allegiance to whoever looked likely to prevail. The dislocations of war, however, also allowed slaves to seek not only liberty from bondage but also autonomy from colonial society or imperial authorities. The many maroon communities dispersed throughout the American tropics presented an important precedent. At the close of the Seven Years War, before any revolution was enacted in the Americas, there were independent communities of escaped slaves and their descendants occupying the hinterlands of Brazil, the Guianas, Jamaica, Saint-Domingue, and the Caribbean shore of North America. Their very existence marked out the perimeters of colonial authority, represented a standing rebuke to slave societies, and presented slaves with an alternative model to arduous plantation life.[18] During the American Revolution and also during the Spanish American Wars of Independence, enslaved men and women took flight in substantial numbers during the years of turmoil, and not always to assist one set of combatants or the other. Hundreds of runaways sought refuge in the swamplands of the Carolinas or along the East Florida border during the American Revolution. In the early nineteenth century, many more scattered to the hinterlands or marauded through the countryside in Venezuela and Peru, in regions where control of the slave population, anyway, had been tenuous at best.[19] Warfare at

---

[18] Alvin O. Thompson, *Flight to Freedom: African Runaways and Maroons in the Americas* (Mona, Jamaica, 2006).

[19] Jane Landers, *Black Society in Spanish Florida* (Urbana, IL, 1999), 77–9; Landers, *Atlantic Creoles in the Age of Revolutions* (Cambridge, MA, 2009), 95–100; Adelman, *Sovereignty and Revolution in the Iberian Atlantic*, 362–4.

once provided the opportunity to escape and undermined the capacity of colonial and imperial officials to command the borders of frontier settlements.

The breach within the ruling class across the Atlantic world led men and women not only to seek new allies or to identify new redoubts for independence but also to view themselves in new ways. Throughout the Americas, slaves and former slaves staked claims to political identities newly available to them during the wars for independence. Enslaved men and women in New England who fought for the Continental Army insisted that they be recognized as American patriots. Those who served the British side demanded recognition as loyal subjects of George III. The former French slaves who fought for Spain during the insurrection in Saint-Domingue knew themselves as the Black Auxiliaries of Charles IV. Those whose freedom was recognized by Jacobin France thought of themselves as citizens of the revolutionary Republic. Enslaved men and women declared their love of the *patria* across South America during the Wars of Independence there. For very many former slaves, liberty was not enough. They requested all the rights enjoyed by other free citizens or loyal subjects. They demanded back wages, access to land, the right to pensions, claims to kin.[20] Historians interested in the acquisition of liberty sometimes have underplayed the pursuit of full civic equality by former slaves. The transformation of slaves into citizens was less dramatic in Latin America, where mixed-race men and women long had enjoyed rights and privileges to varying degrees. However, the ideological transformations that accompanied the Age of Revolutions, the emphasis placed on equality and patriotism, meant that everywhere, although to varying degrees, the racial hierarchies that determined social place would be more fragile thereafter in many parts of the Atlantic world. Even before the comprehensive emancipations of the nineteenth century, many peoples of African descent in the Americas had come to think of themselves as possessing a relationship to the nation, state, or empire, rather than lying beyond its reach. That perspective, encouraged by the political languages of liberty and equality, led some free blacks across the Atlantic world, but particularly in the United States and Britain, to campaign for the overthrow of slavery or to settle in the new British colony in Sierra Leone established in 1787.[21]

The turmoil attending the Age of Revolutions, moreover, emboldened those who remained in slavery, transforming the politics of the enslaved even in those environments that held out few immediate opportunities for freedom. It was such evidence that enabled Eugene Genovese, in 1979, to suggest that the Haitian Revolution marked a decisive break in the character and outlook of slave revolts in the Americas. Before the

---

[20] Christopher Leslie Brown, *Moral Capital: Foundations of British Abolitionism* (Chapel Hill, NC, 2006), 294–8; Jane Landers, 'Transforming Bondsmen into Vassals: Arming Slaves in Colonial Spanish America', in Brown and Morgan (eds.), *Arming Slaves*, 129–37; Laurent Dubois, *A Colony of Citizens: Revolution and Slave Emancipation in the French Caribbean* (Chapel Hill, NC, 2004); Blanchard, 'The Languages of Liberation', 495–530; Camilla Townsend, ' "Half my body free, the other half enslaved": The Politics of the Slaves of Guayaquil at the End of the Colonial Era', *Colonial Latin American Review*, 7/1 (1998), 105–28.

[21] Brown, *Moral Capital*, 282–96; Richard S. Newman, *The Transformation of American Abolitionism: Fighting Slavery in the Early Republic* (Chapel Hill, NC, 2002), 86–106.

Saint-Domingue insurrection, he argued, slave rebellions hoped to restore the social and political order that African captives had known before becoming slaves in the Americas, but after the Haitian Revolution enslaved men and women throughout the Atlantic world began to see themselves as important players in the international politics of the era. Therefore, by resisting slavery, he contended, slaves were embracing and participating in the democratic revolutions against the colonial *ancien régime*.[22] This argument is perhaps excessively schematic in at least two respects. It oversimplifies the politics of enslaved men and women before the Saint-Domingue uprising and overlooks the continued importance of royalist politics among many slaves in the Americas after Haitian Independence.[23] The basic point should be endorsed, though. The circulation of revolutionary ideas through print and the movement of people meant that enslaved men and women contemplating violent resistance often understood their causes as one aspect of a much broader insurgency. Some drew inspiration from Haiti.[24] Others saw in the emerging antislavery movements in the United States and the British Isles the possibility of sympathy and assistance. It became possible in these years for slaves to imagine what previously had been inconceivable—that a time had arrived in which a collective pursuit of liberty might yield allies and ideological support in addition to savage repression, that the determined could overthrow slavery because the age seemed to hold out the possibility of its final destruction. By revolting against slavery from within, it might be possible to hasten its abolition from without.[25] The causes, course, and consequences of the antislavery movements of the revolutionary era can only be understood fully against this backdrop of economic growth on the one hand and warfare, both internecine and international, on the other.

ANTISLAVERY IN THE AGE OF REVOLUTIONS

The antislavery opinions that acquired political influence in the Age of Revolutions had important pre-revolutionary precedents. Across the Atlantic world, in both Europe and

---

[22] Eugene Genovese, *From Rebellion to Revolution: Afro-American Slave Revolts in the Making of the Modern World* (Baton Rouge, LA, 1979), 82–125.

[23] See, for example, Stuart Schwartz, 'Cantos and Quilombos: A Hausa Rebellion in Bahia', in Landers and Robinson (eds.), *Slaves, Subjects, and Subversives*, 247–72, and Matt D. Childs, *The 1812 Aponte Rebellion in Cuba and the Struggle against Slavery* (Chapel Hill, NC, 2006), 155–71.

[24] From a large and rapidly growing literature on the impact of the Haitian Revolution on black politics in the Atlantic world, begin with the essays in David Patrick Geggus and David Barry Gaspar (eds.), *A Turbulent Time: The French Revolution and the Greater Caribbean* (Bloomington, IN, 1997): David P. Geggus, *The Impact of the Haitian Revolution in the Atlantic World* (Columbia, SC, 2001); and David Patrick Geggus and Norman Fiering (eds.), *The World of the Haitian Revolution* (Bloomington, IN, 2009), part III.

[25] This theme has been developed at length most recently in Gelien Matthews, *Caribbean Slave Revolts and the British Abolitionist Movement* (Baton Rouge, LA, 2006), although see also Michael Craton, *Testing the Chains: Resistance to Slavery in the British West Indies* (Ithaca, NY, 1982) 241–321.

in the Americas, both in the plantation colonies and in the settlements outside the plantations, particular individuals and groups had declared their hostility to the Atlantic slave trade and colonial slavery. These expressions of discomfort with human bondage were too sporadic and too diffuse, though, to curtail the expansion of the plantation complex in its first two centuries of development in the Americas.[26] The enslavement of Africans in the Americas only became a sustained moral and political issue in the aftermath of the Seven Years War. That global conflict, which brought war to the Caribbean and the hinterlands of North America, called renewed attention to the strategic and economic importance of the American colonies and the difficulties of administering them. There developed in Britain and France in particular a small but important culture of dissent that questioned the means and ends of empire, which extended the historic concern with what colonies had done to Europe in to a broader set of questions about the consequences of allowing colonial settlements to develop without sustained oversight by metropolitan governments. With the new programmes in Britain, France, Spain, and Portugal to improve colonial administration, there emerged among a small few a hope of regulating and mitigating colonial slavery, by subjecting it to the rule of law. These years brought the first efforts to promote the amelioration of slavery, an impulse that reflected too the increasing importance that polite society assigned to sensibility and moral refinement. An exceptional few, notably Anthony Benezet, Granville Sharp, or the Abbé Raynal, imagined a radical overthrow of the entire system. Most reformers were hoping rather to find ways to make slavery more humane, more Christian, and less arbitrary.[27]

These impulses, most broadly felt in France, Britain, and British North America, coursed throughout the Atlantic in the 1760s and 1770s. But only in the Anglo-American world did organized antislavery movements crystallize before the onset of the French Revolution. The particular course of British and British American antislavery owes something to the distinctive social and cultural world of the late eighteenth-century British empire—the comparatively wide space for political participation, the large number of British settlers in the Americas, the open flow of published information about the character of colonial society, and the religious diversity within the empire which allowed for a diversity of views on slavery and abolition. But the crucial fact that explains British divergence from its rivals was the peculiar character of the American Revolution. The political crises that caused the war, and that followed from it, produced an extraordinary outpouring of commentary from both sides of the Atlantic on the proper meaning of liberty and the precise definition of slavery. In both Britain and the

---

[26] David Brion Davis, *The Problem of Slavery in Western Culture* (Oxford, 1988; 2nd edn); Brown, *Moral Capital*, 33–103.

[27] Christopher L. Brown, 'Empire without Slaves: British Concepts of Emancipation in the Age of Revolutions', *William and Mary Quarterly*, 56/2 (1999), 273–306; Celia Azevedo, 'Rocha's *The Ethiopian Redeemed* and the Circulation of Anti-Slavery Ideas', *Slavery and Abolition*, 24/1 (2003), 101–26; Jean Tarrade, 'Is Slavery Reformable? Proposals of Colonial Administrators at the End of the Ancien Regime', in Marcel Dorigny (ed.), *The Abolition of Slavery from L. F. Sonothonax to Victor Schoelcher, 1793, 1794, 1848* (Paris, 1993).

Thirteen Colonies, propagandists confronted the dissonance between professions of commitment to liberty and the institutional reality of human bondage.[28]

As a consequence, a demonstrated commitment to addressing the wrongs of slavery emerged from the American War as a moral imperative, particularly for those whose economies did not rely directly on human bondage. In New England and in the Hudson and Delaware river valleys, there arose collective efforts to abolish slavery gradually, a commitment that set slavery on a course for extinction in the middle and northern states during the half-century after American independence.[29] In Britain, a national antislavery campaign came to fruition in 1787 that transformed this new moral imperative into an active political programme. The British abolitionists proved spectacularly successful in winning public support. They framed the issue as, at once, a question of national pride and elementary moral judgement. They benefited from the enthusiasm of a nation that wished to know itself as a defender and proponent of liberty. It helped, also, that the targets of reform lay outside the British Isles, on the West African coast or in the Caribbean colonies. The House of Commons provided a useful venue for the airing of grievances, for declarations of justice to injured humanity, and for the assessment of evidence.[30] Nowhere else in the Atlantic world, including in the United States of America, was there an institution such as the House of Commons that could enable the abolitionists to make their case on a national scale. Since, in almost every instance, the energy for antislavery reforms came from outside government rather than from within, abolitionists would make progress in the years that followed only in those polities unusually responsive to public opinion.

The French Revolution transformed the direction and character of antislavery organizing, first in France and the French Caribbean colonies and then throughout the Atlantic world. The calling of the Estates General and the subsequent Jacobin ascension to power allowed position and influence to the intellectual coterie most committed to abolitionist principles, a coterie that drew its inspiration from antislavery activists in Britain. In 1789, they granted official recognition and equal civil rights to a delegation of free black men from Saint-Domingue. In 1794, three years after the colonial uprisings began, they authorized the abolition of slavery throughout French dominions. That declaration, the first of its kind in human history, followed at once from both Jacobin political ideology and the hope of restoring French control over the insurrections in the French West Indies.[31] Insurrection and emancipation in the French Caribbean would inspire, in turn, a counter-revolutionary reaction that would retard the progress of antislavery movements across the Atlantic world.

The fear of black Jacobins stretched across the Americas from Philadelphia to Buenos Aires, or in the Caribbean basin, from New Orleans to Cartagena. Imperial

---

[28] Brown, *Moral Capital*, 105–53.

[29] For a helpful overview, see Berlin, *Many Thousands Gone*, 228–55.

[30] Brown, *Moral Capital*, 333–450; Seymour Drescher, *Capitalism and Antislavery: British Mobilization in Comparative Perspective* (New York, 1987), 67–88.

[31] Dubois, *Avengers of the New World*, 60–193.

governments and colonial elites of every stripe scrambled to sustain the plantation order. The British government that had actively considered the abolition of the slave trade in 1792 turned during the next ten years to the project of defending or extending the plantation regime, while public antislavery campaigning quickly became first tentative and then silent. The fear of the next Saint-Domingue inhibited the development of a national campaign to abolish slavery in the new United States from 1790 to 1820. In those years, only the colonization of liberated slaves to the distant shores of West Africa seemed to offer a viable solution. It now seemed as if large-scale emancipation, unless managed carefully, was most likely to end in revolutionary violence. This was the era in which proslavery argument first achieved intellectual maturity. During the initial debates in Britain, spokesmen for the slaveholders and slave traders had been on the defensive. They took the position that abolition and emancipation were desirable in the abstract but impossible in practice. The example of the Haitian Revolution allowed the slave interest to take the argument one step further. There emerged from these years the view that slavery was not only beneficial economically, but that it was a positive good for society and the moral order. For without slavery, the forces of chaos would run amok throughout plantation societies across the Americas. The programme of the abolitionists, it was contended, seemed to point not only to an end of the slave trade and slavery but also to an end to settler societies in the Americas.[32]

It would seem an extraordinary irony, then, that the first significant bans on the Atlantic slave trade should emerge from the United States and Great Britain in precisely these years of counter-revolution, fear, and racial anxiety. But to view the landmark bills that abolished first the British slave trade in 1807 and then the United States slave trade in 1808 as at odds with this reaction against Saint-Domingue is to misunderstand the sources of slave trade abolition or its purposes. From the very beginning, the desire to abolish the slave trade drew upon imperatives only loosely related to humanitarian concern. The first efforts to stop the slave trade developed in the North American colonies in the 1760s and 1770s where concerns about the dangers of slave imports combined with a declining need for new captives from Africa and an emerging interest in demonstrating the sincerity of revolution principles. Only Georgia and South Carolina merchants imported significant numbers of African slaves to North America after 1776. Their recalcitrance prevented a ban on the slave trade to the new United States for two decades after the ratification of the constitution in 1788. But, not long after, the example of Haiti, the rapid growth of the native-born slave population, and a lingering commitment to abolitionist ideology enabled the abolition of the US slave trade in 1808, though an illegal trade would continue for many years after. A similar dynamic was at work in much of mainland Spanish America where economic

---

[32] Gordon K. Lewis, *Main Currents in Caribbean Thought: The Historical Evolution of Caribbean Society in its Ideological Aspects, 1492–1900* (Baltimore, MD, 1983), 94–170; Lacy K. Ford, *Deliver Us from Evil: The Slavery Question in the Old South* (Oxford, 2009). For anxieties about the example of Haiti outside the Anglo-American world, begin with the essay collections on the Haitian Revolution as cited above.

interest, republican ideology, and concerns for social stability contributed to bans on slave imports during the Wars of Independence in the second and third decades of the nineteenth century.[33]

In Britain too, interest and idealism converged to make slave trade abolition possible in the aftermath of the Haitian Revolution. In Britain, however, the attack on the slave trade would also became closely associated with evolving definitions of national identity and imperial purpose. The political meaning of the antislavery ethos changed dramatically with Napoleon's decision to restore French authority in the sugar colonies in 1802. That reversal helped associate the antislavery cause with liberty and justice, and with the war on despotism, rather than with Jacobin radicalism and revolution. By the time of French defeat in Saint-Domingue, the British controlled the Atlantic shipping lanes in and out of the Caribbean. For that reason abolition of the slave trade did not seem to create the same strategic disadvantages that had been expected when abolition had been discussed more than a decade before. Even more, though, the danger that might follow from flooding new settlements with tens of thousands of slaves each year had now become clear in the British Isles, as it had in the United States. The abolition bill of 1807, which eliminated the slave trade of the principal supplier of captives in the Americas, was at once an effort to reclaim the mantle of moral supremacy and part of a strategic effort to undermine the position of European rivals. That element of statecraft apparent in the abolition of 1807 would complicate British efforts to secure international cooperation on slave trade abolition at the Congress of Vienna in 1814 and thereafter, although British diplomats would secure there an agreement that the slave trade was 'an odious commerce' that ought to be suppressed. Still, to outside observers, it often seemed that Britain hoped to secure commercial hegemony through an ostensibly humanitarian campaign to abolish the slave trades of its allies and rivals.[34]

By 1820, then, the Atlantic slave system stood at a pivot. On one side lay the growing influence of antislavery sentiments, particularly in the British Isles but elsewhere in the Atlantic world too, which had curtailed important branches of the Atlantic slave trade, and placed the slaveholding class throughout the Americas on the defensive. First through the American Revolution and its aftermath, and then much more consequentially through the Haitian Revolution, enslaved men and women had begun to insert themselves into the wider political arena, by seeking allies when opportunity presented and seeking autonomy and independence when it did not. Territories rich in potential for staple crop production by enslaved men and women went under-utilized as a result. In the newly independent Haiti, in the British West Indies, on the Caribbean coast of

---

[33] Don E. Fehrenbacher, *The Slaveholding Republic: An Account of the United States Government's Relations to Slavery*, completed and edited by Ward M. McAfee (Oxford, 2001), 135–72; James F. King, 'The Latin-American Republics and the Suppression of the Slave Trade', *Hispanic American Historical Review*, 24/3 (1944), 387–9.

[34] Roger A. Anstey, *The Atlantic Slave Trade and British Abolition, 1760–1810* (London, 1975), part IV. On tensions between hostility to British high-handedness and respect for the British example, see Matthew E. Mason, 'Keeping up Appearances: The International Politics of Slave Trade Abolition in the Nineteenth-Century World', *William and Mary Quarterly*, 66 (2009), 809–32.

South America, plantation production declined because of the combined impacts of war, revolution, and antislavery. Outside the plantation zones, slavery had been set on a course for extinction. Each of the northern and middle Atlantic states had instituted schemes that provided for a gradual emancipation. Similar measures had begun to take shape too in Spanish South America, in the aftermath of the Wars for Independence. Emancipation by degrees, however, paled before emancipation by decree, if one is to measure influence in terms of the number of slaves who achieved their freedom. The spectacular growth in the number of freedmen and freedwomen in the Americas during the Age of Revolution owed most to the offers of liberty extended to slaves in time of war and to the other opportunities for escape that the destabilization of colonial society presented. The tendency to lionize peaceful acts of abolition and emancipation as the engine of change in the revolutionary era obscures the profound importance of violence in the liberation of enslaved men and women from human bondage.

Yet, on the other side of this divide lay a rapidly growing slave economy throughout the Americas, a still powerful slaveholding interest capable of influencing politics both at the colonial and imperial level, and a still flourishing, though now reshaped, transatlantic as well as internal market in African slaves. It was far from apparent in 1820 that the institution of slavery would be extinguished everywhere in the Americas in little more than four generations. This points out, perhaps, a need to keep the sum impact of the age of revolutions in proper perspective. Its legacies for abolitionist and emancipationist politics were profound. But the era marked not the end of the Atlantic slave system but rather its dramatic repositioning. Nonetheless, the Age of Revolutions yielded a new sense of the possible that then, and thenceforth, would influence the aspirations of both enslaved peoples and abolitionists. This expectation of imminent transformation, however unlikely when seen through the prism of the economic facts of the time, would figure importantly in the political struggles that would conclude with the age of emancipation that followed.

BIBLIOGRAPHY

Bergad, Laird W., *The Comparative Histories of Slavery in Brazil, Cuba, and the United States* (Cambridge, 2007).

Blackburn, Robin, *The Overthrow of Colonial Slavery, 1776–1848* (London, 1988).

Blanchard, Peter, *Under the Flags of Freedom: Slave Soldiers and the Wars of Independence in Spanish South America* (Pittsburgh, PA, 2008).

Brown, Christopher Leslie, *Moral Capital: Foundations of British Abolitionism* (Chapel Hill, NC, 2006).

Childs, Matt D., *The 1812 Aponte Rebellion in Cuba and the Struggle against Atlantic Slavery* (Chapel Hill, NC, 2006).

Davis, David Brion, *The Problem of Slavery in the Age of Revolutions, 1770–1823* (Ithaca, NY, 1975).

Dubois, Laurent, *Avengers of the New World: The Story of the Haitian Revolution* (Cambridge, MA, 2004).

Frey, Sylvia, *Water from the Rock: Black Resistance in a Revolutionary Age* (Princeton, NJ, 1991).

Gaspar, David Barry, and David Patrick Geggus, *A Turbulent Time: The French Revolution and the Greater Caribbean* (Bloomington, IN, 1997).

Klein, Herbert S., and Ben Vinson III, *African Slavery in Latin America and the Caribbean* (2nd edn. Oxford, 2007).

CHAPTER 36

....

ATLANTIC WORLD
1760–1820

Economic Impact

....

CRAIG MULDREW

THERE would have been no Atlantic world without trade. The nature of goods produced and manufactured was important, as was the organization of labour and movement of people—treated in other chapters—but this chapter will focus on the circulation of goods and changes in trading patterns. Most discussions of trade have been written from the point of view of single European nations, or their former colonies, rather than from an 'Atlantic' perspective. In part this is because European countries were in competition for wealth in this period, and archives have been organized by states, but there were many similarities between the trading patterns of the various states and the wealth their merchants were able to gain from trade. Throughout this period the consumption of American-produced sugar, tobacco, and coffee, as well as the use of American gold and silver for money, was common throughout Europe. At the same time, the settlement of colonial emigrants and transported slave populations continued to grow and to transform the agriculture and environment of the Americas and western Africa.

By the mid-eighteenth century the characteristic trading patterns of the Atlantic world were well established. The main exports at the beginning of the period from the New World were gold and silver from the mines of Mexico and Peru, as well as sugar and tobacco grown in Brazil, the Caribbean, and the Chesapeake, together with furs and cod from Canada and forest products from New England. Increasingly, cacao, coffee, and cotton also became important, and other natural products such as tropical hardwoods, dyestuffs, rum, and hides were also exported in varying degrees. We should not forget that people were also traded, and David Eltis has described in his chapter how European traders purchased an ever-increasing number of slaves in Africa for export to the Americas. European manufactured goods, notably cloth, iron, copperware, and guns, were traded for slaves in Africa, and were also increasingly exported to the Americas as settler populations grew. Overwhelmingly this trade was organized along mercantilist principles, with most trade taking place between European mother countries and the colonies under their control. There was however considerable inter-regional trade between British American colonies (and later between them and the United States) and also between colonies within the Spanish empire, and there was at all times an active inter-colonial and inter-imperial smuggling trade.

Also, although gold and silver were mined in the New World and minted into the famous Spanish dollar or pieces or eight (reales), most was shipped to Europe with some going also to the Philippines, with the result that most American colonies experienced a shortage of specie throughout the period.[1] There are few estimates of the money supply in Brazil and the Spanish colonies for this time, but, on the eve of the American Revolution, Alexander Hamilton estimated that there were 7,500,000 Spanish dollars circulating in the Thirteen Colonies. However, small change was especially scarce. To make up for this lack, many commodities such as tobacco, sugar, furs, cacao beans were used as currency, and all the Thirteen Colonies issued their own paper currencies.[2] An important result of this situation was that the Atlantic world was held together through ties of interpersonal credit between merchants trading over long distances. In contrast to the great monopoly companies trading to the East, most Atlantic trade was carried out by private merchants who could not rely on the infrastructure of company agents and political alliances. Wherever possible, kinship ties were used to secure credit, but merchants anxious to do business had frequently to trust strangers. In such cases knowledge about trading conditions and society in destination colonies was valuable. Therefore knowledge of the Atlantic was also a vital commodity.[3]

Britain emerged as the dominant trading, military, and investment force by the nineteenth century. In part its rise can be read as a result of the success of the British fiscal-military state in the Seven Years War, and subsequently in the wars of the French Revolution. However, by the third quarter of the eighteenth century the Spanish navy was still strong, and, until their trading networks were all but destroyed by the revolution in Saint-Domingue, the French were importing more sugar and coffee, and at cheaper prices, than the British. Therefore one theme that will be emphasized here is that eighteenth-century Britain enjoyed an advantage over European competitors for Atlantic trade because it had developed a much larger and more successful manufacturing industry. This achievement rested largely on the growth in demand from Atlantic colonial populations. More manufacturing led to higher wages in

---

[1] Andre Gunder Frank, *REORIENT: Global Economy in the Asian Age* (Berkeley, CA, 1998), 142–51.

[2] John J. McCusker and Russell R. Menard, *The Economy of British America, 1607–1789* (Chapel Hill, NC, 1985), 337–41.

[3] Craig Muldrew, *The Economy of Obligation: The Culture of Credit and Social Relations in Early Modern England* (London, 1998), 192–4; Marta C. Vincente, *Clothing the Spanish Empire: Families and the Calico Trade in the Early Modern Atlantic World* (London, 2006), 32–41.

England, which in turn led to a continual and buoyant popular demand for colonial goods.[4] High wages did not, however, make British manufactured goods more expensive, as increasing division of labour continued to reduce costs. Consequently, British manufactures were eventually able to undercut and supplant the production of locally made goods throughout the Atlantic. This argument is not to stress British economic nationalism in any way, but rather to explain how the conceptualization of Atlantic trade can be integrated into a general understanding of the changing world economy.

The first twenty-five years of this period witnessed a general increase in trade across the Atlantic to all parts of the Americas. France was especially successful in establishing sugar production in the Caribbean, and in re-exporting sugar products to other continental European countries. Also, both Spain and Portugal instituted reforms which freed trade within their empires, and as a result commercial volume increased. However, this overall rise in trade was significantly disrupted and altered by global and European warfare, as well as the great political upheavals of the American War of Independence, the revolt in Saint-Domingue in 1791, and the various national uprisings in the colonies of Spain. Although warfare had affected Atlantic trade since the earliest days of privateering, the political and economic consequences of war in the period under consideration here fundamentally changed the Atlantic world.

The period began with the Seven Years War, which saw the French navy crippled, and the loss of the French North American colonies. The British Royal Navy also captured the French sugar colonies of Guadeloupe in 1759 and Martinique in 1762, as well as Havana, before returning them by treaty. This success of the navy in warfare both protected British trading interests and opened up new opportunities which British merchants were eager to capitalize on. The major disruption in the period between the end of the Seven Years War and the beginning of the Napoleonic Wars was Britain's loss of the Thirteen Colonies. Yet the ability of its merchants to repair relations with their counterparts in the new United States after the disruption of the War of Independence, and to continue their important trading links to the Caribbean, meant that, by the late 1780s, both British imports to the United States and American exports to the Caribbean had once again begun to exceed their pre-revolutionary level. But it was British naval success in the long period 1792–1815 of European warfare which had the greatest effect on trade by cutting off the French and Spanish from their American colonies, leading to the decline of France as a participant in the Atlantic world and the eventual break-up of the Spanish empire.

Spain was the oldest of the European powers with established trade to the Americas, so it will be considered first. Before the Seven Years War, Spain had attempted to enforce the most restrictive trade on the Atlantic through a fleet (*flota*) system controlling sailings from Seville (and later Cádiz) to Vera Cruz, Cartagena, and Portobelo, where goods were trans-shipped across the Isthmus of Panama for trade with Lima. The

---

[4] Robert C. Allen, *The British Industrial Revolution in Global Perspective* (Cambridge, 2009), chapter 2.

primary purpose of such fleets was to enforce mercantilist restriction over trade, and to protect the precious metal they carried home to Spain. However, the monopoly nature of the fleet system meant that the Spanish trading system could not operate as a free market. Thus, prior to 1760, trade did little to boost either the Spanish mainland economy or that of its colonies. The limited numbers of sailings, and the easy profits made by Seville (and later Cádiz) merchants from the shipment of gold and silver, meant that the New World market was not one which Spanish manufacturers were ever able to exploit.[5]

In the first half of the eighteenth century Spanish weakness after the War of the Spanish Succession (1701–14), and later losses in the War of Jenkins's Ear (1739–42), meant that French, British, and Dutch traders were able to make inroads into the Spanish trading system, through both legal trade and contraband. In an attempt to reverse this decline Spain, under Charles III, who acceded to the throne in 1759, instituted what has come to be called 'free trade'. Charles and his ministers realized that Spain had suffered a decline in its home production of manufactured goods in comparison to France and Britain, whose output of goods such as silks and woollen cloth had been steadily increasing in the first half of the eighteenth century. As a result, in 1778, Spain abandoned the fleet system and opened up participation in the Atlantic trade to thirteen other Spanish ports besides Seville and Cádiz, and allowed Spanish producers of goods to participate in trade for the first time.[6] This was, however, still 'free trade' within the commercial codes of mercantilist practice, also adhered to by Great Britain and France. Such conventions identified both colonial production and markets as beneficial to the home country only if such trade contributed to that country's balance of payments. In Spain's case, the importation of precious metals met that goal and could be converted into military power. However, other countries' colonies were also seen as producers of goods which could be re-exported to earn foreign profits, creating a favourable balance of trade. This outcome, it was argued, would, in turn, bring valuable gold and silver into the country, creating a situation whereby the state could tax it and pay for its armies and navy.[7]

After 1778, Spanish trade expanded rapidly. Between 1778 and 1796 exports from Spain to America rose about four times what they had been previously. In 1784, for instance, exports were worth 457,700,000 *reales de vellón* or about £3,575,781.[8]

---

[5] John R. Fisher, *The Economic Aspects of Spanish Imperialism in America, 1492–1810* (Liverpool, 1997), 57–9; Mark A. Burkholder and Lyman l. Johnson, *Colonial Latin America* (Oxford, 1998), 148.

[6] Burkholder and Johnson, *Colonial Latin America*, 144–50; Fisher, *Economic Aspects*, 134–40, chapter 8.

[7] David Ormrod, *The Rise of Commercial Empires: England and the Netherlands in the Age of Mercantilism, 1660–1770* (Cambridge, 2003), 15–27.

[8] Wherever possible, weight or volume have been used to measure trade, and to make comparisons between countries, to avoid any distortions arising from the rapid monetary inflation of the years after 1780. The difficulties of devising price series to account for inflation has been rehearsed in detail by Ralph Davis, and his figures of value have been used where possible. Ralph Davis, *The Industrial Revolution: British Overseas Trade* (Leicester, 1979), 77–86. But where only monetary values are available, it has been decided to use the British pound as a standard unit for comparison simply for the reason that this is the

This increase also had the effect of stimulating the production of Spanish products. The most significant of these were Catalonian printed cottons, linens, and silks, especially calicos, which found an important market in the Spanish American colonies.[9] However, the great majority of the exported goods (probably over 80 per cent) produced in Spain remained agricultural, such as oil, nuts, dried fruits, wines, and *aguardiente* (spirits). Most of the manufactured goods shipped through Spain to America originated in other European countries, especially Britain, where cloth was made much more cheaply than in Catalonia. The percentage of such foreign products averaged between 40 and 55 per cent of all goods shipped between 1782 and 1796.[10]

However, imports into Spain from America rose tenfold between 1782 and 1796 and continued at this level afterwards. The vast majority of these imports continued to be composed of gold from Cartagena (14 per cent) and silver from New Spain (42.5 per cent). In total, 293,000,000 pesos (worth £45,781,250) were exported in these years. Through new techniques involving the application of mercury to the smelting of silver, Spain was able greatly to increase its production throughout the eighteenth century.[11] The next most important import was tobacco, which accounted for 13.6 per cent of imports and was worth 74,500,000 pesos (£11,640,625). It was followed by cacao (7.8 per cent), sugar (5.5 per cent), indigo (4.2 per cent), and cochineal (4.2 per cent). The bulk of the tobacco was grown in Cuba, which underwent a spectacular economic expansion after 1760. There, sugar production also expanded eightfold by 1789, and increased further after the slave revolt in Saint-Domingue. The success of this trade led to the creation of the first creole elite of plantation owners. After 1800, production of sugar, coffee, and tobacco also increased in Puerto Rico.[12] Cacao production increased in Venezuela and the area of New Granada, as did the production of livestock to supply the sugar islands in the Caribbean where manure was needed to make intensive cultivation possible. Grazing also expanded in the Río de la Plata supplying an average of 1 million hides to Spain, and salt beef for the sugar islands and the mines in Potosí. This activity enabled Buenos Aries to develop into the major commercial entrepôt of the South Atlantic. However, only Spain's continuing ability to mine precious metals allowed it to pay for manufactured goods from other European countries both for use at home and in America.[13]

---

currency most familiar to the author. To give an idea of what value this might have represented, an English agricultural labourer might have earned £15–25 a year around 1760. An exchange rate of 20 *reales* to one *peso de plata* and 6.4 pesos to the pound has been used here. Fisher, *Economic Aspects*, 154; John J. McCusker, *Money and Exchange in Europe and America, 1600–1775: A Handbook* (London, 1978), 310–12.

   9 Vincente, *Clothing the Spanish Empire*, chapters 4–5.

   10 Fisher, *Economic Aspects*, 143–52.

   11 Ibid. 186–95; John H. Coatsworth, 'The Mexican Mining Industry in the Eighteenth Century', in Nils Jacobson and Hans-Jürgen Puhle (eds.), *The Economies of Mexico and Peru during the Colonial Period, 1760–1810* (Berlin, 1986), 26–45.

   12 Francisco A. Scarano, *Sugar and Slavery in Puerto Rico; The Plantation Economy of Ponce, 1800–1850* (Madison, WI, 1984), 7.

   13 Fisher, *Economic Aspects*, 167–70; Burkholder and Johnson, *Colonial Latin America*, 294–7.

This great increase in production and trade led to a growth in the population of New Spain from 3.3 million to 5.8 million people by the 1790s and also led to increased immigration from Spain.[14] After the ending of the British slave trade in 1807, Spanish colonies began to import slaves from Africa in large numbers for the first time since the seventeenth century. The great increase in foreign manufactured goods allowed people's standards of living to rise, but also led to the decline of local wool production in Peru and New Spain. Unlike the North American colonies, which relied almost exclusively on British imports, Spanish America, because of the irregularity of imports during the fleet system, had developed an indigenous woollen cloth industry especially in New Spain and Peru, to provide clothing for the populations there.[15] But this form of production was unable to compete in price and quality with the cheaper British cloth, which used less expensive wool and was produced more efficiently through the division of labour in the different stages of cloth working.[16] Also, from the 1780s, cotton cloth became much more popular and could be produced more cheaply in Catalonia and England than in America.

This expansion of Spanish Atlantic trade, however, did not survive the seismic disruption of the French Revolutionary and Napoleonic wars. Military weakness in Europe led to the defeat of the Spanish navy, which previously had been able to defend Spanish trade. Spain initially participated in the coalition of countries fighting against the French Revolution, but, after a number of military defeats, signed a treaty with France in 1795. This led to war with Britain and the decisive naval defeats of Cape St Vincent and Trafalgar. Britain successfully blockaded Cádiz from 1796, cutting off Spain from its colonies. From this point on political isolation and high fiscal demands on the part of Spanish colonial administrations led to a series of political challenges to Spanish rule and eventually the dismemberment of the Spanish empire into the countries of Latin America. By the mid-1820s Spain controlled only Cuba and Puerto Rico.

Living standards in many of the Spanish colonies fell as, first the British blockade of Cádiz, and then later the continental blockade, cut off the markets for American exports to Spain, notably silver and tobacco. The shipment of goods from Spain was also halted with the result that aggressive British merchants sought new markets in Spanish America to replace lost continental outlets. British merchants settled in significant numbers in Rio de Janeiro, Buenos Aires, Valparaiso, and Lima, and British exports sent directly to Latin America rose from £79,000 between 1794 and 1796 to £5,000,000 by 1824-6.[17] The United States also increased trade with Latin America.

In 1800 the income per capita in many Latin American colonies was about half that of the United States, but by the 1820s, it had fallen considerably. During the blockade

---

[14] Burkholder and Johnson, *Colonial Latin America*, 288-90; Fisher, *Economic Aspects*, 171-2.

[15] Aurora Gómez-Galvarriato, 'Premodern Manufacturing', in Victor Bulmer-Thomas, John H. Coatsworth, and Roberto Cortés Conde (eds.), *The Cambridge Economic History of Latin America* (Cambridge, 2006), ii. 375-94; Richard J. Salvucci, *Textiles and Capitalism in Mexico: An Economic History of the Obrajes 1539-1840* (Princeton, NJ, 1987).

[16] Salvucci, *Textiles and Capitalism in Mexico*, 151.

[17] Davis, *Industrial Revolution*, 89.

years silver mines in Peru and New Spain were not maintained, making capital accumulation difficult as most money went to pay for imports and the Wars of Independence.[18] Consequently, many of the new countries had to enter into trade treaties with Britain, which further secured markets for its goods.[19] However, after the end of the Napoleonic Wars, sugar production boomed in Cuba and Puerto Rico, where slavery remained legal until the 1850s, reaching almost 150 million pounds by 1820. In 1770 the Spanish produced less than 5 per cent of the total production of the Caribbean. But by 1821 these two Spanish colonies were producing large quantities of sugar, coffee, and tobacco, which by 1850 amounted to 60 per cent of the Caribbean's sugar and 82 per cent of its molasses.[20]

In contrast to Spain, the Portuguese had for a long time been developing the production of sugar—in this case, in Brazil—to supplement output initially begun on their Atlantic islands such as Madeira, even as gold and diamond mines were discovered in the Brazilian interior. Unusually, the Portuguese were also initially little concerned with the enforcement of national trading preferences, but war with the Dutch had led Portugal to institute a protective fleet system akin to that of Spain. In the 1760s and 1770s Portuguese–Brazilian trade was in crisis owing to a number of factors, including the decline of mining output, the Lisbon earthquake, and an expensive war with Spain over the borderland with the Río de la Plata.[21] The Methuen Treaty of 1703 arising from the War of Spanish Succession gave the British the right to supply Portugal and Brazil with British manufactured goods in return for protection of its territorial integrity. By 1750, British manufactured goods, consisting of cloth, ready-made garments, tools, hardware, and metals, shipped to Portugal and Brazil were worth £1,100,000. But, because of the value of gold and sugar exports, Portugal still had a favourable balance of trade in Europe at this time. After 1750, gold and sugar production declined, leaving Portugal with a growing trade deficit.

As a result, the marquis of Pombal, Portugal's prime minister, became convinced of the need for reform. To this end, he established trading companies to attract investment and promote home industry to produce goods for the Brazilian market. Although these companies were short-lived, trade was revived and Brazil underwent what one

[18] Victor Bulmer-Thomas, *The Economic History of Latin America since Independence* (Cambridge, 1994), 19, 28–9; John H. Coatsworth, 'Notes on the Comparative Economic History of Latin America and the United States', in Walter Bernecker and Hans Tobler (eds.), *Development and Underdevelopment in America* (Berlin, 1993), 10–30.

[19] Bulmer-Thomas, *Latin America since Independence*, 33–5.

[20] David Eltis, 'The Slave Economies in the Caribbean: Structure, Performance, Evolution and Significance', in Franklin Knight (ed.), *UNESCO History of the Caribbean* (New York, 1997), iii. 113–19; id., *Economic Growth and the Ending of the Transatlantic Slave Trade* (Oxford, 1987), 283–9; Francisco A. Scarano, *Sugar and Slavery in Puerto Rico; The Plantation Economy of Ponce, 1800–1850* (Madison, WI, 1984), 7, 31.

[21] Stuart B. Schwartz, *Sugar Plantations in the Formation of Brazilian Society: Bahia, 1550–1835* (Cambridge, 1986), 186, 426–7; Dauril Alden, 'Late Colonial Brazil, 1750–1808', in Leslie Bethell (ed.), *The Cambridge History of Latin America*, vol. ii (Cambridge, 1984), 620–5.

historian has termed an 'agricultural renaissance'. Sugar production rose 69 per cent from 1759 to 1807, and stood at 90,000,000 pounds by 1821. Tobacco production also increased to 21,000,000 pounds by 1790, allowing Portuguese merchants to earn money from re-exports in Europe. Brazil also became the second-ranked producer of cacao and a major exporter of coffee, producing 27,500,000 pounds by 1821. It also exported rice and wheat. In addition, Brazil became a key supplier of high-quality raw cotton to the rapidly growing European cotton textile industry. In 1782, England imported about 9,000 pounds of cotton from Brazil, rising to 150,000 pounds per annum soon thereafter. By 1807, Brazil exported over 17 million pounds a year, and 28 million pounds by 1820.[22] In 1800 the Brazilian population exceeded 2 million people, two-thirds of whom were African or of African descent. Within this group, free blacks and mulattos formed 23 per cent, and slaves 38 per cent.[23] Brazil received far more African slaves than any other American colony, principally to work on sugar plantations.[24]

Another reform initiated from the 1760s was the founding of factories within Portugal to produce cotton goods, hats, woollen cloth, china, and hardware. These factories shipped 40 per cent of their produce to the growing Brazilian population, while Brazilian weavers were shut down. The course of Brazilian trade was also changed by the Revolutionary and Napoleonic Wars, after Spain invaded Portugal and Britain sent troops to its ally's defence. The years 1800–7 witnessed a 69 per cent decline in the exports of Portuguese manufactures to Brazil as British ships increasingly defied Portuguese law and shipped British-made goods to Brazilian ports, where they undersold the Portuguese manufactures. After the war, however, agricultural production and exports recovered, especially after the removal of the Portuguese court to Rio de Janeiro in 1808.[25]

The Dutch, after the loss of their territory in Brazil, gained the Caribbean colonial possessions of Suriname, and the islands of Essequibo, Demerara, and Berbice. But, after initial success in the late seventeenth century in the slave trade, the Dutch West India Company was unsuccessful and went bankrupt in 1738. However, private investment in colonial sugar plantations meant that by 1750 they were sending some 18–20 million pounds of sugar and 6 million pounds of coffee to the Dutch Republic annually. The sugar was refined in the Republic for re-export; however, for every pound of colonial sugar imported another two pounds were imported from France. Sugar production never expanded beyond this level, although there was a great investment of some 80 million guilders in coffee production, which expanded six times to 36 million pounds. Yet since Dutch presence in the Caribbean was small in comparison to

[22] Luis Amaral, *Historia geral do agricultura brasileira* (São Paulo, 1959), ii. 302, 636–7; Alden, 'Late Colonial Brazil', 630–9, 643–6.

[23] Burkholder and Johnson, *Colonial Latin America*, 149–50, 261–2, 267–8.

[24] The Trans-Atlantic Slave Trade Database. http://www.slavevoyages.org/tast/assessment/estimates. faces.

[25] Alden, 'Late Colonial Brazil', 627–53; Schwartz, *Sugar Plantations*, 426–7; Bulmer-Thomas, *Economic History of Latin America since Independence*, 36.

other colonial powers, the great investment required in production meant that profit margins were very slim, and this resulted in a great wave of plantation bankruptcies in the 1770s when long-term bonds could not be paid back. Production continued after this, but with the Dutch state subordinated to France after 1795, the British captured Essequibo and Demerara leading to much coffee being re-exported through London. Sugar production persisted in Suriname, but on a reduced scale, throughout the nineteenth century. Dutch sugar production never amounted to more than about 5 per cent of total Caribbean production, and in contrast to other countries, profits were never enough to recoup the large investment needed for it.[26]

By the 1760s France was also a major producer of sugar, coffee, indigo, and cotton grown in the Antilles, particularly Saint-Domingue. Although New France was a much older colony, and had developed a profitable fur trade in the seventeenth century, the supply of new sources of fur had dried up by the mid-eighteenth century due to ecological exploitation. By then, French trade with the West Indies was twenty-five times higher than trade with New France, and Canada also attracted few immigrants. The loss of New France in the Seven Years War therefore appeared more strategic than economic. By the 1720s, sugar production on Saint-Domingue exceeded that in Jamaica, and France remained the major world producer of sugar and coffee until the early 1790s, as can be seen in Table 36.1.

The value of French colonial imports from America had grown from 16.7 million livres tournois in 1716 to 192 million in 1787: on the eve of the French Revolution, colonial trade represented a third of total French imports. In the 1780s, about 2 million pounds of coffee and 6 million pounds of sugar were being consumed annually in Paris, but otherwise France's home market was able to absorb only a limited quantity of the coffee and sugar being imported from the Caribbean. While there were industrial successes in France such as the Paris luxury trades and the silk production of Lyon, real wages did not rise enough to permit a widespread increase in the consumption of imported colonial goods.[27] Most was re-exported to the Netherlands, the German states, and Italy.[28] The French were able to produce sugar more cheaply than the British and thus dominated the market for re-exports in northern Europe (see Table 36.1). Even the trading success France achieved suffered terrible blows from revolutions on both sides of the Atlantic. The slave revolt in Saint-Domingue in 1791 destroyed the main source of colonial production, and the

[26] Jan de Vries and Ad van der Woude, *The First Modern Economy: Success, Failure, and Perseverance of the Dutch Economy, 1500–1815* (Cambridge, 1997), 464–80.

[27] Marzagelli, this volume; Allen, *British Industrial Revolution*, chapter 2; Carlo Poni, 'The Worlds of Work: Formal Knowledge and Practical Abilities in Diderot's *Encyclopédie*', *Jahrbuch für Wirtschaftsgeschichte/Economic History Yearbook*, 50 (2009), 1135–50.

[28] Colin Jones and Rebecca Spang, 'Sans-Culottes, *sans café, sans tabac*: Shifting Realms of Necessity and Luxury in Eighteenth Century France', in Maxine Berg and Helen Clifford (eds.), *Consumers and Luxury: Consumer Culture in Europe 1650–1850* (Manchester, 1999), 43; Jean Tarrade, *Le Commerce colonial de la France à la fin de l'Ancien Régime* (Paris, 1973), ii. 749–55.

Table 36.1. British and French imports of goods produced in the Atlantic for selected dates[29]

Goods	Britain 1760 (lb)	France 1765 (lb)	Britain 1790 (lb)	France 1790 (lb)	Britain 1808 (lb)	Britain 1820 (lb)
Coffee	4,107,824	21,513,016	6,237,392	102,935,810	81,405,072	49,386,266
Sugar	179,755,632	142,660,497	195,634,320	201,518,143	420,390,320	455,259,704
Tobacco	52,347,294	0	46,990,651	0	8,252,452	36,404,120
Cotton	0	4,221,663	28,580,143	9,716,869	43,605,982	152,106,734

Revolutionary and Napoleonic wars meant that French ports lost the profitable re-export trade in colonial goods, which Britain or the United States took over.[30]

Britain, by the mid-eighteenth century, had developed both a successful re-export market in Europe, and an ever-growing home market for its colonial produce largely on sugar and tobacco. By 1760, just over 50,000,000 pounds of tobacco were produced, and over the course of the entire eighteenth century 82 per cent of it was re-exported. Since the mid-seventeenth century British settlers had become major sugar producers, especially on Barbados and later also on Jamaica. By the 1760s, Britain imported almost 180,000,000 pounds, rising to over 455,000,000 pounds by 1820 (Table 36.1).[31] Sugar was the main British import from its American colonies both in terms of amount and value. In 1760, about 20 per cent was re-exported to other countries in Europe, but this proportion dropped to 10 per cent by 1820. High tariffs kept French sugar out of Britain, but British home demand was much greater than in France, because disposable income was higher, and sugar could therefore become an important source of calories for an expanding British population. By the latter half of the eighteenth century a popular market for sugar existed in England, where even poor agricultural labourers and industrial workers consumed significant quantities as a sweetener for tea imported from China and India. British consumption of sugar rose from four pounds per person at the beginning of the eighteenth century to eighteen pounds per person by 1809, while at the same time the population had grown by about 4.5 million people.[32] This increased consumption created a continually increasing demand for British production even at its higher price.

[29] Schumpeter, *Overseas Trade*, tables XV, XVI, XVII; Davis, 'Foreign Trade 1700–1774', 118; Tarrade, *Le Commerce*, ii. 749–55.

[30] Silvia Marzagelli, this volume; Eltis, 'The Slave Economies', 112–13.

[31] As David Elits has shown, the actual production was over 300,000,000 lbs by 1770, indicating that much was consumed in the Americas, although some would have been smuggled into Britain to avoid custom duties. Eltis, 'The Slave Economies', 112–15.

[32] Sidney M. Mintz, *Sweetness and Power: The Place of Sugar in Modern History* (London, 1985), 67.

No other British colonial imports matched the value of tobacco and sugar. The next greatest in value were rice and indigo from South Carolina and Georgia. Fish from the Newfoundland fishery was an important export to southern Europe, but only very small amounts were imported into Britain in the same years. By this time the Canadian trade in beaver furs had declined significantly due to exhaustion of the animal population, and was relatively inconsequential as an import.[33]

Trade also grew within the now geographically sizeable British American empire. By 1770 the population of the combined British American colonies was 2–3 million people.[34] Between 1768 and 1772, on average, the Thirteen Colonies exported £759,000 worth of goods to the West Indies in comparison to £1,615,000 to England and £409,000 to southern Europe. Most consisted of biscuit, flour, rice, and fish to supply food for slaves on the sugar plantations. In return rum, molasses, sugar, cotton, and coffee were imported from the West Indies.[35] New England ports, where shipping was built, organized, and insured, benefited the most. In addition the Thirteen Colonies exported to Britain commodities such as deer skins, whale oil, pine boards, potash, flaxseed, tar, pitch, turpentine, and American rum.[36]

The War of Independence, naturally, led to a severe disruption of trade between the American colonies and Britain. Although Britain fairly successfully blockaded the northern American ports, the American colonies managed to increase their commerce with France, although more imports than exports made it through the blockade. Initially this disruption of trade meant a shortage of currency and rapid inflation in the Thirteen Colonies, which was eventually offset by foreign loans, subsidies, and military investment of £16 million by France and other European countries. The contraction of trade with Britain and the West Indies lasted from the end of the war until 1789, during which time the American economy declined by about 46 per cent because of the fighting.[37] The income and wealth achieved before the Revolution were probably not attained again until the early nineteenth century. Exports from Great Britain to North America (excluding Canada and Newfoundland) declined from £1,825,000 in value 1771–5 to £264,000 1781–5, before recovering to £10,889,000 between 1796 and 1800. This was largely the result of a great increase in the number of manufactured goods such as cloth, wrought iron, and glass being exported.[38] Imports similarly fell by over £2,000,000 during the same period before recovering strongly.[39] However, the strength of the

---

[33] McCusker and Menard, *Economy of British America*, 115, 130, 160, 174, 199.

[34] Ibid. 218.

[35] Gary M. Walton and James F. Shepard, *The Economic Rise of Early America* (Cambridge, 1979), 79–83, 85–6, 193–4.

[36] Ibid. 82–3.

[37] McCusker and Menard, *Economy of British America*, 359–73.

[38] Davis, *Industrial Revolution*, 89; Elizabeth Boody Schumpeter, *English Overseas Trade Statistics 1697–1808* (Oxford, 1960), 64, 68–9; Ronald Findlay and Kevin O'Rourke, *Power and Plenty: Trade, War, and the World Economy in the Second Millennium* (Princeton, NJ, 2007), 352.

[39] Schumpeter, *English Overseas Trade Statistics*, 17.

recovery in trade after 1786 with the new United States shows that British merchants were quickly able to reintegrate themselves into the American market.

Another important development of the period was the continued integration of Ireland as an economic force into Atlantic trade. Ireland had always been involved in the movement of people around the Atlantic, and had exported provisions to the colonies. There was also a long-established cattle trade with England through Chester. However, after 1760, with the development of Liverpool, trade expanded between Ireland and England. During the War of Independence, Ireland became the largest importer by value of British exports, and even in 1800 was the fourth largest market by value for English exports. Also, with the growth of the Irish lace industry, and increasing Irish agricultural production, Ireland became the third largest exporter of goods to England and Wales after the East and West Indies. By the 1830s Irish exports of agricultural produce were equivalent to 13 per cent of English agricultural output.[40]

Britain also exported an increasing number of manufactured goods to its colonies. The origin of this emphasis on the export of manufactures can be traced back to England's situation in the late sixteenth century when it had a relatively underdeveloped manufacturing sector compared to cloth-finishing industries in the Lowlands and Italy, Italian glass making, paper making in France, and metalwork and earthenware from Germany. As a result, successive governments promoted domestic manufacturing.[41] In Atlantic terms, this support manifested itself in the Navigation Acts of the 1650s. Those responsible for legislating for trade argued in favour of supporting English manufacturing as a means of paying for agricultural goods produced in the colonies.[42] Consequently, legislation placed limits on colonial production of manufactured goods. As it transpired, the value of colonial goods proved sufficiently high to enable colonists to purchase quality goods from England or Ireland, thus removing the incentive to manufacture goods within the colonies.[43] Also, increasing sugar production brought a necessary involvement in the slave trade. Again, manufacturing in Britain enabled the exchange of slaves in the trading centres of the African coast for iron and cloth, and the slaves were, in turn, sold in the Caribbean for sugar.

Thus, in economic terms, a virtuous cycle developed for Britain as more labourers moved into manufacturing industries such as cloth making, ironware manufacture, or gun making, which paid higher wages. This development also initially caused wages to rise in agriculture (before the period of the Napoleonic Wars when population rose much more rapidly), as more food had to be produced to feed the manufacturing and other tertiary sectors. In turn, most of the population purchased more imported colonial goods. While Britain was able to increase cloth exports substantially to new markets in Eastern Europe and the Ottoman

[40] Findlay and O'Rourke, *Power and Plenty*, 328.

[41] Barry Supple, *Commercial Crisis and Change in England 1600–1642* (Cambridge, 1959); Joan Thirsk, *Economic Policy and Projects: The Development of a Consumer Society in Early Modern England* (Oxford, 1978).

[42] Nuala Zahedieh, 'Economy', in David Armitage and Michael Braddick, *The British Atlantic World, 1500–1800* (London, 2009).

[43] McCusker and Menard, *Economy of British America*, chapter 15.

empire, the value of these exports was eventually eclipsed by that commanded by manufactured goods such as ironware as well as cheaper cloth, and eventually cottons, in the
Americas.[44] Between 1700 and 1772 goods shipped to the Americas rose from just 11 per cent
of manufactured exports worth £461,000, to 37 per cent of manufactured exports worth
£3,628,000. By 1804–6, this proportion had become fully 54 per cent of exports from Britain,
worth £19,053,000.[45] For instance, exports of glass and earthenware to America and the
West Indies went up from 768,639 pieces in 1700 to 15,785,348 pieces by 1800. Also, pieces of
wrought iron exported there went up from 18,013 pieces in 1700 to 196,549 pieces in 1800,
which accounted for 42 per cent of all wrought-iron exports in that year. By 1800, 84 per cent
of all linen exports, much of which were manufactured in Scotland, and almost half of
the British exports of fustian cloths, wrought silk, short cloths, and flannel were going to
the American colonies.[46] In addition £1–2 million worth of manufactured goods were
exported to Spain and Portugal, many of which were then shipped to their American
colonies. One invoice sent from a firm of Birmingham manufacturers in 1770 to a merchant
in Philadelphia gives an idea of what some of these goods consisted of:

buttons, vests, buckles, boxes, brass buckles, oval buckles, chapes, shovels & tongs, 5 small
br'ad screw gimblett, saws-whet & sett, sash pullies, brass ink potts, hand saw files, inch
shoe rasps, smiths vices, stone wyre, dead stock locks, padlocks, sheep shears, boucles,
candlesticks, dotted awl blades, shoe tacks, steel buckles, pen knives, pistol cap'd pocket
knives, sham buck table knives . . . [47]

Atlantic trade also played a role in supporting the development of Britain's cotton
cloth manufacture. Although increasing home demand for printed calicos in imitation
of Indian imports for women's gowns and mantuas, among other clothes, was the most
important impetus for the development of the industry, the main export trade of
fustians (a cotton/wool mixture) as well as printed cottons and cotton checks was to
the American colonies, and to Africa to purchase slaves. In addition the majority of raw
cotton imports came from the Caribbean islands and Brazil. Imports from the Levant
were also important, but New World cotton was superior.[48] Before the American War
of Independence £66,713 worth of Lancashire cottons were exported to the New World
and £98,699 to Africa, while only £7,975 worth were exported to Europe. With the
disruption caused by the War of Independence new markets were opened up in
Europe, which were soon larger than the Americas. Also, the Caribbean remained an
important supplier of the raw cotton to make the cloth.

To get an idea of the value of this export of manufactured goods we can compare
Britain's East Indian trade with its Atlantic trade. Imports of tea, cotton, silks, and

[44] Herman van der Wee, 'The Western Woollen Industries 1500–1750', in David Jenkins (ed.), *The
Cambridge History of Western Textiles* (Cambridge, 2003), 452 ff.

[45] Davis, *Industrial Revolution*, 88–9; Findlay and O'Rourke, *Power and Plenty*, 314.

[46] Schumpeter, *Trade Statistics*, tables XX–XLV.

[47] Walton and Shepard, *Economic Rise of Early America*, 75, 83–4.

[48] A. Wadsworth and J. De Lacy Mann, *The Cotton Trade and Industrial Lancashire, 1600–1780*
(Manchester, 1965), 145–69, 183–7.

porcelain from Asia were almost as valuable as British imports from the Atlantic, being worth £7,340,000 compared to £11,099,000 imported from its American colonies and the USA in 1794–6. However, exports to Asia were very small in comparison to those sent to the Atlantic.[49] Most Asian imports had to be paid for with precious metals, or with local taxes raised in India. In contrast, imports from the Atlantic could be paid for with profits arising from manufactured goods. Also, although it was the importation of Indian calicos which stimulated the home demand for British manufactured cottons, most of the raw cotton for this industry came from the Atlantic. This was also true of the sugar to sweeten Asian tea. In addition, the British North American colonies and the United States developed service industries to pay for manufactures. In contrast, the Dutch, who in the mid-seventeenth century had exported more manufactured goods within Europe than England, were unable to develop their own colonial markets for manufactures, or to penetrate Iberian markets to the same extent as Britain had done by the late eighteenth century.[50] The Spanish colonies and Brazil also increased their agricultural output significantly in this period, and were thus able to purchase more Spanish manufactured goods and agricultural produce. However, the increasing ability to purchase cheaper British goods eventually undersold manufacturing in Spain and drove local colonial manufacturing out of business.[51]

Statistics provide a sense of the changing scale and integration of countries trading within the Atlantic, but numbers of course do not represent the whole picture. The Atlantic economy should not be conceived in terms of the 'victory' of one country's trade over another, but rather as a system which grew in similar ways in all territories. The exploitation of natural resources such as gold and silver in the south as well as fish, timber, and furs in the north was profitable, but the greatest impact came from the planting of agricultural crops for export, most notably sugar, which also required the enforced migration of millions of Africans to work as slaves in the Americas. Being primarily agricultural, sugar production also allowed the American territories to support growing populations who, in turn, consumed European, and especially British, goods.

As to the overall economic impact of Atlantic trade, the predominant development was the vast increase in the production and consumption of sugar. All the major colonial powers increased their sugar output, and the market for it in Europe, North America, and the Mediterranean continued to grow. Initially demand came from wealthy consumers using sugar to create new desserts and make alcoholic punches with fruit and rum.[52] But the continued growth in demand was sustained once poorer consumers could afford sugar to add to hot drinks such as tea and coffee, or to put in porridge as in England and

[49] By 1794–6 only 14% of British exports were being sent to Asia compared to 51% which were sent to America and 23% to Europe. Davis, *Industrial Revolution*, 89, 112–13.

[50] de Vries and van der Woude, *First Modern Economy*, 495–7.

[51] Vincente, *Clothing the Spanish Empire*, 115–16.

[52] Minz, *Sweetness and Power*, chapter 3; David Vaisey (ed.), *The Diary of Thomas Turner* (Oxford, 1985), 36, 212, 274, 301, 310.

Scotland, or to sweeten fruit pies. This development, of course, had a great effect on African society since it increased the demand for slaves to man the increasing number of sugar plantations. Between 1751 and 1800, almost 4 million slaves were transported across the Atlantic, or 31 per cent of all Africans shipped between 1501 and 1866.[53]

As far as other commodities are concerned, precious metals and tobacco remained valuable exports from the Americas, but they had been equally important before 1760. More novel was the growth in the consumption of coffee, and to a lesser extent chocolate, in continental Europe. Britain also imported increasing amounts of cotton. Apart from sugar, the most important development in the long term was the creation of the market for manufactured goods in the Americas, and to a lesser extent in Africa. This is what T. H. Breen has famously called the 'empire of goods': earthenware, buckles, buttons, silks, cloths, pewter, guns, etc. Most were manufactured in Britain and exported in exchange for agricultural products, as well as for Spanish and Portuguese gold and silver.[54]

Of course cultural practices and ideas also moved with trade, as is reflected in the adoption by colonists of European fashions in clothing and furniture.[55] Questions concerning the relationship between political representation or power and commercial taxation were, of course, central to the origins of the American Revolution. But the most important ideology which emerged directly from the organization of the Atlantic economy was the antislavery movement. The inhumanity of forced labour was directly linked to the consumption of sugar in the famous sugar boycott organized in Britain in the 1790s which led to c.400,000 people abandoning the use of slave-produced sugar.

Ever since 1944, when Eric Williams published his influential book *Capitalism and Slavery*, many historians have also pointed to Atlantic trade, and especially the slave trade, as one cause of the industrial revolution. Williams emphasized the capital generated in north-west England from the symbiosis of the sugar and slave trades, but more recent historians such as Joseph Inikori, Nicholas Crafts, and Pat Hudson have focused more on the Atlantic's role in creating dynamic and rapidly expanding markets for new industrial products after 1750.[56] More recently Findley and O'Rourke have cautioned that this development must be seen as working in tandem with a dynamic home demand and a growing European demand for cotton cloth.[57] Additionally, goods produced in the Atlantic and imported into the European seaboard countries were then re-exported all over Europe for consumption. Tobacco, sugar, and coffee were consumed in Eastern Europe and Italy. In this light, it makes more sense to think of how much European consumption patterns had become dependent

---

[53] The Trans-Atlantic Slave Trade Database: http://www.slavevoyages.org/tast/assessment/estimates. faces.

[54] T. H. Breen, 'An Empire of Goods: The Anglicanization of Colonial America, 1690–1776', *Journal of British Studies*, 25 (1986), 485 ff.

[55] Burkholder and Johnson, *Colonial Latin America*, 204–45; Vincente, *Clothing the Spanish Empire*, chapter 4.

[56] Joseph Inikori, *Africans and the Industrial Revolution in England: A Study in International Trade and Economic Development* (Cambridge, 2002).

[57] Findley and O'Rourke, *Power and Plenty*, chapter 6.

on, and integrated into, the Atlantic economy. In addition much of the expansion of European industrial production was stimulated by demand throughout the Atlantic world. The growth of new populations in the Americas meant that demand grew there as well as Europe. Wars and revolutions, as well as the British ending of the slave trade, disrupted production at different times in different places, but in the long term, by 1850, production increased as David Eltis has shown.[58] The long-term changes in world history wrought by Atlantic trade are enormous; the removal of a large African population from that continent; the adoption of sugar, coffee, chocolate, and tobacco as dietary staples in Europe and then around the world; industrialization; political revolutions; and the antislavery movement were all long-term developments stemming from the scale of trade in this important and tumultuous period of history.

Bibliography

Breen, T. H., 'An Empire of Goods: The Anglicanization of Colonial America, 1690–1776', *Journal of British Studies*, 25 (1986).

Davis, Ralph, *The Industrial Revolution: British Overseas Trade* (Leicester, 1979).

De Vries, Jan, and Ad van der Woude, *The First Modern Economy: Success, Failure, and Perseverance of the Dutch Economy, 1500–1815* (Cambridge, 1997).

Eltis, David, 'The Slave Economies of the Caribbean: Structure, Performance, Evolution and Significance', in Franklin Knight (ed.), *UNESCO History of the Caribbean* (New York, 1997), vol. iii.

Findlay, Ronald, and Kevin O'Rourke, *Power and Plenty: Trade, War, and the World Economy in the Second Millennium* (Princeton, NJ, 2007).

Fisher, John R., *The Economic Aspects of Spanish Imperialism in America, 1492–1810* (Liverpool, 1997).

Inikori, Joseph, *Africans and the Industrial Revolution in England: A Study in International Trade and Economic Development* (Cambridge, 2002).

McCusker, John J., and Russell R. Menard, *The Economy of British America, 1607–1789* (Chapel Hill, NC, 1985).

Schumpeter, Elizabeth Boody, *English Overseas Trade Statistics 1697–1808* (Oxford, 1960).

Tarrade, Jean, *Le Commerce colonial de la France à la fin de l'Ancien Régime* (Paris, 1973), vol. ii.

---

[58] Eltis, 'The Slave Economies', 117–18.

CHAPTER 37

....

LATE ATLANTIC HISTORY

....

EMMA ROTHSCHILD

So where does the story end? Or where does the Atlantic end? And is it a story? The history of the Atlantic world has had an extraordinary and transformative effect on ways of thinking about early modern and modern history, as the chapters in this volume show. 'The dizzying shifts that come from viewing familiar phenomena from different angles, different geographies, and different disciplinary perspectives,' in Eric Slauter's description of the excitement of Atlantic history, have brought lasting changes in the practice and theory of history.[1] There has been a transition in the scale of historical investigation: to the hemispheric or the oceanic, but also to the multiplicity or variability of scales—the variations in distance, from the cosmic to the individual—which is so characteristic of Atlantic history. The 'hemispheric perspective', as Christopher Brown shows in his chapter on slavery, can provide a new view of history, geography, and political economy.[2]

The perspective of Atlantic history has also, in the course of a generation, made it possible to see connections—and discontinuities—which were obscured from view in the established stories of national and imperial history. The history of slavery and the slave trade is again of central importance. The Atlantic world was constituted, Nicholas Canny and Philip Morgan write in their introduction, by the circumstance, starting in the fifteenth century, that people, things, and ideas 'began to move regularly back and forth across the Atlantic Ocean'. But most of the people who moved—and thereby of the ideas and ways of living which moved with them—were in the first four centuries of Atlantic exchanges 'involuntary' migrants. Of these forced sojourners, the 'overwhelming majority', as William O'Reilly shows, were enslaved Africans, most of whom arrived in the Caribbean and Brazil.[3] African slaves were the most Atlantic of all populations in the New World of the fifteenth to the nineteenth centuries. They were

---

[1] Eric Slauter, 'History, Literature, and the Atlantic World', *William and Mary Quarterly*, 3rd Series, 55/1 (January 2008), 135–61, 161.

[2] Chapter by Christopher Brown.

[3] Chapter by William O'Reilly.

the newest Americans, with the shortest lives; the individuals who had the greatest knowledge and the most recent memories of societies on both sides of the Atlantic, and of the traverse between the Old and the New Worlds.[4]

The view from the Atlantic Ocean has even disrupted the familiar chronologies of revolution, independence, and empire. The chapters in this volume refer almost in passing to what would until recently have been startling conclusions; that 'the much-studied English/British presence on mainland America over the course of the seventeenth century was relatively inconsequential', and changed only with the demand for provisions for the slave population in the Caribbean; or that 'the age of revolutions . . . was an era of spectacular growth in the institution of slavery in the Americas', and 'the Haitian Revolution sits at the center of the story'.[5]

The Trans-Atlantic Slave Trade Database, which is the most important statistical resource produced out of a generation (or more) of Atlantic history, reveals a pattern of change in which shifts in perspective in space are disruptive, in turn, of perspectives in time: that the zenith or nadir of the Atlantic slave trade, counted in numbers of slaves embarked in a single year, came in 1829, with more than 117,000 individuals transported, almost all of them in Spanish, French, and Portuguese/Brazilian ships; or that the zenith/nadir of the French slave trade came in the immediately pre-revolutionary and revolutionary period of 1784–92, with 307,000 slaves embarked for the part-island of Saint-Domingue, the modern Haiti (or more slaves than were embarked over the same period for the British Caribbean and mainland North America combined). It also reveals a striking pattern in respect of the African origins of the new Atlantic subjects: that most of the newly landed slaves in Saint-Domingue at the time of the Haitian Revolution—more than a quarter of the entire population of the colony—had arrived in the Americas from the South Atlantic, or from the ports of modern Angola, Mozambique, and the Indian Ocean which were the traditional suppliers of slaves to Brazil, far more than to North America. The South Atlantic and Indian Ocean ports were the places of departure for 55 per cent of the slaves who arrived in Saint-Domingue in 1784–92, compared to only 7 per cent of slaves in the rest of the Caribbean.[6]

---

[4] On the information and memory of slaves in Jamaica, see Vincent Brown, *The Reaper's Garden: Death and Power in the World of Atlantic Slavery* (Cambridge, MA, 2008).

[5] Introduction by Nicholas Canny and Philip Morgan, chapter by Christopher Brown.

[6] The Trans-Atlantic Slave Trade Database; see http://wilson.library.emory.edu:9090/tast/assessment/estimates.faces, accessed on 9 June 2010. Of the 260,000 slaves who landed in Saint-Domingue in 1784–92, according to the Estimates Database, more than 143,000, or 55%, came from the regions identified as 'West Central Africa and St. Helena', and 'South-east Africa and Indian ocean islands'. The important ports, according to the Voyages Database, included Cabinda, Malembo, and Mozambique; see http://wilson.library.emory.edu:9090/tast/database/search.faces. The total population of Saint-Domingue at the time of the French Revolution was estimated at 510,000, including (at least) 450,000 enslaved Africans; a substantial proportion of whom, on the basis of these estimates, had arrived very recently from south-west and south-east Africa. M. L. E. Moreau de Saint-Méry, *Description topographique, physique, civile, politique et historique de la partie francaise de l'isle Saint-Domingue*, 2 vols. (Philadelphia, PA, 1797), i. 5; and see Laurent Dubois, *Avengers of the New World: The Story of the*

These changes in perspective or ways of seeing are irreversible, it seems to me. There is 'no route back from reflectiveness', as the philosopher Bernard Williams wrote of historical understanding; or in this case, from trying to glimpse the consequences of long-distance connections for individuals in the past.[7] But history is not only a perspective, or a vista. There were three large challenges of modern historiography, as described by Bernard Bailyn in an essay of 1982 which was a prelude to much of the Atlantic history of the past generation. All had to do with connections of various sorts: the 'integration of latent and manifest events'; the 'depiction of large-scale spheres and systems'; and the 'description of internal states of mind and their relation to external circumstances and events'. All were identified in the figurative language of perspective, vision, and viewing. But Bailyn also evoked the 'drama of history', as an 'evolving story', or a 'movement through time', and it is this sense of Atlantic history as a story that the editors of the present volume have sought to present.[8]

The narrative of Atlantic history, for Canny and Morgan, is a story of the emergence, consolidation, integration, and transition of an Atlantic world of multiple connections. It begins with the fifteenth-century origins of relatively regular exchanges from east to west, or east to south-west, across an ocean that until then had been a connection, for the most part, in coastal voyages. The story ends, around the time of the zenith/nadir of the Atlantic slave trade in 1829, in the disintegration of Atlantic history into a larger and more worldwide story, as the 'integrity that had emerged in the Atlantic world was threatened by novel political, economic, technological and moral forces'.[9]

The editors have made an outstandingly good case, it seems to me, for the by now well-established chronology of the history of the Atlantic world as extending from the late fifteenth to the early nineteenth centuries. Atlantic history does not end in 'independence': the Inca and the Mali empires were independent long before the innovations of Majorcan cartographers; and the newly independent American republics of the 1780s to the 1820s were dependent, for one or two centuries, on European capital, European commerce, and the European influence of which James Madison was a notably anxious observer. 'Money in all its shapes is influence,' Madison wrote in 1799; 'every shipment, every consignment, every commission, is a channel in which a portion of it flows . . . [as] a stock of British ideas and sentiments proper to be retailed to the people. Thus it is, that our country is penetrated to its remotest corners with a foreign poison vitiating the American sentiment, recolonizing the American character.'[10]

Haitian Revolution (Cambridge, MA, 2004). On the West Central African slave trade, see Joseph C. Miller, *Way of Death: Merchant Capitalism and the Angolan Slave Trade 1730-1830* (Madison, WI, 1988).

[7] Bernard Williams, *Ethics and the Limits of Philosophy* (Cambridge, MA, 1985), 163–4.

[8] Bernard Bailyn, 'The Challenge of Modern Historiography', *American Historical Review*, 87/1 (February 1982), 1–24, 11, 22.

[9] Introduction by Canny and Morgan.

[10] James Madison, 'Foreign Influence', in *The Papers of James Madison*, eds. David B. Mattern, J. C. A. Stagg, Jeanne K. Cross, and Susan Holbrook Perdue (Charlottesville, VA, 1991), xvii. 217–20. On cartography in the early Atlantic world, see chapters by Matthew Edney and Joan-Pau Rubiés.

The formal European empires in the Americas ended only in the late twentieth century, and the informal empires endured throughout the nineteenth century.[11] The rise and fall of Atlantic slavery is at the centre of the narrative of Atlantic history, as this volume shows. But the celebrated landmarks of the almost-end of slavery (the abolition of slavery in most of the French empire in 1793, and again in 1848, the abolition of the slave trade in British ships in 1807 and of slavery in the British empire in 1834, or in 1838) do not mark the end of Atlantic history in any very decisive respect, in a world in which the age of revolutions, and of the rise of antislavery sentiment, was also an age of spectacular increase in slavery; in which the economic thought of much of the American hemisphere, from the 1820s to the 1860s, was in substantial part a reflection on the future of slavery; and in which the formal end of slavery in the Americas came in 1888, in Brazil.

The narrative that is proposed in this volume is economic, technological, and moral, as much as political, in the editors' description. It relates the expansion of the multiple connections that by the eighteenth century constituted a distinctive Atlantic world; and the distintegration of these connections, or at least of the distinctiveness of the Atlantic as a 'world', with the new technologies of transport and communications of the 1830s. Atlantic history ends because the Atlantic is no longer distinct, in a new world of literally worldwide or global connections. Edmund Burke described the Atlantic as 'that uphill Sea', and a century later, all oceans were equal, in the age of steamships (and eventually of aviation).[12] As a British journalist in India wrote in 1857, of the rebellion or mutiny that was enveloping the last days of the East India Company, 'travellers' stories have long since yielded to the powers of steam and of the electric telegraph. We hear no more of an "adversam [sic] mare," an uphill sea,—or of an "ultima thule." '[13]

The economic–technological narrative is a convincing Atlantic story. It has the advantage, in particular, that it corresponds to the stories that contemporaries told each other at the time, about a new world of global connections in which railways and steamships, in François-René de Chateaubriand's description of 1841, 'will have made distances disappear [and] it will not only be commodities which travel, but also ideas which will have wings': a 'universal society', which will be 'neither Indian, nor Chinese, nor American, or rather will be all these societies at the same time'.[14]

But the story of Atlantic integrity and disintegration also raises two interesting and subversive questions about the established limits of Atlantic history. One has to do with the confluence, even in the earliest period of regular connections, of the Atlantic and

[11] Jeremy Adelman, *Republic of Capital: Buenos Aires and the Legal Transformation of the Atlantic World* (Stanford, CA, 1999).

[12] Draft speech on the Stamp Act, January 1766, in *The Writings and Speeches of Edmund Burke*, vol. ii, ed. Paul Langford (Oxford, 1981), 44.

[13] 'Mhairwara in Miniature', *Allen's Indian Mail*, 15/318 (9 June 1857). 'Ultima thule' was a land to the north of the British Isles, and Thule was dimly visible from the Orkneys, in Tacitus' *Agricola*.

[14] François-René de Chateaubriand, *Mémoires d'outre-tombe*, 3 vols. (Paris, 1973), iii. 715, 720.

other oceans; and between short-distance (or coastal), medium-distance (or Atlantic), and long-distance (or worldwide) exchanges. The other has to do with the idea of an Atlantic 'world', or 'world-view', in a cultural or moral sense. These questions may point, in turn, to a continuity of Atlantic history, well into the nineteenth-century age of self-conscious globalism, or distancelessness; and to the possibilities of an extended Atlantic history in relation to histories of information, histories of ideas, economic history, and the history of the natural and invented environment.

Atlantic connections were an extension, as the chapters in the early part of this volume show, of exchanges over shorter distances. There were Atlantic voyages—including the voyage around the British isle described by Tacitus, and the African expeditions of Roman traders—long before there was an Atlantic world. But the Atlantic Ocean was also a route to somewhere else. The great epic poem of the Atlantic, and of fifteenth-century voyages, was a celebration not of Columbus but of Vasco de Gama. The *Lusiads*, by Luis de Camões, was written 'part on the Atlantic Sea, and partly on the Indian shore' (in Voltaire's description), and Camões was said to have swum ashore, holding up his poem in one hand, following a shipwreck on the Mekong River, in modern Cambodia. The Atlantic is to Vasco de Gama's right, as he sets out to 'discover' India. But India is *also* to the right, as well as to the left. In William Julius Mickle's translation of 1776:

> Far to the right the restless ocean roared,
> Whose bounding surges never keel explored;
> If bounding shore, as Reason deems, divide
> The vast Atlantic from the Indian tide.

The bounding shore, there, is America, on the westward route to India. Eventually, Vasco de Gama's expedition reaches the Cape of Good Hope, depicted as an anguished and love-struck giant, turned into a mountain for all eternity. Once beyond, all is different:

> Nor long excursive off at sea we stand,
> A cultured shore invites us to the land.[15]

The Atlantic was on the way to almost everywhere, from the perspective of Portugal, which was a rising Atlantic power at both the beginning and the end of the story recounted in this volume. But it was on the way somewhere for others, as well, and in particular on the way to Europe, as well as to India. The Mesoamerican writer Chimalpahin, in the early seventeenth century, described 'a delegation of Japanese men who came through Mexico City on the way to Europe'.[16] The European trading routes to India and China frequently involved a substantial turn to the *right*, in Camões' terms, as N. A. M. Rodger shows; what would have seemed, in the age of steamships, to be a substantial detour.[17] The un-Atlantic Lord Clive went to Calcutta

---

[15] Luis de Camöens, *The Lusiad; or, the Discovery of India. An Epic Poem*, trans. William Julius Mickle (2nd edn. London, 1778), pp. cc–ccii, 183, 210.

[16] Chapter by Kevin Terraciano.

[17] Chapter by N. A. M. Rodger.

via Brazil, when he returned from England to India in 1765 to assume the diwani or financial administration of eastern India, on the momentous occasion to which could be 'date[d]', in Lord Macaulay's description, 'the purity of the administration of our Eastern empire'.[18] As Louis Dermigny showed in his study of the French commerce with China, it is misleading to think of the geography of the eighteenth-century oceans in terms only of distance; one should think, as contemporaries did, in terms of winds and isochrones, or of journeys which take an equal period of time.[19]

Even in the high period of integration, in the late eighteenth century, the Atlantic Ocean was a sea of egresses, or ways out. There was a fairly widespread view of a single, worldwide system of confluent oceans. The Abbé Raynal, in the *Histoire des deux Indes*, described a 'local correspondence to be found between the isthmus of Suez & that of Panama, between the Cape of Good-Hope and Cape Horn, between the archipelago of the East Indies and that of the Antilles'.[20] There was a sense of the Atlantic as a route to other and more opulent waters: the Indian Ocean, the Gulf of Mexico, the Bay of Honduras, the Pacific Ocean. There was the North-West Passage to the Pacific, which Chateaubriand, himself the son of a slave trader in Ouidah, set out to find in 1791, via the Azores and Niagara Falls. There was also the Jamaica Channel into the Gulf of Mexico, and the Grenada passage to Honduras; the isthmus of Panama and the almost-isthmus of Nicaragua; Río Plata in modern Argentina, and the overland routes from the silver mines of Peru; the Cape of Good Hope.

The naval and diplomatic feints of the American War of Independence provide an interesting illustration. The British embassy in Paris reported to London, in May 1776, that the French anticipated an indiscriminate exchange between empires following the loss of New England, such as a British descent on Mexico or Saint-Domingue; 'we should probably then be tempted to fall upon some of their colonies to repair Our Disgrace.'[21] The oddest expedition of the Revolutionary War, in 1781, was in appearance a convoy of East India ships bound for Madras, and in prospect a plan to capture the Cape of Good Hope, proceed to the East Indies, seize the islands of Ceylon and Celebes, incorporate 2,000 'sepoys' or Indian troops from the private army of the East India Company, and return to capture the Spanish settlements in Río Plata.[22] But the project was uncovered by a French intelligence officer in London (who was later the last person to be hanged, drawn, and quartered for espionage), and the armada was

---

[18] 'Lord Clive' (1840), in Lord Macaulay, *Critical and Historical Essays Contributed to the Edinburgh Review*, 4 vols. (London, 1889), iii. 169.

[19] Louis Dermigny, *La Chine et l'Occident: le commerce à Canton au XVIIIe siècle 1719–1833*, 3 vols. (Paris, 1964), i. 245–51.

[20] [Abbé Raynal], *Histoire philosophique et politique: des établissemens et du commerce des Européens dans les deux Indes*, 7 vols. (Amsterdam and The Hague, 1770–4), vi. 191.

[21] Letter of 1 May 1776 from Mr St Paul to Lord Weymouth, The National Archives (United Kingdom), SP78/299/66ʳ.

[22] G. Rutherford, 'Sidelights on Commodore Johnstone's Expedition to the Cape', *Mariner's Mirror*, 28 (1942), 189–212 and 290–308; Admiral Sir Thomas Pasley, *Private Sea Journals 1778–1782*, ed. Rodney M. S. Pasley (London, 1931); and see Emma Rothschild, *The Inner Life of Empires: An Eighteenth-Century History* (Princeton, NJ, 2011).

engaged in the Cape Verde Islands off the coast of West Africa by the French navy, who reached the Cape of Good Hope before it.[23] A part of the expedition continued eastwards to India, and a ship called the *Jupiter* went westwards towards 'the famous River Plate, which vomits forth half the Riches of the World', later returning, disconsolately, to the uninhabited island of Trinidada.[24] The naval commodore of the expedition had meanwhile been the proponent, four years earlier, of an elaborate plan for the development of cotton plantations in the 'delightful and most valuable country' of Mosquitia, in modern Honduras, with the exciting prospect of access to the Pacific, or the South Seas, 'by the way of the Lake of Nicaragua'.[25]

The other subversive question has to do with the idea of an Atlantic world. The expression is at least as old as Lord Byron's verse dramas of the 1820s: 'Whither wilt thou?... Let's see! Spain—Italy—the new Atlantic world.'[26] But it now has the almost irresistible connotation of a world of thought, or a world-view. This sense of Atlantic history as a history of exchanges of people and things, and also a history of shared or collective ways of thinking, has been part of Atlantic historiography from the outset. Isolation 'is not a matter of distance or the slowness of communication; it is a question of what a dispatch from distant quarters means to the recipient', Perry Miller wrote of the 'New England Mind', in 1953.[27] The history of Atlantic connections, too, or of Atlantic negotiations, has always been, implicitly or explicitly, a history of meaning.[28]

But this is an elusive venture, in modern and post-idealist times. 'Weisst Du was? Vati hat keine Weltanschauung,' the young Albert Hirschman said to his sister, in 1928; 'You know what? Daddy has no world-view!'[29] There are no more world-views, now, or not many, and almost no histories of the world-views of others. The Atlantic world is in any case a particularly troublesome subject, as a set of relationships constituted by endless change, for the now old-fashioned enterprise of the great mid-twentieth-century histories of mentalities, or 'structures' of thought which persist over long periods of time.[30] It is a troublesome subject, too, because of the diversity of Atlantic

[23] *The Annual Register, or a View of the History, Politics, and Literature, for the Year 1782* (London, 1783), 111.

[24] Pasley, *Private Sea Journals*, 170, 202.

[25] Brian Edwards, 'Some Account of the British Settlement on the Musquito Shore', presented to the House of Commons by Governor Johnstone on 25 February 1777. Parliamentary Register, 14th parl., 3rd sess., pp. 281, 328, 336.

[26] Lord Byron, *The Deformed Transformed: A Drama* (Philadelphia, PA, 1824), 33–4.

[27] Perry Miller, *The New England Mind: From Colony to Province* (Cambridge, MA, 1953), quoted in John Clive and Bernard Bailyn, 'England's Cultural Provinces: Scotland and America', *William and Mary Quarterly*, 3rd Series, 11/2 (April 1954), 200–13, 209.

[28] On Atlantic histories of culture and meaning, see Jack P. Greene, *Negotiated Authorities: Essays in Colonial Political and Constitutional History* (Charlottesville, VA, 1994), and Christine Daniels and Michael V. Kennedy (eds.), *Negotiated Empires: Centers and Peripheries in the Americas, 1500–1820* (New York, 2002).

[29] Albert Hirschman, *A Propensity to Self-Subversion* (Cambridge, MA, 1995), 111–12.

[30] On the history of mentalities and stable ways of thinking, see Lucien Lévy-Bruhl, *La Morale et la science des mœurs* (Paris, 1903); Jacques Revel, *Jeux d'échelles: la micro-analyse à l'expérience* (Paris, 1996); G. E. R. Lloyd, *Demystifying Mentalities* (Cambridge, 1990).

experiences, or of the worlds of the mind which were shared by the very different denizens of the Atlantic world: slaves and slave owners; individuals living in the port cities and in the interior lowlands of an Atlantic world which extended, in imagination, from Comancheria to the Upper Danube; individuals who traversed the South Atlantic on East India Company floating palaces, en route to Calcutta, or on slave ships like the Portuguese *St Lazaro*, which in the same autumn as Lord Clive's Atlantic journey embarked 557 slaves in Angola, of whom 144 had perished by the time the ship arrived in Brazil.[31]

There have been remarkable recent descriptions of the inner experiences of the Atlantic world: Stephanie Smallwood's history of slaves at sea, or David Shields' account in this volume of the senses in the Atlantic, or Claire Priest's and Elizabeth Mancke's investigations of landed property in Atlantic law and politics.[32] Karen Ordahl Kupperman's history of the understanding of changes in climate provided a new view of all Atlantic voyages.[33] One distinctive moment of the Atlantic experience—the weather at sea, or the 'sentiments one experiences, when from the ship one can see nothing, in all directions, but the serious aspect of the abyss', in Chateaubriand's description—was an experience common to all individuals, without exception, and it has its own historical record, of sorts, in the captains' logs and storm reports of the maritime Atlantic.[34] The storms were the same, even for the slaves who could never see the sea.

But these interior or interior–exterior histories of the Atlantic world unfold at a very different rhythm from the 'evolving story' of political history, and even from the story of Atlantic integrity and disintegration. For states of mind, like the organization of economic life, change only slowly over time. One of the difficulties for Atlantic history—and this is a quite general difficulty for the 'global' or 'transnational' history which has been so all-conquering in recent years—is to describe the coexistence or jumbling together of short-distance, medium-distance, and long-distance exchanges.[35] The economic and political world constituted by 'local' connections across the English Channel did not disappear, for example, in the new Atlantic economy; or even, as Renaud Morieux has shown, in the high period of Atlantic integrity.[36] The connections

[31] The Trans-Atlantic Slave Trade Database; see http://wilson.library.emory.edu:9090/tast/assessment/estimates.faces, accessed on 9 May 2010.

[32] Stephanie E. Smallwood, *Saltwater Slavery: A Middle Passage from Africa to American Diaspora* (Cambridge, MA, 2008); Claire Priest, 'Creating an American Property Law: Alienability and its Limits in American History', *Harvard Law Review*, 120/2 (December 2006), 386–459; Elizabeth Mancke and David Shields, in this volume; and see, on eighteenth-century ideas of land, Emma Rothschild, 'The Atlantic Worlds of David Hume', in Bernard Bailyn and Patricia L. Denault (eds.), *Soundings in Atlantic History: Latent Structures and Intellectual Currents, 1500–1830* (Cambridge, MA, 2009), 405–48.

[33] Karen Ordahl Kupperman, 'Fear of Hot Climates in the Anglo-American Colonial Experience', *William and Mary Quarterly*, 3rd Series, 41/2 (April 1984), 213–40.

[34] Chateaubriand, *Mémoires d'outre-tombe*, i. 248.

[35] See 'AHR Conversation: On Transnational History', *American Historical Review*, 111/5 (2006), especially comments by Chris Bayly and Sven Beckert.

[36] Renaud Morieux, *Une mer pour deux royaumes: la Manche, frontière franco-anglaise (XVIIe–XVIIIe siècles)* (Rennes, 2008).

of Atlantic commerce and finance did not disappear in a suddenly universal world, in which all exchanges were global (and in which many exchanges were disrupted, in any case, in a nineteenth-century world economy which was increasingly national and imperial, as well as universal).

The closely related difficulty has to do with the coexistence of kinds of exchanges which evolve over different periods of time; short-term, medium-term, and long-term exchanges, as it were, or exchanges of news that have almost instantaneous consequences (like the news of the decision in the James Somerset case which had the effect of gradually ending slavery in England), exchanges of credit information (as in the financing of the Liverpool–Louisiana cotton industry), and the exchanges of religious and moral ideas of which the effect, over more than a century, was the end of Atlantic slavery. But these difficulties are also opportunities, for a transnational history which does not assume that the scale of historical exchanges increases inexorably over time; or that the velocity of exchanges increases inexorably with scale, as well as over time. The story told in this volume, which is an economic–technological–moral story, even has a surprising consequence, it seems to me, for future scholarship. It is that the future of Atlantic history will be in part a history that is permissive in respect of frontiers in time, as well as space: a nineteenth-century history, in particular, or a history that takes seriously the coexistence, so characteristic of the nineteenth century, of local, Atlantic, and worldwide exchanges.

The Atlantic or post-Atlantic history of the nineteenth century is already a flourishing enterprise. There are histories of Cuban–New Orleans families, from the 1790s to the 1890s, which are also histories of the French Atlantic; or revisionist histories of the 'new' French empire in North Africa of the mid-nineteenth century, with its continuity of military, commercial, and administrative experience, from the 'old' empire in Saint-Domingue to Algeria in 1831.[37] Walter Johnson's *River of Dark Dreams* is an Atlantic history of the Mississippi Valley in the mid-nineteenth century, in which the spatial environment of the cotton kingdom is transformed by three traverses: of enslaved individuals, walking, from the Atlantic South to Louisiana; of slaves shipped around the American coast to the south-west; and of cotton, credit, information, and economic ideas, transported on the old shipping routes to the Jamaica Channel, New York, and Liverpool.[38] These are descriptions of a period (a very long period) in which the Atlantic world was continuous, in all directions, with larger worldwide connections; and in which Atlantic ways of thinking, Atlantic financial relationships, and the consequences of four centuries of the Atlantic slave trade, were enduring, in a new and self-consciously universal economy.

---

[37] Rebecca J. Scott, '"She...Refuses to Deliver Up Herself as the Slave of Your Petitioner": Émigrés, Enslavement, and the 1808 Louisiana Digest of the Civil Laws', *Tulane European and Civil Law Forum*, 24 (2009), 115–36; Rebecca J. Scott, 'The Atlantic World and the Road to Plessy v. Ferguson', *Journal of American History*, 94/3 (December 2007), 726–33; David Todd, 'A French Imperial Meridian, 1814–1870', *Past and Present*, 210 (2011), 55–86; David Todd, *L'Identité économique de la France: libre-échange et protectionnisme, 1814–1851* (Paris, 2008).

[38] Walter Johnson, *River of Dark Dreams* (Cambridge, MA, forthcoming 2012).

The history of the Indian Ocean world in the nineteenth century, too, is both continuous with and suggestive for Atlantic history. The scale of the movements of individuals in Asia, between the 1850s and the 1930s, was vast, even in an Atlantic comparison; some 27 million Indians and 19 million Chinese who moved to South-East Asia alone.[39] These migrations were associated with exchanges of commodities, ideas, religious experiences, and environmental practices, in the Indian Ocean and the South China Sea, as in the Atlantic. But the mobility of people and ideas was far more circular in Asia, as Sunil Amrith has shown; a migration of sojourners, from China and India, who came and went and returned home, like so many of the unenslaved emigrants to the Americas, whose own journeys are one of the still underexplored stories of Atlantic history.[40]

The Indian Ocean and South China Sea world of migration was continuous, from the 1830s, with the Atlantic economy, in the long nineteenth century of anxious reflection on the future of slavery and slave-like labour. The 3 million African slaves who arrived in the Americas between the 1810s and 1860s were augmented, and to some extent replaced, by indentured labourers from the British Indian empire, who travelled to the British, French, and Spanish islands, and Guyana; and also by 'Chinese coolies', who travelled across the Atlantic to Puerto Rico and Cuba.[41] A study of 'The Negro in Africa and America', commissioned by the American Economic Association, concluded in 1902 that 'by excluding the Chinese we have avoided one threatening phase of heterogeneity. But unfortunately no African exclusion act was passed in the days when such action might have delivered us from the black peril.'[42]

The intellectual and political history of the nineteenth century is now also Atlantic. The history of American ideas about the future of slavery is in part a history of Atlantic exchanges; as in Drew Gilpin Faust's description of the theorist of slavery John Henry Hammond in his (circular) journey from South Carolina to Florence and the Scottish borders, and into the philosophical origins of the French Revolution.[43] Daniel Rodgers, in *Contested Truths*, followed 'Bentham's reputation across the Atlantic', and to the 'margins' of 'legitimate political talk'. The distinctions between intellectual history, cultural history, and histories of political life are elusive, in these late Atlantic histories. In *Atlantic Crossings*, Rodgers described the individual stories and collective ideas which led to the invention, in the late nineteenth-century epoch of nationalist

---

[39] Sunil Amrith, *Migration and Diaspora in Modern Asia* (Cambridge, 2011).

[40] Sugata Bose, *A Hundred Horizons: The Indian Ocean in the Age of Global Empire* (Cambridge, MA, 2006); Sunil Amrith, 'Indians Overseas? Governing Tamil Migration to Malaya, 1870–1941', *Past and Present* (2010).

[41] On British sources for the history of movements of indentured labourers from Asia to the Americas, see 'Family History Sources for Indian Indentured Labour' available from the National Archives at http://www.nationalarchives.gov.uk/documents/research-guides/indian-indentured-labour-pdf.

[42] Joseph Alexander Tillinghast, 'The Negro in Africa and America', *Publications of the American Economic Association*, 3rd Series, 3/2 (May 1902), 1–231, 1.

[43] Drew Gilpin Faust, *John Henry Hammond and the Old South: A Design for Mastery* (Baton Rouge, LA, 1982).

historicism, of an 'era of transatlantic social politics'; 'movements of politics and ideas throughout the North Atlantic world that trade and capitalism had tied together'.[44]

An Atlantic history which edges into the nineteenth and twentieth centuries might even, finally, be a history which engages with 'different disciplinary perspectives', as well as with different angles of vision and different geographies. One prospect is thus of a new economic history of the Atlantic world. Atlantic history was from the outset concerned with economic life and with the uses of quantitative information.[45] The Atlantic world, in the sense used in this volume, of regular exchanges of people, things, and ideas, was an economic enterprise, with financial costs and commercial consequences. But Atlantic history has, with a few distinguished exceptions, notably in the work of Barbara Solow, had relatively little impact on economic history.[46] This is a consequence, in part, of the odd disciplinary divisions of the times, into economic history (for economists), political histories of economic life, histories of economic thought, social histories (of labour), business history, and the 'economic-cultural history' of nineteenth-century historical political economists. Atlantic history has the potential to traverse these distinctions, as it has traversed so many others.[47] There is even a very large subject of study, in the period of Atlantic integration, or the re-evaluation, in the light of new information about the slave trade, of the economic consequences of Atlantic slavery.

A second, related prospect has to do with the environmental history of the Atlantic world. The classic early works of American environmental history are in different respects Atlantic: William Cronon's *Changes in the Land*, in which the history of the early American-European world of buying and selling and gathering and naming was widened to include 'rocks, trees, and soil; plants and animals, both wild and domestic; insects; and even invisible...microorganisms'; and Richard White's *The Roots of Dependency*, which is a history of Native American and European views of the world, over the long nineteenth century.[48] Atlantic history has itself taken an environmental turn, as John McNeill shows in this volume.[49] An Atlantic-worldwide environmental

[44] Daniel T. Rodgers, *Contested Truths: Keywords in American Politics since Independence* (Cambridge, MA, 1998); id., *Atlantic Crossings: Social Politics in a Progressive Age* (Cambridge, MA, 1998).

[45] Bernard Bailyn, 'Communications and Trade: The Atlantic in the Seventeenth Century', *Journal of Economic History*, 13/4 (1953), 378–87; id., *The New England Merchants in the Seventeenth Century* (Cambridge, MA, 1979).

[46] Barbara L. Solow and Stanley L. Engerman (eds.), *British Capitalism and Caribbean Slavery: The Legacy of Eric Williams* (Cambridge, 1987); Barbara L. Solow (ed.), *Slavery and the Rise of the Atlantic System* (Cambridge, 1991).

[47] See Rodgers, *Atlantic Crossings*, and, on the political history of economic life, Adelman, *Republic of Capital*, 1.

[48] John Demos, 'Foreword', in William Cronon, *Changes in the Land: Indians, Colonists, and the Ecology of New England* (rev. edn. New York, 2003), p. xiii; Richard White, *The Roots of Dependency: Subsistence, Environment, and Social Change among the Choctaws, Pawnees, and Navajos* (Lincoln, NE, 1983).

[49] Chapter by John McNeill; Richard Drayton, *Nature's Government: Science, Imperial Britain, and the 'Improvement' of the World* (New Haven, CT, 2000); Pekka Hämäläinen, *The Comanche Empire*

history could extend the universe of historical enquiry to oceans and winds and the power of the sun (and to the 'perfect Noah's Ark' of cows, rams, turkeys, singing birds and 'grasses of every kind', that the captain of the *Jupiter* was carrying in 1781, en route to the Río Plata from his unsuccessful East Indian expedition).[50] It could also, following Cronon, extend the universe of environmental history to individuals and their ideas, including their understanding of rights in different kinds of property, relationships to different kinds of animals, and the uses of different kinds of energy, or power.

A third direction is the history of Atlantic and Atlantic-worldwide information. The history of information, which has been such a flourishing part of the history of early modern Europe and early British India, has been extended in recent years to the Atlantic world.[51] It has a particular affinity, from an eighteenth-century perspective, to Atlantic exchanges. The British-American official Thomas Pownall, who was himself the grandson of an East India Company official in Bombay, identified 'information and knowledge' as the principal condition for what he described as a 'GRAND MARINE DOMINION', 'IN THE ATLANTIC, AND IN AMERICA'.[52] 'In this new world,' Pownall wrote in 1780, in the assumed person of a friend who had set out from Europe to America, but settled, in the end, in the Azores, 'the acquirement of information . . . forms a *character peculiar to these people*', a 'turn of character which, in the ordinary occurrences of life, is called *inquisitiveness*'.[53]

Even here, the late Atlantic perspective is of interest. There were police spies, British informants, subversive songs, and clandestine book-sellers in the Americas, as in Paris and North India; and their connections extended across the more-than-Atlantic or Atlantic-global world. The history of 'long-distance information', as in early modern Venice, included news of Smyrna and Suez.[54] The 'correspondence of the moneyed and the mercantile world', in Edmund Burke's description of 1796, was part of a 'kind of electric communication everywhere'.[55] The investigations of nineteenth-century

(New Haven, CT, 2008); Pekka Hämäläinen, 'The Politics of Grass: European Expansion, Ecological Change, and Indigenous Power in the Southwest Borderlands', *William and Mary Quarterly*, 3rd Series, 67/2 (April 2010), 173–208.

[50] Pasley, *Private Sea Journals*, 184.

[51] Will Slauter, 'Forward-Looking Statements: News and Speculation in the Age of the American Revolution', *Journal of Modern History*, 81 (December 2009), 759–92; John J. McCusker, *Essays in the Economic History of the Atlantic World* (London, 1997); Mark A. Peterson, 'Theopolis Americana', in *Soundings in Atlantic History*, 329–70; Hugh Amory and David D. Hall (eds.), *The Colonial Book in the Atlantic World* (Cambridge, 2000).

[52] Thomas Pownall, *The Administration of the Colonies, wherein their Rights and Constitution Are Discussed and Stated* (4th edn. London, 1768), 164.

[53] [Thomas Pownall], *A Memorial, most Humbly Addressed to the Sovereigns of Europe, on the Present State of Affairs, between the Old and New World* (2nd edn. London, 1780), 42–3.

[54] C. A. Bayly, *Empire and Information: Intelligence Gathering and Social Communication in India, 1780–1870* (Cambridge, 1996); Robert Darnton, 'An Early Information Society: News and the Media in Eighteenth-Century Paris', *American Historical Review*, 105/1 (February 2000), 1–35; Filippo De Vivo, *Information & Communication in Venice: Rethinking Early Modern Politics* (Oxford, 2007).

[55] Edmund Burke, *Second Letter on a Regicide Peace, The Works of the Right Honourable Edmund Burke*, 12 vols. (London, 1894), v. 380.

mass-market imprints, translations, and the reproduction of images (the reading nation and the seeing nation, in William St Clair's expression) are Atlantic-worldwide histories.[56] The descriptions of oral, visual, and remembered knowledge that have been so important in histories of information in Europe and India are important, too, to a history of the most Atlantic of all Atlantic subjects, or of the information of the enslaved.[57]

The last and most imposing prospect is of a new social or cultural history of ideas or states of mind; of the Atlantic as a world-view or *Weltanschauung*. This is a prospect which is of interest to multiple kinds of history. But it is of particular importance to Atlantic or Atlantic-worldwide history, because of the lasting association of Atlantic history with histories of meaning (including the meaning of the Atlantic as a world). It is a variation of one of the oldest of all Atlantic enquiries: in the Abbé Raynal's expression of 1774, into the 'influence which the connections with the new world have had on the customs, the government, the arts, the opinions of the old'.[58] It is related to histories of information (because to have information about other events in the Atlantic world is a necessary, but not sufficient condition for having been influenced by them); to environmental history (because changes in climate and temperature are an enduring part of the experience of Atlantic crossings); and to economic history. It is related, in particular, to an even larger version of Raynal's question, or the enquiry into how much the Atlantic, or the Atlantic world, meant in the interior of the Americas, Africa, and Europe (or Eurasia); into the multiplier effects of Atlantic exchanges.[59]

Late Atlantic history is in an outstanding position, it seems to me, to contribute to these very old and very general enquiries. Atlantic and other transnational histories have liberated historians from the confining classifications of national historiography; and also from other confining identities, including the classification into political history, economic history, intellectual history, cultural history, and social history (just as the traverse to America transformed the classifications of highbrow and lowbrow, or of 'high', 'medium', and 'low' thought).[60] The increase in scale has freed historians to rediscover biography, prosopography, and narratives of individual lives, as the macro-turn has made possible a micro-turn.

[56] William St Clair, *The Reading Nation in the Romantic Period* (Cambridge, 2004); C. A. Bayly, *The Birth of the Modern World, 1780–1914: Global Connections and Comparisons* (Oxford, 2004).

[57] See Brown, *The Reaper's Garden*; Walter Johnson, *Soul by Soul: Life inside the Antebellum Slave Market* (Cambridge, MA, 1999).

[58] Raynal, *Histoire*, vii. 1–2.

[59] On the multiplier effects of long-distance exchanges, see Rothschild, *The Inner Life of Empires*. The economic historian Jacob Price once asked the question, in relation to eighteenth-century Britain, 'Who cared about the colonies?' But he did not really come very close to an answer in respect of meaning, or caring, or of what Bernard Bailyn and Philip Morgan described as the 'lifeblood' as distinct from the 'skeleton', or the 'structural framework of colonial life'. 'Introduction', in Bernard Bailyn and Philip D. Morgan (eds.), *Strangers within the Realm: Cultural Margins of the First British Empire* (Chapel Hill, NC, 1991), 1–31, 3.

[60] Rodgers, *Contested Truths*.

But the Atlantic world is also an extraordinary source of evidence for a new social history of ideas. Even individuals without property, and without words in which to express themselves, were recorded in their Atlantic exchanges; sometimes they were themselves the objects of exchange. They were caught in the web of the law in a multitude of different ways.[61] The legal status of persons, commodities, and ships changed in the course of movement over long distances. To board a ship in the Atlantic was to cross a frontier, including the frontiers of different national systems of law, or of civil and common law, or of administrative, constitutional, and admiralty law. Individuals married, gave birth, died, and inherited in different systems of law. They were naturalized, or lost their nationalities. They were enslaved, or bought their own emancipation. Entire islands crossed the frontiers of law, and entire plantations of individuals escaped from one legal system to another.[62] The slave law of the diverse empires has been a source of evidence for Atlantic history; so is admiralty law (a closely related subject). So too is the evidence that is produced by families and friendships. The family history of roots and genealogies, the legal history of ordinary life, and literary scholarship—the effort to take seriously, and read closely, the words of individuals who were caught up in Atlantic exchanges—would be intertwined, in an Atlantic history of ideas.[63]

So there is an industrious future for late Atlantic history, in all these respects. I do not mean, by 'late Atlantic', a history that is mostly concerned with the nineteenth century, and one of the achievements of the chapters in this volume is to call into question provincialism in time, as well as space. I do mean a history that is informed by the inventiveness of the Atlantic histories of the nineteenth century; and that takes seriously the Atlantic-worldwide connections that were so important at the end of the large narrative of this volume, and throughout the earlier history of the Atlantic world. The story ends well.

BIBLIOGRAPHY

Adelman, Jeremy, *Republic of Capital: Buenos Aires and the Legal Transformation of the Atlantic World* (Palo Alto, CA, 1999).

Bayly, C. A., *Empire and Information: Intelligence Gathering and Social Communication in India, 1780–1870* (Cambridge, 1996).

Brown, Vincent, *The Reaper's Garden: Death and Power in the World of Atlantic Slavery* (Cambridge, MA, 2008).

De Vivo, Filippo, *Information & Communication in Venice: Rethinking Early Modern Politics* (Oxford, 2007).

[61] Hendrik Hartog, *Man and Wife in America: A History* (Cambridge, MA, 2000), 2, 5.

[62] On citizenship and the law, see Caitlin Anderson, 'Britons Abroad and Aliens at Home: Nationality Law and Policy in Britain, 1815–1870' (Ph.D. dissertation, University of Cambridge, 2004).

[63] Slauter, 'History, Literature, and the Atlantic World'.

Faust, Drew Gilpin, *John Henry Hammond and the Old South: A Design for Mastery* (Baton Rouge, LA, 1982).

Johnson, Walter, *Soul by Soul: Life inside the Antebellum Slave Market* (Cambridge, MA, 1999).

Morieux, Renaud, *Une mer pour deux royaumes: la Manche, frontière franco-anglaise (XVIIe–XVIIIe siècles)* (Rennes, 2008).

Rodgers, Daniel T., *Atlantic Crossings: Social Politics in a Progressive Age* (Cambridge, MA, 1998).

Smallwood, Stephanie E., *Saltwater Slavery: A Middle Passage from Africa to American Diaspora* (Cambridge, MA, 2008).

Todd, David, *L'Identité économique de la France: libre-échange et protectionnisme, 1814–1851* (Paris, 2008).

Index